Jewish Women
in America

An Historical Encyclopedia

edited by

Paula E. Hyman and Deborah Dash Moore

SPONSORED BY THE AMERICAN JEWISH HISTORICAL SOCIETY

◦

VOLUME II
M–Z

◦

Routledge
New York • London
1997

PUBLISHER'S STAFF

PROJECT DIRECTOR
Ralph Carlson

MANAGING EDITORS
Lisa Hacken, Sarah Rosen, Jonathan Korzen

PROJECT ASSOCIATE
Harriet Feinberg

EDITOR-IN-CHIEF
Sarah Silberstein Swartz

EDITORIAL STAFF
C.J. Bartelt, Erin Elizabeth Clune, Joseph E.L. Fortt, Kirsten Fermaglich, Douglas Goertzen, Amy Gottlieb, Lisa Lepson, Cynthia Merman, Michele Siegel

PRODUCTION STAFF
Maud Andrew, C.J. Bartelt, Joseph E.L. Fortt, Cynthia Merman, Phillip Ward

COPYEDITING
Sarah Swartz Consulting Services, India Cooper, Douglas Goertzen, Cynthia Merman, Anita Vanca

PHOTO RESEARCH
Hillary MacAustin, Kirsten Fermaglich, Felicia Hermann, Laura Lieber, Adam Sol

Library of Congress Cataloging-in-Publication Data
Jewish women in America : an historical enyclopedia / edited by Paula
   E. Hyman and Deborah Dash Moore
         p.   cm.
         Included bibliographical references and index.
         ISBN 0-415-91936-3 (cloth : alk. paper)
         1. Jewish women—United States—Biography—Dictionaries.
   2. Jewish Women—United States—History. 3. Jews—United States—
Biography—Dictionaries. 4. Jew—United States—Intellectual life.
   I. Hyman, Paula E., 1946– . II. Moore, Deborah Dash, 1946– .
DS115.2.J49 1997
920.72'089'924073—dc21   97-26842
[B]   CIP

ISBN 0-415-91936-3 (2 volume set)
ISBN 0-415-91934-7 (volume 1)
ISBN 0-415-91935-5 (volume 2)

Published in 1998 by
Routledge
29 West 35th Street
New York, NY 10001

Published in Great Britain by
Routledge
11 New Fetter Lane
London EC4P 4EE

Printed in the United States of America on acid-free paper.

Contents

Volume I

Volume II

Jewish Women in America

M

MADAME ALEXANDER *see* **ALEXANDER, BEATRICE**

MAGNIN, MARY ANN COHEN (1849–1943)

Energetic, stubborn, with an outstanding intuition for business—this was Mary Ann Cohen Magnin, the founder of I. Magnin and Company. Until her death at age ninety-four, Magnin took an active interest in the stores, which specialize in exclusive women's clothes.

Mary Ann Cohen, the daughter of a rabbi, was born in Scheveningen, Holland, in 1850. She immigrated with her parents to London, England. On October 8, 1865, in the Great Synagogue in London, she married Isaac Magnin, born in Assen, Holland, in 1842, a carver and gilder. They had eight children: Samuel, Henrietta, Joseph, Emanuel John, Victor, Lucille, Flora, and Grover.

In 1875, the family traveled around Cape Horn to San Francisco. To help support the family, Magnin opened a small store and began sewing and selling lace-trimmed baby clothes, lingerie, and bridal trousseaux, an art she had learned from her mother. By 1877, she had established I. Magnin and moved to a larger, more prominent location. Although the store was named for her husband Isaac, he took little interest in the business, preferring to spend his days discussing socialism and philosophy. Isaac Magnin died on January 27, 1907.

I. Magnin & Co. moved to even larger and more fashionable quarters as the business district of San Francisco changed. The store always cultivated a wealthy clientele. In 1906, after the earthquake and fire that destroyed much of San Francisco, Magnin moved merchandise from the Customs House, which was not damaged, to her home and continued to operate the store. This not only helped those who had lost everything, but was also a wise business decision, as clothing was in demand.

As her children grew older, the girls were trained in handwork, while the boys were brought into the business. The boys worked in the store, learning every part of the business. Emanuel John, the third son, was singled out by his mother for his business ability and sent to New York to handle the buying for the store. Grover, the youngest, was picked by his mother to head the San Francisco store. Joseph, overlooked by his mother, eventually left I. Magnin's to found his own store. This caused a deep rift in the family.

It is impossible to separate Magnin's business and family life. She ruled her store and her family with strict dedication. Although she officially handed over

The founder of I. Magnin and Company, Mary Ann Cohen Magnin was the daughter of a rabbi. She learned the art of sewing fine clothing from her mother and handed off her already well-established department store to her sons. [American Jewish Historical Society]

the business to her sons forty years before her death on December 15, 1943, she continued to make daily inspection tours of the stores and staff until her last days.

A century later, Mary Ann Magnin would have been widely recognized in the business world. However, because of the conventions of the nineteenth century, her role in the development of the department store chain is little known.

BIBLIOGRAPHY

"Founder of I. Magnin & Co. Dies at 95 [sic]." *San Francisco Chronicle*, December 16, 1943; Magnin, Cyril. Oral history, 1976. Western Jewish History Center, Berkeley, California; Magnin, Cyril, and Cynthia Robins. *Call Me Cyril* (1981); Magnin, Edgar Fogel. Oral history, 1975. Western Jewish History Center; Magnin Family Papers. Archives. Western Jewish History Center.

AVA F. KAHN

MAHLER, MARGARET (1897–1985)

Margaret Schönberger Mahler, a pioneering child analyst, began her career in Vienna but made her most important discoveries in the United States. She became a leading authority on the mother-child relationship and the separation-individuation process, which she examined in her best-known work, *The Psychological Birth of the Human Infant*.

Born on May 10, 1897, in Sopron, Hungary, she spoke German to her mother, Eugenia (Wiener) Schönberger, and Hungarian to her father, Gusztav Schönberger (originally Fertoszentmiklos). Resentful of her beautiful younger sister, who resembled their mother, Margaret decided to follow in her adored father's footsteps by becoming a physician. At sixteen, she left Sopron for Budapest, where she began her medical studies in 1917. After encountering anti-Semitism and discrimination as a foreign student in Munich, Jena, and Heidelberg after World War I, she received her doctorate from the University of Jena in 1922 and then moved to Vienna, where she obtained her medical license and established a private pediatric practice.

Introduced to psychoanalytic theories by Sandor Ferenczi in Budapest, she became affiliated with the Vienna Psychoanalytic Society and underwent training analysis, first with HELENE DEUTSCH and later with August Aichhorn and Willi Hoffer. Having worked as an assistant in two pediatric clinics, she became a municipal youth and welfare physician and conducted research on juvenile delinquents in Aichhorn's child guidance centers. In 1938, after the anschluss, she left Vienna for England together with her husband, Paul Mahler, a Jewish chemist whom she had married two years previously. After a brief stay in London, they immigrated to the United States.

Settling in New York, Mahler passed her state medical boards in 1939 and became a member of the New York Psychoanalytic Society. In the 1940s, she worked as an unsalaried consultant at the New York State Psychiatric Institute and Mount Sinai Hospital and taught psychiatry at Columbia University before joining the faculty of the Albert Einstein College of Medicine in 1950. Commuting from New York to Philadelphia on weekends, she directed the child analysis training program of the Philadelphia Psychoanalytic Institute. In 1956, she established a therapeutic nursery program for psychotic children at Einstein. In 1962, with a grant from the National Institute of Mental Health, she created the Masters Child Center, a laboratory for the study of the interaction between mothers and their children under three.

Margaret Mahler was not an observant Jew; her Jewish identity was shaped by the anti-Semitism she experienced in her youth and her mother's death during the Holocaust. Her last wish before her death on October 2, 1985, was that her ashes, together with those of her husband, be interred in the Jewish cemetery in Sopron, alongside her father's grave.

For almost forty years, Margaret S. Mahler was actively involved in teaching, clinical practice, and research in the United States. She published several books and over a hundred scholarly papers. Among the sizable group of emigrés from Nazi Europe who helped shape American psychoanalysis, she stands out as one of the most highly respected and honored for her major contributions to the development of child psychology.

SELECTED WORKS BY MARGARET MAHLER

The Memoirs of Margaret S. Mahler. Edited by Paul E. Stepansky (1988); *On Human Symbiosis and Vicissitudes of Individuation* (1968); *The Psychological Birth of the Human Infant: Symbiosis and Individuation,* with F. Pine and A. Bergman (1975); *The Selected Papers of Margaret S. Mahler.* Vol. I: *Infantile Psychosis and Early Contribution.* Vol. II: *Separation—Individuation* (1979).

BIBLIOGRAPHY

Dick, Jutta, and Marina Sassenberg, eds. *Jüdische Frauen im 19. und 20. Jahrhundert: Lexikon zu Leben und Werk* (1993); Dickstein, Leah J., and Carol C. Nadelson. *Women Physicians in Leadership Roles* (1986); *EJ; International Biographical Dictionary of Central European Emigrés.* Vol. 2, part 2 (1980): 763; *International Encyclopedia of Psychiatry, Psychology, Psychoanalysis and Neurology.* Vol. 6. Edited by B.B. Wolman (1972); McDevitt, John B., and Calvin F. Settlage, eds. *Separation—Individuation: Essays in Honor of Margaret S. Mahler* (1971); Mahler, Margaret. Papers. Margaret Mahler Collection. A.A. Brill Library, New York Psychoanalytic Society and Institute, New York; Mühlleitner, Elke, ed. *Biographisches Lexikon der Psychoanalyse: Die Mitglieder der Psychoanalytischen Vereinigung 1902–1938* (1992); Obituaries. *NYTimes,* October 3, 1985, and *Züricher Tages-Anzeiger,* October 15, 1985; Peters, Uwe Henrik. *Psychiatrie im Exil* (1992); Stevens, Gwendolyn, and Sheldon Gardner. *The Women of Psychology* 2 (1982): 52–55; Swerdloff, Bluma. Interviews with Margaret Mahler, 1969–1974. Oral History Research Project, Butler Library, Columbia University, NYC.

HARRIET PASS FREIDENREICH

MALINA, JUDITH (b. 1926)

Personifying the 1960s countercultural challenge to traditionalism, self-proclaimed anarchist and pacifist Judith Malina likened herself to a biblical prophet, railing at but never dissociating herself from her people. Founder, with Julian Beck, of the experimental Living Theatre, she aimed at dissolving the separation between actor and character, cast and audience, art and politics.

Born on June 4, 1926, in Kiel, Germany, to Rabbi Max Malina and Rosel Zamora, a retired Polish-Jewish actress, Judith immigrated to New York with her parents in 1928. At age seven she appeared at an anti-Nazi rally in Madison Square Garden and shortly after wrote her first poem, for Manhattan's Central Synagogue. By 1938, she was helping her father send pamphlets to Germany, asking, "Do You Know What Has Happened to Your Jewish Neighbors?" She was naturalized in 1944. Throughout her life, the influence of her family's cultural and religious beliefs continued. Often her diary records the Jewish holidays on which activities took place.

An actor, translator, poet, and teacher, Judith Malina cofounded, with her husband Julian Beck, the experimental Living Theatre. A self-proclaimed anarchist and pacifist, she was profoundly influenced by her Jewish cultural and religious beliefs. [New York Public Library]

Dropping out of high school when her father died in 1940, Malina met and began her association with Beck, held various unskilled jobs, and studied acting and directing with Erwin Piscator at the New School for Social Research, debuting as an actress in August 1945. In April of 1948, she and Beck, to whom she was married from October 30, 1948, until his death in 1985, incorporated the Living Theatre, which eventually produced more than seventy-five plays. Their son, Garrick Maxwell, later an actor, was born on February 17, 1949. Her daughter, Isha Manna (from Genesis "and she shall be called woman"), who later acted with the Living, was born on July 19, 1967. Among her critically acclaimed presentations at the Cherry Hill Theater were Pirandello's *Tonight We Improvise*, GERTRUDE STEIN's *Dr. Faustus Lights the Lights*, and the premiere of William Carlos Williams's *Many Loves*.

Expelled by the Cherry Hill management, the Living Theatre eventually settled in its own Fourteenth Street loft. Malina translated Antonin Artaud's iconoclastic *The Theater and Its Double* and continued developing avant-garde theatrical approaches with Beck, presenting Jack Gelber's *The Connection* (1959) and Kenneth Brown's *The Brig* (1963). Touring Europe, Malina directed the company's collective creations, *The Mysteries* and *Frankenstein*, and in France, influenced by Berkeley's Free Speech Movement, helped create *Paradise Now* (1965). Leaving France after its performances were disrupted by hecklers, the company toured the United States throughout 1968. Self-exiled again in early 1969, Malina celebrated a seder aboard ship en route to Europe. In 1971, the company performed street theater in Brazil until jailed and expelled as incendiary. The company then settled in France until 1983, when it returned to America.

For her work, Malina received the Lola d'Annunzio award (1959); Page One Award (1960); Obie Award (1960, 1964, 1969, 1975, 1987, 1989); Creative Arts Citation, Brandeis University (1961); Grand Prix du Théâtre des Nations (1961); Paris Critics Circle medallion (1961); Prix de L'Université de Paris (1961); New England Theater Conference Award (1962); Olympio Prize (1967); and a Guggenheim fellowship (1985).

Besides teaching at New York University and Columbia University, Malina appeared on the Molly Goldberg series and in such movies as *Enemies: A Love Story*, *Dog Day Afternoon*, and *The Addams Family*. Archivist for the Living Theatre, New York State writer-in-residence, publisher of diaries, translations, essays, and cofounder of Akashic Records, which preserves sacred texts, Malina also wrote poetry throughout her career. In 1982 she issued *Poems of a Wandering Jewess*, adapted as a jazz cycle by Steve Lacey (recorded in 1995).

An antiwar activist since the 1950s, she belonged to Women Strike for Peace, the General Strike for Peace, the U.S. Committee for Latin American Political Prisoners, American Friends of Brazil, the War Resisters League, and the Industrial Workers of the World. Influenced by Dorothy Dix and Martin Buber, she rejected the Bible as "barbarous" but found compassion in the *siddur*; in 1984, the New York Humanist church named her Humanist of the Year.

In 1988, she married Hanon Resnikov, a longtime writer-director in the Living Theatre.

A central figure among the radical New York intelligentsia of the 1960s, Malina opposed American Jewry's hostility toward unity between Palestinian Arabs and Israelis, arguing that all God's creations have to work in concert with Him. In her poetry, Malina powerfully exploits religious imagery as cultural reminiscence and explication of current actions. Best known for using mime, improvisation, and audience participation in the Living's performances, she has continued to encourage innovative new playwrights.

SELECTED WORKS BY JUDITH MALINA

Antigone, by Sophocles. Adapted by Bertolt Brecht based on German translation by Friedrich Hölderlin. Translated into English by Judith Malina (1990); *The Diaries of Judith Malina: 1947–1957* (1984); *The Enormous Despair: The Diary of Judith Malina, August 1968 to April 1969* (1972); *Entretiens avec le Living Theatre*, with Julian Beck and Jean-Jacques Lebel (1969); *The Legacy of Cain: Three Pilot Projects: A Collective Creation of the Living Theatre*, with Julian Beck (1972); *The Life of the Theatre: The Relation of the Artist to the Struggle of the People*, by Julian Beck. Foreword by Judith Malina (1986); *Living theater heisst Leben: von einer, d. Auszog, d. Auszog. D. Leben zu lerner*, with Imke Buchholz (1978); *A Monster Has Stolen the Sun and Other Plays*, by Karen Malpede. Preface by Judith Malina (1987); *Paradise Now: Collective Creation of the Living Theatre*, with Julian Beck (1971); *Poems of a Wandering Jewess* (1982. 2d ed. 1984); *Seven Meditations on Political Sado-Masochism: A Collective Creation of the Living Theatre* (1973); *Theandric: Julian Beck's Last Notebooks*, by Julian Beck. Edited by Erica Builder, notes by Judith Malina (1992); *Theatre Trip*, by Michael Townsend Smith. Introduction by Judith Malina and Julian Beck (1969); *We, the Living Theatre*, by Gianfranco Mantegna. Introduction by a Panel Discussion on Theatre as Revolution Coordinated by Aldo Rostagno, with the Participation of Julian Beck and Judith Malina (1970).

BIBLIOGRAPHY

Biner, Pierre. *The Living Theatre: A History Without Myths*. Translated by Robert Meister (1972); Fedo, David.

William Carlos Williams: A Poet in the American Theatre (1983); Lester, Elenore. "The Living Theatre Presents: Revolution! Joy! Protest! Shock! Etc.!" *NYTimes Magazine* (October 13, 1968. Reprinted April 14, 1996): 96; Neff, Renfreu. *The Living Theatre: USA* (1970); Silvestro, Carlo, ed. *The Living Book of the Living Theatre* (1971); Tytell, John. *The Living Theatre: Art, Exile, and Outrage* (1995).

AMY LEZBERG

MALKIEL, THERESA SERBER
(1874–1949)

Theresa Malkiel was an activist for labor, women's rights, and especially socialism. In one of her many published articles, she wrote, "The socialist regime [is] the only true exponent of complete equality and political economic independence."

Theresa Serber Malkiel, one of four daughters, was born on May 1, 1874, in Bar, Russia. The Serber family immigrated to New York in 1891, and although she had been educated, Theresa worked in a garment factory. Within three years, she helped to found the Infant Cloak Makers' Union.

She fought fiercely for the rights of workers. Several showdowns in her factory resulted in considerable media publicity, and her role in the union was noted. She became the first woman to rise from factory work to leadership in the Socialist Party. She was appointed delegate to the initial convention of the Socialist Trades and Labor Alliance in 1896. From that year, she was considered an insider in the Socialist Labor Party. She broke with them in 1899 and a year later joined the Socialist Party of America.

She stopped working in 1900 to marry Leon Malkiel, a fellow socialist and longtime friend. The couple moved to Yonkers, New York, and Theresa Malkiel took up housekeeping and gave birth to a daughter, Henrietta. But she could not give up her commitment to working women. Malkiel organized the Women's Progressive Society of Yonkers, which later became Branch One of the Socialist Women's Society of Greater New York.

When the general strike of 1909 began, Malkiel went to New York to join the picket line. In the course of that strike, the Socialist Party leaders made an alliance with the Women's Trade Union League. Although suspicious of their antisocialist position, Malkiel worked closely with the WTUL, signing up new members, speaking at meetings, and raising funds. She saw this strike as a chance for women to join with men and become emancipated. In an article that appeared on December 4, 1909, in the *New York Call*, a socialist journal she and her husband founded, she wrote, "Comrades, every movement has its opportunities, this is ours."

Malkiel's high hopes for women in socialism never materialized. Once the strike was over, the unions became the champions of working people, while the Socialist Party lost status. Malkiel blamed this new attitude on middle-class reformers who "came down from their pedestals to preach," and on socialist men, who were rarely committed to women's equality.

Continuing her outreach to immigrant working women, Malkiel headed the party's National Women's Committee. She justified a parallel women's socialist party with the explanation that women are "tired of their [party] positions as official cake-bakers and money collectors." When she was offered the job of setting up a suffrage movement within the party, she followed the instructions of the International and established clubs designed to attract working women. Still, the ultimate goal of bringing more people to socialism remained elusive. By 1914, the party leadership withdrew funds from the Women's National Committee and the program was discontinued.

Malkiel wrote *Diary of a Shirtwaist Maker* a year before the TRIANGLE SHIRTWAIST FIRE in 1911. However, after the fire, the book caught public attention and was credited with helping to reform New York State laws on women in industry. Malkiel continued her political activities through World War I. She went on two nationwide tours for the Socialist Party, speaking for women's rights and against United States participation in the war.

The antiwar position of the socialists, combined with the disillusionment that set in after the Russian Revolution, ended most of the enthusiasm for socialism in the United States. Malkiel's husband was now a lawyer, and had run unsuccessfully for several statewide offices. Then, Theresa Malkiel ran for New York State Assembly in 1920 on the Socialist ticket, but lost by a small margin.

Following that defeat, Malkiel concentrated exclusively on adult education. She founded the Brooklyn Adult Students Association and acted as administrator for its classes and summer camp, working toward the education and naturalization of foreign-born women.

Theresa Serber Malkiel died on November 17, 1949. By that time, her role as a radical socialist and union organizer had been largely forgotten. Instead, she was described as "widow of a well-known New York lawyer" who had devoted the last twenty years of her life to education. The headline to her obituary read: "Retired Writer, A Founder of Old *New York Call*, Aided Adult Study."

BIBLIOGRAPHY

AJHQ 68:189–205; Buhle, Mari Jo. *Women and American Socialism: 1870–1920* (1983); Malkiel, Theresa Serber. *Diary of a Shirtwaist Maker* (1910); Miller, Sally M. "From Sweatshop Worker to Labor Leader: Theresa Malkiel, a Case Study." *American Jewish History* 68 (December 1978): 189–205; Obituary. *NYTimes*, November 18, 1949, 29:3.

EMILY TAITZ

MALSIN, LANE BRYANT (1879–1951)

Lane Bryant Malsin was a fashion entrepreneur and pioneer in the best sense of the word, long before Donna Karan or Liz Claiborne. She pioneered niche marketing and mail-order merchandising, as well as innovative work practices and progressive advertising.

Born Lena Himmelstein in Lithuania in 1879, she came to the United States alone at age sixteen and supported herself as a seamstress, beginning at the weekly wage of one dollar. She soon earned the unusual wage of fifteen dollars per week because of her excellent skills. She married David Bryant, a Russian jeweler, who died shortly after their son, Raphael, was born. She supported both herself and her child with her work as a seamstress. Her specialty was lingerie and bridal sets, and she had earned enough by 1904 to open a store with living quarters in the rear. Lena became Lane because of an error when she first opened a bank account.

One of her early innovations was a garment that was used for maternity wear. While proper women were not seen on the street when pregnant, one of her clients asked her to design a garment she could wear in public—"something presentable but comfortable." This garment, with an elasticized waist and an accordion-pleated skirt, was an instant success and soon became the store's major product.

She remarried in 1909, and her husband, Albert Malsin, became her business partner. They had two children—a son, Theodore, and a daughter, Helen. Lane Bryant Malsin concentrated on the design aspects of the business, while her husband took over the business aspects of the firm, which by 1909 had an annual income of over fifty thousand dollars. While maternity garments were a major source of sales, no newspaper would advertise such a garment. In 1911, the *New York Herald* was induced to accept an advertisement, and the business's entire stock was sold out the next day.

The partnership of Lane Bryant Malsin and her husband Albert produced other retailing innovations. They introduced sales of maternity garments by mail and, in 1911–1912, produced a thirty-two-page catalog. In 1916, the business was incorporated as Lane Bryant, Incorporated; by 1917, the company's sales exceeded one million dollars.

Lane Bryant, Incorporated, also introduced clothing for the stout figure. Since no ready-made garments were on the market for this customer, Lane Bryant Malsin and her husband measured some forty-five hundred individual customers in the store and utilized other statistics on about two hundred thousand women to determine three general types of stoutness, then designed clothes to fit them. By 1923, the large-size business had surpassed the maternity wear, accounting for more than half of the annual five million dollars in sales.

Lane Bryant Malsin was vice president and director of the firm until her death on September 21, 1951. Raphael was president while her other son, Theodore, was secretary of the concern. At the time of her death, the company that bore her name was the sixth-largest mail-order business in the country. The retail stores, which began with a branch in Chicago in 1915, had also expanded rapidly. By 1969, the firm consisted of more than one hundred stores and affiliates, with sales of almost two hundred million dollars. The firm has since been purchased by The Limited and has been integrated into this organization.

Lane Bryant Malsin was also a pioneer in terms of employee relations and customer focus. Prior to her death, the company's thirty-five hundred employees participated in a profit-sharing plan and a pension plan that included protection against permanent disability, free hospitalization, group life insurance, and sickness insurance. This was at a time when neither plan was a common practice, particularly in the retail industry. An initial stock offering also included a 25 percent employee subscription.

In terms of customer focus, any Lane Bryant customer whose wardrobe was destroyed in a disaster was offered a free wardrobe through the American Red Cross. In 1947, after a major explosion and fire in Texas City, Texas, fifty-eight mail-order customers were reattired. In addition, after World War II, the Lane Bryant stores became centers for donations of clothing to Europe's needy. Lane Bryant Malsin was also active in the American Red Cross, the Hebrew Immigrant Aid Society, and the Federation of Jewish Philanthropies.

Lane Bryant Malsin also represents the immigrant worker who, through her own initiative, rose from poverty to wealth, but who did not forget those less fortunate than herself. She combined career, marriage, and motherhood at a time when marriage often marked the end of paid work. She demonstrated, through a life of innovation, hard work, and care for others, a Jewish consciousness and an appreciation for others' needs.

BIBLIOGRAPHY

EJ; Fucini, Joseph J., and Suzy Fucini. *Entrepreneurs: The Men and Women Behind Famous Brand Names and How They Made It* (1985); Mahoney, T. "Independent Woman." *Americana Annual* (1952): 431–432; *National Cyclopaedia of American Biography.* Vol. 47 (1965); Obituary. *NYTimes*, September 27, 1951, 31:1, s.v. "Malsin, Lane B."; O'Neill, Lois Decker, ed. *The Woman's Book of World Records and Achievements* (1979); *World Almanac Biographical Dictionary* (1990).

LOUISE KLABER

"MAMA" CASS *see* ELLIOT, "MAMA" CASS

MANDELBAUM, JUDITH PINTA (1906–1977)

Judith Pinta Mandelbaum was an important part of the Mizrachi Women's Organization of America (American Mizrachi Women) from the 1930s until shortly before her death in 1977, by which time the organization was known as AMIT. She also achieved professional acclaim as an outstanding teacher and is remembered fondly as a woman with a wonderful sense of humor and a rich family life.

Both her ardent Zionism and involvement with education were a natural outgrowth of her family background. She was born on June 30, 1906, in Brooklyn to Eliahu and Rose Pinta, both new immigrants from Russia and both Zionists who also believed in Hebrew education for girls; her mother had been a founding member of Achyos Mizrachi. Judith studied Hebrew and religious subjects in an afternoon Hebrew class full of boys. A natural leader, she headed a Young Judaea group when in her late teens and early twenties; there was no Mizrachi youth group at that time. She attended HUNTER COLLEGE in New York City and, at the same time, continued her Hebrew studies at the Teachers Institute of the Jewish Theological Seminary. She was in great demand as a Hebrew teacher, and Joel Braverman hired her to teach the first grade when he established the Yeshiva of Flatbush in Brooklyn. After a few years at Flatbush,

she traveled to Palestine in the early 1930s to work as the private secretary to Rabbi Meire Berlin (later Bar-Ilan), the leader of the Mizrachi movement and the great scholar for whom Bar-Ilan University is named. She traveled to Israel alone, which was highly unusual in those days and required a great deal of courage and personal strength. It was then that she met her future husband, Mordechai Mandelbaum. After a visit to her parents in Brooklyn, she returned to Jerusalem to marry him in 1936, during a period of Arab riots. Their daughter, Rhea, was born a year later. In 1939, the Mandelbaums traveled to America to visit her family. Because of the dangers of sea travel during World War II, they remained in the United States, eventually deciding to reside there permanently.

Her contributions to American Mizrachi Women were many and varied: member of the national and executive boards; national secretary; national vice president; editor-in-chief of the organization's newspaper, assistant editor of the Yiddish supplement, and special editor of its Hebrew-English column; founder and leader of their Herzl Institute lecture series; chair of their National Cultural Committee for a decade, responsible for publishing the American Mizrachi Women Cultural Guide; and AMIT delegate to the World Zionist Congress in Switzerland in 1955.

Judith Pinta Mandelbaum died in Brooklyn on March 7, 1977. She is buried in Sanhedria in Jerusalem. At the time of her death, she and her husband had been preparing to return to Israel to join their daughter and her family, who had made *aliyah* two years before.

BIBLIOGRAPHY

AJYB 79:370; *NYTimes*, March 8, 1977, 34:4.

ALICE M. BURSTEIN
NAOMI BURSTEIN MAX

MANDL, EMMA B. (1842–1928)

In the Chicago world of humanitarian endeavor her name stands forth as that of a woman of strong personality, of keen powers of observation and of high attainment. She seldom speaks in public or claims credit for the institutions founded by her, yet for nearly twenty-five years she has devoted her life to various benefactions.

These words are part of a biographical sketch of Emma B. Mandl that appeared in the 1914 edition of *Leading Women in Social Service.*

The daughter of Jonas and Charlotte (Goldschei-der) Adler, Emma Adler Mandl was born on December 16, 1842, in Pilsen, Bohemia. At the time of her death in 1928, she was survived by a brother, George. It is unknown whether she had any other siblings. She was educated in Pilsen and immigrated to the United States with her family at age fifteen. During the last sixty-nine years of her life, she lived in Chicago. She married Bernhard Mandl on November 26, 1865; they had two children, Sidney (b. 1868) and Etta (Mrs. Sol Klein) (b. 1870).

For approximately forty years, Mandl was devoted to organizing and founding numerous charitable organizations in Chicago. The vast majority of these philanthropic groups were established by prominent German Jewish women, in response to the growing need to provide social services for the influx of Eastern European Jews to Chicago. These institutions eventually became part of the United Hebrew Charities, the precursor organization to the Jewish Federation of Metropolitan Chicago.

Mandl was one of the founders of the Baron Hirsch Woman's Club in 1889. By 1918, according to *The Chicago Jewish Community Blue Book* of that year, the club was the largest philanthropic organization, irrespective of denomination, in Illinois. Mandl was president of the group for fourteen years, and then was made honorary president. The Baron Hirsch Woman's Club was the mother organization for a variety of service groups that all owed their founding and leadership to Mandl. These offspring organizations included the Home for Jewish Orphans (founded in 1894), the Chicago Home for Jewish Friendless and Working Girls (1901), the Ruth Club (1905), the Jewish Home Finding Society (1907), the Chicago Winfield Tuberculosis Sanitarium (1909), the Baron Hirsch Co-Workers (1910), and the Home for Convalescent Men and Boys (1915).

The Woman's Club motto was "In faith and hope the world will disagree, but all mankind's concern is charity." Its members strove to reach out to the needy in a multitude of ways. For example, prior to the establishment of the Home for Jewish Orphans, Chicago orphans were sent to an orphanage in Cleveland that had been set up by the Chicago B'nai B'rith in 1868. After decades of controversy, the Home for Jewish Orphans was founded to provide for the needs of the Chicago Jewish community. Mandl was given the title of honorary director for the contributions she made to this home.

As the founder and first president of the Home for Jewish Friendless and Working Girls, Mandl created an institution that provided an intermediary home for children before they were placed in the Home for Jewish Orphans or returned to a guardian. The home also supplied living quarters for girls and young women who did not have proper homes.

The founding of the Ruth Club was precipitated by the need for a separate institution to serve the needs of young, self-supporting working women. Mandl was instrumental in establishing an independent home with an appropriate environment for working women and for those wanting to learn a trade. The Baron Hirsch Woman's Club had an educational fund that covered the costs of lodging and education until these young women became self-supporting.

The Jewish Home Finding Society reunited children who had been placed in the orphanage with their mothers. The society also started a mothers' pension program and became a foster family agency providing supplemental funds to foster families. Society workers lobbied for increased funding from the state for foster families.

When a deadly outbreak of tuberculosis hit Chicago, Mandl spearheaded the formation of the Chicago Winfield Tuberculosis Sanitarium and, later, the Home for Convalescent Men and Boys. The latter institution founded Rest Cottage, a long-term health care facility for people recovering from heart disease and other debilitating illnesses.

Mandl was a director of Deborah Verein, a charter member of Sarah Greenebaum Lodge No. 15, a member of the Chicago Association of Jewish Women, and the first vice president of the Illinois Federation of Women's Clubs, Second District. In addition, she was a director of the Bureau of Personal Service and a probation officer for the Juvenile Court of Chicago. Not surprisingly, she also favored woman suffrage.

Emma B. Mandl died in Chicago on July 31, 1928. Her altruistic work within Chicago's Jewish community is her lasting legacy.

BIBLIOGRAPHY

AJYB 7 (1905–1906): 86, 31 (1929–1930): 93; "The Chicago Jewess." *Reform Advocate*, January 30, 1909, 725–729; *The Chicago Jewish Community Blue Book* (1918); Meites, Hyman L., ed. *History of the Jews of Chicago* (1924, 1990); Obituary. *Reform Advocate*, August 4, 1928; *The Sentinel's History of Chicago Jewry 1911–1986* (1986); Stein, Oswald. *Leading Women in Social Service* (1914); *UJE*; *Woman's Who's Who of America: A Biographical Dictionary of Contemporary Women of the United States and Canada, 1914–1915*. Edited by John William Leonard (1914. Reprint, 1976).

SANDRA K. BORNSTEIN

MARCUS, RUTH BARCAN (b. 1921)

A logician and philosopher who made pioneering contributions to modal logic and metaphysics, Ruth Barcan Marcus has for almost fifty years been a key figure in philosophical debates. Early in her career, she proposed the widely discussed Barcan formula, a postulate in quantified modal logic. Her later work includes influential papers in the philosophy of logic and language, epistemology, and ethics. A widely lauded collection of her essays, *Modalities*, was published in 1993.

Ruth Barcan Marcus was born in New York City on August 2, 1921, the third daughter of Samuel and Rose (Post) Barcan. Her parents were secular Eastern European Jews who settled in what was then an uncongested middle-class area of the Bronx. Her mother worked as a homemaker; her father was a printer and contributing writer at the *Jewish Daily Forward*, as well as an active member of the Socialist Party and of the Workmen's Circle (*Arbeiter Ring*). A bust of Eugene V. Debs graced the family's living room, and the three daughters, Esther, Hilda, and Ruth, attended the Workmen's Circle's Yiddish-language neighborhood schools in the afternoons, where they were taught Jewish history, literature, dance, music, and the history of socialist labor.

Marcus attended public school, including Herman Ridder Junior High School (a school for intellectually precocious students) and Evander Childs High School, until the twelfth grade. She went on to receive a B.A. in mathematics and philosophy from New York University in 1941 and a Ph.D. in philosophy from Yale University in 1946. In addition to her academic extracurricular achievements (during college, she edited a literary magazine and presided over the mathematics and the philosophical societies), Ruth was a notable athlete. In 1941, the New York University yearbook featured her photo, with a caption that read: "Ruth Barcan, NYU's attractive fencer, is pictured above. One of the most outstanding fencers ever to come to Washington Square College, Miss Barcan epitomizes what is fine and character building in sports for women."

In 1942, Ruth Barcan married Jules Alexander Marcus, a physicist. They had four children, James (b. 1948), Peter (b. 1949), Katherine (b. 1952), and Elizabeth (b. 1957). The couple was divorced in 1976.

Marcus spent the early years of her career in various postdoctoral fellowships and visiting positions, including a Guggenheim Fellowship (1953–1954). She taught at Roosevelt University from 1959 to 1963, and in 1964 she was appointed head of the philosophy department at the University of Illinois at

Ruth Barcan Marcus changed the world of modal logic and metaphysics. For fifty years she has worked in academia, running philosophy departments and writing influential papers on logic, language, epistemology, and ethics.

Chicago. Under her six-year stewardship, the department grew from a two-member faculty to a full graduate department with a nationally ranked faculty of twenty. She then served for three years as a professor at Northwestern University (1970–1973) and, in 1973, was appointed professor of philosophy at Yale University. She retired as Reuben Post Halleck Professor in 1992, and is currently a senior research scholar at Yale, with a continuing appointment as distinguished visiting professor at the University of California at Irvine during winter quarters.

During her tenure at Yale, Marcus was widely recognized as a leading figure, receiving formal offers from (among others) Princeton, UCLA, Penn, and Stanford. Her numerous fellowships and awards include the Medal of the College de France (1986) and fellowships from the National Science Foundation (1963–1964), the Center for Advanced Study at the University of Illinois (1968–1969), the Center for Advanced Study in the Behavioral Sciences at

Stanford (1979), Wolfson College, Oxford (1985–1986), Clare Hall, Cambridge (1988), and the National Humanities Center (1992–1993), as well as residencies at the Rockefeller Center in Bellagio (1973 and 1990). She is an elected member of the Institut International de Philosophie, where she served as president (1989–1992), is a fellow of the American Academy of Arts and Sciences, and has served as president of the Association for Symbolic Logic (1983–1986) and chair of the board of the American Philosophical Association (1977–1983). In 1995, she was awarded an honorary doctorate of humane letters by the University of Illinois.

BIBLIOGRAPHY

Bacon, John. Review of *Modalities*, by Ruth Barcan Marcus. *Journal of Symbolic Logic* 60, no. 3 (1995): 1005–1009; *Contemporary Authors*; Garrett, Don. Review of *Modalities*. *Review of Metaphysics* 48, no. 3 (1995): 688–689; *International Who's Who*; *International Who's Who of Women*; Kraut, Robert. Review of *Modalities*. *Journal of Philosophy* 93, no. 5 (1996): 243–248; Levine, Shaughan. Review of *Modalities*. *British Journal for Philosophy of Science* 46 (1995): 267–274; Marcus, Ruth Barcan. *Modalities* (1993); Sinnott-Armstrong, Walter, Diana Raffman, and Nicholas Ascher, eds. *Morality, Modality and Belief: Essays in Honor of Ruth Barcan Marcus* (1995); *Who's Who in America*; *Who's Who in the East*; *Who's Who of American Women*; Williamson, Timothy. Review of *Modalities*. *Philosophical Books* 36, no. 2 (1995): 120–122.

TAMAR SZABÓ GENDLER

MARGARETEN, REGINA (1863–1959)

Regina Margareten was known as the "Matzoh Queen" and the "matriarch of the kosher food industry," according to her obituary in the *New York Times*.

Born in Balbona (Miskolcz), Hungary, on December 20 or 25, 1863, she came to America as a young bride in 1883, with her husband, Ignatz Margareten, and her parents, Jacob and Mirel Chayah (Mary) (Brunner) Horowitz. Regina, also known as Rebush and as Hannah Rivka, was the Horowitzes' third child and second daughter.

Although pregnant with her first child, she attended night school to learn English. The newly arrived Horowitz-Margareten family was determined to maintain the traditional Orthodox life they had observed in Hungary, and opened a grocery store on Willett Street on New York's Lower East Side. They baked matzoh for themselves the first Passover they were in the United States, and within a few years the matzoh business became their sole occupation. The initial year they used fifty barrels of flour and baked by hand in a rented bakery. Regina Margareten lit the fires, worked the dough, and found customers. The small family business grew to a company that grossed a million dollars in 1931 and used forty-five thousand barrels of flour in 1932. Much of the Horowitz Brothers & Margareten Company's success is attributed to Regina Margareten, who told her grandchildren that in the early years she never saw the light of day except on the Sabbath.

Jacob Horowitz, Regina's father, died in 1885. Her mother, Mirel Chayah, and her brothers Joseph, Leopold, Moses, and Samuel Horowitz continued the business together with Regina and her husband Ignatz. Mirel Chayah Horowitz died in 1919, and Ignatz passed away in 1923. After his death, Regina formally took over as treasurer and as one of the directors of the company, positions she held for the rest of her life. Her sons Jacob and Frederick later followed her into the business. Until two weeks before she died at age ninety-six, she visited the plant daily. Her particular concern was the taste and quality of the matzoh. She would immediately inspect the matzoh when she arrived at the factory at 8:30 A.M. and would have samples sent to her office throughout the day. She is credited with the idea of combining wheat grown in three different states to ensure a superior matzoh and with the company's expansion into making noodles and other kosher products. As one of the company's directors, she participated in policy-planning meetings and decisions in areas such as advertising, marketing, and real estate. When the city took over the company's Lower East Side location for a housing project in 1945, Margareten encouraged the purchase of a large factory in Long Island City to ensure room for growth.

Margareten was the Horowitz Brothers & Margareten Company's spokesperson for internal and external matters. It was she who dealt with union representatives. Every year before Passover during the 1940s and 1950s, Margareten would appear on the radio program sponsored by the company and greet the Jewish community. She spoke in Yiddish and repeated the message in English, for the "sake of the children who may be listening in." Her speech for Passover 1952 was a patriotic, humanitarian, and Zionist message that expressed gratitude to the United States for the "freedom, prosperity, and happiness we have here," which enable us to help our less fortunate brethren and participate in building the State of Israel.

Margareten embodied these charitable values in her life. She made sure that beggars never went away empty-handed from the doors of the Horowitz Brothers & Margareten Company. She was actively involved in synagogues and in religious and philanthropic organizations. The most notable were the Beth Midrash HaGadol Anshei Hungary; the Ohel Torah Talmud Torah, a Malbish Arumim society that provided indigent students at the Talmud Torah with new clothes for Passover; and the Nashim Rachmonioth Society, which helped needy women during pregnancy and after childbirth. Her obituaries report that she was a member of over a hundred different charitable organizations.

In addition to activities on behalf of the community, Regina Margareten was the matriarch of the extended Horowitz-Margareten family. She bought property in the Hunter Mountain area in the Catskills and established Margareten Park, where each of her six children—Yetta Landau, Jacob, Carrie Unterberger, Frederick, Ella Weiss, and Sadie Wohl—had a summer home. Even while staying there in her later years, she would call the firm daily to discuss the price of wheat and confer on how much to buy. She was one of the founders of the Margareten family association, and traveled to her native Hungary almost every year during the 1920s and 1930s to visit relatives. An adventurous woman, she flew the London-Paris leg of the journey in an airplane or zeppelin (family versions differ) in the 1920s. She encouraged family members to immigrate to the United States and employed them in the factory or helped them until they could establish themselves. On her visit to Hungary in 1924, she entered with a relative into partnership in a coal mine in Edeleny, Hungary. The mine provided jobs for local family members. After World War II began, her son Jacob, under her direction, completed affidavits on behalf of numerous relatives and succeeded in bringing many of them to the United States.

A vibrant, dignified woman, Regina Margareten was a pioneer in the kosher food industry in the United States and an active philanthropist in her family and the Jewish community at large. Her nephew Joel Margaretten immortalized her by registering a lilac he bred under the name "Regina." She died in New York City on January 15, 1959.

BIBLIOGRAPHY

AJYB 61:418; Ginsberg, Miriam. Telephone interview with author, July 19, 1995; Golovensky, Muriel. Telephone interviews with author, May 16 and July 18, 1995; Gomperts, Judy, comp. *Directory & Genealogy of the Horowitz-Margareten Family, 1955–1994* (1994), and correspondence and telephone interviews with author, June 6 and June 18, 1995; Gross, Jack. Telephone interview with author, May 18, 1995; Gross, Shirley. Telephone interviews with author, July 5 and July 18, 1995; Horowitz, A. David. Correspondence with author, July 17, 1995; Horowitz, Herbert. Telephone interview with author, July 5, 1995; Horowitz, Jacob L. Correspondence with author, July 24 and July 30, 1995; *Horowitz-Margareten Family Journal* 4, no. 9 (September 1, 1946), and 4, no. 10 (October 1, 1946), and 17, no. 2 (February 1959), and 17, no. 3 (March 1959); *Jewish Daily Forward*, January 16, 1959, 14; Margareten, Harry. Interview with author, July 11, 1995; Margareten, Jack. Telephone interview with author, May 24, 1995; Margareten, Jerome. Telephone interview with author, July 21, 1995; Margareten, Regina. Tape recording of 1952 Passover message. Courtesy of Mrs. Judy Gomperts; Margaretten, Joel, et al., comps. *Directory and Genealogy of the Horowitz-Margareten Family, 1955* (1955); Margaretten, Joel, comp. *A Directory of the Horowitz-Margaretten Family* (1929), and *A History of the Margaretten Family*. Translated by David Margaretten (1941), and Telephone interview with author, June 29, 1995; *NYTimes*, May 1, 1938, sec. 4, 2:6, and December 14, 1942, 20:6, and December 27, 1954, 34:2, and December 24, 1957, 13:4, and April 11, 1984, C12, and Obituary. January 15, 1959, 33:2; Radkowsky, Florence. Telephone interview with author, June 27, 1995.

SHULAMITH Z. BERGER

MARGOLIN, ANNA (1887–1952)

Rosa Lebensboim, better known by her pen name of Anna Margolin, is regarded by literary critics as one of the finest early twentieth-century Yiddish poets in America. Her poetry, translated by ADRIENNE RICH, Kathryn Hellerstein, and Marcia Falk, among others, appears in many Yiddish poetry anthologies in English. Captivating, temperamental, and intellectually gifted, Anna Margolin influenced the work of several major writers and thinkers of her time.

Anna Margolin was born in the Lithuanian town of Brisk on January 21, 1887, the only child of Dvoyre Leye (Rosenblum) and Menachem Lebensboim, who turned from Hasidism to a more worldly way of life. Under her father's guidance, Margolin received a European secular education. As a child, she lived briefly in Königsberg and Odessa, later moving to Warsaw, where her father resided after her parents' divorce. In 1906, her father sent her to America, where she began her writing career.

In New York, she joined the circle of immigrant Jewish intellectuals who gathered around the Yiddishist Chaim Zhitlovsky. Zhitlovsky was influenced by Margolin, both personally and intellectually, and engaged her as his secretary. Margolin's new connections, in addition to her sharp wit and original writing talent, opened many doors for her, and she soon became a professional journalist for the Yiddish press. Her first piece of fiction appeared in the *Fraye Arbeter Shtime*, and she joined its editorial staff for six months.

Restless, Margolin traveled to London, Paris, and back to Warsaw, where she met the Hebrew writer Moshe Stavski and married him. Together they moved to Palestine, where her only child, Naaman, was born. Unhappy in her marriage and stifled by the lack of intellectual stimulation in small-town Tel Aviv, Margolin returned to Warsaw, leaving behind her husband and infant son. In the spring of 1913, she moved to New York, making it her permanent home.

Upon her return to the United States, she joined the staff of the newly established daily *Der Tog* in 1914, and became a member of the editorial board until 1920. At *Der Tog*, she wrote a weekly women's column entitled "In der Froyen Velt" [In the women's world] and traveled in Europe as a correspondent reporting on women's issues. During this time, she wrote several articles supporting the suffrage movement.

In the offices of *Der Tog*, Margolin met her second husband, Hirsh Leib Gordon. When Gordon left for service in World War I, they became estranged, and Margolin became involved with Yiddish writer Reuben Iceland. Iceland was instrumental in encouraging her writing of poetry, and Margolin, in turn, had an impact on his writing. They became lifelong companions.

Margolin used many pen names during her writing career. Beginning in 1909, she wrote short stories under the names Khave Gros and Khane Barut. She signed some of her journalistic work as Sofia Brandt and later as Clara Lenin. When she began to publish poems in the early 1920s, she used the pseudonym Anna Margolin, and then published all her poetry under this name.

Although her first poems appeared in politically radical papers, she did not limit herself to the politics of one newspaper or to the journals of one literary group. She was published in *Di Naye Velt*, *Fraye Arbeter Shtime*, *Nay Yidish*, *Inzikh*, and *Tzukunft*. Her themes were personal, yet intellectual and unsentimental. Margolin's poetry reveals her as a literary modernist with a secular perspective.

In 1923, Margolin edited a poetry anthology entitled *Dos Yidishe Lid in Amerika*, which showcased the best Yiddish contemporary poetry. It included a broad range of writers from both opposing Yiddish literary groups of the time—Di Yunge and the more contemporary Inzikhistn [Introspectivists]—as well as others.

In 1929, eighty of Margolin's poems were published in a volume entitled *Lider*. In this collection, she examined her relationship with Reuben Iceland, as well as her feelings of isolation as a foreigner and as a woman. In America, her book did not receive the acclaim she had anticipated, but in Warsaw, important critics wrote about her work with enthusiasm.

After the publication of *Lider*, Margolin had six poems published and then became silent. Her last poems appeared in 1932. Although she continued to write, she no longer allowed her works to be published. By age fifty, she suffered from severe depression and chronic minor ailments. For the final years of her life, Margolin became a recluse.

Her epitaph, which she wrote herself years before her death, is a lament for a squandered life. Yet in her short writing career, and with only one volume of poetry published, she became the toast of the Yiddish literati and gained wide recognition for her unique poems.

Anna Margolin died on June 29, 1952, in New York.

SELECTED WORKS BY ANNA MARGOLIN
Anna Margolin: Poems. Edited by Abraham Novershtern (1991); *Lider* (1929); *Dos Yidishe Lid in Amerika—1923: Antologye*, editor (1923).

BIBLIOGRAPHY
Cooper, Adrienne. "About Anna Margolin." In *The Tribe of Dina: A Jewish Women's Anthology*, edited by Melanie Kaye/Kantrowitz and Irene Klepfisz (1989); Cooperman, J., and Sarah Cooperman. *America in Yiddish Poetry* (1967); Howe, Irving, and Eliezer Greenberg, eds. *A Treasury of Yiddish Poetry* (1976); Howe, Irving, Ruth R. Wisse, and Khone Shmeruk, eds. *The Penguin Book of Modern Yiddish Verse* (1987); Iceland, Reuben. *Fun Unzer Friling* [Of our springtime] (1954); Korman, Ezra, ed. *Yidishe Dikhterins* (1928); Kramer, Aaron. *A Century of Yiddish Poetry* (1989); Leftwich, Joseph. *The Golden Peacock: Anthology* (1974); *Leksikon fun der Nayer Yidisher Literatur* [Biographic dictionary of modern Yiddish literature]. Vol. 5 (1963): 478–480; Novershtern, Abraham. "'Who Would Have Believed that a Bronze Statue Can Weep?': The Poetry of Anna Margolin." Introduction to *Anna Margolin: Poems* (1991); Pratt, Norma Fain. "Anna Margolin's *Lider*: A Study in Women's History, Autobiography, and Poetry." *Studies in American Jewish Literature* 3 (1983): 11–25, and "Culture and Radical Politics: Yiddish Women Writers, 1890–1940." *American Jewish History* 70, no. 1 (September 1980): 68–90; Reizen, Zalman. *Leksikon fun der Yidisher Literatur, Prese, un Filologye*. 3rd ed. (1927); *UJE*: Whitman, Ruth, ed. *An Anthology of Modern Poetry* (1995).

SARAH SILBERSTEIN SWARTZ

MARINOFF, FANIA (c. 1890–1971)

Fania Marinoff was associated with one of the most vibrant artistic circles in the United States and Europe. She numbered among her friends writers such as GERTRUDE STEIN, playwrights such as Eugene O'Neill, and artists such as Georgia O'Keeffe. Fania Marinoff and her husband, Carl Van Vechten, played a prominent role in the bohemian social and artistic life of New York, particularly of the Harlem Renaissance.

Born, probably in 1890, in Odessa, Russia, Fania was the thirteenth child and seventh daughter born to Mayer and Leah Marinoff, who died not long after Fania was born. Mayer remarried and immigrated to America in the mid-1890s, when Fania was five or six years old, settling in Boston. At age seven, Fania was sent to live with her older brothers in Denver, Colorado. Although she had little formal schooling, she showed considerable promise as an actor, and by age twelve she was earning her living playing soubrette roles in repertory. Fania first arrived in New York in 1903, finding steady work in theater there. In 1912, she met Carl Van Vechten, the author and photographer, and the two were married in 1914.

Marinoff continued to act on the stage after her marriage, appearing as Ariel in the tercentenary revival of *The Tempest* in 1916, and as a lead in the Greenwich Village Players from 1916 to 1917. She was also a pioneer of the early silent film industry, appearing in *One of Our Girls* (1914), *Nedra* (1915), and *Life's Whirlpool* (1916). In 1942, Marinoff became one of the early volunteers for the Stage-Door Canteen, a troupe established to entertain the armed forces. After the war, she retired from the stage, but remained active. She and her husband continued to entertain a large circle of friends in the arts until his death in 1964. Fania Marinoff died seven years later, on November 16, 1971, in Englewood, New Jersey.

While Fania Marinoff was not a practicing Jew, she was an intensely religious person and Judaism was central to her identity. In her early stage career, she was often cast in foreign roles, and occasionally in a Jewish role, and her immigrant background and experience living in working-class neighborhoods brought a sympathy and realism to these roles that impressed contemporary critics and theater audiences.

BIBLIOGRAPHY
AJYB 24:179; *BEOAJ*; "Fania Marinoff." *NYTimes*, December 9, 1917, 8:7; "Fania Marinoff, Actress, 81, Dead." *NYTimes*, November 17, 1971, 51:1; Kellner, Bruce. "Fania Marinoff." In *Carl Van Vechten and the Irreverent

A pioneer of the early silent film industry and member of the Greenwich Village Players, Fania Marinoff "trod the boards" from age twelve until she retired at fifty-five. Throughout her life, she and her husband, photographer Carl Van Vechten, played a prominent role in the bohemian social and artistic life of New York, particularly during the Harlem Renaissance. [New York Public Library]

Decades (1968); Kellner, Bruce, ed. *Letters of Carl Van Vechten* (1987); "Minute Visits in the Wings." *NYTimes*, September 22, 1918, 4:4; "Who's Who." *NYTimes*, March 9, 1924, 8:2; *WWIAJ* (1926, 1928, 1938).

GILLIAN RODGER

MARMORSTON, JESSIE (1903–1980)

Physician, scientist, and professor of medicine, Jessie Marmorston's research in the connection between hormone secretion and cancer contributed to medical knowledge on the psychophysiological link between stress and disease in humans.

Born in Kiev, Russia, on September 16, 1903, Jessie was the daughter of Aaron and Ethel (Wark) Marmorston. The family immigrated to the United States in 1906. After attending public school, young Jessie enrolled at the University of Buffalo, where she earned her bachelor's and master's degrees. In 1924, she graduated from the University of Buffalo School of Medicine.

Immediately following her academic career in Buffalo, Marmorston began an internship at Montefiore Hospital in New York City. At Montefiore, Marmorston met David Perla, a fellow intern. A shared interest in pathology and immunology grew steadily into a personal relationship. Married in 1933, the couple's professional relationship led to a collaboration which culminated in their publication in 1926 of *The Spleen and Its Relation to Resistance*.

Companions, partners, and collaborators—Perla and Marmorston's future was cut short when Perla died an untimely death in 1940 at age forty. With their three daughters, Edith, Elizabeth, and Norma, Marmorston left her home in New York in 1943 to begin a new life in California, where she joined the faculty of the University of Southern California Medical School. In California, Marmorston met Lawrence Weingarten, a Hollywood producer, whom she married in 1945.

While at USC, Marmorston received a series of research grants from the United States Public Health Service to support her research in endocrinology. Ten years after her appointment at USC, she became professor of experimental medicine. From 1957 until her death in 1980, Marmorston served at USC as clinical professor of medicine.

An accomplished author in the field of medicine and medical research, Marmorston wrote on immunology, endocrinology, bacteriology, pathology, psychoanalysis, experimental medicine, clinical methods, cardiology, and the use of computers in medical research. Among her many publications Marmorston wrote *Natural Resistance and Clinical Medicine* (1941). As coauthor, Marmorston contributed to *Psychoanalysis and the Human Situation* (1984), *Manual of Computer Programs for Preliminary Multivariate Analysis* (1965), and *Scientific Methods in Clinical Studies* (1970).

From 1952 to 1959, Marmorston investigated the relationship between hormone secretion and heart attacks in women, concluding that small amounts of estrogen administered to postmenopausal women could decrease the incidence of heart attack. Continuing her studies on endocrinology in the 1960s, Mar-

morston's work in the connection between lung cancer and hormone secretion revealed a connection between emotional stress, the production of hormones, and how the two created a psychophysiological basis for some cancers.

A member of numerous national, international, and regional medical and scientific organizations, Marmorston served her profession and her community with distinction. For thirty-six years, Marmorston served as an attending physician at Cedars-Sinai Hospital in Los Angeles—a position she also held at Los Angeles County Hospital.

Marmorston died in Los Angeles on October 21, 1980, at age seventy-seven. One of millions of immigrants who arrived in this land during the golden age of immigration, Marmorston's life work serves as an example of the contributions of Eastern European Jewish immigrants—and Jewish women—to arts, science, and letters in the United States in the twentieth century.

BIBLIOGRAPHY

BEOAJ; WWIAJ (1938); *WWWIA* 7.

DAVID REGO

MARRIAGE, MIXED, *see* INTERMARRIAGE AND CONVERSION

MARSHALL, LENORE GUINZBURG (1897–1971)

Lenore Guinzburg Marshall, novelist, poet, and activist, was born in New York City on September 7, 1897. She was the daughter of Harry and Leonie (Kleinert) Guinzburg. A student at Barnard College, class of 1919, where she was an editor of the monthly literary magazine *The Bear*, and a member of the Intercollegiate Socialist Society, Lenore was described in her class yearbook with the following verse: "Our manner toward her's friendly / and even rather gracious, / For no one slings / Such odes and things / As does our lauriger Horatius."

After graduation in 1919, she married James Marshall, an attorney who also served as president of the New York City Board of Education. The couple had two children, Ellen and Jonathan, who became the publisher of the Scottsdale, Arizona, *Daily Progress*.

From 1929 to 1932, Marshall worked as an editor at the publishing firm of Cape and Smith, where she convinced her company to take a chance on William Faulkner's *The Sound and the Fury*, which had been rejected by twelve other publishers. She served as the poetry editor of *American Mercury* in 1938 and during World War II was active in the founding of children's writing clubs in the New York City public schools. Throughout her career, she contributed articles and reviews to New York literary magazines. A poet in her own right, Marshall published *No Boundary* (1943), *Other Knowledge* (1957), and *Latest Will* (1969). She wrote the novels *Only the Fear* (1955), *Hall of Mirrors* (1937), and *The Hill Is Level* (1959). The last of these was the story of three generations of mothers and their daughters in a quest for personal emancipation and happiness. *Unknown Artists* was published in 1947; *The Confrontation and Other Stories* appeared in 1972, shortly after Marshall's death; and *Invented a Person: The Personal Record of a Life* was published in 1979. Marshall was a member and director of PEN, the Poetry Society of America, Pen and Brush, the Authors' League, and the MacDowell Colony in Peterborough, New Hampshire. In 1957, a selection of her poems was recorded on the Spoken Arts label.

Marshall's social concern and political activism were perhaps as important to her career as her literary accomplishments. A member of the Post-War World Council from 1940 to 1962, Marshall expressed profound concerns for the fate of humanity in the wake of world war. She was a founder, in 1956, and member to her death of the Committee for a Sane Nuclear Policy. In 1971, she helped to found and was codirector, with nuclear physicist Charles E. Goodell, of the Committee for Nuclear Responsibility, an organization committed to enhancing public awareness of the dangers of nuclear power. This group targeted as especially dangerous the use of nuclear power for generating electricity and the reliance on nuclear weapons as a major component in foreign policy and national security.

Throughout her life, Marshall championed independence of spirit, both literary and political, and she worked consciously and tirelessly in the literary and political realms for the betterment of humanity. Lenore Guinzburg Marshall died on September 23, 1971 at age seventy-two in the Doylestown (Pennsylvania) Hospital after suffering an embolism.

SELECTED WORKS BY LENORE GUINZBURG MARSHALL

The Confrontation and Other Stories (1972); *Hall of Mirrors* (1937); *The Hill Is Level* (1959); *Invented a Person: The Personal Record of a Life* (1979); *Latest Will* (1969); *No Boundary* (1943); *Only the Fear* (1955); *Other Knowledge* (1957); *Unknown Artists* (1947).

BIBLIOGRAPHY
AJYB 73:634; Obituary. *NYTimes*, September 24, 1971, 34:1; *Who's Who in New York* (1960); *WWIAJ* (1938); *WWWIA* 5.

BARBARA L. TISCHLER

MARY, ROSE *see* SHOSHANA, ROSE

MASLOW, SOPHIE (b. 1910?)

Sophie Maslow is one of those modern dance pioneers who "could march from the Worker's Bookstore to the Martha Graham Studio in no time at all, a fact that made it possible to fight the spiritual wars of revolutionary politics and modern dance almost simultaneously" (Graff).

She was a member of the Martha Graham Company from 1931 to 1940, a leader of the New Dance Group, a choreographer and performer in the Dudley-Maslow-Bales Trio, and director of the the Sophie Maslow Dance Company. Maslow is a founding member of the American Dance Festival and the New York City Center Dance Theater. She is the widow of Ben (Max) Blatt, and has one daughter.

Maslow boasts that her father, a Moscow socialist printer, gave her the revolutionary spirit and ability to work with a group. Like many other modern dance pioneers, Maslow attended the Neighborhood Playhouse, that unique cradle of dance that produced the early Graham Company. She also went to Camp Kinderland, a Workmen's Circle camp. One of several Jewish modern dancers who went to and later worked at Camp Kinderland, Maslow jokes that without Camp Kinderland there would have been no modern dance. As a member of the Martha Graham Company from 1931 to 1940, she appeared in such Graham productions as *Primitive Mysteries* (1931), *American Document* (1938), and *Letter to the World* (1940).

The start of Maslow's dance career coincided with the Great Depression and the labor movement of the 1930s. Workers' groups along a wide political spectrum were formed, and dancers joined, in turn forming the Workers Dance League and the New Dance Group. The dancers, often divided by ideology and allegiances, struggled to reconcile revolutionary and bourgeois dance—dance that proclaimed both the workers' movement of the future and dance inherited from traditional forms, even incorporating the new, personalized forms developed by Martha Graham. "Their muscles (and joints) and sinews were trained to

Sophie Maslow is best known as a choreographer of dance pieces that reflect Jewish themes and history. She danced with the Martha Graham Company for nine years and founded the Sophie Maslow Dance Company. Throughout her life she remained committed to choreographing and dancing work that reflected the artistry of folk dance and folk tradition. [New York Public Library]

express power—artistic and social. Clenched fists, aggressive lunges, and themes of hard physical work were common in revolutionary dance" (Graff).

Maslow sees her work as being inspired by a personal heritage rather than by politics or ideology. Her classes at the INTERNATIONAL LADIES GARMENT WORKERS UNION were devoid of political content. "Movement was not a privileged activity." Although dance could and did communicate left-wing ideology, "dance was perceived as a form of expression that could enrich the lives of workers in and of itself," according to Maslow.

Another controversy that emerged in the 1930s among dancers and critics was the source of dance itself. Most staunch left-wingers believed that folk dance was the ultimate source. Maslow, with her lyric ability and strong Graham training, was able to master an idiom that brought the adaptation of folk dancing to the concert stage. This was folk dancing as only a

trained dancer could perform it. Her earliest solo, *Themes from a Slavic People* (Bartok, 1934), was praised in the left-wing press for its lyricism and evocation of folk culture. Also applauded were *Two Songs About Lenin* (1935), inspired by Soviet music, and the film *Three Songs About Lenin*. Stacey Pricket remarks that, "Even if Maslow herself was not drawn to political themes, the evocation of the Soviet Union in her dances touched a responsive chord in the immigrants and new Americans who were heavily represented among the era's radicals." Maslow's work also received praise from Edna Ocko in the *Daily Worker*. She is described as having "quiet strength and power [that] grows more effective with each successive appearance."

With Anna Sokolow, Maslow participated in Workers Dance League concerts in 1934, choreographing *Death of a Tradition* and *Challenge* to the music of Lopatnikoff. In 1936, she choreographed *May Day March*. With Jane Dudley, another member of the Martha Graham Company, she danced *Satiric Suite* in 1937 and *Women of Spain* in 1938. Ever a good Louis Horst student, she too produced a program of preclassic dances in 1941.

The first example of her signature work was produced in 1941, and featured dances to American folk music that depicted the American experience. To the music of Woody Guthrie, Maslow danced the songs of the migratory workers in *Dust Bowl Ballads*. In 1942, one year later, she developed her first masterpiece, *Folksay*, a folk medley based on verses from Carl Sandburg's *The People, Yes*, interspersed with ballads sung by Woody Guthrie.

What better way to heal the wounds of those difficult war years than the celebration of the American spirit that *Folksay* was—and is? Even fifty years after its premiere, college students still know "On Top of Old Smoky" and "Sweet Betsy from Pike" and identify with the free-swinging, open gestures of greeting and romance, and the down-to-earth feeling that fills the work.

Folksay was performed in 1993 at the New Dance Group Gala Concert, held at La Guardia High School of Performing Arts in New York by the Alvin Ailey Repertory Ensemble. Dance critic Edwin Denby praised the work: "The audience . . . is invariably delighted with *Folksay*. They take it perhaps as the reflection of a lovely summer day, and that is what it really is." Margaret Lloyd, one of the earliest dance writers, called it "radiantly outflung, joyous and free . . . the whole is simple and heart-warming and endearing."

If "popular" means "of the common people," Maslow wants her dances to be popular. She would like to see dance have as direct an impact upon as wide an audience as the theater and film do. She believes that the artists are part of, not apart from, everyone. Because folk dancing grows out of the common experience of large groups of people the world over, she dances in folk terms. Her dances follow instinct with folk feeling. They are modern in form, and lean toward theatrical presentation.

After World War II, the destruction of folk traditions, so revered by Russian-Jewish immigrants, finally had an impact. The people were gone, and with them the traditions were vanishing as well. In 1950, Maslow sought out the writings on Russian-Jewish village life by Sholem Aleichem and choreographed *The Village I Knew.* It was first performed at the American Dance Festival in New London, Connecticut, by the New Dance Group. Long before Jerome Robbins amplified those stories into *Fiddler on the Roof,* Maslow built seven episodes, each depicting village life, the celebration of Shabbat, and the exodus following a pogrom. The program notes state: "In Czarist times Jewish communities were frequently uprooted by the authorities and the people driven from their homes. *The Village I Knew* depicts a series of scenes culminating in the despairing, hopeless flight of people once again made homeless."

Maslow restaged *The Village I Knew* for a variety of companies, including the Batsheva in Israel. She relates that the young Israelis were reluctant to dance these memories of the "old country." "Later," she says, "it became easier for them to accept and enjoy them." *Village* was performed in London in 1991 as part of "After the Ark: A Celebration of Jewish Culture in Dance, Music and Song." The festival was staged by Jane Dudley upon her retirement from the London Contemporary Dance School.

Jane Dudley, Sophie Maslow, and Bill Bales formed a unique trio that emerged from the Bennington Summer School and the New Dance Group. The New Dance Group survived the politicized 1930s, the period in which "dance was a weapon in the class struggle," and went on to fulfill its promises to bring dance to the masses. Only a very few members of the group were professional dancers; most were blue-collar workers who came for recreation. When other classes were unaffordable, the New Dance Group charged only fifty cents a month for membership—and threw in a lesson in Marxism. In the 1940s, one could study many styles of modern dance, ballet, "ethnic dance," choreography and, later, notation. There were children's classes as well. Hundreds of people taught, studied, and even slept in the New Dance Group studios. Maslow was an important part of the New Dance Group, teaching children and adults, choreographing and dancing.

The Dudley-Maslow-Bales Trio brought warmth and humor to modern dance in a way that other choreographers could not. Most notably is *The Lonely Ones,* based on William Steig's cartoons and choreographed by Dudley in collaboration with Maslow and Bales. Other Trio works include *Bach Suite* (1942), *As Poor Richard Says* (1943), *Caprichos* (1942), *Furlough,* and *Passional* (choreographed by Dudley). Each member of the Trio contributed dances "for and about the people."

In later years, Maslow formed the Sophie Maslow Dance Company and continued to develop dances on Jewish themes. After *The Village I Knew,* people assumed she was primarily a Jewish choreographer, often forgetting her years in the Graham Company. In 1956, she commemorated the Warsaw Ghetto in *Anniversary* at the 92nd Street YMHA. Like Sokolow, she staged many "Bonds for Israel" Madison Square Garden productions. In 1965, for the annual Hanukkah festival, she produced her version of *The Dybbuk,* which was later staged for the Harkness Ballet (1965). She has also choreographed from the *Book of Ruth* and *Ladino Suite.* Other works include *Manhattan Transfer* (ADF, 1953); *Celebration,* a suite of dances based on Israeli songs (YMHA, 1954); and *Prologue.* (1959).

Maslow continues her active life. Even in her eighties she is often called upon to stage performances in synagogues and Jewish community centers. She travels to many parts of the world. She enjoys the loyal admiration of students, colleagues, and friends. Maslow is a close friend of choreographer Anna Sokolow, with whom she shared a lifetime of performing. *New York Times* dance critic Anna Kisselgoff gave a rave review of the speech Maslow made at Sokolow's April 1995 birthday tribute. As usual, Sophie Maslow was sharing her splendid spirit with her friends.

BIBLIOGRAPHY

Baum, Charlotte, Paula Hyman, and Sonya Michel. *The Jewish Woman in America* (1975); Chujoy, Anatole, and P.W. Manchester. *The Dance Encyclopedia* (1967); Clarke, Mary, and David Vaughan. *The Encyclopedia of Dance & Ballet* (1977); *Dance Magazine* (June 1956, April 1969, April 1985, and April 1991); *Dance Observer* (November 1943 and October 1946); Denby, Edwin. *Dance Writings* (1986); Graff, Ellen. "Dancing Red: Art and Politics." *Studies in Dance History* 5, no. 1 (1994); Harris, Joanna G. "From Tenement to Theater: Three Dance Pioneers." *Judaism* 45, no. 3 (1996); Lloyd, Margaret. *The Borzoi Book of Modern Dance* (1949); Martin, John. *America Dancing* (1936), and *The Dance* (1946), and *John Martin's Book of the Dance* (1963); McDonagh, Don. *The Complete Guide to Modern Dance* (1976);

Maslow, Sophie. Interview by author. Interview by Elizabeth Kendell. Library and Museum of the Performing Arts at Lincoln Center, September 1976; Morgan, Barbara. *Martha Graham* (1941); The New Dance Group. Souvenir Program. June 11, 1993; Schlundt, Christena L. *Tamiris: A Chronicle of Her Dance Career, 1927–1955* (1972); "The Season in Review." *Dance News* (June 1964 and February 1965); *Studies in Dance History 5*, no. 1 (1994): *Of, By, and For the People: Dancing on the Left in the 1930's*. Warren, Larry. *Anna Sokolow: The Rebellious Spirit* (1991).

JOANNA G. HARRIS

MASTBAUM, ETTA WEDELL
(1886–1953)

Etta Wedell Mastbaum was the scion of a prominent nineteenth- and twentieth-century Philadelphia family. A philanthropist, department store executive, art collector, and director of a national chain of motion picture theaters, Mastbaum donated a collection of Rodin sculptures and ephemera to the city of Philadelphia.

She was born Etta Lit Wedell on September 6, 1866, in Philadelphia, the daughter of Rachel Lit and Philip M. Wedell. Mastbaum's mother established a modest dress and millinery shop in Philadelphia in 1891. With her brothers, Samuel and Jacob Lit, the store expanded and became Lit Brothers Department Store, occupying an entire city block in a new building constructed in 1906. The store was sold in 1928, with the Lit family continuing in an executive role. By the 1960s, Lit Brothers was the largest department store chain in the region.

After graduating from high school, Etta attended the Philadelphia Seminary for Women. On January 19, 1904, she married Jules E. Mastbaum, a proprietor of a chain of motion picture theaters stretching from New York to West Virginia. The marriage was a union of two prominent Philadelphians.

Traveling in Europe in 1924, the Mastbaums discovered the work of sculptor Auguste Rodin. After convincing the curator of the Musée Rodin to sell them a small bronze piece, the Mastbaums' interest in Rodin led to many acquisitions of sculptures in bronze and plaster, bas-reliefs, drawings, ephemera, books, and letters written by Rodin. Acquiring items representing each phase of Rodin's career, Etta and Jules Mastbaum sought to create a collection that would provide a comprehensive view of Rodin's life and work. Their collection became second only to Rodin's own donation to France at his death in 1917.

The Mastbaums were given permission by the government of France to amass this collection with the provision that the objects be exhibited in a permanent structure open to the public. Thus, Jules Mastbaum wrote to the commissioners of Philadelphia's Fairmount Park, offering to build a museum and provide funds to maintain the collection as long as it could be housed there. Permission was granted, and Jules Mastbaum commissioned French architect Jacques Gréber, designer of the Benjamin Franklin Parkway, to work with the Philadelphia firm of Paul Cret in designing a beaux-arts structure to house the collection.

While the French Art Commission sought assurance that the collection would be publicly displayed, there was no requirement that the collection itself be owned by the public. But Jules Mastbaum's unexpected death in 1926 led Etta Mastbaum to donate the collection in its entirety to the people of Philadelphia. Dedicated in 1929, the gift by Etta Mastbaum and her daughters Louisette, Margery, and Elizabeth to the city of Philadelphia in honor of Jules E. Mastbaum helped establish that city as the most important center for the study of nineteenth- and twentieth-century French sculpture in the Americas. Prior to the death of Jules Mastbaum, the Mastbaum family funded repairs to Rodin's house and studio at Meudon, and donated a bronze cast of Rodin's *Gates of Hell*. Never cast in the sculptor's lifetime, *Gates of Hell* was considered one of Rodin's most important works. For these efforts, Etta Mastbaum was decorated by the government of France.

After her husband's death, Etta Mastbaum assumed control of his business and financial interests. A director of the Stanley Company of America, she also served her family's interest as an executive of Lit Brothers. As second vice president of the Mastbaum Loan System, a society providing financial assistance to the needy, Etta Mastbaum furthered her husband's memory. She was also active in the Red Cross and in Emergency Aid of Philadelphia and was a member of Philadelphia's Congregation Mikveh Israel.

Etta Mastbaum died in New York City at her residence in the Waldorf Towers on November 1, 1953, at age sixty-seven.

BIBLIOGRAPHY

EJ, s.v. "Lit family"; Obituary. *NYTimes*, October 3, 1953, 17:6; Riopelle, Christopher [associate curator of European painting before 1900, Philadelphia Museum of Art]. Interview with author, June 1996; Tancock, John L. *The Sculpture of . . . Rodin* (1976); Tschirch, John [architectural historian, Preservation Society of Newport County]. Interview with author, June 1996; Watkins, Fridolyn G., comp. *Catalog of the Rodin Museum of Philadelphia*. Rodin Museum of Philadelphia (1929); *WWIAJ* (1928).

DAVID REGO

MAX, PEARL BERNSTEIN (b. 1904)

An administrator and civic activist, Pearl Bernstein Max was born in New York City on September 2, 1904, the daughter of a silk manufacturer, and grew up in a predominantly Jewish neighborhood at 116th Street and Seventh Avenue. After attending Hunter College High School's uptown annex, she won a Regents Scholarship to Barnard College, where she studied history and political science.

After a brief job with the nonpartisan Citizens Union during the mayoral campaign of 1925, she did substitute teaching and volunteer work for the New York League of Women Voters, which eventually hired her to coordinate its municipal affairs committee. For seven years, Max attended city government meetings and briefed committee members, at the same time becoming active in the Women's City Club of New York and the citizens' budget commission. These civic organizations helped her develop expertise on city fiscal affairs and led to her writing a series of articles on the city's budget for the *Sunday World*. When Fiorello LaGuardia became mayor, the League of Women Voters and Women's City Club recommended her to become secretary of the city's Board of Estimate, a post LaGuardia had created. Restless in this post after four years, she became administrator of the Board of Higher Education, coordinating the affairs of the city's four public colleges (Brooklyn, Queens, City, and HUNTER COLLEGE). In 1960, her role in this work led to the establishment of a chancellorship.

Max retired in 1969. Convinced that what was most wonderful about the United States was "the influence that individual citizens and individual citizen groups could have on the way in which government affairs were managed," she has remained active in civic life. Max's husband, Louis William Max, earned a Ph.D. in psychology from Johns Hopkins and was the first Jewish member of the faculty at New York University at University Heights. They have a daughter, Claire Ellen.

BIBLIOGRAPHY

Max, Pearl Bernstein. Oral History Interview. Women's City Club of New York, January 26, 1988; *NYTimes* articles (1939–1966); *UJE*; *WWIAJ* (1938).

ELISABETH ISRAELS PERRY

MAY, ELAINE (b. 1932)

Elaine May, half of one of the most successful American comic teams of the 1950s and 1960s, became one of Hollywood's first important female directors in the 1970s and 1980s. She has often combined her talents for acting and screenwriting with her role as director.

Born in Philadelphia on April 21, 1932, as Elaine Berlin, May spent her early years moving from city to city because of her father's career in show business. Jack Berlin was an actor in the Yiddish theater, and as a child, Elaine made several stage and radio appearances with him. He died when Elaine was eleven, and she moved to Los Angeles with her mother. When she was sixteen, having quit school the previous year, she married Marvin May, but the marriage ended in divorce after a year. One daughter, the actress Jeannie Berlin (she took May's maiden name), was raised by her grandmother.

Elaine May began her career as a part of one of America's most successful comedy teams, Nichols and May. She went on to be one of the first successful female directors in Hollywood. A brilliant actor, she is shown here as the klutzy botanist, Henrietta, in the film A New Leaf. She also directed the film and wrote the screenplay for it.

May studied Method acting and, in the early 1950s, moved to Chicago, where she attended classes at the University of Chicago, though never formally enrolled. There she met Mike Nichols, a young actor, and together they joined Chicago's Compass Players (later the Second City Company), soon forming their own improvisational comedy act. In 1957, a move to New York brought the team greater popularity, and several television appearances gave them a national audience. Their act, which appeared on Broadway from 1960 to 1961 as *An Evening with Mike Nichols and Elaine May*, drew success from its biting social commentary, its perceptive satire of human relationships, and the improvisational capacity of May and Nichols, who never went on with a written script.

May's partnership with Nichols ended in 1961, and she began to write for the stage and screen with little success. She married lyricist Sheldon Harnack later that year, but that marriage quickly ended in divorce. In 1967, she acted in two movies, Carl Reiner's semiautobiographical *Enter Laughing*, based on the Broadway play of the same name, and *Luv*, directed by Clive Donner, where she played opposite Jack Lemmon and Peter Falk.

In 1969, May wrote a one-act comedy play, *Adaptation*, an Off-Broadway hit which she also directed and for which she won a Drama Desk Award. Her first screenplay was *Such Good Friends* (1971), but she became dissatisfied with the production, and the film was released under a pseudonym, Esther Dale. Frustrated with the changes Hollywood studios often forced on writers, May decided that she would have more creative control as writer-director. For her next film, *A New Leaf* (1971), she not only wrote the screenplay and directed, but played the leading role as well. She appeared as the klutzy botanist, Henrietta, who attracts a gold-digging suitor (Walter Matthau) and succeeds in reforming him. Despite her multifaceted involvement in the project, May came into conflict with Paramount when it cut and edited the film. She sued the studio and publicly disowned the film, despite the fact that it was considered an artistic and financial success.

In 1972, May directed her second film, *The Heartbreak Kid*, with a screenplay by Neil Simon. She cast her daughter, Jeannie Berlin, as a stereotypical Jewish American Princess whose husband (Charles Grodin) leaves her three days into their honeymoon for a non-Jewish society girl played by Cybill Shepherd. The movie was one of May's most acclaimed films, with Berlin winning an Academy Award nomination for best supporting actress. May's next project as director and screenwriter was *Mikey and Nicky* (1976), which explores human relationships by examining the fragile friendship between two criminals.

Over the next several years, May worked as a screenwriter with Warren Beatty on *Heaven Can Wait* (1978), for which they won an Oscar nomination, and made uncredited contributions to the screenplays for *Reds* (1981) and *Tootsie* (1982). In 1987, she directed *Ishtar*, a spoof in which Warren Beatty and Dustin Hoffman, as untalented singer-songwriters booked by a nightclub in Morocco, find themselves unwitting players in a game of Middle Eastern espionage. The film, which received much advance publicity, suffered from several delays in release and was not a critical or financial success.

May has been a groundbreaker as a woman director, and for several years she remained one of the few women Hollywood studios would hire to direct. May, however, rejected the notion that being a woman shaped her approach to filmmaking. "Directing is a way of looking at something and then communicating it," she said in 1972. "It would be hideous to think that either sex took a script and in any way pushed it toward any point of view other than the author's. I don't think it's important whether you're a man, a woman or a chair." Reflecting her origins as a stand-up comic, May developed an improvisational film style. Eschewing rigid direction, she has preferred to give actors maximum space to invent, often shooting several takes to allow them to try different approaches to the scene.

Besides directing, May has also continued to act, appearing in *California Suite* (1978) and *In the Spirit* (1990). On the stage, she reunited with her former partner Mike Nichols in a production of *Who's Afraid of Virginia Woolf?* (1980). During the 1990s she has concentrated on writing, including a collaboration with Woody Allen and David Mamet on *Death Defying Acts*, a trio of one-act plays that appeared Off Broadway. She worked again with Nichols in 1994, when she revised the screenplay for his film *Wolf*, and in 1996, as the screenwriter for *The Birdcage*, the success of which underscored the endurance of their chemistry as a comedy team.

As a comic, writer, and director, May is distinguished by the intellectual sophistication of her satire and the independence and artistic integrity of her work. Jewishness has often provided the material for her comedy, as well as being a source for some of the identity conflicts of her characters. But even when employing this ethnic framework, May has been able to explore essentially human experiences, an approach that has ensured her wide influence as a creative artist.

BIBLIOGRAPHY

Biskind, Peter. "Inside Ishtar." *American Film* 12 (May 1987): 20–27; *Dictionary of Literary Biography* 44: 250–254; *NYTimes Magazine* (May 27, 1984): 42; Smith, Sharon. *Women Who Make Movies* (1975); *Time* (March 20, 1972): 92–93.

ERIC L. GOLDSTEIN

MAY, IRMA (b. 1899)

The years following World War I were a perilous time for the Jews of Eastern Europe. In addition to the devastation caused by the war, the entire continent experienced severe economic depression a decade before the United States. Anti-Semitism grew in the region as Jews were held responsible by local populations for causing the economic downturn. But in truth, the Jews suffered disproportionately from the effects of the depression. With immigration to the United States and other nations of the West severely restricted, the Jews of Poland, Russia, Lithuania, Estonia, Latvia, and surrounding nations faced unemployment, famine, and death.

One activist who had a considerable impact on her fellow Jews in this time of crisis was Irma May (also known as Irma May Abramowicz and Irma Weitzenkorn). She was born in Lemberg, Poland, on June 10, 1899, and came to the United States in 1920. Her own foray into activism on behalf of the Jews of Eastern Europe was motivated by personal tragedy. Shortly after her arrival in the United States, her fiancé, Bernard Cantor of Columbia University, was killed while undertaking relief work in the Ukraine.

Irma May's first public appeal was to benefit Jewish students and professors in Eastern Europe. Speaking at Columbia with Rabbi Stephen Wise on December 16, 1920, May documented the continued anti-Semitism in that region. Professors were being dismissed from Polish universities, and Jewish students were no longer being admitted to institutions of higher learning in Poland, Hungary, and Galicia. A committee was formed from the Columbia University Relief Council to raise funds for both the professors and students.

As the 1920s progressed, the situation in Eastern Europe continued to deteriorate for the Jewish population while immigration restrictions in Western nations remained rigid. Unemployment was rampant, and most industries refused to hire Jews. Housing was in short supply; food was scarce, and many faced starvation. Schools and hospitals began to close. Suicides, a rarity in the Jewish community, became more frequent, especially among those unable to provide for their families. Irma May's major contributions to the cause of Eastern European Jewry came during this difficult period. Working as the special commissioner for Eastern Europe for the United Jewish Campaign, she traveled to the region and made detailed written reports on the conditions of the Jews to David A. Brown, the national chairman.

After her return from her journeys, May made a number of appearances in New York to raise funds for the Jews of Eastern Europe. Her efforts met with great success. Her appearance before the Rabbinate of Greater New York on April 13, 1926, resulted in the group passing a resolution for the Jews of New York to raise six million dollars for their coreligionists. In pursuit of this goal, May's eloquent speaking helped raise an initial pledge of $3,700,000 at a series of dinners held on April 26, 1926, by the United Jewish Campaign.

Irma May was a pioneer in American Jewish philanthropy. Her reports from Eastern Europe motivated social action, while her political and speaking skills moved both the New York and larger Jewish community.

BIBLIOGRAPHY

"Arrives with Plea for Starving Jews." *NYTimes*, April 8, 1926, 4; "Depicts Jews' Plight in Eastern Europe." *NYTimes*, April 14, 1926, 4; "Gifts of $3,700,000 Open Jewish Drive." *NYTimes*, April 26, 1926, 1; "Jewish Plea at Columbia." *NYTimes*, December 17, 1920, 24; "The Jews of Poland Face Period of Want." *NYTimes*, March 26, sec. 9, p. 8; "To Tell Relief Needs." *NYTimes*, April 6, 1926, 4; *WWIAJ* (1926, 1928).

JEROME S. LEGGE, JR.

McCLUSKEY, ELLEN LEHMAN (1914–1984)

Ellen Lehman McCluskey, a firm believer that quality design is a result of close communication between architect and interior designer, built her own design firm into a business with national, international, and professional respect. She worked meticulously and with great energy on each project, as well as for the profession and for the organizations with which she was involved. She was a strong advocate of state legislation to register interior designers and to establish fee structures and educational requirements, thereby creating recognition for the breadth of knowledge and familiarity with the other construction professions and materials necessary to be an interior designer.

Ellen Lehman McCluskey was born in 1914, in New York City, where she lived her entire life. The daughter of Allan Lehman, an investment banker and community leader from a prominent Jewish family, and Evelyn (Schiffer) Lehman, she received a B.A. from Vassar College (1934), an M.A. from Columbia University (1936), and studied at the New York School of Interior Design (1936–1937). She was an associate interior decorator with Adele Dewey (1937–1938), Franklin Hughes (1938–1942), and Ruth Warburton Kaufman (1942–1943), all of whom were innovators in the field. Influences on her choice of profession and design sensibilities began, she said, when she traveled to Europe as a child with her mother, developing an appreciation for the arts from the great museums, palaces, and hotels she visted.

She established Ellen Lehman McCluskey Associates in 1948 and was principal of the firm and its retail showroom until her death on October 21, 1984. The firm's work, which included interior and furniture designs for private homes, hotel and restaurants chains, and corporate clients, was widely recognized and published in design magazines in the United States and Europe. Her work was praised for its innovative design solutions, which were responsive to the local climate, cultures, and traditions, as well as the particular needs of each client.

She married Richard McCluskey in 1942 and had three children, Maureen, Sharon, and Orin. She was divorced from McCluskey in 1952 and married Preston Long in 1958. She divorced Long in 1971.

Together with her brother, Orin Lehman, she founded Just One Break, a foundation providing vocational training and placement for the physically handicapped. She also designed its annual ball. Her other community service activities included working on the acquisitions committee and benefit auctions for the Cooper-Hewitt Museum, serving as chair of the American Society of Interior Designers Education Foundation, and working with the National Committee on Historic Preservation.

Her major projects included the Plaza, Waldorf-Astoria, and Regency hotels (New York); the Charlotte City Club (North Carolina); the Light House Club (British West Indies); the New York Infirmary, with the architecture firm of Skidmore, Owings & Merrill; Washington's Watergate Complex; Paradise Island and Britannia hotels (Nassau); Loew's Monte Carlo Hotel; the New York Life Insurance Company Building; and the Parker House (Boston). Her clients included McGraw-Hill, Allied Chemical Corporation, United Airlines, Howard Johnson's, and Prudential Lines. McCluskey was a fellow of the American Institute of Interior Designers, and its New York City chapter president. She was featured in National Hotel Exhibitions and participated on panel discussions on the "modern home."

Ellen Lehman McCluskey's work developed and maintained an integrity that, never blindly following fashion trends, developed a sense of place, scale, function, comfort, and hospitality in each project. Her professionalism made her a leader in the field for several decades. While her work bears her signature, she never sacrificed the physical context or a client's needs and wishes in producing her final designs. She set an example for all design professionals who strive to create real, human-scale living environments.

BIBLIOGRAPHY

Blackwell, Ed, ed. *Celebrity Register.* 3d ed. (1973); "Decorating Studio Opens." *NYTimes*, May 25, 1949, 39:1; McCluskey, Ellen Lehman. *Interior Design* magazine (April 1960–September 1981 passim), and *Interiors* magazine (May 1955-October 1982 passim); Olin, Norma Ireland. *Index to Women of the World from Ancient to Modern Times: Biographies and Portraits* (1970); "Principality of Monaco." *NYTimes*, February 24, 1974, sec. 8, 10:6; *Who's Who in America* (1978–1984); *The Women's Book of World Records and Achievements* (1979); *WWWIA* 8.

MIRIAM TUCHMAN

MEDNICK, MARTHA TAMARA SCHUCH (b. 1929)

One of the most influential women in the development of the psychology of women is Martha Mednick. She was born on March 31, 1929, in New York City of working-class immigrant parents who "had an almost mystical belief in the power of education to change the condition of life." She described her years through high school as dominated by Hebrew/Yiddish classes and a commitment to the Labor Zionist Youth Movement. She also described herself and both her parents as committed activists.

She completed her undergraduate education at the City College of New York (then a free university), which, although a primarily male engineering school, permitted a few women to enroll in its School of Education. Excited by her psychology classes, she obtained a master's degree in school psychology in order to have a career with which to support herself. In 1952, she joined her husband, Sarnoff Mednick (who later became an important contributor to clinical psychology), at Northwestern University, where he was a graduate student. She obtained her Ph.D. from Northwestern in clinical psychology in 1955.

Mednick's autobiography discusses the extreme sexism in graduate school at that time. For example, during the orientation of the first-year graduate class, the head of the department informed them "that the department did not mind admitting women even though they were not going to use their training." Sexism was even more blatant in her clinical setting. And, of course, few women mentors were available.

After receiving her Ph.D., Mednick moved with her husband to Boston, where he had a job at Harvard. She made a number of moves related to his career during the next few years, had two daughters, and worked at "whatever came up." She did some collaborative work with him—first on a personality textbook and then on the development of a measure of creative thinking. By the time of their divorce in 1964, Mednick was affiliated with the Institute for Social Research at the University of Michigan (tenured positions were unavailable to women in the psychology department there at that time). She moved to Washington, D.C., to become a member of the psychology department of Howard University, was appointed a full professor in 1971, and remained there until her retirement in 1995.

Mednick has been very important as a mentor as well as a pioneer in the psychology of women. In 1972, she coedited with Sandra Tangri a special issue of the *Journal of Social Issues* entitled "New Perspectives on Women," which was later expanded into the book *Women and Achievement* (1975). She chaired the Ad-Hoc Committee on Women in Psychology of the American Psychological Association whose work culminated in the formation of a division on the psychology of women in 1973. She served as president of that division (1976–1977) as well as president of the Society for the Psychological Study of Social Issues from 1980 to 1982. Her research has focused on race, class, and sex issues in the psychology of achievement. Many of these studies have been published with students from Howard University, and a list of these students reads like a *Who's Who* of African-American women psychologists.

Mednick was also important in facilitating contact between American and Israeli feminist psychologists. Her "Social Change and Sex Role Inertia: The Case of the Kibbutz" debunked the myth of sexual equality on kibbutzim. With Marilyn Safir, an American-born Israeli who is in the Department of Psychology at the University of Haifa, she organized the first international, interdisciplinary conference on women at Haifa University in December 1981. The book of papers from this conference, *Women's Worlds*, was particularly important because it combined for the first time research by American, Jewish Israeli, Palestinian, and Arab women scholars.

SELECTED WORKS BY MARTHA TAMARA SCHUCH MEDNICK

"Autobiography." In *Models of Achievement: Reflections of Eminent Women in Psychology*. Vol. 2, edited by Agnes N. O'Connell and Nancy F. Russo (1988): 245–259; "New Perspectives on Women," editor, with Sandra S. Tangri. Special issue of *The Journal of Social Issues* 28, no. 2 (1972); "Social Change and Sex Role Inertia: The Case of the Kibbutz." In *Women and Achievement: Social and Motivational Analyses*, edited by Martha T.S. Mednick, Sandra S. Tangri, and Lois W. Hoffman (1975); *Women's Worlds: From the New Scholarship*, edited with Marilyn P. Safir, Dafna Izraeli, and Jessie Bernard (1985).

BIBLIOGRAPHY

Stevens, Gwendolyn, and Sheldon Gardner. *The Women of Psychology*. Vol. 2 (1982).

RHODA K. UNGER

MEIR, GOLDA (1898–1978)

In the pantheon of illustrious national leaders there exists an even more elite subgroup, female heads of state, among whom stands one Jewish woman: Golda Meir, the prime minister of Israel from 1969 to 1973. Pioneer, visionary, risk-taker, indefatigable fund-raiser, eloquent advocate, she was an activist of the first order, one of the founders of the Jewish state, a woman whose life story is as central to the mythos of modern Zionism as that of Theodor Herzl, Chaim Weizmann, and David Ben-Gurion. Presidents and kings found her willfulness charming, while her grandmotherly appearance and plain-spoken personal style endeared her to ordinary people around the world. In her time, Golda was as admired as Queen Elizabeth and as well known by her first name as Madonna is today. Yet, for all her accomplishments and fame, Golda Meir—like Indira Gandhi of India and Margaret Thatcher of Great Britain—was no particular friend of women. She was, in current parlance, a "queen bee," a woman who climbs to the top, then pulls the ladder up behind her. She did not wield the prerogatives of power to address women's special needs, to promote other women, or to advance women's status in the public sphere. The fact is that at the end of her tenure her Israeli sisters were no better off than they had been before she took office. That a notable female can be simultaneously an inspiration and a disappointment, a source of great pride and of deep frustration, is the unique contribution of the queen bee to women's history in general, and of Golda Meir to Jewish women's history in particular.

Since she was born in Russia and died in Israel, it is important to list the half dozen reasons that entitle her to inclusion in an American encyclopedia: Her formative years were spent in Milwaukee and Denver; she became a familiar presence here as she criss-crossed the country to plead Israel's case to American Jews and the U.S. Government; she spoke Hebrew with such an atrocious American accent that her link to us was obvious; when discussing her colleagues in the fledgling Israeli government, she referred to herself as "the 'American' among us"; in the 1970s, she was voted the Most Admired Woman in America at the same time as she was feminism's poster girl, the face above the caption "But can she type?" Finally, Golda Meir has meaning in an American context because, to this very day, some American Jews cite her success as proof that gender equality is a fait accompli in Jewish life. Needless to say, there is more to the story.

She was born on May 3, 1898, in Kiev, Ukraine. Her father, Moshe Mabovitch, a skilled carpenter, and her mother, Blume Naidtich, named her for her maternal great-grandmother, a domineering matriarch who lived to be ninety-four and who always took salt instead of sugar in her tea to remember the bitterness of the Jewish Diaspora. Golda Meir was pleased with this legacy. She identified most, she said, with her "tenacious," "intransigent" relatives, especially her paternal grandfather, who was kidnapped at age thirteen into the czar's army but resisted conversion to Christianity and refused to eat *traif* [nonkosher food].

The Maboviches kept kosher, observed Jewish holidays, and shared traditional Sabbath meals with their extended family—all later lost in the Holocaust. Meir remembered everyone sitting around the table singing Hebrew songs, yet she described growing up in "a not particularly religious household." She vividly recalled her early childhood as a time of abject poverty and terrifying progroms, and she attributed her lifelong commitment to Jewish security to her memories of anti-Semitic violence and the experience of hiding from the Cossacks. She also remembered her sister Sheyna, nine years her senior, risking her life to attend Labor Zionist meetings, and her sister Zipke, the baby, getting the lion's share of their meager gruel. In 1903, Moshe left for America; three years later, he sent for his family and settled them in a two-room flat in the poor Jewish section of Milwaukee. Golda was eight years old.

On the surface, her life story seems to follow the classic immigrant trajectory toward her rendezvous with destiny. But behind the facts lie years of searing family tensions, conflicts between her goals and others' expectations of her, and painful inner struggles that might have fueled a feminist consciousness had she not interpreted them as problems unique to her.

At fourteen, she graduated from the Fourth Street Elementary School as class valedictorian but had to fight her parents for the right to go to high school. She wanted to be a teacher; they wanted her to find a husband. "It doesn't pay to be too clever," warned her father. "Men don't like smart girls." Defying him, she enrolled in Milwaukee's North Division High School and took after-school jobs to pay her expenses. Still, the arguments raged.

Fed up, Golda ran away to live with her sister and brother-in-law in Denver, where she attended school and spent her evenings listening to Shayna's radical friends—anarchists, Socialist Zionists, and Labor Zionists whose debates helped refine Golda's political philosophy. She also fell in love with Morris Meyerson, a quiet, bespectacled sign-painter who loved poetry and music and exposed her to lectures on literature and history but who never fully shared her Zionist passion. A letter of apology from her parents allowed her to return home after a year, and in 1916 she graduated from high school and registered for a three-year program at the Milwaukee Normal School, a teachers' training college. Three times a week, she taught children reading, writing, and history at a *folkshule*, a Yiddish school at the Jewish Center of Milwaukee, but her real teaching took place on street corners—much to her father's distress—where she lectured on Labor Zionism.

In November 1917, Britain issued the Balfour Declaration supporting "the establishment in Palestine of a National Home for the Jewish people." A month later, on Christmas Eve, Golda Mabovitch married Morris Meyerson on the condition that they would immigrate to Palestine and live on a kibbutz. (A decade before her, the first kibbutz was created by a woman, Manya Shohat.) They chose Merhavia in the Emek, an area of festering malarial swamps, with, as she put it, "no orchards, no meadows, no flowers, nothing." But when they arrived in 1921, the admission committee rejected them, saying the kibbutz was not ready for married couples. Stunned, they applied again and were granted a probationary residency during which Golda picked almonds and planted saplings, Morris worked the fields, and the kibbutz members became enamored of Morris's phonograph and classical records. This time, they were accepted.

Before long, she became a model kibutznik and such an expert on breeding and feeding chickens that

*Including a prime minister of Israel in a book on American women might be questioned.
But seen here playing the Statue of Liberty in the Poale Zion Pageant in Milwaukee, you know
that Golda Mabovitch is a Wisconsin girl in her roots. [American Jewish Historical Society]*

the kibbutz sent her to Haifa for a management course and later chose her as its representative to the Histadrut [General Federation of Labor].

While Golda was flourishing, Morris, who had contracted malaria, felt useless and disconsolate. He flatly refused to have children unless she agreed to rear them in a conventional family setting. After two and a half years ("the happiest of my life"), they left Merhavia for Jerusalem, where Golda—giving birth to a son, Menachem, in 1924, and a daughter, Sarah, in 1926—valiantly tried to be a traditional wife and mother amid a life of grinding poverty. Morris worked as a bookkeeper for the Histadrut Building Office, which didn't always pay its salaries, and Golda scrimped and bartered to make ends meet. In exchange for Menachem's nursery school fees, she did the school's laundry by hand, not minding the work but longing for labor with a Zionist purpose and des-

perate for meaningful community. Now it was her turn to feel useless and disconsolate.

One day in 1928, she ran into an old friend, David Remez, who offered her the job of secretary of Histadrut 's Council for Women Workers. Knowing Morris would never approve, she nonetheless took the job and moved to Tel Aviv with her children and her sister. Morris visited on weekends but, in essence, their marriage was over. The separation became final ten years later—though they were never legally divorced—yet, until Morris's death in 1951, Golda would continue to feel guilty "because I couldn't be the wife he wanted and should have had." She would also worry that she had not done enough for her children. "I was always rushing from one place to another—to work, home, to a meeting, to take Menachem to a music lesson, to keep a doctor's appointment with Sarah, to shop, to cook, to work and back home again. And still to this day," she wrote at age seventy-seven, "I am not sure that I didn't harm the children or neglect them." At the same time, she acknowledged, "There is a type of woman who cannot let her husband and children narrow her horizons."

Moving quickly up the ranks, she became a member of the Executive Committee of the Histadrut in 1934 and head of its political department two years later. During World War II, she held several key posts in the World Zionist Organization and in the Jewish Agency, the highest Jewish authority in British-administered Palestine, which functioned as the government of the *yishuv* [Jewish settlement]. When the male leadership was arrested for smuggling in refugees, she served as acting head of the agency, and until the end of the mandate she was its spokesperson in dealings with the British.

With the establishment of the State of Israel in 1948, it became clear that armed confrontation with the Arabs was inevitable. A vast amount of money was needed to equip the armed forces. Because she spoke perfect English, Golda volunteered to go to the United States to solicit twenty-five million dollars from the American Jewish community. Where others had tried and failed, she succeeded in communicating both a compelling urgency and a sense of shared mission. She raised not twenty-five but fifty million dollars.

Her courage took many forms. In May 1948, with five Arab armies massed on Israel's borders, Golda disguised herself as a Moslem woman and crossed into Trans-Jordan for a secret meeting with King Abdullah, to try to persuade him to stay out of the war. Abdullah, King Hussein's congenial grandfather, with whom she'd already had two clandestine encounters, received her with respect but remained unresponsive to her pleas.

When Israel was just four days old and in the thick of battle, Golda returned to the United States to do more fund-raising for the war effort. A month later, Foreign Minister Moshe Sharett appointed her ambassador to the U.S.S.R.—sweet revenge for the little girl once menaced by the Cossacks and a profound thrill for Soviet Jews who, at great peril to themselves, thronged the Moscow synagogue on Rosh Hashanah to greet her. In 1949, she was elected to the Knesset [Israeli parliament] and appointed by Prime Minister David Ben-Gurion to be the minister of labor, in charge of finding jobs and housing for the nearly seven hundred thousand immigrants who streamed into the country between May 1948 and the end of 1951.

Golda held the Labor portfolio for seven years. She said she would have liked to keep it forever, but in 1956, Ben-Gurion made her foreign minister, the second-highest position in the government. He also insisted she adopt a Hebrew-sounding surname to better represent her Hebrew-speaking nation; thus did Meyerson became Meir. The only female foreign minister in the world, Golda Meir was also the only foreign minister who had no use for formalities, who flew tourist class, who shocked hotel staffs by hand-washing her own underwear and shining her own shoes, and who entertained foreign dignitaries in her kitchen, in an apron, serving them her homemade pastry along with a stern lecture on Israel's security. She also was a foreign minister who refused to obey the color line in Rhodesia, inspiring a full complement of dignitaries to follow suit, and whose proudest accomplishment was the export of Israeli technical and agricultural expertise to the African nations.

In 1966, she decided to retire from government; Abba Eban would take over her post. She was sixty-eight years old, ready to become a full-time grandmother, eager to do more reading, listen to music, bake, visit friends, slow down. A year earlier, she'd been diagnosed with lymphoma, a condition she insisted upon keeping secret and for which she was treated at Hadassah Hospital in the dead of night.

Although Meir considered her public career at an end, she was persuaded to become secretary general of Mapai, her political party, and, in 1967, secretary of the unified Labor Party. Then suddenly, in February 1969, Prime Minister Levi Eshkol died of a heart attack and, to avoid a power struggle between Moshe Dayan and Yigal Allon, the party prevailed upon her to become Israel's leader. Retirement would have to wait.

She might have enjoyed more than four years in power had not Egypt and Syria launched a surprise attack on October 6, 1973, to start the Yom Kippur War. Though Israeli forces were able to regain the offensive, they suffered more than twenty-seven hundred casualties, a profound blow to a small country, and especially to Jews, who measure their collective survival one life at a time. Until the day she died, Meir regretted that she had not followed her instincts to call up the reserves days earlier rather than heeding the advice of military intelligence experts who saw no reason to mobilize. Gripped by a kind of national trauma, the public turned against her; parents of the dead shouted at her in the streets and blamed her and Defense Minister Dayan for the devastating losses. The Labor Party suffered a fatal setback and, on June 4, 1974, unable to form a government, Golda Meir resigned.

For all her grief and remorse over the Yom Kippur War, for all the humiliation and pain of her

Strong, proud, defiant *are three of the words that are often used to describe Golda Meir.*
But she also had a sense of humor. A probably apocryphal but nonetheless typical story
has President Nixon telling her that he would trade any three American generals
for General Moshe Dayan. "Okay," she says, "I'll take General Motors,
General Electric, and General Dynamics." [YIVO Institute]

people's rejection of her, she was nonetheless able in her final years to evolve into an elder statesman and beloved public citizen, a woman whom bus drivers insisted on taking to her front door and whom organizations clamored to honor. In time, her image regained its luster, and her reputation as a philosopher-comedian entered the realm of legend.

As a politician and Jewish nationalist, Meir was consistent, strong in her resolve, and undisturbed by nuance or self-doubts. The Zionist cause to her was a moral, historical, and political imperative. Though she was eager to make peace with "the Arabs," and often begged for Arab recognition and Arab partners, her refusal to acknowledge the existence of "Palestinians" or, consequently, Palestinian suffering, was for many years a stumbling block to progress.

As a woman, on the other hand, Meir was a study in contradictions. Though her public persona was almost neuter, she was reputed to have had many lovers for many years. Foremost among them were David Remez, Israel's minister of transport and then of education, and by some accounts the true passion of her life; and Zalman Shazar, one of the preeminent architects of the Jewish state and eventually its president. Though she exhibited stereotypically feminine attributes—the cooking, the warmth and emotionality, the matronly appearance—those who knew her never fail to mention her toughness.

"To survive Israeli politics she had to become tough, she had no choice; she must have gone through hell to get where she did," says Colette Avital, who began her career in Israel's foreign ministry under Meir's tenure and is now one of her nation's top-ranking foreign service officers and its most senior woman. Avital remembers her old boss as someone who could be rigid and hot-tempered, someone who "disliked women, never really helped women."

Jew, Zionist, Israeli—these were the identities that defined Golda Meir's life and galvanized her loyalties while the female aspect of her being remained devoid of consciousness or commitment. ("Whether women are better than men I cannot say," she once wrote, "but I can say they are certainly no worse.") She acknowledged the important role women played in the founding of the State of Israel but was unwilling to bond in solidarity with her sex. Rather than recognize in her life experience the untenable pressures that plague virtually all achieving women, she attributed her strains and sacrifices to her private feminine or maternal failures, faulting her own aspirations, her love of political work, and her burning ambitions for the Jewish state. As prime minister, she did not focus on child care policy or concern herself with the problems of working women or use her influence to argue for equal gender arrangements in the home or to encourage more women to run for public office. The conflicts that tore her apart helped her to sympathize passively with the "heavy double burden" of working mothers but did not inspire her to politicize that sympathy and identify with feminist goals. In fact, she

"Whether women are better than men I cannot say," Golda Meir once wrote, "but I can say they are certainly no worse." She is shown here with RUTH GRUBER, *another woman known for being "the first" in several fields, in a photograph taken in the late 1960s. [Photo courtesy of Ruth Gruber]*

seemed to go out of her way to criticize feminism and distort the tenets of the women's movement.

She did, however, have her epiphanic moments. When Israel was experiencing an epidemic of violent rapes and someone at a cabinet meeting suggested women be put under curfew until the rapists were caught, Meir shot back, "Men are committing the rapes. Let *them* be put under curfew." When Ben-Gurion first made her a minister in his cabinet, the religious bloc objected to the idea of a woman ruling over men, though they finally acquiesced on the grounds that Deborah, the biblical judge, had been acceptable to God. However, when Meir was a candidate for mayor of Tel Aviv, the religious objections defeated her, to her everlasting fury. When Ben-Gurion described her as "the only man" in his cabinet, Golda was amused that he thought "this was the greatest possible compliment that could be paid to a woman. I very much doubt that any man would have been flattered if I had said about him that he was the only woman in the government!" She noticed the disparity but seemed to miss the larger point. She once said in a speech to the UN that the world might be better off if political leaders allowed themselves to "feel more and think less." Yet she did not deduce that having more women in power might add the missing component to public life.

Just as some Jews choose not to be Jewish-identified because they think they have the option to behave as if peoplehood doesn't matter, Golda Meir chose not to be woman-identified and behaved as if gender doesn't matter. But, of course, when one is Jewish and female, both facts matter. She died on December 8, 1978, at age eighty, a titan of modern Zionism, a history-making national leader, one of the most accomplished women of the twentieth century—still feeling guilty about falling short as a wife and mother.

SELECTED WORKS BY GOLDA MEIR

A Land of Our Own: An Oral Autobiography, edited by Marie Syrkin (1973); *My Life* (1975); *This Is Our Strength*, edited by Henry M. Christman (1962).

BIBLIOGRAPHY

Agress, Eliyahu. *Golda Meir: Portrait of a Prime Minister* (1969); Ander, Richard. *Golda Meir: A Leader in Peace and War* (1990); Ben-Gurion, David. *Memoirs* (1970); Davidson, Margaret. *The Golda Meir Story* (1981); Mann, Peggy. *Golda: The Life of Israel's Prime Minister* (1972); Martin, Ralph G. *Golda: Golda Meir—The Romantic Years* (1988); *A Woman Called Golda*. Feature film. Paramount Pictures (1982).

LETTY COTTIN POGREBIN

MELAMED, DEBORAH MARCUS (1892–1954)

Deborah Marcus Melamed wished that Jewish ceremonies, customs, and symbols would enthrall the hearts of women. She believed that Jewish women could mold Jewish practices and invest them with meaning, and that in doing so they would contribute to the preservation of Judaism. With this hope in mind, as well as a sincere desire to fulfill the wishes of her colleague, MATHILDE SCHECHTER, founder of the National Women's League of the United Synagogue of America now the WOMEN'S LEAGUE FOR CONSERVATIVE JUDAISM, Melamed wrote *The Three Pillars* (1927). This book contained clear descriptions of those observances with which she thought all Jewish women should be familiar. She added interpretive words, desiring to instill in other women the love she felt for Jewish tradition. The popularity of *The Three Pillars* is reflected in the fact that it has been reprinted nine times. This volume also became the cornerstone of the educational philosophy of the National Women's League, an organization established within the Conservative Movement with the purpose of improving the souls of women by inducing them to recognize the greatness of Jewish life and literature. Melamed was vice president of this organization from 1920 to 1930 or 1932.

Deborah Marcus Melamed was born in New York City on July 21, 1892. She was the daughter of Hannah Rebecca (Kimhi) and Abraham Marcus, a doctor. After receiving an education in classics at HUNTER COLLEGE, she became a high school Latin instructor. She moved to Philadelphia in 1915, when she married Raphael Hai Melamed, a graduate of the Jewish Theological Seminary (1909), who was completing his Ph.D. at Dropsie College. They shared a love for ancient languages: Raphael Melamed wrote his Ph.D. dissertation on the Targum to Canticles, an Aramaic commentary on the Song of Songs, and Deborah Melamed became a fellow in Semitic languages at Dropsie College (1915–1917). When the Melameds finally settled in New Jersey in 1923 and Raphael Melamed took a position as the rabbi of the B'nai Israel Congregation in Elizabeth, Deborah Melamed began her work in the New Jersey public schools. She became the supervisor of foreign languages in the Elizabeth public schools, a position she held until 1954. However, her full-time career did not preclude time spent working for the Jewish community. Melamed helped to found the Elizabeth chapter of HADASSAH and played an active role in the National Women's League for many years.

Deborah Marcus Melamed died at age sixty-two on November 4, 1954. She is remembered as a woman able to fulfill her responsibilities as a mother of two children, Judith Tamar and David Joseph, while maintaining a career and contributing to the preservation of the Jewish community.

BIBLIOGRAPHY

Hadassah Archives, NYC and Elizabeth, N.J.; Melamed, Deborah M. *The Three Pillars* (1927); Obituary. *NYTimes*, November 4, 1954, 31:4; Schorsch, Ismar. "A Marriage Made in Heaven." *Outlook* 63 (1993): 15+; National Women's League. *They Dared to Dream: A History of National Women's League, 1918–1968* (1967); Women's League of the United Synagogue of America. *Seventy Five Years of Vision and Voluntarism* (1992); *WWIAJ* (1938).

MARJORIE LEHMAN

MELTON, FLORENCE ZACKS (b. 1911)

Philanthropist and visionary innovator, a lay leader for over fifty years, Florence Zacks Melton has helped build institutions that have improved the quality and broadened the scope of Jewish education throughout North America. Together with her family, she has also been cited for outstanding contributions to the welfare of the Jewish people in Israel, and, in particular, to the support of the Hebrew University.

Born on November 11, 1911, in Philadelphia, Pennsylvania, Florence Melton credits her immigrant *bubbe* [grandmother] who sparked her soul with Jewish values and taught her *menshlikhkayt* [being a decent person]. Music was a vital part of her early life, and she studied music, art, and ballet. She married Aaron Zacks in 1930. They had two sons, Gordon Zacks, who has distinguished himself on a national level through his activities in the United Jewish Appeal, the American Israel Public Affairs Committee (AIPAC), and many other organizations, and Barry, a restaurateur who died in 1990.

In 1946, she and her husband founded the R.G. Barry Corporation, the largest manufacturing company for soled slippers in the world. Her invention of the use of foam in footwear revolutionized the industry, and she continues to serve as a consultant for project development and design. Her love and concern for children have motivated much of her career in the business world as well as her involvement in Jewish education. She established a foundation to provide prostheses for children whose parents could not afford to purchase them. For many years she was a leader in her community, and was the first woman invited to serve on the Board of the Huntington National Bank. She also started the first program for Meals on Wheels in Columbus, Ohio.

Aaron Zacks died in 1965. In 1968, Florence married Samuel Mendel Melton, an engineer who built a highly successful business and became a community leader in Columbus with a special mission for Jewish education. In 1959, he had endowed the Melton Center for Research in Jewish Education at the Jewish Theological Seminary of America.

Melton served as a founding member of CAJE in 1975 and continues to support this effort. She is the creator of Columbus's Discovery Program, which has found innovative ways to keep children involved in Jewish education through their high school years. She is a distinguished member of the Commission on Jewish Education in North America.

Melton is best known for having created and supported the successful community-based two-year program known as the Florence Melton Adult Mini School for adult learners. The program operates in over twenty-five communities in the United States, Canada, and Australia. Its graduates receive certificates from the Hebrew University's Melton Centre, which was responsible for developing the unique curriculum. She is currently working on the establishment of Reading Corners in the Jewish community centers of Boca Raton and Columbus.

In recognition of her many achievements and great contributions, Florence Melton has received many honors and awards from B'nai B'rith, including the Janusz Korczak Humanitarian Award from Kent State University. In 1991, she was awarded an honorary Ph.D. from the Hebrew University in Jerusalem, and the degree of Doctor of Humane Letters, *honoris causa*, from the Jewish Theological Seminary of America.

SYLVIA C. ETTENBERG

MENKEN, ADAH ISAACS (1835–1868)

Internationally famous for her starring role in the equestrian melodrama *Mazeppa*, in which she was stripped on stage to a flesh-colored body stocking, lashed to the back of the "wild horse of Tartary," and sent flying on a narrow ramp above the theater, Adah Isaacs Menken consistently defied social mores. She cropped her black hair and smoked cigarettes, and publicly disparaged conventional married life. Menken represented an early example of the cult of personality, blurring her private life with her public persona. Whether riding in a gaudy carriage through

Adah Isaacs Menken became famous when she appeared "nude" while strapped to a horse in the melodrama Mazeppa *(she was actually wearing a flesh-colored bodystocking). A shameless self-promoter, there is dispute as to whether she was born into Judaism or converted. There is no doubt, however, that she was outspoken about and proud of her Jewish identity. [American Jewish Historical Society]*

Central Park or exploiting the incipient art of photography to place her face in every shop window, Menken was expert at self-promotion and publicity. She married four times in the course of seven years. Her second marriage, in 1859, was to the heavyweight boxing champion of the world, John C. Heenan, with whom she had a son, who died in infancy. Menken had one other child, a son by her fourth husband, who also died in infancy in 1867.

One of the most glamorous celebrities of the 1860s, Menken also cultivated a literary following. She wrote poetry and developed relationships with the likes of Walt Whitman, Charles Dickens, Dante Gabriel Rossetti, Alexandre Dumas, and Algernon Swinburne. George Sand was a close friend to the actress and was godmother to Menken's second child, whom Sand convinced Menken to have baptized. Pictures of the actress with Dumas, circulated in Paris where Menken was performing *The Pirates of the Savannah*, enflamed rumors that she was having an affair with the author, and shortly before her death a similar scandal erupted in London when pictures were circulated of her with Swinburne.

Born in the spring of 1835, in Milneburg, Louisiana, to Auguste and Marie Theodore, Adah Isaacs Menken's origins are ambiguous largely because she told different stories of her life to different audiences. A major bone of contention to this day is the authenticity of her Jewishness. Though scholars have some evidence that Menken was raised a Catholic and converted to Judaism only after marrying her first husband, Menken herself once publicly rebuked a journalist who labeled her a convert by announcing that she was "born in that faith [Judaism], and have adhered to it through all my erratic career. Through that pure and simple religion I have found greatest comfort and blessing." Whatever her origins, it is clear that Menken was fervently Jewish in her adult life. After moving to Cincinnati with her first and only Jewish husband, Alexander Isaacs Menken, Adah learned Hebrew fluently, studied classical Jewish texts, and contributed many poems and essays to *The Israelite*, a weekly founded by Rabbi Isaac M. Wise. Her poems indicate a passionate temperament, deeply committed to a kind of proto-Zionism and even messianism. Many are collected in the posthumously published volume *Infelicia*. Menken viewed herself as a modern Deborah, calling on Jews to rise up against persecution in Turkey and protesting the kidnapping of a six-year-old Jewish boy in Bologna by representatives of the Catholic Church. She was one of the few Jews in America to protest when Lionel Nathan was denied the seat in the English Parliament to which he had been elected. And, at the height of her acting career, she refused to perform on Jewish High Holidays. On her deathbed at age thirty-three, suffering from what may have been peritonitis or tuberculosis (or both), and treated by the personal doctor of Napoleon III, Menken was visited by a rabbi.

Adah Isaacs Menken died on August 10, 1868, in Paris. She is buried in the Jewish section of Montparnasse Cemetery.

BIBLIOGRAPHY

Banner, Lois. *American Beauty* (1983); Falk, Bernard. *The Naked Lady or Storm over Adah: A Biography of Adah Isaacs Menken* (1934); Lesser, Allen. *Enchanting Rebel: The Secret Life of Adah Isaacs Menken* (1947), and "La Belle Menken." In *Weave a Wreath of Laurel: The Lives of Four Contributors to American Civilization* (1938); Lewis, Paul. *Queen of the Plaza: A Biography of Adah Isaacs Menken* (1964); Menken, Adah Isaacs, *Infelicia* (1868); *NAW.*

ALAN ACKERMAN

MENKEN, ALICE DAVIS (1870–1936)

Alice Davis Menken once described her greatest weakness as "a too strongly developed optimism." This optimism—perhaps her greatest strength—guided her volunteer work for over thirty years in the rehabilitation of delinquent girls.

The third of the seven children of Michael Marks and Miriam (Maduro Peixotto) Davis, Alice Davis Menken was born on August 4, 1870, in New York City. Descended from several prominent European Sephardi families, she was also a member of the Daughters of the American Revolution on her mother's side. Her family was closely tied to Manhattan's Spanish and Portuguese synagogue of New York City (Shearith Israel). Alice was the great-granddaughter of one of its earliest cantors, Moses Levi Maduro Peixotto. She married Mortimer Morange Menken, an attorney, on October 17, 1893. They had a son, Harold Davis Menken, in 1895.

Menken helped to establish the Shearith Israel Sisterhood in 1896 and served as its president from 1900 to 1929. She began her social relief work in the sisterhood's settlement house on New York City's Lower East Side, the Neighborhood House, which served the area's predominantly Jewish immigrant community. After 1908, when political upheaval in the Ottoman Empire sparked an influx of Sephardi immigrants to the United States, Neighborhood House shouldered much of the responsibility for these newcomers.

Through her sisterhood and settlement house work, Menken became increasingly interested in the rising problem of delinquency among young female Jewish immigrants. In 1908, at the request of city magistrates, Menken founded a sisterhood committee that cooperated with the New York City Probation Department in the Women's Night Court, assisting Jewish women who had run afoul of the criminal justice system. This project lasted eleven years, until the Women's Night Court was dissolved.

Menken's concern for delinquent women led her to help found the Jewish Board of Guardians in 1907.

Alice Davis Menken dedicated her life to working with delinquent Jewish women. In the course of her work, she helped to change the attitude of the penal system from that of punishment to rehabilitation. She once described her greatest weakness as "a too strongly developed optimism." [American Jewish Historical Society]

This organization lengthened the period of supervision of delinquents to three years beyond the end of probation. Menken served as chair of the Department of Court, Probation, and Parole of the board's women's division, and was the organization's vice president at the time of her death. Menken also chaired a committee of the NATIONAL COUNCIL OF JEWISH WOMEN, working with women paroled from various New York State workhouses and prisons.

In 1920, Governor Alfred E. Smith appointed Menken to the Board of Managers of the New York

State Reformatory for Women. She served as its secretary from 1922 to 1932. During her career, Menken also held memberships in the Florence Crittendon League, the National Committee on Prisons, the National Probation and Parole Association, and the Bureau of Social Service of the New York State Board of Parole. Menken helped to found the Jewish Big Sister movement in 1911. During her travels across the United States gathering information on various services available to delinquent women, she established several Jewish Big Sister chapters.

Alice Davis Menken stood at the forefront of what her *New York Times* obituary calls "the evolution of penology from an attitude of sentimentality and punishment to the broader conception of mercy and rehabilitation." Her many published works argued that therapy, not punishment, was the most effective treatment for young offenders. In addition to the notable impact her work and writing had on the field of penology, Menken effected change on a more personal level. Her commitment to social welfare often led her to take young Jewish female delinquents into her own home. Countless numbers of young Jewish women were encouraged to reform themselves because of Menken's progressive approach to the problem of delinquency.

For Menken and other middle- and upper-class Jewish women of her generation, social service work—through the National Council of Jewish Women, synagogue sisterhoods, and the various ladies' auxiliaries and women's divisions of Jewish communal organizations—provided a means for expressing Jewish values: assisting the community's poor, infirm, and distressed, and in general attempting to strengthen the moral fabric of society in keeping with Jewish ethical precepts.

Menken's last and most important book, *On the Side of Mercy: Problems in Social Readjustment* (1933), summarizes her life's work and her theoretical approach. In the introduction, New York governor Herbert H. Lehman praises both Menken's career and the optimism of which she had once spoken so disparagingly. Lehman lauds Menken's "credo of hope" and her belief that "a real alleviation of many of our social evils" requires only a perfection of social welfare technique and the awareness by the community of the needs of its members.

Alice Davis Menken died on March 23, 1936, in New York City.

SELECTED WORKS BY ALICE DAVIS MENKEN

Hints for Meeting the Problem of Maladjusted Youth: A Study in Social Work for Beginners (1922); *On the Side of Mercy: Problems in Social Readjustment* (1933); "The Rehabilitation of the Morally Handicapped." *Journal of the American Institute of Criminal Law and Criminology* 16 (May 1924): 147–154.

BIBLIOGRAPHY

AYJB 38:432; Benedict, Libbian. "Mrs. Mortimer M. Menken: Juvenile Delinquency Expert." *The American Hebrew* (March 26, 1926): 651; Menken, Alice Davis. Papers, P-23. American Jewish Historical Society, Waltham, Mass.; Obituary. *NYTimes*, March 24, 1936, 23:1; Pool, David de Sola, and Tamar de Sola Pool. *An Old Faith in the New World: Portrait of Shearith Israel* (1965); *UJE* 7; *WWIAJ* (1928).

FELICIA HERMAN

MENKEN, HELEN (1901–1966)

One of the finest actresses of her day, as well as a producer and a philanthropist, Helen Menken devoted her entire life to the American theater. Born on December 12, 1901, to artist Frederick William Menken and Katherine (Moden) in New York City, Menken began her stage career at age three in a production of *Humpty Dumpty*. Within two years, she was playing Peaseblossom in Shakespeare's *A Midsummer Night's Dream*.

Menken continued to perform in plays and musicals throughout her childhood and adolescence. She appeared around the country in stock productions. By 1916, she had acquired enough experience to land the role of Blanche Amory opposite the great John Drew in *Major Pendennis*. Two years later, her success was assured by her widely hailed performance as Miss Fairchild in *Three Wise Fools*. Menken did not limit herself to crowd-pleasing roles in popular favorites. She was a serious actress who challenged herself throughout her life.

Through the mid-1920s, she presented a string of powerful performances in challenging dramas, undertaking such parts as The Rat Wife in *Little Eyolf* and Emila Marty in *The Makropoulos Secret*. In 1926, at the height of her career, she engaged in a controversial and daring role, the lesbian Irene De Montcel in *The Captive*. The New York police raided a performance, arrested Menken, and closed down the production. Shortly thereafter, Menken went to London and was a hit in a West End production of one of her outstanding Broadway successes, *Seventh Heaven*. Returning to New York, she played Dorinda in *The Beaux' Stratagem* in 1928. In 1931, she played a season of Shakespeare, performing the roles of Portia in *The Merchant of Venice*, Ophelia in *Hamlet*, and Calpurnia in *Julius*

An accomplished actress and producer, Helen Menken began her career at age three and acted with such luminaries as John Drew and Helen Hayes. Committed to many social causes, she spent much of her time working for the American Theater Wing. During World War II, she produced the Wing's Stage Door Canteen, *which performed for and served food to U.S. servicemen and women. [New York Public Library]*

Caesar. She continued to act for the rest of her life. Her last important role was in 1933, when she played Queen Elizabeth I opposite Helen Hayes in the title role of *Mary Scotland.*

That same year, Menken began her career as a producer with *Saint Wench,* in which she also starred. Her greatest producing effort was the American Theater Wing's *Stage Door Canteen,* which operated from 1942 to 1946. This was Broadway's contribution to the war effort. In *Stage Door Canteen,* the stars not only performed for servicemen and servicewomen, but also cooked and waited tables for them in a wonderfully deglamorized setting.

Menken had three marriages, including a stormy one-year union with Humphrey Bogart. She was a co-founder and trustee of the American Shakespeare Festival Theater and Academy, a vice president of the Institute for the Crippled and Disabled, and a co-founder and vice president of the Society for the Facially Disfigured.

In the latter part of her career, she devoted most of her energy to the American Theater Wing. Menken was its president and worked tirelessly on behalf of its many programs until her death on March 28, 1966. She was awarded a posthumous Tony Award that year.

BIBLIOGRAPHY

Bordman, Gerald. *The Oxford Companion to the American Theatre.* 2d ed. (1992); Rigdon, Walter, ed. *The Biographical Encyclopedia and Who's Who of the American Theatre* (1966); Obituary. *NYTimes,* March 28, 1966, 33:2; Stevenson, Isabelle, ed. *The Tony Award (1987);* UJE; WWWIA 4.

THOMAS F. CONNOLLY

MENUHIN, HEPHZIBAH (1920–1980)

Hephzibah Menuhin, pianist and social activist, was born in San Francisco, on May 20, 1920, the second of three children. Her parents, Moshe and Marutha (Sher) Menuhin, were Russian Jews who came to the United States by way of Palestine. Neither Moshe nor Marutha was a trained musician, but all of their children—Yehudi, Hephzibah, and Yaltah—showed extraordinary musical gifts. Moshe was a student of mathematics and a Hebrew teacher before he gave his full time and energy to managing his son Yehudi's career as a violinist. Marutha also taught Hebrew before she devoted herself to rearing her family.

Hephzibah's education, like her brother's and sister's, was entirely entrusted to her parents and private tutors. She studied piano with Judith Blockley and Lev Schorr in San Francisco, Marcel Ciampi in Paris, and Rudolf Serkin in Basel. She was also an accomplished linguist, having mastered Hebrew, English, French, German, Italian, Spanish, and Russian by her teen years.

Her debut recital, at which she played works of Beethoven, Bach, Chopin, and Weber, took place in San Francisco in 1928, when she was eight years old. In 1933, she and her brother recorded the Mozart Violin Sonata in A. This recording won the Candide prize for the best recording made in France that year. The prize money was donated to charity. The next year, Hephzibah and Yehudi began to perform together, giving one concert in Paris, one in London, and one in New York. Reviewers were in agreement that Hephzibah's talent as a pianist equaled that of her world-renowned virtuoso violinist brother, but the Menuhin parents were determined that Hephzibah's public appearances would be strictly limited. Her mother told an interviewer for the *San Francisco Chronicle*, "Hephzibah yearns for solo recitals and a career of her own. . . . I tell her that the only immor-

tality to which a woman should aspire is that of a home and children." The youngest Menuhin child, Yaltah, also a skilled pianist, did not perform publicly in her youth at all.

The Menuhin parents were less vigilant in protecting their children from early marriages to people with whom they were only slightly acquainted. In 1938, when Yehudi was twenty-two, Hephzibah was eighteen, and Yaltah was sixteen, all three Menuhin

Early in life, Hephzibah Menuhin was considered as talented as her musician brother.
Had her parents not felt that marriage and motherhood would be more appropriate for her,
she might have achieved the success and celebrity of her famous sibling, violinist Yehudi Menuhin.
They are shown here performing together. [New York Public Library]

children married. These marriages all ended in divorce. Hephzibah's husband, Lindsay Nicholas, was the son of a millionaire Australian analgesic manufacturer and the owner of a 24,000-acre sheep ranch. His sister, Nola Nicholas, was Yehudi's first wife.

Hephzibah spent most of the 1940s in Australia, rearing her two sons, Kronrod and Marston, and concertizing. She liked to perform with chamber groups and with orchestras, and was a persuasive advocate for contemporary music, introducing, among other works, the Bartok piano concerti to Australia. In addition, she founded the first traveling library in Australia to bring works to the Outback. In 1947, after a hiatus of almost a decade, she once again began concertizing with her brother. They gave a series of concerts in Israel in 1950; they also performed together in many cities in the United States and throughout Europe.

After World War II, Hephzibah's marriage to Lindsay Nicholas ended. She married Vienna-born sociologist Robert Hauser and moved with him to England, where their daughter, Clara, was born in 1955. With her husband, Hephzibah worked to assist the poor, the homeless, and those recently ill. She also worked for the causes of peace and disarmament, serving as president of the Women's International League for Peace and Freedom.

Hephzibah Menuhin died at age sixty in 1980, after a long battle with cancer. Her legacy of recordings include performances of works by Bach, Mozart, Beethoven, Schumann, Brahms, Franck, and Enesco. She is also remembered for her devotion to the needy and suffering.

BIBLIOGRAPHY

EJ, s.v. "Menuhin, Yehudi"; Magidoff, Robert. *Yehudi Menuhin: The Story of the Man and the Musician* (1955); Menuhin, Moshe. *The Menuhin Saga: The Autobiograpbhy of Moshe Menuhin* (1984); Menuhin, Yehudi. *Unfinished Journey* (1977); *NYTimes*, January 2, 1981; Palmer, Tony. *Menuhin: A Family Portrait* (1991); Rolfe, Lionel Menuhin. *The Menuhins: A Family Odyssey* (1978); *UJE*, s.v. "Menuhin, Yehudi"; Wymer, Norman. *Yehudi Menuhin* (1961).

CHARLOTTE GREENSPAN

MERRIAM, EVE (1916–1992)

> I've sometimes spent weeks looking for precisely the right word. It's like having a tiny marble in your pocket, you can just feel it. Poetry is great fun. That's what I'd like to stress . . . : the joy of the sound of language.

The tactility and fertility of language, its joys and journeys, are the stuff of Eve Merriam's more than fifty books of poems for children. "Eat a poem," she urged her readers and listeners (for her, poetry was to be "out loud"). "Don't be polite. / Bite in. / Pick it up with your fingers and lick the juice that may run down your chin."

Eve Merriam was born Eva Moskowitz in Philadelphia, on July 19, 1916, one of four children of Jennie (Siegel) and Max Moscowitz, emigrants as children from Russia. The family owned a chain of dress shops, and Eve "grew up with fashion." Her book *Figleaf: The Business of Being in Fashion* (1960) is a wittily devastating critique of the industry for its manipulation of women.

After graduating from the University of Pennsylvania in 1937, she embarked on graduate study at Columbia University. There, a teacher speculated that her lack of success in getting her work published might be the result of her Jewish surname. She chose the writing name Merriam from the *Merriam-Webster Dictionary* on her desk. Although she delighted in travel and loved the sea, Merriam's life and writing career centered on New York. Married four times, she was the mother of two sons, Guy (b. 1951) and Dee (b. 1952), by her second husband, Martin Michel. She raised her children in the city and once commented, "I expect to be the last living inhabitant of Manhattan when everyone else has quit for sub or exurbia."

Though known for her books of children's poetry, there is more to Merriam's remarkable body of work. For children and adults she wrote biographies of women and men whom she saw as models: Franklin D. Roosevelt (1952), EMMA LAZARUS (1956, 1959), and Martin Luther King, Jr. (1971). She transformed a lifelong commitment to progressive political views into poems and plays of urban life and social justice. In *The Inner City Mother Goose* (1969), she transforms nursery rhymes into social commentary. "Hushabye Baby" is not on the treetop but on "the top floor / Project elevator / Won't work any more," and "Mary, Mary / Urban Mary," watches her "sidewalk grow / with chewing gum wads / And cigarette butts." Set to music by Helen Miller, *Inner City: A Street Cantata* opened on Broadway in December 1971.

The Club (1976), a wry and sharply comic satire of male behavior, epitomizes the feminism that had been a motif in Merriam's work long before the contemporary women's movement. In 1951, she and historian GERDA LERNER wrote a revue, *Singing of Women*, for the women's division of the New York Council of the Arts, Sciences, and Professions; the poetry collection *The Double Bed from the Feminine Side* appeared in 1958; one of the first books for children about women's work, *Mommies at Work*, came in 1961; and *After Nora Slammed the Door* (1964) carried the subtitle

American Women in the 1960's, the Unfinished Revolution. A self-descriptive list in Merriam's papers notes, "She claims to have been born a feminist, since her birth date is July 19th, the anniversary of the [Seneca Falls convention] in 1848."

Eve Merriam died on August 11, 1992, in New York City. She was, above all, a poet: "You write poems because you must . . . because you can't live your life without writing them." A posthumously published volume, *Embracing the Dark* (1995), concludes with the "Poems Purgatorio" sequence in which the love of language and poetry struggles with the fact of dying: "It may well be exquisite, as the dictionary notes, / adj. keen, intense, acute."

SELECTED WORKS BY EVE MERRIAM

BOOKS

After Nora Slammed the Door (1964); *The Double Bed from the Feminine Side* (1958); *Embracing the Dark* (1995); *Emma Lazarus, Woman with a Torch* (1956); *Figleaf: The Business of Being in Fashion* (1960); *I Am a Man: Ode to Martin Luther King, Jr.* (1971); *The Inner City Mother Goose* (1969); *Mommies at Work* (1961); *The Real Book About Franklin D. Roosevelt* (1952); *The Story of Ben Franklin* (1965); *The Voice of Liberty: The Story of Emma Lazarus* (1959).

PLAYS

The Club (1976); *Inner City: A Street Cantata* (1971); *Singing of Women*, with Gerda Lerner (1951).

BIBLIOGRAPHY

American Women Writers. Vol. 5, supplement (1995); Merriam, Eve. Papers. Kerlan Collection, University of Minnesota at Minneapolis–St. Paul, and Schlesinger Library, Radcliffe College, Cambridge, Mass.

CAROL HURD GREEN

MESSINGER, RUTH (b. 1940)

Quoting Rabbi Abraham Joshua Heschel's statement that "when terrible things happen in a democracy, some are guilty and all are responsible," Ruth Messinger said, "I take the responsibility of which he spoke very seriously."

"I am a New Yorker born and bred. I walk fast, talk fast, think fast and, most importantly, stand up fast when the best interests of my city are being sold down the river," says Ruth Messinger, Manhattan borough president and candidate for mayor of New York City. She is shown here with a local Girl Scout troop. [Office of the President of the Borough of Manhattan]

Born on November 6, 1940, on the Upper West Side of Manhattan, Ruth Messinger is a third-generation New Yorker. Her great-grandparents arrived from Poland and Germany in the nineteenth century; her parents were Wilfred and MARJORIE (GOLDWASSER) WYLER. Ruth attended the Brearley School, graduated from Radcliffe College, and received a master's degree in social work from the University of Oklahoma. She worked as a teacher, school and college administrator, and social worker. She married Eli C. Messinger (from whom she is now divorced) and raised three children before entering politics as a candidate for the New York State Assembly in 1976. She lost, but won when she ran the following year for a City Council seat from Manhattan's Upper West Side. Reelected in 1982 and 1985 by large majorities, by 1988 she was being mentioned as a mayoral contender.

In 1990 Messinger became Manhattan borough president. She plans to run for mayor of New York City. If elected, she would be the city's first woman mayor. Messinger says of herself, "I am a New Yorker born and bred. I walk fast, talk fast, think fast and, most importantly, stand up fast when the best interests of my city are being sold down the river." Elements of this self-description are evident in her advocacy of many liberal causes and her concerns for diverse groups in the community. She has worked to restrain real estate developers from building projects that, in her view, have deleterious environmental or social impacts, and she protects city agency whistle-blowers. She cast the deciding vote on the 1986 City Council gay rights bill and opposed Columbia University's original plans for a commercial biomedical center on the site of the old Audubon Ballroom in Washington Heights, where Malcolm X was assassinated in 1965.

Besides her commitment to the community at large, Messinger exhibits a dedication to her Jewish roots and to the role and place of women in American society. As a child, through her mother's public relations work for the Jewish Theological Seminary, she was brought into close contact with the Jewish community. She is an active member of the Society for the Advancement of Judaism, an advisory committee member of the Jewish Fund for Justice, a board member of the Jewish Foundation for the Education of Women, a former national chair of the advisory council of the National League of Cities, and president of Women in Municipal Government.

Messinger is married to Andrew J. Lachman, a public school administrator. Her three children from her first marriage have produced four grandchildren. An energetic worker and activist, Ruth Messinger is eclectic in her leisure activities. She rollerblades, reads, skis, and, by her own account, "bake[s] the best chocolate desserts in New York." But leisure time is limited, and first and foremost she keeps Rabbi Heschel's dictum in mind as she strives to be a responsible member of the community in which she lives.

ELISABETH ISRAELS PERRY
RONA HOLUB

MEYER, ANNIE NATHAN (1867–1951)

"Had my ambition been less, the gap between idea and fulfillment would perhaps have been slighter." With these words, Annie Nathan Meyer concluded her autobiography *It's Been Fun* (1951), published just days after her death. Her ambition may have exceeded her achievements, but the latter were neither few nor insignificant. She promoted women's higher education; chronicled women's work; dramatized women's status in plays, novels, and short stories; raised funds for Jewish and black students; wrote hundreds of letters to the editor; published art, drama, and music criticism; and championed physical activity and the outdoors. She was also founder of Barnard College, New York City's first liberal arts college for women.

Descended from the distinguished Gershom Mendes Seixas family of precolonial times, Annie Nathan Meyer, born on February 19, 1867, was the fourth child and second daughter of Robert Weeks and Annie Augusta (Florance) Nathan. Having had less than six months of schooling, she was self-educated, boasting that she had read all of Dickens by the time she was seven years old. The Crash of 1873 damaged her parents' financial status and, in 1875, the family moved from New York to Green Bay, Wisconsin, where one of her mother's admirers controlled railroad interests that allowed him to employ her father and her eldest brother, Robert. Her mother resented being forced from her extensive social life, amateur theater, and large family, and her father resented being dependent on her friend's largess. Neither was comfortable living away from New York City. Their marriage deteriorated, with each bringing admirers home. Although her mother sent Maud and Harold, the two middle children, to public school, she kept Annie home to keep her company, denying Annie normal peer experiences.

After three unhappy years, her father returned to New York, while Annie, her mother, Maud, and Harold moved to Chicago to build a new life. This move was even more disastrous than the first. In

Chicago, she saw her mother invest poorly, suffer depression, and eventually turn to drugs, which led to her death. In 1878, the children returned to New York to live with their maternal grandfather and then with their father.

When Maud married in 1880, Annie took charge of the Nathan household and allowed herself time to read and study. By 1885, she had organized a reading circle modeled after Margaret Fuller's conversations and enrolled in the newly established Columbia College Collegiate Course for Women. Her abiding interest, however, was writing, and she modeled her own writing after the writers she admired most at that time: Ralph Waldo Emerson, Margaret Fuller, George Eliot, Elizabeth Barrett Browning. Another strong interest, music, led her to join a sight-reading piano group, where she met Alfred Meyer, a pulmonologist thirteen years her senior. He claimed love at first sight and convinced her to marry him, promising her explicitly that he would support her writing and her use of Annie Nathan Meyer as her legal name. They married on February 15, 1887, four months after they met, and literally played piano duets for the next sixty years. An assimilated German Jew, Alfred Meyer rejected synagogue affiliation. Annie Nathan Meyer left Congregation Shearith Israel, the synagogue with which her family had been affiliated for generations, and soon joined the Ethical Culture Society. Her interests in anticlericalism and reconciling Judaism and Christianity are reflected in her well-received novel, *Robert Annys, Poor Priest* (1901). The Meyers had one daughter, Margaret, born in 1894, who died tragically and mysteriously from an accidental self-inflicted gunshot wound in 1923, just three months after she married Dr. Ira Cohen.

Because her husband was a Columbia alumnus, Annie Nathan Meyer used the Columbia library, obviating her need to continue with the Columbia correspondence course. However, she wanted to study with the same intellectual rigor that was required of male students. A casual meeting with Columbia chief librarian Melvil Dewey, in 1887, led to planning a strategy to establish an affiliate women's college at Columbia. What was intended as a seven-year plan was accomplished in two. Meyer began her campaign in January 1888, with a memorable 2,500-word letter to *The Nation*, arguing that New York had no real claim to culture because, unlike other major cities, it lacked a liberal arts college for women. As part of the strategy, she then visited each name on a list of potential donors. Together with Dewey, Mary Mapes Dodge, and Ella Weed, she prepared a petition to Columbia's trustees urging the founding of an affili-

A cofounder of Barnard College, Annie Nathan Meyer was an indefatigable champion of women's rights. The title of her autobiography sums up her attitude toward life—It's Been Fun. [Barnard College]

ated self-sustaining liberal arts women's college. Naming the college for Frederick A.P. Barnard, a strong advocate for coeducational education, precluded Mrs. Barnard from objecting to the compromise of a separate but affiliated women's college. On October 7, 1889, Barnard College opened with seven full-time and twenty-nine part-time students at 343 Madison Avenue, with three years' rent guaranteed by the Meyers. Annie Nathan Meyer organized Barnard's first board of trustees, appointed herself, and remained active until 1950, often taking responsibility for promoting the college in the press, informally mentoring students, but mainly fund-raising. She often solicited friends to raise money for Jewish students' tuition and expenses.

Although founding Barnard College was her most important contribution to the higher education of women, her relationship with the college was not without significant problems, primarily because she felt slighted by not being acknowledged as its founder.

By the 1930s, another source of acrimony developed from her insistence in having Barnard Hall renamed for its donor, Jacob H. Schiff. A long correspondence with Nicholas Murray Butler, Columbia University president, and Virginia Gildersleeve, Barnard College dean, regarding the naming of the building was fruitless. Meyer and the Schiffs attributed Butler's refusal to anti-Semitism.

In 1891, Meyer edited *Woman's Work in America*, a book that focused on fields in which women had made some progress: education, law, medicine, journalism, and philanthropy (social welfare). In 1892, Meyer published a short, memorable novel, *Helen Brent, M.D.*, about a woman who faces the agonizing choice between career and marriage, and chooses medicine. In subsequent plays and stories, Meyer dramatized the "woman question" and reflected a "separate spheres" ideology, which evolved into a conservative antisuffrage position. Meyer's best scenes explore the hypocrisy behind the double standard, the dilemmas of working wives and mothers, and the unsupported claim that women's participation in public life ameliorates society's problems. To Meyer, motherhood placed a woman into a protected, if not sacred, class. Childless women were free to pursue the professions, but not vote. Meyer saw no inconsistencies in her indisputable achievement in expanding women's higher education and her antisuffragism. This enigmatic stance may be traced to her intense jealousy of her sister, Maud, who was a progressive activist and well-known suffragist, and her impatience with the suffragists' claims about the social and political changes the women's vote would bring. In a widely reprinted article, "Women's Assumption of Sex Superiority" (1904), she introduced a term to describe these overstated claims—"spreadhenism"—and argued that women could bring about social reforms without suffrage. She supported an educational, not a gender-based, voting criterion. Later, she defended her position by stating that the suffragists should have claimed the vote on the principles of justice and equality, not on unrealistic promises. Nevertheless, she eventually joined the League of Women Voters. Another point of disagreement was the suffragists' pacifism. Supportive of war preparedness, Meyer chaired the Emergency Committee of the American Home Economics Association and supervised the production of the film *Cheating the Garbage Pail* (1917), which addressed home-front food shortages.

Meyer was sincerely interested in minority rights. Because it sanctioned segregation, she resigned from the Daughters of the American Revolution. She worked with Mary White Ovington, Roy Wilkins, E.E. Just, James Weldon Johnson, and others to raise funds for black college students. The National Association for the Advancement of Colored People called her to resolve conflicts between blacks and Jews. After meeting Zora Neale Hurston, she found donors to support Hurston at Barnard, breaking the color barrier. For many years, Meyer and Hurston corresponded about Hurston's academic and social experiences at Barnard, her graduate research in anthropology at Columbia, and their writing. Hurston dedicated *Mules and Men* (1935) to Meyer: "To my dear friend Mrs. Annie Nathan Meyer, who hauled the mud to make me but loves me just the same." Meyer's outspoken antilynching stance is best demonstrated by her play *Black Souls* (1932), which is about miscegenation and bigotry in the Deep South. Never a commercial success, it garnered praise and enjoyed several readings in Harlem churches and one production by the Provincetown Players.

By 1933, Meyer acknowledged and finally confronted the impact of anti-Semitism in American society. In a 1935 series of letters to editors of New York dailies and weeklies, she attempted to expose Madison Grant, president of the New York Zoological Society and board member of the American Museum of Natural History, as a racist and follower of Hitler. The New York papers rejected her letters, but the Jewish press published them. Her campaign to oust Grant from his several key positions in New York museums has been vindicated by subsequent revelations of Grant's anti-Semitism.

From the early 1930s, Meyer attacked Nazi policy toward the Jews. Again she used the letters to the editor columns to sound the trumpet for preparedness, patriotism, and the privilege of fighting for one's country, and to bring attention to the plight of German Jews. In 1933, she fruitlessly urged Nicholas Murray Butler to cancel a university tribute to the German ambassador. By 1940, aged and ailing, Meyer despaired of becoming a successful dramatist or novelist but continued to write: over 350 letters to the editor, many short stories, and unfinished novels and plays. She also earned a respectable reputation as a drama critic, an art critic, a nature writer, and an outdoorswoman.

All her life, Annie Nathan Meyer saw herself as an American Jew, rejecting Zionism as inherently divisive. Her husband Alfred Meyer died at age ninety-six on July 14, 1950, and Annie Nathan Meyer polished her autobiography, concluding that although she had been ahead of her time, her life had been extremely worthwhile and, "above all, it *has* been fun."

Annie Nathan Meyer died on September 23, 1951.

SELECTED WORKS BY
ANNIE NATHAN MEYER

Barnard Beginnings (1935); *Black Souls* (1932); *Helen Brent, M.D.: A Social Study* (1892); *It's Been Fun* (1951); *Robert Annys, Poor Priest* (1901); *Woman's Work in America*, ed. (1891. Reprinted 1972).

BIBLIOGRAPHY

AJYB 6 (1904–1905): 155–156, 24:181, 54:540; Askowith, Dora. *Three Outstanding Women* (1941); *BDEAJ*; Birmingham, Stephen. *The Grandees: America's Sephardic Elite* (1971); *DAB* 5; *EJ* (1972); Gordon, Lynn D. "Annie Nathan Meyer and Barnard College: Mission and Identity in Women's Higher Education, 1889–1950." *History of Education Quarterly* 26 (Winter 1986): 503–522; *JE*; Marr, Phebe Ann. "Trustee Annie Nathan Meyer, College Founder, Wrote Plays." *Barnard Bulletin* (February 8, 1951); Masteller, Jean Carwile. "Annie Nathan Meyer." In *American Women Writers*, edited by Lina Mainiero (1981); McCaughey, Robert. "Barnard's Godmother: Annie Nathan Meyer." *Barnard Alumnae* (Spring 1977); Meyer, Annie Nathan. Papers, 1858–1950. AJA, and Personal files, Dean's Office and Department files. Barnard College Archives. Barnard College, NYC, and Rare Books and Manuscript Library, Columbia University, NYC; Nathan, Maud. *Once Upon a Time and Today* (1933. Reprint, 1974); *NAW* modern; Obituary. *NYTimes*, September 24, 1951, 271:1; Solar, Judith Cohen. "Annie Nathan Meyer: The Writer." *Barnard Alumnae* (Summer 1978); *WE*; *WWIAJ* (1926, 1928, 1938).

MYRNA GOLDENBERG

MEYER, EUGENIA GOODKIND (1878–1967)

A prominent civic leader in Westchester County, New York, Eugenia Goodkind Meyer was a longtime advocate of civil rights. Born in New York City on June 1, 1878, she married Max Meyer at New York's Ethical Culture Society in 1902. The Meyers moved to White Plains, New York, in 1914 and became active in its civic life, helping found the Welfare League for Colored People in 1918 (renamed the Urban League of Westchester in 1935). Max Meyer chaired the organization and Eugenia Meyer served for many years as its corresponding secretary. In May 1965, she was honored for her contributions when she was made honorary director for life.

Meyer's commitment to civil rights was also evidenced by her membership in New York's Community Church, a leftist interracial congregation of Unitarians whose congregants included a number of Jews and whose minister, John Haynes Holmes, had long been in the forefront of social activism and struggles for racial justice. She also served as chair and director of the White Plains branch of the Westchester County Children's Association for twenty-five years, where she helped establish its foster care program. Her husband, a clothing manufacturer and labor mediator, served on several industrial boards and served as president of the Fashion Institute of Technology and as a governor of White Plains Hospital.

On May 16, 1950, Eugenia and Max Meyer received the Human Relations Award for Outstanding Citizenship from the White Plains Human Relations Center. The center had been established in 1948 by the State Commission Against Discrimination and the New York State Department of Education.

Max Meyer died of a heart attack at age seventy-six, on January 31, 1953. Eugenia Meyer moved to Katonah, New York, in 1955 and to Hightstown, New Jersey, in 1966. She died of a heart attack in Princeton, New Jersey, on June 2, 1967, a day after her eighty-ninth birthday. She was survived by one sister, a son, and three daughters. As William Strawbridge, president of the Westchester Urban League, commented on her death, "The Urban League has lost one of its most diligent and dedicated workers. . . . She was greatly concerned with relieving injustice and inequity."

BIBLIOGRAPHY

Obituaries. *NYTimes*, June 3, 1967, 31:4, and *White Plains Reporter-Dispatch*, June 3, 1967.

CHERYL GREENBERG

MICHELES, VERA DEAN *see* DEAN, VERA

MICHELSON, GERTRUDE GERALDINE (b. 1925)

G.G. Michelson is a corporate and civic leader who has been a trailblazer for women. As chair of the trustees of Columbia University from 1989 to 1992, she was the first woman to head the board of an Ivy League institution. She was also the first woman on the New York State Financial Control Board. In her forty-seven-year career at Macy's, she rose from management trainee to senior vice president. She has lived in Manhattan most of her life.

Gertrude Geraldine Michelson was born on June 3, 1925, to Thomas and Celia (Cohen) Rosen in Jamestown, a southwestern New York State town where her parents were part of the small Jewish community. She

G.G. Michelson has been a trailblazer for women. As chair of the trustees of Columbia University from 1989 to 1992, she was the first woman to head the board of an Ivy League institution. [Photograph courtesy of Macy's]

was the youngest child, born after a sister and brother. Michelson's parents had emigrated in their teens from the vicinity of Vilna in Russia, where they received whatever education they had. Her mother, who suffered from tuberculosis, died when Michelson was eleven. Because of her mother's illness and her father's various businesses and curiosity, the family lived in various parts of the United States.

Michelson received a B.A. in industrial psychology from Pennsylvania State University in 1945. In 1947, she received her LL.B. from Columbia Law School, one of a few women in her class. Although her father had disapproved of her studying law, she sought credentials, and was inspired by men she met who were going to law school.

Never intending to practice law, Michelson joined the training program at Macy's in New York, seeing opportunity for advancement in a corporation with a large female workforce. In 1948, she became assistant to the labor relations manager and, in 1963, vice president for employee personnel, at the time the store's only female vice president. In the 1970s, as senior vice president for personnel, labor, and consumer relations, she ran Macy's Bureau of Standards (a precursor of government consumer agencies) and Comparison Shopping Office, and negotiated with the Teamsters and fourteen locals representing a total of twenty thousand employees. Macy's called her their "consumer czarina," and *The Women's Book of Records* named her "the only woman in the United States to deal regularly with a major union." From 1980 to 1992, she was senior vice president for external affairs, afterward becoming a director of Federated Department Stores (which had acquired Macy's) until her retirement in 1996.

By 1976, Michelson was a director of Macy's, Harper and Row, Quaker Oats, Chubb, and General Electric; by 1981, of Stanley Works, Goodyear Tire, and Irving Trust. On these boards, she has seen few women's faces.

A Columbia University trustee beginning in 1980 during Michael Sovern's tenure as president, Michelson was elected vice-chair in 1985 and chair in 1989. She was known for her ability to get disparate groups in the university community to work well together. She is currently chair of the Helena Rubinstein Foundation, a life trustee of Spelman College, director of the Markle Foundation, a member of the advisory council of Catalyst, and chair of the Executive Committee of the Rand Corporation. In 1996, when its chairman left to work for the Dole presidential campaign, she was acting chair of Rand's board.

In 1977, Michelson was one of the most well known members of the New York City Business-Labor Working Group. Her many civic roles have included membership on the New York State Financial Control Board and deputy chair of the New York Federal Reserve Bank. She has been a member of the New York City Interracial Council on Business Opportunity, a director of the executive committee of the American Arbitration Association, and a member of the National Commission on Public Service. She has been on mayoral committees including Edward Koch's controversial commission on commercial rent control. Michelson is currently a public governor of the American Stock Exchange, and vice-chair and director of the New York City Partnership.

Michelson has received honorary doctorates from Adelphi University, New Rochelle College, and Marymount Manhattan College. She has also received

Columbia University Law School's James Kent Award, Barnard College's Frederick Barnard Award, Catalyst's Award for Contribution to Corporate Leadership, the American Women's Economic Development (AWED) Award for Outstanding Contributions to Women's Economic Development, the Girl Scout Women's Achievement Award, and the NOW Legal Defense and Education Fund Equal Opportunity Award.

In 1947, she married Horace Michelson, who is now retired from the law firm of Moses and Singer. Their older daughter, Martha Ann, died in a fire as a student at Goddard College. Their younger daughter, Barbara Jane, attended Cordon Bleu after college and has a mail-order baking business. The Michelsons have three grandchildren.

G.G. Michelson is known for her geniality, sharp intelligence, and resolve. She emphasizes the importance of civic leadership, believes government budgets should be balanced, but not on the hides of the poor, and feels that top law school education for needy, gifted students and those interested in public service merits real support. Her goal as a leader has not been to promote women, but rather to promote the integrity of organizations and the communities they serve. Doing her job well, however, helps women by precedent and example.

BIBLIOGRAPHY

Bender, Marylin. "Problems as Executive Aid Housewife." *NYTimes*, February 6, 1964, 32:6, and "Yankee Fan Confirms a Maxim: Nice Gals Finish First." *NYTimes*, December 20, 1970, sec. 3, p. 5; Cummings, Judith. "Notes on People: First Woman Named to State Financial Control Board." *NYTimes*, June 20, 1980, sec. 2, p. 5; Daniels, Lee A. "Columbia Trustee Head: A Low-Key Trailblazer." *NYTimes*, June 21, 1989, sec. 2, p. 7; "Executive Suite: Gertrude G. Michelson." In "Seventy-Five Most Influential Women," edited by Cynthia Rigg and Pat Wechsler. *Crain's New York Business*, March 25, 1996; Fowler, Elizabeth M. "Women in Careers Are Honored." *NYTimes*, October 20, 1967, 69:3; Haberman, Clyde. "Three on State Panel Challenge Budget for New York City." *NYTimes*, May 12, 1982, 1:1; Michelson, Gertrude G. Interview by author, NYC, June 17, 1996; "Only Woman Executive to Deal Regularly with a Major Union." In *Women's Book of World Records and Achievements*, edited by Lois Decker O'Neill (1979); Prial, Frank J. "Mrs. Michelson Gets Two Posts in One Day." *NYTimes*, January 8, 1979, sec. 4, p. 2; Townsend, Alair. "A View from the Top: Alair Townsend Remembers Her Mentor." *Crain's New York Business* (March 25, 1996); Vescovi, James. "Distinguished Columbian: G.G. Michelson '47." *Columbia Law School Alumni Magazine* (September 1996); *Who's Who in America* (1996).

JANE MUSHABAC

MICHELSON, MIRIAM (1870–1942)

Miriam Michelson began her writing career as a journalist, "interviewing a murderer one week and Paderewski the next" and "writing dramatic criticism of a very fearless and truth-telling sort," according to a 1904 biographical note in *Current Literature*. When she turned to fiction, her prose kept the lively immediacy, the breezy freshness, of someone capturing the present moment, and her novels became popular reading. A wry awareness of the complications faced by single working women runs throughout Michelson's writing.

Miriam Michelson was born in the mining town of Calaveras, California, in 1870. She was the seventh of eight children of Samuel and Rosalie (Przylubska) Michelson, who immigrated to the United States from Poland in 1855. (The oldest child, physicist Albert A. Michelson, was the first United States citizen to win a Nobel Prize for science; and the youngest, journalist Charles Michelson, became a close assistant to Franklin D. Roosevelt.)

Educated in San Francisco, Michelson wrote special features and dramatic criticism for San Francisco and Philadelphia newspapers and short stories that appeared in national magazines. Her first novel, *In the Bishop's Carriage*, published in 1904, is narrated by Nancy Olden, a young thief of great charm but questionable ethics. Though a painful orphanage upbringing provides a rationale for Nancy's choice of profession and though she succeeds in reforming herself to become an actor, Nancy remains a challengingly unconventional heroine. The book caused a sensation.

None of Michelson's subsequent novels was as broad a success, but her lively style and her sense of social realities never went unpraised. She published four more novels between 1904 and 1910, including *A Yellow Journalist* (1905), which centers on a smart-talking, hardworking female reporter who develops a deeper sense of ethical values through conversations with a Jewish grandmother she interviews, and *Anthony Overman* (1906), a romance between another spunky but cynical female journalist and an astonishingly pure-minded reformer that occasioned comparisons with George Eliot's *Daniel Deronda*. *The Awakening of Zojas*, a collection of four novellas published in 1910, earns Michelson a place among early science fiction writers.

Michelson continued as a journalist most of her life, but after 1910 the spate of novels slowed. Her last novel, *Petticoat King*, a story of Elizabeth I, queen of England, was published in 1929.

For her last published book, a history and reminiscence of Virginia City, Nevada, entitled *The Wonderlode of Silver and Gold* (1934), Michelson returned to the mining towns she knew as a child. As described in the *New York Times Book Review* on June 17, 1934, she wrote "with insight and understanding . . . with a mocking humor . . . [and a] crisp level-headedness."

Miriam Michelson died on May 28, 1942, in San Francisco.

SELECTED WORKS BY MIRIAM MICHELSON

Anthony Overman (1906); *The Awakening of Zojas* (1910); "Bygones." *Smart Set* 51 (March 1917): 81–92; "Curiosity of Kitty Cochrane." *Smart Set* 37 (May 1912): 133–142; "Destruction of San Francisco." *Harper's Weekly* 50, no. 2576 (May 5, 1906): 623–624; *The Duchess of Leeds: A Slightly Historical Drama, Careless of Chronology, Indifferent to Facts, and Frankly Fanciful in Four Acts* (c. 1932). Miscellaneous Literary and Historical Manuscript Collection, University of Delaware Library, Newark; *In the Bishop's Carriage* (1904). Available electronically via Project Gutenberg; *The Madigans* (1904); *Michael Thwaite's Wife* (1909); *Petticoat King* (1929); *The Wonderlode of Silver and Gold* (1934); *A Yellow Journalist* (1905).

BIBLIOGRAPHY

AJYB 24:182; *BEOAJ*; *Biographies of California Authors and Indexes of California Literature*. Edited by Edgar J. Hinkel. 2 vols. (1942); Bleiler, Everett F. *Science Fiction: The Early Years* (1990); Burke, W.J., and Will D. Howe. *American Authors and Books, 1640–1940* (1943); Bzowski, Frances Diodato. *American Women Playwrights, 1900–1930: A Checklist* (1992); Daims, Diva, and Janet Grimes. *Toward a Feminist Tradition: An Annotated Bibliography of Novels in English by Women, 1891–1920* (1982); Goodman, Joseph T. Papers (c. 1891–1917). Bancroft Library, University of California, Berkeley; Herzberg, Max J. *Reader's Encyclopedia of American Literature* (1962); Kelly, Florence Finch. "The Golden Age of Virginia City." *NYTimes Book Review*, June 17, 1934, 13; Library of Congress Copyright Office. *Dramatic Compositions Copyrighted in the United States, 1870 to 1916* (1918); Livingston, Dorothy Michelson. *The Master of Light: A Biography of Albert A. Michelson* (1973); Michelson, Charles. *The Ghost Talks* (1944); "Miriam Michelson." *Current Literature* 37 (August 1904): 129–130; "Miriam Michelson, S.F. Novelist." *San Francisco Chronicle*, May 29, 1942; Moss, Mary. "Notes on New Novels." *Atlantic Monthly* 97 (January 1906): 47; Pollock, Channing. *Harvest of My Years: An Autobiography* (1943), and dramatization of *In the Bishop's Carriage*, by Miriam Michelson. Harvard Theatre Collection, Cambridge, Mass.; Robinson, Doris. *Women Novelists, 1891–1920: An Index to Biographical and Autobiographical Sources* (1984); *UJE*; Wallace, W. Stewart. *A Dictionary of North American Authors Deceased Before 1950* (1951); *Woman's Who's Who of America: A Biographical Dictionary of Contemporary Women of the United States and Canada 1914–1915*. Edited by John William Leonard (1914); *WWIAJ* (1926, 1928, 1938); *WWWIA* 2.

PAMELA MATZ

MIDLER, BETTE (b. 1945)

Before there were Jewish princesses, there were bawdy Jewish women. Bette Midler fits into this earlier tradition. She is the latest incarnation of the early twentieth-century bawds such as BELLE BARTH and SOPHIE TUCKER. Indeed, Midler does an imitation of Tucker in her role as Delores De Lago, the lowest form of show business and the toast of Chicago. Born in Honolulu on December 1, 1945, to Fred and Ruth Midler, Bette (named after Bette Davis) learned as a young girl to observe other people's behavior carefully and create her own persona.

She was the third daughter in a family where both parents were frustrated and disappointed with their condition. Midler later remembered screaming and shouting matches between her parents and between her father and older sister Susan. In school, she felt like an outsider as well. She was the only white in school, as she later recalled, and she was Jewish. Neither she nor her classmates knew what that meant. Bette wisecracked that she thought it had something to do with boys. Witty responses, quick retorts, and a ready smile became her defense against unpleasant home and school realities. Although she performed well in school, being elected senior class president and graduating as the class valedictorian, she always felt her physical appearance combined with her outré status made her different from the majority of students.

After a year at the University of Hawaii, she left for New York and a career in show business. Midler viewed herself as a singer and a clown, and hoped that opportunities to perform would materialize. She gained a small part in the chorus of *Fiddler on the Roof* in 1965 and later was given the part of Tevye's eldest daughter, Tsaytl. She stayed with the show for three years. While performing in *Fiddler*, she also sang at the Improvisation Club, where she met Stephen Ostrow, the owner of the Continental Baths, a gay gathering place where entertainers performed while the audience sat around the pool area. It was in this setting that Bette Midler developed many of the outrageous personae that became the standards of her concert show and the basis of her spectacular success.

The Divine Miss M became her central character, a woman who wore a black lace corset and gold lamé pedal pushers while singing songs of the 1940s and 1950s. In between songs, she told off-color jokes, moving constantly around the stage. She made frequent references to male sexual parts, and laughed alongside her audience. Midler took neither herself nor her subject matter seriously and communicated a sense of irreverence to her listeners that may have both shocked and delighted them simultaneously. In

The Divine Miss M has moved from the gay bathhouses of New York to the heights of Hollywood and hasn't lost her sense of humor along the way. Owing more to Mae West than to Bette Davis (after whom she was named), Bette Midler continues to offer the world an alternative to the submissive Hollywood woman; she's funny, smart, strong, and successful. [New York Public Library]

the late 1960s, when Midler flourished at the Continental Baths, the country was experiencing a social upheaval. Midler's enthusiastic willingness to discuss in public topics that had always been reserved to private spaces fit into the revolutionary changes in sexual behavior and discourse. Her support for gay men, who have remained a loyal contingent of fans for her shows and records, added to the image she projected of a free and anarchic spirit.

An appearance on the Johnny Carson Show in 1970 helped to give her a national audience. In 1972, Aaron Russo became her manager and is credited with organizing her career and arranging her tours. They had a tumultuous personal and professional relation-

ship, which resulted in Midler taking a year off in 1974 to recover from the mental and physical pressure of constant touring. In 1979, she made her first movie, *The Rose*. In it, she played a rock performer, reminiscent of both her own experience and Janis Joplin's. The performance, a tour de force of acting and singing, demonstrated the incredible stress associated with touring and the added tension of a domineering manager. Midler broke with Russo in 1979 and took charge of her own career.

The Rose launched Bette Midler's Hollywood career. Unfortunately, she followed up this success with a movie called *Jinxed* (1980), which was exactly that. Her movie career went from a spectacular beginning to a seemingly disastrous end. The next few years were very difficult for Bette Midler, and by her own admission, she experienced a mental breakdown. Rest, therapy, and contemplation, a decided contrast to her usual style and behavior, restored her spirit. The whirlwind 1970s, which had included the winning of a Grammy, a Tony, and an Emmy award, ended with *Jinxed*.

Her personal life got back on track, however, when she met and married a German performance artist named Martin von Haselberg in December 1984. The wedding took place, after a brief romance, in Las Vegas and was performed by an Elvis impersonator. By her account, her new husband was funnier than she was, extremely supportive of her career ambitions, and thoughtful in his guidance.

Midler credits von Haselberg with the turnaround in her career. He suggested that she return to comedy, her natural métier. In what turned out to be a brilliant move, she signed with the Disney Company to make a series of comedies. In 1986, she appeared in two movies, both of which became smash hits: *Down and Out in Beverly Hills* and *Ruthless People*. The former movie was the first R-rated movie to come from Disney. These movies established Bette Midler as a major comic actress. The great success of both movies made her known nationally and internationally. Previously, her concert tours, which took her overseas as well, attracted only the young, enthusiastic fans who enjoyed her outrageous humor. In these movies, though Midler's anarchic bent could occasionally be glimpsed, it was her smirk, her grin, and her swagger, rather than her bawdiness, that appealed to a larger, more mainstream audience.

These two hits were followed in quick succession by *Outrageous Fortune* (1987) and *Big Business* (1988). In 1989, she produced *Beaches* through her own production company, All Girl Productions. Though the movie had a successful musical score, it was a melodrama that did poorly at the box office. Audiences did not seem to want Bette Midler to be anything but funny. However, she had other ideas and plans for her career. In the following three years, she appeared in, and produced, three more melodramas, all of which bombed at the box office: *Stella* (1990), *Scenes from a Mall* (1991), and *For the Boys* (1992).

In her personal life, Bette Midler was feeling more confident and capable of sustaining professional failure. In November 1986, she gave birth to a daughter, Sophie (named after Sophie Tucker). After assessing her career, she decided to return to her roots: concertizing and regaining contact with a live audience and her legion of fans around the country. On September 4, 1993, she opened a five-week stint at Radio City Music Hall in New York City as the first leg of a multicity tour. She broke all records in ticket selling and logged more consecutive performances than any other single performer at Radio City. The tour continued into 1994 and won large audiences and critical praise.

On December 12, 1993, she appeared on television as Mamma Rose in the CBS production of *Gypsy*. She also played a witch in the film *Hocus Pocus*. Midler continues to invent and reinvent herself in both old and new media. Her fans enjoy her standard material, always varied with contemporary commentary. In her 1993–1994 concert tour, Dolores De Lago reappeared along with her backup singers, the Harlettes. Midler jokes about the fact that she is a Jewish woman married to a German and readily identifies herself as a Jewish outsider in a Christian world. She clearly believes that her Jewishness adds to her witty understanding of a confusing world.

Bette Midler raised public consciousness on a very important topic, and she did it in mainstream media such as the movies and television. Midler's image of a bawdy woman, who is both knowledgeable and interested in matters sexual, has rarely had the public airing she provided. She is an independent thinker and an initiator of her romantic encounters. As a successful woman actress, she is also a professional who has resources to aid other women and acts as a role model to women in all fields, not only entertainment.

Humor is an extremely effective tool with which to observe human behavior. When the comic laughs at herself as well as at the foibles of her audience, she creates a connection between people and an opportunity to examine serious subjects in a funny manner. Important and forbidden topics receive airings. Bette Midler's knowing smile, which rarely leaves her face, reminds her audience that a humorous perspec-

tive, on any and all subjects, offers catharsis alongside illumination.

Bette Midler has written two books that capture her dissenting form of humor: *A View from a Broad* (1980) and a children's verse book, *The Saga of Baby Divine* (1983), in which the first word she learned was "more." She creates a persona of a woman who has a strong sense of self and a commitment to both justice and self-satisfaction. In a culture that has traditionally seen women as submissive and subservient to the men in their lives, Bette Midler offers a startling alternative. Her women are pushy, ambitious, often selfish, but they are also generous in spirit, always ready to laugh, and fearless in their contact with life. Because the world always needs the fresh and audacious perspective she has to offer, Bette Midler's future, as she enters her fifties, appears rosy.

SELECTED WORKS BY BETTE MIDLER

The Saga of Baby Divine (1983); *A View from a Broad* (1980).

FILMOGRAPHY

Beaches (1989); *Big Business* (1988); *Down and Out in Beverly Hills* (1986); *First Wives Club* (1996); *For the Boys* (1992); *Hocus Pocus* (1993); *Jinxed* (1980); *Outrageous Fortune* (1987); *The Rose* (1979); *Ruthless People* (1986); *Scenes from a Mall* (1991); *Stella* (1990).

BIBLIOGRAPHY

Baker, Robb. *Bette Midler* (1975); Collins, Nancy. "Bette Midler: The Rolling Stone Interview." *Rolling Stone* (December 9, 1982): 15–21; Dreyfus, Claudia. "The 'Gypsy' in Bette." *TV Guide* (December 11–17, 1993): 10–12+; Petrucelli, Alan W. "What Makes Bette Laugh?" *Redbook* 175 (September 1990): 76+; Richards, Peter. "Talking with Bette Midler: 'I've Had My Share of Hard Knocks.'" *Redbook* 171 (July 1988): 64+; Safran, Claire. "Who Is Bette Midler?" *Redbook* (August 1975): 54–58; Sessums, Kevin. "La Belle Bette." *Vanity Fair* 54 (December 1991): 202–207+; Spada, James. *The Divine Bette Midler* (1984); Steinem, Gloria. "Our Best Bette." *Ms.* 12 (December 1983): 41–46; Weber, Bruce. "Musical Comedy Review: Experience the Divine." *NYTimes*, October 18, 1993, C13+.

JUNE SOCHEN

MIKVAH

The *mikvah* is a ritual bath designed for the Jewish rite of purification. The *mikvah* is not merely a pool of water; it must be composed of stationary, not flowing, waters and must contain a certain percentage of water derived from a natural source, such as a lake, an ocean, or rain. Both men and women have used the *mikvah* for ritual purification, but it has always held special significance for Jewish women. Jewish law prescribes that women immerse themselves in the waters of the *mikvah* following their menstrual periods or after childbirth in order to become ritually pure and permitted to resume sexual activity. The observance of this ritual has declined in modern times, but still remains an important element in the ritual practice of many Jewish women. In the United States, where most Jewish women have not observed the laws of menstrual purity, the *mikvah* continues to be an important institution of Jewish life. The uses and interpretations of the *mikvah* have evolved and changed along with the acculturation and modern sensibilities of contemporary Jewish women.

Before the destruction of the Temple, when ritual purity was intimately connected with the Land of Israel and Temple practices, the laws of purity and impurity [*tumah* and *taharah*] were much more far-reaching than in contemporary times. Ritual impurity might result from contact with the dead, loss of menstrual blood, loss of semen through nocturnal emission, or leprosy. Immersion in the waters of the *mikvah* provided a means of transforming an individual (male or female) from a state of ritual impurity to a state of purity. After the Destruction of the Temple, the rabbis curtailed most of the laws of purity, but elaborated those laws applying to women and menstruation. The laws of *niddah*, which determine the ritual status of a menstruating woman and the prescriptions for her sexual behavior, derive from biblical prohibitions regarding contact with a menstruant. The book of Leviticus declared that a woman would be ritually impure for seven days during her menstrual flow, during which time sexual contact was forbidden. The rabbis increased the period of sexual separation to twelve days, prescribing five days minimum for the menstrual flow and seven "clean" days afterward. Following that twelve-day period, the *niddah*, the menstruating woman, would immerse herself in the *mikvah* and then be permitted to resume sexual activity. Within the corpus of Jewish law, the observance of *niddah* is one of the three key *mitzvoth* [commandments] incumbent upon Jewish women.

Women's state of impurity during their menstrual periods is not a matter of hygienic cleanliness but rather a legal definition of ritual purity. Nevertheless, the laws of *niddah* reflect primitive blood taboos and the sense of fear and danger surrounding menstruation. Moreover, the rabbis interpreted the laws of *niddah* within a broader framework known as *taharat hamishpachah*, the laws of family purity. As the term implies, Jewish law transformed women's observance of *niddah* into a duty that affected the entire family.

Safeguarding the purity of other family members as well as regulating sexual behavior thus became primarily the responsibility of Jewish women. Jewish literature is filled with threats of punishment for intercourse during *niddah*, including assertions that children conceived during menstruation might be born with serious health impairments.

In the modern period, Jews have reinterpreted and reassessed the laws of *niddah*. While some Reformers called for the abolition of such practices as backward and superstitious, modern Orthodox leaders, such as Samson Raphael Hirsch, extolled the virtues of periodic sexual abstinence as a means of moral and spiritual elevation. The personal and private nature of adherence to the laws of family purity makes it particularly difficult to determine accurately how many Jews continued to observe the practice. However, evidence suggests that Jewish women in the modern period gradually left behind the traditional regulations of *niddah*.

Jewish immigrants to the United States appear to have largely abandoned the practice of *niddah*, but many communities in America continued to construct *mikvahs*. As early as 1759 in New York and 1784 in Philadelphia, small Jewish communities began building *mikvahs*, imploring local Jews not to neglect the laws of family purity. Throughout the nineteenth century, several congregations throughout America made the building of a *mikvah* a priority, indicating that communal leaders wanted to encourage the practice of *niddah* and at least some women continued to observe family purity. In the early twentieth century, New York's Lower East Side housed over thirty ritual baths, some sponsored by synagogues and others independently owned. Yet, despite the continuing existence of *mikvahs* in America, Jewish leaders consistently lamented women's indifference to the laws of ritual purity and seemed to be addressing a population in which most Jews had ceased to observe the practice.

While *niddah* remained one of the least observed Jewish rituals, Jewish leaders continued to publish prescriptive literature urging women to return to the traditional practice of ritual purity. In a modern American context, defenses of family purity shifted from an emphasis upon adherence to Jewish law to a new interest in the medical and hygienic benefits of *niddah*. Particularly during the first decades of the twentieth century, during the heyday of scientific positivism and eugenics, Jewish authors relied upon the findings of an emerging scientific literature, claiming that sexual abstinence during a woman's menstrual flow decreased rates of cancer and contributed to the overall health of the Jewish people. Armed with medical evidence indicating lower rates of cancer among Jewish women and supporting the purportedly unique capabilities of the *mikvah* to dispel menstrual toxins, Jewish commentators argued that observance of *niddah* was a modern, scientifically sound practice. While such defenses never succeeded in convincing Jewish women to embrace traditional Jewish practice, they do reflect the ways that *niddah* and *mikvah* were reinterpreted in accordance with modern scientific culture. The supposed health benefits of *niddah* remain a part of contemporary Jewish discourse about *niddah*, but they generally receive much more limited attention, as a fringe benefit of family purity, not its primary intent or result.

The emergence of Jewish feminism in the 1970s brought another reconsideration of the laws of family purity and the use of the *mikvah*. Some Jewish feminists urged women to cast off the restrictions imposed by Jewish law and its emphasis on women's biologic functions, but others reclaimed the practice of *niddah* as a feminist ritual. Arguing that periods of sexual abstinence enhanced the companionate bond in marriage and that the practice of *niddah* celebrated the cycle of the female body, some Jewish feminists have embraced *niddah* as a vehicle for women's spiritual renewal and the *mikvah* as a place devoted exclusively to women's needs. Although the observance of *niddah* and regular attendance at the *mikvah* remain minority practices among contemporary Jewish women, the meaning of this centuries-old Jewish ritual continues to evolve along with the needs and values of Jewish women.

BIBLIOGRAPHY

Adler, Rachel. "*Tumah* and *Taharah*; Ends and Beginnings." In *The Jewish Woman: New Perspectives*, edited by Elizabeth Koltun (1976): 63–71; Diner, Hasia. *A Time for Gathering: The Second Migration, 1820–1880* (1992): 124–125, 136; "The Earliest Extant Minute Book of the Spanish and Portuguese Congregation Shearith Israel in New York." *Publications of the American Jewish Historical Society* 21 (1913): 81; Greenberg, Blu. *On Women and Judaism: A View from Tradition* (1981): 105–123; Heinze, Andrew R. *Adapting to Abundance: Jewish Immigrants, Mass Consumption, and the Search for American Identity* (1990): 57–58; Hutt v'Dodd, Evelyn. "The Ways We Are." *Lilith* (Winter 1976–1977): 7–9; Joselit, Jenna Weissman. *New York's Jewish Jews: The Orthodox Community in the Interwar Years* (1990): 115–122; Josephson, Manuel. "Petition to Build a Mikvah in Philadelphia (1784)." In *The American Jewish Woman: A Documentary History*, edited by Jacob Rader Marcus (1981): 134–136.

BETH WENGER

MILGRIM, SALLY (1898–1994)

Against stiff competition of Paris originals, an American designer won the loudest and longest applause yesterday in the preview of Fall costumes at the custom made salon of Sally Milgrim. The silhouette of classic slimness refuses to be displaced and emphasizes its popularity in the medieval richness and color of its fabrics and the brilliant novelty and gaiety of its trimmings.

So reads a review in the *New York Tribune*'s January 1923 issue of Sally Milgrim's evening wear collection for Milgrim's Department Store. With this collection, and the ones that followed, she became one of the premiere American fashion designers of the early twentieth century.

Born in New York City on April 21, 1898, to Philip and Tillie Noble, Sally Noble was just sixteen years old when she married Charles Milgrim on June 27, 1914. Charles Milgrim was then operating a custom suit business on the Lower East Side of New York City with his father and two brothers. Shortly after World War I, at age seventeen and with little more than a public school education, Sally Milgrim joined the business as a dress designer. By the 1920s the business had grown and moved briefly to Broadway and 72nd Street before moving permanently to 57th Street and Fifth Avenue. Milgrim, at this point, not only designed dresses for the company but had expanded into exclusive evening wear and was marketing her talent for fashion to the "smart society set, political wives as well as stars of the stage." During Milgrim's career, she became a friend of the impressario Florenz Ziegfeld and designed clothing for entertainers such as Marilyn Miller, Ethel Merman, Pearl White, and Mary Pickford. The quality of her ready-to-wear gowns, wraps, furs, negligees, and accessories was rare at a time when high fashion was still a made-to-order industry.

At a time when well-to-do women dressed three or four times a day to carry on their daily social lives, Milgrim designed for any and all of these occasions, always incorporating luxury and detailing into the richness of her designs. Milgrim's signature looks typically included details of cross-stitch embroidery, bands of tucking, slot seaming, and fagoting. Color and high-quality fabrics played a large part in her designs. Lace and chiffon could often be found embroidered with crystals in pink or mauve. Whether working with ruffles, tiers, or layers, as a rule hemlines were thirteen inches from the floor.

In 1933, Milgrim's greatest success came when she designed Eleanor Roosevelt's gown for the inauguration of Franklin D. Roosevelt. The pale blue, floor-length ball gown remains in the collection of the Smithsonian Institution.

By March 1936, Milgrim was one of twenty-four women honored by the New York League of Business and Professional Women at an annual achievement dinner. This honor was remarkable in that it recognized not only her achievements among her peers but also as a woman in a male-dominated industry and world.

With the success of her designs, the Milgrim stores expanded along the East Coast to the Midwest, including Detroit, Cleveland, Columbus, Chicago, White Plains, Miami, Palm Beach, and East Orange, New Jersey. In addition, Milgrim sold a wholesale dress collection to stores throughout the country. She retired in 1960, and in 1967 her husband died. The last Milgrim store was closed in Cleveland in 1990.

In June 1994, at age one hundred and six, Sally Milgrim died in Miami, Florida. She was survived by two sons, Franklin and Paul.

BIBLIOGRAPHY

"At Milgrim Uneven Hemlines for Cocktails and Evening." *Women's Wear Daily* (March 1, 1947); "Designer Sally Milgrim Dead at 104." *Women's Wear Daily* (June 15, 1994): 21; "Sally Milgrim, 103, A Clothes Designer." *NYTimes*, June 16, 1994; *WWIAJ* (1938).

JENNIFER VAFAKOS

MILLER, LINDA ROSENBERG
(1877–1936)

Linda Rosenberg Miller was a patron of the arts and Jewish scholarship.

She was born in 1877 in Wheeling, West Virginia, the youngest of four daughters. Her mother, whose maiden name was Kraft, was Bavarian, but lived her adult life in Wheeling. She died when Linda was eleven years old, and her older sister Clemmie was responsible for her upbringing.

Her father, Victor Rosenberg, was born in the United States. He worked in his family's wholesale notions and dry goods business for more than thirty years. A civic leader and devoted father, he died when Linda was seventeen. During his year of illness, Linda put aside her regular teenage activities in order to care for him.

She was the valedictorian of her high school class and attended the Washington, Pennsylvania, Female Seminary. After completing her studies, she moved to Baltimore, Maryland, where two of her three sisters had married and settled. There she married Nathan J. Miller, who had recently graduated from Johns Hopkins University. Nathan Miller began a financial career in Baltimore, and he and his twenty-year-old bride settled there.

The Millers later moved to New York and had two daughters, Helen and Peggy. Although her husband was involved with the community, Miller did not enjoy life in New York. She, along with her sister Rose Kraus, rented summer cabins in Rangely Lake, Maine, where they took their children. They were pioneers among Jewish women who took long vacations in remote places, away from their husbands.

Miller was not drawn to traditional charity work. She was more attracted to spiritual and artistic activities. She became friends with Rebecca Mahler, who introduced her to the world of art. She bought works by Mahler and they spent time together at art shows in New York. She became a serious collector, purchasing works by Cézanne, Detrain, and Matisse. In her world travels, she collected art and artifacts from India and Egypt.

Miller became an active member of Temple Emanu-el and a great supporter of its rabbi, Hyman G. Enelow. Miller attended his lectures at the temple, heard his weekly sermons, and he taught her at home.

Misfortune struck the Miller family when Nathan Miller's business failed, followed by his death two years later. Miller then moved to New Rochelle, New York, where she lived in seclusion for the rest of her life. Her intellectual and spiritual pursuits flourished. She learned French and studied Hebrew with Rabbi Joseph Marcus in order to be able to study the Bible and prayer book in the original. She studied the Mishnah, as well as works by Judah Halevi and Solomon ibn Gabirol. Miller was also actively involved in the Jewish education of her grandchildren, particularly after the tragic death of her daughter Peggy at age twenty-nine.

Linda Rosenberg Miller died on July 26, 1936, in New Rochelle, New York. Her legacy financed the donation of Rabbi Hyman G. Enelow's collection of rare books and manuscripts to the Library of the Jewish Theological Seminary of America. The collection contains 20,000 volumes, including 1,100 manuscripts. She endowed a foundation at Columbia University devoted to Jewish history and literature that brought Salo Baron to Columbia as the first professor of Jewish history in the United States. She also financed the publication of Israel Davidson's *Thesaurus of Mediaeval Poetry*, and supported the publication on Gaonic commentary of the Talmud, and assisted in and supported the publication of the Hebrew weekly and annual of the Histadrut Ivrith in the United States. Notwithstanding the difficulties and tragedies that Miller encountered in the final years of her life, she was a resilient, dedicated, loyal, and spiritual woman who served as a role model for future generations.

BIBLIOGRAPHY

AJYB 39:594; *Essays and Studies in Memory of Linda R. Miller.* Edited by Israel Davidson (1938); *Great Books from Great Collections* (1996); Hurwitz, Ruth Sapin. "Linda R. Miller: A Memoir." *The Menorah Journal* 25, no. 3 (Autumn 1937): 352–363; Levy, Felix A. *Selected Works of Hyman G. Enelow: A Memoir.* Vol. 1 (1935); *UJE*, s.v. "Miller, Nathan J."

NAOMI M. STEINBERGER

MINIS, ABIGAIL (1701–1794)

Born August 11, 1701, Abigail Minis was a businesswoman and landowner known for her support of the Revolutionary cause. With her husband and two young daughters, she was among the first group of approximately forty Jews who arrived in Savannah on July 11, 1733, some six months after the founding of the colony of Georgia by James Oglethorpe. Between 1733 and 1757, she gave birth to seven more children, one of whom died in infancy. Widowed at age fifty-six, with eight children to support, Minis went on to build a small fortune in land.

Although she never learned to speak English well and could barely sign her name, Minis possessed a sharp business acumen. At the time of her death, she owned real property in four Georgia counties, as well as sheep, cattle, and a sufficient number of slaves to run her large plantation. In addition, Minis was well known in Savannah for her hospitality. In 1763, she applied for a license to operate a tavern. She and her five unmarried daughters conducted this business until 1779. The Minis tavern became the site of "elegant entertainments" for members of the colony's elite, including members of the Georgia assembly, judges, the governor's council, wealthy merchants, and other distinguished citizens.

Minis was widely known as a supporter of the Revolutionary cause, and helped supply provisions for the Continental line, Georgia militia, and French forces in the area. Attempts were made by Loyalists to confiscate her property after Savannah fell to the British in December 1778. However, Minis and her daughters successfully petitioned the governor for safe passage to Charleston and protection of their Savannah property for the remainder of the war. In 1783, Abigail Minis returned to Savannah and resumed her business activities, remaining active in the various enterprises owned by the family until her death on October 11, 1794, at age ninety-three.

BIBLIOGRAPHY

BDEAJ; Kole, Kaye. *The Minis Family of Georgia, 1733–1992* (1992); Levy, B.H. *Savannah's Old Jewish Community Cemeteries* (1983); Marcus, Jacob Rader. *The American Jewish Woman: A Documentary History* (1981), and *Early American Jewry.* Vol. 2 (1953); Stern, Malcolm H. "The Sheftall Diaries: Vital Records of Savannah Jewry, 1733–1808." *AJHQ* 54, no. 3 (March 1965): 242–277.

HOLLY SNYDER

MISCH, MARION SIMON (1869–1941)

Marion Misch participated in a great number of volunteer activities through her lifetime, all the while running a successful business following the death of her husband. Her primary interests centered on education and Judaism, and her volunteerism reflected her concern for these issues.

She was born on May 13, 1869, in Allentown, Pennsylvania (some sources state Newark, New Jersey), to Louis Benjamin and Rachel (Pulaski) Simon. She had a brother, Milton (of Providence, Rhode Island), and two sisters, Marguerite Simon (of East Providence) and Mrs. Aaron Padding (of Albany, New York). Her early years were spent in Pittsfield, Massachusetts, where she attended the public schools and normal school. She also studied privately with Rabbi de Sola Mendes. At age fourteen, Marion organized the first Jewish Sabbath school in Pittsfield. Later, she worked as a schoolteacher. On September 3, 1900 (some sources state 1890), she married Caesar Misch, and the couple had one son, Walter. After their marriage, they moved to Providence, Rhode Island, and opened a department store, which Marion Misch ran after her husband's death in 1921. This store was the only one in New England to be headed by a woman.

Misch was very active in both Jewish and non-Jewish activities in Providence, including serving on the Providence school board for fifteen years. In this position, she oversaw the extension of music education in the schools. She served as president of the Rhode Island Federation of Women's Clubs, the first Jewish woman to hold this post. Her activism in Providence was extremely broad. She was founder of the

Providence Plantation Club, director of the Providence Society for Organizing Charity, director of the Providence District Nursing Association, honorary president of the Providence Section of the NATIONAL COUNCIL OF JEWISH WOMEN, vice president of the Providence Civic and Park Association, president of the Rhode Island Federation of Music Clubs, and director of the Providence Association for the Blind. She was the first woman appointed to the Providence Playground Committee and was in charge of purchasing all supplies. She was reappointed to this position by both Republican and Democratic mayors.

Misch served as president of the National Council of Jewish Women from 1908 to 1913. Her volunteer efforts in the Jewish community also included acting as director of the NATIONAL FEDERATION OF TEMPLE SISTERHOODS, president of the Montefiore Ladies Hebrew Benevolent Association, president of the Sisterhood Temple Beth El, and member of the board of trustees, Temple Beth El. She was also a member of the Miriam Hospital Association, the Jewish Orphanage Association, and the Hebrew Educational Center.

Misch lectured throughout the United States and in Canada, Germany, China, India, and Australia, speaking on such topics as music, education, and women's and Jewish issues. Her publications include *Selections for Homes and Schools* (1911), a collection of Jewish prose and poetry, and a "Children's Service" for the Day of Atonement, which she wrote with Dr. Henry Englander.

She died on January 18, 1941, in Providence, Rhode Island.

BIBLIOGRAPHY

AJYB 24:182, 43:361–362; Obituary. *NYTimes*, January 20, 1941, 17:4; Rogow, Faith. *Gone to Another Meeting: The National Council of Jewish Women, 1893–1993* (1993); *UJE*; *WWIAJ* (1926, 1928).

MARY McCUNE

MIZRACHI WOMEN OF AMERICA
see AMIT

MOERS, ELLEN (1928–1979)

Ellen Moers credits "the new wave of feminism for pulling [her] out of the stacks" and into the material that was to become *Literary Women* (1976). That book, the third and last in her career, is a benchmark of feminist criticism.

Ellen Moers was born on December 9, 1928, to Robert Moers, a lawyer, and Celia Lewis (Kauffman) Moers, a teacher. Her older sister, Mary Wenig, became an attorney and a professor; her niece, a rabbi. Moers was schooled in New York City, earned her B.A. at Vassar (1948), her M.A. at Radcliffe College (1949), and her Ph.D. at Columbia University (1954). She married the writer Martin Mayer in 1949 and had two children, Thomas and James. The family expressed its Jewishness in largely secular ways. Moers taught at HUNTER COLLEGE, Barnard College, Brooklyn College, and the Graduate Center of the City University of New York, and wrote for major newspapers and periodicals. By comparison with *Literary Women*, *The Dandy: Brummell to Beerbohm* (1960) and *Two Dreisers* (1969) seem dutiful academic exercises. *The Dandy* shows the limits of its dissertation origins, but it also exhibits both the author's lifelong focus on cultural and comparative literature and her mastery of French literature, which she would use to perfection in *Literary Women*. Her second book moves far away from the subject of the dandy to Theodore Dreiser's novels *Sister Carrie* and *An American Tragedy*.

In her third book, Moers found her true subject. She was deeply affected by the second wave of feminism then in progress. The marriage of that new approach to her matured criticism resulted in a major work. *Literary Women* demonstrates that by the nineteenth century, English, American, and French women writers had a literature and a culture of their own that has become stronger in the twentieth century. Moers boldly asserts that women have particularly strong insights into issues of work, money, social justice, and the heroic.

A prime example of Moers's critical originality is her interpretation of Mary Shelley's *Frankenstein*. That work had never been read in terms of Shelley's gender, biography, or the female Gothic tradition. From a work that seemed to come out of nowhere, *Frankenstein* becomes under Moers's approach a novel deeply tied to Shelley's life as a teenage unwed mother who had experienced several miscarriages and infant deaths, and whose own birth resulted in the death of her mother, the feminist and novelist Mary Wollstonecraft. Death and birth become painfully intertwined in the novel; it is no accident that Shelley called *Frankenstein* her "hideous progeny."

Some early reviews attacked *Literary Women* for its focus on women, but within a few years it became a classic work that underpins subsequent feminist literary criticism of English and American novels.

At the time of her death on August 25, 1979, Ellen Moers was working on a book about the interrelationship between British and American literary figures of the nineteenth century. Her critical approach remained comparative, cultural, and gendered.

SELECTED WORKS BY ELLEN MOERS

The Dandy: Brummell to Beerbohm (1960); *Literary Women* (1976); *Two Dreisers* (1969).

BIBLIOGRAPHY

Howard, Maureen. "Literary Women." *NYTimes Book Review*, March 7, 1976, 4–6; Lehmann-Haupt, Christopher. "Why Not Literary People?" *NYTimes*, March 12, 1976, 31; Winegarten, Renée. "Ladies of the Desk." *American Scholar* 45 (Autumn 1976): 607–610; Wood, Michael. "Heroine Addiction." *New York Review of Books*, April 1, 1976, 12–13.

CLAIRE SPRAGUE

MOÏSE, PENINA (1797–1880)

"Three cheers for California Mountain Wine! . . . a beverage so pleasant, and exhilarating, as to make one oblivious to temperance pledges, and which possesses a spell, as potent as that of any table rapper, for raising spirits," wrote a poor, nearly blind, and ailing Penina Moïse in a letter dated 1875. Despite her suffering, she demonstrated an unflagging poetic wit and love of life. Moïse, an early Jewish educator, was one of nineteenth-century America's best-known Jewish poets. Appreciated in her own day for her literary skill and sense of humor, Moïse is relatively unknown to present-day readers.

Penina Moïse was born on April 23, 1797, to a large and wealthy family in Charleston, South Carolina. Her father, Abraham, was a successful Alsatian-born merchant. Her mother, Sarah, was the daughter of a wealthy family from the island of St. Eustace, where she met and married Abraham in 1779. They came to Charleston in 1791, fleeing a slave insurrection. Moïse was the sixth of nine children and the youngest daughter. Her brothers, Cherie, Aaron, Hyam, and Benjamin, were born in the Caribbean. Her older sister Rachel and her younger brothers, Jacob, Abraham, and Isaac, were born in the United

One of nineteenth-century America's best-known Jewish poets, Penina Moïse was also a teacher and the first Jewish American woman to contribute to the worship service, writing 190 hymns for Congregation Beth Elohim in Charleston, South Carolina. [American Jewish Archives]

States. She left school at age twelve, after her father's death. Moïse served as the family nurse, caring for her mother and brother Isaac, an asthma sufferer. Always nearsighted, during the Civil War her eyesight deteriorated into blindness.

Moïse grew up in the presence of a diverse, vital, and well-integrated Jewish community, devoting herself to Jewish issues. She was encouraged in her poetry by her brother Jacob and sister Rachel, and her work appeared in both the Jewish and general press. Her 1833 collection of poems, *Fancy's Sketch Book*, was the first by a Jewish American woman. Moïse also wrote columns for newspapers throughout the United States. Her poetry covered a variety of topics, including current events, politics, local life, Judaism, Jewish rights, and Jewish ritual reform.

Along with her literary endeavors, Moïse devoted her life to teaching. In 1845, she became the second superintendent of Congregation Beth Elohim's Sunday school. The Civil War forced Moïse to leave Charleston for Sumter, South Carolina. Returning after the war in much reduced circumstances, she supported herself by running an academy together with her widowed sister and her niece. Though self-conscious about her poverty, she accepted it with humor and grace.

Moïse was the first Jewish American woman to contribute to the worship service, writing 190 hymns for Beth Elohim. The Reform movement's 1932 *Union Hymnal* still contained thirteen of her hymns.

Penina Moïse died on September 13, 1880, in Charleston. Her life, reminiscent of the life of REBECCA GRATZ, exemplifies the choices available to Jewish American women of her era and class. She sustained her deep spiritual commitment to Judaism throughout her life, albeit to a Judaism transformed by Protestant aesthetics and American political thought. Though her poetry did not maintain its popularity, her work attests to her great intellect and indomitable spirit.

BIBLIOGRAPHY

Adams, Charlotte. *Critic* 15 (1895): 327; *AJYB* 7 (1905–1906): 17–31; *Appleton's Cyclopaedia of American Biography* (1887. Reprint 1968); *BDEAJ*; *DAB*; Dinkins, S.A. "Penina Moïse." *American Jews' Annual* 5646 (1885–1886), ch. 5; *EJ*; Elzas, Barnett A. *The Jews of South Carolina* (1905); Hagy, James W. *This Happy Land* (1993); *JE*; Kayserling, M. *Die Jüdischen Frauen* (1879); Markens, Isaac. *The Hebrews in America* (1888); Moïse, Penina. Correspondence File. American Jewish Archives, Cincinnati, Ohio; *NAW*; *UJE*; Zola, Gary Phillip. *Isaac Harby of Charleston, 1788–1828* (1994).

JAY M. EIDELMAN

MOLODOWSKY, KADYA (1894–1974)

And why should this blood without blemish
Be my conscience, like a silken thread
Bound upon my brain,
And my life, a page plucked from a holy book,
The first line torn?

These lines, from Kadya Molodowsky's 1927 sequence "Froyen-Lider" [Women poems] pose a crucial question: How can a Yiddish woman writer reconcile her art with Judaism's definition of a woman's role? Molodowsky's answer to that question in her poems, children's poems, novels, short stories, essays, plays, autobiography, and journalism, published between 1927 and 1974, evolved into even broader questions about the very survival of Jews in the modern world.

Kadya Molodowsky was born in the shtetl Bereza Kartuska, White Russia, located within the czarist

A rarity among Yiddish women poets, Kadya Molodowsky had a successful career that spanned forty-seven years. In her writing, which covered many genres, she explored not only the role of women in Judaism but also the cultural and historical crises faced by Jews in the twentieth century. [YIVO Institute]

Russian province of Grodino (now the Belarus Oblast' of Brest). The second of four children, Kadya had an older sister, Lena, and two younger siblings, a sister, Dora (Dobe), and a brother, Lebyl. Her father, a learned Jew who taught Hebrew and Gemara [commentary on the Mishnah] to young boys in heder [elementary Jewish school], was also an adherent of the Enlightenment and an admirer of Moses Montefiore and Theodor Herzl. Her mother, Itke (the daughter of Kadish Katz/Kaplan, for whom Kadya was named), ran a dry-goods shop, and later opened a factory for making rye kvass.

Molodowsky was taught to read Yiddish by her paternal grandmother, Bobe Shifre. Her father instructed her in the study of the Hebrew Pentateuch and also hired various Russian tutors to teach her Russian language, geography, philosophy, and world history. Such an education, especially the instruction in Hebrew, was highly unusual for a girl in the shtetl, and according to her niece and nephew, Kadya was better educated than either of her sisters.

At seventeen, Molodowsky passed the high school graduation exams in Libave. She tutored students in Bereza until her eighteenth birthday, when she obtained her teaching certificate. From 1911 to 1913, she taught in Sherpetz and in Bialystok, where her mother's sister lived and where she joined a Hebrew-language revivalist group. From 1913 to 1914, she studied under Yehiel Halperin in Warsaw to earn qualification for teaching Hebrew to children. At the start of World War I, Molodowsky worked in Warsaw at a day-home for displaced Jewish children, sponsored by her teacher Yehiel Halperin. Between 1914 and 1916, she worked at teaching and day-home jobs in such towns as Poltave and in such cities as Rommy and Saratov on the Volga. From the summer of 1916 until 1917, Molodowsky taught kindergarten and studied elementary education in Odessa, where Halperin had moved his Hebrew course to escape the war front.

In 1917, after the Bolshevik Revolution, Molodowsky attempted to return to her parents in Bereza, but was halted in Kiev. There, she worked as a private tutor and in a home for Jewish children displaced by the pogroms in the Ukraine. In 1920, having survived the Kiev pogrom, she published her first poem. In Kiev, she met Simkhe Lev, a young scholar and teacher originally from the shtetl of Lekhevitsh. They married in the winter of 1921. The couple lived in Warsaw until 1935, except for a period around 1923, when they worked at a children's home sponsored by the Joint Distribution Committee in Brest-Litovsk.

In Warsaw, Molodowsky taught in two schools: by day in the elementary school of the Central Yid-dish School Organization (known by its acronym, TSHISHO), and in the evenings at a Jewish community school. She was active in the Yiddish Writers Union at Tlomatske Street 13, where she met other writers from Warsaw, Vilna, and America.

In 1927, Molodowsky published her first book of poetry, *Kheshvendike Nekht* [Nights of Heshvan], under the imprint of a prestigious Vilna and Warsaw Yiddish publisher, B. Kletskin. The book's narrator, a woman in her thirties, moves through the landscape of Jewish eastern Europe. Molodowsky contrasts the narrator's modernity with the roles decreed by the Jewish tradition for women, according to law, custom, or history. *Kheshvendike Nekht* received approximately twenty reviews in the Yiddish press, nearly all laudatory.

Molodowsky was deeply aware of the poverty in which many of her students lived. She wrote poems for and about them. Her second book, *Geyen Shikhelekh Avek: Mayselekh* [Little shoes go away: Tales], published in Warsaw in 1930, was awarded a prize by the Warsaw Jewish Community and the Yiddish Pen Club.

Molodowsky's third book of poems, *Dzshike Gas* [Dzshike Street], published in 1933 by the press of the leading Warsaw literary journal, *Literarishe Bleter*, was reviewed negatively on political grounds for being too "aesthetic." Her fourth book, *Freydke* (1935), features a sixteen-part narrative poem about a heroic Jewish working-class woman.

Molodowsky immigrated to the United States in 1935. She settled in New York City, and her husband joined her in 1937 or 1938. Her fifth book, *In Land fun Mayn Gebeyn* [In the country of my bones] (1937), contains fragmented poems that represent an internalization of exile.

Molodowsky's literary endeavors then branched out in several directions. In 1938, she published a new edition of her children's poems, *Afn Barg* [On the mountain]. In 1942, she published *Fun Lublin Biz Nyu-York: Togbukh fun Rivke Zilberg* [From Lublin to New York: Diary of Rivke Zilberg], a novel about a young immigrant woman. At this time, Molodowsky also wrote a series of columns on great Jewish women for the Yiddish daily *Forverts*, using Rivke Zilberg, the name of the novel's protagonist, as her pseudonym.

Fearful for her brother and other family still in Poland in 1944, Molodowsky put aside her editorship of the literary journal *Svive* [Surroundings], which she had cofounded in 1943, publishing seven issues, and began to write the poems of *Der Melekh Dovid Aleyn Iz Geblibn* [Only King David remained] (1946). *Der Melekh Dovid Aleyn Iz Geblibn* contains many *khurbm-lider* [destruction poems] that draw upon traditional Jewish literary responses to catastrophe.

In 1945, another edition of her children's poems, *Yidishe Kinder* [Jewish children], was published in New York. That same year, a book of her children's poems in Hebrew translations by Lea Goldberg, Nathan Alterman, Fanya Bergshteyn, Avraham Levinson, and Yakov Faykhman appeared in Tel Aviv. She published a long poem, *Donna Gracia Mendes;* a play, *Nokhn Got fun Midbar* [After the god of the desert] (1949), which was produced in Chicago and in Israel; a chapbook of poems, *In Yerushalayim Kumen Malokhim* [In Jerusalem, angels come] (1952); and a book of essays, *Af di Vegn fun Tsion* [On the roads of Zion], and a collection of short stories, *A Shtub mit Zibn Fentster* [A house with seven windows], both of which appeared in New York in 1957. She also edited an anthology, *Lider fun Khurbm* [Poems of the Holocaust] (1962). In the 1950s, she revived the literary journal *Svive*.

From 1948 through 1952, Molodowsky and Simkhe Lev lived in Tel Aviv. There, Molodowsky edited a journal for PIONEER WOMEN, *Heym* [Home], which portrayed life in Israel. Molodowsky also began work on a novel, *Baym Toyer: Roman fun dem Lebn in Yisroel* [At the gate: Novel about life in Israel] (1967). At the end of this period, she began to write her autobiography, *Fun Mayn Elter-zeydns Yerushe* [From my great-grandfather's inheritance], which appeared serially in *Svive* between March 1965 and April 1974.

Published in Buenos Aires in 1965, Molodowsky's last book of poems, *Likht fun Dornboym* [Lights of the thorn bush], includes dramatic monologues in the voices of legendary personae from Jewish and non-Jewish traditions and contemporary characters. The book concludes with a section of poems on Israel from the 1950s, which, like the ending of her autobiography, express Molodowsky's Zionism.

In Tel Aviv, in 1971, Molodowsky received the Itzik Manger Prize, the most prestigious award in the world of Yiddish letters, for her achievement in poetry. Kadya Molodowsky died in a nursing home in Philadelphia, Pennsylvania, on March 23, 1974.

SELECTED WORKS BY KADYA MOLODOWSKY

A Shtub mit Zibn Fentster (1957); *Af di Vegn fun Tsion* (1957); *Ale Fentster tsu der Zun: Shpil in Elef Bilder* (1938); *Baym Toyer* (1967); *Der Melekh Dovid Aleyn Iz Geblibn* (1946); *Dzshike Gas: Lider* (1933, 1936); *Freydke: Lider* (1935, 1936); *Fun Lublin biz Nyu-York: Togbukh fun Rivke Zilberg* (1942); *In Land fun Mayn Gebeyn: Lider* (1937); *Kheshvendike Nekht: Lider* (1927); *Lider fun Khurbn: Antologye,* ed. (1962); *Likht fun Dornboym: Lider un Poeme* (1965); *Malokhim Kumen Keyn Yerushalayim: Lider* (1952); *Martsepanes: Mayselekh un*

Lider far Kinder (1970); *Mayn Elterzeydns Yerushe. Svive* (March 1965–April 1974); *Mayselekh* (1930); "Meydlekh, froyen, vayber, un . . . nevue." *Literarishe Bleter* 4, no. 22 (June 3, 1927): 416; *Nokhn Got fun Midbar: Drame* (1949); *Pithu et Hasha'ar: Shirei Yeladim.* Hebrew translations by Nathan Alterman, Lea Goldberg, Fanya Bergshteyn, Avraham Levinson (1979); *Svive,* ed, (1943–1944; 1955–1974); *Yidishe Kinder: Mayselekh* (1945).

BIBLIOGRAPHY

Hellerstein, Kathryn. "Hebraisms as Metaphor in Kadya Molodowsky's *Froyen-Lider* I." In *The Uses of Adversity: Failure and Accommodation in Reader Response,* edited by Ellen Spolsky (1990): 143–152, and "In Exile in the Mother Tongue: Yiddish and the Woman Poet." In *Borders, Boundaries, and Frames: Essays in Cultural Criticism and Cultural Studies (Essays from the English Institute),* edited by Mae G. Henderson (1995), and "Kadya Molodowsky's Froyen-Lider: A Reading." *AJS Review* 13, nos. 1–2 (1988): 47–79, and "A Question of Tradition: Women Poets in Yiddish." In *Handbook of American-Jewish Literature: An Analytical Guide to Topics, Themes, and Sources,* edited by Lewis Fried (1988): 195–237, and "The Subordination of Prayer to Narrative in Modern Yiddish Poems." In *Parable and Story as Sources of Jewish and Christian Theology,* edited by Clemens Thoma and Michael Wyschogrod (1989): 205–236, and "A Yiddish Poet's Response to the Khurbm: Kadya Molodowsky in America." Translated into Hebrew by Shalom Luria. *Chulyot: Journal of Yiddish Research* 3 (Spring 1996): 235–253; Howe, Irving, Ruth R. Wisse, and Khone Shmeruk, eds. *The Penguin Book of Modern Yiddish Verse* (1987); Klepfisz, Irena. "Di Mames, dos Loshn/The Mothers, the Language: Feminism, *Yidishkayt,* and the Politics of Memory." *Bridges* 4, no. 1 (Winter/Spring 1994): 12–47; Peczenik, F. "Encountering the Matriarchy: Kadye Molodowsky's Women Songs." *Yiddish* 7, nos. 2–3 (1988): 170–173; Pratt, Norma Fain. "Culture and Radical Politics: Yiddish Women Writers in America, 1890–1940." In *Women of the Word: Jewish Women and Jewish Writing,* edited by Judith R. Baskin (1994): 111–135; Zucker, Sheva. "Kadye Molodowsky's 'Froyen Lider.'" *Yiddish* 9, no. 2 (1994): 44–51.

KATHRYN HELLERSTEIN

MONK, MEREDITH (b. 1942)

An innovator in mixed-media forms, Meredith Monk uses music, dance, drama, and film in theater pieces that may move between ancient times and modern, between exotic fantasy and everyday reality. In her pieces, the plague of the Middle Ages is seen as the precursor of AIDS, while St. Joan dies as motorcycles speed by her. Acting as composer, choreographer, librettist, and performer, Monk has created a diversity of works, ranging from the media experimentation of *Sixteen Millimeter Earrings* (1966), with

Using dance, drama, music, and film, Meredith Monk says that she creates mixed media events which reach "towards emotion that we have no words for, that we barely remember." Self-described as "Inca-Jewish," she has changed modern performance art and dance through her innovative techniques. [New York Public Library]

its segments of film and taped singing along with live performance, to racial, historical studies, as in the site-specific *Ellis Island* (1983), which dramatically traces the brave immigrants' arrival in the New World at the turn of the century.

She was born on November 20, 1942, to Audrey Lois (Zellman) Monk and Theodore Glenn Monk in Lima, Peru, where her mother, a professional singer, was on tour. She has described herself as "Inca Jewish." She has one sister, Tracy. In 1950, the family moved to Connecticut. Monk continued her early training in music at Sarah Lawrence College, where she also studied modern dance with Bessie Schönberg. Graduating in 1964, she soon began to choreograph to her own music, always starting with an idea, then letting the media and the structure find themselves.

In 1968, Monk formed the House Foundation for the Arts to develop a group of artists committed to an interdisciplinary approach to performance. Working with some twenty performers, who had to be skilled—as she is—in acting, dancing, and singing, Monk proceeded to create a repertory of theater works: devising the dramatic structure, composing the music, choreographing the movement, and acting, dancing, and singing with her group.

In New York City in 1969, the first section of *Juice* used eighty-five performers on the spiral ramp of the Guggenheim Museum. The second section put a smaller number on the stage of the Minor Latham Playhouse, and the third took place in Monk's home loft, where television screens displayed various scenes, but no live performers appeared. In 1971, *Vessel: An Opera Epic*, featuring the character of Joan of Arc, took place on a single evening, beginning in Monk's loft, continuing in the Performing Garage, and concluding in a parking lot. *The Education of the Girlchild* (1972) was an extended solo in a single space, beginning with the dancer as a withered old woman and ending with her as a radiant young girl.

More specific characters appeared in *Quarry* (1976), when a child lying in bed cried, "I don't feel well, I don't feel well," and in lighted corners around her, visions appeared of her present life and her family history: a maid peeling an orange and reading a magazine; an Old Testament couple fleeing as a dictator appears; victims dropping their jewelry and money as Nazis lead them away; a film showing a quarry with bodies emerging and disappearing, then floating on a pond.

In the film *Book of Days* (1989), scenes of an ancient world in black and white intermingle with scenes of the modern world in color. In a medieval ghetto, a child envisions a future of airplanes and television; to her grandfather, they are visions of Noah's Ark. The ancient wisdom of the Jewish heritage is transmitted from generation to generation. Both plague in the medieval world and AIDS in the modern are shown to threaten destruction. In the film, ancient houses crumble as automobile horns are heard in the distance.

Monk has continued to make increasingly complex site-specific works. In 1994, *American Archeology No. 1: Roosevelt Island* featured a cast of sixty on an island in Manhattan's East River. The first act shows happy dancers in a spacious park. The second act, performed at night on the ruins of a smallpox hospital, shows the helpless gestures of convicts and weary patients. But in the end, a peacefully lighted hilltop serves as a sign of hope.

Monk titled the 1996 exhibition of her work at the New York Public Library for the Performing Arts *Archeology of an Artist*. For the brochure she wrote: "In a sense I think of myself as a vocal archeologist, trying to dig down to the most fundamental human utterances, the most elemental forms. . . . In the larger works, I combine forms weaving together music, movement, film object, light and ambiance. This multidimensional approach hopefully creates a poetry of sound, image and movement that increases the luminosity and radiance of the experience."

For her dance-operas, theater pieces, musical compositions, and films, Monk has received a number of awards and honors, including two Guggenheim Fellowships, the Brandeis Creative Arts Award, a MacArthur Foundation Fellowship, three Obie Awards, six ASCAP Awards for Musical Composition, the Dance Magazine Award, and the Samuel H. Scripps American Dance Festival Award.

In a 1983 brochure, Monk defined her goal as creating "an art that breaks down boundaries between disciplines, an art which in turn becomes a metaphor for opening up thought, perception, experience." Her goal has remained constant: "An art which reaches towards emotion that we have no words for, that we barely remember—an art that affirms the world of feeling in time and society where feelings are being systematically eliminated."

SELECTED WORKS BY MEREDITH MONK

American Archeology No. 1: Roosevelt Island (1994): *Archeology of an Artist* (1996): *Book of Days*, film (1989): *The Education of the Girlchild* (1972): *Ellis Island* (1983): *Four Services in Celebration of the Universal Human Quest for Spirituality* (1996); *Juice* (1969); *Quarry* (1976); *Sixteen Millimeter Earrings* (1966); *Vessel: An Opera Epic* (1971).

BIBLIOGRAPHY

Anderson, Jack. "Entering a World Only Meredith Monk Can Map." *NYTimes*, June 16, 1996; *Current Biography*; Dance collection. New York Public Library for the Performing Arts, Lincoln Center; *Encyclopedia Americana*; Jowitt, Deborah. "Ice Demons, Clicks, and Whispers." *NYTimes Magazine*, June 30, 1991; *Who's Who in America*; Zurbrugg, Nicholas. "Meredith Monk: Music That Dances, Dances That Sing." *Dance Theatre Journal* (Winter 1992–1993); Videotape collections. New York Public Library, and the House Foundation for the Arts, NYC.

SELMA JEANNE COHEN

MORDECAI, ROSA (1839–1936)

Rosa Mordecai was born into an important nineteenth-century Jewish American family in Washington, D.C., on February 14, 1839. Little detail is known of her life. One of her biographers noted in 1912 that "Miss Mordecai says of herself . . . she is simply Rose Mordecai, 'without either romance or mystery, but one who loves her fellow men.'" In his introduction to a 1953 republication of Mordecai's recollections of the first Hebrew Sunday school in America, Joshua Bloch said she "was one of the last representatives of that group of pious gentlewomen, who in their days were responsible for the religious training of Jewish youth and who left an indelible impression upon the mind and spirit of all who had come to know them."

Mordecai was a scion of a distinguished family of merchants, physicians, educators, soldiers, philanthropists, and reformers. Faith in education as the path toward equality of opportunity was instilled in Rosa Mordecai by her father, Alfred Mordecai—a distinguished educator and businessman, the first Jewish graduate of West Point, and the foremost expert on munitions in antebellum America—and her mother, Sarah (Hays), niece of REBECCA GRATZ, the founder of the first Hebrew Sunday school in America.

From her mother, Rosa Mordecai inherited her faith in Judaism. Mordecai's contributions to the character of nineteenth-century Judaism was evident in a public and private life dedicated to the idea and practice of merging Jewish American women's spiritual and religious lives within the temporal and secular world of nineteeth-century America. With her sisters, Laura and Miriam, Mordecai established and operated a private school in Philadelphia for girls, which they ran for forty years. No doubt Mordecai's efforts in this direction were a legacy of her paternal grandfather, Jacob Mordecai, who established a seminary for "young ladies" in Warrenton, North Carolina, in 1809. In its day, this seminary was considered one of the better institutions of instruction in the South, drawing its students from many prominent southern families.

Mordecai's contemporary account of the first Hebrew Sunday school in America remains as the most thorough record of religious education of Jewish children in the antebellum United States. This Sunday school, established in Philadelphia in 1838, was founded by Mordecai's maternal great-aunt, Rebecca Gratz. According to Bloch, Mordecai's account of this school "enrich[es] our knowledge of the personality of Rebecca Gratz . . . and of the remarkable role she played in early efforts to strengthen the position of Judaism and to give meaning to its teaching and practices in this country."

A prominent citizen of Philadelphia, Mordecai "contributed, in various ways, to the improvement of civic life." Rosa Mordecai died in Washington, D.C., on October 31, 1936. She is buried in Philadelphia in the cemetery of the Mikveh Israel Congregation.

BIBLIOGRAPHY

AJYB 39:595; Bloch, Joshua. "Rosa Mordecai's Recollections of the First Hebrew Sunday School." *PAJHS* 42, no. 4 (June 1953): 397–406; *DAB*; *JE*; Logan, Mary S. *The Part Taken by Women in American History* (1912. Reprinted 1972); Marcus, Jacob Rader. *Memoirs of American Jews, 1775–1865* (1955–1956), and *United States Jewry, 1776–1985*. Vol. 1 (1989).

BARBARA BRENZEL

MORDECAI, SARA ANN HAYS (1805–1894)

Sara Ann Hays Mordecai was the epitome of Victorian female devotion to literature, art, and domesticity—albeit one of a peculiarly Jewish bent. The sixth of ten children born to Samuel and RICHEA GRATZ of Philadelphia, Sara Ann was born on September 27, 1805, and raised in a household dominated by the figure of her maternal aunt, REBECCA GRATZ, who, for Sara Ann and her siblings, was the primary model of Jewish womanhood. Sara Ann later described the

household adulation of "Aunt Becky." "My beloved mother always looked up to her with affection and pride, and we, her children, were taught to share with her the love and reverence which my aunt inspired from all."

Sara Ann showed an early inclination toward literature and art. As a teenager, she assembled a commonplace book filled with drawings, sketches, paintings, and poetry of her own, as well as that of others in her circle, which included family friends Charlotte Meade Graham, Charles Fenno Hoffman, and Ann Meredith Ogden. The commonplace book reveals that Sara Ann was possessed of a keen sensibility for the natural world, and it is a demonstration of her skills in the visual and literary arts.

On June 1, 1836, at age thirty-one, she married rising young army officer Alfred Mordecai, with whom she had seven children. As the wife of a military officer, she enjoyed a comfortable life-style for many years in Watervliet, New York, where her husband was in charge of ordnance at the arsenal maintained by the United States Army. Her husband, a southerner by birth and upbringing, refused to take sides in the Civil War and resigned his army commission in 1861—a decision for which Sara Ann Hays Mordecai, as a northerner, was unjustly blamed by some of their contemporaries. In reflecting on his personal "great reverse of fortune" following the war's end, however, Alfred Mordecai paid tribute to the equanimity of "my affectionate wife," whose companionship he deemed a solace during a trying time.

The bulk of the family income during the war years was provided by a school run by Mordecai's daughters ROSA, Ellen, and Miriam, who shared her veneration of their great-aunt Rebecca Gratz. In 1870, following the death of Rebecca Gratz, Mordecai penned a short biographical sketch, entitled *Recollections of My Aunt, Rebecca Gratz, by One of Her Nieces*. This piece was finally published anonymously in 1893, just prior to the death of Sara Ann Hays Mordecai in Philadelphia, in 1894, at age eighty-nine.

**SELECTED WORKS BY
SARA ANN HAYS MORDECAI**

Commonplace book. American Jewish Historical Society, Waltham, Mass.; *Recollections of My Aunt, Rebecca Gratz, by One of Her Nieces* (1893).

BIBLIOGRAPHY

Falk, Stanley L. "Divided Loyalties in 1861: The Decision of Major Alfred Mordecai." *Publications of the American Jewish Historical Society* 48, no. 3 (March 1959): 147–169.

HOLLY SNYDER

MORGAN, ROBIN (b. 1941)

If I had to name a single quality characteristic of patriarchy, it would be compartmentalization.... Intellect severed from emotion.... The earth itself divided—national borders.... If I had to name a single quality characteristic of global feminism, it would be connectivity—a capacity dangerous to every status quo, because of its insistence on noticing.

Robin Morgan uses words as ammunition, as one can see in her quote above from *The Word of a Woman* (1992), in a lifetime battle for women's dignity and global change. As poet, novelist, journalist, lecturer, and feminist theorist, she expresses the reality of contemporary women's oppression. Her identification with women knows no borders. She travels far to interview women rebel fighters in the Philippines, Palestinian women activists in the Intifada, and postrevolutionary Iranian women.

Morgan is also a renowned activist. She was one of the key organizers of the 1968 protest at Atlantic City's Miss America Contest, which helped launch the second wave of United States feminism. A decade later, she became a spearhead of the international women's liberation movement.

Morgan has written more than a dozen books, including five books of poetry, two novels, and numerous books of essays. She is best known as editor of two historic anthologies. *Sisterhood Is Powerful: An Anthology of Writings from the Women's Liberation Movement* gives voice to American feminists of the 1960s. These raw and immediate essays cover topics such as female orgasm, the nature of prostitution, the lives of radical lesbians, and the challenge of being black and female.

The second groundbreaking volume she edited, *Sisterhood Is Global: The International Women's Movement Anthology*, compiles articles about the status of women in seventy countries. In 1984, Morgan founded the Sisterhood Is Global Institute (SIGI), bringing together the writers of the anthology at an organizing conference. SIGI functions as a think tank on women's human rights worldwide.

Morgan was born on January 29, 1941, daughter of Faith Berkeley Morgan, in Lake Worth, Florida. She married writer Kenneth Pitchford, whom she

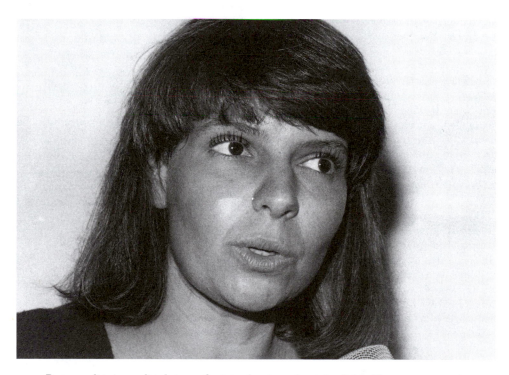

Poet, novelist, journalist, lecturer, feminist theorist and activist, Robin Morgan expresses the reality of contemporary women's oppression worldwide. For more than twenty years she worked as a contributing editor and then editor in chief for Ms. magazine, helping to define that publication. [Bettye Lane]

later divorced. Together they had one son, Blake Morgan-Pitchford, in 1969. She attended Columbia University and remained in New York City. She was a contributing editor to *Ms.* magazine for twenty years, and then became its editor-in-chief from 1990 to 1993, when it was relaunched as an advertising-free publication. She has received numerous awards, including the National Endowment for the Arts prize in poetry, the Feminist Majority Foundation Woman of the Year Award, and the Front Page Award for Distinguished Journalism.

Robin Morgan identifies her religion as Wiccan and/or atheist. She writes: "When compelled to define myself specifically in ethnic terms—I have described myself as being European American of Ashkenazic (with a touch of Sephardic) Jewish ancestry. I respect and understand the desire of others to affirm their ethnic roots as central to their identities, but while I'm quite proud of mine, I feel they're just not particularly central to my identity. And I am deeply opposed to all patriarchal religions, including though not limited to Judaism."

SELECTED WORKS BY ROBIN MORGAN

The Anatomy of Freedom: Feminism, Physics, and Global Politics (1982); *Death Benefits* (1981); *The Demon Lover: On the Sexuality of Terrorism* (1989); *Depth Perception: New Poems and a Masque* (1982); *Dry Your Smile: A Novel* (1987); *Going Too Far: The Personal Chronicle of a Feminist* (1977); *Lady of the Beasts: Poems* (1976); *The Mer-Child: A Legend for Children and Other Adults* (1991); *Monster: Poems* (1972); *The New Woman: An Anthology*, poetry editor (1969); *Sisterhood Is Powerful: An Anthology of Writings from the Women's Liberation Movement*, compiled, edited, and introduction (1970); *Sisterhood Is Global: The International Women's Movement Anthology*, compiled, edited, and introduction (1984); *Upstairs in the Garden: Selected and New Poems, 1968–1988* (1990); *The Word of a Woman: Feminist Dispatches 1968–1992* (1992).

BIBLIOGRAPHY

American Women Writers. Vol. 5, Supplement. Edited by Carol Hurd Green and Mary Grimley Mason (1994); *Contemporary Authors.* Vol. 29 (1990); *Jewish American Women Writers.* Edited by Ann R. Shapiro (1994); *Major Twentieth-Century Writers: A Selection of Sketches from Contemporary Authors.* Edited by Bryan Ryan (1991); Morgan, Robin. Correspondence with author, December 13, 1996.

REENA BERNARDS

MORGENTHAU, ELINOR
(1891–1949)

Elinor Morgenthau was an assimilationist German Jewish success story. Morgenthau achieved prominence by promoting the men around her and by

Elinor Morgenthau worked closely with Eleanor Roosevelt and tirelessly supported her husband Henry's career, helping him to gain the post of secretary of the treasury under Franklin Roosevelt. Focusing on assimilation through most of her life, she began to reassociate herself with Judaism after the Holocaust. [Library of Congress]

camouflaging her Judaism. She was a product of her era and was adept at its political and social strategies.

Elinor ("Ellie" to her friends) Fatman Morgenthau was born in 1891 in New York City to a well-to-do family of German Jewish descent. Her father, Morris Fatman, was a clothing manufacturer, and her mother, Settie (Lehman) Fatman, was from the wealthy Lehman family of banking fame. Elinor had one older sister, Margaret. She attended Miss Jacoby's private school for girls and was unusual for her time in continuing on to college. She enjoyed Vassar College, where she was a standout in theater. She was also athletic, participating enthusiastically in both tennis and horseback riding.

Following her graduation in 1913, she returned to Manhattan, where she taught acting at the Henry Street Settlement House. It was there that she met Henry Morgenthau, Jr., of the influential Morgenthau family. On February 22, 1916, she proposed to him in Central Park, and the couple was married on April 17, 1916. The ceremony was performed by Rabbi Stephen Wise.

The Morgenthaus studiously rejected all Jewish observance. They celebrated both Christmas and Easter, complete with a festive ham. They avoided Jewish social networks and vacation spots. They had three children: Henry III, who became a television producer; Robert, the district attorney for New York; and Joan, a physician. Their sons were not ritually circumcised, and they pointedly violated the Ashkenazi custom of not naming children for living relatives.

The Morgenthaus split their time between New York City and their farm in Dutchess County. Elinor Morgenthau became the speaker for the state Democratic Committee Women's Division. In 1920, she and her husband began their association with Eleanor and Franklin D. Roosevelt, campaigning for him in every election thereafter. The two women became close friends, and it was said that the Morgenthaus were the only Jews the Roosevelts knew socially.

Elinor Morgenthau was a master conversationalist with invaluable political instincts. She took lessons in public speaking and applied her talents toward promoting her husband's career. Her ambition helped propel him to positions of power under Roosevelt, including his appointment as secretary of the treasury. When the family moved to Washington, D.C., she coached her husband in political nuances and operated as his fill-in when he was unavailable to speak. Her successful reading of the political climate enabled the Morgenthaus to straddle the rivalry between the Franklin and Eleanor Roosevelt camps. In 1941, Elinor Morgenthau became Eleanor Roosevelt's assistant in the Office of Civilian Defense. However, in 1942, her activities were drastically curtailed due to health problems.

Morgenthau's involvement with Jewish affairs was consciously minimal. She never attended religious services. Nevertheless, she recognized the impact of the Holocaust when, in 1944, she accompanied Eleanor Roosevelt on a visit to the Oswego, New York, internment camp for displaced persons. Similarly, the Holocaust also affected Henry Morgenthau's political activity. He drew closer to Jewish interests when he became head of the newly created War Refugee Board. Elinor Morgenthau supported her husband's increasing Jewish involvement (after FDR's death), including campaigning on behalf of the new State of Israel.

In 1945, the couple attended a Passover seder for American servicemen, the Morgenthaus' first observance of the ritual meal. Whether this thawing of relations with the Jewish world would have continued can only be guessed. Following a heart attack in 1945, Elinor Morgenthau suffered a stroke and died in New York on September 21, 1949. A master of political maneuvering whose time forced her into the shadow of her husband, Elinor Morgenthau came to her Jewishness only late in life.

BIBLIOGRAPHY
AJYB 52:503; Morgenthau, Elinor. Records, RG 171. Office of Civilian Defense, National Archives, Washington, D.C., and Oral History Transcripts. Library of Congress; Morgenthau, Henry, III. *Mostly Morgenthaus: A Family History* (1991); *National Encyclopedia of American Biography* (1950), s.v. "Morgenthau, Henry, Jr."; *Who's Who in America* (1946), s.v. "Morgenthau, Henry, Jr."

EDNA FRIEDBERG

MORTON, LEAH *see* STERN, ELIZABETH

MORTON, MARTHA (1865–1925)

As a female playwright, Martha Morton faced adversity within the male-dominated New York theater world. Despite repeated rejection, she achieved fame and prosperity. Morton not only got her plays produced, but also directed and cast them herself, completely defying the theater industry's expectations or vision of women's involvement.

Born in New York City to Joseph and Amelia (Marks) Morton on October 10, 1865, Martha attended the city's public schools and Normal College (later HUNTER COLLEGE). She began writing at a young age. "It was fore-ordained by heredity that I should write," Morton explained in a 1904 *Theater Advertiser* interview, citing her mother as the one who "transmitted to me her taste for play reading."

She struggled to get her plays onstage. In her early twenties, when she tried to get her first play, *Helene*, produced, one of several managers who rejected it told Morton, "a woman playwright on my stage, why it would demoralize the entire company." Defiant, she adopted a male pseudonym, Henry Hazleton, in order to find a producer for her second play, *The Merchant*. She won a contest sponsored by the *World*, a New York daily, which offered five thousand dollars and a production of the best play entered. *The Merchant* opened at Union Square Theater in 1891 to positive reviews and immediately sold for fifteen thousand dollars. After the success of her first play, Morton wrote and produced *Brother John* (1893), *His Wife's Father* (1895), and *A Fool of Fortune* (1896), the profits from which totaled over $250,000. Her prosperity did not lead her to lose sight of her convictions. She took her role as a dramatist seriously and approached her work with political and feminist sensibilities.

"Womanhood is a tragedy today," Morton commented in the 1904 interview in the *Theater Advertiser*. "My next play will be one about suffrage for women," she announced. "It is the one thing that American women need, because it will furnish them a balance. They have been so loved and petted and sheltered that they have lacked what suffrage will give them, a sense of responsibility."

In January 1907, after she was refused membership to the American Dramatists Club because of her gender, Morton founded the Society of Dramatic Authors, establishing a basic level of enfranchisement for women in her field. Men were invited to join the new society because, as Morton said, "the drama is universal. . . . All dramatists are one in their work; therefore, as moderns we may make no restrictions of nationality or sex." Morton had a pronounced commitment to women, recognizing the challenges they encountered in all facets of theater.

Martha Morton also resisted stereotypes by creating strong, independent female characters, such as Anna, the protagonist in *On the Eve* (1909), an upperclass woman in Russia during the 1905 Revolution who works for the cause. Morton's artistry followed American drama's movement toward realism and away from melodrama. She was a box office success, but did not always attract critical praise for her plays. In 1897, one Chicago reviewer scathingly wrote that her play *A Bachelor's Romance* was "in texture a flimsy bit of airspun gossamer, but it lacks all the gossamer's dainty grace and airy beauty." That "flimsy bit of air-spun gossamer" netted $250,000 for Morton, less than a quarter of her lifetime's earnings. Morton authored over twenty-five other plays, most notably *The Movers* (1907), a play from midcareer revived several times by popular demand, and *Three of Hearts* (1915), one of her last plays, which was produced in London and elsewhere abroad.

In 1897, at age thirty-two, Morton married Hermann Conheim, a Jewish trader and importer. Though she lived in New York during an era of mass immigration of Eastern European Jews and flourishing Yiddish theater, she did not become involved with Yiddish theater circles or immigrant feminists, and never included overt Jewish content in her work. In 1918, she addressed a group of Jewish women in Brooklyn on the insidiousness of movies. She described how cinema lacked the crucial element of live theater, a direct connection to the written and spoken word.

On February 18, 1925, at age fifty-nine, Martha Morton died of heart disease at her home in New York. Playwriting earned her over a million dollars over the course of her career. She was a trailblazer for women's full participation in the theater, doing them justice by creating good roles onstage and supporting her colleagues offstage. Morton's drive helped her deflect critical attacks on her work. In 1896, she told the *New York Mirror*, "So long as the public approve [the play], I should be satisfied, for, after all, the esteem and approval of the playgoers is the thing that we seek to gain."

SELECTED WORKS BY MARTHA MORTON

A Bachelor's Romance (1896); *Brother John* (1893); *A Fool of Fortune* (1896); *Helene* [also known as *The Refugee's Daughter*] (1888); *His Wife's Father* (1895); *The Merchant* (1890); *The Movers* (1907); *On the Eve* (1909); *Three of Hearts* (1915).

BIBLIOGRAPHY

AJYB 24:184, 27:151; Gipson, Rosemary. "Martha Morton: America's First Professional Woman Playwright." *Theatre Survey* (November 1982): 220; Morton, Martha. Clippings file. New York Public Library at Lincoln Center, and Ser 2. Vol. 281, Robinson Locke Collection, New York Public Library at Lincoln Center; Obituary. *NYTimes*, February 20, 1925, 17:4; *UJE*.

MICHELE SIEGEL

MOSES, BESSIE LOUISE (1893–1965)

Gynecologist, professor, and family planning pioneer, Bessie Louise Moses spent a long professional life as a public health advocate and women's health specialist.

She was born on December 21, 1893, in Baltimore, Maryland, one of three daughters of German Jewish philanthropists Bernard and Bertha (Manko) Moses. She graduated from Goucher College in 1915 and went on to graduate work at Johns Hopkins University, teaching biology at Sophie Newcomb College and zoology at Wellesley College before graduating from the Johns Hopkins University School of Medicine in 1922. Moses completed obstetrics and surgery internships at Johns Hopkins Hospital and at Women's Hospital of Philadelphia before opening a private practice in Baltimore in 1924. As an assistant gynecologist at Sinai Hospital, obstetrics instructor at the Hopkins School of Medicine, and the head of the Maternal Health Clinic at Hopkins Hospital, she gained extensive clinical experience and became passionately concerned with women's health issues.

Moses founded the Bureau for Contraceptive Advice in 1927, the first birth control clinic in Baltimore, serving as its medical director for decades. Using the Bureau for Contraceptive Advice as a base, she organized contraceptive clinics and improved public health standards all over Maryland. She lectured on the medical advantages of planned parenthood and trained both white and African-American doctors in order to spread contraceptive strategies and gynecological techniques to the widest possible audience. As part of her determination to reach a wide audience, Moses wrote *Contraception as a Therapeutic Measure* (1936), a book aimed at a popular readership.

In 1950, Moses received the Lasker Foundation Award in Planned Parenthood in conjunction with Margaret Sanger. Sanger and Moses were the first women to receive the Lasker Award, and the national press resulted in high demand for Moses as a speaker and teacher. She conducted seminars in marital relations at Goucher College, Hood, Randolph Macon, and a number of other women's colleges. Goucher presented her with a citation in 1954 for distinguished scientific achievement, and her other alma mater, Johns Hopkins, elected her president of the Johns Hopkins Women's Medical Association. She was a member of Phi Beta Kappa and Alpha Omega Alpha.

Moses achieved a solid reputation as a sensitive and receptive physician, and she continued her private gynecological practice until the last months of her fatal struggle with cancer. Her years of training doctors, health workers, and young women produced a network of highly trained, informed professionals. Moses's deep involvement in family planning at a time when planned parenthood was a highly controversial subject was recognized when she was posthumously inducted into the Maryland Women's Hall of Fame in 1991.

Bessie Louise Moses died on March 25, 1965, in Baltimore, the urban base from which her influence and innovation built a chain of family planning institutions that contributed to Maryland's public health programs.

BIBLIOGRAPHY

Moses, Bessie Louise. Maryland Room, Enoch Pratt Free Library, Baltimore; *NYTimes*, October 19, 1950; "Personalities and Projects: Social Welfare in Terms of Significant People." *Survey* 86 (December 1950): 564–565; *WWIAJ* (1938).

MELISSA KLAPPER

MOSKOWITZ, BELLE (1877–1933)

Belle Moskowitz's career is unique in American politics. After two decades as a settlement worker, social and civic reformer, and labor mediator, in the early 1920s she became one of New York governor Alfred E. Smith's closest advisers. She organized his campaigns and served as a strategist in his "kitchen cabinet." When he ran for president in 1928, she was by far the most powerful woman in the national Democratic Party—the only Jewish woman and the only woman unconnected to a prominent family to achieve such standing.

She was born on October 5, 1877, in Harlem, New York, to Esther (Freyer) and Isidor Lindner. The Lindners, who had emigrated from East Prussia in 1869, ran a small jewelry shop on Third Avenue. Two older brothers survived into adulthood: Walter, later a corporate lawyer in New York City, and Max, a department store executive in Cleveland, Ohio. Educated at public schools, Horace Mann High School for Girls, and briefly at Teachers College at Columbia University, Belle trained to become a dramatic reader and taught dramatics to children.

In 1900, she took her talents to the Educational Alliance, a Jewish settlement on New York's Lower East Side. After handling assignments such as the roof garden and "women's" work, she became director of entertainments and exhibits. Her job was to organize monthly exhibits and orchestral, choral, and dramatic events. She also taught elocution to youngsters and coached dramatic groups. In the fall of 1903, she resigned from this job to marry Charles Henry Israels, an architect twelve years her senior and a volunteer club leader at the Educational Alliance. Although she agreed with her contemporaries that settlement work and married life were incompatible, after her marriage Belle remained active in social service. As she wrote in "The Jewish Woman's Opportunity for Service," published in the *American Hebrew* in 1917, "To think of others is as natural to the Jewish woman as to breathe. She gives and has been trained for generations to give with all her heart."

Accordingly, even after she bore children, she worked part-time outside the home, earning just enough to pay for child care. Editorial work for the social reform journal *The Survey* allowed her to pursue volunteer work through the United Hebrew Charities, the New York State Conference of Charities and Corrections, and the NATIONAL COUNCIL OF JEWISH WOMEN, New York Section. Working with this last group raised Belle's awareness of a pressing social need, the lack of recreational and vacation resources for urban working girls. Under NCJW sponsorship, she began a drive in 1908 to license, regulate, and create substitutes for New York's commercial dance halls. Social and settlement workers elsewhere later took up this cause, agitating successfully for dance hall regulations across the country.

To Belle and her husband, Judaism meant a shared history and perspective, more than a system of rituals. For a time, they attended New York's Sephardi synagogue, Shearith Israel, but disliked the Orthodox tradition of seating women away from the men. They soon shifted to Felix Adler's Ethical Culture Society. When they moved to Yonkers, they found a synagogue more to their liking, but remained admirers and supporters of Ethical Culture. Later they joined Stephen Wise's Free Synagogue.

In 1911, Charles Israels died suddenly of heart disease. To support her children, Carlos (b. 1904), Miriam (b. 1907), and Josef (b. 1909), Belle turned her volunteer experience into salaried work. She wrote a pamphlet on child care called *The Child* for the Metropolitan Life Insurance Company and then worked as "commercial recreation secretary" for the Playground and Recreation Association. The following year, she became grievance clerk for the Dress and Waist Manufacturers Association. This group had just signed a "Protocol of Peace" with the union in an attempt to halt the strikes then endemic in its industry. During almost four years with the group, Belle settled thousands of worker grievances and rose to head its Labor Department. Her relations with her employers were stormy, however. In November 1916, the association elected a new board and fired her.

She continued her volunteer work during her widowhood. In 1912, two groups invited her involvement: the Committee of Fourteen, formed to rid New York of its brothels, and a "Citizens' Committee" investigating links between gambling and police graft. In 1913, a "fusion" political movement gathered around this latter group and elected a reform city administration. The new mayor, John Purroy Mitchel, appointed several social reformers to city posts. Henry Moskowitz, a settlement worker and industrial mediator, became president of the Municipal Civil Service Commission. The salary that went with this job allowed him to marry Belle.

Henry and Belle's paths had crossed often on the Lower East Side and during her various reform campaigns. A protégé of Felix Adler and LILLIAN WALD, Henry had earned a Ph.D. in philosophy from the University of Erlangen in 1906. He later became head resident at the Downtown Ethical Society (Madison House), which he had founded in 1898 with some college friends. A founder of the National Association for

Belle Moskowitz exercised a level of power in the political realm unprecedented for women in her time. When Alfred Smith ran for president in 1928, she was by far the most powerful woman in the national Democratic Party. [American Jewish Archives]

the Advancement of Colored People in 1909, he was deeply involved in city fusion and state and national Progressive Party movements. Belle and Henry thus shared many interests. They married in November 1914.

After she lost her job with the dress manufacturers, Moskowitz became a private industrial consultant. In 1918, she and Henry made a fateful political decision: They decided to support Alfred E. Smith for governor, despite his links to Tammany Hall, New York's Democratic Party machine. As a member of an "Independent Citizens' Committee," a group of non-Tammany Democrats and former Progressives, Belle Moskowitz organized the woman's vote for Smith (New York women won the vote in 1917). Her work brought her to Smith's attention.

Smith's victory, which came as World War I ended, prompted Moskowitz to suggest that he appoint a "Reconstruction Commission" to plan the course of the state's future. He accepted her idea and appointed her the commission's executive secretary. Its reports, issued between April 1919 and March 1920, covered five areas: labor and industry, the rising cost of living, public health, education, and government reorganization and retrenchment. The reports reflected the fundamental progressive creed of the era, that government should spur business interests to cooperate voluntarily in reform, but when voluntarism failed, the state should step in. Smith followed this creed in developing his Reconstruction Labor Board, a State Highways Transport Committee, expanded powers for the Department of Farms and Markets, and a State Housing Board.

During his first two-year term, Smith relied increasingly on Moskowitz's political judgment and foresight. When he lost the 1920 election, he took her with him to the planning group developing a bistate "authority" for the Port of New York–New Jersey. Moskowitz devised the group's public relations program, which included a pioneering nonfiction motion picture called "Mr. Potato" that explained how a port authority would reduce food costs.

Smith won reelection in 1922, thanks in strong measure to Moskowitz's publicity work. He then offered her a government post, but she refused, choosing instead to create the post of publicity director for the State Democratic Committee. This post allowed her to perform many services for Smith—editing his public papers, writing his speeches, preparing and monitoring legislation, ferreting out information, and finding the right person for a vacant post. Her duties included distributing copies of Smith's speeches and messages, sending out weekly news releases, and planting favorable editorial comment in newspapers. The job made her a central figure in the governor's circle.

Moskowitz's publicity work for Smith had three goals: to win support for Smith's policies, reelect him, and after 1924 make him president. Developing citizens' committees to promote his campaigns, in 1924 she churned out all the publicity and correspondence related to his presidential ambitions. When, in 1926, his fourth gubernatorial victory swelled his out-of-state support, Moskowitz coordinated the response, maintaining a vast correspondence and a card file on every Smith booster. It was this network that, in 1928, won the primaries and, ultimately, Smith's presidential nomination.

But it could not win Smith the presidency. Anti-Catholic sentiment, rejection of his stand against Prohibition, concerns about his inadequate preparation for the job, and his own provincialism combined to defeat him. During the 1928 race, Belle Moskowitz, the only woman on the executive committee of the Democratic National Committee, directed campaign publicity. After Smith lost to Herbert Hoover, Moskowitz stayed on as his press agent as he tried to retain his hold on the Democratic Party. In 1932, she organized his futile bid for the presidential nomination against Franklin Delano Roosevelt. In December, she fell down the front steps of her brownstone on West 94th Street and, while recovering from broken arms, suffered an embolism. Belle Lindner Israels Moskowitz died on January 2, 1933, at age fifty-five.

In an era when women, unless related by blood or marriage to political figures, never achieved proximity to political power, Moskowitz succeeded with Smith by offering him a selfless, nonthreatening loyalty. "She never belittled him," labor reformer Frances Perkins said. "She never in the slightest way betrayed him . . . never grabbed credit for herself. She gave it to the Governor." Indeed, when friends spoke of Smith as her protégé, Moskowitz corrected them by calling him her mentor. This traditionally "feminine" political strategy allowed Moskowitz to exercise a level of power unprecedented for women in her time. It did not make her a "feminist" hero, but it did permit her to have a lasting impact on a major political figure.

BIBLIOGRAPHY

AJYB 24:184, 35:127; *DAB* 1; *EJ*, s.v. "Moskowitz, Henry"; *NAW*; Obituary. *NYTimes*, January 3, 1933, 1:4; Perry, Elisabeth Israels. *Belle Moskowitz: Feminine Politics and the Exercise of Power in the Age of Alfred E. Smith* (1987, 1992); *UJE*; *WWIAJ* (1926, 1928); *WWWIA* 1.

ELISABETH ISRAELS PERRY

MOSS, MARY (1864–1914)

In a portrait published in *Bookman* magazine in 1903, Mary Moss says of herself, "If I . . . knew this 'fame' was to be thrust upon me I'd [have] mis-spend every Saturday afternoon, so as to have a dark past to draw on. As it is, I've . . . never experienced anything in the least noteworthy."

Mary Moss was born in Chestnut Hill, Philadelphia, on September 24, 1864, into an assimilated Jewish family. Her father was Dr. William Moss, a surgeon and a major in the Civil War, and her mother was Mary (Noronha) Moss. Their home was a meeting place for intellectuals, a tradition Mary Moss continued, living in the house her entire life.

Educated in private schools, Mary Moss began publishing in 1900, writing for the *Philadelphia Times* and the *Philadelphia Press*. She covered the Yiddish theater and wrote about subjects such as child care facilities, the lives of insane women, immigrant life, and women who worked in cranberry bogs in New Jersey. She also covered the popular expositions of her day.

Moss published stories, novellas, contemporary criticism, and articles in magazines including *Bookman*, *Atlantic Monthly*, and *The Nation*. Two published novellas, "Julian Meldohla" in *Lippincott's Magazine* (1903) and "Judith Liebestraum" in *Scribner's* (1904), have Jewish themes. She published two novels, *A Sequence in Hearts* (1903) and *The Poet and the Parish* (1906).

Beginning in 1892, Moss and Owen Wister, writer and friend, performed publicly in a piano quartet. Together, they traveled to the 1893 Chicago World's Fair. Moss nursed both parents through fatal illnesses and suffered health problems herself before traveling in Europe. Mary Moss died in Catania, Sicily, on April 2, 1914.

SELECTED WORKS BY MARY MOSS

"Chronicle and Comment." *Bookman* (1903); "Judith Liebestraum." *Scribner's* (1904); "Julian Meldohla." *Lippincott's Magazine* (1903); *The Poet and the Parish* (1906); Scrapbook of articles and stories, 1900–1904. John Hay Library, Brown University, Providence, R.I.; *A Sequence in Hearts* (1903).

BIBLIOGRAPHY

AJYB 6 (1904–1905): 158–159; *JE* 9 (1925); Leonard, John W. *Woman's Who's Who of America: A Biographical Dictionary of Contemporary Women of the United States and Canada, 1914–1915* (1914); Payne, Darwin. *Owen Wister: Chronicler of the West, Gentleman of the East* (1985); Robinson, Doris. *An Index to Biographical and Autobiographical Sources* (1984); *UJE*; Wallace, W. Stewart. *Dictionary of North American Authors Deceased Before 1950* (1951); Wister, Owen. "Mary Moss Died at Catania, April 2." Transcript of memorial service, Baltimore, 1914. Brown University, Providence, R.I., and University of Virginia, Charlottesville; *WWWIA* 1, 1897–1942 (1943).

BETH O'SULLIVAN

MOVIES *see* FILM INDUSTRY; FILMMAKERS, INDEPENDENT; YIDDISH FILM

MUFFS, YOCHEVED [JUDITH] HERSCHLAG (b. 1927)

During much of her tenure (1964–1990) at the Anti-Defamation League (ADL), Judith Herschlag Muffs worked with major book publishers to correct inaccuracies in their accounts of Jews and Judaism. Stressing accuracy and objectivity, she succeeded in modifying dozens of textbooks and reference books. Today, inaccurate depictions of Jews have been largely eliminated from educational materials.

She was born Judith Herschlag (Yocheved is her Hebrew name) on August 5, 1927, and grew up in Jamaica, Queens, the youngest of three children. Her father, Alexander Herschlag, and her uncle together owned a wholesale bread bakery. Her mother, May (Friedman) Herschlag, a homemaker, died when she was thirteen years old. She attended Hebrew school, which she loved, and where, when she was about eleven years old, Hashomer Hadati, a religious Zionist youth group, performed.

In early 1946, she dropped out of New York University and went to the Hashomer Hadati training farm in upstate New York, where she learned to cook, mix concrete, and milk cows. In 1947, when she was nineteen, she immigrated illegally to British-controlled Palestine, arriving by unconverted World War II troop carrier within a day of the famed *Exodus* ship, which carried over forty-five hundred survivors from Nazi Europe to Palestine.

She settled with her *garin* [aliyah group] at a kibbutz, where she eventually became kitchen manager, preparing meals and stretching meager food supplies. The kibbutz fought off several Arab attacks during the Israeli War of Independence in 1947–1949. Judith Herschlag served as a messenger during times of alert, learning to throw grenades and to shoot.

Shortly after her return to the United States in late 1949, she started to work for Young Judaea, an educational movement for Zionist youth. She first served as a group leader and then, beginning in 1954, as national program director. Eventually, she wrote five volumes of "Judaean Leaves," a program guide for group leaders.

While she worked at Young Judaea, she returned to school, attending Queens and Brooklyn colleges. She completed her B.A. degree in sociology in 1952, and went on to do graduate work in sociology and anthropology at New York University.

In 1959, she went to work for the United Synagogue Commission on Jewish Education, an organization that sets policy, develops courses and objectives, and prepares text materials to implement curricula for Jewish religious schools. There, she was editor of a variety of books and publications, including five volumes of *Our Age*, a biweekly for high school students.

She organized and participated in countless interfaith seminars and institutes at Christian seminaries and universities from the 1960s through the 1980s. In the late 1960s she coproduced the ADL–Catholic Archdiocese of New York twelve-part television series

The Image of the Jew in Literature and *Jews and Their Religion*, featuring, among others, Elie Wiesel and Yitz Greenberg. Her study in the 1970s, "Jewish Textbooks on Jesus and Christianity," appears in the Vatican publication *Fifteen Years of Catholic-Jewish Dialogue* (1988). In the 1980s she was on the task force of the National Conference of Catholic Bishops to develop and promote an accurate account of Jews and Judaism in Catholic education.

On April 5, 1970, she married Rabbi Yochanan Muffs, distinguished service professor of Bible studies at the Jewish Theological Seminary of America. The couple has an apartment in Jerusalem, where they spend part of every year, and Muffs has both American and Israeli citizenship.

Muffs was a consultant and a contributor to numerous books, films, and television documentaries on the Holocaust. Her *The Holocaust in Books and Films: A Select and Annotated Bibliography* has been published in three editions since its initial publication in 1978. She also cowrote and acted in the ADL presentation of *Women vs. the System*, produced by ABC-TV.

Muffs considers her work at the ADL a continuation and expansion of her earlier commitments to Judaism, interfaith understanding, and civil rights. At the ADL she has served as director of special projects, associate director of interreligious affairs, director of research and curriculum, and associate director of publications. She retired from the ADL in 1990, and continues to consult for them on major projects.

Throughout her entire professional career, Muffs has striven to promote love of Judaism among Jewish young people, and understanding of Judaism among those of other faiths.

BIBLIOGRAPHY

"ADL Forces Change in Anti-Semitic Book." *Southern Jewish Weekly*, February 15, 1974; "ADL Protest Causes Publishers to Correct School Textbook." *Jewish Ledger*, February 14, 1974; Bole, William. "Textbook Watch: The Image of Jews in Kids' Schoolbooks." *Long Island Jewish World* 10, no. 47 (November 20–26, 1981): 1, 15–17; Fitzgerald, William. "Children of Survivors Meet, Holocaust Offspring Asked to Struggle Against Hatred." *The Dispatch* (Hudson/Bergen Counties, N.J.), May 28, 1984, p. 12; Hyer, Marjorie. "Jewish Leaders Threaten Boycott of Papal Visit." *Washington Post*, June 20, 1987; Jawin, Jess. "ADL—The Watchdog." *Texas Jewish Post*, February 14, 1974; Muffs, Yocheved. Interviews by author, September–December 1996, and personal correspondence and files; "Religious Zionist Pioneers to Remember Early Struggles." *The Jewish Week & The American Examiner*, May 18, 1984, p. 22; "Revised Textbook Result of ADL Representations." *Jewish News*, February 14, 1974.

DIANE M. SHARON

MUSEUMS, JEWISH

Jewish women play prominent roles as founders, directors, curators, artists, and patrons of Jewish museums in the United States. While women have rarely played an exclusive role in the creation of either small community or larger museums, their work as creators and developers of these repositories is critical.

HISTORY

Jewish museums emerged in several European cities over a short span of years in the late nineteenth century. Emancipation and Enlightenment resulted in the transformation of objects of traditional religious practice, intended for home or synagogue use, into artifacts for passive display. Similar motivation led Judge Mayer Sulzberger to donate twenty-five objects to the library of the Jewish Theological Seminary of America (JTS) in 1904. From this seed, and from the 1944 gift of FRIEDA SCHIFF WARBURG of the neo-Gothic mansion at 92nd Street and Fifth Avenue in New York, grew the Jewish Museum.

The first formalized museum in America dedicated to Judaica was established in 1913, when Hebrew Union College (HUC) organized its museum in Cincinnati. (Reorganized, it became the Skirball Museum in Los Angeles, in 1972.) Throughout its history, the NATIONAL FEDERATION OF TEMPLE SISTERHOODS (renamed the Women of Reform Judaism in 1993) has also played a considerable role in creating Jewish museums, even including in its bylaws that one of the five goals of each sisterhood should be the establishment of a Jewish museum in every synagogue. It is particularly since the Holocaust that Jewish museums in America have flourished. When the Judah L. Magnes Museum, named for the San Francisco rabbi who presided over the Hebrew University in Jerusalem, was established in Oakland, California, in 1962, the words of Rebecca Fromer reflected the new consciousness:

> Before the ashes there was life, and that life would be celebrated, and perhaps if we were lucky would constitute restoration of the name and serve to sanctify it. . . . And so, the museum began with a wealth of mind, the desire to share, to make real through something that could be seen and touched, a part of the collective identity we had no other way of knowing.

Across the United States, the new recognition of the need to preserve and document Jewish culture, and through its interpretation to educate a new generation of Jews and non-Jews, motivated founders of Jewish museums. Notable are the B'nai B'rith Klutznick

National Jewish Museum, established in Washington, D.C., in 1957; the Judah L. Magnes Museum, established in Oakland, California, in 1962 and then moved to Berkeley, California; the Spertus Museum of Judaica, established in Chicago in 1967; Yeshiva University Museum, established in New York City in 1973; and the National Museum of American Jewish History, established in Philadelphia, in 1976.

Along with the Jewish Museum in New York and the HUC Skirball Museum in Los Angeles, in 1977 these seven Jewish museums established the Council of American Jewish Museums (CAJM), which later received ongoing administrative support from the National Foundation for Jewish Culture. Membership was made available to other museums in 1987. By 1996, the CAJM had grown to more than fifty member museums, over one-third of which are synagogue museums. Representatives of many of these museums attend annual conferences and are involved in other programmatic activities.

Representing a broad spectrum, from modest synagogue collections to major exhibiting institutions, almost all the members of the CAJM are supported by larger institutions. The Skirball Museum, supported by the Reform Hebrew Union College–Jewish Institute of Religion; the Jewish Museum, supported by the Conservative Jewish Theological Seminary of America; and Yeshiva University Museum, supported by the Orthodox Yeshiva University are projects of the academies of three major American Jewish movements, while the Spertus Museum of Judaica is supported by the independent Spertus College. The B'nai B'rith Klutznick National Jewish Museum, The Judaica Museum of The Hebrew Home for the Aged in Riverdale, in the Bronx, New York, and My Jewish Discovery Center of the Jewish Community Center of Los Angeles illustrate the diversity of parent institutions.

HOLOCAUST INSTITUTIONS

A significant number of Holocaust memorials and museums have been established in the United States. Although dominated by the U.S. Holocaust Memorial Museum in Washington, D.C. (a federal museum supported in part by private funds) and the Museum of Tolerance of the Simon Wiesenthal Center in Los Angeles, the memorial function and specific focus of these centers, along with other members of the Association of Holocaust Organizations, have often separated their path from that of Jewish museums—a fact that provides evidence of Jewish vitality and diversity. Ironically, it has often been more difficult to rally strong public support for Jewish museums, because

contemporary Jewish life has so profoundly identified with the Holocaust.

WOMEN AND JEWISH MUSEUMS

There are many explanations for the contributions of women to the development of Jewish museums. In previous decades, Jewish museums offered them opportunities for recognition not attainable in other fields. For example, in the Western European birthplaces of Jewish museums, educated and culturally alert women could volunteer and enter into careers at the museums. In recent decades, as professional areas such as rabbinate and cantorate have opened to women, and as academic opportunities at university levels have expanded, women's involvement in Jewish museums has increased.

Professional Jewish museum work has been a more recent development. Although the academic field of Jewish art was advanced in pre-Holocaust Europe, its American version was not advanced until RACHEL WISCHNITZER, former curator of the Berlin Jewish Museum, began teaching at STERN COLLEGE FOR WOMEN of Yeshiva University in New York City, at age seventy-one. During a twelve-year span, she served as a role model and inspiration to several generations of students at Stern College.

Access to Jewish arts education remained rare until the development of Jewish studies programs after the 1970s. Many leading Jewish museum professionals trained in related art fields. Olga Weiss, curator of exhibitions at the Spertus Museum of Judaica, worked as a volunteer before earning a master's degree in art history. Susan Goodman studied primitive art, beginning her career at the Guggenheim Museum, later joining the staff of the Jewish Museum, where she serves as chief curator. Female leadership at both these institutions encouraged Goodman's professional development.

Only recently have more options been offered for serious training in the arts, Jewish studies, and education. Vivian Mann, who holds the Morris and Eva Feld Chair of Judaica at the Jewish Museum, directs the first master's program in Jewish art and material culture. In the first year of the program (1994–1995), twelve of fourteen students were female. Joint studies at the Jewish Theological Seminary of America, Columbia University, and the Jewish Museum are creating a new professional standard for future generations of Jewish women museum professionals.

At present, some 80 percent of Jewish museum directors are women. This continues a pattern of women building, creating, and developing these institutions. JOY UNGERLEIDER-MAYERSON directed the

Jewish Museum in the 1970s, later becoming a strong patron of Jewish arts worldwide through the Dorot Foundation. Joan Rosenbaum, who succeeded her in 1980, brought the museum international recognition, guiding a major expansion project in 1992. Under their leadership, the Jewish Museum presented exhibitions that extended far beyond ritual objects and transformed the museum into a center for the study of contemporary art, history, and culture as interpreted in Jewish life.

Other museum directors have continued this pattern. Sylvia Herskowitz, longtime director of the Yeshiva University Museum, nurtured the museum through a period of growth and accomplishment. Margo Bloom has developed and displayed a number of analytical social history exhibitions at the National Museum of American Jewish History in Philadelphia. Anna Cohn spearheaded the evolution of the B'nai B'rith Klutznick National Jewish Museum from a gallery installation to a substantial exhibition facility. She later developed the Precious Legacy Project, a traveling exhibit of Judaica collected at Prague from destroyed Czech and Slovak Jewish communities, and then served as the first director of museum planning for the U.S. Holocaust Memorial Museum. Rebecca Fromer and Ruth Eis played extraordinary roles in the establishment and collection development of the Judah L. Magnes Museum. Nancy Berman, formerly curator at the Jewish Museum, transformed the Skirball Museum after 1972, leading to the 1996 opening of the Skirball Cultural Center.

CURATORS

Grace Cohen Grossman, curator at the Skirball Museum, advanced cataloging of Judaica at the Smithsonian Institution as research collaborator for the National Museum of American History. Her other achievements include the core exhibition and Project Americana of the Skirball Museum, and the publication of the comprehensive *Jewish Art* (1995).

Working in other repositories, such as the library of the JTS, Evelyn Cohen pioneered the creation of the Jewish Art Department. Sharon Liberman Mintz continued this work, which resulted in an extensive collection and exhibition program relating to all aspects of the Hebrew book, manuscripts, and related art objects.

COLLECTORS AND PATRONS

Jewish museums bear testimony to the husbands and wives who have collected Judaica together, and who have, in many cases, made considerable financial contributions. A few donors stand out in generously shaping museums. Abram Kanof and his wife, Frances

Jewish women have played prominent roles as founders, directors, curators, artists, and patrons of Jewish museums in the United States. Pictured above is Joan Rosenbaum, the director of the Jewish Museum in New York City, who has brought the museum international recognition and guided a major expansion project for the institution. [The Jewish Museum, New York]

Pascher, established the Tobe Pascher Workshop at the Jewish Museum as a studio center for the creation of Jewish ceremonial art; Erica Pappenheim Jesselson and her husband, Ludwig Jesselson, have long been identified as the patrons of the Yeshiva University Museum; and Audrey Skirball Kenis, with her support of the new Skirball Cultural Center and Museum, has continued Jack Skirball's vision of a new kind of cultural and educational entity to reinforce Jewish identity.

EDUCATORS

Jewish museums have transformed themselves from repositories to vital centers of Jewish education and identity formation. Esther Netter, of My Jewish Discovery Center, targeted assimilated Jews and inter-married families through a series of traveling exhibitions. Adele Lander Burke, of the Skirball Museum, developed the groundbreaking MUSE program, which uses ethnographic approaches to compare ceremonial objects among diverse cultures. Judith Siegel, of the Jewish Museum, helped develop programs for *Bridges and Boundaries*, an exhibition exploring Jewish and African-American identities.

DOCENTS

Volunteers continue to play a significant role in Jewish museums. Women have predominated as docents, conducting tours and programs. The Skirball Museum has 140 docents, and Yeshiva University Museum has over 30, while the Jewish Museum limits its corps to 40. In recent years, there has been a notable shift toward male retirees whose volunteer efforts mark a search for a fulfilling experience, while new, full-time career opportunities have been made available to women.

Judith Siegel, director of education at the Jewish Museum, feels that the arts offer an opportunity for a richer integration of the volunteer's own education, delving into "Who am I? What can I teach? What audience can I reach? What levels of instruction can I provide?" This search for identity bridges centuries and is "a way [for volunteers] to think creatively about what they know."

SYNAGOGUE MUSEUMS

Since the 1970s, a growing number of synagogue Judaica collections have been made accessible through the establishment of interpretive exhibitions and the creation of gallery space. For the most part, these small museums are projects developed and run by women from the congregation or its sisterhood. Collections range in size from a few pieces in a showcase to several rooms. Efforts like the Sylvia Plotkin Judaica Museum in Phoenix, Arizona, the Temple Judea Museum of Keneseth Israel in Elkins Park, Pennsylvania, and the Mizel Museum of Judaica in Denver, Colorado, are notable: All three have developed their own shows by taking an interpretive approach to the collections.

With the publication of *A Temple Treasury: The Judaica Collection of Congregation Emanu-El of the City of New York* by Reva Goodlove Kirschberg and Cissy Grossman, this collection of New York's Congregation Emanu-El has become well known. It is featured in the newly opened Herbert and Eileen Bernard Museum and includes both the functional objects for-merly used in the synagogue and a formal collection begun in 1928 when the present building at Fifth Avenue and 65th Street was erected. Cissy Grossman, curator of the collection, has also developed numerous Judaica exhibitions as assistant curator at the Jewish Museum and curator of the historic Central Synagogue collection in New York City.

In addition to the numerous synagogues whose buildings have landmark status, significant collections include the Congregation Beth Ahabah Museum and Archives Trust, in Richmond, Virginia, and the Dr. Edgar R. Cofeld Judaic Museum of Temple Beth Zion, in Buffalo, New York. The Elizabeth S. Fine Museum at Congregation Emanu-El, in San Francisco, bears the name of the wife of longtime rabbi Alvin Fine, while the Janice Charach Epstein Museum Gallery of the Jewish Community Center of Metropolitan Detroit bears the name of this young artist, also in memoriam. The mission of this gallery is to show and support the work of young Jewish artists.

CONCLUSION

The traditionally strong presence of women in the Jewish museum field has shaped and defined the scope and influence of these institutions. Women make enormous contributions as builders of institutions. Yet their strong presence fails to give museums priority of place for Jewish communal budgets, where museums struggle to carve their identity against a backdrop of more pressing social service demands. Consequently, even today, Jewish museums occupy a modest position in the Jewish communal roster. Perhaps because women direct them, Jewish museums are compelled to continue to struggle to achieve even a modest degree of visibility within the philanthropic community.

Nonetheless, Jewish museums have played an enhanced role in recent decades as educational and cultural centers, as well as sources of preservation and documentation of significant historical events. Their ability to recognize the changing social and religious needs of their communities assures both an important and vibrant future for these institutions.

BIBLIOGRAPHY

AJYB 91 (1991), s.v. "American Jewish Museums: Trends and Issues"; Bilski, Emily D. "The Art of the Jewish Museum." In *The Jewish Museum New York* (1993); Glaser, Jane R., and Artemis A. Zenetou. *Gender Perspectives: Essays on Women in Museums* (1994); Greenwald, Alice. "Jewish Museums in the U.S.A." *EJ Yearbook* (1988–1989): 167–181; Grossman, Cissy and Reva Goodlove Kirschberg. *A Temple Treasury: The Judaica Collection of Congregation Emanu-El of the City of New York* (1989); Grossman, Grace. *Jewish Art*

(1995); Siegel, Judith. Conversation with author, December 1995; Van Voolen, Edward. "Jewish Museums in Europe." *EJ Yearbook* (1988–1989): 182–188.

KAREN FRANKLIN

MUSIC

JEWISH WOMEN AND JEWISH MUSIC IN AMERICA

Female balladeers and minstrels entertained other women privately and at family celebrations of Sukkoth, Purim, Pesach, and Shavuoth throughout centuries of European Jewish history. Among Sephardic Jews and Near Eastern–Mediterranean groups such as the Yemenites, an age-old custom of funeral wailing women [*endicheras*] continued well into the twentieth century. The injunction concerning *kol isha* [woman's voice], limiting the singing voice of women, prevailed since Talmudic times among all Jewish traditions barring participation in religious rituals and liturgy. Consequently, Jewish women kept to their own separate devotionals, much as did biblical Miriam, who led the women outside the Israelite encampment after crossing the Red Sea, where they intoned what may have been their own version of Moses' Hymn of Triumph.

In the Eastern European areas of Jewish settlement, spurred by the spread of the *haskalah* enlightenment movement during the nineteenth century, Yiddish secular culture began to flourish, creating a tradition of folk artistry among traveling *badkhonim* [bard-troubadours] and *klezmorim* [instrumental musicians]. Although talented women increasingly sought opportunities for active participation, their route to public performance remained either through male entertainers in their families or by separation from Jewish life.

WOMEN AND YIDDISH AMERICAN MUSIC THEATER

Beginning in 1876, Avrom Goldfaden (1840–1908) devised and developed a new genre, the operetta, for his performing troupes of singing actors and instrumentalists who traveled to Jewish communities in Russia, Romania, Austria, and Poland. Performances featured women rather than young boys in the female roles and even had special set pieces for female performers. By the 1880s, this Jewish theatrical art and its artists had found its way to America, where the male actors became matinee idols, and the actresses became role models reflecting the diversity of women's lives and conditions in America.

In America, women from Goldfaden's theatrical company expanded their repertories to include hymns, and liturgical chants. Sophie Karp (1861–1906), who had been discovered and trained for the stage by Goldfaden, became a starring soubrette in Yiddish revues and plays at the Bowery theaters on the Lower East Side of New York City. In 1896, she introduced a Yiddish ballad written especially for her by Peretz Koppel Sandler. That song, "Eili, Eili," a dramatic arietta, became an immediate favorite and soon became a featured solo by BERTHA KALICH (1874–1939) and many other female performers of the day, even some in the general entertainment field. Operatic sopranos SOPHIE BRASLAU (1902–1935) and Rosa Raissa (1893–1963) sang "Eili, Eili" in their programs at the Metropolitan Opera House and other concert halls. BELLE BAKER (1896–1957) featured it in her touring vaudeville presentations, and her photograph adorns several published editions of the song. Soon, Cantor Yossele Rosenblatt was including this song in his concert and recording repertoire, and his photograph in cantorial garb appeared on its sheet music publications. As a result, a song originally presented by women on the Yiddish stage was transformed into a Jewish hymn and consequently considered the musical domain of male singers.

Music was an essential element of the Yiddish musical theater in America, as shaped and given distinctive form by Goldfaden. Songs were the dominating elements in drama as well as comedy, and everyone on the Jewish stage had to sing. The earliest female actor-singer, for whom Goldfaden wrote many operettas featuring heroic women, was Regina Prager (1874–1949). In the course of her long career, she introduced such operetta heroines as Shulamith, a sad maiden of the Second Temple Era, and Dinah, warrior consort of Bar Kokhba. Over the years, Prager went from lovely soubrette and romantic lady to formidable matron in the leading role for Boris Tomashefsky's highly successful musical *Di Khazinte* [The lady cantor]. For almost two decades, her photograph adorned the song sheet covers of numerous musical selections. By World War I, female performers were regularly featured on theater posters and commercial sheet music, usually in costumes and in scenes from the shows.

Early on, resourceful Yiddish theatrical entrepeneurs were presenting their own versions of the "uptown" American musicals. BESSIE THOMASHEFSKY (1873–1962) starred as the "Jewish American Beauty" in her husband Boris Thomashefsky's production of *The Yiddish Yankee Doodle*. In her later years, she enjoyed a busy theatrical life as a director and producer, as well

as performing in her own shows. Although Jacob P. Adler was the abiding theatrical star of his day, the "Adler women" also displayed exceptional talents. Both his daughter CELIA ADLER (1889–1979) and the widely acclaimed performer and teacher STELLA ADLER (1902–1992), daughter of third wife SARA ADLER (1858–1953), appeared in varied dramatic roles well past their eightieth birthdays.

In its heyday, the Yiddish theatricals mirrored immigrant tenement life, presenting issues and problems faced by audiences. Family matters had particular importance in an era of physical accommodation, economic survival, and social acculturation into American life. The nobility of motherhood was celebrated in legions of stories and songs. How could it be possible, balladeers sang, that one mother could take care of ten children and yet ten children would not take care of one mother? Women's woes were discussed and often resolved across the footlights. Reality was presented to an extent not parallelled in the general theatrical world of those years. Theatrical treatments might be comic with songs about suffragists and women's rights, and lyrics jested about women not only as cantors but also as doctors, politicians, even rabbis. Such role reversals were a traditional part of Purim celebrations, but they may also have reflected a feminist agenda. Many were serious expositions, for example on behalf of legislation to protect women workers, especially following upon the TRIANGLE SHIRTWAIST FIRE in 1911 when 146 workers lost their lives.

JENNIE GOLDSTEIN (1895–1960) was a particular favorite in her dramatic portrayals of women struggling to survive despite adversity. Her songs, while musically varied, had a predominant message: "The sun shines but never for me." She began her theatrical career as a vulnerable immigrant waif, progressing from wronged maiden who must give away her baby, to the older girl with a checkered past, and then an exhausted working woman pleading "take me away from the sewing machine." Her photographs in those roles appeared on sheet music covers and souvenir programs, and she filled crowded theaters on the Bowery and then Second Avenue with teary women and sympathetic men.

Women played comic as well as pathos-ridden roles. Two popular comic-soubrettes enjoyed long and illustrious careers: Nellie Casman (1896–1984) and MOLLY PICON (1898–1992). Casman, who wrote her own material and songs, typically played naughty yet wise roles. One of her tunes, "Yosel, Yosel," and its English version, "Joseph, Make Your Mind Up," continues to be sung by non-Jewish as well as Jewish performers worldwide. Molly Picon was a beloved performer on the Yiddish stage, in the general entertainment field, and on recordings. Her characterizations were shaped by her petite physical appearance and warm personal charm. Three leading composers of the Yiddish music theater, Joseph Rumshinsky, Sholom Secunda, and Abraham Ellstein, composed songs for her.

By the second half of the twentieth century, the distinctive qualities of Yiddish theater and most of its gifted artists had moved into the mainstream by means of radio, recordings, movies, and then television. However, in the process they sacrificed their earlier role as role models whose kinship with other immigrant women reflected female concerns in adapting to life in *di goldene medine* [the golden land]. With their unique qualities of communication across the footlights, they had fashioned a night school for women, teaching lessons with songs and stories on how to survive and overcome a multitude of tribulations. In their heyday, the old Yiddish theatricals and their music helped bring women into the forefront of Jewish artistic self-expression.

WOMEN AND AMERICAN JEWISH LITURGICAL MUSIC

Over the three-hundred-year history of Jewish life in America, Jewish sacred music was sung in synagogues and temples throughout this country. In the nineteenth century, Judaic hymnals were published and distributed throughout the United States. Hebrew liturgical texts and their English free translations were set to traditional chant as well as to composed or adapted melodies. Increasingly, Jewish women's voices joined with those of men in choirs and congregational singing in less traditional synagogues. Women also began to participate in the shaping of American Jewish liturgical customs and preparation of hymnals. REBECCA GRATZ (1781–1869) started a formal Sunday school for Jewish children and utilized liturgical texts and hymn tunes for the religious lessons. PENINA MOÏSE (1797–1880) edited and translated the texts and music of German Jewish Reform hymnals, adapting them for American congregations. EMMA LAZARUS (1849–1887) wrote devotional poetry for the Gottheil-Davis hymnal (1875/1887) adopted by Temple Emanu-El in New York City. Members of the Jewish Women's Congress, organized in 1893 at the World's Columbian Exposition in Chicago, commissioned a major American Jewish liturgical publication, *A Collection of the Principal Melodies of the Synagogue from the Earliest Time to the Present*, compiled and edited by Alois Kaiser and William Sparger.

By the turn of the century, Jewish women went beyond traditional familial roles and began to take active roles in their religious communal and cultural life. In 1923, the NATIONAL COUNCIL OF JEWISH WOMEN published a monograph on Jewish music, *An Introduction to Jewish Music, in Eight Illustrated Lectures*, by Angie Irma Cohon (1890–1981). Over the next three decades, Cohon's work was the basic course of Jewish musical study for branches of the council organization and other congregational groups across the country.

In the decades following World War I, Jewish women's choruses sang Yiddish and Hebrew folk songs and holiday melodies at public functions. Moreover, Jewish liturgical music had come into general American performance. Special prayers like *Kol Nidre* [all vows], *El Mole Rahamim* [God of mercy], and familiar Sabbath *zmirot* [spirituals] had become available on player-piano rolls, in published sheet music arrangements, and on commercial recordings that often featured women singers. Not only did women perform Jewish spiritual music, but some also composed and arranged devotional selections. Mana-Zucca (nom de plume of Augusta Zuckerman, 1885–1981) wrote a number of such songs, including two concert-style anthems, "Rakhem" [Have compassion] and "Sholem Aleichem" [Peace to you]. Increasingly, women musicians were participating in the spiritual musical expression of American Jewry.

Clearly, this practice constituted a challenge to the concept of isolating *kol isha* in an observant Jewish life. By the 1930s, except at Orthodox synagogues, women sat together with men as they intoned the responsive prayers in congregational unity. There were mixed choruses, and sopranos sang solos. Women had always sung at home, but now they sang in public, and the music they sang was progressing well beyond that of the usual range of Jewish women's songs. Moreover, the ranks of religious school teachers were rapidly filling with women, many of whom taught the liturgical melodies as well as folk tunes to their students. All of Jewish music was becoming their shared domain.

In the period following World War II, three schools of sacred music were instituted. In 1948, the School of Sacred Music was established at the Hebrew Union College–Jewish Institute of Religion (HUC–JIR) for the academic training of cantors and music educators to serve Reform Judaism. In 1952, the Jewish Theological Seminary of America (JTSA) inaugurated the Cantors Institute and College of Liturgical Music on behalf of its constituency, Conservative Judaism. At about the same time Yeshiva

University began to add courses in Jewish musical study, and in 1964 it formally established the Cantorial Training Institute for Orthodox congregations. Until that time, training of cantors had been by oral transmission from cantor to apprentice.

From its inception, the School of Sacred Music admitted women to Jewish liturgical music studies and offered them accreditation to serve congregations as music educators and choral leaders, but not as cantors. Following the ordination in 1972 of Rabbi SALLY J. PRIESAND, the Reform branch of Judaism began to accept women for training as cantors, and in 1975 Barbara Ostfeld-Horowitz was ordained as the first woman cantor. She received pulpit placement following graduation and was inducted into the American Conference of Cantors. By 1995, when she received a twenty-year honorary award at HUC–JIR graduation services, there had been ninety-four other women cantor graduates from that school. In accepting her award, Ostfeld-Horowitz said, "Women cantors have altered the way in which prayer is offered, heard, and received."

In 1984, the Jewish Theological Seminary of America began accepting of women for rabbinical training in the Conservative branch of Judaism. Meanwhile, women had been students at the seminary's College of Liturgical Music since its establishment, and some had received degrees in sacred music. In 1984, Erica Lipitz and Marla Rosenfeld Barugel applied and were permitted to prepare for ordination as *hazan* [cantor]. They were granted that status by the Cantors Institute in 1987, and both were placed with congregations. Since then, a number of other women have completed and received cantorial designation. However, acceptance or rejection of women cantors in the Conservative Movement depends on the particular congregation and its rabbi. Moreover, until recently, admission was not formally given to women cantorial graduates by the Conservative professional organization, the Cantors Assembly of America. This reflects continuing opposition among some constituents to women's expanded role.

According to age-old Judaic tradition, the rabbi has been the principal religious teacher-scholar and spiritual interpreter-counselor, and only in America has that office assumed a more active ministerial-preacher role at the religious services. In contrast, the traditional role of the American cantor has remained that of *shaliah zibbur*, or leader in ritual duties and musical guide and inspirer of congregational prayer. The issue of women's roles as leaders of prayer are still hotly debated. For example, there remain several significant halakic [legal] issues for interpretive

consideration: mandatory cantorial observance of the 613 principles of faith (traditional male duties); the counting of a minyan [ten Jews] as male for a proper order of service; and, of course, the abiding matter of *kol isha* in divine worship. Women have not been granted admission to Orthodox cantorial training at Yeshiva University, nor is that likely to happen in the foreseeable future.

In the Jewish Ministers Cantors Association, a traditionally oriented group established in America late in the nineteenth century, membership remains entirely male. However, two unaffiliated organizations are concerned with the roles of women in synagogue music: the American Guild of Jewish Organists, which includes male and female liturgical musicians and offers musical guidance to its membership; and the Women Cantors Network, the female counterpart of the Jewish Ministers Cantors group. The network was founded by Cantor Deborah Katchko-Zimmerman in 1981, gathering together a group of twelve women serving as cantors or seeking that professional goal. By 1996, the membership had grown to ninety.

Katchko-Zimmerman typified those who needed such an organization. Granddaughter of an eminent European cantor, most of whose family had perished in the Holocaust, she was trained privately by her cantor father. She secured a full-time active position at a Conservative congregation in Connecticut but felt isolated from the male cantorate. Joining her in spearheading the network organization was another privately trained Cantor, Doris Cohen, formerly a liturgical soloist with composer and conductor Sholom Secunda, who has served at a Reform pulpit in New York City. The network is a support group with annual study conferences and a regular newsletter.

Though debate continues regarding the female cantorial profession, among all the denominations of Judaism, women's voices increasingly are heard in America leading congregations in all the year-round calendar and life-cycle observances of the Jewish faith. These women train and lead choirs, arrange and compose liturgical works, and present special Jewish music programs. They attend to a great many duties as music educators in the religious schools, including the training of girls and boys to assume religious responsibilities of bar and bat mitzvah.

Jewish women are taking advantage of increasing opportunities in Jewish music itself. As performers, many now include works of Judaic relevance on their programs. At temples and synagogues, they are choir singers and choral leaders, as well as organists and music directors. Some have composed music of Jewish inspiration, often on commission for works with Holocaust themes. Complete services have appeared in the past few years, among them those of MIRIAM GIDEON (1906–1996). The growing roster of younger composers of Jewish works includes Judith Berman, Judith Karzen, Lillian Klass, Shulamit Ran, Elizabeth Swados, and Judith Lang Zaimont.

SINGERS OF YIDDISH FOLK MUSIC

RUTH RUBIN and Eleanor Chana Mlotek have led the way over past decades with their achievements as collector-arrangers and performers of Yiddish songs. Among many younger women devoting their talents to Jewish folk music in Hebrew and Yiddish, as well as Ladino and English, are Debbie Friedman and Robyn Helzner, both of whom are also gifted recording artists.

As a pioneer Jewish music educator, JUDITH KAPLAN EISENSTEIN (1909–1996) not only published and composed pedagogical materials for adults as well as children but also taught and inspired a number of women to follow in her footsteps. TZIPORAH JOCHSBERGER (b. 1920) established a music school that focused on the Jewish music education of youngsters. More recently, Leah Abrams, Isabel Ganz, and Judy Caplan Ginsburgh are among a growing number of group music leaders popularizing Jewish music among children and young adults. Significantly for Jewish music in America, most female cantors have also taken on a variety of communal music activities, reaching out to the general public, in addition to fulfilling their usual pastoral and educational duties for their congregations.

Women music educators currently predominate in the Jewish religious schools, and many others who teach at academic institutions and conservatories include Jewish folk music in their curricula. As scholars and writers, they research and publish works treating Jewish music. As supporters and patrons of this music, Jewish women support special programs and musical events offering Jewish music and fill audience seats at such presentations.

WOMEN IN SECULAR MUSIC

American Jewish women in secular music have shared advances and handicaps with the general population of women in the United States. Until the latter part of the nineteenth century, native-born Jewish women suffered from the same Victorian limitations that affected the entire middle-class female population, that is, the belief that professional appearances in public were socially degrading. That attitude was compounded by the lack of a tradition of professional artist-musician families such as prevailed in Europe,

in which women were trained and introduced into professional circles by family members. But the first feminist movement in the United States, powered in large part by the campaign for suffrage, supported women's struggle for a more public role in music as well as in other fields. As a result, in the late nineteenth century, women in music began moving into public life and professional endeavors. Indeed, a startling change had taken place: Women were crowding into the fields of music and music teaching. Their involvement increased from 36 percent in 1870 to 60 percent in 1910, the latter a historic high.

Another favorable element was the traditional Jewish valuing of culture and learning that many families brought with them from Europe, a value system reinforced in America by the nineteenth-century amateur tradition of musical accomplishment. Training in voice and piano made middle-class unmarried women more valuable on the marriage market.

However, the arts have always been a way up for marginalized people. From the 1880s on, anti-Semitism was on the upswing, reaching its high point in the 1920s and continuing until the 1960s. Jewish women's opportunities in other fields were limited during that period, making performance in classical music, musical theater, and popular music an attractive option for the talented.

In music as in other arts, the "aristocracy of talent" has been the criterion for success, not, as in other fields, religion or family credentials or country of origin. Indeed, musicians have benefited from being members of the international musical community. The reasons for this are historical: Beginning in the middle of the nineteenth century, Americans valued European over native-born performers. Indeed, musicians working in the classical tradition, whether or not native-born, were expected to have European training and experience, while those trained in United States were considered inferior.

Much remains unknown about the population of Jewish women in secular music, for whom religion did not play an obvious part in their musical lives. In an age when assimilation was the aim for many, religious differences were suppressed, even at times denied, and names changed, leaving many unidentified as Jews. The investigator risks thrusting on some women an identity they have rejected. (Of course, the reverse is true as well: A number of musicians of Anglo-Saxon descent changed to Slavic-sounding names, e.g., Stokes to Stokowski, Hickenlooper to Samaroff, Liggins to Leginska, in order to appear not Jewish but Eastern European.) Despite these limitations, a picture of female Jewish participation in music begins to evolve.

Singers predominate. For those with musical gifts, careers in opera and musical theater were the only ones in which women are irreplaceable by men. In the first generation of Jewish American opera singers, most were born in Europe: LINA ABARBANELL (1879–1963), ALMA GLUCK (1882–1938), MARIA WINETZKAJA (1888–1956). For these women, being reared in the European tradition of multilingualism was (and is) a distinct advantage. In addition, American audiences have been long been exposed to opera, art, and ethnic songs sung in foreign languages.

Gluck, who began in opera, ultimately chose concert singing, making of it a notable success. ESTELLE LIEBLING (1880–1970) also had a short career in opera. A native-born American, she combined the advantages of fine European training with birth into a professional artist-musician family. Multitalented (she also served as a vocal accompanist), upon her return to the United States in 1902, she made her debut at the Metropolitan Opera. Her two-year stint was followed by extensive tours as soprano soloist with John Philip Sousa's band. Thereafter, although continuing to perform, she concentrated on teaching voice.

Two singers born early in the twentieth century who had brief careers in opera but chose to be lieder and concert rather than opera singers were RUTH KISCH-ARENDT (b. 1906) and JENNIE TOUREL (1910–1973), the latter possibly the greatest of them all. Tourel maintained her interest in Jewish affairs and became an ardent and musically active supporter of Israel, teaching and performing regularly in that country.

Singers born after World War I who have had notable careers in opera include REGINA RESNIK, JUDITH RASKIN, ROBERTA PETERS, and BEVERLY SILLS. Born Belle Silverman in 1929, Sills was a child prodigy: She appeared on radio beginning at age four, started her long years of study with Estelle Liebling at age seven, and began her professional singing career at sixteen. Her career in opera began in her thirties with the New York City Opera, where she became its star. She faced opposition to joining the Metropolitan Opera under Sir Rudolf Bing but finally overcame that as well. Her long and illustrious career as prima donna and remarkable singing actress was crowned by a directorship of the New York City Opera. Her subsequent appointment as president of Lincoln Center for the Performing Arts has been another first for a woman.

Popular music offered opportunities to women, initially as singer/entertainers and only later as instrumentalists. The saloon singer and musical theater actor SYLVIA SYMS, the daughter of an immigrant father, learned her craft by sneaking into saloons to hear jazz greats, overcoming poverty and a minimal education to become one of the outstanding saloon singers of her generation. Among the Jewish women active in the folk music movement was CASS ELLIOT (1941–1974), famous as a member of the Mamas and the Papas. EYDIE GORME (b. 1932), an outstanding popular singer, became famous as a recoding artist and as half of a radio duo with her husband, Steve Lawrence. The daughter of immigrant Turkish Jews, she was fluent in Spanish and recorded and broadcast in that language for the Voice of America. CAROLE KING (b. 1942), middle-class and college-educated, is a much honored singer and songwriter. Three women have had oustanding careers as lyricists in popular music, theater, and film: SYLVIA FINE, DOROTHY FIELDS, and BETTY COMDEN.

Women have had a harder time succeeding as instrumental performers. Among pianists, the earliest Jewish woman to have an international concert career was FANNIE BLOOMFIELD ZEISLER (1863–1927), who also was America's first international star on the concert circuit.

While the number of distinguished professional solo pianists proliferated, no American Jewish woman has quite matched Zeisler's stature in the international concert world. Women of all backgrounds faced handicaps that men were spared. Olga Samaroff (born Hickenlooper, as noted above) wrote of the lower fees traditionally paid to female concert artists. Yet women on the road had greater expenses than men because of the need for companions while young and for multiple expensive concert gowns instead of the one standard outfit for men. Finally, while female wunderkinder have strong audience appeal, that appeal often dwindles with increasing age, something that rarely affects men.

Adherence to socially constructed gender roles as a limiting factor is dramatically illustrated in the life of HEPHZIBAH MENUHIN (1920–1980), gifted sister of Yehudi. Brother and sister both made their first and brilliantly successful public appearances at age eight; however, their father concentrated on promoting his son's career, while Hephzibah, who wished the same support and opportunity, was told that her sphere was home and children. Thus her career, though it flourished sporadically, never equaled her promise as a child. A second sister, Yaltah, also musically gifted, had even less of a performing career.

NADIA REISENBERG (1904–1983) had an international career as a concert pianist. She first studied at the St. Petersburg Conservatory in her native Russia, where she made her debut. In 1922, she immigrated to the United States, where she studied at the Curtis Institute with Josef Hofmann. Her performing career included appearances with major orchestras and ensembles in Europe and the United States. ROSALYN TURECK (b. 1914), who is native born, came from a musical immigrant family who provided her with fine teachers. At sixteen she won entry to the all-scholarship Juilliard School and soon after her debut established her reputation as a Bach specialist with an international career. Others of that generation include Ray Lev and Lonnie Epstein, and in the next generation, Ruth Meckler Laredo (b. 1937). Laredo began as a child prodigy whose first teacher was her mother. After making her debut with the Detroit Symphony Orchestra at age eleven, she studied with Rudolf Serkin, who was a powerful and continuing influence in her musical life.

Whereas piano was the primary instrument for the nineteenth-century female amateur musician, the violin was for American middle-class women a proscribed instrument, one associated with music for dance and thus for accompanying "immodest" movement, and worst of all, one played in sporting houses. Thus the violin was considered an instrument of the devil, not one for the "angel in the house." However, the example of French violinist Camille Urso, who made her debut as a child prodigy in mid-century, together with the later influence of the women's movement, finally changed the violin into an instrument that respectable girls and women might play. By the turn of the century, when the seven-year-old VERA HOCHSTEIN [FONAROFF] arrived in the United States, American women were making careers as concert violinists and as members of women's string quartets and orchestras. A prodigy, she made her debut at nine with the Metropolitan Opera Orchestra, then continued her training in England and the United States. In 1909, she became second violinist in the all-female Olive Mead String Quartet, one of the earliest all-female groups and considered among the finest in the country.

LILLIAN FUCHS was born into a musical family in 1902. She had first-rate conservatory training as a pianist and then as a violinist, and was able to move into the mainstream of musical life in New York, joining her two gifted brothers in chamber music recitals. She was a member of the Perole String Quartet from 1926 to the 1940s, one of the first American women to break the gender barrier in quartet playing.

Playing in professional orchestras and ensembles of all kinds, in concert halls, theaters, cabarets, for radio and television, has been the main source of musicians' livelihoods. Yet women were for many years locked out of these positions. Their first reactions to such discrimination took the form of all-women groups, beginning in the late nineteenth century and coming to a high point between 1925 and 1945, when dozens of such orchestras were active from New York to California. BLANCHE BLOCH (1890–1980) had the advantage of concertizing with her husband, a violinist, beginning with his debut in 1913. She also taught piano, the only other option open to most pianists. However, in the 1930s, Bloch found a niche as pianist in the New York Women's Symphony Orchestra, conducted by Antonia Brico. The concert career of Eudice Shapiro (b. 1914), the daughter of a violist and the granddaughter of a cantor, was aided early by a solo engagement with the New York Women's Symphony Orchestra, with whom she played the Sibelius Violin Concerto in 1938. Some of the women trained in orchestra playing in the all-women groups moved into positions vacated by men during World War II. A few were able to remain after the war was over, beginning the long struggle to integrate community, regional, and in recent years, major American orchestras. This has been one of the most successful and dramatic results of the current women's movement.

Progress for instrumentalists in the fields of jazz and popular music has been slower. Here women found an opportunity during World War II to form their own groups, most notably the International Sweethearts of Rhythm, in order to work and grow as artists. One recording group included Rose Gottesman, drums; June Rotenberg, bass; Mary Lou Williams, piano; Mary Osborne, guitar; and Margie Hyams, vibraharp. Rotenberg was an early crossover artist who later became a member of the New York City Opera Orchestra. On radio, Phil Spitalny's All Girl Orchestra featured "Evelyn [Klein] and her Magic Violin." Klein had graduated from the Institute of Musical Art in New York in 1931.

American composers have had an even longer struggle than performers for recognition, whatever their religious background. Composers who enter the professional music field first as performers have a distinct advantage. Mana Zucca (born Augusta Zuckerman in 1885) was a composer as well as a pianist and singer with an extensive performance record, including appearances with major orchestras. She created a large oeuvre that mixed lighter compositions such as the song "Big Brown Bear" with more serious works including concerti for piano and violin. Her songs

with Yiddish texts are discussed above. JEANNE BEHREND (1911–1988), trained at the Curtis Institute of Music, also combined composition with piano performance, and had early recognition of her creative gifts. However, she stopped composing in the 1940s because of neglect of her music by others, almost as much a problem for Americans as for women.

Not all composers were also performers. MARION BAUER (1882–1955), whose earlier works were considered modern, continued composing almost until her death. Born in Walla Walla, Washington, to immigrant French-Jewish parents, Bauer was especially important for her championing of modern music in books, lectures, and teaching, and through her considerable support of organizations such as the League of Composers.

In recent years, the number of women composers has increased exponentially and includes such outstanding women as Vienna-born Vally Weigl (1889–1982) and the American MIRIAM GIDEON. Born in Greeley, Colorado, in 1906, Gideon earned an M.A. in musicology from Columbia University and a Doctor of Sacred Music degree from the Jewish Theological Seminary in New York. She wrote orchestral and instrumental works, but compositions with texts predominate in her oeuvre. Gideon taught for many years at the City College of New York, the Manhattan College of Music, and the Cantors Institute of the JTSA. Vivian Fine (b. 1913), composer and pianist, wrote for modern dancers Martha Graham, Hanya Holm, Charles Weidman, and José Limón. Other works include opera, chamber, solo instrumental, and vocal genres. Her style has ranged from contrapuntal dissonance to a more lyrical, occasionally humourous style. Ruth Schonthal and Ursula Mamlok, both born in the 1920s in Germany, made their ways by circuitous routes to the United States in the 1940s. Schonthal's style, while modern, reflects her European background, while Mamlok's was early influenced by the music of Arnold Schoenberg. Recently she has combined serial techniques with more lyrical and eloquent writing.

In a traditional nurturant female role in support of the avant garde movement in music beginning in 1921, Minna Lederman (1896–1995) and Claire Raphael Reis (1888–1978), working with Marion Bauer, were publicists for the International Composers Guild, then in 1923 for the League of Composers. Lederman edited its journal, *Modern Music*, and in the process taught a group of modern composers, Aaron Copland among them, how to write about music. Another patron, Minnie Guggenheimer

(1882–1966), was famous for her support of the summer concerts at Lewisohn Stadium in New York and her cheery welcome to audiences during intermissions.

As we enter the twenty-first century, American Jewish music is vastly expanded in variety, range, and quality of activities. Jews had brought to America their secular-folk and sacred-liturgical musical heritage. On these shores, there has been a renascence of age-old traditions that now have become means of the self-expression for Jewish women. Religious freedom in this country has been nourishing to Jewish women's creativity as they increasingly make their marks as composers, organists, singers, instrumentalists, educators, and patrons. Indeed, they are integral to what constitutes an extraordinarily rich American musical environment.

BIBLIOGRAPHY

Block, Adrienne Fried, and Carol Neuls-Bates. *Women in American Music: A Bibliography of Music and Literature* (1979); Heskes, Irene. *The Music of Abraham Goldfaden: Father of the Yiddish Theater* (1990), and *Passport to Jewish Music: Its History, Traditions, and Culture* (1994), and *Yiddish American Popular Songs, 1895 to 1950* (1992); Pendle, Karin, ed. *Women and Music: A History* (1991); Rosenfeld, Lulla Adler. *Bright Star of Exile: Jacob Adler and the Yiddish Theatre* (1988); Sandrow, Nahma. *Vagabond Stars: A World History of Yiddish Theater* (1977); Slobin, Mark. *Tenement Songs: The Popular Music of the Jewish Immigrants* (1982); Tick, Judith. "Women in Music." In *The New Grove Dictionary of American Music*, Vol. 4, edited by H. Wiley Hitchcock and Stanley Sadie (1986).

ADRIENNE FRIED BLOCK
IRENE HESKES

MUSICAL THEATER, YIDDISH *see* YIDDISH MUSICAL THEATER

MYERHOFF, BARBARA (1935–1985)

Anthropologist Barbara Myerhoff looked at the camera in her documentary film *Number Our Days* and explained, "Someday I will be a little old Jewish lady." Giving this as the reason for her study of elderly Jews, she helped to initiate a rethinking of anthropology. Locating herself within her scholarship, she declared that those who are like us—even part of us—are as worthy of study as those cultures thought of as "exotic."

Barbara Gay Siegel Myerhoff was born on February 16, 1935, in Cleveland, Ohio. She was raised there and in Los Angeles by her mother, Florence Siegel, and her stepfather Norman Siegel. She married Lee Myerhoff in 1954 and divorced him in 1982. She had two sons, Nicholas (b. 1968), and Matthew (b. 1971). Always a gifted student and storyteller, she had an outstanding academic career. She receive a bachelor of arts degree in sociology from the University of California at Los Angeles in 1958. At the University of Chicago, she received a master's degree in human development in 1963. She returned to the University of California at Los Angeles to complete a doctorate in anthropology in 1968.

Myerhoff's initial scholarship was devoted to the developing field of ritual and symbolic studies. Her dissertation and subsequent book, *Peyote Hunt: the Sacred Journey of the Huichol Indians* (1974), was a highly regarded work of scholarship for its treatment of pilgrimages and the religious life of a Mexican Indian group. Myerhoff was the first non-Huichol to participate in the sacred annual pilgrimage of the Huichol people, and she used the occasion to understand how rituals and symbols act to communicate the central meanings and memories of a people cut off from their homeland and forced to live within a dominant culture that was hostile to them. The book was nominated for a National Book Award in 1976.

Barbara Myerhoff explored these same themes in her innovative study of elderly Jews in Los Angeles. The work developed as part of a collaborative project on aging at the University of Southern California, where she taught in the department of anthropology for her entire professional career, from 1968 until her death in 1985. She had initially considered work with other ethnic groups, but decided to study Jews for her portion of the project. In 1971, in a period of increasing ethnic pride and militancy, she took seriously comments from leaders in communities of color who told her to "study your own." Neither American Jews nor the elderly had received much attention from anthropologists, and the urban American setting was rarely their subject of study. Myerhoff took a major risk with her career to focus on a group so entirely overlooked by scholars.

Myerhoff's study of elderly Jews who met at a senior center in Venice, California, demonstrated the ways in which rituals, both traditional and invented, gave the aged the visibility of which society and family had deprived them. Performances of all types—storytelling, rituals, even fights—provided a certainty of their place in social interaction that was reassuring and tenuous at the same time, since their ability to hold others' attention could easily be lost. From these observations Myerhoff wrote eloquently and persuasively about the human need to be seen and the ways in which culture offers and withholds that visibility. Myerhoff found and wrote about the resilience, continuity, and innovations in seniors' lives. In articles that appeared in *Secular Ritual*, edited by her and Sally Falk Moore, as well as in other journals and collections, she developed and illustrated these points.

In one of her first publications about the Jewish elderly, she noted that women at the senior center appeared to age with more ease than men. She viewed women whose lives had been devoted to nurturing and caretaking as better able to accept aging, and as more resourceful in finding ways to continue to nurture others through their social activism and mutual support. Women were able to maintain more continuity in their lives than men who were wrenched away from the public world of work.

Another of Myerhoff's most important contributions was her pioneering work on "domestic Judaism" and "women's religion." Her study coincided with the early years of the contemporary women's movement, and she was particularly interested in how women practiced Judaism, a patriarchal religion. She found among the seniors vibrant "domestic" religious practices. Immigrant Jewish women told her about their sense of responsibility to maintain observance in the family and their memories of learning about women's religious duties from mothers and other female relatives. She was a pioneer in challenging the notion that religion can only or best be understood from an elite perspective, usually dominated by males. Rather, her work demonstrated a well-articulated religious system for women that ran parallel to men's sacred worlds. These early insights have been used effectively by a variety of writers and scholars to understand religion from a woman's perspective.

Prior to the publication of her book *Number Our Days*, Barbara Myerhoff made a documentary film about the Jewish seniors with filmmaker Lynn Littman. The film, also entitled *Number Our Days*, was awarded a 1977 Oscar for best short documentary film and two Emmys. Her book was deeply appreciated by both scholars and ordinary readers. It was chosen by both the *New York Times* and *Psychology Today* as among the ten best social science books of 1979. One of its chapters was awarded a Pushcart Prize for 1979, and she was selected as Woman of the Year by the Jewish War Veterans of America in 1980. The book was subsequently adapted as a play and produced by the Mark Taper Forum of Los Angeles in 1981.

Myerhoff's interests in documentary and ethnographic film led her to develop a program in visual anthropology at the University of Southern California, where she chaired the department of anthropology from 1976 to 1980. She collaborated again with Lynn Littman on a second film, *In Her Own Time*, which documented her bout with cancer and the final weeks of her life, as she studied the Jewish community of the Fairfax district in Los Angeles. The film depicted her work with that community and how some of its members helped her to understand and deal with her final illness.

Barbara Myerhoff died on January 7, 1985. She never lived to become "an old Jewish woman," as she imagined she would when she set out to understand what it meant to be aged and Jewish in American society. Not quite fifty years old, she left a remarkable intellectual and personal legacy in her prodigious writing and filmmaking. She reached a wide audience of readers and viewers because of her commitment to tell stories that could help men and women understand their own lives in light of what she saw in communities in "her own backyard," as well as the far reaches of northern Mexico.

Barbara Myerhoff was part of a small group of scholars in the 1970s who introduced the importance of understanding storytelling, who pioneered the study of one's own community, and who paid attention to the relationships among age, ethnic identity, and gender. She was particularly innovative in her scholarship on ritual, exploring how ritual functioned to create its effect, even when participants aided in its invention. Her ideas provided an important foundation for Jewish women to understand aspects of their own religious heritage and to experiment with ritual innovation while defining Jewish feminism.

SELECTED WORKS BY BARBARA MYERHOFF

"Bobbes and Zeydes: Old and New Roles for Elderly Jews." In *Women in Ritual and Symbolic Roles*, edited by Judith Hoch-Smith and Anita Springs (1978); *In Her Own Time*, with Lynn Littman. Film (1984); *Number Our Days*, with Lynn Littman. Film (1977); *Number Our Days* (1979); *Number Our Days* (1981). Play produced by Mark Taper Forum, Los Angeles; *Peyote Hunt: The Sacred Journey of the Huichol Indians* (1974); *Remembered Lives: The Work of Ritual, Storytelling, and Growing Older*, edited by Mark Kaminsky (1992); "We Don't Wrap Herring in a Printed Page: Fusions, Fiction and Continuity in Secular Ritual." In *Secular Ritual: Forms and Meanings*, edited by Sally Falk Moore and Barbara Myerhoff (1977).

BIBLIOGRAPHY

Kaminsky, Mark. Introduction to *Remembered Lives: The Work of Ritual, Storytelling and Growing Older*, by Barbara Myerhoff (1992); Kirshenblatt-Gimblett, Barbara.

Foreword to *Remembered Lives: The Work of Ritual, Story-telling, and Growing Older*, by Barbara Myerhoff (1992); Prell, Riv-Ellen. "The Double Frame of Life History in the Work of Barbara Myerhoff." In *Interpreting Women's Lives: Theory and Personal Narratives*, edited by Personal Narratives Group (1989).

RIV-ELLEN PRELL

MYERS, CARMEL (1900–1980)

Carmel Myers acted in over seventy films, was an early television talk-show host, led a production company that packaged radio and television shows, held a patent for an electronic synchronizer that controlled studio lights, and imported and distributed French perfume. In a Hollywood that encouraged assimilation, she never denied she was Jewish. When offered work by Samuel Goldwyn on the condition that she change her name, she responded, "Oh, Mr. Goldfish, if my career depends upon my hiding the fact that I was born a Jew, I'd rather not have one."

Carmel Myers was born in San Francisco, California, on April 9, 1900. Her parents, Rabbi Isadore and Anna (Jacobson) Myers, moved in 1905 to Los Angeles, where Carmel attended Los Angeles High School and studio schools. She and her brother Zion, a screenwriter, were named for the two holy mountains of Israel. Her father, born in Russia but raised and educated in Australia, was active in campaigns for woman suffrage, abolition of capital punishment, and Zionism. He also was a noted scholar. His character and her mother's careful nurturing of her career led to a life without stereotypical Hollywood behavior.

Myers was working for L-KH Studios in low-budget comedy shorts in 1916 when her father became an unpaid religious consultant for D.W. Griffith's *Intolerance*. Primed by his wife, Rabbi Myers asked for Griffith's help with his daughter's career. After a test reading, Griffith hired her as a contract player for fourteen dollars per week. Contrary to later reports, she did not appear in *Intolerance*. When her employment with Griffith ended, she impressed Carl Laemmele with her reading of a Sarah Bernhardt poem about the death of two sons. Laemmele, who had just lost a beloved nephew, was touched by the subject (but not her reading). Nevertheless, she received a seventy-five-dollars-a-week contract at Laemmele's Universal Studios. She married lawyer-songwriter I. Kornblum in 1920 and divorced him in 1923.

Myers often played a vamp against the top male stars of the era, beginning in *A Daughter of the Poor* in

1917 and ending with cameos in *Gus* and *Won Ton Ton, the Dog That Saved Hollywood* (both 1976). Among her numerous accomplishments were: two-a-day at the Palace Theater in the heyday of vaudeville; a year in Sigmund Romberg musicals, most notably *The Magic Melody*; short fiction and a self-help book, *Don't Think About It* (1952); guest appearances on television; an early television talk show, *The Carmel Myers Show* (1951), hosted from her Park Avenue apartment; and television commercials.

Myers's best known role as Iras in *Ben Hur* (1926) included a nine-month stint in Italy. In Rome, she met Zelda and F. Scott Fitzgerald, with whom she and Ralph Blum, a lawyer and entertainment executive, became close friends. Zelda and Scott often stayed with Myers in Hollywood, and two of Fitzgerald's poems written in her guest book testify to that friendship. The shorter one is:

Orange pajamas and heaven's guitars
Never, oh *never*, the twain shall meet
Never mind, though; the advantage is ours
Reach for a Carmel instead of a sweet

Myers and Ralph H. Blum married in 1929 and had three children: writer and cultural anthropologist Ralph H. Blum (b. 1932) and two adopted daughters, actor Susan Adams Kennedy (b. 1940) and television producer Mary Cossette (b. 1941). After their marriage, they purchased Gloria Swanson's Sunset Boulevard house, and Myers gradually withdrew from films to raise a family. She was a gracious, accomplished, and highly regarded hostess who could arrange dinner parties for three hundred guests at the last minute. She and her husband entertained lavishly and popularized the A and B party-list concept. So extensive was their circle of friends that Cary Grant and Dana Andrews once appeared on the B list for a dinner honoring Ethel Barrymore and Somerset Maugham. They were, however, present for the concert half of the evening that featured Leonard Bernstein. Myers was widowed in 1950 and married film executive Alfred W. Schwalberg in 1951. She was widowed for the second time in 1974.

Carmel Myers's personal life bore no resemblance to her screen persona, the wicked woman she portrayed in so many films. One publisher even refused her memoirs on the grounds that there had been no scandal in her life. In her autobiography *Sunshine and Shadow*, Mary Pickford relates a touching and illustrative encounter with Myers, whom she aptly describes as her "friend . . . beautiful, talented, and of rare intelligence

*A silent screen vamp who acted in more than seventy films, Carmel Myers was also a
successful vaudeville performer and commercial television actress. Best known for her role as
Iras in the 1926 version of* Ben-Hur, *she went counter to the Hollywood tradition of assimilation:
She never changed her name or denied she was a Jew. The above is a still from* Beau Brummel *(1924),
featuring Myers opposite John Barrymore. [Museum of Modern Art Film Archives]*

and character." Pickford made a thoughtless and intolerant remark about German Jews and their fate at Hitler's hands. Myers's calm retort was, "You must never forget that before we are Jewish or gentile, we are all human beings." Remorse for her insult moti-

vated Mary Pickford's four decades of devotion to the Los Angeles Jewish Home for the Aged.

Carmel Myers died on November 9, 1980, in Los Angeles, of a heart attack. The day before she died, she appeared at I. Magnin to endorse her perfume line.

BIBLIOGRAPHY

Adams, Val. "Format: A Ukulele and a Memory." *NYTimes*, September 9, 1951; *AJYB* (1903–1904, 1905–1906, 1921–1922, 1922–1923); Barbanel, Josh. "Carmel Myers, Silent Movie Star Who Played Wicked Women, 80." *NYTimes*, November 19, 1980, A31; Belcher, Jerry. "Carmel Myers, 80, Leading Lady of Silent Films, Dies." *Los Angeles Times*, November 11, 1980; Blum, Ralph H. Telephone interview by author, November 28, 1996; Burtis, Liz. "Vamp of Silent Films Revists Old Haunts." *Los Angeles Mirror News*, July 22, 1956; Byrne, Julie. "Valentino Inspired Smell of Success." *Los Angeles Times*, March 7, 1968, IV: 1, 13; "Carmel Myers." *Variety*, November 12, 1980; "Carmel Myers Buys Hellinger Stories for Radio Series." *Variety*, August 13, 1952; "Carmel Myers Head [sic] TV-Radio Company." *Hollywood Reporter*, September 30, 1952; "Carmel Myers Patents TV Lighting Method, Hurdles 'Can't Do It.'" *Variety*, December 5, 1951, 1; Champlin, Charles. "In Memoriam: Farewell to Notables in the Arts." "Calendar," *Los Angeles Times*, December 28, 1980, 2; Cossette, Mary. Telephone interviews by author, November 18, 1996 and December 11, 1996; Cuskelly, Richard. "Silents Star Carmel Myers: 'I'm Recycling My Life.'" *Los Angeles Herald Examiner*, September 1974; Flynn, Joan King. "How to Beat the Blues." *American Weekly, Los Angeles Examiner*, April 13, 1953; "From 'Ben Hur' to 'Won Ton Ton.'" *Hollywood Reporter*, 46th anniversary ed., September 1977, 30+; Kingsley, Grace. "Tea-cup Tete-a-tete with Stella, the Star-Gazer." *Los Angeles Times*, March 3, 1925, 10; Kramer, William M., and Norton B. Stern. "Mary Pickford: From a Moment of Intolerance to a Lifetime of Compassion." *Western States Jewish Historical Quarterly* 13, no. 3 (1981): 274–281; "L.A. High School Girl Makes Debut as Star in 'Sirens of the Sea,'" *Los Angeles Evening Herald*, September 18, 1917: 17:7; "Looking Back: Carmel Myers." *Hollywood Reporter*, June 5, 1990; "Marriages." *Variety*, October 31, 1951; Pickford, Mary. *Sunshine and Shadow* (1955); *UJE*: 71–72; Robertson, Nan. "Movie Star of Twenties Now Promotes Perfume." *NYTimes*, April 23, 1959, 24; Sullivan, Ed. "The Half World of Those Who Survive Their Mates." *Hollywood Citizen News*, June 15, 1950; Slide, Anthony. "Silent Stars Speak." *Films in Review* 31. no. 3 (March 1980) 129–141; Thomas, Kevin. "Carmel Myers: Vamp to Video." *Los Angeles Times*, January 21, 1975, and "Carmel Myers: Always a Glamorous Personality." "Calendar," *Los Angeles Times*, November 16, 1980, 2; *WWIAJ* (1926, 1938).

DAN GREENBERG

MYERSON, BESS (b. 1924)

The first Jewish Miss America, Bess Myerson transformed the fame bestowed upon her because of her beauty into an illustrious public career.

Born in the Bronx on July 16, 1924, to Louis and Bella Myerson, immigrants from Russia, Myerson grew up during the Depression. Along with her parents

The first Jewish Miss America, Bess Myerson transformed the fame bestowed on her because of her beauty into an illustrious public career. During her year as the reigning Miss America, she witnessed segregation in the South and experienced the humiliation of being turned away by a country club that did not admit Jews.

and her two sisters, the younger Helen and the older Sylvia, she lived in the Sholem Aleichem Cooperative, which housed 250 Jewish working-class, politically liberal families. As a student at the High School of Music and Art, Myerson studied the piano and the flute.

After Myerson graduated from HUNTER COLLEGE in 1945 with a degree in music, her sister Sylvia, seven years her elder, entered her photograph in the Miss America pageant. Although she was advised to change her name so that she wouldn't be recognized as a Jew, Myerson refused, affirming her Jewish identity and becoming the darling of American Jews.

Although some of the judges received anonymous phone calls warning them not to vote for the Jewish contestant, Myerson was the favorite and won over the judges with her dark-haired beauty and musical talent. Encountering anti-Semitism and racism for the first time, she had a difficult and eye-opening year as Miss America. She witnessed segregation in the South and experienced the humiliation of being turned away at a country club that did not admit Jews. For unconfirmed reasons, three out of the five sponsors of the Miss America pageant pulled out of the arrangement that the winner would advertise for them. In response to these experiences, Myerson began to speak out against racial hate for the Anti-Defamation League (ADL) at schools and halls all over the country.

On October 19, 1946, Myerson married Allan Wayne, and on December 31, 1947, gave birth to a daughter, Barbara. Myerson and Wayne divorced in 1956. Although her private life was shaky, with a difficult custody battle, Myerson's public career swung into action in this decade. She began a lucrative television career as the mistress of ceremonies, known as the "Lady in Mink," for *The Big Payoff* from 1951 to 1959. She was also a regular panelist on *I've Got a Secret* from 1958 to 1967. In addition, she hosted the Miss America Pageant from 1954 to 1968, both alone and with such distinguished cohosts as Walter Cronkite.

On May 2, 1962, Myerson married Arnold Grant, a financial and tax attorney who was very well connected. He formally adopted her daughter, now Barra Grant. During this period, Bess Myerson became active in city politics and was appointed commissioner of New York City's Department of Consumer Affairs by Mayor John Lindsay. She became the most visible city official apart from the mayor during the years she served under him, from 1969 to 1973. She cultivated a reputation as the consumer's best friend, setting up a consumer hotline and a Consumer Action Team that conducted daily surprise raids at businesses in high-

complaint areas. Myerson used the media wisely and to her advantage to scare fraudulent businesses and heighten consumer protection awareness. During her years in office, New York City had what was at that time the most far-reaching consumer protection legislation in the country.

Building on her reputation, Myerson wrote *The Complete Consumer* in 1979. In 1982, she coauthored *The I Love New York Diet* with Bill Adler, which reached the *New York Times Book Review* best-seller list.

She continued her career in city politics as the campaign chair for Ed Koch in 1977. After losing the

Bess Myerson has been active in public affairs in many different capacities. She ran unsuccessfully for the Democratic nomination for the United States Senate in 1980 and from 1983 to 1987 was commissioner for cultural affairs in New York City, doubling the budget of the department. She is shown above at a rally to save Grand Central Station in 1975. [Bettye Lane]

Democratic nomination for the United States Senate in 1980, she was again appointed to a city post as the commissioner of cultural affairs from 1983 to 1987, where she doubled the budget, dramatically increasing financial support to many of New York's cultural institutions.

Myerson again was in the news when her boyfriend Andy Capasso was indicted. An investigation was made into Myerson's involvement, which found her guilty of "serious misconduct." She was subsequently indicted on six counts, including conspiracy, obstruction of justice, and mail fraud, on October 3, 1987. However, she was acquitted of all charges in December 1988. Myerson then retired from a long career in the public eye.

Bess Myerson stayed close to the Jewish tradition and people throughout her career, always presenting herself as a Jewish public figure. Besides delivering speeches for the Anti-Defamation League, Myerson acted as a spokeswoman for Israeli Bonds, served as the national commissioner of the ADL, and was honored by United Jewish Appeal. She lives in New York City.

BIBLIOGRAPHY

Alexander, Shana. *When She Was Bad: The Story of Bess, Hortense, Sukhreet and Nancy* (1990); Dworkin, Susan. *Miss America, 1945: Bess Myerson's Own Story* (1987); Preston, Jennifer. *Queen Bess: The Unauthorized Biography of Bess Myerson* (1990).

LISA LEPSON

N

NASSAU, LILLIAN (1899–1995)

Lillian Nassau, the doyenne of New York City antiques dealers, was instrumental in the revival of international interest in the lamps and metalwork created by Louis Comfort Tiffany at the turn of the century. In addition to rehabilitating Tiffany, whose breathtaking glass lamps were still being destroyed for their bronze when she started buying them, she was important in the renewal of interest in art nouveau design. She went on to make a market in decorative arts created by the Bauhaus and during Europe's art deco and art moderne periods, although she never exhibited the same intensity of feeling for these as for Tiffany and art nouveau.

Born Lillian Brimberg on December 25, 1899, she emigrated with her Yiddish-speaking family from Warsaw to New York when she was two years old. She was the oldest of the three daughters of Harry and Sophie Brimberg. Her father held several occupations, including selling furs, china, and real estate. Her mother was a housewife. After graduating from the city's public schools, Lillian attended Columbia University, planning to become a reporter, a goal she abandoned upon her marriage in 1920 to Harry Nassau. Soon she was the mother of two sons. Divorced in the late 1930s, she bought and sold gold and silver jewelry door to door on Long Island to help support her family during the difficult Depression era.

Nassau opened her first Manhattan shop in 1945, plunging into work partly to assuage her grief over the death of her older son, Robert, in the armed forces during World War II. With a general knowledge of antiques gained during a stint in a New York furniture shop and by reading newly published studies of art nouveau, she gradually began to deal in the decorative objects produced in Europe during the late nineteenth and early twentieth centuries. In 1956, she bought her first Tiffany lamp for $175 from a dealer who had paid $100 for it. Today, outstanding genuine examples of these naturalistic lamps can bring more than a thousand times that amount. Soon her shop became the mecca for serious buyers of Tiffany from all over the world.

Nassau's discerning eye did not rest with Tiffany. She acquired objects created by European giants of design such as René Lalique, Georg Jensen, Emile Gallé, Josef Hoffman, Louis Majorelle, and Carlo Bugatti. One could find dazzling Liberty silver and even American art pottery in her shop. While Lillian Nassau dealt in a wide variety of twentieth-century antiques, those she kept for herself were more circumscribed. Harking back to her earliest door-to-door dealing, she collected only art nouveau jewelry, which was sold at auction by Sotheby's after her death.

Although she abandoned active dealership at age eighty-three, leaving her eponymous 57th Street gallery in the care of her son Paul, Nassau remained a sought-after consultant in the field of twentieth-century decorative arts until her illness and subsequent death on October 9, 1995.

BIBLIOGRAPHY

Esmerian, Ralph. Introduction to *Important Works of Art and Jewelry from the Collection of Lillian Nassau, Ltd.* (June 1996); *NYTimes*, December 23, 1979, sec. 2, p. 45, and January 10, 1982, sec. 2, p. 27, and October 9, 1995, p. 21, and May 19, 1996, sec. 2, p. 35; Zuckerman, Doris. Interview with author, May 30, 1996.

JEAN ULITZ MENSCH

NATELSON, RACHEL (1885–1943)

As a young girl, Rachel Natelson corresponded with an uncle who had been studying with HENRIETTA SZOLD. From him, she learned about Palestine and the Zionist movement. These exchanges were to lay the foundation for her extraordinary life as a leader on behalf of the Zionist cause—including being one of the founding members of HADASSAH, the Women's Zionist Organization of America.

Born in Brooklyn in 1885 to Samuel and Mary (Rokeach) Wasserzug Natelson, Rachel Natelson attended Brooklyn public schools, and then went on to Adelphi College in New York. She graduated in 1907 as a teacher of English and was awarded the Barlow Medal for excellence in scholarship.

Natelson taught in New York City high schools from 1908 to 1915. It was during this time that she began what would be thirty years of Zionist activity. In 1912, Natelson and seven other women met with Henrietta Szold, and together they founded Hadassah. The purpose of Hadassah was to provide medical and educational services to all citizens of Palestine, regardless of race, religion, or creed. To date, Hadassah remains one of the largest Jewish organizations in America, and certainly the largest Zionist women's organization. At the time of Rachel Natelson's death in 1943, Hadassah had branches in five hundred cities in forty-six states. Today, it enjoys a total membership of 380,000, with fifteen hundred branches in the United States.

Natelson served Hadassah as the recording secretary for the New York section until 1915, and then transferred her efforts to its Brooklyn division. In this same year, Natelson decided to leave her teaching career in order to devote herself completely to the Zionist movement. For Hadassah, she was the secretary of the Brooklyn section from 1917 to 1923, chair of the Borough Park section from 1919 to 1922, and a member of the national board from 1919 to 1931.

Natelson became a member of the national executive committee of the Zionist Organization of America and was a delegate at the 1923 Zionist Congress in Carlsbad, Czechoslovakia. In 1926, Natelson was the director of the United Palestine Appeal in Greater New York, and, in 1928, she chaired the Jewish National Fund Council of Hadassah. During World War I, Natelson was secretary of the Magen David Adom. Her deep interest in music led her to help found MAILAMM, the American Palestine Music Association, of which she was national secretary from 1933 until her death. In addition to extensive organizational work, her efforts on behalf of Palestine included authoring several articles on Zionism.

Rachel Natelson was also associated with the NATIONAL COUNCIL OF JEWISH WOMEN, the Brooklyn Federation of Jewish Charities, the League of Women Voters, the Non-Partisan Society for the League of Nations, and the Adelphi College Alumni and Auxiliary.

It is a tragic irony that, while this passionate Zionist's work for Hadassah took her traveling throughout the United States, the one trip Rachel Natelson wanted to take most of all, to Palestine, never came to be. Rachel Natelson died in Brooklyn, on May 8, 1943. She was fifty-eight years old.

BIBLIOGRAPHY

AJYB 45:390–391; Obituary. *NYTimes*, May 9, 1943, 40:6; *WWIAJ* (1926, 1938).

ADINA LEWITTES

NATHAN, ADELE GUTMAN (1889–1986)

Adele Gutman Nathan was born on September 15, 1889, in Baltimore, Maryland, to Ida (Newberger) and Louis Kayton Gutman. Her father owned Joel Gutman and Company, a department store founded by his father. She had two siblings, Joel and Elizabeth. She grew up with CLARIBEL and ETTA CONE, friends of her mother, and saw them and GERTRUDE STEIN in Europe in the 1920s. She graduated from (Baltimore) Girls Latin High School and Goucher College (1910) and did graduate work at Johns Hopkins University (M.A.), Columbia University, and the Peabody Institute. She married James Nathan on February 20, 1912, and divorced him about 1920. She was awarded the Freedom Foundation Award (1953), the Vagabond Players Citation (1971), Special Decoration–U.S. Navy, and the Goucher College Alumnae Award. Her clubs and memberships included Gilbert and Sullivan

Association, Lincoln Circle, American Revolution Roundtable (archivist, 1941–1950), The Woman Pays (president, 1967–1968, 1977–1983), the Overseas Press Club of America, and the American Theatre Wing.

Nathan's long-standing interest in theater began in college and continued to her death. She helped found the Vagabond Players (1916) in Baltimore, was involved in children's theater with the Little Lyric Theatre (Baltimore) in the 1920s, directed at the Cellar Players of the Hudson Guild (1920s to 1940s) and the Cherry Lane Theatre (New York City), and headed the Federal Theater Project in New Jersey (1937). She met and produced plays by Theodore Dreiser, H.L. Mencken, Eugene O'Neill, and Elmer Rice. She later directed short nonfiction subjects for Paramount and Grand National Pictures (mid-1930s) and was chief scriptwriter at the U.S. Department of Education (1941). She wrote for newspapers, corresponding from Europe in the mid-1920s about cultural affairs for the *Baltimore Daily Gazette* and writing in the 1950s for the *Cripple Creek Gold Rush* (Colorado). She was feature editor for *St. Nicholas Magazine* (1943–1944) and contributed to *Vogue*, the *Atlantic Monthly*, the *New York Times Magazine*, and the *Encyclopedia Americana*. Nathan had another career as a well-respected writer of nonfiction children's books, publishing fourteen, many of which had multiple printings and were translated into other languages.

Her greatest successes came as a writer and producer of historical pageants. She staged commemorative events for cities, corporations, and groups, including the centenaries of the B&O Railroad (1927) and of International Harvester (1929), the 1933 and 1939 World's Fairs, the cities of Rochester, New York (1934), and Winston-Salem, North Carolina (1949), the American Jewish Tercentenary in Trenton (1955), and the Hundredth Anniversary of the Battle of Gettysburg and Lincoln's Gettysburg Address (1963). In 1974, she wrote *How to Plan and Conduct a Bicentennial Celebration* for the American Bicentennial.

Adele Gutman Nathan, professionally active until the last two years of her life, transmitted American culture and her long-standing interest in technology, especially railroads, to a general public through theater, film, pageants, articles, and books. She died on July 24, 1986, in New York City.

BIBLIOGRAPHY

Adele Gutman Nathan Collection. Bienecke Rare Book and Manuscript Library, Yale University, New Haven, Conn.; *BEOAJ*; Commire, Anne, ed. *Something About the Author* 48: 174; *Contemporary Authors*; Nathan, Adele Gutman. *How to Plan and Conduct a Bicentennial Celebration* (1976); Obituaries. *AB Bookman's Weekly* 78, no. 10: 831, and *NYTimes*; *UJE*; *WWWIA* 9 (1985–1989): 263; *Who's Who in America*. 38th ed.; *WWIAJ* (1938): 770; *Who's Who of American Women*. 8th ed. (1974): 697; Young, Timothy. "Life's Rich Pageant" (1993).

LORAINE HAMMACK

NATHAN, MAUD (1862–1946)

Maud Nathan, social reformer and political activist, lived two distinct lives. She was born on October 20, 1862, into a distinguished old New York Sephardic family (she had relatives who fought in the American Revolution; one of her cousins was Supreme Court Justice Benjamin Cardozo; and another cousin was the poet EMMA LAZARUS) and had a privileged childhood. Her parents were Annie Augusta (Florance) and Robert Weeks Nathan. She had an older brother, Robert Florance Nathan, a younger brother, Harold Nathan, and a younger sister, ANNIE NATHAN MEYER, founder of Barnard College. The family moved to Green Bay, Wisconsin, for four years after her father suffered some business reversals, and Maud Nathan finished her high school education in the local public high school. The Nathan children returned to New York after their mother died in 1878. Two years later, at age seventeen, Maud Nathan married her thirty-five-year-old first cousin Frederick Nathan, and embarked upon the life of a society wife. She served various charitable causes and was, it was said, the life of every party she attended. She and her husband summered in Saratoga Springs, New York, where she was renowned for her beautiful singing voice and her elegant presence at all the glittery social functions.

Maud and Frederick Nathan had one child, Annette Florance Nathan, who died in 1895 at age eight (although Frances Nathan Wolff, Frederick Nathan's sister, gives Annette's age at the time of her death as ten in her *Four Generations: My Life and Memories of New York over Eighty Years*). Her daughter's death brought about a dramatic change in Maud Nathan's life.

A friend, Josephine Shaw Lowell, founder of the New York Consumers League, urged Nathan to take a greater interest in the sufferings of working women in New York City, ostensibly as a way to free herself from her grief over the loss of her child. This was the real beginning of Nathan's distinguished career as a social reformer and political activist. Nathan was president of the New York Consumers League from 1897 to 1927. She served as vice president of the Woman's

Municipal League of New York. From 1902 to 1904, she chaired the industrial committee of the General Federation of Women's Clubs. She was a member of the Daughters of the American Revolution. Her work was not limited to exposing bad working conditions for women and children but also focused on educating consumers. She argued that it was the consumer's responsibility to be aware of conditions in factories and sweatshops, and also to strive to be a responsible shopper on a daily basis. At Christmastime, for example, hints to shoppers published in the New York newspapers included exhortations to shop early and to carry small packages home themselves rather than asking the shop to deliver them.

Nathan also worked tirelessly for woman suffrage, an issue that caused a rift in her relations with her family. Her brothers and sister opposed this reform, while her cousin Benjamin Cardozo supported a constitutional amendment, writing Nathan that his conscience would not allow him to vote against it.

Frederick Nathan shared his wife's views on equal suffrage, leading the Men's League for Equal Suffrage, helping to organize the International Men's League at Stockholm, and marching in the first suffrage parade. Newspaper accounts of conventions and demonstrations often mention his presence at his wife's side (occasionally referring to him as Mr. Maud Nathan).

Nathan was the first woman invited to speak at the Sephardic synagogue Shearith Israel, giving a talk entitled "The Heart of Judaism" in 1897. Simon Nathan, Frederick Nathan's great-grandfather, was president of Shearith Israel at one time, and the Nathan family were an important and powerful influence on the congregation. Maud Nathan called for Jews to abhor "racialism," to be open-minded, and to work for social justice and reform. Her attitude toward members of her religion suggests an antipathy to religious dogma and a strong belief that religious faith is best exemplified by a commitment to social justice and tolerance of all people and faiths. Her writing was not limited to sermons, however. Maud Nathan won the New York Herald Prize in 1913 for the best letter in favor of woman suffrage. She wrote two books, *Story of an Epoch-Making Movement* (1926), on the Consumers League, and *Once Upon a Time and Today* (1933).

The collection of twelve scrapbooks housed at the Schlesinger Library of Radcliffe College, attests to Nathan's astute marketing sense. She employed several clipping services, and thus was able to preserve a variety of letters to the editors of various newspapers, as well as accounts of demonstrations, lectures, marches, and honors. There are newspaper articles about a public meeting at which Nathan was heckled by an antisuffragist ex-assemblyman and the furor that followed. There are accounts of speeches and lectures, almost all of which remark favorably on Nathan's elegant appearance and imposing demeanor, and all of which convey a sense of a lively, interested, intelligent woman and the culture she inhabited.

After Frederick Nathan died in 1919, Maud Nathan and her companion, Corinne Johnson, traveled the world together, continuing to work for the rights of working women, equal suffrage, and the education of consumers. Nathan and Johnson bought a summer home in Litchfield, Connecticut, where they involved themselves in the community. They were instrumental in forming a community action group, and supported the local schools, presenting awards at graduation ceremonies for many years.

Maud Nathan died at home on December 15, 1946, at age eighty-four.

SELECTED WORKS BY MAUD NATHAN
Once Upon a Time and Today (1933); Scrapbooks. Schlesinger Library, Radcliffe College, Cambridge, Mass.; *Story of an Epoch-Making Movement* (1926).

BIBLIOGRAPHY
AJYB 6 (1904–1905): 159–160, 24:185, 49:615; *BEOAJ*; *DAB* 4; *JE*; *NAW*; Obituary. *NYTimes*, December 16, 1946, 23:3; *UJE*; Wolff, Frances Nathan. *Four Generations: My Life and Memories of New York over Eighty Years* (1939); *WWIAJ* (1926, 1928, 1938); *WWWIA* 2.

ANNE KAUFMAN

NATIONAL COUNCIL OF JEWISH WOMEN

Resolved that we, Jewish women, sincerely believing that a closer fellowship will be encouraged, a closer unity of thought and sympathy and purpose, and a nobler accomplishment will result from a widespread organization, do therefore band ourselves together in a union of workers to further the best and highest interests of Judaism and humanity, and do call ourselves the "National Council of Jewish Women."

When the National Council of Jewish Women was founded with these words in 1893, it was the first national organization in history to unite Jewish women to promote the Jewish religion. That its commitment to preserve Jewish heritage in a quickly modernizing America would be fraught with contradictions was not readily apparent in the optimistic surroundings of the World Parliament of Religions, convened as part of the Chicago World Exposition.

The NCJW seemed well suited to embodying the values of the exposition, which was a showcase for the greatest hopes of modernity—especially science, technology, and democracy. The council consistently strove to apply the latest "scientific" methods in its work, whether it was improving religious school instruction or aiding new immigrants. It reflected the influence of democracy in its attempt to adopt a pluralistic approach to Judaism, insisting on active involvement in the religion but not on adherence to particular practices. This approach of Americanizing without giving up Jewish identity was quite popular. In its first five years, more than five thousand American Jewish women, mostly of German descent, joined the fledgling organization. By the time it reached its tenth anniversary, the council had more than doubled

that number. In recent decades, membership has hovered around ninety thousand.

The excitement generated in the council's early years, however, masked significant internal divisions. The organization's mission to "save Judaism" from the internal threat of assimilation as well as the external threat of anti-Semitism attracted a variety of women with very different approaches to furthering "the best and highest interests of Judaism and humanity."

The NCJW's dominant guiding force was represented by its founder, HANNAH G. SOLOMON. Solomon, who served as the organization's first president, was a quintessential American clubwoman. Married to a businessman, she was financially well-off, leaving her with free time to serve in civic organizations. She believed that with status came the responsibility to serve and care for her community, from supporting the arts to serving the needy. Occasionally that meant engaging in activities that seemed to stretch the

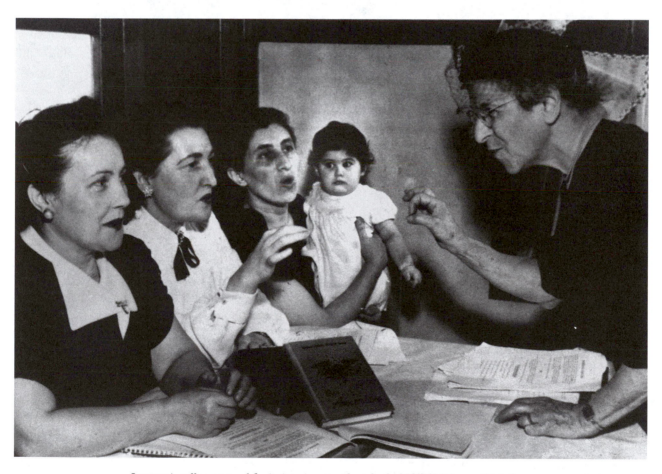

Internationally renowned for its immigrant aid work, the NCJW did everything from welcoming and comforting new arrivals to finding them places to live. The above photograph depicts an NCJW volunteer in Milwaukee teaching English. [National Council of Jewish Women]

MISS JULIA RICHMAN, OF NEW YORK CITY,
Chairman of Committee on Religious Schools.

MRS. HANNAH G. SOLOMON, OF CHICAGO,
President of the Council of Jewish Women.

MRS. SOPHIE BEER, OF NEW YORK CITY,
First Vice-President of the Council.

MRS. CARRIE S. BENJAMIN, OF DENVER, COLORADO,
Chairman of Committee on Philanthropy.

MRS. REBECCA KOHUT, OF NEW YORK CITY,
President of New York Section.

MRS. NELLIE L. MILLER, OF MEMPHIS,
Vice-President of Tennessee Section.

This reproduction from Harper's Bazaar *in 1896 portrays the officers of the council
at the time of their first triennial convention in New York City. [Peter Schweitzer]*

boundaries of "proper" womanhood such as entering politics. In fact, NCJW would prove to be an important political training ground for dozens of political appointees. The most famous was arguably BELLE MOSKOWITZ, who served in the administration of New York governor Alfred Smith.

But such forays into politics were always justified as extensions of motherhood, an ideology now termed by scholars "domestic feminism." Clubwomen believed in a modest form of women's rights, including woman suffrage, but they justified those rights not as the logical outcome of equal citizenry but as necessary to carry out their traditional duties as wives and mothers.

Clubwomen were the greatest influence in the NCJW's early years, with some groups simply trans-forming themselves from literary or sewing circles into NCJW sections. However, also among the founders was a second group that formed an influential minority. Typified by the woman who made the call to organize at the founding convention, SADIE AMERICAN, and the woman who reportedly suggested the organization's name, Julia Felsenthal (daughter of renowned Reform rabbi Bernard Felsenthal), these women were somewhat younger than their club-women counterparts. They were also single, and many worked as social workers. Where clubwomen raised money for settlement houses and occasionally conducted programs there, these women staffed set-tlement houses. For the social workers, belonging to a sewing club or literary circle, even one that substituted Jewish topics for secular ones, was not enough. They steered the organization toward a more active role in the immigrant Jewish community, with emphasis on conducting programs for "clients" rather than on implementing programs for members.

Where the two factions came together was in their commitment to social justice, the preservation of Judaism and the Jewish community in the United States, and a vision of religion that combined the two. Together they made a formidable team—one group with the capacity to raise needed funds (including women from such wealthy and influential families as the deBeerses, the Sulzbergers, and the Harts), and the other with the experience and energy to design and implement the programs for immigrants that would come to be the core of NCJW's organizational identity.

In its early years, however, influenced by a strong group of learned members including the likes of renowned educator JULIA RICHMAN, REBEKAH KOHUT (daughter and widow of prominent rabbis), ROSA SONNESCHEIN (editor of the *American Jewess*), and NINA MORAIS COHEN (daughter of Rabbi Sabato Morais), the NCJW concentrated on combating assimilation by educating Jewish women about Judaism, hoping in the process to strengthen Jewish homes by making council members into better Jewish mothers.

NCJW study circles typified the council's pattern of translating an American practice into a Jewish context. The format of the groups was borrowed from the literary clubs popular among upper-class American women. The council simply replaced discussions of European literature with examinations of Jewish texts and topics. However, in the Jewish community, the NCJW study circles were distinctive because they offered Jewish women a unique opportunity to study their heritage at an advanced level. They also gave women a vehicle through which they could participate in debates formerly reserved for male scholars, on topics such as whether women should be rabbis.

At first, much of America's Jewish leadership applauded the council's efforts. Where rabbis were seemingly fighting a losing battle against assimilation, the NCJW brought a new and powerful weapon to the fray: motherhood. The NCJW declared that motherhood was the primary religious responsibility of every Jewish woman. That traditional stance, however, was tempered by domestic feminism. If mothers were now to be the "saviors" of Judaism in America, as some rabbis declared, then mothers needed a voice in Jewish communal institutions as well as in the home. Members of the NCJW pressed for, and often won, positions on the boards of synagogues and other Jew-

ish agencies. By 1920, the organization had initiated Council Sabbaths, a once-a-year recognition of the NCJW's work in which council members led services at their home congregations. In many cities, Council Sabbaths provided the first opportunity for women to participate in a synagogue service from the *bimah* [stage]. As well, they provided many congregants with their first experience of seeing women lead prayers.

In some areas, the council's efforts were met with a mix of predictable sexist opposition to women going beyond what some saw as their "proper" roles. In most places, however, Jewish leaders saw the NCJW as an ally in the struggle to preserve a vibrant Jewish community in the United States. Eventually, however, as the Jewish community splintered into denominations, the NCJW would be caught in the crossfire of the battle for control of American Jewry. The organization became the target of widespread criticism when its commitment to pluralism prevented it from endorsing any particular interpretation of Judaism.

In fact, the NCJW's commitment to pluralism would nearly result in the organization's demise, but not from outside pressures. Rather, internal divisions would prove to be so contentious that they permanently changed the council's religious character. The NCJW's founding leadership overwhelmingly identified with Reform Judaism. Some, like Solomon and American, were active followers of radical Reform, observing the Sabbath on Sunday rather than the traditional Saturday. These leaders understood that their Jewish practices would not be accepted by everyone, and they did not try to use their positions to recruit support for radical Reform. But neither did they understand that for some members issues like adherence to the traditional Sabbath were nonnegotiable. To cross that line was not merely to Americanize Judaism but to abandon the faith. That the leaders of an influential Jewish organization, especially an organization that often represented the Jewish community to non-Jews, would be perceived as abandoning central Jewish practices was unacceptable. The issue came to a climax at the 1913 convention. Those advocating adherence to a more traditional interpretation of Judaism lost, and many left the organization.

Leaving was made easier by the fact that, by 1913, the NCJW and a few "fraternal" orders were no longer the only options for Jewish women wanting to exercise leadership roles. For women tired of defending their beliefs at NCJW conventions, organizations with clearer commitments, such as HADASSAH's endorsement of Zionism or a sisterhood's attachment to the philosophy of its synagogue, were appealing. The result of this external competition and internal division was an increased focus on social service, especially immigrant aid work. That shift was so powerful that many people still (incorrectly) consider the NCJW a nonreligious, or even antireligious, organization.

In the meantime, however, the NCJW had embodied a profound change in Jewish thinking. Where once men were held primarily responsible for the public expression of Judaism and for passing along the heritage to the next generation, the NCJW's expansion of Jewish motherhood transferred that role to women. The council's position again reflected an Americanization of Judaism. Christian America had long viewed religion as the domain of women. The NCJW, as the conduit through which this view was transmitted to the Jewish community, would begin a process of marked change in what would come to be considered "proper" gender roles for Jews. That change included a new vision of women as active public participants in their religion and their communities.

Though the NCJW came to emphasize social service over more explicit religious expression, it would be inaccurate to portray the organization as abandoning religious work. In fact, the NCJW was the first Jewish organization to develop a vision that social work and political action constituted important religious expression. They even summarized that vision in their motto "faith and humanity." Through the NCJW, Jews adopted the philosophy, common in Christian America's Social Gospel movement, that social work was God's work. This social justice–based religion would significantly influence institutions such as Jewish federations and synagogue social action committees.

The NCJW's actual practice of Jewish social justice reflected turn-of-the-century Progressive politics, a reaction to the deplorable conditions of America's urban poor. The council's broad-ranging work centered around programs to help immigrant Jewish girls and was led by women like Sadie American, ROSE BRENNER (who would serve as national vice president and then president), and CECILIA RAZOVSKY (who would eventually use her skills to lead a variety of American and international Jewish immigrant organizations). The nature of the work was guided by two main forces: a belief in science and a belief in motherhood. Committed to applying the latest scientific methodology to its work, the NCJW replaced the model of benevolent charity common in the Jewish community with preventive philanthropy. Rather than asking individuals to give on an as-needed basis, with recipients returning for handouts as circumstances required, the NCJW stressed efficiency in services designed to help clients become self-sufficient. As

with most Progressive organizations, the council intended to solve problems rather than merely treat symptoms.

In line with their emphasis on motherhood, council members and employees provided services to more than twenty thousand immigrant Jewish girls who arrived on American shores without guardians. They met girls at ports of entry, built settlement houses, provided vocational training and Americanization classes, shared tips on etiquette, provided cultural programs, and fought against the influence of the white slave trade. They visited girls in their homes to see how they were doing and acted as advocates for those in legal trouble.

Members who provided such aid were termed "friendly visitors," reflecting the council's belief that they were providing the stern but loving guidance that would have been provided by a stable home had circumstances allowed. Some recipients of NCJW services viewed "friendly visitors" as annoying interlopers who offered help only because it served their own self-interest to combat anti-Semitism, not because they understood or cared about the immigrants' needs. There is no doubt that "friendly visitors" were separated from the girls they served by a wide economic and social gap.

In addition, many NCJW members were ambivalent about training girls to enter the workforce, doing so because they recognized the economic necessity but regretful that women who worked could not pay "proper" attention to care of children and home. Resulting policies included support of protective legislation for working women and corollary opposition to the Equal Rights Amendment. These policies were easy to adopt from the vantage point of wealthy homes, but they sometimes made life more difficult for the families they were supposed to help. Yet, unlike most other Jewish agencies, the council's model of philanthropy required more than giving money. All "friendly visitors" received training in modern social work, and the personal contact that many members had with the immigrant community humanized the statistics and, in many cases, led to genuine empathy.

Furthermore, the NCJW differed from other (largely Christian) organizations that saw poor immigrant girls as "fallen" and in need of saving. The council believed that their clients were generally good people who merely needed to overcome unfortunate circumstances. The help they provided was therefore material, not spiritual. They did hope that the girls they served would become good Jewish mothers, and sometimes supported religious training toward that end, but their goal was to help the girls preserve their

The NCJW encouraged family life and Jewish activities in all areas of the country.
The sign on the wagon in the above photograph says "This way to kosher picnic."
[National Council of Jewish Women]

ethnicity in ways that were "appropriate" to America, not merely to preserve Judaism.

By most accounts, the NCJW's model of immigrant aid was highly successful. One New York City report credited the council's preventive programs with a 40 percent decrease in Jewish women arraigned for prostitution. NCJW leaders were invited to present sessions at international conferences, and their methods were taught in college classrooms. No organization wielded more influence over immigrant Jewish girls than the NCJW.

Success also produced significant spin-off projects. The most famous was the NCJW's innovative services for the visually impaired. Rather than treating the visually impaired as unemployable and therefore in need of charity, the council approached blindness as a health issue. They encouraged schools to mainstream blind children rather than institutionalize them, and ran an aggressive prevention campaign teaching children how to prevent blindness. They also helped mainstream the visually impaired into Jewish religious life by printing the first Braille prayer book. Most important, the council did not assume that loss of sight meant loss of ability to work. In place of char-

ity, the NCJW created an extensive vocational training program designed especially for the visually impaired and helped find jobs for those who completed the program.

Also unique was the NCJW's Department of Farm and Rural Work, which was exceptionally active in the 1920s. As a response to overcrowding, many resettlement agencies encouraged Jews to live outside urban centers. However, the council was the only agency that provided for the ongoing religious, health, and educational needs of these rural Jewish families, supplying services to more than twenty-five hundred farms in eight states.

The NCJW was innovative in combating anti-Semitism as well. Five years before B'nai Brith established the Anti-Defamation League, the council's Committee for Purity of the Press reviewed newspaper accounts about Jews and publicly objected to stories tainted by anti-Semitism. The council was also one of the first Jewish organizations to find a way formally to involve young people in their work. From 1894 until the 1950s, the council of Jewish Juniors provided an opportunity for teenagers to participate in the council's social welfare projects. Like synagogue youth groups today, junior sections were attached to their adult counterparts in individual communities and often served as feeders for the adult council sections.

The demographic center of the council's immigrant aid work was, not surprisingly, New York City. As the major point of entry for Jewish immigrants, Ellis Island was the natural hub for the NCJW's services. However, New York City had not always been the council's geographic center. Original NCJW sections indicate a significant midwestern presence, with Chicago as the undisputed trendsetter bolstered by strongholds in places like Cincinnati, Cleveland, and Pittsburgh (which provided the council with its second national president, Pauline Rosenberg). As immigrant aid work became more central to the organization, however, so did New York City.

The council's shift in focus and geography was accompanied by a shift in the power of its leaders. American, who had moved from Chicago to New York City, emerged as the clear, if controversial, leader of the council's immigrant aid programs. Her affiliation with the New York section led many to wonder if the New York section and the NCJW were becoming one

and the same, leaving others in subordinate roles as supporting cast members. That concern led to threats of secession by some sections and to a fight between Solomon (who remained in Chicago) and American. Several years of controversy eventually forced American out of the organization, but no one could change the fact that New York City had become the center of American Jewry. To this day, the national offices of the organization remain in New York.

Though internationally renowned for its immigrant aid work, the NCJW was not as clearly committed to other Progressive ideas. For example, though most council leaders personally supported woman suffrage, the organization itself never took an official stand on the issue. This failure to act may have been because a significant number of suffrage leaders were anti-Semitic, because council leaders feared that a debate over suffrage would result in a destructive split reminiscent of disputes over religious policy, or because, for these largely privileged women, suffrage simply did not seem as pressing as helping starving immigrants. Most likely, failure to act on the leading women's issue of the day resulted from all these factors.

Although concentrated in large urban areas, NCJW chapter volunteers throughout the country provided services to their communities. This bookmobile (probably from the 1930s) spreads the habit of reading throughout the Greensboro, North Carolina, area. [National Council of Jewish Women]

Up to World War II, NCJW did not take a stand on Zionism. But after the Holocaust, their Department of Israel Affairs would become one of their largest divisions. One program sent toys to children in Israel. These two women from the Milwaukee section oversee the shipment of toys. [National Council of Jewish Women]

However, the NCJW was a leader on other women's issues. For example, Margaret Sanger credited the council with being the first organization in the United States publicly to demand the legalization of birth control. For the NCJW, support for birth control was not so much an issue of sexuality, or even of women's rights, as it was a natural part of their con-

cern for Jewish immigrants and a belief that family planning was necessary to conquer poverty.

By the end of the 1920s, changing world politics and increasing American restrictions slowed the wave of Jewish immigration, but the new circumstances did not diminish the NCJW's programs or alter its focus. Though reduced in size, the council's immigrant aid

The NCJW's Home Instruction Program for Preschool Youngsters [HIPPY in English, HaETGAR in Hebrew] was begun in 1969. It is designed to provide help and support to parents, who, in turn, provide a learning and nurturing environment for their children. This exhibit explaining the program is being consulted by DR. RUTH WESTHEIMER. *[National Council of Jewish Women]*

programs stayed in place until after World War II, when the organization helped refugees from the Holocaust navigate the necessary bureaucracy to resettle in the United States and offered classes in English and citizenship. They also helped those who stayed in Europe rebuild their lives. In 1945, the NCJW created the Ship-A-Box program, which provided educational materials to European children and teachers. The following year, it established settlement houses in Paris and Athens and offered college scholarships so that European students could study social work in the United States and then return home where their services were so desperately needed.

The council, like the rest of the world's Jewish community, was transformed by the war. Though the group did not change its emphasis on motherhood or social welfare work, it did reflect transformations occurring throughout the American Jewish community. Most noticeable was the organization's growth. Spurred by postwar public proclamations of ideal womanhood that promoted voluntarism and sup-

ported the council's glorification of motherhood, membership in the NCJW nearly doubled between 1945 and 1970, going from 60,000 to 110,000 members in nearly 200 sections.

Another postwar change was the council's adoption of Zionism. Previously unwilling to take an official stand on Zionism for fear of divisiveness, the horrors of the Holocaust overrode members' ambivalence about the need for a Jewish state. In fact, that need seemed so clear that the council's Department of Israel Affairs would quickly surpass the size of its Department of Immigrant Aid and would remain one of its largest departments for more than half a century.

Predictably, the NCJW's support of Israel came in the form of sharing expertise in immigrant aid, social work, education, and child care. Early council efforts centered around Hebrew University, where the NCJW established a library for the School of Education (1949), the University High School (1963), and the Center for Research in the Education of the Disadvantaged (1968). As in Europe, the council offered scholarships to Israeli social work and education students who were willing to study in the United States and return home to share their skills. In the arena of child care, the council introduced the Home Activities for Toddlers and Their Families program in 1972. The council also pioneered the Home Instruction Program for Preschool Youngsters (HIPPY in English, known as HaETGAR in Hebrew), which was implemented nationally by the Israeli government in 1975 and has become one of the most acclaimed parenting programs for at-risk families in the world. HIPPY was followed almost immediately by the creation of the MANOF program, a residential support service for delinquent teens. In recent decades, NCJW's Research Institute for Innovation in Education at Hebrew University has focused attention on resettling Ethiopian and Russian Jews in Israel.

In the United States, council programs also experienced a change. By the end of the 1950s, most Jews displaced by the war had been resettled and, in general, the American Jewish community was financially secure. The NCJW continued to look for needs within the Jewish community and continued its reputation for innovation with its Golden Age project, which created senior centers to provide activities and meals to isolated elderly people. The council's traditional services for the poor, however, began to find a new clientele.

Council programs had always been open to non-Jews, and it had always been NCJW policy to invest resources in starting new programs until others (like government agencies) recognized their importance and took them over. In the Progressive Era, such was the outcome of projects like school lunch programs, installation of public water fountains and sanitation systems, and the creation of juvenile courts. In the 1960s, inspired by the civil rights movement, the council actively fostered the transfer of long-standing programs to other hands. In many cities, council sections turned over settlement houses to civil rights leaders.

Because the NCJW's approach to social welfare work was preventive, the organization always pressed for political change, even as it provided programs.

This 1943 photograph shows NCJW council houses in Washington, D.C. They provided day care for hundreds of children.
[National Council of Jewish Women]

First Lady Hillary Rodham Clinton was the featured speaker at the 1996 NCJW convention.
Here she is being presented with the Faith and Humanity Award by Nan Rich, the 1996–1999 president of NCJW (right)
and Susan Katz, executive director and immediate past president (left). [National Council of Jewish Women]

The council's political approach is most easily labeled as liberal. Where it has sought change, it has called for reform rather than revolution. It has shared a belief with most other Jewish organizations that American democracy is good for Jews, and members' own economic success has provided few reasons to question the basic structure of the American economy. Even in terms of gender roles, the NCJW's consistent emphasis on motherhood has kept it from being a radical organization, leading women back into traditional home structures even as it provided opportunities to act outside of family service.

Yet, the council's liberal politics have led others to label the organization as threatening. In the early years, the criticism came from traditional Jews who questioned the council's expansion of women's roles or apparent acceptance of Reform Judaism. In more recent times, the NCJW's opposition to nuclear weapons, McCarthyism, and the Vietnam War, as well as its advocacy of civil rights, earned the organization an FBI file and the (unwarranted) suspicion that it was a communist front.

The NCJW continues to play an important role as a vehicle for Jewish women to express their political activism in Jewish terms. The organization has had Non-Governmental Organization (NGO) status at the United Nations since the UN's founding. Its Washington bureau functions not only as a vehicle for lobbying but also as a source of political training for council members.

The specifics of the council's political policies continue to be shaped by the organization's emphasis on motherhood and social welfare. To provide an informed foundation for its political positions, the NCJW created The Center for the Child, which conducts research on the effectiveness of programs that serve families. Other motherhood-inspired policies have included advocacy for government support of quality child care and the strengthening of women's economic clout. The latter concern, as well as a shift in feminist thinking influenced by the civil rights movement of the 1960s, led the NCJW to reverse its original opposition to the Equal Rights Amendment. In fact, by the mid-1970s, the council would become one of the strongest Jewish voices in favor of the ERA.

Equally strong has been the NCJW's support for reproductive choice, including the right to abortion. This position—an extension of the council's belief in individual liberty, its support for Planned Parenthood, and its efforts to combat poverty—has included vocal support for Medicaid funding for abortion, as well as a presence on the speaker's platform at national pro-choice rallies.

As in its Progressive past, the NCJW also continues to function as a conduit for the exchange of ideas between secular America and the Jewish community. For example, it has looked for the intersections between feminism and Judaism, creating the Jewish Women's Resource Center (an archive of materials on Jewish women), sponsoring conferences on Jewish feminism, housing drop-in centers for Jewish lesbians, and supporting scholarship about Jewish women. Throughout, it has remained committed to pluralism, refusing to endorse a particular religious position or practice but rather promoting community dialogue.

As with all women's voluntary organizations, membership in the council has declined from its heyday in the 1950s and 1960s as more women have entered the workforce. It has survived, in part, because its structure allows individual sections the flexibility to concentrate efforts on meeting local needs. That flexibility, however, has produced a diversity of activity that has made it difficult for the council to establish a clear national identity. Despite this challenge, the NCJW continues to act as a bridge between traditional motherhood and political activity, between the Jewish community and other women's organizations, between Judaism and politics, and between diverse segments of the Jewish community itself.

BIBLIOGRAPHY

Elwell, Ellen Sue Levi. "The Founding and Early Programs of the National Council of Jewish Women: Study and Practice as Jewish Women's Religious Expression." Ph.D. diss., Indiana University (1982); *National Council of Jewish Women: Proceedings of the First Convention, November 15–19, 1896* (1897); *Papers of the Jewish Women's Congress, 1893* (1894); Rogow, Faith. *Gone to Another Meeting: The National Council of Jewish Women, 1893–1993* (1993); Solomon, Hannah. *Fabric of My Life* (1946).

FAITH ROGOW

NATIONAL FEDERATION OF TEMPLE SISTERHOODS

In 1913, the women of Reform Judaism, who were organized in independent, local synagogue sisterhoods founded in the 1890s and 1900s, united to create a national organization of women dedicated to religion. Reform Jewish women joined the American women of the era who established a host of voluntary associations to further various social and communal agendas. The National Federation of Temple Sisterhoods (NFTS), officially renamed in 1993 the Women of Reform Judaism–The Federation of Temple Sisterhoods, grew from 9,000 members in forty-nine sisterhoods at its founding to 100,000 members in six hundred local affiliates in the United States, Canada, and twelve other countries by 1995.

Recognizing "that the increased power which has come to the modern American Jewess ought to be exercised in congregational life," Reform sisterhood members gathered in 1913 in Cincinnati, at the request of the Union of American Hebrew Congregations, Reform Judaism's synagogal body. After hearing addresses by leading rabbis celebrating Reform's emancipation of Jewish women from the fetters of the oriental synagogue, the NFTS elected CARRIE SIMON, *rebbetzin* of the Washington Hebrew Congregation, founding president. Historian Jacob Marcus has suggested NFTS emerged because the NATIONAL COUNCIL OF JEWISH WOMEN, founded in 1893, had abandoned its original aim of strengthening Jewish religious life in favor of focusing on social service work. Certainly, Simon saw NFTS created not to duplicate existing Jewish women's organizations but to carry the banner of religious spirit necessary to strengthen the congregation. Although she originally invited sisterhood women in "so-called conservative congregations" and even Orthodox Jewish women to join her, within a decade these women would create their own national and denominational organizations.

From its inception, NFTS revealed that it would use the forum of a broad, public organization to further what had become, in America, women's spheres of responsibility within Judaism and the synagogue. Its standing committees demonstrated that domestic responsibilities beyond the home in the congregation, religious school, and community were the paramount tasks of NFTS. First and foremost, NFTS strove to further the religious spirit of Reform Jewish life. Its leaders stated time and again that their chief purpose was religious, fostering Reform's particular expression of modern Judaism. Through circulars sent by the National Committee on Religion and through its biennial conventions, NFTS attempted to orchestrate the directions of its work at a nationwide level.

The NFTS encouraged weekly worship, for example, by convincing local sisterhood women to provide baby-sitting to free young mothers for an hour or by canvassing door-to-door to persuade friends to join them in temple. NFTS encouraged sisterhood women to create in their temples a spirit of welcoming community, reminded members to bridge the distance between pulpit and congregation by sitting in the first row of the sanctuary, and suggested that they sponsor an hour of refreshments and sociability after Friday evening services.

NFTS expected that local sisterhoods would continue the tradition of their foremothers, the women of the nineteenth-century Hebrew ladies' benevolent societies, and buy ritual objects and flowers to beautify their synagogues. Sisterhood women continued to take special responsibility for Jewish holiday celebrations in the synagogue by building and decorating the temporary booths required for Sukkoth, giving religious school children Hanukkah candles and candies, arranging masquerades and carnivals for Purim, and leading the way in simplifying the all-too-elaborate celebrations that had come to characterize their sons' and daughters' confirmations on Shavuoth.

Yet the national organization staunchly resisted relocating all aspects of a home-based Judaism to the temple. While NFTS celebrated sisterhood women organizing communal Passover seders, its leaders wanted the first meal of the holiday reserved for their families and the Friday evening sanctification service also saved for their homes.

As Mothers in Israel concerned with the future of Jewish life in America, education of children and youth work held preeminent places on NFTS's agenda. Its National Committee on Religious Schools paid particular attention to the quality of local congregational schools, staffing and teacher training, the curriculum, and the involvement of school parents. It established a publication fund that began to produce not only textbooks for the classroom but works of adult education as well. NFTS enhanced the education of its members with Bible study classes, courses on the Jewish child, and, after the establishment of the State of Israel, through teaching the Hebrew that the Reform movement had once abandoned, making women Jewishly literate.

Supporting children in religious school through their confirmations at age sixteen did not complete NFTS's mission for youth work, for keeping the next generation tied to Reform Judaism was pivotal to its program. In the late 1920s, NFTS turned its attention to the Young Folk's Temple Leagues, organizations for the eighteen-to-twenty-eight-year-old youth of Reform Jewish communities. The NFTS sought ways to connect these young men and women to Reform Judaism by inviting them to assist in religious schools and suggesting that they have a voice on temple boards. After World War II, NFTS played a founding role in the creation of the North American Federation of Temple Youth, an organization aimed at youth in high school.

Not surprisingly, concern for the future meant that sisterhood women were also determined to forge "a real bond of tradition and sentiment between the boys at the College and the women of the Sisterhood . . . from the earliest days it was always the duty and privilege of the mothers in Israel to provide in their own households for the rabbinic students in the community." With rabbinic students now at Hebrew Union College in Cincinnati, NFTS women adopted modern modes for shouldering this responsibility. First they raised scholarships, boasting, by 1919, twenty-four complete scholarships funded for future rabbis. Then NFTS conducted a campaign to build a dormitory at Hebrew Union College. When it opened in 1925, the dorm housed 100 students and stood as a tribute to NFTS's determination to continue, as Mothers in Israel, to provide for their communities of the future.

Promoting religion in the community, especially to those isolated without a local family base, was a logical extension of this work. NFTS circulated lists of Jewish college students—the 1927 list had 1,330 names—and urged sisterhoods in university communities to invite these young people to services and to their homes. The organization encouraged individual sisterhoods to send Passover foods to Jewish prisoners and took a special interest in providing Jewish materials for the blind. NFTS was a founder of the Jewish Braille Institute of America. Sisterhood women transcribed articles into Braille, supported the monthly *Jewish Braille Review*, and helped develop a Hebrew Braille alphabet.

For many years, NFTS walked a fine line between its commitment to Reform Judaism and its interests in general philanthropic work and contemporary political issues. NFTS presidents, such as Hattie M. Wiesenfeld, urged members not to overextend sisterhood by venturing into social service and political avenues best left to other organizations. Acutely conscious of the extent of the funds they could raise—through the sale of Jewish art calendars, Uniongram occasion cards for birthdays and memorials, and publications—early NFTS presidents were eager to promote the spirit of Reform Judaism by organizing free religious schools for those not affiliated with the synagogue. More often than not, they encouraged sisterhood activities to promote Reform Judaism and discouraged those that redirected energies and monies elsewhere, however worthy the cause.

Nonetheless, in times of national emergency, such as during World War I and World War II, NFTS wholeheartedly joined others in the cause. The organization encouraged members to bring the comfort of religious community to military men stationed far from home. With the Red Cross, the NFTS organized the women of Reform Judaism to aid their nation and those who suffered from the war.

Moreover, NFTS leaders always considered certain issues, notably peace work and separation of church and state in the public schools, at the center of sisterhood's religious mission. Citing the prophet Isaiah, who envisioned a time when swords would become plowshares, NFTS joined other associations in the 1920s, promoting the prevention of war and encouraging the U.S. Government in its pursuit of disarmament. Local NFTS constituents opposed the Bible bills of the 1920s and the release time bills of the 1940s, which gave schoolchildren in some locales time off for religious instruction. NFTS resolutions reveal other political issues Reform Jewish women did agree upon, including funds for the relief of Jewish women in Palestine (1915) and support for the rescue of Ethiopian (Falasha) Jewry (1923).

Furthermore, despite preferring to refrain from politics, NFTS was concerned from its inception with one major political issue—the changing role of women, especially within Reform Judaism. NFTS proceedings are filled with presidents' speeches and the reports of chairmen, as they were then known, celebrating that for woman in Reform Judaism "the day of her inferiority is a memory of the Dark Ages." But NFTS regularly sought to push the limitations of that emancipation farther. In 1925, NFTS president STELLA FREIBERG wondered at the wise man who penned the biblical portrait of the woman of valor: "Could that sage in Israel have foreseen the future? . . . Could he have seen her rise in the realm of her religion, watch her descend from the gallery unto the lower floor and then ascend even into the pulpit?" Within its first decade, NFTS leaders would herald the experiment of electing women to synagogue boards; call for its members, in the absence of vacationing rabbis, to lead summer services; and proclaim Sisterhood Sabbath, a day when, in some congregations, women could lead the service and preach to the entire congregation. NFTS reports contain a record of what its members presumed to be landmarks—the first time a woman trustee sat on the pulpit during services, the first time a woman read scripture on Yom Kippur—celebrating Reform Judaism's emancipation of women in the synagogue. Later, NFTS leaders would turn to these examples of successful female religious leadership as "a revelation of what the women may do if they ever enter the rabbinate."

Despite the exigencies of the Depression, which saw NFTS stabilize at around 350 local affiliates, as some impoverished sisterhoods resigned and few new ones joined, NFTS activities expanded in new directions. The chief reason for these new approaches was the hiring, in 1933, of Jane Evans, "the first lady of Reform Judaism" and NFTS's first full-time executive director. The moving force in charting new directions for NFTS, especially those that extended beyond congregational life and the humanitarian vision Reform Judaism espoused, Evans first turned her attention to enriching and strengthening local sisterhood life. While running an office that handled hundreds of letters every day, she launched new projects: the publication of the newsletter *Topics and Trends*, a radio program of Jewish liturgical music, leadership training institutes, and a speakers' bureau, which guaranteed a volunteer speaker—often Evans herself—to every local affiliate.

Then Evans began to push NFTS beyond its original mandate of service to the congregation, religious school, and community. A particularly keen observer of contemporary affairs and a religious pacifist who offered to resign from NFTS when the United States entered World War II, she demanded that Reform Jewish women voice their opinions on both the issues confronting Reform Judaism and the political challenges of the day. She helped orchestrate NFTS's fund-raising for a home for Reform Judaism's national organizations, the House of Living Judaism, and lobbied to see it built in New York, not in Reform's traditional center, Cincinnati. In 1961, just as President John F. Kennedy was convening the Commission on the Status of Women, Evans brought the question of women's rabbinic ordination before NFTS. Under her guidance, resolutions supporting access to birth control information, civil rights, fair employment practices, child labor legislation, the revision of immigration legislation, the elimination of capital punishment, and the de-escalation of the Vietnam War were all endorsed at NFTS biennial conventions. Evans was particularly interested in promoting peace and caring for worldwide Jewry, including the Jewish community in Palestine and, after 1948, in the new State of Israel. This strong concern for international political affairs pushed NFTS to broaden its mission. The organization that had never adopted a resolution in favor of woman suffrage endorsed the Equal Rights Amendment to the Constitution in 1973; urged sisterhoods during the 1980s, the international decade for women, to form coalitions with other women's organizations for the advancement of all women; and celebrated its support for a woman's right to abortion in the 1992 "March for Women's Lives" in the nation's capital. Under her long administration, Evans and her successors, Eleanor Schwartz (1976–1992) and Ellen Y. Rosenberg (1992–), took the Women of Reform Judaism far beyond the domestic sphere of its founders into the larger Jewish world and the arena of women and politics.

Through NFTS, sisterhood women exercised a collective voice. Although they shared with their husbands and brothers the spaces of their synagogues, the institutional structures of Reform Judaism, and its religious and humanitarian values, NFTS nationally and its individual affiliates locally allowed Jewish women a venue for the creation of a female Reform Jewish culture. Through its programs and shifting interests—weekly worship, synagogue celebrations, education, youth, and, later, expanding women's sphere and roles and extending women's religious and civil rights—NFTS enabled its members to help change the expectations of American Jewish women's proper behavior within the portals of their Reform synagogues and ultimately to enlarge their roles there and in the world.

BIBLIOGRAPHY

Davis, Karen, "The Ascent of Sisterhood: The First Eight Decades." *Reform Judaism* (Fall 1992): 37+; Evans, Jane. Oral history interview with Abraham J. Peck, November 4, 1985. AJA, Cincinnati, Ohio; Hirt-Manheimer, Aron. "Sisterhood for the '90s: A Conversation with Ellen Y. Rosenberg." *Reform Judaism* (Fall 1992): 40–42; Nadell, Pamela S., and Rita J. Simon, "Ladies of the Sisterhood: Women in the American Reform Synagogue, 1900–1930." In *Active Voices: Women in Jewish Culture*, edited by Maurie Sacks (1995); National Federation of Temple Sisterhoods. *Index of Resolutions, Adopted by the National Federation of Temple Sisterhoods, 1913–1985* (1988), and *Proceedings of the National Federation of Temple Sisterhoods* (1913–), and *Topics and Trends* (n.d.); Rosett, Frieda S. Papers, 1924–1987. Mss Collection number 353, folder 1/3, Speeches, 1924–1943. AJA.

PAMELA S. NADELL

NATZLER, GERTRUD AMON (1908–1971)

Gertrud Amon Natzler's collaboration with her husband, Otto Natzler, over almost four decades produced some of the twentieth century's finest ceramics. They are held by over seventy museums throughout the world and by countless private collections. Her nearly twenty-five thousand hand-thrown pots, bowls, and bottles are celebrated for their refinement, delicacy, and proportion. While the body of her work reflects an unending quest for absolute perfection of form, she also produced functional pieces, such as *yahrzeit* [memorial] lamps. Her husband brought exceptional color and texture to the work with the glazes he invented and developed by experimentation, carefully documenting several thousand formulas.

Gertrud Natzler was born on January 7, 1908, to Adolf and Helene (Grünwald) Amon, Viennese Jews who had one older child, Hans. Her father had a stationery manufacturing business and her mother was a homemaker. Educated in Vienna, she studied at the Handelsakademie [commercial school], then worked as a secretary and took courses in painting and drawing. She met Otto Natzler and in 1934 the two began to study ceramics together at the workshop of Franz Iskra. Only one year later, they set up their own studio, devoting themselves full-time to their art. Soon the work of the largely self-taught artists was recognized for its excellence. In March 1938, on the day the Natzlers learned they had been awarded a silver medal at the World Exhibition in Paris, the Nazis took over Austria. They married in June, and in September left their homeland for California.

Settling into a new workshop in Los Angeles, the Natzlers began a prolific American career, distinguished by national and international recognition, innumerable exhibitions, awards, and acclaim. They spent the summers from 1956 to 1960 as artists-in-residence at the Brandeis Institute in Santa Susana, California, conducting ceramics workshops for college-age Jewish participants. Among many institutions where their work is exhibited are the Jewish Museum in New York, Bezalel National Museum in Jerusalem, and the Los Angeles County Museum of Art .

Gertrud Amon Natzler died from cancer on June 3, 1971. For more than a year after her death, Otto Natzler was unable to work, but then he began firing

Gertrud Natzler's collaboration with her husband, Otto, over almost four decades has produced some of the twentieth century's finest ceramics. The above photograph of the two artists was taken in 1958. [Hella Hammid]

and glazing over two hundred pieces she had left. Thus the collaboration continued, as did exhibitions of their work, including retrospective shows in 1973 at the Renwick Gallery of the Smithsonian Institution, Washington, D.C., in 1977 at the Craft and Folk Art Museum in Los Angeles, and in 1993 at the American Craft Museum in New York. The 1994 exhibit at the Jewish Museum in Vienna brought the work of Gertrud Amon Natzler full circle to the place of her birth.

BIBLIOGRAPHY

The Ceramic Art of the Natzlers. Written and directed by Edmund Penney, videocassette, 1967; *The Ceramic Work of Gertrud and Otto Natzler: A Retrospective Exhibition.* Exhibition catalog, Los Angeles County Museum of Art (1966); *The Ceramic Work of Gertrud and Otto Natzler.* Exhibition catalog, M. H. de Young Memorial Museum, San Francisco (1971); *Clay Today: Contemporary Ceramists and Their Work: A Catalogue of the Howard and Gwen Lurie Smits Collection at the Los Angeles County Museum of Art* (1990); *Form and Fire: Natzler Ceramics 1939–1972.* Exhibition catalog, Renwick Gallery, National Collection of Fine Arts, Smithsonian Institution (1973); *Gertrud and Otto Natzler: Collaboration/Solitude.* Exhibition catalog, American Craft Museum, NYC (1993); *Gertrud and Otto Natzler Ceramics: Catalog of the Collection of Mrs. Leonard M. Sperry, and a Monograph by Otto Natzler.* Exhibition catalog, Los Angeles County Museum of Art (1968); *Natzler.* Exhibition catalog, Craft and Folk Art Museum, Los Angeles (1977); Natzler, Otto. Interview by author. Los Angeles, May 11, 1996; *WWWIA* 6.

NANCY L. BARTH

NAUMBURG, ELSIE MARGARET BINGER (1880–1953)

Elsie M.B. Naumburg successfully combined a career in science and active participation in philanthropies, gaining the respect and affection of her many friends and colleagues. Born July 7, 1880, in New York City and educated in private schools, she was the daughter of Frances (Newgass) Binger and Gustav Binger, a wealthy German industrialist who came to New York in 1867. She had three brothers: Robert, Walter D., and Carl. In 1908, she married Victor Reichenberger.

Traveling to Germany in 1912, she studied at the universities of Frankfurt-am-Main and Munich. She began her museum studies at the Senckenberg Museum in Frankfurt and subsequently at the Zoologische Staazmuseum in Munich.

Victor Reichenberger had died in 1913, and the young widow returned to New York in 1916, as the United States was about to enter World War I. Soon thereafter, she volunteered in the Department of Ornithology at the American Museum of Natural History, becoming a staff member in 1918, a research associate in 1923, and an associate benefactor in 1930. In 1923, she married Walter Wehle Naumburg, an amateur cellist and a member of a prominent New York family. They made their home in New York and New Caanan, Connecticut.

Somewhat earlier she had begun studying the birds collected on the Theodore Roosevelt–Colonel Candido Rondon expedition to Brazil, the famous River of Doubt expedition. This enormous task was completed in 1930 with publication of "The Birds of Matto Grosso, Brazil," still a classic.

Her deep interest in the poorly known South American avifauna led her to support fieldwork by Emil Kaempfer in eastern Brazil and Paraguay from 1926 to 1931. After beginning her study of this collection, she found it essential to pinpoint the remote collecting localities, many of which did not appear on available maps. Taking a year off from her ornithological studies, she worked at the American Geographical Society, producing a still-useful gazetteer. She was named a fellow of the Society.

She published several papers in a planned series to cover the entire Kaempfer collection. However, bowing to the humanitarian demands brought about by the outbreak of World War II, she gave up her own research to devote more time to relief projects, especially the Soldiers' Canteen operated by the Salvation Army. Its activities centered around helping refugee and unemployed musicians during wartime.

Only one of many accomplishments, Elsie Naumburg's The Birds of Matto Grosso, Brazil, *is to this day an invaluable classic in the study of birds. A well-known ornithologist, she was also a great philanthropist who contributed to many causes.* [American Museum of Natural History]

In 1946, Naumburg established at the American Museum of Natural History the Frank M. Chapman Memorial Fund in honor of her mentor. It is now a major support of field and museum studies of birds worldwide, reflecting Chapman's broad interests and pioneering studies of bird distribution and diversity.

Naumburg became secretary and treasurer of the Walter W. Naumburg Foundation, founded by her husband in 1925 to support composers and musicians. In addition, she was chairman of the board of An Hour of Music, Inc., established in 1937 to provide promising performers with a professional debut in New York. She was also a fellow of the New York Academy of Sciences and of the American Ornithologists' Union and director (1942–1948) of the National Audubon Society.

Elsie Naumburg was active in several educational projects for children. She was a founder and trustee of the William T. Hornaday Memorial Foundation, established to promote children's museums, and a director of the Greenwich (Connecticut) Nature Center.

Elsie Margaret Binger Naumburg died on November 25, 1953, in New York City.

SELECTED WORKS BY ELSIE M.B NAUMBURG

"Animal 'Building': A Visit Behind the Scenes at the American Museum Where You May See Animals Being Made Ready for Exhibition." *The Junior Natural History* 1, no. 11 (1937): 13–16; "The Bird Fauna of North America in Relation to Its Distribution in South America." *The Auk* 43 (1926):485–492; "The Birds of Matto Grosso, Brazil: A Report on the Birds Secured by the Roosevelt Rondon Expedition." *Bulletin of the American Museum of Natural History* 60 (1930): 1–432; "Descriptions of Proposed New Birds from Brazil and Paraguay," with George K. Cherrie. *American Museum Novitates*, no. 58 (1923): 8 pp.; "Descriptions of Proposed New Birds From Brazil, Paraguay, and Argentina," with George K. Cherrie. *American Museum Novitates*, no. 27 (1921); "Gazetteer and Maps Showing Collecting Stations Visited by Emil Kaempfer in Eastern Brazil and Paraguay." *Bulletin of the American Museum of Natural History* 68 (1935): 449–469; "The Senckenberg Museum, Frankfort-on-Main, Germany." *The Auk* 48 (1931): 379–384; "Studies of Birds from Eastern Brazil and Paraguay, Based on a Collection Made by Emil Kaempfer." *Bulletin of the American Museum of Natural History* 74 (1937): 139–205, and 76 (1939): 231–276; "Three New Birds from Northwestern [=Northeastern] Brazil." *American Museum Novitates*, no. 554 (1932).

BIBLIOGRAPHY

EJ.

MARY LeCROY

NAUMBURG, MARGARET (1890–1983)

Up to the present time, education has missed the real significance of the child's behavior by treating surface actions as isolated conditions. Having failed to recognize the true sources of behavior, it has been unable effectively to correct and guide the impulses of human growth.... The new advances in psychology, however, provide a key to the real understanding of what makes a child tick.

This is a quote from Margaret Naumburg, founder of the Walden School and author of many works on psychology and art therapy. She was born on May 14, 1890, in New York City to German-born Max Naumburg, a successful clothing manufacturer, and American-born Theresa (Kahnweiler) Naumburg. Margaret was the second daughter in a family with three girls and one boy. Although raised in a Jewish home and interested in Jewish mysticism, she identified more closely with the ideologies of Ethical Culture. This organized intellectual and spiritual movement did not require a formal conversion for participation and attracted other German Jews throughout the United States. Naumburg's ideas alienated her from her parents.

While a student at Barnard College, Naumburg roomed with Evelyn Dewey, took courses with John Dewey, was the president of the Socialist Club, and counted Walter Lippmann "as one of her closest men friends." Shortly after graduation, she left for Europe, where she studied economics at the London School of Economics, learned the Delcroze method in music under Alys Bently, and studied child education with Maria Montessori.

Upon her return to New York in 1914, Naumburg settled into the new American bohemian community of Greenwich Village, where she openly lived with Waldo Frank, author of novels and cultural criticism. Frank, a graduate of Yale University, was the son of a successful lawyer. Both Naumburg and Frank became consumed by postimpressionist art and reality and dedicated their lives to reforming society. Naumburg's desire for public recognition and for respect in the field of child development and education eventually led to her marriage to Frank in 1916.

In 1914, Naumburg opened the first Montessori school in the United States. It occupied space at the Henry Street Settlement House. This experience gave Naumburg the opportunity to develop her own educational philosophies, which early on began to conflict with Montessori methods. After only one year, she left the school to establish her own institution, the Walden School.

Naumburg's Walden School opened in a rented room at the Leete School on East 60th Street. It began as a nursery school for two-year-olds, and a new level was added each year. In 1928, the first graduating class included the children of a famous analyst, a university professor, an art teacher, and a well-known writer and suffragist. The school was perceived as part of a movement to "free the arts." It was praised highly in the press and had strong support from the intellectual community. In 1915, the *New York Tribune* described the "very interesting and remarkable" new experiment. The intellectual and cultural atmosphere was further enhanced by the presence of Hendrik Van Loon, Lewis Mumford, and Ernest Bloch, who were invited by Naumburg to work with the students.

Influenced by Freud's theories, the Walden School used psychoanalysis as the base of its educational philosophies. The emphasis at the Walden

School was on "the development of children's capacities," not the "accumulation of knowledge." The first catalog states the school's aim "to develop individuality and initiative" and, through music and art, to stimulate the child's creative activity. The art program, developed by Naumburg's sister Florence Cane, was greatly influenced by Jung.

In 1922, Naumburg and Frank gave birth to a son, Thomas. By 1924, their marriage had dissolved, and, soon after, Naumburg resigned as director of the Walden School. By the late 1920s, she found a new career in writing. In 1928, her book *The Child and the World*, based on her experiences at Walden, was published.

In the 1930s, Naumburg began her work and research in art therapy. While working with children at the New York Psychiatric Institute, she developed her method of diagnosis and therapy by teaching free art expression. She wrote about her philosophies and methods in four texts: *An Introduction to Art Therapy*, *Schizophrenic Art*, *Psychoneurotic Art*, and *Dynamically Oriented Art Therapy*. In the 1940s, Naumburg pursued training in psychiatry at Bellevue Hospital. By the late 1950s, she was lecturing widely and developed the first art therapy courses at the New School for Social Research and at New York University. Naumburg remained at the New School for Social Research until her retirement in 1969.

Naumburg received the Ernest Kris Prize in 1973 and was a fellow of the American Orthopsychiatric Association and the American Psychological Association.

Margaret Naumburg died on February 26, 1983, at age ninety-two.

**SELECTED WORKS BY
MARGARET NAUMBURG**

The Child and the World (1928); *Dynamically Oriented Art Therapy* (1966); *An Introduction to Art Therapy* (1973); *Psychoneurotic Art* (1953); *Schizophrenic Art* (1953).

BIBLIOGRAPHY

American Journal of Art Therapy 22 (October 1982); *EJ*; Frank, Dr. Thomas, and Kate Frank. Conversation with author, February 1995; Karier, Clarence J. *Scientists of the Mind* (1986); Obituary. *NYTimes*, March 6, 1983; *UJE*; *The Walden Story: Forty Years of Living Education* (1954).

JULIE ALTMAN

NCJW *see* NATIONAL COUNCIL OF JEWISH WOMEN

NEIMAN, CARRIE MARCUS (1883–1953)

Dallas's legendary Neiman Marcus specialty store owes its style, its personal brand of service, and its first cache of merchandise to Carrie Marcus Neiman, the fashion authority who helped launch a retailing concept. Until the Texas store opened on September 10,

With her husband, her brother, $25,000, and the dream of a fashionable retail department store, Carrie Marcus Neiman launched a business that is now legendary. She became chair of the board in 1950, after her brother's death. Her brother helped launch a Jewish country club in Dallas, because all the existing clubs were closed to Jews. [Photograph courtesy of Neiman Marcus]

1907, women went to dressmakers for apparel. In the new store, Neiman selected quality ready-to-wear garments that suited her taste and anticipated stylish trends. When the Texas frontier turned rich with oil, Neiman was poised to play Pygmalion for newly wealthy customers whose shopping sprees fueled Texas tales and made Dallas an international fashion capital.

Born on May 5, 1883, in Louisville, Kentucky, Carrie Marcus Neiman was the youngest of three daughters and two sons of German immigrants Delia (Bloomfield) and Jacob Marcus, a cotton broker. In 1895, the family moved to Texas to live with a daughter married to a Hillsboro grocer. In 1899, they moved to Dallas. After high school in 1902, Carrie Neiman became top salesperson at A. Harris and Company. After marrying Abraham Lincoln "Al" Neiman on April 25, 1905, in Dallas, both Neiman and her older brother Herbert Marcus, a buyer for a rival store, joined Al Neiman's salvage business and moved to Atlanta. In 1907, with twenty-five thousand dollars in profits, the trio returned to Dallas to launch their dream store. The Neimans divorced in 1928 because of his infidelities. Herbert Marcus bought out his brother-in-law's ownership in the store. He was chairman of the board from 1923 to 1950. Carrie Neiman became the chair following his death in December 1950. In 1951, the store did a $21 million volume.

Carrie Neiman belonged to Temple Emanu-El and Columbian Club, a Jewish country club, which her brother helped launch because Dallas clubs were closed to Jews.

Carrie Marcus Neiman died in Dallas on March 6, 1953, in the same month that *Holiday* magazine pronounced her a symbol of elegance.

BIBLIOGRAPHY

AJHQ 66:123–136; Harris, Leon. *Merchant Princes: An Intimate History of Jewish Families Who Built Great Department Stores* (1979); Marcus, Stanley [nephew]. Telephone conversation with author, May 2, 1996; Peeler, Tom. "Story of the Store: The Unlikely Marriages of Neiman and Marcus." *D Magazine* (August 1984): 165–171; Smith, Marcus Jerrie [grandniece]. Telephone conversation with author, May 6, 1996; Street, James. "Dazzling Dallas." *Holiday* (March 1953): 102–119; Tolbert, Frank X. "Death Takes Mrs. Neiman at Age of 69." *Dallas Morning News*, March 7, 1953, 1, and "Mrs. Neiman Dead; Store Co-Founder, Chairman of Neiman-Marcus in Dallas Started Business in '07 with Husband and Brother." *NYTimes*, March 8, 1953, 89, and *Neiman-Marcus, Texas: The Story of the Proud Dallas Store* (1953).

HOLLACE AVA WEINER

NEUGARTEN, BERNICE L. (b. 1916)

Academic study of adult development and aging—now a well-established subject essential to social practice and policy and to the clinical professions—can be said to derive from the pioneering scholarship and teaching of Bernice L. Neugarten in the decades since 1950. Working at the border of sociology and psychology, Neugarten contested many of the myths of middle and late life, helped to build and maintain unique academic programs, and trained scores of influential scholars in the field she helped to invent.

Born Bernice Levin in 1916, Neugarten grew up in the small town of Norfolk, Nebraska, where she advanced quickly through the public school system, taking college courses even before she entered her teens. She enrolled as an undergraduate at the University of Chicago during the days of Robert M. Hutchins's reforms that made it possible for students to study for college and then graduate degrees in just a few years. Thus, she earned her B.A. in English and French literature and M.A. in educational psychology by the time she was twenty-one. Her professional life took form as a result of both preparation and accident; perhaps inevitably, Neugarten made the impact of "off-time experiences" and of the discontinuities and continuities in adult experience major themes in her scholarly work.

Neugarten's initial career plans were stalled by her youth, she believes, as she appeared too young to school authorities to be a credible high school teacher. She was "rescued," she says, by the offer of a graduate assistantship at the University of Chicago in the new Committee on Child Development (later Human Development). She earned her Ph.D. in 1943. The next eight years were devoted to family life, raising two children, doing part-time research and consulting, and working with her husband on local community projects aimed at racial integration.

After she returned to full-time academic work in 1951, Neugarten came to play a critical role in the maturation, so to speak, of human development as a subject at the University of Chicago and elsewhere, even though it was by accident that she came to specialize in adult development and aging after she was unexpectedly called upon to design a course in that subject. In 1960, she was the first person at the University of Chicago to gain tenure in that field (without a joint appointment in another department). This period was an unusually fruitful one. The famed Kansas City Studies of Adult Life (1952–1962), conducted with foundation and federal support, were carried out under Neugarten's leadership, jointly with Robert J. Havinghurst and William E. Henry. The project represented the first community-based research to focus on middle age and aging. With a research agenda that was, for its time, uniquely multidisciplinary, the work produced by Neugarten in 1964 and 1968 represents many of the key issues that came to define the field: social role performance, age differences in family, work and leisure patterns, social mobility, age-grading, personality processes, psychological adjustment, and life satisfaction. In Neugarten's own words, the major contribution of the Kansas City studies was "to demonstrate not only that there is no single direction or pattern of social-psychological aging, but no single pattern of optimal aging" (1988).

Neugarten's scholarly work helped to launch the careers of many social and behavioral scientists. She notes with pride that half of her students over the years have been women. During a period of institutional tension at the University of Chicago with regard to the matter of gender and academic appointments, Neugarten served as the first chair of the university's Committee on Women, which, with its research and advocacy, had a considerable impact locally and nationally.

Neugarten is the coauthor or editor of eight books and the author of more than 150 articles. She herself has noted that the pattern of her research has been to open new topic areas rather than follow a single line of inquiry over an extended period—"to map out some of the landscape of what had earlier been the neglected territory of the second half of life." She invented terms now widely used—the "young-old," to identify those in their late years still able to function well, and the "old-old," those who are frail and need support. Perhaps her most important contribution, paradoxically enough, has been to demonstrate that compared to earlier periods in history, age has declined in significance in distinguishing between middle-aged and older people. Aging is a complex and highly individual process in which there are many possibilities for "success."

In 1975 and 1994, Neugarten was recognized by the American Psychological Association for her achievements in research, teaching, and leadership. Late in her career, she made policy her primary interest. Neugarten served a term on the Federal Council on Aging and was instrumental in planning the 1981 White House Conference on Aging. Always an independent thinker, her support of basing government programs on need rather than entitlement put her at odds with senior citizen interest groups. Neugarten has, characteristically, resisted the conventional reaction: "Perhaps the most constructive ways of adapting to an aging society will emerge by focusing not on age at all but on the more relevant dimensions of human needs, human capacities, and human diversity."

SELECTED WORKS BY BERNICE L. NEUGARTEN

Age or Need? Public Policies for Older People (1982); "The Aging Society and My Academic Life." In *Sociological Lives*, edited by Matilda While Riley (1988); "Changing Meanings of Age in the Aging Society," with Dail A. Neugarten. In *Our Aging Society: Paradox and Promise*, edited by Alan Pifer and Lydia Bronte (1986); *The Meanings of Age: Selected Papers of Bernice L. Neugarten* (1996); *Middle Age and Aging* (1968); *Personality in Middle and Late Life* (1964).

STEVEN WEILAND

NEUGASS, MIRIAM DOROTHY NEWMAN *see* NEWMAN, ISADORA

NEVELSON, LOUISE (1900–1988)

If an object is in the right place, it is enhanced to grandeur. More than that, it pleases the inner being and that, I think, is very important. That equals harmony.

Louise Nevelson belongs to a generation of Manhattan-based painters and sculptors who were born at the close of the nineteenth century and whose careers spanned the twentieth, coinciding with the development of modernism in America. Like several of the artists who later became known as abstract expressionist painters and sculptors, in the 1920s Nevelson traveled to Paris and also studied in New York at the Art Students League. In the 1930s, she worked under the auspices of the Federal Art Project of the Works Progress Administration, which allowed her and her colleagues an important opportunity to earn a salary for making and teaching art. The WPA also provided a forum for artists to meet and exchange ideas while acquiring professional credentials. It was in the late 1940s and during the 1950s that modernism came into its own in the United States, and artists who had been working steadily through the 1920s and 1930s developed a mature style. Each of these artists combined the predominant avant-garde influences of cubism and surrealism (imported to New York by European exiles from World War II) as well as the writings of Carl Jung, Sigmund Freud, and Jean-Paul Sartre with their own personal concerns to create the distinctive works for which they are best known. Jackson Pollock's experiments culminated in the famous "drip" paintings, Mark Rothko painted fields of atmospheric color on monumental canvases, and Louise Nevelson's tabletop sculptures collaged from found pieces of wood metamorphosed first into wall sculptures and finally into total environments.

Louise Nevelson was born Leah Berliawsky on September 23, 1900, in Pereyaslav, fifty miles southeast of Kiev. Nevelson's father, Isaac Berliawsky, was born in 1871 in Pereyaslav. Her mother, Minna Ziesel (Smolerank) Berliawsky, was born in 1877 in the village of Shusneky. Louise was one of four children. The family emigrated in 1905 from Russia to Rockland, Maine. When they arrived in the United States, a cousin helped them to Anglicize their names. Thus, Louise's brother Nachman became Nathan (Nate), her sister Chaya became Annie, and the following year another sister, Lillian, was born.

The transition from shtetl life in Russia to a small, Anglo-Saxon community in rural Maine was not an easy one. The Berliawskys were Orthodox Jews who spoke Yiddish at home. However, they seem to have been isolated even from the community of two dozen Jewish families who lived in Rockland at the time. Minna Berliawsky suffered the most, unable ever to fully acclimate. Isaac Berliawsky began as a junk dealer and tradesman, eventually becoming an influential landowner and builder in Rockland. Education was emphasized in the household for the daughters as well as the son. Nate was in fact more athlete and entrepreneur than scholar, and did not finish high school. He was, however, eventually successful in business, running the Thorndike Hotel in Rockland for many years. Like his mother and sisters, Nate supported Louise with gifts of money during her leaner years in New York.

Louise excelled in her art classes in high school and resolved to attend Pratt Institute in New York, as several of her teachers had done, after graduation. However, when presented with the opportunity to marry the wealthy businessman Charles Nevelson and move to New York as a society matron rather than alone as a poor student, she did not hesitate to do so. The Nevelsons were German-speaking Latvian Jews from Riga. Charles was a partner in Nevelson Brothers Shipping Company, based in New York. After a honeymoon in Cuba, the Nevelsons settled at 300 Central Park West.

The 1920s were a turbulent time for Louise Nevelson, which marked her passage from a young matron to an unencumbered bohemian. Her only child, Myron (Mike) Irving Nevelson, was born February 23, 1922,

in New York. Beginning with Mike's birth, the Nevelson domestic situation worsened. Louise Nevelson was profoundly dissatisfied with marriage and motherhood, and Charles Nevelson was under significant stress because the once-successful Nevelson brothers' company was experiencing cash flow problems. During this period Louise Nevelson studied at the Art Students League with Anne Goldthwaite, THERESA BERNSTEIN, William Meyerwitz, and Kenneth Hayes Miller. In 1926, she studied theater with Princess Matchabelli, and began a lifelong study of religious philosophies and spiritualism. In particular Louise Nevelson followed the teachings of Jiddu Krishnamurti. Like the technique of assemblage that Louise Nevelson would later develop as a means of self-expression, she cobbled together elements from various cultures, religions, and philosophies to arrive at a personal worldview.

In 1930 Louise Nevelson studied with Hilla Rebay, whose theory of non-objective art was concerned with the link between spiritual concepts and formal aesthetics.

In 1931, Nevelson went to Munich to study with the well-known modernist painter Hans Hofmann. The political climate in Germany was already uncomfortable for avant-garde artists as well as for Jews, but Nevelson nevertheless counted the experience of studying in Munich a formative one. It was there that she first came in contact with Hofmann's ideas of the "push and pull" of balanced composition, and with cubism, which she said "gave her the key to stability." The element of cubism that Nevelson adopted for her own was the structuring of abstract compositional elements within a geometric grid. This method lent an order to the chaos of the found materials Nevelson later accumulated for sculpture, and for the broad, improvised gestures she used in her lithographs and etchings.

Tiring of Munich, Nevelson traveled around Europe, working as an extra in films in Vienna and Berlin. Back in New York in 1932, she joined Diego Rivera's Rockefeller Center mural project, but she did not lend much practical assistance. When the mural was destroyed by its patron for inflammatory communist content, Nevelson did not participate in the subsequent artist boycotts or protests. If the prevailing concern in intellectual and artistic circles during the 1930s was commitment to social change, Louise Nevelson was in this regard out of step with her contemporaries. The most lasting lesson Nevelson seems to have taken from her time with Rivera was the model of a charismatic leader surrounded by enthusiastic followers. In her later years, Louise Nevelson succeeded in surrounding herself with an army of assistants—artists, students, and friends—who worked in her studio for a few days, weeks, or years, for as long as they were content to serve as subjects in an artistic monarchy.

In 1935, Louise Nevelson showed her work for the first time in a museum exhibition, *Young Sculptors*, at the Brooklyn Museum. Her work during the 1930s was composed largely of small semiabstract figures modeled in clay. In 1937, she landed her first and only steady job, as a WPA-funded teacher at the Educational Alliance School of Art.

The 1940s were a time of building foundations for Louise Nevelson. In a now-famous encounter she marched into the prestigious Nierendorf Gallery one day in 1941 to demand an exhibition from the gallery director. After a studio visit, Karl Nierendorf agreed to represent her, and in September of that year she had her first of four solo shows with him. Although no works were sold from these early exhibitions, they received positive reviews and her relationship with Nierendorf greatly enhanced Louise Nevelson's visibility. She was discouraged by the lack of sales, however, and ended up destroying much of the work. With the help of Nierendorf and funds inherited upon the deaths of her parents (Minna Berliawsky died in 1943, and Isaac Berliawsky in 1946), Nevelson purchased a house on East 30th Street. Having lived in a series of small shared apartments following her separation and eventual divorce from Charles Nevelson, a house and studio of her own marked an important achievement for her as an independent person and as an artist. In 1947, Karl Nierendorf died unexpectedly, depriving Nevelson of her staunchest supporter. In response to these losses, Nevelson became withdrawn, crafting small black boxes with velvet interiors, and exhibiting very rarely. The three themes that scholar Laurie Simon has identified as central to Nevelson's iconography—royalty, marriage, and death—came to the fore in the late 1940s and remained important throughout her career.

In 1949–1950, Louise Nevelson made two trips to Mexico. She was affected by the monumental and totemic qualities of Maya art, elements of which she subsequently incorporated into her own work. Two etchings made shortly after her return demonstrate how Nevelson synthesized a surrealist interest in dream imagery, her experience of Maya art, and her own preoccupations with royalty (she considered herself to have queenly qualities), marriage (to her work), and death (real and symbolic). The totemic figures in *The King and Queen* and the mystical space of *Magic Garden*, two etchings completed in 1950 and 1951,

respectively, were combined by Nevelson in her major sculptural environments of the 1950s.

Ancient Games and Ancient Places, exhibited at Grand Central Moderns Gallery in 1955 incorporated prints and sculptural works. The focal point of this exhibition was *The Bride of the Black Moon*, a wooden sculpture standing three and a half feet high (this work, like much of Nevelson's production from the period, was later destroyed).

The aesthetic and psychological journeys Nevelson undertook in the years immediately following construction of *The Bride of the Black Moon* resulted in the following exhibitions: *Royal Voyage*, 1956; *The Forest*, 1957; *Moon Garden + One*, 1958; and *Sky Columns Presence*, 1959. *Sky Cathedral*, a component of *Moon Garden + One*, was Nevelson's first wall sculpture. Composed of 116 stacked boxes enclosing architectural fragments, *Sky Cathedral* shifted the idea of sculpture as an object one walks around to an environment that surrounds the viewer. These works, all created from scavenged wood and dipped in vats of black house paint to create a uniform surface, addressed, both literally and metaphorically, feared and cherished memories. Nevelson gathered wooden refuse from old buildings and scavenged antique architectural elements rife with the personal histories of strangers and wove them into her own personal mythology and work.

The black environments earned Louise Nevelson her first substantial critical and public success. Through donations from the artist's collectors, the Whitney Museum of American Art acquired *Black Majesty*, the Brooklyn Museum acquired *First Personage*, and the Museum of Modern Art acquired *Sky Cathedral*. Nevelson appeared in a *Life* magazine spread posing with *Moon Garden + One* in 1958. One of the most tangible rewards of recognition was Nevelson's inclusion in a group show at the Museum of Modern Art in 1959. For this exhibition Nevelson created her first white environment, *Dawn's Wedding Feast*.

Dawn's Wedding Feast represented a kind of mystical cosmic marriage. For this installation, Nevelson created several anthropomorphic totems. Other sculptors in New York were experimenting with totemlike sculptures, among them Louise Bourgeois and David Smith, but the inclusion of sculptural walls in Nevelson's environments of this period was both unique and influential. *Dawn's Wedding Feast* transformed the gallery into a shrine. In this sense, *Dawn's Wedding Feast* was important as an early example of what has come to be called installation work, but is also the first full realization of the type of spiritual environments that Nevelson was commissioned to create in the 1960s and 1970s for both Jewish temples and a Christian house of worship.

In 1964 the Jewish Museum in New York acquired Nevelson's wall sculpture *Homage to 6,000,000 #1*, and in 1965 the Israel Museum in Jerusalem acquired *Homage to 6,000,000 #2*. With the sobriety of their titles and the significance of their destinations, the relevance of Nevelson's Jewish identity to these works seems clear enough. However, the formal language of the two versions of *Homage to 6,000,000* does not differ significantly from contemporaneous works such as *Sky Cathedral* (1958) or *An American Tribute to the British People* (1960–1965). Nevelson was typically willing to weave any intriguing material into her personal myth, but she was notably reticent on the subject of her Jewish heritage. When questioned in interviews on this topic she replied that it was too personal to discuss. The spirituality of Louise Nevelson's work might best be understood by considering her repeated emphasis on a search for harmony.

Saint Peter's Lutheran Church in Manhattan commissioned Nevelson to design entirely the interior for their Chapel of the Good Shepherd. For this commission, the artist created a frieze of white wall sculptures referring to the twelve apostles and three suspended columns symbolizing the Trinity. At the front of the chapel, Nevelson hung from the ceiling a gilded abstract crucifix. In addition, she designed white vestments for the chapel clergy. When asked about designing a Christian chapel as a Jew, Nevelson replied, "To me there is no distinction between a church and a synagogue. If you go deep enough into any religion you arrive at the same point of harmony."

In addition to constructing major works, Nevelson spent the 1960s and 1970s engaged in a campaign to expand her reputation in the artistic community. In 1962 alone, she held the following offices: president of National Artists Equity, vice president of the Federation of Modern Painters and Sculptors, member of the National Association of Women Artists, and member of the Sculptors Guild. In this decade she began her affiliation with Arnold Glimcher, who wrote her first major catalog and showed her work frequently at his Pace Gallery, first in Boston and then in New York.

Major commissions during the 1970s included a fifty-five-inch wooden wall for Temple Beth-El in Great Neck, New York (1970), and a sculpture commemorating the bicentennial of the United States for the federal courthouse in Philadelphia (1976). During this period, Nevelson explored the medium of Cor-Ten steel, a durable metal that rusts on the exterior but retains its internal integrity. In this medium, Nevelson was able to design numerous monumental outdoor works, including an exterior wall sculpture for Temple Israel, in Boston (1973); a black monumental work for the Embarcadero Center in San Francisco (1977); and perhaps her most successful steel sculpture, *Atmosphere and Environment XIII: Windows to the West*, for the city of Scottsdale, Arizona. In 1978, a small plot in lower Manhattan was renamed Louise Nevelson Square, and seven tree-shaped monumental steel pieces were installed there by the artist.

In 1979, Louise Nevelson was elected a member of the American Academy and Institute of Arts and Letters in New York. In this capacity she occupied the chair that was originally held by American sculptor Augustus Saint-Gaudens when the organization was founded in 1889.

Louise Nevelson died on April 17, 1988, at her home in New York City. Arnold Glimcher organized a memorial service and collected writings, which he later published, of remembrances from her friends.

Louise Nevelson continues to be eulogized after her death, most recently in the 1994 commemoration of the Nevelson-Berliawsky Gallery of 20th Century Art at the Farnsworth Art Museum in Nevelson's hometown of Rockland, Maine. In Rockland, New York, and museums around the world her presence continues to be felt. Louise Nevelson took her identity as a Russian-born American Jewish woman artist and used it as raw material to construct both a myth and a body of work that speaks hyperbolically to the binary opposites of which she was made: extravagance and asceticism, clarity and confusion, darkness and light.

BIBLIOGRAPHY

Albee, Edward. *Louise Nevelson: Atmospheres and Environments* (1980); Anderson, Wayne. "American Sculpture: The Situation in the Fifties." *ArtForum* (Summer 1967): 60–66; Ashton, Dore. *Art of the 20th Century: A Revelation* (1982); *EJ*; *EJ* (1973-1982); Friedman, Martin. *Nevelson: Wood Sculptures* (1973); Glimcher, Arnold. *Louise Nevelson* (1972), and *Louise Nevelson Remembered: Sculpture and Collages* (1989); Hughes, Robert. "Sculpture's Queen Bee." *Time* (January 12, 1981): 46+; Krauss, Rosalind. *Passages in Modern Sculpture* (1977); McAvoy, Susan Lane. *Louise Nevelson: The Farnsworth Collection: An Exhibition Celebrating the Opening of the Nevelson-Berliawsky Gallery of 20th Century Art* (1994); MacKown, Donna. *Dawns + Dusks: Louise Nevelson* (1976); Murray, Elizabeth. *Artist's Choice: Modern Women* (1995); Wilson, Laurie. "Bride of the Black Moon: An Iconographic Study of the Work of Louise Nevelson." *Arts* (May 1980): 140–148.

ROBIN CLARK

NEWMAN, ESTELLE (1896–1964)

The Estelle R. Newman City Center, Jewish Guild for the Blind in New York City is named in recognition of the tireless efforts of Estelle Newman on behalf of services for the blind. In 1950, Newman was the principal founder of the women's division of the Guild, and she remained an active member of its board until her death.

Under her leadership, the women's division pioneered in gathering public support to enable the blind to integrate their lives more completely into the larger community. The women's division also expanded efforts to develop more advanced methods of treating blindness. At the Guild's Home for the Aged Blind in Yonkers, New York, Newman's work was instrumental in establishing a program of medical, psychiatric, recreational, and physical rehabilitation for the elderly blind. In gratitude, the medical wing was named for her and her husband, Jerome, a financier.

Estelle Reiss Newman was born in New York City on November 24, 1896, to Rose Fassbinder and Elias Reiss. She had an older brother, Arthur, who died in a tragic accident as a young man. Her parents were of German and Austrian origin. From World War I to the 1930s, Elias Reiss was known as the "Dean of Worth Street" (Worth Street was a center for cotton goods and textiles). Estelle received religious schooling at a Reform Sunday school. After high school, she attended and graduated from Adelphi College. On January 12, 1920, Estelle Reiss married Jerome Newman, a pioneer in the securities industry.

In the 1930s, she lived on Long Island with her husband and two children—a son, Howard, and a duaghter, Patricia. Alarmed by the rising danger of Nazism, she helped to found Youth Aliyah, an organization led by HENRIETTA SZOLD to save Jewish children from persecution and bring them shelter and education in Palestine. At that time, Newman also headed the South Shore organizations for the New York Federation of Jewish Philanthropies and the United Jewish Appeal.

When America entered World War II, Newman volunteered to work with the Office of Price Administration. She was awarded a certificate of merit for her efforts. Later, she served on the board of the New York Shakespeare Festival. Although Estelle Newman willingly gave her time and energy to a variety of philanthropic activities, most of her efforts were centered upon the Jewish community. She is particularly known for her creative endeavors for the blind.

Estelle Newman died on July 10, 1964, at her home on Fifth Avenue in New York.

BIBLIOGRAPHY

AJYB 66 (1965): 580; "Mrs. Jerome A. Newman Dead: Benefactor of the Blind Was 65 [sic]." *NYTimes* (July 11, 1964), 25:2.

LOUISE MAYO

NEWMAN, ISADORA (1878–??)

Variously described in the pages of the *New York Times* in the 1920s and 1930s as writer, poet, and artist, Isadora Newman found creative expression in a variety of media. Two themes, however, run through this diversity: a respect for the ability of children to see freshly and a lasting impression of the black and Creole heritage of her native New Orleans.

Born Miriam Dorothy Newman on April 23, 1878, she was the daughter of Rebecca (Kiefer) and Isidore Newman, a respected banker and businessman who later became known for his philanthropy. The Isidore Newman School, named for him in 1913, remains a testament to his activism and generosity within the New Orleans Jewish community, where he was also a founding member of B'nai B'rith.

The young Miriam's delicate health made formal schooling difficult. Her education took place at home under a governess's tutelage. Her path seems to have followed a conventional late nineteenth-century sequence. At twenty-three, she married Edwin A. Neugass. For the next several decades, she focused on home and her three children, Bessie, James, and Edwin.

By 1920, the couple was living in New York, where Neugass had a seat in the Stock Exchange. With the children grown, Newman enrolled in classes at Columbia University. Then Edwin died in October of 1921.

Her first artistic venue was as a storyteller. Initially at the University Settlement, but later in schools and other public places, she made her stories of Creole and black life and legend come alive. She collected folktales from foreign countries, as well. Later, for adult audiences, she included songs in an evening of entertainment. In 1926, her first collection of such tales, *Fairy Flowers*, illustrated by Willy Pogany, was published. This is when Isadora Newman, the writer and artist, was born. Kudos came quickly, and the text was translated into language after language. Praising the book, the French government honored her with Palmes Academiques in 1928.

Under the encouragement of artists, including Pogany, who felt she had natural talent, Isadora Newman took up painting, primarily watercolors, and then traveled to France to study sculpture. She received a degree from La Horde Society. Her work was shown in Europe, as well as regularly exhibited at galleries in New York and Louisiana.

The visual artist, however, did not turn her back on literature. A book of poems, *Shades of Blue*, came out in 1927. Then, in 1930, two books of legends written in German appeared. She was also busy adapting her stories for the stage. One such, *Granny's Garden*, was produced in 1931. Columbia University and the Jewish Art Theater both staged her dramas.

Isadora Newman's seemingly restless creativity flowed from her devotion to children. In 1926, the year of her first publication, the Serbian government honored her for her relief to war orphans. Her art, in all forms, received acclaim for its clear-eyed, childlike vision. Her home state claimed her as its Gauguin. But all children, under the spell of the storyteller, recognized a kindred spirit.

SELECTED WORKS BY ISADORA NEWMAN

Fairy Flowers (1926); *Granny's Garden* (1931); *Neger und Negerlein* (1929); *Shades of Blue* (1927); *Wir Sollin Freundlich* (1930).

BIBLIOGRAPHY

"Author Charges Two with Extortion Plot." *NYTimes*, August 24, 1932, 2:1; Devree, Howard. "A Reviewer's Notebook." *NYTimes*, January 10, 1937, sec. 10, 10:4; *EJ*, s.v. "Newman, Isidore"; "French Honor Mrs. Isidora Newman." *NYTimes*, [1928?] 16:6; Harris, Ruth Green. "Seen in the Galleries." *NYTimes*, February 24, 1929, sec. 10, 19:1; Herman, Kali. *Women in Particular: An Index to American Women*, s.v. "Newman" and "Isadora Newman," and "Neugass, Miriam Dorothy Newman" (1984); Jewell, Edward Alden. "Art in Review." *NYTimes*, May 28, 1932, 9:3; "Mme. Newman in Recital." *NYTimes*, October 14, 1931, 26:4; *National Cyclopaedia of American Biography* 3 (1930), s.v. "Neugass, Miriam Dorothy Newman ('Isidora Newman')"; "Offer to Plaintiff Is Charged to Juror." *NYTimes*, February 9, 1935, 32:3; Review of *Fairy Flowers*, by Isadora Newman. *NYTimes Book Review*, June 26, 1927, 15; Review of *Shades of Blue*, by Isidore Newman. *NYTimes Book Review*, January 15, 1928, 6; *UJE*, s.v. "Newman, Isidora"; "The Week in New York." *NYTimes*, May 29, 1932, sec. 8, 7:5; *Who Was Who in American Art*. 1985 ed. (1898–1947); *WWIAJ* (1938).

MARY ELLEN HENRY

NEWMAN, PAULINE (1890?–1986)

Pauline Newman was a labor pioneer and a diehard union loyalist once described by a colleague as "capable of smoking a cigar with the best of them."

The first woman ever appointed general organizer by the INTERNATIONAL LADIES GARMENT WORKERS UNION (ILGWU), Newman continued to work for the ILGWU for more than seventy years—first as an organizer, then as a labor journalist, a health educator, and a liaison between the union and government officials. Newman played an essential role in galvanizing the early twentieth-century tenant, labor, socialist, and working-class suffrage movements. She also left an important legacy through her writings, as one of the few working-class women of her generation who chronicled the struggles of immigrant working women.

An acerbic woman whose unorthodox tastes ran to cropped hair and tailored tweed jackets, Newman loved the labor movement. She referred to the ILGWU as her "family" and believed that it was, for all its flaws, the best hope for women garment workers. Still, Newman was a pragmatic feminist who understood that most union leaders were only marginally interested in the concerns of working women. So, along with her union work, she campaigned throughout her life for labor legislation to protect women workers, and she forged alliances with progressives of all classes.

Vice president of the New York and National Women's Trade Union League (WTUL) during the 1920s, 1930s, and 1940s, Newman was part of a cross-class circle of women reformers that included Eleanor Roosevelt, ROSE SCHNEIDERMAN, and Frieda Miller. Miller, who was Newman's partner of fifty-six years, was New York State industrial commissioner and later U.S. Women's Bureau chief. This circle of women shaped the body of laws and government protections that most workers now take for granted.

Newman's career was a balancing act. Torn between the gruff, male-dominated Jewish socialist milieu of the ILGWU and the more nurturing "women-centered" Women's Trade Union League, Newman chose, for personal as well as political reasons, to divide her energies between the two. Through the WTUL, she found an alternative family of women who provided the emotional and political support so essential for a woman who eschewed the traditional protections of marriage and family. Through the union, she maintained a connection to the world of Jewish socialism in which she was raised and which was central to her identity.

Pauline Newman was born to deeply religious parents in Kovno, Lithuania, sometime around 1890. (The exact date of her birth was lost when her family emigrated.) She was the youngest of four children, three girls and a boy. Her father taught Talmud to the

Pauline Newman worked for the INTERNATIONAL LADIES GARMENT WORKERS UNION
for more than seventy years—first as an organizer, then as a labor journalist, a health educator,
and a liaison between the union and government officials. In this photograph she is on the right
with three other women attending a labor conference in 1947. [Schlesinger Library]

sons of wealthy men. Her mother supported the family by buying fruit from peasants in the countryside and selling it at the Kovno marketplace.

Her activist career began when, as a child, she had to fight for the right to an education. First the Kovno public school excluded her because her family was Jewish and poor. Newman was rebuffed again by the local rabbi when she requested permission to attend the all-boy *heder* [religious school]. After further lobbying, Newman won the rabbi's permission to attend Sunday school classes, where she learned to read and write Yiddish and Hebrew, but he would not allow her to study religious texts. Undaunted, she begged her father to let her sit in on the Talmud classes that he taught. He relented, but was unable to explain to his daughter's satisfaction why she and other girls and women had to be restricted to a curtained-off balcony in the synagogue. Newman would later recall her resentment at the privileges accorded to males in Jewish education and worship as the spark for her lifelong fight against sex discrimination.

When Newman's father died suddenly in 1901, her mother decided to take her three daughters to New York City, where her son had already settled. At age nine, Newman went to work in a hairbrush factory. Two years later, she began working among other children in the "kindergarten" at the Triangle Shirt-waist Factory, the most infamous of early twentieth-century garment shops.

Depressed by the grim working and living conditions on the Lower East Side, Newman took solace in the worker-poetry she read in the socialist Yiddish press. Like many Jewish immigrants, Newman got her first education in socialism and trade unionism through the popular newspaper the *Jewish Daily Forward*. She joined the Socialist Literary Society at age fifteen and began to school herself in the social realist literature that she hoped to emulate. Charles Dickens was a particular favorite. Through her reading, she perfected her English-language reading and writing skills. Believing that literature would both comfort and radicalize her fellow workers, as it did her, Newman organized after-work study groups at Triangle. These became the basis for the women's unions she would soon organize.

In 1907, with New York City in the grip of a depression and thousands facing eviction, the sixteen-year-old Newman took a group of "self-supporting women" to camp for the summer on the Palisades above the Hudson River. There they planned an assault on the high cost of living. That winter, Newman and her band led a rent strike involving ten thousand families in lower Manhattan. It was the largest rent strike New York City had ever seen, and it catalyzed decades of tenant activism, which eventually led to the establishment of rent control. As the leader of the strike, Newman came to the attention of the Socialist Party, which ran her for secretary of state of New York the following year. Women did not yet have the vote in New York, but Newman used the campaign as an opportunity to stump for woman suffrage.

At this time, she began organizing women garment workers in shops throughout lower Manhattan, paving the way for the UPRISING OF THE 20,000 in 1909—the largest strike by American women workers to that time. During the long, cold months of the strike, Newman met with wealthy women, explaining the horrific conditions under which shirtwaist dresses were manufactured. Drawing on her readings of English literature to come up with images that native-born affluent women could relate to, she won the sympathy of many of New York's wealthiest. Some of them even decided to join the garment workers' picket lines to stop police brutality against the strikers.

In recognition of her key role in organizing and sustaining the strike, Newman was appointed the first woman general organizer for the International Ladies Garment Workers Union. From 1909 to 1913, she toured the United States, organizing garment strikes in Philadelphia, Cleveland, Boston, and Kalamazoo, Michigan. She also stumped for the Socialist Party in the freezing, bleak coal-mining camps of southern Illinois and campaigned for woman suffrage for the Women's Trade Union League. It was a lonely and frustrating few years for Newman, because she felt that the union leadership had little interest in organizing women and that her work was undervalued and undermined at every turn.

Newman was devastated by the TRIANGLE SHIRT-WAIST FIRE of March 25, 1911—in which 146 young workers lost their lives, most of them immigrant Jews and Italians. Newman, who had worked at the factory for seven years, knew many of the victims. Her grief made her anxious to accept a post, in 1913, with the Joint Board of Sanitary Control, established by New York State to improve factory safety standards. Newman inspected industrial shops and lobbied state legislatures for wage, hour, and safety legislation for women workers. Through this job, she met Frances Perkins, then an activist for the Consumers League, later to become Franklin Roosevelt's secretary of labor. Perkins and Newman took state legislators on tours of the worst factories in the state. Newman gained the respect of these political figures, who would call on her for advice or consultation many times over the next half century.

In 1917, the Women's Trade Union League dispatched Newman to Philadelphia, to build a new branch of the league. There she met a young Bryn Mawr economics instructor named Frieda Miller. Miller, who was chafing at the constraints of academic life, gladly left academia to help Newman with her organizing. Within the year, the two were living together. It was the beginning of a turbulent but mutually satisfying relationship that would last until Miller's death in 1974. In 1923, the two women moved to New York's Greenwich Village, where they raised a daughter together. Though lesbian families were not openly discussed in the 1920s, their family seems to have been accepted by government and union colleagues.

In 1923, Newman became educational director for the ILGWU Union Health Center, the first comprehensive medical program created by a union for its members. Newman would retain that position for sixty years, using it to promote worker health care, adult education, and greater visibility for women in the union. She became a beloved and highly respected mentor to young women in the union. She also promoted the cause of women in trade unions through her positions as vice president of the New York and National Women's Trade Union Leagues.

From the late 1920s on, Newman worked for and helped to shape new government agencies charged with the task of improving labor conditions for women workers. She consulted frequently for New York State on minimum wage and safety codes for women workers. She also served on the U.S. Women's Bureau Labor Advisor Board, the United Nations Subcommittee on the Status of Women, and the International Labor Organization Subcommittee on the Status of Domestic Laborers.

Socially, Newman and Miller—who began a successful career in government in the 1920s—were part of the circle of women who surrounded Eleanor Roosevelt in the 1920s and 1930s. They were both regular guests at Val-Kill, the home that Franklin built for Eleanor Roosevelt near the family mansion at Hyde Park. And, during the mid-1930s, Newman visited the White House with some regularity. In 1936, she received national news coverage when Eleanor Roosevelt asked her to bring a group of young women garment and textile workers to stay as guests of the first lady for a week at the White House.

After World War II, Newman and Miller were commissioned by the U.S. Departments of State and Labor to investigate postwar factory conditions in Germany. During the Truman years, Newman addressed the White House Conference on the Child and served as a regular consultant to the U.S. Public

Health Service on matters of child labor and industrial hygiene.

Newman continued to work for the ILGWU until 1983, writing, lecturing, and advising younger women organizers. During her seventy-plus years with the union, she waged a constant struggle to convince male leaders to acknowledge the needs and talents of women workers.

With the revival of the feminist movement in the 1970s, the elderly Newman came to be seen as a feminist heroine. In 1974, the Coalition of Labor Union Women honored her as a foremother of the women's liberation movement. During the 1970s and 1980s, Newman became a living witness to the sweatshop conditions that prevailed during the early part of the twentieth century. She spoke regularly to historians and reporters and to groups of young women workers, her heavily wrinkled face and timeworn voice telling as much as her words about her decades of struggle on behalf of the labor movement. Newman's dedication to writing also made her a valuable resource for scholars of women and trade unionism.

From 1909 to 1913, Newman was a regular contributor to the *New York Daily Call*, *Progressive Woman*, and the WTUL publication *Life and Labor*. From 1913 to 1918, she had a regular column in the *Ladies Garment Worker* entitled "Our Women Workers." She continued to write for WTUL publications until 1950 and for the ILGWU newspaper *Justice* through the 1960s. The stories, columns, and reportage that she left behind form an important part of her historical legacy.

Pauline Newman died in 1986 at the home of her adopted daughter, Elizabeth Burger. She was approximately ninety-six years old. Newman's death evoked a deep sense of loss in the ILGWU and among women trade unionists more generally. She had made her balancing act work and carved out a niche for herself as a liaison. Standing with one foot in the male-dominated labor movement and one foot in the cross-class world of women reformers, she touched a great many people. It is not easy to sum up Newman's career. Her contributions as an organizer, a legislative expert, a writer, and a mentor to younger women activists were profound and wide-ranging. Her historical significance far exceeds any official title that she held.

BIBLIOGRAPHY

Buhle, Mari Jo. *Women and American Socialism, 1870–1920* (1981); Fink 269–270; Kessler-Harris, Alice. "Organizing the Unorganizable: Three Jewish Women and Their Union." *Labor History* (Winter 1976); Neidle, Cecyle. *America's Immigrant Women* (1975); Newman, Pauline M. Oral history interview by Barbara Wertheimer, and Papers. Schlesinger Library, Radcliffe College, Cambridge, Mass.; Orleck, Annelise. *Common Sense and a Little Fire: Women and Working-Class Politics, 1900–1965* (1995).

ANNELISE ORLECK

NFTS *see* NATIONAL FEDERATION OF TEMPLE SISTERHOODS

NIRENSTEIN, BLANCHE COHEN (1885–1972)

A descendant of a family active in Jewish communal life, Blanche Cohen Nirenstein further developed her legacy of leadership in a wide range of social science activities.

She was born in Manhattan on November 24, 1885, to David and Wilhemina (Minnie) Cohen. Her parents named her Bluma, which she formally changed to Blanche upon graduation from high school. She was the fourth of eeven children, seven of whom lived to adulthood. Her maternal grandparents, the Levys, were immigrants from Germany and among the founders of the Hebrew Immigrant Aid Society.

Her father, David Cohen, who had emigrated from Suwalk, Lithuania, at age fourteen, was a descendent of the Vilna Gaon. Cohen worked in the real estate business and devoted considerable energy to Orthodox Jewish educational institutions and synagogues. He served as president of the Rabbi Isaac Elchanan Theological Seminary, the forerunner of Yeshiva University, in its early years. He was a founder of the Rabbi Jacob Joseph School (RJJ), the Uptown Talmud Torah, Beth Israel and Lebanon Hospitals, Bronx Machzikei Talmud Torah, and the Hebrew Teachers' Institute, and was founder and president of the Eldridge Street Synagogue on the Lower East Side.

Blanche Cohen was married in 1906 to Alexander Schlang, a realtor who was a builder of Congregation Sons of Israel in Brooklyn. She founded the Ladies Educational Society of this Orthodox congregation and served as its president. She had a daughter, Hortense (b. 1907), and three sons: Maurice Herbert "Mike" (b. 1909), Joseph (b. 1911), and David (b. 1912). The family moved from Brooklyn to Manhattan in 1929, on the day of the Wall Street crash. Alexander Schlang died on December 31, 1944, and Blanche subsequently married Ellick Nirenstein, a banker.

In 1919, her family founded a kosher summer camp for immigrant children named Camp Tranquility, on farm land in Earlton, New York. Nirenstein was active in Tranquility's Women's League from its inception until the end of her life, supporting its goal of providing quality camp experience for children in need. Yeshiva College Women's Organization also benefited from her leadership; she served as president and raised scholarship money for students of the college. In 1942, Nirenstein founded the Manhattan chapter of Mizrachi Women's Organization of America (later known as AMIT), an organization dedicated to caring for and educating disadvantaged Jewish children in Palestine. As president of the Manhattan chapter, she raised funds to sponsor the creation of youth villages and vocational schools. She was president of the Rabbonim Aid Society for eighteen years, raising and distributing much needed funds to support impoverished rabbis and their widows, particularly victims of the Holocaust, and at the time of her death she was chair of the society's board of directors. The Rabbonim Aid Society was based at The Jewish Center, an Orthodox synagogue on the West Side, where Nirenstein was an active member, as were both her husbands.

Her husband Ellick Nirenstein died on June 21, 1957. Nirenstein's communal activity continued unabated, as an experienced volunteer leader at the helm of charitable social service organizations to promote traditional Jewish life in America and in Israel. Toward the end of her life, Nirenstein was honored as Mother of the Year by the RJJ School Ladies League, the yeshivah day school where she was a life member and a patron.

Blanche Cohen Nirenstein died at age eighty-seven on September 3, 1972, in New York City.

BIBLIOGRAPHY

AJYB 74:558; Andron, Richard (Ricky) [grandson]. Telephone interview by author. Boca Raton, Fla., winter 1996; Andron, Sandy [grandson]. Telephone interview by author. Miami, Fla., winter 1996; Bellovin, Tobi. Telephone interview by author. AMIT National Office, NYC, fall 1996; *EJ*, s.v. "Yeshiva University"; Harstein, Sam, and Sylvia Hershkovits. Telephone interview by author. Yeshiva University, NYC, fall 1996; Klaperman, Gilbert. *The Story of Yeshiva University* (1969); Miller, Pearl [niece]. Telephone interview by author. Miami, Fla., winter 1996; Obituary. *NYTimes*, September 4, 1972, 18:6; Schlang, David. Telephone interview by author. NYC, summer 1996; Schlang, Mike. Telephone interview by author. Palm Beach, Fla., winter 1996; Shick, Rabbi. Telephone interview by author. Rabbi Jacob Joseph School, NYC, fall 1996; Smolowe, Greta [granddaughter]. Telephone interview by author. North Carolina, winter 1996.

DEBBIE KRAM

NOETHER, EMMY (1882–1935)

Emmy Noether, a German mathematician, was the world leader in the twentieth-century development of modern "abstract" algebra. Her writing, the students she inspired, and their books wholly changed the form and content of higher algebra throughout the world.

Noether was born in Erlangen, Germany, on March 23, 1882. Her father, Max Noether, was a professor of mathematics at Erlangen, an expert on algebraic geometry. She received her Ph.D. in mathematics from Erlangen in 1907, with a dissertation on invariant theory (involving what she later would call "computational" algebra). In 1915, she moved to Göttingen, as an assistant to the world-famous mathematician David Hilbert. There, she gave a course in his name (she was not allowed to lecture at the time on her own account) and applied her knowledge of invariant theory to relativity theory in a paper that impressed Einstein.

In 1920, she turned her attention to algebra, with decisive axiomatic treatment of the theory of ideals as they apply to number theory (to factor algebraic integers) and to algebraic geometry (curves and surfaces defined by equations). She inspired many students, in particular the Dutchman B.L. Van der Waerden, who delivered brillant lectures following her ideas and then presented them in his famous text *Modern Algebra*, which revolutionized the subject. As a graduate student in Göttingen (1931–1933), I attended her lectures and learned something of her insights. Subsequently, in 1941, Garrett Birkhoff and I published an undergraduate text, *Survey of Modern Algebra*, which introduced the Noether view of mathematics to English-speaking students. Noether's lectures also influenced many young French mathematicians, several of whom (André Weil, Claude Chevalley) went on to found the Bourbaki group, whose systematic treatise on all of mathematics was much influenced by Noether's methods. She was also active in algebraic topology, a field in which she persuaded the experts (Paul Alexandroff and Heinz Hopf) to describe topological invariants not as "numbers," but instead as algebraic objects (groups). Her own research (with Brauer and Hasse) in 1930 solved a famous problem in the theory of algebras. Her brother was also a mathematician, but Emmy Noether was so well known that she was called "der Noether."

With the rise of Hitler in 1933, Emmy Noether was dismissed from her modest position as Ausserordentliche Professor at Göttingen—she was not only Jewish but a woman and a liberal. The Rockefeller Foundation helped to fund a position for her in the United States at Bryn Mawr College, where there was a long tradition of interest in higher mathematical research. There she was also able to travel once a week to Princeton University, to lecture there and at the Institute for Advanced Study, giving her effective access to one of the great centers of American mathematics. At Bryn Mawr, she helped various young women mathematicians. She advised Marie J. Weiss and guided the Ph.D. thesis of Ruth Stauffer (McKee). She also helped OLGA TAUSSKY-TODD, whom she had known in Göttingen.

Emmy Noether died on April 14, 1935, from complications following surgery. Her ideas about the abstract and conceptual approach of mathematics have been spread throughout the mathematics world by her students, her admirers, and many others who had personal contact with her. In the judgment of many, she is the greatest algebraist of the twentieth century.

SELECTED WORKS BY EMMY NOETHER

"Beweis eines Hauptsatzes in der Theorie der Algebren." With R. Brauer and H. Hasse. *Journ. f.d. reine u. angew. Math.* 167 (1932): 399–401; "Eliminations Theorie und Ideal Theorie." *Math. Annalen* 90 (1923): 177–184; "Nichtkommutative Algebren." *Math. Zeit.* 37 (1932): 514–541; *Scripta Mathematica* 3:201–220, with Hermann Weyl.

BIBLIOGRAPHY

Birkhoff, Garrett, and Saunders Mac Lane. *A Survey of Modern Algebra* (1977); Bourbaki, N. *Eléments de Mathématique* (1941, 1942, 1950, 1997); Brewer, J.W., and Martha K. Smith, eds. *Emmy Noether: A Tribute to Her Life and Work* (1981); Van der Waerden, B.L. *Moderne Algebra*. 2 vols. (1931. Reprint 1933).

SAUNDERS MAC LANE

NURSING

Early in the twentieth century, trained nursing was not considered a suitable profession for a young Jewish woman. Patriarchal values dominated Jewish family culture. Women's personal desires for education were often set aside. Long periods of training were also not acceptable to women who had to consider the economic needs of their families. To quote a Jewish garment worker, Bea Heller, "It didn't pay in the hospitals, so I had to quit and go back to the factory" (Ewen 1985).

It is interesting to ponder what might have motivated members of an ethnic group to enter a profession that, at least on the surface, seemed to embrace an incongruous belief system. Jews are an ethnic minority who first faced quotas in being admitted to nursing schools and then discrimination in being hired by non-Jewish hospitals. Ethnicity could quickly be established with the requirement of a letter of recommendation from a member of the clergy. Jewish hospitals were organized because Jewish physicians frequently could not obtain attending rights at non-Jewish hospitals. Also, Jewish hospitals understood dietary requirements and observances that made Jewish patients more comfortable.

In order to examine the role Jewish nurses played in the establishment of modern American nursing, it is necessary to focus on some early American nursing history. In the United States, in 1839, as a result of an urgent appeal from Dr. Joseph Warrington, director of the Philadelphia Dispensary, a number of women in the community organized themselves into the Nurse Society. As Adelaide Nutting stated in *History of Nursing and Source Book for Nursing* (1904), "The preamble to their constitution stated that . . . the undersigned, . . . do associate for the purpose of providing, sustaining, and causing to be instructed as far as possible, *pious* and prudent women."

The cause of training nurses was advanced by Dr. Samuel Gross, a founder of the American Medical Association. In 1869, Gross submitted a committee report resolving that "every large and well organized hospital should have a school for the training of nurses, not only for the supply of its own necessities, but for private families, the teaching to be furnished by its own medical staff, assisted by the resident physicians." Interest in schools continued to grow, and by 1890 there were more than thirty-five schools of nursing in the United States, modeled along the Nightingale system.

First attempts in nursing care were related to maternity nursing and the care of children. Nursing was seen as an extension of the nurturing and mothering role. Victorian morality prohibited women from caring for male patients who were not related to the household.

Nursing schools were developing in such a way that the demands on a probationer and subsequent nursing student would not permit a marriage relationship or dependent children. The age range most desirable for entering nursing school was the age at which most women made the decision to work or marry. The decision to enter nursing, therefore, meant choosing between a career or marriage. Marriage, a home, and children comprised the sought norm of the time for both Jewish and non-Jewish women. In fact, all activities in social work, hospital boards, and similar projects were seen as an extension of the mothering and nurturing role first exhibited in the home.

Nurses were trained in an arena of Christian spirituality with enormous emphasis on moral character. Christian underpinnings in nursing education continued to be evident in the United States as late as the 1950s. The Jamieson and Sewell series of nursing history texts, widely used in training programs, were written from the socio-Christian perspective. It was common practice to require nursing students to attend prayer time each morning and read aloud from the New Testament. Jewish students were not exempted from this practice, although they may have found it to be objectionable. A student may have been required to stay after prayers and give an explanation to the superintendent of nurses for not reading out loud. This practice continued well into the 1940s.

During the Civil War years, PHOEBE YATES LEVY PEMBER, not a trained nurse, distinguished herself as matron and administrator of the large Chimborazo Hospital in Richmond, Virginia, capital of the Confederacy. During this same time, another Jewish woman, Hanna Sandusky, distinguished herself as a midwife in Pittsburgh, Pennsylvania. Originally trained by her midwife mother in Eastern Europe, she arrived in the United States with her son in 1861 to join her husband. She became involved in attending to mothers delivering babies in the densely populated Hill District. Since grandmothers frequently attended at births, and the Yiddish word for grandmother is *bobba*, she quickly became affectionately known as Bobba Hannah. Her extraordinary skill was noticed by a local physician. He paid the expenses for Bobba Hannah and her son, who had eye problems, to seek medical attention in Germany. There she attended a school of midwifery and worked as a midwife before returning to Pittsburgh with a German diploma. A truly righteous woman, she served as a matchmaker, collected money and linens to marry off poor girls, and sewed shrouds for the dead. She never charged a fee and presided at 3,571 registered births, her last, at age eighty-two, in 1909.

The NATIONAL COUNCIL OF JEWISH WOMEN *established programs not only in urban areas but also in sparsely populated rural areas. The woman pictured above is a visiting nurse, making her rounds on snowshoes. [National Council of Jewish Women]*

In *A Generation of Women: Education in the Lives of Progressive Reformers* (1979), Ellen Lagemann termed her research subjects the "progressive generation" because they were a "pioneer" generation in the history of American women. Early nursing leaders functioned in a male-defined world, on their own terms. Early Jewish American nurses were "pioneers" for entering the field during a time when organized nursing attempted to strengthen its case for a closed profession by establishing entrance requirements and insisting on the registration of its members. Early leaders during this period included LILLIAN WALD, AMELIA GREENWALD, NAOMI DEUTSCH, Blanche Pfefferkorn, and REGINA KAPLAN. RAE LANDY and ROSE KAPLAN were the first American nurses in Palestine as HADASSAH was being established. Another interesting personality, EMMA GOLDMAN, attended midwifery school in Vienna, Austria, and returned to the Lower East Side to work as a midwife among the indigent Jewish immigrants.

JOSEPHINE GOLDMARK's report on the poor state of nursing schools, and often poor conditions for the students, helped reform many nursing programs. Most graduate nurses worked in homes and not hospitals, and tours of duty could often be twenty-four hours. She was an active member of the Henry Street Visiting Nurses Association and probably influenced Lillian Wald.

The New England Hospital for Women and Children in Boston, Massachusetts, was incorporated on March 18, 1863, with a charter calling for the admission of one Negro and one Jew to each class. The first trained African-American nurse, Mary Eliza Mahoney, graduated from that school on August 1, 1879. The names of the first trained Jewish nurses in America, following the tradition of Florence Nightingale, and their contributions are still undocumented. Jewish women, however, became trained nurses, even if they had to attend Catholic nursing schools, which several Jewish women did.

In 1873, Bellevue Hospital in New York City established its school of nursing. That same year, New Haven Hospital and Massachusetts General Hospital also established schools. Mount Sinai Hospital, in

Nurses were essential to the services provided by HADASSAH *in Palestine. This 1936 photograph shows* HENRIETTA SZOLD *with a class of graduating nurses.* [Hadassah Archives]

*This Henry Street Settlement "visiting nurse" is using rooftops
to go from house to house to save climbing up and down stairs.
[American Jewish Historical Society]*

New York City, opened the Mount Sinai Training
School for Nurses in March 1881. The newly formed
school had no difficulty in attracting students. While
the Mount Sinai Training School for Nurses was nonsectarian, constant efforts were made to attract eligi-
ble Jewish girls. Thirty such applications were
received during the first year; seventeen applicants
were accepted into the first class of forty-three. It was
a requirement to pass an examination in reading, penmanship, simple arithmetic, and English or German
dictation. Of course, it was not possible to have Friday
evenings and Saturdays off. These requirements
would have been daunting to many immigrant Jewish
girls, whose schooling and resources were limited. It is
remarkable that young Jewish women became nurses
in a climate where schools began in non-Jewish populated centers, and where young women had to have
"suitable acquirements and character," as well as being
"pious"—terms not generally well defined.

Evelyn Benson, in her research, has found that
Jewish nurses served with distinction in the Spanish-
American War. In fact, Jewish nurses served with

distinction in World War I and World War II, as well as in every instance where American soldiers have been mobilized.

Mathilda Scheuer was president of the American Nurses Association during the time that attempts were made to end racial discrimination within the organization. One area of contention was the scheduling of annual organizational membership meetings during Rosh Hashannah or Yom Kippur. There is evidence of considerable correspondence between the alumni associations of Jewish training schools and the professional organizations trying to remedy this situation. However, some replies were not receptive to considering changing the dates of meetings.

Jewish nurses who have provided leadership to the profession since the middle of the twentieth century include Rachel Bliss, Felissa Cohen, Adele Hurwitz, and Ingeborg Mauksch. Thelma Schorr retired as editor of the *American Journal of Nursing*. June Rothberg, Jacqueline Rose Hott, CLAIRE FAGIN, Harriet Feldman, and Janice Selekman have been, or are, deans at schools of nursing. Nettie Birnbach only recently stepped down as president of the New York State Nurses Association. The list is extensive. Jewish nurses are frequently leaders of nonnursing organizations as well.

Careful Jewish quotas on admittance to nursing school were maintained, probably until the establishment of the U.S. Cadet Nurse Corps in 1943, when the government paid the expenses for the cadet students. In *Making Choices, Taking Chances: Nurse Leaders Tell Their Stories* (1988), Myra Levine, professor emeritus, University of Illinois College of Nursing, described her own experience with quotas in attempting to gain admission to Michael Reese Hospital School of Nursing in 1940.

Moving nursing education into the collegiate setting resulted in an increase in Jewish nurses. The elimination of quotas on school admissions also helped. A college education and being able to live at home made a career in nursing acceptable to Jewish parents. Another factor responsible for increased numbers of Jewish nurses was the large-scale employment of nurses in hospitals and industry, instead of individual employment in private homes, from World War II onward.

HADASSAH Nurses Councils were formed in 1989 to encourage Jewish nurses to join and network together. The Raphael Society of the Association of Orthodox Jewish Scientists also encourages Jewish nurses to join. The many and varied accomplishments of Jewish women in nursing are finally being chronicled.

BIBLIOGRAPHY

Benson, Evelyn R. "Mathilda Scheuer (1890–1974): A Biographical Sketch." *Journal of Nursing History* 2, no. 1 (1986): 36–42; Carnegie, M. Elizabeth. *The Path We Tread: Blacks in Nursing, 1854–1990* (1991); Ewen, Elizabeth. *Immigrant Women in the Land of Dollars: Life and Culture on the Lower East Side, 1890–1925* (1985); Hirsh, Joseph, and Beka Doherty. *The First Hundred Years of The Mount Sinai Hospital of New York: 1852–1952* (1952); Lagemann, Ellen. *A Generation of Women: Education in the Lives of Progressive Reformers* (1979); Levine, Myra. *Making Choices, Taking Chances: Nurse Leaders Tell Their Stories*. Edited by Thelma Schorr and Anne Zimmerman (1988); Maggs, Christopher. *Origins of General Nursing* (1983); Morton, Marian J. *Emma Goldman and the American Left: Nowhere at Home* (1992); Nutting, Adelaide. *History of Nursing and Source Book for Nursing* (1904); Prince, Ethel. Communication with Grace Ryan, September 14, 1947. Archives. Box 6, Folder 12. School of Nursing, Jewish Hospital of Brooklyn, and New York State Nurses Association, Guilderland, N.Y.; Selavan, Ida Cohen. "Bobba Hannah, Midwife." *American Journal of Nursing* 4 (1973): 681–683.

SUSAN MAYER

O

OLSEN, TILLIE (b. c. 1913)

Writer Tillie Olsen is a leading spokesperson for silent and oppressed workers, especially creative women whose daily routine stifles their expression.

Tillie Lerner Olsen was born in Mead or Wahoo, Nebraska, in 1912 or 1913 (the most often used birthday is January 14, 1913). She was the daughter of Samuel and Ida (Goldberg) Lerner, from Odessa and Minsk, and had five siblings, Jan, Harry, Lillian, Eugene, and Vicki.

While in Russia, Samuel Lerner worked for the Bund, a Jewish socialist movement. He and his wife came separately to America after the failure of the 1905 revolution, in which they had participated. They met again in New York, then finally reunited in Mead, Nebraska, where Lerner was a tenant farmer, sometime between 1908 and 1910. By 1917, the family had moved thirty miles to a working-class neighborhood in Omaha. Lerner became a peddler, then ran the Silver Star Confectionery, where Olsen remembers shelling almonds for candies. He then found work as a painter and paperhanger.

Samuel Lerner, who held strong political and economic views, served as secretary of the Nebraska Socialist Party and, in 1928, was its candidate for lieutenant governor. He was an active member of the Workmen's Circle in Omaha and organized regional midwestern events.

Tillie Olsen's Russian Jewish heritage, radical political roots, and Midwest environment left a lasting impression on her. Her sense of class consciousness and social agenda emerged from her radical heritage, which downplayed Jewish religious observance and emphasized the social agenda of *yiddishkeit* [Jewish heritage]. (Her father was an atheist to the end of his life, and she went to Socialist Sunday school.) Olsen claimed that her values came from her *yiddishkeit*.

Tillie attended Central High School in Omaha but dropped out in 1929 in the eleventh grade. Coming from an immigrant working-class background, she saw at school how people from the other side of the track lived. She was alienated and marginalized, a compound of Jewish, working class, immigrant, poor, and female. Although she did not graduate, a humor column she wrote for the high school paper credits the rigorous reading and writing requirements and intellectual excitement of the school, and particularly her teachers Sara Vore Taylor and Autumn Davies, for igniting a passion to read and write. But political activism and birth of a child out of wedlock intervened.

The Depression intensified Tillie's radicalism. In 1931, she joined the Young Communist League. In 1932, active in the Omaha Council of the Unemployed, she was identified in the newspaper under aliases such as Teresa Landale and Theta Larimore. She then moved to Kansas City, where she worked in a tie factory. She was arrested for leafleting and served five months in jail. She worked as a tie presser, hack writer, model, mother's helper, ice-cream packer, book clerk, waitress, punch-press operator, and temporary office helper. She also worked in meat packing in Omaha, Kansas City, and St. Joseph.

In 1933, at the age of nineteen, Tillie left Omaha to recuperate from pleurisy in Faribault, Minnesota, and started writing *Yonnondio: From the Thirties*. She then moved to California, where she was jailed for two weeks following a police raid against radicals. She married Jack Olsen (né Olshansky), a Kiev-born printer and strong union advocate who had also been a member of the Young Communist League. They had four daughters: Carla, Julie, Katherine Jo, and Laurie. Jack Olsen died in 1989 at age seventy-seven.

Olsen returned to writing in the mid-1950s after her children were grown. She was awarded a writing fellowship at Stanford in 1956–1957 and a Ford Foundation grant in literature in 1959. Her short story collection *Tell Me a Riddle* has become an American classic. The title story, "Tell Me a Riddle," won the O. Henry Short Story Award in 1961 and became an Academy Award–winning movie in 1980, starring Melvyn Douglas and Lila Kedrova.

Olsen rediscovered and reprinted the 1861 Rebecca Harding Davis story *Life in the Iron Mills* in 1972. Her Depression novel *Yonnondio: From the Thirties*, started in 1933 and finished in the late 1950s, was published in 1974. The novel is about the lives of the midwestern poor. It follows the Holbrook family's migration from Wyoming to the Dakotas, ending in the south Omaha slaughterhouses. *Silences*, begun in 1962 and published in 1978, narrates the difficulty women writers saddled with the burdens of raising and supporting a family have faced in a patriarchal society. It is a lament for unfulfilled promise and for stunted talent.

Olsen is an internationalist, believing in one human race without religious, racial, or ethnic divisions. Her parents were socialists, but she became a communist, which may have created additional alienation. She joined and quit the Communist Party more than once and has been critical of its policies. During World War II, she was president of the California CIO Women's Auxiliary. She is an outspoken advocate of the Universal Declaration of Human Rights. She exhibits a Jewish "secular messianic utopianism," which came from her immigrant parents. (Lyons in Nelson and Huse, p. 144).

Olsen has taught in writers' programs at Amherst College, Stanford University, and Kenyon College; she was a fellow of the Radcliffe Institute, a writer-in-residence at Massachusetts Institute of Technology, and a regents lecturer at the University of California; and she has received National Endowment for the Arts awards, a Guggenheim Fellowship, and a doctor of arts and letters degree from the University of Nebraska (1979). In 1991, she received the Mari Sandoz Award of the Nebraska Library Association, and she was the winner of the $25,000 Rea Award from the Dungannon Foundation in New York for best short story of 1994. The January 3, 1994, issue of *Newsweek* commemorated the magazine's sixtieth anniversary with an article entitled "The First Sixty Years." In this article, the editors chose authors who were emblematic of the decades: For the 1930s, it was Tillie Olsen. Public acknowledgment has not been universal, however, and Harold Bloom has been criticized for not including Olsen in *The Western Canon: Books and Schools of the Ages* (1994).

Olsen now lives in San Francisco, has traveled widely, and has visited Omaha and Lincoln, Nebraska, several times in the last twenty years. She acknowledges that some of her writing is autobiographical, much of it deriving from her early life in Omaha. Nevertheless, her work addresses deep universal issues of gender, class, religious identity, and social consciousness.

SELECTED WORKS BY TILLIE OLSEN

Silences (1978); *Tell Me a Riddle* (1961. Movie, 1981); *Yonnondio: From the Thirties* (1974).

BIBLIOGRAPHY

Coiner, Constance. *Better Read: The Writing and Resistance of Tillie Olsen and Meridel Le Sueur* (1995); *Contemporary Authors* Vol. 1 (1981): 485; *EJ* 1982–1985; Lyons, Bonnie. "Tillie Olsen: The Writer as a Jewish Woman." *Studies in Jewish American Literature* 5 (1986): 89–102; Nebraska Jewish Historical Society Archives, Omaha; Nelson, Kay Hoyle, and Nancy Huse, eds. *The Critical Response to Tillie Olsen* (1994); Olsen, Tillie. Correspondence with author; *Omaha Jewish Press* (various issues); Orr, Elaine Neil. *Tillie Olsen and the Feminist Spiritual Vision* (1987); Pratt, Linda Ray. "The Circumstances of Silence: Literary Representation and Tillie Olsen's Omaha Past." In *The Critical Response to Tillie Olsen*, edited by Kay Hoyle Nelson and Nancy Huse (1994), and "Tillie Olsen's Omaha Heritage: A History Becomes Literature." *Memories of the Jewish Midwest* 5 (1989): 1–16; "The '30s. A Vision of Fear and Hope. Tillie Olsen." *Newsweek* (January 3, 1994): 26–27.

OLIVER B. POLLAK

ORPHANAGES

In April 1855, the well-known Jewish philanthropist REBECCA GRATZ led a group of Philadelphia

In the late nineteenth and early twentieth centuries, most of the children in Jewish orphanages were girls. The above photograph, taken around the turn of the century, depicts a class of young women studying in a schoolroom at the Cleveland Jewish Orphan Asylum. [Western Reserve Historical Society]

Jewish women in founding the Jewish Foster Home, one of the earliest Jewish orphanages in the United States. The women saw it as their responsibility to provide for Jewish orphans and destitute children who should not be "left to the precarious chance of strangers' beneficence and ... estranged from the religion of their fathers, left with a doubtful morality and with no feeling for the faith of Israel."

The Philadelphia Jewish Foster Home was one of many Jewish orphanages established in the mid-nineteenth century in cities with significant Jewish populations. In this era, known as the "heyday of American orphanages," Jewish philanthropists founded child-care institutions to accommodate growing numbers of dependent Jewish children who, it was feared, would otherwise be reared in non-Jewish asylums and lost to the Jewish community. Until 1940, when most American Jewish orphanages closed their doors, women were highly visible as founders, managers, staff members, and clients of the institutions.

Gratz and her associates remained at the helm of the Jewish Foster Home until 1874, when a male board of directors assumed control of its affairs. This pattern—of women founding orphanages, then displaced by men as the institutions grew in size and sophistication—was replicated at many other American orphanages, Jewish and non-Jewish, of the time. In the nineteenth century, however, orphanages were often described as a "women's sphere of philanthropy." The association of women with orphanages may be attributed to their traditional nurturing role, the greater involvement of women in charitable causes following the Civil War, and the community-based nature of orphanage work. Even when they did not occupy top positions, women were active in the day-to-day operation of the institutions, both as paid staff members and as volunteers. At the Philadelphia Jewish Foster Home, the New York Hebrew Sheltering Guardian Society, the Hebrew Orphan Asylum (HOA) of New York, and the Cleveland Jewish Orphan Asylum, among others, women were instrumental in fund-raising; providing clothing, equipment, and entertainment for the children; counseling youngsters, especially the girls; and supervising recently discharged orphanage wards.

Moreover, in the late nineteenth and early twentieth centuries, Jewish orphanages served a largely female clientele. While orphanages initially housed poor youngsters from the German Jewish community, beginning in the last decades of the nineteenth century, the great majority of their charges were the children of Eastern European immigrants, who arrived in large numbers between 1881 and 1924. Most of those housed in Jewish orphanages in this period were not full orphans, but rather "half orphans," generally the children of widowed or deserted mothers.

These women generally tried to support their children for some time following a family crisis. They took in laundry and boarders, labored in the garment sweatshops that crowded immigrant ghettos, or sought work as cooks, peddlers, or scrubwomen. Some used the little insurance money left to them after their husbands' deaths to establish small grocery or candy stores, which were often unsuccessful. Many left their young children in the care of relatives, neighbors, or older siblings while they went out to work. Hardly any organized child-care programs existed in the late nineteenth century, with the exception of scattered day nurseries, such as those sponsored by the United Hebrew Charities or the Temple Emanuel Sisterhood. The meager subsidies provided to destitute Jews by the United Hebrew Charities and other organizations offered little relief to families in desperate circumstances.

When the mother's income proved insufficient, or relatives caring for a child could no longer do so because of illness, the child's misbehavior, or other factors, it often became necessary to admit children to orphanages. For many women, this was a very painful decision, arrived at after much soul searching. Some vented their anger and frustration in the pages of the Yiddish press, or submitted applications for their children, only to withdraw them after they had changed their minds. Parents who committed children to orphanages tended to divide up their families. In most cases, older youngsters went to work or remained at home to care for infants and small children, while school-age children were sent to orphanages, sometimes to different institutions.

Within the institutions, children received elementary education, vocational training, and religious instruction. In keeping with nineteenth-century norms regarding male and female roles, the educational and

GROUP OF BABES AND I NURSE
We need your generous help.   We ask it for our Asylum.
We ask it for our work.   We ask it for our Babies.
Will you enroll your name in this worthy cause?
THE HEBREW INFANT ASYLUM

Women were usually given the task of raising funds for Jewish orphanages. As the above card demonstrates, some knew exactly what would appeal to potential donors.
[Peter H. Schweitzer]

Jewish orphanages were dedicated to providing for both the spiritual and material needs of the children in their care. This often included a formal program of physical exercise. These young women are doing calisthenics. The photograph was taken around 1915 at the Cleveland Jewish Orphan Asylum. [Western Reserve Historical Society]

vocational programs offered by Jewish orphanages were organized along stereotypical lines. For the most part, orphanage directors prepared boys for vocational and agricultural pursuits, and girls for marriage and motherhood, following temporary stints as dressmakers, milliners, or domestic servants. In addition to performing numerous household chores (generally justified as "vocational training"), youngsters received formal instruction in many areas. While boys were trained in carpentry, farming, shoemaking, ironwork, and printing, girls studied sewing, embroidery, dressmaking, "machine operating," millinery, and, later, typing and stenography.

Following their discharge from the orphanage, many girls were placed in after-care programs, such as the New York Clara de Hirsch Home, the New York Hebrew Orphan Asylum's "Friendly Home" (in which a small group of girls boarded for several months and mastered domestic skills), or a similar facility managed by the Philadelphia Jewish Foster Home. In establishing such programs, orphanage directors sought to prepare their female wards for family life and enable them to earn a livelihood before marriage. These sheltered environments and close personal supervision of female graduates would, it was hoped, protect young girls from the dangers of urban life, especially prostitution, then a significant problem in immigrant Jewish ghettos.

While Jewish orphanages generally succeeded in rearing their wards to be self-supporting, they also limited the young people's sights by directing them to specific fields. For example, they encouraged girls to enter domestic service, an occupation viewed as safe and appropriate for lower-class women in this period. Immigrant Jewish girls, however, tended to reject such positions, regarding them as humiliating. By the turn of the twentieth century, Jewish orphanage directors increasingly recognized the need to widen their wards' horizons, by providing opportunities for higher education to the more talented youngsters. Many Jewish orphanages established scholarship funds to assist students attending high school and college, trade, and professional schools.

At a time when young American women began to attend college in greater numbers, several Jewish orphanages developed special programs to benefit female students. Intellectually gifted girls were encouraged to attend college and become nurses or teachers, some of whom later returned to the orphanages as staff. By 1921, for example, a number of Hebrew Orphan Asylum girls attended HUNTER COLLEGE and Columbia University's Teachers College, and quite a few were enrolled in high school and evening college professional courses. The Jewish Foster Home's Pfaelzer Fund, directed entirely by women, provided gifted girls with scholarships to various industrial, professional, or artistic programs.

Beyond general and vocational education, Jewish orphanage directors saw it as their mission to train their wards to serve the Jewish community as rabbis and teachers. They sent qualified boys to the Hebrew Union College (Reform) or Jewish Theological Seminary (Conservative) to prepare for the rabbinate. Many girls also received higher Jewish education. In 1896, Kaufmann Kohler, a prominent Reform rabbi and instructor at the HOA, urged that promising HOA girls, whom he found to be "as clever and bright as the boys, if not more so," be trained as Sunday school teachers.

Despite their notable successes in some areas, including education, many Jewish orphanages in the nineteenth century were highly regimented institutions that isolated children from the outside world. Most tragically, Jewish orphanage directors, in their zeal to Americanize their wards, often alienated them from their largely foreign-born parents. Many orphanage wards had difficulty relating to their families following discharge. As one Brooklyn Hebrew Orphan Asylum alumnus put it, "[My mother] was almost like a stranger to me. I didn't like the kind of food she cooked because I had never eaten it in the Home. . . . Also she spoke Yiddish most of the time, and I didn't understand that. I think the Fellows should see their parents more while they are in the Home."

The early twentieth century witnessed a significant liberalization of orphanage policies in all areas, including parental visitation. Increasingly, Jewish orphanages served a changing population, composed largely of emotionally disturbed and socially maladjusted youngsters. With the expansion of foster care, the orphanage increasingly became a thing of the past.

Around 1940, most Jewish orphanages were absorbed into umbrella organizations, known as Jewish children's associations, in many cities.

Significant numbers of American Jews spent major portions of their childhoods in Jewish orphanages. Moreover, the institutions' influence reached beyond the youngsters themselves to their parents and relatives, as well as to staff members and those who supported the institutions financially and otherwise. Orphanage stories offer valuable insights into the lives of both middle- and lower-class women in a critical period of American Jewish history.

BIBLIOGRAPHY

Bank, Jules. "A Study of 108 Boys Discharged from the Brooklyn Hebrew Orphan Asylum, 1924–1929. Based on Case Records and Interviews." M.A. thesis, Graduate School for Jewish Social Work (1936); Baum, Charlotte, Paula Hyman, and Sonya Michel. *The Jewish Woman in America* (1976); Bernard, Jacqueline. *The Children You Gave Us: A History of 150 of Service to Children* (1973); Brooklyn Hebrew Orphan Asylum, Annual Reports, 1880–1925, and Hebrew Sheltering Guardian Society, Annual Reports and Minutes, 1880–1925. Collections, Jewish Division, New York Public Library; Child Care Study, NYC, 1922, and Child Care Study, Philadelphia, 1920, and Child Care Study, Philadelphia, 1924. Bureau of Jewish Social Research, New York Kehillah; Cleveland Jewish Orphan Asylum. Annual Reports, 1880–1925, and Records, 1868–1957. Cleveland Jewish Orphan Asylum Manuscript Collection. Cleveland Jewish Archives, Western Reserve Historical Society; Fleischman, S.M. *The History of the Jewish Foster Home and Orphan Asylum of Philadelphia, 1855–1905* (1905); Friedman, Reena Sigman. "'Send Me My Husband Who Lives in New York City': Husband Desertion in the American Jewish Immigrant Community." *Jewish Social Studies* (Winter 1982): 1–18; Goren, Arthur. *New York Jews and the Quest for Community: The Kehillah Experiment, 1908–1922* (1970); Hebrew Orphan Asylum. Annual Reports, 1860–1925, and Records, 1880–1925, and Council of Jewish Federations and Welfare Funds Papers. Hebrew Orphan Asylum Manuscript Collection. American Jewish Historical Society; Lerner, Gerda. *The Majority Finds Its Past: Placing Women in History* (1979); Philadelphia Jewish Foster Home. Annual Reports, 1880–1925, and Records, 1855–1929, and Association for Jewish Children Records. Philadelphia Jewish Foster Home Manuscript Collection. Philadelphia Jewish Archives, Balch Institute; Polster, Gary. "Member of the Herd: Growing Up in the Cleveland Jewish Orphan Asylum, 1868–1919." Ph.D. diss., Case Western Reserve University (1984); Ross, Catherine. "Society's Children: The Care of Indigent Youngsters in New York City, 1875–1903." Ph.D. diss., Yale University (1977); Sharlitt, Michael. *As I Remember: The Home In My Heart* (1959).

REENA SIGMAN FRIEDMAN

ORTHODOX JUDAISM

Orthodox views on the role women may play in their community's religious, educational, and social life have reflected the range of attitudes that religious group has harbored toward American society and culture. Generally, those Orthodox Jews who have resisted Americanization and who have attempted to live religious lives reminiscent of their European past have not countenanced the active participation of women within the synagogue. In the most recent generation, some of these Orthodox men and women have loudly opposed what they perceived to be the deleterious impact feminism has made on American Jewish life. They have censured Conservative, Reform, and Reconstructionist leaders for their broad redefinitions of women's roles. They have also criticized other segments of the Orthodox community who have pressed the halakah to allow women greater activity in public ritual and religious leadership. Yet, even the most traditional of Orthodox Jews have come to recognize that modern conditions have necessitated that girls and young women in America receive a more extensive Jewish education than their mothers and grandmothers had. This understanding has inspired the creation of comprehensive Orthodox school systems for girls, which have produced some outstanding Orthodox women educators. This dynamic approach to women's education reflects, to some extent, Orthodox attitudes that were first expressed in Eastern Europe some eighty years ago.

For many other Orthodox Jews, the opening of synagogue life to greater women's participation, within what they see as the expansive boundaries of halakah, is but another dimension of their accommodationist approach to their encounter with America. Those who have altered the architecture of synagogues to make women comfortable at Orthodox services, who have admitted women to their synagogue boards and ritual committees, and who, beginning in the 1970s, have supported the creation of women's *tefilla* [Orthodox prayer] groups have all acted in accord with their beliefs that for traditional Judaism to remain vital, it had to and could adjust to the American environment. While these accommodationists have not always been of one mind over the extent of female participation in religious life, they have been uniformly in favor of providing women with ever increasing Jewish educational opportunities comparable to those accorded men.

1700–1850

The need to increase room for women within the Orthodox synagogue, as they observed services and rituals, was among the issues congregational leaders faced in the earliest periods of American Jewish history. (It must be remembered that the few synagogues established in this country before approximately 1840 adhered to Orthodox rules.) Jewish officials from New York to Philadelphia to Newport to Charleston were concerned that their services and edifices merit the approbation of their non-Jewish friends. They were apprehensive that gentile visitors might look askance at women segregated behind a closed latticed partition, "like a hen coop" as one visitor in 1744 described the women's section in New York's Shearith Israel. Accordingly, they designed open galleries that would improve women's sight lines, without making men immediately aware of their presence. Often, these synagogues engaged Christian architects to facilitate their plans and to implicitly ensure that their synagogues were built for American-style worship. There were no religious discussions about the permissibility of this architectural innovation. It was a generally accepted Jewish adjustment to American life. Likewise, there were no calls, until the 1850s, for men and women to sit together. In colonial New England and elsewhere, separate seating was not uncommon in churches and meeting houses. Thus, the accommodating Orthodox synagogue was in consonance with American mores in having its modern gallery.

But even as women of this period, and men too for that matter, were unconcerned with advocating a role for females in synagogue ritual, some women were interested in greater recognition as members of these congregations. Typically, women's identities within congregations were subsumed beneath those of their fathers and husbands. Many congregations did accord widows rights as "members" to retain their seats in the synagogue, to be buried in the congregational burial ground, and possibly to send their children to the Jewish school. But women could not vote on synagogue plans and policies. Ultimately, those women who wanted a sense of empowerment and participation within communal life established their own separate benevolent societies that were sometimes affiliated with, and other times separate from, synagogue life. The Female Hebrew Benevolent Society of Philadelphia was one of the most important of these independent organizations. Led by REBECCA GRATZ and other women of that city's Mikveh Israel, it established in 1838 the first Jewish Sunday school in the United States. Offering classes conducted initially by an all-female faculty, it attracted by its second year some eighty boys and girls and was praised by Rabbi Isaac Leeser, the most important Orthodox spokesperson of the pre–Civil War period.

Generally, Jewish education during this time was based in congregational schools where preference in enrollment was given to male applicants. Still, by the 1840s, most synagogue schools were coeducational, although both sexes received little more than rudimentary training in Jewish studies.

1850–1900

With the emergence of Reform congregations in the 1850s, policies on whether men and women could sit together during services was one of the essential points of demarcation between liberal and Orthodox congregations. In the pre-1880 period, membership disagreements over instituting family pews probably caused more splits in once-Orthodox congregations than any other proposed reform. Proponents of change spoke of their respect for women's equality, and the need to attract young people to services, and above all the importance of their synagogue conforming to American social trends. The accommodating Orthodox of that era also wanted to project a modern image to the larger world and were troubled by widespread disaffection from Judaism. But, for most Orthodox groups, mixed seating was a violation of Jewish law that could not be countenanced. It was also, to their minds, a harbinger of other ritual reforms that would further undermine traditional Judaism.

Despite the halakic constraints, not all late nineteenth-century American congregations that defined themselves as Orthodox kept the genders apart during prayer. Indeed, when the Union of Orthodox Jewish Congregations of America was founded in 1898, a number of its charter constituents had family pews.

Nonetheless, consistent with American Orthodox political traditions, these synagogues, whether they countenanced mixed seating or not, did not ordinarily admit women as members. But, in continuing to deny women, except an occasional widow, congregational suffrage, they seemingly differed little from their liberal religious counterparts who polemicized in favor of women's equality but who denied them membership in their synagogues.

The issue of synagogue membership for women did not concern those Orthodox Jews from Eastern Europe who began arriving in this country as early as the 1850s, intent on transplanting the religious civilization they remembered from the old country to these shores. In the ephemeral *landsmanshaft* synagogues as well as in the larger, more established shuls on New York's Lower East Side and elsewhere, women had no role in ritual life. Possibly as a concession to the American religious environment on the part of men just beginning to acculturate—or maybe

because the gentile architectural firm they hired deemed it appropriate—in landmark synagogues like the Lower East Side's Eldridge Street's Kehal Adath Jeshurun, women were able to see services very well from the large open galleries. And women could be of service to their congregation and community through their ladies' auxiliary fund-raising and mutual aid. Still, at least in the public sphere, men remained the focus of religious attention. For most immigrant rabbis, the key women's issue had to do with the traditional requirement that proper *mikvahs* [ritual baths] be established for those who might use them. Leaders were also worried that poorly trained colleagues often issued improperly written *gittim* [writs of divorce]. Their great fear was that if remarriage occurred, children from a second union would be Jewishly illegitimate. In 1902, when the Agudath ha-Rabbanim [Union of Orthodox Rabbis of the United States and Canada] was founded, solving the problem of *gitten* was identified as an important organizational objective.

The central place men occupied in the worldview of those who tried to resist Americanization is best illustrated, however, in their attitudes toward Jewish education and the preventive socialization of their second-generation youngsters. In 1886, a group of the most religious downtowners pooled their limited funds to establish Yeshiva Etz Chaim, a small heder for boys. Its mission was to train boys the way young men had been traditionally educated in Eastern Europe and, as important, to keep them away from the assimilatory pressures imposed upon youngsters by this country's public schools. Analogizing as they did from their Old World pasts, they assumed that in America, too, girls would receive their Jewish training as they always had: informally, at home, from their mothers or from a private tutor. In Russia, most Jewish girls did not go to the government schools. In America, however, they attended the public schools en masse. Because they were thus exposed to systematic English-language and secular training, the pace of acculturation of daughters from the most religious downtown families was far greater than it was for the small number of male scholars who were sent to Etz Chaim and its other yeshivah counterparts that were established around the turn of the twentieth century.

The transplanted Orthodox community's sense that formal education was for boys alone was also reflected in early admission policies of both the ephemeral, independent *heder melameds* and of the metropolises' first afternoon Talmud Torahs. Thus it was a major departure when, in 1894, leaders of the Machzike Talmud Torah, some of whom were also prime supporters of the Etz Chaim endeavor, instituted classes for girls. It was a signal recognition that American conditions required some new approaches toward indoctrinating and socializing young women into the traditional faith.

Outside of New York and other large Orthodox enclaves, where the pool of potential students was very limited, school officials could not as easily stand on law or ceremony in restricting education to boys. While *heder melameds* usually trained only boys in preparation for the youngsters' bar mitzvahs, classes in fledgling congregational or communal schools were often coeducational.

1900–PRESENT

In the first decade of the twentieth century, acculturating Orthodox Jews from Eastern Europe and their second-generation children revisited the role women might play in congregational life and emphasized the need to train both girls and boys in the basic principles and practices of Judaism. For example, the Orthodox Union and its youth wing, the Jewish Endeavor Society, which operated both on the Lower East Side and in Philadelphia, offered Americans new modern Orthodox services. As always, men and women were separated by a *mehitzah* during services. But now women, including Miriam Jacobs, Frances Lunevsky, Ida Mearson, and Irene Stern, who were students of Jewish education at the Jewish Theological Seminary, served as members of the board of directors of the society and taught in that organization's religious schools, which offered classes to both boys and girls. The union and its society's philosophy was that it was not so important how much girls and boys learned about their faith through their encounter with the synagogue and school. Rather, it was essential for young women and men to be inculcated with an interest in being part of the Orthodox community. Thus, the Orthodox Union supported the New York Kehillah's educational innovations that were directed at both girls and boys. It was, likewise, the stance of Orthodox schools like the Uptown Talmud Torah and the Rabbi Israel Salanter Talmud Torah, both in Harlem, which worked with the New York Kehillah's bureau of education and offered separate classes for girls and boys in their neighborhoods.

Concomitant with these efforts, a different strain of transplanted Orthodoxy began to evolve in immigrant neighborhoods, first in Brooklyn and then downtown, which advocated still another way girls might be educated. The first Mizrachi [Religious Zionist] National Hebrew School for Girls was founded in Williamsburg in 1905. Analogizing itself from the modern heders of Eastern Europe (the so-called *heder metukkan*), these American schools offered girls a supplementary school curriculum that emphasized Hebrew language, grammar, conversation, and literature. In 1910, a sister school was created on Madison Street in Lower Manhattan. According to one contemporary observer, the "school was confined to the teaching of girls, for two reasons; first, because it was easier to get Jewish parents to permit the teaching of these modern 'fads' [that is, Hebrew language and religious Zionism] to girls than to boys, and second, because the nationalist movement made the education of Jewish women an essential part of its program" (Dushkin, p. 83).

In 1929, the scope of Mizrachi-style education for girls took an additional step forward when the Shulamith School, the first American all-day Orthodox school for girls, was established in Brooklyn. In this "girls' yeshivah," elementary school students were exposed to a Hebrew-intensive curriculum that was integrated with their general studies. Interestingly enough, in organizing their school, American Mizrachiites drew upon a newly nascent Eastern European model, the BAIS YA'ACOV movement, that was being sponsored by their ideological opponents within the Orthodox world, the anti-Zionist Agudat Yisrael.

Beginning in 1917, at the instigation of Sarah Schenirer, some of Poland's most Orthodox Jews addressed the problem that their counterparts in America failed to address: the growing dichotomy between the socialization of girls and boys. As Schenirer saw it, the best young men were still under the safe influence of the yeshivah. But girls, bereft of formal Jewish education, were drifting away from ancient traditions. The Bais Ya'acov answer was the creation of a new women's yeshivah system that, in its heyday, offered girls a seven-year curriculum that included prayers, the Bible, and Jewish laws and customs, all taught in Yiddish. Secular subjects were also offered as required by Polish law.

The American Shulamith group agreed with Schenirer's assumptions and believed that, in this secularized country, yeshivah education for girls was essential. They differed, of course, over the ideological messages to be proffered. As Mizrachiites, they wanted, above all, for students to be inculcated with the love of Hebrew and of Zion, teachings that the Agudists disdained.

Some years later, with the approach of World War II, in 1937, the Bais Ya'acov girls' yeshivah movement put down roots in Brooklyn's hospitable Orthodox soil. And with its Yiddish-based, anti-Zionist Jewish ideology, its providing of only minimal general studies, and its pedigree as having merited the approbation of the great Torah sages of Eastern Europe, it quickly became one of the most favored organizations of the Agudath ha-Rabbanim and other comparable resistant Orthodox organizations. Still, when these American-based groups backed the Bais Ya'acov concept, they tacitly admitted that modern conditions necessitated that girls and young women in America receive a more extensive Jewish education than had their mothers and grandmothers.

Meanwhile, Mizrachi influences were strongly apparent and unchallenged in the mission and outlook of the Yeshiva of Flatbush and the Ramaz School, founded in 1928 and 1936 respectively. These first coeducational modern yeshivahs in the United States emphasized to girls and boys both the importance of modern Hebrew studies and culture even as they disdained the Talmud-predominant or Talmud-exclusive curriculum that had characterized earlier boys' yeshivahs in this country and put a high premium on Orthodox accommodation to the secular world. Eventually, in the 1940s, as both the Mizrachi- and Agudist-influenced schools and their first students matured, each of these institutions would add high school programs to their offerings. Until that time, if New York Orthodox girls wanted training beyond elementary school under their denomination's auspices, they had only the supplementary Hebrew Teachers Training School for Girls, sponsored by the women's branch of the Orthodox Union. That is, of course, if these ambitious youngsters did not opt for pedagogic studies at the more established Conservative Jewish Theological Seminary of America, a school that welcomed both men and women.

Still, in all, through the interwar period, intensive Orthodox Jewish education remained the preserve of an elite, usually New York–based, group of women who had access to these schools. For most Orthodox women, both in the city and elsewhere, the synagogue, and specifically the synagogue sisterhood, was the locus of their public Orthodox Jewish lives and the source of their education and communal participation. Sisterhood educational and social activities were expanded dramatically for a middle-class female constituency that had time to devote to religious volunteer work. Women were told that they had a role to play and a particular talent in improving the aesthetic beauty of the sanctuary. And sisterhood classes were the place where many adult women acquired the Jewish knowledge that had been withheld from them as youngsters. Moreover, with the help of materials often produced by the national Women's Branch of the Orthodox Union, major attempts were made to convince women that observance of commandments that they were learning about could be consonant with good middle-class life-styles.

For example, pamphlets and books that spoke of the importance of Jewish women maintaining kosher kitchens advocated for the faith on the basis that "nothing has refined the Jewish character as much as the dietary laws," that "abstinence from foods permitted to others . . . develop[s] and strengthens self mastery and control," and of course builds strong, healthy youngsters (Joselit, *NY's Jewish* . . . , p. 110). The observance of laws of family purity (menstrual restrictions) was projected as contributory to family happiness, mental health, and beauty. And maybe as important, efforts were made to build beauty parlor–like modern ritual facilities that made purification more attractive.

What was done by, with, and for women as part of the modern Orthodox synagogue remained circumscribed within their own "special sphere," the sisterhood. There, women assumed leadership roles and demonstrated their abilities and commitments. They were not part of the synagogue's overall governance structure. Even the most avant-garde interwar synagogues emulated neither the example of the Jewish Endeavor Society nor of Harlem's Congregation Mikveh Israel, which when founded in 1905 admitted two women to its original board of directors. However, it seems that Orthodox women of this period were not overly perturbed by their absence from the congregation's power base. As one historian of interwar Orthodoxy has pointed out, "the guidebooks of the Women's Branch of the Orthodox Union" do not evidence "even a hint of implied criticism or demurral" about the "special sphere." Middle-class Orthodox women and men apparently agreed that in the end, women's "chief characteristic was that of 'homemaker'" and their "overriding objective in life was to beautify the Jewish home (Joselit, "The Special Sphere . . . ," p. 223).

Educational opportunities for women under Orthodox auspices grew enormously in the postwar period as the varying styles of day school or yeshivah schooling for girls and boys became an expanding norm within that community. For those within the resisting segment, made up now primarily of those who had fled Hitler or survived the Holocaust, the Bais Ya'acov schools offered a curriculum that bolstered adherence to Old World ways and consciously underplayed the importance of general education. By 1948, it was possible for a young woman to stay within that educational system from elementary school through high school and through the seminary. At that most advanced level, the best and most committed students were offered their own Hebrew teachers' training course, essential for that movement to produce its next generation of instructors. Significantly, their teacher certification did not mandate a college degree. Quite to the contrary, Bais Ya'acov women, like their brothers in old-line yeshivahs, were actively discouraged from entering that world of higher secular education. In all events, by the early 1960s, seminary graduates were running some sixteen Bais Ya'acov elementary and secondary schools and seminaries in New York and two sister schools outside the metropolis. Complementing the Bais Ya'acov system that attracted religious girls of all types were those smaller Hasidic girls' yeshivahs, like the Lubavitcher's Beth Rivkah schools, that were controlled by the specific groups that established themselves in postwar America.

Of course, girls' yeshivahs were comparable to yeshivahs for boys and men primarily in their common goal of socializing their students against the perceived evils of general society. For example, as noted above, neither group of school leaders wanted their students to attend college. However, their Jewish educational missions were fundamentally different, befitting their adherence to Old World views of what Jewish men and women had to know. Simply put, the ideal male student was the one most proficient in Talmud. And, since the entire thrust of yeshivah training had always been to produce Talmudic scholars, that highly valued goal had to be continued in America. Women, on the other hand, were not to be taught Talmud since ordinarily they had not been exposed to such advanced learning in the past. And, in the minds of many Orthodox rabbinical leaders, it was a useless endeavor or, at worst, an evil pursuit. Practically, that meant that female yeshivah graduates were restricted to the types of studies their female ancestors were exposed to—with Bible being the most advanced subject—although they would learn their Torah with greater intensity and sophistication.

The different ways these young men and women spent their long educational days has had its own significant impact within these separatist communities. Freed from, or denied, the burden or opportunity of studying Talmud all day, female yeshivah students became more exposed to their American environment. Typically, these women emerged from school worldlier than their fathers, brothers, and, maybe most important, their husbands, a change that had no small impact upon how the sexes related to one another within their communities.

Meanwhile, in very different, third-generation Americanized Orthodox communities, coeducational schools flourished as the groundbreaking Flatbush and Ramaz models were emulated nationally. By the early 1960s, there were some ninety coeducational schools and ten high schools under Orthodox auspices throughout the United States. In these institutions, girls and boys studied general subjects together and in some schools learned religious studies, including Talmud, in coed groups. After high school, girls and boys, possessed of prep school–level secular training, were expected to pursue American professional careers as that group increasingly found acceptance and felt comfortable in gentile environments.

In these same postwar years, the model of women's education, first seen in the Shulamith School, was very attractive, in its own right, to Orthodox young women whose families identified with Yeshiva University. Although Yeshiva University pioneered a comprehensive modern yeshivah educational system for men, it paid, through 1945, scant attention to the needs of Orthodox Jewish women. As early as 1929, it was possible for a male student to receive a quality, Talmud-intensive Jewish education, and more-than-adequate secular academic training, through his college years under one Orthodox roof. And if he then wanted to complete his schooling with *semicha* [ordination], as a modern Orthodox rabbi, he could finish his studies within Yeshiva's Rabbi Isaac Elchanan Theological Seminary (RIETS). There was no comparable girls' high school or Orthodox college and certainly no rabbinical training school available for female counterparts. During the interwar period, daylong Jewish education for girls was only beginning, for a small elite, at the elementary school. The typical female counterpart of a yeshivah boy went to the public schools, and the most committed, among those who were lucky enough to live in New York, availed themselves of advanced supplementary Jewish training through high school at either the Conservative seminary or the Orthodox Union's Hebrew Teachers Training School.

To be sure, Yeshiva University officials were sometimes criticized for their myopia toward young women. As early as 1925, one outspoken editorialist in the Orthodox monthly, the *Jewish Forum*, called upon the school "to submerge our prejudiced views of former days . . . let us think of our children, girls as well as boys—we regret that Dr. Revel [Yeshiva University's president] seems to make no provision for the Jewish education of our girls" (Gurock, *The Men . . .*, pp. 190–191). Nonetheless, such criticisms had no discernible effect upon Yeshiva University's policy makers because there was no significant demand for separate but equal training for young women emanating from its constituent families.

Most parents of Yeshiva University's students believed that their daughters could handle, as they always had, the social pressures and the sometimes anti-Jewish sentiments that were expressed in the religiously heterogeneous public schools. And as far as college was concerned, there was no need for a women's Yeshiva College because the overwhelming majority of Orthodox families did not consider post-secondary education a necessary, or even a warranted, final educational step for their daughters.

After World War II, Yeshiva University moved to provide Orthodox women with advanced educational opportunities largely because the women in their community and their families were then beginning to attend college. The first step toward the creation of an Orthodox women's college was the establishment in 1948 of the Central Yeshiva High school for girls in Manhattan. Several years later, a Brooklyn branch was opened. In 1952, Yeshiva University absorbed the Orthodox Union's Hebrew Teachers Training School as its own Teachers Institute for Women. Finally, in 1954, STERN COLLEGE FOR WOMEN began making its singular contribution to Orthodox women's education.

From a social and religious ideological perspective, Stern, like Yeshiva College before it, affirmed a secular college education as permissible, indeed as warranted, for American Orthodox Jews. It also said to its prospective women, as Yeshiva University had always said to its men, that they could imbibe much of the best of American college social life without challenge to their patterns of Orthodox observance. And it suggested to these women's families that Stern's particular niche included preparation for careers, graduate study, and "management of a Jewish home and family." Implicit too was the understanding that this women's college, placed within the world's largest Jewish community, would provide its students, particularly those from smaller Jewish communities, with abundant opportunities for social engagements with potential marriage mates. From its inception, Stern College enrolled, in almost equal numbers, women from within and without the metropolitan area, a trend that continues to this day.

From a Jewish educational point of view, Central and Stern occupied a middle ground distinctive from both Ramaz and Flatbush and from Bais Ya'acov, even as the women's college was flexible enough to attract a minority of students from these very different types of schools. For example, Talmudic study was always available as an option for students. And in the last fifteen or twenty years, Talmud has become increasingly popular, certainly among its college-age students. As an Orthodox, single-sex school, Stern's classes were always closed to men, although many of its faculty were males, as were its first three deans. In 1977, a Stern alumna, Karen Bacon, was appointed dean.

By the 1970s, there would emerge from among the many graduates of these girls' yeshivahs, seminaries, and day schools and Stern College for Women a coterie of highly educated and motivated women destined to make a significant impact upon their variegated community. The resisting segment within Orthodoxy benefited from the works of women dedicated to upholding traditional ideas and the status quo. For example, learned women writers for the Lubavitcher movement articulated counterattacks against Jewish feminists' calls for change within Orthodox Judaism. Some of these spokeswomen also engaged in discussions and debates on college campuses in furtherance of their movement's outreach programs to unaffiliated Jews.

Meanwhile, other women, products of Orthodox day schools and then secular university training or Stern College, or sometimes defectors from Bais Ya'acov schools, challenged the Orthodox community to address what they perceived to be disabilities imposed upon them by halakah and to accord them a greater role in synagogue life and public Orthodox ritual. Often defining themselves as Orthodox feminists and attuned to the rhetoric and successes of their sisters elsewhere, they saw no place for a "special sphere" within congregational governance, explored the ways in which women might participate in the Orthodox service within the bounds of Jewish law, and demanded that Orthodox rabbis revisit the laws and consequences that govern the *agunah* [a woman who has been denied a Jewish divorce by her husband and is thus unable to remarry within Jewish law].

Accordingly, over the past twenty years, many modern Orthodox congregations have changed, without profound religious debate, their long-standing rules governing membership and board leadership. Since century-old exclusions were rooted primarily in political custom and social mores and not Jewish law, it was a relatively simple matter to accommodate what women and some men wanted. In most instances, it was only a question of whether other men in the synagogue would be comfortable with women in positions of power within the congregation.

At the same time, the successful efforts of women to forward their participation within the Orthodox service have provoked immense discussion and debate within Orthodox ranks. Probably, the Hebrew Institute of Religion is the nation's most avant-garde congregation in its championing of women's involvement. There, with the expressed imprimatur of its rabbi,

Avraham Weiss, worshipers regularly pass the Torah scroll from the men's to the women's sections during services. The parents and siblings of bar and bat mitzvah children stand together on the *bimah* during services to offer a family blessing. Women and men recite the megillah at special egalitarian readings. And for close to twenty years, this synagogue has been home to a monthly women's *tefilla*, which begins its year's calendar with women's *hakafot* and a Torah reading during Simchat Torah. The organizers of these women's services have included Ronnie Becher, Cheryl Harris, Nancy Lerea, and Miriam Schacter. The Riverdale Women's *tefilla* is actually one of thirteen such prayer groups that, according to a 1996 WOMEN'S *TEFILLAH* MOVEMENT survey, meet regularly in synagogues and homes in the metropolitan area. Seven other groups meet in other communities across the United States. It is estimated that college campuses are home to an additional eight prayer groups.

While types of public bat mitzvah experiences have become part of the contemporary Orthodox girl's coming of age, most Orthodox congregations have neither accepted nor integrated most other Orthodox feminist activities or groups into their synagogues' lives. Indeed, women's *tefillas* have been castigated by both the Agudath ha-Rabbanim and by a group of five *roshei yeshiva* [professors of Talmud] at Yeshiva University's Orthodox seminary. As early as 1982, leaders of old-line Orthodoxy in this country told Orthodox feminists and their supporters, "Do not make a comedy out of Torah" (Gurock, *American Jewish Orthodoxy* . . . , p. 61). More significantly, three years later, in 1985, colleagues of Rabbi Weiss and Rabbi Saul Berman, another spokesman for feminist Orthodoxy at this centrist Orthodox school, unequivocally declared that prayer groups were a "total and complete deviation from tradition" (Wertheimer, p. 133).

To date, most Stern College students and alumnae have adopted a personal position of benign neglect toward the women's *tefilla* debate. Stern College student organizations and publications have not aligned themselves with the opponents of women's *tefilla* but neither have they established such groups within their own schools. And most members of the prayer groups from Riverdale, Manhattan, Brooklyn, and so on are not part of Yeshiva University's community. Though Stern women increasingly desire advanced training in Talmud and allied rabbinic texts, they have not become advocates for greater participation in ritual life or professional leadership in the synagogue. More typically, the best students want to be intellectual resources for the Orthodox community in schools and women's yeshivahs in both America and Israel. They often seek out postbaccalaureate training either in Yeshiva University's graduate school of Judaica or at schools like New York's DRISHA INSTITUTE FOR JEWISH EDUCATION.

Thus, while BLU GREENBERG and her husband, Rabbi Yitz Greenberg, two of the staunchest backers of Orthodox feminism who are not affiliated with Yeshiva University, have spoken about the eventuality of women earning Orthodox ordination, to date only one woman has sought admission to RIETS. But Haviva Krasner-Davidson was a graduate of Ramaz, then Columbia University and the University of Maryland, and was not a Stern College alumna. RIETS leaders did not respond officially to this potential applicant's request. In all events, by the mid-1990s, attitudes toward women's *tefilla* had become a litmus test for the degree of resistance or accommodation harbored by both Orthodox rabbis and their laity, male and female, toward both feminism and other aspects of contemporary American Jewish life.

In February 1997, an international conference on "Feminism and Orthodoxy" was held in New York City that brought together the variegated groups that advocate greater women's participation in synagogue life. This gathering caused their critics to redouble their public opposition to feminist-Orthodox agendas.

Finally, while Orthodox rabbis have staunchly denied feminist allegations that halakah is inflexible and incapable of effectively addressing the tragic predicament of the *agunah*, they have been moved by wide-ranging social pressures to look again at this long-standing problem. For example, in 1981, Agunah was founded by Orthodox feminists Rivka Haut, Susan Aaronoff, and their supporters to advance this issue and cause within their own community. The battle has been engaged on two fronts. In some individual cases and communities, pulpit rabbis and communal leaders have excoriated men who have refused to grant their wives the necessary writ of divorce that would permit them to resume normal lives and social relationships. Various religious legal remedies have been explored to appropriately bend halakic rules. Their solutions have ranged from ex post facto annulments of marriages to prenuptial agreements. In 1993, the Rabbinical Council of America, the national organization of Orthodox rabbis made up primarily of men ordained by Yeshiva University, approved an innovative prenuptial document. Still, these efforts have received mixed reviews among Orthodox feminists who want their rabbis and men's organizations to more aggressively ostracize recalcitrant husbands.

Prospectively, the next decades will probably witness, within Orthodoxy's resisting as well as accommodating camps, the continued efflorescence of advanced women's education and the emergence within these groups' ranks of highly educated and committed female Torah scholars. It will be interesting to observe, particularly within the most modern of Orthodox elements, whether those who will be acknowledged and respected for their knowledge of Jewish law and tradition will aspire, in significant numbers, to greater formal and professional leadership roles within their communities. It will likewise be intriguing to see to what extent modern Orthodox male authorities will accommodate these desires and aspirations, and if men and women together will develop new models of community leadership and power relationships within their communities.

BIBLIOGRAPHY

Dushkin, Alexander M. *Jewish Education in New York City* (1918); Fine, Jo Renee, and Gerard Wolfe. *The Synagogues of New York's Lower East Side* (1978); Goldman, Karla Ann. "Beyond the Gallery: The Place of Women in the Development of American Judaism." Ph.D. diss., Harvard University (1993); Grinstein, Hyman B. *The Rise of the Jewish Community of New York, 1654–1860* (1945); Gurock, Jeffrey S. *American Jewish Orthodoxy in Historical Perspective* (1996), and *The Men and Women of Yeshiva: Higher Education, Orthodoxy and American Judaism* (1988), and *Ramaz: School, Community, Scholarship and Orthodoxy* (1989), and *When Harlem Was Jewish* (1979); Joselit, Jenna Weissman. *New York's Jewish Jews: The Orthodox Community in the Interwar Years* (1990), and "The Special Sphere of the Middle-Class American Jewish Woman: The Synagogue Sisterhood." In *The American Synagogue: A Sanctuary Transformed*, edited by Jack Wertheimer (1987); Lerner, Anne Lapidus. "'Who Has Not Made Me a Man': The Movement for Equal Rights for Women in American Jewry." *AJYB* 77 (1977): 11–16; Poll, Solomon. *The Hasidic Community of Williamsburg* (1962); Rakeffet-Rothkoff, Aaron. *The Silver Years in American Jewish Orthodoxy: Rabbi Eliezer Silver and His Generation* (1981); Sarna, Jonathan D. "The Debate over Mixed Seating in the American Synagogue." In *The American Synagogue: A Sanctuary Transformed*, edited by Jack Wertheimer (1987); Sussman, Lance. *Isaac Leeser and the Making of American Judaism* (1995); Wertheimer, Jack. *A People Divided: Judaism in Contemporary America* (1993); *Women's Tefillah Network Newsletter* (August 1996).

JEFFREY S. GUROCK

OSTERMAN, ROSANNA DYER
(1809–1866)

One of Texas's earliest benefactors was German-born Rosanna Dyer Osterman. Born February 26, 1809, she married Joseph Osterman in Baltimore in 1825 and moved to Galveston, Texas, in 1838. Together, the couple operated a general mercantile and import business. Osterman was instrumental in the founding of the first Jewish community in Texas. She brought the first rabbi to Texas in 1852 to consecrate the state's first Jewish cemetery, and the first-known Jewish service in the state was held at the home of her brother Isadore Dyer in 1856.

Osterman was known throughout Galveston Island for her talent, energy, and generosity. In one famous instsance, she gave her recipe for meat biscuits to Gail Borden, a family friend. Her biscuit, which allowed travelers on the frontier to carry a nonperishable food item, was made from dried, powdered buffalo meat, beans, and cornmeal, ingredients Osterman obtained from trading with the Comanche Indians. Her husband financed Gail Borden's experiments to perfect the biscuit, which led to Borden's most important discovery—condensed milk.

During the 1853 Galveston yellow fever epidemic, Osterman's abilities as a nurse became well known. She set up tents on the grounds of her home to care for the sick and dying. During the Civil War, Galveston was occupied by the Union army. Most residents fled the island, but Osterman, by now a widow, remained. She turned her home into a hospital where she cared for Union soldiers and later for Confederate soldiers. Carpets became slippers and sheets became bandages.

According to a popular story, Osterman helped the Confederates retake the island. She learned from a wounded Union soldier that the Confederates' plans to retake the island on January 12, 1863, had been revealed to the Union troops by a runaway slave. Osterman alerted the Confederate general in Houston, who moved his attack to January 1. Galveston once again became a Confederate port.

Rosanna Dyer Osterman died in the explosion of a Mississippi River steamboat in 1866. She left her considerable fortune to charities around the United States. At her death, a local newspaper stated that the history of Rosanna Osterman was more eloquently written in the untold charities that had been helped by her liberal hands than in any eulogy a person could bestow.

BIBLIOGRAPHY

Fornell, Earl Wesley. *The Galveston Era: The Texas Crescent on the Eve of Secession* (1961); Hewitt, W. Phil, researcher. *The Jewish Texans* (1974); Ornish, Natalie. *Pioneer Jewish Texans: Their Impact on Texas and American History for Four Hundred Years, 1590–1990* (1989); Osterman, Rosanna. Papers. Rosenberg Library, Galveston, Tex., and Texas Jewish Archives. Barker Texas History Center,

University of Texas, Austin; *UJE*, s.v. "Dyer, Isadore"; Winegarten, Ruthe, and Cathy Schechter. *Deep in the Heart: The Lives and Legends of Texas Jews* (1990).

SUZANNE CAMPBELL

OSTRIKER, ALICIA SUSKIN (b. 1937)

Alicia Ostriker is a feminist revolutionary. She has been in revolt since her 1986 groundbreaking book, *Stealing the Language: The Emergence of Women's Poetry in America*, in which she shows how women, from the beginning of writing poetry in America, were forced to deal with the prejudice and strictures of male-dominated criticism. Eight years later, in *The Nakedness of the Fathers*, she extends her passionate inquiry to the situation of the Jewish woman, who for thousands of years has been denied her selfhood and forbidden to speculate about the meaning of biblical myth and legend. Neither book relies on vain complaint. Both show how women can overleap the traditional bonds imposed on them. With anger, blasphemy, and invention, women poets have transformed history and reality. Both books are personal and universal. As a poet, a Jew, and a woman, Ostriker starts from her own beginnings and shows how she has gathered the courage to move out into the clear new air of freedom and autonomy. Full of passionate daring and personal chutzpah, only a poet could have written *The Nakedness of the Fathers*.

In order to understand Ostriker's development, it is necessary to go back to her early work on Blake. In her 1965 book, *Vision and Verse in William Blake*, and culminating in 1977 in her edition of *The Complete Poems*, Ostriker learned about Blake's suspicion of authoritarianism as well as his liberating, imaginative vitality. The word "visionary" became a watchword of the highest order in Ostriker's vocabulary.

If we go back to her early books of poetry, from the 1969 *Songs* to the sophistication of *Green Age* twenty years later, we can see her transformation from a poet of the quotidian to a poet of the sacred. In the poem "A Meditation in Seven Days" she writes, "Fearful, I see my hand on the latch / I am the woman, and about to enter."

Alicia Suskin Ostriker was born in New York City on November 11, 1937. She married Jeremiah P. Ostriker in 1958, and had three children: Rebecca (b. 1963), Eve (b. 1965), and Gabriel (b. 1970). Her father, David Suskin, was a playground director for the New York City Department of Parks. Her mother, Beatrice (Linnick) Suskin, was a folk dancer. She has one sister, Amy David, born in 1948. She received her B.A. from Brandeis University in 1955, and her M.A. and Ph.D. from the University of Wisconsin in 1961 and 1964, respectively. In 1965, she began to teach in the Rutgers University English department, where she is now a full professor.

As she was quoted in Catherine Blair's 1993 critical work *Feminist Revision and the Bible*, ". . . having oscillated all my life between criticism and poetry, I'm trying in *The Nakedness of the Fathers* . . . to produce a work in which both these modes go on simultaneously and interact. Layers of biblical textuality come into play with layers of my own identity and family history; I interpret the Bible while it interprets me."

In *A Woman Under the Surface* (1982), she writes about women in crisis, confronting both personal and political disaster. It is important to note the double meaning in the title. But this is not the first time she has juxtaposed the personal and the political. In *The*

Being a poet, a Jew, and a woman defines all of Alicia Ostriker's work. She approaches the history of both poetry and Judaism from an unorthodox, feminist point of view.

Mother/Child Papers (1980), she movingly juxtaposes the birth of her third child, a son, with the Vietnam War. In *The Imaginary Lover* (1986), she continues to write boldly about domesticity and marriage, but in "An Army of Lovers" and "Warning" she starts to assert her Jewishness more personally: "She is like Abraham arguing with God . . . / She wants everyone to escape."

In her 1983 book of critical essays, *Writing Like a Woman*, we see who her spiritual mothers are: H.D., Sylvia Plath, Anne Sexton, May Swenson, and ADRIENNE RICH. But she has gone a step beyond them, calling on her spiritual father, William Blake. Now, in her vatic vision of the world as a Jew, she wants to see women healed and changed with the restoration of the goddess in her many forms.

What does such a wide-ranging successful career have to tell us about Jewish studies? Alicia Ostriker is one of an increasing number of women writers who have the courage to approach biblical history and legend from an unorthodox, feminist point of view. This is not to say that Ostriker follows any path other than her own. Brought up in an assimilated household, regarding herself as an ex-atheist, she enters into every legendary life, both male and female, with a personal vision. Nothing received is sacrosanct; everything is subject to history and experience.

SELECTED WORKS BY ALICIA OSTRIKER

CRITICAL AND SCHOLARLY BOOKS

The Bible and Feminist Revision: The Bucknell Lectures on Literary Theory (1993); *Stealing the Language: The Emergence of Women's Poetry in America* (1986); *Vision and Verse in William Blake* (1965); *William Blake: The Complete Poems* (1977); *Writing Like a Woman* (1983).

POETRY AND PROSE POETRY BOOKS

The Crack in Everything (1996); *A Dream of Springtime: Poems 1970–78* (1979); *Green Age* (1989); *The Imaginary Lover* (1986); *The Mother/Child Papers* (1980); *The Nakedness of the Fathers: Biblical Visions and Revisions* (1994); *Once More Out of Darkness and Other Poems* (1974); *Songs: A Book of Poems* (1969); *A Woman Under the Surface* (1982).

RUTH WHITMAN

OVED, MARGALIT (b. c. 1934)

Margalit Oved—dancer, choreographer, singer, actress, musician—is the epitome of a performance artist. She has left an indelible mark on twentieth-century Jewish culture through her inventive and modern interpretations of ancient biblical tales.

Margalit Oved explores biblical, familial, and mystical themes in her choreography and dancing. Incredibly versatile, she also writes her own music and sings as part of her performances, which reflect her background as a Jewish Yemenite who lived in Israel then settled in the United States. [New York Public Library]

Oved, an emigrant from Yemen, began her career in her teens as one of the original members of Sarah Levi-Tanai's ethnic Inbal Dance Company in Tel Aviv, Israel. Her creative roots go further back, however, to her native Aden, where as a child she danced barefoot and carefree. Her story, told through her dances, is that of a Jewish Yemenite turned Israeli and then American. Despite her several transformations, she did not abandon her earliest influences. At the same time, she has internalized her experiences in the United States, including the raising of an American-born family, and used them to inform her more recent work.

Born around 1934, Oved attended Catholic school because her mother believed that she would receive the best education there. In an interview with *The Jerusalem Post* in 1995, Oved said that her mother's concept of God was "sincerity, compassion and honesty."

In her fifteen years with the Inbal Dance Company, Oved choreographed dances based on the rhythms and traditions of Yemen, Arabia, Africa, India, and Spain. She worked closely with Inbal's students, as well as with its director, Levi-Tanai. Oved rose to the status of principal dancer before quitting the company in 1965 to strike out on her own.

In 1967, she settled in Los Angeles. She met and married Melvin Marshall, whom she has called a "prince of the Bronx." Together, they have two sons.

Oved began teaching in the dance department at UCLA. She started building her solo repertoire, creating *Yemenite Wedding*, *The Dybbuk of Aden*, *The Birth of a Drum*, and *Kingdom of Spirit*. Other dances from that period include *Gestures of Sands* (made into a documentary film), *A Donkey Stepped on a Flower*, *The Prophetess*, *Tamar*, *In Memory of Jeanie Irwin*, *A Dancer*, and *My Father* (later renamed *The Family of Man*). *Landscape* brought her to the attention of the American public when it was performed at the Los Angeles Dance Festival in 1972. *Dance Magazine* wrote, "[Oved is] a radiant performer who moves with calculated economy yet conveys an impression of dancing with extravagant panache. Oved is also a highly original choreographer."

In 1973, she created *Through the Gate of Aden*, the tale of her own life writ large. Through music and movement, she portrayed life in her native town.

Biblical, familial, and mystical themes occupy center stage in Oved's work. Through these themes, she expresses her beliefs about life's basic virtues and values: honesty, simplicity, and the importance of human relationships. For example, her work *In the Beginning* enacts the burgeoning awareness of Adam and Eve. *Dance Magazine*, in September 1974, described the work as portraying "the discovery of all expression for the first time . . . the journey from the paradise of non-knowledge to the hell of knowledge."

Another work, *David and Goliath*, portrays the saga of the Israelite shepherd who slew the giant Philistine. Oved, dancing both roles, created a play on the multiple facets of the two characters and how they interacted with one another. By incorporating elements of the slain Goliath, through his gestures and facial expressions, into the triumphant David, she depicted the evolution of the youthful shepherd into a powerful monarch.

Oved created her own music for most of her dances, relying heavily on percussion instruments. These instruments, she feels, mimic the sounds of her childhood when she played with tin cans given to her by her mother. Oved also learned how to use her own voice as another instrument. One of her performance signatures was the combination of taped voice and instrumentation serving as background music for live singing. Through song and percussion, she sought to reflect the totality of human and animal sound. She told *Dance Magazine* in 1974, "it is the climate, philosophy, human concerns, birth, death, and above all, feeling."

During her nearly thirty years in Los Angeles, Oved formed her own company, the Margalit Dance Theatre Company. Besides dancing and choreographing, she acted in such films as *The Greatest Story Ever Told* (1965) and *Hill 24 Doesn't Answer* (1955).

In 1994, she returned to Tel Aviv to revitalize the Inbal Dance Company, taking her twenty-six-year-old son Barak Marshall with her. Reviews in *The Jerusalem Post* gave Oved high marks for her effort.

Oved's professional accomplishments have been recognized with three choreography awards from the National Endowment for the Arts. HADASSAH, the Women's Zionist Organization, honored her for her contributions to Jewish culture with its prestigious Myrtle Wreath Award in 1973.

BIBLIOGRAPHY

Attitude 1, no. 4 (August/September 1982): 4; *Dance Magazine* (August 1972): 25–26, and (September 1974): 44–46; *The Jerusalem Post*, October 25, 1994, and May 15, 1995, and June 12, 1995, and February 16, 1996; Oved, Margalit. Program notes. Margalit Dance Theatre Company, Los Angeles, October 31, 1975–November 2, 1975.

JANE ROSEN

OZICK, CYNTHIA (b. 1928)

In conversation, one hears a soft, youthful tinkle, clear as a bell. Then there is the unfailing Old World politeness, the refinement of language, and a bright eagerness in the voice to share her thoughts, to hold nothing back. Yet, if the voice is poetry, the words are prophecy. One will hear this in the deep insights, the well-wrought thought, the keen incisiveness, and the sharp wit. These will come later—but they will come.

There is simultaneously something very young and something decidedly hoary about the persona of Cynthia Ozick. She herself recognizes this duality. In "The Break," a virtuoso comic performance that first appeared in the Spring 1994 issue of *Antaeus*, her younger self (who goes by the Hebrew name of Shoshana) solemnly announces her disengagement from the "white-haired, dewlapped, thick-waisted, thick-lensed hag" (who goes by the Greek name of Cynthia)—a writer disgustingly devoid of that hunger

Winner of numerous literary awards, writer Cynthia Ozick has created classic characters and stories of Jewish life. A successful essayist as well as novelist, short story writer, and playwright, her fictional works on the Holocaust are among her most moving. [American Jewish Archives]

region. That is a tradition of skepticism, rationalism, and antimysticism, opposed to the exuberant emotionalism of the Hasidic community that flourished in the Galitzianer [Galician] portion of Eastern Europe. This explains, perhaps, why the Hasidic rebbe in Ozick's story "Bloodshed" is such a reasonable man, almost a Litvak. Ozick herself, she does not tire of repeating, is a *misnaged*, an opponent of mystic religion. In her stories, however, she wallows in mysticism.

Ozick describes the life of her parents with reverence. It was not unusual for them to put in a fourteen-hour day at the drugstore, often closing the store at one in the morning. Cynthia herself served as the delivery girl of prescriptions. Ozick describes her mother's life as a life of total generosity, of lavishness, of exuberance, of untrammeled laughter. Her father, a discreet, quiet man, a *talmid khokhem* [a Jewish scholar], who also knew both Latin and German from his Russian gymnasium years, ground and mixed powders and entered prescriptions meticulously in his record book. It is not without interest that, according to his daughter, he wrote beautiful Hebrew paragraphs and had a Talmudist's rationalism.

However, life was not without its childhood pain. At the age of five and a half, Ozick entered heder, the Yiddish-Hebrew "room" where, in the America of those years, Jewish pupils were sent for religious instruction. There she was confronted by a rabbi who told Cynthia's *bobe* [grandmother], who had accompanied her granddaughter to school, in Yiddish, "Take her home; a girl doesn't have to study." Ozick dates her feminism to that time and is especially grateful to her grandmother for bringing her back to school the very next day and insisting that she be accepted. Even the rabbi, to whom Ozick appears to bear no lasting animosity, had occasion to be grateful, for this girl had, as the rabbi would quickly learn, a *goldene kepele* [golden little head] that caught on quickly to the lessons. Ozick owes her knowledge of Yiddish to a certain Rabbi Meskin, a teacher who "taught girls as zealously as he taught boys," and to her grandmother.

At P.S. 71 in the Bronx, the hurt was of a different order. At home and in heder, the young girl was considered intelligent. In school, on the contrary, she was made to feel inadequate. She was, however, excellent in the bookish arts, such as grammar, spelling, reading, and writing. While Ozick describes the Pelham Bay section of the Bronx as a lovely place, she found it "brutally difficult to be a Jew" there. She remembers having stones thrown at her and being called a Christ-killer as she ran past the two churches in her neighborhood. She was particularly uncomfortable in

for success that drives great artists. What does this "seventeen-to-twenty-two-year-old" energetic, ambitious writer, who sees a whole row of luminescent novels on the horizon, have in common with this sixty-six-year-old woman who is resigned to her failures? "I would not trade places with her," shouts Shoshana, "for all the china in Teaneck."

Cynthia Ozick was born in New York City on April 17, 1928, the second of two children. She subsequently moved to the Bronx with her parents, Celia (Regelson) and William Ozick, who were the proprietors of the Park View Pharmacy in the Pelham Bay section. Her parents had come to America from the severe northwest region of Russia. More important for an insight into Ozick's temperament, they came from the Litvak [Lithuanian] Jewish tradition of that school because she would not, on principle, sing the particularly Christian Christmas carols, and was made "a humiliated public example for that." While writing *The Cannibal Galaxy*, a novel set in a Jewish all-day school, she asserts, "I thought of my own suffering, deeply suffering wormlike childhood in grade school; and of my mother's endurances in grade school as an immigrant child. . . . Carelessness in a teacher of small children can burn in impotence for life, like a brand or horrible sign."

All was not dreariness in her childhood, however, for there remained the world of books. In "A Drugstore in Winter," Ozick describes how reading and "certain drugstore winter dusks" came together thanks to the traveling library that arrived in her neighborhood every other week. She recalls that the librarians would come into the Park View Pharmacy after their rounds to have a cup of hot coffee at the fountain. Ozick would come in behind them, having chosen the two fattest volumes from the boxes of books and magazines offered to her. With these books in her hands, she was transported to another world.

She began her reading with fairy tales. From her older brother, she received the perfect birthday present—books. These books had a magical effect, transforming her from a doltish schoolgirl into "who I am"—a reader, and perhaps a writer. "Some day when I am free of P.S. 71, I will write stories. Meanwhile, in winter dusk, in the Park View, in the secret bliss of the Violet Fairy Book, I both see and do not see how these grains of life will stay forever."

Ozick owes her metamorphosis into a writer to the fact that her mother's brother, Abraham Regelson, was a Hebrew poet of no mean reputation. She feels that, somehow, he paved the way for her to embark on such a "strange" career—writer. Because of him, she says, "it seemed quite natural to belong to the secular world of literature." At one time, she attributed her freedom to choose such a "frivolous" career as writer to her gender. "My father loved me," she told an interviewer, "but I think one of the reasons from earliest childhood I felt free to be a writer is that if I had been a boy, I would have had to go be something else."

School became a serious pursuit for Ozick when she entered HUNTER COLLEGE High School in Manhattan. There she was made to feel part of an elite, a Hunter girl, in a place where academic excellence set one apart. Ozick describes this feeling fleetingly in the short story "An Education," in which Una Meyer excels in Latin, and in the long novel, *Trust*, contrasting the heroine's fruitful academic experience with her mother's empty-headed schooling at Miss Jewett's finishing school.

In a reminiscence she entitled "Washington Square, 1946," she tells how, eager for the new life awaiting her in college, she arrived a day early at the as yet unpopulated and therefore desolate campus of Washington Square College of New York University in Greenwich Village. In the Village, she discovers a newsstand that carries the *Partisan Review*, the journal of the literary avant-garde. Ozick will purchase her first non-textbook-book and browse through the Village's secondhand bookstores with the literary longing of youth. She will become a writer.

But first she would have to become an "old man." On graduation from college, Ozick set out for Columbus, Ohio, where, at Ohio State University, she pursued a graduate degree in English literature, earning a master's degree with the thesis "Parable in the Later Novels of Henry James." As she confesses in "The Lesson of the Master," she "became Henry James." She explains how she was influenced by him to become a worshiper of literature, one who, having to choose between ordinary human entanglement—real life—and exclusive devotion to art, chooses art. She chose art over life, she says, to her eternal regret. Ozick asserts that she acted on the teaching of her mentor at the wrong time, while still a youth. It is not clear, however, that she did in fact abandon *la vraie vie*, as Proust puts it, for, at the age of twenty-four, in 1952, she married Bernard Hallote. Upon receiving his degree, he would become a lawyer for the city of New York.

It is true, nevertheless, that during the first thirteen years of her marriage Ozick devoted herself exclusively to what she called "High Art," working on a philosophical novel, *Mercy, Pity, Peace, and Love*, called "MPPL" for short. Ozick would abandon this effort after several years, "a long suck on that Mippel," she would remark wryly. She also spent six and a half years, from 1957 to 1963, on *Trust*, another massive novel, published in 1966.

Ozick underwent a cultural transformation during that time. She became a Jewish autodidact, mastering for herself much of the Jewish textual tradition. Having read, at age twenty-five, Leo Baeck's "Romantic Religion," an essay that "seemed to decode the universe for me," she was further influenced, by Heinrich Graetz's *History of the Jews*, to add a Jewish nuance to *Trust*.

By becoming a "Jewish writer," Ozick did not abandon the world. But she did begin to wrestle with the term "Jewish writer." In 1965, the same year her daughter Rachel—today a Ph.D. in biblical archaeology—was born, she published several poems on Jewish themes in *Judaism* and produced "The Pagan

Rabbi," published in 1966. She also wrote a hilarious short story based loosely on the career of Isaac Bashevis Singer, "Envy; or Yiddish in America," published in *Commentary* in 1969.

Her stature grew quickly. Three of her stories have won first prize in the O. Henry competition, and five of her stories were chosen for republication in the yearly anthologies of *Best American Short Stories*. The editor of the 1984 volume called her one of the three greatest American writers of stories living today. She was nominated for the National Book Award and the PEN/Faulkner Award and won half a dozen coveted awards and grants, including both a Guggenheim and a National Endowment for the Arts Fellowship. She was also given the precious commodity of time in the form of the American Academy of Arts and Letters Mildred and Harold Strauss Living Award for five years to pursue her craft. She has received several honorary doctorates and was invited to deliver the Phi Beta Kappa Oration at Harvard University. In 1986, she was the first recipient of the Michael Rea Award for career contributions to the short story.

After *Trust*, Ozick shied away from the novel, publishing at regular intervals *The Pagan Rabbi and Other Stories* (1971), *Bloodshed and Three Novellas* (1976), and *Levitation: Five Fictions* (1982). She returned to the novel quirkily, as the result of the settlement of a threatened lawsuit by a Jewish day school headmaster who had read himself, justifiably or not, into the 1980 short story, "The Laughter of Akiva." That story, enlarged and completely rewritten, became the novel *The Cannibal Galaxy* (1983). Another novel, *The Messiah of Stockholm* (1987), is sandwiched between two volumes of essays, *Art and Ardor* (1983) and *Metaphor and Memory* (1989). A third volume of essays, *Fame and Folly*, containing pieces on T.S. Eliot, Anthony Trollope, and Isaac Babel, was published in 1996. Meanwhile, in England, an essay collection called *Portrait of the Artist as a Bad Character* has been published.

Of Ozick's fascinating female characters—from Sheindel, the *sheytl*-wearing *rebbetzin* [bewigged rabbi's wife] in "The Pagan Rabbi," to Hester Lilt, the "imagistic linguistic logician" of *The Cannibal Galaxy*, to Rosa, the bag-lady Holocaust survivor of "The Shawl"—none is more beloved by admiring readers than Ruth Puttermesser, the protean heroine of Ozick's 1997 novel, *The Puttermesser Papers*. At first glance, one would characterize Puttermesser neither as heroine nor as beloved. She certainly would not be taken as a role model in either of the worlds to which she clings: the legal profession and the Jewish community, writ large. Most likely modeled on Ozick's

lawyer-husband as much as on the writer herself, Ozick's Puttermesser is beloved for her intelligent and exemplary readings of the Jewish textual tradition, for her practical involvement in the repair of the world, and for her ability to mingle the law with the lore. She is beloved because, although she is finally defeated, like all of us, by entropy, she teaches, by example, that every innocuous butter knife (the meaning of *Puttermesser*) can cut through life to its core of meaning. As Ozick stated in a piece published in a special edition of *Life* magazine on "The Meaning of Life," "Our task is to clothe nature, . . . to impose meaning on being. . . . Our task is the discipline of standing against nature when nature-within-us counsels terrorizing. . . . Our task is to invent civilization."

That is Puttermesser speaking, but it is also Rosa. In 1980, Ozick published, in the *New Yorker*, "The Shawl," two thousand words of finely honed impressionism, a rendering in miniature of the Holocaust in all its horror. A movingly dramatic reading of "The Shawl" by actress Claire Bloom was featured in 1995 on *Jewish Short Stories from Eastern Europe and Beyond*, a National Public Radio series subsequently published on audiocassette by the National Yiddish Book Center. In 1983, again in the *New Yorker*, Ozick published a sequel to "The Shawl," expanding it into "Rosa," a novella whose heft permitted her publisher to issue *The Shawl* (1989) as a separate volume, consisting of the story and the novella. Probably the most widely accessible of Ozick's demanding prose works, it is now found on the reading lists of most college courses on the literature of the Holocaust, along with works by Elie Wiesel and Primo Levi. Ozick told the *Paris Review* in an interview that she would prefer not to make art out of the Holocaust. "I don't want to tamper or invent or imagine, and yet I have done it. I can't not do it. It comes. It invades."

If the Holocaust has invaded Ozick's consciousness—it is present in different guises in "The Pagan Rabbi," "Levitation," and *The Messiah of Stockholm* as well—all the more so has the ugly phenomenon of Holocaust denial invaded her conscience. In an article in the *Washington Post Book World* (January 15, 1995), explaining how she came to write the play *Blue Light* (1994), she relates how, as early as 1961, she came to realize that the world had attenuated the Holocaust into the "Second World War," as though Zyklon B, the deadly gas used to murder Jews, were nothing more than an artifact of war. The road from attenuation to revisionism to Holocaust denial became an increasingly simple one for her to trace.

During her fifth decade as a writer, Ozick became what she has called an "elderly novice." She had long before promised herself that she would one day write for the theater. Eager to wallow in the "delectable theatrical dark," she decided in 1990 to dramatize for the stage "The Shawl" and "Rosa." The play was originally scheduled to be produced by Robert Brustein at the American Repertory Theatre in Cambridge, Massachusetts. Ozick did several rewrites—making the figure of the denier more and more "satanic"—but the production was canceled for budgetary reasons. In 1992, after more revisions, the play received two staged readings in New York at Playwrights Horizons. Its first full-blown production, under the direction of Sidney Lumet, took place at Sag Harbor's Bay Street Theatre. Finally, after fifteen or so revisions, *The Shawl* was produced off-Broadway, at Playhouse 91 of the American Jewish Repertory Theatre, in 1996.

Given Ozick's stature in the literary world, the play received considerable critical attention. Ben Brantley, reviewing it in the *New York Times* (June 21, 1996), was awed by Ozick's power "to let us temporarily, but thoroughly, inhabit someone else's mind." What Brantley missed, however, was Ozick's intention "not to be merciful to the cruel," that is, to the Holocaust deniers.

Although Ozick has only good things to say about Sidney Lumet and the other theater people she has worked with, she has expressed regret that she had to spend so much time on the mechanics and staging of this play, time that otherwise might have been spent "breathing inside a blaze of words," practicing the solitary art of the prose writer. Her recent return to the essay and to prose fiction marks yet another beginning for Ozick, and the product is as fresh as the work of a young experimental novelist. Witness her entry into cyberspace in the fall of 1996 with a ten-day "Diary" on Michael Kinsley's Internet magazine *Slate*. (In the "Diary," Ozick reveals that she has been keeping a private diary since 1953, when she was twenty-five years old.) She has also had pieces on *The Portrait of a Lady* and GERTRUDE STEIN, as well as a fictional account of a visit from a Muscovite cousin published in her regular outlets, the *New York Times Book Review*, the *New York Times Magazine*, and the *New Yorker*. Telling much about the heights that she reaches in American literature today, in 1997 the *New Yorker* published a major essay by Ozick on Dostoyevsky. Posterity will judge whether Fyodor and Shoshana-Cynthia are playing in the same Garden.

SELECTED WORKS BY CYNTHIA OZICK

Art and Ardor (1983); *Bloodshed and Three Novellas* (1976); *Blue Light* (1994); *A Cynthia Ozick Reader* (1996); *Fame and Folly* (1996); *The Cannibal Galaxy* (1983); *Levitation: Five Fictions* (1982); *The Messiah of Stockholm* (1987); *Metaphor and Memory* (1989); *The Pagan Rabbi and Other Stories* (1971); *The Puttermesser Papers* (1997); *The Shawl* (play) (1996); *The Shawl: A Story and Novella* (1989); *Trust* (1966).

BIBLIOGRAPHY

Currier, Susan, and Daniel J. Cahill. "A Bibliography of the Writings of Cynthia Ozick." *Texas Studies in Literature and Language* 25, no. 2 (Summer 1983): 313–321; Lowin, Joseph. *Cynthia Ozick* (1988); Moyers, Bill. "Heritage Conversation with Cynthia Ozick." Transcript, WNET-TV, New York, April 3, 1986; Teicholz, Tom. "[*Paris Review* Interview with] Cynthia Ozick." *Paris Review* 102 (Spring 1987): 154–190.

JOSEPH LOWIN

P

PAKTOR, VERA (1949–1995)

Vera Paktor, who contributed to United States maritime policy as a journalist, lawyer, and administrator, could well be called the "first lady" of the seaways; certainly, at many points in her career, she was the "first woman."

Paktor was born in Budapest, Hungary, on June 14, 1949, to Julian and Serena (Moskovitz) Paktor. She had an older sister, Natalie. The family emigrated to escape the 1956 revolution and came to Chicago; she became a naturalized citizen in 1966. She obtained a degree in journalism from Southern Illinois University at Carbondale in 1972 and certification to practice maritime law in Washington, D.C., in 1981.

In 1977, Paktor was appointed a vice president of Great Lakes and European Lines, the youngest person and first woman to be named a corporate officer in that field. She was district director of the Federal Maritime Commission—again, the first woman appointed to that position—from 1978 to 1981, receiving an award for meritorious service. In 1994, she was the first woman ever to be considered as a candidate for administrator of the commission, a presidential appointment (a retired rear admiral received the position). Paktor also established Communicore Inc., a public relations firm based in Evanston, Illinois, that dealt in maritime issues, served as executive vice president of the United States Great Lakes Shipping Association, and was instrumental in writing the 1985 Maritime Act. She was one of the crew that brought a vintage tugboat via the St. Lawrence Seaway to Chicago in the early 1980s for the Chicago Yacht Club's clubhouse on Lake Michigan. In 1982, she became the first woman elected president of the Propeller Club of the United States, a trade organization for executives in the international maritime industry.

Paktor was a contributing editor for *Seaway Review* and wrote more than a hundred articles on maritime subjects for that publication, including "The U.S. Merchant Marine Academy of Kings Point" (1981), "The Emerging National Maritime Policy" (1982), and "Policy Reform in the U.S. Will Come Only When the Great Lakes Region Mobilizes Its Legislators" (1995). Her *Federal Regulations and the Freight Forwarders* (1992) was the first manual for ships dealing with freight forwarding; this benchmark publication was translated into Spanish in 1995.

In addition, Vera Paktor was active in politics and devoted a great deal of time to the Jewish community in the Chicago area. She managed campaigns for politicians at local and state level, stood for election as Cook County commissioner in 1994 (finishing a close second), and was the youngest member of Mayor Richard M. Daley's Council on Manpower and Economic Advisory Board. She served on the boards of the Bernard Horwich Jewish Community Center, the Mayer Kaplan Jewish Community Center, Temple

Beth El, and Beth Hillel Congregation and also acted as a mentor to many young Jewish individuals.

In 1994, Paktor married Allen Gross, of Chicago. She died on November 15, 1995, in Skokie, Illinois.

BIBLIOGRAPHY

Gross, Allen [husband]. Interview with author, Chicago, Ill., 1996; Nelson, Natalie [sister]. Interview with author, Maggie Valley, N.C., 1996; Obituary. *Skokie News*, November 15, 1995.

ANNETTE MUFFS BOTNICK

PALEY, GRACE (b. 1922)

"'Men are different than women,' said Joanna, 'and it's the only thing she says in this entire story'" ("A Woman, Young and Old"). Much of Paley's fiction elaborates this apparently simple observation, calling attention to the act of writing, which complicates all such simplicities.

Paley has written highly acclaimed short stories, poetry, and reflections on contemporary politics and culture. Her settings are primarily urban, taking her readers to the apartments, playgrounds, and streets of New York. Her characters are usually women who speak in the first person. Often they are Jewish, and always they are concerned with questions of relationship. The protagonists she creates are not heroic in the traditional sense of the word, but they manage surprisingly well in a world that seems less than friendly.

Paley's literary prominence is the result of almost three decades of writing during which she has produced three volumes of short stories critics invariably describe as highly crafted. After *The Little Disturbances of Man* appeared in 1959, she received a Guggenheim Fellowship (1961) and a National Endowment for the Arts Award (1966). *Enormous Changes at the Last Minute* was published in 1974, followed by *Later the Same Day* in 1985, the year in which her first collection of poems, *Leaning Forward*, appeared. In 1980, she was elected to the American Academy of Arts and Letters. In 1986, she was awarded a PEN/Faulkner Prize for fiction and also named the first State Author of New York. In 1987, she received a National Endowment for the Arts Senior Fellowship. In addition to Paley's *New and Collected Poems* (1992), she and her friend Vera B. Williams produced two volumes of stories, poems, reflections on contemporary life, and illustrations; *365 Reasons Not to Have Another War* was first published as a date book by the War Resisters League and New Society Publishers (1988) and reis-

sued with additions by the Feminist Press as *Long Walks and Intimate Talks* (1991).

The youngest of three children, Grace Goodside Paley was born into a comfortably middle-class family living in the Bronx. Her parents were Ukrainian socialists who came to the United States in 1906, after both had been arrested for participating in workers' demonstrations and one year after her father's brother had been killed by the czarist police. (Paley memorialized this event in her story "In This Country, but in Another Language, My Aunt Refuses to Marry the Men Everyone Wants Her To.") Within a few months, the couple's first child, Victor, was born, followed two years later by a daughter, Jeanne. Grace was born fourteen years later, on December 11, 1922. By then, her working-class father had gone to medical school and established a successful practice. His mother and two sisters had followed the young couple to America and lived with them. The family's native Russian was augmented by the Yiddish spoken by the elder Mrs. Goodside and on the Bronx streets, where English vied for prominence with other languages. The cadences of Russian and Yiddish speech continue to resonate in Paley's fiction.

Following an undistinguished period of study in high school and college, Grace dropped out of school and held various office jobs, occasionally taking courses as well. A class she took with W.H. Auden at the New School for Social Research was to prove especially significant. Auden read his young student's poetry and advised her to echo the spoken language in which she lived rather than the language of some literary ideal about which she may have read. She took his advice both in the poetry she continued to write and the short stories she began writing more than a decade later.

In 1942, Grace married Jess Paley. They had two children (Nora, born in 1949, and Danny, born in 1951). The couple separated in the late 1960s and divorced in 1972, the year in which she married Bob Nichols, a family friend and political ally. She has taught briefly at a number of New York universities (Columbia, NYU, Syracuse, and City) and for twenty-two years (1966–1988) at Sarah Lawrence, whose Bronxville campus is geographically near but socially remote from the Bronx neighborhood of her childhood.

Recognized as an accomplished writer of short fiction, Paley is equally renowned as a political activist, a role that began, as it might have for many of the characters she has created, as an extension of PTA activities in her children's school. The combination of neighborhood and, increasingly, global concerns led her to a prominent role in the peace movement of the

Grace Paley is not only an accomplished writer of short fiction but also a political activist. When she was arrested in 1977 for unfurling an antinuclear armaments banner on the White House lawn, the judge asked her, "When will you stop [protesting]?" "I'm getting old. Pretty soon, I'll stop," replied Paley. She hasn't stopped yet. The above photo was taken at an antinuclear speak-out in February of 1979. [Bettye Lane]

1960s and a series of often controversial trips to some of the world's most troubled nations, among them North Vietnam in 1969, Chile in 1972, the Soviet Union in 1973, Nicaragua and El Salvador in 1985, and Israel in 1987.

Paley was one of the founders in 1987 of the Jewish Women's Committee to End the Occupation of the Left Bank and Gaza and has been an outspoken advocate of Palestinian rights. That activity is significant as an indication of her engagement in women's issues, as well as her recent concern with Israel. In her fiction, she has created characters who speak eloquently on behalf of the diaspora. One of the most explicit and often-cited examples of such views can be found in "The Used-Boy Raisers," written in the 1950s, when Israel was barely a decade old. In this story, Faith, the central character of a cycle of short stories that span Paley's writing career, reflects on her relationship to her two husbands and to Jewish concerns. Denying any knowledge of the significance of the kaddish, Faith rejects Israel "on technical grounds" as well. "I believe in the Diaspora," she tells her former and present husband, insisting that once Jews are "huddled in one little corner of a desert, they're like anyone else.... Jews have one hope only—to remain a remnant in the basement of world affairs . . . a splinter in the toe of civilizations, a victim to aggravate the conscience," a function Paley herself has certainly served in her political life.

Paley's stories often reflect on a range of Jewish identity issues of concern to contemporary, largely assimilated urban American communities. She has not created characters who are religiously observant, or Zionists, or committed to particularly Jewish causes. No matter what their age, marital status, or work, her Jewish characters are liberal, modern figures. Those who are immigrants speak a Yiddish-inflected English. Their offspring speak in less foreign tones but share the political and social commitments of the elders with whom they may nonetheless argue. In "Zagrowsky Tells," for example, readers once again meet Faith, this time confronting the old pharmacist Zagrowsky and the black child whom Faith cannot believe is his grandson. Faith reminds Zagrowsky that in the past he was considered a racist and sexist, asserting that the only reason his attitudes were tolerated was that "it wasn't time yet in history to holler." His rejoinder is to note parenthetically "(an American-born girl has some nerve to mention history)." In such invocations of the Eastern European Jewish past, readers encounter a characteristic of Paley's writing that may be thought of as oblique confrontation. Differences between opposing figures—men and women, parents and children, young and old, police and demonstrators—are not minimized in Paley's stories. Rather, conflicts are resolved or left suspended among pithy, trenchant verbal exchanges that activate a psychic or physical world the interlocutor may not have considered.

Most often, Paley's speakers are women pondering the nature of friendship, love, or family. The stories in which we find them frequently parody traditional romantic tales, as the subtitle of her first volume would indicate. When *The Little Disturbances of Man* appeared in 1959, it carried the subtitle "Stories of Women and Men at Love," calling attention to the deliberate skewing of established tropes. (When it was reissued, that bold title was tamed, rendered into the less oppositional "Stories of Men and Women in Love.") Paley's protagonists speak in equally irreverent, earthy tones about social and sexual intercourse, "that noisy disturbance," as the latter is called in "Enormous Changes at the Last Minute." At the same time, such women also take enormous pleasure in love. Despite their abandonment by men, their struggles to raise children alone in a community of other mothers, or the presence of men who are able to father children but not to raise them, these women revel in the life of the body. Only on the last page of her most recent volume of stories has Paley admitted a character whose physical life has nothing to do with men. In "Listening," Cassie complains that Faith is willing to tell "everyone's story but mine." Rather than the insistent focus on women and men, she asks, "Where the hell is my woman and woman, woman-loving life in all this? . . . Why have you left me out of everybody's life?" It is an accusation that Faith, often a stand-in for the writer herself, immediately accepts as just. To be left out of the story, silenced or unheard, is a wrong individuals must counter as if their very lives depended on it.

Although questions about both Jewish and female identity are significant in Paley's stories, they yield to the unmistakable precedence she gives to speech. Central to the structure and themes of every text Paley has written is talk: the words of anger, uncertainty or, more commonly, love and acceptance that characters utter to one another, to themselves, and to the reader.

The ability to reconcile the sounds of Yiddish, Russian, Polish, and English, along with the signs of Jewish and Christian culture, depends on the ability to speak up loudly and clearly. In their commonsense approach to the world around them, as in their use of irony and clever banter, Paley's characters give new, quite literal significance to the idea of living by one's wits.

Telling stories is, then, an enterprise that matters tremendously in Paley's stories, and she includes frequent allusions to the craft of writing. The autobiographical narrator of "A Conversation with My Father" wants to please her father, who wishes she would write "a simple story . . . just recognizable people and then write down what happened to them next." But she cannot write a story driven by plot, "the absolute line between two points," because such a construction "takes all hope away. Everyone, real or invented, deserves the open destiny of life." It is certainly not simplicity or comprehensibility that Paley disavows, but rather the determinism of conclusive, linear stories. As another autobiographical narrator in "Debts" explains, uttering what may sound like Grace Paley's literary manifesto, the storyteller's obligation to family and friends is "to tell their stories as simply as possible, in order, you might say, to save a few lives."

SELECTED WORKS BY GRACE PALEY

The Collected Stories (1994); *Enormous Changes at the Last Minute* (1974); *Later the Same Day* (1985); *Leaning Forward: Poems* (1985); *The Little Disturbances of Man* (1959); *Long*

Walks and Intimate Talks (1991); *New and Collected Poems* (1992); *365 Reasons Not to Have Another War* (1988).

BIBLIOGRAPHY

Aarons, Victoria. "A Perfect Marginality: Public and Private Telling in the Stories of Grace Paley." *Studies in Short Fiction* 27, no. 1 (Winter 1990): 35–43; Areana, Judith. *Grace Paley's Life Stories: A Literary Biography* (1993); Baba, Minako. "Faith Darwin as Writer-Heroine: A Study of Grace Paley's Short Stories." *Studies in American Jewish Literature* 7, no. 1 (Spring 1988): 40–54; Kamel, Rose. "To Aggravate the Conscience: Grace Paley's Loud Voice." *Journal of Ethnic Studies* 11 (1989): 305–319; Lyons, Bonnie. "Grace Paley's Jewish Miniatures." *Studies in American Jewish Literature* 8, no. 1 (Spring 1989): 26–33; Satz, Martha. "Looking at Disparities: An Interview with Grace Paley." *Southwest Review* 72 (Autumn 1987): 478–489; Taylor, Jacqueline. *Grace Paley: Illuminating the Dark Lives* (1990).

ANITA NORICH

PARKER, DOROTHY ROTHSCHILD (1893–1967)

Brilliant, unrelenting, and fiercely witty, Dorothy Rothschild Parker came to signify the urbane and irreverent sensibility of New York City in the 1920s. As an adult, Parker rarely spoke of her family and Upper West Side upbringing, although she often hinted that her past had been tragic. The youngest of three siblings by many years, Dorothy was born on August 22, 1893 to a Jewish father, J. Henry Rothschild, and a Scottish mother, Eliza (Marston) Rothschild. Eliza Rothschild died when Parker was five years old, an event that devastated the child. Soon thereafter, her father, who had made a small fortune in the garment industry, married a strict Roman Catholic, whom Dorothy bitterly disliked.

As a young girl, she attended, and despised, a Catholic school in Manhattan, later transferring to Miss Dana's, a boarding school. Henry Rothschild told the school authorities that his daughter was Episcopalian, but her dark Jewishness marked her as an outsider. She would always maintain this image of herself, and in the face of early alienation and many disappointments, she developed a biting and irreverent sense of humor. Late in life, she described herself as "one of those awful children who wrote verses," but despite her writerly inclinations, she left school abruptly at age fourteen, never to return, to take care of her ill father, who was once again a widower. When he died in 1913, the twenty-year-old Dorothy made a living by playing piano at a Manhattan dance school.

In 1917, she married Edwin Pond Parker II; it was a marriage doomed to years of alcohol-soaked pain and eventual dissolution. A stockbroker from a prestigious Hartford, Connecticut, family, the handsome Edwin Parker shared Dorothy's love of excitement and had the advantage of what she later termed "a nice, clean name." Shortly after their wedding, Edwin went off to war, leaving Dorothy alone in New York. That same year, she became a staff writer at *Vanity Fair* magazine, and quickly distinguished herself there with her cutting and well-turned humor. In 1918, at age twenty-five and with little tolerance for the popular theater (although she would later write four plays herself), she succeeded P.G. Wodehouse as *Vanity Fair*'s drama critic. It was an unprecedented position for a woman of any age at that time. Parker was an immediate success: notoriously vicious, and notoriously funny. "If you don't knit, bring a book,"

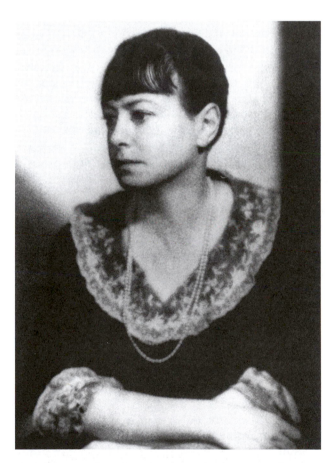

One of the most shrewdly sensitive and elegant satirists of the twentieth century, Dorothy Rothschild Parker wrote best-selling poetry, successful short stories, and classic screenplays but was never satisfied with her work. Most commonly connected with the famous Algonquin Round Table, at the end of her life she disparaged it and the decadent life-style she and other Round Table members led. [New York Public Library]

she moaned in one review. When she lost her job in 1920, after her famously tart reviews offended the sensibilities of the theater elite, Robert Benchley, her close friend and fellow *Vanity Fair* writer, resigned in protest. It was, Parker said, "the greatest act of friendship I'd known."

Parker, Benchley, and Robert Sherwood (also of *Vanity Fair*) lunched regularly at the Algonquin Hotel with a small group of self-publicizing writers eager to create a legend out of their own banter, bons mots, insults, and decrees. In addition to the *Vanity Fair* trio, the "Algonquin Round Table" included newspapermen Alexander Woollcott and Harold Ross (who would found the *New Yorker* magazine in 1925) and, in subsequent years, EDNA FERBER, Harpo Marx, Tallulah Bankhead, and other notable figures in literary and theatrical circles. The Round Table was the perfect forum for Parker's incomparably quick tongue, and soon her quietly dropped words became those most listened for. Asked during this period to use the word "horticulture" in a sentence, she famously responded, "You can lead a horticulture, but you can't make her think." She rarely failed to surprise and delight her eager audience, and her droll asides were circulated throughout sophisticated New York circles.

But despite her growing fame and the endless parties where she always took center stage, Parker was miserable. Lurking behind her quest for fun was a growing sense of desperation, as her short poem "The Flaw in Paganism" indicates:

> Drink and dance and laugh and lie,
> Love, the reeling midnight through,
> For tomorrow we shall die!
> (But, alas, we never do.)

Her insistent hopefulness always seemed to be sideswiped by catastrophe or disappointment—as she put it, "laughter, hope and a sock in the eye." She was deeply dissatisfied with the free-lance magazine writing she did in the 1920s, had serious money problems, and was involved in a succession of painfully brief love affairs with men who cared little for her. All these troubles led to two failed suicide attempts, in 1923 (following an abortion) and 1925. Her marriage to the morphine- and alcohol-addicted Edwin Parker finally ended in 1928. Through her worst years, Parker maintained a tough-talking and hard-drinking public exterior, scoffing at her own misery with blasé humor.

At the suggestion of a friend, she collected a volume of her poetry in 1926 to pay for an overseas trip, although she herself felt her verse was not good enough for a book. To her great surprise, *Enough Rope* became an instant best-seller, rare for a book of poems. In this and subsequent successful volumes of poetry—*Sunset Gun* (1928), *Death and Taxes* (1931), and *Not So Deep as a Well* (1936)—Parker poked fun at her own heartbreak, masochism, and hopefulness. Her most effective verse captures the breadth of her dreams and disappointments with bitter irony and perfect turns of phrase, but only hints at their depths.

Parker's stories, like her poetry, resonate with heartache and disenchantment, and reflect her obsessions: incessant alcohol consumption, spoiled romance, social injustice, and the follies of the rich. Her most acclaimed story, "Big Blond," won the O. Henry Prize in 1929. It depicts the drunken loneliness, male dependence, and increasing desperation of an aging "kept woman." Like many of Parker's stories, it highlights, with intense and desolate intimacy, the lack of possibilities faced by many women. Other stories have been collected in *Laments for the Living* (1930), *After Such Pleasures* (1933), and *Here Lies* (1939). Parker also produced a great deal of literary criticism, published over many decades in the *New Yorker* (under the title "Constant Reader") and, from 1958 to 1963, in *Esquire*. These reviews were often penned with the same unblinking brutality as her earlier drama reviews (of A.A. Milne's *The House at Pooh Corner*, she said, "Tonstant Weader Fwowed Up"), although as often they were generously sensitive and enthusiastic.

Despite her cynicism, Parker was deeply earnest about politics and maintained a lifelong, if intermittent, commitment to activism. She surprised her New York friends in the 1920s when she was arrested while marching for the release of the anarchists Sacco and Vanzetti. In later years, she went to Spain to work against Franco in the Spanish Civil War ("the proudest thing" she ever did), organized Hollywood screenwriters, and was blacklisted in the 1950s for her pro-Left views. While she still spent many weekends at the homes of rich friends, the pleasures she took in wealth were always mingled with fierce disdain.

In 1934, at age forty, Parker married the writer Alan Campbell, who was eleven years her junior. The couple became a Hollywood screenwriting team whose credits included the original *A Star Is Born* (1937). Although she found it hard to refuse the huge paychecks, Parker was not proud of her work in Hollywood and felt (as she did about reviewing) that screenwriting kept her from serious literary engagement. She was able to produce stories and poems only sporadically in the 1930s and later years, and never reached the level of productivity to which she aspired nor wrote the novel she had always dreamed of writing. Campbell, who was also half-Jewish, adored her, but was often eclipsed by her powerful talent and personality. Their relationship was complicated by economic woes, as well as their ongoing alcoholism and his homosexuality. The couple divorced in 1947, remarried in 1950, separated in 1953, and reconciled again in 1956, staying together until Campbell's death in 1963.

Before her lonely death in New York on June 7, 1967, Parker disparaged the life that she and other Round Tablers had led. She also judged her own writing harshly as derivative and not living up to her promise. "I was following in the exquisite footsteps of Miss Edna St. Vincent Millay," she once claimed, "unhappily in my own horrible sneakers." Elsewhere she said that she had been "just a little Jewish girl trying to be cute." However, her work uniquely catalogued society's random pretensions and her own tough, intimate longings. She remains one of the most shrewdly sensitive and elegant satirists of the twentieth century.

SELECTED WORKS BY DOROTHY PARKER

After Such Pleasures (1933); *Death and Taxes* (1931); *Enough Rope* (1926); *Here Lies* (1939); *Laments for the Living* (1930); *Not So Deep as a Well* (1936); *The Portable Dorothy Parker* (1976); *Sunset Gun* (1928); *A Star Is Born*, with Alan Campbell (screenplay) (1939).

BIBLIOGRAPHY

BEOAJ; Cooper, Wyatt. "Remembering Dorothy Parker." *Esquire* (July 1968); *DAB* 8; *EJ*; Gaines, James R. *Wits End: Days and Nights of the Algonquin Round Table* (1977); Harriman, Margaret Case. *The Vicious Circle: The Story of the Algonquin Round Table* (1951); Hellman, Lillian. *An Unfinished Woman: A Memoir* (1969); Keats, John. *You Might as Well Live: The Life and Times of Dorothy Parker* (1970); Meade, Marion. *Dorothy Parker: What Fresh Hell Is This?* (1989); *NAW* modern; Obituary. *NYTimes*, June 8, 1967, 1:2; Parker, Dorothy. Interview, June 1959. Oral History Collection, Columbia University, NYC, and Interview. In *Writers at Work: The Paris Review Interviews*, edited by Malcolm Cowley (1958); *UJE*; Woollcott, Alexander. "Our Mrs. Parker." In *The Portable Woollcott* (1946); *WWWIA* 4.

DANIEL ITZKOVITZ

PARNIS, MOLLIE (c. 1905–1992)

Mollie Parnis's wit and fashion savvy made her clothing designs a must among many first ladies during her tenure as fashion legend. Throughout her reign on Seventh Avenue in New York's fashion district, Parnis often gave voice to a very spirited manifesto that strongly expressed how she governed her fashion house. She explained her idea of fashion with a mix of practical theory and a disciplined manner of observation. "Fashion is individual, not a series of rules," she maintained staunchly, when defining the standards necessary in beautifying the female body. Fashion was meant to enhance the intrinsic beauty of a woman, not overpower her. Adhering to this philosophy allowed her to uphold her reputation as a directed and driven perfectionist, not interested in starting fads, but instead in complimenting and assisting the very essence of a woman. "My clothes have a little sex. Too much is obvious. And anyway, I have put the sexiest dresses on some dames and nothing helps," she once stated.

Parnis never discussed her age in public or validated any dates ever proposed by journalists. However, the most accurate and probable date of her birth was March 18, 1905. Born in Brooklyn, but raised mostly in Manhattan's Lower East Side, Mollie, her three sisters, and brother experienced a lower-middle-class upbringing, with very few extras to help ignite the eventual fashion careers of three of the siblings. In later years, her sister Jerry, with husband Ben Cahane, headed the design firm of Jerry Parnis, Incorporated, an apparel manufacturing company that mass-produced moderately priced dresses. Peggy Parnis married Sol Hochman, owner of Chevette, Incorporated, and became head designer of his lingerie company.

Both parents, Abraham and Sara (Rosen) Parnis, were Jews who had emigrated from Linberg, Austria, at the turn of the century. Her father sold butter and eggs wholesale until he died when Mollie was ten. At that point, the family's finances were the responsibility of her mother, who went to work immediately. The older children worked as well. At age eight, Mollie Parnis began her first career as an English tutor to foreigners for twenty-five cents per hour. With the support of her family she attended Wadleigh High, on the Upper West Side, and soon after graduation her first and only pursuit at formal education came with her enrollment at HUNTER COLLEGE. Her intention was to study law, but her attempt was overshadowed by her ultimate vocation.

Her interest in fashion may have been precipitated in part by an incident in high school. Since amenities were few, ingenuity and necessity prevailed when a high school classmate asked her to a party after a football rally. Having no other dress than the navy blue serge she had been wearing at the rally, she quickly raced home to rearrange and redesign the only day dress she owned. While snipping the neckline, adding lace, and sewing on the finishing touch of an artificial flower, her first creation was realized. This momentary scene in Parnis's young adult life may have been the subconscious stimulus for her entry into an industry that she would, in due time, enrich and influence on many levels.

With the help and encouragement of a family connection, at age eighteen Parnis was hired to work as an assistant saleswoman for a wholesale blouse manufacturer. At the blouse company, she impressed the owners with her eye for detail and her ability to satisfy the needs of retail buyers by adding finishing touches on blouses to create distinction and a variety of style. Instead of giving Parnis a raise, the owners added her name to the building directory, arousing her first taste of fame. "Well, you don't know what that did for me," she said. "I got so excited over it, I had all my friends come over to Seventh Avenue to look at 'Mollie Parnis, 4th Floor.' It was like an actress having her name up in lights for the first time."

Her next position, in 1929, was as a stylist for the dress house of David Westheim. This was a particularly auspicious move, as she met there Leon Livingston (originally Levinson), a textile salesman, and married him on June 26, 1930. For three years, Parnis was a wife and a mother to her only child, Robert. By 1933, during the height of the Depression, when most manufacturers were going out of business, Parnis and her husband opened the doors of Parnis Livingston, Incorporated.

In the beginning, Livingston was the business talent, while Parnis dominated the creative direction of the company. Their success was due in part to Parnis's ability to oversee a staff of designers who could interpret and carry to fruition her vision of fashion. Although unable to cut, sew, or draw herself, having never had any type of design education, Parnis engineered her business with an astute eye for detail and knowledge of what the American woman wanted in her wardrobe. In no time, the husband and wife business partnership secured for Parnis Livingston the position of a major silk-dress house on Seventh Avenue.

From this point on, Mollie Parnis's designs were characterized by quality, fit, and the essential use of refined fabrics. Her unique styling sense gave women over the age of thirty the opportunity to dress with elegance and beauty without compromising the integrity of the form and function of the dress or the individual body. Throughout the 1940s and 1950s, and even until the early 1980s, Parnis's creations graced the style and advertising pages of *Vogue, Harper's Bazaar, Vanity Fair,* and *Life,* among other magazines. Her designs were photographed by fashion giants such as Horst P. Horst, Toni Frissell, and Louise Dahl-Wolfe. By 1966, a Parnis dress had made the cover of *Harper's Bazaar* with the caption, "50 great American dresses for the year of the dress." Parnis had arrived.

The death of her husband in 1962 ended the Parnis Livingston business partnership. However, within three months the company reopened its doors and evolved. The strategy for the second phase of the dress house was engineered, in part, to fulfill the economic and life-style needs of the metamorphic American woman. Secondary lines, such as the "Mollie Parnis Boutique Collection," debuted in 1970, under the direction of Mollie Parnis and with the design talent of Morty Sussman. At this time, two new labels were developed in response to a rising informal popular culture that had expanded the roles and demands of women in the home and in the workplace. The "Mollie Robert" label was formed to provide working women with affordable styling, while "Mollie Parnis Studio" directed its efforts toward the younger, independent consumer just entering the work force.

The prestige house of Mollie Parnis remained strong with the design influence of George Samen, until 1984, when Parnis closed her doors on Seventh Avenue for the last time. Unable to completely leave the business she had grown up in, she developed "Mollie Parnis at Home," a lounge-wear collection for Chevette Lingerie in the fall of 1985. Regardless of the price points of her creations, an overview of Parnis's work shows a strict adherence to a very contemporary and constantly reinventive outlook. She never strayed from her policy of excellence in her vision of elegant clothing. She knew better than most that fashion is a temporal medium that expresses itself most succinctly within a particular period and, although she did not believe in creating curiosities, she always seized the opportunity to present the height of fine fashion to the American woman.

Aside from her devotion to her profession, Parnis's famous Sunday evening salons were the highlight and the result of her commitment to sustain a broad life-style. Complete with art and music, and featuring an intimate circle of prominent politicians, journalists, (of particular interest to her), writers, artists, and New York socialites, an evening with Parnis was designed to capture the spirit of a true epicurean. Her gracious manner allowed her guests the freedom and ease to speak candidly with regard to all topics. Parnis was noted for her art collecting; her salon evenings would end with a viewing of a Matisse (her most prized possession), or an Utrillo or Cézanne, bought with great admiration for the beauty they bestowed on her private surroundings, both on Park Avenue and her weekend home in Katonah, New York.

Her generosity was often reciprocated, with dinner invitations extended from a roster of famous homes. Frequently chosen to visit the White House, Parnis often said that she wished her friends could see her now, shaking hands with the president and dressing the first lady. On one occasion in 1955, Mamie Eisenhower reportedly wore a green and blue silk taffeta Parnis dress to a Washington dinner, only to be met in the receiving line by a duplicate worn by a guest. In response to the fanfare at the time, Parnis declared that her designs were not singular in nature but were analogous to the great democracy of the United States. This incident did not dissuade Mrs. Eisenhower from purchasing future Parnis dresses, nor Bess Truman, Lady Bird Johnson, or Patricia Nixon.

Parnis also was a noted humanitarian. In 1971, she donated prize money to city programs such as "Dress up Your Neighborhood" and helped to create and promote vest-pocket parks throughout the New York boroughs. The success of these efforts led to her funding of a sister program in Jerusalem in 1973, to help beautify one of the oldest cities in the world.

In 1984, Parnis established the Mollie Parnis Livingston Foundation, which gave over $1.5 million to various charities. She contributed scholarships to fashion schools throughout the city and became a board member of the Parsons School of Design, which presented her with an honorary doctorate in 1989. In addition, Parnis was a founding member of the Council of Fashion Designers of America, and she also served on the board.

Perhaps her most availing philanthropic effort was the formation of the Livingston Awards, in honor of her son, Robert Livingston, publisher of *More Magazine*. His death in 1979 precipitated the development of three annual grants and citations for excellence for journalists under the age of thirty-five in all branches of media. Although Parnis never accomplished her dream of completing college, she made it possible for others to achieve their goals and hopes for the future.

Mollie Parnis died on July 18, 1992.

BIBLIOGRAPHY

Bender, Marilyn. *The Beautiful People* (1967); "Blue-Green on the National Scene." *Life* (April 25, 1955); *Current Biography* (1956); "Dead, Mollie Parnis." *NYTimes*, August 3, 1992; Friedman, Arthur. "Memories of Mollie Parnis." *Women's Wear Daily*, September 16, 1992; Lambert, Eleanor. *World of Fashion* (1965); Lurie, Diana. "Close-Up: When Mollie Parnis Thinks a Dress Will Sell, It Goes." *Life* (June 17, 1966); *McDowell's Dictionary of Twentieth Century Fashion* (1985); Martin, Richard, ed. *Contemporary Fashion* (1995); Morris, Bernadine, and Barbara Walz. *The Fashion Makers* (1978); Murrow, Edward R. "Mollie Parnis at Home." *Person to Person*. CBS, September 1955. Video; Naylor, Colin, ed. *Contemporary Designers*. 2nd ed. (1991); Parnis, Mollie. Costume collections. Costume Institute, Metropolitan Museum of Art, NYC, and Fashion Institute of Technology Museum, NYC. Designer files. Costume Institute Library; Stagemeyer, Anne. *Who's Who in Fashion* (1996); "A Woman of Many Modes: Mollie Parnis Dead at 93." *Women's Wear Daily*, July 20, 1992.

DIANE LADA

PEACE MOVEMENT

Throughout the twentieth century, Jewish women have played a major role in American peace organizations and movements. In the 1980s, they began to form a Jewish women's peace movement in their own name.

The contemporary American Jewish women's peace movement draws its roots from several earlier movements and organizations: the early work of the NATIONAL COUNCIL OF JEWISH WOMEN (NCJW); women's peace groups such as the Women's International League for Peace and Freedom (WILPF) and Women Strike for Peace (WSP); the various movements for social justice in the United States, especially the civil rights and anti–Vietnam War movements; the feminist movement, and the development of a specifically *Jewish* feminism; Jewish groups in the diaspora formed to question Israeli policies regarding war, peace, and the Palestinians; and, especially, the Israeli women's peace movement.

A LONG HISTORY OF ORGANIZING FOR PEACE

As early as 1908, more than a decade before other national Jewish organizations addressed the problem, the National Council of Jewish Women created a Committee on Peace and Arbitration to study the causes of war. Under the leadership of FANNY BRIN, the committee brought pacifist ideas before the membership through articles placed in NCJW publications, resolutions calling for the abolition of war, and speeches by well-known pacifists. Among the keynote speakers at NCJW assemblies were Jeannette Rankin, the first woman member of Congress and a pacifist who voted against World War I, and suffragist Carrie Chapman Catt.

NCJW affiliated with the Women's International League for Peace and Freedom, founded in 1915 to promote cooperation among women of all nations in pursuing peace based on social and economic justice. In 1925, NCJW participated with eleven other women's organizations in a National Conference on the Cause and Cure of War. Representing millions of women, the coalition lobbied for United States endorsement of the World Court and the League of Nations and called for international legislation against war. With WILPF, NCJW called on the government to reduce military budgets, worked for passage of a law outlawing chemical and biological weapons, and demanded a prohibition against United States declarations of war without a national referendum.

In addition to the NCJW's organizational involvement in peace efforts, individual Jewish women have long been active in peace organizations such as WILPF, WSP, and the movement to end American involvement in the Vietnam War.

Women Strike for Peace began on November 1, 1961, when thousands of mothers staged a national one-day protest to "End the Arms Race, Not the Human Race." WSP protested the toxic effects of nuclear testing and was influential in the signing of the first international test ban treaty; initiated the measurement of radiation resulting from nuclear test emissions and focused public attention on the radia-

tion contamination of milk; established a Clearing House on the Economics of Disarmament, which challenged the popular belief that military spending is good for the economy; and demonstrated the benefits of conversion to a peace-oriented economy.

When the House Committee on Un-American Activities (HUAC), attempting to discredit the peace movement, served subpoenas on fourteen members of WSP in 1962, the organization used media savvy, ridicule, humor, and theater so creatively that they struck a crucial blow at HUAC itself. WSP members filled the audience, brought babies into the hearing room, gave roses to the subpoenaed witnesses, and scolded the hearing officers in schoolmarm tones, simultaneously proclaiming their moral opposition to the arms race. Portions of the press, already becoming critical of HUAC, gave WSP substantial and favorable coverage.

By 1967, WSP was demonstrating against the Vietnam War, uniting its antiwar activities with the struggle for civil rights, and occasionally practicing civil disobedience. They formed a new women's antiwar coalition named the Jeannette Rankin Brigade

Women Strike for Peace began on November 1, 1961, when thousands of mothers staged a national one-day protest to "End the Arms Race, Not the Human Race." Jewish women have from the beginning been extremely active in the organization. This May 1978 photograph shows BELLA ABZUG, *one of the founders of WSP, leading a march against the Vietnam War. [Bettye Lane]*

in honor of the eighty-seven-year-old pacifist's militant nonviolent stance against war and conducted a "die-in," a sit-in, and a Women's March on the Pentagon.

Among the notable Jewish members of Women Strike for Peace were AMY SWERDLOW, BELLA ABZUG (who won election to Congress with WSP support), PEARL WILLEN (former president of the NCJW), and Cora Weiss, a leading member of WILPF. They joined such prominent civil rights leaders as Rosa Parks, Fannie Lou Hamer, and Coretta Scott King in the endeavor.

WSP explicitly stressed women's concerns, practices, and philosophical approaches to questions of war and peace. Having begun with conventional, middle-class housewives' conceptions of the social role of women, basing their political efforts outside the home on their roles as mothers, WSP members gradually came to question those traditional definitions. By the 1970s, their daughters' generation was forming the second wave of the American feminist movement and challenging war as "masculinist" behavior, related to the subordination of women.

Simultaneously, Jewish women, many of whom were participants in the feminist second wave, began to challenge the subordination of women within the Jewish religion, American Jewish communities and organizations, and Israeli society. As a peace movement developed within Israel, Israeli women expressed dissatisfaction with their exclusion from important roles within it.

JEWISH PEACE MOVEMENTS AND THE ISRAELI-PALESTINIAN CONFLICT

An explicitly Jewish peace movement emerged out of a confluence of forces in the 1970s. The 1967 war and Israel's annexation of the West Bank, Gaza, Sinai, and Golan changed the physical and political terrain of Israel. It altered the relationship between the United States and Israel, newly focusing the attention of United States Jews on Israel. It transformed the nature of Palestinian political movements and fostered peace movements within Israel and the diaspora.

Although Tandi, the "Movement of [Palestinian and Jewish] Democratic Women in Israel," had formed as early as 1948 to work for peace and equal rights for women and children, it stood largely alone until a number of Israeli peace movements organized in the 1970s. In 1975, Marsha Freedman, an American-born member of the Israeli Knesset elected with the support of the Israeli women's movement, advocated a "two-state solution" to the Israeli-Palestinian conflict, that is, negotiations toward a Palestinian state along-

side Israel. In 1978, Peace Now formed in Israel, and American Friends of Peace Now in the United States.

Within the United States, Jews began to form organizations such as Breira (1973–1978), proposing that the Israeli Labor Party pursue peace more affirmatively. In 1980, New Jewish Agenda formed as "a progressive voice within the Jewish community and a Jewish voice within the Left community." A multi-issue group, it, too, soon focused on promoting the two-state solution.

The 1982 war in Lebanon created a turning point in the formation of Israeli-Palestinian peace movements. The massacres at Sabra and Shatilla refugee camps of hundreds of Palestinians, predominantly women and children, by Lebanese Falange forces under Israeli military supervision caused painful soul-searching and protest demonstrations by Jewish women and men in Israel and in the diaspora. Four hundred thousand Israelis, constituting 10 percent of the Israeli people, demonstrated against the war and the massacres. Thousands of Jews and non-Jews demonstrated throughout the diaspora.

The International Jewish Peace Union (IJPU), formed in Paris in 1982 in response to the Lebanon War, was quite male-oriented. Among the organizers of American chapters, however, were Ellen Siegel, who had practiced nursing (and seen conditions firsthand) in Lebanon, Hannah Davis (also a member of New Jewish Agenda), and Ellisa Sampson, an observant Jew with a long history of activism and political analysis dating back to her experiences living in Israel from 1972 to 1978. Sampson led the New York chapter.

The IJPU initially concentrated on the Israeli incursion into Lebanon and supported Yesh Gvul, a movement of Israeli soldiers who refused to serve in the occupied territories. Later, influenced by an increasingly female membership and by the activities of the Israeli, Palestinian, and Jewish American women's peace movements, the IJPU also organized medical relief in Lebanon and the territories, most of whose recipients were women.

FEMINISM, PEACE, AND THE ISRAELI-PALESTINIAN CONFLICT

In the 1970s and 1980s, the Israeli-Palestinian conflict moved Jewish women to act for peace in their own name as Jews and as women. Initially, however, the response to this conflict brought about splintering within the feminist movement, within peace groups, and among Jews themselves. Many Jews who had been very active in fighting against the Vietnam War were disturbed when their fellow peace activists championed

In the 1970s and 1980s, the Israeli-Palestinian conflict moved Jewish women to act for peace in their own name as Jews and as women. This Israeli woman is a Holocaust survivor demanding peace. [Photo courtesy Sherry Gorelick]

Palestinian rights, criticized Israeli policies, or attacked Zionism.

Confrontations regarding Zionism and Palestinian-Israeli relations roiled the United Nations Decade for Women conferences in Mexico (1975) and Copenhagen (1980), and numerous other feminist conferences, newspapers, and other institutions. Fierce disagreements agitated the Jewish caucus of the (U.S.) National Women's Studies Association and several International Women's Day celebrations. Eventually, however, although strong disagreement remained, many Jewish women (along with Arab women) took leading roles in promoting peace in the Middle East.

In 1985 Reena Bernards, executive director of New Jewish Agenda, LETTY COTTIN POGREBIN, an editor of *Ms.* magazine, and Gail Pressberg, director of Middle East programs at the American Friends Service Committee, organized a Dialogue Project to plan for more constructive relations between Jews and Arabs at the forthcoming "End-of-Decade" UN Conference on Women. They invited prominent Jewish women from mainstream United States Jewish organizations, women from the Arab-American Anti-Discrimination Committee, and leaders of the Feminist Arab Network. They succeeded in creating a model for discussion of grievances allowing for genuine communication.

By then American Jewish feminists and lesbian feminists had published a number of influential anthologies, poems, and essays on various themes. Letty Cottin Pogrebin's pivotal article "Anti-Semitism in the Women's Movement" addressed controversies about the Israeli-Palestinian conflict. Six prominent poets and writers formed Di Vilde Chayes to express their support for Israel as a Jewish state, their chagrin at Israeli treatment of Palestinians (particularly within the "occupied territories" of the West Bank and Gaza), and their anger at anti-Semitism expressed among some of those activists opposing the occupation and the war in Lebanon.

EVELYN TORTON BECK published *Nice Jewish Girls: A Lesbian Anthology*, including some reflections by United States and Israeli Jews about Israel. In *The Tribe of Dina: A Jewish Women's Anthology*, Melanie Kaye/Kantrowitz and Irena Klepfisz published interviews with Israeli peace activists Chaya Shalom, Galia Golan, and Lil Moed.

INFLUENCE OF THE
ISRAELI WOMEN'S PEACE MOVEMENT

A specifically Jewish women's peace movement in the United States formed in support of women in Israel organizing against the Israeli occupation of the West Bank and Gaza, and in favor of a negotiated settlement of the Israeli-Palestinian conflict. Israeli Women in Black formed in response to the Israeli government's reaction to the Palestinian Intifada. A popular uprising in the West Bank and Gaza, the Intifada began December 9, 1987, in response to an incident between a Jewish driver and Palestinian workers. Begun by children throwing stones at Israeli soldiers in the occupied territories, it continued as coordinated strikes in which Palestinian shopkeepers closed stores, and workers periodically stayed away from their jobs within green-line Israel.

When Yitzhak Rabin, who was then defense minister, declared an "Iron Fist" policy of "force, might, the breaking of bones" against young Palestinian stone-throwing protesters (a policy articulated and demonstrated on international TV), a group of Jerusalem women dressed in black held a vigil demanding an end to the violence. They also demanded negotiations between Israel and the PLO toward peace.

The initial Jerusalem vigil—a line of women dressed in black, standing for one hour every Friday, holding banners and placards saying "Stop the Occupation," "Stop the Violence," and "Negotiate"—spread to Tel Aviv, Haifa, and eventually to twenty-four different locations throughout Israel. Within a few months it had spread to the United States, Canada, Europe, and Australia. In the United States, after the beginning of the Intifada, Letty Pogrebin, Hanan Ashrawi, and others revived the Dialogue Project for mutual understanding.

While for some time North American Jewish visitors to Israel had returned to the United States with concerns regarding the state of perpetual military alert and the militarization of Israeli society, and while some American Jewish travelers had long questioned Israeli governmental policies toward Palestinians, once the Israeli peace movement gained ground, and particularly after the formation of Women in Black, the influence of the Israeli women's peace movement on North American Jewish women intensified. Guest lec-

turers—first Israeli Jews, then Israeli Jews with Israeli Palestinians, and finally Palestinian women leaders from the West Bank—toured the United States, Canada, and Europe speaking before Jewish women's groups and at synagogues and peace organizations. Among the visiting speakers were Edna Zaretski and Mariam Mar'i (sponsored by the Feminist Task Force of the New Jewish Agenda), Dalia Sachs and Nabila Espanioli, Alice Shalvi, Zehira Kamal, Naomi Chazan, and Rita Giacomen.

In New York City in April 1988, Clare Kinberg, Irena Klepfisz, and GRACE PALEY, activists and poets, founded the Jewish Women's Committee to End the Occupation of the West Bank and Gaza (JWCEO). They were encouraged by Lil Moed, an American Jewish feminist who had helped organize a precursor to the Los Angeles New Jewish Agenda, then moved to Israel and was active in forming SHANI. Formed "in solidarity with Women in Black and other Israeli and Palestinian women's groups working for peace," the JWCEO held weekly vigils, carrying signs and banners similar to those of the Israeli Women in Black, in front of the offices of major United States Jewish organizations and in Jewish neighborhoods.

JWCEO's aim was "to promote dialogue in the U.S. Jewish community, and to support negotiations between the Israeli government and the PLO toward

This "Stop the Occupation" demonstration took place in Haifa in January of 1989. [Photo courtesy Sherry Gorelick]

the establishment of a Palestinian state alongside Israel." Similar groups formed in twenty-four locations throughout the United States; others were organized in Canada, Italy, Scandinavia, and Australia. Beginning in 1988, the New York JWCEO published the *Jewish Women's Peace Bulletin*, reporting on the activities of the Jewish women's peace movement in Israel and the diaspora. Jewish women's peace groups, sometimes calling themselves Women in Black, were active in Boston, Berkeley, Chicago, Minneapolis, Los Angeles, Ann Arbor, Palo Alto, Santa Cruz, San Francisco, Tucson, Syracuse, Philadelphia, Seattle, and Washington, D.C. In 1990 JWCEO published *Jewish Women's Call For Peace*, an organizing handbook.

Although holding weekly vigils was their major activity, both the Israeli Women in Black and their international solidarity organizations engaged in a variety of other political activities. In 1988, when Israeli women organized Women's Organization for Women Political Prisoners (WOFPP) to investigate sexual harassment and other forms of mistreatment of Palestinian women prisoners and began a telegram protest campaign, they urged diaspora Jewish groups to transmit the information and send their own telegrams.

Accordingly, in the United States, women from JWCEO, NJA, and the IJPU organized the Human Rights Rapid Response Network to send monthly telegrams to the Israeli government, prison wardens, or the military administration of the occupied territories, in concord with WOFPP and the Israeli Women in Black. In a number of cases the lives of severely ill Palestinian women prisoners were saved by this mobilization of international attention.

WOMEN AND PEACE CONFERENCES

Demonstrations, retreats, and conferences played a major role in Jewish women's peace activities, both in Israel and the diaspora. These activities encouraged introspection, consciousness-raising, mutual influence, and public education.

There were four major international women's peace conferences between 1987 and 1991, and two major nongovernmental international conferences within the United States. Through the four women's conferences, Israeli and Palestinian women developed an increasing amount of mutual understanding and ability to work together, and Jewish women in the diaspora learned of their work.

The First International Jewish Feminist Conference, organized by United States Jewish women, brought Jewish women from around the world to Jerusalem in November 1988 to discuss "The Empowerment of Jewish Women." With the outbreak of the Intifada and the crisis of Israeli governmental policy, members of the planning group split over the question of whether to permit discussion of the effect of the Intifada on women. The newly formed Women in Black and SHANI organized a demonstration at the conference, inviting participants to attend a "Post-Conference," entitled "Occupation or Peace?—A Feminist Response."

The Post-Conference included testimony by two Palestinian women from the West Bank about their conditions as women and as Palestinians. This was the first time that most of the participants had heard from Palestinian women directly, and it was the first time that many of the diaspora women met the Israeli women's peace movement and were able to hear their point of view.

As a result of these conferences in late 1988, Israeli Jewish women began to have greater contact with Palestinian women, both within the Israeli green line and in visits to the West Bank and Gaza. They began to plan, in coordination with one of the four major Palestinian women's organizations, a Women Go for Peace Conference for the following December.

The 1989 Women Go for Peace Conference was significant for several reasons. For the first time, representatives of major Israeli Jewish women's social service organizations committed themselves to combining the quest for Israeli-Palestinian peace into their program of furthering the status and condition of women in Israel. Also for the first time, the Israelis shared the podium with leaders of a Palestinian women's organization. In drawing American and other diaspora women back to Israel for an explicitly women's peace conference, it furthered their understanding and therefore their work in Jewish women's peace movements at home. Coinciding with a major international effort by the Israeli Peace Now organization to draw people from around the world to join local Israelis and Palestinians in a "Hands Around Jerusalem" peace chain, it gave the Israeli and Palestinian women's peace movements worldwide press coverage. Like their international counterparts, American Jewish women returned with reports about the conference, which they shared with other Jewish women at meetings organized by the JWCEO, the NCJW, NJA, and various synagogues and women's organizations.

The success of the 1989 conference led the Israeli and Palestinian women's organizations to plan together a Women's International Conference for Israeli-Palestinian Peace for December 1990. Assistance in funding and planning was elicited from

Swedish WILPF and from Jewish women's peace organizations in other countries. American women played an important role.

The process of planning the 1990 conference added three new dimensions to the Jewish women's peace efforts. (1) *Joint planning.* Whereas the 1988 Post-Conference had been organized by the Israeli women, with invitations to Palestinian women to participate, and the 1989 conference had been planned separately, with Israelis organizing the morning session and Palestinians the afternoon, the 1990 conference was planned together. The Israeli Women's Peace Coalition (composed of eight different women's peace groups), the Israeli Women's Peace Network (Reshet), and three of the four Palestinian women's organizations caucused separately, but the monthly planning meetings were integrated. (2) *Modeling of a conflict resolution process.* As the planners put it: "We hope that the 1990 conference, and the process by which we are mutually planning for it, may serve as a model for making peace in the Middle East and as a demonstration of the possibility for a peaceful settlement of the conflict." (3) *The articulation of a feminist orientation to peace.* In contrast with the typical absence of women from official peace conferences, the Women's International Conference was to demand women's participation in the peace process, provide women's perspectives on the issues dividing Palestinians and Israelis (utilization of resources, Law of Return, etc.), and address women's issues typically neglected in men's considerations of war and peace, among them the effects of militarization on women's rights, the relationship between war and the levels of sexual harassment and domestic violence, and the many other ways that war differently affects women and men.

The women intended to model and push for actual internationally backed negotiations between the official Palestinian leadership and the Israeli government. Consequently, they wished to have the participation of representatives who were as highly placed as possible. Because it was still illegal for members of the PLO to enter Israel-Palestine, and illegal for Israelis to meet with members of the PLO, a double conference was planned. Part would take place at the United Nations offices in Geneva, Switzerland, and part would take place in Jerusalem.

These plans were interrupted by the Iraqi invasion of Kuwait on August 2, 1990, and the Persian Gulf War. The war virtually silenced peace groups in Israel. Although both the Israeli and Palestinian women proclaimed that "now, more than ever, we must work for peace," the war forced the planners to have a much smaller conference in Jerusalem in December and to postpone the Geneva portion of the conference. American Jewish women spoke and observed at the December conference and reported back afterward.

In May 1991, the second half of the Women's International Conference for Israeli-Palestinian Peace convened at the Palais des Nations in Geneva, attended by seventy-five women from thirteen countries. Among the representatives were members of the European and Swedish parliaments, high-level members of the PLO, six other Palestinians from the territories, and ten Israelis, two of them members of the Israeli Knesset, including Yael Dayan, daughter of Israeli general Moshe Dayan.

Three days of intensive discussion and negotiation produced a three-page consensus document covering most of the major issues in the Israeli-Palestinian conflict. The document called for official negotiations, regional security and arms control, human rights, and attention to the economic and social consequences of the occupation. "We are women talking to each other while war is going on between our two peoples," said the PLO ambassador in her closing remarks. "It is very important for our people to know that we can meet together to work for peace."

News of the Geneva conference was transmitted by the participants and observers returning to their countries, in the form of speeches (primarily before women's organizations, including JWCEO, the National Jewish Women's Resource Center, the American Association of University Women, NJA, and various synagogues), radio programs on such stations as KPFA (part of the Pacifica Network), and articles in such journals as *BRIDGES* and *New Directions for Women*.

The conference coincided with U.S. Secretary of State James Baker's as yet fruitless efforts to get Israel and the Palestinians to agree on terms for an international peace conference. Four months later, an official international peace conference began in Madrid, Spain, with Israeli and Palestinian participation. Women in Black as a symbol and activity of women's direct action for peace was later adopted by Serbian women protesting the war in Bosnia and by American women expressing their support for the victims of that war. It became an international symbol and resource for women's work for peace.

BIBLIOGRAPHY

Adams, Judith Porter. *Peacework: Oral Histories of Women Peace Activists* (1991); Balka, Christie, and Reena Bernards. "Israeli and Palestinian Women in Dialogue: A Model for Nairobi. New Jewish Agenda's Role at the UN 'Decade for Women' Conference Forum '85 in Nairobi:

Final Report." 4107 v.f. Jewish Women's Resource Center, National Council for Jewish Women, NYC; Beck, Evelyn Torton, ed. *Nice Jewish Girls: A Lesbian Anthology* (1982. Revised and expanded 1989); Brettschneider, Marla. *Cornerstones of Peace: Jewish Identity Politics and Democratic Theory* (1996); Bulkin, Elly. "Hard Ground: Perspectives on Jewish Identity, Racism, and Anti-Semitism." In *Yours in Struggle: Three Feminist Perspectives on Anti-Semitism and Racism*, edited by Elly Bulkin, Minnie Bruce Pratt, and Barbara Smith (1984); Chazan, Naomi. "Israeli Women and Peace Activism." In *Calling the Equality Bluff: Women in Israel*, edited by Barbara Swirski and Marilyn P. Safir (1991); Degan, Marie Louise. *The History of the Women's Peace Party* (1939); Espanioli, Nabila, and Dalia Sachs. "Peace Process: Israeli and Palestinian Women." *Bridges: A Journal for Jewish Feminists and Our Friends* 2 (1991): 112–119; Falbel, Rita. "Jewish Women." *New Directions for Women* (March/April 1989), and "Women's Vigil Against the Occupation." *Genesis* 19, no. 2 (Summer 1988): 7; Falbel, Rita, Irena Klepfisz, and Donna Nevel. *Jewish Women's Call for Peace: A Handbook for Jewish Women on the Israeli/Palestinian Conflict* (1990); Foster, Catherine. *Women for All Seasons: The Story of the Women's International League for Peace and Freedom* (1989); Freedman, Marcia. *Exile in the Promised Land: A Memoir* (1990); Gorelick, Sherry. "The Changer and the Changed: Methodological Reflections on Studying Jewish Feminists." In *Gender/Body/Knowledge: Feminist Reconstructions of Being and Knowing*, edited by Alison M. Jaggar and Susan R. Bordo (1989); "Doing the Impossible for Peace." *New Directions for Women* 2, no. 5 (September/October 1991), and "Geneva Conference: History and Goals." *Bridges* 2 (1991): 120–123; Kaye/Kantrowitz, Melanie, and Irena Klepfisz, eds. *The Tribe of Dina: A Jewish Women's Anthology*; Klepfisz, Irena. *Dreams of an Insomniac: Jewish Feminist Essays, Speeches and Diatribes* (1990); "An Open Letter to Women Attending the American Jewish Congress Conference 'Empowerment of Jewish Women' from SHANI—Israeli Women Against the Occupation." #4288. Jewish Women's Resource Center, National Council for Jewish Women, NYC; Pogrebin, Letty Cottin. "Anti-Semitism in the Women's Movement" *Ms.* (June 1982, and see "Letters Forum: Anti-Semitism" in the February 1983 issue for responses). (Reprinted in *Eye* 9, no. 2, March 1983), and *Deborah, Golda and Me: Being Female and Jewish in America* (1991), and "Going Public as a Jew: How I Was 'Born Again' to My Own People." *Ms.* (July/August 1987); *The Road to Peace: Israeli-Palestinian Dialogue in New York*. Special edition, *New Outlook* 32, no. 3–4 (March–April 1989); Rogow, Faith. *Gone to Another Meeting: The National Council of Jewish Women, 1893–1993* (1993); Swerdlow, Amy. *Women Strike for Peace: Traditional Motherhood and Radical Politics in the 1960s* (1993); Sharoni, Simona. *Gender and the Israeli-Palestinian Conflict: The Politics of Women's Resistance* (1995).

ARCHIVAL MATERIALS
 The files of the Jewish Women's Committee to End the Occupation of the West Bank and Gaza are available to researchers at the Swathmore College Peace Collection.

IN POSSESSION OF THE AUTHOR
 "Final Document." Women's Geneva Conference for Israeli-Palestinian Peace. Palais des Nations, Geneva, Switzerland, May 13–15, 1991. 3 pages; Sachs, Dalia. Speech given (in Hebrew; English translation by its author) at the panel on women and their contribution to peace. Women Go for Peace Conference, Jerusalem, Israel, December 29, 1989.

SHERRY GORELICK

PEIXOTTO, JESSICA BLANCHE (1864–1941)

Jessica Blanche Peixotto, a member of a prominent Sephardic family distinguished for its long history of intellectual, philanthropic, and cultural contributions to the United States, broke gender boundaries throughout her career as a social economist and university professor. She was born in 1864 in New York City, the only daughter and oldest child of Raphael Peixotto, a prosperous Ohioan involved in trade with the South, and Myrtilla Jessica (Davis) Peixotto, originally of Virginia. In 1870, Raphael Peixotto moved his family and business to San Francisco. Jessica Peixotto's four brothers were Edgar, a San Francisco attorney; Ernest Clifford, an artist and author; Eustace, director of public school athletics in San Francisco; and Sidney Salzado, a social worker.

After high school graduation in 1880, Peixotto acquiesced to family disapproval of her ambitions for higher education, continuing her studies at home through private instruction. In 1891, however, she enrolled at the University of California at Berkeley, receiving a bachelor's degree in 1894, and continued on to graduate study in political science and economics. She received a Ph.D. in 1900, the second given to a woman at the University of California. Peixotto's thesis *The French Revolution and Modern French Socialism*, published in 1901, was based on independent research undertaken at the Sorbonne in 1896–1897.

In 1904, Jessica Peixotto joined the faculty of the University of California at Berkeley as a lecturer in sociology. Her appointment was soon transferred to the economics department, where she taught until her retirement in 1935. In 1918, Peixotto was the first woman to earn the rank of full professor at Berkeley. Her service as head of her department was also a first for a woman there. National honors include her election as vice president of the American Economic Association in 1928. Following her retirement, Peixotto received honorary doctorates in law from Mills College in 1935 and from the University of California in 1936.

Peixotto's published works include *Getting and Spending at the Professional Standard of Living: A Study of the Costs of Living an Academic Life* (1927), and *Cost of Living Studies. II. How Workers Spend a Living Wage: A Study of the Incomes and Expenditures of Eighty-Two Typographers' Families in San Francisco* (1929). A collection of papers and comments *Essays in Social Economics in Honor of Jessica Blanche Peixotto* (1935) provides full details of her life and published writings.

Throughout her career, Peixotto was deeply committed to social causes, serving for twelve years on the California State Board of Charities and Correction. During World War I, she worked in Washington, first as executive chairman of the child welfare department of the Women's Committee of the Council of National Defense, and then as chief of the council's child conservation section. She was also a member of the Consumers' Advisory Board of the National Recovery Administration in 1933. At the University of California, Peixotto founded a program within the economics department that ultimately led to a professional school of social work.

Jessica Peixotto died in October 1941. While proud of her Jewish background, she was not involved in the Jewish community or any Jewish causes. Her funeral service, followed by cremation, was conducted by a representative of the Unitarian Society, together with the vice president and provost of the University of California.

SELECTED WORKS BY
JESSICA BLANCHE PEIXOTTO

Getting and Spending at the Professional Standard of Living: A Study of the Costs of Living an Academic Life (1927); *Cost of Living Studies. II. How Workers Spend a Living Wage: A Study of Incomes and Expenditures of Eighty-Two Typographers' Families in San Francisco* (1929); *The French Revolution and Modern French Socialism* (1901).

BIBLIOGRAPHY

AJYB 24:189, 44:342; *JE*; *NAW*; Obituary. *NYTimes*, October 21, 1941, 23:5; *UJE*; *WWWIA* 1; *WWIAJ* (1928, 1938); *Essays in Social Economics in Honor of Jessica Blanche Peixotto* (1935).

JUDITH R. BASKIN

PEIXOTTO, JUDITH (1823–1881)

In 1918 a writer for the American Jewish Historical Society noted that while "To-day a goodly proportion of the teachers in the public schools of New York are Jews. . . . this was not always the case." Seventy-one years earlier, Judith Peixotto, a twenty-four-year-old public school teacher of Sephardic origin, among the earliest Jewish educators in America, earned the distinction of becoming the first Jewish principal in the city of New York.

Judith Salzedo Peixotto was the daughter of the Amsterdam-born physician Dr. Daniel Levy Maduro Peixotto (1799–1843) and New York–born Rachel (Seixas) Peixotto (1798–1861), both of Spanish and Portuguese origin. Judith's paternal grandfather, Curaçao-born Moses Levi Maduro Peixotto (1767–1828), who immigrated to New York in 1807, served as hazan at Shearith Israel, the Spanish and Portuguese synagogue of New York, from 1820 until his death. Daniel and Rachel Peixotto were married in March 1823, and Judith was born on December 30 of that year in New York. The Peixottos had seven more children: Zipporah (b. 1826), Sarah Naar (b. 1828), Moses Levi Maduro II (b. 1830), Rebecca (b. 1832), Benjamin Franklin (b. 1834), Raphael (b. 1837), and Miriam Maduro (b. 1842). According to the 1830 census the Peixotto family had four boarders and/or members of the extended family living with them in their home.

Her father's premature death in 1843 left twenty-four-year-old Judith with most of the responsibility for supporting the family. That year, Judith entered the teaching profession in the New York public schools, where she and her sisters Zipporah and Sarah Naar seem to have been the only Jewish teachers.

Judith Peixotto was a teacher at the Ward School No. 10, Fourth Ward, for girls at 32 James Street from 1847 to 1850. In 1848, fourteen of her students, aged seven to sixteen, were selected to have their writing published in the *Excelsior Annual*, the student body's annual report. The New York *Sun*, on April 15, 1850, called her "a thorough scholar and teacher" and mentioned "the great excellence of her classes."

From 1849 to 1850, Peixotto served as principal of the Female Evening School No. 10, Fourth Ward, where students from ages twelve to fifty were instructed in literacy and rudimentary arithmetic. In 1849, she wrote to the school's committee: "We do not speak without foundation when we tell you that from our Evening School many will go forth determined to cultivate the soil in which, we trust, seeds have been sown that will produce fruit of uncommon excellence; nor should we be surprised if among them there should be those who will become teachers, strong in mental energy, rich in an education implanted by your noble efforts, and inspirited by the desire to do good."

Peixotto's name does not appear on the New York City Board of Education rolls after 1850. She apparently gave up teaching when she married David Solis

Hays (1820–1897) at 12 Bedford Street on September 17, 1851. David Hays, originally from Pleasantville, New York, was a well-known pharmacist, and served as treasurer of the College of Pharmacy in New York City. For several years, he and Peixotto's brother Moses operated a pharmacy business, with stores at 207 Division Street and 543 Fifth Avenue.

Judith and David Hays had eight children: Sarah Rosalie (b. 1852), Daniel Peixotto (b. 1854), Rebecca Touro (b. 1855), Benjamin Franklin (b. 1857), George Davis (b. 1859), Rachel Peixotto (b. 1861), David Solis, Jr. (b. 1863), and Cora Florence (b. 1870). Judith Peixotto Hays died on March 1, 1881, and is buried at the Shearith Israel Cypress Hills Street Cemetery in Queens, New York.

BIBLIOGRAPHY

Cowen, Elfrida D. "Judith Salzedo Peixotto." *AJHS* 26 (1918): 249–250; de Sola Pool, David, and Tamara de Sola Pool. *An Old Faith in the New World: Portrait of Shearith Israel, 1654–1954* (1955); "Excerpts from Scrap Books." *AJHS* 27 (1920): 507; Hays, Daniel Peixotto. "Daniel L.M. Peixotto, M.D." *AJHSQ* 26 (1918): 219–230; *Jewish Encyclopedia* 9 (1912): 582; Lyons Collection IV. Phillips sketch pamplets and scrapbooks. Scrap Book No. 1, American Jewish Items, p. 40; *PAJHS* 26: 249–250; Stern, Malcolm H. *First American Jewish Families: 600 Genealogies, 1654–1988.* 3d ed. (1991).

AVIVA BEN-UR

PEMBER, PHOEBE YATES LEVY (1823–1913)

The life of Phoebe Yates Levy Pember, Confederate administrator of Chimborazo Hospital outside Richmond, Virginia, in many ways epitomizes the high level of acculturation, regional identity, and acceptance into Christian society that characterized second- and third-generation southern Jews in the nineteenth century. She was born on August 18, 1823, in Charleston, South Carolina, to Jacob Clavius Levy, the son of Polish immigrants, and Fanny (Yates) Levy, of Liverpool, England. For over three decades, Jacob Levy operated a successful mercantile establishment, and his wife enjoyed a highly acclaimed acting career in the Charleston theater. Their wealth and stature in the community enabled the Levys to move among the city's social elite. Following financial setbacks in the late 1840s, the family moved to Savannah, Georgia.

The fourth of seven children, six of them girls, Phoebe followed in the footsteps of other siblings who embraced the Confederate cause. Her older sister, Eugenia, married Philip Phillips, a lawyer and United States congressman from Mobile, Alabama. Eugenia Phillips's outspoken support for southern nationalism resulted in her imprisonment and subsequent exile from Washington, D.C., in August 1861, and a second incarceration in the summer of 1862, following the Union occupation of New Orleans. Her younger brother, Samuel Yates Levy, served as a major in the Georgia infantry before his capture and confinement in 1864–1865 at a United States military prison on Johnson's Island in Ohio. Following his release, Samuel returned to Savannah, where he edited the *Savannah Advertiser* for a short time in 1868. His hostility to the federal occupation of Georgia brought him into repeated conflict with military officials, and he ultimately was forced to resign from the newspaper.

Little is known of Phoebe's life before the Civil War. She received some formal schooling, as her memoirs and personal letters reveal an articulate, sophisticated mind. In 1856, she married a non-Jew, Thomas Noyes Pember of Boston, but their marriage lasted only five years and produced no children. Thomas contracted tuberculosis. After an unsuccessful convalescence in the South, he died in Aiken, South Carolina, on July 9, 1861. A young widow, Phoebe Pember moved back with her parents, who had fled Savannah for the safety of Marietta, Georgia. But here she felt confined and unproductive and quarreled with her father, whom she described as indifferent to her needs. In November 1862, Phoebe Pember accepted an invitation from her friend Mrs. George W. Randolph, wife of the Confederate secretary of war, to serve as the matron of Chimborazo Hospital.

Under the supervision of a senior medical officer and with the help of numerous assistants, she oversaw nursing operations in the second of the hospital's five divisions and attended to the housekeeping, dietary needs, and comfort of over fifteen thousand men. As the first female administrator appointed to Chimborazo, Pember offered the warmth and femininity craved by the soldiers, but she also fought against repeated attempts to undermine her authority. Much of the time this meant blocking efforts by the staff to pilfer supplies, especially whiskey, placed under her control. On one occasion, she threatened a would-be thief with a gun she kept hidden nearby. Her self-assurance and commitment to caring for the sick and wounded earned praise among Richmond society. In his book *Belles, Beaux and Brains of the 60's* (1907), Thomas C. DeLeon described Phoebe as a "brisk and brilliant matron" with "a will of steel under a suave refinement."

A Southern Woman's Story: Life in Confederate Richmond (1879), Phoebe Pember's account of her experiences at Chimborazo from December 1862 until April 1865, provides a valuable resource for Southern, gender, and American Jewish historians. Sensitively written and anecdotal in style, her memoirs detail day-to-day life in the wards, describe the poor state of Confederate medical facilities, reveal the attitudes of and toward southern women, and offer a glimpse into the mind-set of a highly acculturated southern Jewish woman. Throughout her adult life, Pember remained conscious of her high social status and moved freely among the South's elite families, suggesting that Jews could enjoy complete acceptance in Christian society. Although she married outside Judaism and apparently did not practice her faith, she spoke openly and proudly of her Jewish heritage. Following the Civil War, Pember traveled extensively throughout the United States and Europe. She died on March 4, 1913, at age eighty-nine, while visiting Pittsburgh, Pennsylvania, and is buried beside her husband in Savannah's Laurel Grove Cemetery.

BIBLIOGRAPHY

DeLeon, Thomas C. *Belles, Beaux and Brains of the 60's* (1907); Gamble, Thomas. *Savannah Duels and Duellists, 1733–1877* (1923); Hagy, James William. *This Happy Land: The Jews of Colonial and Antebellum Charleston* (1993); Marcus, Jacob R. *The American Jewish Woman: A Documentary History* (1981), and *The American Jewish Woman, 1654–1980* (1981), and *Memoirs of American Jews, 1775–1865*. 3 vols. (1956); *NAW*; Pember, Phoebe Yates. *A Southern Woman's Story: Life in Confederate Richmond*. Edited by Bell Irvin Wiley (1879. Reprint 1959); Phillips-Myers Family Papers. Collection 596, Southern Historical Collection. University of North Carolina at Chapel Hill; Stern, Malcolm H. *First American Jewish Families: Six Hundred Genealogies, 1654–1988*. 3d ed. (1991).

MARK I. GREENBERG

PERLMAN, FLORENCE (1896–1975)

One of the women responsible for shaping HADASSAH into its role of national prominence was Florence Bierman Perlman. A national board member of Hadassah from 1938 until her death, Perlman also held many other important positions within the organization. She served as chair of Hadassah Israel Education Services (HIES) and of YA'AL, the women's auxiliary of the Hadassah–Hebrew University Medical Center. She was national membership chair (from 1962), national vice president, chair of the building commission for erection of Hadassah House in New York, as well as convention chair and delegate to the World Zionist Congress.

Perlman served as president of the New York chapter of National Jewish Women's Organizations, and as the first chair for national American affairs. She was chair of its national vocational education committee and of the conferences committee. Perlman was also active in other Zionist organizations. She chaired the Jewish National Fund, membership and public relations committees, and was a member of the General Council of the Women's International Zionist Organization.

Her activities in the wider community included appointments by Governor Thomas E. Dewey of New York to the board of visitors, New York State Training School for Girls in Hudson, New York, and membership on the State Committee for Human Rights. She also served on the New York City Council and on the New York State Prison Committee.

Born in New York City on July 28, 1896, Florence Bierman was the daughter of Max and Dora (Schneck) Bierman. She graduated from Barnard College in 1918, a year after marrying Nathan D. Perlman. In addition to her work for Jewish and community endeavors, she managed her husband's successive political campaigns for Congress, New York State Supreme Court, and attorney general of New York. The Perlmans had a son, Jack M. Perlman. At her death in New York on September 24, 1975, she was survived by her two brothers, Samuel and Maurice Bierman, a sister, Lena Hausman, and three grandchildren.

BIBLIOGRAPHY

AJYB 77:597; Obituary. *NYTimes*, September 25, 1975; *Who's Who in World Jewry* (1965).

AVIS DIMOND MILLER

PERLMAN, HELEN HARRIS (b. 1905)

Helen Harris Perlman, with almost seventy years as a social work practitioner, supervisor, teacher, consultant, and author to her credit, is a legend in her field. She is Samuel Deutsch Distinguished Service Professor Emeritus in the School of Social Service Administration at the University of Chicago, and she has served on national policy committees, lectured around the world, and participated in pioneering social work programs and research.

Born on December 20, 1905, in St. Paul, Minnesota, she was the oldest of seven children, four of whom survived to adulthood. Her parents had come to St. Paul from Eastern Europe, and her father was a factory manager whose sympathies were often with his socialist and union workers rather than with his employer. Helen earned a B.A. in English literature and education from the University of Minnesota in 1926, a certificate in psychiatric social work from the New York School of Social Work in 1934, and an M.S. from the Columbia University School of Social Work in 1943. She married Max Perlman in 1935 and they had one son, Jonathan Harris Perlman (b. 1942).

Perlman originally hoped to teach college English, but she found that in the 1920s opportunities in academia for women, and for Jews, were scarce. She went to Chicago to look for a job as an advertising copywriter, but instead found a summer job as a counselor at the Jewish Social Service. "I had no training, but I used the ways I had developed as a writer to understand people's actions and behaviors and feelings and problems," she explained. When she was finally offered an advertising job that fall, she turned it down to stay in social work. She spent eighteen years as a social caseworker in family service agencies, schools, a child guidance clinic, and a psychiatric hospital, lectured part-time at the Columbia University School of Social Work from 1938 to 1945, and in 1945 became an assistant professor at the University of Chicago, where she taught until her retirement. She has also taught and lectured in Canada, England, Hawaii, Hong Kong, Scotland, India, and Puerto Rico.

Perlman's areas of study have included ego psychology and its implications for clinical work; lifetime personality growth and development resulting from a person's daily transactions at work, at home, and in society; therapeutic and educational problem-solving processes; and how social values and value conflicts affect future planning. She has also taught social casework: its governing principles, ethics, values, and methods of helping and enabling people suffering from stress, disability, and other social or psychological problems.

Perlman is the author of *Social Casework: A Problem-Solving Process*, which is based on the premise that the "social surround" of our society and its value systems affect what is and is not possible, and that certain kinds of solutions breed new problems. It has sold over a hundred thousand copies in English and been translated into eight languages. She has written eight books, in all, which have been translated into eleven foreign languages, as well as over eighty published articles. She returned to her first love, literature, in her 1989 book *The Dancing Clock*. It offers a collection of her childhood memories to help others "explore and remember how they reacted to and were marked by events in their youth." Her many honors range

from the undergraduate Drama Prize for Best Playwright and the Best Writing of the Year award from the Department of English Literature at the University of Minnesota in the 1920s to her Lifetime Achievement Award presented by the Council on Social Work Education in 1992.

Helen Harris Perlman continued to teach single graduate courses for nine years after her retirement, including "The Minority Child in Twentieth Century Literature" and "Utopias and Human Welfare," in which she sought to establish how present-day social workers and thinkers can, and should, connect with humanists of the past.

SELECTED WORKS BY HELEN HARRIS PERLMAN

The Dancing Clock (1989); *Helping: Charlotte Towle on Social Work and Social Casework* (1969); *Looking Back To See Ahead* (1989); *Persona: Social Role and Personality* (1968); *Perspectives in Social Casework* (1971); *Relationship: The Heart of Helping People* (1979); *So You Want To Be A Social Worker* (1962, rev. ed. 1970); *Social Casework: A Problem-Solving Process* (1957).

BIBLIOGRAPHY
EJ.

RHODA LEWIN

PESOTTA, ROSE (1896–1965)

Shortly before her death, Rose Pesotta was asked how she would live her life if she could live it over again. She replied, "I have no regrets of my chosen path of the past. I would choose the same path, trying perhaps to avoid some of the mistakes of the past. But always having the vision before me—in the words of Thomas Paine, 'The world is my country. To do good is my religion.'" The sweeping idealism of that statement tells us much about Pesotta, anarchist, labor activist, immigrant, internationalist. Known primarily as one of the first female vice presidents of the INTERNATIONAL LADIES GARMENT WORKERS UNION (ILGWU), Pesotta saw her union organizing as an opportunity to fulfill the anarchist mandate "to be among the people and teach them our ideal in practice."

Rose Pesotta was born in 1896, the second of eight children, into a middle-class family in Derazhnya, a railroad town in the Russian Ukraine. Her father, Itsaak Peisoty, was a grain merchant, and her mother, Masya, was active in the family business. Pesotta attributed her lifelong concern for social justice to her "dynamic and unconventional" father, but seemed unaware that the shtetl tradition of women's work outside the home

Rose Pesotta, known primarily as one of the first female vice presidents of the INTERNATIONAL LADIES
GARMENT WORKERS UNION, *brought charisma, energy, and, most important, empathy to everything
and everyone she approached in life. A fervent anarchist, she saw her politics as a natural outgrowth
of her Jewish background and Jewish culture in general. She is shown here bringing bread
to striking workers. [Rose Pesotta Papers, New York Public Library]*

represented by her mother may have also facilitated
her career.

Pesotta attended Rosalia Davidovna's school for
girls, with its Russian curriculum and its clandestine
classes in Jewish history and Hebrew. After two years
at the school, she was needed at home to help care for
her siblings, and home tutoring replaced formal
schooling. But her political apprenticeship in one of
the many leftist groups in the Russian Pale of Settlement was as important as her formal education. She
joined her older sister, Esther, in the local anarchist
underground. The group's discussion of well-known
leftists Pyotr Kropotkin, Mikhail Bakunin, and Pierre-

Joseph Proudhon, and the political activities of young
radicals, opened a window on the possibilities of a
wider world.

Her parents' plan to marry her to an ordinary village boy precipitated her decision to join her sister in
America. In 1913, her parents gave her permission to
embark for the New World. Once in New York,
Pesotta began working in various shirtwaist factories,
and struggled to learn English. Soon, she joined Local
25 of the ILGWU. The local became a base for her
union career. In 1915, she helped the local form the
first education department in the ILGWU, and in
1920 she was elected to Local 25's executive board. In

1922, Pesotta completed the program at the Bryn Mawr Summer School for Workers, and between 1924 and 1926, she was a student at Brookwood Labor College. During the 1920s, she played a key role in the union's chronic struggles with communists. Grateful union officials recognized Pesotta's contributions by appointing her as an organizer in the late 1920s.

Pesotta brought a charismatic personality, boundless energy, and a unique ability to empathize with the downtrodden to the organizing field. In 1933, she spearheaded the Dressmakers General Strike in Los Angeles in the face of antipicketing injunctions, hired thugs, and communist dual unions. She mobilized the largely Mexican labor force through Spanish-language radio broadcasts and ads in ethnic newspapers. Although the strike was not successful, Pesotta's leadership established her as one of the most gifted organizers of the union.

Pesotta's visibility in California led to her election in 1934 as a vice president of the ILGWU, serving on the general executive board. Pesotta was conflicted about her ten years of service in that position. Sexism and a loss of personal independence continually troubled her, until she finally resigned from the position in 1942.

Between 1934 and 1944, though, Pesotta was one of the most successful organizers in the United States. She carried the union message to workers in Puerto Rico, Detroit, Montreal, Cleveland, Buffalo, Boston, Salt Lake City, and Los Angeles. On loan from the ILGWU to the Congress of Industrial Organizations (CIO), she joined the great labor upheavals of the 1930s in Akron, Ohio, and Flint, Michigan. In 1944, Pesotta refused a fourth term on the CIO General Executive Board, with a brief critical statement that "one woman vice president could not adequately represent the women who now make up 85 percent of the International's membership of 305,000."

Following her resignation from union office, Pesotta published two memoirs: *Bread upon the Waters* (1945) and *Days of Our Lives* (1958). She worked briefly for the B'nai B'rith Anti-Defamation League and for the American Trade Union Council for Histadrut, Israel's labor organization. But she supported herself during those years largely as a factory operative. Her life, in a sense, had come full circle—she embraced what she called "the freedom of a plain rank and file member of the union."

Anarchism and Judaism are key to understanding Pesotta's identity and sense of self. Although first introduced to anarchist philosophy in Europe, Pesotta found community and support for her libertarian beliefs in the alternative culture of American anarchism. Anarchism was her ethical center. It celebrated the inherent goodness of the individual and rejected private property, the state, and authority. Like EMMA GOLDMAN and other women attracted to the movement, Pesotta found support for a sexually free life-style embedded in anarchist tenets of personal freedom. She was secretary of the anarchist paper *The Road to Freedom* and was a key member of the Sacco-Vanzetti Defense Committee.

For Pesotta, anarchism was inextricably enmeshed with Jewish culture and communities. Although not religiously observant, Pesotta always identified herself as Jewish. The Holocaust and the foundation of Israel deepened her sense of herself as a Jew. It seems ironic that her second memoir casts Judaism in a central role after a lifetime spent in secular activism and outside of the family roles critical to Jewish practice. Closer scrutiny reveals the congruence between Pesotta's idealized past and her American life. In her books, her need to understand "external power relationships" as a Jew in czarist Russia meshed neatly with the Jewish labor union in tension with American culture.

In the fall of 1965, Pesotta was diagnosed with cancer of the spleen. Quietly she resigned from her job and went to Miami to "recuperate in the sun." On December 4, 1965, she died alone in a Miami hospital.

SELECTED WORKS BY ROSE PESOTTA
Bread upon the Waters (1945); *Days of Our Lives* (1958).

BIBLIOGRAPHY
Glenn, Susan A. *Daughters of the Shtetl: Life and Labor in the Immigrant Generation* (1990); International Institute of Social History. Archives. Amsterdam, Netherlands; International Ladies Garment Workers Union. Archives. Cornell School of Industrial and Labor Relations, Ithaca, New York; Kessler-Harris, Alice. "Organizing the Unorganizable: Three Jewish Women and Their Union," *Labor History* 17 (Winter 1976); Leeder, Elaine. *The Gentle General: Rose Pesotta, Anarchist and Labor Organizer* (1993); *NAW* modern; Obituary. *NYTimes*, December 8, 1965, 43:3; Pesotta, Rose. Papers. Rare Books and Manuscripts Division, New York Public Library, Astor, Lenox and Tilden Foundations, NYC; Shepard, Naomi. *A Price Below Rubies: Jewish Women as Rebels and Radicals* (1993).

ANN SCHOFIELD

PETERS, ROBERTA (b. 1930)

When Roberta Peters was just thirteen, famed tenor Jan Peerce suggested she take lessons to cultivate her amazing natural voice. Six years later, she made her debut on the stage of the Metropolitan Opera—and has been dazzling international audiences ever since.

Roberta Peters was born on May 4, 1930, in New York City. Despite their modest means, her parents, Ruth (Hirsch), a milliner, and Sol Peterman, a shoe salesman, arranged the private tutoring in language, piano, drama, and ballet that made possible their only child's remarkable career. In 1949, after hearing her audition in the studio of her teacher, William Herman, the late renowned impresario Sol Hurok took Peters under his wing, despite her youthful nineteen years and complete lack of performing experience. Hurok arranged her audition for Rudolf Bing, then general manager of the Metropolitan Opera, which led to a contract to appear as the Queen of the Night in Mozart's *The Magic Flute*. As fate would have it, the young singer was called upon several weeks earlier, on November 17, 1950—with just six hours' notice—to replace an indisposed colleague as Zerlina in Mozart's *Don Giovanni*. Since then, Peters has earned acclaim singing such coloratura heroines as Lucia in *Lucia di Lammermoor*, Gilda in *Rigoletto*, and Rosina in *The Barber of Seville*, as well as roles in other styles: Mozart's Zerlina, Susanna, Despina, and Queen of the Night; Richard Strauss's Zerbinetta; Johann Strauss's Adele; Donizetti's Adina and Norina; and Menotti's Kitty, a role she created for the American premiere of *The Last Savage* at the Metropolitan Opera. She also added roles in romantic operas, including *La Traviata* and *La Bohème*, to her repertoire, with much success. In fact, Peters has achieved the longest tenure of any soprano in the history of the Metropolitan Opera. A performer in fifty-seven Texaco radio broadcasts heard live from the Met, she also made an unprecedented sixty-five appearances on the Ed Sullivan television show.

Beyond her success on American stages, the renowned singer has performed in operas, concerts, and recitals with some of the world's greatest conductors and orchestras. Peters made her European debut as the Bohemian Girl under the direction of Sir Thomas Beecham at London's Covent Garden. Her performance as Queen of the Night under the direction of Karl Böhm at the Salzburg Festival won high praise, as did her appearances at the Kirov Theater in Leningrad and the Bolshoi Theater in Moscow, where she became the first American-born artist to receive the coveted Bolshoi Medal.

With varied repertoire ranging from baroque masterworks of Bach and Handel through German lieder, French, Italian, Spanish, and English art songs, and American folk songs, Peters has presented recitals and master classes throughout the world. In 1979, she

Roberta Peters has thrilled audiences all over the world with an incredibly varied repertoire including Jewish folk music and modern operas by Israeli composers. She had the longest tenure of any soprano in the history of the Metropolitan Opera. [New York Public Library]

traveled to the People's Republic of China. Tours of Japan, Korea, Hong Kong, and Taiwan followed in 1987, 1988, and 1990.

Peters is also a popular recitalist and master teacher on the American college and university scene. Her successes there—and throughout the world—have been acknowledged with the awarding of honorary doctorates from Lehigh, St. John's, and Rhode Island universities, as well as from Elmira, Ithaca,

Westminster, Colby, and New Rochelle colleges. She also serves as trustee emeritus of Ithaca College, an overseer of Colby College, and an overseer of the Brooklyn College Performing Arts Center.

While maintaining a schedule averaging forty concert appearances each year, Roberta Peters has also lent her efforts to a variety of social causes. She served as chairman of the National Cystic Fibrosis Foundation for several years and has recently appeared in concerts benefiting AIDS research. She has taken an active role in efforts to promote government funding for the arts and serves on the boards of the Metropolitan Opera Guild and the Carnegie Hall Corporation. In 1991, she was appointed by President George Bush to a five-year term on the National Council on the Arts. Peters is also an avid tennis player and has appeared in several celebrity tournaments.

Roberta Peters has made Israel and music of Jewish interest an important priority in her life. Although she received no formal Jewish education, she learned to speak Yiddish as a child from her grandmother, who spent most of the year living with the Peterman family while her husband served as maitre d' at Grossinger's Hotel in the Catskill Mountains, and with whom the young Roberta attended an Orthodox synagogue. Peters continues to include Yiddish folk songs in her many performances for synagogue audiences and other Jewish groups. She is a member of the board of the Anti-Defamation League and devoted to the cause of Israel Bonds. Peters has appeared often in Israel, performing in a benefit concert for the Roberta Peters Scholarship Fund of Hebrew University, and for soldiers in 1967, when she and her colleague Richard Tucker were caught in Israel during the Six-Day War. In addition to performing contemporary works by leading composers Aram Khatchaturian, Paul Creston, and Roy Harris, Peters appeared in the 1973 Carnegie Hall premiere of Darius Milhaud's *Ani Ma'amin* (with libretto by Elie Wiesel) and in the 1982 premiere of Abraham Kaplan's *Kedushah Symphony*.

Roberta Peters is the author of her own memoir, *Debut at the Met* (with Louis Biancolli, 1967) and has earned critical acclaim for her many recordings for RCA, Deutsche Grammophon, CBS, and London Decca. Her famous interpretations of Gilda, the Queen of the Night, and Rosina have recently been rereleased on compact disc.

Peters was married to fellow opera star Robert Merrill in a 1952 ceremony at New York's Park Avenue Synagogue, but the young couple divorced later that same year. Since April 10, 1955, the star performer and teacher, and dedicated servant of a host of worthy causes, has been married to prominent real estate investor Bertram Fields. They are the parents of Paul, a businessman, and Bruce, a banker.

SELECTED DISCOGRAPHY
Il Barbiere di Siviglia. RCA 6502; *Rigoletto*. RCA 60172; *Die Zauberflote*. Deutsche Grammophon 435395.

BIBLIOGRAPHY
Lyman, Darryl. *Great Jews in Music* (1986); Slonimsky, Nicolas. *Baker's Biographical Dictionary of Musicians*. 8th ed. (1993).

MARSHA BRYAN EDELMAN

PETLUCK, ALICE S. (1873–1953)

Alice S. Petluck was one of the earliest women legal pioneers. An immigrant from Russia, she became one of the first women in the United States to attend law school and to practice in New York. She was a prominent New York social reformer, who, through her example, was able to open the door for generations of future female lawyers.

Alice Serber Petluck was born on July 23, 1873, in Bar, Russia. One of at least three sisters, she immigrated to the United States in 1892 at nineteen. Remarkably, although she spoke no English at the time of her arrival, she graduated from New York University Law School a mere six years later. For the most part, the late 1800s were a time of widespread opposition to women attending law school, and the majority of law schools adopted formal measures to keep them out. New York University was one of the few law schools in the country to admit women. Alice Serber was one of only six women in her class.

After graduation, she married Dr. Joseph Petluck, a physician. In 1918, she became president of the Mothers Welfare League of the Bronx, an organization that addressed the needs of largely poor women and children in the Bronx. As president, Petluck was instrumental in establishing an alimony bureau, which operated through New York's magistrate courts to obtain payments for families with absent husbands. Through her work with the league, Petluck became concerned with the problem of juvenile delinquency. She advocated an increase in the number of home visits by visiting teachers to troubled families so that the teachers could work with families to prevent future occurrences. The league also operated as an employment bureau for young women during the Depression.

Alice Petluck was one of the first women lawyers to practice in the Federal District Court in the Southern District of New York and is believed to be the first woman lawyer to argue a case in New York's intermediate court of appeals. In 1928, Petluck was refused admittance to the Bronx Bar Association because she was a woman. In response, she and other women lawyers created the Bronx Women's Bar Association. Petluck served as a director of the association and was chair of its grievance committee at her death.

Petluck served her community in a number of other ways. She was president of the Parents Association of Junior School 55 in the Bronx, which was largely responsible for establishing the school's first dental clinic in 1923. She was also active in numerous Jewish causes, such as the WOMEN'S AMERICAN ORT, the Mizrachi Women's Organization of America (AMIT), the Federation of Jewish Women's Organizations, the Sisterhood of Congregation B'nai Jeshurun, and Ebra, Inc. Her work in the community was so well respected that a 1931 newspaper poll in the Bronx named her one of the borough's twenty leading citizens.

The Petlucks had three children, all lawyers: Charles A. Petluck, who served in the state attorney general's office; Ann Poses, an assistant executive director of the United Service for New Americans; and Robert Petluck, a principal in the Bronx.

Alice Petluck broke with convention by creating a career for herself at a time when most women were relegated to the household. A civic leader and innovator, she used her training to improve the lot of women and children.

She died on December 4, 1953, at age eighty.

BIBLIOGRAPHY

AJYB 56 (1956): 571; *NYTimes*, December 30, 1928; Obituary. *NYTimes*, December 11, 1953, 31:2; "One Hundred Years of Women at NYU School of Law." Centennial materials, NYU Law School, 1992; "Restless Women: The Pioneering Alumnae of New York University School of Law." 66 *NYU Law Review* 1996 (1991).

LAURA J. LEVINE

PHILANTHROPY

Jewish law and custom, secular culture, and economic and social roles have shaped Jewish women's involvement in philanthropic activities. Although the term is often associated with the beneficence of the wealthy, philanthropy refers to a broad range of activities—giving time as well as giving money—that are intended to enhance the quality of life in a community or a society. The concept of philanthropy is broader than charity, which is primarily directed to those in need. Philanthropic activities include charitable actions as well as support for self-help and mutual benefit organizations, and efforts that sustain communal institutions.

Jewish tradition specifies that men and women are expected to perform philanthropic acts of *chesed* [loving-kindness] and *tzedaka* [social justice]. Both are obligated to visit the sick, prepare the dead for burial, comfort mourners, give to the poor and the needy, support widows and orphans, offer hospitality, provide dowries for brides, and support community institutions. There are, however, qualitative differences in the ways that men and women have fulfilled these requirements at different times and in different contexts. Under strict interpretation of Jewish law, which governed most Jewish communities until this century, Jewish women were not held to the same standards of ritual performance as men or expected to devote significant amounts of time to learning Torah. Consequently, philanthropy has been a principal vehicle for religious expression for Jewish women, in contrast to Jewish men who have also been expected to devote themselves to prayer and study. Involvement in philanthropic endeavors has also provided Jewish women with a separate sphere, an arena in which they can contribute to community life, often serving as a context for exercising influence in the larger community or society, what historian Kathleen D. McCarthy calls a parallel power structure. Philanthropic activities have served yet another purpose. In social settings where Jewish women have been discouraged from active or fulfilling careers in paid jobs, philanthropic work provided them with "invisible careers."

Over the course of Jewish history, groups and organizations have been created to ensure that charitable purposes are carried out: A great deal of philanthropic activity occurs within voluntary groups rather than being done by individuals in a solo and informal fashion. Jacob R. Marcus's *Communal Sick-Care in the German Ghetto* describes the development of burial and sick-care associations, including the division of labor between men and women, that evolved as more German Jews became city dwellers. For medieval German Jews, the community as a whole or paid beadles were responsible for burial, and communal alms were given to the sick. Burial societies, organized by men but with women participants, were developed in the sixteenth century, and women-only burial societies were organized during the seventeenth century. Caring for the sick represented an expanded function of the burial society. The first women's organization in Germany that was specifically devoted to caring for the sick was founded in Berlin in 1745. Today, in the United States, burial societies for men and women exist as autonomous entities but are often attached to synagogues. An allied function, ensuring that mourners obtain their first meal after a burial or even all of their meals throughout the period of mourning, is frequently the province of informal groups of women in a community or formal groups within a synagogue.

Histories of Jewish philanthropy during the nineteenth and twentieth centuries describe four different organizational patterns: autonomous women's organizations, women's organizations that included some men, women's auxiliaries of male-dominated groups, and male-dominated communitywide organizations with token but increasing participation and influence by women.

AUTONOMOUS WOMEN'S ORGANIZATIONS

In some charitable endeavors, women created autonomous organizations where men were excluded. Often, these were parallel to men's organizations. In the United States, the most common types were ladies' benevolent societies, which existed in most communities during the nineteenth century. According to historian Rudolph Glanz, ladies' benevolent societies were transplanted, but expanded, versions of the female benevolent societies that existed throughout Germany. There, their role was more circumscribed, since they were part of a broader network of communal institutions. In America, they played a major role before large Hebrew charities were formed in the latter half of the nineteenth century. In small towns and cities, it was common for the synagogue and the benevolent society to be the only two Jewish communal institutions. Even into the twentieth century, as W. Lloyd Warner's study of "Yankee City" (Newburyport, Massachusetts) observed, the Jewish Ladies' Aid Society was the main Jewish charitable organization.

Women have also been the founders and donors of free loan societies. The Ladies' Hebrew Free Loan Society of Providence lent money only to women, but groups in Seattle and Chicago assisted both men and women. In major centers of Jewish life, another type of free loan society, called *gemachim*, lent goods. This is an understudied area: The only systematic discussion is Julia Bernstein's survey of *gemachim* in Jerusalem. Bernstein found that most *gemachim* are started by one person and operate on a small scale, usually out of the founder's home, sometimes with the assistance of a few friends. They tend to specialize in lending certain types of objects, such as bridal gowns, ritual objects, and tables and chairs. One *gemach* in Jerusalem, Yad Sarah, started out in this fashion and has grown into a large charitable organization that provides medical supplies and equipment. Regrettably, sociological studies of major Jewish communities in the United States such as Borough Park have overlooked *gemachim*.

Some nineteenth- and early twentieth-century Jewish women's organizations channeled domestic skills into philanthropic activities, for example, sewing societies that supplied immigrants, orphans, and soldiers with clothing and blankets. Today, in Orthodox and Hasidic communities, autonomous women's *bikur holim* societies visit hospitalized patients, attending to their needs for ritual objects and kosher food and ensuring that their relatives have housing and meals, usually for Shabbat but also at other times if patients are hospitalized at great distances from home.

Starting in the late nineteenth century in the United States, the United Kingdom, Germany, and Australia, Jewish women established what eventually became large, autonomous, national, and in several instances international organizations that played a central role in domestic and international philanthropy. They continue to provide health care, education, and social services in Israel. The first large national organization in the United States was the NATIONAL COUNCIL OF JEWISH WOMEN (NCJW), founded in 1893 as part of the World Congress of Religions of the Columbian Exposition in Chicago. NCJW was shaped by secular and religious forces. Paralleling events in the broader society, where American women established clubs and became involved in settlement houses and social reform movements during the late nineteenth century, NCJW provided an important mechanism for women to exercise public roles at a time when relatively few middle-class women were employed and when women had limited formal political influence since they were unable to vote. NCJW's members collaborated with other women's groups in various social reform efforts, including international activities designed to reduce the white slave trade. At the same time, NCJW institutionalized traditional kinds of communal activities of Jewish women: assisting immigrants by meeting them on arrival at Ellis Island, especially young women without families who might fall under the wrong influences; organizing Sabbath schools and Jewish study groups; visiting patients; establishing a kosher kitchen and later a synagogue in public hospitals on New York's Welfare (now Roosevelt) Island; and, in 1946, founding one of the first senior citizen centers in the United States.

HADASSAH, the largest Jewish women's organization in the United States, was founded by HENRIETTA SZOLD in 1912 to raise money for health and medical care in Palestine, starting with a nursing service in 1913. By the 1930s, Hadassah was a major provider of health care and social services, including Youth Aliyah, the resettlement of Jewish children from Europe. With increasing commitment to Zionism and a rise in migration to Palestine, a number of other organizations were established during the 1920s, including American Mizrachi Women (now AMIT, founded in 1925), PIONEER WOMEN (1925), WOMEN'S AMERICAN ORT (1927), and the Women's League for Israel (1928). A different ideology and constellation of functions were evident in the EMMA LAZARUS CLUBS. This organization, founded by CLARA LEMLICH SHAVELSON, a union activist, included women who were interested in expressing their progressive political ideology on domestic political issues in a Jewish context. Joyce Antler observes that the clubs "developed an agenda for collective action that linked women's rights and human rights to historical models."

It is important to recognize that these organizations drew on an expanding population of Jewish women who were more affluent and had more discretionary time than earlier generations. Immigrant women worked in factories, took in boarders, and created home-based businesses. Ewa Morawska's profile of the Jewish community of Johnstown, Pennsylvania, notes that even when families gained an economic foothold, Jewish women continued to work in family-owned businesses and had relatively little leisure time. Yet these women combined paid work and volunteer activities. The rise of large, autonomous Jewish women's organizations in the early twentieth century occurred at a historical moment when more Jewish women were able to spend time volunteering and when they mainly chose to devote their time to Jewish organizations. This process was amplified and expanded after World War II as Jewish families achieved even greater economic prosperity and moved to the suburbs where numerous groups were created.

WOMEN'S ORGANIZATIONS THAT INCLUDED SOME MEN

A second pattern of organizational arrangements included Jewish women's groups that included male donors and participants. Isaac Rontch and the Yiddish Writer's Group surveyed home town societies [*landsmanschaftn*] during the 1930s in a Work Projects Administration–supported project. Excerpts of this larger work are included in *Jewish Hometown Associations and Family Circles in New York*. A small number of the twenty-five hundred *landsmanschaftn* that responded to the survey were "ladies' societies": 71 were founded by women and 287 were women's auxiliaries. A majority of the women's *landsmanschaftn* had male

presidents or secretaries. For example, the Proskurover Ladies Benevolent Society was founded in 1909 and incorporated in 1916 by five women and one man. These mutual benefit societies served as an important context for sociability, sponsoring numerous social functions and providing immigrants social and economic capital as well as social welfare benefits. They offered members interest-free loans, burial plots, funeral expenses, and sickness and disability benefits. Like free loan societies, they had an enormous impact on the social and economic mobility of immigrants and were important building blocks in the development of viable Jewish communities in large cities as well as small towns.

Some organizations established by women recruited men as donors and board members, often as a way to sustain an enterprise that needed more money or organizational expertise. The Philadelphia Jewish Foster Home, established in 1855, and the Brooklyn Ladies Hebrew Home for the Aged, founded in Williamsburg in 1907 (and relocated to Brownsville), were established by women but later recruited male donors and board members. Philadelphia's Ezrath Nashim [Helping Women], founded in 1873, was reorganized as the Jewish Maternity Home and expanded its activities to personal visiting, a sewing circle to produce clothing and other items, a Nurses' Training School, a seaside Home for Invalid Women and Children, and a temporary nursery. However, the inclusion of men as donors and board members did not inevitably lead to male dominance. Regarding the addition of men to Ezrath Nashim's board, Evelyn Bodek noted, "The men added to the Board never controlled the society."

WOMEN'S AUXILIARIES OF MALE-DOMINATED GROUPS

A third type of organizational arrangement is the women's division of a larger, male-dominated organization. In some cases, these were affiliates of national or international groups, such as B'nai Brith Women's Organization and the Women's Divisions of the AMERICAN JEWISH CONGRESS and the United Jewish Appeal. Usually they were auxiliaries, a separate sphere for women within a small local group, often a synagogue, that served as a vehicle where women carried out charitable and communal work without necessarily being included in the organization's power structure. Frequently, women's auxiliaries were represented on an organization's board, but membership did not always lead to authority or influence.

Many women's auxiliaries were benevolent societies and sisterhoods that were part of synagogues.

The Atlanta Hebrew Ladies' Benevolent Society was established by members of the city's major Reform congregation. It provided immigrants with food, coal, clothing, and financial assistance as well as cooking lessons, temporary housing, and cash assistance. Over the course of the late nineteenth century and during the early twentieth century, benevolent societies changed their names and altered their functions, becoming sisterhoods. According to Jacob Marcus, the first Jewish women's group given the title of "sisterhood" was established as the Unabhaegiger Orden Treuer Schwestern [the Independent Order of True Sisters] at New York City's Temple Emanu-El during the 1840s. By the 1890s, the number of sisterhoods in the United States had expanded. Many were involved in community service, including, in New York City, recruiting volunteers who served as "friendly visitors" for the United Hebrew Charities, offering instruction, guidance, and financial assistance. New York's Shearith Israel, the Spanish and Portuguese synagogue's sisterhood, formed an Oriental Committee to serve the small and impoverished population of Sephardic immigrants moving to the Lower East Side during the early part of this century. Parallel to the immigrants' own institutions, these women sponsored a synagogue, religious school, and settlement house. Their efforts were severely criticized by Morris Gadol, editor of the Ladino newspaper *La America*, who indicated that the members of the sisterhood were only pretending to help and suggested that 86 Orchard Street, the building where all of these organizations were located, ought to be excommunicated.

The transition from benevolent society to sisterhood involved a shift in focus. Jenna Joselit points out that sisterhoods became less involved in charitable work because of the expanded role of professional social workers. Instead of concentrating on charitable work, these groups turned their attention toward serving their congregations rather than the community at large. They spent time raising money for congregations, organizing social events, supporting Hebrew schools, and establishing gift shops whose ostensible purpose was to raise money but also encouraged members to use the ritual objects and read the books that were sold.

Women's auxiliaries also played an important role in many of the Jewish orphanages and children's institutions that were established during the second half of the nineteenth century. In addition to fund-raising, women provided or underwrote the cost of services that enhanced the quality of the children's lives. In the Rochester Jewish Children's Home, a Mother's Club of neighborhood women prepared a Kiddush for each bar mitzvah and provided each child with clothing, including new outfits for major Jewish holidays. In 1950, the Hebrew Orphan Asylum in New York City founded a Godmother's Association, which was "a society of clubs led by women who would take on the role of confidante for a small number of children." They met in their homes to "give the children a taste of family life" and provided visits to concert halls, art galleries, parks, and the theater as well as to the women's country homes.

WOMEN'S INCREASING PARTICIPATION AND INFLUENCE IN MALE-DOMINATED COMMUNITY GROUPS

A final type of organizational arrangement includes large communitywide organizations dominated by men, where women had token involvement in the past but are currently increasing their participation and influence. Although there have been exceptional women who played key roles in male-dominated institutions, such as REBECCA GRATZ of Philadelphia, who started several important organizations such as the Jewish Orphan Society in 1815 and the Hebrew Sunday School Society in 1838, and PAULINE PERLMUTTER STEINEM, president of the Toledo, Ohio, Hebrew Free Loan Society, large Jewish communal institutions have been dominated by men. This situation has been steadily changing in the past two and a half decades as more women have entered professions and challenged gender roles. Rather than accept second-class citizenship or involvement in parallel organizations, Jewish women have been challenging the male dominance of many communal institutions, including synagogues. In 1979, Aviva Cantor charged that volunteering served as a "sheltered workshop" in the sense that women were engaged in tasks providing a sense of participation but had little influence over the direction of communal affairs. These challenges have begun to alter the governance of Jewish communal institutions, particularly Jewish Federations, where the proportion of women on boards and key committees has increased and more women are involved in top leadership roles. In 1975, 17 percent of Federation board members were women as compared to 32 percent in 1993. Interestingly, Jewish women have made greater strides in small communities than in large ones. More women are taking their place in these organizations based on their own talents and track record of giving, and not just on their husbands'.

A great deal more has been written about Jewish philanthropic organizations than about patterns of individual giving and volunteering. A study of wealthy donors done by Francie Ostrower, which included a sizable number of Jews, pointed out that they viewed giving to Jewish causes as a communal tax—obligatory giving expected of all members of the Jewish community. Limited but compelling evidence suggests that men and women carry out their charitable commitments in different ways. Ewa Morawska observes that much of the daily informal and regular giving of *tzedaka* [charity] was the province of women since they had primary responsibility for the *pushkes* [charity boxes] that were found in the homes of most Jews in Johnstown, Pennsylvania, during the first half of this century. More needs to be learned about gender differences in face-to-face giving within Orthodox communities, some of it at daily minyan but much of it through house-to-house solicitation by fund-raisers, beggars, and beggars pretending to be fund-raisers. Susan Weidman Schneider's two-part series in *LILITH* points out that men and women have different philanthropic styles. Women are more drawn to causes and issues; men are more influenced by the social recognition and prestige they gain from the public announcement of donations that occurs in Jewish fund-raising events featuring "card calling." When Jewish women support an organization, they tend to give money and time, in contrast to men whose support is more often limited to writing a check.

In contemporary secular societies, involvement in philanthropic endeavors is an important form of Jewish affiliation, a way that people express their Jewish identity and commitment to Jewish continuity. In the past, Jewish philanthropic institutions were successful in relying on a combination of religious motivations, peer pressure, a sense of communal responsibility, support for the State of Israel, and concern for the survival of the Jewish people. Recruiting and fund-raising techniques also account for the fact that American Jews are more generous than their non-Jewish peers. However, a number of trends suggest that this situation is changing. There is considerable evidence that the Jewish civil religion that evolved during this century will not continue in its present form. In response, Jewish organizations and conferences now include opportunities for Torah study and ritual observance. Several cultural and social changes—decreased barriers toward Jews in employment and social relations, decreased religious observance, increased intermarriage, changes in the nature of Israeli society, and the attractiveness of Israel as a focus of giving—are altering the nature of Jewish philanthropy. There are strong signs that Jewish philanthropic and organizational life will not continue in its present form without conscious changes in both the structure of organizations and in the techniques they employ to motivate donors and volunteers. Although Jewish philanthropy has experienced considerable

changes over the course of this century, some trends suggest a greater amount of discontinuity. In the past, there were significant generational differences in the types of organizations people chose, but involvement remained almost exclusively focused in the Jewish community. Today, more and more organizational affiliations and donations by each succeeding generation are to organizations outside the Jewish community.

Empirical data from a number of studies indicate that Jews are becoming more integrated into the philanthropic organizations of the general society. They are less exclusively involved in Jewish organizations and direct more of their donations to non-Jewish organizations. Warner's community study of Newburyport observed that each generation of Jewish women selected a different set of activities from the previous one. Immigrants joined the Jewish Ladies' Aid Society and their daughters joined Hadassah. To further the analogy, were Warner to revisit, he might find some of their granddaughters in Hadassah but others in the Junior League, an organization once closed to Jewish women. Data from the 1990 National Jewish Population survey, discussed in *American Jewish Philanthropy in the '90's*, reveal that 70 percent of first- and second-generation American Jews contributed to Jewish philanthropies. By the third generation, this declined to 50 percent, and it was reduced further to 36 percent in the fourth generation. Declining social barriers combined with an increase in the number of very wealthy and philanthropic Jewish families has meant that Jews are being courted as donors and board members for mainstream institutions that excluded them in the past, such as non-Jewish hospitals, art museums, orchestras, and public libraries. Alice Goldstein points out that women's involvement in Jewish and non-Jewish activities should not be assumed to be mutually exclusive, but that organizations need to provide different types of volunteer opportunities to attract better-educated women and those more likely to have careers. Susan Weidman Schneider points out that women are themselves spearheading major changes, since younger Jewish women are supporting alternative funds, like the New Israel Fund and the Shefa Fund, organizations outside the traditional Federation structure that combine their feminism and their commitment to Jewish community life.

Jewish women's philanthropy, then, represents the nexus of women's roles in the Jewish community and the societies in which they have lived, and reflects the influence of religious and secular values. Although some critics see philanthropic endeavors as ways to keep women from real work in the form of paid jobs, and keep them subordinate and marginal, providing an illusion of participation but little real influence, other observers have noted the myriad other functions of philanthropy. It is important to recognize that much of the routine philanthropic work of Jewish women has enhanced the quality of their lives, enabled many to find meaningful careers albeit in unpaid work, cemented their relations with other women, provided emotional support and built social capital in Jewish communities, supported institutions, and promoted Jewish continuity.

BIBLIOGRAPHY

Angel, Marc D. *La America: The Sephardic Experience in the United States* (1982); Antler, Joyce. "Between Culture and Politics: The Emma Lazarus Federation of Jewish Women's Clubs and the Promulgation of Women's History, 1944–1989." In *U.S. History as Women's History*, edited by Linda Kerber and Alice Kessler-Harris (1995); Baum, Charlotte, Paula Hyman, and Sonya Michel. *The Jewish Women in America* (1976); Bernstein, Julia. "The Trend to Lend: Gemachim in Action." *Jerusalem Post* 12 (March 1993): 11; Bodek, Evelyn. "'Making Do': Jewish Women and Philanthropy." In *Jewish Life in Philadelphia, 1830–1940*, edited by Murray Friedman (1983); Bogin, Hyman. *The Luckiest Orphans* (1992); Cantor, Aviva. "The Sheltered Workshop." *Lilith* (Spring 1979); Chambré, Susan M. "Parallel Power Structures, Invisible Careers, Benevolence and Reform: Implications of Women's Philanthropy." *Nonprofit Management and Leadership* 4 (1993): 233–239; Daniels, Arlene Kaplan. *Invisible Careers* (1988); Glanz, Rudolph. *The Jewish Woman in America: Two Female Immigrant Generations, 1820–1929.* Vol. 2: The German Jewish Woman (1975); Goldstein, Alice. "New Roles, New Commitments? Jewish Women's Involvement in the Community's Organizational Structure." *Contemporary Jewry* 11, no. 1 (1990): 49–76; Goldstein, Howard. *The Home on Gorham Street and the Voices of Its Children* (1996); Joselit, Jenna. "The Special Sphere of the Middle-Class American Jewish Woman: The Synagogue Sisterhood, 1890–1940." In *The American Synagogue: A Sanctuary Transformed*, edited by Jack Wertheimer (1987); Kliger, Hannah, ed. *Jewish Hometown Associations and Family Circles in New York: The WPA Yiddish Writers' Group Study* (1992); Kosmin, Barry A. *The Status of Women in Lay and Professional Leadership Positions of Federations* (1994); Kosmin, Barry A., and Paul Ritterband. *Contemporary Jewish Philanthropy in America* (1991); Landesman, Alter F. *Brownsville: The Birth, Development and Passing of a Jewish Community in New York* (1971); McCarthy, Kathleen D. "Parallel Power Structures: Women and the Voluntary Sphere." In *Lady Bountiful Revisited: Women, Philanthropy, and Power*, edited by Kathleen D. McCarthy (1990); Marcus, Jacob R. *Communal Sick-Care in the German Ghetto* (1947); Milamed, Susan. "Proskurover Landsmanschaftn: A Case Study in Jewish Communal Development." *AJH* 76: 40–55; Moore, Deborah Dash. *To the Golden Cities: Pursuing the American Jewish Dream in Miami and LA* (1994); New York Section, National Council of Jewish Women. *All Our Yesterdays, All Our Tomorrows* (1974); Ostrower, Francie. *Why the Wealthy Give* (1996); Rogow, Faith. *Gone to Another Meeting: The National Council of Jewish Women, 1893–1993* (1993); Schneider, Susan Weidman. "Feminist Jewish Philanthropy." *Lilith* (Fall 1993): 14–17, and "Jewish Women's Philanthropy." *Lilith* (Winter 1992): 1–10; Tenenbaum, Shelley. *A Credit to Their Community: Jewish Loan Societies in the United States, 1880–1945* (1993); Tobin, Gary A., and Adam Z. Tobin. *American Jewish Philanthropy in the 1990's* (1995); Warner, W. Lloyd. *The Social System of American Ethnic Groups* (1945); Wenger, Beth S. "Jewish Women of the Club: The Changing Public Role of Atlanta's Jewish Women (1870–1930)." *AJH* 76: 311–333.

SUSAN CHAMBRÉ

PHILLIPS, ELLEN (1821–1891)

Ellen Phillips influenced generations of young Jewish girls and boys in nineteenth-century Philadelphia. One of the founding members of the Hebrew Sunday School Society in 1838, Phillips donated her time, family wealth, and religious convictions to several Jewish and sectarian philanthropic organizations.

Ellen Phillips, born on October 30, 1821, was the tenth of eleven children of Zalegman Phillips, a lawyer and president of Congregation Mikveh Israel (1806–1807, 1822–1834), and Arabella Solomans. The Phillipses, one of Philadelphia's original Jewish families, had established themselves as a part of nineteenth-century Philadelphia's Jewish elite through their wealth, charitable activities, and association with Congregation Mikveh Israel.

Phillips and REBECCA GRATZ, her contemporary, were deeply influenced by their Jewish heritage. Her desire to preserve and instill the tenets of her religion in the young, especially as the number of Jews entering America from Europe increased, resulted in Phillips, Gratz, Louis B. Hart, and Simha Peixotto establishing the Hebrew Sunday School Society in 1838 under the aegis of the Hebrew Benevolent Society. The school was to provide supplementary religious education to all Jewish children. This was significant because, until that time, girls received no formal training. Phillips served the society from its inception to her death in 1891 as a creator and signer of the Society's constitution, a teacher, school superintendent (1871–1886), and vice president and manager of the Benevolent Society. Phillips contributed to other charities helping poor and immigrant Jews by making considerable donations to the Jewish Maternity Association, the Jewish Theological Seminary, the Young Women's Union (est. 1885), and the building of Touro Hall, a permanent residence for the Sunday School, in 1891. Consequently, Ellen Phillips's good works were honored through a memorial bed at the Maternity Association's home in 1891, and a tablet in the main hall of Touro Hall in the same year.

Ellen Phillips died on August 2, 1891, continuing her philanthropy even in her will. She left donations of over $110,000 to the Jewish organizations named above and to secular organizations such as the American Philosophical Society and the Fairmount Park Art Gallery, to which she donated artwork that she had inherited from her brother, Henry Mayer, a former congressman and president of the board of Fairmount Park Commissioners.

By dedicating her life to preserving and instilling Jewish heritage in the young, Ellen Phillips used her position and faith to educate generations of individuals. At the same time, she occupied a place of authority and social significance within the Jewish community of nineteenth-century Philadelphia. Phillips typified the "elite Jewess" of the antebellum era who, as a privileged woman, dominated the female realm of community service that would eventually be overcome by professionalism and dominated by men by the turn of the century.

BIBLIOGRAPHY

Ashton, Dianne. "Souls Have No Sex." In *When Philadelphia Was the Capital of Jewish America*, edited by Murray Friedman (1993); Bodek, Evelyn "'Making Do': Jewish Women and Philanthropy." In *Jewish Life in Philadelphia, 1830–1940*, edited by Murray Friedman (1983); Morais, Henry Samuel. *The Jews of Philadelphia: Their history from the Earliest Settlements to the Present Time . . .* (1894); Phillips, Ellen. Papers. Hebrew Sunday School Society Collection, Rolls 1–4. Jewish American Archives, Balch Institute of Ethnic Studies, Philadelphia; Rezneck, Samuel. *The Saga of an American Jewish Family Since the Revolution: A History of the Family of Jonas Phillips* (1980); Sussman, Lance. *Isaac Leeser and the Making of American Judaism* (1995); *UJE*; Wolf, Simon. *The American Jew as Patriot, Soldier, and Citizen* (1972).

ERIKA PIOLA

PHILLIPS, IRNA (1901–1973)

Millions of people helped popularize the radio and television soap operas created by scriptwriter Irna Phillips. Born in Chicago, Illinois, on July 1, 1901, to William S. and Betty (Buxbaum) Phillips, she had nine older siblings. Her father, a grocer born to Polish immigrant parents, died when Irna was eight years old, leaving her mother, a Jewish immigrant from Germany, to keep the large family together with income from several rental properties.

A sickly and sensitive child, Phillips sought refuge in books and a world of make-believe. She attended public schools in Chicago before matriculating at Northwestern University in 1918. The following year, she transferred to the University of Illinois, where the aspiring actress studied drama. When an acting position failed to materialize, Phillips took her B.S. in education in 1923 and embarked on a teaching career. With the exception of one year of graduate study at the University of Wisconsin, she spent the next seven years teaching English, public speaking, and drama at a junior college in Fulton, Missouri, and at a teachers' college in Dayton, Ohio.

During summer vacations, Phillips worked without pay for radio station WGN in Chicago. She briefly hosted the inspirational program *A Thought for Today* before turning her attention to scriptwriting. In 1930, she created *Painted Dreams*, one of the earliest radio soap operas. Phillips and another woman played the parts for the serial's six characters and provided the sound effects. The program's immediate popularity encouraged Phillips, who became eager for network sponsorship. When WGN refused to give Phillips the rights to *Painted Dreams*, she simply created a new program, *Today's Children*, which aired on NBC beginning in 1932. Both serials featured a wise motherly character, modeled on Betty Buxbaum Phillips. Phillips retired this highly popular serial in 1938, shortly after her mother's death.

Working with a full-time secretary and staff of writers and researchers, Phillips produced five daytime serials during the early 1940s. Among her most popular radio soap operas were *The Guiding Light*, *Woman in White*, *The Right to Happiness*, *Lonely Women*, and *The "New" Today's Children*. Known for her trademark cliff-hangers, the use of organ music to create moods, and the "crossover" (when characters from one show appeared on another), she was among the first scriptwriters to utilize the amnesia victim and the murder trial. Shunning sensationalism, Phillips preferred to focus on real-life families as they coped with such socially significant issues as juvenile delinquency during World War II, the adjustments of returning war veterans, adultery, adoption, and divorce. In contrast with other radio soap operas, which typically endorsed traditional visions of domesticity and femininity, Phillips's serials frequently conveyed the complexities of modern women's choices.

Television brought an end to many of radio's soap operas, but Phillips proved adaptable to the new format. Her first effort (*These Are My Children*) flopped, but in 1952, *The Guiding Light* became the first daytime radio serial to make the transition to television. Phillips also wrote for such programs as *The Brighter Day, The Road to Life, As the World Turns, Another World, Days of Our Lives,* and *Love Is a Many Splendour'd Thing.* In 1964, she also served as a consultant for the prime-time series *Peyton Place.*

Phillips, who never married, adopted two children, Thomas Dirk (b. 1941) and Katherine Louise (b. 1943). Phillips suffered a heart attack and died in Chicago on December 23, 1973.

BIBLIOGRAPHY

Current Biography Yearbook (1943, 1974); "Irna Phillips, 72, Serials Writer." *NYTimes*, December 30, 1973, 31:1; "Life as a Soap Opera: The Story of Irna." *Chicago Daily News*, January 12, 1974; *NAW* modern; Phillips, Irna. Papers. State Historical Society of Wisconsin, Madison; "Script Queen." *Time* 35 (June 10, 1940): 66+; "Writing On: Irna Phillips Mends with Tradition." *Broadcasting* 83 (November 6, 1972): 75; *WWWIA* (1974–1976); Wyden, Peter. "'As the World Turns' They Suffer and Suffer." *Saturday Evening Post* (June 25, 1960), 30+.

JOANNE PASSET

PHILLIPS, PAULINE ESTHER FRIEDMAN *see* VAN BUREN, ABIGAIL

PHILLIPS, REBECCA MACHADO (1746–1831)

Rebecca Phillips's life embodies the overlapping of the mundane and the exceptional: She not only was a mother, but also served as a pioneering leader in Jewish and secular American communal life.

Rebecca Machado Phillips was born in Reading, Pennsylvania, on November 21, 1746. She was the elder of two daughters born to María Caetana (Zipporah) and Rev. David Mendez Machado. Both of her parents were born in Portugal, and their families had been secret Jews in Lisbon for generations.

Her parents settled in New York, where David Machado served as hazan of Shearith Israel, the Spanish and Portuguese synagogue. He died a year after Rebecca's birth, on December 4, 1747. Her mother remarried shortly thereafter to Israel Jacobs, producing Rebecca's half-sister Rachel. Sixteen-year-old Rebecca Machado was married on November 10, 1762, in Hickory Town, Plymouth Township, Montgomery County, Pennsylvania, to Jonas Phillips, a merchant eleven years her senior.

Shortly after their marriage, the couple moved to New York, and by the next autumn, the first of their children was born. The early years of marriage were financially strained, though by the second decade of their marriage, the Phillips family became prosperous. According to Philadelphia tax records of 1781 and 1782, Jonas Phillips, who worked as a merchant during the Revolution, was the second wealthiest Jew of the city. From age seventeen to forty-six, Rebecca Phillips bore twenty-one children. Later Rebecca and Jonas Phillips also demonstrated their philanthropy through the adoption of their orphaned grandchildren, Mordecai Manuel and Judith Noah.

The Phillips family remained in New York until the occupation of that city by the British army in 1774 prompted their move to Philadelphia. Dr. Benjamin Rush's letter to his wife, describing the marriage ceremony of eighteen-year old Rachel, the fifth child of Jonas and Rebecca, is the only surviving account of an eighteenth-century Jewish wedding.

In 1782, Phillips and Grace Nathan undertook to raise and collect funds for the purchase of ritual objects for the newly founded Mikveh Israel synagogue of Philadelphia. In 1801, Phillips was one of the founding members of the Female Association for the Relief of Women and Children in Reduced Circumstances, an organization dedicated to assisting yellow fever victims in Baltimore, supporting a soup house for the poor, and generally providing food and clothing to indigent women and children. Phillips's philanthropy is also evident in her bequest of a large scroll of the Book of Esther, the megillah from which the hazan at Congregation Shearith Israel has traditionally read.

In 1820, at age seventy-four, Rebecca Phillips served as "first directress" and one of thirteen managers on the board of the Female Hebrew Benevolent Society of Philadelphia. The society, founded in 1819 to assist the Jewish indigent, was the first Jewish charitable society in America not associated with a synagogue. Phillips's responsibilities are delineated in the Society's constitution: "The first Directress shall preside at the meetings of the Board of Managers, preserve order, appoint committees, call special meetings, and give the casting vote in questions where the board are equally divided."

The society held two general meetings yearly, while managers met once every two weeks during the winter and more frequently if needed. In 1820, Phillips paid the society an annual subscription of three dollars (two dollars annually was required for membership). The last record of Phillips's public involvement dates to 1825, when she donated thirty dollars to Mikveh Israel's Building Committee.

Jonas Phillips died in 1803. Rebecca spent the last twenty-eight years of her life as a widow. The engraving on the tomb of Jonas Phillips in the burial grounds of Shearith Israel reads: "Jonas Phillips, Merchant / son of Aaron Uriah Phillips / and husband of Rebecca Mendez Machado." According to an unconfirmed source, the tombstone had originally depicted Rebecca seated at her late husband's grave, accompanied by a small child.

Rebecca Phillips died at age eighty-five on June 25, 1831, in Philadelphia and is buried in the Mikveh Israel Cemetery of that city.

BIBLIOGRAPHY

Ashton, Dianne. "'Souls Have No Sex': Philadelphia Jewish Women and the American Challenge." In *When Philadelphia Was the Capital of Jewish America*, edited by Murray Friedman (1993); Barnett, Richard D. "Zipra Nunes's Story." In *A Bicentennial Festschrift for Jacob Rader Marcus*, edited by Bertram Wallace Korn (1976); *BDEAJ*; Butterfield, L.H., ed. *Letters of Benjamin Rush. Vol. 1, 1761–1792* (1951); *The Constitution of the Female Hebrew Benevolent Society of Philadelphia* (1825); Elmaleh, L.H., and J. Bunford Samuel, comps. *The Jewish Cemetery: Ninth and Spruce Street, Philadelphia* (1962?); Genealogical Publishing Co. *First Census of the United States Taken in the Year 1790, Pennsylvania* (1992); Kohut, George Alexander. "The Oldest Tombstone Inscriptions of Philadelphia and Richmond." *AJHS* 6 (1897): 107–111; Morais, Henry Samuel. *The Jews of Philadelphia: Their History From the Earliest Settlements to the Present Time* (1894); Phillips, N. Taylor. "Family History of the Reverend David Mendez Machado." *AJHS* 2 (1894): 45–61; Phillips, Rosalie S. "A Burial Place for the Jewish Nation Forever." *AJHS* 18 (1909): 106; Pool, David de Sola. *Portraits Etched in Stone: Early Jewish Settlers, 1682–1831* (1952); Pool, David de Sola, and Tamar de Sola Pool. *An Old Faith in the New World: Portrait of Shearith Israel, 1654–1954* (1955); Sarna, Jonathan D. *Jacksonian Jew: The Two Worlds of Mordecai Manuel Noah* (1981); Shearith Israel. Trustee minutes and other records of the Congregation, anno 5523, p. 20, AJA; Stern, Malcolm H. *First American Jewish Families: 600 Genealogies, 1654–1988* (1991); Wolf, Edwin, II, and Maxwell Whiteman. *The History of the Jews of Philadelphia from Colonial Times to the Age of Jackson* (1957).

AVIVA BEN-UR

PHILLIPS, ROSALIE SOLOMONS
(c. 1867–1946)

When, in 1912, a tiny Jewish women's study group known as the Hadassah Circle announced its intention to form an international organization addressing social conditions in Palestine, one of its founders, along with HENRIETTA SZOLD, was Rosalie

Along with helping to found HADASSAH, *Rosalie Solomons Phillips served many mainstream secular American causes, including the New York State Democratic Committee.* [American Jewish Historical Society]

Phillips, a woman whose name was already well known in Jewish American philanthropy and politics. Through her involvement in the fledgling organization, Phillips offered a wide range of resources and connections critical to its success.

Born around 1867, in Washington, D.C., Rosalie was the daughter of Adolphus S. Solomons, founder of the Montefiore and Mount Sinai hospitals in New York and the Providence Hospital in Washington. Rosalie's life story, like her father's, is one of intense involvement in and service to both American and Jewish concerns and causes.

A founding member and the first chair of HADASSAH, she was also president of the Columbia Religious and Industrial School for Jewish Girls, a vice president of the NATIONAL COUNCIL OF JEWISH WOMEN, New York Section, honorary vice president of the Union of Orthodox Jewish Congregations of America, honorary president of Young Judaea, and a member of the board of directors of the Young Women, a Jewish organization. Additionally, she was deeply involved in the maintenance and workings of the Spanish and Portuguese synagogue in New York.

A descendant of Haym Salomon, a financier of the American War of Independence, Rosalie expressed her ardent patriotism through numerous avenues of mainstream political involvement. Married to Captain N. Taylor Phillips, an attorney who was likewise a leader in democratic politics, Rosalie Phillips assumed her first political post in 1918. This position, as coleader of New York's Seventh District, was augmented by her membership in the Democratic County Committee for the Fifth Assembly District.

In 1928, Phillips was made vice-chair of the Women's Division of the New York State Democratic Committee, a position she held until 1943. Prior to that time, in 1920, she had already been named an official delegate for New York and, in that capacity, attended six consecutive conventions between 1920 and 1936.

In addition to her professional political involvement, Phillips was a lifetime member of both the American Flag Association and of the Daughters of the American Revolution, Knickerbocker Chapter, for which she also served as president. A charter member of the National Society of Patriotic Women of America, she functioned as that organization's organizational historian.

Rosalie Phillips died in New York City on February 5, 1946, at her home on the Upper West Side.

BIBLIOGRAPHY

AJYB 48: 496; "Mrs. N.T. Phillips, Figure in City, 79." *NY Times*, February 7, 1946, 23:3; *WWIAJ* (1928).

DAWN ROBINSON ROSE

PHOTOGRAPHERS

There is no simple way to categorize Jewish American women photographers—they are too diverse a group. They come from distinctly different political periods, economic strata, and even cultures (some were born abroad). They share neither mindset nor style, their subjects and interests vary widely, and their worldview and art seem to have little to do with their Jewish identity.

Links, however, may exist among some of them. For example, a significant number of Jewish American women photographers seem to have a strong social conscience—whether they were born to wealth as were DORIS ULMANN and DIANE ARBUS, or in working-class neighborhoods, as were Helen Levitt and Rebecca Lepkoff, or come from abroad, as did Sandra Weiner. Many seem to reject obviously pretty or pleasing subjects, and sometimes conventional techniques, in favor of work that is intellectually probing, wryly amusing, radical, provocative, or even profoundly disturbing. And many appear to want their work to serve some moral, historic, or humane purpose, however subtly expressed. Even ANNIE LEIBOVITZ, the ultimate "celebrity photographer," documented the tragedy of Sarajevo, where she traveled with noted photography critic SUSAN SONTAG. Finally, many went to art school to study sculpture or painting and only later, often by accident, found their way to photography. Many seemed to feel it was a much less demanding medium to master than other art forms.

From the time of its invention in 1839, and for some period thereafter, photography was regarded more as a scientific invention and curiosity than a new and valued fine art—the talents of women, therefore, were deemed appropriate for it. What is more, women found in photography fewer obstacles to their progress than in the traditional fine arts of painting, sculpture, and architecture. Photography, then, offered women a career, a way to earn a living, and a medium for artistic expression.

PORTRAITURE

With the advent of photography, portraits suddenly became a reality for the middle class and even for the masses. Portraiture was a genre many women found congenial, including many Jewish American women photographers, and some specialized in it—at least for periods within their careers.

It must be understood, however, that "portraits" come in many guises and depend on many factors: the motive of the photographer, the complicity (or lack of it) of the sitter, and the variables of lighting, focus, and composition.

Doris Ulmann (1882–1934), was born to wealth and raised on New York City's Park Avenue. Like other women of means, she took up photography as a hobby and as a creative outlet. A student of sociologist/photographer Louis Hine (who used photography to make people aware of social injustice—like child labor) and later of photographer Clarence White, Ulmann established her reputation by publishing portfolios of the medical faculties of Columbia and Johns Hopkins universities. Because she worked to please herself, she rarely photographed anyone in whom she was not interested. Her subjects in the early 1920s were prominent urban artists and intellectuals (Albert Einstein, Thornton Wilder, Paul Robeson, for example), who posed at Ulmann's request and expense.

Later in the decade, her work took a new direction as she set out to document rural life. Traveling to New England, New York, and Pennsylvania, she photographed Mennonites and various Shaker settlements. Later, in the rural South, she recorded South Carolina's Gullah people, Creoles, and Appalachian mountaineers. Why the interest in cultural anthropology? The early death of Ulmann's mother and the photographer's own delicate health as a youngster, as well as the influence of Hine, no doubt sensitized her to the dignity of human struggle. Also, she wanted to record a disappearing way of life and to serve some social purpose. However, this body of work could never be mistaken for an objective record; although handsome, the images romanticize and idealize their subjects.

Trude Fleischmann (1895–1990), who took up photography at age nine, grew up in a prosperous Jewish family in Vienna. On returning there in 1918 after studying art history in Paris, she opened a thriving portrait studio, drawing her subjects mainly from the world of actors (Hedy Lamarr, Katharine Cornell), dancers, and musicians (Bruno Walter). While her early work was brown-tinted and soft-focused, she later favored a more "modern" sharp-focused approach. LOTTE JACOBI (1896–1990), born in Germany, likewise specialized in portraits of artistic and scientific achievers (Einstein, Thomas Mann, J.D. Salinger).

Rebecca Lepkoff's (b. 1916) work evolved in ways similar to Doris Ulmann's. Born on New York City's Lower East Side, she concentrated on the city's streets in her early work, producing portraits and city views. After moving to Vermont, she photographed the local people (farmers, homemakers) in their world.

During her career, Ruth Orkin (1921–1985) did portraits, photojournalism, and street photography, and also codirected films (*The Little Fugitive, Lovers and Lollipops*). In the 1950s, she photographed illustrious actors and musicians (Marlon Brando, Woody Allen, Leonard Bernstein, Isaac Stern). One of her more interesting later projects was to take pictures throughout the year from the window of her Central Park West apartment. Given the limitations of her perch, the variety of images is impressive—she documented shifts in light, clouds, weather, and a parade or two.

The best portraits by Austrian-born photographer Inge Morath (b. 1923) have a satiric edge. For his sitting with her, artist/cartoonist Saul Steinberg made droll paper masks that the sitters (presumably Steinberg and his wife) wear. Masks aside, their demeanor and dress are entirely proper, stiff, even decorous—the contrast is whimsical and disquieting. Morath's dim view of social distinction based solely on wealth is revealed in her photo of "Mrs. Eveleigh Nash, Buckingham Palace Mall" (1953). The subject, who is laden with a mink coat and a chinchilla lap blanket and wears a marvelously baroque hat, is seen seated in her open-air carriage, her chauffeur at her side. Like Margaret Dumont, Groucho Marx's straight woman, Mrs. Nash is a perfect parody of a dowager. Morath became a widely published photojournalist and in 1953 was invited by Robert Capa to join the photo-cooperative Magnum Photos.

There is an unmistakable feminist slant to the work of Judy Dater (b. 1941). Using herself and others costumed or nude as models, she explores woman's roles, strengths, and vulnerabilities. At its best, her work displays a caustic humor as in the images: "Elephant Woman Steps Out" or "Death by Ironing." In her earlier work, content was clearly emphasized (women's identities, stereotypes, and sexual roles); aesthetics were not a major consideration. More recently, she has experimented with constructions consisting of portraits and various evocative scenes arranged in differently configured grids. She has also been experimenting with computer-altered images.

ANNIE LEIBOVITZ (b. 1949), whose own celebrity rivals that of many of her sitters, is one of today's highest-paid and most sought-after commercial photographers. Her specialty is portraits of celebrities, and, as critic Charles Harding observes, "a startling number of her images have become icons of popular culture." Some critics have dismissed her work on the arbitrary grounds that it is commercial, deals with popular culture, and rarely seems to get "below the surface."

Her portraits are unidealized and striking for their sharp wit, for her inventive use of props, and for her habit of parodying what she sees as her subject's persona. She photographed Whoopi Goldberg submerged in a milk bath, roaring with laughter; Demi Moore nude and very pregnant for a cover of *Vanity Fair*; Roseanne and Tom Arnold wrestling in the mud (*Vanity Fair*). Her portrait of artist Keith Haring is particularly apt. Nude, he becomes a piece with the room he poses in—his body, the walls, couch, lamp, and even the coffee table on which he stands are all white and painted with his trademark black "primitive" writing.

Leibovitz's childhood was unique for a Jewish youngster because her father was an Air Force colonel. She lived in many places, including a year in Israel on a kibbutz. Like many woman photographers, she began as a painting student (in the 1960s, at the San Francisco Art Institute) but was seduced by the immediacy of photography. In 1991, she was the second living photographer ever to be featured in an exhibit at the National Portrait Gallery in Washington, D.C.

ADVERTISING

Foto Ringl + Pit was the name of a photographic studio founded in 1930 in Berlin by Ellen Auerbach (b. 1906) and Grete Stern (b. 1904), which produced witty, prize-winning, avant-garde advertising work. As Juan Mandelbaum's film on the studio reveals, Ringl + Pit was a name derived from the photographers' childhood nicknames: Pit for Auerbach and Ringl for Stern. (Their last names, they believed, sounded too much like a firm of Jewish merchants). The two, raised in bourgeois Jewish homes in Germany, rejected the constraining values of their families. They studied photography with Bauhaus Professor Walter Peterhans, adopted a bohemian life-style, and

Foto Ringl + Pit was a photographic studio that produced witty, prize-winning, avant-garde advertising work. This ad features a mannequin. The hand that displays the lotion bottle belongs to one of the photographers. [ringl + pit. Courtesy of Robert Mann Gallery]

came to epitomize the "new woman"—that is, they were emancipated, independent women who cropped their hair, wore trousers, took lovers, and answered only to themselves.

Auerbach (who now lives in New York City) and Stern (who lives in Argentina) have recently been "rediscovered" and are enjoying much critical and scholarly attention. Although they won advertising assignments and worked on other artistic projects, their collaboration had only limited commercial success, probably because of their avant-garde style and lack of interest in business. One of their prize-winning photographs advertises the hair lotion Petrole Hahn (1931). Typically, it employs props and features a female mannequin, whose creamy skin, cupid mouth, kohl-rimmed eyes, and simpering smile are obviously artificial. The dummy's eyebrows and wavy stylish wig, however, are made of human hair, and the hand that displays the lotion bottle belongs to one of the photographers. This surreal blend of reality and fantasy startles at first, then coaxes the viewer toward deeper philosophical musings.

DOCUMENTATION—FORMAL INTERESTS

Alma Lavenson's (1897–1989) father was a successful businessman, philanthropist, and community leader in the San Francisco area. Reflecting his era's attitudes, he felt that it was wrong to take a job from someone who needed it and also believed that a working daughter reflected on his ability to support his family. Because her father disapproved of women working if they didn't have to, it is no wonder that Lavenson consistently referred to herself as an amateur, and after her marriage in 1933 continued to think of photography only as an avocation. Her work is unique in that she concentrated on industrial and architectural themes, subjects traditionally favored by men. Interested mainly in formal design, textural elements, and tonalities, she did studies of dams ("Calaveras Dam II," 1932) and dying or defunct mines and mining towns. In the 1920s and 1930s, "Precisionists" Charles Sheeler, Niles Spencer, and others, whose work Lavenson may have known and certainly was in sympathy with, also favored machine imagery and sharply defined, clearly rendered compositions.

DOCUMENTATION—SOCIAL AND ANTHROPOLOGICAL

Helen Levitt (b. 1913) is a native New Yorker. Born and raised in the Italian-Jewish Bensonhurst section of Brooklyn (her father was Jewish, her mother Italian), she currently lives in Manhattan. Her best-known pictures were produced in the 1940s, when she combed the streets, generally of poorer neighborhoods, catching her subjects unawares—especially children at play. Her work celebrates the inventiveness and spontaneity of childhood. Her black-and-white photographs have repeatedly been described as lyrical documents of city life, and while they may stir nostalgia for a less complex time, her work is emphatically realistic and nonidealized. She seems to have shared with Ben Shahn (an acknowledged influence, along with Henri Cartier-Bresson and Walker Evans) not only a strong social consciousness and sympathy with working people and their offspring but also an aesthetic inclination for dramatic cropping and empty or decaying urban landscape.

Although Sandra Weiner (b. 1921) was born in Poland, she immigrated to the United States with her parents in 1938 and is now a New Yorker. Weiner shares Levitt's interest in taking photographs of generally poorer city children at play in the city's streets. She also has written books for children, illustrating them with her photographs (*It's Wings That Make Birds Fly*).

Lynne Cohen (b. 1944) seems as much a cultural anthropologist as a photographer, but it isn't people she scrutinizes—only their environments and artifacts. Her photographs reveal what strange, amusing,

and sometimes haunting places these environments are—lobbies, waiting rooms, beauty parlors, pools in health spas, classrooms, shooting ranges, and labs of all kinds. But Cohen is an artist, not a scientist, and she has no compunction about moving the odd chair or hat rack to make her constructions more effective or evocative. She is sensitive to textures, and her generally large-scale, sharp black-and-white images have strongly defined horizontals and verticals. She also frames her prints in "real" marbled Formica. So clear is this photographer's vision and imagery that a particularly sterile or pathetically "enhanced" public place might well be thought of as "a Lynne Cohen place."

Rosalind Solomon (b. 1930) has traveled widely to document exotic cultures. Sandi Fellman (b. 1952) is likewise interested in remote places. She published a book, *The Japanese Tattoo* (1986), about the tattooed body. One particularly winning image, "Horiyoshi III and his son" (1984), is of a cherubic, smiling golden-skinned infant held by his father. So as not to distract from the child and the dense and gorgeously tattooed chest of his father, only the man's torso and hand are visible—all else has been cropped.

Lauren Greenfield is among the younger and talented social documentary photographers working today. In a very interesting recent project, she studied

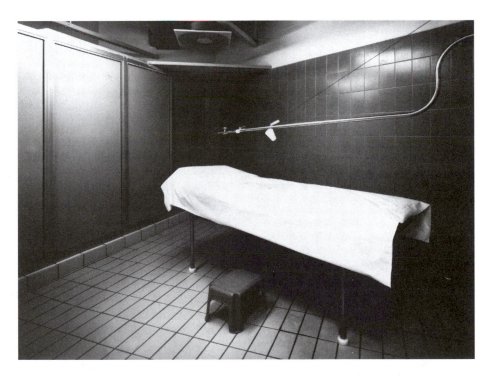

Lynne Cohen seems as much a cultural anthropologist as a photographer,
but it isn't people she scrutinizes—only their environments and artifacts.
The title of this photograph is "Spa." [Lynne Cohen. Courtesy of the P.P.O.W. Gallery]

the rites of passage of teenagers in Southern California. Her print "Ashleigh, 13, weighs herself the morning of her bat mitzvah" (1995) speaks volumes about budding girls, American society's obsession with weight, and the lurking horror of anorexia. A lovely young girl, waif-thin and elegantly dressed in black with pearls, is seen standing on a scale in a very well-appointed bathroom. As she solemnly stares down at the scale's pronouncement, her robed parents hover in the doorway and a sister sits on the edge of the whirlpool, also anxiously awaiting the results. Greenfield, who grew up around Santa Monica, knows the life-styles and rituals of affluent teens. Her sensitivity to social and psychological issues is probably "inherited" from her mother, a professor of psychology. The photographer herself studied anthropology and photography at Harvard.

REPORTAGE—TABOO SUBJECTS

Documentation and photojournalism imply a certain neutrality and emotional distance, but it is unlikely that the work is ever completely objective—a photographer's involvement with and attitude toward a subject, however subtle, is always present. Jewish American women photographers—including Lisette Model, Diane Arbus, Nan Goldin, and Merry Alpern—occupy an important place in the tradition of sociological reportage that examines intense, disturbing, even shocking subjects.

Lisette (Stern) Model (1901–1983), born in Vienna to a cultivated and prosperous family, studied her first love, music, with Arnold Shönberg. She took up photography later in Paris only "as a way to make a living." Her mordant view of her fellow human beings was already evident in a suite of her early prints called *Promenade des Anglais* (1934–1937). Her unsuspecting prosperous bourgeois subjects lounging on the boardwalk at Nice seem transformed into a gallery of freaks—self-indulgent, ridiculous, and solitary. Among her later work in New York (where she immigrated with her husband, painter Evsa Model) are shots of people who function far outside society's norms: dwarfs, the obese, transvestites, and derelicts.

Diane Arbus (1923–1971) studied with Lisette Model, and like her teacher was born to wealth (her family owned Russeks Furs). She, too, was fascinated by freaks and by the freakishness in all of us. Freaks reminded her of fairy-tale characters who stopped passersby and demanded an answer to a riddle. As she explained to Janet Malcolm, she saw them as life's "aristocrats" because they had already "passed their test in life"—they were born with some terrible trauma that other people constantly fear may befall them. She felt

she succeeded in presenting images (transvestites, the mentally retarded, twins, triplets, celebrities—Mae West and Norman Mailer, for example) that "nobody would see" unless she had photographed them. Considered one of the century's preeminent photographers, Arbus achieved what most artists only aspire to—she expanded our collective perception of the world.

Nan Goldin (b. 1953), called "a Piaf with a camera," also documents those who live on life's margins. The difference in her work, however, is that she records her own world. She and her circle—artists, transsexuals, drag queens, and lovers of both sexes, some people wasting with AIDS—are often caught in particularly vulnerable moments (she photographed herself, eyes bloodied, after having been beaten by a boyfriend). Emotionally fragile and disconnected, all her subjects seem to suffer. Few (her parents excepted) ever laugh or smile, and most are shot in vivid warm tones and exclusively in interiors; bars, bedrooms, and bathrooms seem their natural habitat. An Edward Hopper sensibility haunts Goldin's work. Despite proximity and yearnings, her subjects cannot seem to connect. In her book *The Ballad of Sexual Dependency*, the photographer states her fear that "men and women are irrevocably strangers to each other, irreconcilably unsuited." Goldin's work has been influenced by photographers Weegee, August Sander, and Diane Arbus. In late 1996, the Whitney Museum mounted a much discussed exhibition of Goldin's work. According to an article in the *New York Times*, fashion photography of the 1990s (for example, ads for Calvin Klein) has appropriated the documentary-style realism of Goldin and others, and brought the "transgressive fringes into the mainstream."

Merry Alpern (b. 1955), child of a mixed marriage, studied sociology at Grinnell College, which may help explain her interest in documenting the flotsam of the urban environment. Fascinated by the homeless, she "started hanging out" with a couple she observed on the traffic islands of Manhattan's Upper West Side and began to record their lives. The woman, AJ, who attracted Alpern visually, was a hooker and a drug user; her companion (not lover) was Jim Bob. Alpern asked and got AJ's permission to photograph her at work. As the photographer explained to Simi Horowitz, she was willing to put herself in such taboo and possibly dangerous situations because, like Arbus, she felt that her camera functioned as a kind of protective barrier between her and her subjects.

More recently, with a zoom lens, she photographed exchanges between upscale clients and anonymous prostitutes at a sex club in the Wall Street area.

Merry Alpern's series of photographs taken with a zoom lens of exchanges between upscale clients and anonymous prostitutes at a sex club in the Wall Street area is curiously unsexy. Nonetheless, it earned her the disapprobation of congressional conservatives when she submitted images from the series as part of a National Endowment for the Arts grant application. She was turned down. [Merry Alpern]

The series, shot over a six-month period across an air shaft and through a dirty window divided into four panes, is curiously unsexy. Nevertheless it became a sort of cause célèbre. When Alpern submitted fifteen pieces from the series as part of a National Endowment for the Arts grant application, her application was rejected. Conservative congressional forces were outraged that government monies were being spent on what they considered smut (the work of Alpern and others).

EXPRESSIONISTS

Judith Golden (b. 1934) combines media (paint, graphite) and various printmaking techniques to create powerful, expressive images that often center on woman, her various masks, personas, and powers. At times, she paints (with theatrical makeup and metallic pigments) and powders her models before photographing them. Likewise, Nina Glaser manipulates media and alters her models before creating photographic "staged" tableaux. In one work (untitled) she conjures up visions of the dead and dying in concentration camps. Nude models, who have been coated with a muddy white substance, lie in constrictive cubicles. Only their shoulders and heads, tilted at disconcerting angles, can be seen. Like grotesque mannequins, they seem wooden, deathly.

Historically, women have been excluded and marginalized, and women artists have been particularly sensitive to the restrictions imposed on them. This has probably affected the sort of subject and work they choose to explore. Women photographers, like women artists in general, have been insufficiently studied. Only recently have their contributions begun to be acknowledged in books, exhibitions, and scholarly essays.

BIBLIOGRAPHY

Als, Hilton. "Unmasked." *The New* Yorker (November 29, 1995): 92; Bosworth, Patricia. *Diane Arbus: A Biography* (1984); Cohen, Lynne. *Lost and Found* (1992), and *Occupied Territory* (1987); Dater, Judy. *Cycles* (1992); Dater, Judy, and Jack Welpott. *Women and Other Visions* (1975); Ehrens, Susan. *Alma Lavenson* (1990); Enyeart, James, L. *Judy Dater: Twenty Years* (1988); Fellman, Sandi. *The Japanese Tattoo* (1986); Goldin, Nan. *The Ballad of Sexual Dependency* (1986); *Nan Goldin: I'll Be Your Mirror* (1996); Gover, Jane. *The Positive Image* (1988); Hogan, Charles. "Annie Leibovitz." *Art News* (March 1990): 91–95; *Helen Levitt* (1980); *High Heels and Ground Glass: Pioneering Women Photography*. Video, written and produced by Deborah Irmas and Barbara Kasten (c. 1990); Horowitz, Simi. "Life on the Street." *American Photographer* (July 1989): 79; Lavin, Maud. "Ringl and Pit: The Representation of Women in German Advertising, 1929–1937. *The Print Collector's Newsletter* 16, no. 3 (1985): 92; *Lisette Model* (1979); McEven, Melissa A. "Doris Ulmann and Marion Post Wolcott: The Appalachian South." *History of Photography* 19, no. 1 (1995): 5; Malcolm, Janet. "Aristocrats." *The New York Review of Books* (February 1, 1996): 7; Meyerowitz, Joel, ed. *Street Photography* (1994); Mitchell, Margarette. *Recollections: Ten Women of Photography* (1979); Morath, Inge. *Portraits* (1986); Naef, Weston. *The Collection of Alfred Stieglitz: Fifty Pioneers of Modern Photography* (1978); Newhall, Beaumont. *The History of Photography from 1839 to the Present Day* (1982); Orkin, Ruth. *Ruth Orkin: More Pictures from My Window* (1983); *Ringl and Pit*. Video, produced and directed by Juan Mandelbaum (1995); Rosenblum, Naomi. *A History of Women Photographers* (1994); Solomon, Rosalind. *Portraits in the Time of AIDS* (1988); Sontag, Susan. *On Photography* (1978); Spindler, Amy. "Nineties' Attitude: Visual and Raw." *NYTimes,*

November 26, 1996; Sullivan, Constance. *Women Photographers* (1990); Thomas, Ann. *Lisette Model* (1990); Tucker, Anne, ed. *The Woman's Eye* (1973).

HELEN GOODMAN

PICON, MOLLY (1898–1992)

A drunk's dare to a five-year-old on a trolley car initiated the career of Molly Picon, the petite darling of the Yiddish musical theater. Later, with her *geneyvishe oygen* [mischievous eyes], dark bob, and endearing acrobatics, she won hearts on tours across the United States, Europe, Palestine and Israel, South Africa, and Australia. In over eighty years of performing, "Our Molly" would also delight audiences in radio, film, and television. Despite being told by an English director not to use her hands too much, as it was "too Jewish," Picon used every one of her fifty-eight inches to convey the humor, poignancy, and passion for performance that glowed beneath her physical pranks. For much of her career, her forte was the adorable waif, often a motherless boy, who, with naive gumption, a charming display of tears, laughter, somersaults, splits, songs, cartwheels, and musical instruments, accompanied by an occasional farm animal and good luck, managed to make it in the adult world.

Hers was a limber, adaptable *sekhl* [smarts]: versatile, gallant, indomitable. She seemed simultaneously all-American in her winsome tomboy persona, the irresistible scamp whose good sense and unabashed virtue led to fame and fortune, and entirely Jewish in her devotion to Yiddish and efforts on behalf of Jewish refugees and the State of Israel. A staunch Roosevelt supporter, she was a candle to the world's conscience during and after World War II. Wherever she performed, as well as in her own home, she gave solace through awareness, fun, and compassion. To her audiences, she brought both laughter and tears; to her foster children she offered a *haimish* [homey] present and the vision of a humane future.

She was born Margaret Pyekoon on Broome Street on the Lower East Side of Manhattan on February 28, 1898. Her grandmother, who cherished a fantasy romance of her own, claimed that Molly's birthday was a sweltering first of June, allowing Molly, who never seemed to age onstage, to celebrate two birthdays a year. Molly's mother, Clara Ostrovsky (later Ostrow), had left Rizshishtchov ("a little town that looks like a sneeze and sounds it") near Kiev, Russia, in 1890, just ahead of the pogroms, with her brothers and sisters (eleven, eventually); her father, Aaron, a wheat grower; her mother, Sarah; a feath-

erbed; and a samovar. Molly's father, Louis (or Lewis) Pyekoon (later Picon), had studied for the rabbinate in Warsaw, where he married his first wife, whom he neglected to divorce before emigrating. Louis was unhappy that his first child, his "Molly Dolly," was a girl. He came and went; after his second daughter, Helen, was born, he left for good. Molly, Helen, Clara, and Clara's mother, Sarah, moved to Philadelphia, where Clara was a seamstress at Kessler's Theater and took in boarders, reputable and otherwise.

In 1903, Clara took five-year-old Margaret, dressed in red and sporting an elegant fake-fur muff, to the Bijou Theater for a contest. A drunk on the trolley demanded that she do her act then and there. She consented, concluding with an imitation of the drunk himself. Impressed, he collected pennies for her from the other passengers. At the contest, she would add to them the first-prize five-dollar gold piece and the loose change that her first legitimate audience had spontaneously tossed onstage. Molly Picon had begun her theatrical career.

Molly studied piano with Fanny Thomashefsky. (She would continue to acquire skills throughout her life, including improvisation from Commedia Dell'Arte and, in her thirties, rope-climbing from an Arab acrobatic troupe.) She performed with Michael Thomashefsky's Yiddish repertory troupe at the Arch Street Theater (including, at age fifteen, *Uncle Tom's Cabin*, with alternate performances in Yiddish and English) and in cabaret from 1912 to 1915. She left William Penn High School before graduation. In 1918 she was cast as Winter in a touring English-language vaudeville act, *The Four Seasons*. A flu epidemic in 1919 in Boston closed the theaters, leaving Molly stranded. Only a Yiddish theater the authorities had apparently overlooked, the Boston Grand Opera House, managed by Jacob Kalich, remained open.

Molly Picon answered his advertisement for a *flaam feierdig soubrettin* [lively ingenue]. He cast her. Within a year, after his proposals in five fluent languages and broken English, Picon and Kalich announced their engagement onstage. They married on June 29, 1919, in the back of a Philadelphia grocery store, the bride in a dress stitched by Mama Clara from a theater curtain.

On Friday, August 13, 1920, Picon gave birth to a stillborn baby girl. "Peculiar that a perfect love should bear dead fruit," she wrote. Pelvic disease left her unable to bear more children.

Yonkel, as Picon called Kalich, took her to Europe for two years, "to perfect my Yiddish, to get my star legs, and not to be inhibited by working with people who knew me" and to enhance her reputation in America. Kalich brought Picon to the great theaters of Europe, the Vilna Troupe, and many non-Jewish companies. He directed Picon in his adaptation of *Tzipke*, in which she played a plucky ragamuffin

Molly Picon seemed simultaneously all-American in her winsome tomboy persona, the irresistible scamp whose good sense and unabashed virtue led to fame and fortune, and entirely Jewish in her devotion to Yiddish and efforts on behalf of Jewish refugees and the State of Israel. [American Jewish Archives]

much like Yankele, her signature role (performed, she hyperbolized, "3,000 times").

Thrown out of Romania because of anti-Semitism and competition with the Romanian National Theater, Picon and Kalich returned to New York, where they teamed with composer Joseph Rumshinsky to create operettas scripted and directed by Kalich with lyrics often by Picon. From 1922 to 1925, Picon appeared on Second Avenue in *Yankele* and more, including *Mamale, Raizele, Oy Is Dus a Meydl* [Oh, what a girl], and *The Circus Girl*, in which Picon dangled by one foot from a rope. D.W. Griffith, calling her "the most interesting actress in America," tried but failed to raise money for a film for Picon, *The Yiddisher Baby*.

Her first films were made in Europe. She debuted in *Das Judenmadel* by Otto Freister, filmed in Austria in 1921, followed by *Hutet Eure Tochter*, which had no Jewish content, in 1922. In Kalich's Yiddish film *Ost und West* (1923) [East and West, also known as *Mizrakh un Mayrev*], Picon is an American girl who, when not disguised as a Hasidic boy, mistakenly marries a Talmudist, played by Kalich, eventually happily secularized. A censored version was shown in America; in 1932, viewing a restored version with Yiddish dubbing and sound effects added, a critic opined that "it breathes Jewish character, but does not satisfy . . . thank God . . . high literary expectations." In 1925, *Yidn Fun Sibir*, a reworking of existing films, linked Clara Young, glamorous star of Eastern European operetta, with Picon. In 1929's *Little Girl with Big Ideas*, her talkie debut, Picon acted in English with a put-on heavy Yiddish accent. For *Yidl Mitn Fidl* (1937), directed by Joseph Green with songs by Ellstein and Itsik Manger, Picon, playing a girl who dresses as a boy at her father's bidding, was paid ten thousand dollars, the highest salary for a Yiddish movie; dubbed into English in 1961, it was retitled *Castles in the Air*. In *Mamele* (1938), a comic melodrama from a play by Meyer Schwartz, Picon, over forty, played Khavtski, an energetic twelve-year-old gamin who cares for her widowed father and six siblings. This was the last Jewish film made in Poland before the Nazi onslaught.

In the fall of 1930, back at the Second Avenue Theatre, by now renamed the Molly Picon Theatre, she was performing in *The Girl of Yesterday* (entering via a rope) and *The Love Thief* to twenty-seven hundred patrons a week. Following a tour of the States, Picon and Kalich went to Palestine, where Chaim Nachman Bialik hosted them on a kibbutz. Her first American musical, *Birdie*, was in 1933, the year that Kalich began his long-running column for the *Jewish Daily Forward*.

In 1936, Picon contracted for a radio show, which continued for many years, first sponsored by Jell-O, later by Maxwell House Coffee. She toured South Africa, where she sang Negro spirituals to Zulu dancers, and where the poverty stunned her as it had in Poland. On her return, she played harmonica in *Bublichki*. At the close of the 1930s, worrying that Yiddish was dying out, Picon took the role of a sophisticated Jewish woman in Sylvia Regan's English-language drama *Morningstar*, which, despite STELLA ADLER's directing, closed in eight weeks.

After Picon translated her husband's Yiddish play, *Schmendrick* [Nincompoop], she and Kalich briefly separated, reuniting as personal and professional equals, no longer mentor and student. In her autobiography, Picon, who decried "toilet" comics, is frank about their sexual problems, as she is about the cancer that later invaded Kalich's intestinal tract. Kalich wrote *Oy Is Dus a Lebn* [What a life], a musical about his and Molly's life together, and in 1942 they sponsored their foster child, George Weinstein, a seventeen-year-old Belgian Jew living in London.

During the war, Picon performed in refugee camps in Canada. Immediately at war's end, she and Kalich sailed on a barebones vessel to perform in camps and orphanages with the Jewish Labor Committee in Europe, taking chocolates, sewing items, makeup, new costume jewelry, and sanitary products, so that survivors "might feel like (men and) women again." In one camp audience a three-year-old heard his first sounds of laughter. Back in America, while Picon translated songs from French and German, she and Kalich worked for the United Nations Relief and Rehabilitation Administration and sold bonds for Israel and the Children's Fund.

In 1947, Kalich and Picon moved from University Place in Manhattan to their country home, Chez Schmendrick, in Mahomac, New York. There, after a *shvim, shvitz, und schnaps* [skinny-swim, sweat, and snort], they felt refreshed to "fly, fly, fly."

At fifty, Picon somersaulted again as the thirteen-year-old Yankele, as she would to the age of eighty. "Deep down within me, I was Yankele. I still am," she claimed. She appeared in *For Heaven's Sake, Mother*, in which she played a seamstress, *Abi Gesunt* [So long as you're healthy], *Sadie Is a Lady*, *Mazel Tov, Molly*, and *Pavolye, Tage* [Slowly, Daddy], a rewrite of *Hello, Molly*, in which *Variety* called Picon "a bean-sized Bernhardt." *The Molly Picon Show* began on television in 1949.

In 1953, the year of her pre-Broadway flop *Make Mama Happy*, Picon's mother died after a heart attack; Picon did not sing "My Yiddishe Momme" for a year.

For more than eighty years Molly Picon charmed the public and helped keep the Yiddish theater alive. Known best for her portrayals of "the adorable waif" (often a boy) in Yiddish plays, she also acted, sang, and danced her way through English plays. She appeared in several films and television shows and on Broadway. [American Jewish Historical Society]

Kalich began a memoir, *I'm Talking About Molly*, using Picon's diaries. He wrote *Farblondjete* [mixed up] *Honeymoon*, in which Picon played a young servant who eventually marries the lord of the manor, and *Ghetto Gayeties*, for which Picon translated the songs; he starred in *The World of Shalom Aleichem*, in which Picon sang a small role. They wintered in Miami, where Picon did four vaudeville shows a day.

Picon sang for the Knesset in Israel in 1955, where she and Kalich adopted Meira, the daughter of Picon's deceased stepbrother by her father's first wife. In America, Picon broke her wrist onstage, continued the show, and completed the run in a cast. After another American tour, Picon was asked to audition for the first time in her life, for Mrs. Jacoby in *A Majority of One*. She was offended by the test, and by the performance of GERTRUDE BERG, who won the role. Years later, Picon got her "sweet revenge," playing the part in London. Helen Hayes, on learning that Picon had been dubbed "the Yiddish Helen Hayes," responded: "From now on I will be proud to be the shiksa Molly Picon."

A surprising revival of Yiddish theater in 1959 was Kalich's *The Kosher Widow*, their first completely dramatic play, which she called "the biggest thing since the Zionist movement." Picon assumed two roles, wife and sweetheart.

Soon thereafter, Picon first refused then accepted the role of an Italian mother whose sons live in the fast lane, in the film version of Neil Simon's *Come Blow Your Horn*, for which she was nominated for an Academy Award for best supporting actress in 1964. She appeared on television in *A Family Affair*, *The Jack Paar Show*, *Car 54, Where Are You?* (in which she sang Warshawsky's "Der Alef Bays"), and *Dr. Kildare*. After a bout with appendicitis on tour, Picon wrote her "mish-mosh" family biography, *So Laugh a Little*, with Ethel Rosenberg.

The role of the genteel widow Clara Weiss in *Milk and Honey* (originally *Shalom*), somersaulting with sheep and goats at age sixty-four, was her only original Broadway success. "Thank God for Molly," wrote critic Phil Adler. Picon then chose uncharacteristic stage roles: a nagging mother-in-law in *Madame Moussez*, *The Rubiyat of Sophie Klein*, and the lead in *Chu Chem*, which a critic called "The King and Oy," an absurd piece about a search for Jews in China.

After The Six-Day War and more bond sales for Israel, Picon accepted the role of Yente the Matchmaker in Norman Jewison's movie *Fiddler on the Roof*, in which Kalich had a small role. *How to Be a Jewish Mother*, a revue in which she appeared with Godfrey Cambridge, was considered insulting by many blacks and ill-conceived by many whites. Picon, who had twice been the only white performer in Harlem, was stunned.

Picon performed *Solid Gold Cadillac* in Chicago in 1969 without Kalich, whose health had begun to deteriorate, but at a gala hosted by the Hebrew Actors Union at the Commodore Hotel in New York, they celebrated their fiftieth wedding anniversary together. On Broadway, in an apt coincidence, Picon took over Helen Hayes's role in *The Front Page* and was received with cheers. On the other hand, *Will It Last*, later called *Paris Is Out*, closed after a hundred uncomfortable performances.

Picon was honored in 1975 at the Hundredth Anniversary of the Yiddish Theater at the Museum of the City of New York; the museum maintains a collection of her costumes, pictures, programs, and scripts.

On October 12, 1975, she performed at Carnegie Hall before a background of slides of her life.

In 1976, a year after Kalich's death, Picon sold Chez Schmendrick, giving pictures, plaques, and books to YIVO, and rented a house in Cortland. She performed her one-woman show *Hello Molly* in 1979, selected Jean Grillo Benjamin as coauthor for her autobiography *Molly!*, and moved near Lincoln Center with her widowed sister Helen Silverblatt, who had also been a child actress. They vowed to speak only Yiddish to each other for the rest of their lives.

The Philadelphia Public Library presented a major exhibit on her work while she was performing *Milk and Honey* there. On June 28, 1980, Picon received the Creative Achievement Award of the Performing Arts Unit of B'nai B'rith. For her lifetime contribution to Jewish performing arts, in 1985 the Congress of Jewish Culture awarded her a Goldie, named for the "father" of the Yiddish theater, Abraham Goldfaden. She accepted wearing a tuxedo in homage to the boy's hand-me-downs she had worn in her early films.

Molly Picon's role as Yente the Matchmaker in Norman Jewison's 1971 movie of Fiddler on the Roof *helped garner the film a nomination for an Academy Award as Best Picture.*

Molly Picon, "the girl who gets older every year and younger every day," remained zestful until Alzheimer's disease gripped her final few years. She died on April 6, 1992. Throughout her career, she had lived up to her beloved Yonkel's admonition: "Molly, that's our job. Make them laugh."

BIBLIOGRAPHY

BEOAJ; EJ; Slater, Elinor, and Richard Slater. *Great Jewish Women* (1994); *UJE; WWIAJ* (1926, 1928, 1938).

JOANN GREEN

PIERCY, MARGE (b. 1936)

In an autobiographical essay, novelist and poet Marge Piercy admonishes, "Pay sharp attention to that trouble looming, but don't let it taint your Sabbath celebration." This tension between celebration and disquietude marks Piercy's life and work. Grounded in feminism, political activism, and Jewish spirituality, more than twenty-five volumes comprise Piercy's oeuvre. Above all else, Piercy wishes her work to be useful to people's inner and political lives. By articulating their experiences, poetry gives "validation and dignity" to the disenfranchised. Novels persuade readers "to cross those borders of alienation and mistrust" and empathize with "characters whom the reader would refuse to know in ordinary life." Piercy's poetry fuses the political, domestic, and autobiographical spheres with imagery drawn from nature, sensual and dream memories, and Jewish mysticism. Her novels explore "the choices people make, out of their characters and their time and their class and their social circumstances."

Piercy was born on March 31, 1936, in Detroit, Michigan. She and her brother, Grant, grew up in a working-class neighborhood marked by racial tension. Her father, Robert Douglas Piercy, from a working-class Presbyterian family in a coal-mining town in Pennsylvania, installed and repaired heavy machinery for Westinghouse. Her mother, Bert Bernice (Bunnin) Piercy, from an observant, working-class Jewish family in Cleveland, had only a tenth-grade education. Remembering her as deeply intuitive and imaginative, Piercy credits her mother with making her a poet. Piercy developed her love of Judaism from her Orthodox, Yiddish-speaking maternal grandmother, Hannah. Indeed, Piercy's earliest memories of Jewish ritual are bound up with the scent of Hannah's clothes and kitchen. Her grandfather, a union worker, was murdered while organizing bakery workers.

From an early age, Piercy grappled with issues of identity. In race-torn Detroit, her Jewishness set her apart, eliciting anti-Semitic bullying. At home, her discomfited father "told me I wasn't Jewish and . . . mother . . . would wait till he went to work and tell me of course I was." She notes wryly, "All my husbands were Jewish. . . . I felt a mixed marriage was more than I personally could handle. Marrying a man is mixed enough." Central to her commitments to both Judaism and political activism is the knowledge of the Holocaust. Shaken by her Lithuanian-born grandmother's grief over relatives murdered by the Nazis, at age ten Piercy vowed that she would always remain Jewish. The Holocaust also made clear the necessity of political engagement.

The first in her family to attend college, Piercy earned a scholarship to the University of Michigan (B.A., 1957), winning several Hopwood awards for writing. At Northwestern University (M.A., 1958), she married Michel Schiff, a French Jewish exchange student in physics. Schiff's family had survived the Holocaust by crossing illegally into Switzerland. Her encounter with them informed the French Jewish family in *Gone*

Marge Piercy's life as a poet and novelist has been informed by her political activism, her feminism, and her Judaism. Her work is marked by humanity and empathy, focusing frequently on the disenfranchised and the alienated in society. [Library of Congress]

to *Soldiers*, her 1987 novel about World War II. Divorced at age twenty-three, Piercy struggled financially, writing poetry and fiction. Her first six novels remained unpublished, in part because of their feminist content. In 1962, Piercy married Robert Shapiro, a computer scientist. The couple lived in Cambridge, San Francisco, Brooklyn, and the Upper West Side of Manhattan. Their unconventional open marriage ended in divorce in 1980. Piercy's first book of poetry was accepted in 1966 and published in 1968, the year her first novel was accepted. On June 2, 1982, she married writer Ira Wood, whom she had known for six years. They live in Wellfleet, Massachusetts. They have cowritten a play, *The Last White Class* (1979).

Although no longer a student, Piercy was active in the radical Students for a Democratic Society (SDS) in the late 1960s. By 1970, however, she had become disillusioned with the devaluation of women, of Judaism and Zionism, and of creative writing by the New Left. Fearing the censure of her fellow activists, she curtailed her own Jewish practice. Finally, she left the SDS and became actively involved in the women's movement, a commitment that continues to fuel and validate her artistic work. Saying kaddish for her mother, who died on Hanukkah in 1981, renewed her creative interest in Jewish practice—in "the female lunar side of Judaism," sparking a desire to live as "a full Jew again, but with my entire being, my history, my intelligence, my knowledge, and aesthetics." She began to compose liturgical poems and rituals, contributing actively to the Reconstructionist Movement's prayer book, *Hadesh Yameinu: A Siddur for Shabbat and Festivals.* She was part of the committee that produced *Or Chadash*, the siddur of *P'nai Or* (a Philadelphia-based renewal center), where her liturgical poems also appear. In addition, she contributes regularly to Jewish journals such as *Tikkun*, where she served as poetry editor, and *Kerem*. She was one of the founders of the havurah Am ha-Yam on Cape Cod and has served on its board of directors and in various offices.

As fictions that "help us make sense of our lives," Piercy's novels focus on the possibility for radical social change. They are characterized by exhaustive background research and a close and imaginative attention to the details of domestic arrangements. In *Woman on the Edge of Time* (1976), an impoverished Hispanic woman time travels to a future society whose genderlessness and social organization embody the ideas of radical feminism. *He, She, and It* (1991) intertwines the sixteenth-century legend of the Golem of Prague with a cyberpunk depiction of a cyborg created to protect an embattled Jewish community in a futuristic dystopia. *Gone to Soldiers* (1987) creates a counter-

war story by focusing on women's experiences of World War II from multiple perspectives, including a Jewish heroine of the French Resistance, Jewish twin girls (one dies on a death march, the other escapes to America but encounters sexual abuse), a romance writer turned foreign correspondent, and a lesbian fighter pilot. Piercy's poems explore ecofeminism, love, political awareness, spirituality. The "Chuppah" section of *My Mother's Body* (1985) contains selections from her 1982 wedding ceremony to Wood. Some of her liturgical poems appear in *Available Light* (1988), *Mars and Her Children* (1992), and *What Are Big Girls Made Of?* (1997).

While most feminist critics show a strong appreciation for Piercy's work, mainstream critics have tended to favor her poetry over her novels, which are sometimes seen as too political. Piercy notes, "People tend to define 'political' or 'polemical' in terms of what is not congruent with their ideas." Piercy's awards include the Arthur C. Clarke Award for science fiction (1992), Brit ha-Dorot Award, Shalom Center (1992), Golden Rose Poetry Prize, New England Poetry Club (1990), Carolyn Kizer Poetry Prize (1986, 1990), and a National Endowment for the Arts award (1978). Her manuscripts are housed at the University of Michigan, Harlan Hatcher Graduate Library.

SELECTED WORKS BY MARGE PIERCY

"Autobiography." In *Contemporary Authors Autobiography Series*, edited by Dedria Bryfonski (1984); *Available Light* (1988); *Braided Lives* (1982); *Breaking Camp* (1968); *Circles on the Water* (1982); *City of Darkness* (1996); *Dance the Eagle to Sleep* (1970); "The Dark Thread in the Weave." In *Testimony: Contemporary Writers Make the Holocaust Personal*, edited by David Rosenberg (1989); *The Earth Shines Secretly: A Book of Days* (1990); *Fly Away Home* (1984); *Going Down Fast* (1969); *Gone to Soldiers* (1987); *Hard Loving* (1969); *He, She, and It* (1991); *The High Cost of Living* (1978); *The Last White Class*, with Ira Wood (1979); *Living in the Open* (1976); *The Longings of Women* (1994); *Mars and Her Children* (1992); *The Moon Is Always Female* (1980); *My Mother's Body* (1985); *Parti-Colored Blocks for a Quilt* (1982); *Small Changes* (1973); *Stone, Paper, Knife* (1983); *Summer People* (1989); *To Be of Use* (1973); *The Twelve-Spoked Wheel Flashing* (1978); *Vida* (1980); *What Are Big Girls Made Of?* (1997); *Woman on the Edge of Time* (1976).

BIBLIOGRAPHY

Contemporary Authors. New Revisions Series 43: 359–365; Montresor, Jaye Berman. "Marge Piercy." In *Jewish American Women Writers: A Bio-Bibliographical and Critical Sourcebook*, edited by Ann Shapiro et al. (1994).

SARA R. HOROWITZ

PILPEL, HARRIET FLEISCHL
(1911–1991)

Harriet Fleischl Pilpel was a prominent participant and strategist in women's rights, birth control, and reproductive freedom litigation for over half a century. During her long career as an active civil libertarian, she served as general counsel to both the Planned Parenthood Foundation of America (PPFA) and the American Civil Liberties Union (ACLU), and assisted numerous other organizations concerned with civil liberties, censorship, reproductive freedom, the status of women, and related areas. Pilpel served on several committees of the AMERICAN JEWISH CONGRESS.

Harriet Fleischl Pilpel was born on December 2, 1911, in the Bronx, New York. She was the oldest of three daughters born to Julius and Ethel (Loewy) Fleischl. She graduated from Vassar College in 1932 and received a master's degree in international relations (1933) and a law degree (1936) from Columbia University. She married Robert C. Pilpel in 1933 and had two children, Judith and Robert. She and her husband were active members of the Ethical Culture Society. After graduating from Columbia, Pilpel joined the firm of Greenbaum, Wolff and Ernst. There, through her association with Morris Ernst, attorney for Margaret Sanger, Pilpel became deeply involved with reproductive freedom litigation, first in the birth control movement and then in the abortion rights movement. Among the birth control cases she worked on with Ernst and others were *State* v. *Nelson* (1940), decided in the Connecticut Supreme Court, and *Tileston* v. *Ullman* (1943), *Poe* v. *Ullman* (1961), and *Griswold* v. *Connecticut* (1965), all of which were decided by the Supreme Court of the United States. Pilpel authored Planned Parenthood's amicus curiae briefs in the latter two cases.

Pilpel's career encompassed both the pre-*Griswold* phase of birth control advocacy and the extraordinary developments that would link the Supreme Court's rulings on contraception to the abortion issue. Thus, she could lay claim to having worked closely with Margaret Sanger and other birth control advocates in their efforts to repeal or overturn state-level birth control laws, and also to having strategized with Linda Coffee, Sarah Weddington, and numerous others concerning *Roe* v. *Wade* and related cases. Pilpel was profoundly influenced by arguments that the right to privacy holding in *Griswold*—the state may not peek into the bedroom and forbid the use of birth control—could be extended to contend that a woman had a fundamental right to abortion, and she participated in the swell of activism and litigation that sought to

A lawyer's lawyer, Harriet Pilpel served as general counsel to both Planned Parenthood and the American Civil Liberties Union. A lifelong advocate of a woman's right to choose, she was actively involved in the entire panoply of litigation that led to Roe v. Wade. *[New York Times Pictures]*

link the two issues in legislatures, in courts, and in the public imagination. Finally, as the abortion issue came to the forefront in the late 1960s and early 1970s, she helped to shift the emphasis of activists from reform to repeal of legislative restrictions on abortion.

Through her association with the ACLU, PPFA, and similiar organizations, Pilpel was a mentor and adviser to many young attorneys involved with the abortion rights struggle. At Sarah Weddington's request, for instance, Pilpel organized a challenging moot court practice before both argument and reargument phases of *Roe* v. *Wade*. Pilpel also authored the Planned Parenthood Foundation of America's amicus curiae brief in the case. She was a member of the Association for the Study of Abortion, a scholarly group devoted to the study of various reform measures, and she testified before both state and federal legislatures on abortion concerns. Pilpel favored locating a woman's constitutional right to control her reproductive choices in the Ninth and Fourteenth Amendments, rather than the First. Her PPFA briefs concerning abortion emphasized the linkage between the right to privacy in decisions and actions concerning contraception and fertility, established in *Griswold*, and the putative right to a safe, legal abortion, which would be established in *Roe*.

Pilpel's interest in reproductive freedom was matched by her concern for First Amendment issues. She had an active practice in intellectual property and copyright law, and served as attorney to many writers and publishers, handling general contract work, as well as cases relating to freedom of expression. Her clients included such figures as EDNA FERBER, BETTY FRIEDAN, Billy Graham, Jerome Kern, Alfred Kinsey, Erich Maria Remarque, Mel Brooks, and Svetlana Alliluyeva (Stalin's daughter). Pilpel also specialized in matrimonial law. With Theodora S. Zavin, she coauthored two books, *Your Marriage and the Law* (1952) and *Rights and Writers: A Handbook of Literary and Entertainment Law* (1960). She was also coauthor (with Morton D. Goldberg) of *A Copyright Guide* (1960) and (with Minna Post Peyser) of *Know Your Rights* (1965). She was a frequent guest on William F. Buckley's *Firing Line* and served on several national commissions devoted to the status of women. In 1965, she represented pediatrician Benjamin Spock in an unsuccessful effort to block advertising included in copies of his best-selling *Baby and Child Care*. Between 1982 and 1991, she was associated with the law firm of Weil, Gotshal and Manges. In 1989, several years after the death of Robert Pilpel, she married Irwin Schwartz, a lifelong friend with whom she had gone to high school.

Harriet Fleischl Pilpel died on April 23, 1991.

SELECTED WORKS BY
HARRIET FLEISCHL PILPEL

"Birth Control and a New Birth of Freedom." *Ohio State Law Journal* 27 (Fall 1966): 679–690; "The Challenge of Privacy." In *The Price of Liberty: Perspectives on Civil Liberties by Members of the ACLU*, edited by Alan Reitman (1968); *A Copyright Guide*, with Morton D. Goldberg (1960); *Know Your Rights*, with Minna Post Peyser (1965); "The Right of Abortion." *Atlantic* 223 (June 1969): 69–71; *Rights and Writers: A Handbook of Literary and Entertainment Law*, with Theodora S. Zavin (1960); "Sex vs. the Law: A Study in Hypocrisy." *Harper's* 230 (January 1965): 35–40; *Your Marriage and the Law*, with Theodora S. Zavin (1952).

BIBLIOGRAPHY

Faux, Marian. *Roe v Wade: The Untold Story of the Landmark Supreme Court Decision That Made Abortion Legal* (1988); Garrow, David J. *Liberty and Sexuality: The Right to Privacy and the Making of Roe v Wade* (1994); Gilbert, Julie. *Opposite Attractions: The Lives of Erich Maria Remarque and Paulette Goddard* (1995); Pilpel, Harriet F. Papers. Schlesinger Library, Radcliffe College, Cambridge, Mass., and Sophia Smith Collection, Smith College, Northampton, Mass.; Weddington, Sarah. *A Question of Choice* (1992).

BERNARD UNTI

PIONEER WOMEN

Pioneer Women, the Labor Zionist women's organization in the United States—today called Na'amat—was officially founded in 1925. The new group sought to elevate the public profile of the *halutzot* [Zionist women pioneers] in the *yishuv* [Palestine Jewish settlement community] and to help the pioneer women's cooperatives in Palestine through American-based philanthropic efforts. Pioneer Women considered itself the sister movement in the diaspora of Moezet Hapoalot, the Palestine women workers' movement. It embraced the latter's vision of "expand[ing] the boundaries of the Jewish woman's role" in the *yishuv* and "secur[ing] her full and equal participation in the process of Jewish national reconstruction."

Pioneer Women also emphasized the importance of women in the American Zionist enterprise and provided a forum for working-class Jewish immigrant women who sympathized with the aims and ideals of socialist Zionism and the nascent *yishuv*. In time, the organization opened up new channels of communication between the Palestine labor movement and the Jewish community in America. It became a significant force in American Jewish life and played a central role in American Zionism in the decades preceding the establishment of the State of Israel in 1948.

THE WORK OF MANYA SHOHAT

"The entire movement here is worthless!" lamented the Zionist leader Manya Shohat in 1921. Thus Shohat, a member of the first Histadrut [General Federation of Jewish Workers in the Land of Israel] delegation to the United States, described the American branch of Poale Zion [Workers of Zion], an offshoot of the Russian socialist Zionist party. Shohat decried the inactivity of the local party and informed her Palestine comrades that the American movement was but a "tempest in a teacup." Under current circumstances, she advised, the American party could not be depended upon to promote investment in Palestine. Additionally, as she quickly discovered, any fundraising conducted by Histadrut delegates inadvertently

*Pioneer Women, the Labor Zionist women's organization in the United States, was officially founded in 1925.
This portrait taken at the 1934 convention includes* GOLDA MEIR, *then national secretary, second row,
fourth from the right. [G. Gross. Photograph courtesy Na'amat, USA]*

competed with the American movement's existing drive to send tools and farm machinery to the Palestinian *kvutzoh* [workers' colonies] as well as the World Zionist Organization's ongoing Keren Heyesod [Palestine Foundation] campaign.

In order to avoid overtaxing the American party's scarce resources, Shohat created an ad hoc committee of female Poale Zion members to raise $10,000 worth of kitchen and laundry equipment for the struggling *kvutzoh* in Palestine. The women's committee elicited the interest of a cadre of female Zionist activists who worked hard to achieve their fund-raising goal. Neither the campaign nor the committee, however, was a top priority for Shohat. In fact, she devoted most of her energy to clandestine efforts to procure weapons for Hashomer [the Watchman], the Jewish self-defense organization of the Palestine labor movement. Nonetheless, Shohat's efforts did lay the groundwork for the creation of Pioneer Women three years later.

FROM TREE NURSERIES TO
LABOR ZIONIST WOMEN'S ORGANIZATION

In 1924, when the Zionist leader Rahel Yanait (later Ben-Zvi) sought American Jewish financial support, she turned to the women who previously partici-

pated in the ad hoc committee organized by Shohat. Yanait was director of a girls' agricultural school and tree nursery near the Ratisbonne monastery in Jerusalem. The nursery was one of several such projects organized by the Palestine labor movement. Yanait requested financial assistance for the construction of a well. The Mandate administration, which implemented Britain's irregular policies in Palestine, severely curtailed the water supply available to the nursery.

Yanait drew up plans for a well with the assistance of the Jewish National Fund, the Zionist agency responsible for land acquisition and development in the *yishuv*. Next she enlisted the support of SOPHIE UDIN and six other Poale Zion activists: Eva Berg, Leah Brown, Chaya Ehrenreich, Luba Hurwitz, Rahel Siegel, and Nina Zuckerman. The women recognized the potent political value of such an undertaking for the Palestine labor movement. They also sought to exploit Yanait's call for help in order to assert their own agenda within the male-dominated Poale Zion Party. Like many of their contemporaries who experienced the swift social, economic, and political transformation of American women in the 1920s, the cohort grouped around Udin reasoned that their objectives would be best advanced through an autonomous Labor Zionist women's organization. To this end, on March 8, 1924, they published a carefully crafted letter written by Yanait in *Der Tog* [The day]. In the letter, Yanait opined that "our tree nursery cannot exist without a well" and that during the previous two years "more than 130,000 saplings from our *kvutzah* have been planted in 17 points in Galilee and Judaea." The letter, in its endearing simplicity, proved highly effective. The image of Jewish female pioneers tending "saplings" and reclaiming the wilderness of the *yishuv* struck a responsive chord among working-class Jewish immigrant women. Udin and her followers succeeded not only in raising an initial $500; they also exploited the enthusiastic communal response to Yanait's letter in order to buttress their campaign for an independent Labor Zionist women's organization.

Poale Zion's male leadership was generally opposed to the creation of a separate women's organization. The leaders feared that such a structure would undermine the party's credibility in the eyes of the immigrant community. Having long since "emancipated" Poale Zion's female members and endowed them with equal rights, they argued there was no need to sponsor a new women's organization. However, such specious reasoning did not deter Udin, Berg, Brown, Ehrenreich, Hurwitz, Segal, and Zuckerman. They asserted that the minuscule number of women in Poale Zion—and their subservient roles as caretakers and child-care providers within the party framework—actually inhibited women from joining the movement. Only an autonomous Labor Zionist women's organization, they believed, would enable them to assume greater responsibility for the movement and fully realize their potential.

Finally, in 1925, Udin appealed to the fifteenth annual Poale Zion convention to approve the formation of a separate women's organization. "I explained, in the name of a small group of members," she later recalled in modest but revealing terms, "our desire to be a part of the party, an organic part, *but independent*" (emphasis added). With the support of Manya Shohat, Rahel Yanait, Goldie Meyerson (later GOLDA MEIR), and other key figures in Moezet Hapoalot, the American women's group officially seceded from Poale Zion.

THE CREATION OF PIONEER WOMEN

During the interwar period, an increasing number of American Jewish women became active in the Zionist movement. In fact, between the end of World War I and the establishment of the State in Israel in 1948, the number of women enrolled in the American Zionist movement grew tenfold, from approximately thirty thousand to over three hundred thousand. In this period, HADASSAH (originally the women's auxiliary of the Zionist Organization of America) became the largest Zionist group in the United States with 250,000 members. Meanwhile, Pioneer Women grew from three thousand to twenty-eight thousand members.

In 1926, the first convention of the newly established Women's Organization for the Pioneer Women of Palestine was held in New York City. Leah Biskin was elected the group's national president. The convention declared the new women's organization to be completely autonomous in its political and educational work. It adopted a socialist Zionist platform and affiliated with the World Union of Poale Zion, the Socialist International, and the World Zionist Organization. The group stressed the importance of ideological and political tasks over philanthropic activities. The convention articulated the following goals: "(1) to help create a homeland in Palestine based on cooperation and social justice; (2) to give moral and material support to the Moezet Hapoalot; and (3) to strive through systematic cultural and propaganda work to educate the American Jewish woman to a more conscious role as coworker in the establishment of a better and more just society in America and throughout the world."

At the outset, Pioneer Women—the organization was officially renamed in 1939—mobilized twenty clubs with nine hundred members. The movement's ranks were initially comprised of Yiddish-speaking immigrant women who possessed an exceptional esprit de corps. These idealistic, committed, and liberal young working women made time for political and fund-raising activities for girls' agricultural training schools in Petah Tikvah, Nahalat Yehuda, and Hadera, places most of them never expected to see themselves.

In contrast to other American Jewish women's organizations, Pioneer Women stressed a philosophical orientation attuned to the Jewish immigrant milieu. The organization upheld the notions of *yiddishkeit* [Jewishness], class consciousness, and feminism as its central values. Moreover, Pioneer Women's membership, deeply proud of its cultural identity, shunned what it perceived to be the bourgeois trappings of Americanized groups like Hadassah and the NATIONAL COUNCIL OF JEWISH WOMEN. Pioneer Women "is not just one more organization of women," the movement leaders proclaimed. "It is an organization of women with the distinct task of furthering the economic emancipation and the national rehabilitation of the Jewish masses." In fact, the members of Pioneer Women worked hard to distinguish themselves from other women's groups. Golda Meir, who was sent by Moezet Hapoalot as an emissary to Pioneer Women from 1928 to 1929 and from 1932 to 1934, later recalled: "Suspicious of frivolity, it was a long time before the earnest women tolerated purely social gatherings where the ladies might play bridge instead of listening to a lecture on A.D. Gordon, Borochov or other socialist Zionist theoreticians."

THE GROWTH OF PIONEER WOMEN

Golda Meir and other leaders of the women workers' movement in Palestine, including Beba Idelson, Hana Hisik, Rahel Katznelson-Rubashov (later Shazar), Elisheva Kaplan, and Ada Maimon, played conspicuous roles in the life of the organization in the 1930s. They spent extended time in the United States as emissaries of Moezet Hapoalot and regularly toured Pioneer Women clubs in cities around the country, where they also promoted the Histadrut and the Zionist cause to general Jewish audiences. "They were really the soul of the organization," recalled Dvorah Rothbard, head of Pioneer Women from 1942 to 1945. "Around them there was such a holy feeling! They were the ones who gave [Pioneer Women] content, who gave it wings, who gave it imagination."

As the Jewish immigrant milieu steadily succumbed to the pressures and the allure of Americanization during the interwar years, Pioneer Women sought to strengthen its base by tapping the vast reservoir of potential American Jewish female support for Labor Zionism. This approach mirrored the general trend of the wider American Labor Zionist movement. With respect to Pioneer Women, however, much public relations groundwork was inadvertently laid by the INTERNATIONAL LADIES GARMENT WORKERS UNION and several highly placed Hadassah members who publicly endorsed the Histadrut program in election campaigns for the Eighteenth and Nineteenth Zionist Congresses (1933 and 1935).

In the 1930s, Pioneer Women's American leadership, together with the Palestinian shlichim, undertook a campaign aimed at both Yiddish- and English-speaking Jewish women in the United States and Canada. In 1931, for example, the organization published Vos arbeterns dertseyln [The woman worker speaks], an anthology of personal reminiscences by halutzot about their experiences in Palestine. The book included essays about the early years in several kvutzeh; life in Palestine during World War I; impressions of A.D. Gordon, Rachel Blaustein, and other notable figures in the yishuv; Jewish family life in agricultural colonies; and several hitherto unpublished photographs of halutzim and Jewish colonies.

The volume was so well received that in 1932, Pioneer Women published an English translation entitled The Plough Woman. The latter opened a window on Jewish life in the Palestine to a largely uninformed English-reading audience. The well-known writer and Labor Zionist advocate Maurice Samuel translated the material. Explaining the alleged profundity of "word-symbols" such as kvuzeh, kibbutz, halutz, and meshek hapoalot [women's training farm], Samuel asserted that the yishuv revealed the "extraordinary folk-depths of the [Zionist] movement, the deep and inexhaustible sources of a renaissance which, in effect, is only at its beginning." As Samuel's comments imply, The Plough Woman was intended to be more than a straightforward translation of Vos arbeterns dertseyln. Appearing at the height of the Depression, a period that coincided with the yishuv's rapid growth and economic expansion, the volume presented a poignant alternative to the hardship and, in many instances, misery of American Jews. It pointed the way to individual fulfillment and collective redemption.

As Pioneer Women's membership became increasingly Americanized, the organization gradually became less doctrinaire and shifted to an English-speaking orientation. The organization steadily grew, and so did the proceeds of its fund-raising campaign on behalf of Moezet Hapoalot. In its first decade, Pioneer Women transmitted over $383,000 to Histadrut-related projects in Palestine. By 1939, it had 170 chapters in 70 cities and approximately 7,000 members. Of the 170 clubs, 85 were categorized as "Yiddish-speaking" and contained 4,500 members. It was nevertheless clear that the English-speaking clubs provided the point of entry for new and younger members between the ages of thirty and thirty-five, including a preponderance of recruits from outside the movement ranks.

THE BROADENING OF
PIONEER WOMEN'S ACTIVISM

In 1941, Pioneer Women maintained 250 clubs with a total membership of 10,000. In addition to its traditional Zionist orientation and support for the Palestine labor movement, the organization now concentrated on bringing in "women from all walks of life" and imitating the social norms of other American Jewish women's organizations. The younger acculturated members, wrote Rose Kaufman (national president from 1965 to 1969) in 1942, "like teas, attractive settings, flowers on the table, luncheons in a hotel—why not?" In a similar vein, new ventures like the Tozeret Haarez Consumers' League—intended to support

The English "White Paper" of 1945 on immigration to Israel was anathema to Zionists, and Pioneer Women mounted a concerted protest. [American Jewish Historical Society]

the *yishuv*'s commercial industries—gradually replaced the strident political campaigns of previous decades.

But Pioneer Women did not abandon its record of social activism. During World War II, it mobilized a countrywide network of volunteers who participated in civil defense efforts, Red Cross activities, war bond sales, blood drives, salvage work, and victory gardens. Such activities demonstrated Pioneer Women's commitment to American Jewry's wartime efforts and enhanced the organization's national visibility. The wartime campaign, explained the June 1944 issue of *Pioneer Women*, also benefited the organization by "add[ing] zest to the Eretz Israel program." It appealed to a broad range of non-Yiddish speakers and attracted new members who previously assumed that "we were interested in only the Eretz Israel program." In this period, when news of the destruction of European Jewry became well known, the organization also created emergency fund-raising initiatives such as the Child Rescue Fund of 1943 and the Building Fund of 1944, both of which were targeted at the needs of European Jewish refugee children in the *yishuv*. After the war, the campaign was widened to include orphans and children born in displaced persons camps.

With the establishment of the State of Israel in 1948, Pioneer Women expanded the range of its American activities. It embraced a cultural educational agenda that revealed growing concern about Jewish continuity in the New World. It moderated much of its original socialist and feminist ideology as well as its philosophical and political orientation. In this way, the organization reflected the changing character and concerns of a sizable segment of American Jewish women while continuing its work with labor and progressive groups on behalf of liberal causes.

After the establishment of the State of Israel, Pioneer Women proved to be an important partner for the Labor Zionist movement in Israel as well as a key player in American Zionism. The organization worked very closely with Moezet Hapoalot and the Jewish Agency for Israel. It promoted American Jewish tourism to the new state, conducted numerous independent and collaborative fund-raising campaigns, spearheaded efforts on behalf of vocational and educational centers for Jewish and Arab women and girls, helped create a vast network of day-care centers for Israeli working families, actively participated in Zionist political affairs, and served as a conduit to American Jewish society for Israel's rising women's movement.

On the American front, too, Pioneer Women assumed responsibility for a multiplicity of Labor Zionist causes that encompassed the movement's ongoing cultural, political, and educational concerns in the United States. Over the years, one of Pioneer Women's most favored projects has been the Habonim Labor Zionist youth movement. Created in 1935, Habonim sustains a network of coeducational year-round activities and summer camps. It espouses Labor Zionist values and ideals and serves as a training ground for many future leaders of American Labor Zionism.

In recent decades, Pioneer Women (reestablished as Na'amat in 1981, the name of its sister organization in Israel) has experienced a gradual decline in membership. From a peak of approximately fifty thousand members in the 1970s, the organization has been reduced by nearly half, or roughly the size of Pioneer Women in 1948. This trend is due, in part, to the fact that many of Naamat's functions and goals—like those of the Zionist Organization of America, Hadassah, Mizrachi, and other American Zionist groups—have been steadily adopted by mainstream American Jewish groups and institutions.

To sum up, before the establishment of the State of Israel, Pioneer Women anticipated the shift in American Jewish priorities vis-à-vis the Jewish national home and the increasing importance of Labor Zionism in world Jewish affairs. It was distinguished in the American context by the fact that it alone served as a channel for Jewish immigrant women who sympathized with aims and ideals of the labor movement in Palestine. It also provided a unique foothold for many Zionist leaders in the decades before the cause of the State of Israel became an integral component of the American Jewish consensus. In more recent decades, however, as Naamat and other Zionist groups struggle to maintain their place in the evolving American Jewish landscape, the organization has gradually shed much of its distinctive character. Nevertheless, it remains the voice of Labor Zionist women on American soil and the outpost of a progressive and egalitarian Zionist vision of diaspora Jewry.

After the establishment of the State of Israel, Pioneer Women was an important partner
of the Labor Zionist movement in Israel. This photograph shows the organization
shipping much-needed supplies to the women in the new state. [Na'amat, USA]

BIBLIOGRAPHY

AJYB; American Jewish Historical Society Archives. Brandeis University, Waltham, Mass.; Bernstein, Deborah S., ed. *Pioneers and Homemakers: Jewish Women in Pre-State Israel* (1992); Cohen, Moshe. *Labor Zionist Handbook: The Aims, Activities and History of the Labor Zionist Movement in America* (1939); *EJ* 13 (1971): 555; Halperin, Samuel. *The Political World of American Zionism* (1985); Katznelson-Rubashov, Rachel. *Vos Arbeterns Derzeyln: A Eretz Israel Bukh* (1931); Katznelson-Shazar, Rahel. *Adam Kmo Shehu: Prakei Yomanim Vereshimot.* Edited by Michal Hagitti (1989), and *The Plough Woman: Memoirs of the Pioneer Women of Palestine.* Translated by Maurice Samuel. 2d ed. (1975); Keren, Thea. *Sophie Udin: Portrait of a Pioneer* (1984); Mandelkern, Nick. "The Story of Pioneer Women." Parts 1–4. *Pioneer Women* (September 1980): 20–29, (November 1980): 6–8+ (January/February 1981): 13–16, (March/April 1981): 6–9; Meir, Golda. *My Life* (1975); Naamat USA. Archives. YIVO Institute for Jewish Research, NYC; Raider, Mark A. *American Jews and the Zionist Movement* (forthcoming); Reinharz, Jehuda, and Shulamit Reinharz, eds. *The Letters and Papers of Manya Shohat* (forthcoming); Shapira, Anita. *Berl: The Biography of a Socialist Zionist* (1984); Sokoloff, Judith A. "Naamat USA Through the Decades." Parts 1 and 2. *Naamat Woman* (September/October 1995): 16–27, (November/December 1995): 12–18; Spizman, Leib, ed. *Geshikte fun der Zionistisher Arbeter Bavegung in Zfon Amerike.* 2 vols. (1955); Stein, Kenneth W. *The Land Question in Palestine, 1917–1939* (1984); Weinberg, Sydney Stahl. *World of Our Mothers: The Lives of Jewish Immigrant Women* (1988); Yanait Ben-Zvi, Rahel. *Before Golda: Manya Shohat.* Translated by Sandra Shurin (1989), and *Drakhai Sifrati* (1971).

MARK A. RAIDER

PISKO, SERAPHINE EPPSTEIN (1861–1942)

Like so many middle-class Jewish women at the turn of the century, Seraphine Eppstein Pisko used her longtime experience in volunteer charitable work and her organizational talents to move into the realm of the professional workplace. In 1911, Pisko was appointed secretary of National Jewish Hospital (NJH) for Consumptives in Denver. She was later appointed executive secretary as well as vice president, and remained in control of day-to-day affairs at the hospital until her retirement twenty-seven years later in 1938. National Jewish had opened in 1899 as a nonsectarian sanatorium for indigent tuberculosis victims, although the majority of patients in the early years were Jewish. At the administrative helm of NJH, Pisko was probably the first woman in the United States to assume the position of chief executive of a national Jewish institution.

Seraphine Eppstein Pisko was born in St. Joseph, Missouri, on January 1, 1861, to Max and Bertha Eppstein, and moved to Denver in 1875 with her parents when she was fourteen years old. She was the eldest of six, followed by her sisters Julia and Carrie, her brother Arthur, and twin sisters Lillian and Helen. Seraphine attended local Denver public schools. In 1878, at age seventeen, she married prominent Jewish Denver businessman Edward Pisko, who was eighteen years older and headed a thriving liquor business. An Austrian immigrant who had been elected to the Colorado State Legislature in 1876 and had served as president of Denver's B'nai B'rith in 1877, Pisko was a leader in Denver's growing Jewish community. After they were married, the couple resided in New York City for a period, but Seraphine Pisko returned to Denver as a widow after the untimely death of her husband just a few years after they were married. Back in Denver, she made her home with her sister and brother-in-law, Lillian and Ernest Morris, who were active members of Denver's Jewish community.

Pisko then embarked on a renewed lifelong commitment to local Jewish and general charitable work. She served as president of the Hebrew Ladies Benevolent Society in Denver, which was renamed the Jewish Relief Society in 1901, and attended the first national Conference of Jewish Charities as a delegate. Prominent in Denver club work as well, she represented the Women's Club of Denver at the 1899 National Conference of Charities and Corrections in Cincinnati. After retiring as president of the Jewish Relief Society, she accepted the paid position of the first field secretary (traveling fund-raiser) for National Jewish Hospital, which eventually evolved into her appointment as secretary. Pisko also served as president of the local chapter of the NATIONAL COUNCIL OF JEWISH WOMEN, where she helped organize the Denver Jewish Settlement House and free kindergarten to benefit Eastern European Jewish immigrants living on Denver's west side. Although of German Jewish descent and a staunch Reform Jew, Pisko was frequently sensitive to the religious and cultural needs of the Eastern European immigrants, and helped introduce a kosher kitchen at NJH in 1923. A cultured woman of cosmopolitan sensibilities, she was well known in many American Jewish communities, and she became a national director of the National Council of Jewish Women as well.

Seraphine Eppstein Pisko was an exceptionally capable woman, who earned a national reputation for her organizational expertise. Her experience in managing local Jewish charitable organizations made her particularly suitable to embark on a professional career in hospital fund-raising and administration. Her contacts with Jewish communities throughout the country also served her well in developing national support for the growing sanatorium. In 1925, National Jewish Hospital honored her by renaming the Women's Pavilion the Seraphine Pisko Pavilion. At the dedication, Pisko was described as a woman of "extraordinary ability," "remarkable powers of organization," "splendid judgment," "fine tact," and "all-embracing sympathy."

Failing health forced Pisko to retire in 1938, but she continued as an honorary officer until her death on July 27, 1942, at age eighty-one. Seraphine Eppstein Pisko served as a role model for generations of Jewish women that followed, combining a clear professional vision with unswerving commitment to the Jewish community.

BIBLIOGRAPHY

AJYB 7 (1905–1906): 94, 45:391; Breck, Allen. *A Centennial History of the Jews of Colorado* (1960); Fitzharris, Mary Ann. *A Place to Heal: The History of National Jewish Center for Immunology and Respiratory Medicine* (1989); Friedenthal, S. "The Story of the Jews of Denver." *The Reform Advocate* (1908); National Jewish Hospital Collection. Beck Archives of Rocky Mountain Jewish History, University of Denver; Obituary. *NYTimes*, July 31, 1942, 15:4; Toll, William. "Gender and the Origins of Philanthropic Professionalism: Seraphine Pisko at the National Jewish Hospital." *Rocky Mountain Jewish Historical Notes* 11, nos. 1 and 2 (Winter/Spring 1991); Uchill, Ida. *Pioneers, Peddlers, and Tsadikim* (1959); *UJE*; *WWIAJ* (1928, 1938).

JEANNE ABRAMS

POETRY

What is a Jewish poem? Does it wear a yarmulke
and a tallis?
Does it live
in the diaspora
and yearn for homeland?

Myra Sklarew's poem entitled "What Is a Jewish poem?" frames the question within the traditionally male stereotypes of what it is to be Jewish. Since she herself is a contemporary Jewish woman poet, a survivor of the Holocaust living in America, her poem forces the reader to confront a deeper, unspoken question: What constitutes a Jewish poem written by a woman in America? The male-centered attitude of Sklarew's poem, which ludicrously refers to the Jewish poem as "little *yeshiva bokher*," is, unfortunately, a fairly accurate assessment of the way in which literary critics have defined Jewish poetry.

In the essay "American-Jewish Poetry: An Overview," R. Barbara Gitenstein points out the narrow focus of critics. She suggests that a student conducting an overview of American-Jewish literature might conclude that "there are no American-Jewish writers who are women, no writers who have lived in towns smaller than Chicago—and surely no writers who are poets." Even among the few anthologies and literary surveys that emphasize poetry over prose, editors and scholars have favored primarily male poets, with token references to women. Few have attempted to evaluate the poetry of Jewish American women as a collective. While in the nineteenth and early twentieth centuries Jewish women poets dotted the landscape of American poetry, there has been a recent flourishing of women poets, many of whom choose to write on Jewish themes. Recent efforts, mostly by Jewish women poets and scholars, to anthologize and examine the tremendous range of these works have been the first tentative explorations in this rich and complex territory.

The question remains: What makes a poem "Jewish"? Is it enough that the poet is Jewish? Must the theme be Jewish? Is there such a thing as a Jewish "sensibility" or attitude in poetry? From the nineteenth century to the present, Jewish American women have written poetry to varied audiences in a dramatic range of form, style, and theme. To look exclusively at poems with Jewish content would be misleading. It ignores the possibility that the desire to write poetry that is not thematically Jewish may itself be a defining feature of the complex position of Jewish American women, and it overlooks poets whose Judaism influences their writing in more subtle ways. Just as poets whose work is not primarily Jewish deserve attention, it is also important to address women poets who identify themselves as Jews, although they may not be considered Jewish by halakic law. A poet of such force and popularity as ADRIENNE RICH, for example, is often left out of anthologies because her mother was not Jewish.

The tremendous diversity of Jewish American women's poetry is caused by a balancing act, or, in some cases, a full-scale war, between the three parts that make up the identity of the poet: Jewish, American, and female. What value does the poet place on each of these attributes? How is the poem able to integrate or juxtapose them? How does each poet define herself as a Jew, a woman, and an American? The compatibility of these three competing identities changes most significantly over historical time, but is also affected by the poet's position in society and religious commitment. Of course, the relationship among the Jewish, female, and American identities of a poet can shift from one poem to the next. One of the virtues of poetry is that it allows for such contradiction, so that a poet may argue with traditional Judaism in one poem, and celebrate it in another.

To take a closer look at the history of Jewish poetry by American women, then, is to bring together a collection of poets rarely considered to have anything to do with each other. There is, however, a common thread: The poets share a sense of marginality, of viewing the world from outside the mainstream. Jewish women's poetry is often transformational, whether it is from within the Jewish world, or in American society at large. Writing from the margins—as Jews, as women—these poets often become the modern equivalent of prophets, critically evaluating and condemning existing circumstances, and envisioning better ones. It is worth noting how many Jewish women poets write with a strong sense of social responsibility, a desire to create poetry that can shape reality, perhaps drawing on the Jewish teachings of *tikkun olam* [repairing the world]. In addition, the poet's place on the outskirts of literary movements and circles has led in many cases to greater innovation and experimentation.

Most scholars name EMMA LAZARUS as the first American Jewish poet, male or female, to be recognized by mainstream America. Born in 1849 to an established American family, Lazarus differed from many other Jewish women poets of her time due to her privileged background and the support of her influential father. Her early poems did not reflect a Jewish awareness, but were rooted in classical texts and clearly inspired by the great male poets of her time. The collection of poems that proudly pronounced Lazarus a Jewish poet was *Songs of a Semite*. Published in 1882, the book coincides with the influx of Russian immigrants to America in response to harsh pogroms, an event that profoundly affected Lazarus.

The poetry of Emma Lazarus embraced the many diverse and often contradictory parts of her identity—the American citizen praising tolerance and liberty, the secular Jew concerned about a Jewish homeland as well as growing anti-Semitism at home, and the woman who, "late-born and woman-souled," chose a career in writing over marriage. Despite her traditional use of poetic form, she was in many ways a forerunner to the vocal activism of Jewish women poets writing in the 1960s and 1970s.

Lazarus is best known for her poem "The New Colossus" (1883), engraved at the base of the Statue of Liberty. Most Americans are familiar only with "Give me your tired, your poor, / Your huddled masses yearning to breathe free," but the poem as a whole hints at the three parts of Lazarus's identity—the powerful figure of the welcoming mother, the theme of exile, and the affirmation of America's tolerance. The Statue of Liberty becomes "A mighty woman with a torch, whose flame / Is the imprisoned lightning, and her name / Mother of Exiles." It may be that Lazarus's genuine belief in America as the land of opportunity allowed her to embrace her Jewish heritage publicly, partly out of an idealist hope that America could not harbor anti-Semitism, and partly as a defiant stand in the face of anti-Semitism when she could no longer ignore it.

While Lazarus remains the best-known Jewish woman poet of the nineteenth century, there were many other Jewish women writing poetry, many of whom did not venture beyond traditional Jewish themes. Diane Lichtenstein's book *Writing Their Nations: The Tradition of Nineteenth-Century American Jewish Women Writers* (1992) is the first book to examine critically the writing of early Jewish women poets. Lichtenstein views the poets in the context of American and Jewish cultural myths, making the claim that these poets attempted to synthesize the American and Jewish ideals of womanhood. PENINA MOÏSE (1797–1880) wrote the first Jewish hymnal, as well as one of the first volumes of poetry published by a Jew in America, *Fancy's Sketch Book* (1833). Her poem "Daughters of Israel" calls, as Lazarus did, Jewish women into action, but here it is a battle to maintain and uphold traditional Jewish roles. "Wife! mother! sister! on ye all / A tender task devolves / Child husband, brother, o ye all, / To nerve their best resolves." She also wrote poems reflecting the immigrant's dream of acceptance in the New Land. That there was a need for lines such as "Oh! not as Strangers shall your welcome be / Come to the homes and bosoms of the free" suggests wishful thinking, an attempt to comfort and inspire those new immigrants who, perhaps, did not receive such a warm welcome. It is difficult to know whether poets like Lazarus and Moïse wrote these poems out of pride and conviction, or out of fear of anti-Semitism and a desire, conscious or not, to align with the American side.

Lichtenstein includes many lesser-known poets in the "tradition" of Jewish women's poetry. REBEKAH GUMPERT HYNEMAN (1812–1875) wrote poems in praise of biblical women, celebrating rather than questioning them, as modern poets would later begin to do. Octavia Harby Moses (1823–1904) was another poet who accepted her position as the traditional Jewish mother and wife. In the 1890s, Jewish women's poetry gained greater prominence, as Jewish women took advantage of the expanded freedoms offered to all white American women.

There was, of course, another group of women poets writing in the early twentieth century who offered tremendous innovations of musicality and form. Immigrating to the United States from Eastern Europe, these poets wrote poems in Yiddish clearly inspired by modernist trends in Europe. Despite the nonpolitical nature of most Yiddish American poetry by women, socialist and communist journals often published their work, as well as the elitist literary journals of the Yunge and Inzikh movements. While women writers hovered on the fringes of the Yunge, a literary movement that emphasized personal voice over nationalistic rhetoric, experimention with mood and language over traditional form and the aesthetic beauty of the poem independent of political associations, they incorporated many of its values. In fact, women poets had an ironic advantage. Their marginal position allowed them the freedom to explore unique variations of meter and sound as well as personal subject matter, surpassing some of the more well-known male poets in originality and intensity of mood.

ANNA MARGOLIN (1887–1952) and CELIA DROPKIN (1888–1956) were two of the most significant and inventive women poets writing in Yiddish. Margolin's poetry characterizes the modernist leanings of Yiddish American poets in its attention to form, sound, and intimate subject matter. Mysterious, empassioned, and linguistically complex, her poems mirror the writing of European modernists with their references to classical texts. She herself lived a modern life unrestricted by traditional roles; she had several lovers and allowed her son to be raised by his father. While Celia Dropkin's life was more suited to traditional family values— she married and raised five children—her poetry was not. Her poems seem to dance along the edge of the acceptable, with an almost erotic fascination with the dark and dangerous. In "I Am a Circus Lady," the speaker of the poem dances between knives, lured by the danger of touching them, of falling. FRADL SHTOK (b. 1890) was another poet of exceptional originality, although her work is more difficult to find in translation. She couched striking imagery in a brashly erotic tone and highly experimental poetic forms.

Yiddish women poets were generally well-versed in European literary trends, but they also lived their daily lives immersed in the rich cultural texture of *yiddishkeit*. They were twice alienated—as immigrants to America and as women on the outskirts of Yiddish politics and the literary elite. Thus their poetry reflects an even greater complexity in terms of identity than that found in the poetry of the early poets writing in English. Yid-

dish women poets grappled with their changing relationship to traditional Jewish roles as well as to a traditional God. KADYA MOLODOWSKY (1894–1974) was already an established poet when she immigrated to America in 1935. Respected for her poetry, journalism, and scholarship, she fought through her poetry against the condescending treatment of women poets by the male-dominated intellectual circles of the time. Playing off the concept of the Jews as the chosen people, in the poem "God of Mercy," she asks God in an ironic, but seriously plaintive tone to "choose another people." While not doubting the existence of God, she is able to argue with the injustice and tragedy God allows the Jewish people to suffer: "O God of Mercy / For the time being / Choose another people. / We are tired of death, tired of corpses, / We have no more prayers." She asks God to "grant us one more blessing—/ Take back the gift of our separateness."

MALKA HEIFETZ TUSSMAN (1893–1987), whose work was published in *Insikh*, the journal of the radical Introspectivists, also engaged in a dialogue with God through humor as well as debate and plea. She speaks to God intimately, finding connection to the divine through nature. To her, a sunset is a "Godset." She views the creative process of the poet as a divine process and at one point writes simply that "The Holy One is a poem." This intimate and playful battle of words captures a uniquely Yiddish approach to the divine—celebrating, teasing, and questioning in the same breath.

In addition to the more literary poets, many Yiddish women chose to write politically and socially motivated poetry for communist presses. These poets were less concerned with God and poetics, and more concerned with the need to change the place of women in society. Speaking out against the oppression of women, poets such as Esther Shumiatcher, Sara Barkan, and Shifre Weiss wrote poetry designed to motivate and inspire.

When looking at the Yiddish poetry of women in America, it is important to acknowledge the Jewish women, many of them poets themselves, who have made Yiddish poetry the subject of literary criticism through research and translation. Given the emphasis on sound and form, it is unfortunate that most Jewish readers are unable to read the poems in their original language. Norma Fain Pratt, Kathryn Hellerstein, Adrienne Rich, RUTH WHITMAN, and Marcia Falk have done invaluable work in making these poems accessible through careful translation and scholarship.

The well-known modernist poet GERTRUDE STEIN shares in common with the Yiddish poets a devotion to stylistic experimentation. But how is it possible to compare this first major poet of the twentieth century to her predecessors, poets such as Lazarus and Moïse, who exemplified the ideals of Judaism, womanhood, and America? Rather than attempting to balance or reconcile the Jewish, female, and American aspects of her identity, Stein chose to disregard them. She lived her life in antithesis to all expectations and stereotypes—a Jew who bordered on anti-Semitism, a lesbian who played out the traditional male role of husband to ALICE B. TOKLAS, and an American who chose to live and write in Paris. She was also an art collector and hostess of a successful salon, maintaining close connections with painters and composers as well as poets. As the child of prosperous German Jewish immigrants, this appreciation for art and culture was itself a trait of the Jewish upper middle class from which she came. Yet Stein was determined to forge her own unique path. Her defiance of traditional rules and boundaries was applied with equal enthusiasm and conviction to her poetry. She was one of the greatest modernist writers of her time, experimenting with form, language, and musicality, attempting to rid herself of nouns as she rid herself of any preconception of how she must behave. It was precisely her ability to follow her own unique path that earned her a prominent place in American literary history.

Naomi Replansky, another noteworthy Jewish poet of the early twentieth century, did not achieve such fame. Her first book of poems, *Ring Song*, was not published until 1952, although it included poems written as early as 1934, when Replansky was just sixteen years old. Replansky wrote lyrical, carefully worded poems that belied their intensity. A few of these poems centered around Jewish themes, such as the poem entitled "The Six Million," which recounts a godless Holocaust, but other poems reflect a related theme of otherness. In "Housing Shortage," published in *The Dangerous World*, the speaker of the poem feels she is taking up too much emotional space. "I tried to live small / I took a narrow bed. I held my elbows to my sides. I tried to step carefully / And to breathe shallowly / In my portion of air / And to disturb no one." Replansky was not a prolific writer, publishing only two collections, but her accomplished voice and quietly intense response to the Holocaust are worth further exploration.

MURIEL RUKEYSER (1913–1980), one of the most significant Jewish American poets in history, who is only recently gaining the recognition she deserves, grappled fully and passionately with all aspects of her identity. Hers is not only the story of a tremendously gifted, driven, and prolific writer, but it is the story of twentieth-century America, told from the point of view of one Jewish activist. Born on the eve of World War I, Rukeyser witnessed and condemned a host of injustices around the world. Despite Rukeyser's contribution as a modern writer, her story is also one of invisibility; she is rarely included in the all-male roster of modernists such as Wallace Stevens, William Carlos Williams, and Ezra Pound. Her inventive writing style, range of themes, and unique capacity for embracing contradiction make her work difficult to classify, and many critics have dismissed her for that reason. Jewish poets such as Adrienne Rich and Denise Levertov, however, praise Rukeyser as a mentor and role model. Rich, in her introduction to *A Muriel Rukeyser Reader* (1994), writes,

> To enter this book is to enter a life of tremendous scope, the consciousness of a woman who was a full actor and creator in many ways. Muriel Rukeyser was beyond her time—and seems, at the edge of the twenty-first century, to have grasped resources we are only now beginning to reach for: connections between history and the body, memory and politics, sexuality and public space, poetry and physical science, and much else.

Rukeyser, like Lazarus and many of the poets to follow, was not only a poet, but a brilliant and persuasive essayist. In addition to publishing fifteen collections of poetry, Rukeyser wrote numerous articles and books of prose. But writing in the mid-twentieth century as a lesbian, she chose very different means of expressing the conflict between her Jewish and female identities. Her first book of poems, *Theory of Flight*, written when she was twenty-one, was awarded the Yale Younger Poets Prize. Already in this early collection she writes in her "Poem of Children," "Breathe-in experience, breathe-out poetry." This is precisely what she continues to do in her work, chronicling her personal experiences alongside those of the entire planet. Her rich and inspiring life led her to Alabama to report on the Scottsboro trial, to Spain on the eve of Civil War, and to North Vietnam to speak out in the 1960s. Every one of her political actions was recorded in poetry. "The Book of the Dead," a poem written in response to miners in West Virginia, represents a new way of writing poetry, in which Rukeyser's voice intertwines with the minutes of meetings, workers' letters, graphs and equations, stock quotations, and even X-rays. Rukeyser saw poetry as a necessary way to combat the terrible silence of nations in the face of Word War II and other tragedies.

While she experimented with a range of traditional and new forms, her most innovative work captures the rapid, disjunctive movements of modern life. Rukeyser herself compared this type of writing to the collage of camera angles used in film. In her book *The Life of Poetry* (1949), Rukeyser is able to contain the full multiplicity of the self—vast, paradoxical, and infinitely rich. The book not only offers up a philosophy of what poetry can mean, but also a unique perspective on what poetry can do. As Rich wrote, "What does poetry have to do with democracy? Read it here."

Muriel Rukeyser wrote openly of her experiences as a woman and a Jew, tossing her Jewish identity into the complex range of ideas present in her poetry. The poem "Letter to the Front," published in 1944, merges the atrocities of the Holocaust with a long list of political injustices occurring during her lifetime. "To be a Jew in the twentieth century," she writes, "Is to be offered a gift." But the second stanza continues, "The gift is torment." What makes being a Jew in the twentieth century "torment"? That it requires living as the whole self, feeling a sense of responsibility for all those in need, and daring to "live for the impossible." Rukeyser is a key poet in the course of Jewish women's poetry, not only because her poetry stands as a memoir to a dramatic and volatile era in American history, but because Rukeyser so willingly accepted the "gift" of her Judaism at a time when, as Stein demonstrates, it was possible to ignore it.

It is hard to imagine a feminist anthology or university course that would not include the poetry of Adrienne Rich. Much of the praise she has extended to Rukeyser's body of work could be applied to her own. She, too, is a passionate and prolific writer, unleashing the possibilities of poetic form and subject matter to meet her needs. Like Rukeyser, she takes on the role of poet-prophet, refusing to shy away from the most difficult and painful events and emotions. And yet the all-consuming passion with which she writes and lives, sometimes manifesting as rage, sometimes love, suggest that Rich is hopeful about our capacity to effect change. Her involvement in the political and feminist movements of the 1960s led her to write with eloquence about the relationship between the personal and political, power and powerlessness. Much of Rich's poetry is an attempt to break down the barriers between sexual identity and politics, "between Vietnam and the lover's bed." The poem "Diving into the Wreck," which marked a turning point in Rich's poetry, perhaps best describes the way in which Rich bravely delves into the "wreck" of flawed societal structures that reside around and within her: "I came to explore the wreck. / The words are purposes. / The words are maps. / I came to see the damage that was done / and the treasures that prevail."

While Rich is best known for the fragmented, often angry poems inspired by her changing politics in the 1960s and 1970s, her poetry had a very different beginning. Like Rukeyser, she was awarded the Yale Younger Poets Prize in her early twenties. This first collection of poems, *A Change of World* (1951), was carefully shaped and structured, the poems neatly worded and understated. Even in this early work, however, Rich was beginning to write about the hierarchy of male-female roles in poems such as "Aunt Jennifer's Tigers," but through implication and metaphor rather than direct statement. That Rich began writing in the tight, controlled forms of modern American writing in the 1950s suggests that the open, fragmented style of her later work is equally controlled and deliberate, a style chosen by Rich to encompass a rage and a vision that could no longer be contained in more traditional forms.

What makes Rich such a central figure in terms of Jewish American poetry is that she writes openly about her divided self in her later work. Rich pushes the already marginal status of the Jewish American women even further than her predecessors, presenting herself as the half-Jewish American woman, ostracized by and struggling to come to terms with both halves. In an essay in *Nice Jewish Girls: A Lesbian Anthology* (1982), Rich challenges herself to confront her relationship to the Jewish part of her heritage and identity. The essay "Split at the Root: An Essay on Jewish Identity" grapples with Rich's relationship with her secular Jewish father, her own latent anti-Semitism, and her process of growing awareness and commitment as a Jew. Her father was relatively silent about his Judaism, and Rich grew up in a Christian environment of proper manners and hidden racism. "Sometimes I feel I have seen too long from too many disconnected angles: white, Jewish, anti-Semite, racist, anti-racist, once-married, lesbian, middle-class, feminist, exmatriate southerner, split at the root—that I will never bring them whole."

Rich's prose work can articulate and break down the inconsistencies of the whole self, but only a poem can bring them together in one fragile effort of will, like a broken vase whose pieces are put back together without glue, threatening to shatter at any moment. In a longer poem, "Sources," Rich engages in a poetic battle with her contradictory roots. The phrase "split at the root" forms the haunting chorus of this difficult poem; *"From where does your strength come, you Southern Jew? / split at the root, raised in a castle of air?"* Rich holds her life up against the Jews of the Holocaust—

"All during World War II / I told myself I had some special destiny ... there had to be a reason / I was growing up safe, American / with sugar rationed in a Mason jar" and the Zionist women who forged a new life in Palestine—"socialists, anarchists, jeered / as excitable, sharp of tongue / too filled with life / wanting equality in the promised land," trying to map out her place among them, a way to connect. In another poem in the same collection, "Yom Kippur 1984," Rich does not distinguish her Jewish identity from social consciousness. She interrelates a move cross-country, the renewal and communal spirit of Yom Kippur, and the daily injustices she reads in the paper into a textured collage reminiscent of Walt Whitman. "What is a Jew in solitude?" she asks, then immediately extends the question: "What is a woman in solitude: a Queer woman or man?"

While the impetus of her writing is often raw emotion—need, anger, sorrow, love—it is examined from a highly intellectual perspective that exposes the pain, but also distances from it. Mind and heart, like Jew and gentile, woman and American, personal and political, wrestle in her poems. Although Rich's background may be more ambivalent than some other Jewish writers, her work is profoundly Jewish in that she dares to ask the question, and to take responsibility for a heritage she must seek out for herself. She became a strong advocate of peace between Palestinians and Jews in Israel, and cofounded the Jewish women's journal *BRIDGES*.

Many Jewish poets writing poetry from the 1970s to the present have aligned themselves with the feminist movement and believed in the poetic power to make changes in terms of gender equality and political justice. Denise Levertov shares Rich's tenuous relationship with her Jewish heritage, feminist approach, and sense of social responsibility, but these elements enter her poetry in a more subtle way. Her father was raised a Hasidic Jew, then converted to Christianity before she was born. Her Irish mother treasured story, magic, and mysticism. This connection to the spiritual and to myth is evident in Levertov's poetry. Levertov wrote several poems drawing on biblical texts. "The Jacob's Ladder," which is shaped like a series of steps, uses the the biblical image as metaphor. In Levertov's version, the ladder is made of stone, and the angels must hop down, while "a man climbing / must scrape his knees." This interchange of human effort and spiritual visitation becomes a metaphor for writing poetry. "Wings brush past him. / The poem ascends."

Other feminist writers, such as Erica Jong and MARGE PIERCY, wrote poetic commentary on the rela-

tionship between women and men in society. Many of Piercy's poems revolve around cultural notions of beauty, and the tension between the individual identity and societal expectations. In "Barbie Doll," the "girlchild," criticized by a classmate, eventually cuts off the offending body parts and dies. Made to look beautiful in her coffin, the guests exclaim over how pretty she looks. Other fiction writers who have also published books of poetry include GRACE PALEY and CYNTHIA OZICK.

Piercy and other feminist poets have attempted to rewrite the cultural myths held by the society in which they live. But the changes in the 1970s moved beyond a heightened awareness of universal political and social injustice. The celebration of ethnic culture and emphasis on individual awareness and discovery in the past few decades have drawn many Jewish poets to look openly at what makes them Jewish, examining their relationship with the past as well as present Jewish community.

Poets such as Myra Sklarew and Irena Klepfisz write poetry that attempts to repair the ties to ancestors and the culture of Eastern European Jewry severed by the Holocaust. Other poets write from the perspective of outsiders, not to America, but to the land of Israel. Irena Klepfisz is emerging as a powerful and significant voice in Jewish women's poetry. As a lesbian Jewish poet, she writes about themes of feminism and lesbianism, as well as activist poetry about Israel. Her poetry is most notable, however, for her struggles to revive the Yiddish culture that has been lost both through the Holocaust and through assimilation in America. Klepfisz attempts to make peace with the duality of her immigrant status, further complicated by the reality that Yiddish was not, as she was told, her *mame loshen* [mother tongue], by juxtaposing Yiddish and English on the page in a fascinating dance of dualing identities. These lyrical poems do not translate the Yiddish, but engage with it, bringing it back to life and making the poem, like the poet, incomplete without both halves interwoven. She writes that "this Yiddish of mine, this fragmentary language ... might prove worth salvaging and sheltering." The revival of the Yiddish language, then, is in some way a tribute to the sustaining life force of a culture and people who have survived, and a way for the poet to remember and reach out to them. She expresses this in "Di Rayze Aheym / The Journey Home":

Zi shemt zikh.
She has forgotten
alts fargesn
forgotten it all.

Myra Sklarew also writes about the Holocaust from a personal perspective. Her poems reflect a playfulness with language even as the content is intensely serious. Those who died in the Holocaust continue to walk through her thoughts and poems. In "Benediction," she writes, "Sometimes I see them coming / and going along the road / where they were swallowed up / carrying their empty luggage." Having written seven books of poetry, including *From the Backyard of the Diaspora* (1976), Sklarew's greatest accomplishment is her recent collection entitled *Lithuania* (1995). The poem "Lithuania," written in ten sections that interweave Sklarew's return to the sites of massacres with documentation and story drawn from accounts by Holocaust survivors and Lithuanian citizens, family letters and diaries, is a moving account of both the suffering and loss of Lithuanian Jewry, and the effort of one Jewish woman in America to record and remember it as her own experience. Sklarew, disturbed by the beauty of the landscapes where such horror took place, writes that "the poem attempts to penetrate beneath the pastoral beauty of these habitations of death, to peel back the layers of earth and time, to touch the places where our people once lived and, by so doing, to touch them."

American women living in Israel and beyond grapple with their relationship to Israel during times of political tension. The desire for a just and peaceful world wrestles at times with love and support for a Jewish homeland. There are several women poets writing in English in Israel, but the work of Shirley Kaufman, Linda Zisquit, and Rachel Tvia Back is read here in America, providing through the intensity of poetry an account of the events and mood of Israel.

Shirley Kaufman is often included in anthologies of contemporary American poetry, though she resides primarily in Israel. One of her most significant and powerful poems, "Looking at Henry Moore's Elephant Skull Etchings in Jerusalem During the War," is a long poem that records the fear and alienation of living in Israel in wartime through fragments of image and dream. "There is a way to enter / if you remember / where you came from / how to breathe under water / make love in a trap."

In the first collection of poems by Linda Zisquit, sparse and elusive poems rest uneasily against a backdrop of war and tension. "When war broke out I was unloosed," she begins in a sensual and disturbing poem about love entitled "Summer at War," written in 1982. Zisquit is not only an American Jew living in Israel, but a modern Orthodox Jewish woman, coping with the hurt and alienation of being a woman in a male-dominated tradition, revisiting Talmudic and biblical texts. The voice in her poems is distant and restrained, giving a sense of barely controlled emotion. "My body like a poem / admires itself, tries to make itself / perfect," she states in the poem "In Hebrew the Word Compassion Is Plural for Womb." Rachel Tvia Back presents a newly emerging voice, experimenting with language and collage to transpose the experiences of the Gulf War onto the page. In "Notes from a Sealed Room," the room becomes a cave, a womb: "*place of hiding and hidden (heart's / cave, heart's caution: calcareous regions).*" Women writers living in America also write poems about Israel, some describing how it feels to be there, others writing from a more political point of view. The anthology *Without a Single Answer: Poems on Contemporary Israel* (1990), edited by the poets Elaine Marcus Starkman and Leah Schweitzer, includes beautifully written poems on a variety of perspectives and from a surprising range of voices, such as a poem by Julia Vinograd, a Berkeley street personality and poet, on a Jerusalem she has never seen.

As women poets are turning their attention toward their heritage and culture, they are taking a new look at traditional texts. The poet Deena Metzger, inspired by quests for spiritual fulfillment, also drew on the fertile environment of the 1970s. Her spiritual poetry is framed within a primarily Jewish mystical perspective, drawing on the teachings and language of the Cabala. Through poetry, Jewish women have both criticized and reconnected with the texts and rituals that excluded them for so long. A growing trend, one that is rooted in the English and Yiddish poetry of the late nineteenth and early twentieth centuries, is for Jewish women poets to add their voices to the sacred texts of Judaism through poetry that takes the form of midrash on biblical sources in the form of stories.

ALICIA OSTRIKER is one of the more playful experimenters with poetic midrash. Ostriker has contributed to the face of women's poetry in America through her feminist critiques and political poetry. Her critical work *Stealing the Language: The Emergence of Women's Poetry in America* (1986) analyzes an astounding range of poetry by women, drawing connections between them and highlighting their compromised position in the essentially male literary world. Ostriker's midrash-inspired poetry wages a similar war within the boundaries of Jewish tradition. These poems are angry and forthright, but are often laced with humor and absurdity. Retelling the story of the covenant with Abraham, for example, she writes from the perspective of a modern-day Abraham, reading over a slightly fishy contract. The poem "The Story of Abraham," included in David Curzon's anthology *Modern Poems on the Bible* (1994), presents a bold headline that paraphrases the biblical rendition of the blessings promised to Abraham. But the small print adds several conditions, including "a mark of absolute / Distinction," circumcision. When Abraham interrupts, saying, "I'd like to check / Some of this out with my wife," God responds: "NO WAY. THIS IS BETWEEN US MEN." Ostriker's humorous but telling reenvisioning of biblical text is fully explored in her book *The Nakedness of the Fathers* (1994), a book that integrates poetry and critical prose.

Ostriker's midrashic poem speaks through the voice of a man, but many poems by Jewish women allow the women in the Bible, who often play a secondary role to the men, a chance to speak, sometimes for the first time. The act of re-creating the voices of these women provides a new and rich connection to biblical sources for women by either allowing the contemporary woman to enter into the biblical story, or drawing the biblical character into a modern context. The titles of recent anthologies of Jewish women's writing are evidence in themselves of this trend. One anthology, entitled *Sarah's Daughters Sing* (1990), brings together poems by Jewish women writing in America and beyond. It is an important work because it draws together poetry on Jewish themes, such as poetic midrash, and poetry by Jewish women on non-Jewish themes, such as love and the home. The anthology of work by lesbian Jewish writers, edited by Melanie Kaye/Kantrowitz and Irena Klepfisz, alludes to the forgotten sister of the male leaders of the twelve tribes of Israel in its title, *The Tribe of Dina* (1986). And the Jewish women's magazine LILITH celebrates in its title the recent reclaiming of the first wife of Adam. Seen through male eyes as a traitor, temptress, and demoness, Lilith is hailed by contemporary women as a feminist visionary. Women poets rescue the figure of Lilith, reinvent Eve and the matriarchs, and take over the role previously granted to Adam to observe and name the world around them.

In 1984, Shirley Kaufman wrote a poem in which the biblical Sarah and Hagar become two women living in modern Jerusalem. Entitled "Deja Vu," the poem imagines a meeting at the Dome of the Rock, the place Muslims believe Abraham brought Ishmael to be sacrificed. Sarah is "showing the tourists with their Minoltas / around their necks the place / where Mohammed flew up to heaven," while Hagar prays in the women's section.

They bump into each other at the door,
the dark still heavy on their backs
like the future always coming after them.
Sarah wants to find out what happened
to Ishmael but is afraid to ask.
Hagar's lips make a crooked seam
over her accusations.

The juxtaposition of the two stories provides a powerful commentary on the lives of Jewish and Palestinian women in contemporary Israel, while adding a creative and beautifully written midrash to the rabbinic commentaries.

Poets such as Chana Bloch and Linda Pastan do not confront directly their Jewish selves in their work, but their Jewish identities and love of biblical text are simply an integral part of who they are and what they write about. Bloch, who is also well known as a translator of Israeli poets, writes poems that have been whittled down to the core like the smallest Russian doll in her poem "The Family." Writing about family and personal experience, Bloch is able to enter the remembered world of the child. In a poem recalling the small joys of childhood, she asks innocently, "If we were so happy / why weren't we happy?" When writing on biblical themes, Bloch imaginatively enters biblical texts, making startling leaps of imagery with grace and skill. Her midrashic poems are not political commentaries about the stories, but paths for the reader to follow into the story itself, captured through sound, mood, and image.

Linda Pastan's poetic world is also a small one, as she keenly observes and delights in the simple pleasures and common experiences of her life. She describes the everyday, from the stationary bicycle to an article of clothing, with such a fresh approach and skilled crafting of language that it becomes memorable and meaningful. "Long after Eden, the imagination flourishes with all of its unruly weeds." Among these daily experiences, she writes of setting the Passover table and visiting Jerusalem, and constantly draws hints of biblical story into her poems. A poem entitled "Lumberjacks" views the cutting down of the forest as a symbolic destruction of Eden, as Eve watches their work until "even the complicitous apple was felled, and the smell / of sawdust was like death / in the nostrils" (*An Early Afterlife*).

Two of the most significant women poets of the 1980s and 1990s, Louise Glück and MAXINE KUMIN, write poetry that renders their Jewish backgrounds practically invisible. This is not to say that they reject their Jewish heritage, only that it does not appear as a theme in their poems. Louise Glück, who won the Pulitzer Prize for *The Wild Iris* (1992), does explore biblical mythology along with Greek, but does not do so from a particularly Jewish perspective. Glück's tight, meticulously crafted, and lyrical poetry uses paradox and deliberate ambiguity to describe the "thrust and ache" of the human condition. An earlier poem, "The Garden," encompasses the human fear of birth, love, and burial in the creation myth. Her later collection, *The Wild Iris*, returns to the scene of the garden, but in this work it is the modern-day garden superimposed on the mythological. In this poem, everyone speaks—the gardener, the flowers, even a God who is voiced by seasons and changes of weather. Despite allusions to Eden and Moses, the structure of the book revolves around the daily Christian prayers of Matins and Vespers. It is an ambitious and moving work, merging the eternal resonance of the mythological garden with the present-tense urgency of caring for an actual garden, in which there is constant change, and all movement is overshadowed by inevitable winter.

Although she was "raised on the Old Testament," the closest thing to God in the poems of Maxine Kumin is the natural world, which she turns to for signs of survival and regeneration. Often mesmerized by the everyday, Kumin places humans, animals, and vegetables on equal footing in her poems. Ordinary places become magical, the kitchen "a harem of good smells / where we have bumped hips and / cracked the cupboards with our talk." Like Pastan, the gift of her poetry lies in the balance of powerful observation and skilled shaping of line and experience. Inside a pea pod, "nine little fetuses / nod their cloned heads" ("The Pea Patch").

While Jewish women can forge new links with sacred text through poetic midrash, Jewish women poets have returned to the timeless ritual of prayer. Poets such as Ruth Whitman in her collection *The Marriage Wig* (1968) challenge traditional women's roles and ritual in the Jewish community. The need for new liturgy to accompany changing approaches to women's ritual has led women rabbis and leaders to seek out poems and songs to replace and supplement traditional prayers. There is traditionally in Judaism a fine line between poetry and prayer, and Jewish women in recent years have crossed over it. A diverse collection of poems edited by Marcia Cohn Spiegel and Deborah Lipton Kremsdorf, *Women Speak to God: The Prayers and Poems of Jewish Women* (1987), contains in one book Miriam's Song of the Sea, poems by Yiddish and English poets that address, question, and rebel against God, and newly written prayers by women for a variety of occasions. Marge Piercy has written several poems that work as more inclusive and relevant alternatives to traditional prayers, such as the Amidah [the central section of prayer at each service].

Marcia Falk's *Book of Blessings: New Jewish Prayers for Daily Life, the Sabbath and the New Moon Festival* (1996), renders poetry and prayer nearly indistinguishable. It may seem strange to include a prayer book in a survey of Jewish women's poetry, but this siddur is also a collection of poems. Falk's quiet, meditative poems, along with her lyrical translations and adaptations of Israeli and Yiddish poets and traditional psalms, serve as prayers and meditations. Even her genderless re-creations of blessings demonstrate a movement and lilting lyricism, clearly written through the eyes and ears of a poet. Poetic devices such as line breaks, alliteration, and rhyme are used when necessary to highlight the theme of each blessing. Marcia Falk has been noted for her poetry and scholarship, as well as her translations of the Hebrew poet Zelda and the Yiddish poet Malka Heifetz Tussman, but this work may prove to be her crowning achievement. It reminds us of the power of poetry to lift us out of the material world into a more sacred and awesome space, and makes prayer more relevant and accessible to contemporary Jews, particularly women, who have been alienated by traditional liturgy.

The contributions of Jewish women poets to American literary history and political activism, as well as to the enrichment of Jewish culture and practice, are astounding. With the recent flourishing of Jewish women poets, it is impossible to name them all. Feminist Jewish journals such as *Lilith* and *Bridges* feature their work, as does the Jewish literary journal *Agada*, edited by Reuven Goldfarb, and the politically based magazine *Tikkun*, of which Marge Piercy is poetry editor. But these glimpses at the poetry of Jewish women in feminist anthologies and Jewish journals do not tell the whole story. A definitive anthology of poetry by Jewish American women poets has yet to be published.

BIBLIOGRAPHY

ANTHOLOGIES OF JEWISH WOMEN POETS

Kaye/Kantrowitz, Melanie, and Irena Klepfisz, eds. *The Tribe of Dina: A Jewish Women's Anthology* (1986); Spiegel, Marcia Cohn, and Deborah Lipton Kremsdorf. *Women Speak to God: The Prayers and Poems of Jewish Women* (1987); Wenkart, Henny, ed. *Sarah's Daughters Sing* (1990).

LITERARY CRITICISM

Baskin, Judith. *Women of the Word: Jewish Women and Jewish Writing* (1994); Gittenstein, R. Barbara. "American-Jewish Poetry: An Overview." In *Handbook of American-Jewish Literature: An Anlaytical Guide to Topics, Themes, and*

Sources, edited by Lewis Fried (1988); Hellerstein, Kathryn. "Poetry." In "Jewish American Writing." *Oxford Companion to Women's Writing in the United States*, edited by Cathy Davidson and Linda Wagoner-Martin; Lichtenstein, Diane Marilyn. *Writing Their Nations: The Tradition of Nineteenth-Century American Jewish Women Writers* (1992); Ostriker, Alicia Suskin. *Stealing the Language: The Emergence of Women's Poetry in America* (1986); Stern, Gerald. "Poetry." In *Jewish American History and Culture: An Encyclopedia* (1992).

JESSICA ROSENFELD

POGREBIN, LETTY COTTIN
(b. 1939)

Letty Cottin Pogrebin is a liberal Jew who names anti-Semitism when she senses it and an outspoken feminist on issues of women's rights as well as responsibilities to children.

Pogrebin's significant impact and appeal in the Jewish community have been as a crossover star; she first gained national recognition in the general women's movement and after that as a Jewish activist. Primarily a writer, she is also a peace activist, magazine editor, conference organizer, founding member of organizations, and spokesperson for numerous causes—women's workplace rights, feminist advocacy journalism (she's a founding editor of *Ms.* magazine), nonsexist child rearing (her book *Growing Up Free* was for a while the baby boomers' Dr. Spock), social justice (as a cofounder of the National Women's Political Caucus), the expansion of women's rites in Judaism, Jewish inclusion in the women's movement, black/Jewish rapprochement, and Mideast peace efforts (as a past president of Americans for Peace Now).

Born on June 9, 1939, in Queens, New York, Letty Cottin grew up in a religiously observant Conservative household. Her father, Jacob Cottin, a lawyer, was active in the Jewish community and the synagogue, and her mother, Cyral (Halpern) Cottin, was a designer. She was educated at the Yeshiva of Central Queens, the Jamaica Jewish Center Hebrew High School, and Brandeis University, where she received a B.A. cum laude in 1959. She married Bertrand Pogrebin, a lawyer, in 1963.

Keenly aware of the exclusion of women from the Jewish religious tradition, by age fifteen Letty had turned her back on organized Judaism because she was not allowed to attend the kaddish minyan when her mother died in 1955. Despite her anger at Jewish law and custom that excluded women, she still celebrates Hanukkah with elaborate festivities with her husband and children—twin daughters Robin and Abigail and

son David. As she explains it in *Deborah, Golda, and Me*, "Rebellion was one thing; giving up the Jewish holidays was something else. I wasn't going to let my alienation from my father's religious institutions cut me off from the rituals . . . associated with my mother and the home-based Judaism in which my heritage seemed . . . most real."

Pogrebin has written honestly about her own life, intensely focused on the stages she has passed and is passing through. Thus she has been able to articulate certain dislocations on behalf of women who came of

Letty Cottin Pogrebin is omnipresent. A liberal Jew who names anti-Semitism when she senses it and an outspoken feminist on issues of women's rights as well as responsibilities to children, it is hard to think of a good cause in which she is not effectively involved. [Bettye Lane]

age in the late 1950s and early 1960s and whose experiences paralleled her own. And because she has been ahead of the wave on so many issues, she has been able to represent the concerns of younger women as well. She has researched and presented subjects of consequence in all women's lives: the job market (*Getting Yours: How to Make the System Work for the Working Woman*), parenthood (*Growing Up Free: Raising Your Child in the '80s*), friendship (*Among Friends*), how personal and national politics interact (*Family Politics: Love and Power on an Intimate Frontier*), and aging (*Getting Over Getting Older*).

In her early analytical books, Pogrebin tackled subjects that drew on her own experience—sex, motherhood, daughterhood, national politics—to illustrate her positions on various issues. In *Deborah, Golda, and Me*, the method shifts. No longer are her own experiences cited as anecdotal evidence to buttress her positions; instead, she uses her own life experience as a window onto "being female and Jewish in America." She fosters a degree of intimacy with her readers and lecture audiences that surely derives from her comfortable self-disclosure. This book put a public face on Jewish feminism, rendering the movement less parochial in the eyes of many who might have been self-conscious about their own identification as Jews. Because of high visibility as an outspoken feminist organizer—and through her longtime identification with *Ms.* (her name has been on the masthead since 1971)—her narration of her encounters with religious and communal sexism and her determination to remain attached to a more inclusive Judaism have drawn audiences of disaffected Jewish women all across the country who have welcomed her frank critiques.

For Jewish women attempting to incorporate their Judaism into an already strong feminism, *Deborah, Golda, and Me* was a landmark book, illuminating one Jewish woman's life as almost no other contemporary nonfiction work had done. Letty Cottin Pogrebin became the voice most clearly identified with secular Jewish women's concerns. She addressed subjects that have shamed or troubled many thoughtful Jews—patriarchal religious traditions, anti-Semitism, tensions between blacks and Jews, Israel's troubled relationship with the Palestinians—and comes out of these struggles hoping that she has changed things for the better.

Pogrebin has merged her political activism, her feminism, and her strong Jewish identity to help create or shape MAZON: A Jewish Response to Hunger, the Jewish Fund for Justice, the New Israel Fund, the American Jewish Congress Commission on Women's Equality, and the civil rights movement of Israel. She

Committed to the rights of women throughout the world, Letty Pogrebin can be counted on to be where her presence is required. The above photograph was taken at the 1995 Fourth World Congress on Women in Beijing, China. [Joan Roth]

has also become an adept of the interface—between Jews and Christians, between feminists and lawmakers, between black feminists and Jewish feminists, between Jewish women and Palestinian women.

It is in her personal mode, either relating an experience or observation or "confessing" an aspect of her own personal search, that Pogrebin is at her strongest and most original. She is the feminist who wasn't afraid to say she "adored" her husband, the liberated woman who'd stitched a needlepoint pillow with the addresses of all the houses they'd lived in together, the working mother who voiced the worries of her ideological sisters over raising children (she seems to have given her own offspring tenderness *and* independence), the feminist who was a friend of heads of state yet who still cared about crisp potato latkes and a well-set table. In her most recent book, *Getting Over Getting Older*, she is also the terrific-looking woman who is not afraid to talk candidly about aging: the sags in the body, the slips of memory, and the onset of existential angst.

Letty Cottin Pogrebin has a voice that is both strong and sweet. Her place in our Pantheon is guaranteed by the fact that hardly any public Jewish feminist event feels complete without her presence.

SELECTED WORKS BY LETTY COTTIN POGREBIN

Among Friends: Who We Like, Why We Like Them, and What We Do with Them (1986); *Deborah, Golda, and Me: Being Female and Jewish in America* (1991); *Family Politics:*

Love and Power on an Intimate Frontier (1983); *Getting Over Getting Older: An Intimate Journey* (1996); *Getting Yours: How to Make the System Work for the Working Woman* (1975); *Growing Up Free: Raising Your Child in the '80s* (1980); *How to Make It in a Man's World* (1970); *Stories for Free Children,* editor (1981).

SUSAN WEIDMAN SCHNEIDER

POLIER, JUSTINE WISE (1903–1987)

A distinguished judge of the New York City Family Court for thirty-eight years, Justine Wise Polier promoted the rights of children inside and outside of the judiciary. Espousing an activist concept of the law and a rehabilitative rather than a punitive model of judicial process, she pioneered the establishment of mental health, educational, and other rehabilitative services for troubled children. She also took a leading role in opposing racial and religious discrimination in public and private facilities. As a committed Jewish leader, she spoke out against anti-Semitism, urging Jews to lead the battle for human rights for all minorities.

Polier's passionate advocacy for the rights of children, the poor, and minorities was a family legacy. Born on April 12, 1903, in Portland, Oregon, where her father, Rabbi Stephen Wise, accepted his first pulpit and became Oregon's first (unpaid) commissioner of child welfare, Justine was much influenced by her father's social concerns and those of her mother LOUISE WATERMAN WISE, a painter and social reformer. Louise Wise organized the Free Nurses' Association in Portland to provide free medical and nursing care for poor mothers and children. She continued her charitable work on behalf of women and children when the Wises moved to New York City in 1905. Most notably, Louise Wise founded the Child Adoption Agency of the Free Synagogue in 1916, which her husband had established nine years earlier, to find homes for Jewish orphans and other hard-to-place children. Eventually known as the Louise Wise Services, the agency also provided services to unmarried pregnant women. In later years, Polier would succeed her mother as chairman of the agency's board; she also succeeded her mother as president of the Women's Division of the AMERICAN JEWISH CONGRESS. Polier also served as national vice president of the congress.

After attending the Horace Mann High School, Justine enrolled in Bryn Mawr College in 1920, transferring to Radcliffe College for her third year. While at Radcliffe, she worked at the Elizabeth Peabody Set-

tlement House in Boston, teaching English to foreign residents. She spent her last year at Barnard College, graduating in 1924. Although an economics major, she took philosophy courses with John Dewey and educational psychology with William Kilpatrick at Teachers College. At Barnard, she took part in a New York State Labor Department investigation of industrial accidents suffered by women workers, a project that furthered her interest in women and the labor movement.

After college, she obtained a job in the textile mills in Passaic, New Jersey, to learn about factory life firsthand. Fearing that she would not be hired if she was identified as the daughter of Rabbi Wise, well known for his pro-union sentiments, she used her

A fighter throughout her life for the rights of children and minorities, Justine Wise Polier was a judge of the New York City Family Court for thirty-eight years. She attributed her main goals of fighting injustice and "speaking truly . . . without fear" to the influence of the Hebrew prophets and her father, Rabbi Stephen Wise. [American Jewish Historical Society]

mother's maiden name. When her identity was discovered, she was fired and blacklisted. She then studied briefly at the International Labor Office of the League of Nations in Geneva, Switzerland.

Heeding her father's advice to study law if she wanted to foster social justice, Justine enrolled in Yale University Law School in 1925. One of a handful of women law students, she was elected to Coif, the honorary legal society, and became an editor of the *Yale Law Journal.* Midway through her second year, several thousand workers went out on strike at the Passaic textile mills. Much to the displeasure of Yale's president, she became deeply involved in the strike, commuting back and forth between New Haven and Passaic. With her father's encouragement, she addressed strike rallies, urging workers to persist in their fight. Newspapers wrote about her as the "Joan of Arc of the mills," and provided interviews and photos of this "rabbi's daughter . . . threatened with arrest" because of her role in the strike.

At the end of her second year at Yale, she married a young law school professor, Leon A. Tulin. He died from leukemia in 1932, leaving her with a young son, Stephen. She married her second husband, Shad Polier, a civil liberties lawyer, four years later; their children are Jonathan Wise Polier and Trudy (Polier) Festinger.

From 1929 to 1934, Polier served as the first woman referee in the Workmen's Compensation Division of the New York State Department of Labor, directing a critical study of New York City's referee system. This work led to her appointment as head of a Commonwealth Fund research survey on national labor laws. She became secretary and counsel to the Mayor's Committee on Unemployment Relief, producing what the *New Republic* called the "best report on the problem of relief for the unemployed ever issued in the United States."

In 1934, New York mayor Fiorello La Guardia appointed Polier to the post of assistant corporation counsel, heading the Workmen's Compensation Division. In the following year, he appointed her to a judgeship in the city's domestic relations court (the predecessor to the family court)—the first woman in New York State to hold a judicial post above magistrate and the youngest municipal justice in the country. She took a leave of absence in 1941–1942 to serve as special counsel and deputy chairman of the Office of Civilian Defense, working closely with Eleanor Roosevelt. With Eleanor Roosevelt and others, Polier founded in 1942 the Wiltwyck School for Boys for emotionally disturbed black youngsters; the school soon became nonsectarian. Under her leadership, the Louise Wise Services adoption agency also became a nonsectarian provider.

Polier was an activist judge who believed that the law should be used as an agent of social change. Calling on the resources of the social and behavioral sciences to aid judges in treating offenders, she made her court into a national laboratory of communication between the legal system, the behavioral sciences, and the human services delivery system. She vigorously opposed race and religion as being the predominant criteria for determining placement and other services for children. In the Skipwirth attendance case (1958–1961), she found that de facto segregation existed in schools in Harlem. She helped initiate a class action suit (*Wilder* v. *Sugarman*, 1971–1978), against all private and public foster care agencies (including the Louise Wise Services) for racial discrimination. With her husband, she wrote New York State's first antidiscrimination law.

Polier was the guiding force behind the formation of the Citizens Committee for Children, a powerful advocacy group for children. A meeting at her home in 1960 set in motion a sustained effort for welfare reform. She also helped to mobilize lawyers on behalf of the poor. As vice president of the American Jewish Congress, Polier participated in social action, civil rights, education, and welfare initiatives. With her husband, who drafted much of the Congress's civil liberties legislation, she set the organization on a course that combined a passionate commitment to Jewish life with an equally passionate concern for the rights of minorities.

After retiring from the bench in 1973, Polier served as the director of the Juvenile Justice Division of the Children's Defense Fund, advocating enhanced services and protections for children throughout the United States. She was president of the Marion E. Kenworthy–Sarah H. Swift Foundation, and served on the boards of the Tappanz Foundation, the Field Foundation, and the Eleanor Roosevelt Institute. She died on July 31, 1987, at the Columbia-Presbyterian Medical Center in New York City.

As a "fighting judge" and in her extrajudicial work, Polier consistently challenged practices that she considered not to be in the best interests of the child—"best interests" being a concept she helped to develop. In her leadership of the American Jewish Congress, she sought to further Jewish interests, including those of women, while also working to foster civil liberties for minorities. She attributed her main goals—fighting injustice and "speaking truly . . .

without fear"—to the influence of the Hebrew prophets and her father Stephen Wise. Like both her parents, Polier was widely considered to be a voice of conscience for her era.

SELECTED WORKS BY JUSTINE WISE POLIER

Back to That Woodshed (1956); *Everybody's Child, Nobody's Child* (1943); *Juvenile Justice in Double Jeopardy: The Distanced Community and Vengeful Retribution* (1989); *The Rule of Law and the Role of Psychiatry* (1968); *A View from the Bench* (1964).

BIBLIOGRAPHY

Antler, Joyce. *The Journey Home: Jewish Women and the American Century* (1997); *BEOAJ*; *UJE*; *WWIAJ* (1938).

JOYCE ANTLER

POLLAK, VIRGINIA MORRIS (1898–1967)

During World War II, sculptor Virginia Morris Pollak discovered that her training in casting methods and her family's tradition of community service dovetailed perfectly. Working with plastic surgeons at Halloran Hospital on Staten Island, Pollak not only developed a superior modeling material for reconstructive surgery but also modeled plates for skull replacements from the notoriously difficult metal tantalum. One of these, at ninety-five square inches the largest metal cranial replacement ever made, allowed a seriously wounded serviceman to recover within weeks, winning the sculptor a deserved place in medical history and a presidential citation.

Born in Norfolk, Virginia, on October 16, 1898, to Arther and Sadie (Spagat) Morris, Virginia Leigh Morris Pollak belonged to a family committed to the city's aesthetic improvement. Her father, one of three founding members of Norfolk's Beautifying Commission, attempted to establish a city park system, a pursuit to which his daughter would contribute almost thirty years after his death in 1929. But long before she became active in such natural aesthetic matters, she devoted her talents to sculpture, studying at Harriet Whitney Frishmuth's and Gutzon Borglum's studios, as well as at the fledgling Art Students League in New York and at Yale. Her own professional ambitions were sidelined, however, by her father's death, and Virginia returned to Norfolk to assume the director's post at his women's clothing firm, the House of Arther Morris. She left there in January 1939 to marry Leo L. Pollak, an engineer whose New Jersey company would soon be manufacturing precision aviation and marine instruments for the war effort.

With her husband absorbed in war work and her young son at school, Pollak volunteered with the Red Cross, teaching arts and crafts to wounded servicemen at Halloran. But surgeons soon encouraged her to establish the hospital's Medical Moulage Laboratory, where she improved the clay negocolle with the addition of an alginate that sped setting by thirty-two minutes, enabling patients to escape the uncomfortable body molds in fewer than four minutes.

Pollak's companion in this research, the Viennese artist Alfred Wokenberg, later joined her in forming Alva Studios, which created high-quality sculptural replicas from originals in major museums. After the war, while visiting flower shows with her husband, a passionate gardener and president of the Dahlia Society of America, Pollak's attention turned to the possibility of such reproductions for public consumption. Though these pieces were initially created for gardens and smaller museums, in the postwar years of the Marshall Plan portrait busts of the nation's first leaders were commissioned by the government for international embassies.

Although Pollak was appointed by President Kennedy to his Commission for the Employment of the Handicapped and to the advisory councils of the planned Kennedy Center and the Smithsonian Institution, she found time in the 1960s to complete her father's dreams for Norfolk's beautification. Chairing the Fine Arts Commission, she created an outdoor sculpture museum at the Botanical Garden, which wraps around the region's largest airport, near Chesapeake Bay. Weathered figures, scattered throughout the lush plantings and culminating in the Avenue of American Naval Heroes, the site for the city's NATO-sponsored Azalea Festival, are a legacy left by an artist-philanthropist who lived in New York until her death on January 1, 1967, but whose heart never really left the city of her birth.

BIBLIOGRAPHY

Norfolk Ledger-Dispatch, July 5, 1947; Obituary. *NYTimes*, February 1, 1967, 40:1; *Virginian-Pilot and Ledger-Star*, November 12–13, 1950, December 1–2, 1957, August 30, 1963, February 1, 1967; *WWWIA* 4 (1961–1968).

LINDA F. McGREEVY

POLLITZER, ANITA (1894–1975)

Born on October 31, 1894, in Charleston, South Carolina, the fourth child of second-generation Eastern European immigrant parents, Clara (Ginzburg) and Gustave Morris Pollitzer, Anita Pollitzer devoted her public life to feminist politics and artistic patronage. Pollitzer's most prominent contribution to feminism came in 1945, when she became Alice Paul's hand-picked successor for the chairmanship of the National Woman's Party (NWP). Pollitzer also gained recognition for her close friendship with Georgia O'Keeffe, whose artistic career blossomed when Pollitzer showed Alfred Stieglitz a series of her paintings. A biography of O'Keeffe by Pollitzer, entitled *A Woman on Paper: Georgia O'Keeffe*, published after Pollitzer's death and against O'Keeffe's wishes, has added significantly to information on the artist's personal life.

After graduating from Memminger High and Normal School, Pollitzer entered Teachers College at Columbia University, where she majored in art and education. Soon after her graduation in 1916, she became interested in the woman suffrage movement, met Alice Paul, and joined the NWP. As a party organizer traveling through the states for the NWP, she helped ratify the Nineteenth Amendment to the Constitution. Pollitzer demonstrated her commitment to woman suffrage in 1917 by being arrested as a Silent Sentinal picketing the Woodrow Wilson White House. In August 1920, Pollitzer used her considerable charm to convince legislator Harry T. Burn of Tennessee to cast the deciding vote for the amendment. In 1933, Pollitzer received a master's degree in international law from Columbia University. Soon after this achievement, she became vice-chair of the World Woman's Party with Alice Paul.

Pollitzer married Elie Charlier Edson, a free-lance press agent, in 1928. The couple settled in New York City for the duration of both of their lives. Neither earned a substantial salary, causing them to depend upon securities bestowed on her from her relatives and an inheritance from his mother. She remained active both in the arts and in feminist politics throughout most of her life. In 1971, the same year her husband died, she suffered a stroke. She died four years later, on July 3, 1975, in New York City.

BIBLIOGRAPHY

BEOAJ; Geboire, Clive, ed. *Lovingly, Georgia: The Complete Correspondence of Georgia O'Keeffe and Anita Pollitzer* (1990); Irwin, Inez Haynes. *The Story of the Woman's Party* (1921); National Woman's Party. Papers. Library of Congress; *NAW* modern; Obituary. *NYTimes*, July 5, 1975, 20:3; Pollitzer, Anita. Correspondence with Georgia O'Keeffe. Beinecke Library, Yale University, New Haven, Conn., and Correspondence with Miriam Holden. Princeton University, Princeton, N.J., and *A Woman on Paper: Georgia O'Keeffe* (1988); *WWIAJ* (1928, 1938); *WWWIA* 6.

JENNIFER NELSON

POLYKOFF, SHIRLEY (b. 1908)

"Does she . . . or doesn't she?" asked advertising copywriter Shirley Polykoff in 1955, in the first advertising campaign ever to try to sell hair dye to a mass audience. The campaign worked. The number of women in America using hair dye rose from 7 percent to 50 percent within a few years, the phrase "Does she . . . or doesn't she?" became part of the American lexicon, and Shirley Polykoff was credited with having helped create the hair-dye industry.

Shirley Polykoff was born on January 18, 1908, in Brooklyn, New York, the second of the three daughters of Hyman Raphael and Rose (Lieberman) Polykoff. Originally from Odessa and Kiev, respectively, the couple had married in Russia and immigrated to the United States in 1905 to avoid conscription. The son of a lumber merchant, Hyman had received some formal schooling in mathematics and literature. Rose was self-taught and could read and write Yiddish and Russian. Upon arrival in the United States, she went to night school and learned to read and write English. Hyman first worked in a lumberyard, then became a sales representative for necktie manufacturers, and was successful enough to enable the family to move from the Jewish ghetto of Brownsville to the Irish ghetto of Williamsburg, and ultimately to middle-class Flatbush, Brooklyn. The girls attended Sunday school in order to learn about their Jewish heritage, but more emphasis was placed on public schooling, which would open up future opportunities. This applied particularly to Shirley.

Rose Polykoff, in her eagernesss for a son, had named her second child Leo before the child's birth. "Leo," renamed Sheryl, later modified to Sadie, Sarah, and finally Shirley (as the most American equivalent), was raised as the boy of the family. Being a boy meant becoming a *fardiner*, or money-earner, the ultimate achievement in a struggling immigrant family. Shirley embraced the role, taking every opportunity to dress in boy's clothing and getting her first job at age eleven, selling women's coats in a department store before Christmas.

In the Polykoff family, alongside the emphasis on upward mobility was the drive to become American. To Shirley Polykoff, this was embodied in the advertisements in magazines showing how to do everything from cleaning one's teeth to ordering in restaurants. At age twelve, she entered a competition to create an ad for Campbell's Soup. She did not win, but the letter of acknowledgment from the advertising agency awoke her to the fact that people actually earned a living by writing ads. Nine years later, she got her first job as advertising copywriter for a women's fashion and specialty store in Brooklyn, starting at nineteen dollars a week. Writing headlines like, "Look like you're going to the races when you're only racing to the grocers" and "Rhinestones, a girl's next best friend," she quadrupled her salary within months. She subsequently became lead fashion writer for the major department stores, Bambergers and Kresges, in New Jersey.

In 1933, while working for the Fifth Avenue furrier I.J. Fox in New York City, Shirley met George Halperin. They were married three weeks later, on May 10, 1933. A lawyer with a degree from New York University, Halperin was unusual for the times in understanding and supporting his wife's need for her own career. Despite the logistical and emotional difficulties of juggling family and career, Polykoff continued to work after the births of their daughters Alix (b. 1938) and Laurie (b. 1944).

In 1955, at an age where most people in the creative departments of advertising agencies were considered past their prime, Shirley Polykoff got her big break. She was hired by the major advertising agency of Foote, Cone & Belding to work on their newly acquired Clairol account. The challenge was to make it respectable for anyone to dye her hair, at a time when the only women who colored their hair were models, actresses, part of the jet set, or women simply considered to be "fast." The "Does she ... or doesn't she?" campaign Polykoff created brilliantly juxtaposed this risqué headline with wholesomer-than-thou mother and child photographs. Significantly, the ads ran in *Life*, a family magazine, instead of the fashion and beauty publications. For the first time in history, Shirley Polykoff made it possible for millions of women to color their hair—and still belong to the PTA.

She continued to create memorable and effective, as well as award-winning, campaigns for Clairol, including lines like, "Is it true blondes have more fun?," "If I've only one life, let me live it as a blonde!," and "The closer he gets, the better you look." She also wrote the line "Chock Full o' Nuts, the heavenly coffee." In 1961, George Halperin died, and Foote, Cone & Belding raised Polykoff's salary, making her the highest-paid employee in what was then the seventh-largest advertising agency in the world. She became a senior vice president, chairman of the creative board for the New York office, and the first woman member of the board of directors. In 1967, she was named National Advertising Woman of the Year.

In 1973, she became president of her own creative advertising agency, Shirley Polykoff Advertising, Inc., with major clients like Houbigant Perfumes, Kimberly-Clark, and Schering-Plough, as well as

Bristol-Myers, makers of Clairol. This was also the year she was inducted into the New York Copywriters' Hall of Fame. In 1980, she became the first living woman ever elected to the National American Advertising Federation Hall of Fame. In 1983, the National Council of Women of the United States gave her the Lifetime Achievement Award for her pioneering accomplishments in communications.

In 1984, Shirley Polykoff retired. In the course of her career, she appeared numerous times on national television and radio and gave lectures on advertising and general business practices at colleges and universities throughout the country, including Princeton University, Syracuse University, and the University of Chicago. She was called to Washington, D.C., by Secretary of State William P. Rogers to participate in a business convention and by President Jimmy Carter to create an advertising campaign for the Equal Rights Amendment.

At a time when women's liberation was still in its infancy, in a profession open neither to women nor to Jews, Shirley Polykoff, in becoming the *fardiner* her mother had dreamed of, also became an inspiration and role model for several generations of young women.

BIBLIOGRAPHY

Polykoff, Shirley. *Does She . . . or Doesn't She?* (1975), and Interview by author, NYC, April 6, 1996.

TESSA FISHER

POMERANCE, JOSEPHINE WERTHEIM (1910–1980)

Josephine Wertheim Pomerance was a leading advocate of nuclear arms control and the United Nations. Born on October 2, 1910, to Alma (Morgenthau) and Maurice Wertheim, she was the eldest of three daughters and the granddaughter of Henry Morgenthau, Sr. She earned a B.A. from Smith College in 1933 and married the architect Ralph Pomerance on June 4 of that year. They had two sons and a daughter.

In 1950, Pomerance cofounded the Committee for World Development and World Disarmament (CWDWD). Under Pomerance's leadership, and through her generous yearly contributions, the CWDWD worked to convince the American public to support programs for global development. The CWDWD also helped lay the foundation for the late-1950s movement opposed to nuclear testing, a fact the newly founded Committee for a Sane Nuclear Policy acknowledged by selecting Pomerance as one of only three women to sign its initial November 1957 *New York Times* advertisement, as well as one of the three female board members.

In 1959, Pomerance shifted her attention. She joined the staff of the American Association for the United Nations and, in 1961, secured a post with the John F. Kennedy administration as a UN adviser to nongovernmental organizations. In 1962, Pomerance helped initiate the Citizens Committee for a Nuclear Test Ban, an elite lobby effort directly supervised by the White House. Thereafter, Pomerance helped lead the Non-Governmental Committee on Disarmament, a group that played a major role in promoting disarmament at the UN in the ensuing decades. Following her death on July 15, 1980, the organization established the Josephine Pomerance award for outstanding contributions in the field of disarmament.

BIBLIOGRAPHY

Cousins, Norman. *The Improbable Triumvirate: John F. Kennedy, Pope John, Nikita Khrushchev* (1972); Lepper, Mary Millins. *Foreign Policy Formation: A Case Study of the Nuclear Test Ban* (1971); Obituary. *NYTimes*, July 17, 1980; Pomerance, Josephine. Papers. Swarthmore College Peace Collection, Swarthmore, Pa.

ALLEN SMITH

POOL, JUDITH GRAHAM
(1919–1975)

Judith Graham Pool was a physiologist whose scientific discoveries revolutionized the treatment of hemophilia.

She was born in Queens, New York City, on June 1, 1919, to Nellie (Baron) Graham, a schoolteacher, and Leon Graham, a stockbroker. After graduating from Jamaica High School, she attended the University of Chicago, where she was a member of Phi Beta Kappa and Sigma Xi. In 1938, she married Ithiel de Sola Pool. Together they had two sons, Jonathan Robert (b. 1942) and Jeremy David (b. 1945). In 1946, Pool received her Ph.D. from the University of Chicago.

When the couple moved to California in 1949, Pool began both her lifelong relationship with Stanford University and her illustrious career as a research scientist. Pool started out as a research associate at Stanford Research Institute in 1950. In 1953, she joined the staff at Stanford's School of Medicine as a research fellow, supported by a Bank of America-Giannini Foundation grant for hemophilia research. That same year, she and her husband divorced.

Pool then initiated her extensive research on blood coagulation, publishing her first paper on the topic in 1954. Working with two associates, Pool developed a method for separating the antihemophilic factor (AHF), or factor VIII, which is used for transfusion to correct the bleeding defect in hemophilia, from blood plasma. She was then able to create cryoprecipitate, a cold-insoluble protein fraction of whole blood plasma, which was available to the public in 1965. This concentrate could be made without special equipment, left in a plastic bag, and refrozen and stored up to a year, thereby allowing hemophiliacs to be treated with more ease than ever before in their homes or in any hospital or medical facility.

Her work on muscle physiology was also noteworthy. Pool developed techniques to measure the electric potential of a single muscle fiber within a membrane. These techniques are used all over the world.

Pool earned the title of senior research associate in 1956, senior scientist in 1970, and full professor in 1972, without ever going through the lower professorial ranks. The value of her contributions was widely recognized, and she was invited to lecture at numerous institutions and congresses. She was a member of the scientific advisory committees of the National Institutes of Health and the National Hemophilia Foundation, which renamed its research fellowship the Judith Graham Pool Research Fellowship in her honor.

In her later years, Pool devoted much time and effort to increasing opportunities for women in the field of science, both by publishing articles on the topic and by serving as the co-president of the Association of Women in Science and as the first chairwoman of Professional Women of Stanford University Medical Center.

Pool gave birth to one daughter Lorna (b. 1964). In 1972, she married Maurice Sokolow, professor of medicine and hematology at the University of California, San Francisco. They were divorced in 1975.

Judith Graham Pool died at age fifty-six on July 13, 1975, in Palo Alto, of a brain tumor.

BIBLIOGRAPHY

Massie, Robert K., and Suzanne Massie. *Journey* (1975); Obituary. *NYTimes*, July 15, 1975, 36:2; *NAW* modern; *WWWIA* 6.

LISA LEPSON

POOL, TAMAR DE SOLA (1890–1981)

Tamar de Sola Pool dreamt of a socially and economically just world where people consistently acted toward one another with good will, fairness, and faith. She believed that a solution to the world's problems would lead to the eradication of Jewish persecution and a global understanding that the Jewish people needed an independent state. She entreated the nations of the world to cooperate with one another, to live together peacefully before God, and to create a new world order. In pursuit of the Zionist ideal, she also encouraged a reconciliation between Jews and Arabs.

A visionary, an inspirer as well as an activist, Tamar de Sola Pool was born on August 4, 1890, in Jerusalem, to Rabbi Chaim Hirschenson, originally of Safed, and Eva (Cohen) Hirschenson. The Hirschenson family immigrated to the United States in 1904, settling in New Jersey, where Rabbi Hirschenson became a congregational rabbi. As supporters of Eliezer Ben-Yehuda's efforts to revive the Hebrew language, the Hirschensons decided to converse with their children only in Hebrew, even while living in the United States. Tamar had four siblings: Dr. NIMA ADLERBLUM, a noted scholar and philosopher; Esther Taubenhaus, the first woman director of the B'nai B'rith Hillel at Texas A and M University; TEHILLA LICHTENSTEIN, who founded the Society of Jewish Science with her husband, Rabbi Morris Lichtenstein; and Benjamin Hirschenson, an engineer.

In 1913, Tamar graduated from HUNTER COLLEGE, where she studied Latin, Greek, and French. Following a year spent doing graduate work at the University of Paris, she became an instructor of comparative literature at Hunter College (1914–1917). At a Young Judaea convention during the summer of 1916, Tamar Hirschenson met David de Sola Pool, who was then president of the organization. David de Sola Pool, who was born in London in 1885, had immigrated to the United States in 1907 to become the rabbi of Congregation Shearith Israel in New York City, a position he held until his death in 1970. On February 6, 1917, Tamar Hirshenson and Pool married and together shared a life of commitment to Jewish religious, social, and political causes. They traveled wherever they thought they were needed, including Jewish communities in the Far East and Europe. The Pools had two children: Naomi and Ithiel.

As a married woman, Tamar de Sola Pool volunteered her services to the Jewish community, believing that an American woman's commitment to world causes was among her most important responsibilities. She became an active member of HADASSAH, the Women's Zionist Organization, founded in 1912 by

A visionary, an inspirer, and an activist, Tamar de Sola Pool believed that an American woman's commitment to world causes was among her most important responsibilities. Deeply involved in HADASSAH, *she also wrote two books and was a member of many organizations, including the Sisterhood of Shearith Israel, the* NATIONAL COUNCIL OF JEWISH WOMEN, *and the World Zionist Organization.* [Hadassah Archives]

HENRIETTA SZOLD. As part of Hadassah, Tamar de Sola Pool joined other women in helping to build a homeland for Jews in Palestine. She continued Szold's commitment to bringing modern medical care to Palestine, aiding and continuously promoting the expansion of the Hadassah Medical Center. She became the president of the New York chapter of Hadassah (1929–1935) and later became the national president (1939–1943). She raised funds, increased Hadassah's membership, and transformed the Hadassah newsletter into a Zionist magazine of wider scope. Pool also joined Szold's struggle to save Europe's Jewish children from Nazi persecution. Beginning in 1934, through a project entitled Youth Aliyah, Pool endeavored to rescue and resettle children safely in Palestine. As Pool continued her efforts for Youth Aliyah following World War II, her concern grew for children placed in detention camps in Cyprus by the British. She was so disturbed that she traveled to Cyprus to celebrate Passover at a children's camp. She also organized training centers in Cyprus to provide these children with teachers and textbooks. Pool's activism was not limited to Hadassah. She became involved in many organizations throughout her life, including the Sisterhood of Shearith Israel; the NATIONAL COUNCIL OF JEWISH WOMEN, an organization of which she became the director; and the World Zionist Organization.

Although a witness to the world's atrocities, she maintained a deep faith in God. Her views were expressed in a book, which she coauthored with her husband, *Is There an Answer?* Pool also never lost sight of the meaning of Jewish tradition. For example, she never allowed grave historical circumstances to challenge her belief in the idea of freedom indigenous to the celebration of the holiday of Passover. Passover served as a continuous reminder of God and humanity's redemptive powers, and that the struggle for freedom should never be abandoned. Demonstrating her concern for the men and women fighting for freedom from fascism, she edited a Haggadah [Jewish allegorical material] translation with her husband, which was distributed to American soldiers fighting throughout the world. Her involvement in the life of the synagogue, combined with her passion for preserving the Jewish past, motivated her to join her husband in writing *An Old Faith in the New World*, which surveyed the history of Congregation Shearith Israel of New York City from 1654 to 1954.

When Tamar de Sola Pool passed away on June 1, 1981, the world Jewish community lost one of its most altruistic supporters.

SELECTED WORKS BY TAMAR DE SOLA POOL

"Children to Palestine," *The Women's Press* (1948): 5+; "Exiles on Cyprus," *Highroad* (1948): 24–28; *The Haggadah of Passover*, with David de Sola Pool (1955); *Is There an Answer?*, with David de Sola Pool (1966); *An Old Faith in the New World*, with David de Sola Pool (1955).

BIBLIOGRAPHY

AJYB 83:360–361; *EJ* s.v. "Hirschenson; Pool"; Hadassah Archives, NYC; Horowitz, Gloria Goldreich. *The Hadassah Idea: History and Development* (1986); *Hudson Observer*, November 15, 1916; *The Jewish Week–American Examiner*, June 7, 1981: 2; *Kinosha News*, January 25, 1946; *JTA-DNB*, June 3, 1981; Mizruchi, Ephraim H. "Filling the Moral Vacuum," *Hadassah Magazine* 48 (1966): 20; *NYTimes*, September 15, 1933, and Obituary. June 3, 1981; Spanish and Portuguese Center. Archives. Congregation Shearith Israel, NYC; Szold, Henrietta. Correspondence, Hadassah Archives, NYC; *UJE*; *WWIAJ* (1938); *Who's Who in the World*. 5th ed.; *WWIA* 7.

MARJORIE LEHMAN

PORITZ, DEBORAH T. (b. 1936)

With the exception of Governor Christine Todd Whitman, Deborah T. Poritz is the most visible woman in New Jersey politics. She was the first woman to serve as the state's attorney general, and on July 10, 1996, she was sworn in as the first woman chief justice of the New Jersey Supreme Court. She was nominated by Governor Whitman on June 13, 1996, and is the first Republican chief justice to serve in twenty-five years.

Born in Brooklyn, New York, in 1936, Deborah Tobias was also raised there. She received her B.A. degree magna cum laude from Brooklyn College in 1958 and was elected to Phi Beta Kappa. As a Woodrow Wilson fellow, she studied English and American literature at Columbia University, and then pursued graduate studies at Brandeis University from 1959 to 1962.

For three years, she taught composition and literature at Ursinus College outside of Philadelphia, Pennsylvania. But when her husband, Alan Poritz, a mathematician, got a job in Princeton, New Jersey, she decided to go to law school. She received her law degree from the University of Pennsylvania in 1977, shortly after turning forty.

Her first job as a lawyer was in environmental law. She joined the office of the New Jersey attorney general as a deputy attorney general in the Division of Law in the Environmental Protection Section. In 1981, she was appointed deputy attorney general in charge of appeals and chief of the Banking, Insurance, and Public Securities Section. From 1986 to 1989, she served as assistant attorney general and director of the Division of Law, where she supervised more than three hundred attorneys for the state.

From 1989 to the beginning of 1990, she served as the principal advisor to Governor Thomas H. Kean on legal and policy matters. When Governor Kean left office in 1990, she joined the Princeton law firm of Jamieson, Moore, Peskin & Spicer, where she was a partner. She left there in 1994 to become attorney general.

When she was appointed chief justice, the president of the New Jersey State Bar Association, Cynthia M. Jacob, told the *New York Times*, "She has played an

As she was growing up she was just a "nice Jewish girl from Brooklyn," but now Deborah Poritz is the chief justice of the New Jersey Supreme Court. When Governor Christine Todd Whitman announced her appointment, she quipped that you could hear the "glass ceiling" being shattered as she spoke. [Laura Pedrick/NYT Pictures]

active role in virtually every public issue that has been litigated through the Attorney General's office for many years."

Poritz and her husband have two adult sons, Mark and Jonathan.

BIBLIOGRAPHY

New Jersey Department of Law and Public Safety, Office of the Attorney General. Press release, June 17, 1996; *NYTimes*, June 14, 1996, and July 11, 1996.

ALEXANDRA J. WALL

PORTER, SYLVIA FIELD
(1913–1991)

As the first woman on the financial desk of a big-city newspaper and the first woman to break into the world of writing about finance, Sylvia Field Porter, economist, columnist, and best-selling author, was a pioneer for over half a century in educating the American consumer about money matters.

Sylvia (Feldman) Porter, the only daughter and second child of Russian Jewish immigrants, was born Sylvia Feldman on June 18, 1913, in Patchogue, New York, to Louis Feldman, a physician, and Rose (Maisel) Feldman. The middle-class, cultured family moved to Brooklyn, New York, where Sylvia's father continued to practice medicine until he died of a sudden heart attack in 1925. After trying other jobs to support the children, her energetic and resourceful mother, who decided to change the family name to Field, became a successful milliner. She also insisted that Sylvia prepare herself for a career. Sylvia attended P.S. 99, skipping the sixth grade, and graduated from James Madison High School at age sixteen. Since Cornell University would not award her a scholarship because of her young age, Sylvia enrolled at tuition-free HUNTER COLLEGE in Manhattan as an English and history major, while continuing to live at home.

The stock market crash in the fall of 1929 severely affected the Field family when Sylvia's mother lost an investment of $30,000. Shocked by the family's loss of financial security and determined to understand what had occurred, Sylvia switched her major to economics. She earned a Phi Beta Kappa key as a junior and the bachelor's degree magna cum laude in 1932. Her involvement in the world of finance heightened in 1931 when she married bank employee Reed R. Porter. Unable to obtain work because of the Depression and because she was a woman, Porter apprenticed at a new investment counseling firm. Through this position and others on Wall Street, Porter acquired broad financial experience, augmenting her knowledge with business courses at New York University. Then, using the byline "S.F. Porter" to disguise her gender—her superiors did not want it known that she was a woman—she began to write articles for financial journals and a column for the *American Banker*. This enabled her to combine her love of writing with her growing expertise in investments.

For several years, when Porter applied for jobs in person, she could not break the barriers surrounding the male-dominated business and financial world. Eventually, she obtained a free-lance position with the *New York Evening Post* in 1935, simply because the managing editor considered hiring a woman amusing. Readers, however, increasingly turned to Porter's articles, since they explained economic issues and injustices in lay terms. In 1938, the *Post* made her its financial editor, and she began to write a daily column, "Financial Post Marks," later changed to "S.F. Porter Says."

When the *Post* realized that Porter's gender was an asset, it changed her byline on July 15, 1942, to

Sylvia Porter has been a pioneer for more than half a century in educating the American consumer about money matters. She was the first woman to succeed in this highly competitive business. [Bettye Lane]

"Sylvia F. Porter" and added her photograph to the column. In an interview for *New Women in Social Sciences*, Porter reflected, "On that day I became a woman." The revelation that S.F. Porter was a woman resulted in more requests for lectures and for columns in other magazines. While she did not neglect the experts—she founded *Reporting on Governments*, a weekly newsletter for the banking and securities community, in 1944—Porter had the greatest impact on her popular audience. In 1947, her column became nationally syndicated, and she began to publish comprehensive yet commonsense guidebooks on personal finance. With tax expert Jacob Kay Lasser, Sylvia Porter wrote *How to Live Within Your Income* (1948), *Money and You* (1949), and *Managing Your Money* (1953, 1962). From 1960 until her death in 1991, *Sylvia Porter's Income Tax Guide* appeared annually.

She educated the public about investments and money management, partially by eliminating "baffle-gab," her term for the cryptic terminology of government and finance, and she devoted much of her work to consumer advocacy. In an interview in *Particular Passions: Talks with Women Who Have Shaped Our Times*, Porter said, "I like to think I've contributed in some way to the increasing willingness of the American public to take on the responsibilities of the econ-omy." She steered clear of involvement in politics, but consented to participate in President Gerald Ford's economic summit in 1974 and to serve as chair of his nonpartisan Citizens Action Committee.

Over the next two decades, Porter issued several books to assist the American consumer in navigating the maze of available financial choices. *Sylvia Porter's Money Book: How to Earn It, Spend It, Save It, Invest It, Borrow It, and Use It to Better Your Life* was a 1,105-page handbook based partially on a quarter century of her columns. It promptly made the best-seller list of the *New York Times* in 1975 and sold more than a million copies. *Sylvia Porter's New Money Book for the Eighties: How to Beat the High Cost of Living—And Use Your Earnings, Credit, Savings, and Investments to Better Your Life* was also a best-seller. Previously, economists and financial advisers had assumed that money was handled by men, so women didn't need to know the ins and outs of money management (some even thought money was too complicated for women to grasp). Sylvia Porter was the first to say (actually, shout) that women had a responsibility to understand—and to enjoy—money. In 1978, after more than three decades with the *Post*, Porter's five-times-a-week column moved to the *New York Daily News*. Through the Field Newspaper Syndicate, it appeared in 450 newspapers and reached 40 million readers around the world.

Her accolades included numerous honorary doctorates and awards. Sylvia Field Porter was a trailblazer as a female journalist and economist in the traditionally male-dominated field of finance. For more than five decades, financiers and laypersons alike utilized Porter's counsel in making business and money decisions, earning her the designation of one of America's most influential women.

Sylvia and Reed Porter divorced in 1941. She married G. Sumner Collins in 1943. Collins died in 1977. They had one daughter, Cris Sarah Del Cuore, a classical pianist and music teacher, now of Norway, Maine. Porter also had a stepson, Sumner C. Collins, of Medical Lake, Washington. On January 2, 1979, Sylvia Porter married James F. Fox, a public relations executive. She died of emphysema on June 5, 1991, in Pound Ridge, New York, survived by her husband, daughter, two grandchildren, stepson, and brother, Dr. John Feldman, a California physician.

SELECTED WORKS BY SYLVIA FIELD PORTER

How to Get More for Your Money (1961); *How to Live Within Your Income*, with Jacob Kay Lasser (1948); *How to*

Make Money in Government Bonds (1939); *If War Comes to the American Home, How to Prepare for the Inevitable Adjustment* (1941); *Love and Money* (1985); *Managing Your Money*, with Jacob Kay Lasser (1953. Revised 1962); *Money and You*, with Jacob Kay Lasser (1949); *The Nazi Chemical Trust in the United States* (1942); *Sylvia Porter's A Home of Your Own* (1989); *Sylvia Porter's Financial Almanac for 1983* (1982); *Sylvia Porter's Guide to Your Health Care: How You Can Have the Best Health Care for Less* (1990); *Sylvia Porter's . . . Income Tax Book* (1981–. Annual); *Sylvia Porter's Income Tax Guide* (1960–1991. Annual); *Sylvia Porter's Money Book: How to Earn It, Spend It, Save It, Invest It, Borrow It, and Use It to Better Your Life* (1975); *Sylvia Porter's New Money Book for the Eighties: How to Beat the High Cost of Living—And Use Your Earnings, Credit, Savings, and Investments to Better Your Life* (1979); *Sylvia Porter's Personal Finance Magazine* (1983–1989); *Sylvia Porter's Planning Your Retirement* (1991); *Sylvia Porter's Tax Saving Tips* (1988–1990. Annual); *Sylvia Porter's Your Finances in the 1990s* (1990); *Sylvia Porter's Your Own Money: Earning It, Spending It, Saving It, Investing It, and Living on It in Your First Independent Years* (1983); *Your Financial Security* (1987).

BIBLIOGRAPHY

American Jewish Biographies (1982); *The Annual Obituary 1991* (1991); Bird, Caroline. *Enterprising Women* (1976); Bowman, Kathleen. *New Women in Social Sciences* (1976); *Current Biography Yearbook* (1980, 1991); Fowler, Glen. "Sylvia F. Porter, Financial Columnist, Dies at 77." *NYTimes Biographical Service* 22, no. 6 (June 1991): 571; Gilbert, Lynne, and Gaylen Moore. *Particular Passions: Talks with Women Who Have Shaped Our Times* (1981); Mooney, Louise, ed. *Newsmakers: The People Behind Today's Headlines* (1991); *New York Daily News,* July 24, 1979, 39; Obituary. *NYTimes,* June 7, 1991, B6; *People Magazine* (October 29, 1979): 35–39; *Time* (November 28, 1960): 46–52; *Woman Alive!* KERA-TV, WNET/13 (1972). Schlesinger Library, Radcliffe College, Cambridge, Mass.

PEGGY PEARLSTEIN

POWDERMAKER, HORTENSE (1896–1970)

In her memoir, aptly entitled *Stranger and Friend: The Way of an Anthropologist* (1968), Hortense Powdermaker explored the balance of involvement and detachment necessary for participant-observer fieldwork in cultural anthropology, stressing the ability to "step in and out of society." Her secular Jewish identity was apparently a factor in learning this skill, exemplified in an academic career that included thirty years of college teaching and the writing of five major books based on widely diverse fieldwork studies. Her choice of projects and her writing reflected a concern for social equality, which at times stretched her commitment to impartiality.

The daughter of Louis and Minnie (Jacoby) Powdermaker, she was part of the second generation of her family to be born in the United States. Except for her English Jewish maternal grandmother, relatives on both sides were of German Jewish ancestry. Both grandfathers were prosperous businessmen in Philadelphia, where Hortense Powdermaker was born on December 24, 1896, the second of four children. Their father was also in business, sometimes more and sometimes less successfully. Her older sister Florence Powdermaker became a well-known psychiatrist. She also had a younger brother and sister. The family moved to Reading, Pennsylvania, when Hortense was five, and to Baltimore seven or eight years later.

Stranger and Friend touches only briefly on Powdermaker's Jewish identity. Although her maternal grandfather was president of a Reform synagogue in Pennsylvania and she was confirmed in Baltimore, she reports not sensing "much religious feeling" in the family. As a teenager she rebelled against what she called the boring "Americanized business culture" of her relatives, criticizing their attachment to material things, their concern with subtle class distinctions within the family, and their negative view of more recent Jewish immigrants from Eastern Europe. Later, she sought out acquaintances among Eastern European Jews, appreciating their sense of cultural roots and their socialist ideology.

Powdermaker's first personal encounter with anti-Semitism came as a day student at Goucher College, when she was not invited to join a sorority because she was Jewish. In the 1930s, she found it necessary to "pass" as a Methodist while doing fieldwork in a small Mississippi town, but she also contacted the Jewish community in a larger town nearby.

At Goucher, Powdermaker was an enthusiastic history major interested in socialism and the labor movement. She worked one spring vacation as a machine laborer in a shirt factory, then became active in the Women's Trade Union League. After graduating in 1919, she was employed for several years as a labor organizer for the Amalgamated Clothing Workers in New York, Cleveland, and Rochester. Conscious of her role as a middle-class outsider, she kept a detailed diary, precursor to the field notes that would later form the basis for her anthropological work.

Moving to England in 1925, Powdermaker began studying anthropology with the noted Polish-born scholar Bronislaw Malinowski at the London School of Economics. Profoundly influenced by his teaching, she lived in Bloomsbury and was active in his small circle of graduate students. She earned her Ph.D. in 1928, then spent ten months in the southwest Pacific, studying firsthand the social structure of a small coastal fishing village on the island of New Ireland. Her first book, *Life in Lesu*, appeared in 1933.

Between 1930 and 1937, Powdermaker was associated with the Institute of Human Relations at Yale University, where her interest in psychological anthropology was encouraged by its director Edward Sapir. During 1932–1934 she lived in the small town of Indianola, Mississippi, carrying out one of the earliest participant-observer community studies in the Deep South. Her book *After Freedom* (1939) was a pioneering work on United States race relations, praised for its portrayal of the black church, of cultural and class diversity within the African-American community, and of cultural patterns and psychological attitudes among both blacks and whites.

In 1944, she wrote a book for high school students, *Probing Our Prejudices*, an anthropological and psychological discussion of the causes and dynamics of racism, anti-Semitism, and discrimination against immigrants in the United States. It was infused with her commitment to tolerance, which she saw as inherent to American democracy, in contrast to the tyrannies of Nazism.

A devotion to democratic ideals was also reflected in her next fieldwork site—Hollywood—where she studied the social structure of the film industry and its effect on the content of contemporary films. Though she aimed to achieve an impartial view of various components of the industry, her popular book *Hollywood, the Dream Factory* (1950) criticized screenwriters, management, and what she called the "totalitarianism" pervading Hollywood culture, with its "concept of man as a passive creature to be manipulated." In retrospect, she criticized her methodology during this study, regretting that she had allowed her own values to dominate her research.

In her last major fieldwork project (1953–1954), Powdermaker continued to study mass communication, examining the interaction of media and social change among copper miners in Northern Rhodesia (now Zambia). Her book *Copper Town* appeared in 1962.

From 1938 to 1968, Powdermaker taught anthropology at Queens College in New York, where she was made full professor in 1954, received the Distinguished Teacher Award in 1965, and retired as professor emeritus. While teaching at Queens, she also lectured at the William Alanson White Institute of Psychiatry, Psychoanalysis, and Psychology (1944–

1952); the New York College of Medicine (1958); and, during World War II, at Yale, in an Army Specialized Training Program for the South Pacific. She was vice president of the New York Academy of Sciences (1944–1946) and vice president (1945–1946) and president (1946–1947) of the American Ethnological Society. In 1957, Goucher College awarded her an honorary doctorate of science.

Powdermaker spent the last two years of her life in California. She had begun research on the youth culture of Berkeley, when she died of a heart attack on June 15, 1970.

Hortense Powdermaker had close relations with many colleagues and students, and lived for a number of years with a foster son, Won Mo Kim. Perhaps her most enduring legacy is her final book *Stranger and Friend*. It is a candid account of her fieldwork in terms of her cultural background and psychological makeup (informed by psychoanalysis), including her multiple roles as a woman stepping in and out of diverse societies. The first book of its kind, it came at a time when anthropology was emphasizing "scientific method" rather than the humanistic and reflexive approach she exemplified. From the 1990s perspective of social scientists telling their own stories and acknowledging their cultural position in relation to their subjects, her work can be seen as groundbreaking.

SELECTED WORKS BY HORTENSE POWDERMAKER

After Freedom: A Cultural Study in the Deep South (1939); "The Channeling of Negro Aggression by the Cultural Process." *American Journal of Sociology* 48 (1943): 122–130; *Copper Town: Changing Africa, the Human Situation on the Rhodesian Copperbelt* (1962); "Fieldwork." In *International Encyclopedia of the Social Sciences*, edited by David L. Sills. Vol. 5 (1968): 418–424; "From the Diary of a Girl Organizer." *The Amalgamated Illustrated Almanac* (1924); *Hollywood, the Dream Factory: An Anthropologist Studies the Movie Makers* (1950); *Life in Lesu: The Study of a Melanesian Society in New Ireland* (1933); *Probing Our Prejudices: A Unit for High School Students* (1944); *Stranger and Friend: The Way of an Anthropologist* (1968).

BIBLIOGRAPHY

Current Biography Yearbook (1961): 372–373; *DAB* 8; *NAW* modern; Obituary. *NYTimes*, June 17, 1970, 47:3; "Powdermaker, Hortense." In *Notable Maryland Women*, edited by Winifred G. Helmes (1977): 285–289; Trager, George L. "Hortense Powdermaker: A Tribute." *American Anthropologist* 73 (1971): 786–787; Wolf, Eric R. "Obituaries: Hortense Powdermaker." *American Anthropologist* 73 (1971): 783–786; *WWWIA* 5.

BARBARA C. JOHNSON

PRAG, MARY GOLDSMITH
(1846–1935)

One of California's first Jewish educators, Mary Goldsmith Prag came to San Francisco as a young child during the Gold Rush. She became a religious and secular teacher, an administrator, a fighter for equal rights for women, and the mother of the first Jewish congresswoman, FLORENCE PRAG KAHN.

Born in Poland in 1846, Prag reached San Francisco in 1852, having crossed the Atlantic to New York, then continuing to Central America, crossing the Isthmus of Nicaragua by mule and canoe, and finally arriving in California on a crowded steamship. With Mary were her mother, Sarah Goldsmith, her father, Isaac Goldsmith, who would become a ritual butcher for the young Jewish community, and an older brother and sister. Soon there would be six children in the family. She attended both public school and the religious schools of Congregation Emanu-El (founded in 1851) and Hephzibah, a community religious school. After graduating from San Jose State Normal School, she married Conrad Prag on October 3, 1865, in San Francisco. Born in 1831 in Poland, Conrad Prag was a forty-niner, a merchant, and a founding member of San Francisco's and Salt Lake City's Jewish communities.

Establishing a home in Salt Lake City, where Conrad Prag then lived, Mary Goldsmith Prag gave birth to two children, Florence (b. 1866) and Jessie (b. 1869). Jessie died at age ten. Florence would marry Congressman Julius Kahn and, upon his death, succeed him in Congress. Conrad Prag died on December 17, 1883.

The family returned to San Francisco in 1869. Prag taught for twenty-eight years at Temple Emanu-El, and also taught in and served as head of the history department of Girls' High School. In 1905, she was appointed vice-principal of the school. Upon her retirement in 1921, Prag was named the first Jewish member of the San Francisco Board of Education, where she served until her death on March 17, 1935, at age eighty-nine. Known for her progessive educational methods, tenacity, and sense of humor, Prag had among her many accomplishments the passage of the Teachers' Pension Bill and a bill that guaranteed women teachers were paid the same as men. She was affiliated with the Federation of Jewish Charities, the Jewish Education Society, the Jewish Community Center, and Temple Emanu-El.

Prag's writings describe the early history of San Francisco's and Utah's Jewish and secular communities, painting vivid pictures of individuals and events that shaped the West. Her unpublished manuscripts include "Early Days," a memoir of the chaotic days of Gold Rush San Francisco, and "My Life Among the Mormons," describing her life in Utah. Her reminiscences of Jewish education in San Francisco are published in Jacob Voorsanger's *The Chronicles of Emanu-El.*

Both by example and in her writings, Prag left a record of Jewish life in the nineteenth century Far West, demonstrating how a woman and a practicing Jew could play a leadership role in religious and public life, a model followed by her daughter, Florence Prag Kahn.

Mary Goldsmith Prag was one the first Jewish educators in California. She was also the mother of the first Jewish congresswoman, FLORENCE PRAG KAHN. *[Western Jewish History Center]*

BIBLIOGRAPHY

AJYB 37:260; "Mary Prag (1846–1935)." Memorial Meeting, San Francisco Board of Education (March 1935); Meyer, Martin. *Western Jewry: An Account of the Achievements of the Jews and Judaism in California* (1916); Prag, Mary Goldsmith. Manuscripts. Western Jewish History Center, Judah Magnes Museum. Berkeley, Calif.; Stern, Norton B. "The Prags in Brief." *Western States Jewish History* 17 (1985): 163–169; Voorsanger, Jacob. *The Chronicles of Emanu-El* (1900), and "Random Thoughts." *Emanu-El* 8 (1899): 1; "Who's Who in Politics." *Emanu-El* 9 (1929): 14.

AVA F. KAHN

PRIESAND, SALLY JANE (b. 1946)

On June 3, 1972, Sally Jane Priesand became the first female ordained rabbi in America.

The daughter of Irving Theodore and Rose Elizabeth (Welch) Priesand, she was born on June 27, 1946, in Cleveland, Ohio. As a teenager at Beth Israel-West Temple, a Reform congregation on Cleveland's West Side, she began to display an intense commitment to Judaism and Jewish life. Deeply spiritual and affected by the vision of Reform Judaism epitomized in its camps and youth groups in the early 1960s, she set her sights on becoming a rabbi long before an emerging women's liberation movement raised anew the call for women's access to traditionally male professions.

In 1964, Priesand entered the University of Cincinnati. She knew that its joint undergraduate program with neighboring Hebrew Union College–Jewish Institute of Religion (HUC–JIR) would allow her to complete the first year of rabbinic school as an undergraduate. Accordingly, upon graduation from the University of Cincinnati in 1968, she was admitted to HUC–JIR's rabbinic school.

As a rabbinic student, Priesand began to enjoy the rewards and experience the frustrations that would mark her career as the first female rabbi. Media attention swelled to a crescendo as she approached ordination, with headlines such as one reported in 1964, "Girl Sets Her Goal to be First Woman Rabbi." Quickly, Priesand found herself standing before a wide spectrum of Jewish women as a symbol of the emerging feminism they were just then confronting. Her rabbinic thesis, published as *Judaism and the New Woman* (1975), highlighted the changing role of women in Jewish history and was meant to advance their emancipation in Jewish religious life.

As Priesand sought student pulpits and performed fieldwork in congregations unable to hire full-time rabbis, she discovered that synagogues refused to interview her—or interviewed her only for the nov-

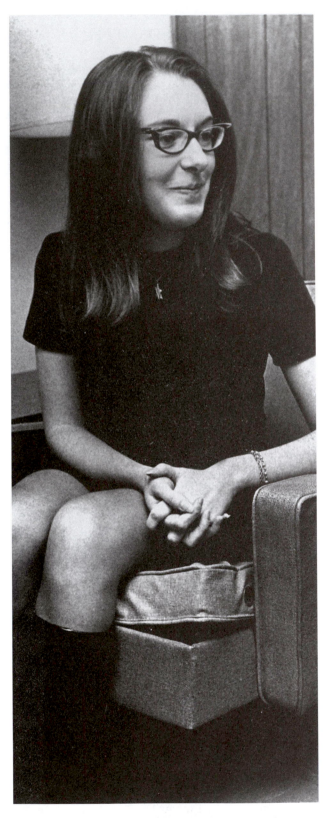

Sally Jane Priesand, the first female ordained rabbi in America, faced a difficult struggle to be accepted. [American Jewish Archives]

elty—claiming they could not possibly have a woman rabbi. Experiences in student pulpits in Milwaukee, Wisconsin; Champaign, Illinois; Hattiesburg, Mississippi; and at Cincinnati's Isaac Mayer Wise Temple conveyed what Priesand would soon describe as "the unbelievable and almost unbearable pressures of being the first woman rabbi."

In June 1972, when Alfred Gottschalk, president of HUC–JIR, ordained her as a rabbi, Priesand became the first woman in Judaism ever to earn seminary ordination. She found her first job at New York City's Stephen Wise Free Synagogue as assistant and then associate rabbi (1972–1979). In 1979, she left the congregation when she was not promised that she would succeed its ailing senior rabbi.

In the next years, Priesand again found temple boards using her gender as an excuse not to hire her. Unable to secure a new position commensurate with her experience in the rabbinate, she took a part-time pulpit at Temple Beth El in Elizabeth, New Jersey (1979–1981) and worked as a chaplain at Manhattan's Lenox Hill Hospital. In 1981, she came to her current

congregation, Monmouth Reform Temple, in Tinton Falls, New Jersey. There Priesand forged a creative partnership with the 285 families in her congregation, acting upon her belief that a rabbi's primary task is to help Jews take responsibility for their Judaism.

In the larger Reform Movement, she worked with the Central Conference of American Rabbis Task Force on Women in the Rabbinate to try to smooth the way for the women who followed her. Celebrating the twentieth anniversary of her rabbinate in 1993, Priesand again voiced her long-standing critique that the institutions of Reform Judaism have still not fulfilled Reform's historic commitment to equality of the sexes. As the first female rabbi, Priesand has always stood in the forefront of those who have struggled to carve a place for women and their perspectives in contemporary Judaism.

SELECTED WORKS BY SALLY JANE PRIESAND

Judaism and the New Woman (1975); "Postscript." In *Women Rabbis: Exploration and Celebration.* Papers Delivered at an Academic Conference Honoring Twenty years of

What is history to one generation is commonplace to another. Here is Sally Priesand (center) on her visit to Hebrew Union College—Jewish Institute of Religion on the twenty-fifth anniversary of her graduation. Everyone else in the picture is a rabbinical student, except for Karla Goldman, second from right, a faculty member. [Photograph courtesy of Karla Goldman]

Women in the Rabbinate, 1972–1992, edited by Gary P. Zola (1996); "Preparation for the Rabbinate—Yesterday, Tomorrow." *Central Conference of American Rabbis Yearbook* 85 (1975): 162–164.

BIBLIOGRAPHY

Hume, Jack. "Girl Sets Her Goal to Be First Woman Rabbi." *Cleveland Plain Dealer*, March/April 1964; Mirsky, Norman. *Unorthodox Judaism* (1978); Proctor, Priscilla, and William Proctor. *Women in the Pulpit: Is God an Equal Opportunity Employer?* (1976).

PAMELA S. NADELL

PRINCE, JANE (1896–1969)

Jane Prince dedicated her life to furthering the economic, social, and educational opportunities of young people in Palestine and Israel through her involvement in the Women's League for Palestine and its successor, the Women's League for Israel, and with the American Friends of Hebrew University.

Born in New York City on January 19, 1896, Jane Gottfried married William Prince, the president of the Gottfried Baking Company. They had three children, Richard, Cynthia, and Doris, all of whom continued in their mother's footsteps by being active members in a number of Zionist groups and charities.

As the Women's League president (1932–1957) and chair of finance (1957–1969), Jane Prince worked earnestly to provide vocational training and social adjustment to young women, many of whom were refugees, in Palestine and Israel. The Women's League built and supported four different homes in Tel Aviv, Haifa, Jerusalem, and Netanya, which housed and educated these women, while also training them to contribute to the war effort in Palestine. Prince was also the Israel Bond chair of the Women's League, the director of the Federation of Jewish Women's Organizations, the director of the Women's Division for State of Israel Bonds, and vice president of the American Medical Center.

Prince's philanthropy was not limited to women, for she was an active member in the American Friends of Hebrew University, which provided higher education to women and men in Palestine and Israel. In 1941, the Jane G. Prince Scholarship Fund was established at Hebrew University, where there is a dormitory in her name. Prince was awarded Woman of the Year by the Women's Institute of Jewish Studies of the Jewish Theological Seminary in 1954. She was a committee member for the Scopus Award Dinner in 1962 and was made a fellow of Hebrew University in 1964.

Jane Prince died on January 7, 1969, in New York City, leaving behind her son and two daughters and a legacy of dedication to the lives of women and Zionism.

BIBLIOGRAPHY

AJYB 71:607; American Friends of Hebrew University. Newsletters. American Jewish Historical Society, Waltham, Mass; Obituary. *NYTimes*, January 8, 1969, 47:1.

KAYLA SHIP

PSYCHOLOGY

Although both Jewish men and women have made significant contributions to American psychology from its earliest beginnings, it is exceedingly difficult to determine who is Jewish. More than other social sciences, psychology has identified itself with scientific objectivity—holding that the sex and race of its practitioners are irrelevant to their research and practice. Religious identity and social class are even less likely to be noted.

It is surprising, nevertheless, how invisible Jews, as Jews, are in the field of psychology; because, in absolute terms, a disproportionate number have contributed to the field as theorists, researchers, and practitioners. Jewish women are well represented in the field but are not necessarily named as Jews or, with a few exceptions, appear to be concerned with Jewish issues. As EVELYN TORTON BECK notes, "To be visible as a woman, a feminist, and a Jew makes you multiply vulnerable to attack on those counts. No wonder major Jewish theorists are stripped of their Jewishness in histories of psychology."

It is clear that generational differences in self-naming also exist. Those women who came to the United States as part of the wave of intellectuals fleeing Nazism in the mid- and late 1930s spoke openly about their Jewishness and the anti-Semitism they were attempting to escape. The American-born women of their generation also mentioned anti-Semitism as part of their professional lives. However, those women who began their professional lives in the 1960s or 1970s, when anti-Semitism had diminished or become less overt, were less likely to mention their Jewish identity.

Younger women appear to be more willing to identify themselves as Jewish. Many of these women are also feminists. They are particularly likely to be found among the leaders in the new field of the psychology of women. It is not surprising, however, that many are activists for other forms of social justice as well. In this, they resemble their male counterparts, who have been found in disproportionate numbers among the presidents of the Society for the Psychological Study of Social Issues (SPSSI).

Many of these women have working-class origins. Many mention their sense of class, as well as ethnic marginality. Some attribute their activism to their parents' values. Sandra Tangri speaks for these women in her tribute to her father on his ninetieth birthday, "I got more than love from my father. I got my most important values and the basis for my politics from him. I got my sense of place, of belonging to an historic stream of thinkers and 'tooers' (activists), and the confidence to be my own person from him. . . . His passionate commitment to the idea of social justice planted in me the seeds of my feminism." Other women speak out for all those older women who have been silenced. And some, because no autobiographical material exists, do not tell us why they have spoken or why they have remained silent.

THE EARLY PIONEERS

Like their male counterparts, the first generation of American women psychologists (educated in the nineteenth century) were almost all native-born Protestants. In contrast, the first major Jewish women contributors to psychology were trained in Europe more than a generation later and fled to the United States to escape the Nazis in the mid- or late 1930s. Like their male counterparts, many of these women made their most important contributions in psychoanalytic and psychodynamic theory. For example, FRIEDA FROMM-REICHMANN and ELSE FRENKEL-BRUNSWICK (who were placed among the group of 228 psychologists living between 1600 and 1967 who had made eminent contributions to the field) were both psychoanalysts.

Many of the other women who immigrated to the United States during this period also had an impact on the developing field of clinical psychology. They included Eugenia Hanfmann (1905–1983) who, as a child, moved with her family to Lithuania and later Germany because of the Russian revolution. Hanfmann's career was supported by a network of male Jewish mentors. She reported that a mentor sent her to work with Kurt Koffka at Smith College in 1930 and that she then remained underemployed until another Jewish man helped her to get a clinical position at Worcester State Hospital where she did research with Tamara Dembo on new patients' reaction to the hospital. Her major contributions to clinical psychology during this period involved the study of conceptual thinking in schizophrenics and of the role of projective tests in the assessment of personality.

Hanfmann worked for the Office of Strategic Services during World War II and was later appointed a lecturer in clinical psychology at Harvard University. Like a number of women in her cohort, she was unable to obtain a permanent faculty position after World War II. In 1952, Abraham Maslow invited her to start a counseling service for students at the newly formed Brandeis University, a position she described as her last and longest lasting.

Erika Fromm (b. 1910) is another Jewish woman trained in Europe who has made important contributions to clinical psychology. In her autobiography, she described herself as the oldest of eight children born in Germany of an Orthodox Jewish family with intellectual and artistic interests. She received her Ph.D. in psychology from the University of Frankfurt in December 1933 and, two weeks later, left Germany for Holland. She immigrated to the United States with her husband in 1938, narrowly avoiding the Holocaust. Fromm believes that sexism hindered her career and delayed for nine years the attainment of a full professorship that had been promised her at a well-known university. She has had, nevertheless, an important impact on psychoanalysis through her work on dream interpretation and on hypnosis as a key to the unconscious.

Another important European-educated contributor to psychoanalytic theory was MARGARET MAHLER, who was born in Hungary in 1897. Mahler's work involved object relations theory—an area that also interested later Jewish scholars such as Nancy Chodorow, Jean Baker Miller, and Jessica Benjamin.

Tamara Dembo (1902–1993) made important contributions to both clinical and social psychology. She was educated at the University of Berlin, where she soon became a member of the study group that formed around Kurt Lewin. Her early career closely paralleled that of Eugenia Hanfmann. She came to the United States to work with Kurt Koffka (an important Gestalt psychologist) at Smith College and, as conditions in Germany deteriorated, remained and worked at the Worcester State Hospital from 1932 to 1934. After moving through a number of temporary positions, she finally became a full member of the faculty at Clark University.

Dembo's major contributions were in the field of rehabilitation psychology, where she advocated adapting environments to people rather than the other way around. She taught the field to see that disabilities are in the environment rather than in the person. She worked with a large range of handicapped individuals, including children with cerebral palsy and veterans who had lost limbs or been blinded in World War II, as well as institutionalized retarded patients.

These female (and male) refugees from Nazism helped to change the focus of American social psychology by giving it a more "outsider" perspective. Psychology was no longer the domain of a privileged white male establishment. This increased ethnic diversity helped shift the field from an emphasis on the differences between individuals and groups to an emphasis on the social forces that induce the perception of such differences. These women were also early activists for various social causes. This was especially true of MARIE JAHODA (b. 1907), who spent the war years in England but had an illustrious career in the United States beginning in 1945.

THE INDIGENOUS PIONEERS

The four American-born Jewish women whose contributions to psychology began shortly after the end of World War II were more diverse in their focus than the women discussed above. Mary Henle, who was born in Cleveland, Ohio, in 1913, resembles the immigrant group most—probably because she became interested in Gestalt psychology after studying under Wolfgang Kohler as an undergraduate at Smith College.

Henle remained committed to experimental and theoretical issues involving Gestalt psychology throughout her graduate studies at Bryn Mawr. In her autobiography, Henle made an explicit statement about the sexism and anti-Semitism that were prevalent in psychology during the Depression of the 1930s and later. "It is hard to say whether, as a woman, I had special difficulty in finding employment, though I suppose I did. In addition to the scarcity of positions, anti-Semitism was prevalent and often explicit. Thus, if I did not get a job for which I applied, I could not know for sure whether I lacked the qualifications, or whether it was because I was a woman or Jewish."

Thelma Alper (b. 1908) described herself in her autobiography as having grown up in a very achievement-oriented, but not at all college-oriented, Jewish family in Massachusetts. In 1939, she applied to the Ph.D. program in psychology at Harvard University. Her account of her interview with its chairman is illustrative of the difficulties women in psychology faced during this period.

It was not without trepidation, however, that I asked for an appointment with the chairman of the psychology department, Dr. Edwin G. Boring. Set up for thirty minutes, the interview

lasted almost three hours. Dr. Boring was polite but not very encouraging. He told me that the department did not really welcome female graduate students, that they had accepted very few over the years and that only a handful had survived. But at the end he agreed that if I was ready to "throw myself to the lions," the department would accept me on my terms as a part-time student, beginning in the fall of 1939.

Alper persevered and in 1943 became the eleventh woman (and the first Jewish woman) to be granted a Ph.D. in psychology from Harvard.

She was appointed a lecturer (due, partly, to the scarcity of men available for non-war-related positions) and remained the only woman in the department until she was joined by Eugenia Hanfmann in 1946. However, Harvard was not prepared to offer tenure to women, and eventually both left. Alper finally accepted a tenured position at her alma mater, Wellesley, in 1952, where she remained for the rest of her career.

Alper's research combined elements of clinical and social psychology. Her social psychological research was greatly influenced by Kurt Lewin, whose class she had taken at Harvard, and focused primarily on memory for completed and uncompleted tasks.

BERNICE LEVIN NEUGARTEN (b. 1916) was born in a small town in Nebraska where her father, who had emigrated from Lithuania, bought and sold goods from farmers and ranchers. She moved to Chicago at age seventeen to attend the University of Chicago and never left—receiving all of her degrees there.

Despite taking eight years off to raise two children, Neugarten wrote or edited eight books and wrote more than 150 professional articles and monographs. She pioneered the field of adult development and aging and originated the important concepts of "social clocks" and "age norms."

Jane Loevinger (b. 1918) received an offer of an assistantship at the Institute of Child Welfare of the University of Minnesota, but this was later withdrawn. In her autobiography, Loevinger indicates that having politically radical sympathies and being Jewish were probably more important to this decision than her gender. Loevinger finally completed her graduate work at Berkeley where, she noted, she was never aware of any prejudice against Jews, women, or sympathizers with left-wing movements.

During World War II, Loevinger had a series of teaching appointments at first-class universities. When the war ended, however, women were expected to retire from their careers to leave room for the returning men to resume theirs. Unable to obtain an academic position in St. Louis where her husband was on the faculty of Washington University, Loevinger conducted a variety of research studies supported by grants to others and, eventually, to her. In 1971, twenty-five years after she had arrived in St. Louis, Loevinger (at her own request) finally became a tenured professor at Washington University.

Loevinger's work involved the areas of measurement and psychoanalysis. She published work on the construction of projective tests as well as on the meaning and measurement of ego development.

A GENERATION OF SOCIAL ACTIVISTS

Although the first generation of women often mentioned anti-Semitism in their accounts of their lives, there are fewer comments about anti-Jewish prejudice in later women's accounts. This group of women (born in the 1920s or early 1930s) embarked on their careers after World War II when discrimination against Jews had become less overt. Instead of their Jewishness, social activism appears to have been the important focus for their professional lives.

With the exception of ETHEL TOBACH (b. 1921), all of these women were born in the United States. As the feminist movement in the late 1960s and early 1970s made positions of leadership for women more acceptable, a number of Jewish women became presidents of the Society for the Psychological Study of Social Issues.

Marcia Guttentag (1932–1977) became the second female president of SPSSI in 1971, fifteen years after the election of its first female president, Marie Jahoda. Her career was cut short by her early death. Nevertheless, she managed to write or edit many books during her short life. Several of these books focused on mental health evaluation. She was also interested in gender inequity in education and in 1983 coauthored with her husband, Paul Secord (also a psychologist), a book on the societal implications of varying male:female ratios that is still cited.

Gordon Derner's conclusion to Guttentag's obituary in the *American Psychologist* sums up Guttentag's impact on public policy as well as on the people with whom she worked.

> Marcia was ever the activist. She vigorously insisted on strict moral, professional, and personal standards. Her writings, her speeches, her direct action, and her untiring interest in people encouraged concern for others and helped improve standards of human interaction. Her book *Undoing Sex Stereotypes* helped in making provisions in the Career Incentive Act of 1977

for the elimination of sex stereotyping in elementary and secondary career education efforts. In 1970 she was the first scholar in residence at the U.S. Commission on Civil Rights where she was able to study and appraise public laws and policies with respect to equal protection of all without regard to color, race, religion, national origin, or sex. The reports of the Commission were submitted to the President and Congress for action in civil rights.

The election of June Louin Tapp in 1979 marked what James Capshew called the beginning of an "informal affirmative action" program within SPSSI. Between 1978 and 1988, seven women were elected president (about 30 percent of the membership during this period were women). Six of these women were Jewish or part Jewish.

June Tapp (1929–1992) did her major research on psychology, law, and public policy. As is usual for women within this cohort, Tapp held a number of short-term positions in several cities before "settling in" as a professor at the Institute of Child Development at the University of Minnesota in 1972.

Tapp was a leader within several divisions of the American Psychological Association (APA). She was one of the founders of the Psychology-Law Society (now a division of APA). She was also the coauthor/editor of two books: *Ambivalent America* (1971) and *Law, Justice, and the Individual in Society* (1977). But, for Tapp, justice was not simply an abstract concept. During the 1960s, she worked with Saul Alinsky and studied African-American men in Woodlawn (one of the most impoverished communities in Chicago), and in the 1970s, she worked with a team of graduate students on the Wounded Knee Trial (as adviser as well as researcher-scholar).

Tapp was succeeded by Cynthia Deutsch (b. 1928), who reported that there was some concern among the male SPSSI leadership about the election of two women presidents in a row. Deutsch has been primarily concerned with the psychological consequences of early intervention in the lives of children at risk. Her presidential address to SPSSI, titled "The Behavioral Scientist: Insider and Outsider," seems to summarize the sense of marginality in this cohort of socially activist women.

After a year with a male president, Clara Weiss Mayo (1931–1981) was elected president of SPSSI in 1982. Mayo's father was Jewish, and she acknowledged both her Jewishness and the anti-Semitism that had caused her parents to flee Austria in 1938. Unfortunately, Mayo died before she could serve her year in office. She acquired her applied social interests from

Tamara Dembo during the period she was a graduate student at Clark University.

After she joined the faculty at Boston University, Mayo was involved in one of the first studies to examine the effect of busing on school integration. She was also interested in the way nonverbal communication patterns helped or hindered relationships between individuals from different social groups.

Mayo's term was filled by MARTHA MEDNICK (b. 1929), the president-elect of SPSSI. Born and educated in New York City, Mednick was an influential pioneer in the study of women and gender.

Mednick was succeeded by another Jewish woman, Lois Wladis Hoffman (b. 1929). She spent most of her professional career at the University of Michigan where she became a professor of psychology in 1975. Hoffman's earliest work was on child development, much of it conducted with Martin Hoffman, her former husband. Hoffman also maintained a long-standing interest in the effect of maternal employment on children which began with her doctoral dissertation. She wrote two important books in this area: *The Employed Mother in America* (1963) and *Working Mothers* (1974). Later, Hoffman teamed up with Martha Mednick and Sandra Tangri to edit *Women and Achievement: Social and Motivational Analyses* (1975).

The final individual in this group of Jewish female presidents of SPSSI is Phyllis Katz (b. 1938). Katz has worked against both racism and sexism. She founded the feminist journal *Sex Roles* and served as its editor from 1975 to 1990. She is currently editor of the *Journal of Social Issues*, SPSSI's major journal. She was a professor at the Graduate Center of the City University of New York, but since 1975 she has maintained her own research institute in Boulder, Colorado. Katz's major work in psychology has been on the socialization of gender roles in children. She has also edited two books on eliminating racism.

OTHER ROUTES OF PROFESSIONAL ACCOMPLISHMENT

Not all members of this cohort have had the same educational and career trajectory. Although she was born in New York City, Frances Degen Horowitz (b. 1932) received her undergraduate education at Antioch in 1954 and her Ph.D. from the University of Iowa in 1959. Much of her professional career was spent at the University of Kansas, where she was vice chancellor for Research, Graduate Studies and Public Service and dean of the Graduate School. Furthermore, she was professor of psychology but, more centrally, she started the department of and was professor of Human Development and Family Life. She has been president of the Graduate Center of the City University of New York since 1991. Horowitz's research has focused on early childhood development and children in poverty. She received the APA Outstanding Contribution to the Science Directorate Award and has been on the committee to select the Weizmann Institute's Women in Science Award since 1994. She was president of the APA Division of Developmental Psychology in 1977–1978 and president-elect of the Society for Research in Child Development in 1995–1997, and is the current president of the organization (1997–1999).

Judith Seitz Rodin (b. 1944) is another college president who had an illustrious academic career before moving into administration. Rodin did important work on obesity, aging, and social control while a professor of psychology at Yale, where she also became dean of the Graduate School before moving to her present position as president of the University of Pennsylvania. She has been an important contributor to research and policy issues involving women's health.

Judith Alpert (b. 1944) has made her primary contributions to psychology in the areas of school psychology and, more recently, psychoanalysis.

It is sometimes difficult to decide where to place women chronologically, since their professional careers are frequently interrupted. Thus, Sylvia Scribner's (1923–1991) year of birth should place her among an earlier generation of contributors to psychology. But Scribner's career was frequently interrupted by her political activities. After graduating with honors from Smith College in 1943, Scribner worked as a union organizer and an indefatigable antiestablishment activist for many years. While she worked as assistant to the director and operational research analyst for the Jewish Board of Guardians in New York City (1958–1962), she enrolled as a graduate student at the New School for Social Research. She finally received her Ph.D. in 1970 under the direction of Mary Henle. Scribner's scholarly contributions were primarily in the area of cross-cultural psychology. During the 1970s, she traveled frequently to Liberia to study the relationship between culture and thought. Her body of scholarship is a remarkable accomplishment for someone who received her only full-time faculty appointment at the age of fifty-nine.

A GENERATION OF FEMINIST ACTIVISTS

While many women were involved in the study of social issues during this period, in the 1970s and 1980s many activist women focused their energies on the study of women and gender and on feminist organizational activities within APA. One such leader in the development and legitimization of the psychology of women is FLORENCE DENMARK (b. 1932). Her career also shows some of the discontinuities familiar from other women's life histories. Despite a somewhat late start, however, Denmark has held virtually every elected office in the profession of psychology. In 1980, she was the first Jewish woman to be elected president of the American Psychological Association.

A disproportionate number of Jewish women have been active scholars and practitioners in the field of the psychology of women. For example, the 1996 APA membership directory lists 209 fellows of this division (a status conferred by APA as a whole through evidence of unusual or outstanding contribution or performance in the field of psychology). By name, fifty-six of these individuals appear to be Jewish, and this figure does not include deceased individuals or those who are no longer members of APA. Since 1985, the Committee on Women in Psychology has given distinguished career awards to thirty-one women; twelve of these awards were given to Jewish women. Jewish women (not all of them psychologists) have also received all but one of the Association for Women in Psychology's distinguished career awards.

Barbara Strudler Wallston (1943–1987), a fine feminist scholar who died young, was the recipient of many awards. Wallston possessed awesome organizational skills and rose to early leadership in organizations fostering women's careers within psychology and the development of the psychology of women. She was a leader in the Association for Women in Psychology as well as the sixth president of the APA's Division on the Psychology of Women.

Wallston also made important contributions to psychological research. She developed a health locus of control scale with her then husband, Kenneth Wallston, which is used internationally to measure people's beliefs about what controls their health status. She also worked in the area of dual-career couples, stereotyping, and feminist methodology in psychology.

A number of other Jewish women have also served as president of the APA's division on women. Annette Brodsky (b. 1938) followed Florence Denmark and Martha Mednick as its fifth president (1977–1978). She originated the feminist therapists' roster for the Association for Women in Psychology in 1970.

Brodsky was the coeditor of the first book on psychotherapy and women and has conducted important research on sexual contact between therapists and clients. She currently lives in Los Angeles, where she is a director of clinical training for a large hospital and an expert witness on sexual abuse in psychotherapy.

Rhoda Kesler Unger (b. 1939) was the eighth president of the division (1980–1981). Like many of the other women in this group, she was born of working-class parents and educated in New York City. She taught for a few years at Hofstra University, where her interests changed from physiological to social psychology. During this period she met Florence Denmark and coauthored an early text on the psychology of women with her. Since 1972, she has been a professor of psychology at Montclair State University in New Jersey and director of the All-College Honors Program. Unger's primary work has been on the relationship between ideological values, theory, and methodology within psychology. She has also written and/or edited four textbooks in the psychology of women.

Hannah Lerman (b. 1936) was the twelfth president of the Division of the Psychology of Women (1984–1985). Unlike many of the women discussed in this article, Lerman has been in private practice as a therapist for all of her working career (mostly in the Los Angeles area). She is a cofounder of the Feminist Therapy Institute. Unusual among psychologists in private practice, Lerman has contributed extensively to the research literature on psychotherapy.

Lenore Walker (b. 1942) was the seventeenth president of the division (1989–1990) and is best known for her groundbreaking work on battered women.

Another important contributor to the psychology of women who has also been president of the APA Division on the Psychology of Women (1990–1991) is Bernice Lott (b. 1930). Lott began her professional activities in behalf of women somewhat later than usual because she did not obtain a full-time tenure track position (at the University of Rhode Island) until 1977—twenty-four years after she had received her doctorate in social psychology from UCLA. Lott's autobiography contains striking similarities to other important Jewish women psychologists' accounts of the social activism of their parents and in their own social activism. Lott's career also shows discontinuities similar to those of other women who are/were married to prominent men in the field. She taught in the extension division of the university where her husband had a regular appointment and then as a special education teacher in junior high school. Following her second marriage, to Albert Lott, she began to publish research regularly both in collaboration with him and by herself. Her work has focused on prejudice and discrimination against women and on the social learning of gender.

One of the most recent Jewish presidents of the Division of the Psychology of Women, Laura Brown

(b. 1952), is also one of the only women in this group to discuss explicitly what being Jewish means for her: "Feminist therapy has joined at the root with my Jewish heritage so that, an hour at a time, a life at a time, I can participate in the revolutionary activity of 'Tikkun olam' healing the world through the transformative work of feminism that takes shape for me in the practice of feminist therapy." Brown describes herself in her autobiography as coming from a large family of Jewish women in which women's intellect and education were specifically valued and encouraged. She has lived in Seattle since 1977, where she has a full-time private practice and serves as a clinical professor of psychology at the University of Washington. In 1991, Brown became the first openly lesbian licensed psychologist in Seattle. Before becoming president of the Division on the Psychology of Women, Brown was also president of APA's Division on Gay and Lesbian Psychology. Brown has been a precocious and prolific contributor to the professional literature on psychotherapy and women. She has written a compelling book in this area, *Subversive Dialogues* (1994).

Judith Worell (b. 1928), the president-elect of the Division on the Psychology of Women, is another New York City–born woman who has contributed extensively to this field as well as to counseling psychology. In addition to her active administrative responsibilities and scholarly work, Worell recently completed a five-year term as editor of the *Psychology of Women Quarterly*. Worell's research interests focus on the development of a feminist model for counseling psychology. She coauthored a widely used textbook in this area and is a leading figure in the pursuit of a feminist transformation of psychological education, research, and practice. She has also conducted extensive research on women's roles throughout the lifespan and on their satisfaction with their close relationships.

There are many other women born during the late 1930s and early 1940s who have made important contributions to psychology. Some of them identify themselves as Jewish in biographical statements, while others do not. Very few have been directly involved with Jewish religious issues or Jewish cultural life. PHYLLIS CHESLER (b. 1940)—who wrote the challenging book *Women and Madness* (1972) during the early days of the feminist movement—is an exception in this area.

So, too, was Nancy Datan (1941–1987), who had a significant impact on both anthropology and psychology during her short life. Datan immigrated to Israel in 1963 but completed her Ph.D. in the human development program at the University of Chicago while in Israel and returned to the United States in 1973 because, she said, there was no place there for a divorced woman with three young children. Datan and several colleagues conducted a pioneering study of aging among women from five subcultures in Israel, which ranged from traditional to modern in their conceptions of women's roles. Datan's work consistently reflected her concerns about Jewish identity, marginality, and sexuality and love—the latter two terms were interchangeable in her lexicon. She also edited an important series of books on adult development and aging. In the final year of her life, she wrote a moving (and surprisingly humorous) account of her experiences with breast cancer and her reservations about breast reconstruction.

Sandra Schwartz Tangri (b. 1937) also has written about her Jewish ethnicity. She describes herself "as a highly educated daughter of Jewish immigrants one of whom was a Yiddish poet and wallpaper-hanger, and neither of whom finished high school. . . ." She also noted that as a child she always knew that being Jewish meant being different and that California in the 1940s and 1950s was not a land of unbounded tolerance. Her parents, however, worked to make her working-class Jewish identity a source of pride. She attended a Jewish school three days a week until she finished high school, where she learned to read, write, and speak Yiddish as well as a little Hebrew and a lot of Jewish history. While a graduate student at the University of Michigan, Tangri met Martha Mednick with whom she collaborated on important research in the psychology of women. Between academic jobs, she was director of the Office of Research for the U.S. Commission on Civil Rights for four years and senior research associate at the Urban Institute for three years. She eventually returned to academia and is currently professor of psychology at Howard University. She conducted longitudinal research on women's career development for her Ph.D. dissertation and has returned to the original group several times during her career to examine long-term changes. She has also studied sexual harassment in the federal work force and ethical issues in population programs.

Other important Jewish contributors to the psychology of women have been less involved in organizational activities. However, these women have contributed much to the field. Indeed, the first and still classic article in this area is "Psychology Constructs the Female" (1968) by Naomi Weisstein (b. 1940). Weisstein was born into a passionately antiauthoritarian family in New York City—she has, in fact, described herself as a "red diaper baby." She received her Ph.D. in cognitive psychology from Harvard University in only three years in spite of that university's enormous sexism, which she described wittily in the article "How Can a Little Girl Like You Teach a Great Big Class of Men?" (1977). Sexism within psychology led her to "the only position I could find"—a lectureship at the University of Chicago, which she described as "a position tailored for overqualified faculty wives" that did not even carry library privileges. She finally joined the faculty of the State University of New York at Buffalo in 1973, where her research life was cut short by chronic fatigue and immune dysfunction syndrome. Despite her relatively short life as a researcher, Weisstein contributed to the understanding of the neuropsychology of visual perception as well as to feminist scholarship.

Marilyn Safir (b. 1938) has also been relatively uninvolved in organizational issues within APA—probably because she immigrated to Israel shortly after receiving her Ph.D. in clinical psychology from Syracuse University. She had become disenchanted with the treatment of women here and went to Israel because she believed that there would be more sexual equality there. In Israel, she became an early advocate of feminism and has fostered dialogue between American and Israeli scholars. She wrote an article on nature versus nurture issues in sex differences on cognitive tests and recently coedited a collection of works challenging myths of sexual equality in Israel.

Sandra Lipshitz Bem (b. 1944) is another important figure in the study of the psychology of women. Bem was born to a working class family in Pittsburgh and attended an Orthodox Jewish day school throughout her childhood. She and her husband, Darryl Bem, did early collaborative work on the internalization of gender stereotypes as a source of gender inequality, which served as evidence in a major sex discrimination case. She also originated the concept of androgyny as a measure of personality that views "masculine" and "feminine" traits as independent of each other. Her recent book, *The Lenses of Gender* (1993), examines the way gender is constructed by societal constraints.

Michelle Fine (b. 1953) has contributed an astonishing body of work on psychology and education in the past few years. Although some of Fine's work is on women, it is probably better characterized as being on social justice. Fine is especially challenging and exciting when she looks at marginality and the way issues of race, class, and disability "braid" with one another. Fine was the Goldie Anna Charitable Trust Professor of Education at the University of Pennsylvania, but she resigned that position, in part because of the unwillingness of that institution to offer tenure to qualified women. She is currently professor of psychology at the Graduate Center of the City University of New York. Fine is a passionate social activist. She has coedited a book on women and disability, written a book on African-American and Latina high school drop-outs, and coedited a book on problematizing whiteness. Her book of essays, *Disruptive Voices* (1992), provides a comprehensive view of her articles in the professional literature—ranging from analysis of theory and method to hands-on descriptions of rape and rape counseling.

SOME CONCLUSIONS

Jewish women in psychology have made their most important contributions in two areas—clinical psychology and the social psychology of intergroup relationships, especially as it involves groups marginalized in our society. Their interest in psychodynamic issues is consistent with findings on psychologists as a whole, which suggest that those who identify themselves as Jewish are more likely to have a subjectivist theoretical orientation than other psychologists. Recent immigrant status (parents or grandparents) has also been found to be associated with social rather than biological explanations for group differences. And various forms of social marginality appear to be related to researchers' interest in "real-life" aspects of power rather than laboratory-based demonstrations of social influence.

The marginality of women within psychology has been ameliorated by the important influence women have had on one another. Many mentor/student relationships exist. As the field of the psychology of women became an organized structure within psychology, collaborative efforts appear to have multiplied exponentially.

Feminist women in psychology value environmental rather than biological explanations for behavior, the important role of historical and cultural circumstances, and the significance of subjectivity in psychological research. Since many of these feminist women are also Jews from working-class immigrant backgrounds, their social activism as well as their concentration in certain areas of psychology make a great deal of sense. Psychology would be poorer without their perspective.

WORKS BY AND ABOUT PSYCHOLOGISTS DISCUSSED

Addelston, Judi, and Michelle Fine. "'Fag Hags,' Firemen, and Feminist Theory: Girl Talk on Amtrak." In Chesler, Rothman, and Cole (1995); Alper, Thelma G. "Autobiography." In O'Connell and Russo (1983): 189–199; Alpert, Judith, ed. *Psychoanalysis and Women: Contemporary Reappraisals* (1986); Alpert, Judith, et al. *Psychological Consultation in Educational Settings* (1982); *American Psychologist* 31

(1976): 83–86; 33 (1978): 77–80; 43 (1988): 243–244; Bem, Sandra L. *The Lenses of Gender* (1993); Bem, Sandra L., and Darryl J. Bem. "Training the Woman to Know Her Place: The Power of a Nonconscious Ideology." In *Roles Women Play: Readings Toward Women's Liberation*, edited by M.H. Garskof (1970): 84–96; Bohan, Janis S. *Re-placing Women in Psychology: Readings Toward a More Inclusive History* (1992); Brodsky, Annette M., and Rachel T. Hare-Mustin, eds. *Women and Psychotherapy* (1980); Brown, Laura S. "Notes of a Feminist Therapy 'Foredaughter.'" In Chesler, Rothman, and Cole (1995), and *Subversive Dialogues: Theory in Feminist Therapy* (1994); Brown, Laura S., and Mary Ballou, eds. *Personality and Psychopathology: Feminist Reappraisals* (1992); Brown, Laura S., and Maria P.P. Root, eds. *Diversity and Complexity in Feminist Therapy* (1990); Chesler, Phyllis. *Women and Madness* (1972); Chesler, Phyllis, Esther D. Rothman, and Ellen Cole. *Feminist Foremothers in Women's Studies, Psychology, and Mental Health* (1995); Crawford, Mary, and Rhoda K. Unger, eds. In *Our Own Words: Readings on Women and Gender* (1997); Datan, Nancy. "Corpses, Lepers, and Menstruating Women: Tradition, Transition, and the Sociology of Knowledge." *Sex Roles* 14 (1986): 693–703, and "Illness and Imagery: Feminist Cognition, Socialization, and Gender Identity." In *Gender and Thought: Psychological Perspectives*, edited by Mary Crawford and Margaret Gentry (1989): 175–187; Datan, Nancy, A. Antonovsky, and B. Maoz. *A Time to Reap: The Middle Age of Women in Five Israeli Subcultures* (1981); de Rivera, Joseph. "Obituary of Tamara Dembo (1902–1993)." *American Psychologist* 50 (1995): 386; Derner, Gordon F. "Obituary of Marcia Guttentag (1932–1977)." *American Psychologist* 35 (1980): 1138–1139; Deutsch, Cynthia P. "The Behavioral Scientist: Insider and Outsider." *Journal of Social Issues* 37 (1981): 172–191, and "Gender Discrimination as an Intergroup Issue: Comment on Capshew and Lazlo." *Journal of Social Issues* 42 (1986): 185–189; Fine, Michelle. *Disruptive Voices: The Possibilities of Feminist Research* (1992), and *Framing Drop-Outs: Notes on the Politics of an Urban High School* (1991); Fine, Michelle, and Adrienne Asch, eds. *Women with Disabilities: Essays in Psychology, Culture, and Politics* (1988); Fine, Michelle, Lois Weis, Linda C. Powell, and L. Mun Wong, eds. *Off White: Readings on Race, Power, and Society* (1997); Fromm, Erika. "Autobiography." In O'Connell and Russo (1988): 87–101; Guttentag, Marcia. "Children in Harlem's Community Controlled Schools." *Journal of Social Issues* 28 (1972): 1–20, and *Undoing Sex Stereotypes: Research and Resources for Educators* (1976); Guttentag, Marcia, and Paul Secord. *Too Many Women: The Sex Ratio Question* (1983); Guttentag, Marcia, et al., eds. *The Evaluation of Training in Mental Health* (1975); Hanfmann, Eugenia. "Autobiography." In O'Connell and Russo (1983): 141–152; Henle, Mary. "Autobiography." In O'Connell and Russo (1983): 221–232; Hoffman, Lois W. *Working Mothers: An Evaluative Review of the Consequences for Wife, Husband, and Child* (1974); Hoffman, Martin H., and Lois W. Hoffman. *Review of Child Development Research* (1964); Holroyd, Jean C., and Annette M. Brodsky. "Psychologists' Attitudes and Practices Regarding Erotic and Nonerotic Physical Contact with Patients." *American Psychologist* 32 (1977): 843–849; Horowitz, Frances D. *Exploring Developmental Theories: Toward a Structural Behavioral Model to Account for Behavioral Development* (1987), and *The Gifted and Talented: Developmental Perspectives* (1985), and *Visual Attention, Auditory Stimulation, and Language Discrimination in Young Infants* (1975); Katz, Phyllis A. "Modification of Children's Gender-Stereotypical Behavior: General Issues and Research Considerations." *Sex Roles* 14 (1986): 591–602; Katz, Phyllis A., ed. *Toward the Elimination of Racism* (1976); Katz, Phyllis A., and S. Boswell. "Flexibility and Traditionality in Children's Gender Roles." *Genetic, Social, and General Psychology Monographs* 112 (1986): 103–147; Katz, Phyllis A., and Dalmas A. Taylor, eds. *Eliminating Racism: Profiles in Controversy, Perspectives in Social Psychology* (1988); LaFrance, Marianne. "Clara Mayo." In O'Connell and Russo (1990): 238–245; Lemisch, Jesse, and Naomi Weisstein. "How We Learned to Love Our White Rabbit Hats: Cornucopia Isn't Consumerism." *Against the Current* (January/February 1992): 31–34; Lerman, Hannah. *A Mote in Freud's Eye: From Psychoanalysis to the Psychology of Women* (1986), and *Pigeonholing Women's Misery: History and Political Analysis of the Psychodiagnosis of Women in the Twentieth Century* (1997); Lerman, Hannah, and Natalie Porter, eds. *Feminist Ethics in Psychotherapy* (1990); Levine, Felice J. "Obituary of June Louin Tapp (1929–1992)." *American Psychologist* 49 (1994): 965; Loevinger, Jane. "Autobiography." In O'Connell and Russo (1988): 155–166; Lott, Bernice. *Becoming a Woman: The Socialization of Gender* (1981), and "Who Ever Thought I'd Grow Up to be a Feminist Foremother?" In Chesler, Rothman, and Cole (1995), and *Women's Lives: Themes and Variations in Gender Learning* (1987, rev. ed. 1994); Lott, Bernice, and Diane Maluso, eds. *The Social Psychology of Interpersonal Discrimination* (1995); Makosky, Vivian P. "Sandra Lipsitz Bem." In O'Connell and Russo (1990): 30–39; Mayo, Clara W. "Training for Positive Marginality." In *Applied Social Psychology Annual*, edited by Leonard Bickman. Vol. 3 (1982); Mednick, Martha T.S., and Sandra S. Tangri, eds. "New Directions on Women." *Journal of Social Issues* 28, no. 2 (1972); Mednick, Martha T.S., Sandra S. Tangri, and Lois W. Hoffman, eds. *Women and Achievement: Social and Motivational Analyses* (1975); Nye, F. Ivan, and Lois W. Hoffman. *The Employed Mother in America* (1963, 2d ed. 1976); O'Connell, Agnes N., and Nancy F. Russo, eds. *Models of Achievement: Reflections of Eminent Women in Psychology* Vol. 1 (1983), and Vol. 2 (1988), and *Women in Psychology: A Bio-Bibliographic Sourcebook* (1990); O'Leary, Virginia E. "Obituary of Barbara Strudler Wallston (1943–1987)." *American Psychologist* 43 (1988): 817; O'Leary, Virginia E., Rhoda K. Unger, and Barbara S. Wallston, eds. *Women, Gender, and Social Psychology* (1985); Rodin, Judith, and Jeanette R. Ickovics. "Women's Health: Review and Research Agenda as We Approach the 21st Century." *American Psychologist* 45 (1990): 1018–1034; Safir, Marilyn P. "The Effects of Nature or of Nurture on Sex Differences in Intellectual Functioning: Israeli Findings." *Sex Roles* 14

(1986): 581–590; Safir, Marilyn P., Martha S. Mednick, Dafna Izraeli, and Jessie Bernard, eds. *Women's Worlds: From the New Scholarship* (1985); Schlossberg, Nancy K., and Lillian E. Troll. "Bernice L. Neugarten." In O'Connell and Russo (1990): 256–265; Stevens, Gwendolyn, and Sheldon Gardner. *The Women of Psychology.* Vols. 1–2 (1982); Swirski, Barbara, and Marilyn P. Safir, eds. *Calling the Equality Bluff: Women in Israel* (1991); Tangri, Sandra S. "A Feminist Perspective on the Ethical Issues in Population Programs." *Signs* 1 (1974): 895–904, and "Some Contributions to Feminist Research in Psychology." In Chesler, Rothman, and Cole (1995); Tangri, Sandra S., Martha R. Burt, and L.B. Johnson, "Sexual Harassment at Work: Three Explanatory Models." *Journal of Social Issues* 38, no. 4 (1982): 33–54; Tapp, June L. "Psychological and Policy Perspectives on the Law: Reflections on a Decade." *Journal of Social Issues* 36 (1980): 165–192; Tapp, June L., and Fred Krinsky. "Ambivalent America: A Psycho-political Dialogue (1971); Tapp, June L., and Felice J. Levine, eds. *Law, Justice, and the Individual in Society: Psychology and Legal Issues* (1977); Tobach, Ethel, Rachel J. Falmagne, Mary B. Parlee, Laura W.W. Martin, and A.S. Kapelman, eds. *Mind and Social Practice: Selected Writings of Sylvia Scribner* (1997); Unger, Rhoda K. *Female and Male: Psychological Perspectives* (1979), and "From the Heart and the Mind: Nancy Datan." *Feminism and Psychology* 5 (1995): 441–448, and "Making a Feminist: A Personal History." In Crawford and Unger (1997): 10–14, and "Using the Master's Tools: Epistemology and Empiricism." In *Feminist Social Psychologies: International Perspectives*, edited by Sue Wilkinson (1996): 165–181; Unger, Rhoda, K., ed. *Representations: Social Constructions of Gender* (1989); Unger, Rhoda K., and Mary Crawford. *Women and Gender: A Feminist Psychology* (1992, 1996); Unger, Rhoda K., and Florence L. Denmark. *Woman: Dependent or Independent Variable?* (1975); Walker, Lenore. *The Battered Woman* (1979), and "The Transmogrification of a Feminist Foremother." In Chesler, Rothman, and Cole (1995); Wallston, Barbara S. "What are the Questions in Psychology of Women? A Feminist Approach to Research." *Psychology of Women Quarterly* 5 (1981): 597–617; Wallston, Barbara S., and Kathleen E. Grady. "Integrating the Feminist Critique and the Crisis in Social Psychology: Another Look at Research Methods." In O'Leary, Unger, and Wallston (1985): 7–34; Wallston, Barbara S., and Virginia E. O'Leary. "Sex Makes a Difference: Differential Perceptions of Women and Men." In *Review of Personality and Social Psychology*, Vol. 2, edited by L. Wheeler (1981); Weisstein, Naomi. "'How Can a Little Girl Like You Teach a Great Big Class of Men?' the Chairman Said and Other Tales of a Woman in Science." In *Working It Out*, edited by Sarah Ruddick and Pamela Daniels (1977): 241–250, and *Kinder, Kirche, Kuche as Scientific Law: Psychology Constructs the Female* (1968), and "Neural Symbolic Activity: A Psychophysical Measure." *Science* 168 (1970): 1489–1491; Wong, E., and Naomi Weisstein. "A New Perceptual Context-Superiority Effect: Line Segments are More Visible Against a Figure than Against a Ground." *Science* 218 (1982): 587–589; Worell, Judith, and Claire Etaugh, eds. "Transformations: Reconceptualizing Theory and Research with Women." *Psychology of Women Quarterly* 18, no. 4 (1994); Worell, Judith, and Norine Johnson. *Feminist Visions in Psychology: Education, Research, and Practice* (1997); Worell, Judith, and Patricia Remer. *Feminist Perspectives in Therapy: An Empowerment Model for Women* (1992).

BIBLIOGRAPHY

Association for Women in Psychology Newsletter (Winter 1997); Beck, Evelyn T. "Judaism, Feminism, and Psychology: Making the Links Visible." In *Jewish Women Speak Out*, edited by Kayla Weiner and Arinna Moon (1995): 11–26; Capshew, James H. "Networks on Leadership: A Quantitative Study of SPSSI Presidents, 1936–1986." *Journal of Social Issues* 42 (1986): 75–106; Coan, Richard W. *Psychologists: Personal and Theoretical Pathways* (1979); Deutsch, Cynthia P. "Gender Discrimination as an Intergroup Issue: Comment on Capshew and Lazlo." *Journal of Social Issues* 42 (1986): 185–189; Fine, Michelle. *Disruptive Voices: The Possibilities of Feminist Research* (1992); Morawski, Jill G. "White Experimenters, White Blood, and Other White Conditions: Locating the Psychologist's Race." In *Off White: Readings on Race, Power, and Society*, edited by Michelle Fine, Lois Weis, Linda C. Powell, and L. Mun Wong (1997): 13–28; Russo, Nancy F., and Angela duMont. "Division 35: Origins, Activities, Future." In *A History of Divisions in the American Psychological Association*, edited by Donald Dewsbury (1997); Russo, Nancy F., and Florence L. Denmark. "Contributions of Women to Psychology." *Annual Review of Psychology* 38 (1987): 279–298; Samelson, Franz. "From 'Race Psychology' to 'Studies in Prejudice': Some Observations on the Thematic Reversals in Social Psychology." *Journal of the History of the Behavioral Sciences* 14 (1978): 265–278; Scarborough, Elizabeth, and Laurel Furumoto. *Untold Lives: The First Generation of American Women Psychologists* (1987); Sherwood, J. J., and M. Nataupsky. "Predicting the Conclusions of Negro-White Intelligence Research from Biographical Characteristics of the Investigator." *Journal of Personality and Social Psychology* 8 (1968): 53–58; Stevens, Gwendolyn, and Sheldon Gardner. *The Women of Psychology* (1982); Tangri, Sandra S. "Living with Anomalies: Sojourns of a White American Jew." In *Women's Ethnicities: Journeys through Psychology*, edited by Karen F. Wyche and Faye J. Crosby (1996): 129–143; Tiefer, Leonore. *A Brief History of the Association for Women in Psychology (AWP), 1969–1991* (1991); Unger, Rhoda K. "Explorations in Feminist Methodology: Surprising Consistencies and Unexamined Conflicts." *Imagination, Cognition, and Personality* 4 (1984–1985): 387–405, and "Looking toward the Future by Looking at the Past: Social Activism and Social History." *Journal of Social Issues* 42 (1986): 215–227, and "Through the Looking Glass: No Wonderland Yet! (The Reciprocal Relationship between Methodology and Models of Reality)." *Psychology of Women Quarterly* 8 (1983): 9–32; *Who's Who of American Women* (1997–1998).

RHODA K. UNGER

PURVIN, JENNIE FRANKLIN
(1873–1958)

Jennie Franklin Purvin was one of a few Jewish women to become prominent in both civic and Jewish communal work in Progressive Era Chicago.

Born in Chicago on August 23, 1873, Jennie had one sister and three brothers. Her mother, Hannah Mayer, the daughter of German Jewish immigrants, was born in and graduated from high school in Chicago. Her father, Henry B. Franklin, came to Chicago from Germany in 1867.

Jennie Franklin graduated from high school in 1891, putting aside college plans to assist in her father's cigar-manufacturing business. In 1899, she married businessman Moses L. Purvin. They had two daughters, Nata and Janet.

Active in many women's civic groups, she also chaired women's committees in support of Chicago mayoral candidates. She was most prominent in the campaign to create clean and accessible bathing beaches on Lake Michigan. Although disappointed in her hopes of being appointed to Chicago's Board of Education, she was appointed the sole woman member of the public library's board of directors in 1933. She served as president of the Chicago section of the NATIONAL COUNCIL OF JEWISH WOMEN (1920–1922) and of the Sisterhood of Chicago's Sinai congregation (1925–1927). In her later years, she worked in association with Mandel Brothers Department Store to create the Club Women's Bureau, an art exhibition space for Chicago artists, and a camp advisory bureau to advise parents about summer camps.

Jennie Franklin Purvin retired in 1955 and died in Chicago on November 1, 1958. Notable for combining her work in Jewish women's organizations with a prominent role in Chicago's general civic life, Purvin's legacy remains Chicago's beautiful beachfront.

BIBLIOGRAPHY

Kominsky, Neil. "Jennie Franklin Purvin: A Study in Womanpower." In *The American Jewish Woman: A Documentary History* (1981); Purvin, Jennie Franklin. Collection. AJA, Cincinnati, Ohio; *WWIAJ* (1938).

KARLA GOLDMAN

Jennie Purvin was one of the essential people without whom the striking beachfront of Chicago would not exist. [American Jewish Archives]

R

RABBIS

In 1972, SALLY PRIESAND became the first woman ordained a rabbi, teacher, and preacher in America. Since then more than 350 women have become rabbis in the Reform, Reconstructionist, and Conservative branches of American Judaism.

Jewish women's recent entrance to the brotherhood of the rabbinate masks a lengthy history of the question of women's ordination. In fact, in almost every decade since the 1890s the challenge to the male hegemony over the rabbinate was raised among some sector of American Jewry. At times discussions surfaced in the Anglo-Jewish press and at meetings of various Jewish organizations. But generally in these settings the question was an abstract one. Not only would its outcome scarcely affect the lives of those engaged in the debate, but as one observer noticed in 1897, there were no women then—or so she assumed—who wanted to be rabbis.

Yet parallel to this hypothetical debate and often removed from it were those who, beginning in the 1920s, sought rabbinical ordination for themselves, as Sally Priesand later would. Like the nineteenth-century pioneers who tried to crash the barriers against women in American medicine, law, and the ministry, these women enrolled in rabbinical school, hoping to complete the curriculum and, alongside their fellow students, receive ordination.

In 1889, the journalist Mary M. Cohen, a leading member of her traditional Philadelphia synagogue, broached the topic of women rabbis in "A Problem for Purim" on the front page of *The Jewish Exponent*. In this short story crafted for the Jewish holiday of masquerade, Cohen asked whether or not women could contribute to the development of American Judaism by becoming rabbis. The arguments she gave revealed a climate of rising expectations for changing female roles in American Judaism.

From the 1890s forward, the question eddied out to American Jewry, striking a particularly responsive chord among its more liberal sectors, namely Reform Jews. Yet, in these early years, the issue, as Mary M. Cohen had shown, was by no means confined to Reform Judaism. By the beginning of the twentieth century, those at more traditional institutions, such as Conservative Judaism's Jewish Theological Seminary, were well aware of the emerging debate. In 1903, when HENRIETTA SZOLD, the foremost Jewish woman of her day, went to meet with seminary president Solomon Schechter about studying there, the subject came up. As she subsequently wrote: "After he was assured that I was not an aspirant after Rabbinical honors, he agreed to put no obstacles in my way."

From time to time over the course of the next century, committed American Jews—rabbis and *rebbetzins* [rabbis' wives], sisterhood presidents and seminary

*This formal photograph of Sally Priesand in 1972 when she became a rabbi
had to be included in this book. Since then more than 350 women have been
ordained as rabbis in America. History changes quickly. [American Jewish Archives]*

professors, and men and women committed to shaping Judaism in the spirit of democratic egalitarianism—continued their often theoretical debate about the question of women's ordination. As they did, they could point to a small number of trailblazers who, at times, presented Americans with examples of women functioning—albeit unofficially—as rabbis.

Although Jewish history offers a long list of erudite women some deemed "well-nigh . . . lady rabbi[s]" (Frank, p. 59), the first American paradigm was the "girl rabbi of the Golden West" (Clar and Kramer), RAY FRANK. In 1890, learning that there were to be no High Holiday services in Spokane, Washington, Frank, a Sabbath school principal, agreed to preach. From then

until shortly before her marriage a decade later, she preached and led religious services, studied for a time at Reform Judaism's Hebrew Union College, and wrote about what she would do if she were a rabbi, explaining that she did not desire to be one.

While Frank may be considered the first American Jewish woman functioning, without formal ordination, as a rabbi, she was by no means the last. In fact, she was followed by a number of women, mostly—but not exclusively—in the more liberal settings of Reform Judaism, who from time to time found themselves leading and preaching as if they were rabbis. Among them was *rebbetzin* PAULA ACKERMAN of Meridian, Mississippi. In 1950, when her husband,

Rabbi William Ackerman, died, the president of the congregation asked her to fill in—temporarily. For the next three years, until Temple Beth Israel hired a man to replace her, she conducted weddings and funerals, led services, and preached. Ackerman's practical rabbinate gave Reform Judaism's leaders the opportunity to reiterate what, by 1950, had long been its official stance: In principle, women could be rabbis; in practice, none were.

Reform Jewish leaders had not come to this position from observing the informal, but nevertheless real, religious leadership of women like Ray Frank and Paula Ackerman. Rather this posture evolved in the 1920s and 1930s after a series of formal challenges to the seminaries of Reform Judaism, Hebrew Union College and the Jewish Institute of Religion (the two merged in 1950). In the 1920s, following the Nineteenth Amendment granting women the right to vote and the heightened expectation that now all barriers to woman's full equality would fall in American life, a small number of women entered rabbinical school, hoping to become rabbis.

The first was Martha Neumark. In 1921, the seventeen-year-old student at Hebrew Union College launched a two-year-long debate over whether or not the college would ordain women rabbis. In the course of that debate Reform rabbis affirmed, in principle, that "woman cannot justly be denied the privilege of ordination" (Central Conf. of Amer. Rabbis, p. 51). But the college's board of governors, fearing this act would constitute an irrevocable break with the more traditional sectors of American Jewry, prevented her from achieving her goal.

Neumark was not the only woman in the interwar years to challenge the exclusion of females from the rabbinate. IRMA LEVY LINDHEIM, DORA ASKOWITH, and, most important, Helen Levinthal (later Lyons) raised the very same challenge. In 1939, the Jewish Institute of Religion awarded Helen Levinthal a master of Hebrew literature, not the rabbinical ordination she had sought. By then she had completed the entire rabbinical curriculum and written a thesis on woman suffrage from the point of view of Jewish law. Subsequently, like Ray Frank, Levinthal for a time exercised informal rabbinic leadership, preaching at High Holiday services in Brooklyn in 1939. But eventually she, like many of the other pioneers before and after her, settled down to a life as wife, mother, and exemplary Jewish volunteer.

The failure of each of these women to become a rabbi illustrates the roles—student, teacher, and principal; volunteer, especially for Jewish women's organizations; and most importantly, wife and mother—

sanctioned for American Jewish women at mid-century. Women could do many things in American Judaism, but they could not become rabbis.

Within the next quarter century, however, this would change. In 1972 in Reform Judaism, in 1974 in Reconstructionist Judaism, and in 1985 in Conservative Judaism, the first women received rabbinic ordination. That these women succeeded where those before them had failed reflected the coalescence of several factors in American Jewish life in the second half of the twentieth century. Surely, the long history of the consideration of women's ordination paved the way, especially in Reform Judaism, for its leaders to accept women rabbis at last. Of inestimable significance, too, was the new wave of American feminism, launched in the 1960s, which renewed the nineteenth-century call for women's access to the professions. The elite seminaries producing rabbis thus became another of the exclusive male institutions and restricted professions then under siege, as, in a changing political climate, women fought and won access to places historically closed to them. As American Judaism—especially its more liberal sectors—continued to accommodate to the changing tempo of the lives of its members, equal rights for women came to sit squarely on its agenda in the 1970s and the 1980s. These factors and others, including the increasing numbers of American—and American Jewish—women, especially married women with children, entering the workforce, help to account for the dismantling of the barricade to women's ordination. Yet in the 1970s and 1980s, the successful resolution to the question continued to depend, as it had since 1897, upon the perseverance of individual women who continued to push for ordination for themselves.

In 1964, when Sally Priesand crossed the threshold of the Cincinnati campus of the Hebrew Union College–Jewish Institute of Religion as a freshman in its undergraduate program, she followed the path of the pioneers, like Martha Neumark, who had already raised the question in the very same halls. But while the earlier unsuccessful challengers stood largely in isolation, the future Rabbi Priesand found an ever-widening circle of supporters, whose imaginations were sparked by the nascent feminist movement. Most important, she won the favor of Hebrew Union College president Nelson Glueck, who decided to act on what his predecessors had simply asserted, woman's right to ordination. At the same time, both the Anglo-Jewish and the national press carefully monitored Priesand's progress as a symbol of women's liberation and the inroads it was making in American religion. In June 1972, Priesand became the first woman in America ordained a rabbi. (In 1935, in Germany, Regina Jonas,

*Of course, there are many ways to change history. Pictured above in July of 1973 are newlyweds
Deborah and Mark Hurvitz, the first husband and wife team studying for the rabbinate.
They are talking to Dr. Alfred Gottschalk, the president of the Hebrew Union College.
They attended the college's California branch. [American Jewish Archives]*

who later perished in the Holocaust, had received private Reform ordination.) Already it was clear she would not be the last.

In Philadelphia at the same time, a new rabbinical school, the Reconstructionist Rabbinical College, had also admitted its first students. Once the liberal wing of Conservative Judaism, Reconstructionist Judaism had since split off. In 1968 its rabbinical school opened, and women were among its first students. In 1974, Sandy Eisenberg Sasso achieved rabbinic ordination there.

While the lengthy battle for women's rabbinic ordination was fought largely on the ground of Reform Judaism, the campaign blazed fiercely in Conservative Judaism. In fact, Conservatism was never utterly removed from the topic. Each time the debate about women's ordination swelled in Reform Judaism, Conservative leaders found themselves reacting to the

issue, much as Solomon Schechter had in his meeting with Henrietta Szold. But as Seminary officials routinely diverted women interested in rabbinical school to teacher-training programs, Conservative Judaism failed to develop a pioneering core of challengers to the historic status quo.

The question surfaced again in Conservatism in 1972, at the height of the contemporary wave of American feminism, and this time it refused to go away. In the spring of 1972, a group of committed Conservative Jewish—and passionately feminist—women, well aware of Priesand's impending ordination, vociferously demanded equality in their branch of American Judaism. At the same time, a handful of other women found their requests for rabbinical school applications from the Jewish Theological Seminary denied. National media attention involved a wide audience in the debate. In particular, in these years the *New York Times* published feature-length articles on the first women in Conservative synagogues in pararabbinic jobs and those who abandoned Conservative Judaism to become Reform and Reconstructionist rabbis.

The result was that Conservative Jewish leaders found themselves inextricably entangled in the issue of women's rabbinic ordination. For a long decade between 1972 and 1983, they engaged in an intricate political dance of shifting alliances, studies undertaken, commissions formed, hearings held, motions tabled, and votes counted. Finally, in 1983, over the objection of a number of colleagues who boycotted the vote, the faculty of Jewish Theological Seminary agreed to admit women to the rabbinical school. In 1985, Amy Eilberg, one of a cluster of women waiting in the wings for a favorable decision, biding their time by taking the curriculum necessary for rabbinic ordination, was ordained.

The debate around women rabbis, whether divorced from the women contending for the honor or raised by those who were its pioneers, reveals an unexpectedly long and broad history of this question within American Judaism. That no sector of American Judaism has been immune from the challenge of women's religious equality, symbolically represented by female ordination, is evident from the recent emergence of this old question among a new sector of American Jewry, the modern Orthodox. In the 1990s, the first advocates of women's rabbinic ordination in Orthodoxy and the first women seeking admission to its rabbinical school, Yeshiva University, have roused some of America's most traditional Jews to realize that here too the debate is underway.

The prehistory of women rabbis opened with the raising of the question over a century ago and closed with the ordination of the very first women. By 1996, 255 women had been ordained at Reform Judaism's Hebrew Union College–Jewish Institute of Religion, including, starting in 1992, the first women ordained in Israel. Of the 184 rabbis ordained at the Reconstructionist Rabbinical College between 1973 and 1996, seventy-three were women. Between 1985 and 1996, Conservatism's Jewish Theological Seminary ordained fifty-one women.

Just as Mary M. Cohen's character had stunned her audience by posing the very notion of women in the rabbinate, this first generation of female rabbis has jolted American Judaism. Not content with simply replicating what they found in synagogue life, the first women rabbis self-consciously perceived themselves trailblazers. They voiced, to some ears stridently, a critique of Judaism's status quo, arguing that it was largely created by men and that, for far too long, it had marginalized women. Standing in their own eyes as pathbreakers, these rabbis have striven collectively to push American Judaism toward an egalitarian future, one which fully incorporates women's many different voices.

But before the very first female rabbis could begin to raise their particular concerns, they had to win approval from a wide swath of American Jewry. The very first women in the rabbinate discovered that ordination was but the first hurdle. Those ordained in the 1970s and early 1980s, before a significant cohort of women rabbis emerged, found themselves struggling for acceptance. Congregations refused to interview them for jobs. Community boards of rabbis opposed their participation. Conservatism's Rabbinical Assembly, the collective of rabbis that for years had routinely admitted to its ranks rabbis trained at Reform seminaries, turned away qualified female applicants.

At the same time, the new rabbis found themselves struggling to overcome the conviction that this was one job women could not possibly do. Congregants worried that women rabbis could not carry heavy Torah scrolls. They feared the rabbis would be too soft-spoken for the job, or alternatively that they would always preach on feminism. Unaccustomed to seeing women in the ritual garb of *kippot* and *tallith*, the congregants displayed their sense that women rabbis disturbed the traditions they knew.

Drawing upon the strategies pioneered by the feminist movement, the first female rabbis organized to challenge these objections. Via Reform's Women's Rabbinic Network and the Central Conference of American Rabbis Task Force on Women in the Rabbinate, they began addressing these and a host of other issues, like maternity-leave policies, which had never concerned an all-male rabbinate.

As more and more women entered the ranks of the rabbinate, some of the initial difficulties waned and new questions emerged. Among them was whether or not women rabbis perform their roles differently than their male colleagues; and, if so, what bodes for the future of American Judaism. Extensive interviews reveal that the first generation of women rabbis contend—although their male peers by and large deny this—that, as women, they offer a different model for the rabbinate. Self-consciously reflecting the influential work of psychologist CAROL GILLIGAN, the female rabbis describe themselves as more approachable, prone to involve their congregants, and likely to speak sermons in a different voice.

Determined to bring their perspectives as American and Jewish—and often as feminist—women to bear upon American Judaism, many in this first generation have sharply critiqued Judaism's historical marginalization of women's religious activities. They have sought to mark the major milestones of women's biological lives, to push for female-inclusive and gender-neutral liturgy, and to seek new interpretations for texts read largely in the past through male eyes. In particular, several have written for children, believing that the key to change lies in shaping the next generation's perspective on gender and Judaism.

In so doing, these new leaders of American Judaism have pioneered and challenged not only the institution of the rabbinate but also American Jews and American Judaism to listen, at long last, to the voices of women.

BIBLIOGRAPHY

Central Conference of American Rabbis. *Yearbook*, Vol. 32 (1922); Clar, Reva, and William M. Kramer. "The Girl Rabbi of the Golden West: The Adventurous Life of Ray Frank in Nevada, California and the Northwest." *Western States Jewish History* 18 (1986): 99–111, 23–236, 336–351; Fishman, Sylvia Barack. *A Breath of Life: Feminism in the American Jewish Community* (1993); Frank, Ray. "Women in the Synagogue." In *Papers of the Jewish Women's Congress* (1894); Greenberg, Simon, ed. *The Ordination of Women as Rabbis: Studies and Responsa* (1988); Nadell, Pamela S. "'Top Down' or 'Bottom Up': Two Movements for Women's Rabbinic Ordination." In *An Inventory of Promises: Essays in Honor of Moses Rischin*, edited by Jeffrey Gurock and Marc Lee Raphael (1995), and "The Women Who Would Be Rabbis." In *Gender and Judaism*, edited by T.M. Rudavsky (1995); Nadell, Pamela S., and Rita J. Simon. "Ladies of the Sisterhood: Women in the American Reform Synagogue, 1900–1930." In *Active Voices: Women in Jewish Culture*, edited by Maurie Sacks (1985); Portnoy, Mindy Avra. *Ima on the Bimah: My Mommy Is a Rabbi*. Steffi Karen Rubin, illustrator (1986); Simon, Rita J., and Pamela S. Nadell. "In the Same Voice or Is It Different? Gender and the Clergy." *Sociology of Religion* 56, 1 (1995): 63–70, and "Lay Leaders' Views About Female Rabbis and Ministers." *Shofar* 13, 4 (Summer 1995): 52–58, and "Teachers, Preachers, and Feminists in America: Women Rabbis," *Shofar* 10, 1 (Fall 1991): 2–10; Simon, Rita J., Angela Scanlan, and Pamela S. Nadell. "Rabbis and Ministers: Women of the Book and the Cloth." In *Gender and Religion*, edited by William Swatos (1993), also in Rita Simon, *Rabbis, Lawyers, Immigrants, Thieves: Exploring Women's Roles* (1993); Szold, Henrietta. Letter to Judge Mayer Sulzberger, February 14, 1903. Henrietta Zold [sic] Papers, Jewish Historical Society of Maryland; Wertheimer, Jack. *A People Divided: Judaism in Contemporary America* (1993).

PAMELA S. NADELL

RABINOFF, SOPHIE (1889–1957)

Sophie Rabinoff was a pediatrician and professor of medicine whose innovative work helped to establish the fields of public health and preventive medicine in the United States and Palestine. In a career that spanned five decades, she brought basic health care and disease control to the struggling residents of Palestine and to some of the poorest urban populations in America.

Born in Mogileff, Russia, on May 19, 1889, Rabinoff was barely a year old when her parents, Louis and Rose Rabinoff, immigrated to the United States. The family settled in New York City, where Rabinoff was educated in public schools and eventually at HUNTER COLLEGE (1906–1908). She went on to study medicine at the Women's Medical College of Pennsylvania, in Philadelphia. After her graduation in 1913, she became the first female intern at the Beth Israel Hospital in New York. She completed a three-year residency in pediatrics at the New York Home for Infants, where she participated in important research on childhood diseases such as rickets, scurvy, and diphtheria. She also conducted research on infant feedings and nutrition.

With this specialized training, Rabinoff was selected by HADASSAH founder HENRIETTA SZOLD to be part of the first American Zionist Medical Unit (1918–1919), a team of doctors and nurses sent by Hadassah to Palestine. The unit's mission was to treat emergency medical needs and introduce basic principles of health care. Rabinoff, the only female physician in the group, organized the region's first clinic for the treatment of Jewish and Arab children.

After returning to the United States in 1919, Rabinoff briefly pursued private medical practice, but her interest in public health eventually prevailed. By 1921, she was working as a pediatrician for the New York Department of Health. In 1934, she was appointed a health officer for New York City and assigned to organize the new health districts of the Lower West Side and the Lower East Side. In 1938, she became the health officer for the East Harlem district, one of the most overcrowded and underprivileged areas of the city. Her success led to her appointment as senior health officer for three districts of the Bronx, an area encompassing half a million people, in 1944. That same year, she received a master of science in public health from Columbia University.

In 1947, Rabinoff decided to return to East Harlem and address the alarming rates of tuberculosis, venereal disease, and infant mortality among the growing population of Puerto Rican immigrants. Earning the trust and respect of local community leaders, she gradually involved them in establishing programs of health education, inoculations, and other basic medical care.

Rabinoff joined the faculty of New York Medical College as a clinical instructor in public health in 1939. At the college, she supervised the fieldwork of senior medical students. In 1951, she was made a full professor and the director of the college's department of public health and industrial medicine, a post she held until her retirement in 1957. She died in October 1957 at the hospital where she helped to train many future physicians.

Rabinoff was the author of several articles, including "Nutrition Problems in a Community Health Program" (1939) and "Progress in Public Health During the Last Half Century" (1955). She was a diplomate of the American Board of Preventive Medicine and Public Health, a fellow of the American Medical Association and the American Public Health Association, and a member of numerous other professional organizations. In 1957, the Women's Medical College of Pennsylvania presented her with its Alumnae Achievement Award in recognition of her long and creative medical career.

SELECTED WORKS BY SOPHIE RABINOFF

"Nutrition Problems in a Community Health Program." *Women's Medical Journal* (May 1939); "Progress in Public Health During the Last Half Century." *Journal of the American Medical Association* (February 1955).

BIBLIOGRAPHY

Journal of the American Medical Association 165, no. 14 (December 7, 1957); *NYTimes*, July 8, 1951, and Obituary. *NYTimes*, October 3, 1957, 29:2; Women's Medical College of Pennsylvania, Philadelphia. Alumnae questionnaire, April 1953, and News release, June 4, 1957; *WWIAJ* (1938).

SHEILA SEGAL

RADNER, GILDA (1946–1989)

Known to television audiences as bumbling Emily Litella, scatterbrained Roseanne Roseannadanna, and nerdy Lisa Loopner, comedian Gilda Radner shot to stardom on NBC's *Saturday Night Live* (SNL). Hailed by critics as the next Lucille Ball, Radner's success in television in the 1970s led to a brief film career, tragically cut short by cancer at age forty-two.

Gilda Radner was born June 28, 1946, into the prosperous Detroit Jewish family of Herman and Henrietta (Dworkin) Radner and older brother Michael. Herman's father, George Ratkowsky, had emigrated from Lithuania to New York City, and later to Detroit, where he established a successful kosher meat business. Herman, despite only a fifth-grade education, made the

The ditziness of her Saturday Night Live *characters belied the shrewdness of her comedy. Gilda Radner went on to a make several successful movies, but her promising career was cut short when she died of cancer in 1989. She is shown here as her character Roseanne Roseannadanna. [New York Public Library]*

family fortune from an Ontario brewery he purchased in the 1920s. Radner's mother, Henrietta, was an aspiring ballet dancer who worked as a legal secretary until she married Herman in October 1937.

Radner remembers her childhood as one of the most difficult periods of her life. Because her mother could not tolerate the Detroit winters, the family spent four months each year in Florida, disrupting the school year, and preventing Radner from making close friends. Radner became attached instead to her governess, "Dibby" (Elizabeth Clementine Gillies), the model for her SNL character Emily Litella. When schoolchildren teased Radner for being overweight, "Dibby" provided Radner with her first lesson in comedy, telling her to "say you're fat before they can. Just make a joke about it and laugh." Her relationship with her mother was distant and somewhat competitive, but Radner felt very close to her father, who died of brain cancer when she was fourteen years old. Indulging his own show-business fantasies, Herman encouraged her to perform, gave her dancing lessons, and often took her to Broadway road shows in downtown Detroit. While not religiously observant in her adult life, Radner had a clearly Jewish upbringing. Her brother had a bar mitzvah, she attended Sunday and Hebrew school, and sat shiva for her father when he died. For comic material, she often drew on the Jewish community in which she grew up—in skits about the gum-cracking Jewish coed Rhonda Weiss or in her famous "fake" commercial for skin-tight "Jewess jeans."

Radner attended the University of Michigan, majoring in drama, but never graduated. She moved with a boyfriend to Toronto and landed a part in the musical *Godspell.* She later joined the Toronto company of Second City Comedy, an improvisational comedy troupe, where she worked with Dan Aykroyd, John Belushi, and Bill Murray.

Radner moved to New York in 1973, joining many of her Second City friends in "The National Lampoon Show," an Off-Broadway cabaret. In 1975, producer Lorne Michaels chose Radner (whom he had seen perform in Toronto) and other members of the Second City company for his new late-night comedy/variety show. Gilda Radner premiered with the Not Ready for Prime Time Players on *Saturday Night Live* in October 1975, and continued to perform with the troupe until 1980, garnering a 1978 Emmy Award for her work on the show.

While life as a television star was glamorous and fulfilling, Radner suffered from the pitfalls that can accompany fame. Under constant public scrutiny, her lifelong insecurity about her appearance resurfaced, manifesting itself in bouts of bulimia. And although Radner clung to the SNL crowd as a surrogate "family," she often voiced her desire for marriage and a family of her own. Radner took her SNL act to Broadway in 1979 (*Gilda Radner—Live from New York*), where she received mixed reviews from critics, but met her first husband, G.E. Smith, the bandleader for the show, whom she married in a civil ceremony in 1980.

Radner appeared in Buck Henry's film *First Family* (1980), and then in *Hanky Panky* (1982), during which she met Gene Wilder. She described the meeting as love at first sight. She soon divorced Smith (1982), and made a second movie with Wilder, *The Woman in Red* (1984). Wilder and Radner were married in the south of France in September 1984. They made one more movie together, *Haunted Honeymoon* (1986), before Radner was diagnosed with ovarian cancer. Between chemotherapy treatments, Radner wrote her autobiography, *It's Always Something,* in which she detailed her struggle with cancer and the aid she received from the Wellness Community.

Gilda Radner died in Los Angeles on May 20, 1989. She employed her Jewish identity as an essential element in her comedy, and her affectionate and incisive characterizations represented an important breakthrough in the visibility of Jewish women on television.

FILMOGRAPHY

All You Need Is Cash (1978); *First Family* (1980); *Gilda Live* [film and record] (1980); *Hanky Panky* (1982); *Haunted Honeymoon* (1986); *The Last Detail* (1973); *Mr. Mike's Mondo Video* (1979); *Movers and Shakers* (1985); *The Woman in Red* (1984).

BIBLIOGRAPHY

Current Biography (February 1980): 29–32; Hevesi, Dennis. "Gilda Radner, 42, Comic Original of 'Saturday Night Live' Zaniness." *NYTimes,* May 21, 1989, 46; Kaplan, Robert. "Gilda, I Can't Forget You." *NYTimes,* June 2, 1989, A31; Radner, Gilda. *It's Always Something* (1989); Saltman, David. *Gilda: An Intimate Portrait* (1992); Stone, Elizabeth. "Gilda Radner: Goodbye; Roseanne, Hello, Broadway." *NYTimes Magazine,* November 9, 1980, sec. 6, p. 42; Young, Tracy. "America's Last Sweetheart." *Mirabella* (September 1989): 122.

ANDREA MOST

RAINER, LUISE (b. 1910)

Largely forgotten today, Luise Rainer arguably is as notable for her meteoric rise to stardom in 1930s Hollywood as she is for her subsequent obscurity. Born in Vienna, Austria, on January 12, 1910, she had already achieved acclaim on the European stage and screen in her twenties. She arrived in Hollywood amid a wave of European artists, writers, scientists, and other intellectuals fleeing Nazi persecution. A protégé of the legendary Max Reinhardt, German theatrical director and fellow refugee, she played in her most memorable roles opposite William Powell in *The Great Ziegfeld* (MGM, 1936) and Paul Muni in *The Good Earth* (MGM, 1937). Her performances in these films earned her both raves and an unprecedented two successive Oscars. As part of the gallery of Metro-Goldwyn-Mayer luminaries, she also helped define the studio's reputation as the "Tiffany" of motion picture companies in Depression-era America.

Within three years, however, Rainer's career had vaporized almost as quickly as its success had taken shape. Columnist Louella Parsons diagnosed Rainer with what the influential Hollywood reporter called the "Oscar curse." In both *The Great Ziegfeld* and *The Good Earth*, Rainer had played a long-suffering, indefatigable, and loyal wife to celebrated impresario Florenz Ziegfeld and a Chinese peasant, respectively. Although MGM had touted her as the next Garbo, her subsequent roles typecast her as an obedient, supportive spouse. For her part, Rainer claims that she tried to pursue roles featuring stronger, more independent women. In a 1988 interview, for example, she told *People Weekly* that she attempted to convince MGM to give her the role of Marie Curie. Greer Garson eventually played the famous French scientist.

While a poor succession of studio-imposed roles and a disastrous marriage to playwright Clifford Odets have been proffered as explanations for the quick demise of Rainer's career, the roles that had garnered Rainer such acclaim were themselves becoming anachronistic. As the Roosevelt administration prepared the country for war, encouraging industry to usher women into a burgeoning wartime workforce, the image of the obedient, long-suffering wife appeared increasingly out of step with this new social reality. Today, one of Rainer's greatest roles labors under condescending ethnic stereotyping as well. However compelling, the performances of both Paul Muni and Rainer evidence that Asians and other minorities were largely visible only through stereotypes rendered by white actors and actresses.

In offscreen life, Rainer hardly fit the image of the lachrymose heroines she often portrayed. Along with Odets, Rainer joined other Hollywood talents as a part of the Popular Front, a broad-based coalition of leftist political activism that emerged out of Los Angeles during the 1930s. She served as one of the founding members (along with Muni, journalist DOROTHY PARKER, novelist and playwright LILLIAN HELLMAN, actress Gale Sondergaard, and other Hollywood notables) of the Motion Picture Artists Committee and the Joint Anti-Fascist Refugee Committee, organizations devoted to the cause of Republican Spain against the totalitarian forces of Generalissimo Francisco Franco.

With the collapse of the Popular Front by the late 1930s and her divorce of Odets in 1940, however, Rainer increasingly eluded public view. Her last Hollywood film—*Hostages* (1943)—about the underground resistance movement, received a lukewarm reception. Rainer continued to make infrequent guest appearances on American television throughout the 1950s and 1960s, including an episode for the thriller anthology series *Suspense* ("Torment," March 30, 1954) and opposite silent film star Ramon Navarro in the World War II series *Combat* ("Finest Hour," Decem-

During her heyday in the 1930s, Luise Rainer helped MGM gain its reputation as the Tiffany of the motion picture industry. One of the few artists ever to receive two successive Oscars, she won the Best Actress award for her performances in The Great Ziegfeld *(1936) and* The Good Earth *(1937). [New York Public Library]*

ber 21, 1965), in which she plays a sympathetic countess. In 1988, she appeared in "A Dancer," a short film produced for Italian television.

Aside from the initial publicity Rainer received in the popular press for *The Great Ziegfeld* and *The Good Earth*, very little information on her exists. Indiana University at Bloomington has some of her personal papers catalogued in the Clifford Odets collection. For the sixtieth anniversary of the Oscars, in 1988, *People Weekly* interviewed Rainer. At that time she was living in Switzerland with her second husband, publisher Robert Knittel.

FILMOGRAPHY

The Big City/Skyscraper Wilderness (1937); *Dramatic School* (1938); *The Emperor's Candlesticks* (1937); *Escapade* (1935); *The Good Earth* (1937); *The Great Waltz* (1938); *The Great Ziegfeld* (1936); *Heute kommt's drauf an* (1933);

Hostages (1943); *Ja der Himmel über Wien* (1930); *Sehnsucht 202* (1932); *The Toy Wife* (1938).

BIBLIOGRAPHY

Baskette, K. "Know Luise Rainer." *Photoplay* 48, no. 5 (1935): 44; Bronner, E. "Luise Rainer." *Films in Review* 6, no. 8 (1955): 390; Ceplair, Larry, and Steven Englund. *The Inquisition in Hollywood: Politics in the Film Community, 1930–1960* (1983); Crichton, K. "Girl Who Hates Movies." *Collier's*, May 23, 1936: 36; Daugherty, F. "Luise Rainer in a New Role." *Christian Science Monitor Magazine*, August 24, 1938: 4; Fletcher, A.W. "The Tempestuous Life Story of Luise Rainer." *Photoplay* 50, no. 1 (1936): 24, and 50, no. 2 (1936): 74; Hall, L. "The Romantic Story of Luise Rainer's Surprise Marriage." *Photoplay* 51, no. 3 (1937): 50; Hamilton, S. "What's Happened to Rainer?" *Photoplay* 52, no. 6 (1938): 22; "Happy 60th Oscar," *People Weekly* (April 11, 1988): 85. Reprinted in Academic Index Database; Katz, Ephraim. "Luise Rainer." *Katz's Film Encyclopedia*. Reprinted in Microsoft Corp., *Cinemania* CD-ROM (1996); "Thank Offering; Shaw's Saint Joan." *Time* (March 18, 1940): 68; "Where Are They Now?" *Newsweek* (April 15, 1963): 20.

STEVEN CARR

RAND, AYN (1905–1982)

The life and work of Ayn Rand, the novelist and philosopher who promoted an ethics called "Objectivism," provide ample evidence for those who believe that human beings are inherently self-contradictory and illogical. In her novels, Rand glorified the self-made man who aggressively demonstrated his superiority over the masses through his business acumen. As a writer, Rand had little to do with entrepreneurial activities. While she did eventually make money from her writing, she always lived frugally. Her husband of fifty years was a quiet and reserved man, never financially successful, who was happiest in his garden or painting at his easel. Her ideal physical types were tall, blond, muscular men and delicate, graceful blonde women—she herself was small, dark, and never at ease with her body. She believed passionately in the importance of the individual, yet her books developed a cultlike following among the millions of people who read them. The chief irony is that Rand became best known for her insistence on the primacy of human reason.

The eldest of three sisters, Ayn Rand was born Alissa Rosenbaum on February 2, 1905, in St. Petersburg, Russia, to Fronz and Anna Rosenbaum. Her father, a pharmacist, had his own shop, a rare position for Jews in Russia. A precocious child, Alyssa declared herself an atheist in her early teens, and while she never denied her Jewish heritage, she also never softened her opposition to religion or any other form of "mysticism." The privations she and her family endured as a result of the Russian Revolution, including the Bolsheviks taking possession of her father's business, affected her deeply. Somehow she managed to survive the purges of bourgeois students long enough to obtain a degree in history from the University of Leningrad in 1924. At the university, she took a few classes in American political history and found the principles expressed in the Declaration of Independence fascinating.

Despite the progressively isolationist policy of the Soviets, some Western exports still found their way to Russia in the 1920s. For Alyssa, the most important were American movies. Conditions in the United States—at least as depicted on the screen—impressed her as strongly as conditions at home repelled her, so when distant cousins provided the miraculous opportunity to travel to the United States, she did not hesitate. She turned twenty-one in Berlin, on her way to America. At immigration, she announced that her first name was Ayn (pronounced to rhyme with "pine"). Shortly after, she chose the second part of her beloved typewriter's brand name for her surname.

Deciding that Chicago, her cousins' home, was too provincial, she moved to California to write for the movies. A fluke encounter with Cecil B. DeMille on her second day in Hollywood led to a job as an extra in the film *The King of Kings*. This gave her a glimpse of a bit player named Frank O'Connor, the man she would marry in April 1929. But her ambition to write for the movies was not so easily fulfilled, and she scraped by for years on the salary she earned working in RKO's wardrobe department, writing in her spare time. Her first break came with a stage play *Night of January 16th*, which was produced on Broadway during the 1935 season. Royalties from the modestly successful play gave her the freedom to concentrate on her writing.

Rand's first novel, *We the Living*, appeared in 1936. A melodrama dismissed by most reviewers as overbearingly anti-Soviet, it quickly went out of print. Since her husband rarely worked, Rand had little but her own passion to support her during her next major project, the novel that was to become *The Fountainhead*. While writing *The Fountainhead*, Rand wrote a futuristic novella entitled *Anthem* about the struggle of two lovers in a collective society to reclaim the concept of a self. At the time, only a British publisher would touch it. A stage version of *We the Living* called *The Unconquered* also failed. Eventually Rand found

Known best for her two novels, The Fountainhead *and* Atlas Shrugged, *Ayn Rand was never taken seriously by critics or philosophers. Despite this, her books are still best-sellers, and her philosophy of ethics, called "objectivism," is still debated by her fans. [New York Public Library]*

studio work again, reading screenplays for Paramount. This job provided the contact with an editor at Bobbs-Merrill who, on the strength of the first several chapters, promised to publish *The Fountainhead.*

After a slow start and generally unsympathetic reviews upon its publication in May 1943, the book became a best-seller, and by the end of 1949, it had sold half a million copies. The protagonist, an architect named Howard Roark, embodied Rand's ideal man, an individualist who would assert his own convictions in the face of complete social opposition. In the novel's climactic scene, Roark blows up a public housing project (before occupation) rather than see his vision and plans grossly distorted. Yet Roark is not the thorough outcast he might seem. At his subsequent trial, he speaks so eloquently about his beliefs that the jury refuses to convict him. Rand wrote the screenplay for the movie version, starring Gary Cooper and Patricia Neal, which was released in

1949. The popular success of *The Fountainhead* established Rand's career as a novelist and put her on secure financial ground for the first time in her life.

Her increasing fame brought her hundreds of fan letters and enlarged her social circle. By the early 1950s, she had cultivated a devoted coterie consisting mostly of college students and recent graduates eager to emulate her fictional heroes. Two of them, Nathan Blumenthal and his eventual wife, Barbara Weidman, apparently became so important to Rand that, in 1951, she and her husband followed them to New York City, where Rand and her husband spent the rest of their lives. In New York, Rand continued to work on what would be her last novel, *Atlas Shrugged.* In regular Saturday night salons, she would share portions of her work-in-progress with her group.

Rand and her husband served as witnesses at Blumenthal and Weidman's wedding in 1953, testifying to their close relationship. In her 1986 biography of Rand, Weidman claims the dubious distinction of naming the sexual attraction between her own husband and Rand in late 1954. Once that element was acknowledged, both Rand and Blumenthal (now named Nathaniel Branden) evidently felt justified by Rand's own tenets in embarking on an intense secret affair. According to Rand, sexual desire should go hand-in-hand with intellectual respect and shared ideals. Given their mutual interests and commitments, it was inevitable for a physical passion to develop between them—and unthinkable for it not to be fulfilled, despite their marriages and the twenty-five-year age difference. When *Atlas Shrugged* appeared—through Random House, after a search for a publishing house that would not cut her work—it carried a joint dedication to her husband and to Branden.

Like *The Fountainhead, Atlas Shrugged* eventually became a best-seller. Like the earlier novel, it attracted negative reviews. Most critics found the premise of the novel—that the most gifted, creative, and successful members of a society are exploited by the untalented and unappreciative masses—only slightly less implausible than the major action of the novel, a strike of geniuses to force an end to their abuse.

Devastated by the poor critical response, exhausted from twelve years of effort, and discouraged by the thought that she might have written all she had to say, Rand withdrew. It was Branden who succeeded in restoring her confidence and supporting her second crest of fame by inaugurating regular lectures on Rand's philosophy. Under the auspices of the Nathaniel Branden Institute, he and several other faithful students offered talks on "The Basic Principles of Objectivism," covering subjects such as "The Nature of Emotions," "Social Metaphysics," "The Ethics of Altruism," and "What is Reason?" The lectures soon drew hundreds of people in New York and expanded to several sites around the country. Sales of *Atlas Shrugged* continued to build—its opening sentence, "Who is John Galt?" became a popular password for those in the know—and Rand flourished in the attention. Although she herself delivered few lectures at Nathaniel Branden Institute, she did tour the country to speak on numerous college campuses. With Branden, she began a monthly called *The Objectivist Newsletter*, later expanded and renamed simply *The Objectivist*. Both versions contained essays by Rand, Branden, and other associates (including perhaps her most celebrated admirer, the economist Alan Greenspan, now chairman of the Federal Reserve Board) that analyzed current political events and applied the principles of Objectivism to everyday life. The last books Rand published were collections of essays taken from the Objectivist periodicals.

The cohesion of the Objectivist movement shattered irrevocably, however, in 1968 when Branden finally admitted to Rand that he would not resume their long-suspended affair. In response, Rand denounced Branden, accusing him of betraying essential Objectivist principles, and forced him to sever all connections with Objectivist activities, including the institute bearing his name. Most devotees accepted her judgment and condemned Branden, even without particulars, but the upheaval occurred at a particularly inopportune moment. Rand had begun to lose her primary audience, usually young, idealistic adults, to other causes, and her customary argumentativeness in public appearances became less refreshing, more defensive and alienating. Criticism of Rand's sexual politics began to figure as prominently as attacks on her doctrine of "rational selfishness." The first sexual encounter in *The Fountainhead* between Howard Roark and Dominique Francon became emblematic of a peculiarly American romanticization of rape, at least according to feminists like Susan Brownmiller. Circulation losses pushed her to reduce *The Objectivist* to a smaller form again, called *The Ayn Rand Letter*, which appeared more and more irregularly until she ended publication in 1975.

Other personal losses took a toll as well: Her husband began to show signs of dementia years before his death in 1979, and the joyous news that her youngest and favorite sister Nora still lived led only to a brief and painfully disappointing reunion in 1973. She made a strong recovery from surgery for lung cancer in 1974, but she no longer had the stamina or the focus to devote herself to any large writing project.

Apart from intermittent appearances in television interviews, Ayn Rand's last regular speaking engagement was her annual lecture at Boston's Ford Hall Forum. Nevertheless, she had completed about one-fourth of a screenplay for a television miniseries of *Atlas Shrugged* and was in the midst of preparing her next Ford Hall lecture at the time of her death, on March 6, 1982. Several hundred mourners waited in the cold to enter the Manhattan funeral home where her body was laid out, alongside a six-foot floral dollar sign, the following day. The graveside service in Valhalla, New York, consisted only of a reading of Kipling's poem "If" before Rand was buried beside her husband.

An assessment of Rand's reputation a decade and a half after her death must account for several contradictory factors. Few professional philosophers take her work at all seriously, yet many groups of readers and fans still debate and write about her theories. Her work continues to appeal to those who search for non-religious answers about human progress and agency. Certainly her declaration that selfishness is a virtue and altruism a vice is contrary to traditional Jewish values—yet her exaltation of personal ambition is not so different from that of many Russian Jewish immigrants of her generation who savored the relative freedom of America. Despite their dismissal by the critical establishment, her books continue to sell. Together, her novels have sold approximately twenty-five million copies, a figure that still grows by about 250,000 every year. Rand might not have succeeded in achieving the immediate influence of a crusading novelist like Harriet Beecher Stowe, as she had hoped, but her popularity today testifies to an enduring appeal.

SELECTED WORKS BY AYN RAND

Anthem (1938); *Atlas Shrugged* (1957); *The Fountainhead* (1943); *Night of January 16th* (1936); *The Virtue of Selfishness* (1965); *We the Living* (1936).

BIBLIOGRAPHY

Branden, Barbara. *The Passion of Ayn Rand* (1986); Branden, Nathaniel. *Judgment Day: My Years with Ayn Rand* (1989); Den Uyl, Douglas J., and Douglas B. Rasmussen, eds. *The Philosophic Thought of Ayn Rand* (1984); Gladstein, Mimi Reiser. *The Ayn Rand Companion* (1984); McDowell, Edwin. "Ayn Rand: Novelist with a Message." *NYTimes*, March 9, 1982, sec. 2, 6; Pierpont, Claudia Roth. "Twilight of the Goddess." *New Yorker* (July 24, 1995): 70–81; Saxon, Wolfgang. "Ayn Rand, 'Fountainhead' Author, Dies." *NYTimes*, March 7, 1982, 36; Sciabarra, Chris M. *Ayn Rand: The Russian Radical* (1995).

CATHERINE DALIGGA

RAPOPORT, LYDIA (1923–1971)

Lydia Rapoport was a social worker, professor, caseworker, and advocate of social change. Her contribution to crisis theory shaped current treatment. She was born in Vienna on March 8, 1923. Eugenia Margulies, her mother, was born in Poland and trained as a teacher. Her father, Samuel Rapoport, studied law in Vienna, but his real interests were in language and music. He was a gifted linguist, competent in seventeen languages. He played the violin and wrote music reviews for a newspaper. Lydia shared his affinity for music, becoming a skilled harpsichordist and pianist. In 1906, Samuel had immigrated to Philadelphia, Pennsylvania, but finding American society lacking in cultural resources, he returned to Vienna, where he found work as a grain trader. Responding to increased anti-Semitism and resurgent German nationalism, he immigrated again in 1928, this time to New York City, and became a translator. The rest of the family remained in Vienna until 1932, while Emanuel, Lydia's older brother, finished academic high school.

Lydia Rapoport attended New York public schools, and graduated from HUNTER COLLEGE, Phi Beta Kappa, at age nineteen. After receiving her master's degree from Smith College Graduate School of Social Work at age twenty-one, she became a caseworker in Chicago, and later a supervisor at the Jewish Children's Bureau and at Michael Reese Hospital. She trained in working with emotionally disturbed children, receiving a certificate in child therapy from the Institute of Psychoanalysis. Rapoport earned a Fulbright scholarship in 1952 to the London School of Economics. She lectured extensively, promoting the strengthening of social work training in Britain. She developed an association with the renowned Tavistock Clinic, a mental health training institute.

In 1954, Rapoport moved to California, where Emanuel lived with his family. She worked as a field supervisor for students at the University of California at Berkeley. She joined the faculty a year later, received tenure in 1963, and became a full professor in 1969.

Rapoport spent a year at the Harvard School of Public Health in 1959–1960, studying with Eric Lindemann, an authority on the effects of crisis and trauma. Rapoport's work is an integral part of the foundation of current crisis intervention and crisis-oriented brief therapy. She identified the goals of crisis intervention: relief of symptoms, restoration of precrisis functioning, understanding of precipitants, and identification of remedial measures. This model continues in use today. While at Harvard, she also studied the crisis reaction of parents of premature infants with Gerald Caplan, who had done postwar studies on the impact of crisis on immigrant children in Israel. Rapoport did research and casework with families of premature infants.

On her return to Berkeley, she studied the use of mental health consultation as a way to extend the practices of mental health professionals. Rapoport advocated for advanced training and postgraduate programs for community mental health personnel, both to train them for leadership positions and to bring about social change. In 1969, she established the Community Mental Health Training Program at the School of Social Welfare, University of California at Berkeley.

Rapoport took a leave from Berkeley when she was appointed educational consultant at Hebrew University Paul Baerwald School of Social Work in Jerusalem in 1963. She concentrated on cross-cultural family planning projects.

Rapoport was not religious, but she became attached to Israel and the Israeli social work community. She returned often, and began a collection of contemporary Israeli art. She accepted a position as the first United Nations interregional family welfare and planning adviser in 1971. Although it meant a temporary move from Berkeley to New York, Rapoport took the position because it promised international travel. Early in the year, and in spite of illness, she revisited Israel and England. Shortly after her return to New York in July, Rapoport underwent emergency intestinal surgery. While the operation itself was a success, postoperative treatment was not, and she died seven weeks later of bacterial endocarditis on September 6, 1971.

In her brief lifetime, Rapoport added much to current theory and knowledge on crisis intervention, community mental health consultation, social work education, and international family planning. A collection of her works, *Creativity in Social Work*, was published in 1975. Her friends established the Lydia Rapoport Endowment Fund at the Smith College School of Social Work, which supports the Lydia Rapoport Distinguished Visiting Professorship.

BIBLIOGRAPHY

Greenwood, Ernest, Gertrude Wilson, and Robert Apte. "Lydia Rapoport." In Memoriam. University of California at Berkeley, July 1975; Katz, Sanford N., ed. *Creativity in Social Work: Selected Writings of Lydia Rapoport* (1975); *NAW* modern; Trattner, Walter J., ed. *Biographical Dictionary of Social Welfare in America* (1986); *Who's Who of American Women*. 7th ed. (1972–1973).

SUSAN MEDYN

RASKIN, JUDITH (1928–1984)

A lyric soprano whose vocal talent blossomed while she was in college, Judith Raskin developed into one of the outstanding musical artists of the twentieth century. Her impeccable musicianship, convincing acting, and striking beauty kept her in constant demand as an opera performer, as a recitalist, and as a teacher, and she was famous for the absence of ego-centricity often found in prima donnas.

Judith Raskin was born in Yonkers, New York, on June 21, 1928, the only child of American-born parents. Both were public school teachers and strong labor-movement sympathizers. Her father, Harry A. Raskin, a graduate of City College, was an accomplished pianist and chaired the music department at Evander Childs High School. Her mother, Lillian (Mendelson) Raskin, who graduated from HUNTER COLLEGE, taught at Public School 64 in the Bronx.

As a child, Raskin studied piano and violin. She graduated from Roosevelt High School in Yonkers, where she sang in the glee club. After her junior year at Smith College, she married Raymond A. Raskin, a distant cousin, then a navy doctor and later a psychiatrist and psychoanalyst. The ceremony, which took place July 11, 1948, in New York, was performed by the Smith College rabbi, since neither Raskin family was affiliated with a synagogue. Raskin graduated from Smith in 1949. Raymond and Judith Raskin had two children: Jonathan Marvin (b. 1951), a physician in New York, and Lisa Abby (b. 1953), professor of psychology and dean of faculty at Amherst College in Massachusetts.

At Smith, Raskin majored in music (receiving the Harriet Dey Barnum voice scholarship), and studied under Anna Hamlin, with whom she continued to study after graduation. Her first important operatic role was Sister Constance in the December 1957 NBC-TV Opera production of Poulenc's *Dialogues of the Carmelites.* For her 1957 debut with NBC, she had sung Susanna in Mozart's *The Marriage of Figaro* in Ann Arbor, Michigan. Three other major debuts were also in Mozart roles: in 1959, for the New York City Opera, Raskin sang Despina in *Così fan tutte;* in 1962, at the Metropolitan Opera, she repeated the role of Susanna; and in 1963, at Glyndebourne, England, she sang Pamina in *The Magic Flute.*

Baroque opera was another specialty: Raskin appeared in Monteverdi's *The Coronation of Poppea,* and in *Orfeo* (recorded by RCA in Rome in 1965), as well as in Purcell's *The Fairy Queen,* and Rameau's *Les Indes galantes* [The amorous Indies]. Equally comfortable with twentieth-century opera, she created the role

A lyric soprano, Judith Raskin developed into one of the outstanding musical artists of the twentieth century. Emphasizing the poetic approach to music over a purely vocal one, she sang a large variety of concert music including Yiddish songs and the work of Jewish composers. [New York Public Library]

of the bride in the televised 1963 premiere of Gian Carlo Menotti's *Labyrinth,* commissioned by NBC-TV Opera, and the title role in Douglas Moore's *The Ballad of Baby Doe* in Central City, Colorado, in 1956. She also sang Anna Trulove in Igor Stravinsky's *The Rake's Progress* (recorded by CBS in London in 1964). In the course of her operatic career, Raskin sang about twenty roles and performed with the Chicago Lyric Opera, the Santa Fe Opera, the Opera Company of Boston, and the Opera Society of Washington.

Raskin also had an important career singing lieder and orchestral works, especially after leaving the Metropolitan (where her final performance was March 16, 1972). On October 9, 1964, she made her New York recital debut as the eighth Ford Foundation soloist.

Her program included the New York premiere of *Songs of Eve*, a thirty-minute song cycle commissioned from Ezra Laderman. She also premiered Hugo Weisgall's Yiddish song cycle *The Golden Peacock* and songs by MIRIAM GIDEON. In the 1970s, she recorded works by all three Jewish American composers. She sang with the New York Philharmonic, the Boston Symphony, the Philadelphia Orchestra, and the London Symphony, among others. With the Cleveland Orchestra under George Szell, she recorded Mahler's Fourth Symphony.

Her other recordings include a performance of *Così fan tutte*, made in London for RCA Victor in 1967, and numerous recordings for RCA, Decca, Columbia, London, C.R.I., and Epic Records. In addition to the Ford Foundation grant, she received the Marian Anderson Award in 1952 and 1953, and a London Grammy in 1967. Raskin was awarded honorary degrees by Smith College (1963) and Ithaca College (1979). She published an article entitled "American Bel Canto" in *Opera News* in 1966.

Beginning in 1975, Raskin taught at the Manhattan School of Music and the 92nd Street Y School of Music in New York, where a master class for opera singers bears her name. The following year, she started teaching at Mannes College of Music. She also taught at City College in New York. From 1972–1976, she cochaired the music panel of the National Endowment for the Arts, and until her death served as a judge for the Metropolitan Opera auditions. Raskin frequently contributed her talent to State of Israel Bonds. From 1962 to 1965, and again in 1968 and 1969, she appeared at the "Chanukah Festival for Israel," held in Madison Square Garden. She also sang in Miami Beach in 1973, and in Indianapolis in 1973.

Harold C. Schonberg's *New York Times* obituary quotes an interview in which Raskin describes her own singing: "I've tried to make up in depth what I don't have in quantity. There is a kind of singer who has a poetic approach to music rather than a purely vocal approach." Her teaching reflected the same attitude. Singers who studied with her emphasize that she never considered—or referred to—"the voice," as many teachers do, as an entity separate from the person.

Raskin was diagnosed with breast cancer in 1962, but after a radical mastectomy she returned to full activity. In 1982, she developed ovarian cancer and died Friday, December 21, 1984. That Sunday, more than a thousand people crowded the sanctuary at Stephen Wise Free Synagogue in New York for her funeral. That synagogue, in which she had begun her professional career more than thirty years earlier, singing second soprano in the choir, now hosts a yearly recital endowed in Raskin's memory by her family.

BIBLIOGRAPHY

Baker's Biographical Dictionary of Musicians. Edited by Nicolas Slonimsky. 8th ed. (1992); *Current Biography Yearbook, 1964.* Edited by Charles Moritz (1966): 366–368, and *Current Biography Yearbook, 1984* (1985): 472–473; Hague, Amy, and Jonathan M. Raskin, and Lisa A. Raskin, and Raymond A. Raskin, and Ellen Stettner. Telephone conversations with author, December 1995–January 1996; Herman, Kali. *Women in Particular: An Index to American Women* (1984); Ireland, Norma Glin. *Index to Women of the World from Ancient to Modern Times: Biographies and Portraits* (1970), and *Index to Women of the World from Ancient to Modern Times: A Supplement* (1988); *New Grove Dictionary of American Music.* Edited by H. Wiley Hitchcock and Stanley Sadie (1986); *New Grove Dictionary of Music and Musicians.* Edited by Stanley Sadie (1980); *New Grove Dictionary of Opera.* Edited by Stanley Sadie (1992); Obituary. *Opera News* (June 1985): 42; Polner, Murray. *American Jewish Biographies* (1982): 341–342; Raskin, Judith. Papers. Sophia Smith Collection, Smith College, Northampton, Mass.; Schonberg, Harold C. "Judith Raskin, Lyric Soprano Acclaimed for Musicianship." *NYTimes*, December 22, 1984, sec. 1, p. 29; *Who's Who in America.* Vols. 34–43 (1984); *Who's Who in American Music: Classical.* Edited by Jaques Cattell Press (1983); *WWWIA* 8:331.

PAULA EISENSTEIN BAKER

RAUSHENBUSH, ELIZABETH BRANDEIS (1896–1984)

Following in the footsteps of her famous father, Elizabeth Brandeis Raushenbush became an expert on labor legislation in the United States and one of its strongest defenders. Born on April 25, 1896, to Louis and ALICE GOLDMARK BRANDEIS, her childhood memories were etched by her father's rapid success as a prominent attorney. In her adult life, Raushenbush defended the constitutionality of protective legislation as the most effective way to ensure wage and hours standards for working men and women, to regulate child labor, and to protect the well-being of the injured and unemployed. She based her support for such laws on empirical evidence that revealed the economic, political, and sociological implications of unregulated working conditions and on her belief that government should work with community groups to pass legislation that equalized the rights of labor and employers.

College training and firsthand community service shaped Raushenbush's understanding of the need for labor laws. After receiving her B.A. from Radcliffe College in 1918, she was employed for the next five years by the Washington, D.C., Minimum Wage Board, a regulatory body created to enforce a local law that protected women and minors from conditions detrimental to their health and morals resulting from wages inadequate to maintain decent standards of living. As the board's secretaries, Raushenbush and her lifelong friend Clara Beyer paid for and conducted the important research that exposed businesses that underpaid women and employees who were minors. As secretary, Raushenbush not only played an instrumental role in enabling the board to fulfill its duties, but also enjoyed a useful apprenticeship that established the foundation of her graduate work.

Raushenbush pursued graduate-level studies of social and economic conditions in the department of economics at the University of Wisconsin, Madison. She continued the process of linking scholarly inquiry with the formation and implementation of public policy under the direction of her mentor, John R. Commons. After graduating with a Ph.D. in 1928, Raushenbush taught courses in the economics department at Madison for over forty years and worked with Commons and carried on his traditions after he retired.

Raushenbush contributed the section on labor legislation in volume three of Commons's famous series, *History of Labor in the United States*, documenting the historical evolution of maximum hours, minimum wage, child labor, and unemployment compensation laws. In her study "Organized Labor and Protective Labor Legislation" she summarized labor laws passed during the New Deal, especially the National Industrial Recovery Act and Fair Labor Standards Act. In these and other sources, Raushenbush provided both a thorough study of the interaction among the courts, organized labor, and lobby groups in the history of labor laws and an informative resource for current understandings of public policy formation.

Raushenbush's academic accomplishments did not keep her from active community service. After World War II, she dedicated her time to child labor issues and to the passage of legislation for unemployment insurance. She served on the governor's Committee on Migratory Labor in Wisconsin and on the United States Labor Department's Advisory Committee on Young Workers, studying the earnings, working conditions, housing, and education of child laborers and migratory workers. She was particularly concerned with the enforcement of legislation that set minimum age and maximum hours requirements for agricultural workers and that regulated living conditions.

Elizabeth Raushenbush and her husband, Paul Raushenbush, led the fight for the adoption of unemployment insurance in Wisconsin and succeeded in developing a model law that was used by other state governments. Passed in January 1932, the Groves Bill, as it was called, provided workers with ten weeks of benefits each year. Elizabeth Raushenbush supported the law because it compelled employers to accumulate the funds to provide unemployment payments to their employees at a rate based on existing salaries. She described the bill as invaluable because its provisions placed the burden on employers as a way to induce them to stabilize employment and to find jobs for the workers they laid off. The first of its kind, the Groves Bill provided the foundation for the Social Security Act of the New Deal.

In her written work, Raushenbush did not link her reform interests to her religious background. She identified herself as an educator and labor activist. Elizabeth Raushenbush died in April 1984, survived by her son, Walter. Her colleagues remembered her integrity and devotion to a wide range of public problems. Her generosity and ability to target serious social issues, to organize the necessary research, to galvanize others to her cause, and to pursue legislative measures enabled her to leave an indelible mark on late twentieth-century understanding of labor legislation in the United States.

SELECTED WORKS BY ELIZABETH BRANDEIS RAUSHENBUSH

Governor's Commission on Human Rights. "The Migrant Problem, Past and Future, in Wisconsin." *Proceedings of the Migrant Labor Conference* (December 4, 1964): 4–10; "Labor Legislation." In *History of Labor in the United States, 1896–1932*. Vol. 3, edited by John R. Commons (reprint, 1966); "Organized Labor and Protective Labor Legislation." In *Labor and the New Deal* (1958); "Our 'UC' Story," with Paul Raushenbush. Oral History Project, Columbia University (1979).

BIBLIOGRAPHY

BEOAJ; Beyer, Clara M. Interview by Vivien Hart, 1983. Schlesinger Library, Radcliffe College, Cambridge, Mass.; Haferbecker, Gordon M. *Wisconsin Labor Laws* (1958); Mason, Alpheus Thomas. *Brandeis: A Free Man's Life* (1946); Munts, Raymond. "Unemployment Compensation in Wisconsin: Origins and Performance." In *Unemployment Insurance: The Second Half-Century*, edited by James F. Byers and W. Lee Hanson (1990); Raushenbush, Elizabeth Brandeis. Papers, 1920–1967. Schlesinger Library, Radcliffe College; Raushenbush, Elizabeth Brandeis, and Paul Raushenbush. Papers. State Historical Society of Wisconsin; *WWIAJ* (1938).

AMY BUTLER

RAZOVSKY, CECILIA (1891–1968)

Cecilia Razovsky was a remarkably active woman who spent her life striving to assist immigrants in adapting to life in the United States and other countries. This interest in immigrant issues motivated her involvement in the NATIONAL COUNCIL OF JEWISH WOMEN (NCJW) and a variety of other organizations.

Razovsky was born on May 4, 1891, in St. Louis, Missouri, to Jonas and Minna (Meyerson) Razovsky. She received her education from Washington University, St. Louis (1911), the Corliss School of Law (1912), the St. Louis School of Economics (1913), and the Chicago School of Civics and Philanthropy (1919). She also pursued graduate work in sociology at the University of Chicago. Razovsky worked as a legal secretary in St. Louis from 1909 to 1911. From 1911 to 1917, she taught English to foreigners in the public evening schools. In 1917, she moved to Washington, D.C., to become an inspector in the child labor division of the United States Children's Bureau, a post she filled until 1920. In 1927, Razovsky married Dr. Morris Davidson, and the couple had one son, David L. Davidson.

Razovsky performed important work for the National Council of Jewish Women and was very active in that organization, serving on the national board throughout the 1930s. She served as secretary for the immigrant aid department from 1920 to 1932, and became associate director in 1932. In 1923, Razovsky represented the NCJW at the World Conference of Jewish Women in Vienna and spoke on immigration restriction in the United States.

Her interest in immigration issues influenced her involvement in other organizations as well, including posts in the National Conference of Social Work from 1926 to 1929. She was chair of the Conference on Immigration Policy in 1928. The following year, she was the official delegate, representing ten national American organizations at the International Conference for Protection of Migrants in Geneva. She became the executive director of the National Coordinating Committee for Aid to Refugees and Emigrants coming from Germany, and executive secretary of German-Jewish Children's Aid in 1934. She was a member of a committee on contact with Jewish communal agencies and the committee for social work for aliens at the International Conference on Social Work, held at Frankfurt-am-Main, Germany, in 1932. In 1933, she was chair of a committee of twelve specialists appointed by Secretary of Labor Frances Perkins to advise the Committee of Forty-Eight on conditions at Ellis Island and other ports. She served on the General Committee of Immigrant Aid at Ellis

Cecilia Razovsky spent her life striving to assist immigrants in adapting to life in the United States and other countries. She was an influential member of many organizations, including the NATIONAL COUNCIL OF JEWISH WOMEN. *Her writing on and study of immigration issues helped to define elements of United States policy. [American Jewish Historical Society]*

Island and New York Harbor, both as chair, from 1933 to 1936, and as secretary, in 1937. Throughout this period, she conducted a number of studies on the lives of Jewish refugees, including studies of conditions in European port cities (1923, 1935), Cuba (1924), Mexico (1926, 1930), Canada (1926), and Brazil and Argentina (1937).

Razovsky was the editor of the NCJW publication *The Immigrant* from 1922 to 1930. She wrote a number of articles, plays, and pamphlets on immigration and conditions of Jews in Latin America, including *Handicaps in Naturalization*, which influenced Congress to reduce naturalization fees. Other publications, which were prepared for the NCJW, include *What Every Emigrant Should Know* (1922), *What Every*

Woman Should Know About Citizenship (1926), and *Making Americans* (1938).

SELECTED WORKS BY CECILIA RAZOVSKY

Handicaps in Naturalization (1932); *Making Americans* (1938); *What Every Emigrant Should Know* (1922); *What Every Woman Should Know About Citizenship* (1926).

BIBLIOGRAPHY

EJ; Rogow, Faith. *Gone to Another Meeting: The National Council of Jewish Women, 1893–1993* (1993); *UJE*; *WWIAJ* (1938).

MARY McCUNE

RECONSTRUCTIONIST JUDAISM

Unlike other branches of American Judaism, Reconstructionism originated in the philosophy of one individual, Mordecai Kaplan (1881–1982). Kaplan is renowned for his definition of Judaism as an evolving religious civilization. The term "Reconstructionism" comes from his notion that Judaism should neither be reformed nor conserved, but reconstructed. Reconstructionists use the foundation and building blocks they have inherited from the past, reordering and adding to them so that they fit the needs, values, and tastes of current generations, but without altering them in ways that would make them unrecognizable or sap their richness. As part of his program for reconstruction, Kaplan rejected a supernatural theology and repudiated the concept of the chosen people.

Kaplan was a controversial figure in American Jewish history because of his willingness to confront difficult issues. Among his bold new ideas was advocacy for changes in women's roles in Jewish life. Kaplan was a principal architect of women's equality in Judaism. While the philosophy of Reconstructionism has undergone significant changes since Kaplan's death, the equality of women remains a central tenet and hallmark of the newest movement in Judaism.

KAPLAN'S LIFE AND THOUGHT

The concepts and teachings of Mordecai Kaplan form the basis for understanding Reconstructionism's pioneering role in the struggle for women's equality in Judaism. Kaplan's commitment to the equality of women was an essential part of his life and thought. Born in Lithuania, he was the son of an Orthodox rabbi who immigrated to the United States to assist Rabbi Jacob Joseph in his work as chief rabbi of New York. As a young man, Kaplan served an Orthodox congregation, the Jewish Center in New York City, as rabbi. He left this position to found the Society for the Advancement of Judaism (SAJ) in New York City

in 1922. Part of Kaplan's motivation for founding the SAJ was the insistence of the Jewish Center's membership on retaining the traditional practice of separate seating for women and men, and its refusal to set up a women's organization in the synagogue. Those who joined the SAJ did so to follow Kaplan's leadership. Yet he had to struggle with the new congregation over the mixed seating issue. For the first High Holiday services at the SAJ, he demanded mixed seating, achieving his goal despite opposition from congregants and members of his own family, male and female. Also that spring, Kaplan orchestrated the now famous first bat mitzvah, during which his twelve-year-old daughter JUDITH KAPLAN [EISENSTEIN] recited the blessings and read from the Torah at Sabbath morning services. Until that event, there had been no puberty ceremony for girls in American Judaism comparable to the bar mitzvah.

THE EQUALITY OF WOMEN IN JUDAISM

In the 1920s, Kaplan frequently sermonized in support of women's recently gained political emancipation, using biblical texts to prove his point. In 1936, Kaplan's blueprint for women's equality in Judaism, including ordination, was published in *The Reconstructionist Papers*. Perhaps his most insightful comment in that essay was that equality could come about only through woman's "own efforts and initiative. Whatever liberal-minded men do in her behalf is bound to remain but a futile and meaningless gesture. The Jewish woman must demand the equality due her as a right to which she is fully entitled." Kaplan went on to present his critique of the status of women in Jewish life. He argued that the Jewish community would drive women out if it did not provide vehicles for their self-fulfillment. Cautioning women not to be fooled by those who argued that they already had an elevated role in Judaism, he made reference to the many negative comments in rabbinic literature about women's intelligence and abilities. He ridiculed "The Woman of Valor," the verses in Proverbs that extol women's domestic virtues, as "the flattery of a parasitic husband."

The essay goes on to discuss the ways Jewish law defines women as of inferior status to men and chronicles the religious and juridical disabilities inherent in that status: the exemption from the performance of mitzvahs and the denial of the rights of women to lead prayer services, act as witnesses, inherit property, and initiate divorce. Kaplan concluded that Jewish law had to be changed to rid Judaism of these inequities. It is remarkable that he made these suggestions more than thirty years before the movement for the equality of women in Judaism put them on the Jewish agenda.

In addition to Kaplan's commitment to the equality of women in Judaism, several other elements of his philosophy play a significant role in Reconstructionism's leadership on this issue. Reconstructionism is distinguished from other branches of Judaism by its base in Kaplan's theology. Influenced by the popular religious naturalism of his time, Kaplan did not accept the concept of God as person but understood God as the Power in the universe that makes for righteousness and salvation. Kaplan understood God as a process inherent in nature and humanity that brings about good in the world. Kaplan's God is not an actor, controlling history, but rather can be perceived in the world through the best endeavors of human beings, acting *b'tselem elohim* [in the image of God]. Kaplan's theology is therefore a useful tool in dealing with the problem feminists confront when they face a prayer service replete with male God language. Although Kaplan himself never removed male references to God—such as the pronouns He or Him, or masculine concepts like King or Lord—his theology renders God "gender-neutral" and suggests that the use of male God language reflects human perceptions, not divine reality.

LIVING IN TWO CIVILIZATIONS

Kaplan believed that to function effectively, American Jews need to live in what he called two civilizations, the Jewish and the American. He was convinced that Jewish life would flourish if immigrant Jews understood that they did not have to give up their heritage and traditions to consider themselves fully American. In this regard, Kaplan became an early proponent of cultural pluralism. He was able to look back on Jewish history and see the continuous interpenetration of the ideas and norms of the larger civilizations in which Jews dwelled and the accommodations that Judaism made to these realities. He taught that Judaism is a continuously evolving civilization, not a static, immutable religious system. It was this understanding that allowed Kaplan to make innovations in women's roles and to embrace philosophies, like democracy, that had not previously been dominant in the Jewish experience. To Kaplan's way of thinking, democratic principles required universal suffrage, including equality for women in Judaism.

JEWISH LAW

Kaplan understood halakah as a component of the nonbinding, but sacred, inherited traditions of the Jewish people. Kaplan was himself observant of traditional ritual practices, but he also held Jewish law accountable to contemporary ethical standards. It was on this basis that Kaplan had no problem calling for the full equality of women, despite the obvious difficulties reconciling this stance with traditional halakah and norms of Jewish practice. He also vigorously supported creative approaches to ritual. Because of Kaplan's affinity for Jewish tradition, however, the changes he made in his own congregation and recommended in his writings were much less radical than those of the Reform Jewish thinkers of his era, who usually dismissed halakic considerations. Even so, his attitude eventually proved too flexible even for the denomination that would come to be called Conservative, into which he had moved after his early years in Orthodoxy.

THE CHOSEN PEOPLE

By far, the most significant element in Kaplan's thought in relation to feminist principles was his passionate opposition to hierarchy. This was most boldly expressed in Kaplan's decision to remove the chosen people doctrine from Jewish liturgy. Kaplan maintained that such a claim to divine election was inseparable from a claim to superiority. He advocated the recognition that all peoples have unique and important destinies, which inherently invalidates the idea of one particular chosen people. This antihierarchical orientation is part of a larger worldview that does not give advantage to one group of people over another. It lends support to feminist endeavors in Judaism, for just as the Jewish people cannot claim a superior status over other nations, men cannot claim a superior status over women.

THE NEED FOR A SEPARATE MOVEMENT?

Kaplan himself saw no need to start a separate movement to achieve his goals. In fact, he opposed the idea of creating a Reconstructionist movement to carry out his philosophy. His goal was to create a unified American Judaism without denominational factionalism. Yet it became clear to his followers that if Kaplan's visions were to be realized, a separate movement was needed. The debate over becoming a movement lasted for several decades, during which time more and more small groups around the United States and Canada began to develop and label themselves Reconstructionists. In the 1950s, these groups began including women in the minyan and allowing them to come up to the Torah for aliyot, as had been the case at the SAJ since the mid 1940s. They also continued the practice of bat mitzvah. But other changes in the role of women that Kaplan had endorsed in his writings, such as serving as witnesses, leading services, public Torah reading, and wearing ritual prayer garments like *kippot* [skullcaps] and *tallitot* [prayer shawls] did not come about until the late 1960s when women themselves began demanding changes, as Kaplan had predicted would be necessary back in 1936. Another major step took place in 1967 when a convention of Reconstructionists took the bold step of deciding to open a college for training rabbis in Philadelphia.

THE RECONSTRUCTIONIST
RABBINICAL COLLEGE ORDAINS WOMEN

The question of the ordination of women to the rabbinate certainly was in the public consciousness at the time the Reconstructionist Rabbinical College was founded in 1968. The women's liberation movement was asking questions about women's complete equality that had not seriously been considered previously. Although none was yet ordained, several women candidates were then studying at the Reform Movement's Hebrew Union College. Despite the open discussion of this issue, the founders of the Reconstructionist Rabbinical College decided not to create added controversy by recruiting women for its first class. In its second year, however, when the founders advertised for students, they received one inquiry from a woman. Sandy Eisenberg Sasso was accepted without debate or subsequent controversy. For the next several years, only a few women applied, and all were accepted. The class that entered in 1974, the year of Sandy Sasso's graduation, was half women, and that trend has continued ever since. The rabbinical college has had women as part of upper-level administration and full-time faculty since the mid-1970s. It currently houses Kolot: the Center for Jewish Women's and Gender Studies, a resource center for curricular and liturgical materials.

THE RECONSTRUCTIONIST RABBINICAL
ASSOCIATION: NEW MODELS FOR RABBIS

Based on Kaplan's passion for democracy and his antipathy toward hierarchy, Reconstructionism encourages new and diverse models for the rabbinate. The Reconstructionist rabbi is not prepared to be the distant "father figure" or authoritarian leader. Reconstructionist rabbis are trained to see themselves as facilitators in Jewish life. The Reconstructionist rabbi is still "the teacher," but one who understands the importance of learning from and listening to students. The goal is to promote the growth of others as knowledgeable Jews, to empower them, to engage fully in Jewish life, and to bring ideas from the secular world into creative and productive encounter with Judaism. Many Reconstructionist innovations around women's issues in Judaism have been facilitated by women in the Reconstruction-

ist rabbinate, in concert with other women Reconstructionists.

WOMEN RABBIS RECLAIM TRADITION

Reconstructionist women rabbis have been instrumental in the creation of rituals, stories, music, and theologies that have begun to give women's experience a voice in Judaism. Most of the focus has been on rituals for life-cycle events. New ceremonies have been created for births, heterosexual weddings and lesbian commitment ceremonies, divorces, conversions, weaning, and the onset of menarche and menopause. The movement as a whole has been committed to creating liturgy that is in consonance with feminist ideas and practices and that reflects a new role for women's celebration and creativity. This is reflected in the prayer books and rabbinic manuals that have been published. Kaplan himself took bold steps at mid-century to publish prayer books that reflected his philosophy. Under the leadership of David Teutsch, president of the Reconstructionist Rabbinical Colllege, this liturgy is now being reconceptualized for a new generation. Gender-neutral language and the presence of women's commentaries and poetic visions are central to this effort.

Another central focus of the Reconstructionist movement has been on the arts, and contemporary Jewish women's music in particular. Kaplan's eldest daughter, Judith Kaplan Eisenstein, a leading musicologist and teacher of Jewish music, made a considerable contribution in this area.

FOCUS ON WOMEN'S ISSUES

Reconstructionist women rabbis have also found their voices through raising consciousness in their congregations and schools about issues related to women's lives. Some have focused on issues like domestic violence or reproductive rights as these affect the Jewish community. Others have devoted energy to helping Orthodox women to gain the right of divorce in traditional communities in Israel. Many have spoken out for the right of Jewish women to pray aloud and read from the Torah when at the Western Wall in Israel.

WOMEN RABBIS' LIVES AND
THE FAMILY ETHIC

By far, the most difficult problem facing women in the Reconstructionist rabbinate today is finding a balance between their professional and personal commitments. Some women have found the rabbinate congenial because motherhood is expected of Jewish women and, for the most part, the community accommodates. But what for some is a positive synthesis of their professional and private lives is for others an experience of living without healthy limits between work and family life. Most experience the dilemmas common among women who have taken on professional commitment while at the same time attempting to raise children, run a household, care for elderly relatives, or have a meaningful life outside of work. The problems of balancing career and home life are particularly acute in a calling such as the rabbinate, which is still defined and experienced as much as a personal commitment as it is a professional commitment.

Even Kaplan's forward-looking philosophy did not encompass an analysis of the family that would be helpful to this generation of women. The majority of Reconstructionist women rabbis are in heterosexual marriages and have children. There are several single parents and lesbian couples with children as well. For those who have remained single or childless, their choices have been complicated by pressure from the Jewish community to be "fruitful and multiply." Although the technical commandment to continue the survival of the Jewish people is addressed to men, women in the rabbinate feel the responsibility as heavily incumbent upon them. While accepting their choices, or lack of them in some cases, most have internalized the sense that to be complete as Jewish women they must have children. There is little support for the idea that they are in fact building up the Jewish people through their contributions as teachers of children rather than necessarily as biological parents.

LESBIAN RABBIS

Another focus of Reconstructionist concern in the current era has been an interest in rethinking ethics from a Jewish perspective. A focus on sexual and reproductive ethics has been a major part of this trend. In 1987, in an article on women in the rabbinate, Anne Lapidus Lerner credited the Reconstructionist Movement with being the first to champion egalitarianism as an underlying principle. The main issue for Reconstructionism, she asserted, was that the movement also "openly espoused non-heterosexuality" and would have to come to terms with the presence of lesbians in the rabbinate. The Reconstructionist Rabbinical College has been admitting lesbians and gay men to the rabbinate since 1984. The Federation of Reconstructionist Congregations and Havurot has also developed educational programs that lead toward the full acceptance of lesbian rabbis and teachers, as well as rituals that affirm lesbian relationships. But this full accep-

tance has yet to be attained, even for lesbian rabbis who fulfill the obligation of motherhood.

MEN'S ROLES

The logical result of women's demand for changes in Judaism must include thinking about changed roles for men as well. With their advocacy of patrilineal descent in the 1970s, the Reconstructionist Rabbinical Association supported the principle that a man who takes responsibility for raising a Jewish child can pass Judaism on to the next generation as well as a woman. This policy statement is part of a larger understanding within Reconstructionist Judaism that the real message of feminism for the Jewish people is a reassessment of how we structure our lives to provide opportunities for all human beings to flourish, personally and professionally.

FEMINISM AND RECONSTRUCTIONISM

The Reconstructionist Movement has played a significant role in creating an environment of equality for women in Judaism. Predicated on Kaplan's vision of a reconstructed Jewish community, his followers have made equality for women in all aspects of Jewish religious and juridical life an absolute value. The Reconstructionist Movement has moved beyond Kaplan's original vision of equality toward a reconceptualization of Judaism through a feminist lens. The movement has been a home for Jewish women's creativity and celebration through music, creation of resources for curricula and liturgy, the development of pioneering questions on feminist ethics, a home for gay and lesbian Jews, and a place where men's roles are also being redefined. Mordecai Kaplan's legacy of finding bold responses to difficult questions has remained alive in the Reconstructionist Movement.

BIBLIOGRAPHY

Alpert, Rebecca T. "A Feminist Takes Stock of Reconstructionism." *Reconstructionist* 54 (1989): 17–22; Alpert, Rebecca T., and Goldie Milgram. "Women in the Reconstructionist Rabbinate." In *Religious Institutions and Women's Leadership: New Roles Inside the Mainstream*, edited by Catherine Wessinger (1996); Alpert, Rebecca T., and Jacob Staub. *Exploring Judaism: A Reconstructionist Approach* (1985); Kaplan, Mordecai. "The Status of Woman in Jewish Law." In *The Reconstructionist Papers* (1936), and in *The Future of the American Jew* (1948), and *The Kaplan Journal*. Archives, JTS (1922); Kessner, Carole. "Kaplan and the Role of Women in Judaism." In *The American Judaism of Mordecai M. Kaplan*, edited by Emanuel S. Goldsmith, Mel Scult, and Robert M. Seltzer (1990); Scult, Mel. *Judaism Faces the Twentieth Century: A Biography of Mordecai M. Kaplan* (1993).

REBECCA T. ALPERT

RECREATION *see*
LEISURE AND RECREATION;
SUMMER CAMPING

REFORM JUDAISM

Leaders of Reform Judaism in the United States have often celebrated their movement's role in emancipating women from the many restrictions that Judaism has traditionally imposed upon their ability to participate and lead public worship. Although Reform thinkers in Germany made the case for women's equality in Judaism and the abolition of anachronistic laws and customs that stifled the public expression of women's religiosity, it was only in the United States that practical innovations adopted by the Reform Movement actively redefined the nature of women's participation in public worship. Chief among Reform Judaism's liberating innovations have been the abolition of a separate women's gallery within the synagogue in the 1850s and the ordination of the first American female rabbi in 1972. Reform congregations have also provided important sites for Jewish women to work out the tensions between evolving societal expectations for women and the roles identified with traditional Jewish practice.

Many common innovations in early American synagogues helped to redefine women's place in Jewish worship even before the emergence of a formal Reform movement. American synagogue builders had, for the most part, done away with the partition barriers that kept women out of sight, in traditional women's galleries. Many congregations employed choirs of mixed male and female voices, challenging the usual Orthodox prohibitions against allowing women's voices to be heard within worship services. In addition, the introduction of confirmation services in many Jewish congregations signified, in part, an effort to solemnize the Jewish education and identity of girls as well as boys.

FAMILY PEWS

Family pews, the innovation connected with women's status most explicitly identified with the nineteenth-century Reform Movement, may have arisen as a matter of convenience. When Rabbi Isaac Mayer Wise's Anshe Emeth Congregation in Albany occupied a church building in 1851 and when New York's Temple Emanu-El bought a former church in 1854, both congregations determined that rather than build new galleries, they would seat men and women together in the pews that had been used by the

churches. The prominence of Temple Emanu-El's Reform program and of its elite congregants helped place family pews on the Reform agenda.

With Reform's emergence as the dominant tendency among America's acculturating Jews in the 1860s and 1870s, the family pew became a requisite feature of the imposing temples and synagogues added to the post–Civil War urban landscape. Offered a place in the sanctuary, Jewish women continued a trend that had marked early nineteenth-century American synagogues. In a departure from the traditional pattern of synagogue worship, women quickly came to dominate attendance at weekly Sabbath services. Women's access to the sanctuary floor, however, came at a moment when the content of congregational participation had been radically redefined. The Judaism championed by American Reformers placed the rabbi or service reader in a prominent elevated location at the front of the congregation. Women did not need more Jewish education to participate in Reform services that were premised upon the limited knowledge and involvement of all the congregants.

Although Reform leaders often celebrated their introduction of the family pew in bringing gender equality to Jewish religious life, the second half of the nineteenth century brought mixed results in forwarding the public position of women in America's Reform congregations. Although Jewish women's attendance patterns may have emulated the pew dominance of American Christian women, mid-nineteenth-century Jewish women did not participate in the explosion of voluntary and organizational activity identified with women in Protestant churches of the same era. The Reform synagogue's emphasis upon worship undermined the existence of the many synagogue-affiliated groups, like female benevolent societies, which had earlier been part of broadly defined synagogue communities. As the purposes of the congregation narrowed to the limited sphere of worship, women found little to do except sit and listen quietly. Those active synagogue affiliations that remained—spiritual leadership and lay governance—were exclusively in male hands.

STRUCTURAL CHANGES AFFECTING WOMEN'S ROLES

Formal organization of the Reform Movement grew from the founding of the Union of American Hebrew Congregations (UAHC) in 1872 and the Hebrew Union College (HUC) in 1875. Women contributed some money, but otherwise played little role in these institutional developments. Although HUC president Isaac Mayer Wise had often called for the creation of a "female theological seminary," nothing along these lines ever emerged. A few female students did enroll at the early Hebrew Union College, but none advanced very far in their studies.

One area in which women continued to expand their involvement in synagogue life was in congregational religious schools, in which they often served as teachers and supporters. But even in these settings, women were often explicitly excluded from leadership roles and could not serve on the congregational boards overseeing the schools. Late nineteenth-century Reform congregations rejected the exclusively male bar mitzvah, adopting the confirmation ritual observed on Shavuoth as the primary adolescent rite of passage, thus hoping to demonstrate their regard for the religious education of girls. During confirmation services, girls, together with boys, offered prayers and speeches, and testified to their learning and commitment.

It was not until the late 1880s that new structures emerged to absorb the latent energies of the women within Reform congregations. The first Jewish SISTERHOOD OF PERSONAL SERVICE organized by Rabbi Gustav Gottheil of New York's Reform Temple Emanu-El provided the prototype for a women's organization that was quickly emulated in Jewish congregations throughout the country. At first, these groups of Americanized Jewish women focused their energies on the impoverished Eastern European Jewish multitudes lately arrived in the United States. As numerous organizations emerged around the turn of the century to tend to the needs of these immigrants and as the professionalization of social work displaced "lady visitors" in immigrant work, women's synagogue organizations often turned their now-organized energies back to their own communities. Women's groups offered services in whatever ways congregations would allow them to participate, often in areas such as schools and temple decoration. The expansion of women's energies in this direction was also facilitated by attempts to expand the ambit of the synagogue beyond the narrow worship-centered sanctuary of early Reformers. The massive temple edifices built in the early twentieth century hosted a broad range of community-oriented activities.

Congregational governance structures yielded slowly to women's participation. A few Reform congregations responded to calls from the NATIONAL COUNCIL OF JEWISH WOMEN in the 1890s to open up the category of synagogue membership to women who were not widows of deceased members. Yet, for the most part, the call to grant women access to both membership and positions on congregational boards met stony resistance. It was not until the Nineteenth Amendment to the Constitution was passed in 1920,

granting female suffrage, that most Reform congregations offered formal membership to women who were not widows or who were unmarried, and began to invite sisterhood presidents to serve on congregational lay leadership boards.

Women affiliated with the Reform Movement were first organized into a national movement in 1913 when the NATIONAL FEDERATION OF TEMPLE SISTERHOODS (NFTS) was formed at a special meeting of 156 representatives from 52 congregations, held in conjunction with the UAHC meeting held in Cincinnati. The moving forces behind creation of the NFTS were Rabbi George Zepin of the UAHC and CARRIE SIMON, a civic leader who was the wife of a Washington, D.C., rabbi. Simon served as the organization's founding president and Zepin as its executive secretary. Organization of the NFTS at a national level prompted many congregations that had not yet created women's membership organizations to found local synagogue sisterhoods. Once founded, these groups encouraged thousands of women to focus their energies on congregational life.

In the interwar years, sisterhood members elaborated their congregational roles, assuming responsibility for a wide range of temple, school, and communal activities, as well as for certain liturgical events. Sisterhoods organized community seders and summer services. At annual sisterhood Sabbaths, women took public pulpit roles, delivering sermons and often conducting the services themselves. On a national level, the NFTS took a leading role in supporting the movement's rabbinic school, raising student scholarships, and supplying funds to build the Sisterhood Dormitory in Cincinnati. NFTS was also instrumental in founding the National Braille Institute and the National Federation of Temple Youth.

CHANGING PERCEPTIONS OF WOMEN'S ROLES

The presence, contributions, energy, and activities that women brought to the Reform Movement, nationally and locally, contributed to growing expectations that women should be recognized as full participants in the work of Reform Judaism. Through the sisterhood, women were beginning to have a say in both local synagogue governance and the national movement. The growth of a cadre of local and national sisterhood leaders, together with the logic implicit in the woman suffrage amendment, confronted Reform leaders with the question of female religious leadership.

In 1922, facing the possibility that Martha Neumark, a female student at Hebrew Union College, might continue her studies and become a candidate for ordination, HUC's board of governors and faculty and the Reform Movement's federation of rabbis, the Central Conference of American Rabbis (CCAR), all took up the question of whether to approve, in principle, the ordination of female rabbis. Some traditionalist-leaning members of the HUC faculty expressed misgivings as to whether the Reform Movement, in ordaining women, would irreparably sunder itself from the other movements in Judaism. Nonetheless, the faculty unanimously agreed that this innovation was consistent with the inclusive and progressive tenets of the Reform Movement and was equivalent to other major breaks with tradition accepted by the movement. Consideration of the issue at the 1922 CCAR convention was especially noteworthy for the decision of the delegates to include female members of the audience, mainly wives of the rabbis in attendance, in the discussion. Although the faculty and the CCAR both voted to support the proposed change, HUC's board of governors, which had to make the final decision, ultimately rejected the proposal.

The question of whether women should serve as rabbis lay dormant over the next few decades as the energy and creativity of women within the movement provided their communities with a rich congregational life. During World War II, as had been the case during World War I, many women looked to the sisterhood to formalize their contribution to the war effort. They knitted, crocheted, baked cookies, organized blood banks, sold bonds, conducted first-aid classes, and resettled Jewish refugees, all under the auspices of their congregational sisterhoods. Continued postwar growth in synagogue activity reflected a nationwide return to religion that enlivened both churches and synagogues through the 1950s. As synagogue organizational life flourished, sisterhoods were critical in sustaining synagogue life in older congregations and in creating new frameworks for community as old and new congregations found their way to the suburbs.

The confirmation service, with its egalitarian commitment to Jewish education for both boys and girls, had been an early aspect of the Reform Movement's agenda. As the bar mitzvah ceremony regained popularity in Reform congregations after World War I, however, confirmation ceremonies became increasingly a province for girls alone. The feminization of the group confirmation service, together with the bar mitzvah ceremony's emphasis on individual Jewish ritual skills and obligations, highlighted the gender inequity within Jewish worship that confirmation was meant to neutralize. The first bat mitzvah ceremony, as a female counterpart to the bar mitzvah, was introduced by Mordecai Kaplan, founder of the Reconstructionist Movement, for his daughter JUDITH KAPLAN [EISENSTEIN] in 1922. The bat mitzvah ceremony slowly took root within the Conservative Movement in the 1930s and 1940s. The Reform Movement's commitment to the confirmation rite, however, slowed acceptance of the bat mitzvah in Reform temples. Bat mitzvah ceremonies began to appear in Reform congregations in the 1950s and made more general progress in the 1960s. Varying in format, a Reform bat mitzvah was often celebrated with a reading of the haftarah on Friday night rather than with the standard bar mitzvah Saturday morning Torah service. By the early 1970s, a Saturday morning bat mitzvah service, identical in its requirements with the ceremony held for boys, was in place in most Reform congregations.

In the years surrounding the publication of BETTY FRIEDAN's *The Feminine Mystique* (1963), the rhetoric of gender egalitarianism and equality of opportunity became more familiar in the broader culture. The idea of sustaining distinctive rituals to mark the religious obligations and duties of boys and girls, or of men and women, within Judaism became untenable. No one within the Reform Movement questioned the decision of Meridian, Mississippi's Reform congregation to appoint the widow of their deceased rabbi to serve as the community's spiritual leader from 1951 to 1953. In 1956, the CCAR's Barnett Brickner asked the CCAR to declare a commitment to the principle of female ordination. Although his proposal received general approval, the question was "laid on the table" until those with opposing views could present their case—or, as it turned out, indefinitely. In 1963, the women of the NFTS reflected shifting cultural currents and renewed attention to questions of women's equality by again requesting the governing (male) bodies of Reform Judaism to take up the question of women's ordination.

Ultimately, the issue was resolved without grand statements from the movement's organizing bodies. As SALLY PRIESAND advanced through the course of study at the Hebrew Union College–Jewish Institute of Religion (HUC–JIR) in Cincinnati, the question was no longer one of abstract commitments but of practical realities. HUC–JIR president Nelson Glueck made clear that he would ordain a female candidate when the opportunity arose. Following Glueck's death in 1971, the honor of ordaining America's first female rabbi devolved upon Alfred Gottschalk, Glueck's successor as president of HUC–JIR. The Reform Movement's accomplishment was soon followed by the Reconstructionist Rabbinical College, which ordained its first female rabbi in 1973. The Conservative

Movement's Jewish Theological Seminary did not ordain a woman as rabbi until 1985.

The ordination of Sally Priesand was seen by some as the ultimate realization of women's religious equality by the Reform Movement. As additional female colleagues joined in numbers that by the early 1980s approached equity with the number of male ordainees, the movement continued to celebrate its commitment to female religious equality. On one level, the advent of female rabbis did address the question of women's equal authority and status within the movement. Yet, despite a general commitment to gender equity, differentials in male and female rabbinic salaries indicate that there are still limits to equality. Even though female rabbis have now been in the field long enough to qualify for positions requiring seniority, a survey of rabbinic posts at large congregations, of faculty positions at HUC–JIR campuses, and of leadership roles within the movement reveals strikingly few women in the central roles that will continue to determine the future of the movement.

Changing societal roles for women have also reshaped congregational life. Although sisterhoods remain important membership organizations, congregational leaders no longer assume that they can draw on the unlimited energies and time of a cadre of talented female volunteers. As a result, much of the responsibility for sustaining a more limited range of congregational activities falls increasingly upon paid (male and female) staff members. Meanwhile, some women now become involved in synagogue life and governance without first rising through the sisterhood. As women take on lay leadership roles that were once monopolized by men, many are wary of the subsidiary role often ascribed to sisterhoods. This same concern was reflected in the National Federation of Temple Sisterhoods' 1993 decision to change its name to Women of Reform Judaism, the Federation of Temple Sisterhoods (WRJ). The change of name reflects a desire to be seen not merely as an ancillary service group but as an organization that puts its members and their interests at the center of the Reform Movement. Although WRJ continues to fulfill many of NFTS's traditional roles within the movement, current efforts such as campaigns against breast cancer and in areas of social action, as well as sponsorship of a new bible commentary written by women, demonstrate a commitment to redefining the tradition and texts of Jewish life.

As the WRJ's Torah commentary project suggests, the desire to offer women full access to Judaism is complicated by the indelibly patriarchal sources of Jewish tradition. Gender-inclusive liturgical reform, for example, is slowed by desires to preserve the language of Jewish tradition, worries about how to keep texts familiar to congregants who are poorly educated in Hebrew, and differing perceptions of the extent to which Jewish prayer and practice are formulated as expressions of male religiosity. In 1993, the movement published a "gender-sensitive" liturgy meant to supplement *Gates of Prayer*, which appeared in 1975. The new edition does not employ male pronouns to refer to God, and it offers gender-neutral English prayers and translations. Changes in the Hebrew text, however, are limited to adding the names of the matriarchs to liturgical references to the patriarchs. Although some within the movement would like to see more efforts to challenge the patriarchal language and roots of Judaism, others choose to reject or ignore the changes that have already been offered.

The particular adaptations necessary to realize Reform Judaism's rhetorical commitment to the principle of religious equality for men and women have evolved along with the broader society's often-confusing mix of expectations of proper gender roles. Contemporary Reform Judaism, for instance, struggles with how to redefine notions of rabbinic authority in ways that can do justice to both the men and women who fill rabbinic roles. At the same time, the movement must also accommodate those who believe that there should be a way to sustain distinctive religious roles and responsibilities for men and women. Discrete and significant advances, like the ordination of female rabbis or efforts to demasculinize Jewish prayer, often tend to raise awareness that even more change is necessary. Current efforts to push Reform practice and liturgy to respond to gender concerns often draws upon the creative work of progressive Jews from outside the Reform Movement. Yet, the recognition that a vibrant and relevant Judaism must respond to the challenges raised by the position of women in American life derives from the earliest days and concerns of America's Reform Movement.

BIBLIOGRAPHY

Evans, Jane. "Intertwining Yesterday, Today, and Tomorrow: The Union of American Hebrew Congregations." In *The Jewish Condition: Essays on Contemporary Judaism Honoring Rabbi Alexander M. Schindler*, edited by Aron Hirt-Manheimer (1995); Goldman, Karla. "Beyond the Gallery: The Place of Women in the Development of American Judaism." Ph.D. diss., Harvard University, 1993; Joselit, Jenna Weissman. *The Wonders of America: Reinventing Jewish Culture, 1880–1950* (1994); Nadell, Pamela S. "'Top Down' or 'Bottom Up': Two Movements for Women's Rabbinic Ordination." In *An Inventory of Promises: Essays on American Jewish History in Honor of Moses Rischin*, edited by Jeffrey S. Gurock and Marc Lee Raphael (1995); Nadell,

Pamela S., and Rita J. Simon. "Ladies of the Sisterhood: Women in the American Reform Synagogue, 1900–1930." In *Active Voices: Women in Jewish Culture*, edited by Maurie Sacks (1995); National Federation of Temple Sisterhoods. *The Days of Our Years: Service through Sisterhood, 1913–1963* (1963); Umansky, Ellen M. "Women in Judaism: From the Reform Movement to Contemporary Jewish Religious Feminism." In *Women of Spirit: Female Leadership in the Jewish and Christian Traditions*, edited by Rosemary Radford Ruether and Eleanor McLaughlin (1979), and "Women's Journey toward Rabbinic Ordination." In *Women Rabbis: Exploration and Celebration*, edited by Gary P. Zola (1996).

KARLA GOLDMAN

REICHENBERGER, ELSIE MARGARET BINGER *see* NAUMBERG, ELSIE MARGARET BINGER

REISEN, SARAH (1885–1974)

Sarah Reisen was a member of an illustrious Yiddishist literary family whose reputation she maintained by her multiple talents as a poet, fiction writer, translator, and children's author. Recognized by contemporaries for her humane literary sensibility, she brought to Yiddish literature not only her own creative works, but also her translations, which introduced readers of all ages to world literature.

Reisen was born in 1885 in Koydenov, White Russia, to a distinguished family. She received a rich and varied education: a rabbi's wife taught her basic Hebrew; her father, Kalmen Rayzen, a writer and freethinker, instructed her in the weekly Torah portions; from her scholarly and pious mother, Kreyne Epshtayn, she learned German; and a shtetl teacher tutored her in Russian.

Her mother died when Reisen was ten. Briefly, she lived in Vinitze with her father and brothers, Abraham and Zalmen, and then with her older sister in Mohilne. In 1899, at fourteen, she moved to Minsk, where she worked as a seamstress, concurrently continuing her studies. Thereafter, she earned a precarious livelihood as a tutor of Russian. Reisen married the writer David Kasel in 1904 and had a son, Moishe Reisen-Kasel; the marriage ended in divorce. She shuttled between Warsaw, Minsk, and Vilna, and finally, in 1933, immigrated to New York.

Reisen's literary career was launched in Minsk, when she was seventeen, with the publication of a sketch in Russian and a translation of I.L. Peretz. She joined the Yiddish literary circle, which included Rokhl Brokhes.

Sometimes under the pen name of Sarah Kalmens (derived from her father's name), her sketches, short stories, and poems appeared in such periodicals as the Bundist *Di Folkstzaytung, Der Veg, Der Fraynd,* and her brother Abraham's publication, *Eyropeyishe Literatur.* Her work also appeared in the Yiddish presses of London and New York: the *Forward* (which serialized her novels), *Di Tsukunft, Amerikaner,* and *Feder.* She also wrote, translated, and performed in theater pieces.

Reisen's first Yiddish translation was published by her brother Abraham in *Dos Yidishe Vort* [The Yiddish word], followed by her highly acclaimed translation of Gogol's "The Overcoat." Between 1922 and 1929, she translated the works of Turgenev, Pushkin, Andreyev, Tagore, and Tolstoy, among others.

Her contribution to children's literature was significant, and included original stories and adaptations, legends, and poetry. Her books for children included *Der Ber un dem Veshuvniks Dray Techter* [The bear and the villager's three daughters] and *Bobe Yakhne un Meyshele.* Once a teacher herself, Reisen adapted works by Oscar Wilde and Daniel Defoe for use in Yiddish schools.

Her poetry was published in Korman's *Yidishe Dikhterins Antologye,* Basin's *Amerikaner Yidishe Poezye,* and Rozhansky's *Di Froy in der Yidisher Poezye. Kholem un Vor* [Dream and reality] is a collection of her early writings. Her first poetry collection, *Lider,* appeared in 1924 in Vilna; another volume, *Lider fun Sore Reyzen,* was published in 1955 in New York.

Reisen was a lyrical poet who spoke from the heart in the unmediated, modest language of love, abandonment, loneliness, and the wonders of the world—natural and human. A maternal figure in the Yiddish literary world, she stands as a sustaining link in the chain of Yiddish literature.

Sarah Reisen died in New York City on October 25, 1974.

BIBLIOGRAPHY

Basin, Moyshe. *Amerikaner Yidishe Poezye* [American Yiddish poetry] (1940); Grobard, B. "Lider fun Sore Reyzen" [Poems by Sarah Reisen]. *Di Tsunkunft* [The future] 61, no. 3 (March 1956): 138; Korman, E. *Yidishe Dikhterins Antologye* [Yiddish poetesses anthology] (1928); *Leksikon fun der nayer yidisher literatur* [Lexicon of new Yiddish literature]. Vol. 8 (1968); Rawitch, Melech. *Mayn Leksikon* [My Lexicon]. Vol. 4, Book 2 (1982); Reizen, Zalman. *Leksikon fun der Yidisher Literatur, Prese, un Filologye* [Lexicon of Yiddish literature, press, and philology]. 2d ed. (1929); Rozhansky, Shmuel, ed. *Di Froy in der Yidisher Poezye* [The woman in Yiddish poetry] (1966); *UJE.*

FRIEDA FORMAN

REISENBERG, NADIA (1904–1983)

Whether recording a Brahms sonata with clarinetist Benny Goodman, enjoying her three grandsons, or giving a master class in Jerusalem, pianist Nadia Reisenberg's joy in relationships radiated from her.

Born on July 14, 1904, in Vilna, in what is now Lithuania, Nadia Reisenberg was the eldest of three daughters of Aaron and Rachel (Grad) Reisenberg. Her father was an accountant for several publishing houses; the family was comfortably middle class. Because she and her sister Clara were clearly musically talented, her parents moved to St. Petersburg when she was eleven so that the two girls could attend the renowned Imperial Conservatory. There, Reisenberg studied with noted piano pedagogue Leonid Nikolayev.

Due to the upheavals of the Russian Revolution, Reisenberg's family left Russia in 1920. They traveled in Lithuania, Poland, and Germany with many adventures and hardships, and with many musical successes for the two sisters. Arriving in New York in 1922, they were welcomed and assisted by a family contact, Isaac J. ("Sasha") Sherman.

Nadia Reisenberg initially performed in private homes while studying privately with Alexander Lambert. She made her American debut on December 17, 1922, playing Ignace Paderewski's Polish Fantasy for piano and orchestra in the presence of the composer, and she gave a successful debut recital at New York's Aolian Hall on February 6, 1924. On June 24, 1924, she married Isaac Sherman, who later had an import-export business. The couple had two sons. The elder son, Alexander, became an engineer, while the younger son, Robert, was for many years the executive producer of WQXR, a classical music radio station in New York.

Reisenberg energetically combined a happy family life with a flourishing concert career: solo recitals, performances with orchestras, and touring. In 1930, invited by celebrated pianist Josef Hofmann to the Curtis Institute in Philadelphia, she began studying with him. She received her Curtis Institute diploma in 1935 and continued postgraduate study until 1938. She also taught at Curtis from 1934 to 1938. From 1938 to 1940, she made radio history in an acclaimed series of weekly concerts with the WOR Radio Orchestra, conducted by Alfred Wallenstein, performing all the piano concertos of Mozart.

Meanwhile her sister Clara Rockmore, whose debut as a violinist was thwarted by arm problems, had developed an extraordinary career playing the theremin, an electronic instrument that is played without being touched, named after its inventor, Leon

Pianist Nadia Reisenberg made radio history in an acclaimed series of weekly concerts with the WOR Radio Orchestra, performing all the piano concertos of Mozart. An accomplished solo and chamber performer, she also devoted much of her energy to teaching and maintained a long-term relationship with the Rubin Academy of Music in Jerusalem. [International Piano Archives, University of Maryland]

Theremin. At times the two sisters performed together; a peak of their shared work was Clara's Town Hall recital on October 27, 1938, which included the challenging A Major sonata of Cesar Franck.

In the early 1950s, Reisenberg shifted from a solo career to one focused on teaching, which she loved, and chamber music, to which she had been especially drawn from her youth. From the testimony of her students and from her own remarks, it is clear that she was an extraordinary teacher—kind yet demanding, often letting her relationships with students flower into deep personal connections. Reisenberg taught at Mannes beginning in 1955, at Juilliard beginning in

1974, and privately. In chamber music, she appeared many times with the Budapest String Quartet and with numerous other artists, including clarinetist Simeon Bellison, violinist William Kroll, and cellist Joseph Schuster. She judged many competitions, including the prestigious Leventritt Award. Reisenberg maintained a vigorous schedule of teaching and performing almost until her death, celebrating her seventy-fifth birthday in a performance with violinist Erick Friedman at the Caramoor Festival. A range of LP recordings, most made for Westminster in the 1950s, capture her lucid, lyric musicality. These include Chopin nocturnes and mazurkas, Haydn sonatas, and works of Mussorgsky, Kabalevsky, Rachmaninoff, and Tchaikovsky.

Reisenberg identified herself as a Jew, but without any ritual observance. She had a strong attachment to Israel, giving six summer seminars at the Rubin Academy of Music in Jerusalem, the last one only two years before her death. Many of Israel's leading musicians studied with her.

Family was central to Reisenberg: her intimate relations with her sisters, her fulfilling marriage to her husband, who died in 1955, and her delight in her two sons and three grandsons. Yet many students and musical colleagues also became "family" for her. Upon Nadia Reisenberg's death on June 10, 1983, she was mourned by a broad circle of associates whose lives she had enriched.

BIBLIOGRAPHY

Baker's Biographical Dictionary of Musicians; Martin, Steven M. *Theremin: an Electronic Odyssey.* Film. (1995); Neidle, Cecile. *America's Immigrant Women* (1975); *New Grove Dictionary of American Music.* Edited by H. Wiley Hitchcock and Stanley Sadie (1986); Obituary. *NYTimes,* June 12, 1983; Reisenberg, Nadia. Collection. International Piano Archives at Maryland (IPAM), University of Maryland, College Park; Saleski, Gdal. *Famous Musicians of Jewish Origin* (1949); Sherman, Robert, and Alexander Sherman, eds. *Nadia Reisenberg: A Musician's Scrapbook* (1985); Sherman, Robert. Telephone interview by author, December 5, 1996; *UJE; Who's Who of American Women; WWIAJ* (1926); *WWWIA* 8.

HARRIET FEINBERG

RESNIK, JUDITH (1949–1986)

One of the seven crew members who died in the tragic explosion of the space shuttle *Challenger* on January 28, 1986, Judith ("J.R.") Resnik was a pioneer for women entering NASA's space program, and the second American woman astronaut to travel in space.

A talented scientist and a private individual, Resnik gave her deepest loyalties to her father, her career, and her close friends. Although she avoided publicity whenever possible, she was fun-loving and spirited; her romantic crush on actor Tom Selleck was often a source of good-natured teasing among her coworkers.

Born Judith Arlene Resnik on April 5, 1949, in Akron, Ohio, to first-generation Jewish Russian parents, Judith was a bright, curious child who, by kindergarten, could both read and solve simple math problems. Her father, Marvin, was an optometrist and a part-time cantor when he married Sarah Polensky, a former legal secretary from Cleveland Heights. After Judith was born, the Resniks had a son, Charles.

The Resniks were an upper middle-class Jewish family devoted to their religion and to all learning. Gifted in math and science, Resnik excelled in academics from a young age. She also attended Hebrew school and, by her teenage years, was an accomplished classical pianist. Teachers and friends described her as extremely bright, disciplined, perfectionistic, and personable.

With a score of 800 on her math SAT tests, Resnik was accepted to Carnegie Tech (now Carnegie-Mellon) in Pittsburgh, where she majored in electrical engineering. After graduating in 1970, she married Michael Oldak, a fellow engineering student. The couple moved to New Jersey, where Resnik was employed in the missile and surface radar division of RCA. In 1971, they moved to Washington, D.C. Resnik received her master's degree in engineering from the University of Maryland, and began work on her Ph.D. while employed as a biomedical engineer in the neurophysics lab at the National Institutes of Health. She and Oldak divorced in 1975.

In 1977, while she was finishing work on her doctorate, NASA began recruiting minorities and women to the space program. Though Resnik had never shown particular interest in the space program, she decided to apply. After receiving academic honors for her doctoral work in electrical engineering, she accepted a job with Xerox. She moved to Redondo Beach near Los Angeles, where she continued to train for the NASA tryouts. In 1978, at age twenty-nine, Resnik was one of six women accepted into the program.

She would be the second American woman to fly in space (after Sally Ride in 1983), and the fourth woman worldwide. During her first six years at NASA, she specialized in the operation of a remote-control

A gifted student, Judith Resnik not only made a perfect 800 on her math SAT test, but also excelled at Hebrew school and was an accomplished classical pianist. She was the second American woman to travel in space and, along with schoolteacher Christa McAuliffe, lost her life in the Challenger *disaster.*
[CORBIS/BETTMANN]

mechanical arm that moved objects located outside the spacecraft. In 1984, on her first space flight on the shuttle *Discovery*, Resnik was responsible for unfurling a 102-foot-long solar sail, which, on future missions, would be used to capture the sun's energy.

NASA's *Challenger*, Flight 51-L, was Resnik's second space launch. She was to have assisted in photographing Halley's comet. Famous for its civilian crew member, teacher Christa McAuliffe, the mission endured three delays before taking off at 11:38 A.M. on January 28, 1986. Seventy-three seconds into the flight, the space shuttle exploded in midair due to hydrogen leakage caused by faulty O-ring seals. Along with her six crew members, Resnik died in the worst space disaster in history.

BIBLIOGRAPHY

Bernstein, Joanne E., and Rose Blue with Alan Jay Gerber. *Judith Resnik, Challenger Astronaut* (1990); "For Women Only: Resnik Scholarship." *Flying* (January 1991); Hauck, Richard. Telephone interview by author, June 27, 1996; Sherr, Lynn. "Remember Judy." *Ms.* (June 1986); Spencer, Scott, and Chris Spolar. "The Epic Flight of Judith Resnik: An Investigative Obituary." *Esquire* (December 1986).

LYNN COHEN

RESNIK, REGINA (b. 1922)

Regina Resnik, world-famous opera singer and leading lady at New York's Metropolitan Opera House, was born on August 30, 1922, in the Bronx, New York. From an early age, Resnik knew that she wanted to be an opera singer. Although her Jewish Russian immigrant parents could not afford to pay for singing lessons, Resnik began instruction at age thirteen with Rosalie Miller, who offered her free lessons. The match proved successful, and Resnik continued her studies with Miller during her college years and her professional career.

The singer was as precocious and disciplined in her academic studies as she was in her music. After skipping several grades, she attended a special junior high school where she could study German and Italian in preparation for her chosen vocation. Despite her ambitions, Resnik and her family knew that she faced difficult odds. She turned down a scholarship to the Juilliard School of Music, and instead attended HUNTER COLLEGE in New York. There, she could earn a bachelor's degree in music education that would allow her to teach if she could not support herself as a professional singer.

Resnik need not have worried. In the early 1940s, her singing career took several definitive steps forward. She made her concert debut at the Brooklyn Academy of Music on October 27, 1942. In the same year, she made her operatic debut, portraying Lady Macbeth in the New Opera Company's production of Verdi's *Macbeth* in New York City. She also embarked on a national tour of the United States under the auspices of Pryor Concert Management of Council Bluffs, Iowa, giving forty concerts with choral societies, in university towns, and at women's clubs and churches. She made her international debut in 1943 in Mexico City, singing Leonora in Beethoven's *Fidelio*.

The following year, Resnik achieved a milestone in her career. She won the Metropolitan Opera auditions, and debuted at the Met on December 6, 1944, as a last-minute replacement for Zinka Milanov. The role was Leonora in Verdi's *Il Trovatore*. Other leading roles that Resnik performed during her first season with the Met included the title role in Puccini's *Tosca*, Santuzza in Mascagni's *Cavalleria Rusticana*, and Leonora in *Fidelio*. Personal happiness coincided with public success when, in 1947, Resnik married lawyer Harry W. Davies, with whom she later had a son.

Following the triumph of her first season, Resnik became a leading soprano at the Met. Her roles from the mid-1940s to the mid-1950s included Ellen Orford in the New York premiere of Britten's *Peter Grimes*, Alice Ford in Verdi's *Falstaff*, Sieglinde in Wagner's *Die Walküre*, and both Donna Anna and Donna Elvira in Mozart's *Don Giovanni*. She also sang Sieglinde at the Bayreuth Opera House in Germany in 1953. During this period, she worked with many renowned conductors, including Edward Johnson, Jean Morel, Sir Thomas Beecham, and Bruno Walter. In addition, she learned a great deal about singing and the business of music from her manager, William Stein, and her accompanist, Leo Taubman.

Resnik excelled in a wide variety of soprano roles at an unusually early age. However, in the mid-1950s, she faced an unexpected and traumatic challenge, which caused her career to change direction. Her voice gradually acquired the darker qualities of the lower mezzo-soprano, causing her difficulty in performance. When Rosalie Miller proved unable to help her through the transition from soprano to mezzo-soprano, Resnik sought the advice of Giuseppe Danise, who became her new teacher. Under his guidance, she abandoned her large repertoire of soprano roles and learned new mezzo parts that brought out the warm vocal color for which she became famous.

This vocal adjustment also caused problems with the Metropolitan Opera management. Resnik was shunned by the Met's new director, Sir Rudolf Bing, who offered her only minor roles. This lack of appreciation forced her to go abroad to sing the leading roles she desired. The result was a highly successful career in Europe. She achieved particular success at Covent Garden in London, where she made her debut in the title role of Bizet's *Carmen* in 1957, under the direction of David Webster. Her other London roles included Marina in Mussorgsky's *Boris Godunov*, Mistress Quickly in Verdi's *Falstaff*, and Klytamnestra in Strauss's *Salome*. She sang Carmen in Vienna under the direction of Herbert von Karajan in 1957 and 1958, followed by performances in Berlin, Paris, and Stuttgart. Other successful roles in Europe included Amneris in Verdi's *Aïda*, Fricka in Wagner's *Das Rheingold* and *Die Walküre*, and Herodius in *Salome*. Despite occasional performances with the Metropolitan Opera, Resnik resigned in protest from the Met roster in 1967 when she was not cast as Carmen in the Met's production of the opera. She later returned when the Met's management recanted and offered her the role.

Throughout her career, critics praised Resnik for her superb acting. She strove to add new dimensions to every role and to create dramatic force and subtlety. Carmen, Klytamnestra, Mistress Quickly, and the title role in Tchaikovsky's *The Queen of Spades* were her favorite acting challenges. She was named Commander of the French Academy of Arts, Sciences and Letters, was named *Kammersängerin* in Austria, and was awarded the President's Medal in the United States.

The 1970s and 1980s brought new pleasures and successes for Resnik. She married her second husband, painter Arbit Blatas, in 1975, and expanded her creativity to other areas of the opera. In the early 1970s, she began directing opera productions around the world. She has directed twelve productions in total, in San Francisco, Hamburg, Warsaw, Lisbon, Venice, Sydney, and Strasbourg. She explored her Jewish heritage in a documentary on the Venetian ghetto, which aired on public television in the spring of 1983.

BIBLIOGRAPHY

Bloomfield, Arthur. "Our Critics Abroad: San Francisco." *Opera* 34, no. 1 (February 1983): 179–182; Cummings, David M. *International Who's Who in Music and Musicians Directory* (1992); *EJ* (1973–1982); Mayer, Martin. "Our Critics Abroad: America, Mozart, and Sondheim: New York." *Opera* 41, no. 1 (November 1990): 1313–1316; "Reflected Glory: A Century at the Met." *Opera News* 48, no. 4 (October 1983): 64–80; "Regina Reflects: Forty Years After Her Met Debut, Mezzo Resnik Tells of Her Turbulent But Ultimately Fulfilling Career." *Opera News* 49 (December 1984): 10–14, 58–60; Resnik, Regina. *Geto: The Historic Ghetto of Venice*. Documentary, KQED San Francisco (1983); Rich, Maria F., ed. *Who's Who in Opera* (1976); Rosenthal, Harold. "Regina Resnik." In *The New Grove Dictionary of Music and Musicians*, edited by Stanley Sadie (1988); Slominsky, Nicolas, ed. *Baker's Biographical Dictionary of Musicians* (1984).

JENNIFER STINSON

RESNIKOFF, FREDA (1880–1965)

Freda Resnikoff was a founder and dedicated leader of the Mizrachi Women's Organization and mother, mother-in-law, and grandmother-in-law of three of its national presidents. The matriarch of a family of ten children, Resnikoff was well known in Orthodox circles for her volunteer work, fund-raising, and unending hospitality.

Freda (Wolfson) Resnikoff was born in Kazhimirov, Russia, to Lifsa Krachek and Rabbi Meir Wolfson, a renowned scholar. Reb Meir headed the town's elementary yeshivah, while his wife ran the general store. Freda had one sister, Baila, and three brothers, Elimelech, Beryl, and Shlomo.

In 1897, Freda married twenty-two-year-old Hyman (Chaim Yitzchak) Resnikoff, a scholar and, by profession, a barber who manufactured a kosher shaving powder. He escaped the czar's army in 1905 and fled to the United States. Freda Resnikoff, with an infant and three young children, arrived in New York in 1907. The family settled on New York's Lower East Side.

In 1910, Resnikoff helped to found Bnos Mizrachi, serving as secretary and treasurer. This group marked the origins of the educational network that was incorporated as Mizrachi Women in 1925 and is today called AMIT.

In 1922, the family moved to a four-story brownstone on South Tenth Street in Williamsburg, Brooklyn. There, Resnikoff organized a chapter involving the women of Young Israel and of Yeshivah Torah Vodaas. Her Yiddish handwritten book of meeting minutes and records of more than a decade is a family treasure.

The Resnikoff home was a center of family life and holiday gatherings for relatives, with a constant flow of visitors from Europe and Israel. Freda Resnikoff's philanthropies included Yeshivah Torah Vodaas and the Chofetz Chaim Yeshivah in Brooklyn, which her husband helped to found. Out-of-town students or those fleeing from Russia were taken in as boarders, and some stayed for years. Resnikoff instilled in her children a great respect for scholarship, a fierce sense of loyalty to family, and a strong belief in acts of loving-kindness.

All of Resnikoff's daughters, as they married, became members of their local Mizrachi Women chapter, as did her daughters-in-law. Her daughter-in-law Nathalie Resnikoff and daughter Dvorah Rabinowitz Masovetsky became national presidents, a position held today by Evelyn Blachor, Resnikoff's granddaughter-in-law. Elissa Chesir, her granddaughter, is a current national vice president.

When her husband died at age sixty in 1935 as the result of an accident, Resnikoff, with the three youngest children still living at home, kept the family together and her home intact. Freda Resnikoff died at age eighty-five on April 29, 1965, in Brooklyn, New York.

BIBLIOGRAPHY

AJYB, 67:540; AMIT Women. Jerusalem Chug I and Jerusalem Chug II Souvenir Journal. June 2, 1996; Blachor, Isaac [grandson]. Interview by author, July 15, 1996; Obituary. *NYTimes*, April 30, 1965; Resnikoff Family Tree. August 1965; Septimus, Helen Wilkenfeld [daughter]. Interview by author, July 24, 1996.

ESTHER FARBER

RICH, ADRIENNE CECILE (b. 1929)

Adrienne Rich, one of the best American poets of our time, is not someone who would take pride in the description, "not just a woman poet." She has shown that, far from being a limiting or qualifying word, "woman" can be a badge of honor. It can speak of possibilities too long unexplored and passions once turned away. It can be a declaration of freedom and of power.

Adrienne Rich was born on May 16, 1929, in Baltimore, Maryland. Her mother, Helen Elizabeth Rich, a composer and pianist, taught her at home until the fourth grade. Her father, Arnold Rich, a physician with a great love of books, encouraged Adrienne in her ambitions to be a writer. She attended Radcliffe College, where she graduated cum laude in 1951.

It was also in 1951 that Rich published her first book of poetry, *A Change of World*, which received immediate acclaim. Indeed, poet W.H. Auden had chosen it to be published in the Yale Series of Younger Poets, a great honor in itself. Two years later, Rich married economist Alfred Haskell Conrad and, within six years, had given birth to three sons. In 1955, her book *The Diamond Cutters and Other Poems* garnered even more positive critical attention.

Speaking of her early work, critics use such words as "formal," "elegant," and "controlled." She had that combination of consummate skill and great talent—even genius—that compels the predominantly white male literary establishment to make exceptions.

"When the Civil Rights movement came along in the late fifties, early sixties," Rich said in a 1991 interview, "and I began to hear Black voices describing and analyzing what were the concrete issues for Black people, like segregation, like racism, it came to me as a great relief. It was like finding language for something that I'd needed a language for all along. That was the first place where I heard a language to name oppression. And it was an enormous relief, even as it threw up a lot of questions for me as to where I stood with all this."

In 1963, *Snapshots of a Daughter-in-Law: Poems 1954–1962* was published. Speaking in a 1994 interview with Matthew Rothschild, Rich said, "When I was putting together the manuscript of my third book . . . which contains what I think of as my first overtly feminist poem, called "Snapshots of a Daughter-in-Law," some friends of mine looked at the manuscript and said, 'Now don't give it this title. People will think it's some sort of female diatribe or complaint.' I wanted that title and I wanted that poem." Rich's friends were right in their predictions. Previously laudatory critics censured the book for being "too personal, too bitter." But the poet had found an essential part of her voice. She was a not a good girl; she was a dangerous woman.

Dangerous or not, Rich was too fine a poet to be ignored. She continued to be an important figure in American poetry. She also continued to work out the issues of feminism and womanhood in her personal life. In 1966, she separated from her husband of thirteen years. When he committed suicide four years later, she was left with three adolescent boys to rear on her own. She was also deeply involved in the major political struggles of the time—the antiwar movement and the civil rights movement.

The response to *Diving into the Wreck: Poems 1971–1972* reflected the tension of Rich's position as a poet. It was unabashedly, even militantly, feminist—and it won the National Book Award. It was a hard pill for many literary men—and some women—to swallow. One of the best poets of the day was, at one and the same time, one of those loudmouthed "women's liberationists." And there was worse to come. Rich declined to accept the National Book Award in her own name, deploring the idea of competition among poets. Instead, she accepted it in the name of all women and donated the money to charity.

She then attacked motherhood. At any rate, she attacked the patriarchal underpinnings of our conception of motherhood. This time her medium was prose, a book entitled *Of Woman Born: Motherhood as Experience and Institution.*

By this time Rich was as controversial a figure as contemporary literature has produced. Helen Vendler, in *Parnassus: Poetry in Review*, singled out the poem "Rape" in *Diving into the Wreck* for particular damnation. "This poem," she wrote, "like some others [in the book], is a deliberate refusal of the modulations of intelligence in favor of . . . propaganda." *Harvard Magazine*'s RUTH WHITMAN, on the other hand, called the title poem of the volume "one of the great poems of our time."

In the late 1970s, another segment of the "unheard" found representation in Rich's work as her lesbianism became a more important element in her poetic voice. *The Dream of a Common Language: Poems 1974–1977* incorporated an earlier work, *Twenty-One Love Poems*. This collection was followed by *A Wild Patience Has Taken Me This Far: Poems 1978–1981*. During the same period, Rich wrote numerous essays, addressing issues in literature and in lesbian-feminist politics. These were collected in *Lies, Secrets and Silence: Selected Prose 1966–1978* and *Blood, Bread and Poetry: Selected Prose 1979–1986*

Rich and poet/novelist Michelle Cliff, who would become her life companion, coedited a lesbian-feminist

It is impossible to overestimate the impact of Adrienne Rich on poetry in America in the last few decades. Too richly talented to be ignored by the literary establishment, she has at the same time been too politically oriented to be comfortably digested. This photograph was taken at a pro-choice rally in Union Square in New York City in March of 1979. [Bettye Lane]

journal entitled *Sinister Wisdom* from 1980 to 1984. Also in 1980, Rich published *Compulsory Heterosexuality and Lesbian Existence*, another prose work.

Beginning in the 1980s, Rich began increasingly to speak of her Jewish heritage, as in *Your Native Land, Your Life*, published in 1986. In *An Atlas of the Difficult World: Poems 1988–1991*, she continues this theme as it embraces the necessity of poet and citizen to remain grounded in reality, in the difficulties and struggles of the world. There is no honorable escape into "pure art."

In 1994, Rich published *What Is Found There: Notebooks on Poetry and Politics*. The title is from a poem by William Carlos Williams, which states quite clearly a belief the two poets share. "It is difficult / to get the news from poems / yet men die miserably every day for lack / of what is found there." To Rich, as to Williams, poetry is a necessary thing, a source of essential nourishment and a force for change. In the book, she laments that "poetry is banned in the United States" and "under house arrest." It has been neutralized by the assumption that it is obscure, effete and written for other poets.

Rich's poetry is none of those things. It is rich in the beauty of language, but at the same time enormously accessible. It is filled with passion and compassion. And it is always grounded in the realities of life in this time and this country, although its very concreteness helps it to transcend the boundaries of time and place.

In *What Is Found There*, Rich addresses the issue of Jewishness and "whiteness." Peter Erickson in the *Kenyon Review* says that Rich "does not find that her Jewishness cancels or mitigates her whiteness but instead explores both as valid aspects of her identity. Although Rich's Jewish affiliation is strongly in evidence here, she is also eloquent about the effects of her own whiteness." She acknowledges that being white has sometimes kept her from noticing the diversity around her, or of noticing when it disappeared and the faces around her became uniformly white.

In her latest volume, *Dark Fields of the Republic: Poems 1991–1995*, Rich affirms the value of the personal, the individual, the intimate. But at the same time, she declares that "the great dark birds of history screamed and plunged / into our personal weather."

Rich made headlines when she turned down the 1979 National Medal for the Arts. She protested a "democracy" in which so much wealth and power is in the hands of a few. Art, she stated, "means nothing if it simply decorates the dinner-table of power which holds it hostage."

Throughout her life, Rich has taught at a number of colleges and universities, beginning as a lecturer at Swarthmore College in 1967 and continuing through the Graduate School of the Arts of Columbia University and on to City College of the City University of New York. In 1972, she left New York to teach at Brandeis University in Waltham, Massachusetts. Among the other institutions where Rich carried on her work as both poet and teachers are Bryn Mawr, Rutgers, Cornell, Scripps, Pacific Oaks, and Stanford. She has also been a member of the advisory board of the Boston Woman's Fund and New Jewish Agenda.

Rich lives in Santa Cruz, California, with her partner, Michelle Cliff.

**SELECTED WORKS
BY ADRIENNE CECILE RICH**

A Change of World (1951); *A Wild Patience Has Taken Me This Far: Poems 1978–1981* (1981); *An Atlas of the Difficult World: Poems 1988–1991* (1991); *Blood, Bread and Poetry: Selected Prose 1979–1986* (1986); *Compulsory Heterosexuality and Lesbian Existence* (1980); *Dark Fields of the Republic: Poems 1991–1995* (1995); *Diving into the Wreck: Poems 1971–1972* (1973); *Lies, Secrets and Silence: Selected Prose 1966–1978* (1979); *Of Woman Born: Motherhood as Experience and Institution* (1976); *Snapshots of a Daughter-in-Law: Poems 1954–1962* (1963); *The Diamond Cutters and Other Poems* (1955); *The Dream of a Common Language: Poems 1974–1977* (1978); *What Is Found There: Notebooks on Poetry and Politics* (1994); *Your Native Land, Your Life* (1986).

BIBLIOGRAPHY

"Adrienne Cecile Rich." In *Her Heritage: A Biographical Encyclopedia of Famous American Women* (1994); Baker, David. "Against Mastery." *Kenyon Review* (June 1, 1992); *Contemporary Authors, New Revision Series.* Vol. 20; Erickson, Peter. "Singing America: From Walt Whitman to Adrienne Rich." *Kenyon Review* (January 1, 1995); Rothschild, Matthew. "Adrienne Rich." *Progressive* (January 1, 1994); St. John, David. "Brightening the Landscape: Dark Fields of the Republic, Poems 1991–1995." *Los Angeles Times* (February 25, 1996).

KATHLEEN THOMPSON

RICHARDSON, ROIPHE ANNE
see **ROIPHE, ANNE**

RICHMAN, JULIA (1855–1912)

When Julia Richman was eleven years old, she told her family, "I am not pretty . . . and I am not going to marry, but before I die, all New York will know my name!" When she died, her "promises" had come to pass: She did not marry, and a great many New Yorkers knew her name.

Born on October 12, 1855, Julia Richman was the third child of Moses and Theresa (Melis) Richman, German-speaking Jewish immigrants from Prague, Bohemia. Her middle-class family lived first in the Chelsea section of Manhattan, then moved to "Kleindeutschland," a heavily German district later known as the Lower East Side, and finally settled on Central Park West.

Richman was an excellent student who enjoyed school and wanted to continue her education beyond the eighth grade, but her parents did not see any need for her to do so. A family battle ensued, which Richman won, permitting her to enroll at the newly organized Female Normal College, later renamed HUNTER COLLEGE. At age seventeen, she graduated and began a forty-year career in the New York City schools as a teacher at Public School 59.

In addition to her work at the public school, Richman began to teach in the Sabbath school of the Reform Temple Ahawath Chesed, where she and her family were members. This connection led to her involvement in another aspect of Jewish communal life, charitable work. Together with a few other middle-class German Jewish women, she organized the Young Ladies Charitable Union, which after five years was absorbed into the Hebrew Free School Association, of which Richman became a trustee.

As was her wont, Richman worked hard for the association, primarily as a fund-raiser, but she also found time to organize another group, the YOUNG WOMEN'S HEBREW ASSOCIATION, which began as an adjunct of the Young Men's Hebrew Association. In 1885, when the influx of Eastern European Jews pouring into the Lower East Side caused considerable alarm in the established German Jewish community, several of the groups in which Richman was active joined together to form the Educational Alliance, which became the most important organization of uptown Jews working to Americanize their newly arrived downtown brethren.

In accord with the majority of people concerned with the arrival of thousands of foreigners during the late nineteenth century, Julia Richman saw great danger for the United States if the newcomers did not learn the English language and American ways. Fearing balkanization and fragmentation, she argued that the school must "wrest" immigrant children from the language and customs of their homeland. Her work at the Educational Alliance was one road to this end. In addition to holding English as a second language classes, the alliance offered instruction in American sports, cooking, dressing, and other activities.

Julia Richman, who by 1884 had become the first Jew and first Normal College graduate to be named a grammar school principal, advocated all such efforts. First at the alliance and then in the public schools attended by immigrant children, she developed a language program under which foreign-born children would be tested for knowledge of English and then placed in an appropriate class in which they could remain for six to eight months. During this period, they would be immersed in English, forbidden to use their first language even when at play or in the washrooms. If they disobeyed, their mouths would be washed out with soap (kosher, if appropriate).

Learning the language of America came first, but Julia Richman wanted the schools to do much more. On her list were the establishment of kindergartens; cheap, nutritious lunches; playgrounds; health examinations; instruction in domestic science for girls and manual training for boys. She was not alone in advocating these initiatives, but when she was elevated to district superintendent of the Lower East Side schools in 1903, she was in a better position than most to put them into effect.

Richman saw her assignment as multifaceted. In her view, the bursting classes, dilapidated buildings, and high dropout rate in her district were only part of a dismal picture. If immigrant children were to become good American citizens, she believed that conditions in the teeming streets surrounding her schools must also be addressed. Settlement house workers, with whom she worked closely, had managed to convince the city to level and erect a fence around a plot of land near Allen Street and thus create a much-needed oasis, but the space was neglected and unsupervised and, as a result, soon became as much of a slum as the blocks around it. Julia Richman, using the clout of her fellow Educational Alliance trustees, forced the Parks Department to live up to its responsibilities. Many residents of the Lower East Side appreciated her efforts on their behalf, but there were also others who resented her "lady bountiful approach" and her public opposition to some East Side institutions, such as street peddling.

Considering the weight of her other activities, it is surprising that Julia Richman was also an author. In addition to her many articles in social service publications such as *Outlook*, she coauthored *The Pupil's Arithmetic* (1909) and *Good Citizenship* (1908). The first is a text for elementary school teachers, the second for use in civics classes. Other articles presented new educational ideas such as homogeneous grouping and continuous promotion. She also wrote books for Sabbath school teachers, laying out model lessons even an untrained volunteer could follow.

During this same period, Julia Richman raised enough money from her wealthy German Jewish associates, such as Felix Warburg, to establish a settlement, Teachers' House, which, among other activities, dispatched "visitors" to the homes of truant children and used other methods, including stipends, to enable them to return to school. A placement counselor was also installed at Teachers' House, responsible for finding jobs for those youngsters who could not be induced to return to the classroom.

In many ways, Julia Richman was a liberated woman while conforming to the rules established by the society in which she lived. Because teaching young children and caring for the unfortunate were permissible female activities, these were the arenas in which she performed. On the other hand, she would not settle for being just an ordinary teacher or charity volunteer. That would not have satisfied her ambition and desire for fame. Within the parameters of acceptable female behavior, she struggled to achieve the power and prominence denied to all but a handful of women of her day.

Julia Richman died in Paris on June 24, 1912.

BIBLIOGRAPHY

AJHQ 70:35–51; *AJYB* 6 (1904–1905): 169, 14 (1912–1913): 128; Altman, Addie R., and Bertha R. Proskauer. *Julia Richman: An Appreciation of a Great Educator* (1916); Berrol, Selma. *Julia Richman: A Notable Woman* (1993); *JE*; *NAW*; Obituary. *NYTimes*, June 26, 1912, 13:5; *UJE*.

SELMA BERROL

RIDING, LAURA (1901–1991)

Laura Riding, also known as Laura Riding Jackson, was an unconventional poet and critic who is credited with helping shape modern poetry. She worked closely with a number of the leading writers and later in near-isolation. Her career moved from literary circles in New York and London to a modest citrus farm in Florida. Helping to define modern poetry, she gave up writing poetry herself for a time but later began publishing again after a silence of thirty years. Her poetry is intellectual and introspective, often dealing with abstract questions like the role of the poet in confronting truth. Her work was never widely read nor popular; yet she was an influential figure among other writers and thinkers, exerting, from all accounts, a dynamic, forceful, often eccentric personality.

Riding was born in New York City on January 16, 1901, the daughter of Nathaniel S. and Sarah (Edersheim) Reichenthal; she described her parents as Jewish but not very religious. Judaism seems to have had little influence on her life, personal or professional, and biographers note her rejection of both Judaism and her father's socialism. Scholars have also noted that her various name changes accompany major transition points in her life.

A promising student, she attended Cornell University on a scholarship, but did not complete her degree. In 1920, she married a Cornell history instructor, Louis Gottschalk, and then moved with him first to Illinois and then to Kentucky. At this point, she decided to pursue a career as a poet, and her early work was acclaimed by the "Fugitive" writers. Her marriage was dissolved in 1925. No longer married to Gottschalk, she nonetheless changed her name to Laura Riding Gottschalk, the name under which she published her first two volumes of poetry.

After a brief period in New York, her name now Anglicized to Laura Riding, she went to England, where she lived with the poet Robert Graves and his family. In 1929, during an emotionally tumultuous period, Riding attempted suicide. After her recovery, she and Graves settled in Majorca, where they ran the Seizin Press, produced a journal called *Epilogue*, and collaborated on books including *A Survey of Modernist Poetry*. Between 1926 and 1938, she wrote prolifically and published numerous volumes of poetry. The peak of her career came with the publication of *Collected Poems* in 1938, and in fact soon afterward she renounced poetry. With the start of the Spanish Civil War, she and Graves went to the United States, where their relationship ended.

Riding later married Schuyler Jackson, the poetry reviewer for *Time* magazine. Moving to Florida, they raised fruit and pursued independent scholarship in linguistics. After Jackson's death in 1968, Riding continued working on their lexicography project, assisted by a Guggenheim Fellowship awarded in 1973. Riding continued to write, and there was a resurgence of interest in her work in the 1970s and 1980s when she published new critical works and revised editions of her poetry. She received a fellowship from the National Endowment for the Arts in 1979, and was awarded a Bollingen Prize in early 1991 for her lifelong devotion to the art and ideals of poetry.

Laura Riding died of heart failure in Florida on September 2, 1991.

BIBLIOGRAPHY

Adams, Barbara. *The Enemy Self: Poetry and Criticism of Laura Riding* (1990); *Annual Obituary 1991*, edited by Deborah Andrews (1992); Baker, Deborah. *In Extremis: The Life of Laura Riding* (1993); *Contemporary Authors, New Revised Series* 28:251–253; *Contemporary Literary Criticism* 373, 377; Nye, Robert, ed. *A Selection of the Poems of Laura Riding* (1994); Riding, Laura. Papers. Laura and Schuyler B. Jackson Collection, Cornell University, Ithaca, New York, and Joint University Libraries, Nashville, Tenn., and Northwestern University, Evanston, Ill., and State University of New York, Buffalo, N.Y.; Wallace, Jo-Ann. "Laura Riding." In *The Oxford Companion to Women's Writing in the United States*, edited by Cathy Davidson and Linda Wagner-Martin (1995); Wexler, Joyce Piell. "Laura Riding." In *Dictionary of Literary Biography* 48: 236–245, and *Laura Riding: A Bibliography* (1981), and *Laura Riding's Pursuit of Truth* (1979).

JANE GABIN

RITUAL

Ritual is an act or a set of actions that employs symbols meaningful to the participants in a formal, repetitive, and stylized fashion. Ritual frames significant moments and important new realities. It is often used to effect transition from one state of being to another, as in weddings, funerals, or graduations. It is one of the most fundamental ways that human beings mark meaning in their personal lives and in the lives of their families and societies. Ritual is created in response to primal human terror that the universe is not inherently ordered and that human existence is ultimately physical and nothing more. Its power lies in the fact that it addresses and engages the body. In the words of the anthropologist BARBARA MYERHOFF, "Rituals persuade the body . . . ; [in ritual] the entire human sensorium [is involved] through dramatic presentation."

Ritual behavior is universal and innate—witness how young children ritualize accidental behaviors at bedtime, a time of transition from waking to sleep, by insisting on their subsequent precise repetition. It is one of the primary ways an individual or a culture conveys understanding of self to itself or to others and is one of the chief means of conveying that message to future generations. As the anthropologist Joseph Campbell wrote, "Ritual is mythology made alive." Thus, ritual transmits traditions and can be a powerful agent of cultural conservation. However, precisely because of the dynamic human need it addresses and because material and cultural circumstance change, ritual is constantly being invented, sculpting new meaning for a changed present and for the future. Ritual therefore, can also be a powerful vehicle for social and cultural change.

Ritual behavior is one of the fundamental pillars of Judaism, and of all religions, whose concern is precisely with ultimate meaning and purpose. Men in normative (rabbinic) Judaism have far more access to the sacred through personal ritual than do women. Under Jewish law (halakah), males are required to don ritual garments (*tzitzit*, tallith), which symbolically represent all 613 commandments of the Torah. Males over age thirteen are required to strap miniscrolls containing key verses of the Torah to the head and arm (phylacteries, or tefillin) and to make repeated signs of the letter *shin*, which represents one of God's names, with the straps, thus literally, binding themselves to Torah and emblazoning God's name on their bodies. A ritualized way of shearing hair leaves the "corners" of the male head conspicuously uncut (*peot*). Ritual covering of the head is required of all males, as is the growth of full, untrimmed beards. The only time that ritual bodily cutting is not only allowed but enjoined in Judaism is ritual circumcision (Brith Milah), performed as a sign of covenant with God. These ritualized behaviors effectively sacralize the male body, making it a carrier of the sacred and a vehicle for public demonstration of connectedness to God and Torah.

There is no analogous sacralization of the female body in traditional Judaism. On the contrary, such quintessentially female biological functions as menstruation and childbirth plunge women into a state of ritual impurity (*niddah*), meaning "separate," "outcast," "ostracized." Although technically, all Jews are considered ritually impure since loss of the sacrificial system of purification in the Temple, *niddah* is by far the most elaborate of all the functional remnants of the purity laws, and the one with the greatest behavioral consequences, requiring sexual abstinence and physical separation for a minimum of twelve days a cycle, and even longer after a birth. Female head covering, enjoined for married women only, is not, like that of men, referenced to God. Rather, it signals sexual unavailability to any male but the husband and derives from a male-centered perception of women as sexual objects to men.

The extensive world of family and public ritual in normative Judaism is also a male preserve. By religious law or social custom, such fundamental acts as sanctifying the wine and ritually cutting and blessing the bread on the Sabbath and festivals, performing the ritual which formally ends the Sabbath and holidays, lighting Hanukkah candles, leading the Passover seder, dwelling in the Tabernacle, blessing and waving the Four Species on Tabernacles, counting in a prayer quorum, leading services, making blessings over the Torah reading, public reading of the Torah and rejoicing with the Torah on the Festival of the Torah (Simhas Torah), are all restricted to men.

While women are obligated to observe many of the laws of the Sabbath, festivals, and mourning, especially those forbidding certain acts, and all those concerning the ritual diet, there are only three female-specific rituals in rabbinic Judaism. These are removing and burning a portion of bread before it is baked, lighting the Sabbath and holiday candles, and observing the laws of *niddah*, which culminate in the women's immersion in a ritual bath (*mikvah*), after which sexual relations between husband and wife may resume. In fact, however, anyone baking bread is obligated to the dough ritual, and in the absence of a woman, men are

Feminist rituals have become an essential part of the participation of contemporary women in Judaism. This Tashlich *ceremony in Riverside Park in New York City was sponsored by MA'YAN: The Jewish Women's Project. The cantor is Naomi Hirsch. [Joan Roth]*

obligated to light holiday candles, making the only true female-specific rituals those surrounding uterine or vaginal bleeding, with its attendant connotations. By contrast, men's immersion in the *mikvah* is voluntary, performed to ready themselves for the Sabbath, holidays, or other sacred pursuits. This leads to the feminist plaint that through *mikvah*, men ready themselves for God and women ready themselves for men.

Over the centuries, Jewish women elaborated a rich set of personal rituals with which they sacralized their daily lives, major life-cycle events, and holidays. Intensely meaningful to them, these rituals nevertheless did not enjoy the status of those ordained by the rabbis. The world of female ritual was almost completely obliterated in modern times as women's forms of spiritual expression, always seen as unlearned and superstitious, were also condemned as unmodern and a threat to Jewish efforts to achieve equality and acceptance in non-Jewish society. As a result, the earliest wave of Jewish feminists perceived only the paucity of normative ritual for women in Judaism. This paucity, the negative associations of some existing ritual, and the utter male-centeredness of most ritual in normative Judaism became the prime area of protest and the spur for creative adaptation and innovation in Jewish feminism.

In the past twenty-five years, feminists have elaborated a host of new rituals for women. Some of these, like the bat mitzvah for girls (actually initiated by the founder of Reconstructionism, Mordecai Kaplan, in 1922), parallel the established ritual for boys, celebrating attainment of the age of adult responsibility for the commandments of Judaism through various synagogue rituals. Complementarity, appropriating male-identified ritual for females, is not always possible or desirable, however. A prime example is feminist birth rituals for girls. Traditionally, the birth of a daughter is marked by the father reciting blessings over the Torah in the synagogue, at which point he names the baby, in the presence of neither mother nor child. The flagrant imbalance between this modest ritual and that of the Brith Milah for boys was one of the first that Jewish feminists addressed. Since few have accepted the suggestion of ritual rupture of the hymen as a physical analogue to circumcision, however, feminists have created other ceremonies to celebrate the birth of girls and initiate them into the community. Among the most common rituals used are immersion of the baby in a *mikvah*, washing her feet as a sign of welcome, wrapping the child in a prayer shawl and lighting of candles. Birth ceremonies and bat mitzvahs for girls have now become ubiquitous on the Jewish scene, including Orthodoxy, attesting the strength of the

feminist critique and the degree to which it has been internalized in a remarkably short time even by those who claim to reject feminism and the larger culture from which Jewish feminism has borrowed its impulse.

The "first phase" of Jewish feminism, in the 1970s, focused on equality: gaining access to and appropriating male-identified rituals and rights, such as donning sacred garments and counting in a prayer quorum. Innovation, however, has become the predominant Jewish feminist expression. In the metaphor of the Jewish feminist theologian Judith Plaskow, feminists want to bake a new pie rather than merely get a piece of the old one. The quest for equality, Plaskow and others argue, is inherently inegalitarian because women seek male-identified roles but men do not value or appropriate traditionally female rituals or spirituality. It is also assimilatory, since ritual and spiritual traditions developed by women are seen as inferior and unworthy of perpetuation. Thus, the quest for equality is based on and reinscribes male normativeness in Judaism, while suppressing specifically female spiritual expression. This situation is analogous to that of Jews or other minorities seeking equality who adopt the majority culture, but forsake their own. As Jews have moved from seeking only equality in the larger society to seeking continued Jewish identity as well as equality, Jewish feminists have evolved from merely adopting male-identified ritual to also elaborating a specifically female ritual expression. Thus, while women in all the movements but Orthodoxy, and even this exclusion is no longer hermetic, now discharge the same traditional functions as men, a host of new rituals have been created to frame female experience. These include rituals for menarche, menopause, pregnancy, labor, birth, infertility, miscarriage, stillbirth, abortion, adoption, weaning, hysterectomy, and attaining older-age wisdom.

Many of these rituals celebrate female biological functions. Most feminists have rejected the criticism that this defines women biologically, diminishing their full humanity, as patriarchy historically has done. Rather, they argue, these rituals have assigned positive value to functions that traditionally were ignored or despised and have given Jewish women a means to affirm their bodies in a religion that blesses such other bodily functions as bladder and intestinal evacuation.

Feminists have also modified existing rituals to reflect women's full personhood in Judaism, fashioning egalitarian marriage and divorce ceremonies. They have created feminist Passover seders and *ushpizin* ceremonies in the Tabernacle to welcome the matriarchs, paralleling the traditional invitation to the patriarchs. Some feminists have reclaimed *mikvah*, rejected out of

This photograph was taken at MA'YAN's first Community Feminist Seder,
which was held in 1994. More than two hundred women attended. [Joan Roth]

hand by many, seeing in its waters a primal symbol of creation and nurturing, reminiscent of amniotic waters. Feminists use *mikvah*, however, to affirm female biological functions with no reference to men or to sex, to mark other beginnings or ends, such as birth or divorce, or in rituals for physical or emotional healing. Lesbians have created commitment and divorce ceremonies to solemnize lesbian relationships and bring them into the fold of Jewish celebration. In dethroning the centrality of the male in Judaism, these are the most radical of feminist rituals.

Feminists have reclaimed rosh hodesh, the new moon (celebration of the new month), traditionally a semiholiday for women, making rosh hodesh groups the chief venue for creating and transmitting new rituals and for female experience of what anthropologists call "communitas," radical bonding of those sharing a liminal state or moment. Feminists have reworked the language of ritual by including the matriarchs, feminizing God language or creating grammatically neutral forms to address and name God, and by changing divine images from ones of hierarchy and dominion to ones of immanence, creation, and nurturing. Many have reclaimed and

reworked traditional forms of female spiritual expression, such as *tkhines*, private petitionary prayers recited at candlelighting, immersion in the *mikvah*, bread baking, or other sacred acts. Core male rituals have been feminized, the participation of the mother and other women, for example, being added to the traditional circumcision ritual. Feminists have also created new rituals to mark the birth of boys, in addition to circumcision, in which the male organ is not the center of attention or sacralization. In this, they have brought feminist ritual creativity to the religious socialization of Jewish men.

In all this activity, women have laid claim not just to perpetuate Judaism as elaborated by male authorities but to fashion it themselves, in their image, as men historically have fashioned Judaism in male image, and have begun to create a feminist Judaism. Their efforts are a prime example of ritual operating as an agent of fundamental cultural change and the rapidity with which such change can occur.

For all the unabashed innovation of feminist ritual, feminists have sought and found much precedent for female-specific ritual by women in traditional Jewish societies. They point to Sephardi birth rituals for girls, which were routinely printed in Sephardi prayer books, as well as rosh hodesh festivities. Scholars such as Chava Weissler and Susan Starr Sered have brought to light rich worlds of female spirituality and ritual within traditional Ashkenazi and Kurdish Jewries, respectively. They have shown how traditional women who completely accepted and indeed venerated rabbinic authority nevertheless authorized themselves to become, in Sered's words, "ritual experts." These women sacralized every imaginable aspect of their lives through rituals they created and then successfully communicated as binding for the women of the community—as close an analogue to halakah [rabbinic law and authority] as one could have. While feminists reject the segregation and marginalization that was the context for creation of traditional women's ritual, they welcome a "usable past" within Judaism to mitigate the sense of breach with Jewish tradition, to validate their own ritual creativity and to contribute one of the essential elements of successful ritual: a sense of naturalness, seamlessness, and harmony.

Jewish feminist rituals reject, create, and also integrate, since the vast majority of Jewish feminists choose to remain within the Jewish community and in remaining, profoundly affect the rest of Judaism. If, in Evan M. Zuesse's words, rituals "rescue [profane activity] from the terror of inconsequentiality and meaninglessness," Jewish feminist rituals also rescue feminists from invisibility and derogation in their religious tradition and thus, for all their newness, indeed, because of it, are a prime agent of continued identification. They are without doubt one of the richest creative streams in contemporary Judaism.

BIBLIOGRAPHY

Adelman, Penina V. *Miriam's Well. Rituals for Jewish Women Around the Year* (1986); Adler, Rachel. "In Your Blood, Live: Revisions of a Theology of Purity." *Tikkun* 8/1 (January/February 1993): 38–41; Alexander, Bobby C. "Ceremony." *Encyclopedia of Religion* 3:179–183; Alpert, Rebecca T. "Exploring Jewish Women's Rituals." *Bridges* 2/1 (Spring 1991/5791): 66–80; Balka, Christie, and Andy Rose, eds. *Twice Blessed: On Being Lesbians Gay and Jewish* (1991); Berman, Phyllis. "Enter: A Woman." *Menorah* 6, 1–2 (November/December 1984); Broner, E.M. *A Weave of Women* (1978); Campbell, Joseph. *The Masks of God: Primitive Mythology* (1970); Cantor, Debra, and Rebecca Jacobs. "Brit Banot: Covenant Ceremonies for Daughters." *Kerem* (Winter 1992–1993): 45–55; Coppet, Daniel, ed. *Understanding Rituals* (1992); Diamant, Anita. *The New Jewish Wedding* (1985); Falk, Marcia. *The Book of Blessings: A Feminist Reconstruction of Prayer* (1992), and "Notes on Composing New Blessings: Toward a Feminist/Jewish Reconstruction of Prayer." *Journal of Feminist Studies in Religion* 3 (Spring 1978): 39–53; Gross, Rita M. "Female God Language in a Jewish Context." In *Womanspirit Rising: A Feminist Reader in Religion*, edited by Carol P. Christ and Judith Plaskow (1979); Heschel, Sussannah, ed. *On Being a Jewish Feminist* (1983); Kaye/Kantrowitz, Melanie, and Irena Klepfisz. *The Tribe of Dina: A Jewish Woman's Anthology* (1986); *Kerem: Creative Explorations in Judaism*; Koltun, Elizabeth, ed. *The Jewish Woman: An Anthology*. Special Issue of *Response*, no. 17 (Summer 1973), and *The Jewish Woman: New Perspectives* (1976); Levine, Elizabeth Resnick, ed. *A Ceremonies Sampler: New Rites, Celebrations and Observances of Jewish Women* (1991); Lewin, Ellen. "'Why in the World Would You Want to Do That?' Claiming Community in Lesbian Commitment Ceremonies." In *Inventing Lesbian Cultures in America*, edited by E. Lewin (1996); *Lilith: The Independent Jewish Woman's Magazine*; Magnus, Shulamit S. "More Light on Menarche." *New Menorah*, 2d series, 1 (Winter 1985), and "Reinventing Miriam's Well: Feminist Jewish Ceremonials." In *The Uses of Tradition*, edited by Jack Wertheimer (1992); Meiselman, Moshe. *Jewish Women in Jewish Law* (1978); Myerhoff, Barbara. "Rites of Passage: Process and Paradox." In *Celebration: Studies in Festivity*, edited by Victor Turner (1982); Myerhoff, Barbara, et al. "Rites of Passage." *Encyclopedia of Religion* 12: 380–387; Orenstein, Debra, ed. *Lifecycles: Jewish Women on Life Passages and Personal Milestones* (1994); Plaskow, Judith. "God and Feminism." *Menorah* 3/2 (February 1982), and *Standing Again at Sinai* (1990); *The Reconstructionist: A Journal of Contemporary Jewish Thought and Practice*; Reifman, Toby Fishbein, ed. *Blessing the Birth of a Daughter: Jewish Naming Ceremonies for Girls* (1976); *Response: A Contemporary Jewish Review*; Sered, Susan Starr. *Women as Ritual Experts: The Religious Life of Elderly Jewish Women in Jerusalem* (1992); Turner, Kay. "Contemporary Feminist Rituals." In *The Politics of Women's Spirituality*, edited by Charlene Spretnak (1982); Turner, Victor. *Ritual Process: Structure and Anti-Structure* (1977); Weidman Schneider, Susan. *Jewish and Female: Choices and Changes in Our Lives Today* (1985); Weissler, Chava, "Images of the Matriarchs in Yiddish Supplicatory Prayers." *Bulletin of the Center for the Study of World Relations* 14/1 (1988): 45–51, and "The Traditional Piety of Ashkenazic Women." In *Jewish Spirituality from the Sixteenth Century Revival to the Present*, edited by Arthur Green. Vol. 2 (1987): 245–275, and "Traditional Yiddish Literature: A Source for the Study of Women's Religious Lives." The Jacob Pat Memorial Lecture, Harvard College Library, 1987; Zuesse, Evan M. "Ritual." *The Encyclopedia of Religion* (1987).

SHULAMIT MAGNUS

RIVERS, JOAN (b. 1933)

"Can we talk?" In the minds of millions of Americans, this common phrase conjures up the image of Joan Rivers, the woman who realized in the mid-1960s that "the country was ready for something new—a woman comedian talking about life from a woman's point of view" (*Enter Talking* 340).

In revues, nightclub acts, and concert halls (in the early 1960s), and to a vast new audience via television in the 1970s and 1980s, Rivers popularized and perfected a genre of comedy that challenged reigning social conventions. Her willingness to "say what is really on everyone's mind" was coupled with an ingenue quality. This made her a less-than-threatening figure and enabled her to popularize the type of monologue that had previously been the domain of male comedians: Their acts combined social criticism with sharp wit, and Rivers was soon to join them. She paid homage to these pioneers in her 1986 autobiography, *Enter Talking*. Hearing Lenny Bruce perform in the village was for her "an event that forever changed my comedy life. . . . Boom! there he was, an obscenity among the pleasant routines of the Establishment" (*Enter Talking* 305). Influenced by Bruce, Rivers worked assiduously on her own routines and became a skillful crafter of comedic scripts for herself and others. Among her early writing credits are routines for the *Phyllis Diller Show*, episodes of *Candid Camera*, and material for Johnny Carson's *Tonight Show*. It was on the *Tonight Show*, in 1965, that Rivers got her big national break. Introduced as one of the writers for the show, she and Carson engaged in a hilariously funny dialogue. As Rivers remembered it, "At the end of the show he was wiping his eyes. He said, right on the air, 'God you're funny. You're going to be a star'" (*Enter Talking* 359).

Born in Brooklyn, New York, as Joan Alexandra Molinsky on June 8, 1933, Rivers was the youngest daughter of Beatrice (Grushman) and Meyer Molinsky, a doctor. Both of her parents were Russian Jewish immigrants from the Odessa area. Despite the geographical proximity of their origins, Rivers's parents came from vastly different socioeconomic circumstances. Meyer Molinsky's family had been poverty-stricken in Russia, and they remained poor in their early years in America. Molinsky's entry into the medical profession propelled the family into the emergent Jewish middle class of Brooklyn. Beatrice Molinsky's family had been very wealthy merchants in Odessa but left everything behind in the Old Country. That loss of status forever haunted Beatrice Molinsky, and she continually pushed her husband—a struggling general practitioner in the heavily Jewish Brownsville section of Brooklyn—to earn more money. The conflict between her parents ("My mother wanted M.D. to stand for Make Dollars") was the inspiration for many of Rivers's early routines. The constant arguments in the family about money left her with a permanent sense of insecurity that she mined for its comedic value. The epilogue to *Enter Talking* concludes in this way: "She lives the

In the mid-1960s, Joan Rivers introduced people in America to something new: a woman comedian talking about life from a woman's point of view. Rising from the comedy clubs, she moved on to host the Tonight Show and write several books and plays, helping to redefine modern comedy. [New York Public Library]

life her mother longed to have—but still believes that next week everything will disappear."

From earliest childhood, Rivers wanted to be an actor. Her mother wanted her youngest daughter to prepare herself for marriage and entry into polite society. The tension between these aspirations deeply influenced the young woman's life and craft. Educated in Brooklyn's Ethical Culture School and Adelphi Academy, Rivers was an enthusiastic participant in the school drama and writing programs. At Adelphi, she founded the school newspaper. At Connecticut College and later at Barnard, she read widely in the classics and took courses in the history of the theater. Though she was later to project a scatterbrain image, the key to her craft lies in her classical education and her ability to turn out witty monologues and dialogues. In 1954, Rivers graduated from Barnard College with a degree in English literature and was awarded membership in Phi Beta Kappa. After college, she took an entry-level job at a firm in the New York fashion industry. She soon gave it up for a short-lived (and disastrous) marriage to the boss's son. "Our marriage license turned out to be a learner's permit" (*Enter Talking* 68).

Determined to succeed in the theater, Rivers did temporary office work while auditioning for roles in Off- and Off-Off-Broadway plays. In 1960, she developed comedy routines that gained some attention and in 1961 got her first big break when she joined the Second City Comedy troupe of Chicago. Her improvisational and writing skills shone at Second City. Within a few years, she was a regular at New York City comedy clubs, foremost among them the Duplex and the Bitter End. In her act, she joked about sex in a way that was both shocking and endearing. Women comedians had not spoken with such frankness before. "I knew nothing about sex. All my mother told me was that the man gets on top and the woman gets on the bottom. I bought bunk beds" (*Still Talking* 50). It was from these clubs that Rivers was catapulted to fame by her appearances on national television. Throughout the first decade of her career she continued to write, perform in clubs, and appear on television.

The 1970s saw Rivers venture into other entertainment media. While her Broadway play *Fun City* was greeted with a mixed reaction, her comic 1973 TV movie, *The Girl Most Likely To*, was the most successful made-for-TV movie of its time. Its theme—the revenge of a woman jilted for her looks—was the harbinger of a new direction in writing about women's issues. Two books, *Having a Baby Can Be a Scream* (1975) and *The Life and Times of Heidi Abramowitz*, were also great successes—as were her 1986 autobiography, *Enter Talking*, and its sequel, *Still Talking* (1991).

During her rise from stand-up comic to television personality, Rivers married producer Edgar Rosenberg. He became her de facto manager, and together they embarked on a number of entertainment ventures, including the ill-fated *The Late Show Starring Joan Rivers*. Their marriage, described in some detail in *Still Talking*, was inextricably linked to both of their careers. They had one child, Melissa Rosenberg. In

1987, Edgar Rosenberg committed suicide. Rivers's reaction was feisty and characteristic: "The best therapy for me would have been to go right from the mortuary to the stage, but my advisers agreed it would have been unseemly." Seven years later, in 1994, Rivers dealt with this tragedy and its aftermath in her NBC movie *Tears and Laughter*. In this film, Rivers and her daughter Melissa play themselves and demonstrate, as Gina Bellafante noted in *Time* magazine, "the sunny conviction that the saga of their cruel lives will serve as a morality tale. . . . It also manages to convey a message about the capacity for survival." In that same year, Rivers wrote and produced a Broadway play, *Sally Marr and Her Escorts*. Based on the life of Lenny Bruce's mother, it too deals with the cruel price that celebrity and talent exact from those blessed and cursed with its gifts.

Joan Rivers has been supportive of Jewish philanthropic and social causes and is a former HADASSAH Woman of the Year. In her books, she makes reference to Jewish holidays and rituals, as well as very trenchant and witty remarks about American Jewish social phenomena—including the Catskill Mountains Borscht Belt, where she performed early in her career. In *Enter Talking*, there is a particularly moving account of her first Yom Kippur away from the warmth—and fury—of her family. Her portrayal of her own family's Jewish life provides us with confirmation of Jenna Weissman Joselit's observation in *The Wonders of America* (1994) that, for American Jews, "the Jewish home was now placed at the core of Jewish identity, often becoming indistinguishable from Jewishness itself."

SELECTED WORKS BY JOAN RIVERS

BROADWAY AND TELEVISION
Fun City (1972); *The Girl Most Likely To* (1973); *The Late Show Starring Joan Rivers* (1986–1987); *Sally Marr and Her Escorts* (1994); *Tears and Laughter* (1994).

FILMS
The Muppets Take Manhattan (1984); *Rabbit Test* (director, 1978); *Serial Mom* (1994); *Spaceballs* (1987); *The Swimmer* (1968).

BOOKS
Enter Talking (1986); *Having a Baby Can Be a Scream* (1975); *The Life and Times of Heidi Abramowitz* (1984); *Still Talking* (1991).

BIBLIOGRAPHY
Current Biography Yearbook (1987); "Joan in Full Throat." *Time* (May 16, 1994); Joselit, Jenna Weissman. *The Wonders of America* (1994).

SHALOM GOLDMAN

RIVKIN, NACHA (1900–1988)

Orthodox Jewish education for women in America began with the work of Nacha Rivkin, a founder of Shulamith School for Girls, the first girls' yeshivah in the United States. Nacha (Heber) Rivkin was born on May 5, 1900, in Kalisch, Poland, the long-awaited first child of Yaakov Tuvia and Shaina Sora (Sytner) Heber. Rivkin's father, an Alexanderer Hasid, owned one of the first lace factories in Eastern Europe. Her mother was also active in managing the business. Nacha attended the local Polish school and received private tutoring in Hebrew, Judaic studies, French, German, art, and music.

With the outbreak of World War I, the Heber family (by this time Rivkin had two younger brothers, Shlomo David and Aryeh Leib) was forced to flee Poland and settled in Rostov, Russia. There they met the Lubavitcher rebbe, Rabbi Sholom Ber Schneerson, known as the "Rashab," and his daughters Chana and Chaya Moussia. The Schneerson sisters became Nacha's most intimate lifelong friends.

In 1920, Nacha Rivkin married Rabbi Moshe Ber Rivkin, a protégé of the Rashab, who was then dean of Yeshiva Tomchei Temimim in Lubavitch. Their first child, Ella (who later married Rabbi Aaron B. Shurin, author, journalist, and professor of Judaic studies at Stern College, Yeshiva University), was born in 1921. In 1924, Rabbi Rivkin was sent by the Rashab to Palestine to administer the Yeshivas Toras Emes. In Palestine, Nacha Rivkin continued to study Hebrew and began studying early childhood education, leading to an accredited teacher's license. In 1926, the Rivkin's second child, Sholom, was born. Rabbi Sholom Rivkin is the chief rabbi of St. Louis, Missouri, and chief judge of the Rabbinical Court of America. He is an international authority on Jewish divorce law.

In 1929, Nacha Rivkin and her children immigrated to America, joining Rabbi Rivkin, who had already gone to become dean of Yeshiva Torah Vodaath. The Rivkins settled in Brownsville, Brooklyn. To their distress, there was no Jewish girls' school, so their daughter, then age eight, attended public school, and Nacha Rivkin taught her Hebrew and Judaic studies at home. Rivkin was soon approached by Rabbi M.G. Volk, who was seeking Hebrew-speaking teachers to help him open a school for girls. In 1929, together with Rabbi Volk, Rivkin and two other teachers started the Shulamith School for Girls in Borough Park, Brooklyn. Rivkin was responsible for curriculum development and taught kindergarten and first grade.

Rivkin is best known for her innovative approach to teaching Hebrew to young children. Influenced by Maria Montessori and Jean Piaget, she rejected the monotonous rote method used at the time and instead used games, songs, pictures, and stories to teach Hebrew language and Judaic studies. She made concepts such as Shabbat, Jewish holidays, and Jewish ethics an integral part of her Hebrew lessons. The mimeographed sheets, which she wrote and illustrated to help teach her pupils, eventually became the primer *Reishis Chochma*, which was published by Torah Umesorah in 1954. It was followed by a companion workbook in 1955 and the second volume, *Reishis Chochma-Bet*, in 1967. The books are in their nineteenth printing and are used as the official primer for 550 Torah Umesorah day schools.

Music was important to Rivkin's pedagogy. She made up songs to celebrate holidays and birthdays, as well as to teach the Hebrew alphabet. With the help of her daughter, who had musical training, these songs ultimately became the *Shiru Li* record series.

Rivkin was also a talented artist who painted over two hundred canvases during her lifetime. While mostly self-taught, she also studied under the noted Jewish artists Henoch Leiberman and Saul Raskin. With a preferred medium of oil paints, she created nature scenes and still lifes, while other paintings portray Jewish themes.

Rivkin continued to influence Jewish education even after her retirement. She was a major resource for books on Jewish early childhood education. In her early eighties, she taught pedagogic methods at the Sarah Schenirer Teachers Seminary in Brooklyn. In 1980, Rivkin was honored by Yeshiva Torah Vodaath for her accomplishments in education.

Nacha Rivkin died on July 17, 1988 (third of Av), leaving two children, five grandchildren, and fourteen great-grandchildren. After her death, a group of educators founded the Machon Nacha Rivkin Seminary for Advanced Torah Studies for women, in her honor. The seminary, located in Bayit Vegan, Jerusalem, opened in the fall of 1989.

Nacha Rivkin dedicated her life to advancing Jewish education. Much beloved by students and teachers alike, her influence spread far beyond the halls of the Shulamith school. A courageous and proficient "doer," she broke out of the mold of the passive, retiring, religious *baleboosteh* [homemaker]. Her willingness to infuse her lessons with Orthodox Jewish values at a time when public expressions of Jewishness were muted demonstrates her commitment to her faith. Through her music and artwork, she expanded the range of career possibilities for Orthodox women of her time. In all parts of her life, Nacha Rivkin exemplified the ideals of the *Eyshet Hayil* [Woman of Valor, from Proverbs]: "She girds herself with strength, and performs her tasks with vigor. . . . Her mouth is full of wisdom, her tongue with kindly teaching."

SELECTED WORKS BY NACHA RIVKIN

Reishis Chochma (1954); *Reishis Chochma-Bet* (1967); *Shiru Li*, with Ella Shurin (1960).

BIBLIOGRAPHY

Rivkin, Jacqueline. "Nacha Rivkin." Manuscript in progress, June 1996, and interview by author, July 15, 1996; Shurin, Ella. Interview by author, June 3 and July 3, 1996.

SUSAN SAPIRO

ROBBINS, BETTY (b. 1924)

Amid great worldwide controversy, the first female cantor in Jewish history, Betty Robbins, was appointed by the Board of Trustees and Congregation of Temple Avodah in Oceanside, New York, in July 1955. A young woman of thirty-one, Betty Robbins, with four young children, husband, and new homeland, shattered five thousand years of Jewish tradition and history when she was designated a cantor. Never before had a woman worn the garb and performed the traditional role of hazan in a Jewish synagogue anywhere in the world.

Betty Robbins was born Berta Abramson on April 9, 1924, in Cavala, Greece, to Russian parents Ida (Nathanson) and Samuel Abramson. In 1928, the Abramsons moved with their daughter and older son Moishe to Sopot, Poland, where Samuel Abramson went into business with relatives. Inspired by recordings of the great cantor Yossele Rosenblatt, Betty dreamed of joining the boys' choir in the German Jewish shul she attended. When the cantor refused to permit Betty to sing in the boys' choir during services, she decided to sit opposite the choir in the upstairs balcony and try to outsing them. Eventually the cantor agreed to teach Betty and allow her to sing if she would cut her braids off and wear a simple boy's haircut. Betty was soloist in the choir of the German Jewish Synagogue for six years until 1938. She also dared to enter the religious heder of the Polish Synagogue of Sopot. Again the rabbi relented and allowed her to study if she would sit in the hallway behind a curtain during the lessons.

In 1938, the family went into hiding for many months. Moishe Abramson had already left Poland in 1933 as a young Zionist. Betty's father finally managed to arrange the family's escape. After some time in

The first female cantor, Betty Robbins, was appointed by the board of trustees and congregation of Temple Avodah in Oceanside, New York, in July 1955. [Betty Robbins]

London, Samuel Abramson was offered an opportunity to immigrate to Australia or Madagascar. He chose Australia because the city of Sydney sounded Jewish to him.

In April 1942 at a dance arranged by Rabbi Max Schenk at Temple Emanuel in Sydney, Betty met Sheldon Robbins, a corporal in the medical division of the U.S. Army Air Corps who was on leave from his New Guinea station. They were married in a civil ceremony in Mackay, Queensland, on September 18, 1943 and in a religious ceremony at the Brisbane Hebrew Congregation, Queensland, on October 25, 1943. On August 8, 1944, Robbins came to the United States on the first boat transporting war brides from Australia.

After the war, Sheldon Robbins began working for the New York City health department. Judd Robbins was born in 1946, Sandra Robbins in 1949, Jacqueline Robbins in 1950, and Steven Robbins in 1954. Around 1951, the Robbins family moved to Oceanside, New York, where they became members of the Reform Jewish congregation of Temple Avodah.

In 1955, Temple Avodah was without a cantor for the High Holidays. After much consultation with their rabbi, Charles Ozer, and other eminent Jewish authorities, the board of trustees in August unanimously appointed Betty Robbins the new cantor of this congregation.

A front-page article in the *New York Times* on August 3, 1955, states, "A spokesman for the School of Sacred Music of Hebrew Union College-Jewish Institute of Religion said she might well be the first woman cantor in 5,000 years of Jewish history." The article continues, "The spokesman for the School of Sacred Music, founded in 1947 as the first training school for cantors in this country, said today there was no religious law, merely a tradition, against women becoming cantors."

Robbins taught religious school for eighteen years at Sinai Reform Temple in Bay Shore, Long Island, and earned a teaching certificate from Hebrew Union College in 1962. She tutored bar and bat mitzvah students, taught Israeli dancing, and formed and directed adult and children's choirs. As a teacher for the Association for Retarded Children, Robbins used music therapy long before it was recognized as a specialty.

After Sheldon Robbins retired in 1979, he and Betty Robbins moved to Lake Worth, Florida. In Palm Beach County, Betty Robbins served as cantor, tutored bar and bat mitzvah students, taught religious school, organized choirs, and created a yearly *zimriah* [songfest] for schoolchildren. As a member of the clergy, she conducted religious services on dozens of worldwide Jewish holiday cruises.

The little girl from Greece, Berta Abramson, who went all alone in her new homeland, Poland, to hear the cantor sing melodies she loved, was a rebel with a heart and mind of her own. The innate sense of equality and independence that existed inside this eight-year-old became the pioneering spirit of the female cantor Betty Robbins.

BIBLIOGRAPHY

"Greek Holocaust Refugee at 16, She Revisits Birth Place, Teaches in U.S." *Jewish Week-American Examiner*, February 13–19, 1977; "Making Musical History." *Australian Jewish News*, Sydney edition, life/style, April 24, 1992, section 2, 1–2; Robbins, Betty. Interviews and correspondence with author; *Temple Topics*. Temple Avodah, Oceanside, N.Y., September 1955, October 1955; "Woman Cantor." *Time* (August 15, 1955): 36–37; "Woman Named Cantor of Jewish Synagogue." *Long Island Star-Journal*, August 2, 1955; "Woman Named Temple Cantor, Perhaps First in Jewish History." *NYTimes*, August 3, 1955, 1.

SANDRA ROBBINS

ROBERTS, COLETTE (1910–1971)

Colette Jacqueline (Levy Rothschild) Roberts devoted her life to increasing people's understanding and appreciation of modern art. She was born in Paris on September 16, 1910. She graduated from the University of Paris and then attended the École du Louvre and the Academy Ranson where she studied painting with Roger Bissière. She also studied at the Institut d'Art et Archéologie with Henri Focillon.

In 1934, when Colette was twenty-four, she married Edward Sherrill Roberts, an American engineer (they later divorced). During World War II, she moved alone with her young son, Richard Barclay, to the United States, where she became a citizen. She settled in New York City and worked as a lecturer and writer for the French press. In the early 1940s, she was instrumental in organizing Franco-American cultural exchanges and exhibitions, and in the late 1940s became the director of the National Association of Women Artists. Simultaneously, she served for a short time as secretary to the curator of Far Eastern art at the Metropolitan Museum of Art. For the remainder of her career, she lived in Manhattan and continued to focus her versatile talents in the field of the visual arts.

The influence of her former teacher Roger Bissière was so stimulating to Roberts's understanding of the art of her day that in 1952 she decided to continue her studies, specializing in modern American art. From 1957, while continuing to exhibit her work in France, through 1968, she worked at New York University (NYU) as an instructor in the Division of Education (now the School of Continuing Education). Her popular course, "Meet the Artist," was listed as "a rare opportunity to visit the studios of artists with national and international reputations, to view the artists' work and to ask questions of the artists themselves." The artists her students visited included Adolph Gottlieb, Willem de Kooning, Roy Lichtenstein, LOUISE NEVELSON, and Ilya Bolotovsky. In 1968, she was an assistant professor at NYU, and the following year became the director of the Hofstra University Art Gallery, which was affiliated with NYU.

From 1960 to 1967, Roberts wrote reviews of Manhattan gallery exhibitions for the highly respected Parisian journal *Architecture d'Aujourd'hui*. In addition, she contributed articles to *France-Amérique* and *Art and Architecture*, and was the author of two monographs, *Mark Tobey* (1960) and *Louise Nevelson, Sculptor* (1961). Her other book, *Pocket Museum*, was written in 1964. In 1960, Roberts received the Palmes Académiques award from the French government for her work as chair of the French section of the American Red Cross and was selected to become a writer-in-residence at the

MacDowell Colony in Peterborough, New Hampshire. From 1952 to 1968, while working as an art critic and teaching a course at the university, Roberts continued to gain respect as gallery director of the Grand Central Moderns. She developed a reputation for giving a start to many unfashionable artists. One of them, Louise Nevelson, became a major international figure. Roberts first showed Nevelson's work in the mid-1950s, alerting John Canaday, the *New York Times* art critic, to her great potential as a sculptor. Canaday wrote that Louise Nevelson "has become one of the best sculptors of our half of the century, a potential that Mrs. Roberts recognized."

Roberts's identification with France was lifelong. It was in the American Hospital in Paris on August 9, 1971, that Colette Roberts died of congestive heart failure.

The main focus of Roberts's life was modern art. The success she earned as a gallery director, art critic, and educator influenced the art world of the mid-twentieth century in New York and Paris and throughout the world.

SELECTED WORKS BY COLETTE ROBERTS

Louise Nevelson, Sculptor (1961); *Mark Tobey* (1960); *Pocket Museum* (1964).

BIBLIOGRAPHY

Obituaries. *NYTimes*, August 12, 1971, 36:4, and *Architecture d'Aujourd'hui*, 157 (August 1971): 17; *Who's Who in American Art* (1966, 1973, 1976, 1978); *Who's Who in American Women* (1966, 1968, 1970, 1972); *WWWIA* 5.

CARLA MUNSAT

ROBISON, SOPHIA MOSES
(1888–1969)

Sophia Moses Robison was the first to document the class, racial, and moral judgments that determined who would be labeled a "juvenile delinquent" and how variations in description distorted data accumulated on delinquency. She also believed that social research carried the obligation to help correct the problems studied. A highly social woman, Robison was known for her Sabbath night parties, which brought together people of opposing views or different expertise, or simply those she felt would benefit by meeting.

She was born on November 28, 1888, the eldest of seven children—five girls and two boys—born to Minnie (Herman) and Morris Moses, he a Jewish immigrant from Germany and she from a prosperous third-generation American Jewish family. The family's strong tradition of learning ensured a solid education, both secular and Talmudic, for all their children. Sophia won a scholarship to Wellesley, graduating Phi Beta Kappa in 1909. There, she discovered pacifism, woman suffrage, and her own identity as a Jew, having been exposed for the first time to a world of non-Jews. While teaching high school, she earned an M.A. in German literature from Columbia in 1913. She also taught Sabbath school in the Reform synagogue, built in part by her parents' efforts, in Mount Vernon, New York.

In 1913, she married Sylvan Robison, the son of Russian Jewish immigrants and an ardent Zionist and Orthodox Jew. She had five children between 1915 and 1923, while she also began to study for her Ph.D. in sociology. During World War I, Robison was an active volunteer in many organizations, including a Zionist study group organized by HENRIETTA SZOLD, which also included Margaret Sanger. After the war, her husband's business began to decline and she became the family breadwinner, moving from volunteer to paid employment.

Robison became a social worker at the Hebrew Sheltering Guardian Society, then the executive secretary of the Brooklyn chapter of the NATIONAL COUNCIL OF JEWISH WOMEN. She earned a graduate certificate in social work at the New York School of Social Work (now the Columbia University School of Social Work) in 1929.

Robison then began her career in research, first as part of Columbia's Social Science Research Council's study of Greenwich Village in 1930, and then in focusing on her lifelong concern with delinquency in the research for her Ph.D., working under Robert MacIver. Her work culminated in her book *Juvenile Delinquency: Can It Be Measured?*, which broke new ground by documenting the variation in youth actions labeled delinquent depending on the race, class, ethnic group, and neighborhood of the child. She demonstrated the class and social bias in both definition and reporting of delinquency that skewed all official data. She also showed the strong link between "delinquent" and "dependent" labels. Robison received her doctorate from Columbia in 1936. From 1931 to 1940, she served as director of the Division of Neighborhood Statistics of the New York City Welfare Council. In 1937, her husband died.

Robison was the executive director of the National Council of Jewish Women from 1940 to 1942 and then served two years in the Survey Division of the Office of Civilian Defense. She then moved to head the Statistical Research Division on Delinquency of the U.S. Children's Bureau. At the end of World War II, the White House asked Robison to study the economic impact of the influx of refugees to America, in order to allay fears that these people were lowering wages and costing taxpayers. Her resulting book, *Refugees at Work*, with an introduction by Eleanor Roosevelt, documented the positive economic and cultural impact of these new Americans. Next, she spent five years as director of the Harlem Project on Delinquency in the Schools. In 1950 she was named consultant on juvenile delinquency to the Mid-Century White House Conference. During this period, Robison taught research and corrections at various colleges, including the Smith College School of Social Work. In 1946, she was appointed a full-time professor of research at the New York School of Social Work, a post she held until her retirement in 1954.

After retirement, Robison continued her dual research interests in delinquency and in Jewish demography, using her skillful statistical analyses as well as her ability to engage the subjects of the research in order to improve services or change practices. She added her interest of civil rights, especially in housing, to her research agenda. She continued her Friday evening Sabbath parties, bringing leading social thinkers and activists together.

In all, Robison wrote twelve research monographs, seven books, twenty-five publications in scholarly journals, and many reviews and papers. Sophia Moses Robison died in New York on August 4, 1969.

BIBLIOGRAPHY
Saul, Shura. *Sophia Moses Robison, Woman of the Twentieth Century* (1981).

MIRIAM DINERMAN

ROCK, LILLIAN (1896–1974)

Lillian Rock had great energy, enthusiasm, creativity, and willingness to give money and time to the causes that concerned her: equality for women, advancement of the poor, and Jewish organizations.

Rock was born in New York City on August 6, 1896, to Joel and Ida Libby (Gross) Rock and had at least two brothers and a sister. She graduated with an LL.B. from Brooklyn Law School in 1923. In 1925, at age twenty-nine, she was admitted to the New York bar and began to practice. When her brother Nathaniel was admitted to the bar, Rock took him in and became the senior partner of Rock and Rock in New York City. After eleven years of practice, she claimed to have handled over five thousand cases. The exact nature of most of these cases is unknown, but some involved landlord/tenant matters.

Rock focused her attention outside of work on promoting the election of women to public office. With a highly developed sense of public relations, she dealt well and frequently with the press. She wrote for popular magazines and was far ahead of her time in her opinions on social policy.

In 1935, she founded the League for a Woman President and Vice President, with membership open to both women and men. The name was later revised to the League for a Woman for President and Other Offices, and its membership grew to three thousand. Its aim was to convince one of the major parties to name a woman candidate for vice president or president of the United States. Rock proposed Florence E. Allen, a judge on the U.S. Circuit Court of Appeals, as president of the United States, and backed Josephine Roche, Assistant Secretary of the Treasury, for higher office. In July 1939, Rock embarked on a month-long plane tour of South American countries with Mrs. Lionel Sutro to research the status of women in those countries.

Rock joined dozens of organizations and was counsel to some of them. She was a member of the New York County Lawyers Association, the Bronx Women's Bar Association, the International Federation of Women Lawyers, and other women's professional and Jewish organizations. She served as vice president of the National Association of Women Lawyers and was the legal adviser for the Virginia Gildersleeve International Fund for University Women, an organization that supported third-world women's projects. The size of her membership responsibilities was so vast that, at times, she mistakenly thought that she held certain offices and made unauthorized changes.

A Reform Jew, she was an organizer of the Bronx division of the American Jewish Congress and a member of Congregation Temple Beth Elohim and Montefiore Congregation.

With her remarkable abilities, Rock enjoyed associating with other women of achievement. Her direct gaze reflected her inner strength and unequivocal determination. Flamboyant in dress, particularly in her hats, she lived luxuriously at Sutton Place in Manhattan, collecting art objects and rare books. Death came suddenly on May 13, 1974. She was buried in Mt. Hebron Cemetery in Queens, New York, survived by two brothers, a sister, and two nephews.

BIBLIOGRAPHY
NYTimes, July 20, 1939, and Obituary. May 15, 1974, 48:3; *UJE*; *WWIAJ* 3 (1938): 862.

DOROTHY THOMAS

ROIPHE, ANNE (b. 1935)

Novelist, journalist, and essayist Anne Roiphe was a respected contributor to the world of letters before moving away from assimilation toward an exploration of Jews and Jewish subjects.

Roiphe was born December 25, 1935, to Blanche (Phillips) and Eugene Roth, a lawyer, and grew up in affluence in New York City. She graduated from Sarah Lawrence College in 1957, married Jack Richardson the next year, and divorced in 1963. She had one child from that marriage, as well as two children and two stepchildren with Herman Roiphe, a psychoanalyst whom she married in 1967.

Roiphe is probably best known as a novelist. Her first novel, *Digging Out*, appeared in 1966 to good reviews, although as a whole her work has met with mixed critical success. Most of Roiphe's protagonists are women driven by issues of personal identity: mother-daughter conflicts, struggles over middle-class values, and clashes between women's personal aspirations and societal expectations. While her early novels often had Jewish protagonists, Jewish issues were decidedly incidental to the themes and plots of the novels.

Ironically, Roiphe's return to Judaism was instigated by her family's "celebration" of Christmas. In 1978, Roiphe wrote an article in the *New York Times* on how her family displayed a Christmas tree each year. The article became something of a cause célèbre, provoking a torrent of contemptuous and reproachful criticism from the Jewish community. In response—although perhaps more as a personal search than as an answer to her critics—Roiphe wrote her first nonfiction book, *Generation Without Memory* (1981). An account of a late twentieth-century American Jew detailing, reevaluating, and occasionally defending her assimilated life, *Generation Without Memory* is at turns insightful and shallow, raising tough questions without always necessarily engaging them head-on. At the end of the book, however, Roiphe declares her intention to search out a more meaningful form of Jewish life for herself.

Not surprisingly, Roiphe's work since that time has been devoted largely, although not exclusively, to Jewish themes. As a journalist, Roiphe has been a frequent contributor to liberal Jewish magazines such as *Present Tense* and *Tikkun*, while continuing to write for the secular press, including a regular column in the *New York Observer*. Most recently, she has been a contributing editor to the *Jerusalem Report*. Her novels since the *Times* piece have focused largely on Jewish themes: *Lovingkindness* is a story of a mother coming to terms with her *ba'alot teshuva* daughter, while *Pur-suit of Happiness* is a thinly veiled depiction of Roiphe's own family history. Roiphe also wrote *A Season for Healing*, an extended rumination on balancing the universal and the particular implications of the Holocaust. Many critics, however, felt that Roiphe went too far by actually indicting Jewish "obsession" with the Holocaust for a host of problems facing the Jewish communities of America and Israel. Despite such criticisms, Anne Roiphe has become an important voice for those Jews who, while perhaps uncomfortable with organized religion, nevertheless feel an attraction and a commitment toward their Jewish heritage.

SELECTED WORKS BY ANNE ROIPHE

Digging Out (1966); *Generation Without Memory: A Jewish Journey in Christian America* (1981); *Lovingkindess* (1987); *A Season for Healing: Reflections on the Holocaust* (1988); *Up the Sandbox!* (1970)

BIBLIOGRAPHY

Hoyt, Carolyn. "Anne Roiphe" *Jewish Americam Women Writers: A Bio-Bibliographical and Critical Sourcebook* (1994); Ross, Jean W. "Roiphe, Anne Richardson." *Contemporary Authors* 89–92 (1980); Steinberg, Sybil S. "Anne Roiphe." *Publishers Weekly* (August 2, 1993): 57–58; Strickland, Ruth L. "Anne Roiphe." *Dictionary of Literary Biography. Yearbook: 1980* (1981); Winter-Damon, Tim. "Roiphe, Anne (Richardson)." *Contemporary Authors* 45 (1995); Zelechow, Bernard. "The Odyssey of Anne Roiphe: Anatomy of an Alienated Jew." *Midstream* 35 (August/September 1989): 43–47.

SETH KORELITZ

ROME, ESTHER (1945–1995)

A coauthor of *Our Bodies, Ourselves*, a classic women's resource book, Esther Rome came of age with the onset of the modern feminist movement and was a leader in shaping modern American notions of self-help and advocacy for women's physical and mental health.

Esther Rachel (Seidman) Rome was born in Norwich, Connecticut, on September 8, 1945, the youngest child of Leo and Rose (Deutsch) Seidman. Her parents operated a five-and-ten-cent store in Plainfield, Connecticut, a small textile mill town where Esther grew up. She had two brothers, Aaron and Abe Seidman, and a sister, Sara Levine. She graduated from Brandeis University in 1966 and earned a M.A. from Harvard University's Graduate School of Education in 1968. She was married to Nathan Rome in 1967, and had two sons, Judah and Micah, in respectively 1977 and 1982.

Rome and the women who founded the Boston Women's Health Book Collective began to meet in

1969, following one of the first women's liberation conferences, held in Boston. Their book *Our Bodies, Ourselves* evolved from a collection of articles distributed on newsprint, starting in 1970, to progressively expanded and updated versions. By 1996, *Our Bodies, Ourselves* was over seven hundred pages and sold nearly four million copies in over fifteen languages. It is considered an indispensable reference work by several generations of women around the world.

Rome was a member and served on the staff of the Boston Women's Health Book Collective for over twenty-five years. She was also a board member of the collective. Rome's perspective, that women's health difficulties require broad solutions that include social, economic, and political responses as well as medical ones, was reflected in the work of the collective. All of their written work juxtaposed first-person narratives of women's experiences with medical information garnered from published research.

The collective's approach was reflected in Rome's grounded outlook on all facets of her life and work. Her major contributions focused on sexuality, menstruation, food and nutrition, and the beauty industry.

Her menstruation brochure, printed in red ink, was one of the collective's first spin-off publishing projects. It grew into a related long-term project when toxic shock syndrome, a strep infection that causes serious illness and in some cases death, was first identified in the 1970s. When it became apparent that the disease was most prevalent among young women who used high-absorbency tampons, Rome began a campaign to institute uniform labeling on tampon packages. During a long stint on the American Society for Testing and Materials' Tampon Task Force, Rome held her ground against persistent opposition from tampon manufacturers. Today tampon boxes include a warning—much like that on cigarettes—and contain a flyer describing possible risks and how to use the product safely.

One of Rome's last projects was to assure appropriate regulation of silicone-gel breast implants by the United States Food and Drug Administration. Between 1988 and the end of her life, she was involved in every facet of the struggle to assure sound research on the long-term safety of these devices. Her greatest contributions were an astute understanding of the science related to the use of silicone in the body and the communication of that information in commonsense language. Rome formed and ran a support group of women with breast implants in the Boston area, provided information to print and television reporters so that consumers would be educated on the issues, and placed the struggle in a larger context of the social pressure on women to alter their physical appearance.

At the time of her death, Rome was completing the editing of a book, *Sacrificing Our Selves for Love*, coauthored with Jane Wegscheider Hyman (1996), that analyzes significant women's health issues, including cosmetic surgery, dieting, domestic violence, and HIV infection, that relate to women's desire to accommodate partners in intimate relationships.

Rome's own domestic life illustrated the grace with which she blended domestic and advocacy careers. A devoted mother, she reserved Friday nights to be with her family to celebrate the Sabbath. She helped to keep a kosher home, and was an active member of Temple B'nai Brith in Somerville, Massachusetts, where she lived with her family.

Rome lived her life as she would have wished for all women—with the power of decision over its structure and its details. She loved to seek and absorb information, to digest it thoughtfully, and to share it broadly. Although she embraced visibility when it advanced her cause, she did not seek the limelight, but always shared the work and its rewards. Esther Rome died of breast cancer on June 24, 1995.

BIBLIOGRAPHY

Boston Women's Health Book Collective. *The New Our Bodies, Ourselves* (1992); "Esther Rome, Author, Dies at 49; Sought Better Health for Women." *NYTimes*, June 27, 1995, D21; Hyman, Jane Wegscheider, and Esther Rome. *Sacrificing Our Selves for Love* (1996); Rome, Nathan [husband]. Personal communication with author, January 1997; Sanford, Wendy. "In Memoriam: Esther Rome." *A Gala Celebration—Our Bodies, Ourselves* (March 8, 1996): 24–26; Zones, Jane. "Esther Rome: 1945–1995." *Network News* (September/October 1995): 8.

JANE SPRAGUE ZONES

ROME, EVA SCHOCKEN *see* GLASER, EVA SCHOCKEN

ROSE, ERNESTINE (1810–1892)

"I was a rebel at the age of five," said Ernestine Rose. She was born in the Jewish quarter of Piotkrow, Russian Poland, on January 13, 1810, to a rabbi whose religious duties and scholarly pursuits were supported by the generous dowry of his wife, the daughter of a wealthy businessman. Her family name was Potowski and her given name, Ernestine Louise, was acquired only after she moved to England. As their only offspring, Ernestine received an unusual education for a female child of that time and place, including the

Lecturer Ernestine Rose became famous in America speaking about religious freedom, public education, abolition, and women's rights. Dubbed the first Jewish feminist, she devoted her life to the cause of women's rights and suffrage. [Schlesinger Library]

study of scriptures in the original Hebrew. Her first rebellious act was to question the justice of a God who would exact hardships such as her father's frequent religious fasts. At age fourteen she rejected both the idea that women were inferior to men and the Jewish texts and traditions that supported this belief. Two years later, following her mother's death, she refused to marry the man her father chose. She brought her case before the civil court, an unusual act at a time when Jews abided by the decisions of rabbinic authorities. She traveled many hours in severe weather to argue on her own behalf and recovered the inheritance that had been promised by her father to her betrothed. Justice received, she returned most of the money to her father, taking only what she needed to leave Poland.

She arrived in Prussia to find that Polish Jews were unwelcome. Again she sought justice, this time appealing to the king of Prussia, who exempted her from a law that required sponsorship of Jews by a German property holder. While in Berlin, she invented a room deodorizer, the proceeds of which allowed her to support herself in Holland, Belgium, and France. She advocated for the oppressed wherever she traveled. In England in 1832, she met Robert Dale Owen, a utopian socialist whose ideas on human rights and equality informed her future activism. Owen encouraged her to speak at meetings of the Association of All Classes of All Nations, which they cofounded, launching her brilliant career as an orator. In 1835, she married William Ella Rose, a jeweler and fellow Owenite, and the following year the couple settled in New York.

In the United States, Rose's extemporaneous speeches on religious freedom, public education, abolition, and women's rights earned her the title "Queen of the Platform." She lectured frequently in New York and nearby states. However, she also traveled to the South, where she confronted a slaveholder who vowed he would have tarred and feathered her if she were not a woman, and as far west as Michigan, where she is credited with beginning "the agitation on the question of woman suffrage."

From 1850 to 1869, when she and her husband returned to England, Rose attended and played a major role in nearly every New York and national convention on women's rights. She toured with Susan B. Anthony, who adopted Rose's slogan "Agitate, agitate." In the 1840s and 1850s, when antislavery and women's struggles overlapped, she worked closely with Elizabeth Cady Stanton, Lucretia Mott, Paulina Wright, Sojourner Truth, William Lloyd Garrison, and Frederick Douglass. After the Civil War, some political strategists urged that women delay their quest for the vote and focus on the rights of African Americans, but Rose consistently maintained that the struggles be conjoined, stating "emancipation from every kind of human bondage is my principle."

Rose abandoned her Jewish religious practices, but she responded with immediacy when the editor of the *Boston Investigator*, a free-thought journal for which she frequently wrote, attacked the Jewish people. A ten-week letter exchange ensued, during which Rose presented a strenuous critique of anti-Semitism and a defense of Jews based on their historical contributions to secular as well as religious culture. This prompted the editor of the *Jewish Record* to write in an article on the controversy that Rose showed "some of the old leaven of the Jewish spirit."

Rose's eloquent advocacy of a sweeping agenda for social change produced mixed results. She failed to achieve her dream of a utopian socialist community in Skaneateles, New York, but was successful in 1869, after nearly fifteen years' work, in securing New York legislation that allowed married women to retain their own property and have equal guardianship of children. Although American women did not gain the vote until more than a quarter-century after Rose's death, Susan B. Anthony considered her, with Mary Wollstonecraft and Frances Wright, to have pioneered the cause of woman suffrage.

Despite ill health, Ernestine Rose continued to work for social justice until her death in Brighton, England, on August 4, 1892. Although she left no personal memoirs or letters, her eloquent words, spoken in thirty-two states and abroad, justify the assessment of her as the "first Jewish feminist."

BIBLIOGRAPHY

Anthony, Susan B. Diary, 1854. Schlesinger Library, Radcliffe College, Cambridge, Mass.; *DAB*; Eiseman, Alberta. *Rebels and Reformers: Biographies of Four Jewish Americans: Uriah Phillips Levy, Ernestine L. Rose, Louis D. Brandeis, Lillian Wald* (1976); *EJ*; Gray, Carole. "Nineteenth Century Women of Free Thought." *Free Inquiry* (Spring 1995); Harper, Ida Husted. *The Life and Work of Susan B. Anthony.* 3 vols. (1898–1908); *History of Woman Suffrage*, 1848–1900. Vols. 1–3 edited by Elizabeth Cady Stanton, Susan B. Anthony, and Matilda Joselyn Gage. Vol. 4 edited by Susan B. Anthony and Ida Husted Harper (1881–1902); *NAW*; Suhi, Yuri. *Eloquent Crusader: Ernestine Rose* (1970), and *Ernestine Rose and the Battle for Human Rights* (1959); *UJE*.

JANET FREEDMAN

ROSE, HANNAH TOBY (1909–1976)

The Brooklyn Museum was one of the pioneers of a comprehensive relationship between museum and public, and Hannah Toby Rose was the chief architect of that alliance.

Born in New York City on April 12, 1909, Rose arrived at the Brooklyn Museum in February 1931 to work as a docent. By 1943, she was supervisor of education—a position she held through many administrative shifts until her retirement in 1972—and had already begun implementing the revolutionary changes that irrevocably altered the way that the public regards the museum experience.

Hannah Rose was able to disseminate her progressive programs as a member of many prominent national and international groups, including the International Committee on Education in Museums, of which she was president from 1953 to 1962. Rose's words from her speech accepting the first annual Katherine Coffey Award accurately reflect her vision: "A museum is a very, very unique place. It is an educational institution, but it's not a school. It's a place of reference for children, and research for scholars, but it's not a library." Recognizing the need for a new strategy to incorporate the museum into a comprehensive public educational matrix, Rose conceived of novel and effective means of forging this coalition. Her perspicacity is confirmed by the fact that today such links between the museum and the public are taken for granted.

Rose's innovations broke down boundaries, eliminating the invisible barrier between the museum's collections and the outside world. She instituted programs to teach classes directly in the galleries—called the "Mobile Classroom"—in an attempt to recast the museum as a site of exploration, not merely of entertainment. Augmenting the experience beyond the galleries themselves was the policy of lending films, sound recordings, and slides to public schools for use in educating students about the museum, either before or after an actual visit to the museum. Rose also initiated a television series highlighting various strengths of the museum's collections and organized music concerts relevant to specific exhibits, which were performed both at the museum and broadcast on New York public radio.

In a 1955 report, Rose summed up the goals of the museum's education department, stressing the need to provide information that would enhance classroom studies, arouse appreciation for humankind's relations through many eras and periods, and encourage the habit of visiting museums. She was acutely aware of the need to resist the concept of a museum as existing in a vacuum and believed that to assure an institution's existence in perpetuity, one must appeal to the younger generations and instill in them a sense of the museum's potential role in their lives.

Hannah Toby Rose died on December 14, 1976.

SELECTED WORKS BY HANNAH TOBY ROSE

"The Brooklyn Museum Study Tours." *Brooklyn Museum Annual* 9 (1967–1968): 28–29; "Education Division." *Brooklyn Museum Bulletin* 16, no. 4 (1955): 4–10, and *Brooklyn Museum Bulletin* 20, no. 1 (1959): 23–24, and *Brooklyn Museum Bulletin* 21, no. 1 (1960): 23–25; "The First Families of North America," with Michelle Murphy. *Brooklyn Museum Quarterly* 22, no. 4 (1935): 183–189; *Museums and Teachers* (1956); "Museum's Role in Education." *Art Digest* 29 (February 15, 1954): 24; *Role of the Arts in Meeting the Social and Educational Needs of the Disadvantaged* (1967).

BIBLIOGRAPHY

Obituary. *NYTimes*, December 21, 1976, 36:1; *WWWIA* 7.

NOAH CHASIN

ROSEANNE (b. 1952)

Surely the most controversial American comedian since Lenny Bruce, Roseanne exists at the intersection of feminism and the working class. Although her comedy comes directly from the leftist feminism of the 1970s, Roseanne enjoyed her greatest success from an eponymous sitcom broadcast on ABC-TV beginning in 1988 when the working class had become otherwise invisible to popular culture. In its nine-year run, *Roseanne* garnered high ratings and the attention of media critics and political writers. Barbara Ehrenreich found in the program "the neglected underside of the eighties, bringing together its great themes of poverty, obesity, and defiance." Though its star was never honored by the television establishment for her work, the success of the program launched this inelegant stand-up comedian to a highly visible platform for her own working-class feminism.

Born November 3, 1952, in Salt Lake City, the eldest child of Jerry and Helen Barr, Roseanne spent her early years aware that she belonged to a vocal minority. The Barr family, which included Roseanne's siblings Geraldine and Benjamin, identified with Jewish culture to define itself against its neighbors in largely Mormon Salt Lake City. One window of exposure to Judaism came through Roseanne's grandmother, Bobbe Mary, who forced herself to listen to anti-Semitic radio broadcasts, then phoned in her objections to the radio station. Jerry Barr inspired in his daughter an interest in comedy, and all three Barr children learned to heed his call of "comedian, comedian" when one appeared on television.

Comedy, Roseanne says in her autobiography, "was something that Jews really owned and knew about and did better than almost anyone else. It was the Midrash, it was about connection, and the symbolic murder of the status quo, and the blurring of what is sacred and what is profane . . . a place on earth where Jews are not threatening to non-Jews and people in Utah." With only comedians as positive role models, comedy became a lifeline for Roseanne (as it does, she suspects, for all Jewish people), and murdering the status quo, a reason for living. This is an easy motif to detect in her comedy, and it is no surprise that among those she cites as inspirations are FANNY BRICE, DOROTHY PARKER, Lenny Bruce, and JOAN RIVERS.

Married to Bill Pentland in 1974, Roseanne was raising three children in Denver on an unsteady income when she stumbled upon the Woman to Woman Bookstore and made a few inquiries about a working-class housewife's role in the women's movement. The first outlet for her comedy came at a restaurant in Denver where Roseanne served cocktails and rebuttals to men's routine sexist comments. In both cases, Roseanne found a gift for using the politics of the women's movement as comedy. From the restaurant to a local comedy club to L.A.'s Comedy Store and, in 1985, to *The Tonight Show*, Roseanne's rise as a stand-up comedian was brisk enough to demonstrate that even in the most cynical quarter of the entertainment business, her message would be heard.

On *Roseanne*'s opening credits, a blaring saxophone plays as the camera follows the Conner family around the kitchen table. They are laughing and eating pizza, Chinese food, potato chips—nothing to suggest the carefully planned repasts of other television mothers. The Conners move through the half-hour episode turning conventional images of maternity, marriage, wage-earning, and sexuality on their ears. The sitcom, a genre not generally recognized as one that challenges established social ideas, became for Roseanne a national forum for questioning the role of women. Unlike earlier sitcom moms, Roseanne Conner celebrated the vulgar. Whole installments of *Roseanne* were devoted to public flatulence, masturbation, and breast-feeding. Roseanne and her husband, Dan, lie to the IRS, default on bank loans, and, on an annual Halloween episode, dunk their neighbors in simulated blood while laughing from the sanctuary of the Conner kitchen.

Roseanne Conner was an incarnation of the comedian's "domestic goddess," her alter ego who Roseanne insists will someday be asked to rule the world. An early episode of *Roseanne* featured Roseanne Conner's fantasy of taking a bath in her own tub alone, with no interruptions from her children or husband. During the course of the episode, Roseanne nonchalantly murders her family, is tried, and is ultimately exonerated because everyone realizes, amid a chorus of praise to motherhood, that the systematic denial of five minutes of privacy for Roseanne justifies her acts of carnage. The domestic goddess always wins in the end.

One of the few performers who need no last name, Roseanne brought working-class women into the television world of the 1980s. Finding her roots in the long tradition of Jewish comedy, her stand-up comedy and her television show turned the "mom" stereotype on its ear, giving the public a new image of how a woman and a mother sounds, looks, and acts. [New York Public Library]

Roseanne, who has abandoned her second names for their patriarchal assumptions, has never been far from public scrutiny. A four-year marriage to comedian Tom Arnold became the darling story of supermarket tabloids, as did her third marriage to former chauffeur Ben Thomas, with whom she had her fourth child in 1995. Roseanne's performance of the national anthem on a televised baseball game, when she rubbed her crotch, attracted national attention. When *New Yorker* editor-in-chief Tina Brown named Roseanne as a guest editor of a special women's issue, several writers associated with the magazine quit in noisy disgust. (The magazine once referred to Roseanne's life as "one big unpopularity contest.") In a 1996 interview, Roseanne reported, not for the first time, that her work as a comedian, a mother, and an activist has been a lengthy indenture to the one job for which she feels best qualified, queen of the United States. Her campaign slogan is a case in point for her subversive comedy: "Vote for Rosie and put some new blood in the White House— every 28 days."

SELECTED WORKS BY ROSEANNE
Roseanne: My Life as a Woman (1989); *My Lives* (1994).

BIBLIOGRAPHY
Carswell, Sue. "Roseanne for Queen of the Universe." *Out* (February 1996): 62; Cole, Lewis. "Roseanne." *The Nation* (June 21, 1993): 878–880; Dowd, Maureen. "Eustace Silly." *NYTimes*, September 3, 1995, 4:11; Dutka, Elaine. "Slightly to the Left of Normal." *Time* (May 8, 1989): 82–83; Ehrenreich, Barbara. "The Wretched of the Hearth." *The New Republic* (April 2, 1990): 28–31; Horowitz, Joy. "June Cleaver Without Pearls." *NYTimes*, October 10, 1988, 1, 10; Lahr, John. "Dealing with Roseanne." *New Yorker* (July 17, 1995): 42–61; Sessums, Kevin. "Really Roseanne." *Vanity Fair* (February 1994): 58+; Wolcott, James. "Roseanne Hits Home." *New Yorker* (October 26, 1992): 123–124, and "With Respect to Roseanne." *New Yorker* (March 4, 1996), 134–135.

PETER TABACK

ROSEN, GLADYS (b. 1924)

Researcher and historian in Judaic studies, Gladys Rosen wrote the following about her childhood home: "Our house was filled with Hebrew books and dictionaries. We never had a living room, just a dining room with a book-covered table. Until I was 4 or 5, I thought that's what dining room tables were for—books, not eating."

Born on August 15, 1924, to Morris Ben-Zion and Mildred (Buckstein) Levine, Gladys grew up in Queens, New York. She graduated from Brooklyn College in 1943 with honors in classics, and two years later received a degree from the Jewish Theological Seminary. In 1944, she married chemist Murray Rosen, and they had two sons, David and Jonathan. In 1948, Gladys Rosen earned a Ph.D. in Semitic languages and literature from Columbia University. After teaching Hebrew and Judaic studies at Brooklyn College, she became an executive associate at the American Jewish History Center of the Jewish Theological Seminary from 1960 to 1970.

Shortly after, Rosen became the program specialist at the American Jewish Committee (AJC) and published a groundbreaking manual, *Guidelines to Jewish History and Social Studies Instructional Materials*. This publication provided important information for the teaching of Jewish history in American secondary schools. In addition to writing other AJC publications, she helped organize conferences on the Jewish family, Jewish education, and the changing role of the Jewish American woman.

An active advocate of lifelong learning, she served as the assistant director of the Academy for Jewish

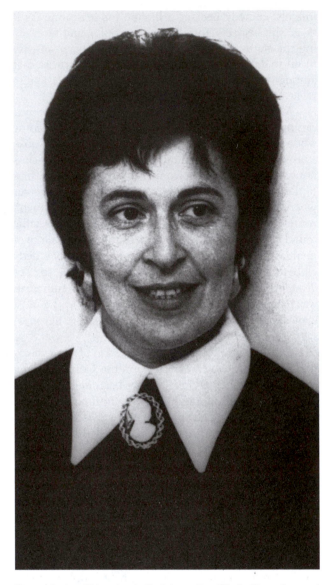

Researcher and historian in Judaic studies, Gladys Rosen has used her knowledge and experience to broaden the appeal and approach of Jewish history. She helped bring the study of Jewish history into the nation's high schools and has also influenced the field of continuing education in Jewish studies. [American Jewish Historical Society]

Studies Without Walls and the successful Jewish Studies Summer Seminar series held at various college campuses. A frequent lecturer, she was also an interviewer for a nationally syndicated radio program, *Jewish Viewpoint*.

Rosen edited *Jewish Life in America: Historical Perspectives* (1978) and coedited with Steven Bayme *Jewish Family and Jewish Continuity* (1994).

DONALD ALTSCHILLER

ROSEN, NORMA (b. 1925)

In a 1974 essay, "The Holocaust and the American-Jewish Novelist," Norma Rosen asked rhetorically: "Must we tell stories that reflect the Holocaust . . . ? Can't we just leave it out?" Among the earliest American novels to grapple with the impact of the Nazi genocide upon Jews and Western culture, Rosen's most celebrated novel, *Touching Evil* (1969), is part of the author's growing body of work that imaginatively explores being a Jew and a woman in contemporary urban America. Compelled, as a Jewish writer, by the injunction to remember, "*Zakhor*," Rosen's fiction and essays examine ethics, motherhood, and faith after the Holocaust, as well as Jewish identity, feminism, texts, and practices.

Born on August 11, 1925, in the Jewish neighborhood of Borough Park in Brooklyn, New York, she was a product of what she describes as "an immaculate Jewish conception. . . . My parents, who were Jews by birth, refrained from intercourse with the Jewish religion and proudly passed me, in an untainted state, into the world." The only child of American-born Louis Gangel, a businessman, and Rose (Miller) Gangel, Norma absorbed Jewish culture and cadences from the Brooklyn milieu of her early childhood, and from her grandparents' Yiddish-speaking household. She received no formal Jewish education, and her parents discouraged questions about European roots or Jewish practice. Her mother resented the diminished role of women in the synagogue and refused to attend services on High Holidays.

Norma moved to Manhattan with her parents and attended Julia Richmond High School. She studied literature and dance at Mount Holyoke College, graduating cum laude and Phi Beta Kappa in 1946. She continued to study dance with José Limón and Martha Graham and taught English and dance at the private Riverdale School. In 1953, she received an M.A. in English from Columbia University for her thesis on the novels of Graham Greene. She began working in book production at Harper & Row in 1954, quitting to write full-time in 1959 when her first two published stories appeared in *Commentary* and *Mademoiselle*. (Initially she published briefly under the name of Norma Stahl.) Her first novel, *Joy to Levine!*, was published three years later under the name Norma Stahl Rosen.

On August 23, 1960, after a brief first marriage, she married Robert S. Rosen, a professor of modern languages at Baruch College. Their daughter, Anne Beth, was born in 1961, and their son, Jonathan Aaron, in 1963. Since 1965, Rosen has taught creative writing at the New School for Social Research in New York, the University of Pennsylvania, Harvard University, Yale University, Columbia University, and the Tisch School of Dramatic Writing at New York University, and other institutions. From 1971 to 1973, she was a fellow at Radcliffe College's prestigious Bunting Institute. She received the Eugene F. Saxton Award and in 1975, she was awarded the New York State Creative Artists Public Service Grant. Rosen currently lives in New York City.

Born in Vienna in 1924, Rosen's husband escaped the Nazi genocide on a children's transport to England in November 1938. His parents did not survive. In contrast to Norma Rosen, Richard Rosen observed kashrut [dietary laws] and attended synagogue; moreover, he had received an extensive Jewish education. His experiences impelled his wife to confront the Jewish past, and she began to study Jewish philosophy and history, becoming interested in Jewishness not only as a demographic accident but as an ongoing search for meaning. Rosen moved to Brookline, Massachusetts, where she attended the weekly *shiurim* [study sessions] of Rabbi Joseph Solovietchik, encountered a women's prayer service, and began to incorporate Jewish concepts into her writing.

Rosen's novels are governed by ethical and philosophical issues in concrete contexts, as well as the intricacies of domestic life and intimate relationships. A sharp sense of observation and a keen sense of humor inform much of her writing. In *Touching Evil*, which took Rosen six years to write, the two non-Jewish protagonists become what she calls "witnesses-through-the-imagination" by watching the Adolf Eichmann war-crime trials on television or seeing photos of a death camp. Central to the novel is the question Rosen articulates elsewhere: "How can we live now?" *At the Center* (1982) utilizes traditional Jewish texts and motifs such as the *Akedah* [the binding of Isaac] to explore the theological crisis of a daughter of Holocaust survivors who are later murdered in New York. Set in an abortion clinic, the novel also examines those ethical issues related to abortion, and the effect on the domestic and inner lives of physicians and patients. The novel emerged out of a series of interviews Rosen conducted for the *New York Times Magazine*, which led her to study rabbinic responses on abortion. Struck by the rabbinic compassion for, rather than judgment of, the woman's situation, Rosen came to see Judaism afresh.

In 1973, Rosen left the safety of fiction to write "unprotected" essays. Her first collection, *Accidents of Influence: Writing as a Woman and a Jew in America* (1992), charts her growing self-awareness as a Jew, a feminist, and an intellectual. In a remarkable range of subject matter, Rosen reflects on the difference between urban and suburban motherhood, the absence of Jewish content in Western culture, the impact of the Holocaust, the evolution of a distinct Jewish American culture, and Jewish feminism. In one essay, she imagines French philosopher and apostate Simone Weil entering a synagogue as did Franz Rozenzweig, but instead of becoming inspired, as he was, to reclaim Judaism, she emerges resentful of the subservience of women.

A member since its inception in 1987 of the Genesis Seminar for writers and scholars at the Jewish Theological Seminary, Rosen completed a collection of midrashim on biblical women, *Biblical Women Unbound: Counter-Tales* (1996). Citing a biblical passage and its textual problems, each midrash enacts a dialogue with ancient rabbinic writers, while engaging with contemporary questions. The book explores midrash as both a literary genre and a theological inquiry.

SELECTED WORKS BY NORMA ROSEN

Accidents of Influence: Writing as a Woman and a Jew in America (1992); *At the Center* (1982. Reprint, 1996); *Biblical Women Unbound: Counter-Tales* (1996); *A Family Passover*, with Anne Rosen and Jonathan Rosen (1980); *Green: A Novella and Eight Stories* (1967); *John and Anzia: An American Romance* (1989. Reprint, 1997); *Joy to Levine!* (1962); "The Lovemaking of I.B. Singer." *Commentary* (March 1996); *Touching Evil* (1969. Reprint 1990).

BIBLIOGRAPHY

Goldberg, Marilyn. "The Soul-Searching of Norma Rosen." *Studies in American Jewish Literature* 3 (1983): 202–211; Klingenstein, Suzanne. "Norma Rosen." In *Jewish American Women Writers: A Bio-Bibliographical and Critical Sourcebook*, edited by Ann Shapiro et al. (1994); Rosenberg, Ruth. "Norma Rosen." *Dictionary of Literary Biography*. Vol. 28: *Twentieth Century American Jewish Writers*, edited by Dan Walden (1954): 248–252.

SARA R. HOROWITZ

ROSEN, ORA MENDELSOHN (1935–1990)

A brilliant research physician, Ora Mendelsohn Rosen tragically died of cancer, the disease whose processes her researches in cell biology had helped to explain. A leading investigator of how hormones control the growth of cells, Rosen held the Abby Rockefeller Mauz Chair of Experimental Therapeutics at Memorial Sloan-Kettering Cancer Center in New York City. Although her initial research involved insulin, not cancer cells, the implications of her discoveries reverberated throughout biochemical and genetic research, including cancer research. Rosen's work allowed scientists to understand for the first time how insulin interacts with a cell and opened the way for detailed investigation of how an insulin receptor molecule transmits signals from the cell's surface to its interior. The topic of communication within a cell is significant not just for diabetes research but also for understanding cancer.

Born and bred in New York, Ora was the first child and only daughter of Isaac and Fanny (Soier) Mendelsohn. Her parents, both born in Russia, met and married in Palestine in 1925. Several years later, they came to the United States. Isaac Mendelsohn became a professor of Semitic languages at Columbia University; Fanny Mendelsohn specialized in remedial reading.

Ora Rosen was born on October 26, 1935, and grew up on Manhattan's Upper West Side in an intellectual household. Her parents had high expectations for her and her younger brother, Ezra, who later became a professor at the Hebrew University of Jerusalem. The Mendelsohns were Zionists and immersed in Jewish culture. Ora joined the left-wing Zionist youth movement Hashomer Hatzair as a teenager, but did not receive a formal Jewish education.

She attended public schools and then entered Barnard College, majoring in biology as a premed student. In 1956, she graduated and married Samuel Rosen, a physician who later became a dean at the Albert Einstein College of Medicine in New York. The Rosens had two sons, Isaac and Gideon. Despite her decision, typical of young women in the 1950s, to marry after graduation and have children, Rosen atypically did not let marriage or children deflect her from pursuing a career in medical research. In 1960, she received her medical degree from Columbia University's College of Physicians and Surgeons. After additional study of cell biology and biochemistry at New York University and the Albert Einstein College of Medicine, she joined the latter institution in 1966 as an assistant professor of medicine. Just a year later, she was made an associate professor. In 1975, her promotion to full professor signaled the importance of her research. In 1976, she was appointed professor and chair of the department of molecular pharmacology, and in 1977, she became director of the division of endocrinology.

After joining the faculty of Memorial Sloan-Kettering in 1984, Rosen, working with researchers at Genentech, cloned the gene for the human insulin receptor in 1985. The insulin receptor is the cell-surface molecule to which the hormone insulin binds. The receptor, in effect, turns the key to transmit signals into a cell, thus activating information inside the cell. Prior to Rosen's research, scientists did not know how insulin got into the cell. Her findings led to further inquiry into the role of insulin in normal cell function as well as in such cell disorders as diabetes.

In recognition of her work, Rosen received awards from the American Medical Women's Association and the Albert Einstein College of Medicine. In 1989, she was elected a member of the National Academy of Sciences, a rare honor for a woman.

Personal tragedy interrupted her brilliant career, when her husband, Samuel, died in the early 1980s. She subsequently married Jerard Hurwitz, an American Cancer Society research professor working at Sloan-Kettering in DNA replication.

On May 30, 1990, on the Jewish holiday of Shavuoth, Ora Mendelsohn Rosen, age fifty-four, died of breast cancer at her home on Manhattan's Upper East Side.

BIBLIOGRAPHY

American Men and Women of Science. 16th ed. (1986); Mendelsohn, Ezra. Interview by author, November 29, 1996; Obituary. *NYTimes,* June 1, 1990.

DEBORAH DASH MOORE

ROSENBERG, ANNA LEDERER
(1899–1983)

The first woman to serve as assistant secretary of defense, Anna Lederer Rosenberg achieved distinction in government and business. Born on July 19, 1899, to Albert and Charlotte (Bacskai) Lederer in Budapest, Hungary, she came to the United States with her family in 1912, after her father's business failed. She was naturalized in 1919. She attended Wadleigh High School in Manhattan. During World War I, as an adolescent, Anna sold Liberty Bonds and was a volunteer nurse in an embarkation hospital. Later, she held some of the highest government posts ever occupied by a woman and received recognition for her efficiency, intelligence, energy, and for a certain brashness. She married Julius Rosenberg, a rug merchant, at age twenty and had a son, Thomas, at age twenty-one.

During the 1920s, Rosenberg gained experience in politics and philanthropy. A speech she made advocating woman suffrage brought her to the attention of Jim Hagan, a Tammany district leader. Rosenberg became active in Manhattan's seventh Assembly District Democratic Party Organization. She got her start managing campaigns for Walter Hagan (for alderman)

and John Buckley (for assemblyman) in 1922. She also managed James J. Hagan's campaign to retain leadership of the seventh Assembly District and Saul Streit's run for the Assembly.

Rosenberg held increasingly important government roles during the 1930s. A committed Democrat, she served in the New Deal administration and became a trusted adviser to Franklin Roosevelt, Harry Truman, New York Mayor Fiorello LaGuardia, and New York Governor Herbert Lehman. She ran congressional campaigns for Louis Brodsky in 1930 and Theodore Peyser in 1932. She also ran Nathan Straus, Jr.'s 1933

The first woman to serve as assistant secretary of defense and the first woman awarded the Medal for Merit, Anna Lederer Rosenberg succeeded in two male-dominated worlds, government and business. She relied on humor, diplomacy, and, often, direct or strong language when her authority and knowledge were challenged. She is shown here with General Omar Bradley in France in 1944. [Courtesy of Thomas Rosenberg]

In 1944, Anna Rosenberg served as President Roosevelt's personal representative in Europe and, in 1945, President Truman sent her to the European theater to study military personnel problems. This 1951 photograph with General George C. Marshall and Lyndon Johnson was taken in Washington, D.C. [Courtesy of Thomas Rosenberg]

campaign for aldermanic president, and served as assistant to Nathan Straus, regional director of the National Recovery Administration (NRA). In 1934, she replaced Straus, becoming acting state NRA compliance director. Between 1934 and 1945, Rosenberg held positions as regional director of the NRA; the Social Security Board; Defense, Health, and Welfare Services; and the War Manpower Commission.

During the 1940s, Rosenberg combined government work and private consulting. In 1945, she left government and started her public relations firm, Anna M. Rosenberg Associates. Rosenberg continued her service to the country during the 1940s. Governor Lehman appointed her to the New York State War Council during World War II. In 1944, she served as President Roosevelt's personal representative in Europe and, in 1945, Truman sent her to the European theater to study military manpower problems.

From 1946 to 1950, she was a member of the American Commission to UNESCO and, from 1944 to 1947, a member of the advisory board of the Office of War Mobilization and Reconversion. During these years, she received numerous honors, including an honorary degree from Russell Sage College, a commendation from the Navy for outstanding voluntary service, the Medal of Freedom (1945), and the Congressional Medal of Honor (1946). She was the first woman awarded the Medal for Merit (1947).

Rosenberg reached the peak of her government career in the 1950s. In 1950, George Marshall called on Rosenberg to be assistant secretary of defense in charge of military manpower requirements, a position that involved procurement, utilization, and policymaking.

Rosenberg's nomination ran into trouble when rumors spread about her supposed un-American activity and Communist Party membership. Investigators found nothing to substantiate these rumors. Jewish groups, the Anti-Defamation League among them, raised questions over Rosenberg's treatment. They pointed to her thirty years of loyal service and claimed her detractors were "a rogues' gallery of anti-Semites" that included a confessed Ku Klux Klan leader. The Senate confirmed her nomination after clearing her name.

In 1951, Rosenberg received a citation from the Federation of Jewish Women's Organizations and an honorary Doctor of Laws from Tufts University. She also received the Department of Defense Certificate of Appreciation, its highest civilian honor, for her service as assistant secretary of defense. Next to Eleanor Roosevelt, she was the second most famous American woman with the troops in Korea.

In 1953, Rosenberg returned to her firm and continued to work for nearly thirty years. Her son, Thomas, was a business partner. Respected by labor and management, her clients included the American Hospital Association, *Encyclopaedia Britannica*, Studebaker, the Rockefeller brothers, John Hay Whitney, Marshall Field, and MARY LASKER. She was, however, still a woman in a man's world. In 1954, *Fortune* magazine claimed she exploited her sex, evident "in her choice of bizarre hats, her clanking gold bracelets [Madame Bangles was her nickname in the Pentagon], and her soignée appearance." Regular references in the press to her appearance, jewelry, and petite stature underscore the attitudes she faced. She used people's assumptions about her coyness and femininity to her advantage, but also relied upon humor and diplomacy or utilized direct or strong language when dealing with those who challenged her authority and knowledge. Her success and the admiration she garnered from military and government leaders indicate how skillfully she negotiated the male-dominated arenas in which she worked. In a 1966 article on women's work in *The Great Ideas Today*, Rosenberg noted that even after "forty years of public and private business life, the situation—vis-à-vis women in careers—has not changed substantially."

After her departure from government, Rosenberg remained an active citizen, mediating a major transit strike in 1960 and serving as a member of the New York City Board of Education and the United Nations Association. Hers was a powerful voice in urban action and civil rights. In 1962, after forty-two years of marriage, she and Julius Rosenberg divorced. She later married former Marshall Plan administrator, Paul Hoffman. The *New York Post* noted (February 7, 1965) that when she and Hoffman married, they "pledged only to love and honor," not to obey one another. In 1964, Rosenberg received the second annual Eleanor Roosevelt Political and Public Service Memorial Award. At the dinner in her honor, Robert Lovett, who served with Rosenberg when she was assistant secretary of defense, noted that she brought to the position "a wide experience, a professional competence, and a compassionate understanding that was a model of administrative accomplishment." Others acclaimed her talents as a labor mediator, diplomat, adviser of presidents, troubleshooter, administrator, mother, and grandmother. In 1966, Rosenberg was awarded the medallion of the City of New York and a Congressional Certificate of Appreciation in 1972.

Rosenberg's activities included numerous Jewish causes. She served as director of the Women's Division of the United Palestine Appeal in New York, the Women's Division of the Joint Distribution Committee, and the Federation of Jewish Philanthropies. She was involved in the NATIONAL COUNCIL OF JEWISH WOMEN, the ORT Reconstruction Fund, and in 1930, was business manager of the *Hakoah* soccer football team, the first all-Jewish team to play in the United States.

Anna Rosenberg developed cancer toward the end of her life and died of pneumonia on May 9, 1983.

BIBLIOGRAPHY

AJYB 85: 415–416; "Anna Goes to Washington." *Reader's Digest* (February 1951); "Anna M. Rosenberg—She Sells Intuitions." *Fortune* 50, no. 5 (1954): 74; "Busiest Woman in U. S." *Life* 32, no. 3 (January 21, 1952): 79+; *The Continuum Dictionary of Women's Biography* (1989); *Current Biography* (1943): 631–634, and (January 1951): 538–540; *Current Biography Yearbook* (1983): 467, s.v. "Hoffman"; *EJ*; Frantz, Joe. Oral history interview with Anna Rosenberg Hoffman, November 2, 1973. Lyndon Baines Johnson Library and Museum, Austin, Tex.; Hoffman, Anna Rosenberg. "A New Look at Women's Work." *The Great Ideas Today* (1966), and Oral History. Eleanor Roosevelt Oral History Transcripts, Franklin Delano Roosevelt Library, Hyde Park, N.Y., and Papers. Schlesinger Library, Radcliffe College, Cambridge, Mass.; Kaster, Greg. "Anna Marie Lederer Rosenberg." In *European Immigrant Women in the United States*, edited by J. Litoff and J. McDonnell (1994); Marcus, Jacob. *United States Jewry, 1776–1985*. Vol. 4 (1993): 241; Michaelson, Judy. "Women in the News." *New York Post-Weekend Magazine*, February 7, 1965, sec. 2; Neidle, Cecyle. *America's Immigrant Women* (1976); Obituary. *NYTimes*, May 10, 1983, D25; "Outgoing Directrix." *New Yorker* 21 (September 15, 1945): 20–21; Svonkin, Stuart G. "Jews Against Prejudice." Ph.D. Diss., Columbia University (1995); *UJE*; U.S. Senate Committee on Armed Services. *Nomination of Anna M. Rosenberg to be Assistant Secretary of Defense: Hearings before the Committee on Armed Services.* 81st

Cong., part 2, 1950; Wall, Joseph. "Reminiscences of Anna M. Rosenberg." Interview. Oral History Collection, Columbia University, NYC; *WWIAJ* (1938).

SUSAN L. TANANBAUM

ROSENBERG, ETHEL (1915–1953)

Few Jewish American women evoke as varied and passionate a response as Ethel Rosenberg. To some she was an arch-villain, to others a crass ideologue, and yet to others a hapless victim. Convicted and executed on June 19, 1953, with her husband Julius Rosenberg, for conspiracy to divulge atomic secrets to the Soviet Union, Rosenberg was only the second woman in the United States to be executed by the federal government.

The trial and execution of the Rosenbergs was a direct outgrowth of the political and social climate of the early 1950s. The increasing hostility and hysterics of Cold War politics assumed its most virulent form in the anticommunist witch-hunts of the House on Un-American Activities Committee and Senator Joseph McCarthy's Subcommittee on Investigations. Jews from various walks of life were particularly targeted because of their disproportionately large affiliation and/or sympathies with leftist politics during the 1930s and 1940s. The Jewish establishment's fear of anti-Semitic backlash in the wake of anticommunist sentiment resulted in a further distancing between itself and the accused. And finally, the escalating casualties in the Korean War created a highly charged political atmosphere of distrust and obsessive fear of communism, and the need to ascribe blame for postwar gains by the communist bloc.

When conferring the death penalty on the Rosenbergs, Judge Irving Kaufman described the defendants' crime as "worse than murder ... causing the communist aggression in Korea with resultant casualties exceeding 50,000 and who knows but what that [sic] millions more, innocent people may pay the price of your treason...."

Esther Ethel (Greenglass) Rosenberg was born on September 28, 1915, in the squalor and poverty of New York's Lower East Side, the first-born child of Barney and Tessie (Feit) Greenglass. The two-room, cold-water tenement apartment where they lived with Barney Greenglass's eight-year-old son, Sammy, from his first marriage was located at 64 Sheriff Street, half a block from the Williamsburg Bridge. Barney Greenglass, an immigrant from Russia, had a sewing machine repair shop in the front room of their apartment. Tessie Greenglass, according to Rosenberg's

biographer Ilene Philipson, was a dour, embittered woman who inexplicably resented her only daughter. Ethel would maintain a troubled and conflict-ridden relationship with her mother throughout her life. Two other brothers, Bernard and David, followed, two and a half and six years younger than Ethel, respectively.

Ethel attended neighborhood schools, proving a more diligent and successful student than her brothers. At Seward Park High School, although shy and often reticent, she showed early promise as an actor, and starred in several school theatrical productions by the time of her graduation in 1931. With her eyes on broader horizons than the Lower East Side, she opted for all college preparatory courses rather than the secretarial curriculum of most of the other female students.

However, when she graduated from high school at the beginning of the Depression, she decided to go to work to assist with family expenses. She nevertheless maintained her theater activities with the experimental theater at the Clark Settlement House. During this time, she also began studying music seriously and was eventually invited to join the prestigious Schola Cantorum, which sometimes performed at Carnegie Hall and the Metropolitan Opera House. Through the end of 1931, she was intent upon making a career for herself in music or theater. Radical politics, although widespread and eagerly embraced by Jews in New York City, were not part of the Greenglass family's world.

Ethel's introduction to leftist radicalism came with her first job at the National New York Packing and Shipping Company, located at West 36th Street. She held this job for three and a half years, and the experience introduced her, for the first time, to non-Jews, underpaid and exploited workers, union organizers, and active members of the Communist Party. She soon found coworkers who shared her love of music and theater, with whom she spent her evenings, and her days were filled with discussion of radical political philosophy. She discovered herself to be in sympathy with the party's ideological opposition to fascism, racism, and anti-Semitism, its support of unionism, and its idealization of the Soviet experiment. In the early 1930s, many American radicals still viewed Stalinist Russia as a noble and successful attempt to improve government. Jewish disillusionment would come only with the signing of the Ribbentrop-Molotov Pact in 1939 and with news of Stalinist anti-Semitic purges.

In August 1935, the workers of the Shipping Clerk's Union called a general strike. Ethel was the only woman on the four-person strike committee. At the conclusion of the strike, she and the other leaders of the strike committee were fired. They appealed to the newly formed National Labor Relations Board (NLRB) and were subsequently vindicated by the NLRB for their union activities.

Still hoping for a career in singing and theater, she focused her energies on entertaining at Popular Front activities. These included public demonstrations that supported relief for the needy, union organizations, and antifascist forces in the Spanish Civil War. In December 1936, while singing for a Seaman's Union benefit, Ethel was introduced to Julius Rosenberg, the man who would soon become her husband and change the course of her life.

Julius Rosenberg, also the son of immigrant parents, was an engineering student at City College and an ardent communist. As a child growing up on the Lower East Side, he zealously embraced Judaism and wanted to study for the rabbinate. While a student at City College, which was a hotbed of radical Jewish politics, Julius eagerly exchanged his religious fervor for political zealotry.

Julius and Ethel married on June 18, 1939. They had two sons, Michael in 1943 and Robert in 1947. During the early years of their marriage, they lived in an apartment in the Knickerbocker Village on the Lower East Side. Julius Rosenberg worked first as a civilian for the United States Signal Corps and later for Emerson Radio and Phonographic Company. While he continued his communist activities, including recruitment of coworkers, Ethel Rosenberg committed herself wholeheartedly to raising her two small children, abandoning all interest in politics and the theater.

The sequence of events leading to the arrest of Ethel and Julius Rosenberg began, like falling dominoes, with the arrest in February 1950 of Klaus Fuchs, a German-born physicist who had worked on the Manhattan Project and was then residing in England. Fuchs named his American courier, "Raymond" Harry Gold, who in turn identified his unnamed contact in Albuquerque as a young, dark-haired machinist working at Los Alamos. This young machinist was David Greenglass, Ethel Rosenberg's youngest brother.

David Greenglass's wife, Ruth, was also implicated by Gold. To ensure his wife's immunity from imprisonment, Greenglass led the FBI to his brother-in-law Julius Rosenberg. Julius Rosenberg was arrested on June 16, 1950, and on July 17 Ethel Rosenberg was arrested by the FBI, never to return home.

It is well documented that the government's case against Ethel Rosenberg was tenuous, and recently decoded KGB documents confirm that her role in an espionage network was negligible at best. Analysts of the case now agree that Ethel Rosenberg was arrested in order to force her husband to continue the chain of disclosures. Julius Rosenberg's refusal forced the government's hand, and Ethel Rosenberg assumed her husband's posture of maintaining their innocence and refused to admit any knowledge of espionage activities. At a February 1951 meeting of the Joint Congressional Committee on Atomic Energy, United States attorney Myles Lane stated: "The case is not strong against Mrs. Rosenberg. But for the purpose of acting as a deterrent, I think it is very important that she be convicted, too, and given a stiff sentence."

The high-profile case began in March 1951 in the district court for the Southern District of New York in Manhattan. To ensure that the trial would not be delegitimized as an anti-Semitic charade, all of the government's players, Judge Irving Kaufman, and the prosecutors Irving Saypol and Roy Cohn were Jewish. Both Saypol and Cohn would prove themselves to be "loyal" American Jews, earning reputations for successfully prosecuting communists. Of the twelve randomly selected jurors, however, not one was Jewish.

David Greenglass, the government's key witness, did not hesitate to present very damaging testimony concerning his sister's role in the transfer of Greenglass' crudely drawn implosion-type lens design to a Soviet courier. Ethel Rosenberg's own performance under cross-examination caused irreparable damage to her own defense. In addition to her frequent invocations of the Fifth Amendment, her cool, dispassionate responses to even her own brother's accusations were interpreted as superciliousness and disdain for the proceedings. Her refusal to show emotion during the reading of the guilty verdict and the pronouncement of the death penalty only confirmed the belief of the government, press, and supporters of the verdict that she was a fanatical ideologue, emotionless, and devoid of womanly and maternal instincts. She was accused of being more committed to communist ideology than to her own children. Ethel Rosenberg's refusal to accommodate gender convention and dissolve into a hysterical or weeping victim suggested to many, including President Dwight Eisenhower and FBI director J. Edgar Hoover, that she was in fact the dominant force in the spy network. Cartoons and illustrations of the Rosenbergs often depicted the diminutive Ethel Rosenberg, barely reaching five feet in her high heels, as towering over her bespectacled, stoop-shouldered husband.

The Rosenbergs were moved to Sing Sing prison to await the appeals that their attorney, Emmanuel Bloch, filed. The United States Court of Appeals rejected the first appeal in February 1952. The United States Supreme Court turned down the subsequent application for writ of certiorari, although Justice Felix Frankfurter dissented on the grounds that the Rosenbergs were tried for conspiracy but sentenced for treason.

While the appeals were in progress, supporters of the Rosenbergs began to reach a wide audience in the court of public opinion. The National Committee to Secure Justice for the Rosenbergs was gaining momentum in the United States and abroad. While most of the pro-Rosenberg forces were leftist-leaning organizations, nonleftist support was beginning to question the excessive penalty.

The issue of anti-Semitism was a constant undercurrent during the trial and its aftermath. As support for the Rosenbergs rose within the ranks of leftist organizations, there were renewed attempts by the Rosenberg defenders to link anti-Semitism with the Rosenbergs' prosecution. The established Jewish community, fearing that an association with Jewish radicalism might result in an anti-Semitic backlash, rejected this charge. Jewish leaders and intellectuals, the American Jewish Committee, and the American Civil Liberties Union, with its large Jewish membership, publicly endorsed the guilty verdict.

In a last-minute attempt to have the case heard again before the Supreme Court, Rosenberg attorneys presented enough new argumentation that Justice Douglas granted a stay of execution on the court's last day before its summer recess. They were elated by the Douglas stay of execution, fully confident that over the summer the pro-Rosenberg momentum would be able to yield enough worldwide support for clemency. However, in a nearly unprecedented move, Chief Justice Fred Vinson reconvened the court to annul Justice Douglas's stay. Massive rallies in Times Square, petitions, letters, marches, and a last-minute appeal to President Eisenhower by Michael Rosenberg could not forestall the government's haste to execute the Rosenbergs. Julius and Ethel Rosenberg were executed shortly after 8:00 P.M. on Friday, June 18, 1953. Like her husband, Ethel Rosenberg died quietly, with dignity, and to her last breath maintained her innocence and love for her children.

Thousands of mourners came to honor Julius and Ethel Rosenberg, but not one of Ethel's family came, including her mother, who never forgave her daughter for involving her younger brother David in her communist activities.

Ethel Rosenberg's Jewish identity was forged not by her childhood ties to traditional Judaism but by her political radicalism. As was common with Jewish radicals, the abandonment of religious belief and affiliation was a necessary step in the assumption of a transcendent universalist ideology. The prison letters Rosenberg wrote suggest that, while she had an adequate understanding and appreciation of Jewish values and customs, she first and foremost saw herself as a martyr for political oppression.

Few legal cases in United States history have raised as many questions as the Rosenbergs'. Regardless of questions concerning the guilt or innocence of the accused, legal scholars now agree that some of the actions on the part of government players, from ex-parte discussions between Judge Kaufman and the prosecution to Chief Justice Vinson's politicizing of the final appeal, would today have seriously compromised the integrity of the government's case.

At the end of the twentieth century, with the terrors of McCarthyism a distant historical nightmare, many Americans still believe that Julius and Ethel Rosenberg were guilty because they were un-American. Others believe them guilty although the punishment did not fit the crime. And many believe even more strongly than before that they were the hapless victims of gross governmental misconduct.

BIBLIOGRAPHY

Coover, Robert. *The Public Burning* (1976); *DAB* 5; Doctorow, E.L. *The Book of Daniel* (1971); *EJ*, s.v. "Rosenberg Case"; Garber, Marjorie, and Rebecca Walkowitz, eds. *Secret Agents: The Rosenberg Case, McCarthyism, and Fifties America* (1995); Goldstein, Alvin H. *The Unquiet Death of Julius and Ethel Rosenberg* (1975); Meeropol, Michael, ed. *The Rosenberg Letters: A Complete Edition of the Prison Correspondence of Julius and Ethel Rosenberg* (1994); Meeropol, Robert, and Michael Meeropol. *We Are Your Sons: The Legacy of Ethel and Julius Rosenberg* (1975); Moore, Deborah Dash. "Reconsidering the Rosenbergs: Symbol and Substance in Second Generation American Jewish Consciousness." *Journal of American Ethnic History* (Fall 1988); Nason, Tema. *Ethel: The Fictional Autobiography* (1990); *NAW* modern; Philipson, Ilene. *Ethel Rosenberg: Beyond the Myth* (1988); Radosh, Ronald, and Joyce Milton. *The Rosenberg File: A Search for the Truth* (1973); Schneir, Walter, and Miriam Schneir. *Invitation to an Inquest: A New Look at the Rosenberg-Sobel Case* (1968); Sharlitt, Joseph H. *Fatal Error: The Miscarriage of Justice that Sealed the Rosenbergs' Fate* (1989).

LISA KOGEN

ROSENBERG, SOPHIE SONIA
(b. 1888)

Dress designer Sophie Rosenberg was born in Odessa, Russia, on December 21, 1888, to Benjamin and Leah Daschew. At age twenty she immigrated to the United States and came to New York City, where she was to live the rest of her life. Shortly after her immigration, on April 20, 1908, she married Abraham Jacob Rosenberg.

Her first job in the United States was as a forelady at the Eureka Dress Company in 1908. By 1916, she started her own dress company at 161 West 44th Street. In 1926, the partnership of S. Goodstein and Sophie Rosenberg became known as Sonia Inc., using Rosenberg's middle name as title to the company. Later that year, Sonia Inc. became formally known as Rosenberg-Goodstein Inc., only to be changed to Sonia Rosenberg Inc. by 1929. The final and most remembered name of Sophie Rosenberg's company came to be Sonia Gowns Inc. in 1935, when she entered into the business with Gloria Morgan Vanderbilt.

Under the terms of this business alliance, Gloria Vanderbilt was president of the company, and her twin sister, Thelma Furness, its vice president, while Sophie Rosenberg was secretary, and Jacob Rosenberg was treasurer. They were all to have equal authority in the management of the company. Unfortunately, this business alliance was short-lived and unprofitable for all parties involved by 1938. The *New York Times* reported that Gloria Vanderbilt sued to close the gown shop and reported losing all of her initial $40,000 investment, plus an additional $10,000 requested by Rosenberg for the business.

Though her business venture with the Vanderbilt family was brief, she never left the dress design business, and within a few short years, in 1944, she went into business once again, retaining the name of Sonia Gowns Inc. This time, she made herself president of the company and was in partnership with Ethel D. Arkin and George Arkin at 25 West 57th Street in New York. Rosenberg remained there until she closed the shop in 1956 at age sixty-eight.

BIBLIOGRAPHY

"Vanderbilt Sues Gown Shop." *NYTimes*, June 12, 1938; *WWIAJ* (1938).

JENNIFER VAFAKOS

ROSENBLATT, GERTRUDE
(1891–1955)

On February 24, 1912, a group of approximately thirty young women, who called themselves Bnoth Zion, or the Daughters of Zion, met together at the urging of HENRIETTA SZOLD with the intent of founding HADASSAH. Gertrude Rosenblatt was one of those women, and on March 7, 1912, when the officers were elected, she became one of the first directors of Hadassah, the Women's Zionist Organization. Her involvement in this new organization was only the beginning of her philanthropic activities aimed at helping those in need in Palestine and Israel.

Born in 1891, Gertrude (Goldsmith) Rosenblatt married Bernard A. Rosenblatt, a prominent lawyer from New York City and an ardent Zionist (he was founder and/or president of a number of Zionist organizations) who helped Szold draft the constitution for Hadassah. They had two sons, David and Jonathan. The couple settled in Palestine, but later returned to New York City.

Rosenblatt was an organizer of Young Judaea and, while in Israel, a founder of Ruhamah, a Haifa orphanage. In 1926, she organized clothing distribution in Haifa, and in 1934 she received a citation from the British high commissioner in Palestine for her role in providing aid to flood victims in Tiberias, Israel. Upon her return to the United States, she became a key member in the Hebrew-Speaking Society of New York, which was formed in 1949.

Gertrude Rosenblatt died on October 9, 1955, and was buried in Haifa, Israel. She truly was a Daughter of Zion whose passion for Israel was surpassed only by her passion to improve life for those who lived there.

BIBLIOGRAPHY

AJYB, 58:478, s.v. "Gertrude Rosenblatt," and 71:608, s.v. "Bernard Rosenblatt"; Beth Hatefutsoth, *Women of Valor: The Story of Hadassah, 1912–1987* (1987); Kutscher, Carol Bosworth. "The Early Years of Hadassah, 1912–1921." Ph.D. diss., Brandeis University (1976); Miller, Donald H. *A History of Hadassah, 1912–1935* (1968); Obituary. *NYTimes*, October 10, 1955, 27:6.

KAYLA SHIP

ROSENCRANTZ, ESTHER
(1876–1950)

An accomplished physician in her own right, Esther Rosencrantz is remembered most for an intense interest in Sir William Osler, her mentor, which pervaded her adulthood and was her legacy. Rosencrantz was born on November 18, 1876, in San Francisco, California, the daughter of John and Bertha (Wertheimer) Rosencrantz. She grew up on Sixth Street, in a working-class Jewish neighborhood. A graduate of Stanford University (1899), Rosencrantz studied chest diseases with Osler at the Johns Hopkins School of Medicine. In 1904, she became the second California woman to receive a Johns Hopkins medical diploma. She interned at the New York Infirmary for Women and Children, and for the next decade pursued clinical research and practice in the field of tuberculosis in London, Berlin, Paris, and Bern.

In 1913, Rosencrantz began a long career as a clinical professor of medicine at the University of California, San Francisco (UCSF), where she served as a specialist in pulmonary diseases. She was in charge of the University of California Tuberculosis Clinic at the San Francisco Hospital, and was a trustee or consultant for a number of tuberculosis treatment facilities in northern and central California. Rosencrantz often visited needy patients at home, providing them with food, milk, and medications at her own expense. At the end of World War I, she was a member of the Red Cross Tuberculosis Commission in Italy, serving overseas for two years, and was honored by the Italian government for her work there.

In addition to her medical research, practice, and teaching, Rosencrantz became a member of the Division of Medical History and Bibliography at UCSF, focusing on William Osler (1849–1919), who was the most prominent and respected American physician in modern medical education. She collected any materials she could lay her hands on that were related to her beloved teacher. Earl Nation, M.D., of the American Osler Society refers to Rosencrantz as "Osler mad," noting that she saved "tufts of grass and shrubs on which Osler had trod!"

Rosencrantz retired as associate professor of medicine in 1943 after several years of being edged out of financial and office support. She registered her displeasure in letters to university officials, offended by their treatment in light of her long and successful service to the university. She continued to work as a volunteer in the Division of Medical History, expanding and cataloguing her Osler collection. By 1948, she had apparently resigned herself to her constrained circumstances in the medical school, writing to the dean: "in spite of all—and in the words of Osler . . . to have striven, to have made an effort, and to have been true to certain ideals—this alone is worth the struggle."

Little is known of Rosencrantz's life as a Jew. Her collected papers, maintained by the UCSF Library Archives and Special Collections, reveal little interest in or contact with Jewish people or institutions. Her death from heart disease on December 18, 1950, however, was written up in San Francisco's *Jewish Community Bulletin*, and Alvin Fine, rabbi of Temple Emanu-El, the city's largest Reform congregation, officiated at her funeral service.

Rosencrantz led a remarkably adventurous life for a woman born in late nineteenth-century America.

Attending Johns Hopkins when it was the foremost institution at the dawn of scientific medical education in the United States, her work was with the disease that was the major cause of morbidity and mortality of the era. Her coerced retirement coincided with the decline of tuberculosis. She assimilated into the dominant culture, like many California Jews, and a great man became her heritage.

BIBLIOGRAPHY

BEOAJ; "Esther Rosencrantz, Medical Educator, 74." *NYTimes*, December 19, 1950: 29:4; Gilcreest, Edgar Lorrington. "In Memoriam—Esther Rosencrantz." *Bulletin of the San Francisco County Medical Society* (March 1951): 18+; Nation, Earl F. *Ester Rosenkrantz, MD and Her Collection of Osleriana* (1996); "Obituary—Dr. Esther Rosencrantz." *Jewish Community Bulletin* (December 22, 1950): 6; Rosencrantz, Esther, Papers. Special Collections/University Archives, The Library and Center for Knowledge Management, University of California, San Francisco, and "Posthumous Tributes to Sir William Osler." *Archives of Internal Medicine* 84 (1949): 170–197; Sigerist, Henry E. "William Osler (1849–1919)." In *The Great Doctors* (1958); *UJE; Who's Who in California, 1942–43* I (1943): 784 *WWIAJ* (1938).

JANE SPRAGUE ZONES

ROSENSOHN, ETTA LASKER
(1885–1966)

On September 25, 1966, David Ben-Gurion drafted a letter to a leading member of HADASSAH, the Women's Zionist Organization of America. "I just learned with sorrow the passing of my dear friend, Etta Rosensohn," Ben-Gurion wrote. "I always admired her intellect and devotion for Hadassah and for the Jewish People. It is a great loss for Hadassah and for American Jewry." Ben-Gurion's handwritten letter of condolence offers testament to the prominence and success of Etta Lasker Rosensohn's many years of work for Hadassah. Though Rosensohn geared much of her philanthropic career toward Jewish and Zionist affairs in New York City, her involvement with Hadassah proved to be the great passion of both her personal and professional life.

Henrietta (Etta) Lasker was born in August 1885, in Galveston, Texas, one year after the birth of her older sister, Florina, and one year before the birth of her younger sister, Loula. Both of her parents came from educated German Jewish backgrounds. Her father, the well-known businessman Morris Lasker, immigrated to the United States from East Prussia in 1856 at age sixteen. Her mother, Nettie Davis, was a third-generation Jewish American, who hailed from a

An influential philanthropist and social activist, Etta Lasker Rosensohn focused most of her energy on Jewish and Zionist affairs in New York City. Her great passion was HADASSAH, *where she served on the national board for more than two decades and as the national president. [Hadassah Archives]*

town near Rochester, New York. Except for a brief stint living in Germany in 1893, Etta, her sisters, and three brothers came of age in a wealthy Galveston community. After attending college at the University of Texas, she moved to New York City and, like so many other elite women of her day, devoted her life to social and philanthropic work.

Etta and her sisters attended the New York School of Social Work and became trained social workers interested in working for the Jewish community. In 1918, they authored a study for the Bureau of Philanthropic Research called *Care and Treatment of the Jewish Blind in the City of New York*. That same year, Etta met and married Major Samuel J. Rosensohn, a lawyer and an assistant in labor relations to Secretary of War Newton Baker during World War I. They raised two children, William and Janet. Samuel Rosensohn died in 1939.

After World War I, Rosensohn and her sisters became affiliated with the NATIONAL COUNCIL OF JEWISH WOMEN, where Rosensohn served until 1930 as chairperson of the Department of Service to the Foreign-Born and founded that department's newspaper, *The Immigrant*.

Although Rosensohn also pursued a wide diversity of philanthropic activities in the interwar years, her central commitment to Hadassah was confirmed as early as August 1939 by her election as Hadassah's representative to the board of governors of the Hebrew University of Jerusalem. HENRIETTA SZOLD, founder of Hadassah, was the only other female member elected at this time to the university's governing body. A member of the national board of Hadassah for more than two decades, Rosensohn also served as national president from 1952 to 1953. Immediately before her tenure as president, she served as chair of the Hadassah Medical Organization Committee. Of all of her interests, Rosensohn ultimately considered Hadassah's medical work to be her top professional priority. From 1939, for instance, Rosensohn played an integral role in the founding and expansion of the Hebrew University–Hadassah Medical School in Jerusalem. In 1959, Hebrew University honored her for her longtime commitment to Hadassah's medical work by establishing the Etta Lasker Rosensohn Chair of Bacteriology at the Hebrew University Medical School.

When Etta Lasker Rosensohn died on September 20, 1966, in New York City, many social and political activists agreed with David Ben-Gurion's sentiment that her death represented a great loss for Hadassah and for American Jews.

BIBLIOGRAPHY

AJYB 68:532; *EJ*; Gunther, John. *Taken at the Flood: The Story of Albert Lasker* (1960); Obituary. *NYTimes*, September 21, 1966, 47:2; Obituary of Florina Lasker. *NYTimes*, September 2, 1949, 17; Rosensohn, Etta Lasker, *Care and Treatment of the Jewish Blind in the City of New York*, with Florina Lasker and Loula Lasker (1918), and Papers. Hadassah Archives, NYC; *UJE* 7; *WWIAJ* (1926, 1928, 1938); *WWWIA* 4.

ERIN ELIZABETH CLUNE

ROSENSTEIN, NETTIE (1890–1980)

Fashion designer Nettie Rosenstein was instrumental in the popularization of the "little black dress" in America. She observed the trend in French couture and used the power of the ready-to-wear industry to popularize the look in America. Her career developed through the 1930s and 1940s, at a time when France lost some of its influence as the world's fashion center. Rosenstein was one of many American dressmakers to gain from this change.

The youngest of three children, Nettie moved from Salzburg, Austria, to New York City with her parents, Joseph and Sarah Rosencrans, in the 1890s. Her parents opened a dry-goods store at 118th Street and Lenox Avenue. Dressmaking was a skill that she began to develop at a very early age. Her interest in and exposure to the fabrics in her parents' store formed the backbone of her career. Nettie's sister, Pauline, ran a millinery business known as Madame Pauline in the Rosencrans family house, next to the dry-goods store. Nettie began her career as a custom dressmaker for her sister's clients.

In 1913, Nettie married Saul Rosenstein. They had two children, Jerome (b. 1914) and Claire (b. 1925). In 1916, Nettié Rosenstein started a custom dressmaking business in her home on West 117th Street. By 1921, she employed fifty dressmakers and had moved her business to a more fashionable address at East 56th Street. During the 1920s, Rosenstein switched to selling wholesale. By the late 1920s, I. Magnin, Neiman-Marcus, Nan Duskin, and Bonwit Teller were some of the stores that carried her clothing.

When Saul Rosenstein retired from his successful women's underwear business in the late 1920s, Nettie Rosenstein tried retirement, too. Two years later, however, she began working for the dressmaking firm Corbeau & Cie. In 1931, she reopened her own dressmaking firm on West 47th Street with her sister-in-law, Eva Rosencrans, and her former boss at Corbeau & Cie., Charles Gumprecht. In spite of the Depression, Rosenstein's business flourished, grossing $1 million in 1937. By 1942, she had moved her business again, to 550 Seventh Avenue.

Rosenstein's designs were among the highest-priced wholesale clothes in New York City. Because they were so widely copied, the influence of her work went far beyond those who could afford her clothing. The reasons for her high prices were her use of high-quality materials and construction techniques, and her precise fit process. Each of her designs was first conceived on a showroom model, and then adapted in fit and proportion five times to five different-sized workroom models that represented the average figure. Rosenstein, who was given a design award in 1938 by the department store Lord & Taylor and who received the fashion industry's Coty Award in 1947, contributed largely to the movement of the democratization of fashion in America during the first half of the twentieth century by making good-quality clothing of sophisticated design available for the ready-to-wear

customer. Nettie Rosenstein died, after a long illness, at age ninety on March 13, 1980.

BIBLIOGRAPHY
Harriman, Margret Case. "Very Terrific, Very Divine." *New Yorker* (October 19, 1940): 28–34; Obituary. *NYTimes*, March 15, 1980; Steele, Valerie. *Women of Fashion* (1991); *WWWIA* 7.

DENNITA SEWELL

ROSENTHAL, DORIS (c. 1895–1971)

Doris Rosenthal was a daring explorer, a dedicated educator, and a painter of colorful and expressive yet unromanticized work representing the everyday life of Mexican Indians at a time when anti-Mexican sentiment in the United States was rife.

Born in Riverside, California, around 1895, Rosenthal was raised on a ranch by her parents, Emil J. and Anne (Unruh) Rosenthal. She won a scholarship in 1918 to study with George Bellows and John Sloane at the New York Art Students League.

Rosenthal was educated at Los Angeles State Teachers College, followed by graduate studies at Columbia University. She then worked briefly as a commercial designer of silks, saving enough money to tour Europe, where she continued the study of painting from 1920 to 1922. After returning from Europe, she married Jack Charash, a theater agent, and her early work depicted backstage scenes and New York department store dressing rooms. While teaching at Columbia Teachers College from 1924 to 1931, Rosenthal actively pursued her painting career and had her first solo show at Morton Galleries in 1928.

In the late 1920s, Rosenthal published a unique series of unbound plates, *The Prim-Art Series*. These portfolios consist of graphic images from all over the world executed by Rosenthal and based on designs acquired from objects in museums. Arranged around thematic motifs such as transportation, costumes, and birds rather than by country or time, the portfolios were a teaching tool and a resource for the professional designer. Each portfolio came with a lesson plan and method of application. The transportation portfolio included images of Russian carriages, railroad cars, bicycles, balloons, Egyptian triumphal cars, planes and zeppelins, representing everything from the fantastical to flash-in-the-pan industrial designs. Delightfully random, the portfolios were part of an emerging modernist art that looked to the so-called primitive for inspiration, hoping to return art to simple production unpolluted by industrialism and the factory.

The *Prim-Art* portfolios were instrumental in winning her two Guggenheim fellowships, in 1931 and 1936, to travel to Mexico. These trips changed the course of her life and art. By 1934, Rosenthal was a nationally and internationally recognized "regionalist" painter of Mexican themes, noted for her skill in composition and draughtmanship. Articles describing "the *Gringa*" painter appeared frequently. She maintained a studio in Silvermine, Norwalk, Connecticut, while teaching art at James Monroe High School in the Bronx. In the summers, Rosenthal traveled by burro into the remote states of Mexico, carrying sketchpads and a Flit gun, and using tequila as a fixative when necessary. Returning from her thirteenth summer in Latin America in 1944, Rosenthal compared the devastating effects of the military dictatorship on the arts in Guatemala to the flourishing Mexican art tradition. She concluded, "I feel pretty certain that systemization is sterilization as far as the arts go." Two months later, contributing to the national debate on art education in the United States, she warned against bureaucracy, echoing her earlier strong words: "Systemization is the greatest evil."

Mostly figurative, Rosenthal's paintings, based on hundreds of sketches from her travels, focus on domestic detail and daily gestures, inviting the viewer to experience the intricacies of ordinary life with the Mexican Indians, especially the lives of children. The Sanchezes of Cherán, Mexico, was one of the families that accepted Rosenthal into their homes. Their sons are depicted in "TOPS," one of her most famous paintings. Another painting, "The Source," shows Tarascan Indians bathing in water piped for miles in hollowed-out tree trunks. Mexican critic Guillermo Rivas wrote of her work in 1934: "Doris Rosenthal is not striving to escape life, but rather does she go out to meet it." Rosenthal sought not to work as a *tourista*-artist, capturing mere picturesque impressions of a place, but to engage in the culture, coming to a deeper appreciation of people's everyday lives.

By the time Doris Rosenthal died in November 1971, she had made Oaxaca, Mexico, her permanent home.

SELECTED WORKS BY DORIS ROSENTHAL

Pertaining to Birds: How to Use Bird Motifs in Design, compiler (1929); *Pertaining to Boats,* compiler (1928); *Pertaining to Costume: How to Use Historic Costumes in Design,* compiler (1930); *Pertaining to Flowers and Trees: How to Use Nature Motifs in Design,* compiler (1930); *Pertaining to Man: How to Use Figure Motifs in Design,* compiler (1930); *Pertaining to Transportation: How to Use Transportation Motifs in Design,* compiler (1929); *Prim-Art Series. Vol. 1: Animal Motifs* (1926); " 'System Is Greatest Evil': What Is Wrong with American Art Education?" *The Arts Digest* (August 1, 1944): 12.

BIBLIOGRAPHY

"Doris Rosenthal: Mentor Plus Mexico." *Art News* (February 15, 1943): 20; "Doris Rosenthal Paints Mexico in an Original Idiom." *Art News* (April 1, 1939): 13; "Doris 'the *Gringa*' in Guatemala." *American Artist* 8, no. 6 (June 1944): 22–26; Henkes, Robert. *American Women Painters of the 1930's and 1940's: The Lives and Works of Ten Artists* (1991); Obituary. *NYTimes*, November 28, 1971, 72:7; Pagano, Grace, ed. *Encyclopaedia Britannica Collection of Contemporary American Painting* (1946); Rosenthal, Doris. Papers, 1932–1965. Archives of American Art, Smithsonian Institution, Washington, D.C.; "Seen in Old Mexico." *Art Digest* (March 1, 1941): 9; "Shows Fruits of a Scholarship in Mexico." *The Art Digest* (February 15, 1934): 29; *WWIAJ* (1928); *WWWIA* 5.

JEANNE SCHEPER

ROSENTHAL, IDA COHEN
(1886–1973)

Ida Cohen Rosenthal, in partnership with her husband, not only reinvented the modern bra, but launched the company that became the world's largest bra manufacturer. Born on January 9, 1886, in Rakov, Russia, Ida was the eldest of the seven children of Abraham and Sarah (Shapiro) Kaganovich (changed to Cohen when the family immigrated to the United States). Her father was a scribe, and her mother ran a small general store. As a girl, Ida was apprenticed to a dressmaker. At age sixteen, she moved to Warsaw, where she worked and took classes in Russian and mathematics.

Returning to Rakov, Ida met and fell in love with William Rosenthal, son of Solomon and Sarah (Botwinick) Rosenthal. His father was a teacher and collector of Hebrew books. Ida and William became active in the socialist movement, which drew them to the attention of the local police. Then, in 1905, facing the prospect of being drafted to fight Japan, William decided the time had come to leave for America. A few months later, Ida joined him.

Setting up shop in Hoboken, New Jersey, Ida Rosenthal supported herself as a dressmaker. In 1906, she and William were married. In 1907, their son Lewis was born; Beatrice followed nine years later. The Rosenthals formed a successful business partnership that lasted until William's death in 1958. They worked together in Ida's dress shop, moving it to Manhattan in 1918. In 1921, the Rosenthals began working with Enid Bissett, who had a shop called Enid Frocks. Fashions of the day demanded a boyish look, so early brassieres were designed to flatten the figure. But for many women, this was not a flattering style. Enid cut apart one of the "bandeaus" then in fashion, and made a brassiere for a fuller figure. William improved on her idea, designing brassieres in different sizes, and the modern bra was born. At first they were given away with the dresses sold in the shop, but when demand for the brassieres increased, the Enid Manufacturing Company was set up to make them. In 1930, the Maiden Form Brassiere Company was founded. Enid was soon forced to withdraw because of ill health. In 1960, the company name was changed to Maidenform, Inc., to conform with the trade name of the company's product.

The company grew more successful every year. William was president, overseeing design and production, and Ida handled the financial side of the business, often traveling to visit the stores that carried their products. In 1949, a copywriter for a New York ad agency created the slogan used in the now-famous "I dreamed" ads. The ads began with "I dreamed I went shopping in my Maidenform bra," but also featured women in less traditional roles, such as winning an election and going to work.

When William died in 1958, Ida became president. A year later she became chair of the board, and her son-in-law, Joseph Coleman, took over the presidency. Suffering a stroke in 1966, Ida was no longer able to actively run the company, and Beatrice succeeded her husband upon his death in 1968. Ida Rosenthal died in New York City on March 28, 1973. Today, the company is run by Elizabeth Coleman, Beatrice's daughter.

Ida and William Rosenthal were involved in many Jewish causes, such as the Anti-Defamation League of B'nai B'rith and the United Jewish Appeal. In 1942, they presented Solomon Rosenthal's collection of Hebrew books to New York University, establishing the William and Ida Rosenthal Collection. A foundation established ten years later, in honor of Ida Rosenthal, ensured that a librarian would be paid to care for the collection. In 1943, they established Camp Lewis for the Boy Scouts of America, in memory of their son, who had died in 1930.

Always independent and willing to take chances, Ida Cohen Rosenthal was a business leader at a time when women were not easily accepted in leadership roles. She and her husband left an impressive record of innovation and success in the world of women's fashion.

BIBLIOGRAPHY

Bird, Caroline. *Enterprising Women* (1976); *Catalogue of the William and Ida Rosenthal Collection of Judaica and Hebraica including the Solomon Rosenthal Hebraica Collection,* New York University Library of Judaica and Hebraica (1955); *Great Lives from History: American Women* (1995); "I Dreamed I Was A Tycoon in My . . ." *Time* 76 (October 24, 1960): 92; "Maidenform's Mrs. R." *Fortune* 42 (July 1950): 75-76; Morris, Michele. "The Mother Figure of Maidenform," *Working Woman* 12 (April 1987): 82+; *National Cyclopedia of American Biography* 57 (1977): 339-340; *NAW* modern; Obituary. *NYTimes,* March 30, 1973, 42:2; Vare, Ethlie Ann, and Greg Ptacek. *Mothers of Invention. From the Bra to the Bomb: Forgotten Women and Their Unforgettable Ideas* (1988); *WWWIA* 5.

JOY A. KINGSOLVER

ROSENTHAL, JEAN (1912–1969)

Jean Rosenthal was a pioneer in theater lighting design. "Light is quite tactile to me. It has shape and dimension." Inspired by the paintings of Rembrandt and Monet, Rosenthal mastered the technical and poetic aspects of stage lighting. She used light's form, color, and movement to express the intention of a performance. Carefully integrating light into the overall texture of a piece, Rosenthal believed that "the most successful and brilliant work a lighting designer can do is usually the least noticeable."

Born Eugenie Rosenthal in New York City, on March 16, 1912, she was the only daughter and second of three children of Pauline (Scharfman) and Morris Rosenthal. Her parents, who emigrated from Romania in the 1880s, were both children of Jewish tailors. An unconventional family for the time, both parents worked as medical doctors, her father as an ear, nose, and throat specialist, her mother, as a psychiatrist.

Following her mother's progressive educational beliefs, Jean and her brothers attended the Ethical Culture School in the Bronx and later enrolled in the experimental Manumit School in Pawling, New York. With good humor, Rosenthal described the unorthodox yet holistic education she received at Manumit: "We . . . learned how to enter a chicken coop without scaring the chickens. Very valuable thing to know when you work in the theatre." For high school, Rosenthal studied at the Friends Seminary in Manhattan, a more formal educational environment, where she had a difficult time fitting in. At age sixteen, Rosenthal barely graduated from the school.

With her grades too low for her to be accepted at a prestigious college, Rosenthal enrolled in the Neighborhood Playhouse School of the Theatre in Manhattan. She was soon captivated by the experimental dance work of one faculty member, Martha Graham. Between 1928 and 1930, Rosenthal immersed herself

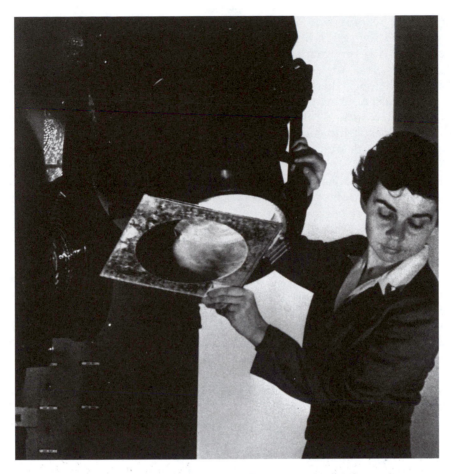

A pioneer in theater lighting design, Jean Rosenthal used light's form, color, and movement to express the intention of a performance. Most famous for her unconventional lighting of dance and opera, especially the works of Martha Graham, she also designed the lighting for some of Broadway's classic productions, including West Side Story *and* Cabaret. *[Schlesinger Library]*

in Graham's work, doing all aspects of production and technical assistance. In order to get more rigorous technical training, Rosenthal enrolled in the Yale University School of Drama from 1931 to 1934. There, she studied closely with the well-known stage lighting instructor Stanley McCandless. In 1932, Rosenthal received the Henrietta Lord Memorial Award for her work at Yale.

Rosenthal's first professional job was in 1935 as production supervisor for a WPA theater project in New York City. In this setting, she worked with John Houseman and Orsen Welles and, in 1937, became a production assistant for Welles's Mercury Theatre. During Welles's production of *Julius Caesar* in 1937, Rosenthal made a name for herself as an inventive lighting designer, bringing her a succession of jobs on Broadway. To supplement this production work, Rosenthal founded her own company in 1940, the

Theatre Production Service, which ran a mail-order catalog for theatrical equipment.

Rosenthal did the stage lighting for a number of well-known Broadway plays and musicals, such as *West Side Story* (1957), *Becket* (1960), *Hello, Dolly!* (1964), *Hamlet* (1964), *Fiddler on the Roof* (1964), *The Odd Couple* (1965), and *Cabaret* (1966). She is most famous for her unconventional lighting of dance and opera performances, including long-term collaborations with Gian Carlo Menotti, the New York City Ballet and its predecessor the Ballet Society, Martha Graham, and the New York City Opera. Rosenthal also worked as an illumination, theater, and restoration consultant, assisting on such projects as the Pan-American terminal at the John F. Kennedy Airport in New York, the Los Angeles Music Center, the American Shakespeare Festival Theater in Connecticut, as well as theaters in Canada and Australia.

A small, dark-haired woman with large blue eyes, Rosenthal confronted the sexism of her male-dominated profession by being very courteous, commonly referring to her crew of electricians as "darling" and "honey." She spent her free time in the company of close friends, disliking the more formal social life of cocktail parties. A lifelong New Yorker, Rosenthal shared her apartment, as well as her home on Martha's Vineyard, with artist Marion Kinsella.

Throughout her career, Rosenthal favored dance performances, particularly the abstract works of Martha Graham. In contrast to Broadway musicals and plays, which required a relatively standardized lighting design, Graham's dances allowed for imaginative and experimental illumination. Rosenthal used dramatic side lighting, giving dancers a sculptural quality. She made Graham's performances a professional priority: "To do one or two new works for Martha a year was a part of my life and a renewal of my own interior spirit." In the last weeks of her life, suffering from cancer and confined to a wheelchair, Rosenthal designed the lighting for her final Graham piece. Until her death in New York City, on May 1, 1969, Rosenthal lived a "lifetime in light."

BIBLIOGRAPHY

Billy Rose Theatre Collection. New York Public Library; Lael Wertenbaker Collection. Mugar Library, Boston University; *NAW* modern; Obituary. *NYTimes*, May 2, 1969, 43:1; Ridgon, Walter, ed. *Biographical Encyclopaedia and Who's Who of American Theatre* (1966); Rosenthal, Jean. Papers. Wisconsin Center for Film and Theater Research, University of Wisconsin, Madison; Rosenthal, Jean, and Lael Wertenbaker. *The Magic of Light: The Career and Craft of Jean Rosenthal, Pioneer in Lighting for the Modern Stage* (1972); Sargeant, Winthrop. "Please, Darling, Bring Three to Seven." *The New Yorker* (February 4, 1956): 33–59; *WWWIA* 5.

CAROL FIPPIN

ROSS, BETTY (1900–1964)

Journalist Betty Ross, best known for her interviews with celebrities, was born on July 15, 1900. Her parents, Polish immigrants Joseph and Ida (Cantor) Rosenblum, settled in Hartford, Connecticut, shortly before their daughter's birth. During the next four decades, Joseph Rosenblum established himself as a real estate broker and, with his wife, raised five sons and two daughters.

After attending public schools in Hartford, Betty worked for the *Hartford Post* and became interested in a writing career. She studied journalism and literature at Columbia University from 1920 to 1923, and, beginning in 1923, published feature articles in the *New York World* under the name Betty Ross. In subsequent years, her byline appeared in major city newspapers, including *The New York Times* and Philadelphia's *Public Ledger,* and in such widely read magazines as *Outlook, Popular Science,* and *Success.*

Extensive travel in Asia, Europe, the Middle East, and Russia during the mid-1920s provided Ross with much of the material she used in her syndicated columns and articles. During these years, she interviewed such noted literary, political, and religious personalities as Helen Fraser (a Liberal candidate for the British Parliament in 1923), author John Galsworthy, and Grand Rabbi Haim Nahoun of Egypt. In addition to profiling these men and women in print, Ross was among the first journalists to conduct radio interviews, in a program called "Peeps at Celebrities."

Ross published two accounts of her career as a journalist: *Heads and Tales* (1934), about her interviews with noted individuals, and *Reporter in Petticoats* (1947). She also explored aspects of her Jewish heritage in print. The United Jewish Campaign published her pamphlet "A Visit to the David Brown Colony in Crimea" in the late 1920s, and a fictionalized account of life in a Jewish settlement in Russia appeared under the title *Bread and Love* in 1930.

By 1939, Ross had settled in London, where she would spend the remainder of her life. There, she continued to write and also became involved with the British Broadcasting Corporation, working in both radio and television. Her work on Mexican documentary films resulted in several publications, including *With Cortez in Mexico,* which was serialized by UNESCO. The Mexican government awarded Ross the Aztec Eagle, in recognition of her documentation of the country's heritage.

Ross died in London, her home of twenty-five years, on December 31, 1964, survived by her husband, Maurice Arram, a London attorney.

SELECTED WORKS BY BETTY ROSS

Heads and Tales (1934); *Reporter in Petticoats* (1947); *True Adventures Great Explorers Told Me* (1959); "A Visit to the David Brown Colony in Crimea" (1929).

BIBLIOGRAPHY

McGinley, Art. "Good Afternoon." *Hartford Times,* June 26, 1962; Silverman, Morris. *Hartford Jews, 1659–1970* (1970); *Who Was Who in Journalism 1925–1928* (1978); *WWIAJ* (1928).

JOANNE PASSET

ROTH, LILLIAN (1910–1980)

Lillian Roth, singer-actress whose career met with early success but was eventually sidetracked by alcoholism and mental illness, was born in Boston on December 13, 1910. At age five, she was pushed into show business by her stagestruck parents, Arthur and Katie (Silverman) Rutstein, and a year later, she was cast in a Broadway play. As a child, she attended the Professional Children's School with classmates Ruby Keeler and Milton Berle; the latter would remain a lifelong friend. Throughout her childhood Roth's father's alcoholism resulted in his periodic lengthy separations from the family. As a result, her ambitious mother molded her and her younger sister Ann (born in 1913) into vaudeville headliners known as "The Roth Kids" on the Keith-Orpheum circuit.

When Roth was fourteen, she was signed by the Shuberts for *Artists and Models*. She was soon transfered to the Chicago company of the show because New York legal authorities considered her too young to be in a "risqué" show. By age seventeen, she was appearing in *Earl Carroll's Vanities of 1928* and *Ziegfeld's Midnight Follies*. *Variety* and New York City newspapers praised Roth's singing voice and stage personality. Her next step was to go to Hollywood, where she signed a seven-year contract with Paramount Pictures in 1929. Her movie career coincided with the beginning of the talkies. Her first film was *The Love Parade* (1929), starring Maurice Chevalier and Jeanette MacDonald. In 1930, she made *The Vagabond King, Honey, Animal Crackers* with the Marx Brothers, and *Madame Satan*. These films were followed by *Ladies They Talk About* and *Take a Chance* in 1933.

The early 1930s were a series of professional triumphs and personal disasters for Roth. She acknowledged that she earned over one million dollars, and lost it all. During this period, she drank heavily and married and divorced four husbands, including New York judge Ben Shalleck. By the early 1940s, people regarded her career as over. In 1945, she committed herself to a New York mental institution, but the treatment did not provide a permanent cure for her illness. In 1947 she joined Alcoholics Anonymous, where she met her fifth husband, Burt McGuire, who was a Catholic. Roth's personal and spiritual feelings led her to convert to Catholicism in 1948. Friends accused her of forsaking Judaism; however, in her autobiography, *I'll Cry Tomorrow* (1954), Roth observed that although her parents had believed in God, she and her sister had not been brought up religiously. Roth declared that she was so inherently Jewish that she could not really forget her heritage and thought that she was "the richer" because of it.

On February 4, 1953, Roth told her tragic story to millions of Americans on the popular television program *This Is Your Life*. The favorable response she received encouraged her to write her autobiography, which described her struggle against alcoholism and mental illness; it became an international best-seller. The book was made into a film in 1955, starring Susan Hayward. As a result of the publicity, Roth was able to make a modest comeback in nightclubs, on television, and on the stage. In the 1960s, she appeared in the theatrical production *I Can Get It for You Wholesale* and in the touring company of *Funny Girl*. Her last movie was *Communion* in 1977.

Lillian Roth died in New York City on May 5, 1980, at age sixty-nine.

FILMOGRAPHY

Animal Crackers (1930); *Communion* (1977); *Honey* (1930); *Ladies They Talk About* (1933); *The Love Parade* (1929); *Madame Satan* (1930); *Take a Chance* (1933); *The Vagabond King* (1930).

BIBLIOGRAPHY

Contemporary Authors (1981); "Lillian Roth, Actress and Singer Dies." *NYTimes*, May 5, 1980, C20; Obituaries. *Newsweek* (May 26, 1980): 93, and *Time* (May 26, 1980): 89, and *Variety Weekly* (May 14, 1980): 14; Roth, Lillian. *I'll Cry Tomorrow* (1954); Smith, Cecil. "She Won't Cry Tomorrow." *Los Angeles Times*, January 8, 1956, sec. 4, p. 1:4

BONNIE STARK

RUBIN, GAIL (1938–1978)

In 1979, Rabbi Michael Graetz wrote that the photographer Gail Rubin "had a sense of being present at the day of creation.... Development of life was her deepest inspiration. Her animals are less often seen alone than in families or groups—she discerned within nature a love pervading all the universe, a love which for her was expressed even in rock formations and trees." The work of Gail Rubin reflects a love and respect for all aspects of the Israeli landscape as much as it reflects a passion for life.

Gail Rubin's photographic career ended tragically at age thirty-nine when, on March 11, 1978, she was murdered by Arab terrorists on a beach near Ma'agan Michael, near Tel Aviv. At the time, Rubin was photographing rare birds. When the terrorists landed on the beach in rubber boats, they discovered Rubin. After asking her a number of questions, they shot her.

Rubin was born in New York City, on April 12, 1938, the only child of Jonathan and Estelle Rubin. Jonathan Rubin was a vice president and treasurer of

Krasdale Foods. Estelle Rubin was a psychotherapist. In New York, Rubin attended the Dalton School, graduating in 1956, and began her undergraduate career at the University of Michigan. Rubin completed her undergraduate studies at Finch College in New York in 1960. Upon completing her degree, Rubin began working in an editorial position at Viking Press and New Directions, until she became managing editor at Delacorte Books.

In June of 1969, Rubin traveled to Israel for a short vacation. Fascinated by the land and the people, she decided to remain in Israel. In Israel, Rubin began working as a press photographer. At this time, Rubin primarily used black-and-white photos. She was one of the first civilians to travel to Egypt with Israeli soldiers during the Yom Kippur War in 1973. In 1973, Rubin began to concentrate her work on the natural landscape, using color photos. According to her parents, Rubin had intended eventually to return to the United States.

In her photos of Israeli nature, Rubin focused her attention on diverse objects, including birds, water buffalo, butterflies, mountains, and bodies of water. Rubin complemented her photographs with a knowledge of local history and detailed observations. For example, accompanying her stunning photo of the Hula Lake in the Hula Nature Reserve in the Galil in northern Israel, Rubin discusses the history of the tension between the *halutzim*, the pioneer settlers in Israel, and those individuals whose concern for natural conservation led to the creation of the reserve. Rubin comments on the effect of the settlers on the land: "The balance of life was upset. The natural order destroyed. The interrelationship of amphibian, mammal, and birdlife and swamp vegetation vanished. . . . The vast swamplands, once the scene of constantly changing birdlife—ducks, herons, pelicans—fell silent." Rubin's work reflects her love of the land of Israel and her desire to capture its uniqueness and beauty.

SELECTED WORKS BY GAIL RUBIN

Psalmist with a Camera (1979).

Rubin's photographs appeared in the December 1977 publication of *Natural History* in the article "Eucalyptus Bark" by Edward S. Ayensu and in the January 1978 publication of *Natural History* in the article "Ibex in Israel" by Len Aronson. Rubin's work can also be found in *U.S. Camera*, Time-Life's *Nature Science Annual 1976*, Time-Life's *Birds of Sea, Shore and Stream, Life in Zoos and Preserves*, and Time-Life's *Photography Annual 1979*. Rubin's photographs were exhibited at the Jewish Museum in New York in February of 1977, the Magnes Museum in Berkeley, California, and the Israel Museum in Jerusalem.

BIBLIOGRAPHY

AJYB 80:371; "Israelis at Funeral for Gail Rubin." *NYTimes*, March 18, 1978, 26:4; "Memorial Meeting Is Held for U.S. Victim of P.L.O. Attack on Israel." *NYTimes*, March 17, 1978, 9:2; *Natural History* 87 (June 1978): 4; "U.S. Born Photographer Was First Victim in the Raid." *NYTimes*, March 13, 1978, 11:1.

JESSICA ZELLNER

RUBIN, RUTH (b. 1906)

Ruth Rubin has devoted a lifetime to the collection and preservation of Yiddish folklore in poetics and songs. Her writings include books, articles, and music collections. As a popular performer-folklorist, she would describe the background of her selections and then sing them in a simple, unaccompanied style.

Born Rifkele Royzenblatt in Montreal in 1906, to immigrants from Bessarabia, she grew up in a Canadian multilingual household of books and music. In the early 1920s, she went to New York City, where she worked as a secretary and wrote Yiddish poetry, a collection of which was published by the end of that decade. In 1932, she married Harry Rubin and in 1937, her son Michael was born. Meanwhile, she embarked upon Yiddish folklore studies and taught literature and music at several Yiddish schools. During World War II, Rubin translated and had published Yiddish diaries that had been smuggled out of the ghettos and concentration camps of Europe.

The Holocaust defined Rubin's mission to collect, document, and perform the Jewish legacy of Eastern European folk song. She became an active member of the American Folklore Society, the Canadian Folk Music Society, and the International Folk Music Society, and served on the editorial board of the *New York Folklore Quarterly*. She participated in programs with other folk song performers at many concerts, including Carnegie Hall performances. In 1945, she began to make recordings for Folkways Records, and then she became a busy lecturer-performer for religious organizations and educational institutions. In 1959, her son died tragically, and Ruth Rubin's world stood still for a while.

In the 1970s, following the death of her husband, Ruth Rubin reemerged and resumed her mission on behalf of Yiddish folk songs. For use in her entertaining lectures and in her many published articles in Yiddish and English periodicals, she shaped sensitive translations into English so as to make those materials more accessible to a wider public. Her book *Voices of a People: The Story of Yiddish Folksong* explored the

Ruth Rubin devoted her life to collecting, documenting, and performing the Jewish legacy of Eastern European folk songs. During the Holocaust, she translated and published Yiddish diaries that had been smuggled out of the concentration camps and ghettos of Europe. This experience only helped define her commitment to preserving the beauty of Yiddish music. [YIVO Institute]

historical background and ethnic meaning of the song texts, treating them as important literary materials. Her song collections *A Treasury of Jewish Folksong, in Yiddish and Hebrew* and *Jewish Folk Songs, in Yiddish and English* also included valuable discussions of the origins of the lyrics and melodies. A 1983 grant from the National Endowment for the Humanities, and another from the Memorial Foundation for Jewish Culture, enabled her to complete the organization of her extensive field collections. Her materials have been placed in various libraries: the AMLI (Americans for Libraries in Israel) in Tel Aviv, Israel, the Library of Congress in Washington, D.C., and the YIVO Institute for Jewish Research in New York City.

BIBLIOGRAPHY

Rubin, Ruth. Papers. AMLI, Tel Aviv, Israel, and Library of Congress, Washington, D.C., and YIVO Institute for Jewish Research, NYC; *WWIAJ* (1938).

IRENE HESKES

RUBIN, VERA COOPER (b. 1928)

Vera Cooper Rubin has forever changed our fundamental view of the cosmos, from a universe dominated by starlight to one dominated by dark matter. Rubin was born on July 23, 1928, in Philadelphia, Pennsylvania, the younger of two daughters of electrical engineer Philip Cooper and his wife Rose (Applebaum). Philip Cooper encouraged his daughter's interest in astronomy, taking her to amateur astronomy meetings after the family moved to Washington, D.C., and assisting in her first homemade telescope when she was fourteen.

Vera discovered early that women science students were not accepted at some universities. Her early experiences shaped her later work for women's equality in the sciences, especially astronomy. Rubin received her B.A. from Vassar in 1948 and her M.A. from Cornell University in 1951, where she met and married Robert Rubin, a graduate student in physical chemistry. Her controversial master's thesis examined the possibility of a bulk rotation in the universe by looking for "non-Hubble flow." At that time, the redshifts (lengthening of light waves due to the motion of an object, such as a star or a galaxy) for only 109 galaxies had been obtained, yet her analysis seemed to show an extra, "sideways" motion of galaxies independent of the normal Hubble recession caused by the expansion of the universe. The paper got a cold reception and was rejected by both *Astronomical Journal* and *Astrophysical Journal*. Although Rubin later agreed that perhaps her data were too skimpy, her thesis was a factor in Gerald de Vaucouleur's claim for evidence of the "Local Supercluster."

Rubin's doctoral work was conducted at Georgetown University under the auspices of George Gamow. Her thesis (1954) was one of the earliest works on the clustering of galaxies. She concluded that galaxies were not randomly distributed over the sky, but instead there was a definite clumping. Her results were not followed up by the scientific community, as the subject of large-scale structure was not studied seriously until the late 1970s.

From 1955 to 1965, Rubin rose from research associate to assistant professor at Georgetown, and from 1963 to 1964 she engaged in work on the rotation of galaxies with the famed husband-wife team of Geoffrey and Margaret Burbidge. In 1965, Rubin joined the staff of the Department of Terrestrial Magnetism of the Carnegie Institution of Washington, where she remains today. It was during this year that Rubin became the first woman to "legally" observe at Mount Palomar Observatory under her own name as a guest investigator.

In the early 1970s, Rubin renewed her interest in non-Hubble flow, and, with W. Kent Ford, she found evidence again for extra motion. The "Rubin-Ford effect" has been called spurious by some and well-established by others. Rubin is perhaps best-known for her work with Ford and others on the rotation curves of spiral galaxies, using newer technology to update the groundbreaking work of the Burbidges. Rubin found that spiral galaxies have "flat rotation curves." Unlike our solar system, in which the majority of the matter is contained in the sun, and thus the planets follow Keplerian motion with Mercury having a much faster orbital velocity than Pluto, the luminous matter in spiral galaxies has a high orbital velocity out to the visible edge. This is usually explained as due to the fact that the bulk of the galaxy's mass is not clustered at the center, where the visible bulge of the galaxy is, but there exists a halo of dark matter extending at least to the visible edge, if not farther. Thus, Rubin and her collaborators provided some of the first direct evidence for the existence of dark matter, verifying the earlier theoretical work of Jeremy Ostriker and James Peebles. Since 1978, Rubin has analyzed the spectra of over two hundred galaxies and found that nearly all contain copious amounts of dark matter.

Rubin holds four honorary doctorates, a 1993 Presidential National Medal of Science, the 1994 Dickson Prize in Science from Carnegie-Mellon University, and the 1994 Russell Lectureship Prize of the American Astronomical Society. In 1981, she became the second woman astronomer to be elected to the National Academy of Sciences. She served as associate editor of *Astronomical Journal* from 1972 to 1977 and of *Astrophysical Journal Letters* from 1977 to 1982. The Rubins have four children: David M., Judith S., Karl C., and Allan M.—all of whom have Ph.D.s in the sciences, including daughter Judith S. Young, a noted astronomer in her own right.

Remembering what it was like to be a lone woman staring at galaxies, Vera Rubin considers it a responsibilty and a privilege to be a mentor. "It is well known," she says, "that I am available twenty-four hours a day to women astronomers."

SELECTED WORKS BY VERA RUBIN

"Extended Rotation Curves of High-Luminosity Spiral Galaxies. Vol. 4, Systematic Dynamical Properties, Sa to Sc," with W. Kent Ford, Jr., and N. Thonnard. *Astrophysical Journal Letters* 225 (1978): L101–111; "Fluctuations in the Space Distribution of the Galaxies." *Proceedings of the National Academy of Sciences* 40 (1954): 541–549; "Rotational Properties of 21 Sc Galaxies with a Large Range of Luminosities and Radii, from NGC 4605 (R = 4 kpc) to NGC 2885 (R = 122 kpc)," with W. Kent Ford, Jr., and N. Thonnard. *Astrophysical Journal* 238 (1980): 471–487; "Weighing the Universe: Dark Matter and Missing Mass." In *Bubbles, Voids and Bumps in Time: The New Cosmology*, edited by James R. Cornell (1989); "Women's Work." *Science* 86 (July/August 1986): 58–65.

BIBLIOGRAPHY

Bartusiak, Marcia. *Through a Universe Darkly* (1993), and "The Woman Who Spins the Stars." *Discover* (October 1990): 88–94; Lightman, Alan, and Roberta Brawer. *Origins* (1990); Stille, Darlene R. *Extraordinary Women Scientists* (1995); *Who's Who in America 1996*. Vol. 2 (1996); Yount, Lisa. *Contemporary Women Scientists* (1994).

KRISTINE LARSEN

RUBINSTEIN, HELENA (1870–1965)

My Life for Beauty, Helena Rubinstein's autobiography, was published in 1966, a year after her death. In the introduction, her son Roy Titus called his mother's life and work "so inseparable that a book dealing with one aspect without the other would seem incomplete." Thus, the first half recounts "My Life," and the second half, "For Beauty," includes advice for achieving beautiful skin, hair, nails, and so on. The title is poignant and very appropriate. In addition to her son's assessment that Rubinstein's life and work were "inseparable," the title also lends credence to the theory that she gave her life for beauty. Late in life, she expressed numerous doubts about the wisdom of her absorption in her career in beauty, blaming this involvement for painful costs in her personal life.

Helena Rubinstein was born to Jewish parents in Crakow, Poland, on December 25, 1870. Her father, Horace, a not very successful wholesale food broker, was very strict. The beautiful Mama Rubinstein, Augusta (Silberfield) Rubinstein, had a tremendous impact on Helena and her seven sisters (Pauline, Rosa, Regina, Stella, Ceska, Manka, and Erna). Their mother insisted her daughters would gain power and influence through beauty and love. In fact, Helena Rubinstein's beauty industry began with jars of Modjeska cream, named after her mother's friend, actress

When she left her home in Poland to live with relatives in Australia, Helena Rubinstein
took with her twelve pots of face cream her mother had gotten from a Cracow chemist.
She offered them for sale, and the rest is history. [American Jewish Archives]

Helena Modjeska. The actress had introduced Mama to the chemist who created the cream, Dr. Jacob Lykusky, a Hungarian chemist living in Crakow. He made the cream from a formula of herbs, essence of almonds, and extract from the bark of the Carpathian fir tree.

As the oldest daughter, Helena was often put in charge of her siblings. As she recounted the story, since her father had no sons (two boys had died as babies), and since she was good with figures, she helped her father with bookkeeping. She attended her first business meeting at age fifteen, substituting for her ill father. Her mother advised her, "If you want to be really clever, listen well and talk little."

Her father decided that Helena should study medical science. While she enjoyed the laboratory work, the sights and odors of the hospital sickened her. When she became very thin and unhappy, her father agreed that she could end her medical studies, but insisted that she marry. He picked out a thirty-five-year-old wealthy widower for his eighteen-year-old daughter. She refused to marry him and brought home her own choice,

Stanislaw, a non-Jewish University of Crakow medical student. Papa refused. Helena wrote to her Uncle Louis, her mother's brother, asking if she could stay with him and his family in Australia. Helena Rubinstein left Poland for Australia with twelve pots of her mother's beauty cream.

The Australian women, who suffered from sun-damaged skin, were awed by Helena Rubinstein's beautiful skin. Soon Rubinstein had given away almost all of her cream. Her mother kept providing more until Helena decided to open a shop to sell the cream. She got financial backing from Helen MacDonald, a woman whose complexion improved using Helena's cream. MacDonald loaned her £250, about $1,500, which Rubinstein used to buy a large quantity of the cream and to rent and furnish a shop in Melbourne. After doing the painting and making the curtains and the sign herself, she opened Helena Rubinstein, Beauty Salon. She began experimenting with creams for different kinds of skin in her kitchen. Woman's page editor Eugenia Stone came from Sydney, some five hundred miles away, to interview Rubinstein. The country-wide publicity resulted in a deluge of orders. She made enough money to bring over Dr. Lykusky to develop related products.

In her autobiography, she says she turned the £250 debt into a £12,000 credit by working eighteen-hour days for two years. Other sources indicate that it took her about eight years, from 1890 to 1898. In Australia, she started the practice of putting one of her sisters or another relative in charge of various parts of her business. She sent first for Ceska, the third youngest sister. She also began her hands-on training by spending a year in Europe, studying with experts to learn about skin treatments, facial surgery, and good dietary practices. For example, she studied dermatology in Paris with Dr. Berthelot.

She put her personal life on hold while she developed her career in business. Meeting and falling in love with American newspaperman Edward William Titus rattled her, as she had never imagined falling in love. When he asked her to marry him, she acknowledged her love, but said she first wanted to establish a salon in London, England. She opened a salon on Grafton Street in Lord Salisbury's previous home. She continued training in beauty and skin care in Europe and recruited Dr. Emmie List from Vienna to join her London staff. Edward came to London and proposed again. This time she accepted. She was thirty-eight when they married in a private civil ceremony in 1908. Titus continued to write and also advised her in the business, even creating clever advertising for her salon.

Her first pregnancy forced her to focus on her personal life rather than her business. She created what she called a "real home . . . with garden." With the birth of Roy in 1909 and Horace in 1912, she focused her attention on the children. When Horace was about two, Rubinstein convinced Titus to move to Paris, where she purchased a salon from Madame Chambaron. This salon specialized in herbal preparations. Rubinstein found Paris women more receptive to her innovations in makeup.

In 1915, a year into World War I, Titus finally convinced her to move to the safety of the United States—to New York City. They moved first to West End Avenue on Manhattan's Upper West Side, and then one block west to Riverside Drive. Thus began her career in America, where her advertisements promised scientific benefits. She opened her New York salon, the Maison de Beauté Valaze, at 8 East 49th Street. Starting in 1916, she expanded her operations, opening salons in San Francisco and Philadelphia. The next year she opened salons in Boston, Los Angeles, Washington, D.C., Chicago, and Toronto. In the twenties, Helena Rubinstein went to Hollywood and taught movie stars THEDA BARA and Pola Negri how to use mascara, which emphasized their eyes and created their images as "vamps." Rubinstein continued her makeup line and also began to train salespeople to sell her products at selected stores. In 1928, she moved her New York salon to the east side at 57th Street.

She wrote of her intensive involvement in her business. Her children went to boarding school. Her husband complained, but she didn't listen at first. Finally, he told her he was in love with a younger woman. She sold her business to Lehman Brothers in order to win Edward back by showing him how important their marriage was, but it was too late. Meanwhile, the new owners had no luck with the business. Earlier, Rubinstein had developed friendships with store owners during her frequent instructional tours, and these store owners kept in touch with her to report their dismay with Lehman Brothers. Secretly, Helena Rubinstein began to buy stock on the open market. She also wrote to other stockholders, urging them to complain about how the new owners were running the business. Finally, the stock market crash enabled her to buy back her business at a fraction of what Lehman Brothers had paid for it.

Her personal life did not go as well. Both of her ailing parents died before she had the chance to see them again. She suffered terribly. A physician friend insisted that she recover from her grief by traveling to Switzerland, where she could recoup and study diet treatment with Dr. Bircher-Benner. She came back to the United States ten pounds lighter and full of energy, with the idea of bringing this treatment to her salons. "A Day of Beauty" at the Helena Rubinstein salons became popular all over the world.

In 1935, at a party at the home of Comtesse de Polignac, daughter of Jeanne Lanvin, whose haute couture studio was located near her salon, Helena Rubinstein met a Georgian named Prince Artchil Gourielli-Tchkonia. They married three years later, in 1938. They lived in New York City during the winter and in Europe in spring and summer. They were lucky to get out of their Paris apartment in 1939, following the outbreak of World War II.

During the war, some critics suggested that her business products were unnecessary during such hard times, but Rubinstein argued to the contrary. She insisted that during times of trouble and depression, women needed the added lift of makeup. She said that President Franklin Roosevelt agreed, once telling her, "Your war effort . . . is to help keep up the morale of our women. And you are doing it splendidly."

In the late 1940s, Rubinstein opened the House of Gourielli for men, complete with ticker tape from Wall Street, but this venture of selling colognes and facials for men was ahead of its time, although she anticipated the lucrative market of men's products in the 1990s.

She was profoundly affected by the death of her second husband in 1956, but was able to rebound from this grief to continue her active business life. In addition to using her products, Helena Rubinstein urged women not to smoke, to drink lightly, if at all, and to pay particular attention to physical exercise, proper diet, and inner peace.

Helena Rubinstein died of natural causes on April 1, 1965, at age ninety-four. She was said to have a cosmetics business worth somewhere between $17.5 million and $60 million, with international holdings, including laboratories, factories, and salons in fourteen countries. Helena Rubinstein established the Helena Rubinstein Foundation to provide money for the arts and to charitable institutions. While she did not support Jewish causes in particular, she did donate $500,000 to create the Helena Rubinstein Pavilion at the Tel Aviv Museum. Her entire collection of miniature rooms is on display there.

BIBLIOGRAPHY

AJYB 67:541; Allen, Margaret. *Selling Dreams: Inside the Beauty Business* (1981); *BEOAJ*; *DAB* 7; *EJ*; Fabe, Maxene. *Beauty Millionaire: The Life of Helena Rubinstein* (1972); O'Higgins, Patrick. *Madame: An Intimate Biography of Helena Rubinstein* (1971); Obituary. *NYTimes*, April 2, 1965, 1:2; *NAW* modern; Rubinstein, Helena. *My Life for Beauty* (1966); Slater, Elinor, and Robert Slater. "Helena Rubinstein." In *Great Jewish Women* (1994); *WWIAJ* (1938); *WWWIA* 4.

SARA ALPERN

RUKEYSER, MURIEL (1913–1980)

> To be a Jew in the twentieth century
> Is to be offered a gift. If you refuse,
> Wishing to be invisible, you choose
> Death of the spirit . . .
> Accepting, take full life.

Muriel Rukeyser's poetry faces the challenge expressed in these lines from "Letter to the Front" by trying to embody, with striking verbal and thematic juxtapositions, the unity she believed underlies a world seemingly disconnected.

During her life, Rukeyser was often the center of controversy. Critics either loved or hated her; there was seemingly no middle ground. Rukeyser won the Yale Younger Poets Award in 1935, at age twenty-one, with the publication of her first book, *Theory of Flight*. She continued to earn praise throughout her career, winning the first Hariet Monroe Poetry Award, the Levinson Prize, the Copernicus Prize, and a Guggenheim Fellowship. But Rukeyser did not lack unenthusiastic readers. Critics such as Weldon Kees, the editors of *Partisan Review*, and Louise Bogan continually published negative reviews of her books. However, despite the red-baiting of the 1950s and the relentless jabs of critics such as Randall Jarrell—who wrote in 1953, "if my reader will get as woolly-headed and as oracularly emotional as he can . . . he will get the raw material of one of Miss Rukeyser's elegies"—Rukeyser never succcumbed to political pressures.

Muriel Rukeyser was born on December 15, 1913, into a middle-class Jewish family living in New York. Her father, Lawrence B. Rukeyser, was born in Wisconsin, where his grandfather had moved in 1848, but left for New York to work as a construction engineer. Lawrence cofounded Colonial Sand and Stone, a sand and gravel company, with Generoso Pope, an Italian-American fascist, and thus, in Rukeyser's words, was involved in "the building of New York." When Lawrence went bankrupt in 1932, Rukeyser's college education at Vassar and Columbia University came to an end. Her mother, Myra (Lyons) Rukeyser, was born in Yonkers and for some time worked as a bookkeeper.

"It was the silence at home" that first influenced Rukeyser to become a writer. This silence manifested itself not only in a lack of verbal communication among family members—"there were three things that were never talked about: sex and money and death"—but also in a spiritual and intellectual void. There were no books in Rukeyser's home (when her sister Frances was born in 1921, Rukeyser's books were thrown away to make room in the nursery), with the exception of Shakespeare and the Bible. Furthermore, there was not a trace of Jewish culture in the home with the exception of a silver Kiddush cup and a legend that Rukeyser's mother was a direct descendant of Rabbi Akiba. Lawrence Rukeyser had been brought up among the "Western stories," and Myra rebelled against the religious values of her "studious and improvident" father.

When her mother suddenly turned to religion, Muriel Rukeyser noticed that the Jews around her spent much energy trying to assimilate into the mainstream of American culture. They tried "to be invisible . . . quiet and polite." Like life in her home, the Jews of Rukeyser's parents' generation were silent, refusing to be involved in "suffering that demanded resistance." For Rukeyser, the life-style of the Jews was in contradiction with the message of the Bible, with its "clash and poetry and nakedness, its fiery vision of conflict resolved only in God."

In love with the clashing of ideas, with parallel events in life and history that enable "contradictions to be contained and synthesis to be achieved," Rukeyser took upon herself the role of poet-prophet. Important for her was not the finding of an answer, but the process of searching itself, for Rukeyser did not desire "a sense of Oneness with the One so much as a sense of the Many-ness with the Many." Rukeyser's is an oracular voice, a clarion for the oppressed and silenced, that demands from humanity acts and expressions of love.

Rukeyser dove into the world and changed it from within by remaking its myths, its shared stories of experience. "Breathe-in experience, breathe-out poetry," she wrote in "Poem out of Childhood." Indeed, Rukeyser's poetry is informed by her remarkably active life. By age forty, Rukeyser had been arrested while covering the second Scottsboro trial for a student newspaper (and caught typhoid fever in an Alabama police station), traveled to Gauley, West Virginia, for hearings on a silicon mining disaster (the subject of her long poem in her second book, *U.S. 1*),

witnessed the beginning of the Spanish Civil War in 1936, saw the opening of the Golden Gate Bridge, worked at the graphics division of the Office of War Information, trained as a film editor, and taken ground school instruction at Roosevelt School of Aviation. In the latter half of her life, Rukeyser taught at Sarah Lawrence College, traveled to Hanoi on an unofficial peace mission with Denise Levertov and Jane Hart, and was arrested and jailed in Washington, D.C., for protesting the Vietnam War. She was also elected president of PEN in 1975, and traveled to Korea to protest the incarceration of poet Kim Chi-Ha. Rukeyser's politics correspond with her poetics in that both stress the interconnectedness of people and events.

Rukeyser typically wrote long poetic sequences, in which she mixed the lyric with the prosaic, making use of every form of language, including minutes of shareholders' meetings, equations for falling water, stock quotations, journalistic interviews, and courtroom depositions. By combining these voices, Rukeyser sought to create a new, previously unheard voice. It is no accident, then, that although she often used the space on the page in innovative ways—playing with punctuation and adding extra spaces between words—she never used it for silence or stillness. It also becomes clear why Rukeyser wrote about historical figures such as the physicist Willard Gibbs, the painter Albert Ryder, the composer Charles Ives, the labor organizer Ann Burlak, Rabbi Akiba, and Herman Melville. All of these important figures share common unifying visions of the world.

As a woman, Rukeyser was a courageous precursor to the feminist movement of the 1960s. She was independent enough to marry and divorce painter Glynn Collins (the marriage lasted only six weeks) and to give birth to William, first named Laurie, out of wedlock. She was brave and daring enough to write about such issues as pregnancy and the possibilities of loving another woman. She wrote, in "Ann Burlak," on behalf of the "ten greatest American women":

> The anonymous farmer's wife, the anonymous
>   clubbed picket,
> the anonymous Negro woman who held off
>   the guns,
> the anonymous prisoner, anonymous cotton-picker
> trailing her robe of sack in a proud train,
> anonymous writer of these and mill-hand,
>   anonymous city walker,
> anonymous organizer, anonymous binder of the
>   illegally wounded,
> anonymous feeder and speaker to anonymous
>   squares.

As a Jew, she wrote about Akiba and what it means to "love / your belief with all your life" ("The Gates"). And as the person Anne Sexton called "beautiful Muriel, mother of everyone," she wrote about the need to affirm and embrace life simply by saying yes: "Say yes, people. / Say yes. / YES." ("Theory of Flight").

SELECTED WORKS BY MURIEL RUKEYSER

Beast in View (1944); *Body of Waking* (1958); *Breaking Open* (1973); *Bubbles* (1967); *The Collected Poems of Muriel Rukeyser* (1979); *The Colors of the Day: A Celebration of the Vassar Centenial* (1961). Play; *Come Back, Paul* (1955); *Elegies* (1949); *The Gates* (1976); *The Green Wave* (1948); *I Go Out* (1961); *The Life of Poetry* (1949, 1974); *Mazes* (1970); *One Life* (1970); *The Orgy* (1965, 1966); *Selected Poems* (1951); *The Speed of Darkness* (1968); *Theory of Flight* (1935); *The Traces of Thomas Hariot* (1971, 1972); *A Turning Wind* (1939); *29 Poems* (1972); *U.S. 1.* (1938); *Wake Island* (1942); *Waterlily Fire: Poems, 1935–62* (1962); *Willard Gibbs* (1942).

BIBLIOGRAPHY

Barber, David S. "Finding Her Voice: Muriel Rukeyser's Poetic Development." *Modern Poetry Studies* 11, no. 1 (1982): 127–138, and "'The Poet of Unity': Muriel Rukeyser's *Willard Gibbs*." *CLIO: A Journal of Literature, History and the Philosophy of History* 12 (Fall 1982): 1–15; "Craft Interview with Muriel Rukeyser." *New York Quarterly* 11 (Summer 1972) and in *The Craft of Poetry*, edited by William Packard (1974); Daniels, Kate, ed. *Out of Silence: Selected Poems of Muriel Rukeyser* (1992), and "Searching/Not Searching: Writing the Biography of Muriel Rukeyser." *Poetry East* 16/17 (Spring/Summer 1985): 70–93; Gardinier, Suzanne. "'A World That Will Hold All The People': On Muriel Rukeyser." *Kenyon Review* 14 (Summer 1992): 88–105; Jarrell, Randall. *Poetry and the Age* (1953); Kertesz, Louise. *The Poetic Vision of Muriel Rukeyser* (1980); Levi, Jan Heller, ed. *A Muriel Rukeyser Reader* (1994); Pacernick, Gary. "Muriel Rukeyser: Prophet of Social and Political Justice." *Memory and Fire: Ten American Jewish Poets* (1989); Rich, Adrienne. "Beginners." *Kenyon Review* 15 (Summer 1993): 12–19; Rosenthal, M.L. "Muriel Rukeyser: The Longer Poems." In *New Directions in Prose and Poetry*, edited by James Laughlin. Vol. 14 (1953): 202–229; "A Special Issue on Muriel Rukeyser." *Poetry East* 16/17 (Spring/Summer 1985); Turner, Alberta. "Muriel Rukeyser." In *Dictionary of Literary Biography* 48, s.v. "American Poets, 1880–1945" (1986): 370–375; *UJE*; "Under Forty." *Contemporary Jewish Record* 7 (February 1944): 4–9; Ware, Michele S. "Opening 'The Gates': Muriel Rukeyser and the Poetry of Witness." *Women's Studies: An Introductory Journal* 22, no. 3 (1993): 297–308; *WWWIA*, 7.

MICHAEL J. SCHWARTZ

RUSKAY, ESTHER JANE (1857–1910)

Esther Jane Ruskay was a distinguished and outstanding writer and speaker in the Jewish community before the turn of the century. Her articles on Jewish life appeared in numerous newspapers, and a collection of her writings, *Hearth and Home Essays*, was published in 1902 by the Jewish Publication Society.

Born in New York City in 1857 to Goldie (Webster) and Abraham Baum, Esther, a second-generation American, was the eldest of ten children. As an adult, she was actively involved in establishing many Jewish communal institutions including the New York section of the NATIONAL COUNCIL OF JEWISH WOMEN, the Educational Alliance of the Lower East Side, and the YOUNG WOMEN'S HEBREW ASSOCIATION. Ruskay has many firsts to her credit, including being a member of the first graduating class of Normal College (now HUNTER COLLEGE) in 1875, and being the first woman to speak from the pulpit of New York's flagship Reform synagogue, Temple Emanu-El. She was a vocal supporter of conservative Jewish values at a time when Judaism and Jewish ritual practice were being criticized as out-of-step with the modern world. Ruskay's views are most forcefully expressed in a talk she delivered to the founding meeting of the New York section of the National Council of Jewish Women on May 9, 1893. She opened her talk by chiding the topic assigned her, "The Revival of Judaism":

> Before starting to write my paper, I looked up the definition of "revival" and found it to mean "a return to life—an awakening." Clearly then, Judaism was either dead or sleeping and needed to be awakened and to me was deputed the task. I did not look up the word "Judaism," I thought I knew what that meant and if I did not there was no danger of my remaining unenlightened.

Ruskay continued by criticizing those who look elsewhere for ethics and comfort:

> We have in Judaism and the Jewish life all of divine comfort and consolation—yet we pass it by and seek in Ethical Culture and its kindred cults an answer to our prayers. Ethical Culture is neither more nor less than the expression of the wide humanitarianism of the Mosaic creed, as the ethics of all religions are the outcome of their faiths. Ethics is the tail of the kite. Religion is the kite itself.

In defense of Hebrew as the language of prayer, she went on:

> You say, Hebrew is a mere jumble of words without meaning. It should not be. It ought not be. Why not teach it, beginning the study in the Jewish home under Jewish teachers as in the olden days? It can be taught to our children and it should be given them in the same spirit of educational fervor that we give the Latin and Greek for their classical training. . . . Now then, must we wait until other nations have taken it up and made the language theirs? Will there be value in Hebrew only after we recognize the value to the outside world? I trust not since the study of Hebrew would do more to foster in us soulful sentiment for the Bible and respect for the noble traditions of our race than all the so-called culture of all the universities combined.

Esther Ruskay was married to Samuel J. Ruskay. They had three sons, Burrill, Ceil, and Everett. Esther Jane Ruskay died in 1910 at age fifty-three of a brain tumor.

SELECTED WORKS BY ESTHER JANE RUSKAY

Hearth and Home Essays (1902); "The Revival of Judaism." Speech delivered at founding meeting, New York section, National Council of Jewish Women, May 9, 1893.

BIBLIOGRAPHY

AJYB 6 (1904–1905):178, 10 (1908–1909):127.

R. LORI FORMAN

S

SAARINEN, ALINE (1914–1972)

Interestingly, although Aline Saarinen served as the chief of the National Broadcasting Company's Paris news bureau, the first woman to hold a position of this type, she did not intend to pursue a career in television. She was first and foremost an art critic.

Aline (Bernstein) Saarinen was born to two amateur painters, Allen and Irma (Lewyn) Bernstein, in New York City, on March 25, 1914. It did not take long for her parents to take their daughter on her first of many European art tours. Her upbringing clearly encouraged her to major in art and English at Vassar College, where she served as an art critic for the college's newspaper. Graduating in 1935 Phi Beta Kappa, she soon enrolled at New York University's Institute of Fine Arts and received an M.A. in 1939.

During World War II, Saarinen took a few years off from the art world to play an active role on the home front. She served as executive secretary to the Allegheny County Rationing Board in Pittsburgh and as a nurse's aide in Washington. However, the art world pulled her back, and in 1944 Saarinen contributed to *Art News*, thus beginning her professional career as an art critic.

It did not take Saarinen long to prove that she had a great deal to offer the art world. Soon after contributing to *Art News*, she became its managing editor. Then in 1947, Saarinen became an associate art editor for the *New York Times*. She served in this position until 1954, and remained with the *Times* as an associate art critic until 1959. While with the *Times*, Saarinen wrote numerous articles and reviews. In addition, in 1958, she wrote *The Proud Possessors*, a best-selling book that dealt with American art collectors.

In 1962, the Metropolitan Museum of Art exhibited Rembrandt's *Aristotle Contemplating the Bust of Homer*. Since she had established herself as a respected critic in print, television reporters sought Saarinen's insight on this portrait. Her television career had begun. Saarinen's style was simple, informal, and pleasant. People liked her. Just as she rose quickly as an art critic in the world of written media, Saarinen soon gained prominence in the world of television, becoming a well-known on-air personality.

As a television art critic, Saarinen's commentaries were both entertaining and informative. She felt that the more that people knew about art, the better off both they and the art world would be. Therefore, she examined a wide variety of topics from Vatican art to postage stamp design. Saarinen often resorted to unorthodox means of criticism—at one point comparing a bronze sculpture of a runner to film clips of an actual sprinter. She did not hesitate to express her view on art and architecture she did not like, developing a list of the six worst human creations: the Pan Am building, Salvador Dali's *Last Supper*, the typical suburban house, glass sculpture at Lincoln Center, a lamp with a violin base, and the faces on Mount Rushmore.

Saarinen also had no problem cutting off individuals she interviewed if she found them to be either unexciting or too talkative.

Given Saarinen's bold nature, it is not surprising that the National Broadcasting Company appointed her as the chief of its Paris news bureau. Furthermore, her boldness made her the perfect candidate to host *For Women Only*, a panel talk show that addressed questions from the audience. The show dealt with a wide range of issues, from abortion to the generation gap. As host of this program, Saarinen was not interested in being didactic. She simply wanted to arouse concern in her audience.

Saarinen was married twice. Her first husband was public welfare administrator Joseph H. Loucheim, whom she married in 1935. She and Loucheim had two children, Donald (b. 1937) and Harry (b. 1939). The couple divorced in 1951. Three years later, she married the Finnish architect Eero Saarinen, with whom she had one child, Eames (b. 1954). Eero Saarinen died in 1961.

Saarinen had the opportunity to delve into the political arena. President Lyndon B. Johnson asked the art critic to serve as ambassador to Finland, a position that certainly appealed to Saarinen given that Finland was her second husband's homeland and a country that was concerned about its architecture. However, Saarinen turned down the president's offer.

Aline Saarinen left a tremendous mark on both the art world and the world of the media. As a Jewish-American woman, her success opened many doors to Jews, women, and other minority groups who hoped to follow in her footsteps.

Aline Saarinen died on July 13, 1972, in New York City.

BIBLIOGRAPHY

NAW modern; *NYTimes*, November 7, 1958, 25:3; Obituary. *NYTimes* July 15, 1972, 26:1; Saarinen, Aline. *The Proud Possessors* (1958); *WWWIA* 5.

ANDREW JACOBS

SACK, SALLYANN AMDUR (b. 1936)

"I had never quite experienced serendipity until the Jewish genealogy 'bug' bit me in 1977. Then I knew that this was what I had been seeking all my life. The pursuit of Jewish genealogy combines my love of being Jewish, my passion for history, my curiosity about people, and my addiction to mysteries. It offers the opportunity to research and write my own personal mystery—my specific family's history. The bug bit hard, and nothing in my life has been the same

Widely regarded as the "godmother" of Jewish genealogy, Sallyann Amdur Sack was first encouraged to explore her family's roots by her daughter Kathryn.

since," says Sallyann Amdur Sack, reflecting on twenty years' involvement with the topic.

The contemporary pursuit of Jewish genealogy as a popular, worldwide movement began in the 1970s. Sometimes called the "godmother" of Jewish genealogy, Sack has played a major role in its development as a pioneer, leader, and creative force.

Born on March 13, 1936, in Cleveland, Ohio, she is the older of two daughters of Max and Frances (Steinsnider) Amdur. Her parents, though born in the United States, were children of Eastern European immigrants who had come here during the first decade of this century, the Amdurs from Lithuania, the Steinsniders from Poland and Hungary with a detour through Canada. Max Amdur, an organizer of the Amalgamated Clothing Workers Union, taught his daughters the importance of taking responsibility for making important things happen, an influence Sack cites as seminal to her leadership in the field of genealogical research.

She was valedictorian of her class at Cleveland Heights High School and attended Radcliffe College, where she was elected to Phi Beta Kappa and graduated magna cum laude in 1957. She married Lawrence C. Sack in Cleveland, Ohio, in 1956. They raised three children. Their son, Robert Ira Sack, M.D., is a psychiatrist like his father. Daughter Elizabeth Felber is an attorney. The youngest daughter, Kathryn Solomon (who first stimulated Sack's interest in tracing the family roots), is a radiologist-in-training.

In 1972, Sack earned a Ph.D. in clinical psychology from the George Washington University and ever since has been in full-time private practice in Bethesda, Maryland.

In 1980, Sack founded the Jewish Genealogy Society of Greater Washington and served as its first president. In 1984, she organized the first international seminar on Jewish genealogy, held in Jerusalem. In 1985, she cofounded *Avotaynu: The International Review of Jewish Genealogy*, widely considered the "voice" of Jewish genealogy. She is president of Avotaynu, Inc., the parent company of the journal, which publishes books, monographs, and microfilm publications on Jewish genealogy.

Among other activities, Sack has conducted a week-long seminar in Moscow and has served on a number of advisory boards, including the Dorot Genealogy Center at Beth Hatefutsoth Museum in Tel Aviv. Sack was also active in the groundbreaking effort of the U.S. National Archives to open former Soviet archives to Jewish genealogical researchers.

SELECTED WORKS BY SALLYANN AMDUR SACK

Guide to Jewish Genealogical Research in Israel (1987. Rev. ed. 1995); *Index and Catalog to the Russian Consular Records*, with Suzan Wynne (1987); *Search for the Family*, with Mark Shulkin (1980); *Where Once We Walked: A Guide to the Jewish Communities Destroyed in the Holocaust*, with Gary Mokotoff (1991).

GARY MOKOTOFF

SALBER, EVA (1916–1990)

Eva Salber devoted her life to working on behalf of the world's poor and oppressed people. The ancient Jewish commandment "Be kind to the stranger" characterizes the ideals that Eva Salber pursued in her work as a physician, researcher, and writer.

Eva Salber was born in Cape Town, South Africa, on January 5, 1916, the second of three daughters of Lithuanian parents, Moses and Fannie (Srolowitz) Salber. From the University of Cape Town Medical School, she received an M.B.Ch.B. (the equivalent of an M.D.) in 1938, a diploma in public health in 1945, and a doctorate in medicine (M.D.) in 1955. She married physician Harry T. Phillips in 1939, and the couple had four children: David (b. 1943), a sociologist; Mark (b. 1946), a historian; Rosalie (b. 1950), a health care administrator; and Philip (b. 1954), an investment adviser. She taught at the Harvard School of Public Health (1957–1966) and at Duke University Medical School (1971–1982). Her honors included terms as a Radcliffe Scholar, Radcliffe Institute for Independent Study (1966–1967), as a Macy Fellow (1969–1970), and as Senior International Fellow of the Fogarty International Center, National Institutes of Health (1980).

As a physician, she promoted the health of poor communities by empowering patients and populations. Many of those she assisted became leaders and organizers in their own communities. Her work in a housing project in Boston and with poor rural populations in North Carolina grew out of lessons learned in South Africa, where she and her husband were pioneers in establishing community health centers after World War II. In the United States, as in South Africa, she believed fervently that health and well-being stem from one's total life circumstances, in which medical care plays an important but limited role. Because they opposed apartheid, Eva Salber and her family left South Africa in 1956.

In her scientific research, Eva Salber published close to a hundred articles in a wide variety of medical journals in Britain, South Africa, and the United States, primarily on epidemiological studies relating social factors and health, as well as related community health issues. Among her contributions were studies on infant growth in different races, socioeconomic patterns in breastfeeding, smoking behavior in schoolchildren, lactation and breast cancer, and social factors in the utilization of health services.

In a more literary genre, she used her intimate knowledge of several communities to produce two rich oral histories, *Caring and Curing: Community Participation in Health Services*, and *Don't Send Me Flowers When I'm Dead*. All her work, both scientific and literary, is reviewed in her autobiography, *The Mind Is Not the Heart: Recollections of a Woman Physician*.

Eva Salber died in Chapel Hill, North Carolina, on November 18, 1990. Throughout her life, she displayed the generosity and drive for improvement of social conditions characteristic of her Jewish home and community.

SELECTED WORKS BY EVA J. SALBER

Caring and Curing: Community Participation in Health Services (1975); *Don't Send Me Flowers When I'm Dead: Voices of Rural Elderly* (1983); *The Mind Is Not the Heart: Recollections of a Woman Physician* (1989).

BIBLIOGRAPHY

American Men and Women of Science (1966–1982, 1989); *Contemporary Authors* (1989); *Dictionary of International Biography* (1976); *The International Authors and Writers Who's Who* (1990); Salber, Eva J. Papers. William R. Perkins Library, Duke University, Durham, N.C.; *Who's Who in America* (1983–1989); *Who's Who in Health Care* (1977–1990); *The World Who's Who of Women* (1973–1990).

HARRY T. PHILLIPS

SALOMON, ALICE (1872–1948)

Alice Salomon, social worker and pedagogue, was born in Berlin, Germany, on April 19, 1872, the second of three children. Her father, a leather trader, and her mother raised Salomon in a practicing Jewish home, giving her an education appropriate to a daughter of the upper middle class.

Full emancipation in 1871 weakened Jewish group cohesion. Young Jews, among them Salomon, were now free to seek training beyond the expectations of their sex, class, and community. After a trip to England, where she was impressed by the social work of British women, Salomon studied pedagogy and accepted Protestant baptism. In 1893, after a visit to Jeanette Schwerin's educational service group for women, Salomon became engaged in group work. Indeed, Schwerin herself became Salomon's mentor.

In 1933, the Nazis labeled Salomon a "non-Aryan Christian." In response to the race laws, Salomon closed her world-famous Women's Academy in Berlin—where she introduced the American "case study" method into Europe—rather than remove Jewish faculty and students. She then began to work with Jewish social work organizations to help other baptized Jews. In 1936, Salomon made a second tour of America. Upon her return, the Nazi police interrogated her, giving her three weeks to leave Germany.

On June 12, 1937, Salomon arrived in the New York City, where she lived and worked for the last decade of her life. In 1944, she was named honorary president of the International Association of Schools of Social Work; she had served as chairperson in 1929. Although a lecture tour left her in ill health, Salomon carried on a lively correspondence with coworkers and students and continued to work for the training and professional recognition of women in social work

Though baptized a Protestant as a young woman, social worker Alice Salomon shut down her famous Women's Academy in Berlin rather than remove Jewish faculty and students as the Nazis demanded. [Library of Congress]

until her death in her New York apartment during a heat wave on August 30, 1948.

SELECTED WORKS BY ALICE SALOMON

Character Is Destiny (1983); *Die Ausbildung zum sozialen Beruf* (1927); *Leitfaden der Wohlfahrtspflege*, with S. Wronsky (1921); *Soziale Diagnose*, with S. Wronsky (1926); *Soziale Therapie*, with E. Glese (1926).

BIBLIOGRAPHY

Muthesius, Hans, ed. *Alice Salomon. Die Begründerin des sozialen Frauenberufs in Deutschland. Ihr Leben und Ihr Werk* (1958); Obituary. *NYTimes*, September 1, 1948, 23:1; *UJE*; Walk, Joseph. *Kurzbiographien zur Geschichte der Juden 1918–1945* (1988); Wieler, Joachim. *Erinnerung eines zerstörten Lebensabends. Alice Salomon während der NS-Zeit (1933–1937) und in Exil (1937–1948)* (1987).

ANN MANN MILLIN

SAMPTER, JESSIE ETHEL (1883–1938)

Jessie Ethel Sampter, poet, Zionist thinker and educator, social reformer, and pacifist, was a member of the inner circle of HENRIETTA SZOLD's female friends in Palestine during the 1920s and 1930s.

Like Szold, she was raised in a family of girls and never married. The Sampter family had two children, Jessie and Elvie.

Jessie Sampter was born in New York City, on March 22, 1883, to Rudolph and Virginia (Kohlberg) Sampter, prosperous second-generation German Jews, and raised in an elaborately decorated mansion on Fifth Avenue in Harlem, housing three generations of an extended family. She was a sensitive, frail child, partially crippled by polio at age thirteen. Because illness prevented her from attending school, her family engaged tutors. Later, she audited courses at Columbia University, but most of her education was acquired through extensive reading at home.

Poems written in her twenties reflected the humanitarian standpoint of her Ethical Culture background and of the Unitarian Church, which she joined. Ever the "Seeker" (the title of an early poetry collection and a youth group under her supervision), Sampter maintained a lifelong quest for respite from physical pain, emotional distress, and spiritual longing. Five people raised her Jewish consciousness and introduced her to Zionism. JOSEPHINE LAZARUS, sister and biographer of the poet EMMA LAZARUS, and the writer MARY ANTIN, kindled the spark; poet Hyman Segal uncovered residual national feelings; Professor Mordecai Kaplan presented the idealism of the biblical prophets and the evolutionary development of Judaism. In the home of Henrietta Szold, her most influential mentor, Sampter absorbed the power and the beauty of Jewish ritual. Through Szold, she learned to appreciate New York's Eastern European Jews. Soon she moved into a settlement house on the Lower East Side, and then to a YMHA. The two women embraced a religious and philosophical pacifism that proved unpopular after the United States entered World War I. Ultimately, they surrendered to pressure from Zionist leaders, who feared the taint of disloyalty, and resigned from a pacifist organization.

During the war years, Sampter became American Zionism's educator par excellence. She organized HADASSAH's School of Zionism, training young leaders for Zionist girls' clubs and adult speakers for Hadassah and the general Zionist organizations, first the Federation of American Zionists, then the Zionist Organization of America. She was director of the school and conducted its class on Zionism. In 1917, three hundred students enrolled in correspondence courses. To further disseminate the Zionist message, Sampter composed "propaganda" (educational) manuals with ALICE SELIGSBERG and edited a textbook on Zionism that went through three editions.

In 1919, Sampter found a permanent home in Palestine, with a commitment so strong that she relinquished her American citizenship. At first she lived in Jerusalem, hosting Sabbath services along progressive lines. The participants—including Szold, educator Alexander Dushkin, and Norman Bentwich, attorney general of the British mandate—were as exceptional as the services they conducted. They omitted prayers for the restoration of Temple sacrifice, and encouraged female participation in the reading and communal singing of uplifting songs of all kinds.

Preferring country to city life and a classless society to capitalism, Sampter built a cottage in the village of Rehovot, then joined Kibbutz Givat Brenner. With the proceeds from her house, she constructed Bet Yesha, a vegetarian convalescent home, on kibbutz land and lived in one of the rooms.

Atypically for Jews from Europe and America, Sampter displayed active concern for the Yemenite Jews then trickling into Palestine. She chafed at their inferior position in Jewish society and tried to remedy the unjust treatment of females in their polygamous community. Girls and women were usually denied an education and confined to menial occupations. From the start, Sampter undertook the education of Yemenite girls in classes and clubs. She adopted a foundling Yemenite child and educated her in a progressive fashion.

Sampter channeled her pacifist convictions into advocacy of peaceable relations between Jews and Arabs. Her poems and stories envisioned Ishmael and Isaac dwelling fraternally in the land of a common ancestor. Even after terrorist incidents, which she reported in all their brutality, she advocated a policy of nonreprisal, blaming the British for criminal negligence of administrative duties.

Never physically strong and always emotionally fragile, Sampter succumbed to malaria and heart disease on November 11, 1938, and was interred in Givat Brenner. A sorrowful Henrietta Szold presided over the funeral, then urged kibbutz youth to emulate Sampter's idealism.

Jesse Sampter was an active writer, a skillful Zionist propagandist, and a seminal Zionist educator. At the time of her untimely death, her poetry manifested a new muscularity as she abandoned conventional forms for common speech and free verse. Today, however, her poems, stories, and articles are more valuable as signs of their time than as literature. Sampter's principal legacy is personal rather than literary: her exemplary courage in overcoming illness and standing by her convictions, her attempts to advance the regeneration of Judaism on its native soil and to further economic and social justice, and her vision of a mixed population of Jews and Arabs, living side by side in peace and harmony.

SELECTED WORKS BY
JESSIE ETHEL SAMPTER

Around the Year in Rhymes for the Jewish Child (1920); *The Book of Nations* (1917); *Brand Plucked from the Fire* (1937); *The Coming of Peace* (1919); *A Course in Zionism* (1915. Revised as *A Guide to Zionism*, 1920, and *Modern Palestine: A Symposium*, 1933); *The Emek* (1927); *Far over the Sea: Poems and Jingles for Children by H.N. Bialik.* Translated by Jesse Sampter (1939). Issued in Hebrew as *Ud Muzal Ma'aish.* Translated by Pinchas Lander (1944); *In the Beginning* (unpublished autobiography); *Nationalism and Universal Brotherhood* (1914); *The Seekers* (1910); *The Speaking Heart* (unpublished autobiography).

BIBLIOGRAPHY

AJYB 24:198; Badt-Strauss, Bertha. *White Fire: The Life and Works of Jessie Sampter* (1956); *Bet Yesha: Thirty Years* (1965–1966); *EJ*; Lowenthal, Marvin. *Henrietta Szold: Life and Letters* (1942); *NAW* modern; Obituary. *NYTimes*, November 26, 1938; 16:3; *UJE*; *WWIAJ* (1926, 1928, 1938).

BAILA R. SHARGEL

SCHAEFER, BERTHA (1895–1971)

By profession, Bertha Schaefer was an interior decorator, but she broadened the definition of decorator to designer, innovator, and pioneer in integrating fine arts and architecture with interior design. In the 1940s, she challenged architects who were rethinking the traditional home to translate two-dimensional design into three dimensions and to work collaboratively with interior designers, craftspeople, and fine artists in developing a comprehensive plan for postwar, contemporary living.

Bertha Schaefer was born in Yazoo City, Mississippi, in 1895. She, her parents, Emil and Julia (Marx) Schaefer, and her sister lived in a house designed by her father that was "untraditional" in construction and, unfortunately, poorly suited to the southern climate. Schaefer obtained a B.A. from Mississippi State College for Women and a diploma in interior decorating from the Parsons School of Design. In New York City, she opened two businesses, Bertha Schaefer, Interiors (1924) and the Bertha Schaefer Gallery of Contemporary Art (1944). Her firm and gallery featured American and European painting and sculpture, and launched the careers of many artists and designers. She was both owner and principal of the firm and gallery until her death. She masterminded a series of exhibitions called "The Modern House Comes Alive" (1947–1948), which presented what she considered to be the American parallel to the European modern arts and crafts movement, especially Germany's Bauhaus school. The exhibitions focused on economical designs that possessed craftmanship as well as beauty and were suited to the postwar era in which the ready availability of labor and materials would facilitate mass production. In particular, Schaefer promoted functional and economical lighting fixtures. As early as 1939, she was using decorative interior fluorescent lighting.

Her firm's work included interior and furniture design for private homes, apartments, hotel lobbies, and restaurants. Other projects ranged from creating a model bathroom for General Electric (1954) to designing the interior of a new Temple Washington Hebrew Congregation (1954).

Schaefer's innovative interiors and furniture designs caught the attention of Joe Singer of M. Singer and Sons Furniture Company in New York City. Singer appreciated Schaefer's unique ability to marry the fine arts with the commercial arts, both in her furniture design and in her gallery. In a week-long trade show, twenty-one pieces of furniture from Italy and fifteen pieces by Bertha Schaefer debuted in an impressive showroom designed by Schaefer and Richard Kelly, an accomplished lighting designer. Schaefer continued to design furniture for Singer from 1950 to 1961.

Her professional accomplishments and academic contributions brought her invitations to participate in many round-table discussions and design juries sponsored by museums and universities. She won design awards from the Museum of Modern Art (1952) and the Decorators Club of New York (1959), the latter an organization for which she served two terms as president (1947–1948 and 1955–1957). She was also a member of the American Institute of Decorators, the Home Lighting Forum, the Illuminating Engineers Society, the Architectural League of New York, the American Federation of the Arts, and the Art Dealers Association of America.

Schaefer recognized the impact that modern imagination, technology, and industrial means of production would have on the creation of living and working environments. "These were the new areas for living, the reports of which had so quickened our imaginations, that were to expand our lives while simplifying our chores," she explained in an article in *Crafts Horizon* magazine. Her constant alertness to new ideas and her professional contributions made a significant impact on the history of postwar American living, architecture, and design.

Bertha Schaefer died on May 24, 1971.

BIBLIOGRAPHY

"Across the Seas of Collaboration for the New Singer Collection." *Interiors* 110 (December 1951): 120–129; "Bertha Schaefer, A.I.D., Respects an Assemblage of Abstract Art in a Softly Lighted Living Room." *Interiors* 119 (August 1959): 81; "Bertha Schaefer's Lobby for an Apartment House." *Interiors* 111 (April 1952): 104–105; "Bertha Schaefer Wins Award." *Interiors* 118 (June 1959): 20; "Case of Ambidexterity." *Interiors* 116 (December 1956): 118–121; "Focalite." *NYTimes*, February 4, 1945, sec. 6, p. 12:5; "Integrating the Arts: Newark." *Interiors* 114 (June 1955): 20; Madison, Mary. "Decorator Favors Buying Paintings First and Building Color Scheme Around Them." *NYTimes*, September 30, 1944, 18:3; "Modern House Comes Alive." *Crafts Horizon* 13 (September 1953): 30–33; Obituaries. *Crafts Horizon* 31 (August 1971): 4, and *NYTimes*, May 26, 1971, 46:1; "Portraits." *Interiors* 114 (May 1955): 100+; Roche, Mary. "A Lift From Lighting." *NYTimes*, January 14, 1945, sec. 6, p. 28:2, and "New Ideas and Inventions." *NYTimes*, June 8, 1947, sec. 6, p. 39:1; "Trials of Jurying." *Crafts Horizon* 16 (March 1956): 30–35; *Who's Who of American Women* (1958–1971); *WWWIA* 5.

MIRIAM TUCHMAN

SCHECHTER, MATHILDE
(1857–1924)

Mathilde Roth Schechter, founder of the WOMEN'S LEAGUE FOR CONSERVATIVE JUDAISM and the wife of Solomon Schechter, the well-known Jewish scholar, was born in Guttentag, a small town in Silesia, and orphaned at an early age.

Little is known about her parents or family background. Indeed, she exemplifies the difficulties of learning about the wives of famous men, frequently women of talent, who are overshadowed by their better-known spouses. Like so many women of her day, her energy was expended primarily in the private sphere, and thus the task of reconstructing her life is difficult. Despite the fact that she was intent on creating a life rather than building an empire, she founded what became one of the largest Jewish women's organizations in the United States.

Having grown up in the Jewish home for orphans in Breslau, Mathilde was educated in local schools and attended the Breslau Teacher's Seminary. Home to a thriving Jewish community, Breslau was also the site of the Jewish Theological Seminary, an eminent scholarly and rabbinical institution. After teaching in Breslau for a number of years, Mathilde moved to England to study at Queens College in London and to "read in the treasures of the British Museum, the National Gallery and the endless private collections."

In 1887, she met and married Solomon Schechter, the Jewish scholar who discovered the large cache of ancient Jewish manuscripts in a Cairo synagogue. The collection became known as the Cairo Geniza.

The Schechter home quickly became the center of the young intellectual Jewish elite in London. Mathilde Schechter's hospitality was legendary, and she maintained her reputation when the couple moved to Cambridge and later to the United States. She had a strong Jewish identity and contributed significantly to the Jewish community. While her husband taught at Cambridge and traveled around Europe and the Middle East collecting manuscripts, Mathilde Schechter brought up their three children, edited the works of local scholars, and engaged in various literary pursuits including a translation of the Jewish poet Heinrich Heine. Furthermore, she edited almost everything her famous husband wrote and is primarily responsible for the felicitous English style of his essays.

In 1902, the Schechter family came to America when Solomon Schechter was appointed president of the Jewish Theological Seminary in New York. Again the Schechter home became an intellectual center for a diverse group of people. HENRIETTA SZOLD in writing to Frank Schechter later described the Schechter home and "those full vivid days when she [Mathilde Schechter] and your father and your house were a stimulating creative center, in whose genial warmth we—so many, many of us—basked and were transformed."

Mathilde Schechter pursued serious interests outside the home. She established a Jewish vocational school for girls on the Lower East Side, which not only prepared young women for the world of work but also helped to strengthen their Jewish identity. Her musical talent and interest in congregational singing (new at that time) led to the organization of a Society for Ancient Hebrew Melodies as well as the publication of a hymn book titled *Kol Rina—Hebrew Hymnal for School and Home*. The crowning achievement of her public career was the establishment of the Women's League of the United Synagogue of America (today called the Women's League for Conservative Judaism). The United Synagogue, organized by Solomon Schechter a few years before his death in 1915, was designed to include all types of synagogues. However, it virtually marked the beginning of the Conservative Movement in America. The establishment of the Women's League was a way for Mathilde Schechter to pay tribute to her husband. The league was at first a constituent body of the United Synagogue, but Mathilde Schechter strongly advocated its

Mathilde Schechter was the founder of the WOMEN'S LEAGUE FOR CONSERVATIVE JUDAISM.
*Her home in New York City became the intellectual center of a diverse group of Jewish scholars
and activists, including her friend* HENRIETTA SZOLD. *[Ratner Center, Jewish Theological Seminary]*

autonomy, lest "the organization be swallowed into the United Synagogue entirely." The Women's League, whose chapters were within the synagogue, expanded quickly, and within a few years there were thirty-four chapters all over the country.

One of the first projects of the Women's League was the establishment in 1918 of a Student House in the Columbia University area that served as a center for Jewish students as well as for Jewish soldiers and sailors on leave. The concept of a Student House was a true expression of Mathilde Schechter's values as a caretaking person. It fulfilled an important function as a recreational and cultural center before the existence of the B'nai B'rith Hillel university system.

Speaking on Mother's Day 1919, at Mordecai Kaplan's Jewish Center in New York, Mathilde Schechter stressed the "absolute unselfishness and utter forgiveness of mother-love," at the same time emphasizing the needs of mothers to retain a sense of themselves apart from their maternal role. She believed strongly in the power of Judaism to soothe and to comfort. The Mitzvot [commandments] and especially the rituals were indeed "the song of our soul's communion with God." Defending the ancient idea of ritual, she eloquently stated her belief that "a living religion needs the spirit and the red-blooded warmth of forms, forms tenderly kissed into life by the spirit."

Mathilde Schechter lived in an age when domesticity was the ideal for women. She was a multifaceted individual, creative both in her home and in the public arena. As an organizational person, she developed herself fully, in line with the traditional women's roles of the times, yet stretching them in new and creative ways.

Mathilde Schechter died in August 1924.

BIBLIOGRAPHY

AJYB, 27:151; *NYTimes*, August 28, 1924, 17:5; Scult, Mel. "The Baale Boste Reconsidered: The Life of Mathilde Roth Schechter (M.R.S.)." *Modern Judaism* 7 (February 1987): 1–29.

MEL SCULT

SCHENK, FAYE LIBBY (1909–1981)

Faye Libby Herz Schenk rose to national and international prominence as a Jewish leader. Born on August 17, 1909, in Des Moines, Iowa, to Rebecca (Zeichick) and Haphtah Herz, she received her B.A. and M.A. in genetics from Drake University, where she was offered a chair in zoology. A committed Zionist, she chose instead to direct her considerable talents and energies into organizing and strengthening Zionist organizations worldwide. From 1939 to 1949, she and her husband, Morris Schenk, lived in Australia, where she became active in the Women's International Zionist Organization. Upon her return to New York, she became active in HADASSAH and founded the Washington Heights Group for its New York chapter. Schenk went on to hold every major portfolio in Hadassah and eventually served as national president from 1968 to 1972. During her term as president, Hadassah initiated the rebuilding of its hospital on Mount Scopus and created its Institute of Oncology in Jerusalem.

While her primary organizational commitment was to Hadassah, Schenk's enormous energy led her to assume leadership roles throughout the Jewish world, including president of the American Zionist Federation, cochair of Keren Hayesod–United Jewish Appeal, vice-chair of the National Council of the American-Israel Public Committee, and member of the board of governors for the Hebrew University and the Jewish Agency. In 1974, the Hebrew Union College–Jewish

Institute of Religion conferred the degree of doctor of humane letters on Schenk.

After a full life of activity and accomplishments, Schenk made aliyah in April 1978. Here her career reached its peak when she was elected to represent the World Confederation of United Zionists on the Zionist executive and was placed at the head of the organization department of the executive.

Faye Libby Schenk married Morris Schenk, a Reform rabbi, in 1933. They had two children, Mina and Raphael, and five grandchildren. Faye Schenk's charisma and warm personality drew people from all walks of Jewish life into the Schenk home, where she melded together her Orthodox upbringing with her Reform commitments and Zionist ideology. She was fluent in Yiddish and conversant in Hebrew, and her spirit embodied her deep love for Judaism and the Jewish people.

After surviving the September 1970 El Al airplane hijacking, Schenk declared, "Life owes me nothing more. I owe life everything." Faye Libby Schenk died on her birthday, August 17, 1981, at age seventy-two and was buried on the Mount of Olives in Jerusalem.

BIBLIOGRAPHY

AJYB, 83:362; *EJ* (1973–1982); "In Memoriam: Faye Schenk." Published in Jerusalem by Hadassah (August 1982).

R. LORI FORMAN

SCHIFF, DOROTHY (1903–1989)

Married four times before resuming her maiden name, Dorothy Schiff, owner and publisher of the *New York Post* newspaper for thirty-seven years, was perhaps most accurately described as "Mrs. *Post*." Her publishing philosophy was simple: The *Post* must avoid "narrow-mindedness, prejudice, and all the things it is the business of liberals to fight." Her private life was more complex. Besides having four husbands, Schiff was romantically linked with a Rothschild, Serge Obolensky, the Vicomte Sebastien Foy, Averell Harriman, Lord Beaverbrook, Leslie Hore-Belisha, H.G. Wells, and (erroneously, she insisted) Franklin Delano Roosevelt. Revealingly, she once said, "A lot of my life was a search for love—to love and be loved."

A paradox, Schiff was attractive, socially prominent, and politically influential—but plagued by depression and anxiety. Raised a Jew, she read the New Testament, attended Christian services, and called the bat and bar mitzvah ceremony a rabbi conducted for her and her younger brother her "confirmation."

Received into the Episcopal church before her first marriage, she reverted to Judaism before her second, favored the establishment of Israel but disapproved of her third husband's support of the *Irgun*, and visited Israel with her fourth husband—a place that was "grimmer" than she expected but impressive in its dedication to the kibbutz movement.

Schiff was born on March 11, 1903. Her grandfather Jacob Schiff, who had emigrated from Frankfurt in 1865, was a director of Kuhn, Loeb & Co., a founder of Temple Emanu-El, and a devout Jew who visited his grandchildren each Friday to confer Sabbath blessings. He contributed generously to the INTERNATIONAL LADIES GARMENT WORKERS UNION because of his concern for Eastern European immigrants and set up Hebrew schools in all five boroughs of New York City. Schiff's father, Mortimer Schiff—dispatched to a Great Northern road gang to learn the railroad business, and then to Europe to learn banking—preferred racehorses. Her mother, Alice Neustadt, shared her husband's aversion to German Jews as well as his social aspirations. The couple accepted Jacob Schiff's wedding gift—a Fifth Avenue mansion—but fled the family enclave for Northwood, the Schiff estate in Oyster Bay, New York. In 1904, they were finally admitted into the social register.

Schiff's early years were scarred by parental coldness and a lonely education at home, due to her mother's fear of infection. During her single year at Brearley School, she felt isolated by her wealth and her Jewishness. Nor was she successful during a year at Bryn Mawr, failing every course before she left to prepare for her debut. She studied typing and shorthand, took correspondence courses, and enrolled in the New School University in Exile, but, as she observed years later, she was desperate to be free, and "marriage was the only escape."

At seventeen, she met Richard B. Hall, a salesman who was perennially in debt but was listed in the social register. Despite parental disapproval, she married him in 1923. A son, Morti, was born in 1924 and a daughter, Adele, thirteen months later; but the marriage was doomed. Schiff's family allowance was twenty times Hall's salary; even worse, he was a drinker, a philanderer, and an anti-Semite who complained that his wife's origins barred him from the best clubs. In 1931, when her parents' deaths within a few months of each other gave her an inheritance of well over fifteen million dollars, Schiff announced, "Dick, I'm rich at last—and now I'm going to divorce you!"

She had already met George Backer, the son of Eastern European immigrants. After a Nevada divorce, she married him in 1932. On her three-hundred-acre

share of the Northwood estate, Schiff built, at the height of the Depression, the mansion where her third child, Sarah-Ann, was born in 1934. Her deepening emotional depression led her into intensive therapy and back to New York City, where she became involved in community and political activities. She attended the 1933 Inaugural Ball and, inspired by President Roosevelt's speech, expanded her interests. She participated in a Madison Square rally to boycott German goods, became director of the Women's Trade Union League, joined organizations helping the underprivileged, and was appointed to the Board of Child Welfare.

Introduced to President Roosevelt by his daughter, Anna, Schiff became a frequent guest at Hyde Park, the Roosevelt estate on the Hudson. She was often driven about by FDR in his specially constructed automobile. When he bought an adjoining ninety-acre tract, she purchased half at his urging and constructed the modest Red House in a style she dubbed "Franklin the First."

In 1938, Schiff ran for Nassau County delegate to the New York State Constitutional Convention but lost to Robert Moses. The following June, at her husband's urging, she purchased the *Post*.

The country's oldest continuously published daily, the *New York Post* was founded by Alexander Hamilton in 1801. In 1939, its owner, J. David Stern, was compelled to sell the debt-ridden paper. Backer became president and editor, while Schiff became vice president and treasurer. The feature editor, whom Schiff later promoted to executive editor, was Theodore O. Thackrey, destined to be her third husband. After the change in ownership, the *Post* continued to lose money and readers—a situation that exacerbated marital conflicts. In 1942, Schiff decided to take over the newspaper, ending both her collaboration and her marriage with Backer. After a 1943 Nevada divorce, she married Thackrey.

The 1940s brought publishing triumphs and personal trials. In 1946, the *Post* bought the *Bronx Home News* (circulation: 124,000) and went on to acquire radio and television stations. The *Post* itself was refurbished with added popular features, syndication services, new columnists, a foreign bureau, a Paris edition (the *Paris-Post*, published from 1945 to 1948), and a tabloid format. But Schiff suffered a miscarriage in 1944, and her marriage foundered. Thackrey argued that her friendship with the president gave rise to rumors and endangered the *Post*'s independence. Husband and wife also disagreed politically: In 1948, Thackrey supported Henry Wallace for president, while Schiff, disliking Harry Truman, endorsed

Thomas E. Dewey. The couple published their differences in a series of columns. After the election, Schiff attended the United Nations session in Paris. When she returned home to find that Thackrey had written a critique of conservative policy around the world, she forbade him to publish it. In July 1950, they were divorced.

Thereafter, the *Post* became Schiff's primary focus. She cut costs, developed new advertising accounts, and encouraged a wider spectrum of views, supporting her staff's investigation of Robert Moses (an old friend) and coverage critical of such conservative icons as Walter Winchell, Joseph McCarthy, and J. Edgar Hoover. In September 1951, she began publishing a series of columns on various issues; in the following year, she won election as anti-Tammany candidate for the Democratic State Committee from the Ninth Assembly District. She supported Adlai Stevenson, but her friendship with Nelson Rockefeller caused problems. In 1958, for instance, the *Post* endorsed Democratic gubernatorial candidate Averell Harriman. But the day before the election, Schiff commandeered the final edition's front page to rebuke Harriman for calling Rockefeller anti-Israeli. The criticism alienated liberals and Schiff's longtime friends; later that year, she abandoned the column. Meanwhile, her personal life had entered a new stage. In April 1951, she had met Rudolf G. Sonneborn, a Jewish German industrialist and Zionist from Baltimore. Schiff accompanied him to Israel, and in 1953 announced their marriage in her column. The marriage endured through his slow recovery from a massive stroke in 1959, but in 1965 they were divorced.

The 1960s brought a revival of political attention as Schiff returned to the Democratic fold by endorsing John F. Kennedy. She was a guest at the White House during his administration and after the accession of Lyndon B. Johnson—although she refused the latter's request to serve as ambassador to Liberia. But Schiff was not impressed with the 1972 Democratic candidate George McGovern, being generally skeptical of reformers. As she confided in a "Dear Reader" column, "Politics doesn't consist in being right. It's in making other people think you are."

The 1960s also brought the 114-day newspaper strike that, on December 7, 1962, closed down four New York papers: the *New York Times*, the *Daily News*, the *World-Telegram*, and the *Journal-American*. In a show of unity, workers at the *Herald Tribune*, the *Mirror*, and the *Post* also went on strike. The *Post* had weathered a seventeen-day strike in 1958, but it was too small and liberal for a strong voice in the Publisher's Association, which opposed the strikers, and

its financial balance was precarious. Outvoted on critical points and afraid that the strike would hasten the *Post*'s demise, Schiff resigned from the association and resumed publication. She antagonized her fellow publishers, but the *Post* seemed secure. It survived, even when the *World-Telegram*, the *Journal-American*, and the *Herald Tribune* merged into the *World Journal Tribune* in 1966, with a combined circulation of nearly seven hundred thousand. Less than a year later, the *Post* announced that the *World Journal Tribune* had published its last issue.

To expand production, the *Post*—now the only evening paper in New York City—purchased automated equipment and moved from West Street to the larger quarters vacated by the *Journal-American* on South Street. But television had begun to have an effect. By the mid-1970s, the *Post* was running a deficit, and in December 1976, Schiff announced that the paper had been sold to Rupert Murdoch.

Though her career was not immune to criticism—some people alleged that she confused gossip with political commentary—Schiff had no illusions about her role. "Influence, not power," she commented, "is what interests me," and she explained her many invitations in this way: "It's only because I'm Dorothy Schiff of the *New York Post*; otherwise I wouldn't be [there]." Nor did she sentimentalize her devotion to the paper. In an interview shortly before her death on August 30, 1989, she said "The men I was in love with were in love with someone else, and the men who were in love with me were a nuisance. And so I have given that side of me to things—my newspaper, really. I had to . . ."

BIBLIOGRAPHY

Adler, Cyrus. *Jacob H. Schiff: His Life and Letters* (1928); "Dorothy Schiff, 86, Ex-Post Owner, Dies." *NYTimes*, August 31, 1989; *EJ*; *Foremost Women in Communications: A Biographical Reference Work on Accomplished Women in Broadcasting, Publishing, Advertising, Public Relations, and Allied Professions* (1970); Hellman, G.T. Profiles. *The New Yorker*, 44 (August 10, 1968): 37+; Ingham, John N., ed. *Biographical Dictionary of American Business Leaders* (1983); Potter, Jeffrey. *Men, Money and Magic: The Story of Dorothy Schiff* (1976); Schiff, Dorothy. Papers, 1904–1989. New York Public Library.

FRANCESCA TILLONA

SCHIFF, THERESE LOEB (1854–1933)

Among her diverse activities, Therese Loeb Schiff organized a literary series for wealthy German Jewish women, donated ten thousand dollars to the

NATIONAL COUNCIL OF JEWISH WOMEN to help cope with Jewish prostitution among young immigrant women, and lectured for the Consumers League in support of protective legislation to end child labor and the exploitation of women. Schiff was a paradigm of the intellectual, religious, and cultural activities and also the social service and even political endeavors of upper-middle-class German Jewish women during the late nineteenth and early twentieth centuries.

Her father, Solomon Loeb, emigrated from Worms, Germany, after the 1848 revolution and settled in Cincinnati, where he joined a relative in the clothing firm Kuhn, Netter. Loeb married Fanny Kuhn, the sister of his cousin Abraham, and became a partner in the firm, which was renamed Kuhn, Loeb. On November 6, 1854, Fanny Loeb gave birth to Therese, Solomon's oldest child. Fanny died before giving birth to her second child, and in 1860 Solomon traveled to Germany, where he married Betty Gallenberg. Betty raised Therese as her own daughter, and she and Solomon had four children of their own: Morris, Guta, James, and Nina. At Betty's urging, in 1867 Solomon Loeb moved the firm to New York, where the family became part of the elite group of German Jewish financiers known among themselves as "Our Crowd."

In 1873, Therese met Jacob Schiff. Schiff, born in 1847 in Frankfurt, Germany, had immigrated to the United States at the age of eighteen and had become a successful financier. Kuhn, Loeb had recently invited Schiff to join the firm, and with Betty Loeb's encouragement he had become a frequent guest at the Loeb home. In 1875, he and Therese were married. Jacob and Therese's first child, Frieda, was born in 1876, and their son, Mortimer, was born a year later.

After his eldest daughter's wedding, Solomon Loeb gave his son-in-law, Jacob, a full partnership in Kuhn, Loeb. Schiff and Loeb had very different strategies for investment, and Therese Schiff was often caught in the middle of their arguments. Schiff prevailed, however, and within ten years had taken over as president of the firm. Under Schiff's leadership, Kuhn, Loeb prospered. It became one of the most powerful investment houses in the United States, and Schiff one of the most influential Jewish men of his generation.

Therese Schiff was raised in an agnostic household, and Jacob Schiff was an Orthodox Jew who prayed daily and would not conduct business on the Sabbath. Nevertheless, like most of the other members of their set, they were actively involved in American Reform Judaism and were members of Temple Emmanu-El in New York. In 1890, on the occasion of

Therese Schiff epitomized the intellectual, religious, philanthropic, and cultural activities of upper-middle-class German Jewish American women during the late nineteenth and early twentieth centuries. [American Jewish Archives]

their daughter Frieda's confirmation, the Schiffs donated to the synagogue a set of Torah ornaments decorated with an American flag and an American eagle—a symbol of their commitment to American Jewry and the United States.

As a devout Jew, Jacob Schiff donated 10 percent of his income to charity. Jacob's funds enabled Therese to become involved in the many volunteer and philanthropic activities that characterized the lives of upper-middle-class German Jewish women. By the late 1880s, the German Jewish community in New York was financially very comfortable and used its wealth to build Jewish institutions and establish organizations to help the newly arriving and less fortunate Eastern European immigrants. Freed by servants of domestic responsibilities, these Jewish women took upon themselves the task of creating and staffing the new organizations, which were often funded by their husbands' money. Jewish women in the late nineteenth and early twentieth centuries, for the most part, conformed to expectations that they would marry and raise families. Volunteerism and philanthropy offered them an opportunity to act beyond their homes in a way that did not contradict their gender defined roles.

During his lifetime, Jacob Schiff directed much of his wife's philanthropic activity. After Jacob's death in 1920, Therese Schiff became more independent and continued her philanthropy on her own, often as leader or participant. Schiff gave three hundred thousand dollars to the Henry Street Settlement as a memorial to her husband, whose funds had allowed LILLIAN WALD to open the settlement house in 1895. Schiff was particularly involved with the Emanuel SISTERHOOD OF PERSONAL SERVICE of which she was an honorary vice president and a member of the advisory board. In 1926, when she was the honorary chair of the women's division, she donated thirty thousand dollars to the United Jewish Campaign. Schiff also made generous donations to other Jewish charities and organizations including the Montefiore Hospital for Chronic Diseases, the Loeb Convalescent Home, and the YMHA. In 1931, in memory of her son, Mortimer, who had died while he was national chairman of the Boy Scouts of America, Schiff gave money to that organization to purchase land for a national training center.

Therese Loeb Schiff died of a cerebral thrombosis on February 26, 1933, at her home on Fifth Avenue. She was remembered for her personal dedication and charitable contributions as "a mother in Israel." In 1874, Jacob Schiff had written to reassure his mother that his future bride was neither uncultured nor a feminist like other American women, but could have been raised in the best of German families. Schiff undoubtedly would not have characterized herself as a "feminist" either, yet her activities demonstrated a commitment and concern not only for the Jewish people and the less fortunate in general, but for the intellectual and personal well-being of American Jewish women in particular.

BIBLIOGRAPHY

Adler, Cyrus. *Jacob H. Schiff: His Life and Letters*. Vol. 1 (1929); *AJYB* 35:128; Baum, Charlotte, Paula Hyman, and Sonya Michel. *The Jewish Woman in America* (1976); Berrol, Selma. "Class or Ethnicity: The Americanized German Jewish Woman and Her Middle Class Sisters in 1895." *Jewish Social Studies* 47, no. 1 (1985): 21–31; Birmingham, Stephen. *Our Crowd* (1967); Chernow, Ron. *The Warburgs: The Twentieth-Century Odyssey of a Remarkable Jewish Family* (1993); *EJ*; Kuzmack, Linda Gordon. *Woman's Cause: The Jewish Women's Movement in England and the United States* (1990); *NYTimes*, February 26, 1933, 20:3, and February 27, 1933, 15:1, and February 28, 1933, 20:5; Slesin, Susan. "Tiffany Glass to Torah Pointers: Looking Beyond the Surface." *NYTimes*, October 21, 1993, C1; Sochen, June. *Consecrate Every Day: The Public Lives of Jewish American Women, 1880–1980* (1981); Sorel, Nancy Caldwell. "Kuhn, Loeb Calls on the House of Morgan." *Forbes* (October 27, 1986), 64; Supple, Barry E. "A Business Elite: German Jewish Financiers in Nineteenth-Century New York." In *The American Jewish Experience*, edited by Jonathan D. Sarna (1997).

IDANA GOLDBERG

SCHLAMME, MARTHA (1925–1985)

Once described as a "Viennese Mary Martin," Martha Schlamme began her American career singing Yiddish and Hebrew songs in the resort hotels of the Catskills in the late 1940s. She earned a national reputation in the 1950s as a performer of "Songs of Many Lands" (the title of her concert program and of a 1954 Vanguard record), and later won acclaim for her interpretations of Kurt Weill songs.

Martha Haftel Schlamme, born in Vienna in 1925, was the only child of restaurateur Meier Haftel and Gisa (Braten) Haftel. As a child, she studied the piano and learned Yiddish and German songs from her family. After the Nazi annexation of Austria in 1938, her parents sent her to live with relatives in France. She later joined her parents in England. There she continued her education, begun in Viennese public schools, in a Jewish school. When her parents were interned as enemy aliens in a camp on the Isle of Man, she chose to remain with them. While in the camp, she studied English and secretarial subjects, and first performed onstage in a German-language production of Shakespeare's *As You Like It*.

It was also in the internment camp that she decided to pursue a musical career after hearing the Icelandic singer Engel Lund perform folk songs in several languages, including Yiddish. She studied piano and voice in London after the war, supporting herself with office work, and began to perform

She sang songs in a dozen languages, including Yiddish and Hebrew.
Ultimately, Martha Schlamme's interpretation of the works of Kurt Weill
made her an "overnight" success and led to a long Broadway career.

onstage and for BBC radio. After coming to the United States in 1948, she continued her musical education and, despite discouragement from mezzosoprano JENNIE TOUREL, began a performing career that took her to concert halls and nightclubs from coast to coast. Her repertoire included songs in over a dozen languages. Among her recordings are five collections of Yiddish songs (for Vanguard, MGM, and Tikva), one each of Israeli songs and of French Christmas carols (for Vanguard), one record of German songs (with accompaniment by Pete Seeger, for Folkways), and several live performance records (for Vanguard and MGM).

In 1959, on the eve of the opening of the Edinburgh Festival, Schlamme first performed a program of Kurt Weill songs in a tiny Edinburgh club. The enthusiastic reaction of reporters in town for the festival, she later recalled, made her "a star overnight." Her *World of Kurt Weill in Song* (with Will Holt, later recorded for MGM) began a long Off-Broadway run in 1963 and led to other Weill performances, including roles in *The Threepenny Opera* and *Mahagonny*, as well as *A Kurt Weill Cabaret* (with Alvin Epstein, also recorded for MGM). She also appeared onstage in productions ranging from *Fiddler on the Roof* to plays by Maxim Gorky, and performed in such one-woman shows as *A Woman Without a Man Is . . .* and *The Jewish Woman*.

Schlamme's two marriages, to Hans Schlamme and to Mark Lane, ended in divorce. Martha Schlamme died in Jamestown, New York, on October 6, 1985, two months after suffering a stroke while onstage. In her nearly forty years of performing in the United States, she helped to popularize Yiddish and international folk songs, and to remind Americans of the legacy of composer Kurt Weill.

BIBLIOGRAPHY

AJYB 87:443; *Current Biography Yearbook 1964* (1965); Lawless, Ray M. *Folksingers and Folksongs in America* (1965. Reprint 1981); Pareles, Jon. "Martha Schlamme, Singer, 60." *NYTimes*, October 8, 1985, sec. 1, p. 24; *Who's Who of American Women.* 12th ed. (1981); Wilson, John S. "Schlamme Evokes Weill Cabaret Style." *NYTimes*, August 13, 1976, sec. 3, p. 19.

ROBERT A. ROTHSTEIN

SCHNEIDERMAN, ROSE (1882–1972)

"The woman worker needs bread, but she needs roses too," Rose Schneiderman said in 1911. This most famous of Schneiderman's lines captures the essence of the political philosophy that guided her long and extraordinary career as an internationally recognized leader of American working women. For nearly half a century, Rose Schneiderman worked tirelessly to improve wages, hours, and safety standards for American working women. She saw those things as "bread," the very basic human rights to which working women were entitled. But she also worked for such "roses" as schools, recreational facilities, and professional networks for trade union women, because she believed that working women deserved much more than a grim subsistence.

Only four feet nine inches tall, with flaming red hair, the diminutive Polish Jewish immigrant possessed legendary power as an orator. From 1904 through the 1950s, the militant trade unionist and women's rights advocate spoke on street corners, soapboxes, lecture platforms, and over the radio, impressing even those who did not share her political views. In an age when political oratory was a leading form of entertainment, many contemporaries described her as the most moving speaker they had ever heard. Even her enemies evoked a sense of her emotional punch—dubbing her "the Red Rose of Anarchy."

Schneiderman's powers of persuasion won her many influential admirers. A close friend and adviser to Franklin and Eleanor Roosevelt, Schneiderman taught them most of what they knew about working people. As president of the New York Women's Trade Union League (NYWTUL) from 1917 to 1949, and of the National WTUL from 1926 to 1950, Schneiderman served both presidents and governors as a liaison to organized women workers. She was the only woman on FDR's National Recovery Administration

Labor Advisory Board. She played a key role in shaping the landmark legislation of the New Deal: the National Labor Relations Act, the Social Security Act, and the Fair Labor Standards Act. She also helped make New York State a national laboratory for labor and social welfare legislation, first as a lobbyist for the NYWTUL from 1911 to 1932, and then as New York secretary of labor from 1937 to 1943.

Schneiderman had a strong Jewish identity and was active on behalf of Jewish causes throughout her career, particularly during the 1930s and 1940s. Her speeches and letter-writing campaigns mobilized the resources of the labor movement to help Jewish refugees escape from Nazi-occupied Europe. She was also a major fund-raiser for the Labor-Zionist Leon Blum Colony in Palestine.

For her socialist views and her union organizing efforts on behalf of working women—not to mention her flaming red hair—Rose Schneiderman's enemies dubbed her "the Red Rose of Anarchy." That didn't stop her from getting the ear of Eleanor Roosevelt and becoming a key adviser on FDR's New Deal policies. [Kheel Center, Cornell University]

Rose Schneiderman was born on April 16, 1882, to devout Jewish parents in Saven, Poland. Her father, Samuel, was a tailor. Her mother, Deborah (Rothman), did a little bit of everything; she took in sewing, baked ritual breads, sewed uniforms for the Russian Army, treated the sick with herbal medicines, and even tended the bar at a local inn when the barkeep was too drunk to do it herself. Strong believers in education for girls, Schneiderman's parents bucked Jewish tradition to send her to school. When she was four, they enrolled her in a heder. At six, they moved to the city of Chelm so that Schneiderman could attend a Russian public school.

The Schneiderman family migrated to New York City in 1890. Two years later, Samuel died of meningitis, leaving three children and a pregnant wife. Deborah Schneiderman did the best she could to support her children. She took in boarders, sewed and washed for neighbors, and even worked as a handywoman. Still, for a time, she was forced to place her three children in an orphanage. When Rose Schneiderman returned home, her mother worked nights so that Rose could attend school during the days. But, in 1895, when her mother lost her night job, thirteen-year-old Rose was forced to leave school and enter the paid workforce.

Deborah Schneiderman begged United Hebrew Charities, an organization run by middle-class German Jews, to find her daughter a "respectable" job at a department store. Retail jobs were deemed more respectable than factory work because the environment was more pleasant and sexual harassment was thought to be less common. Deborah Schneiderman worried that factory work would sully her daughter's reputation. She hoped that a job as a fashionable salesgirl would usher Schneiderman into the middle class. The single mother who had fed her children on charity food baskets was grimly determined to help them escape poverty. Perhaps self-conscious about a childhood that was poor even by Lower East Side standards, Schneiderman latched onto her mother's obsession with respectability. That preoccupation lasted throughout her life, shaping and limiting her political choices.

But respectability didn't pay the rent. Then, as now, blue-collar work paid a great deal better than pink-collar jobs. After three years as a salesgirl, Schneiderman asked a friend to train her as a cap maker. She did earn higher wages than in the department store, but, like many women garment workers, Schneiderman quickly grew frustrated by the gender hierarchy in her shop that reserved the best-paying positions for men while relegating women to the worst jobs. When she expressed her frustration, more seasoned women workers began to teach her about three political ideologies that would change her life: trade unionism, socialism, and feminism.

In 1903, the twenty-one-year-old Schneiderman organized her shop for the United Cloth Hat and Cap Makers' Union, a union founded and run by socialist Jews, most of whom were Eastern European immigrants like herself. Initially skeptical of the ability of young women to organize, male union leaders were deeply impressed by Schneiderman's skill as an organizer and her charismatic speaking style. Within a year, she became the first woman elected to national office in an American labor union.

The following year, as leader of a general strike of cap makers, Schneiderman was offered aid by the NYWTUL, an organization founded by progressive reformers to help working women unionize. Although the women who ran the NYWTUL were sincere, they lacked credibility among the working classes. They hoped to change that by attracting respected women unionists like Schneiderman.

By 1906, Schneiderman's talents as an organizer had won her the vice presidency of the NYWTUL. In 1908, German Jewish philanthropist IRENE LEWISOHN offered Schneiderman money to finish her schooling. Schneiderman refused the scholarship on the grounds that she could not accept a privilege that so few working women had. However, she did accept Lewisohn's amended offer to pay her a salary to organize working women. Schneiderman became chief organizer for the NYWTUL, a post she held until 1914.

Organizing furiously in garment shops throughout Lower Manhattan, Schneiderman helped pave the way for the great UPRISING OF THE 20,000 of New York's shirtwaist makers in 1909–1910, the largest strike by American women workers to that time. That strike, led largely by young Eastern European Jewish women, galvanized the fledgling INTERNATIONAL LADIES GARMENT WORKERS UNION (ILGWU) and gave the NYWTUL a national reputation. But it also generated tensions between Jewish women and men in the ILGWU, and between working-class Jews and the middle-class Christian women who dominated the NYWTUL. In both cases, the more powerful group chastised the immigrant Jewish women strikers for being too fervent and too uncontrollable.

In the years after the shirtwaist strike, Schneiderman's relationship with the league's founders deteriorated. Believing them to be both anti-Semitic and antisocialist, Schneiderman resigned in 1914. For the next two years she worked as general organizer for the ILGWU. That position had its frustrations as well.

The male leadership of the ILGWU showed little interest in organizing women. Feeling undermined and angry, Schneiderman left the ILGWU and became chair of the Industrial Wing of the New York Woman Suffrage Party in 1917.

Long an ardent suffragist, Schneiderman had helped found the Wage Earner's League for Woman Suffrage in 1911 and toured for the Ohio suffrage referendum in 1912. In January 1917, she launched one final, successful drive to win the vote for New York women. That same year, she was elected president of the NYWTUL. By the end of World War I, Schneiderman was a leading figure in both labor and feminist politics in New York State. Her socialist activism and her campaign during the war to prevent the state assembly from suspending labor laws protecting women workers won her the lasting enmity of conservative members of the state legislature. They investigated her officially and publicly dubbed her "the Red Rose of Anarchy."

Schneiderman fought back by organizing newly enfranchised women to defeat antilabor legislators in the 1918 election. And, in 1920, Schneiderman ran for the United States Senate on the New York State Labor Party ticket. Though she lost, her campaign highlighted issues of importance to American working people. Her broad platform called for the construction of nonprofit housing for workers, improved neighborhood schools, publicly owned power utilities and staple food markets, and state-funded health and unemployment insurance for all Americans.

By the mid-1920s, Schneiderman was a nationally known figure. In 1926, she was elected president of the National WTUL, a post she retained until her retirement in 1950. Her growing interest in labor legislation had also brought her into a circle of women reformers surrounding a new friend of the NYWTUL, Eleanor Roosevelt. In 1921, when Roosevelt began to stake out a political career separate from her husband's, she became involved in the NYWTUL. Before long, Schneiderman became a regular guest at the scrambled egg dinners that Roosevelt liked to cook for her friends, and Roosevelt came into contact for the first time with the world of the working class. Her friendship with Schneiderman deepened quickly, and, by the mid-1920s, she was inviting Schneiderman to Hyde Park to spend time with Franklin. These conversations between FDR and Schneiderman laid the foundations for many of the ideas about labor that would become law during his presidency.

In 1933, after his inauguration, Roosevelt named Schneiderman as the only woman on the National Labor Advisory Board. Schneiderman wrote the NRA codes for every industry with a predominantly female workforce. It was a heady experience for a Polish immigrant whose formal schooling had ended at age thirteen. After leaving Washington, Schneiderman was appointed secretary of labor for New York State. In that post, she campaigned hard for the extension of social security to domestic workers, for equal pay for women workers, and for comparable worth. She also used state laws to aid the union drives of the state's growing legion of service workers: hotel maids, restaurant workers, and beauty parlor workers.

During the late 1930s and early 1940s, Schneiderman became deeply involved in efforts to rescue European Jews and to resettle them in the United States and Palestine. Her work won her the praise of Albert Einstein, who wrote: "It must be a source of deep gratification to you to be making so important a contribution to rescuing our persecuted fellow Jews from their calamitous peril and leading them toward a better future." Schneiderman ultimately could rescue only a small number, and she described herself as "sick with worry" for the duration of the war years.

In 1949, she retired from public life, devoting her time to writing her memoirs and making radio speeches and occasional appearances for various labor unions. Schneiderman never married, but she had a long-term relationship with labor movement colleague Maud Swartz.

Rose Schneiderman died in New York City on August 11, 1972, at age ninety.

Long before the most recent wave of feminist activism, Schneiderman attacked sexual segregation in the workplace, tried to unionize not only industrial women but also white-collar and domestic workers, called for state regulation not only of factory and office working conditions but also of working conditions in the home. She argued for comparable worth laws, government-funded child care, and maternity insurance. And, for more than half a century, she organized women to fight—not just for economic independence but also for the right to have meaning and beauty in their lives. She died just as a new women's movement was gaining strength. Many of her ideas were taken up by that movement and are still being debated in classrooms, courtrooms, and congressional chambers. Those ideas and dreams, as much as the government protections that most American workers now take for granted, are the legacy of Rose Schneiderman.

BIBLIOGRAPHY

AJYB 24:200, 74:559; *EJ*; Endelman, Gary. *Solidarity Forever: Rose Schneiderman and the Women's Trade Union*

League (1982); Fink, 321–322; Kessler-Harris, Alice. "Rose Schneiderman." In *American Labor Leaders*, edited by Warren Van Tine and Melvyn Dubofsky (1987); *NAW* modern; Obituary. *NYTimes* August 12, 1972, 26:3; Orleck, Annelise. *Common Sense and a Little Fire: Women and Working-Class Politics in the United States, 1900–1965* (1995), and "Rose Schneiderman." In *Portraits of American Women From Settlement to the Present*, edited by G.J. Barker-Benfield and Catherine Clinton (1991); Schneiderman, Rose. *All For One* (1967), and Papers. Tamiment Library, NYC; *UJE*; *WWIAJ* (1926, 1928, 1938).

ANNELISE ORLECK

SCHOCKEN, EVA (1918–1982)

Eva (Chawa) Schocken was born near the end of World War I on September 29, 1918, in the small city of Zwickau, Germany. Her father was Salman Schocken, a businessman who, with his brother, had built up a chain of department stores across Germany. Her mother was Lili Schocken.

Salman was a leader in the Zionist movement and was deeply involved in Jewish culture and intellectual history. In the late 1920s, when the German branch of Zionist publishing failed, Salman took it over, calling it Schocken Books. In 1934, after the Nazis decreed that Aryan publishers would not be allowed to publish Jewish writers, he added to his stable of authors such noted Jewish intellectuals as Franz Kafka and Martin Buber.

The family left Germany at the end of 1933 and immigrated to Jerusalem. Around the time the family had to leave Germany, Eva was sent to a boarding school in England. Later, she joined her family in Palestine. In Jerusalem, her mother took a dislike to a boy her daughter was seeing and presented Eva with a steamship ticket to join her brother in the United States.

In the late 1930s, Eva Schocken arrived in New York City, where she attended college at the Bank Street School. In 1941 she married Theodore Herzl Rome, and later had four children. She eventually completed her bachelor's degree at Bank Street and went on to get a master's degree from Columbia University in early childhood education and remedial reading. When her father brought Schocken Books to New York in 1946, she became involved as an education consultant. When Salman died in 1960, Eva's husband Herzl took over as president of Schocken Books. Eva became an editor.

This was the period during which Eva Schocken did her most influential work. She expanded Schocken's scope to include books in her own areas of interest, education and women's studies. She reissued a series of works by Maria Montessori, who had been nearly forgotten in this country by the 1960s. She kept Schocken Books in the forefront of the educational revolution of the 1960s with works by Herbert Kohl and books on the "open classroom" concept.

Eva Schocken also spearheaded the first women's studies series in books, including both reissues and original works. Her consulting editor was GERDA LERNER, a scholar and historian of the women's movement. The reprints included suffragists and feminists such as Elizabeth Cady Stanton. One of the new books in the series—*Women's Diaries of the Westward Journey*, by Lillian Schlissel—was a minor best-seller.

After Herzl died in 1965, Eva's brother Theodore Schocken became president of Schocken Books. In 1968, Eva married Julius Glaser, who later became chairman of the company. When her brother died in 1975, Eva became president and led the firm until her death.

Although Eva Schocken seemed to prefer the role of editor, Schocken Books reached its peak under her leadership as president. It was during this period that she brought out what was to be Schocken's foremost best-seller *When Bad Things Happen to Good People*, by Rabbi Lawrence Kushner. She also imported from England a children's book, *Masquerade*, that became an American best-seller. She died on January 12, 1982, at age sixty-four.

BIBLIOGRAPHY
Obituary. *NYTimes*, January 13, 1982; Rome, David. Interview by author, May 2, 1997.

ANDRA MEDEA

SCHOOLMAN, BERTHA SINGER (1897–1974)

Like her friend and mentor HENRIETTA SZOLD Bertha Schoolman gave a lifetime of service to the betterment of Jewish education and to the cause of Youth Aliyah, the movement to bring Jewish youth out of Germany to live in children's villages in Israel. In the words of her friend and eulogist Marian G. Greenberg, Schoolman was "a woman of moral and intellectual integrity, who had the courage to live in accordance with her convictions."

Bertha Schoolman was born in New York City on December 9, 1897. She graduated from HUNTER COLLEGE in 1919 and from the Teachers Institute of the Jewish Theological Seminary of America in 1921. A committed Jewish educator, Bertha Schoolman taught at the Central Jewish Institute of New York, the first American Jewish community center with an educational focus. Throughout her life, she would also play an important role in the administration and educational programs of the Cejwin Camps, founded in 1919 by her husband, Albert.

A lifelong Zionist, Bertha Schoolman acted on her convictions by taking her two young daughters to Palestine for extended visits and schooling as early as 1931 and again in 1937–1938. In the United States, Schoolman implemented her Zionist beliefs through her active involvement in HADASSAH, the Women's Zionist Organization of America. She served as national secretary from 1940 to 1941 and as vice president from 1941 to 1943. For six years (1921–1927), she headed the Hadassah Palestine Committee, which then supervised all of Hadassah's educational and medical projects. She chaired other important Hadassah

committees, including the Jewish National Fund (Keren Kayemet) Hadassah Medical Organization committee, Zionist relations, and political relations. She also wrote articles for the *Hadassah Newsletter* (now *Magazine*), the *Jewish Social Service Quarterly*, and the *Reconstructionist Magazine*. In 1947, she received the Outstanding Alumni Award from the Teachers Institute of the Jewish Theological Seminary of America.

It was in 1947, too, that Schoolman's vital service to Youth Aliyah began when she accepted the Jewish Agency's urgent call to act as cochair of its Youth Aliyah Management Committee. Bertha Schoolman responded to the emergency summons, despite potential physical danger and personal sacrifice. She arrived in Palestine on November 28, 1947, the day before the United Nations General Assembly voted for the Partition Plan for Palestine and Jewish statehood. From 1947 to 1953, she spent six months of each year

Bertha Schoolman was a lifelong Zionist activist, serving in HADASSAH *for many years and even risking her life in the cause of Youth Aliyah. She is shown here with Mr. Mintz, the deputy speaker of the Knesset, at the Anne Frank Haven dedication ceremony at Shaarei Avraham (Poale Agudah) in 1960. [Hadassah Archives]*

in Israel, away from her family, helping Youth Aliyah to cope with the enormous task of caring for hundreds of young survivors of European extermination camps and ghettos. On one occasion, while riding in a convoy to welcome refugees, she narrowly escaped death from the weapons that killed Hans Beyth, acting director of Youth Aliyah. It was fitting that on the occasion of naming the reception center at Ramat Hadassah-Szold in Bertha Schoolman's honor, Moshe Kol compared her service to that of "a soldier in the front lines for whom no place is too remote, no duty too dangerous." In recognition of her service in Israel prior to the establishment of the state, Schoolman was given the Fighter for the State Award by the Israel Ministry of Defense on Independence Day in 1969.

During the difficult days of 1947–1948, when Hadassah Hospital on Mount Scopus had to be abandoned and medical services reorganized, Schoolman joined a small group of Hadassah leaders from America to assist the directors of the Hadassah Medical Organization. Her creative concern for the future of the young refugees led to her involvement in the founding in 1949 of the Neve Hadassah Youth Village near Kibbutz Tel Yitzchak in Central Sharon.

Bertha Schoolman, who had been a member of the World Zionist Actions Committee from 1937, attended historic sessions of the World Zionist Congress in Europe and Israel. She was the first American Jewish woman to chair the Actions Committee and Congress Commissions and deliver reports to the plenary sessions in fluent Hebrew.

A member of the Society for the Advancement of Judaism and of the board of directors of the Jewish Reconstructionist Foundation, Bertha Schoolman's educational philosophy was rooted in the Reconstructionist approach to Judaism. She died on January 6, 1974, after a long illness.

BIBLIOGRAPHY

AJYB 76:517; *EJ*; Obituary. *NYTimes*, January 9, 1974, 38:2; Schoolman, Bertha Singer. Papers. Hadassah Archives, NYC.

GLADYS ROSEN

SCHULBERG, ADELINE (1895–1977)

Adeline Schulberg was a successful talent and literary agent. A committed socialist in her youth, she later became involved in child welfare, education, and other social issues.

She was born Adeline Jaffe on April 14, 1895, and arrived in the United States from Russia as an infant. Following the rise of anti-Semitic pogroms that swept Eastern Europe at the turn of the century, she, along with her mother, Hannah, and her two older brothers, Joseph and David, joined the two million Jews who would make the trip to the United States over a twenty-year period. The Jaffes were met in New York by Adeline's father, Max, and they moved to Madison Street on the Lower East Side, a densely packed neighborhood filled with Jewish immigrants. Poverty was widespread on the Lower East Side, and the Jaffes were no exception. These early surroundings influenced Schulberg's political views, and she became an active socialist who knew many of the movement's leaders, including Leon Trotsky and George Sokolsky.

In 1913, she married an ambitious *New York World* reporter, B.P. Schulberg. Her husband soon got a job working for Adolph Zukor's Famous Players, but it was Adeline Schulberg's work in the suffrage movement that got B.P. his first assignment, a film documentary about the English suffragist leader Sylvia Pankhurst. The couple moved uptown to Harlem and Schulberg soon gave birth to a son, Budd. From a very young age she had a love for books and had dreamed of becoming a librarian. Although this dream was never fulfilled, this slight woman with boundless energy was determined to educate her son, taking him to lectures at nearby Columbia University and making sure that he was never without a book to read.

Five years after the Schulbergs were married, they moved to Hollywood, a young city in California that a small group of Eastern European immigrants had been rapidly turning into the motion picture capital of the world. When her husband got a job as a producer at Paramount Pictures, Schulberg became active in child welfare and education, and received a degree from the University of California in 1926. Drawing upon her socialist roots, Schulberg organized birth control clinics throughout the West. In 1929, Schulberg helped to found the first progressive school in California, which was based on the philosophies of educational innovator John Dewey.

Her marriage to B.P. Schulberg lasted for twenty years. They divorced in 1933, and Schulberg thrived in her new-found independence. Using the connections she had made in the Hollywood community, Schulberg set up the Ad Schulberg Agency and represented some of Hollywood's biggest stars, including Marlene Dietrich, Fredric March, and Herbert Marshall. Schulberg sold the agency in the 1930s, and since the terms of the agreement barred her from practicing in the United States, she moved to England. When World War II began in 1939, Schulberg set up an "underground railroad" in London for refugee talent from Nazi-occupied Europe.

After the war, Schulberg returned to New York City and became a talent scout for Columbia Pictures. SHELLEY WINTERS was her best-known discovery. Seeking to reestablish the control she had wielded as head of the Ad Schulberg Agency, she formed a literary agency. Her clients included her son, Budd, whose most famous work was *What Makes Sammy Run?*, novelists Vicki Baum, FANNIE HURST, and Ruth McKenney, author *of My Sister Eileen*, Roger Price, Mark Harris, and Rex Reed.

Adeline Schulberg died in New York City on July 15, 1977.

BIBLIOGRAPHY

Obituary. *NYTimes*, July 16, 1977, 24:1; *WWIAJ* (1938).

MIK MOORE

SCHULMAN, GRACE (b. 1935)

When asked about the role Judaism played in her life, Grace Schulman responded that being Jewish "is an immense cultural privilege . . . [because] it leads to knowledge of other languages and cultures." Schulman's poetry reflects this sentiment, for it is in her poems that the reader may travel to a variety of edifying spheres wherein time and space evanesce. Though her cultural identity is significantly connected with much of her writing, the environment in which Schulman was raised cultivated her as a poet and thinker.

Grace Waldman Schulman was born in 1935, in New York City, to Marcella and Bernard Waldman. Marcella, a sixth-generation American Jew, was educated in Portugal. Bernard, an immigrant from Poland, studied at University College, London, and in Germany. The Waldmans raised Grace on West 86th Street, in an environment about which she now reflects, "The sophistication of it was stifling in a way, but kind and encouraging." Her home was frequented by various intellectuals who, along with her parents, stimulated Grace to write poetry by the age of seven. At the age of fourteen, she met Marianne Moore, about whom she later wrote her doctoral dissertation. Moore remained an influential figure upon Grace—and a "miraculous" friend—until her death in 1972. Marcella Waldman, also a writer, fostered her daughter's interests and taught her how to type.

Schulman attended American University (B.S., 1954), Bard College, and the Johns Hopkins Writing Seminars. Between earning her master's and doctoral degrees (1960 and 1971, respectively) from New York University, she worked briefly as a reporter. She

became the poetry editor of the *Nation* in 1972 and a professor of English at Baruch College, CUNY, in 1973. During that year, she won fellowships from Yaddo, the Karolyi Foundation, and the MacDowell Colony. She worked as the director of the Poetry Center at the 92nd Street YM-YWHA from 1974 until 1984. In 1975, Schulman won the Lucille Medwick Memorial Award from International PEN. Since then, she has contributed significantly to studies in poetry with her writings on Marianne Moore, Ezra Pound, and May Swenson and her translations of T. Carmi.

Schulman's first collection of poems, *Burn Down the Icons* (1976), is a creative response to Christian symbolism and poets who attracted her as a young writer. Her second, *Hemispheres* (1984), is largely about Israel and includes a poem ("Songs of My Fathers") about her grandmother's grandfather, Shmuel, a Romanian Jewish immigrant. Similarly in *For That Day Only* (1994), Schulman recalls the memory of her immigrant grandfather, David, from whom she acquired both her love of New York and her love of walking, in a salient poem, "Footsteps on Lower Broadway." In this poem, Schulman expertly draws together three visions of New York—her grandfather's, Walt Whitman's, and her own—invoking a shared sacred space wherein certain "haunts" are experienced in various ways. The narrative itself is a tour through parts of the city sanctified by Whitman's and Grandfather Dave's meanderings, and develops out of a comparison of their perspectives on aspects of New York (e.g., a synagogue on Crosby Street).

Schulman lives with her husband, Jerome Schulman, a research scientist and professor, in New York and East Hampton.

SELECTED WORKS BY GRACE SCHULMAN

Burn Down the Icons (1976); *For That Day Only* (1994); *Hemispheres* (1984); "Grace Schulman." (1984). Recording; "Literature, *The Nation*, and the World." In *The Art of Literary Publishing: Editors and Their Craft*. Edited by Bill Henderson (1980); "Marianne Moore and E. McKnight Kauffer: Their Friendship, Their Concerns." *Conversant Essays: Contemporary Poets on Poetry* (1990); "Marianne Moore and E. McKnight Kauffer: Two Characteristic Americans." *Twentieth-Century Literature: A Scholarly and Critical Journal* 30, no. 2–3 (Summer/Fall 1984): 175–180; "Sylvia Plath and Yaddo." *Ariel Ascending: Writings About Sylvia Plath*. Edited by Alexander Paul (1985); "'The Voice Inside': Translating the Poetry of T. Carmi." In *Translating Poetry: The Double Labyrinth*, edited by Daniel Weissbort (1989); *Two Decades of New Poets* (1983); "Women as Literary Innovators." (1976). Recording.

MONICA HILLER

SCHURZ, MARGARETHE MEYER
(1833–1876)

Credited with establishing the first kindergarten in the United States, Margarethe Meyer Schurz was born on August 27, 1833, in Hamburg, Germany, the youngest of four children. Her mother died at her birth. Her father, Heinrich Meyer, a prosperous, socially liberal Jewish merchant, opened his home to artists and intellectuals. Margarethe grew up immersed in progressive ideas, such as uniting the small autonomous German states into one democratic country.

When Friedrich Froebel came to Hamburg to lecture on his new theories of educating children, Margarethe and her older sister, Bertha, attended his classes, becoming kindergarten enthusiasts. Bertha and her husband, Johannes Ronge, an ex-priest and revolutionary, were forced to leave Hamburg after the 1848 German revolution failed. Settling in London, in an area populated by German refugees, they opened a kindergarten. In 1851, Margarethe came to assist.

Carl Schurz, also exiled from Germany for revolutionary activities, arrived in London the same year. Visiting his friend Johannes Ronge, he met Margarethe, whom he described in his *Reminiscences* as a girl "of fine stature, a curly head, something childlike in her beautiful features, and large, dark, truthful eyes." Carl and Margarethe fell in love at first sight and were married on July 5, 1852, sailing in August for America. They lived first in Pennsylvania, where their first child, Agatha, was born in 1853.

Margarethe, troubled by a lung ailment, returned to England with Agatha in 1855 for a water cure. Carl rejoined his family at the end of the year, taking them to Switzerland, where a second daughter, Marianne, was born. The family moved to Watertown, Wisconsin, in August 1856, where Carl's parents, sisters, several other Schurz relatives, and many German immigrants had settled.

In the fall of 1856, Margarethe Schurz opened a kindergarten in her living room for Agatha and four young cousins, teaching them the songs and games she had learned from Froebel. She soon moved her German-speaking kindergarten to the center of Watertown, so that more children could conveniently attend. Schurz continued as director until 1858, when she and Carl moved to Milwaukee. The Watertown kindergarten remained in operation—although moved to another building—until prejudice against the German language during World War I forced it to close.

Traveling to Boston with Carl in the fall of 1859, Schurz met Elizabeth Peabody and explained Froebel's principles to her, inspiring Peabody to set up the first English-speaking kindergarten in 1860 and to devote the rest of her life to promoting the kindergarten movement.

In 1867, when her third daughter, two-year-old Emma Savannah, died, Margarethe, her health weakened by grief, left for Europe with Agatha and Marianne. They stayed for over two years, returning to live in Washington, D.C., after Carl had been elected to the U.S. Senate. In 1871, a son, Carl Lincoln Schurz, was born and, in 1876, a second son, Herbert. Two days later, on March 15, 1876, Margarethe Meyer Schurz died at age forty-three.

BIBLIOGRAPHY

Baylor, Ruth M. *Elizabeth Palmer Peabody: Kindergarten Pioneer* (1965); Ellsworth, Edward. *The Froebelian Kindergarten Movement, 1850–1880: An International Crusade for Political and Social Progress* (1988); Fuess, Claude Moore. *Carl Schurz: Reformer* (1963); *NAW*; Obituary. *NYTimes*, March 19, 1876, 12:2; Quam, Dr. S. *First Kindergarten in the United States*. 3d ed. (1967); Shapiro, Michael Steven. *Child's Garden: The Kindergarten Movement from Froebel to Dewey* (1983); Snyder, Agnes. *Dauntless Women in Childhood Education, 1856–1931* (1972); Swart, Hannah Werwath. *Margarethe Meyer Schurz* (1989).

SUSAN FLEMING

SCHWARTZ, ANNA JACOBSON
(b. 1915)

Anna Jacobson Schwartz is "a leading authority on economic history, monetary economics, international monetary systems, and monetary statistics," according to the citation honoring her as a Distinguished Fellow of the American Economic Association (AEA) in 1993. Her voluminous publications in these areas have so far spanned a period of more than fifty years.

Anna Jacobson Schwartz was born on November 11, 1915, in New York City to Pauline (Shainmark) Jacobson and Hillel Jacobson, both of whom had immigrated to the United States from Eastern Europe during the first decade of the century. Hillel Jacobson was a manager and responsible for rabbinical supervision of the kosher meat department of Swift and Co. Anna was the third of five children, including an older sister and brother and two younger brothers. At Camp Achvah, a Hebrew camp associated with a Hebrew afternoon high school, which she attended from 1930 to 1936, she met Isaac Schwartz, whom she married in 1936. Isaac Schwartz was, until his retirement, controller for an importing firm. The Schwartzes have four children—Jonathan, Paula, Naomi, and Joel.

After graduation from Barnard College and beginning graduate study at the Graduate Faculties of Columbia University, from which she received her M.A. in 1935 and her Ph.D. in 1964, Schwartz worked briefly at the U.S. Department of Agriculture in 1936 and then at the Columbia University Social Science Research Council, from 1936 to 1941. She then joined the National Bureau of Economic Research, where she has done most of her research and writing and where she remains a research associate. She has had a number of part-time academic associations, including Baruch, Brooklyn, and HUNTER COLLEGE of the City University of New York and New York University, and has been adjunct professor of economics at the Graduate School and University Center of the City University of New York since 1986. One unusual interlude in her career occurred in 1981–1982, when she was staff director of the U.S. Gold Commission, a group of mostly political appointees charged with making recommendations on the future role of gold in the American monetary system.

Schwartz initially made her reputation in the field of quantitative economic history. That was the subject of her first journal article, in 1940, of a two-volume work coauthored with Arthur D. Gayer and Walt W. Rostow, published in 1953, and many papers since then. She is most widely known for three monumental books on American and British monetary history, coauthored with Milton Friedman. These books were described in the AEA citation as "the major force in reorienting the profession's thinking ... about the importance of the stock of money in cyclical fluctuations," to the point where she was described by a critic as "the high priestess of monetarism." A book consisting of appraisals of her work, edited by Michael D. Bordo, was published in 1989.

Schwartz has received many honors during her career. She was elected to Phi Beta Kappa in 1934 and received the Murray Fellowship awarded by Barnard College in 1934–1935. She was elected president of the Western Economic Association in 1987–1988, and has received honorary degrees from the University of Florida (1987), Stonehill College (1989), and Iona College (1992). The most recent honor was the citation by the American Economic Association in 1993.

Throughout her career, Anna Schwartz's work has been distinguished by meticulous attention to detail and unsurpassed knowledge of data and sources of information on monetary and financial matters. She is always helpful to scholars needing help with such questions and exceptionally generous in reading manuscripts sent to her for advice and criticism.

BIBLIOGRAPHY

American Economic Review 84, no. 4 (September 1994); Bordo, Michael D., ed. *Money, History, and International Finance: Essays in Honor of Anna J. Schwartz* (1989); Crittendon, Ann. "Baptism of Fire at Gold Panel." *NYTimes*, January 20, 1982; Schwartz, Anna. Conversations with author, and Curriculum Vitae. National Bureau of Economic Research, Cambridge, Mass.

ROBERT LIPSEY

SCHWARTZ, FELICE NIERENBERG (1925–1996)

Felice Nierenberg Schwartz, a pioneer advocate for the advancement of women in the workplace, was born in New York City on January 16, 1925, the daughter of Albert and Rose (Kaplan) Nierenberg. Her father owned Etched Products Corporation, a metal engraving and etching plant. Upon her father's death in 1951, Schwartz joined her brother Theodore in an effort to rescue the then-failing business. After three and a half years as vice president of production, years she would later refer to as the equivalent of a master's degree in manufacturing, Schwartz and her brother sold the business at a modest profit. Married to Irving Schwartz, a physician, in 1946, Schwartz spent the next eight years raising their three children, Cornelia Ann, Tony, and James Oliver.

The decade dedicated to saving the family business and raising her own family was bracketed by Schwartz's founding of two national organizations. In 1945, shortly after graduating from Smith College, Schwartz founded the National Scholarship Service and Fund for Negro Students (NSSFNS), an organization dedicated to opening the doors of higher education to African-American students. In 1962, when her youngest child entered nursery school, she founded Catalyst, an organization dedicated to opening the doors of business to women.

The founding of NSSFNS bore some of the same marks as the founding of Catalyst seventeen years later. After attending Knox School in Cooperstown, New York, Schwartz was "greatly relieved" to arrive at Smith College and see so many Jewish girls around. (At the time, Jewish students made up about seven and a half percent of her class at Smith.) The safety in numbers that allowed her to stop "being afraid to be Jewish" sensitized her to the loneliness, isolation, and fear of her few fellow African-American students, who made up only an extremely small percent of Smith's enrollment. After graduating from Smith, which she did in three years through an accelerated program,

Schwartz worked briefly for the National Association for the Advancement of Colored People. Within a year after graduation, she founded the NSSFNS. Her efforts to boost African-American enrollment focused on encouraging and enabling African-American students to apply to college rather than on confronting institutions of higher education with their continuing legacy of discrimination. To that end, she published *A Guide for Negro College Students to Interracial Colleges*, the first directory of its kind. In addition to identifying and cataloging the over $14 million in available scholarships, she established a fund to increase the funds available to African-American students.

The founding of Catalyst was similarly rooted in Schwartz's appreciation of options open to her but closed to others. During her years as a full-time mother, Schwartz was frustrated by how few educated family women believed, let alone shared her confidence, that they could return to the work world whenever they chose. Schwartz formed a board of five college presidents, Thomas C. Mendendahll of Smith College, Margaret Clapp of Wellesley College, Paul Ward of Sarah Lawrence College, Douglas Knight of Lawrence College, and C. Easton Rothwell of Mills College, and began operating Catalyst out of her suburban home in Westchester County, New York. Its original mission was "to bring to our country's needs the unused abilities of intelligent women who want to combine work and family." As with NSSFNS, Schwartz was determined to put Catalyst's definition "in terms that were acceptable and non-threatening."

In the three decades in which she served as its president, Catalyst grew and expanded its focus to respond to emerging trends in the marketplace as well as in women's lives. In its first decade, Catalyst developed a nationwide network of 250 resource centers and focused its efforts on counseling women who wished to combine family duties with part-time work. Concentrating on placing women in the public sector, the organization pioneered several job-sharing pilot projects in which two women shared a full-time job. In 1972, with her colleagues at Catalyst, Margaret H. Schifter and Susan S. Gillotti, she coauthored *How to Go to Work When Your Husband Is Against It, Your Children Aren't Old Enough*, and *There's Nothing You Can Do Anyhow*.

In the 1970s and 1980s, responding to a changing economy in which increasing numbers of women were forced to seek full-time work, Catalyst's focus shifted from the public sector to the private sector and from counseling to research and advocacy. Catalyst began promoting the participation of women in corporations and their recruitment on corporate boards.

These years saw the production of numerous groundbreaking studies on child care, parental leave, and dual-career families. Schwartz became a widely respected expert on work and family issues, lauded by both business executives and feminists, and Catalyst increasingly served in an advisory capacity to major companies and firms.

Schwartz's final years at Catalyst were colored by the national controversy ignited over an article she published in 1989 in the *Harvard Business Review*. Schwartz intended the article, "Management Women and the New Facts of Life," as a call to action to corporate leaders to remove the barriers to productivity and advancement still facing female managers. Among the barriers she highlighted was the failure of corporations to exhibit the flexibility necessary to accommodate different types of women within the corporate environment. Schwartz proposed two ends of a spectrum along which corporate women fall: the "career primary" woman and "career family" woman. She suggested that creating policies to accommodate the "career family" woman was good business. As a result of a *New York Times* article on her idea headlined "'Mommy Career Track' Sets Off a Furor," Schwartz became known as the "mommy track author" and the subject of hundreds of articles on the "mommy track controversy." Ironically, after twenty-seven years dedicated to the advancement of women, the founder of Catalyst came under attack for establishing barriers to women's advancement. In *Breaking with Tradition: Women and Work, The New Facts of Life*, Schwartz grounded the often painful controversy surrounding her article in "the conspiracy of silence" on the part of feminists as well as business that too often "conceals the experience of women in business" and prevents problems from getting addressed.

One year after the publication of the *New York Times* article on the "mommy track," Felice Nierenberg Schwartz was featured in *Fortune* magazine's sixtieth anniversary issue as one of 126 world leaders, thinkers, and trendsetters. Honorary degrees were bestowed on her by Pace University (1980), Smith College (1981), Marietta College (1989), and Chatham College (1990). Schwartz left Catalyst in 1993 and died at her home on February 8, 1996, just one month after completing her third book, *The Armchair Activist: Simple Yet Powerful Ways to Fight the Radical Right*.

SELECTED WORKS BY FELICE NIERENBERG SCHWARTZ

The Armchair Activist: Simple Yet Powerful Ways to Fight the Radical Right (1996); *Breaking with Tradition: Women and Work, The New Facts of Life* (1992); *A Guide for Negro College*

Students to Interracial Colleges (n.d.); *How to Go to Work When Your Husband Is Against It, Your Children Aren't Old Enough, and There's Nothing You Can Do Anyhow*, with Margaret H. Schifter and Susan S. Gillotti (1972); "Management Women and the New Facts of Life." *Harvard Business Review* (January/February 1989).

BIBLIOGRAPHY

Current Biography Yearbook (1993); Hopkins, Ellen. "Who Is Felice Schwartz and Why Is She Saying Those Terrible Things about Us?" *Working Woman* 15 (October 1990): 116+; Lewin, Tamar. "'Mommy Track' Sets Off a Furor." *NYTimes*, March 8, 1989; Obituary. *NYTimes*, February 10, 1996, 52; Schwartz, Felice Nierenberg. Smith Centennial Study. Oral History Project, Transcript recorded September 13, 1971. Smith College Archives, Northampton, Mass.; *Who's Who of American Women* (1992–1993).

GAIL TWERSKY REIMER

SCHWEITZER, REBECCA
(1880–1938)

Rebecca Schweitzer had a heart as big as her pocketbook. She was born Vera Garbovitsky on April 7, 1880, to Hirsch and Hannah (Levine) Garbovitsky in Kremai, Russia. Her wealthy parents provided private tutoring for their daughter. Eighteen years later, Rebecca married Peter Schweitzer in 1898, in Russia. The couple had two sons (Louis and William) and two daughters (Sarah Grinberg and Elizabeth Licht). In 1904, the Schweitzers immigrated to the United States, where Peter created Peter J. Schweitzer, Inc. The firm eventually became the largest importer and exporter of cigarette paper in the United States. Schweitzer, Inc., had factories in Elizabeth, New Jersey, and Vanduss, France.

The success of Schweitzer, Inc. allowed the Schweitzers to become leading Jewish American philanthropists. Both Rebecca and Peter were dedicated Zionists. In 1921, they provided the initial capital through HADASSAH to build the first hospital in Tiberias, Palestine. Nine years later, in May 1930, work was completed. The hospital was named the Peter J. Schweitzer Memorial Hospital in his memory (he had died in 1923).

In addition to her support for Hadassah, Rebecca Schweitzer contributed to other Zionist organizations, including Keren Hayesod [Foundation Fund] when it was created in 1920 to provide all Jews with a means to further the goal of a Jewish state through monetary contributions. In 1920 the Women's International Zionist Organization (WIZO) established an avenue

Rebecca Schweitzer was an international philanthropist who made key contributions to the Zionist cause. [American Jewish Archives]

for female participation in Keren Hayesod through the "Jewel Fund." The concept was that women who were not as wealthy as Rebecca Schweitzer could donate their jewelry. Proceeds from the sale of the jewelry would be divided between Keren Hayesod (two-thirds) and WIZO (one-third). This idea eventually led to the creation of a separate women's division involved with fund-raising campaigns. Schweitzer's interest in Zionism extended beyond philanthropy to politics. She attended the Fourteenth World Zionist Congress in Vienna in 1925 as a delegate.

Schweitzer was also a principal shareholder in the Palestine Development Council, sponsored through money from the Jewish Colonial Trust. The Jewish Colonial Trust was created with the intention of becoming a large financial clearinghouse (bank) to back projects that would further the Zionist dream of a Jewish state.

Rebecca Schweitzer's philanthropic work crossed international boundaries. In 1926, the French government made her a knight in the Legion of Honor; two years later, she received honorary French citizenship. Both of these acts resulted from her philanthropy in Malancene, France. The success of Schweitzer, Inc., also probably prompted the French government to make these gestures.

After her husband's death, beginning in 1925 Schweitzer played an integral part as president of the Home of the Daughters of Jacob. She also served as a charter member of the American Friends to the Jewish Blind of Palestine. In that year, Schweitzer organized and became the first president of the Palestine Lighthouse for the Blind's New York City chapter.

Rebecca Schweitzer died on March 20, 1938, at Mount Sinai Hospital after an emergency operation. She was fifty-seven years old at the time of her death, but had made contributions to the financial well-being of the yet unformed Israeli state that would be felt by many future generations.

BIBLIOGRAPHY

AJYB 40: 391; Obituary. *NYTimes*, March 21, 1938; *WWIAJ* (1926, 1938).

MORDECAI MOORE

SCHWIMMER, ROSIKA (1877–1948)

Rosika Schwimmer was a leader in the international pacifist and feminist movements, a passionate and forceful advocate of pacifism in a time of war. Schwimmer's career soared during the early twentieth century, but, by the 1920s, she was caught in the backlash of antifeminism and anti-Semitism that swept the United States. A complicated and fiery public figure, Schwimmer remained resolute in her political and ideological commitments throughout her controversial career.

Born on September 11, 1877, in Budapest, Hungary, to Max and Bertha (Katscher) Schwimmer, Rosika Schwimmer grew up in a secular, middle-class Jewish family. She married Paul Bédy, a journalist, in 1911, but the couple divorced after two years. At age eighteen, when her father's business failed, Schwimmer took a job as a bookkeeper. As a young clerical employee, she began organizing women workers. She founded the National Association of Women Office Workers in 1897, the Hungarian Association of Working Women in 1903, and the Hungarian Council of Women a year later. An advocate of women's economic, social, and political equality, Schwimmer earned a reputation as a leading proponent of women's rights in Hungary before she reached age thirty. Schwimmer participated in a host of political campaigns, lobbying for marriage reform and birth control and campaigning against child labor. She organized the Hungarian Feminist Association, which succeeded in winning woman suffrage in 1920. She also edited the Hungarian feminist journal *A Nö* [The woman] and published works of fiction.

Schwimmer attracted international attention when she addressed the 1904 International Women's Congress in Berlin, Germany. Later, she became press secretary of the International Woman Suffrage Alliance and moved to London, England, to fulfill her duties.

Schwimmer was living in London when Britain entered World War I in 1914. In addition to her feminist activities, Schwimmer had always been an ardent pacifist. When the European countries declared war, she devoted all of her energies to opposing the war and urging a peaceful settlement. She issued a proposal calling for the neutral nations to meet and formulate a plan for mediation. Shortly after the war began, she traveled to the United States and met with President Woodrow Wilson and Secretary of State William Jennings Bryan, attempting (without success) to convince them to convene a United States–sponsored neutral mediation conference.

Schwimmer spent the early war years in the United States, traveling the country as a lecturer and political activist. Already a well-known public figure, Schwimmer addressed a wide range of constituencies, including Jewish and feminist groups. Carrie Chapman Catt, leader of the American suffrage movement and president of the International Woman Suffrage Alliance, recruited Schwimmer as a speaker and organizer in the campaign for woman suffrage in America. While promoting suffrage, Schwimmer continued to broadcast her opposition to war. In 1915, Schwimmer helped to create the Women's Peace Party, becoming the organization's international secretary. At the Hague Congress of Women held later that year, Schwimmer convinced the conference to send representatives to meet with leaders of both neutral and belligerent nations and encourage peaceful mediation. Jane Addams led the delegation to the belligerents, and Schwimmer took responsibility for meeting with leaders of the neutral countries.

When international leaders refused to take action on mediation, Schwimmer began making plans for an unofficial, privately sponsored international meeting. In November 1915, Henry Ford, the leading American automobile manufacturer, agreed to back Schwimmer's plan. The Ford Neutral Mediation Conference convened in Stockholm on February 8, 1916, with Schwimmer serving as expert adviser. The American delegation sailed to Stockholm on the *Oscar II*, popularly known as the Peace Ship. The American press published harsh editorials about the Peace Ship Expedition, ridiculing the project and its goals, criticizing the female delegates, and attacking Schwimmer's leadership. While the press issued its negatively biased reports, the mission suffered several setbacks. Many delegates resented Schwimmer's authoritative tactics and accused her of financial mismanagement. Henry Ford returned home before the ship reached its destination. As the criticism against her mounted, Schwimmer resigned her position as adviser to the expedition. Schwimmer was indeed a stubborn and uncompromising leader. She focused entirely on the ultimate goal of ending the war and displayed little patience for others who differed with her approach. While her commitment to pacifist goals never wavered, her leadership style alienated many participants, and the press portrayal of her severely damaged her public reputation.

Schwimmer remained in Europe following the Ford Conference and emerged as an active political player after World War I. In November 1918, when her native Hungary became a democratic republic, Schwimmer assumed a post as minister to Switzerland. However, the democratic government lasted only five months, overthrown by Béla Kun's Communist regime. The new Communist government persecuted Schwimmer and prohibited her from leaving the country. In 1920, she succeeded in escaping to Vienna.

One year later, Rosika Schwimmer gained readmission to the United States. Unlike her first visit, her arrival in 1921 was not met with speaking engagements and public meetings. Schwimmer found her public career destroyed by negative publicity and her former allies in the feminist and suffrage movements unwilling to risk the political consequences of association with her. She was attacked by antifeminist and anticommunist forces. Several right-wing organizations as well as congressional committees accused her of having served as a German spy during the war. At the same time, they charged her with being a Bolshevik agent. In the wake of the right-wing backlash in post–World War I America, Schwimmer was attacked for her feminism, pacifism, and political radicalism. With xenophobia and anti-Semitism on the rise, she also faced discrimination as a foreigner and a Jew. Jewish groups were hardly more welcoming of Rosika

Rosika Schwimmer began her public career in her native Hungary as a labor organizer and suffragist, then entered the international arena as a pacifist with the outbreak of World War I. The disastrous "Peace Ship" expedition severely damaged her reputation, and she was ultimately denied United States citizenship. [Rosika Schwimmer Collection, New York Public Library]

Schwimmer. Following the Peace Ship Expedition and Ford's subsequent publication of anti-Semitic literature, the Jewish press had printed several stories indicating that Schwimmer had tricked Ford into sponsoring the Peace Ship, thus inciting his anti-Semitic hatred.

Schwimmer petitioned for American citizenship in 1928, but a Chicago federal district court denied her request, citing her refusal to bear arms in defense of the country. As a pacifist, Schwimmer would not agree to the clause in the citizenship application that required such an oath. In 1929, the United States Supreme Court upheld the lower court decision. The Court declared her unworthy of citizenship, not only because she refused to bear arms (despite the fact that women had never been required to fight and she was well beyond the age of conscription), but also because she ardently advocated world government and made her living as a public activist and speaker. Schwimmer never received American citizenship, but lived in the United States as a resident alien until her death in 1948.

Schwimmer continued to work in the feminist and pacifist movements, although she never succeeded in reviving her public reputation or career. She joined Mary Ritter Beard in planning a World Center for Women's Archives. She also cooperated with her close friend and leading pacifist Lola Maverick Lloyd in sponsoring a Campaign for World Government. Schwimmer retained the ultimate goal of achieving world peace through the creation of a world federation of governments. As an acknowledgment of her work, Schwimmer's associates awarded her a privately sponsored World Peace Prize. In 1948 she received a nomination for the Nobel Peace Prize.

Schwimmer remained committed to the causes of feminism and pacifism throughout her life. She could be uncompromising and stubborn in pursuing her political goals, traits that earned her devoted allies but also alienated many coworkers. She emerged as one of the most powerful political players in the international feminist and pacifist movements, but she also paid the price for living in an era of right-wing backlash, xenophobia, and anti-Semitism. Despite her many challenges and setbacks, Rosika Schwimmer never abandoned her unshakable devotion to achieving the goals of world peace and equality.

Rosika Schwimmer died on August 3, 1948.

BIBLIOGRAPHY

The American Jewish Woman, 1654–1980, s.v. "Rosika Schwimmer"; AJYB, 51:524; American Reformers; BEOAJ; DAB, Supp. 4; EJ; Hershey, Burnet. The Odyssey of Henry Ford and the Great Peace Ship (1967); Kraft, Barbara S. The Peace Ship: Henry Ford's Pacifist Adventure in the First World War (1978); Lee, Albert. Henry Ford and the Jews (1980); NAW; Rosika Schwimmer, World Patriot (1937. Revised 1947); Obituary. NYTimes, August 4, 1948, 21:1; Schwimmer, Rosika. Papers. Hoover Institution, Stanford University, Stanford, Calif., and Rosika Schwimmer-Lola Maverick Lloyd Collection, Rare Books and Manuscripts Division, New York Public Library, NYC; Steinson, Barbara J. American Women's Activism in World War I (1982); UJE; United States v. Rosika Schwimmer, 279 US 644 (1929); Wenger, Beth S. "Radical Politics in a Reactionary Age: The Unmaking of Rosika Schwimmer, 1914–1930." Journal of Women's History 2, no. 2 (Fall 1990): 66–99; Wiltsher, Anne. Most Dangerous Women: Feminist Peace Campaigns of the Great War (1985); WWIAJ (1928, 1938).

BETH WENGER

SCOTT, MIRIAM FINN (c. 1882–1944)

Miriam Finn Scott, a child diagnostician and specialist in parent education, advocated that "the soil of a child's life was his home" and that parents could ensure the proper growth of their children if only they transformed their homes into "gardens." Scott's belief that good parenting was not instinctual fueled her desire to provide advice to parents in child rearing. She mourned the loss to humanity of contributions that could have been made by children had their parents enabled them to explore and develop all of their inherent qualities.

Born in Vilna, Russia, around 1882, she immigrated to the United States in 1893 with her parents, Moses and Gittel (Selechnyck) Finn. Motivated by the need to support her family, the young Miriam began working at a roof playground for children in 1898. In 1899, she began to manage the roof playground at the University Settlement, an institution established in 1886 to ease the adjustment of immigrants into New York City's Lower East Side. The foundations of her future career were formulated at the settlement as she embarked on a mission to better the world by contributing to the growth and development of its children. She married Leroy Scott on June 24, 1904. He was an author who devoted his life to writing after leaving his position as assistant headworker at the University Settlement in 1903. He was born in Fairmount, Indiana, on May 11, 1875, and died tragically on July 21, 1929, by drowning. The Scotts had three children: Helen (Waltz Jr.), Hilda (Lass), and David Scott.

From 1903 to 1906, Miriam Scott, prompted by her concern for the plight of the children of the urban poor, worked for the Speyer School. Initially, this school was established so that the faculty and students of Columbia University's Teachers College could examine and test new educational methods. However, one of the terms of Mr. and Mrs. James Speyer's gift to enlarge the early twentieth-century quarters of the school was that the school's role be expanded to that of a neighborhood settlement in Harlem. Scott continued her work for the University Settlement at this location. According to Scott, the chief objective of this settlement was to reach as many families as possible and make them recognize the need for substituting degrading influences from their environments with forces that would enable them to live better lives. Therefore, clubs and activities were set up for children as well as for adults. Miriam Finn Scott was the director of the "children's and girl's club work." "Children's work" was carried on each afternoon and consisted of a playroom for children age one to eleven. Scott's commitment to the education of children through play led to the introduction into the playroom of games, which were carefully chosen for their educational as well as recreational value. A small supervisory staff was present to ensure that the children played honestly and unselfishly, learning to be considerate of one another. Girl's club work provided classes for young women in cooking, sewing, and home nursing. In an entry in the *Speyer News* from 1904, Scott commented on the success of the settlement at the Speyer School, remarking that large numbers of people not only took advantage of its services, but also volunteered to help promote many of its programs.

While working for the University Settlement, Scott also attended HUNTER COLLEGE, receiving her bachelor's degree in 1903. She did postgraduate work in the field of educational psychology at Columbia University, New York State University, Moscow University, Zurich University, the University of Bern, and the University of Berlin. Her advanced education and confidence in her ability to make independent contributions to the field of parent education led her to found a clinic in 1915 called the Children's Garden. This institution, located originally at 125 East 57th Street in Manhattan and later in her home at 208 East 16th Street, became one of the first laboratory clinics where the relationship between parents and their children was explored. Scott's approach centered upon the idea that children's problems were often the result of the improper attitudes and habits of their parents. As a result, she worked intently with parents in an attempt to make them recognize where improvements in their own behavior could be made so that they, in turn, could aid their children.

Scott's suggestions to parents can be found in her books, *How to Know Your Child* (1915) and *Meeting Your Child's Problems* (1922). Her substantial observations became even more widely available to colleagues and parents throughout the United States and the world via translations of *How to Know Your Child* into Russian, German, and French, through lectures she gave at universities such as the University of Moscow (summer of 1928), and through radio broadcasts.

To assist parents in understanding the natures of their children Scott also became the director of the School for Parents at the YMHA (Young Men's Hebrew Association, today the 92nd Street Y). There she offered courses entitled "Practical Guidance for Parents" and "Preparation for Parenthood." Her course descriptions invited the married as well as the unmarried to attend, reflecting her desire to see all adults develop qualities necessary for fostering harmonious marriages with sound foundations. She hoped to make the world better for children through the education of their parents, while conveying the feeling that parenthood could become "the most enriching and inspiring business in life." Unfortunately, by the spring of 1939, a limited enrollment forced the YMHA to cancel her classes. She did, however, continue to work at the Children's Garden until her death on January 6, 1944.

SELECTED WORKS BY MIRIAM FINN SCOTT

How to Know Your Child (1915); *Meeting Your Child's Problems* (1922).

BIBLIOGRAPHY

Cremin, Lawrence. *A History of Teachers College* (1954): 104–106; Obituary. *New York Times*, January 7, 1944; Scheuer, Jeffrey. *Legacy of Light: University Settlement's First Century* (1985); *Speyer News 2*, No. 19 (1903–1904) [entry March 8, 1904]: 3, and [entry June 4, 1904]: 3–4, and *Teachers College Record 3* (1902): 1–12. Special Collections. Teachers College, Columbia University, NYC; *UJE*; University Settlement, NYC. Archives. State Historical Society of Wisconsin, University of Wisconsin, Madison; *WWIAJ* (1938); *WWWIA 2*; Young Men's Hebrew Association. Correspondence, and *Education Bulletin* (1937–1938). YMHA Archives. 92nd Street Y, NYC.

MARJORIE LEHMAN

SEAMAN, SYLVIA BERNSTEIN (1900–1995)

"I'm still capable of marching. I marched sixty years ago. I just hope my granddaughter doesn't have to march into the next century." So said Sylvia Bernstein Seaman to a *New York Times* reporter on the occasion of the tenth anniversary of the 1970 women's Strike for Equality and the coinciding sixtieth anniversary of woman suffrage. During her long life, she was not only a witness to but a catalyst for the dramatic changes in women's roles and status over the course of this century.

Sylvia Bernstein was born on November 8, 1900, to Nathan Bernstein and Fanny (Bleat) Bernstein. She had one sibling, a younger brother Steven. She was active in the women's movement from a very young age and first marched for suffrage in 1915. While a student at Cornell University, she marched in the celebratory parades of 1920 when the Nineteenth Amendment was passed and was arrested for publicly wearing riding britches. This was, however, only the beginning of her career as a feminist. After spending several years teaching high school English in New York City, and marrying chemist William Seaman in 1925, she began writing professionally.

From marching for woman suffrage in 1915 to her groundbreaking book on breast cancer
fifty years later to How to Be a Jewish Grandmother, *Sylvia Seaman candidly and courageously*
explored a wide range of feminist issues. She is shown here at a women's rights march in August of 1980.
[Bettye Lane]

Her first books were novels written in collaboration with her college roommate Frances Schwartz and published under the pen name Francis Sylvin. In 1965, she published *Always a Woman: What Every Woman Should Know About Breast Cancer,* a book based on her own experience of a mastectomy. This was the first book written about breast cancer by someone outside the medical profession. The topic, about which Seaman also wrote magazine and newspaper articles, was rarely discussed publicly in the early 1960s. In a 1980 interview, Seaman recalled, "It was considered daring at the time, but it changed attitudes, I think. . . . As for me, I got so much fan mail on that book, you'd have thought I was a movie star."

How to Be a Jewish Grandmother (1979) is a humorous book of advice and anecdotes. Any topic was fair game for Seaman: vasectomies, daughters-in-law, even her own drinking habits. Besides the discussion of what it meant to be Jewish, a woman, and a grandmother, the book was an indication of the changes American culture had undergone in this century. *How to Be a Jewish Grandmother* is a record of the shifting social order of the 1970s, presented from the point of view of one who had herself rebelled against the norms of an earlier generation, but who may have been just a little bit bewildered by the transformations she was witnessing.

Seaman was not the only political activist in her family. Her son, Gideon Seaman, and daughter-in-law, Barbara Seaman, coauthored *Women and the Crisis in Sex Hormones* in 1977; Barbara was also a co-founder of the National Women's Health Network. It was she who had encouraged Sylvia to write *Always a Woman.*

It was breast cancer that many years later caused Sylvia Bernstein Seaman's death, on January 8, 1995.

**SELECTED WRITINGS BY
SYLVIA BERNSTEIN SEAMAN**

Always a Woman: What Every Woman Should Know About Breast Cancer (1965); *How to Be a Jewish Grandmother* (1979).

BIBLIOGRAPHY

Dullea, Georgia. "For Family's Three Generations of Feminists, A Memorable Day." *NYTimes,* August 25, 1980; Saxon, Wolfgang. "Sylvia B. Seaman, 94: A Writer and a Suffragist." *NYTimes,* January 11, 1995.

KAREN BEKKER

SEGAL, LORE (b. 1928)

Lore Segal is a respected writer whose unique background informs much of her work. Born on March 8, 1928, the only child of solidly middle-class parents in Vienna—Lore's father, Ignatz Groszmann, was chief accountant at a bank; her mother, Franzi (Stern), was a homemaker—she experienced a dramatic change when, shortly after Hitler's annexation of Austria, she was one of a group of five hundred Jewish schoolchildren quickly sent to England. For the next thirteen years, she lived in several countries and with many different families—earning a B.A. from Bedford College, London, along the way—before achieving her independence and settling in New York. In 1961, Lore Groszmann married David Segal, an editor; they had two children, Beatrice and Jacob, before David's sudden death in 1970.

Segal's experiences as a refugee formed the basis of her first significant publication, the novelistic autobiography *Other People's Houses* (1964). As the book had been serialized in *The New Yorker*, Segal began to be noticed. She received a Guggenheim Fellowship and a grant from the corporation at Yaddo. Her second novel, *Lucinella* (1976), a fantasy/satire, is set at a writers' retreat similar to Yaddo. Since then, Segal has held teaching appointments at Columbia University, Princeton University, Bennington College, Sarah Lawrence College, the University of Illinois at Chicago, and Ohio State University. She has published another novel, short stories, several books of translation, and a number of books for children.

Segal's most important work to date is her third full-length text, *Her First American* (1985). Although considered a novel, it is, in fact, a sequel to *Other People's Houses*; Lore Groszmann has been renamed Ilka Weissnix, but Carter Bayoux appears in both books under the same name. A black intellectual, Carter is a minor figure toward the end of *Other People's Houses*, but he becomes the central focus of *Her First American*. Carter acclimatizes Ilka to the American way of life, in all its peculiarities. While there is an idyllic interracial retreat in the middle part of the novel, the ending is one of disillusionment. Carter's blackness and Ilka's Jewishness become problematic, not so much for them as for those around them. *Her First American* is a masterful text, and one that is becoming increasingly acknowledged.

One of Segal's primary interests is in storytelling itself, as seen in her translations and children's books. Segal has translated books of the Bible, which she sees as adventure stories, as well as fairy tales from Grimm. Her books for children are in a contemporary fairy-tale mode; her award-winning *Tell Me a Mitzi* (1970)

features stories she had told her own children, all of which begin, "Once upon a time there was a Mitzi." Storytelling also seems to be a theme in Segal's current project, a novel entitled *An Absence of Cousins*, which again draws on her experiences as an ex-refugee. A number of short stories related to this project, including one with that title, have appeared in *The New Yorker*. Judging from these excerpts, such as the O. Henry Award–winning story "The Reverse Bug," the novel may bring Segal the reading public she deserves. Lore Segal is a gifted writer whose finely wrought prose brings to light a unique personal story, a story inseparable from her Jewish heritage.

SELECTED WORKS BY LORE SEGAL

FOR ADULTS
Her First American (1985); *Lucinella* (1976); *Other People's Houses* (1964).

FOR CHILDREN
The Story of Old Mrs. Brubeck and How She Looked for Trouble and Where She Found Him (1981); *Tell Me a Mitzi* (1970); *Tell Me a Trudy* (1977).

TRANSLATIONS
The Book of Adam to Moses (1987); *The Juniper Tree and Other Tales from Grimm* (1973); *The Story of King Saul and King David* (1991).

BIBLIOGRAPHY

Berger, Alan L. "Jewish Identity and Jewish Destiny, the Holocaust in Refugee Writing: Lore Segal and Karen Gershon." *Studies in American Jewish Literature* 11 (1992): 82–95; Cavenaugh, Philip. "The Present Is a Foreign Country: Lore Segal's Fiction." *Contemporary Literature* 34 (1993): 475–511; Earnest, Cathy. "A Conversation." *Another Chicago Magazine* 20 (1989): 153–167; Meyer, Adam. "Lore Segal." In *Jewish American Women Writers*, edited by Ann R. Shapiro (1994): 387–396.

ADAM MEYER

SEGAL, VIVIENNE (1897–1992)

A talented singer/actor and superb comedian, Vivienne Segal enjoyed a lengthy career. She was best known for her role as Vera Simpson, the older woman in love with the "heel," Joey (played by Gene Kelly), in the 1940 Rodgers and Hart musical *Pal Joey*. It was in this musical that Segal introduced her showstopping number, "Bewitched, Bothered and Bewildered," a song that described her love for the younger man. The show catapulted Kelly to fame and gave Segal the chance to get away from the sweet ingenue roles that she had been playing.

Vivenne Segal was born on April 19, 1897, in Philadelphia, Pennsylvania, the daughter of prominent physician Bernard Segal and Paula (Hahn) Segal. Vivienne and her younger sister Louise were encouraged by their mother to pursue show business careers. Segal went to school at the Sisters of Mercy Academy, where she studied music and drama. After singing in several amateur productions for the Philadelphia Opera Society, she appeared on Broadway in 1915 at the Casino Theater in the Schubert production of *The Blue Paradise*, which established her in New York. It was rumored that her well-to-do father underwrote the cost of the production; however, Segal had the looks and talent to continue on her own. After touring with this show for two years, she returned to New York and appeared in many reviews, musicals, and operettas, including *Tangerine* (1921), *The Yankee Princess* (1922), *Adrienne* (1923), the *1924 Ziegfeld Follies*, *The Desert Song* (1926), and *The Three Musketeers* (1928).

In the 1930s and 1940s, Segal's most notable roles were as Nanette in *No, No Nanette* (1938), the countess in *I Married an Angel* (1938), and Queen Morgan Le Fay in *A Connecticut Yankee* (1943). Then in 1952, she appeared in the revival of *Pal Joey*, for which she won the Donaldson Award and the New York Drama Critics Award for best actress. Segal performed in early sound shorts and feature films from 1929 to 1934, on the radio in the 1930s, and on television in the 1950s. Her last public performance was in *Alfred Hitchcock Presents* in 1961. Her long career demonstrated her staying power in show business and her ability to adapt to different media.

Segal married twice. In 1923, she eloped with twice-divorced actor Robert D. Ames. Their marriage ended in 1926. In 1950, Segal married Hubbell Robinson, Jr., a television executive who died in 1974.

Vivienne Segal lived in Beverly Hills until December 29, 1992, when she died of heart failure at age ninety-five.

BIBLIOGRAPHY

AJYB 24:201; Boardman, Gerald. *Oxford Companion to American Theater* (1992); Folkart, Burt A. "Vivienne Segal: Veteran of Musical Theater Roles." *Los Angeles Times*, December 31, 1992, B6; Grimes, William. "Vivienne Segal, 95, a Stage Star in Roles, Sweet to Cynical, Is Dead." *NYTimes*, December 30, 1992, A13:1; Harris, Dale. "Unbothered and Bewitching." *Guardian* 2, January 2, 1993, 24:2; Hewitt, Pamela. *Notable Women in the American Theatre* (1989); Parker, John. *Who's Who in the Theatre* (1961), and *Who Was Who in the Theatre*. Vol. 4 (1978); Rigdon, Walter. *The Biographical Encyclopaedia and Who's Who of the American Theatre* (1966), and *Notable Names in the American Theatre* (1976); Segal, Vivienne. Scrapbook. New York Public Library for the Performing Arts at Lincoln Center, NYC; *WWIAJ* (1926, 1928).

BONNIE STARK

SEID, RUTH *see* SINCLAIR, JO

SEIXAS NATHAN, GRACE (1752–1831)

Grace Seixas was born in Stratford, Connecticut, on November 11, 1752, into a family that loved both America and Jewishness and encouraged learning for all of its members. Sister of literary, skilled, and learned men, she herself evinced a lifelong love of writing. She began writing poetry as a young woman and continued this pursuit until her death, although none of her work was published during her lifetime.

Many of her poems reflect Jewish themes, such as "Reflections on Passing Our New Burial Ground," written on the occasion of the establishment of a new cemetery by New York's Congregation Shearith Israel in 1829. She also maintained a lively correspondence. A favorite correspondent was her niece Sarah Abigail Seixas, who later married Israel Baer Kursheedt. Through her letters to Sarah, Seixas Nathan reveals her concern for the health and well-being of the members of the extended family, as well as a vivacious sense of humor. She was especially attached to her brother Gershom, longtime hazan for New York's Congregation Shearith Israel. Five years after his death at age seventy, she continued to wear the colors of "deep mourning" in memory of "our Blessed Sainted reverend relative."

In addition to her literary gifts, Seixas Nathan shared her brothers' ardent patriotism. Gershom, Benjamin, and Abraham Seixas had all been strong supporters of the Patriot cause during the Revolution. She wrote of herself, during the War of 1812: "I am so true an American—so warm a Patriot that I hold these mighty Armies—and their proud-arrogant-presumptuous and over-powering Nation as Beings that we have Conquered and *shall* Conquer again—this I persuade myself will be so. And may the Lord of Battles grant that it may be so" (November 14, 1814).

Grace Seixas married Simon Nathan, a merchant and like-minded supporter of the Patriot cause, in 1780. Their marriage was a long and happy one. They had one child, (Isaac Mendes) Seixas Nathan, born in 1785.

Grace Seixas Nathan died in New York on November 8, 1831.

BIBLIOGRAPHY

De Sola Pool, David. "Some Letters of Grace Seixas Nathan." *Publications of the American Jewish Historical Society* 37 (1947): 203–211; Marcus, Jacob Rader. *The American Jewish Woman: A Documentary History* (1981), and *United States Jewry, 1776–1985*. Vol. I (1989).

HOLLY SNYDER

SELIGSBERG, ALICE LILLIE (1873–1940)

Alice Lillie Seligsberg, an American Zionist, social worker, civic leader, and HADASSAH president, gave of herself to the orphaned and needy of her people, and influenced thousands of Jewish girls and women for more than a generation. It was in her love for Judaism, and by its extension, Zionism, that Seligsberg made her greatest contributions.

She was born to Louis and Lillian (Wolff) Seligsberg on August 8, 1873. She had one sister and one brother, and the family lived in New York City. Among the first graduates of Barnard College, Seligsberg did graduate work at Columbia University and in Berlin, Germany. It was to poor and underprivileged children that Seligsberg gave her earliest energies. Beginning her career as a social worker and youth leader, she formed a girls' club on the Lower East Side, where she had a great influence upon the members.

After serving as a club worker at the Hebrew Sheltering Guardian Society, Seligsberg established Fellowship House, an institution that placed poor and orphaned children in suitable homes and positions. She was its president from 1913 to 1918.

Seligsberg was responsible for many original contributions to the field of social services. For example, she recommended that the boarding-out department of the Hebrew Sheltering Guardian Society become independent of any institutional control, responsible only to the directors of the parent program. According to experts in the field, this idea completely changed the course of Jewish child care, not only in New York, but throughout the country as well. From 1922 until 1936, Seligsberg served as executive director of the Jewish Children's Clearing Bureau, which placed children in homes and/or orphanages based on the needs of the individual child.

As she grew older, Seligsberg realized that the Ethical Culture Movement, with which her family had been affiliated, did not offer her what she needed. She turned to Rabbi Mordecai Kaplan of the Society for the Advancement of Judaism for help in her return to Judaism. She began studying the Bible and the

Her work with HADASSAH *was only one of the ways social worker Alice Seligsberg contributed to the well-being of orphaned and underprivileged children throughout her life. [Hadassah Archives]*

Prophets, Hebrew, and Jewish history. She also began lively correspondence with Rabbi Judah Magnes, Felix Adler, HENRIETTA SZOLD, and JESSIE SAMPTER, among others. She discussed her philosophical ideas and perceptions about Judaism and its place in her life. According to ROSE JACOBS, "She found in the wisdom of the Jewish sages and prophets something her soul had been seeking, and she identified herself completely with the Jewish community." The culmination of this identification was in her work with Hadassah, the Women's Zionist Organization of America. In 1913, Seligsberg joined the original study group and thus began a lifelong association with Szold, Zionism, and Hadassah.

In 1917, Seligsberg helped with the organization of the first group of Hadassah nurses being sent to Palestine. By the time this group was ready to leave, in June of 1918, she was asked to take the place of E.W. Lewin-Epstein, its business administrator, who had suffered a heart attack.

After a year in Palestine, David de Sola Pool, of the American Joint Distribution Committee, asked Seligsberg to head the Orphans Committee, which was formed to aid Jewish victims of war. But her work in Palestine extended beyond her daily involvement with the Orphans Committee—she also served as a board member of the Institute for the Blind in Jerusalem. While in Palestine, Seligsberg also found time to write several articles and reports about Jewish orphans and other areas of social work in Palestine.

After returning to New York in 1920, Seligsberg immediately resumed her career in social work. In 1922, she was named executive director of the Jewish Children's Clearing Bureau of New York, and, from 1921 to 1923, she served as the national president of Hadassah. Upon completion of her presidency, she became the Palestine advisor to the Junior Hadassah Organization, a position she held until shortly before her death. During her tenure as advisor, Junior Hadassah launched a number of significant projects in Palestine, including the revitalization of Meier Shefeyah, a Youth Aliyah village that housed many war orphans. In a letter to Junior Hadassah, she wrote of her vision for Hadassah and Palestine: "[W]e must say that we think of tasks not merely as medical enterprises or children's services, but as educational projects in the highest sense for Palestine as a whole. . . . Our ultimate task—the Zionist hope—however, is the upbuilding of the Jewish Homeland as a socially just and creative community, creative in every domain, in science, in art, in religion, a community in which every person may develop to the utmost of his power."

When Alice Lillie Seligsberg died on August 27, 1940, Hadassah immediately allocated $25,000 to build a memorial to her in Palestine. This memorial, dedicated by Henrietta Szold on October 15, 1940, established a clinic at the Children's Village. The Alice L. Seligsberg Vocational High School for Girls, which later became the Seligsberg-Brandeis Community College, was also established as a lasting memorial.

BIBLIOGRAPHY

AJYB, 43:364, 431–436; *EJ*; Obituary. *NYTimes*, August 29, 1940, 19:1; *UJE*; *WWIAJ* (1926, 1928, 1938).

MARILYN J. SLADOWSKY

SELZNICK, IRENE MAYER (1907–1990)

Irene Mayer Selznick's career as a producer in the New York theater began in 1947 as Act III of her life. She writes in her memoir, *A Private View* (1983), that

As the daughter of Louis B. Mayer, Irene Selznick was a true child of show business who united two Hollywood dynasties when she married movie mogul David O. Selznick. Her best was yet to come, however, as she became a Broadway giant in her own right, producing plays such as A Streetcar Named Desire. *[New York Public Library]*

Act I was spent under the shadow of her father, the film executive Louis B. Mayer; Act II was marriage to David O. Selznick, producer of *Gone With the Wind*; and Act III consisted of her role as herself and her career as a Broadway producer. She is perhaps best known as producer of Tennessee Williams's *A Streetcar Named Desire* (1947). She also produced *Bell, Book and Candle* (1950), *The Chalk Garden* (1955), and *The Complaisant Lover* (1961), among others.

Irene Mayer Selznick was born on April 2, 1907, to Louis B. and Margaret (Shenberg) Mayer. Her paternal and maternal grandparents had come to New

Brunswick, Canada, in the early 1880s from Vilna and Kovno on the then Russian-Polish border. Her family lived in Haverhill, Massachusetts, where she and her older sister, Edie, attended public school. Then in 1918, the year of the Spanish influenza epidemic, the family moved to California. There her father built MGM into the most respected studio in Hollywood. Despite Louis B. Mayer's intentions, the family succumbed to the rarefied atmosphere of early Hollywood as it existed for wealthy movie executives. They met and socialized with the famous people of the day, which was a problem for Irene Mayer because of a stutter, acquired at school where, as a left-hander, she was forced to write with her right hand.

Her marriage to David O. Selznick, son of Lewis J. Selznick, in 1930 united two of Hollywood's dynasties. "Movies were like a great cause to us," she writes in her autobiography. "We had one romance with each other and another with the movies." Visits to New York in the 1930s forged the real beginning of Selznick's connections in the theater, and laid the groundwork for her career as producer. With David Selznick, she met George and BEATRICE KAUFMAN, Philip Barry, Robert Sherwood, John Hay Whitney, Henry Luce, and William Paley.

Irene Selznick was an executive of her husband's production company, founded in 1936 following the success of *Dinner at Eight*, which was made in three and a half weeks. When Selznick told her husband she was "sick of phony films about Hollywood," he produced *A Star Is Born* in 1937, starring Janet Gaynor and Fredric March. *Gone With the Wind* was released in 1939 to enormous acclaim.

During the war, Irene Selznick underwent psychoanalysis in Los Angeles with Dr. May Romm, and took a wartime job as a Los Angeles County juvenile probation officer. After she moved east, she sat on the board of directors for the New York Citizen Council on Crime and Delinquency.

"I wasn't looking for independence or freedom," she wrote about the end of her marriage. "I preferred protection; I had had it all my life." But in 1945, she and David Selznick were separated, though they were not divorced until 1948. Their marriage produced two sons, Lewis Jeffrey Selznick and Daniel M. Selznick.

She was "shoved into the theater" by her friend Moss Hart, who urged her to hang out her producer's shingle. Her first play was *Heartsong* (1947) by Arthur Laurents, which closed out of town, but the one that followed later that same year was Tennessee Williams's *A Streetcar Named Desire*. Mel Gussow, *New York Times* drama critic, in writing about Selznick's Broadway career, said, "When she produced *Streetcar* and other

plays, she worked hand in glove with the playwright in insuring that the work was seen absolutely to its best advantage." Lifelong awareness of drama and character in movies enabled her to listen for and value the voice of the writer.

From 1985 to her death in New York on October 10, 1990, at age eighty-three, Irene Mayer Selznick was president of the Louis B. Mayer Foundation. Breaking the foundation's tradition of gifts to film schools and institutes, she was responsible for a gift of five million dollars to the Dana-Farber Cancer Institute of Boston. In her will, she left a hundred thousand dollars to the Young Playwrights Foundation to provide income for travel and housing for talented new writers. In this way she ensured her continued involvement in the new young voices of theater and screen.

BIBLIOGRAPHY

Notable Names in the American Theatre (1976); Rigdon, Walter, ed. *The Biographical Encyclopedia and Who's Who of the American Theatre* (1966); Selznick, Irene Mayer. Papers. Boston University Library, Boston University, and *A Private View* (1983).

ANGELA WIGAN MARVIN

SEPHARDI WOMEN

Sephardic Jews constitute only a small proportion of American Jewry. Although they comprised the majority of American Jewry during the colonial period, that majority never exceeded twenty-five hundred prior to the American Revolution. The Sephardim of Holland, the Caribbean, and England may have formed the vanguard of colonial pioneering, yet it is difficult to isolate any special role of Sephardi women or even to arrive at more than an estimate of their numbers. Although the first settlers and their congregations were Sephardic, the notable economic, political, and organizational achievements of the pioneering generation are largely devoid of Sephardi female luminaries. Achievements of Jewish women were not generally documented. To the extent that Jewish women rose to prominence in the colonial period, it was Ashkenazi women whom history remembers.

By the nineteenth century, the Sephardi community was vastly outnumbered by Ashkenazim. Nevertheless, a few outstanding Sephardi personalities captured public notice. PENINA MOÏSE (1797–1880), the first American Jew to publish a volume of poetry, also conducted a private school and wrote movingly of the travails of the Jews at the time of the Damascus Blood Libel (1840). Her hymnal was published and utilized by Congregation Beth Elohim of Charleston, South Carolina. MAUD NATHAN (1862–1946) was a multitalented woman, distinguished for her active involvement in the life of the Spanish and Portuguese synagogue of New York, Congregation Shearith Israel, as well as in the wider New York community. She served as a founder of the Consumers League of New York and the movement for woman suffrage. During her short life, EMMA LAZARUS (1849–1887) gained immortality through her evocation of the immigrant's dream of America in her poem "The New Colossus." Her Sephardi connection was through the prominence of her family in Congregation Shearith Israel rather than through any distinguishable attachment on her part to Sephardi tradition.

The colonial family of the Nathans included another significant public figure, ANNIE NATHAN MEYER (1867–1951). A playwright, novelist, and editor, Meyer left her mark through her active campaign at Columbia University that led to the founding of Barnard College in 1889. In 1891, she edited the volume *Woman's Work in America*.

With the twentieth-century Sephardi migrations to America, a new Sephardi sensibility emerges in American Jewish history. Immigrants from the Arab world and the disintegrating Ottoman Empire arrived with a knowledge of Ladino, a language essentially the domain of women at the time. Unlike earlier Sephardi immigrants, this wave of immigration came from traditional Near Eastern societies, where women's roles had been severely circumscribed. In the newfound Ladino press, some of the hopes and aspirations of anonymous Sephardi women emerge—their fascination with the social activism and economic productivity of Ashkenazi women, their awareness of the greater literacy and synagogue skills of their Ashkenazi counterparts, and their self-consciousness about "Old World" mores. The new Sephardi immigrants were assisted in their efforts at Americanization by the Sisterhood of the Spanish and Portuguese synagogue of New York.

Post–World War II Sephardi immigration from Muslim lands has brought a critical mass of Sephardim to American shores. Although Jewish women were largely confined to the domestic sphere in places such as Syria or Central Asia, the organized Sephardi community in America (the American Sephardi Federation, founded in 1972) has enjoyed new professional and leadership opportunities. Access to higher education has enabled Sephardi women to overcome traditional limitations on their involvement in the broader society. The second president of the American Sephardi Federation, Liliane Shalom, has assumed a leadership position within what was essentially an exclusively male organization. With the expansion of the Sephardi day-school educational network, it may be only a matter of time before Sephardi women have a significant impact on Jewish cultural life in America.

BIBLIOGRAPHY
Angel, Marc D. *La America: The Sephardic Experience in the United States* (1982); Papo, Joseph. *Sephardim in Twentieth Century America* (1987).

JANE S. GERBER

SERDATSKY, YENTE (1877–1962)

Proud, independent, enterprising, and contentious, Yente Serdatsky exemplifies the enormous difficulties experienced by Yiddish women writers in achieving recognition. Her long-neglected work has consequently engaged the attention of contemporary Jewish feminist literary critics.

Serdatsky was born Yente Raybman on September 15, 1877, in Aleksat, near Kovne (Kaunas), Lithuania. Her scholarly father, Yehoshua, dealt in used furniture and provided his daughters with a basic Jewish education including attendance at a Jewish girls' school whose teachers were young men from a nearby yeshivah. At thirteen, she was apprenticed to a seamstress, then worked in a grocery store in Kovne and eventually owned her own grocery store there. She continued to read books in German, Hebrew, and Russian during those years.

In 1905, she left her husband and three children and went to Warsaw to pursue a literary career. Her first story, "Mirl," was published in 1905 in *Der Veg* [The way], a journal edited by Bal-Makhshoves. She was also encouraged by I.L. Peretz, whose home was a gathering place for budding literary talent.

In 1907, she came to America. At first, she lived in Chicago, where, according to Moyshe Weissman, she ran a café where impoverished immigrant would-be writers could eat homemade meals. In New York, her eating place was described as a soup kitchen. At the same time, she published stories, one-act plays, and dramatic sketches in various Yiddish periodicals, including the anarchist *Fraye Arbeter Shtime* [Free voice of labor], the socialist *Fraye Gezelshaft* [Free society], *Fraynd* [Friend], *Di Tsukunft* [The future], and Avrom Reisin's *Dos Naye Land* [The new land]. Her only published volume, *Geklibene Shriftn* [Selected works], including stories, novellas, and dramatic sketches, was published in 1913. She was on the staff of the influential *Forverts*, and her work appeared regularly until 1922, when she quarreled over money matters with

Abraham Cahan, the formidable editor of the paper. She was removed from the editorial staff and seems not to have published for over twenty-five years. Without income from her writing, she lived partly on welfare and partly from renting furnished rooms.

In 1949, she began writing again, primarily in the *Nyu Yorker Vokhnblat* [New York weekly] to which she contributed some thirty stories and reminiscences of I.L. Peretz. Shea Tenenbaum's memoir of Serdatsky suggests that she was morbidly obsessed by Peretz throughout her career.

Serdatsky's fiction and dramatic works focus mainly on women like herself, immigrants who emerged from European, mainly Russian, left-wing political movements. These women, though committed to change and the future, frequently long for the traditional Jewish past they supposedly abandoned. They came to America seeking to build an ideal society together with like-minded male comrades. Instead, they face alienation and loneliness in a society that has little place for radical intellectual women. Serdatsky's heroines who are involved in liaisons are inevitably exploited by lovers and husbands, Nevertheless, her narratives abound in lonely women searching for love and faith. Most are doomed to disappointment. Serdatsky died on May 1, the workers' holiday, in 1962, at age eighty-five.

Poet-critic Yankev Glatshteyn, writing shortly after her death, acknowledged that her considerable talent had been largely unappreciated. He proposed an edition of her uncollected writings as a fitting memorial for Serdatsky, whom he characterized as an "angry" writer. While it conveys Serdatsky's rage and faults her for wasting time shouting and protesting instead of quietly writing, critic Shea Tenenbaum's memoir also portrays her commanding presence and her powerful, intense character.

BIBLIOGRAPHY

Tenenbaum, Shea. *Ayzik Ashmeday* (1964).

DOROTHY BILIK

SETTLEMENT HOUSES

Jewish women have played significant roles as benefactors, organizers, administrators, and participants in American settlement houses. Settlement houses, founded in the 1880s in impoverished urban neighborhoods, provided recreation, education, and medical and social service programs, primarily for immigrants. Although the popularity of settlement houses peaked prior to World War I, the organizations continue to serve low-income families in cities across the United States. From the start of the movement to the present, Jewish women of all backgrounds have found the settlements a congenial place to learn, teach, court, launch careers, and consolidate political power.

The settlement house movement began in America in 1886 when Stanton Coit, a disciple of Felix Adler, established Neighborhood Guild on the Lower East Side of Manhattan. Residents of the guild organized clubs for Jewish and Italian immigrant boys. A sister organization, College Settlement on Rivington Street, offered programs for immigrant girls. Supported in large part by Jewish benefactors, the organizations merged to form University Settlement. Within twenty-eight years of the Neighborhood Guild's founding, reformers established more than four hundred settlement houses in the United States. Though most settlements claimed to be nondenominational, prior to World War II only a few houses successfully integrated Jewish and Christian workers. In 1911, settlement worker Boris D. Bogen estimated that there were seventy-five Jewish settlements (or neighborhood centers, so called because the staff did not live there) in addition to fifty-seven non-Jewish settlements or centers dedicated to serving a Jewish population.

The reaction of Eastern European Jewish women to settlement houses varied considerably according to their expectations, the personality of the settlement workers they encountered, and the quality of the programs. For some female Jewish immigrants, the settlements provided opportunities unparalleled by other institutions. In Boston, Celia Stanetsky Cohen idolized her club leader, Julia Frothingham, at the North End Union, and Cohen spent hours listening to her read literature or discuss suffrage and equal rights. American democracy came alive for Cohen when she and her friends first traveled to Washington, D.C., with the club leader. Undaunted by the club leader's Christianity, Cohen proclaimed that Frothingham had shown her the beauty of life.

Unlike Cohen, many Jewish children were forbidden to cross a settlement house's threshold by parents who feared Christian missionaries. In 1896, Hilda Satt Polacheck of Chicago resisted an invitation to the Hull House Christmas party for fear she might be killed. When she finally entered Hull House, Jane Addams's warm welcome and the fellowship of strangers astonished her. "Bigotry faded," she later recalled. "I became an American at that party." When work took Polacheck from school, Hull House became her classroom at night. For ten years, her social and educational development revolved around

The Chicago Hebrew Institute opened in 1903, specifically to provide social services to Jews.
This 1915 photograph depicts the contestants in a "baby contest." [Chicago Historical Society]

the settlement, and in 1904 Jane Addams arranged for Polacheck to attend the University of Chicago. Six months later, Polacheck began teaching English at Hull House, and she delighted in the transition from program participant to instructor.

Polacheck's experience was unique. The majority of Chicago's Jewish residents avoided Hull House but wanted similar opportunities in a Jewish context. In November 1903, the Chicago Hebrew Institute began promoting the social advancement of the Jewish residents of Chicago. This institute enabled Eastern European immigrants and German Jewish residents to work together. Goldie Tuvin Stone, a middle-class woman from Lithuania, enlisted as a volunteer and was befriended by German Jewish philanthropists, among them Julius Rosenwald, founder of Sears Roebuck.

In addition to friendship, Jewish women found romance at the settlements. When Mary Ryshpan became a student of Thomas Davidson's at the Educational Alliance in New York City, she fell in love with and married fellow student Morris Raphael Cohen, later a renowned philosopher. Anne Schroeder, whose family could not afford the clothes necessary to send her to school at the same time as her sister, met and married fellow club member Louis Abrons at the Henry Street Settlement. With help from mentors, Herbert Lehman in particular, the Abrons family prospered and became leading benefactors of the Henry Street Settlement.

Immigrant journalist ROSE PASTOR STOKES embarked on an ill-fated marriage to patrician James Graham Phelps Stokes after they met at University Settlement in New York City. She later became one of the settlement's most outspoken critics. She ridiculed altruists who patronized working women at settlement houses, and she blamed the settlements for increasing alienation between social classes.

Stokes was not the sole critic. Well-known figures such as ANZIA YEZIERSKA and EMMA GOLDMAN scorned the settlements as well. Yezierska worked briefly at the Emanu-El Sisterhood of Personal Service settlement in Manhattan on 82nd Street, but loathed the job. Radical reformer Emma Goldman scoffed that "settlement work was teaching the poor to eat with a fork." Other reformers thought Americanization programs failed to address the fundamental economic inequalities facing immigrants. Union member Gertrude Barnum declared that the settlements' efforts to provide books, flowers, and music did little to raise wages or shorten working hours. But some settlement workers did confront economic issues. Jane Addams and Florence Kelley at Hull House conducted sociological investigations, and they, as well as others, lobbied politicians and supported labor unions. Early meetings of the Women's Trade Union League were held at University Settlement.

Many women's lives were changed by the meaningful work they found at the settlements. Widow REBEKAH BETTELHEIM KOHUT briefly supported her family by teaching classes at the Educational Alliance, where her success brought her to the attention of reformers at the national level. She later became active in the NATIONAL COUNCIL OF JEWISH WOMEN and served as the first president of the New York Section (1894 to 1898). Later she participated in Woodrow Wilson's Federal Employment Committee and in Governor Franklin D. Roosevelt's Advisory Council on Employment in 1931, where she was one of a few recommending unemployment insurance.

BELLE MOSKOWITZ's career began at New York's Educational Alliance in 1900 when she was hired as the director of entertainments and exhibits. She met architect Charles Israels, who led a boys' club at the alliance, and they were married in 1903. Ties forged during her employment at Educational Alliance led to many other opportunities. After Charles Israels's death in 1911, she chaired a task force to study and combat immorality in dance halls, part of the campaign against white slavery, and she worked for the Dress and Waist Manufacturers Association, serving as manager of the labor department from 1914 to 1916. In 1914, she married Henry Moskowitz, an acquaintance from the Educational Alliance. Moskowitz was a former headworker of Madison Street Settlement in Manhattan and a former resident of University Settlement. Later Belle Moskowitz became Alfred Smith's political adviser. She credited the settlements with providing an opportunity for Jewish women to combine "true womanhood," Jewish traditions, and employment.

For the parents of city children, supervised recreation was a major service of settlement houses. This 1924 photo was taken on the "roof playground" of the Irene Kaufman Settlement. [American Jewish Historical Society]

*Settlement houses also provided a wide range of services for adults. This worker
at the Irene Kaufman Settlement is helping a man fill out his application for citizenship.
[American Jewish Historical Society]*

A settlement house launched Belle Moskowitz's career in public service, but for LILLIAN WALD, founder of the famous House on Henry Street, the settlement was not merely the starting point, it was the root that sustained forty years of social reform initiative in public health, education, recreation, civil rights, housing, and employment. Raised in an affluent German-Jewish family, first in Cincinnati, Ohio, and then in Rochester, New York, Wald longed for meaningful work. From 1889 to 1891, she studied at the New York Hospital training school for nurses. In 1893, she enrolled in the Women's Medical College in New York City and organized home nursing classes for Lower East Side immigrants. In the spring of 1893, after visiting a patient's squalid tenement apartment, she pledged herself to public health nursing, left medical school, and moved with Mary Brewster to College Settlement on the Lower East Side. Later they moved to their own apartment and then, with funds from Elizabeth Loeb and Jacob Schiff, Lillian Wald established the Nurses Settlement at 265 Henry Street, in 1895.

Wald welcomed immigrants from all over the world, Jews and non-Jews alike. She did not envision Henry Street as a Jewish settlement, but she relied on Jewish philanthropists to support her work. The programs attracted many Jewish immigrants who knew that there would be no missionizing at Henry Street. At times, Wald's lack of emphasis on Jewish traditions angered her benefactors. Jacob Schiff, an observant Jew, was outraged when he learned that there had been a Christmas party with a Christmas tree at Henry Street. For the most part, however, he and his family lent their unconditional support.

Wald demonstrated that settlements could be a powerful political base for women. As a popular and knowledgeable advocate for her neighbors, Wald forged alliances with powerful reformers and politicians. She influenced significant legislation at the local, state, and national levels. Her accomplishments include convincing the New York City Board of Health to establish the first public school nursing program in the United States; helping to establish the department of nursing and health at Teachers College of Columbia University; serving as the first president of the National Organization for Public Health Nursing; founding, with Florence Kelley, the National Child Labor Committee; and playing a leading role in the creation of the federal Children's Bureau. At Henry Street, through membership in United Neighborhood Houses of New York City and in the National Federation of Settlements, Wald set high standards for other settlements to follow. Lillian Wald's charisma and dedication attracted many nurses and fellow reformers to Henry Street and other settlements.

German Jewish philanthropists, committed to taking care of their own people and combating anti-Semitism, often served on the boards of directors of settlement houses, raising money, overseeing programs, and hiring key personnel. Though these philanthropists rarely spent much time at the settlement, their contribution cannot be exaggerated. Without the support of Elizabeth Loeb and her daughters Nina Warburg and THERESE LOEB SCHIFF, Lillian Wald would not have been able to rent or purchase buildings, pay the nurses, or staff other programs. Major supporters include Alice and IRENE LEWISOHN, who built, funded, and ran the Neighborhood Playhouse, a theater in the Henry Street Complex. In 1927, the playhouse closed and the settlement took it over. A year later, Irene Lewisohn, in collaboration with Rita Wallach Morgenthau, another one of Wald's close friends and supporters, founded the Neighborhood Playhouse School of the Theatre.

Board members were important for leadership as well as donations. Educator JULIA RICHMAN played a key role in creating New York City's Educational Alliance, the first Jewish social service organization to conceive of itself as a settlement house. As a member of the board of directors of the Hebrew Free School Association, Richman demonstrated the compatibility of Americanization programs, English classes, a lending library, after-school activities, summer camp, art and music classes, and literary clubs, with Hebrew classes and efforts to preserve Jewish heritage. When the Free School Association merged with other organizations on the Lower East Side, including the New York Hebrew Institute (founded by members of the YMHA), Richman expanded the Free School to accommodate and "Americanize" Orthodox Jews arriving each year from Eastern Europe. Incorporated in 1893, and supported by German Jews from uptown, the Educational Alliance provided a model for Jewish philanthropists in other cities. By 1915, Atlanta, Baltimore, Chicago, Cleveland, Columbus (Ohio), Kansas City (Missouri), Los Angeles, and St. Louis had Educational Alliances of their own.

Richman was an active board member from 1891 to 1912, and the only female board member of the Educational Alliance until 1901. She became a mentor to many Jewish women who gravitated toward settlement work, including Belle Moskowitz and Rebekah Kohut. Although the alliance's board rarely ceded power to women, many women joined the auxiliary committee and did important work.

Middle-class Jewish women contributed to the settlement movement through a variety of organizations. The SISTERHOODS OF PERSONAL SERVICE, dedicated to "overcoming the estrangement of one class of the Jewish population from another," was founded by women of Temple Emanu-El in 1887 and was led by HANNAH BACHMAN EINSTEIN. Spreading to nearly every Jewish congregation in New York City, San Francisco, and St. Louis, the sisterhoods established mission schools that came to mirror programs at settlement houses. The Emanu-El Sisterhood had its own settlement at 318 East 82nd Street, as did Temple Israel, whose sisterhood founded, in 1905, the Harlem Federation for Jewish Communal Work, later renamed Federation Settlement. Einstein, who was active in many reform circles, emerged in 1909 as president of the Widowed Mothers Fund Association, a powerful proponent of widows' pension legislation. She had many ties to settlements through her service on the Women's Auxiliary of University Settlement from 1909 to 1912 and her agreement with SOPHIE AXMAN of Educational Alliance to help with delinquent children. In Milwaukee, sisterhood member LIZZIE BLACK KANDER established and served as the first president of the settlement. Kander and Fannie Greenbaum later compiled and published the *Settlement Cook Book*. With the proceeds, board members purchased a new building for the settlement.

Another group of Jewish women reformers came to the settlements via the National Council of Jewish Women (NCJW). The council's founding in 1893 solidified the growing dedication of upper-middle-class Jewish women to the settlement movement. Julia Felsenthal of Philadelphia and Julia Richman attended the first meeting in Chicago to educate their sisters about settlements. The NCJW's threefold mission of philanthropy, religion, and education was ideally suited to settlement work. In Chicago, HANNAH SOLOMON and SADIE AMERICAN rode the NCJW's momentum to establish Maxwell Street Settlement in a Jewish neighborhood on the West Side. In New York, Belle Moskowitz drew on her settlement background to lead the NCJW chapter in a fight against white slavery. Through the NCJW, Jewish women supported settlements run by and for Jewish women.

Mrs. A. Leo Weil of the Pittsburgh Section of the NCJW organized the Columbian School, later called the Columbian Council School, in 1895. In 1909, the name changed to the Irene Kaufmann Settlement as a memorial to the daughter of Mr. and Mrs. Henry Kaufmann. With generous support from the Kaufmann family, the settlement blossomed, offering a district nursing service beginning in 1902, as well as a kindergarten, an employment bureau, an art school, a music school and theater program, and housing reform campaigns. The board hired its first full-time director, Sidney Teller in 1916, and by the time he and his wife Julia Pines Teller resigned in 1941, the annual budget had grown to ninety-seven thousand dollars.

The second president of New York City's NCJW section, RACHEL HAYS SULZBERGER chaired the committee that established Recreation Rooms for Girls at 79 Orchard Street in 1898. Its purpose was to Ameri-

LILLIAN WALD *welcomed immigrants from all over the world, Jews and non-Jews alike, to her settlement house. In fact, her lack of emphasis on Jewish traditions angered some of her benefactors. The reproduction above is the frontispiece of her anecdotal autobiography* The House on Henry Street *(1915).* [Peter H. Schweitzer]

canize while preserving Jewish traditions. After moving to 186 Chrystie Street in 1899, the director, Bertha F. Lubitz guided the girls to form self-help clubs that raised money for summer outings. Opposed to Jewish participation in Christian settlement houses, Rachel Hays Sulzberger and fellow board members Mrs. Aaron Kohn, Ida Blum Straus, Theresa Loeb Schiff, and FLORENCE GUGGENHEIM ensured that recreation rooms provided programs such as Friday evening talks on Jewish history and literature, Saturday evening dances, and Bible and Hebrew classes run by the Jewish Endeavor Society on Sunday. In 1900, Rebekah Kohut endorsed the work of Recreation Rooms in the *American Hebrew*, declaring the program successful because Jewish girls were being helped by their Jewish sisters.

After 1914, with the waning of Jewish immigration and the outbreak of war in Europe, Jewish leaders began to question the scope and content of settlement work. Community chests organized in most cities, except for Chicago and New York, began to control dependent agencies. When the "red scare" of 1919 labeled many progressive settlement leaders as communist traitors, contributions fell. Furthermore, the settlements' sympathy with labor unions and other radical organizations led to a decline in popularity and support. The federal income tax legislation passed in 1914 also eroded contributions to private social service organizations. Most important, settlement neighborhoods were changing. As African Americans replaced Jewish residents of American ghettos, Jewish social workers and philanthropists debated their mission. Should settlements follow Jewish people out of the neighborhood or adapt their programs for newcomers?

In 1914, Miriam Blaustein, widow of David Blaustein, renowned leader of Educational Alliance and then Chicago Hebrew Institute, praised the ideal Jewish settlement, a place that "breathes the Jewish spirit . . . [and] brings home to the Hebrew an historic consciousness." She saw Jewish settlements as the place where Jewish girls could learn about the superiority of Jewish domesticity and about other Jewish women. Settlement worker Walter Solomon objected to Blaustein's remarks, insisting that there could be no such thing as a Jewish settlement because a settlement by definition must be nonsectarian. He argued that only a community center could be Jewish, and that the settlement's purpose was to prepare Jewish children for participation in American life rather than for the resurrection of a Jewish nation. The debate continued without resolution. Meanwhile, people moved. In 1926–1927, at eighteen representative settlements in New York City, 56 percent of program participants were Jewish. A few years later, the number dropped precipitously as the neighborhood changed.

The developments at Council House, founded in Manhattan by the New York Section of the NCJW in 1917, illustrate one group's response to the dilemma. Opened at 74 St. Marks Place, Council House offered a meeting space for mothers and children, and classes in English, dancing, and singing. As the Jewish population began to migrate from Lower Manhattan to the Bronx, Council House moved as well. In 1929, board members erected a three-story building with a gym and playground at 1122 Forest Avenue. Council House continued until the early 1940s, when African Americans began to outnumber Jewish children in the settlement programs. In response, the NCJW drafted a lengthy report concluding that the organization should be turned over to the African-American community, with its own board and programs. At a meeting in New York City, attended by Eleanor Roosevelt, NCJW members, and local leaders from the East Bronx, Council House was renamed Forest House, with a board of directors elected from the neighborhood. The decline in Jewish program participants had weakened the commitment of Jewish supporters, and the settlement's identity changed accordingly.

By World War II, with exceptions such as Educational Alliance in Manhattan and the Irene Kaufmann Settlement in Pittsburgh (which became a community center in 1988), most Jewish settlements had become community centers. At the same time, many Jewish women continued to work in nondenominational settlement houses as administrators, volunteers, and board members.

BIBLIOGRAPHY

Bellow, Adam. *The Educational Alliance: A Centennial Celebration* (1990); Berrol, Selma. "When Uptown Met Downtown: Julia Richman's Work in the Jewish Community of New York, 1880–1912." *American Jewish History* 8, no. 1 (June 1981); Blaustein, Miriam. "Settlements in Small Southern Communities." *Jewish Charities* 5, no. 1 (August 1914); Bogen, Boris D. "Jewish Settlements." *Jewish Charities: Bulletin of the National Conference of Jewish Charities* 2, no. 1 (August 1911); "A Brief History of the Irene Kaufmann Settlement, 1895–1942." Archives. 92nd Street Y, NYC; Bristow, Edward J. *Prostitution and Prejudice: The Jewish Fight Against White Slavery, 1870–1939* (1983); Cremin, Lawrence A. *American Education: The Metropolitan Experience, 1876–1980* (1988); Dye, Nancy Schrom. *As Equals and as Sisters: Feminism, the Labor Movement, and the Women's Trade Union League of New York* (1980); H.B.E. [Hannah Bachman Einstein]. "Sisterhoods of Personal Service." *The Jewish Encyclopedia* (1901); Ewen, Elizabeth. *Immigrant Women in the Land of Dollars: Life and Culture on the Lower East Side, 1890–1925* (1985); Gans, Herbert J. "Redefining the Settlement's Function for the War on Poverty." *Social Work* (October 1964); Gurock, Jeffrey S. "Jacob S. Riis: Christian Friend or Missionary Foe? Two Jewish Views." *American Jewish History* 71, no. 1 (September 1981); Henriksen, Louise Levitas. *Anzia Yezierska: A Writer's Life* (1988); Kennedy, Albert J., Kathryn Farra, et al. *Social Settlements in New York City: Their Activities, Policies and Administration* (1935); Kirshenblatt-Gimblett, Barbara. "Kitchen Judaism." In *Getting Comfortable in New York: The American Jewish Home, 1880–1950* (1990); Lissak, Rivka Shpak. *Pluralism and Progressives: Hull House and the New Immigrants, 1890–1919* (1989); Marcus, Jacob R., ed. *The American Jewish Woman: A Documentary History* (1981); Moore, Deborah Dash. *At Home in America: Second-Generation New York Jews* (1981); Moske, James. "Recreation Rooms and Settlement Collection." Guide to Brooklyn Historical Society collection (1994); *NAW*, s.v. "Belle Lindner Israels Moskowitz," "Hannah Bachman Einstein," and "Lillian D. Wald"; *NAW* modern, s.v. "Rebekah Bettelheim Kohut"; Perry, Elisabeth Israels. *Belle Moskowitz: Feminine Politics and the Exercise of Power in the Age of Alfred E. Smith* (1987); Polacheck, Hilda Satt. *I Came a Stranger: The Story of a Hull-House Girl.* Edited by Dena J. Polacheck Epstein (1989); Rabinowitz, Benjamin. *The Young Men's Hebrew Associations, 1854–1913* (1948); Rogow, Faith. *Gone to Another Meeting: The National Council of Jewish Women, 1893–1993* (1993); Rothenberg, Flora R. "Story of Council House." Unpublished paper (1985); Siegel, Beatrice. *Lillian Wald of Henry Street* (1983); Solomon, Walter Leo. "The Jewish Settlement Again." *Jewish Charities* 5, nos. 8 and 10 (1915); Straus, Mrs. Isidor. "The Recreation Room for Girls." *Jewish Charity: A Monthly Review of General Jewish Charity* 4, no. 4 (January 1905); Trolander, Judith Ann. *Professionalism and Social Change: From the Settlement House Movement to Neighborhood Centers, 1886 to the Present* (1987), and *Settlement Houses and the Great Depression* (1975); University Settlement. *Annual Reports* (1909–1912).

SARAH HENRY LEDERMAN

SHAPIRO, NORMA LEVY (b. 1928)

Once, following a landmark decision in a prisoners' rights case, federal judge Norma Levy Shapiro was described by a detractor as Philadelphia's "Public Enemy Number One." Her many advocates argue that her opinions are merely guided by the law. Such have been the dichotomous views regarding the difficult, often divisive, legal and social issues decided by senior members of the federal judiciary, such as Shapiro.

She was born Norma Sondra Levy on July 27, 1928, in Philadelphia. She and her brother Robert (now a law school professor) were raised in Cheltenham, a Philadelphia suburb. Their father, Bert, a furniture salesman, was born in Russia and immigrated to the United States around 1900. Their mother, Jane Kotkin, was a teacher. Norma graduated with honors from Cheltenham High School and from the University of Michigan in 1948 with a B.A. in political theory. At Michigan, she was elected to Phi Beta Kappa, Phi Beta Phi, and Alpha Lambda Delta. After college, she entered the Law School of the University of Pennsylvania, from which she graduated in 1951, magna cum laude, Order of the Coif, and the only woman in her class. While at law school, she was editor of the *Law Review*, and married Bernard Shapiro, a doctor specializing in the emerging field of nuclear medicine.

Following graduation, Shapiro served as a clerk (1951–1952) for Justice Horace Stern of the Pennsylvania Supreme Court. In 1954, she returned to the Law School of the University of Pennsylvania for a one-year graduate fellowship in criminal law, with an emphasis on juvenile court law.

During the early 1950s, Shapiro taught a number of law courses at the University of Pennsylvania and, in 1956, she joined the prestigious Philadelphia law firm of Dechert, Price and Rhoads as an associate. In 1973, despite leaving the firm as a full-time lawyer for nine years to raise her three sons (Finley, an electrical engineer; Neil, an attorney; and Aaron, a surgeon) and working part-time instead, she was made partner. On August 11, 1978, President Jimmy Carter nominated her to be the first woman judge on the United States Third Circuit District Court.

Several court decisions have gained Judge Shapiro national recognition. Perhaps the most famous was *Harris* v. *Reeves*, filed by a group of prisoners in 1982, complaining that prison overcrowding violated their constitutional guarantee against cruel and unusual punishment. Shapiro agreed with the plaintiffs, established a limit on Philadelphia prison populations, and became the *de facto* overseer of the prisons. In 1993, she ruled in favor of public housing in Chester, Pennsylvania, and placed the Chester Housing Authority in receivership, with the goal of improving public housing conditions.

Shapiro has received many awards for her legal, civic, and philanthropic service from organizations as diverse as the American Bar Association, the Federal Bar Association, the Philadelphia Bar Association, the Golden Slipper Club, and the NATIONAL COUNCIL OF JEWISH WOMEN. She has served as a member or as the chair of Philadelphia and American Bar Association committees, and on the boards of professional societies and judicial bodies, the Jewish Publication Society, the University of Pennsylvania Law School, the Albert Einstein Medical Center, the Women's Law

Project, the Lower Merion [Pa.] School Board, the Jewish Community Relations Council of Greater Philadelphia, and the Philadelphia Federation of Jewish Agencies.

Shapiro believes that her Jewish education and upbringing led her to the pursuit of justice under the law, and have added a spiritual dimension to her everyday life. Her background has given her a greater understanding of the evils of discrimination and social injustice, the blessings of liberty, and the importance of each individual's efforts to make the world better.

BIBLIOGRAPHY

Camden Courier-Post, October 28, 1993; *NYTimes*, August 14, 1996; *Philadelphia Inquirer Magazine* (December 25, 1994); *Philadelphia Magazine* (October 1995).

PAUL E. WALLNER

SHAVELSON, CLARA LEMLICH (1886–1982)

Clara Lemlich has made cameo appearances in histories of the United States, the labor movement, and American Jewry as the young firebrand whose impassioned Yiddish speech set off the 1909 UPRISING OF THE 20,000, the largest strike by women workers in the United States to that time. She has even appeared in that context in the hit Broadway play and movie *I'm Not Rappaport*. But Clara Lemlich's career as a revolutionary and activist began well before that famous speech and extended for more than half a century afterward. The most famous of the *fabrente Yidishe meydlekh* [fiery Jewish girls] whose militancy helped to galvanize the labor movement, she was also a suffragist, communist, community organizer, and peace activist. Clara Lemlich Shavelson lived and breathed politics from her childhood in revolutionary Russia to her last years in a nursing home in California—where she organized the orderlies.

Clara Lemlich was born in 1886 in Gorodok, Ukraine, to deeply religious parents. Like most girls, she was taught Yiddish but was offered no further Jewish schooling. Her parents were willing to send her to public school, but found that Gorodok's only school excluded Jews. Angered by the Russian government's anti-Semitism, her parents forbade her to speak Russian or to bring Russian books into their home. The headstrong child continued her study of Russian secretly, teaching Russian folk songs to older Jewish girls in exchange for their volumes of Tolstoy, Gorky, and Turgenev.

Before she was in her teens, Clara was sewing buttonholes on shirts to pay for her reading habit. Already fluent in written Yiddish, she fattened her book fund by writing letters for illiterate mothers to send to their children in America. When her father found a cache of books hidden beneath a meat pan in the kitchen, he burned the whole lot and Clara had to start collecting again. She began storing books in the attic, where she would perch on a bare beam to read. One Sabbath afternoon, while her family dozed, she was discovered by a neighbor. He not only kept her secret, but lent her revolutionary tracts from his own collection. By the time the Kishinev pogrom of 1903 convinced her parents to emigrate to the United States, seventeen-year-old Clara was a committed revolutionary.

Like so many young immigrant girls, Clara Lemlich found work in a Lower East Side garment shop. Infuriated by working conditions that, she said, reduced human beings to the status of machines, she began organizing women into the fledgling INTERNATIONAL LADIES GARMENT WORKERS UNION (ILGWU) soon after her arrival in New York in 1905. The older, skilled male workers who dominated the union resisted her efforts, but whenever they attempted to strike without informing the women, Clara brazenly warned them that their union would never get off the ground until they made an effort to include women. Over the men's objections, she brought her women coworkers out on strike again and again in various garment shops between 1907 and 1909.

In November 1909, despite the warnings of male union officers and of the middle-class reformers of the Women's Trade Union League who believed that young girls could not sustain a general strike, Clara decided to ignite the long-simmering resentment of tens of thousands of young immigrant working girls like herself. Insisting that she be allowed to address a strike meeting at New York's Cooper Union, she said: "I am one of those who suffers from the abuses described here, and I move that we go on a general strike." To the surprise of almost everyone, between thirty and forty thousand young women garment workers—predominantly Jewish immigrants—walked off their jobs over the next few weeks. It was a bitter, only partially successful strike. It galvanized the fledgling ILGWU and set off a wave of women's strikes between 1909 and 1915 that spread from New York to Philadelphia, Cleveland, Chicago, Iowa, and Kalamazoo, Michigan. But it also set the stage for tragedy when union negotiators failed to advance the young women's demand for safer working conditions. That lapse would come back to haunt the union on March

This undated photograph of Clara Lemlich must have been taken around the time she burst on the national scene with her 1909 speech that led to the UPRISING OF THE 20,000. *[Kheel Center, Cornell University]*

25, 1911, when the TRIANGLE SHIRTWAIST FIRE in New York City killed 146 workers, mostly immigrant Jewish and Italian women.

After the strike Clara was blacklisted from New York garment shops. She turned her energies to the suffrage movement, helping to found the Wage Earners League for Woman Suffrage, a working-class suffrage group. A fiery and effective agitator for the vote, she was eventually fired from her paid position as organizer for refusing to moderate her radical politics to suit the reform vision of most middle-class suffragists.

In 1913, Clara married printer Joe Shavelson and moved to Brownsville, in Brooklyn, where they had three children—Irving, Martha, and Rita. Far from the shop floor, Clara Shavelson began organizing wives and mothers around such issues as housing, food, and public education. She was a leader in the kosher meat boycotts of 1917, called to protest rapid price increases, and in the rent strike movement that swept New York City in 1919 when a postwar housing shortage dramatically raised the cost of decent housing.

In 1926, Shavelson joined the Communist Party and, along with other CP women, founded the United Council of Working-Class Housewives. The council helped the wives of striking workers raise funds, gather food, and set up community kitchens and cooperative child care. Organizing housewives proved so effective that, in 1929, Shavelson and white-goods worker Rose Nelson created the United Council of Working-Class Women (UCWW). The UCWW led rent strikes; anti-eviction demonstrations; meat, bread, and milk boycotts; sit-ins; and marches on Washington. Shavelson argued that consumption was intimately linked to production, and that the working-class housewife was as important a participant in the class struggle as her wage-earning husband, sisters, sons, and daughters.

In 1935, the UCWW changed its name to the Progressive Women's Councils and began building a coalition with a wide range of women's organizations not affiliated with the Community Party to protest the increasing cost of staple foods and housing. With Clara Shavelson as its president, the Progressive Women's Councils mounted a meat boycott that shut down forty-five hundred New York City butcher shops. Though in New York the strike was centered in Jewish and African-American neighborhoods, it soon spread to Chicago, Detroit, Los Angeles, St. Louis, Minneapolis, Cleveland, and several towns in Pennsylvania, involving women of all races, religions, and ethnic backgrounds.

This housewives' coalition alleviated the worst effects of the Great Depression in many working-class communities: bringing down food prices, rent, and utility costs; preventing evictions; and spurring the construction of more public housing, schools, and parks. By the end of World War II, the housewives' movement had forced the federal government to regulate food and housing costs and to investigate profiteering on staple goods. Decades of intense antieviction struggles and years of lobbying for public housing helped convince many municipalities to pass rent control laws, and increased support in Congress for federally funded public housing. It also paved the way for the modern consumer and tenant movements and brought gender politics into the working-class home, shining a bright light on hidden power relations between husbands and wives, parents and children—long before the feminists of the 1960s and 1970s popularized the thesis that the personal is political By demanding to be seen and respected in their own right, Clara Lemlich Shavelson and the housewife-activists laid the groundwork for the personal politics of the 1960s and 1970s.

In 1944, after her husband became ill, the fifty-eight-year-old Shavelson returned to the garment trade and to the union movement. During the 1940s she served on the American Committee to Survey Trade Union Conditions in Europe and spoke out against nuclear weapons as an organizer for the American League Against War and Fascism. After a visit to the Soviet Union with the American Committee, she and the other members had their passports revoked. In 1951, the year her husband died, Shavelson was summoned to Washington to testify before the House Committee on Un-American Activities. Her son and her husband were also investigated; indeed, her family remained under surveillance for the next two decades. Government harassment did not silence Shavelson. She actively protested the executions of Julius and ETHEL ROSENBERG in 1953 and the United States intervention in Guatemala in 1954.

When she retired from the ILGWU in 1954, the unrepentant radical was denied a pension on a technicality. After a long battle she was awarded two honorary stipends by ILGWU president David Dubinsky, but she never did receive a pension from the union she helped to found—and which hails her as a pioneer on every major anniversary.

Clara Lemlich Shavelson lived and breathed politics from her childhood in revolutionary Russia to her last years in a California nursing home—where she organized the orderlies. [YIVO Institute]

In 1960, Shavelson married an old labor movement acquaintance, Abe Goldman, with whom she lived until his death in 1967. At age eighty-one, Shavelson moved into the Jewish Home for the Aged in Los Angeles. During her years there, she persuaded the administrators to honor the grape and lettuce boycott then being promoted by the United Farm Workers and helped the orderlies to organize a union. She died at the home on July 12, 1982, at age ninety-six.

BIBLIOGRAPHY

The only full-length treatment of Shavelson's life can be found in Annelise Orleck, *Common Sense and a Little Fire: Women and Working-Class Politics in the United States, 1900–1965* (Chapel Hill: University of North Carolina Press, 1995). A brief sketch of her life may be found in Paula Scheier, "Clara Lemlich: 50 Years in Labor's Front Line," *Jewish Life* (November 1954), reprinted in part in *The American Jewish Woman, 1654–1980*, edited by Jacob Rader Marcus (New York: K'Tav Publishing, 1981). She is also discussed in Meredith Tax, *The Rising of the Women: Feminist Solidarity and Clas Conflict, 1880–1917* (New York: Monthly Review Press, 1980); and Mari Jo Buhle, *Women and American Socialism, 1870–1920* (Urbana: University of Illinois Press, 1981).

Clara Lemlich Shavelson wrote scores of articles over the years for the Communist Party press. Some are in the personal possession of her family. Interviews with colleagues, friends, and family of Shavelson are in the possession of her grandson Joel Schaffer and her daughter Martha Schaffer.

ANNELISE ORLECK

SHEFTALL, FRANCES HART
(1740–?)

A colonial wife, mother, and housekeeper, Frances Hart Sheftall became something of a public figure during and after the Revolutionary War, in spite of her own intentions.

She was born in the Hague, in the Netherlands, to Moses and Esther Hart in July 1740, and raised in an Ashkenazi home. Little is known of her life before her arrival in Charleston with her brother Joshua, who soon became a prosperous merchant.

The earliest surviving documents that mention her concern her marriage to Mordecai Sheftall of Savannah, Georgia, in October 1761. Frances (also called Fanny) Sheftall was twenty-one years old when she arrived in Savannah as a new bride. Her twenty-six-year-old husband had been born in Georgia to two of the original Jewish arrivals of July 1733, Benjamin and Perla Sheftall. Mordecai and Frances Sheftall were at the center of the Savannah Jewish community

Before the Revolutionary War, the Sheftall house was the scene of regular religious services for the local Jewish congregation. After the fall of Savannah, Frances Hart Sheftall petitioned Continental officers to intercede on behalf of her captured husband and son, all the while finding ways to keep her four children fed and clothed. [American Jewish Archives]

before the Revolution, with regular religious services for the local congregation taking place at their home by 1774.

Frances Sheftall, as the wife and mother of ardent patriots, had occasion to experience the Revolutionary War in a very personal way when her husband and eldest son Sheftall were captured by the British in December 1778, at the fall of Savannah. Having taken refuge from the fighting in nearby Charleston, she found herself in the position of supporting four young children, aged seven, nine, eleven, and fifteen, without recourse to the family resources, which remained in Savannah under British control. She took on an unaccustomed public role during this trying time, petitioning Continental officers such as General Benjamin Lincoln to intercede on behalf of her captive husband and son. She also wrote cheerful letters to help her husband and son keep up their spirits while in prison, and found the wherewithal to rent a house for herself and the younger children and to send them to school, in addition to putting food on the table and clothing on their backs—all while maintaining a kosher household. Sheftall was left on her own with the children for close to a year and a half. In March 1780, she wrote to Mordecai that she had "received the two thousand pounds of Mr. Cape, with which I make exceeding well out by doing a little business." What sort of business she conducted with this money is not divulged. A subsequent letter informed her husband that she was "obliged to take in needle worke to make a living for my family," and a letter written in late 1780 by her son mentions that she was supporting the family by taking in washing and ironing.

By the time she and the children were reunited with Mordecai and Sheftall in Philadelphia in April 1781, Frances Sheftall had managed to bring her household through epidemics of smallpox and yellow fever, the four-month cannon siege of Charleston waged by the British navy, and the humiliation of having the family clothing impounded to pay their passage from Charleston to Philadelphia. Following the war's end, Sheftall returned to Savannah and her former domestic role. Nevertheless, following her husband's death in 1792, she resumed her public activities on her children's behalf, petitioning Congress for redress of the loss suffered by the family as a result of Mordecai Sheftall's financial sacrifices for the patriot cause.

Frances Hart Sheftall died at Beaufort while on retreat from an epidemic of "pestilential fever" in Savannah.

BIBLIOGRAPHY

Hagy, James William. *This Happy Land: The Jews of Colonial and Antebellum Charleston* (1993); Levy, B.H. *Savannah's Old Jewish Community Cemeteries* (1983); Marcus, Jacob Rader, ed. *American Jewry—Documents, Eighteenth Century: Primarily Hitherto Unpublished Manuscripts* (1959), and *Early American Jewry*. Vol. 2 (1953); Stern, Malcolm H. "The Sheftall Diaries: Vital Records of Savannah Jewry, 1733–1808." *American Jewish Historical Quarterly* 54, no. 3 (March 1965): 242–277.

HOLLY SNYDER

SHEPS, MINDEL CHERNIACK (1913–1973)

As a physician, biostatistician, and demographer, Mindel Cherniack Sheps was acutely aware of the role science could play as a powerful social force. She taught that peace, social justice, and science were inextricably bound; humanism in any field must be based on social equity *and* knowledge. Of incisive intellect, firm conviction, and great humor, despising hypocrisy and dishonesty, she was a superb teacher and an avid learner.

She was born in Winnipeg, Manitoba, Canada on May 20, 1913. Her parents, Joseph and Fania (Goldin) Cherniack, emigrés from southern Russia, were committed socialist Zionists and were instrumental in enhancing the *yiddishkeit* movement in Canada. Her father was a lawyer, widely respected in the Canadian Jewish community for his comprehensive knowledge of Yiddish and his application of the wisdom of that literature to law and society. Mindel Sheps was later to apply this knowledge to science. Her brother, Saul Charniack, became minister of finance in the New Democratic Party government in the early 1970s.

After attending I.L. Peretz Shule and St. Johns High School, Mindel was one of the few Jewish women admitted, under a strict quota system, to medical school at the University of Manitoba, graduating in 1936. Later in life, she received a master's degree in public health from the University of North Carolina in 1950 and an honorary doctorate of science from the University of Manitoba in 1971.

She married Cecil George Sheps in 1937, after interning in Saskatoon in 1935. As a resident at the Children's Hospital in Winnipeg in 1937, she became acutely aware of the social issues underlying maternal and child health. In 1938, she and her husband went to London, England, where she worked at the Marie Curie Hospital in Whitechapel, further observing the effects of poverty on health. When she returned to Winnipeg, she went into general practice from 1939 to 1944, joined the socialist Cooperative Commonwealth Federation (CCF) Party, and ran successfully for the Winnipeg School Board in 1942.

In 1944, after a CCF electoral victory in Saskatchewan, Sheps became secretary to the Health Commission in that province. In this position, she surveyed hospital services and strongly supported the hospital insurance scheme enacted in 1945, the first in North America, giving political expression to her experiences and leading her toward a broader vision of epidemiology and the social factors influencing the health of individuals and populations. In this vision she was firmly supported by her husband, who was also trained in public health, health administration, and health services research. Their only child, Samuel, adopted when they were in Saskatchewan, later continued in their footsteps as a physician, epidemiologist, and health services researcher.

Further training in public health established Sheps as a leading thinker in the fields of statistics and demography. She held academic positions at the University of North Carolina, Columbia University, and the University of Pittsburgh. She was also highly regarded in numerous professional associations, including the American Population Association, the Biometrics Association, the American Association for the Advancement of Science, the American Public Health Association, and the International Union for the Scientific Study of Populations.

While trained in mathematics and biostatistics, Sheps was largely self-taught in demography, publishing in that field almost exclusively after 1963 and achieving an international reputation. Her interest in demography stemmed from a strong social conscience, from her experience in the 1940s as a physician, school board member, and particularly from the struggle of Planned Parenthood for recognition in Winnipeg. She was intellectually stimulated by biostatistical applications in demography, and a critical element of her work was her recognition of the links among poverty, fundamental social inequality, and population growth. For Sheps, demography became a science that could achieve social justice and clarify issues of women's rights and equality. Her statistical and demographic research was innovative and insightful, founded on solid mathematical principles; however, it was the social application of this knowledge that she believed to be crucial. A major prize in her name, recognizing the importance of such application, was established by the American Population Association in 1974.

When receiving her honorary doctorate of science degree, Sheps said: "The only hope of solving the problems of this planet lies in the application of scientific understanding and skills in the service of human dignity, freedom, and welfare. . . . I suggest it would be well to approach all human problems with humanity, with a strong sense of the limitation of our knowledge and of the existence of large areas of ignorance, and with readiness to admit the errors we made. In short, we must approach human problems in the best traditions of science."

Mindel Sheps died on January 15, 1973, in Durham, North Carolina. Although short, her epitaph, "To see things plain and still to care," summed up her conviction that cynicism, particularly for a scientist, was an abdication of responsibility.

SELECTED WORKS BY MINDEL CHERNIACK SHEPS

ARTICLES

"An Analytic Simulation Model for Human Reproduction with Demographic and Biologic Components," with C.J. Ridley. *Population Studies* 19 (1966): 297–310; "Approaches to the Quality of Hospital Care." *Public Health Reports* 70 (1955): 877–886; "Changes in Birth Rates as a Function of Contraceptive Effectiveness: Some Applications of a Stochastic Model," with E.B. Perrin. *American Journal of Public Health* 53 (1963): 1031–1046; "An Examination of Some Methods of Comparing Several Rates or Proportions." *Biometrics* 15 (1959): 87–97; "Health Reform in Saskatchewan." *Public Affairs* (Winter 1945): 79–83; "A Model for Studying Birth Rates Given Time Dependent Changes in Reproductive Parameters," with J.A. Menken. *Biometrics* 27 (1971): 325–343; "On Estimating the Risk of Conception from Censored Data," with J.A. Menken. In *Population Dynamics*, edited by T.N.E. Greville (1972); "Probability Models for Family Building: An Analytic Review," with J.A. Menken and A.P. Radnick. *Demography* 6 (1969): 161–183; "Saskatchewan Plans for Health Services." *California Journal of Public Health* 36 (1945): 175–180; "Shall We Count the Living or the Dead." *New England Journal of Medicine* 259 (1958): 1210–1214.

BOOKS

Mathematical Models of Conception and Birth, with J.A. Menken (1973); *On the Measurement of Human Fertility: Selected Writings of Louis Henry*, coedited with E. Lapierre-Adamcyk (1972); *Public Health and Population Change: Current Research Issues*, coedited with J.C. Ridley (1965).

BIBLIOGRAPHY

Obituary. *NYTimes*, January 17, 1973, 42:1; *WWWIA* 6.

CECIL SHEPS
SAM SHEPS

SHORE, DINAH (1917–1994)

Dinah Shore, the quintessential American girl, was both America's sweetheart in the 1940s and 1950s and a leading example of an independent woman in the 1970s. Her career spanned over forty years and included stints on the radio and in the movies. Her most enduring legacy, however, is her impressive vocal recordings and television shows.

Born in Winchester, Tennessee, on March 1, 1917, to Anna (Stein) and Solomon Shore, she was named Frances "Fanny" Rose Stein. Her sister, Bessie, was eight years older. When Fanny was six years old, the family moved to Nashville. Two important childhood experiences affected the person who became the personality called Dinah. First, she suffered an attack of polio when she was eighteen months old, which left her with a paralyzed right leg. Her mother played a crucial role in her rehabilitation, massaging the leg regularly and insisting on a rigorous exercise program. As a result, she overcame the disability and, as a young child, learned to swim, play tennis, and dance ballet.

First as a popular recording artist, then on radio and finally television, Dinah Shore became a favorite of several generations of Americans. Her warm, intelligent, and self-confident presence made her especially suited for television, where she performed for more than twenty-five years. [New York Public Library]

The second major factor was the family's Jewishness. In Winchester, particularly, the Shores were conspicuously out of place as the only Jewish family in a Protestant environment. Even in Nashville, Jews were a small minority, and Shore noted in early interviews that she felt that she always had to be exemplary in her behavior and outstanding in her performance. When she graduated from Hume Fogg High School in 1934, she was voted "the Best All-Around Girl in the Class." By that time, she and her father (her mother had died when she was fifteen) lived with her older sister, who was married.

Shore went to Vanderbilt University, an unusual pathway for a young woman in the 1930s, but appropriate for a middle-class daughter of a businessman who wanted to give his daughter every opportunity for success. Shore majored in sociology at Vanderbilt, where she headed the women's government club and was president of her sorority. She graduated in 1938. During the summer of 1937, she went to New York City with her sorority sisters and fulfilled an ambition to sing on the radio. After her college graduation, she returned to New York and got a job singing on radio station WNEW. This experience led to others, and in January 1939 she became a singer with the Leo Reisman Orchestra. Though *Variety* noted her singing, the reviewer was not overly impressed with her pleasant but unexceptional style.

By this time, she called herself "Dinah," the name of a song she had sung on the radio, and began to enjoy some success. In September 1940, she went on the very popular Eddie Cantor radio show. Cantor later remarked on her hard work, her exceedingly pleasant style, and her easy manner, traits that would be noted throughout her long career. Shore sang on the Cantor show for three years, while also hosting radio musical variety series of her own. In fact, until 1955, she would rarely be off the airwaves for long.

In 1940, her recording of "Yes, My Darling Daughter" sold half a million copies. In 1944, her rendition of "I'll Walk Alone" was one of the year's biggest hits. In all, Dinah Shore had seventy-five hit recordings. Her contralto voice conveyed an image of sincerity and goodwill. Her personal appearances during World War II were enthusiastically received, and only Frank Sinatra exceeded her popularity. On December 5, 1943, she married actor George Montgomery. In 1948, she gave birth to a daughter, Melissa Ann.

In 1951, she made the transition from radio to television and appeared twice weekly for fifteen minutes each. During this period, she also appeared in six movies, the most notable being *Up in Arms* with Danny Kaye. Shore did not enjoy moviemaking and did not think she was particularly effective in that medium. She was right. Television turned out to be the perfect medium; the small screen allowed her personal warmth and intimate manner to be showcased. During the history of *The Dinah Shore Show*, from 1951 to 1956, Shore sang and had guests who performed. In 1956, *The Dinah Shore Chevrolet Show*, a one-hour weekly musical variety show, came into being, and she became even more famous singing her trademark song: "See the U.S.A. in Your Chevrolet." The show remained high in the ratings for seven seasons.

Shore's marriage to George Montgomery ended in divorce in May 1962, and she decided to retire temporarily from a weekly television show so that she could spend more time with her children. Besides her daughter, she had adopted a son, John David, in 1954. Shore moved her family from Beverly Hills to Palm Springs, California, and though she appeared occasionally in concerts and in Las Vegas, she stayed out of the public eye until 1970, when she returned to a new variety show called *Dinah*. This show lasted from 1970 to 1974 and was followed by an afternoon talk show called *Dinah's Place*. On this show, she talked to her guests, shared recipes and cooked with them, and sang. *Dinah's Place* was on the air from 1974 to 1979. Dinah Shore hosted successful television shows for over twenty years, something of a record in an industry where ratings and profitability often lead to quick series cancellations.

Sponsoring a major women's golf tournament beginning in the 1980s, Dinah Shore remained active. In 1981, she did a multicity concert tour for the first time in over a decade. Dinah Shore died of ovarian cancer just short of her seventy-seventh birthday, on February 24, 1994.

Dinah Shore contributed to America's entertainment for over forty years. During wartime, she projected an image of home, love, and family for the American soldiers overseas and for their families at home. In early television, she displayed great skill in the very American format of a variety show, encouraging her guests and introducing new talent. As a talk show hostess in the 1970s, she allowed her guests to share their views in a nonconfrontational setting. While some television critics of the 1970s compared her unfavorably to the more combative Phil Donahue, her supporters pointed out the need for civility in an increasingly tendentious and hostile world.

Dinah Shore was the perfect transitional figure for women in changing times. She was independent, intelligent, self-confident, and accomplished while, at the same time, she projected an image of warmth and femininity. She matured nicely on television, proving to older women that aging was not a curse or a disease. Thanks to audio and video recordings, her legacy continues.

BIBLIOGRAPHY

Cassidy, Bruce. *Dinah! A Biography* (1979); *Current Biography* (1966): 376–378, and (1994): 60; "Dinah's Showcase." *Newsweek* (December 8, 1952): 54; Holden, Stephen. Obituary. *NYTimes*, February 25, 1994, B16; Hubler, Richard G. "The Indestructible Dinah." *Coronet* 47 (November 1959): 143–148; "Is There Anyone Finah?" *Time* (December 16, 1957): 60; Johnson, Grady. "Dinah Shore Story." *Coronet* 33 (November 1952): 92–97; Morehead, A. "For Fifteen Years Nobody Finer." *Cosmopolitan* (August 1955): 44–49; "It's Tough To Be a Woman." *TV Guide* (December 15, 1956): 13; Stewart, Phyllis. "Dinah Shore Is Back on the Road Doing What She Loves to Do Best." *Chicago Sun-Times*, May 17, 1981, 10; "Ten Years for Dinah." *TV Guide* (October l, 1960).

JUNE SOCHEN

SHORE, VIOLA BROTHERS (1890–1970)

In 1920, in the *Saturday Evening Post*, Viola Brothers Shore wrote, "Someday I hope to live the kind of life where I'll have nothing to think about but writing. Where I won't have to scribble my poems in the subway on the back of the delicatessen bill, where if I file the darn thing under bills I'm out a poem and if I file it under poetry the delicatessen man has me in a tight place." This statement characterizes the early struggles of Viola Brothers Shore, a writer of extraordinary versatility.

Born in New York City on May 26, 1890, she was the first child of Dr. Abram Brothers, a well-known surgeon who was also a writer, an actor, and a violinist who taught his daughter to play the violin. According to family lore, her mother, Minnie Epstein Brothers, descended from the first kosher butcher in New York, was born following a dramatic escape from the New Orleans region where her father had shot a southern gentleman who was attacking his pregnant wife. He fled and later Minnie's mother followed in a canoe paddled by a Native American guide. Viola had a sister, Madeleine, and a brother, Arthur J. Brothers, a lawyer.

Educated in public schools and at Normal College (now HUNTER COLLEGE), Viola left school at sixteen with musical aspirations. After these were cut short by her father's illness, she enrolled in business school, then worked in an office, and started an electrical contracting business with William Shore, an engineer whom she'd married in 1912. Daughter WILMA SHORE, who also became a successful writer, was born on October 12, 1913.

While attending New York University, Viola Brothers Shore began her career as a writer in a range of disciplines. She wrote poetry, biography (*Stage Struck John Golden*, 1930), stories and articles published in *College Humor*, *Collier's*, and *Saturday Evening Post*; plays, including *We Must Recruit!* (1930) with Jeanne Manookian, *Stage Struck* (1930) with John Golden, *Fools Rush In*, and sketches for *New Faces*, produced on Broadway in 1934. Her short stories, many about Jewish American lives of the day, were collected in *The Heritage and Other Stories* (1921).

Shore wrote silent movie titles and original stories for many motion pictures including *The Kibitzer* (1929) and *Walking on Air* (1936). She also collaborated on movies with other writers, including Charles Kaufman, with whom she wrote *Breakfast for Two* (1937). She wrote numerous mystery stories, including *The Beauty Mask Murder* (1930) and *Murder on the Glass Floor* (1932) and won several Ellery Queen awards.

Divorced from William Shore in 1926, she later married Henry Braxton, a print dealer. In 1931, they moved to Hollywood and were divorced in 1933. In 1939, Shore married Haskoll Gleichman, a union activist; they divorced in 1945. She, Haskoll Gleichman, and her daughter Wilma were named during testimonies in the House Committee on Un-American Activities hearings.

In 1954, Shore moved back to New York City where she taught writing at New York University. Her papers indicate that in her latter years she was working on books about women in the writing business and about teaching. Viola Brothers Shore died in New York City on March 27, 1970.

SELECTED WORKS BY
VIOLA BROTHERS SHORE

The Beauty Mask Murder (1930); *Breakfast for Two*, with Charles Kaufman (1937); *The Heritage and Other Stories* (1921); *The Kibitzer* (1929); *Murder on the Glass Floor* (1932); *New Faces: An Intimate Review*, with Warburton Guilbert (1934); *No Limit*, with Frank Tuttle (1930); *Stage Struck*, with John Golden (1930); *Walking on Air* (1936); *We Must Recruit!*, with Jeanne Manookian (1930).

BIBLIOGRAPHY

AJYB 24:203; Ask, M.N., and S. Gershanek. *Who Was Who in Journalism 1925–1928* (1978); Bzowski, Francis Diodato. *American Women Playwrights, 1900–1930* (1992); *Contemporary Authors*. Vol. 16 (1975); Coven, Brenda. *American Women Dramatists of the Twentieth Century* (1982); Kalmar, Bert. *The Life of The Party* (1937); Obituary.

NYTimes, March 31, 1970, 41:3; O'Brien, Edward J., ed. *The Best Short Stories of 1919* (1919), and *The Best Short Stories of 1920* (1920), and *The Best Short Stories of 1921* (1921); Queen, Ellery. *One-Hundred-and-One Years' Entertainment: The Great Detective Stories, 1841–1941* (1945), and *The Queen's Awards, 1947* (1947); Shore, Viola Brothers. Papers, 1912–1970. Archives, The American Heritage Center, University of Wyoming, Laramie; Vaughn, Robert. *Only Victims* (1972); "Who's Who and Why." *Saturday Evening Post* (September 18, 1920); *WWIAJ* (1926, 1928, 1938).

BETH O'SULLIVAN

SHORE, WILMA (b. 1913)

In 1929, at age sixteen, Wilma Shore went to Paris to study painting. Leo Stein, GERTRUDE STEIN's brother, declared her a leading talent of her generation. Years later, this prediction came true, but in another artistic area: Shore became a writer.

Wilma Shore was born in New York City on October 12, 1913, to William J. Shore, an engineer, and VIOLA BROTHERS SHORE, a fiction and screen writer. Raised in an assimilated Jewish home, she was educated at the Walden School in New York and in high schools in California, and attended the Otis Art Institute in Los Angeles.

In 1932, Shore married Charles Hancock, an unemployed actor, had a daughter, Hilary, and abandoned her painting career. Following the dissolution of her marriage, she returned to New York City and married writer Lou Solomon in 1935. They moved to California in 1940, and in 1942, her daughter Dinah was born.

As talented a writer as she was a painter, Shore's second story *The Butcher* was included in *The Best Short Stories of 1941*, and she continued to receive their honor call mention in subsequent years. Shore published widely in magazines, including *The New Yorker*, *Cosmopolitan*, *Story Magazine*, *The Saturday Evening Post*, *The Writer*, *Ladies' Home Journal*, *The Antioch Review*, *McCalls*, and *The Nation*. In 1950, her story "The Cow on the Roof" was included in the *O. Henry Awards Prize Stories* and in 1965, *Women Should Be Allowed*, a collection of short stories, was published. Shore also wrote for television, was commissioned to write a song for Carol Channing, and was included in the anthology *Best From Fantasy and Science Fiction* in 1965 and 1973. She also published autobiographical pieces in the *New York Times Sunday Magazine* and the *Women's Studies Quarterly*.

A dedicated teacher, Shore taught at the League of American Writers' School from 1942 to 1944 and at the People's Education Center until its dissolution. She then taught from her home.

Shore's involvement with these schools, her work on the editorial board of the *California Quarterly*, a politically progressive publication, and other left-wing political activity caused her and her husband to be blacklisted during the House Committee on Un-American Activities hearings.

They returned to New York in 1954. Wilma Shore is currently at work on her memoirs.

SELECTED WORKS BY WILMA SHORE

"The Butcher." In *The Best Short Stories of 1941*, edited by Edward J. O'Brien (1941); "The Cow on the Roof." In *O. Henry Awards Prize Stories* (1950); *Women Should Be Allowed* (1965).

BIBLIOGRAPHY

Contemporary Authors. Vol. 16 (1975); Vaughn, Robert. *Only Victims* (1972).

BETH O'SULLIVAN

SHOSHANA, ROSE (1895–1968)

The journey from Lodz, Poland, where Rose Shoshana was born on June 25, 1895, to New York was not an unusual one for an Eastern European Jewish woman of her time. This was, however, only one of many journeys Rose Shoshana made in her long career as a Yiddish actress, theater director, dramatist, writer, and translator. Born Esther Ruda Yakubovitch, she lost her father, a doctor, at age eight and was raised in poverty by her mother. At age twelve, she had to sew to earn money, but continued her studies in the evening at the Folk University at Geyer's Market in Lodz.

As a child she began reciting poetry and acting in plays in school. In 1908, she made her dramatic debut with the Harfe troupe at the Groyses Teater as Manke in Sholem Asch's *Got fun Nekome* [God of vengeance]. In 1912, she married Lazar Kahan, a Yiddish writer, theater person, and Bundist political activist, who would be her partner in many theatrical and literary ventures. They had a daughter, Lila Kalianis, a singer. Throughout her long career, Shoshana performed with many theater troupes both in Europe and America.

A tour of Poland, begun in 1939, was interrupted by World War II. She and her husband fled to Vilna and then to Kovno in Lithuania. In 1941, they made their way through Siberia to Kobe, Japan, where Shoshana performed on the very night of her arrival. At the end of 1941, the couple went with the Bundist refugee group to Shanghai. There, they lived in the ghetto from 1942 to 1945, continuing their theatrical work. In 1946, her husband died of typhus in Shanghai. Their two sons, who remained behind in Europe, disappeared in Soviet territory. It was this experience of Warsaw under siege and, later, her life in the Shanghai ghetto that Shoshana described in her memoir, *In Fayer un in Flamen* [In fire and in flames], her only work to appear in book form, published in 1949 in Buenos Aires under the name R. Shoshana-Kahan, as part of the series *Dos Poylishe Yidntum* [Polish Jewry].

At the end of 1946, after recovering from typhus, Shoshana was brought to America, where she immediately became active as both an actress and journalist. She performed in the National Theater in 1946, in Dos Naye Pleytim Teater [New refugee theater], which she helped to create, and in Maurice Schwartz's Art Theater in 1955. In 1957, she directed the Ensemble Theater.

Her career as a writer was no less prolific. She made her literary debut, according to Zilbercweig, in 1915, with a translation in *Lodzer Tageblat* of Morbeau's "Death of a Dog." From 1924 to 1930 she published novels and contributed to the women's pages of Yiddish newspapers in Poland as well as to the Polish *Pionta Rana*.

In America, she continued her literary activity and was among the first to write about Nazi terror in the Yiddish press. In 1940 she published *"Bletlekh fun a Togbukh"* [Pages from a diary] in the *Forverts* under her own name. In 1941, the Kharbin Russian newspaper *Yevreyski Zhizn* [Jewish life] published her war notes, *In Fayer un in Flamen*, which later appeared as the Yiddish book mentioned above. In 1946, she published a series of articles about life in China in the *Forverts* and in the *Amerikaner.* Between February 1947 and October 1968, she published twelve novels in the *Forverts*. She also edited a daily column for the paper, "Di Froy un di Heym" [The woman and the home], under the name of Rose Mary. Although many of her novels were reprinted in newspapers in Lithuania, Argentina, and elsewhere, none of them was ever published in book form.

Shoshana's work as a translator and dramatist includes translations of Karl Shener's drama *Tayvl's Vayb* [Devil's wife], *Der Friling* [Springtime] by Heinreich Tsimerman, *Yener* [The other] by Gabriela Zapolska, *Di Froy Vos Hot Derharget* [The wife who killed] by Herricks, and *Di Reter fun Moral* [The saviors of morality] by Propan, in collaboration with her husband. She translated and dramatized *Zind un Shtrof* [Sin and punishment] by Zola and Farberovich's *Urke Nakhalnik*, and dramatized her own novels *Bashke* and

Ven dos Harts Iz Yung [When the heart is young], *Zeyer Tsveyter Friling* [Their second springtime], and *Dos Geyeg Nokh Glik* [The hunt for happiness].

Her film appearances include *Lamed Vov* [The thirty-six just men] and Joseph Opatoshu's *In Poylishe Velder* [In Polish woods], both in 1926.

Rose Shoshana died on November 2, 1968.

SELECTED WORKS BY ROSE SHOSHANA

Bletlekh fun a Togbukh [Pages from a diary] (1940); *Dos Geyeg Nokh Glik* [The hunt for happiness] (1948); *Far Zeyere Zind* [For their sins] (1957); *In Fayer un in Flamen* [In fire and in flames] (1941. In book form, 1949); *Ir Mames Sod* [Her mother's secret] (1954); *Kinder on Tates* [Children without fathers] (1951); *Libe un Has* [Love and hate] (1955); *Nakhes fun Kinder* [Joy from children] (1956); *Panna do Zhietchi* [The children's governess] (n.d.); *Plonter fun Lebn* [The tangle of life] (1953); *Ven a Harts Iz Yung* [When a heart is young] (1947); *Ven a Mame Muz Shvaygn* [When a mother must be silent] (1949); *Ver Iz di Mame?* [Who is the mother] (1953); *Yung Blut* [Young blood] (1958); *Zeyer Tsveyter Friling* [Their second springtime] (1950).

BIBLIOGRAPHY

AJYB 70:525; Botoshanski, Y. "Tsvishn yo un neyn" [Between yes and no]. *Di Prese* (Buenos Aires), April 25, 1949/50; *Leksikon fun der Nayer Yidisher Literatur* [Lexicon of new Yiddish literature] (1959), s.v. "Kahan, Shoshana"; Obituaries. *Forverts*, November 4, 1968, and *NYTimes*, November 3, 1968, 89:1; Rogoff, Hillel. "In Fayer un in Flamen—Togbukh fun di Milkhome Yorn." *Forverts*, May 7, 1950; Zilbercweig, Zalmen, ed. *Leksikon fun Yidishn Teater* [Lexicon of Yiddish theater]. Vol. 3 (1959).

SHEVA ZUCKER

SHOSTAK, MARJORIE (1945–1996)

Although not trained as an anthropologist, Marjorie Shostak authored an anthropological classic, the internationally acclaimed *Nisa: The Life and Words of a !Kung Woman*, the life history of a woman of the !Kung San (or Bushmen) people of Africa's Kalahari Desert. She also coauthored another important work, *The Palaeolithic Prescription*, and wrote over twenty scholarly papers on Kalahari ethnography and art, and on the methods of transcribing and writing a life history.

Born in Brooklyn, on May 11, 1945, Shostak was the younger of two daughters born to Jerome Shostak, an educator and author of more than forty English textbooks, and Edna (Schiff) Shostak, a high school teacher. Her forebears originally came from Eastern Europe and England. Shostak studied English literature at Brooklyn College (B.A. 1966), where she met Melvin Konner. Moving to Cambridge, Massachusetts,

they were married in 1968, and Shostak became an associate of Harvard's Peabody Museum. They had three children: Susanne, Adam, and Sarah.

When the couple traveled to Botswana in 1969 for Konner's doctoral research, Shostak spent her time photographing, audiotaping music, and studying women's artistic productions such as beadwork. Well into her fieldwork, she turned her tape recorder toward recording the life stories of women in the Dobe camp. She had taped several histories with varying results when she was introduced to a feisty and outspoken woman in her early fifties, to whom Marjorie gave the pseudonym "!Nisa" (later shortened to "Nisa" by a publisher reluctant to foist click symbols on the public).

The great strength of Marjorie Shostak's *Nisa* is its ability to speak to people across cultural boundaries, a credit both to Nisa herself, a storyteller of great depth and candor, and to Shostak, who framed Nisa's words with insight into their shared womanhood and the human condition.

When *Nisa* appeared in 1981, it quickly became an anthropological classic, reprinted in a paperback edition in 1983 and translated into many languages. Presenting the life history of ethnographic subjects is a well-established tradition in anthropology, an effective vehicle for conveying the life experience of members of of another culture in the subject's own idiom. Shostak's *Nisa* became the most widely read life history in the annals of anthropology. Selling well over 150,000 copies, it became the entrée into anthropology for tens of thousands of students, as well as a foundational text in contemporary feminist anthropology. Shostak's life histories anticipated by a decade the reflexive turn in American anthropology. Her presentation of the words of a woman of the "Fourth World" gave agency and voice to one who was triply disempowered. Shostak's work continues to draw critical attention among scholars even while it delights students and lay readers.

In 1983, Shostak and Konner moved to Atlanta, where Shostak became a research associate at the Institute of Liberal Arts at Emory University and a faculty member in anthropology, teaching courses in life history methods and Kalahari ethnography. Diagnosed with breast cancer in April 1988, she resolved to return to the Kalahari to see Nisa once again, and did so in 1989. She recorded another series of interviews that form the basis of "Nisa Revisited," a manuscript that Shostak had almost completed before her death.

Marjorie Shostak's long and complex relationship with Nisa became the subject of a play, *My Heart Is Still Shaking*, written by Atlanta playwright Brenda

Bynum. The play, directly addressing the issue of Shostak's illness with power and honesty, was a dramatic tour de force.

Raised in the secular humanistic tradition of Judaism, Shostak was appreciative of older traditions expressed in Friday family dinners and her children's bar and bat mitzvahs. Her personal philosophy combined insights from African cultures, her own Judaism, and other spiritual sources.

Marjories Shostak died on October 6, 1996, at age fifty-one.

SELECTED WRITINGS BY MARJORIE SHOSTAK

Nisa: The Life and Words of a !Kung Woman (1981); *Nisa Revisited* (forthcoming); *The Paleolithic Prescription*, with Boyd Eaton and Melvin Konner (1988).

RICHARD B. LEE

SHTOK, FRADEL (b. 1890)

Fradel Shtok holds a place among the pioneers of modern Yiddish literature for her treatment of the inner sensual lives of Jewish women. Although her work showed great promise, her career as a Yiddish writer was brief. Very little biographical information is available about her. Born in Skale, Galicia, in 1890, she was a lively child, musically talented and academically gifted, but her early childhood was marred by the death of her mother when Shtok was two years old. A few years later, her father, Shimen, was sent to prison for his involvement in a murder and died there when Shtok was ten. Thereafter, she was raised by an aunt.

Immigrating to New York in 1907, Shtok published poems and short stories in a variety of anthologies and literary journals, especially those of the literary group Di Yunge [The young generation]. A number of her poems appeared in Moyshe Bassin's landmark anthology *Antologye fun Finf Hundert Yor Yidishe Poezye* [Anthology of five hundred years of Yiddish poetry] (1917). She is one of the first poets to write sonnets in Yiddish.

In 1919, Shtok published a collection of thirty-eight stories entitled *Gezamlte Ertseylungen* [Collected stories], in which the themes of female eroticism and sexual repression are prominent. Responses from critics were mixed. The book was acclaimed by Shmuel Niger in the literary journal *Di Tsukunft* [The future], but a somewhat negative review by the poet Aaron Glanz (Leyeles) appeared in *Der Tog* [The day]. Glanz praised Shtok's writing style and talent, but complained that, as a whole, the collection was monotonous, and advised the author to stop writing about the

shtetl and the sweatshop. Shtok was deeply angered by Glanz's review, and is reputed to have abandoned writing in Yiddish because of it. A harsh review of *Gezamlte Ertseylungen* by Moissaye Olgin appeared in the socialist weekly *Di Naye Velt* [The new world]. Olgin accused Shtok of taking a condescending attitude toward the characters in her stories and writing with a great deal of pessimism. None of the three critics took note of the innovative thematic content in the collection.

During the 1920s, Shtok switched to writing in English and published one work, *Musicians Only* (1927), which received little critical attention.

By the early 1930s, Shtok had disappeared from the Yiddish literary scene. She is thought to have spent her last years in a sanatorium. The date and place of her death remain unknown.

SELECTED WORKS BY FRADEL SHTOK

Antologye fun Finf Hundert Yor Yidishe Poezye [Anthology of five hundred years of Yiddish poetry]. Edited by Moyshe Basin (1917); *Gezamlte Ertseylungen* [Collected stories] (1919); *Found Treasures: Stories by Yiddish Women Writers*. Edited by Frieda Forman, Ethel Raicus, Sarah Silberstein Swartz, and Margie Wolfe (1995); *Musicians Only* (1927); *The Tribe of Dina: A Jewish Women's Anthology*. Edited by Melanie Kaye/Kantrowitz and Irena Klepfisz (1989).

BIBLIOGRAPHY

"Fradl Shtok." *Leksikon fun der Nayer Yidisher Literatur* 8, no. 608 (1981): 39–45; Glanz, Aaron. "Temperament." *Der Tog* (December 7, 1919): 9; Glatshteyn, Yankev. "Tsu der Biografye fun a Dikhterin" [Toward the biography of a woman writer]. *Tog-Morgn-zhurnal*. Sunday supplement (September 19, 1965), 14: 7; Hofshteyn, D., and P. Shames. "Poetik: Elementn fun Ritm un Stil" [Poetics: Elements of rhythm and style]. In *Literatur Kentenish (Ershter Teyl)* (1928); Niger, Sh. "Di Ertseylungen fun Fradl Shtok" [The short stories of Fradel Shtok]. *Tsukunft* (October 1920): 608–609; Olgin, Moissaye. "Pesimizm" [Pessimism]. *Di Naye Velt* (January 9, 1920): 16–17; Reyzen, Zalmen. "Fradl Shtok." *Leksikon fun der Yidisher Literatur, Prese un Filologye* 4 (1929): 572–574; Tabatshnik, Avrom. "Fradl Shtok un der Sonet" [Fradel Shtok and the sonnet]. In *Dikhter un Dikhtung* (1965).

ELLEN KELLMAN

SHULTZ, LILLIE (1904–1981)

Victor H. Bernstein, managing editor of the *Nation* during her years there, described Lillie Shultz as the magazine's "dynamo—a tireless bundle of energy." "Lillie had two passions," he said, "the *Nation* and Israel." This energetic journalist was a Zionist, a champion of the oppressed, a skilled administrator, and a businesswoman.

Born in 1904, Lillie Shultz was raised in Philadelphia with two brothers and three sisters. She attended Philadelphia public schools and the University of Pennsylvania, majoring in education.

Her first job as a journalist was with the *Philadelphia Jewish World* as the editor of the English-language section. In an article entitled "Why I Was Jealous: A Sukkoth Memory," she illustrates her love of Jewish culture and the influence of her grandfather on her future Zionist activism. "Always toward the end," she relates of her grandfather's storytelling in the sukkah, "there crept into his voice a tone of sorrow, as if he saw in the long procession the endless hordes of exiles banished from Palestine to a life of misery and misfortune. And when he finished, he always offered up a prayer for the speedy restoration of Palestine."

Her grandfather's prayer became her own. She moved to New York City and, after a stint as a cable editor and reporter at the Jewish Telegraphic Service, joined the staff of the AMERICAN JEWISH CONGRESS. From 1933 to 1944, Lillie Shultz was chief administrative officer and director of publicity (appointed by Rabbi Stephen Wise himself), and the only woman on staff. She served on the governing council, was an editor of the *Congress Bulletin*, was an active member of a committee dealing with the 1936 Olympics, and was instrumental in encouraging the American Jewish Congress to assert itself in the boycott of goods manufactured in Nazi Germany. Ever committed to the end of oppression and discrimination, she was also instrumental in establishing a commission to investigate economic discrimination against Jews in the United States.

Her political intelligence and skilled writing were best displayed during her tenure as a writer, member of the editorial board, and director of the Nation Associates, an advocacy group at the *Nation*. From 1944 to 1955, Shultz wrote hard-hitting, politically sophisticated articles for the *Nation* from her vantage point as a reporter at the United Nations. In articles such as "U.S.-Israel Crisis: Peace or Appeasement," "Peace: Why It Was By-Passed," and "Democracy's Betrayal of Spain," she commented critically on United Nations actions on matters affecting the Middle East, China, and Franco's Spain. During these years, she also lobbied tirelessly for the partition of Palestine and against nuclear expansion.

In 1956, Lillie Shultz opened her own public relations firm, Kenmore Associates, whose main client was the State of Israel. From 1966 to 1975, she was

director of public relations for the Weizmann Institute of Science in Israel.

Lillie Shultz died in April 1981 after a long illness. Victor H. Bernstein wrote in an obituary for the *Nation* that Lillie Shultz was a "gallant and fighting soul." She had dedicated her life to Zionism and the annihilation of the oppression of all people through action and the written word.

SELECTED WORKS BY LILLIE SHULTZ
"Edge of a Precipice: A Report from Lake Success." *Nation* (1950): 159–161; "The Jerusalem Story: A Victory for the Vatican." *Nation* (1949): 589–592; "Peace or Blackmail: The U.N.'s Chance in the Middle East." *Nation* (1951): 204–207.

BIBLIOGRAPHY
AJYB 83: 363; Gottlieb, Moshe R. *American Anti-Nazi Resistance, 1933–1941* (1982); *NYTimes Biographical Service* 12, no. 1 (January 1981).

RONA HOLUB

SHUVAL, JUDITH TANNENBAUM (b. 1926)

Judith Shuval is one of the main scholars in the field of the sociology of health in Israel. Her research on migration and health, inequality in health, self-care in health, the doctor-patient relationship, and the processes of professional socialization has been based in concrete life in Israel and has broader implications for such topics cross-culturally.

Judith Tannenbaum Shuval was born in New York in 1926. She is a graduate of HUNTER COLLEGE. In 1947, she earned a bachelor of Hebrew letters from the Jewish Theological Seminary and, in 1955, a Ph.D. in sociology from Harvard University. In 1949, she made aliyah to Israel and was appointed senior research associate and project director at the Israel Institute of Applied Social Research. There she directed studies in the areas of ethnic relations, immigrant absorption, housing and urban settlement, medical sociology, occupational sociology, and the sociology of nursing. She also served as adviser on immigrant absorption for UNESCO from 1955 to 1956. She has been a fellow of the American Sociological Association and served as treasurer in the Israeli Sociological Association.

In 1972, Shuval secured an appointment as associate professor in sociology at the Hebrew University in Jerusalem and became the Louis and Pearl Rose Professor of Medical Sociology. She has also served as the director of the Programme on Medical Sociology at the School of Public Health at the Hebrew University. During the academic year 1978–1979, she was a visiting professor of sociology at the University of Michigan at Ann Arbor.

Shuval is the author of many books, including a study on immigration during Israel's first years, *Immigrants on the Threshold* (1963), *The Dynamics of Transition: Entering Medicine* (1979), and *Social Functions of Medical Practice*, written with A. Antonovsky and A.M. Davies (1970), *Newcomers and Colleagues: Soviet Immigrant Physicians in Israel* (1984), and *Social Dimensions of Health: The Israeli Experience* (1992).

Judith Tannenbaum Shuval is Phi Beta Kappa and received the Israel Prize for social sciences in 1965.

BIBLIOGRAPHY

EJ (1973–1982).

MARLA BRETTSCHNEIDER

SIDNEY, SYLVIA (b. 1910)

Feisty and opinionated, Sylvia Sidney in her prime was quite the opposite of the waiflike, even pathetic, victim of social oppression she played in Hollywood's Depression Era films.

Born in the Bronx, New York, on August 8, 1910, Sylvia Kosow Sidney was the daughter of Jewish immigrants from Russia and Romania. She attended New York public schools, then the Theatre Guild School in Manhattan from 1921 to 1925.

Following her Broadway debut at age sixteen in *The Squall*, Sidney graduated to leading-role status and soon attracted Hollywood's interest. She did a short stint with Fox Film—where she made *Thru Different Eyes*—before returning to Broadway. Back onstage in New York, she was discovered by Paramount mogul B.P. Schulberg, who offered her a contract. At Paramount, Sidney made the film that launched her career as a star, *City Streets*, directed by Rouben Mamoulian, who had taught and directed her at the Theatre Guild in New York. Shortly thereafter, she played the weepy pregnant girl in Joseph von Sternberg's *An American Tragedy* and a similarly vulnerable character in King Vidor's *Street Scene*.

In the films Sidney made for Paramount during the 1930s, she was often typecast—against her will—as the wistful, teary-eyed sufferer of hardship. Her characters were either wrongly convicted of crimes, sent to jail, or both. Though she may have lamented being cast in such roles, Sidney's screen personae exemplified heartfelt, working-class, urban heroines with whom similarly metropolitan Jewish audiences could identify.

From An American Tragedy *to* Beetlejuice, *Sylvia Sidney has performed on the silver screen for sixty years. Along the way, the fiery, opinionated actress (who, ironically, often portrayed sympathetically meek characters) has locked horns with such directors as Josef von Sternberg, King Vidor, and Alfred Hitchcock. [New York Public Library]*

A notoriously stubborn personality offscreen, Sidney worked and fought with such luminary directors as von Sternberg, Vidor, Fritz Lang (in whose first three American films she starred), Alfred Hitchcock (for whom she traveled to England), and William Wyler. Her onscreen leading men included Humphrey Bogart, James Cagney, Gary Cooper, Henry Fonda, Cary Grant, and Spencer Tracy, all of whom, like Sidney herself, were rising to stardom during the 1930s.

After her Paramount contract expired, Sidney signed with independent producer Walter Wanger. During this period, she was the first American star to work with Hitchcock—whom she found as difficult as his Hollywood counterparts—on *Sabotage/A Woman Alone*. Among the directors she worked with under Wanger, William K. Howard (with whom she made *Mary Burns—Fugitive*, 1935) remained her favorite.

In 1956, well beyond the heyday of the 1930s social injustice films with which she is so often identified, Sidney left Hollywood and returned to the New York stage. Among her numerous theatrical appearances in the 1950s and 1960s, she played the title role in *Auntie Mame* and Mrs. Kolowitz in *Enter Laughing*. Returning to film in 1973, she appeared in *Summer Wishes, Winter Dreams* as Joanne Woodward's mother. Her comeback performance garnered her an Oscar nomination for best supporting actress. Teenagers today recognize her as the caseworker, Juno, from *Beetlejuice* (1988).

Sidney was married to publisher Bennett A. Cerf from 1935 to 1936, to actor Luther Adler from 1938 to 1947, and to Carlton Alsop from 1947 to 1950. Her second husband, the son of Jacob P. and SARA ADLER, was a member of the famous Adler acting clan of the Yiddish stage. Her son by Luther Adler, Jody, died in 1985 from Lou Gehrig's disease during Sidney's filming of one of the first AIDS television films, *An Early Frost*. In the film, she plays the sympathetic grandmother of a young man with AIDS. Sidney is involved in AIDS research and is a member of the national board of ALS.

Sidney has written two books on one of her favorite pastimes, needlepoint: *The Sylvia Sidney Needlepoint Book* and *The Sylvia Sidney Question and Answer Book on Needlepoint*. She breeds pug dogs at her home in Danbury, Connecticut.

FILMOGRAPHY

Accent on Youth (1935); *An American Tragedy* (1931); *Andre's Mother* (1991); *Beetlejuice* (1988); *Behind the High Wall* (1956); *Behold My Wife* (1935); *Blood on the Sun* (1945); *City Streets* (1931); *Confessions of a Co-Ed* (1931); *Damien: Omen II* (1978); *Dead End* (1937); *The Exorcist III* (1990); *Fury* (1936); *God Told Me So* (1976); *Good Dame* (1934); *Hammett* (1983); *I Never Promised You a Rose Garden* (1977); *Jennie Gerhardt* (1933); *Ladies of the Big House* (1931); *Love from a Stranger* (1947); *Madame Butterfly* (1932); *Mary Burns—Fugitive* (1935); *Merrily We Go to Hell* (1932); *The Miracle Man* (1932); *Les Misérables* (1952); *Mr. Ace* (1946); *One Third of a Nation* (1939); *Order of Death* (1983); *Pick Up* (1933); *Sabotage/A Woman Alone* (1936); *The Searching Wind* (1946); *Street Scene* (1931); *Summer Wishes, Winter Dreams* (1973); *Thirty Day Princess* (1934); *The Trail of the Lonesome Pine* (1936); *Thru Different Eyes* (1929); *Used People* (1993); *Violent Saturday* (1955); *The Wagons Roll at Night* (1941); *You and Me* (1938); *You Only Live Once* (1937).

TELEVISION

An Early Frost (1986); *F.D.R.: The Last Year* (1980); *Finnegan Begin Again* (1985); *The Gossip Columnist* (1979); *Having It All* (1982); *Pals* (1987); *Raid on Entebbe* (1976); *The Shadow Box* (1980); *A Small Killing* (1981).

BIBLIOGRAPHY

Catsos, Gregory J.M. "An Interview with the Outspoken Sylvia Sidney." *Filmfax Magazine* (1990); *Current Biography* (1981); Katz, Ephraim. *The Film Encyclopedia* (1979); Laffel, Jeff. "Sylvia Sidney." *Films in Review* 45, nos. 9–10 (September 1994): 2–19; Quinlan, David. *Quinlan's Illustrated Registry of Film Stars* (1981); Rigdon, Walter, ed. *Who's Who of the American Theatre* (1966); Sidney, Sylvia. Clippings file. New York Public Library for the Performing Arts, and video interview by Robert Sklar, c. 1985. American Museum of the Moving Image, Astoria, Queens; Thomas, Nicholas, ed. *International Dictionary of Films and Filmmakers*. Vol. 3: *Actors and Actresses* (1992); Thomson, David. *A Biographical Dictionary of Film*. 3d ed. (1994); *UJE*; *WWIAJ* (1938).

ALYSSA GALLIN

SILLS, BEVERLY (b. 1929)

A heroine who succeeds against all odds is a perennial favorite of Americans. Opera singer and manager Beverly Sills fits this description. A precocious singer since the age of three, she did not debut at the Metropolitan Opera House until she was almost forty-six years old, way beyond her prime as an opera singer. Yet her career exemplifies a fighter who carved out her own niche in the opera world singing unusual repertory in less well known and less well regarded houses before the official Metropolitan Opera world acknowledged her. Sills defied the odds and, as in the best of American traditions, she succeeded. Further, she was a groundbreaker in her role as director of the New York City Opera Company (NYCO), a position neither a woman nor a singer had ever held before.

Sills's great ability and charming personality showed itself early in her life. Born Belle Miriam

Now known as America's ambassador to opera and the arts in general, Beverly Sills triumphed over many difficulties and prejudices on her way to becoming a major star. Her boundless enthusiasm and egalitarian approach were hallmarks of her tenure as the first woman and first singer to manage the New York City Opera. [New York Public Library]

Silverman on May 25, 1929, in Brooklyn to Shirley (Bahn) and Morris Silverman, she displayed an interest in music as a baby. She listened to her mother's old recordings of Amelita Galli-Curci, the legendary soprano, and by age seven had memorized twenty-two arias. Her Italian was mechanically produced, but her stage presence and bubbly demeanor won over her early audiences. A family friend named her Beverly Sills, because she thought that it had better marquee value than Belle Silverman. Sills performed for family, friends, and whoever would listen. The actress and performer were already in evidence.

As a four- and five-year-old, she sang on the *Uncle Bob's Rainbow Hour* radio show. The self-confident and articulate manner that would be so evident in the adult Beverly Sills was already manifesting itself in the child performer. At age seven, she became the student of ESTELLE LIEBLING, a noted and experienced singing teacher. Liebling remained Sills's only teacher until Liebling's death in 1970. From ages nine until twelve, under Liebling's guidance, Sills was a regular performer on *Major Bowes' Amateur Hour*. Every Sunday,

she and her mother traveled from Brooklyn to Manhattan and the Capitol Theater Building to appear with Major Bowes. After three years, she retired to lead a more normal life in Brooklyn. However, the desire to perform remained an active ambition, though it was temporarily suppressed.

In Sills's second autobiography, called *Beverly*, she described her large, extended Jewish family, particularly her father's side of the family. Morris Silverman had eight brothers and three sisters, while Shirley Silverman had one brother and four sisters. Sundays were often visiting days when the Silverman clan would gather. Beverly and her two older brothers, Stanley and Sydney, visited with their cousins, aunts, and uncles. In her neighborhood, called Sea Gate, Jewish families were in the majority and frequent socializing of family and neighbors was common. Sills easily acknowledges her Jewish heritage, though she had little formal Jewish education. When Sills's father died in 1949 at the age of fifty-three, the connection with his side of the family weakened. By her account, neither the Silverman family nor the rabbi behaved in a comforting or supportive manner. Her mother turned to Christian Science for solace and saw no conflict between her Jewish heritage and her newfound philosophy.

Sills's father played a dominant role in shaping her behavior. He wanted her to complete her education, including college, before she returned to a singing career. Sills was a very good student whose IQ was 155, and she displayed talent for mathematics as well as music, a not unlikely combination of skills. In 1942, she graduated from P.S. 91 in Brooklyn; then, while she continued her singing lessons in French and Italian, she attended Erasmus Hall High School in Brooklyn and the Professional Children's School in Manhattan. By the time she was fifteen years old, she had mastered twenty operatic roles and, in her mind, had set her future course.

While her father wanted her to have a college education, Sills was determined to begin her professional singing career. She convinced her father to let her sing, and in the fall of 1945, at age sixteen, she went to work for the producer J.J. Shubert, touring with his Gilbert and Sullivan repertory company. In February 1947, she debuted in grand opera in the role of the Spanish gypsy Frasquita in Bizet's *Carmen* with the Philadelphia Civic Opera. Although Sills had begun her singing career earlier than many other sopranos, she had little success breaking into a major company's roster. By this time, she had more than fifty roles in her repertoire, but few opportunities to demonstrate her talent.

When her father died of lung cancer in 1949, she was both personally devastated by the loss and professionally frustrated at the lack of progress in her career. She continued searching for parts and often found herself touring in second-rate companies. In 1952, she spent the summer at the Concord Hotel in the Catskills, singing for an audience she called "appreciative Jews." From 1952 to 1955, she auditioned for Joseph Rosenstock, the director of the NYCO, and finally, in 1955, he agreed to let her join the company. This association became a fortunate union for both Sills's career and the company. The NYCO was considered to be the "second" opera house in the city and had neither the budget nor the prestige of the Metropolitan. However, Sills's presence would change that situation. In October 1955, she debuted in Strauss's *Die Fledermaus*, a role that displayed her charm, acting ability, and virtuoso singing. Her skillful coloratura voice, which had been in training for so many years, was now public knowledge.

While touring in Cleveland in 1956, she met the associate editor of the *Cleveland Plain Dealer*, Peter Greenough, and fell in love with him. The romance, courtship, and marriage, however, had many obstacles to overcome. Greenough was married at the time, a father of three daughters, Episcopalian, and thirteen years older than the twenty-six-year-old Sills. When Sills told her mother about Peter, Mrs. Silverman cried and wondered why her baby could not enjoy total happiness and success. Greenough courted Mrs. Silverman while wooing Beverly, and the couple were married on November 17, 1956. They established residence in Cleveland, and Sills commuted to New York to perform. The upper-class WASP society of Cleveland did not open its arms to Sills, a fact that astonished her. Her comfortable New York Jewish world had not prepared her for the sometimes overtly anti-Semitic world of Cleveland's upper crust. Her father-in-law's second wife was openly hostile to her, and Sills noted in her autobiography that she simply did not understand anti-Semitism, which judged people by predetermined labels, not as individuals. In 1959, the couple moved to Boston, where, in 1959, she gave birth to a daughter, Meredith (Muffy) Greenough. Some years later, they moved to New York City.

The Greenoughs learned that Muffy was deaf, a serious blow to an opera singer who had hoped to sing to her daughter. In 1961, Sills gave birth to a son, Peter Jr. (Bucky). Unfortunately, the child was severely retarded and required institutionalization. By her own admission, this was a very difficult period for Sills. She stopped singing professionally and concentrated on caring for her daughter. It was through the persistence of conductor Julius Rudel, her good friend and colleague, that she was persuaded to resume her career in 1962. By 1965, Sills at thirty-six years of age had become the New York City Opera's prima donna. The following year, when the company moved into its new house at Lincoln Center, Sills performed in what she later considered her finest role: as Cleopatra in Handel's *Julius Caesar* with Norman Treigle as her costar.

During the late 1960s, she gained fame and prominence in roles that had not been performed in many years. She was Pamira in Rossini's *The Siege of Corinth*, Elvira in Bellini's *I Puritani*, and three queens in Donizetti's *Roberto Devereux, Maria Stuarda,* and *Anna Bolena*. Sills's superb acting skills and her sparkling personality were well illustrated in these unusual and difficult roles. Critic Winthrop Sargeant called her one of the wonders of New York. She later stated that her Queen Elizabeth in *Roberto Devereux* was her proudest achievement.

On April 8, 1975, at age forty-five, she debuted at the Metropolitan Opera Company as Pamira in *The Siege of Corinth*. The following year, she sang *Lucia* at

Educated in both a Jewish and an American environment that encouraged and rewarded achievement, Beverly Sills is a role model for American women. Hers is certainly the most recognized woman's face in the world of opera. [New York Public Library]

the Met; in 1978, *Thaïs*. But Sills's singing days were soon to be over. As she neared age fifty, she considered other career moves. Her long association with the NYCO remained an interest, and in 1979, she became the first woman and the first singer to manage that opera company. She joined a small group of women opera directors: Carol Fox at the Lyric Opera in Chicago and Sarah Caldwell in Boston. Sills announced her retirement from singing in 1979, and her farewell gala, on October 27, 1980, was televised on PBS. It was twenty-five years to the day since she had first sung with the NYCO. Two thousand fans came to Lincoln Center to pay her tribute, and the company raised $1 million.

During the next ten years, Beverly Sills ran the NYCO. When she began, the company had a $5 million deficit. By 1987, she had eliminated the debt, demonstrating her awesome ability as a fund-raiser and public relations spokesperson for opera. Indeed,

during the 1980s, thanks to her television appearances, Beverly Sills became a national spokesperson for the arts. She also displayed her easy laughter and charming nature on a special with Carol Burnett and in frequent appearances on *The Tonight Show Starring Johnny Carson*. Sills sang for President Ronald Reagan and became a frequently quoted celebrity on matters related to the arts.

Though she acquired critics as well as fans in her new role as manager, Sills innovated in many areas. In 1983, she introduced supertitles in English, making opera more accessible to more people. She introduced sign language as well. Part of Sills's philosophy was to encourage American singers and to provide opportunities for American operas. In the mid-1950s, she had sung in Douglas Moore's *The Ballad of Baby Doe*, and in her tenure as director of the New York City Opera, she mounted productions of Stephen Sondheim, Dominick Argento, and Anthony Davis. Opera audiences saw, for the first time, an opera about Malcolm X (Davis's *X*), as well as a modern treatment of Casanova (Argento's *Casanova*). They heard new American singers such as Jerry Hadley, Samuel Ramey, and Carol Van Ness, all of whom went on to have major international careers. Sills's leadership demonstrated to the opera world that American singers, trained in the United States, could make significant careers for themselves here without apprenticing in Europe, a new phenomenon.

In 1984, Christopher Keene became music director of the company, and Sills concentrated on recruiting new singers and fund-raising. In 1989, she retired from her post but continued speaking and writing about the arts in America. In 1994, she became the chair of the Lincoln Center board, another first as no woman or performer had ever held this position before. Sills said that she planned to develop more programs for teenagers so that the young could be introduced to opera, classical music, and theater.

During the 1980s, she had received many honors, including the Presidential Medal of Freedom. In 1987, she was one of four inductees into the Working Woman's Hall of Fame.

Beverly Sills's contribution to the world of opera and the fine arts has been impressive. Her groundbreaking role as an opera director as well as her career as a singer have been notable. Her audio and video recordings, particularly from her 1950s performances in such delicate roles as Lucia, Manon, Thaïs, and the three Queens, will always preserve her legacy. Sills's singing was known for its delicacy and fine interpretation. Her coloratura voice did not have the range or the endurance of lyric sopranos. It was only the early recordings that captured her voice's beauty. Her video performances of *La Traviata* and *Manon* will ensure future generations the opportunity to see her effective acting technique. Her democratic interest in making opera available to large numbers of people reflects her egalitarian philosophy and her commitment to Americans of all ages, races, and backgrounds.

Indeed, in her autobiographical discussions of her beliefs, Sills talked about her cultural connection to Judaism and America. While she views herself as a religious person, she does not practice any ritual (other than to light a memorial candle for the anniversaries of her parents' deaths). She does not attend prayer services at a synagogue or temple and stated in her autobiography that her daughter, Muffy, could choose any religion she wished. In 1970, she visited Israel and was enormously impressed. She performed with Julius Rudel and the Israel Philharmonic and found the experience to be exuberant, stimulating, and exciting. But her connection to Israel and Judaism, she wrote, is historical and temperamental, not philosophical or spiritual. She believes that one can believe in God and be religious without membership in a particular religion.

As a Jewish American, Sills shares the very American commitment to equal opportunity for all and to the respect for and tolerance of religious and cultural differences. She enjoys the diversity of peoples in this country and considers the artistic freedoms and protections that America offers critical to creative success. As a self-confident woman, educated in both a Jewish and American environment that encouraged and rewarded achievement, Beverly Sills acts as a role model for American women. As someone who overcame many obstacles in her career, she exemplifies the enduring American image of the underdog succeeding against all odds. As an articulate advocate for the arts, Beverly Sills, along with the famous tenors, is possibly the most recognized face from the world of opera. In her new capacity as chair of Lincoln Center, she preserves her vital role in the cultural life of New York City.

BIBLIOGRAPHY

Current Biography. "Beverly Sills." (1982): 392–396; Davis, Peter G. "Devil's Disciple." *New York* 21 (October 8, 1988): 64+; Heymont, George. "Bravo NYCO!" *Horizon* 29 (April 1986): 33–34; McNally, Terence. "Patience Is a Virtue." *Horizon* 28 (July/August, 1985): 58; Rich, Alan. "High Notes at the City Opera." *Newsweek* 104 (October 8, 1984): 80+; Sills, Beverly. *Bubbles: A Self Portrait*, with Lawrence Linderman (1976), and *Beverly: An Autobiography* (1987), and "Make Ours a World of Love, Not Hate and War." *McCall's* 118 (May 1991): 68+.

JUNE SOCHEN

SILVER, JOAN MICKLIN (b. 1935)

With the release of her critically acclaimed film *Hester Street* in 1985, Joan Micklin Silver established herself as one of the country's premier independent film directors. Working with her husband, Raphael Silver, as producer, Joan Silver defied film industry insiders who insisted that women were "one more problem" they didn't need and that Jewish films would never reach a general audience. *Hester Street*, made without studio backing for a budget of $400,000, grossed $5 million in the United States. It garnered for Silver a Writers Guild nomination for best screenplay and for actress Carol Kane an Academy Award nomination for best actress.

Joan Micklin Silver was born in Omaha, Nebraska, on May 24, 1935, to Russian Jewish parents Maurice David and Doris (Shoshone) Micklin. She graduated from Omaha Central High School in 1952 and Sarah Lawrence College in 1956. Fresh out of college, she married Raphael D. Silver, son of Rabbi Abba Hillel Silver of Cleveland. The Silvers lived in Cleveland from 1956 to 1967 and raised three daughters there: Dina, (b. 1958), Marisa, (b. 1960), and Claudia, (b. 1963). Two of the three daughters now work in film, Marisa as a director and Dina as a producer.

In Cleveland, Silver taught music and wrote plays, five of which were performed at Cleveland theaters. Then in 1967, the Silvers moved to New York, and Silver began to write films for educational film companies. One of those companies, the Learning Corporation of America, commissioned her to write and direct films, among them *The Immigrant Experience*, which went on to win several awards. She wrote an original screenplay, *Limbo*, about the wives of prisoners of war in Vietnam, which was purchased by Universal Pictures and made into a film directed by Mark Robson. Silver clashed with the director over the character of the film's heroine, whom she had scripted as a "spunky, terrific gal." Refusing to do a rewrite to "soften" the character, Silver was fired, though she received story and coscripting credit in the final film.

When her success as a writer and director failed to bring her work in feature films, Silver decided to write and direct her own film. Her husband agreed to raise the money for the film and serve as its producer. The film became *Hester Street*, adapted by Silver from the 1890s novella *Yekl* by Abraham Cahan, later the editor of the *Jewish Daily Forward*. Interviewed by *American Film* magazine in 1989, Silver spoke about her choice of subject for *Hester Street*. "I thought, I'm going to make one that will count for my family. My parents were Russian Jewish, and my father was no longer living, but I cared a lot about the ties I had to that world. So that was how *Hester Street* started."

Turned down by every major studio as an "ethnic oddity . . . a lovely film, but for a Jewish audience," *Hester Street* was distributed by the Silvers, who had formed their own production and distribution company, Midwest Film Productions. Seen worldwide by Jewish and non-Jewish audiences, *Hester Street* sparked the beginning of renewed interest in the lives of immigrant Jews.

Despite the success of *Hester Street*, major studios still would not back Silver's next film. Her second feature, *Between the Lines* (1977), about a group of people who work for an alternative newspaper in Boston, was once again produced by her husband. Her third feature, *Chilly Scenes of Winter* (originally released by United Artists as *Head Over Heels* in 1979, but retitled and rereleased by United Artists Classics in 1981), based on a short story by Ann Beattie, marked the beginning of Silver's work with a movie studio.

Her next film with a Jewish topic, *Crossing Delancey*, a romantic comedy about an assimilated Jewish Manhattanite single (played by Amy Irving) and her Lower East Side pickle-selling boyfriend (played by Peter Riegert), was produced for Warner Brothers and released in 1988. Other films include *Loverboy* (1989) for Tri-Star and *Big Girls Don't Cry . . . They Get Even* (1992) for New Line.

Silver's directing extends to theater as well. Her works include *A . . . My Name Is Alice* (1984), *A . . . My Name Is Still Alice* (1992), *Album* (1980), and *Maybe I'm Doing It Wrong* (1982). She has directed several films for television, among them *Bernice Bobs Her Hair* (1975), *Finnegan Begin Again* (1984), *Parole Board* (1990), *A Private Matter* (1992), and *In the Presence of Mine Enemies* (1997), which takes place in the Warsaw Ghetto.

In 1995, Silver directed a radio series (coproduced by the National Yiddish Book Center) for National Public Radio, *Great Jewish Stories from Eastern Europe and Beyond*.

As a successful director who often works outside the Hollywood studio system, Silver has been a pathbreaker. Garnering both awards and box office successes, she has shown not only that women can direct films but that films about Jewish topics can succeed with Jews and non-Jews alike. With a critical reputation for presenting characters with quirky intelligence, grace, and humor, Joan Micklin Silver has pursued a versatile career in film, television, theater, and radio and has opened doors for others who are seen by movie studios as "outsiders."

The major motion picture studios rejected Joan Micklin Silver's film about Jewish immigrants, Hester Street, *as "an ethnic oddity." She and her husband marketed it themselves, grossing five million dollars and establishing her as one of the country's premiere independent filmmakers. [Bettye Lane]*

BIBLIOGRAPHY

Acker, Ally. *Reel Women: Pioneers of the Cinema, 1896 to the Present* (1991); *Contemporary Authors.* Vol. 121 (1987); *Contemporary Literary Criticism.* Vol. 20 (1982); *Contemporary Theatre, Film, and Television.* Vol. 4 (1987); "Dialogue on Film: Joan Micklin Silver," *American Film* (May 1989): 22–27; Gallagher, John Andrew. *Film Directors on Directing* (1989); Halliwell, Leslie. *Halliwell's Filmgoer's Companion.* 9th ed. (1988); Haskell, Molly. "How an Independent Filmmaker Beat the System (with Her Husband's Help)." *Village Voice* (September 22, 1975): 83–86; *International Dictionary of Films and Filmmakers.* 2d ed. Vol. 2: *Directors.* Edited by Nicholas Thomas (1991); *International Who's Who.* 57th ed.

(1993); Kent, Leticia. "They Were Behind the Scenes of 'Between the Lines.'" *NYTimes*, June 12, 1977; Monush, Barry, ed. *International Motion Picture Almanac*. 67th ed. (1996); Singer, Michael, ed. *Michael Singer's Film Directors: A Complete Guide*. 9th ed. (1992); Wakeman, John, ed. *World Film Directors. Vol. 2: 1945–1985* (1988); *Who's Who in America*. 50th ed. (1996); *Who's Who in Entertainment*. 2d ed. (1992); *Who's Who of American Women*. 19th ed. (1996); Wood, Robin. *Hollywood from Vietnam to Reagan* (1986).

MARLENE BOOTH

SILVERSTEIN, ELIZABETH BLUME (1892–1991)

Elizabeth Blume Silverstein's long and productive life revolved around her work in criminal law, real estate management, and Jewish life.

Born on November 2, 1892, in Newark, New Jersey, Elizabeth was Selig and Goldie R. (Aranowitz) Blume's oldest child, followed by three brothers and three sisters. Selig owned two successful dry-goods stores in Newark. Money was thus available for Elizabeth's education. They were Conservative Jews.

At fourteen, Elizabeth said she wanted to be a lawyer. At sixteen, in 1908, she entered New Jersey Law School, graduating with an LL.B. in 1911, nearly three years before she could be admitted to practice. A law clerk until she was twenty-one, she was admitted as an attorney in November 1913 and began a criminal law practice. In February 1917, she was admitted as a counselor. Her practice grew slowly until April 1918 when, without co-counsel, she successfully defended Orzio Ricotta on a homicide charge, a first for a New Jersey woman lawyer. Her celebrity was established. She was admitted to practice before the United States Supreme Court in 1921. In fifty years of practice she is said to have handled more than five thousand cases.

An activist, leader, and magnetic speaker, organizations welcomed her. She was a member of the American Bar Association; vice president of the Women Lawyers Association, predecessor to the National Association of Women Lawyers; and first woman member of the Essex County Legal Advisory Board and the Essex County Bar Association. Before suffrage, she joined the Women's Political Union and afterward the League of Women Voters and the Business Women's League. She was president of the Heinberg Republican Club and the first woman delegate from the Twelfth Congressional District to the Republican National Convention in 1932. But her greatest efforts were devoted to Zionism.

Elected to the AMERICAN JEWISH CONGRESS in 1916, she was chosen to lead a parade of forty thousand protesting Senate ratification of a treaty discriminating against Polish people and later led twenty-five thousand marchers in Newark's Balfour parade. In 1923, she was elected a delegate to the second American Jewish Congress. For years, she chaired fundraising drives. In 1926, as president of the Louis D. Brandeis Lodge, Independent Order B'rith Abraham, she was the first woman president of a men's fraternal organization.

In the early 1920s, she met Max Silverstein, an Orthodox Jew thirteen years her senior. He was a lawyer, real estate investor, general counsel to banks, and a Jewish community leader in Borough Park, Brooklyn. With Rabbi Stephen Wise, he was a co-organizer of the American Jewish Congress and a founder and patron of Yeshiva University. Max, caring for his aged mother, did not feel free to marry until his mother died in 1933. On August 23, 1934, Elizabeth and Max were married. Against all odds, in 1938, at age forty-six, Elizabeth Silverstein gave birth to a son, Nathan Royce. She reduced her law practice. Max died on August 10, 1955, at seventy-six, of a heart ailment and stroke. Elizabeth continued his real estate practice and investments.

Elizabeth Silverstein worked until her early eighties. She and her son, an architect and real estate lawyer, moved to New York's Fifth Avenue. After years of deteriorating health, Elizabeth Blume Silverstein died of heart failure on February 3, 1991, at age ninety-eight. She was buried in Mt. Hebron Cemetery, Queens, New York.

BIBLIOGRAPHY
Thomas, Dorothy. *Women Lawyers in the U.S.* (1957); Folsom, Joseph, ed. *The Municipalities of Essex County New Jersey 1666–1924*. Vol. 3 (1925); *NYTimes*, August 17, 1955, and Obituary. February 5, 1991; Silverstein, Nathan Royce. Interview by author, October 1996; *WWIAJ* (1938).

DOROTHY THOMAS

SIMON, CAROLINE KLEIN (1900–1993)

Attorney Caroline Klein Simon's long career included state office and judicial posts and lifelong efforts in partisan and nonpartisan politics and Jewish philanthropy. Born on November 12, 1900, in New York City, she grew up in Mount Vernon and attended Columbia University. She graduated from New York

Though she claimed she was not a feminist, attorney and later judge Caroline Klein Simon said that for a woman to succeed she "must look like a girl, act like a lady, think like a man, and work like a dog." Her hard work was evident in her long career as a politician and public servant. [American Jewish Archives]

University Law School in 1925. Married, Jewish, and female, she at first could not find a firm that would hire her as an attorney. Advised by friends that volunteer work might lead to remunerative work, she became an unpaid law clerk in the firm of Greenbaum, Wolff, and Ernst and became active in city women's organizations, especially in the Women's City Club and the League of Women Voters.

Simon focused her organizational work on legislative affairs and issues of crime prevention and correction. Spearheading a campaign to place women on juries in New York, with the help of newly elected women in the New York state legislature she finally won nonmandatory service in 1937. Among her other public causes was reforming the Women's Court, which she called "a tragic place," "a circus at which

the participants were human misery in its final form, and the onlookers were those who were so depraved as to find this to their taste." She worked to make the court a place that no one could enter without legitimate purpose. She also worked closely with Jewish groups, including the NATIONAL COUNCIL OF JEWISH WOMEN and the Women's Division of the Federation of Jewish Philanthropies.

Eventually Simon found paid work, first in public relations and later in administration. In 1935, she became executive director of the New York State Council of Jewish Women. Between 1939 and 1940, she edited the *Birth Control Review*. She also took up partisan politics, in the 1930s supporting Franklin D. Roosevelt, even though she was a registered Republican. She directed the Women's Division of a Non-Partisan Committee for the Election of Thomas E. Dewey (first as district attorney in 1937, then as governor in 1944) and in 1942 chaired the Women's Division of the United City Party for Fiorello LaGuardia.

During World War II, she received her first state government posts. In August 1943, she became a member of the State War Council's Committee on Discrimination in Employment; as a member of the Workmen's Compensation Board from 1944 to 1945, she heard workers' appeals. After 1945, she was the only woman member of the State Commission Against Discrimination, a post she held for more than ten years and in which she helped draft the state law against racial discrimination. Governor Dewey made her a member of the State Industrial Board in January 1945. Considering her an expert on crime prevention and the problems of children's and women's courts, Governor Averell Harriman named Simon a member of the State Youth Commission in 1956.

In 1957, Simon made a brief foray into electoral politics. The first woman to be nominated for citywide office, she ran for president of the New York City Council, losing but polling 100,000 more votes than the Republican candidate for mayor. Governor Nelson Rockefeller then named her secretary of state of New York, a post she held from 1959 to 1963, after which she occupied a seat on the New York Court of Claims until 1971. In the late 1960s, Simon was a leader of the National Council on Crime and Delinquency.

Simon spoke and wrote widely on legal and public issues, especially on racial and sexual discrimination. Like many women of her generation, she would precede remarks about discrimination against women with the phrase "I am not a feminist," but would also quip that to succeed in modern times "a woman . . .

must look like a girl, act like a lady, think like a man, and work like a dog."

She divorced her first husband, Leopold King Simon, with whom she had two children; her second husband, Irving W. Halpern, chief probation officer of the New York State Supreme Court, died in 1966. Active in legal work into her nineties, Catherine Klein Simon died on June 29, 1993.

BIBLIOGRAPHY

Simon, Caroline Klein. Papers. Schlesinger Library, Radcliffe College, Cambridge, Mass.; *WWIAJ*.

ELISABETH ISRAELS PERRY

SIMON, CARRIE OBENDORFER (1872–1961)

In an era in which Victorian social conventions limited most women to the private sphere of home and family, Carrie Obendorfer Simon broke important ground for American Jewish women by founding the NATIONAL FEDERATION OF TEMPLE SISTERHOODS (NFTS) in the Union of American Hebrew Congregations (UAHC). Under her leadership, the federation expanded the scope of women's social roles and offered new opportunities and rewarding experiences within the Reform Movement for those committed to Jewish and synagogue life.

Two years after Carrie Obendorfer Simon founded the NATIONAL FEDERATION OF TEMPLE SISTERHOODS *in 1913, it had become the largest Jewish woman's religious organization in the United States.*
[American Jewish Archives]

Carrie Obendorfer Simon was born on March 5, 1872, in Uniontown, Alabama, to Leo and Mary (Wise) Obendorfer. Within a few years of her birth, she moved with her family to Cincinnati, Ohio, where her father began a successful jewelry store and where Carrie graduated from the Cincinnati Conservatory of Music. While still a young woman, she became involved in a local chapter of the NATIONAL COUNCIL OF JEWISH WOMEN (NCJW), founded by her mother in 1895. Through its emphasis on self-education, public socializing, and charity work, the organization offered middle-class and upper-class German Jews like the Obendorfers an opportunity to enter the public arena without substantially challenging established gender roles.

On August 5, 1896, Carrie wed Abram Simon, whom she had met while he was a rabbinical student at Cincinnati's Hebrew Union College (HUC). They had two sons, Leo and David. Following Abram's graduation, he accepted a position in Sacramento, California, and the young couple moved out west. Between 1899 and 1904, Rabbi Simon served the Jewish community of Omaha, Nebraska, and in 1904 he was elected to the pulpit of the Washington (D.C.) Hebrew Congregation, where he remained until his death. As the wife of a rabbi, Carrie Simon took an increasingly active part in synagogue affairs and held a strong desire to enhance Jews' devotion to their heritage. Because the NCJW had proved unable to unite its Orthodox and Reform elements and began instead to avoid religious issues, Simon focused her energies on strengthening temple sisterhoods.

With the support of Rabbi George Zepin, director of synagogue and school extension of the UAHC, Rabbi David Philipson, dean of American reform rabbis, and UAHC president Julius Walter Frieberg, Simon founded the National Federation of Temple Sisterhoods in January 1913 in order to promote Jewish social service and the home. The new body brought together chapters from around the country and doubled in size by 1915, thereby making NFTS the largest Jewish woman's religious organization in the United States. As president of the federation from 1913 to 1919, Simon established the National Committee on Religion, which organized religious schools, increased synagogue attendance, and collected and displayed Jewish ceremonial objects. The Committee on Hebrew Union College Scholarships enabled young men of limited economic means to attend rabbinical school and raised funds for religious educational work by UAHC laypeople. Simon also used her position to encourage the UAHC to include more women on synagogue boards and to welcome intermarried couples into the temple and its sisterhood.

When her tenure as president ended in 1919, Simon continued as an active leader in the federation. She served as honorary president and spoke around the country on its behalf. In the early 1920s, she chaired a committee to raise funds for a student dormitory at HUC and devoted herself to the Jewish Braille Institute of America, founded in 1931, where sisterhood volunteers gave countless hours transcribing English, Yiddish, and Hebrew books for the blind. During her lifetime, Simon watched as the National Federation of Temple Sisterhoods grew from five thousand women in forty-nine American chapters to a hundred thousand women in 585 chapters throughout nine countries.

Carrie Obendorfer Simon died on March 3, 1961, in Washington, D.C.

BIBLIOGRAPHY

AJYB 63: 562; Marcus, Jacob R. *The American Jewish Woman, 1654–1980* (1981), and *The American Jewish Woman: A Documentary History* (1981); *National Cyclopaedia of American Biography* 28 (1940): 54, s.v. "Abram Simon"; Nadell, Pamela S., and Rita J. Simon. "Ladies of the Sisterhood: Women in the American Reform Synagogue, 1900–1930." In *Active Voices: Women in Jewish Culture*, edited by Maurie Sacks (1985); Obituary. *NYTimes*, March 4, 1961, 23:5; Rogow, Faith. *Gone to Another Meeting: The National Council of Jewish Women, 1893–1993* (1993); Umansky, Ellen M. "Carrie Obendorfer Simon." In *Reform Judaism in America: A Biographical Dictionary and Sourcebook*, edited by Kerry M. Olitzky, Lance J. Sussman, and Malcolm H. Stern (1993); *UJE*; *Washington Post*, March 4, 1961, C3; *WWIAJ*, 1926.

MARK I. GREENBERG

SIMON, KATE (1912–1990)

In the 1980s, Kate Simon published three volumes of memoirs of her remarkable life as an immigrant, Yiddish leftist, bohemian, travel writer, and sexual adventurer. Told from a uniquely ironic and feminist perspective, these volumes together form what Doris Grumbach in the *New York Times Book Review* called "a classic of autobiography."

In *Bronx Primitive: Portraits of a Childhood* (1982), Simon re-creates her girlhood in a Jewish-Italian Bronx neighborhood. Born in Warsaw in 1912 to Lonia (Babicz), a corset maker, and David Simon, a cobbler, Simon was named Kaila after her maternal grandmother. When Simon was four, she, her mother, and her younger brother journeyed to America, her father having gone to prepare the way three years earlier. Her childhood memories focus on her struggles against her father, who pressured her to practice the piano for hours a day, urging her to quit school and fulfill his own ambitions of becoming a concert pianist. She also records her initiation into sexuality: her traumatic initial reaction to her sister Sylvia's birth, her thrill at the onset of menstruation, her dawning awareness of sex, her mother's thirteen abortions, and her resourcefulness in the face of sexual abuse at the hands of two cousins, as well as her barber, the neighborhood pedophile and one of her father's close friends. Suspecting her father's tacit complicity with the abusive incidents, Simon spent more and more time away from her parents' apartment.

In *A Wider World: Portraits of an Adolescence* (1986), Simon continues to gain independence from her family. Against her father's will, she switched from vocational school to James Monroe High School, where she studied English literature. On a vacation at a Yiddish leftist encampment in the Catskills with her mother and siblings, she met the Bergsons, who served as surrogate parents for her and for whose children she served as nanny. During the school year, she began to live in various friends' homes and took odd jobs to support herself. An English teacher at Monroe introduced her to opera, Russian films, and the "free love" community. Graduating and finding her own apartment, Simon became an English major at HUNTER COLLEGE. Her time at Hunter consisted of experiments in bohemian fashions, sisterhood with other Hunter girls, leftist political causes such as the Spanish Civil War, poetry readings, exploratory trips to Harlem, and sexual experimentation. While cohabiting with a lover (much to her father's chagrin), she became pregnant by another man and had her first of three abortions.

While the first two volumes of memoirs are cautiously optimistic, the final volume, *Etchings in an Hourglass* (1990), is filled with bitterness and frustration. Simon repeatedly describes God as "the Great Joker" with a malicious sense of humor. Her bitterness is due to the deaths—all from brain tumors—of her first husband, Steve, a deaf endocrinologist whom she had met at Hunter; their daughter, Lexie; and her younger sister, Sylvia. The depression into which these deaths send her is not alleviated by an affair between 1941 and 1946 with a married man, or by a loveless marriage in 1947 to a businessman she hopes will serve as a father figure for Lexie. The marriage would drag on for thirteen years, until their divorce in 1959.

By the end of the 1950s, Simon had already traveled widely. She wrote occasional articles about these experiences, but her career as a travel writer began in earnest in 1958 when a publisher from Meridian Books offered her an advance to write a guidebook of New York City. Between 1959 and 1978, she produced guidebooks for New York, Mexico, Paris, London, and Italy in a series called *Places and Pleasures*. Noted for their vivid descriptions of destinations beyond the usual tourist haunts, the New York and Mexico guides expanded through four editions each. Simon traveled for the rest of her life, stopping for brief annual stints in New York. She recalls her wide acquaintance and adventures (often sexual in nature) in Israel, the Soviet Union, Yugoslavia, Haiti, St. Dominique, India, Tanzania, Tunis, China, Spain, and Japan. She cultivated a broad spectrum of cross-cultural experiences until her death in New York in 1990.

Spanning the twentieth century, Kate Simon's memoirs are the records of a lifetime devoted to migration. The themes of her work—a young woman's search for independence and selfhood, her discovery and attitudes toward sexuality, her loving and ironic stance toward the secular Jewish left, and her encounters with a wide array of "places and pleasures"—make hers a unique voice among memoirists and Jewish immigrant writers.

SELECTED WORKS BY KATE SIMON

Bronx Primitive: Portraits of a Childhood (1982); *England's Green and Pleasant Land* (1974); *Etchings in an Hourglass* (1990); *Fifth Avenue: A Very Social History* (1978); *Italy: The Places in Between* (1970); *London: Places and Pleasures* (1968); *Mexico: Places and Pleasures* (1963); *New York*. Photographs by Andreas Feininger (1964); *New York: Places and Pleasures* (1959); *Paris: Places and Pleasures* (1967); *A Renaissance Tapestry: The Gonzaga of Mantua* (1988); *Rome: Places and Pleasures* (1972); *A Wider World: Portraits of an Adolescence* (1986).

BIBLIOGRAPHY

Grumbach, Doris. Review of *Etchings in an Hourglass*, by Kate Simon. *NYTimes*, August 19, 1990, sec. 7; Neuman, Shirley. "'An Appearance Walking in a Forest the Sexes Burn': Autobiography and the Construction of the Feminine Body." *Signature: A Journal of Theory and Canadian Literature* 2 (1989): 1–26; Phillips, Mark. Review of *A Renaissance Tapestry*, by Kate Simon. *NYTimes*, April 10, 1988, sec. 7, and Review of *A Wider World*, by Kate Simon. *NYTimes*, February 23, 1986, sec. 7.

MICHAEL GALCHINSKY

SINCLAIR, JO (1913–1995)

"The spirit can be the most intolerable ghetto of all," Jo Sinclair asserts in her autobiography, *The*

Seasons: Death and Transfiguration (1992). The statement encapsulates Sinclair's work as a writer, as well as her life as a working-class Jewish American woman struggling with poverty, anti-Semitism, and sexism. Sinclair was ahead of her time in her treatment of such complex themes as Jewish and sexual identity, marginalization, and the internalization of prejudice. In her writing, which has gained increased critical attention since the 1980s, the ghetto not only connotes the physical space and limited social and economic horizons of oppressed minorities, but also serves as a metaphor for the sense of inner constraints that hamper people's well-being.

Born Ruth Seid in Brooklyn, July 1, 1913, she was the last of the five children of Ida (Kravetsky) and Nathan Seid, Russian immigrants who had fled pogroms. When she was three, the family moved to Cleveland. Her father, a carpenter who supported his family with difficulty, never felt at ease in the United States and with the English language. His daughter felt ashamed of his Old World ways and lack of success. Although a superb student, she attended a commercial rather than an academic high school because she was expected to work to help support the family. While working in a factory, she read voraciously and began to write. In the mid-1930s, she met Helen Buchman, who was to be a lifelong friend, mentor, and patron. Buchman invited Ruth to move in with her husband and family, helped her to leave factory work for a position with the Red Cross, and encouraged her writing. She later obtained work with the WPA writers' project.

With her first published story, "Noon Lynching" (1936), Ruth Seid adopted the pseudonym Jo Sinclair, which veiled her Jewishness and introduced an element of gender ambivalence, two issues central to her life and work. The tension between her identities as Seid and Sinclair continued to trouble her throughout her lifetime. In her first novel, *Wasteland* (1946), which focuses on the fictional Braunowitz family and is based in part on her own family, Sinclair explores her mixed emotions regarding Jewish identity. To attain financial success and social acceptance, the protagonist, Jake Braunowitz, passes as the gentile photojournalist John Brown. At the urging of his lesbian sister, whose own struggles enable her to understand her brother, Jake sees a psychiatrist to deal with the toll of anti-Semitism, Jewish self-hatred, and childhood deprivation on his inner life and emotional well-being. Ironically, Sinclair herself continued to write under her ethnically neutral pseudonym. The novel won the 1946 Harper Prize for new writers, and the ten-thousand-dollar award allowed Sinclair to write full time. Sinclair produced novels, stories, radio and television scripts, and an autobiography, and also worked as a ghostwriter. *Harper's* editor Ed Aswell nurtured her talent until his death in 1958.

Sinclair's works explore the repercussions of oppression in many forms: self-denial and self-destruction, anti-Semitism and Jewish self-hatred, continued psychic pain due to childhood suffering and dysfunctional family relations, repression of women's sexual energy and sexual orientation, racism and the internalization of prejudice, poverty, and other forms of marginalization. Her work looks to self-knowledge as a means of emerging from one's internalized ghetto.

While many of Sinclair's works explore the difficulties of being Jewish, she often uses her knowledge of anti-Semitism as a touchstone for examining other prejudices. Considered her best work, *The Changelings* (1955) compares the long history of Jewish oppression with the history of slavery and contemporary discrimination against African Americans in the United States. The novel was awarded the 1956 Jewish Book Council of America annual fiction award. Regarded as her most important script, *Play the Long Moment* (1951) reiterates the inner toll of discrimination by exploring the dilemma of an African-American musician torn between passing as white and acknowledging his identity and heritage.

With the burgeoning interest in ethnic and women's writing, Sinclair's work has gained a growing audience. Several of her volumes have been reissued in the late 1980s and 1990s by the Jewish Publication Society and by the Feminist Press.

Jo Sinclair died of cancer on July 4, 1995, in Jenkintown, Pennsylvania. She was survived by her companion, Joan Soffer.

SELECTED WORKS BY JO SINCLAIR

Anna Teller (1960. Reprint, 1992); *The Changelings* (1955. Reprint, 1983); *The Seasons: Death and Transfiguration* (1992); *Sing at My Wake* (1951); *Wasteland* (1946. Reprint, 1987).

BIBLIOGRAPHY

Contemporary Authors. 2d ed. Vols. 21–24, s.v. "Ruth Seid"; Gitenstein, R. Barbara. "Jo Sinclair (Ruth Seid)." *Dictionary of Literary Biography* 28:295–297; McKay, Nellie. Afterword to *The Changelings*, by Jo Sinclair (1983); Wilentz, Gay. "Jo Sinclair (Ruth Seid)." *Jewish American Women Writers: A Bio-Bibliographical and Critical Sourcebook*, edited by Ann Shapiro et al. (1994).

SARA R. HOROWITZ

SISTERHOODS OF PERSONAL SERVICE

In his 1892 history of Congregation Rodeph Sholom of New York City, Aaron Wise lavishes praise upon the women of the synagogue's sisterhood. Founded two years earlier, the sisterhood had, in Wise's words, "achieved the greatest measure of success through the combined and individual efforts . . . in behalf of all the needy and distressed" of the city. The "indefatigable zeal and ardor they have displayed in the pursuit of their 'task of love'" earned the women of Rodeph Sholom a place of pride in the synagogue's history.

Thousands of middle-class Jewish women throughout the United States took up this "task of love" in the late decades of the nineteenth century, forming Sisterhoods of Personal Service at synagogues across the country. Gustav Gottheil, the rabbi of Temple Emanu-El in New York City, organized the first sisterhood, primarily to aid the masses of Jewish immigrants pouring into the city. By 1905, HANNAH B. EINSTEIN could report in the *Jewish Encyclopedia* that most of the large congregations in New York City boasted Sisterhoods of Personal Service, and that a Federation of Sisterhoods had been established there in 1896 to coordinate sisterhood work with that of the United Hebrew Charities (UHC). The UHC assigned each sisterhood to a district of Manhattan, spreading their work throughout the city.

The Sisterhoods of Personal Service constituted a significant unit within the constellation of Jewish social welfare organizations, personally assisting a considerable number of immigrants through a variety of financial, vocational, educational, and social programs. Though each sisterhood carried out its responsibilities in its own fashion, many opened offices in the districts they were assigned to serve, and some established their own settlement houses, modeled on such institutions as Jane Addams's Hull House and LILLIAN WALD's Henry Street Settlement. Sisterhood settlement houses offered an array of services: kindergartens and nurseries for the children of working mothers; clubs for children; recreation activities; adult classes in English, American citizenship, and, for women, in housekeeping, cooking, and sewing; libraries; employment bureaus; and opportunities for both children and adults to spend summer vacations outside of the city.

In addition, many sisterhoods operated religious schools, both to teach Jewish children the principles of Judaism and to combat the influence of the Christian missionaries flooding immigrant areas seeking converts. The sisterhood of New York's Shearith Israel (the Spanish and Portuguese synagogue) even organized a synagogue, B'rith Shalom, in its neighborhood house at 86 Orchard Street, a move which the sisterhood claimed made it "the only settlement house in the country in which a fully organized synagogue, holding the old traditional services on Sabbath, the festivals and the holy days, is an integral part of the work."

The Sisterhoods of Personal Service drew on an existing tradition of women's benevolence in American synagogues. Modeling themselves on the numerous middle-class Protestant women's organizations formed during the nineteenth century, and inspired by the notion that women were responsible for the moral upkeep of society, antebellum Jewish women had formed ladies' auxiliaries, ladies' fuel committees, and ladies' benevolent or aid societies, offering financial assistance to both their synagogues and the Jewish poor.

Only with the sudden influx of Eastern European immigrants in the 1880s and 1890s, however, did these organizations become fully devoted to what the Shearith Israel Sisterhood called "philanthropic and educational work by personal service and other practicable methods," focusing their attentions almost entirely on serving society rather than the synagogue. The difference between the new Sisterhoods of Personal Service and previous women's organizations, Einstein noted in 1899, was that rather than being merely a "subscriber" to charitable organizations, each sisterhood member "was to devote a certain fixed portion of her time to a definite task and attend it herself; the chief object being the bringing together of the well-to-do and the poor—the 'haves and the have nots'—by means of friendly visiting."

Such attention often met with reluctance or even outright hostility from those the sisterhoods hoped to aid. The significant class schisms between the working-class or poor immigrants, on the one hand, and the middle- and even upper-class sisterhood women, on the other, did not escape either group, and the line was often crossed between helping the poor to help themselves and offering charity to and trying to Americanize the "teeming masses." Some immigrant leaders exhorted their peers to become self-sufficient and to reject what they perceived as the condescending charity offered by sisterhood women.

Despite the hostility of some of those whom they attempted to assist, the Sisterhoods of Personal Service achieved much during their three decades of existence. Their religious schools and English classes were often filled to capacity, the waiting lists for their

*Many sisterhoods operated religious schools, both to teach Jewish children the
principles of Judaism and to combat the influence of the omnipresent Christian community.
This Succoth Pageant was put on by students at the Emanuel Sisterhood for Personal Service (c. 1916)
in San Francisco. [Western Jewish History Center]*

programs and services were generally long, and thousands of immigrants received financial, emotional, educational, or spiritual assistance from sisterhood women. B'nai Jeshurun's historian records that in 1907 alone, over five hundred families received relief from the synagogue's sisterhood, and sisterhood members personally visited almost half of those families.

Though it is difficult to pinpoint the terminus of the period of the Sisterhoods of Personal Service, a significant event took place in 1918 in New York City, when the UHC and the city's sisterhoods amicably severed their relationship. Both sides cited the need for greater control over social welfare in the city, including the standardization of practice and the creation of a professional class of social workers. While some sisterhoods continued to operate through an affiliation with the Federation for the Support of Jewish Philanthropic Societies in New York City, this step toward the professionalization of social work left many sisterhoods without the credentials to continue their work.

Also influential in the demise of the sisterhoods were the sharp curtailment of immigration in the interwar period, the increasing financial solvency of the generation of immigrants who had once relied on the sisterhoods for assistance, and the competing financial and social demands of the two world wars. At the very latest, the Sisterhoods of Personal Service existed until the 1930s. These organizations did not simply disappear, however. Most of them evolved into modern-day synagogue sisterhoods, turning their attentions inward to the synagogue rather than outward to society.

BIBLIOGRAPHY

Einstein, Hannah. "The Federation of Sisterhoods." *Twenty-Fifth Annual Report of the United Hebrew Charities* (1899), and "Sisterhoods of Personal Service." *JE* (1905); Federation of Jewish Women's Organizations. Papers. American Jewish Historical Society, Waltham, Mass.; *Fifty Years of Social Service: The History of the United Hebrew Charities of the City of New York* (1926); Goldstein, Israel. *A Century of Judaism in New York: B'nai Jeshurun, 1825–1925* (1930); Joselit, Jenna Weissman. "The Special Sphere of the Middle-Class American Jewish Woman: The Synagogue Sisterhood, 1890–1940." In *The American Synagogue: A Sanctuary Transformed*, edited by Jack Wertheimer (1987); Menken, Alice Davis. Annual Report, 1916–1917. Sisterhood Papers. Archives of Congregation Shearith Israel,

NYC; Pool, David de Sola, and Tamar de Sola Pool. *An Old Faith in the New World: Portrait of Shearith Israel, 1654–1954* (1955); Wise, Aaron. *The History of Congregation Rodeph Sholom of New York* (1892).

FELICIA HERMAN

SKIDELSKY, RACHEL (c. 1856–1909)

In 1894, at a time when "working mother" was a contradiction in terms for middle-class women, Rachel Skidelsky, a Russian immigrant with a husband and two children under age ten, graduated from the prestigious Women's Medical College of Pennsylvania to become an eminent physician in the city of Philadelphia. Not content to live the life of an average late nineteenth-century woman, Skidelsky believed that as a woman she was just as essential to the progress of society as a man. As a doctor and reformer at the turn of the century, she strove to improve the moral and health conditions of Jewish immigrants in South Philadelphia through improving their environment. Skidelsky sought to alter the environmental conditions, social conditions, and image of downtown Jews through education, work, and access to free bathhouses, swimming pools, fresh water, and fresh air.

Rachel Skidelsky was born Rachel Noar in Vilna, Russia, around 1856, and educated at the gymnasium in Vilna. In the early 1880s, her critical views of the Russian government caused her to flee to the United States to avoid persecution. Arriving first in New York, she later moved to Philadelphia, where she graduated from medical school and raised her family with husband Simon S. Skidelsky, a political commentator, translator, and botanist who is most recognized for his translation of Nikolay Chernyshevsky's *What Is to Be Done?* Skidelsky's children also led notable lives. Her son, Sidney Skidelsky (b. 1886), became a lawyer, and her daughter, Berenice (b. 1887), became a writer, political activist, and lecturer who specialized in American-Soviet relations, similar to her father.

Within two years of attaining her medical degree, Skidelsky became associated with the Women's Health Protective Association. As president of the downtown Health Protective League, she sought to increase the health standards of the Jewish residents of South Philadelphia through cleaner water, streets, and dwellings. She utilized her medical skills through the Hebrew Ladies Emergency Society, often providing free medical attention to those who could not afford such services, and she advocated the implementation of work and education programs to end the cycle of poverty in which many Jewish immigrants in South Philadelphia were trapped. Around 1897, she was nominated to be a factory inspector for the southern section of Philadelphia. Her medical background, ability to speak Russian, and development of two piers on the Delaware River for area residents to use as "breathing spots" made her a viable candidate. Apparently, her appointment never came to fruition.

As a woman physician and an immigrant Russian Jew assisting other immigrant Jews, Rachel Skidelsky dedicated her life to overcoming stereotypes of her gender and her ethnicity. She died on May 13, 1909, with her daughter by her side after a two-week bout with pneumonia. She is buried at Mount Sinai Cemetery in Philadelphia.

BIBLIOGRAPHY

Abram, Ruth J. "Private Practice: Taking Every Case to Heart." In *Send Us A Lady Physician: Women Doctors in America, 1835–1920*, edited by Ruth J. Abram (1985); *AJYB*, 11 (1909–1910): 109; Bernheimer, Charles Seligmen. *The Russian Jew in the United States: Studies of Social Conditions in New York, Philadelphia, and Chicago* (1905); *Childhood in Poetry*. Edited by John MacKay Shaw (1967); Friedman, Murray. *Jewish Life in Philadelphia, 1850–1930* (1983); Morais, Henry Simon. *The Jews of Philadelphia* (1894); Skidelsky, Berenice. Papers, Boxes 1, 3, 12, and 13. Rare Books and Manuscripts Division, New York Public Library; "Well Known Female Physician Dies." *Philadelphia Inquirer,* March 15, 1909, 4.

ERIKA PIOLA

SLESINGER, TESS (1905–1945)

Dedicating her 1934 novel *The Unpossessed* "to my contemporaries" and titling her 1935 collection of stories *Time: The Present* may have been eerily prescient of Tess Slesinger. Not only did her fiction embrace the cross-currents of the lived moment, but her life was cut short by cancer. As a parodic historian of her own times, Slesinger wrote fiction that combined jazzy, up-to-the-minute reports on the state of marriage, sexuality, political culture, and work in 1930s America with a biting, yet emotionally revealing style typical of *Vanity Fair* and the *New Yorker* where she published frequently. Her brief life spanned the continent from the heady world of New York left-wing intellectuals to Hollywood's sunshine as a screenwriter.

Born on July 16, 1905, to well-to-do Hungarian-Russian Jewish parents, Slesinger grew up with three older brothers on New York's Upper West Side. Educated at the Ethical Culture Society School, Swarthmore College, and the Columbia School of Journalism, where in 1925 she received a B.A. in English, Slesinger moved quickly from the sheltered world of wealthy, assimilated Jews into the internecine warfare of New York's Left after her 1928 marriage to classmate Herbert Solow. After working as a journalist for a few years, Slesinger began writing book reviews for the *Menorah Journal*, a left-wing cultural magazine founded and edited by Solow and Columbia professor Elliot Cohen. This world of radicalized, educated Jews offered Slesinger the material she satirized in *The Unpossessed*, published two years after her divorce from Solow.

Slesinger's early childhood was atypical for her class, ethnicity, and era; both her mother and father worked outside the home. Anthony Slesinger had dropped out of law school to help run his father-in-law's garment business, while Augusta (Singer) Slesinger worked in social service agencies, eventually becoming executive secretary of the Jewish Big Sisters. Augusta Slesinger was one of the founders of the New School for Social Research, where she trained as a lay analyst with Erich Fromm and Karen Horney in the mid-1930s. The awareness of psychological ambivalence and her parents' unconventional relationship contributed to Tess Slesinger's pointed irony about her husband's group of radical Jewish humanists. It certainly shaped her vision of marriage and work and the vexed battle between the sexes that was the subject of much of her fiction and screenwriting.

Slesinger began publishing early, but her first big success came in 1932, the year she and Solow divorced, when *Story* published "Missis Flinders," an arch and wicked yet moving tale of a young wife's decision to have an abortion in order to keep her activist husband "free." The notoriety this quasi-autobiographical story received convinced Slesinger to expand the piece into a complex novel tracing not only the Flinderses' disintegrating marriage but the ravaged lives of a group of left-wing writers and artists gathered around a charismatic Jewish professor to start a magazine. Critics immediately praised Slesinger's novel, calling it "impeccable," "brilliantly written," and "sheer genius," and began sorting out the characters of this roman à clef convinced that, in Murray Kempton's words, *The Unpossessed* was a "document" about 1930s literary radicals. However, though the novel and the story collection published the next year were based on Slesinger's experiences, the portraits of the many characters who swirl in and out of universities, society galas, street demonstrations, offices, and abortion clinics describe and set into context a wide variety of that quintessential 1930s type: "the people."

On the strength of her acclaimed fiction, in mid-1935 Irving Thalberg offered Slesinger a salary of a thousand dollars a week as a Hollywood screenwriter. Her first major assignment was to cowrite the screen

An unconventional childhood and her association with Jewish left-wing literary radicals shaped the biting satire of Tess Slesinger's novels and short stories. Her subsequent conquest of Hollywood as a screenwriter was cut short by her untimely death at age thirty-nine. [American Jewish Archives]

adaptation of Pearl S. Buck's *The Good Earth*. On the set, she met her second husband, assistant producer Frank Davis. They married in Mexico in 1936. The two collaborated on scripts, eventually cowriting or adapting four films during the 1940s, including the original screenplay for Dorothy Arzner's feminist musical comedy *Dance, Girl, Dance* and the screen adaptation of Betty Smith's working-class novel *A Tree Grows in Brooklyn*. Like her fiction, Slesinger's screenplays dealt with class differences, sexual competition, gender inequality, and the problems of the artist in contemporary society.

After leaving the New York circle of left-wing anti-Stalinists, Slesinger, unlike many men in the anti-Stalinist Left, did not move right. Instead, after

Germany invaded the Soviet Union and the United States entered World War II, she forged strong connections to the Communist Party through the Anti-Nazi League, the League of American Writers, and the Screen Writers Guild, which she helped found. Slesinger did not live to see the premiere of *A Tree Grows in Brooklyn;* on February 21, 1945, she died of cancer at age thirty-nine, leaving two children, Peter, born in January 1937, and Jane, born in March 1938. Peter Davis continues his family's commitment to politics and film, directing powerful documentaries such as the antiwar film *Hearts and Minds.*

SELECTED WORKS BY TESS SLESINGER

FICTION

"After the Cure." *Vanity Fair* 43 (1935): 48, 65–66; "Ben Grader Makes a Call." *Vanity Fair* 42 (1934): 40, 70; "The Best Things in Life Are Three." *Vanity Fair* 44 (1935): 16, 52b; "Brother to the Happy." *Pagany* 3 (1932): 77–82; "For Better, for Worse." *Delineator* 28 (1936): 18–19; "A Hollywood Gallery." *Michigan Quarterly Review* 18 (1979): 439–454; "Kleine Frau." *Modern Youth* 1 (1933): 28–32; "The Lonelier Eve." *New Yorker* 10 (28 April 1934): 32–33; "Mr. Palmer's Party." *New Yorker* 11 (27 April 1935): 30–32; "The Old Lady Counts Her Injuries." *Vanity Fair* 43 (1934): 23, 79; *Time: The Present* (1935). Reprinted with the addition of "A Life in the Day of a Writer," from *Story* (November 1935) as *On Being Told That Her Second Husband Has Taken His First Lover and Other Stories* (1971); *The Unpossessed* (1934); "You Gi-i-ive Yourself or Drop the Handkerchief." *Vanity Fair* 44 (1935): 41, 60b; "Young Wife." *This Quarter* 3 (1931): 698–708.

NONFICTION

"How to Throw a Cocktail Party." *Vanity Fair* 44 (1935): 46–47, 59; "Memoirs of an Ex-Flapper." *Vanity Fair* 43 (1934): 26–27, 74, 76; "Where the Dear and the Antelope Roam . . ." *Vanity Fair* 44 (1935): 42–43; "Writers on the Volcano." *Clipper: A Western Review* 2 (1941): 4–6.

SCREENPLAYS

Are Husbands Necessary? with Frank Davis. Paramount (1941); *The Bride Wore Red,* with F. Bradbury Foote. MGM (1937); *Dance, Girl, Dance,* with Frank Davis. RKO (1940); *Girl's School,* with Richard Sherman. Columbia (1938); *The Good Earth,* with Talbot Jennings and Claudine West. MGM (1937); *His Brother's Wife.* MGM (1936); *Remember the Day,* with Frank Davis and Allan Scott. Twentieth Century–Fox (1941); *A Tree Grows in Brooklyn,* with Frank Davis, additions by Anita Loos. Twentieth Century–Fox (1945).

BIBLIOGRAPHY

Biagi, Shirley. "Forgive Me for Dying." *Antioch Review* 35 (1977): 224–236; *Jewish American Women Writers: A Bio-
Bibliographical and Critical Sourcebook. Edited by Ann R. Shapiro (1994); Kempton, Murray. *Part of Our Time* (1955); Rabinowitz, Paula. *Labor and Desire: Women's Revolutionary Fiction in Depression America* (1991); Sharistanian, Janet. "Afterword." *The Unpossessed* (1984), and "Tess Slesinger's Hollywood Sketches." *Michigan Quarterly Review* 18 (1979): 439–454; Teres, Harvey. *Renewing the Left: Politics, Imagination, and the New York Intellectuals* (1996); Trilling, Lionel. "Young in the Thirties." *Commentary* 41 (1966): 43–51. Reprinted as "Afterword." *The Unpossessed* (1966); Wald, Alan. *The New York Intellectuals* (1987); *WWIAJ* (1938).

PAULA RABINOWITZ

SLOTT, MOLLIE (1893–1967)

"Gasoline Alley," "Little Orphan Annie," "Dick Tracy," "Moon Mullins," and "Terry and the Pirates" were among the comic strips Mollie Slott supervised during her fifty-six-year tenure with the Chicago Tribune–New York Daily News Syndicate. There she guided the daily operation of a nationwide news distribution service that, in addition to the comics, included columns of advice, sports, politics, and serialized fiction.

Born in Chicago, on April 19, 1893, to Lee Slott and Sarah (Herlinger) Slott, she spent two years at the Academy of Fine Arts in Chicago. Then, concealing her true age, at seventeen she went to work for the *Chicago Tribune.* Her marriage to Charles Levinson on May 29, 1917, produced two sons, William A. and Lee Slott.

In 1921, Slott helped the syndicate achieve a coup when *Tribune* photographers, carrying photos of the Dempsey-Carpentier fight, were blocked from a plane by rivals' chicanery. Resourceful as always, she sent the pictures—the first photos so transmitted—by wire.

In 1946, she became the first female manager in syndicate history. She was later promoted to vice president (1955) and then to director (1961). A member of the National Women's Press Club, the New York Newspaper Women's Club, and the Overseas Press Club, Mollie Slott died on January 24, 1967, in New York City.

BIBLIOGRAPHY

Biography Index; Index to Women of the World from Ancient to Modern Times: Biographies and Portraits; Obituary. *NYTimes,* January 25, 1967, 43:2; Ross, Ishbel. *Ladies of the Press* (1936); "Who's Mollie Slott?" *Newsweek* 27 (January 7, 1946): 64–67; *Who's Who of American Women; WWWIA.*

ALEISA FISHMAN

SOCIALISM

Disproportionate numbers of Jewish immigrant women in America were associated with socialism in the first decades of the twentieth century. Their ideological commitment was expressed in activism in left-leaning garment workers' unions and in the Socialist Party. Their radicalism appears to have grown out of the same sources as male radicalism—the changes experienced by the Jewish community in late nineteenth-century Europe and America, including proletarianization and the secularization of Jewish religious values. But Jewish working women's radical consciousness and their militant collective action in America emerged in the face of extraordinary obstacles.

The women often lacked marketable skills and were more economically vulnerable than men. Moreover, in their attempts to organize, they came up against the cyclical nature of household, as well as wage, labor. The women also struggled against the indifference of men, and even against outright hostility from organized labor, including male-dominated socialist unions, and from the male-led Socialist Party. In addition they confronted competing claims of feminism and socialism, as well as significant cultural expectations, Jewish and American, about the "proper" place and role of women. By the 1930s, although they had not achieved equality in the unions or the party, and although they continued to steer an uneasy course between class solidarity and feminist reform, Jewish working women had made a significant, long-term contribution to the labor movement and social welfare.

Most of the Jewish women who went on to become socialists had had little or no experience with actual factory or shop work. Many of them came to America when they were young teenagers, but most were aware of the growing numbers of Jewish women workers in the old countries, including their mothers. The Russian census of 1897 indicated that 15 percent of Jewish artisans were female and more than 20 percent of Jewish women were employed outside the home. Although much of the work was drudgery and necessary for economic survival, employment expanded the environment of many females beyond the narrow domesticity of the shtetl.

The women were also aware of growing educational opportunities. Despite the official preference in traditional Jewish families for the male child, many of the women who were socialists in America had, as girls, received some formal education in Eastern Europe. Increasing aspirations, stimulated in part by new opportunities, moved many Jews, especially previously hemmed-in girls and young women, to demand even more change.

Significant numbers of women took part in the Jewish revolutionary movements as these developed in Eastern Europe. Young, unmarried women appear to have constituted one-third of the Bund's membership from its beginning in 1897, and they held the organization together after the mass arrests of 1898. In the 1900s, increasing numbers of Jewish women were arrested for political activities. Several who were socialists and militant trade unionists in the United States had been radicalized during this period in Eastern Europe, including Social Democrat ROSE PESOTTA, Bundist Flora Weiss, Socialist-Territorialist Marsha Farbman, and Social Revolutionary FANNIA COHN. When hopes for revolution in Russia ebbed or pogroms intensified, desire for refuge in America, and for an opportunity to fulfill raised aspirations, increased for many, whether or not they were already activists.

The aspirations of young Jewish women were reflected in the large numbers who pursued education after their arrival in the United States while working ten or more hours a day in the garment shops. Going to school at night and working for wages, these women could dream of self-sufficiency, even though a good part of their wages went to supplement family income or to support brothers in higher education. Jobs in the garment industry, however, were oppressive and demoralizing, and threatened the women's dreams. Bosses often took advantage of girls, most of whom they assumed were timid and "green." Females were paid less for the same work, timed when they left to go to the toilet, and subjected to speedups. Sexual harassment was also a serious problem. It is reported in a significant number of memoirs, and once women were organized and union grievance procedures established, charges of sexual abuse were prevalent.

These conditions, and the presence of a cadre of radical Jewish women and men in America, led to a flurry of socialist and union organizing activity by the late 1880s. For a long time, socialism and unionism could not sustain coherent movements among immigrant workers. Socialism was, however, a vital theme in Jewish immigrant life almost from the beginning. As early as 1890, twenty-seven unions and socialist organizations from New York, with a membership close to fourteen thousand, were represented at a United Hebrew Trades conference. It was possible for an American journalist to believe by 1909 that "most of the Jews of the East Side though not all acknowledged socialists are strongly inclined toward socialism."

The journalist exaggerated. But in that same year, the shirtwaistmakers' strike, known as the UPRISING OF THE 20,000, set off a decade of labor unrest in the garment trades, which brought ever-larger numbers into the battle for economic and social justice. On November 22, 1909, CLARA LEMLICH [SHAVELSON], a feisty and courageous working girl and daughter of an Orthodox Jewish scholar, met with tumultuous enthusiasm when she proposed the general strike. At least twenty thousand shirtwaistmakers, mostly Jewish girls and women between the ages of sixteen and twenty-five, joined the "uprising." Only the tiniest minority of them were members of the socialist INTERNATIONAL LADIES GARMENT WORKERS UNION (ILGWU). In the year following the strike, Local 25 alone counted over ten thousand members. The largest strike by women in the United States to that time, the shirtwaistmakers' rebellion stimulated subsequent struggles and victories that led to the formation of stable and relatively powerful socialist unions.

Clara Lemlich was no stranger to militancy. From the time she was ten in the Ukraine, she had been reading Turgenev, Gorky, and revolutionary literature. Like many others, she fled the Kishinev pogrom of 1903. Within a week of her arrival in the United States, fifteen-year-old Clara was at work as a skilled and relatively well-paid draper. She was saving money for medical school when in 1906, as she put it, "some of us girls who were more class-conscious . . . organized the first local." Lemlich was one of seven young women and six men who founded Local 25 of the ILGWU. She participated thereafter in a number of strikes that led up to the major conflict of 1909, by which time she had become well known in activist trade unionist and Socialist Party circles. Clara Lemlich was part of a growing and important cadre. In many shops, there were women like her who influenced significant numbers of others through persistent discussion, invoking a sense of sisterhood, and example.

Perhaps no single development galvanized Jewish immigrants for militant unionism and socialism more than the TRIANGLE SHIRTWAIST FIRE of 1911, which killed 146 workers. The Yiddish press repeated the harrowing details of locked doors, inadequate fire escapes, and burning bodies. And as several women reported, the word "socialism" kept recurring in speeches memorializing the Triangle fire. The fire and its aftermath left a deep impression. Even those who had been radicalized in the Old Country credit the Triangle fire with reinforcing their activist commitments. Fannia Cohn, who in Russia "imbibed and participated in the revolutionary spirit," said "it was the Triangle fire that decided my life's course." After a stirring mass funeral for the victims of the fire, organizers and activists, like ROSE SCHNEIDERMAN, hammered home the message: "I know from . . . experience it is up to the working people to save themselves. The only way they can . . . is by a strong working-class movement."

Between 1909 and 1920, numerous strikes and organizational campaigns changed a largely unorganized industry into a union stronghold. Jewish immigrant women played a major role in this development, and in the process they transformed their shops and themselves. Not all, but a measurably disproportionate number were politicized. The strikes had linked workplace complaints with larger communal concerns for social justice, and reflected a complex mixture of personal goals and collective consciousness. Flora Weiss, for example, wanted to learn dressmaking "to earn a lot of money." But she also "wanted to organize the workers around me . . . to do something for mankind."

By 1920, the ILGWU had become the sixth largest union in the American Federation of Labor. Of the 102,000 dues-paying members, two-thirds were women. Women also constituted one-third of the membership of the Amalgamated Clothing Workers of America (ACWA). In 1920, only 15 percent of women in all manufacturing industries were unionized, while more than 45 percent of female laborers in the garment industry were in unions. This exceptional development was the result of a combination of immediate shop-floor abuses, women's evolving concerns about their dignity as females and workers, and the influence of a highly visible and vocal group of Jewish socialists and other leftist radicals.

In addition, the Jewish immigrant community was generally sympathetic to labor organization. The Jewish socialists, most of whom were deeply rooted in *yiddishkeit*, and in Jewish ethical and prophetic tradition, came to embody a socialism partly derived from Jewish culture and secular messianism. They were dedicated not only to class struggle and the establishment of the "Cooperative Commonwealth," but also to the protection and preservation of Jewish life. Their class consciousness and well-developed ethic of social justice, as well as the prophetic and traditional teachings within which they couched the labor and political conflict, were well understood in the Jewish community. Even Eastern European Jewish Orthodox leaders and newspapers who denounced the socialist leaders of the garment unions as demagogues gave their blessing to striking workers and affirmed the idea of unionization. This kind of support helped Jewish daughters stay in the movement. It legitimized their presence among the strikers and helped build a context of community and family sympathy for female activism.

Despite the supportive environment and outstanding contribution of women to socialist union strength, many male union leaders regarded the women workers, and especially women organizers, with suspicion and hostility. Discrimination was rampant. Neither the ILGWU nor the ACWA stood strongly for the principle of equal pay for equal work, and women workers generally fared less well in contracts. Neither union was receptive to female leadership. Executive positions at the local level continued to be monopolized by men. These conditions existed even where women outnumbered men as in White Goods Local 62 and Shirtwaistmakers Local 25, both of whose presidents were men. Furthermore, despite their majority in the ILGWU and their significant representation in the ACWA, only a small number of women rose to positions at the national level. Between 1916 and 1924, Fannia Cohn served as the only female voice on the ILGWU general executive board (GEB). BESSIE ABRAMOWITZ [HILLMAN] secured a seat on ACWA's GEB after serving as secretary-treasurer of District Council no. 6 in Chicago. And twenty-two-year-old Latvian-born DOROTHY JACOBS [BELLANCA], an organizer of the buttonhole makers' local in Baltimore, succeeded Abramowitz on the ACWA board.

Even those who achieved some distinction, however, revealed the difficulties involved in being the only women on the unions' boards. Fannia Cohn said that although she lived "a full, interesting, and satisfying life," it was "not easy for a woman to be in a leading position, especially in the labor movement." The prejudice and insensitivity of male leadership was not a monopoly of the socialist unions. The Socialist Party also took a long time to support women's unionism without reluctance.

A disproportionate number of Jewish women were members and active recruiters for the party, and a small number were actually Socialist candidates, like Esther Friedman, who ran for the New York State Assembly several times. They were heavily involved despite the fact that the Socialist Party posture toward women was marked, for the most part, by disinterest and condescension. The party never wholeheartedly encouraged women to organize, and even when it officially recognized women in 1908 as a constituent element in the class struggle, it failed to understand the "Woman Question." Socialists never fully faced the issues of women's low position in the labor market, the nature and significance of household labor for women, or the unique cultural baggage that women carried into the workplace. The "problems" of women

were rooted, the party argued, in the system of private property—emancipation for everyone, including women, would arrive with the Cooperative Commonwealth. On tactical questions the Second Socialist International had already spoken the final word in the late nineteenth century: Socialist women were to remain loyal to the party and resist the temptation to make cross-class alliances with other women. Class-consciousness was to be the ultimate loyalty, not gender.

While the recruitment of Jewish women into the Socialist Party outpaced recruitment in many other groups, the process was slow. A Jewish Woman's Progressive Society, a socialist group, emerged in New York and in Chicago in the 1890s, and attracted an impressive roster of radical speakers before it disappeared during the depression of 1893. When the socialist Workmen's Circle (WC) was established in 1892, it formally endorsed participation of women, but did little to encourage it. The WC reorganized in 1901, and separate ladies' branches were recognized for the first time. These branches attracted a sizable membership, but they were mostly extensions of the social networks among women married to Socialist Party men. The ladies' branches were not pathways for those ambitious to make significant contributions, and they failed to integrate women into the party's mainstream.

Only after 1909, when tens of thousands of Jewish women fought successfully for union recognition, did women leaders play an important part in the Socialist Party. The Women's National Committee (WNC), established in 1908, set out to recruit women directly into the party. But in order to maintain centralized party discipline, the WNC also sought to eradicate independent socialist women's organizations. They recruited successfully among the strike leaders and at the same time placed Socialist Party functionaries in important positions in the garment unions and in the Women's Trade Union League (WTUL), a reformist, middle-class organization that had proven a valuable ally in the women's labor movement.

ROSE SCHNEIDERMAN, who had achieved recognition during the 1909 strike, was one of several prominent recruits. And more long-standing socialists, including PAULINE NEWMAN and Clara Lemlich, also used their new, strike-gained visibility to the party's benefit. Newman became a paid organizer for the ILGWU and for several years preached the socialist message to union audiences. Lemlich joined the WTUL executive board and devoted herself to politics, especially the Socialist Party's woman suffrage campaign. There was, however, no increase in party membership. Instead, women trade unionists, including Jewish radicals, committed themselves even more deeply to their union duties.

Some Socialist Party stalwarts like Yiddish journalist THERESA MALKIEL, who had been a member of the WTUL, turned on the middle-class women of that organization, blaming them for distracting women from socialism with the "false consciousness" of feminism. WTUL officials did acknowledge the Socialist Party's contributions to the labor movement in its internal reports, but they rarely praised socialists openly. And the WTUL, not the Socialist Party, emerged as the public champion of working women. Malkiel warned against continuing to cooperate with the "bourgeois" reformers, but of all the reform groups that rallied to the cause of labor, none was more effective in organizing women than the WTUL.

The WTUL, an organization that had provided funds, meeting space, and publicity, and whose middle-class women sometimes picketed, risking police arrest and assault, had helped secure important victories and roused many women to political activism. Socialists Pauline Newman and Rose Schneiderman, therefore, continued to work for the WTUL, even as they experienced some tension in the attempt to synthesize feminism and socialism. A male correspondent warned Schneiderman about her work in the feminist movement: "You either work for Socialism, and as a consequence for the equality of the sexes, or you work for women . . . only and neglect Socialism. Then you act like a bad doctor who pretends to cure his patient by removing the symptoms instead of removing the disease itself."

Jewish socialist women, however, did not work for women only. They did not become full-fledged feminists, at least not to the extent of putting the oppression of women above all else. The more radical and active women steered an uneasy course between their commitment to class solidarity and the promises of feminist reform. Jewish working women's politics grew out of their role as breadwinners, class-conscious Jews, and members of an ethnic community, and they appeared genuinely excited partners in a labor movement that included both sexes. Not only were the women demonstrating their ability to fight side by side with men; there was also the promise that the authentic comradeship and partnership of the day-to-day labor movement could be translated into romantic, respectable, companionate marriages. In the unions and in the party, women remained "junior" partners to be sure, but for most Jewish women this was preferable to a return to restrictive gender separation that had

circumscribed their lives in the shtetls of Eastern Europe.

Yet, while they stressed the common ground they shared with men in the working-class community, the vast majority, possibly as high as 75 percent of Jewish women, favored female suffrage. The women of the Lower East Side of New York, between 1915 and 1917, produced more support for suffrage referenda than almost all other districts, including middle-class Protestant districts. And they did this in the face of the Socialist Party's lukewarm response to female suffrage, and despite the position of the *Jewish Daily Forward*, which carried columns by Jewish socialist luminaries warning women against placing too much emphasis on "political emancipation."

These women stayed with socialism, even though the party continued in the main to treat women's issues as marginal "symptoms" of the class system. But in many places, and especially in Chicago and New York, Jewish women joined, and became prime leaders of, the many women's committees of the Socialist Party. They also stayed with socialist trade unionism even though their union brothers continued to be chauvinistic. But from 1913 on, a small group of Jewish women pressed for a greater measure of equality in the ILGWU and the ACWA, and semiautonomous women's institutions within the garment unions. Pauline Newman and Dorothy Jacobs Bellanca, among other Jewish leaders, argued persuasively that the mixed-gender branches were losing participation of female members who felt intimidated. In the ACWA, women activists eventually withdrew from the established locals and founded separate women's branches that cut across ethnic and occupational lines, bringing together all female workers in the men's clothing industry in a particular city.

Gender segregation had been advocated not as an ideological expression of "female difference," but as a "tactical expedient" toward integration. By 1920, however, left-wing Jewish women in the ILGWU recognized that gender segregation not only had little attraction to the rank and file, Jewish or otherwise, but could actually lead to further exclusion of women, and so they promoted abolition of sex divisions. Even long-term advocates of women's rights, like Fannia Cohn and others, insisted that women and men had "much in common" and ought not to be segregated.

The decision by Jewish women to stay with the Socialist Party and garment unions, despite their second-class status in those institutions, meant that socialist women had the opportunity to prove what so many male comrades previously doubted—the ability of a militant minority to organize working women, and to mobilize these women for battle. Socialist Jewish women made strikes even over the objections of male leadership. And in the unions, they initiated important and enduring education, health, and recreation programs despite the doubts of male colleagues.

Between feminism and socialism, between the desire for civic participation and the equally compelling desire for domestic respectability, most Jewish immigrant daughters had found a middle way. Even when they married, as most did, Jewish women did not leave their politics behind. Among the leadership Cohn, Schneiderman, and Newman never married, but Abramowitz, Jacobs, and Malkiel did. In 1900, Malkiel organized married housekeepers into the Woman's Progressive Society of Yonkers, which later became Branch One of the Socialist Women's Society of Greater New York. Although for most radical Jewish women, home and family pushed sustained activism to the background, many nonetheless retained their union membership and participated as organizers, fund-raisers, and campaigners. And in the Great Depression of the 1930s, when political hopes for the Left flared again, many of the married women valiantly fought against evictions of the down and out, and struggled for the rights of the unemployed.

Women also participated in the extensive Jewish organizational network that was spawned by socialism and communism as these movements grew. Here they managed to combine family and community obligations with a dimension of personal independence. Former working women (and future working women too) found jobs as teachers and administrators in Socialist Sunday schools and Yiddish-language *shuln*, and special places in children's camps, consumer and tenant committees, and labor defense and foreign relief societies. These activities were not direct political participation, but they represented an extraordinary contribution to the socialist labor movement and to social welfare in general. And they offered the Jewish woman a temporarily viable synthesis of her desire for self-sufficiency and fulfillment, her energy, her idealism, her class-consciousness, and the traditional culture out of which some of these aspirations and attitudes emerged.

BIBLIOGRAPHY

Baum, Charlotte. "What Made Yetta Work? The Economic Role of Eastern European Jewish Women in the Family." *Response* 18 (Summer 1973): 32–38; Buhle, Mary Jo. *Women and American Socialism, 1870–1920* (1981); Cohen, Rose. *Out of the Shadow* (1918); Davis-Kram, Harriet. "Jewish Women in Russian Revolutionary Movements." M.A. thesis, Hunter College, City University of New York (1974); Dye, Nancy. "Creating a Feminist Alliance: Sisterhood and Class Conflict in the New York WTUL." *Feminist Studies* 2, no. 2 (1975): 361–375; Endelman, Gary E. "Solidarity Forever: Rose Schneiderman and the Women's Trade Union League." Diss., University of Delaware (1978); Glenn, Susan A. *Daughters of the Shtetl: Life and Labor in the Immigrant Generation* (1990); Kennedy, Susan Estabrook. *If All We Did Was to Weep at Home* (1979); Kessler-Harris, Alice. "Organizing the Unorganizable: Three Jewish Women and Their Union." *Labor History* 17, no. 1 (Winter 1976): 5–23; Kramer, Sydelle, and Jenny Masur, eds. *Jewish Grandmothers* (1976); Levine, Louis. *The Women Garment Workers* (1924); Malkiel, Theresa. *Diary of a Shirtwaist Striker* (1910); Miller, Sally M. "From Sweatshop Worker to Labor Leader: Theresa Malkiel, a Case Study." *American Jewish History* 68, no. 2 (December 1978): 189–205; Pesotta, Rose. *Bread upon the Waters* (1944), and *Days of Our Lives* (1958); Quint, Howard. *The Forging of American Socialism* (1953); Scheier, Paula. "Clara Lemlich Shavelson: Fifty Years in Labor's Front Line." In *The American Jewish Woman: A Documentary History*, edited by Jacob R. Marcus (1981); Schneiderman, Rose. *All for One* (1967); Shannon, David. *The Socialist Party of America* (1955); Shavelson, Clara Lemlich. "Remembering the Waistmakers' General Strike, 1909." *Jewish Currents* 36, no. 10 (November 1982): 9–15; Miller, Sally M. "Other Socialists: Native Born and Immigrant Women in the Socialist Party of America, 1901–1917." *Labor History* 24, no. 1 (Winter 1983): 84–102; Sorin, Gerald. *The Prophetic Minority: American Jewish Immigrant Radicals, 1880–1920* (1985); Wolfson, Theresa. *The Woman Worker and the Trade Unions* (1926).

MANUSCRIPT AND
ORAL HISTORY COLLECTIONS
Amerikaner-Yiddishe Geshichte Bel Pe [American Jewish Oral History]. YIVO, NYC; Cohn, Fannia. Papers. New York Public Library; Oral History of the American Left. Tamiment Institute, NYC; Pesotta, Rose. Papers. New York Public Library; Schneiderman, Rose. Papers. Tamiment Institute; Socialist Party. New York Papers and Minute Books. Tamiment Institute.

GERALD SORIN

SOCIOLOGY

Sociological theory suggests that Jews are likely to be good sociologists, because people positioned on the margins of society (i.e., social outsiders) tend to be astute social observers (Park 1950). Since Jews historically have been the quintessential outsiders, many great sociologists have, in fact, been Jews—particularly Jewish men (e.g., Lewis Coser, Emile Durkheim, Erving Goffman, Irving Louis Horowitz, Herbert Marcuse, Karl Marx, Karl Mannheim, Robert K. Merton, and Georg Simmel), although some did not acknowledge their Jewishness.

The disproportionate contribution by Jews to sociology is clear both in European and American sociology (Fine 1995). Despite this record of Jewish contribution, many analyses of the history of sociology stress the Protestant tradition. Also forgotten is the fact that in order to contribute intellectually, one has to have the *opportunity* to do so. Until recently, faculty positions were perhaps difficult to attain for Jewish men, but they were systematically denied to women, particularly Jewish women, except in marginal academic milieux such as women's colleges.

Theoretically, being a Jew and a woman could constitute "double marginality" (i.e., being doubly positive, leading to particularly profound sociological sensitivity) or paralysis, where the value of belonging to one marginal group is canceled out by belonging to two. In my view, "double marginality" is an asset, because American Jewish women have, indeed, made considerable contributions to the discipline of sociology and to its various subfields (see Reinharz 1993).

When doing historical research on American Jewish women sociologists, it is difficult to determine who is a sociologist. If we use the criteria of a Ph.D. in sociology and faculty appointment in a department of sociology, then many women will be eliminated from the potential group of early sociologists. Although scores of women worked in settlement houses in Chicago, Pittsburgh, New York, and other cities and conducted superb sociological research, they are overlooked in histories of sociology or mislabeled as social workers (Fitzpatrick 1990). Many organizations that spun off from settlement houses—juvenile courts, probation offices, social service agencies—were begun by Jewish women such as Chicagoan MINNIE LOW, whose work straddled the fields of social work and social research. Higher education for women was nearly inaccessible until the turn of the century, and appointment to faculty positions took longer still. Many academic institutions other than women's colleges were altogether closed to women and had quotas for Jews.

Only since 1985 has research been done on women's sociological achievements, let alone on Jewish women's sociological work. One of the earliest books to provide systematic information about women sociologists was published as late as 1991 and labeled by the editor as "the first extensive reference book on great female sociologists." The volume was sixteen years in preparation because the information on early women sociologists was so difficult to locate, and because the academy has "structural barriers to [such] an enterprise. . . . Rewards for writing and teaching about women intellectuals are still problematic" (Deegan 1991, pp. xiii–xv). Deegan claims that American women have functioned as sociologists from 1840 on, even though most nonfeminist historians of sociology believe that women did not enter the profession until after 1930. Thus, the majority of sociologists may not recognize the fact that women sociologists, let alone Jewish women sociologists, existed before the current wave of feminism opened the academy to women in a significant way. As sociologist Helen MacGill Hughes documented (1975) and, later, historian of sociology Mary Jo Deegan, wrote, "White, Anglo-Saxon, Protestant women from the middle and upper middle classes predominate in the marginal world of women sociologists" (1991, p. 11). Only now are people beginning to acknowledge the history of Jewish women sociologists.

The unusual achievements of Jewish women in sociology is recognized only anecdotally. The fact that sociologists are not identified by religion within the American Sociological Association makes it difficult to know empirically which American women sociologists are Jewish and which are not. The influential report on "The Status of Women in Sociology, 1968–1972," commissioned and published by the American Sociological Association in 1973, does not discuss religion at all. Therefore, it is impossible to assess the percentage of current or past sociologists who were American Jewish women, or the percentage of American Jewish sociologists who were women. Whereas books have been written about black sociologists, the Protestant roots of sociology, and women sociologists, there is no analysis by religion of the work of American sociologists, and no work on Jewish American women sociologists as a group. This encyclopedia entry, written more than 150 years after the coining of the term "sociology," is likely the first discussion of the topic.

One factor explaining Jewish women's likely overrepresentation in sociology relative to non-Jews is the value Jews place on education and the scholarly life. Using data from 526 respondents to the 1990 National Jewish Population Survey who were between ages twenty-one and sixty-four, and employed, Rela Geffen found that Jewish women are the most highly educated women in the United States, and their receipt of advanced degrees continues to increase (cited in Sales, Shavelson, and Lasken 1994).

The few anthologies that discuss female sociologists do contain quite a few chapters by Jewish women, but several of these entries (e.g., Kanter 1988) do not mention the author's Jewishness. Some anthologies include a chapter in which an American Jewish female reflects on her work but does not necessarily even mention that she is Jewish (e.g., Daniels

1967). Others include a brief reference to the author's being Jewish, but do not connect this fact to the author's sociological work (e.g., Cavan 1994, Hess 1995, Rubin 1994). Only a few highlight the significant way in which being Jewish shaped the person's life and work (Keller 1995, Reinharz 1995, Tuchman 1995, Wartenberg 1995). Thus, it is ironic that Jews are supposed to be unusually socially aware, yet they do not always recognize the way their Jewishness affects their sociological work.

Because sociologists frequently study subject matter close to their personal concerns or identity, an alternative way to locate American Jewish women sociologists is to locate women who study the American Jewish community. The study of the American Jewish community, however, is so recent that very few individuals are involved (e.g. Lynn Davidman, Debra Renee Kaufman, Rela Geffen Monson, Shelly Tenenbaum, and others). Some women may also be doing *sociological* research about the Jewish community who actually are trained as psychologists (e.g., Bethamie Horowitz, Amy Sales) or literary critics (e.g., Sylvia Barack Fishman). Therefore, the first challenge in understanding the contribution and experience of American Jewish women sociologists is to identify these women.

Jewish feminist sociologists' interest in ethnicity and multiculturalism ironically does not always include an interest in the lives or oppression of Jews. Eminent sociologist Mirra Komarovsky (b. 1905), the second woman president of the American Sociological Association, mentioned briefly that when she graduated from Barnard, her professors warned her that she would face difficulties pursuing an academic career in sociology, as a woman, a Jew, and someone who was foreign-born, a topic about which she does not write or speak. Her vast corpus of writing includes pioneering studies of women, masculinity, cultural contradictions, and self-disclosure, but does not deal with any Jewish issues or Jewish communities. The typical triad of contemporary sociological concerns—race, class, and gender—does not usually address religion or ethnicity. An early exception is Pauline Bart, the only sociologist who contributed an essay ("How a Nice Jewish Girl Like Me Could") to EVELYN TORTON BECK's *Nice Jewish Girls: A Lesbian Anthology* (1982). Moreover, realizing that being women put them in a tenuous position, some Jewish women sociologists may have hidden their Jewish identity to fit in somewhat better. Thus, it is possible that Ruth Shonle Cavan (b. 1896) may have some Jewish roots, given her name and the fact that she wrote about intermarriage, including an article entitled "Jewish Student Attitudes Toward Interreligious and Intra-Jewish Marriage," *American Journal of Sociology* 76 (May 1971): 1064–1071. In an interview, however, Cavan identified herself as Protestant.

The presence of many Jewish women among current sociologists is likely to be noted, if at all, not because these women study Jewish themes but because of their Jewish-sounding names (e.g., Muriel Cantor, Nancy Chodorow, Janet Saltzman Chafetz, Roberta S. Cohen, Arlene Kaplan Daniels, Eva Etzioni, Zelda Gamson, Nona Glazer, Ruth Jacobs, Charlotte Schwartz, and Lenore Weitzman). In fact, locating Jews for research purposes by identifying Jewish-sounding names is an accepted practice among sociologists.

One of the earliest Jewish American women sociologists is Austrian-born FAY B. KARPF (1893–1981), who received her Ph.D. at age thirty-two in 1925 from the University of Chicago, the then preeminent department and home of the distinctive "Chicago school of sociology" (Reinharz 1994). Her German-speaking Orthodox parents sent her to public schools and gave her a profound respect for the spiritual and intellectual life. In late-life interviews, she remembered having her Jewish heritage appreciated as a graduate student, both because several senior male scholars were studying Jewish and other ethnic urban enclaves, and because the presence of many foreign students reduced the ethnocentrism found in other universities. She also claimed, however, that her pioneering work in community studies and "ecological maps" was attributed to men who went on to regular academic careers, unavailable to her.

While a graduate student, Karpf conducted social welfare research at the Chicago Jewish Charities (1922–1923). Her first major work, *American Social Psychology: Its Origins, Development and European Background* (1932), became the standard textbook in social psychology until the early 1960s. Thus, it should be acknowledged that American sociologists from 1932 through the early 1960s learned social psychology through Fay Karpf's work. She later became the first chair of the Division of Social Psychology of the American Sociological Association.

After earning her Ph.D., Karpf went to Paris to study with psychoanalyst Otto Rank, and then moved to New York to teach social work at the Training School for Jewish Social Work, not a university department of sociology. She never had an opportunity to train Ph.D. sociologists who might have sustained her legacy. Inevitably, she has become invisible in the history of the discipline. Like many women, Karpf moved because of an opportunity offered her husband—to direct the newly created Training School for Jewish Social Work, a response to the Jewish community's need for professionally educated social workers to perform Jewish social service. One of the school's goals was to encourage its students to become leaders in the Jewish community and to end the high turnover rate of Jewish social workers. In 1932, the Training School's name was changed to the Graduate School for Jewish Social Work and its curriculum revised to provide knowledge and appreciation of Jewish culture as well as understanding of the general, non-Jewish society.

The Graduate School for Jewish Social Work highlighted differences between the Jewish and non-Jewish communities and emphasized the changing needs of the Jewish community. Fay Karpf's training as a sociologist and position as wife of the director influenced the values and mission of the school. By the early 1930s, she rose to the rank of professor, and by the end of the decade, she chaired a department, teaching courses on the development and theory of social investigation, primarily research courses. Her teaching career ended when the school closed in 1940, a mere fifteen years after she earned the Ph.D.

All of Karpf's writing after her first volume concerns the different schools of psychotherapy, culminating in a book published by the Philosophical Library in New York, *The Psychology and Psychotherapy of Otto Rank* (1953). As a sociologist, she rejected Freudian reliance on instincts in favor of Rank's more sociological views. Later, however, she became disillusioned with Rank for his denying his Jewishness and blaming Jews for the faults of German culture. Rank condemned repressed Jews and gentiles for creating the conditions of general malaise and saw anti-Semitism as a positive force in Jewish cultural development (Klein 1981).

With the demise of the school, Maurice and Fay Karpf moved to Los Angeles where he was appointed executive director of the Federation of Jewish Welfare Organizations of Los Angeles and executive secretary of the Los Angeles Jewish Community Council. She, on the other hand, switched fields from sociology and social work to counseling and psychotherapy, which she practiced in Los Angeles for the last forty years of her life. In 1973, thirty-three years after she left New York, she listed herself in the University of Chicago alumni directory as a clinical psychologist.

Beyond the difficulty of identifying "who is Jewish" are the problems of defining "who is American" and "who is a sociologist." A case in point is HANNAH ARENDT (1906–1975), a woman born in Hanover, Germany, who endured internment during the Holocaust and arrived in New York in May 1941, becoming a citizen only in 1951. Because she lived in the United States for her remaining thirty-four years, she could be considered an American Jewish scholar. Was she, however, a sociologist or a political scientist? Deegan's 1991 reference work on women sociologists contains a chapter on Arendt, yet she is known as a political theorist. Arendt did not have an academic appontment, yet a major sociologist, Irving Louis Horowitz, is the Hannah Arendt Distinguished Professor of Sociology and Political Science at Rutgers University.

Hannah Arendt had a strong identity as a Jew, shaped both by her secular Jewish upbringing and her experiences during the Holocaust. Although she admired the idea of the State of Israel as a refuge for Jews, she was concerned that Jewish nationalism would prove no different from any other form of nationalism, an inherently dangerous phenomenon. Being a Jew in non-Jewish society was, however, not a viable alternative. Her first and last books, *Origins of Totalitarianism* (1951) and *The Jew as Pariah: Jewish Identity and Politics in the Modern Age* (1978), deal squarely with this dilemma. One of her earliest books, *Rahel Varhnhagen: The Life of a Jewish Woman* (1958), concerns the oldest daughter of a prosperous Berlin merchant, raised in Orthodox surroundings, who always suffered from a sense of social inferiority because of her Jewish origin. After marrying into aristocracy, Varnhagen converted to Protestanism, and then came to admire her Jewish heritage, which formerly she had despised.

Many of the Jewish women who were able to enter the profession and be recognized as sociologists were married to sociologists (e.g., ROSE COSER and her husband Lewis, Jessie and Luther Lee Bernard, Caroline and Arnold Rose), as was true of their gentile sisters (e.g., Helen and Everett Hughes, Elizabeth and Alfred McClung Lee, Helen and Robert Lynd, Alva and Gunnar Myrdal) (for biographical descriptions on each of these women, see Deegan 1991). Wives of eminent sociologists became part of the networks of male sociologists and thus gained some access to information and professional opportunities. At the same time, however, they remained in the shadow of their famous husbands and relegated to minor positions, or barred from them altogether because of nepotism rules (see Hughes 1975).

With the renewal of the Ameircan women's movement in the mid-1960s and increased governmental funding for higher education, women, including large numbers of Jewish women, began to seek advanced degrees in greater numbers. Many of these individuals focused their dissertation research on problems relating to women's lives (e.g., Cynthia Fuchs Epstein's "Women and Professional Careers: The Case of the

Woman Lawyer," Columbia University, 1968). The basic concepts concerning sex role socialization (Weitzman 1979), the caste system of the sexes, the "feminine mystique," comparable worth, the unequal distribution of labor in the household, and others were developed by American Jewish women sociologists. Most of the research they undertook concerned inequality and injustice in some form. Most Jewish American female sociologists were feminists and contributed to a large body of literature in feminist sociology. Much of this work was also the underpinning of women's studies courses and programs.

Until the 1970s, tenure was largely unattainable even in those rare circumstances when Jewish women had faculty appointments. Those women who did earn a tenured position were largely in women's colleges rather than at major research universities (e.g., Mirra Komarovsky at Barnard College rather than Columbia Univerity). Women were kept primarily on the outside of academia or in marginal positions within. After the 1970s and the establishment of Sociologists for Women in Society (SWS), a professional group of feminist sociologists, the position of female sociologists improved enormously. Among the leaders of the feminist sociologists are American Jewish women such as Judith Lorber, founding editor of SWS's academic journal, *Gender & Society*. The journal has not yet published much about Jewish life. Currently, the Sex and Gender Section of the American Sociological Association, a section to which many women sociologists belong because of their research interests, is the largest in the association. There is even some "fear" among conservative thinkers that sociology is becoming a "feminized" discipline and profession.

One other factor complicates the attempt to identify American Jewish women sociologists and their contributions—some of these women moved to Israel. These women include Deborah Bernstein, Brenda Danet, Dasna Izraeli (originally Canadian), Beverly Mizrachi, Judith Shuval, and several others. Deborah Bernstein, at the University of Haifa, has conducted pioneering studies of women's political roles in the pre-State period (1987, 1982), and Beverly Mizrachi has studied women of achievement. Judith Shuval has focused on immigration, the health care system, and Russian physicians, winning the prestigious Israel Prize for her first book (1963). Brenda Danet has focused on Israeli bureaucracy (1989).

In sum, there were three types of American Jewish women sociologists in the period before the current wave of feminism: (1) women who were trained as sociologists but whose work was marginalized (e.g.,

Fay Karpf); (2) women who were married to famous sociologists and developed a career of their own (e.g., Jessie Bernard); and (3) women who were not married to sociologists and developed a strong career in sociology (e.g., Mirra Komarovsky). Few of these women mentioned their Jewishness in print, and almost none studied any aspect of Jewish life. Many, however, focused on women's concerns.

After the reemergence of the women's movement, the creative potential of Jewish women sociologists was unleashed, and Jewish women social researchers harnessed all the available research methods to conduct studies that could reshape American society. Their careers could unfold regardless of their marital status, even if they faced discrimination as women. When positions in academia became available, American Jewish women sociologists eagerly sought them and went on to form feminist sociological professional associations. Although their research output has been formidable and influential, it is still the case that very little of it has been devoted to studying Jewish life, and very little autobiographical writing by these women has discussed their lives as Jews.

BIBLIOGRAPHY

Beck, Evelyn Torton. *Nice Jewish Girls: A Lesbian Anthology* (1982); Bernstein, Deborah. *The Struggle for Equality: Urban Women Workers in Prestate Israeli Society* (1987); Bernstein, Deborah S., ed. *Pioneers and Homemakers: Jewish Women in Prestate Israel* (1992); Cavan, Sherri. "Being an Ethnographer." In *Gender and the Academic Experience: Berkeley Women Sociologists*, edited by Kathryn Orlans and Ruth Wallace (1994); Danet, Brenda. *Pulling Strings: Biculturalism in Israeli Bureaucracy* (1989); Daniels, Arlene Kaplan. "The Low-Caste Stranger in Social Research." In *Ethics, Politics, and Social Research*, edited by Gideon Sjoberg (1967); Davidman, Lynn. *Tradition in a Rootless World: Women Turn to Orthodox Judaism* (1991); Deegan, Mary Jo, ed. *Women in Sociology: A Bio-Biographical Sourcebook* (1991); Fine, Gary Alan, ed. *A Second Chicago School? The Development of a Postwar American Sociology* (1995); Fitzpatrick, Ellen. *Endless Crusade: Women Social Scientists and Progressive Reform* (1990); Hess, Beth. "An Accidental Sociologist." In *Individual Voices, Collective Visions: Fifty Years of Women in Sociology*, edited by Ann Goetting and Sarah Fenstermaker (1995); Hughes, Helen MacGill. "Women in Academic Sociology, 1925–1975." *Sociological Focus* 8, no. 3 (1975): 215–222; Kanter, Rosabeth Moss. "Phases of Societal and Sociological Inquiry in an Age of Discontinuity." In *Sociological Lives*, edited by Matilda White Riley (1988); Karpf, Fay B. *American Social Psychology: Its Origins, Development and European Background* (1932); Kaufman, Debra Renee. *Rachel's Daughters: Newly Orthodox Jewish Women* (1991); Keller, Suzanne. "Bridging Worlds: A Sociologist's Memoir." In *Individual Voices, Collective Visions: Fifty Years of Women in Sociology*, edited by Ann Goetting and Sarah

Fenstermaker (1995); Klein, Dennis B. *Jewish Origins of the Psychoanalytic Movement* (1981); Park, Robert Ezra. *Race and Culture* (1950); Reinharz, Shulamit. *A Contextualized Chronology of Women's Sociological Work* (February 1993), and "Fay Karpf: Synthesizer Par Excellence." Paper presented at the annual meetings of the American Sociological Association, Los Angeles, Calif. (August 1994), and "Finding a Sociological Voice: The Work of Mirra Komarovsky." *Sociological Inquiry* 59, no. 4 (1989): 374–395, and "Marginality, Motherhood and Method: Paths to a Social Science Career and Community." In *Individual Voices, Collective Visions: Fifty Years of Women in Sociology*, edited by Ann Goetting and Sarah Fenstermaker (1995); Rubin, Lillian B. "An Unanticipated Life." In *Gender and the Academic Experience: Berkeley Women Sociologists*, edited by Kathryn Orlans and Ruth Wallace (1994); Sales, Amy L., Susanne Shavelson, and Diane Lasken, eds. *Data Book: A Summary of Current Research and Writing on American Jewish Women* (1994, draft); Shuval, Judith. *Immigrants on the Threshold* (1963); Tuchman, Gaye. "Kaddish and Renewal." In *Individual Voices, Collective Visions: Fifty Years of Women in Sociology*, edited by Ann Goetting and Sarah Fenstermaker (1995); Wartenberg, Hannah Schiller. "Obstacles and Opportunities en Route to a Career in Sociology." In *Individual Voices, Collective Visions: Fifty Years of Women in Sociology*, edited by Ann Goetting and Sarah Fenstermaker (1995); Weitzman, Lenore J. *Sex Role Socialization* (1979).

SHULAMIT REINHARZ

SOKOLOW, ANNA (b. 1910)

Anna Sokolow, the "rebellious spirit" of modern dance, was a member of the Martha Graham Company (1937–1940), on the faculty of the Juilliard School of Music, Dance Division (1958–1988), founder and director of La Paloma Azul Company (Mexico, 1940), the Lyric Theater (Israel, 1962), the Anna Sokolow Dance Company (1967), and the Players Project (1971), adviser to Inbal (1953), choreographer of hundreds of dance works, plays, operas, Broadway musicals, and festivals. Her partners included musician Alex North, painter Ignacio Aguirre, and actor John Silvester White. In celebration of her eighty-fifth birthday, in 1995, the dance world joined in tribute to her accomplishments and service, her pioneer work in Mexico and Israel, and, above all, her "blazing force and integrity."

Anna Sokolow, the child of Russian immigrants Samuel and Sara Sokolowski, was born in Hartford, Connecticut, in 1910. The family moved to New York in 1912. Sara became the breadwinner for the family, working in the garment trade, active in the ILGWU and the Socialist Party. At the Emanu-El Sisterhood of Personal Service, Anna took her first dance classes

Anna Sokolow is a dancer and choreographer whose hundreds of dance works, plays, operas, and festivals have reflected the social, political, and human conflicts of her time. Her associations have included the Martha Graham Company, La Poloma Azul Company of Mexico, and the Lyric Theater of Israel. [New York Public Library]

with Elsa Pohl, who taught interpretive dancing in the style of Isadora Duncan. Anna attended the Henry Street Settlement House, the original Neighborhood Playhouse, established by Alice and IRENE LEWISOHN, wealthy Jewish women who were interested in dance and theater. Sokolow studied with Blanche Talmud, Irene Lewisohn, and Bird Larson. Given a full scholarship in 1928, she was invited to join the special classes of the Junior Festival Players when the Playhouse School opened on West 46th Street. There, her teachers included Martha Graham, Louis Horst, Michio Ito, and Benjamin Zemach, an exponent of Hebraic dance. Sokolow's first theater appearance was in Ernest Bloch's *Israel Symphony* in May 1928, staged by Irene Lewisohn.

Sokolow's choreography closely reflects her intense commitment to the social, political, and human conflicts of her times. *City Rhythms*, a student work staged in 1931, reflected currents of her life, the rhythms of New York City, Moscow, Mexico City, and Tel Aviv. Other early works include the *Anti-War Trilogy (Anti-War Cycle)* of 1933. Performed with the Theater Union Dance Group, the piece was staged in three parts: I. *Depression, Starvation*, II. *Diplomacy—War*, and III. *Protest (Defiance)*. This was the first use of the music of Alex North (Soifer), who was Sokolow's partner. She received critical albeit high praise, since, from a Marxist position, "this piece proved that an individual, rather than collective creator, could produce work of high quality."

In the Depression years, Sokolow, SOPHIE MASLOW, and HELEN TAMIRIS, dancers with Jewish working-class origins, were mobilized by the union movement. Sokolow says, "The unions were really my first audience. Poets or writers would read their work, singers and dancers would perform in their halls."

Sokolow was regarded as an outstanding figure of the radical dance era. For the WPA, she created the dances for *Sing for Your Supper*, a variety show that is primarily remembered because it contained the great narrative *Ballad for Americans*.

Invited to Mexico, a land fighting its artistic and social revolution, in 1939 by Carlos Mérida, Sokolow became a pioneer teacher and choreographer. Rita Morgenthau helped get her company to Mexico. Mexico City audiences accepted her dancing, although the work was neither ballet nor folk dance. Away from New York, with a different tempo and culture, her work turned toward lyricism. Her company, La Paloma Azul [The blue dove], received acclaim, as did her production of the *Antigone Symphony* by Carlos Chavez.

With the circumstances of World War II, she began to choreograph Jewish material. She used passages from the Old Testament in 1943 as part of a Montreal Festival performance and *Songs of a Semite*, from a book of poems by EMMA LAZARUS, for a 1943 Y performance. In 1945 and 1946, she danced *The Bride* to "traditional Jewish music" and *Kaddish*, wrapped in tefillin.

Drawn to theater work, she choreographed dances for the drama *Street Scene* (1946) by Elmer Rice, to music by Kurt Weill, lyrics by Langston Hughes. Set in a crowded tenement in the Lower East Side, it was a natural idiom to her. She used the jitterbug and children's games, dance vernacular now fully accepted but

then very innovative. Sokolow had brought a popular social dance swing idiom to the Broadway stage. Theater brought her to the Actors Studio, Elia Kazan's training school. A dance version of Ansky's *The Dybbuk* marked her last concert appearance in 1951.

In the Netherlands, she created *The Seven Deadly Sins* (1967) for the Netherlands Dance Theater, and in Israel, *The Treasure* (1962), a play based on a story by Itzchak Peretz. She staged the vast festivals and fund-raising events after World War II on behalf of the Jewish National Fund and Bonds for Israel. These included the 1952 Purim Festival (with Sholom Secunda) at Madison Square Garden, the 1953 Fund-Raising for Israel Bonds: 3,000th Anniversary of Jerusalem, and the 1954 Hanukkah Festival pageant (with Kim Stanley and Joseph Schildkraut). She staged opera at the New York City Center in 1956, including *Orpheus, La Traviata, The Tempest, L'Histoire du Soldat*, and *Carmen*.

Rooms (1955) grew from sessions at the Actors Studio. It depicts the isolation of the urban dweller. Each dancer sits in a chair, reaching into space, close to one another, yet out of touch. The theme of the withdrawn sufferer appeared again in *Session '58, Opus '50, Opus Jazz 1958* in Israel, *Opus '60*, and, finally, *Opus '65* in the Joffrey Ballet Company's repertory to Teo Macero's jazz score.

Two works are worth special note. *Lyric Suite* (1953), choreographed to Alban Berg's score, was premiered in Mexico and then performed at the Y in 1954 with such notables as Donald McKayle, Jeff Duncan, Ethel Winter, and Mary Antony. The use of Berg's music and the emotive yet nonnarrative choreography made this a landmark in modern dance works. Louis Horst said, "Anna, now you are a choreographer." *Dreams* (1961), an "allegory of time and helplessness," used concentration camp images. In Holland, audiences responded with the silence of recognition. On the fiftieth anniversary of the liberation, *Dreams* still had enormous impact.

In Israel, Sokolow brought Inbal, the Yemenite Company led by Sarah Levi-Tanai, her professional skills. For Inbal, she staged the *Song of Songs* in 1976. With the Juilliard Dance Theater, she built a work called *Ellis Island*; for Batsheva, *Poems of Ecstasy*. In 1979, she choreographed *The Bible in Dance* in Jerusalem, using a setting of the *Song of Songs* by Rachmaninoff and *Psalms* by Mahler. In 1982, she created *Los Marranos* to Ladino folk songs. This versatile woman also did the original choreography for *Hair*, a mime-dance of Beckett's *Act Without Words, Magritte, Magritte*, based on images from the painter's works, and *From the Diaries of Franz Kafka*, a dance-theater work.

At the conference "Jews and Judaism in Dance" at the Joyce Theater in 1986, Anna Sokolow was celebrated as a prime mover in the dance world. Her work has been kept alive through the Player's Project, directed by John and Lory May. Sokolow has dedicated her works to such diverse people as Isadora Duncan, Anne Frank, Louis Horst, Langston Hughes, Franz Kafka, GOLDA MEIR, Nijinsky, Bishop Pike, Aleksandr Scriabin, Hanna Senesh, and her parents. She has given dance and theater a heroism and passion exemplified by those she honors.

BIBLIOGRAPHY

Baum, Charlotte, Paula Hyman, and Sonya Michel. *The Jewish Woman in America* (1975); Clarke, Mary, and David Vaughan. *The Encyclopedia of Dance and Ballet* (1977); *Dance Magazine* (June 1956, April 1969, April 1985, April 1991); *Dance News: The Season in Review* (June 1964, February 1965); *Dance Observer* (November 1943, October 1946); Denby, Edwin. *Dance Writings* (1986); Jowitt, Deborah. "Anna at Eighty-five." *Dance Magazine* 64, no. 8 (August 1995); Lloyd, Margaret. *The Borzoi Book of Modern Dance* (1949); Martin, John. *America Dancing* (1936), and *The Dance* (1946), and *John Martin's Book of the Dance* (1963); McDonagh, Don. *The Complete Guide to Modern Dance* (1976); Morgan, Barbara. *Martha Graham* (1941); New Dance Group. *Souvenir Program*, June 11, 1993; *Studies in Dance History* 5, no. 1. *Of, by, and for the People: Dancing on the Left in the 1930s*. Articles by Pricket, Graff, Ocko; Warren, Larry. *Anna Sokolow: The Rebellious Spirit* (1991).

JOANNA G. HARRIS

SOLIS-COHEN, EMILY (1886–1966)

Prize-winning poet, author, translator, historian, and communal leader Emily Solis-Cohen was born on March 20, 1886, into one of Philadelphia's most distinguished Jewish families, whose presence in America dated from the colonial era. Solis-Cohen was named after her mother, Emily Grace Solis. Her father, Solomon Solis-Cohen, was a prominent medical doctor and influential Jewish communal figure. Her cousin JUDITH SOLIS-COHEN was well known for creating Jewish literature for the blind. Emily, the oldest of four children, had three younger brothers: David Hays, Leon, and Francis Solis-Cohen. She was educated in Philadelphia and attended the University of Pennsylvania. In keeping with a pattern of Philadelphia Jewish women leaders dating from the early nineteenth century, Solis-Cohen never married. She became involved in Philadelphia Jewish communal affairs and is credited with organizing and promoting the YOUNG WOMEN'S HEBREW ASSOCIATION and social

centers around the United States. She worked for the Jewish Welfare Board in Philadelphia, serving as a field secretary and consultant on women's activities. She was also a board member of the Hebrew Sunday School Society and a member of the National Conference of Christians and Jews.

From an early age, Solis-Cohen came into contact with many of American Jewry's most influential personalities. She corresponded with two United States Supreme Court justices, Louis D. Brandeis and Benjamin N. Cardozo. She also exchanged letters with the author FANNIE HURST, the art historian RACHEL WISCHNITZER, and HENRIETTA SZOLD, the founder of HADASSAH, who was one of her childhood teachers. Solis-Cohen served as chair of the Philadelphia committee and was a member of the national committee that planned Szold's seventieth birthday celebration.

Many of Solis-Cohen's literary efforts aimed at the entertainment and edification of Jewish children. Early in her career, Solis-Cohen wrote *David the Giant-Killer, and Other Tales of Grandma Lopez* (1908), and translated from Hebrew a selection of allegorical tales designed for young people by the Russian Hebraist Judah Steinberg, published under the title *The Breakfast of the Birds and Other Stories* (1917). She created "puppet plays" focusing on biblical themes, a "children's Bible"—*The Holy Scriptures: An Abridgment for Use in the Jewish School and Home* (1931)—and compiled and edited *Hanukkah: The Feast of Lights* (1937). Solis-Cohen wrote poetry and received a prize in 1909 for the sonnet "Have We Not One Father" (quoting from Mal. 2:10), based on a rabbinic legend. The sonnet was published in 1922, and later included in an anthology of American Jewish poetry. She also reviewed books for various journals and edited a children's column for the weekly *American Hebrew*.

Solis-Cohen was a pioneer in conducting American Jewish historical research. Her most ambitious scholarly effort was a biography of Isaac Leeser, today recognized as one of nineteenth-century America's most outstanding Jewish leaders. Leeser had led Philadelphia's Mikveh Israel Congregation, the prestigious, traditional Sephardic synagogue her family attended. Solis-Cohen assembled extensive primary sources and worked with the historian Solomon Grayzel to translate into English many of the earliest extant specimens of Yiddish in America in the Leeser collection. Her groundbreaking study yielded two valuable manuscripts: "Isaac Leeser: The Man and his Destiny" and "Isaac Leeser: An American Beginner." Despite her arduous efforts, the project never was completed, though she did write the entry on Leeser for the *Universal Jewish Encyclopedia* (1942). As a historian, Solis-Cohen collected notes on a variety of topics, including the founding in 1875 of a Philadelphia Jewish relief group, Ezrat Nashim, whose purpose she records as "to care for poor Jewish women during confinement and to combat the danger that menaced with the operation of midwives."

Solis-Cohen also wrote specifically for and about Jewish women. In 1925, she published an article called "The Jewish Girl's Thoughts on Jewish Life" based on "my record of three years' work with women's organizations in at least fifty Jewish communities of the Atlantic States," featuring excerpts from letters received from around the United States and Canada. An abbreviated version appeared in a collection of essays called *Jewish Experiences in America: Suggestions for the Study of Jewish Relations with Non-Jews* (1930). Solis-Cohen, one of only two women contributors, also provided an appendix: "Suggested Adaptations of General Discussion Outline for Women's Groups Without Trained Leadership." She authored *Women in Jewish Law and Life* (1932) and a religious collection for Jewish women entitled *Friday Night Stories* (1949), and coauthored works called *Women in Religion* (1936–1941) and *The Magic Top*.

Emily Solis-Cohen was one of the last representatives of a distinguished group of Jewish women and men sometimes referred to as the Philadelphia Group. She shared with them a fervent patriotism, a belief in noblesse oblige, and a commitment to both strengthening traditional Jewish life in America and fostering Jewish-Christian understanding. She devoted her life, as an author and as a communal leader, to improving the living conditions, both material and spiritual, of all Jewish women. She died on April 19, 1966 at age eighty.

SELECTED WORKS BY EMILY SOLIS-COHEN

The Breakfast of the Birds and Other Stories (1917); *David the Giant Killer, and Other Tales of Grandma Lopez* (1908); *Friday Night Stories* (1949); *Hanukkah: The Feast of Lights* (1937); *The Holy Scriptures: An Abridgment for Use in the Jewish School and Home* (1931); *Woman in Jewish Law and Life* (1932).

BIBLIOGRAPHY

AJYB 24:128; Angelo, F. Michael. "The Professional and Personal Papers of Emily Solis-Cohen, Jr." Private collection; Ashton, Dianne. *The Philadelphia Group: A Guide to Archival and Bibliographical Collections* (1991), and "Souls Have No Sex: Philadelphia Jewish Women and the American Challenge." In *When Philadelphia Was the Capital of Jewish America*, edited by Murray Friedman (1993); *EJ*, s.v. "Solis-Cohen"; *Jewish Experiences in America: Suggestions for the Study of Jewish Relations with Non-Jews*. Edited by Bruno Lasker (1930); Leeser, Isaac. Papers. Isaac Leeser Collection, Center for Judaic Studies, University of Pennsylvania, Philadelphia; Solis-Cohen, Emily. Papers, 1923–1936. American Jewish Historical Society, Waltham, Mass.; Solis-Cohen Family. Papers. Solis-Cohen Family Collection, Center for Judaic Studies, University of Pennsylvania; *UJE*.

ARTHUR KIRON

SOLIS-COHEN, JUDITH (1876–1927)

Judith Solis-Cohen, an author and editor, was a feminist by name and in action. According to family legend, her last name reflected her grandmother Judith's demonstration that women wield power. In 1837, when Myer David Cohen asked Judith Solis to be his wife, she agreed to marry him only after he agreed that their names would be hyphenated.

The Solis-Cohen family in Philadelphia traces itself back to Jacob da Silva Solis, who immigrated to the United States in 1803. Over the generations, Solis-Cohens, through their work, have ensured that their family name is remembered. For example, EMILY SOLIS-COHEN, the first cousin of the younger Judith Solis-Cohen, was a well-known writer in her time. Judith Solis-Cohen's father was a renowned physician who did research in laryngology and served as a surgeon in the Union army during the Civil War. Her brother Myer Solis-Cohen was also a doctor, an internist and a pediatrician, who contributed prolifically to medical literature. While her family members' roles in history have been recorded, Judith Solis-Cohen's name is largely unmentioned.

Judith Solis-Cohen was born in Philadelphia in 1876. She was the eldest of the eight children of Jacob da Silva Solis-Cohen and Miriam Binswanger. Judith Solis-Cohen attended Drexel University. She studied art with Colin Campbell Cooper, an artist best known for his paintings of skyscrapers, and she was an expert on dressmaking and costumes. She is also credited with introducing literature on Jewish subjects for the blind in the United States.

Solis-Cohen was an active participant in Philadelphia Jewish intellectual circles. When the Young Men's Hebrew Association of Philadelphia admitted women to membership in 1878, she immediately became involved in organizing educational activities. The "Evening Literary Chats," an example of such activities, were attended by an elite audience.

Solis-Cohen is best remembered for her writing. Her articles about nature, dressmaking, and writing appeared in periodicals and newspapers such as *Writer's Monthly*, *Little Folk's Magazine*, *Little Men and Women*, and *Toilettes*. The Philadelphia *Jewish Exponent* published articles by Solis-Cohen, including "Religious-School Pedagogics: Is the Paid Teacher Superior to the Volunteer?" and "How Immigrants Make Their Entry into the United States: A Glimpse of the New York Barge Office."

Solis-Cohen also wrote fiction. Her story "The Lost Magazine," which appeared in the *Jewish Forum* in 1922, and "Desdemona of the Ghetto," which was published in *Designer* in 1925, were listed among the best short stories for those years.

Beginning on December 3, 1897, and for at least the next ten years, Solis-Cohen edited the weekly "Womankind" column in the *Jewish Exponent*. In these columns, which covered such topics as "What Women Can Earn," "Coeducation," "Women Zionists," "The Woman Suffrage Movement," and "The Council of Jewish Women," Solis-Cohen lived up to her feminist name. She assumed the pen name Giuditta [Italian for Judith] for these columns. According to her sister Elinor, their father thought it was improper for a woman to attach her own name to her writing; however, Solis-Cohen did sign her own name to some of her other published work.

Judith Solis-Cohen died in Atlantic City on October 8, 1927.

SELECTED WORKS BY JUDITH SOLIS-COHEN

"Desdemona of the Ghetto." *Designer* (1925); *Jewish Exponent* (December 1897–April 1907); "The Lost Magazine." *Jewish Forum* (1922).

BIBLIOGRAPHY

AJYB 16 (1914–1915): 162; *EJ*; Friedman, Murray, ed. *Jewish Life in Philadelphia, 1830–1940* (1983); Kramer, William M. "David Solis-Cohen of Portland: Patriot, Pietist, Litterateur and Lawyer." *Western States Jewish Historical Quarterly* 14 (1982): 139–166; Langfeld, William. *The Young Men's Hebrew Association of Philadelphia: A Fifty Year Chronicle* (1928); *National Cyclopaedia of American Biography* 48 (1902): 168; *NYTimes*, November 7, 1937, 9; *Public Ledger* (October 10, 1927); Solis-Cohen, Judith. Solis and Solis-Cohen Papers (1808–1990). American Jewish Historical Society, Waltham, Mass.; *UJE*.

KAREN PHILIPPS

SOLOMON, BARBARA MILLER (1919–1992)

Barbara Miller Solomon, educator and pioneer in women's history, suggests the transformative role that education could play in individual women's lives, a theme that also shaped much of her writing. Her insights about the rich history of educated women helped lay the foundations of modern women's history.

Born Barbara Leah Miller in Boston on February 12, 1919, she was the only child of Bessie (Pinsky) and Benjamin Allen Miller, second-generation Russian Jewish immigrants. Growing up in an aspiring middle-class family (her father was an insurance salesman), she graduated from Boston Girls' Latin School and then entered Radcliffe College in 1936. Radcliffe opened new worlds for her, intellectually and socially. Just before her 1940 graduation, she eloped with Peter Herman Solomon, Harvard '40, the son of Harry Solomon, professor of psychiatry at Harvard Medical School, and MAIDA HERMAN SOLOMON, a pioneer in psychiatric social work. Rabbi Stephen Wise married the couple in New York.

On their return to Cambridge, Peter began his career as a shoe company executive and Barbara took graduate classes at Harvard, while they raised three children, Peter Jr. (b. 1942), Maida (b. 1946), and Daniel (b. 1950). Under the direction of Oscar Handlin, she earned her doctorate in American history from Harvard in 1953. Her revised dissertation, which was published in 1956 as *Ancestors and Immigrants: A Changing New England Tradition*, examined the attitudes of New England Brahmins toward recent immigrants, including Jews, from the 1850s to the 1920s.

Solomon remembered little anti-Semitism at Radcliffe and remained grateful to the school for providing her with generous scholarship support after her father died unexpectedly during her freshman year. Yet, after graduation, she was dismayed to see herself described in her employment file as "one of the better kind" of Jewish students. While Jewish history was never her primary focus, in 1956 she published a history of the Associated Jewish Philanthropies of Boston, entitled *Pioneers in Service*.

Demonstrating how many women combined family life with careers in the 1950s, Barbara Miller Solomon began teaching at Wheelock College in 1957. In 1959, she became head of the Women's Archives at Radcliffe, later the Arthur and Elizabeth Schlesinger Library on the History of Women in America. In 1963, she was named associate dean of Radcliffe College, and in 1970, she became the first woman dean at Harvard College, an event that received national publicity.

Teaching and research were just as important to Solomon as administration. In 1972, she offered the first lecture course on the history of American women at Harvard, laying the groundwork for the formal establishment of women's studies there in 1983. The importance of higher education for women was a central theme in her prize-winning book *In the Company*

Through her writing and her positions at Radcliffe and Harvard colleges, Barbara Miller Solomon was an important figure in the establishment of the study of women's history. Among her many positions, she was head of the Women's Archives at Radcliffe College, later the Arthur and Elizabeth Schlesinger Library on the History of Women in America. [Schlesinger Library]

of *Educated Women: A History of Women and Higher Education in America*, published in 1985, the year she retired from Harvard. She died of cancer on August 20, 1992.

Barbara Miller Solomon's significant impact on the emergence of women's history was matched by her role as a mentor to several generations of graduate and undergraduate students at Harvard and Radcliffe. She forged a professional style that was consciously feminist, but also effective within male-dominated institutions. Being Jewish was a formative part of her intellectual identity throughout her life, although her professional work followed broader themes inclusive

of this strand. Her scholarship, first on the history of immigration and then on women's history, continues to influence new generations of readers and students.

SELECTED WORKS BY BARBARA MILLER SOLOMON

Ancestors and Immigrants: A Changing New England Tradition (1956); *The Evolution of an Educator: An Anthology of Published Writings of Ada Louise Comstock*, editor (1987); *In the Company of Educated Women: A History of Women and Higher Education in America* (1985); "Memories of a Jewish Undergraduate at Radcliffe in the 1930's." In *The Jewish Experience at Harvard and Radcliffe*, edited by Nitza Rosovsky (1986); *Pioneers in Service* (1956); *Travels in New England and New York by Timothy Dwight, 1752–1817*, editor (1969).

BIBLIOGRAPHY

Boston Globe, August 21, 1992; Obituary. *NYTimes*, August 23, 1992; Solomon, Barbara Miller. Papers. Radcliffe College Archives; Schlesinger Library, Radcliffe College, Cambridge, Mass.

SUSAN WARE

SOLOMON, HANNAH GREENEBAUM (1858–1942)

Hannah Greenebaum Solomon founded and served as the first president of the NATIONAL COUNCIL OF JEWISH WOMEN (NCJW). Solomon brought both leadership and ideological vision to the NCJW, helping it become the premier Jewish women's organization of the late nineteenth and early twentieth centuries.

The fourth daughter and one of ten children, she was born on January 14, 1858, to Sarah (Spiegel) and Michael Greenebaum, a successful merchant. She attended both temple school and public school, including two years at Chicago's West Division High School. She also studied piano with Carl Wolfsohn. In 1879, she married Henry Solomon. The couple had three children, Herbert, Helen, and Frank.

Solomon and her sister Henrietta Frank became the first Jewish members of the prestigious Chicago Woman's Club in 1876. A member of Chicago's most prominent Reform synagogue, Temple Sinai, Hannah Solomon belonged to a solidly middle-class community with a strong commitment to Jewish life. Already accomplished and well known in secular women's groups and in the Jewish community, Solomon emerged as an obvious choice to chair the Jewish Women's Committee when Chicago hosted the 1893 World's Columbian Exposition. Although Jewish women had originally been expected to hold their meeting in the Woman's Building, Solomon chose instead to convene Jewish women under the auspices

"Woman's sphere is the whole wide world, without limit," said Hannah Greenebaum Solomon, who proved that statement by founding and serving as the first president of the NATIONAL COUNCIL OF JEWISH WOMEN. *At the same time, as one of the premier civic leaders of Chicago, she emphasized the responsibilities of women in the home. [American Jewish Archives]*

In the late nineteenth century, few Jewish women had access to Jewish education; NCJW sections organized study circles designed to teach Jewish women about the fundamentals of Jewish religion and practice. The women of the NCJW joined their non-Jewish counterparts in supporting the notion that women shouldered responsibility for safeguarding religion in the home and teaching children moral values. Viewing themselves as guardians of Jewish faith, NCJW women attempted to enhance commitment to Judaism through their organization. They also celebrated motherhood as a sacred institution and consistently emphasized the importance of women's role in perpetuating Judaism within the home.

Hannah Solomon recognized that the founding of a national Jewish women's organization, the public nature of NCJW programming, and the leadership of women would not be immediately accepted by the Jewish community. Solomon explained that "to join an organization of 'women'—not ladies—and one which bore the title 'club' rather than 'society,' was in itself a radical step." She warned members to be prepared for critics to "mourn over our neglected children, and wonder how our husbands manage without us." Indeed, Solomon recalled later in her life that in the 1890s she "was considered quite radical" for her public speaking and organizational activity. In the NCJW's early years, Solomon and other leaders often confounded expectations about proper behavior for a woman. As NCJW president, Solomon was the first woman to speak from several synagogue pulpits throughout the country. More often than not, Solomon and NCJW women justified their public roles as an extension of their duties as wives and mothers. "Woman's sphere is in the home, they told us. The last thirty years have been devoted to proof of our boast that woman's sphere is the whole wide world, without limit," declared Solomon, reflecting in 1920 upon the accomplishments of the NCJW in the *American Hebrew*. Like other NCJW leaders, Solomon advocated significant alterations in Jewish women's behavior, but she often masked the nature of that change by underlining the continuity of women's obligation to home and family.

The NCJW pioneered many arenas of Jewish philanthropy and immigrant aid. Its New York section assumed a leading role in aiding new arrivals at Ellis Island and was particularly attentive to the needs of female immigrants.

While New York remained the hub of the NCJW's immigrant aid programs, Solomon also sponsored an extensive array of immigrant services in the Chicago community. Even before assuming the

of the World Parliament of Religions at the Exposition. In the course of the four-day Jewish Women's Congress, a large gathering of Jewish women discussed the multiple possibilities and goals for a national Jewish women's organization. At the conclusion of the congress, delegates founded the National Council of Jewish Women and unanimously elected Hannah Solomon as president.

At its founding, the NCJW dedicated itself to religious, philanthropic, and educational endeavors. Initially composed of ninety-three members, by 1896, the NCJW had organized local sections in fifty cities and had attracted a membership of over four thousand women; by 1925, over fifty thousand women had joined its ranks. One of the NCJW's primary objectives was to educate its own members about Judaism.

presidency of the NCJW, Solomon had worked with the Chicago Woman's Club in several philanthropic endeavors. During her tenure as NCJW president (1893–1905), Solomon founded the Bureau of Personal Service, an agency that served Jewish immigrants in Chicago's seventh ward. Established in 1896 with funds from the Chicago NCJW section, the bureau provided family counseling, supervised loan programs, worked to improve housing conditions, and directed new immigrants to appropriate social service organizations. Many NCJW members volunteered at the bureau's agencies, acting as social workers, visiting prisons, and providing instruction in the English language and American mores. Hannah Solomon chaired the Bureau of Personal Service until 1910, when it became part of Chicago's Associated Jewish Charities, a citywide organization coordinating Jewish philanthropy. Like so many women's projects, the volunteer programs of the bureau and the NCJW predated the establishment of a coordinated Jewish philanthropic effort in the city. The Associated Jewish Charities was founded in 1900, several years after the bureau and NCJW had pioneered volunteer social service programs. Through her presidency of the NCJW and directorship of the bureau, Solomon established herself as one of the premier community leaders of Chicago. She served for years as the only woman on the executive board of the Associated Jewish Charities. Solomon's work placed her squarely in the middle of an active social service network that included both Jewish and gentile agencies. She maintained close connections to Jane Addams and Hull House, the Maxwell Street Settlement, and the Chicago Civic Federation.

Solomon always considered herself a passionate advocate of Judaism and Jewish values. Under her leadership, the Chicago NCJW chapter created a Sabbath school for girls. Solomon and the NCJW considered it particularly important to inculcate Jewish values in young girls and provide them with educational opportunities. The school eventually became so popular that, like so may other ventures initially sponsored by the NCJW, it became absorbed within a larger Jewish institution, adopted by Temple Sinai as part of its regular educational program. In establishing Jewish communal projects as well as building secular organizations, Solomon always considered philanthropy, education, and social service as an extension of religious obligation.

However, Hannah Solomon's personal definition of Judaism did not always correspond with the Jewish values of other NCJW members and provided a source of conflict within the organization. A committed Reform Jew, Solomon supported a movement within Reform Jewry to move the Saturday Sabbath to Sunday as a means of conforming with American standards and encouraging greater Sabbath observance within the Jewish community. While the NCJW primarily attracted Reform women, many of its members were also Conservative and Orthodox, and even its Reform constituents did not unanimously support the Sunday Sabbath movement. Sabbath observance had been a consistent NCJW goal, and many members actively opposed Solomon's support of the Sunday Sabbath. At the 1896 convention, a group of women challenged Solomon's leadership and attempted to remove her from the presidency, citing her endorsement of the Sunday Sabbath. During the contentious debate, Solomon issued her often quoted statement, "I do consecrate the Sabbath. I consecrate every day in the week." Solomon and her allies managed to keep the opposition from ousting her as president and steered the NCJW toward a pluralistic position that supported Sabbath observance without taking an official position on the Sunday Sabbath issue. However, Solomon's stance on Sabbath observance remained a source of divisiveness during her tenure as NCJW president.

In 1905, Solomon declined to be renominated as president of the NCJW, claiming that she was suffering from poor health. However, in that same year she began working with the Illinois Industrial School for Girls, later renamed the Park Ridge School for Girls, which became one of Solomon's most cherished projects. She continued to hold her positions on the boards of the Associated Jewish Charities, the Chicago Civic Federation, and the Illinois Federation of Women's Clubs, and to participate as a leader in several other organizations. As a prominent civic reformer and a representative of the Women's City Club, she investigated problems with Chicago's waste disposal system. Throughout her career, Solomon was an ardent advocate of woman suffrage, although the NCJW itself never formally endorsed the movement. Also interested in international women's issues, she served as a delegate to the 1904 International Council of Women conference in Berlin. She visited Palestine in 1923 and, though she never became a Zionist, she did support Palestine as a refuge for Eastern European Jews. In the last years of her life, she wrote her autobiography and several other works that reflect upon her career. She died on December 7, 1942.

Hannah Solomon represented a generation of middle-class Jewish women who paved the road for women's voice in the public affairs of the Jewish community. A consummate leader and administrator,

Solomon made a career out of voluntarism and social reform. In her secular as well as her Jewish activities, Solomon used her commitment to home and motherhood to redefine proper female behavior and reshape the boundaries between the public and private spheres.

BIBLIOGRAPHY

AJYB 7 (1905–1906): 103, 45:395; "American Jewish Women in 1890 and 1920: An Interview with Mrs. Hannah G. Solomon." *American Hebrew*, April 23, 1920; *EJ*; Golomb, Deborah Grand. "The 1893 Congress of Jewish Women: Evolution or Revolution in American Jewish Women's History?" *American Jewish History* 70 (September 1980): 52–67; *NAW*; Rogow, Faith. *Gone to Another Meeting: The National Council of Jewish Women, 1893–1993* (1993); Sochen, June. *Consecrate Every Day: The Public Lives of Jewish American Women, 1880–1980* (1981), 48–61; Solomon, Hannah. *Fabric of My Life* (1946), and *A Sheaf of Leaves* (1911); *UJE*; Wenger, Beth S. "Jewish Women and Voluntarism: Beyond the Myth of Enablers." *American Jewish History* 79 (Autumn 1989): 16–36; *WWIAJ*.

BETH WENGER

SOLOMON, MAIDA HERMAN (1891–1988)

"The idea of myself as being independent, personally independent . . . I was clear that I wanted to marry, that I wanted a career, that I wanted to have children *and I wanted to combine them all* . . . this was 1912. I also felt . . . believed, rather, that women were equal to any man whom I knew . . . in ability, in power to make my own decisions in regard to work, life, and sex!" For Maida Herman Solomon these words became her hallmark and the guiding principles of her long and illustrious life.

Born in Boston in 1891, Maida was the third daughter and last child of Joseph and Hannah (called Hennie) (Adler) Herman. Having come from Baltimore and married at age nineteen, Hennie was taken under the wing of her aunt LINA HECHT, an important philanthropist.

Lina Hecht was indeed a mentor to the impressionable Maida Herman, as much as to her mother. "It was with horror that I discovered that I didn't originate good works on my own," she would later say, "I inherited good works."

Maida attended the Boston Girls' Latin School, where the education was rigorous. When she graduated in 1908, she had no intention of following her sister Bess to Radcliffe. Bess helped Maida influence their father to allow her to break new ground and go

off to Smith College. Perhaps a factor in her father's decision to allow his youngest daughter to go away to school was Bess's report of ethnic discrimination at Radcliffe. Joseph Herman helped set in motion a process of ethical development that started Maida on a journey toward greater independence and maturity.

She greatly valued her four years at Smith—she said that going to Smith was a "frightfully" important thing. She graduated in 1912, and throughout her life spoke proudly of her experience there. So too, Smith College was justly proud of its distinguished alumna, presenting Maida with the Smith College Medal and with the Day-Garrett Award from its School for Social Work.

The years from 1914 to 1916 were transitional. Maida was openly involved with Jewish organizations. She was accepted to the secretarial program at Simmons College, where she learned stenography and typing, graduating with a B.S. degree in 1914. In 1915, the suffrage movement became a focus in her life: Maida carried a banner at the head of a parade in downtown Boston.

She married Harry Caesar Solomon, M.D., on June 27, 1916. Instead of moving away from the work force, she was drawn into a deeper involvement through the direction she found in her husband's work, by entering the world of psychiatry. With him, she attended many staff meetings at the Boston Psychopathic Hospital (later renamed the Massachusetts Mental Health Center). She met Mary Garrett, the first social service director, who suggested that she join Harry Solomon in his research on neurosyphilitic patients, resulting in one of twenty-eight books and papers she would coauthor. *Syphilis of the Innocent* became a classic in its field.

It was in this setting that Maida Solomon and several others in the social service department received on-the-job training. Here, she learned the importance of integrating the theory of the classroom with practice in the clinical setting.

After starting a career that was to cover a span of over seventy years, Solomon gave birth to four children: Peter Herman, Joseph Herman, Babette, and Eric, between September 1918 and October 1928. Thus, her determination to combine marriage, a career, and a family became a reality.

Solomon's career began to shift in the 1920s: The hospital-based psychiatric social worker and researcher became a community activist and educator. She was recruited by the Simmons College School of Social Work, with the mandate to "beef up" the mental health and psychiatric social work program at the school, a task she undertook with intelligence and

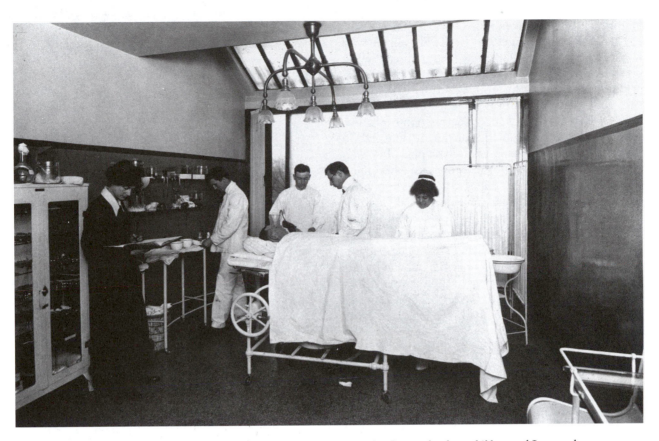

"I was clear that I wanted to marry, that I wanted a career, that I wanted to have children and I wanted to combine them all." One of the small group of social work professionals who "invented" the field of psychiatric social work and the mother of four, Maida Herman Solomon did "combine them all." She is shown here on the left with her husband (second from right) with a neurosyphilitic patient. [Countway Library of Medicine, Harvard Medical School]

gusto in 1934. Her academic title was professor of social economy.

Solomon was increasingly recognized as a pioneer in the field, along with a very small group of social work professionals who "invented" the field of psychiatric social work and oversaw its definition, its development of standards, and its integration with the other institutions of modern American medicine and education—in short, its professionalism. She helped to develop a curriculum that moved social work at Simmons from an undergraduate to a two-year graduate program with a master of science degree.

Upon her retirement from Simmons in 1957, at age sixty-five, Harry suggested that Maida return to the hospital as a consultant in social psychiatry and social work research. In this role, in which she worked into her early nineties, she helped many young professional social workers to combine their careers with marriage and children, thus transplanting her own belief system to those of her young colleagues.

After a long life and a distinguished career, Maida Herman Solomon died in January 1988 at age ninety-six.

BIBLIOGRAPHY

Solomon, Maida Herman. Papers. Schlesinger Library, Radcliffe College, Cambridge, Mass., and Maida Herman Solomon Collection. Simmons College Archives, Boston, Mass., and Mrs. Maida Herman Solomon Oral Memoir. William E. Weiner Oral History Library, American Jewish Committee, New York Public Library, and *Syphilis of the Innocent* (1920).

ANNE S. EVANS

SOLOMONS, HANNAH MARKS (1835–1909)

Hannah Marks Solomons was an influential San Francisco educator and civic worker, as well as the wife of a leading member of the Jewish community.

She was born in Bromberg, Germany, on September 29, 1835, to Gertrude and Lewis Fleishman, who were en route from Poland to the United States, where they changed their name to Marks. The family, including three-year-old brother Bernhard, settled in New Bedford, Massachusetts, where Lewis worked as a furrier. However, the children were soon orphaned, and Hannah was raised by her uncle and aunt, David and JUDITH SOLIS-COHEN, in Philadelphia. In 1852, Bernhard joined the California gold rush, becoming in succession a merchant, miner, teacher, school principal, and farmer. Hannah traveled to California in 1853 for an arranged marriage, but decided against entering into a loveless union. Instead, she began teaching at Temple Emanu-El and at a public elementary school. She became the youngest and only woman principal in San Francisco. Living in a kosher boardinghouse, far from her place of work, Hannah, like many Jews in the West, had to struggle with her commitment to Jewish law.

In 1862, Hannah married Gershom Mendes Seixas Solomons. Born in 1828 to Selina and Lucius Levy Solomons, he was an heir of the well-known Sephardi family; his maternal grandfather, Gershom Mendes Seixas, participated in the 1789 inauguration of George Washington. Seixas Solomons came to San Francisco in 1852. Highly respected, he was a founding member of many Jewish organizations, the secretary of Congregation Emanu-El, an accountant, and a journalist. They had seven children: Selina (b. 1862) became a writer and advocate for woman suffrage; Lucius Levy (b. 1863) became a lawyer and public speaker; Gertrude Marks (b. 1866) died at a young age; Adele Rosa (b. 1868) became a doctor; Theodore Seixas (b. 1870) became an explorer and journalist; Leon Mendes (b. 1873) became a scholar; Frank Benjamin (b. 1875) died as an infant. When the marriage failed, possibly due to Gershom's alcoholism, Hannah was forced to support the family. She returned to teaching in the public schools and at the Hebrew Orphan Asylum.

Admired for her community involvement, Solomons was president of the Ladies Fair Association of Temple Emanu-El (1868, the first Jewish fair in San Francisco), one of the founders and president of the Woman's Educational and Industrial Union of San Francisco, and the representative of San Francisco's Jewish women at an 1888 meeting to decide if women should be allowed on the Board of Education.

Hannah Marks Solomons died on August 4, 1909. Her independence and her accomplishments as an educator and mother were amplified in the West, where family support was limited. Although Judaism had been important to her for most of her life, in her later years she became a follower of Theosophy.

BIBLIOGRAPHY

"Noted Educator Passes Away." *Emanu-El*, August 13, 1909, 10; Rochlin, Harriet, and Fred Rochlin. *Pioneer Jews: A New Life in the Far West* (1984); Sargent, Shirley. *Solomons of the Sierra* (1989); Seixas Family Genealogy. Archives. Western Jewish History Center, Berkeley, Calif.; Solis-Cohen, J., Jr., ed. "A California Pioneer: Bernhard Marks." *PAJHS* 44 (1954): 12–57; Stern, Norton B., and William M. Kramer. "The Historical Recovery of the Pioneer Sephardic Jews of California." *Western States Jewish Historical Quarterly* 8 (1975): 3–25; Voorsanger, Jacob. "Leon Mendez Solomons (1873–1900)." *Western States Jewish Historical Quarterly* 10 (1978): 138–145.

AVA F. KAHN

SOMMERS, ESTELLE JOAN (1919–1994)

When Estelle Sommers died, on March 21, 1994, in Manhattan, the international dance world eulogized one of its most enthusiastic advocates and patrons as "empress of dance" and "an inspiration to women everywhere." Since taking ballet and tap classes as a child, dance had been her passion, professionally and socially. For nearly fifty years—particularly during her long spell at Capezio, a leading manufacturer of dance and fitness wear—her designs helped performers look exquisite and her philanthropy promoted their cause.

Estelle Joan Sommers was born on October 12, 1919, in Baltimore, Maryland, the youngest of seven children, to Mary Agnes (Curland), a homemaker, and David Isaac Goldstein, a union organizer, who died when she was eight months old. She grew up in a poor household, supported first by charities and later by older siblings. Her long affiliation with Israel started when the ardent Zionist teenager joined Young Judaea. A high school graduate, Estelle later extended her education by taking night courses in business and law. She married her first husband, Julian Loshin, in 1942, lived in Cincinnati, Ohio, and had three daughters—Gayle Joan, Cathy Harriet, and Debbie Jane. Following a divorce in 1962, she moved to Manhattan; in December of that same year, she married Ben Sommers (nicknamed "Mr. Capezio"). Their love story was known in dance circles as "the romance of the decade," and so it remained until Ben's death on April 30, 1985.

Sommers made her career in retail dancewear as a designer, business executive, and owner of various

Dancewear designer and innovator, Estelle Joan Sommers revolutionized the field of fitness clothing by introducing the fabric Antron-Lycron/Spandex. She was an entrepreneurial whiz long before her "romance of the decade" and business association with "Mr. Capezio," Ben Sommers. [Kenn Duncan]

ventures. She revolutionized the field of fitness clothing by introducing a new fabric, Antron-Lycra/Spandex, into her innovative designs for Capezio's bodywear. "We saw the fitness boom coming and we encouraged it," she said. Sommers started out in 1947, when, with her first husband, she transformed his piece-goods retail store, Loshin's, into a dance-outfit enterprise and sold her designs to dance studios. In New York, her career was linked with that of her husband. She was the owner-manager of Capezio Fashion Shop from 1964 to 1975; designer-owner of Estar Ltd., from 1969 to 1979; and vice president and head administrator for six Capezio Dance-Theatre Shops nationwide, from 1970 to 1994. From 1975, she co-managed the stores with her daughter Gayle Miller, who became a partner.

Sommers supported many dance organizations in elected capacities, especially during the 1980s and 1990s. Because of the nature of her business, she refrained from publicly promoting one dance company over another, but sustained general dance causes. Of special significance was her tenure from 1979 to 1994 as the United States Chair of the International Committee for the Dance Library of Israel. She was indispensable in establishing this Tel Aviv library as the second most important dance collection worldwide.

Maintaining that she "always cherished my family, Israel, and dance," Sommers successfully fulfilled the roles of a full-time career woman, devoted mother, wife, and companion, undertaking an impressive amount of charitable activities. An ardent traveler, she often tracked major dance events, festivals, and international ballet competitions. Passionately Jewish, Sommers belonged to a Reform congregation and even tried to "convert" others to Judaism. Estelle Joan Sommers was a genuine early embodiment of the contemporary woman.

BIBLIOGRAPHY

Burrows, Roberta. "Estar Is Born." *After Dark* (April 1970); Manion, David. "Estelle Sommers: An Appreciation." *Dance Magazine* (June 1994): 28; Reich, Holly. "Looking Nifty After Fifty." *Daily News*, August 8, 1988, p. 33; Romo, Kenneth. "Estelle Sommers: Unsung Lady of Dance." *Dance Pages* (Spring 1994): 53; Swoden, Dora. "Good, Bad News for Dance Library." *Jerusalem Post* (Israel), June 6, 1990; *Who's Who in the East* (1989, 1991).

MEIRA ELIASH-CHAIN

SONNESCHEIN, ROSA (1847–1932)

On April 13, 1895, the *Chicago Evening Journal* welcomed the premiere of the AMERICAN JEWESS and praised its editor, Rosa Sonneschein. "Until three years ago," the *Journal* effused, she was "one of the best known society women in St. Louis, a prominent figure in literary circles, and an active worker in the field of charity, independent of creed or nationality." Writer, journalist, and clubwoman, Rosa Sonneschein founded the *American Jewess*, the first English-language magazine for Jewish women in the United States, to be a voice and forum for American Jewish clubwomen. Through it, Sonneschein strongly supported, as well as criticized, the NATIONAL COUNCIL OF JEWISH WOMEN and crusaded for women's membership and expanded roles in the synagogue and for Zionism.

Born in Prostejov, Moravia, Austria, on March 12, 1847, Rosa Sonneschein was the daughter of Fannie (Sternfeld) and Hirsch Bär Fassel, a respected scholar and moderate Reform rabbi. Rosa grew up as the youngest daughter in an upper-middle-class home in Nagykanizsa, Hungary, and received an education at home and the local high school that was remarkably thorough for a nineteenth-century girl. In 1864, she married Solomon Hirsch Sonneschein, a young radical Reform rabbi with a congregation in Warasdin, Croatia. In the next five years, the Sonnescheins moved to successive posts in Prague, New York City, and finally, in 1869, St. Louis, where they remained for about twenty years.

Rosa and Solomon Sonneschein had four children: Ben, born in Warasdin in 1865; Fanny (Loth), born in Prague in 1866; Leontine (Pomeroy), born in Prague in 1868; and Monroe, born in St. Louis in 1873. Fanny followed her mother to become active in women's literary clubs. Monroe contributed several poems, stories, and articles to the *American Jewess.*

During the years Rosa Sonneschein spent as a *rebbetzin* [rabbi's wife] in St. Louis, she was a public figure in the city's Jewish community. She helped lead the "Ladies' Meetings" and organized the choral society at the two St. Louis congregations Solomon Sonneschein served. Her position as a *rebbetzin* also enabled her to move beyond the Jewish community, participating in literary circles and the city's German cultural life. In 1879, she founded the Pioneers, a Jewish women's literary society. Modeled on similar Christian women's clubs, the Pioneers devoted themselves not to studying Jewish literature, but to cultivating general literary taste and knowledge. Perhaps encouraged by club experiences, Sonneschein began to publish stories in Jewish periodicals at least as early as the mid-1880s. Her standing in both the German and Jewish communities and her frequent European travels positioned Sonneschein well as a correspondent for the German-language press, and her reports on world expositions in Paris, St. Louis, and Chicago gained her some prominence.

During their years in St. Louis, Rosa and Solomon Sonneschein projected the image of a united couple, but quarreled frequently. They had intellectual disagreements, most notably over the wisdom of Zionism, but personal problems overshadowed these in plaguing their relationship. Mutual charges of infidelity and financial irresponsibility, exacerbated by their roles as public figures in the Jewish community and representatives of it to those outside, made the Sonnescheins' marriage untenable, and they separated in 1891. Rosa first broached the idea of divorce, but ultimately allowed Solomon to sue, wishing "to be rid

An ardent Zionist and advocate for expanded roles for women in the synagogue and religious community, Rosa Sonneschein founded and edited THE AMERICAN JEWESS, *which, though short-lived, gave her a forum for those views. [American Jewish Archives]*

of him, not ruin him." Their divorce was finalized in April 1893.

After the divorce, Rosa Sonneschein's journalistic skills proved essential, as she received no alimony. Through writing, she not only supported herself, but also gained some fame. At a panel of representative presswomen during the May 1893 Press Congress, held as part of the World's Columbian Exposition in Chicago, she spoke on "Newspaperwomen in Austria." During this speech Sonneschein articulated the need for a magazine specifically addressing American Jewish women.

The exposition also featured the Jewish Women's Congress, held in September 1893. The congress brought together prominent middle-class Jewish women from Chicago and across the country to discuss literary, philanthropic, and religious questions. Here, Sonneschein likely garnered support for her proposed magazine, and lent her support to the permanent organization the congress created, the National Council of Jewish Women (NCJW).

Sonneschein remained in Chicago after the exposition, and in April 1895 she began editing the *American Jewess*. At first she also published and managed the business affairs of the magazine. Finding the workload too heavy and the finances too tight, she hired a business manager and opened additional offices in New York in 1896. Financial troubles persisted, however, leading Sonneschein to sell the magazine in 1898, though she retained editorship. Despite the efforts of the new owners, the *American Jewess*'s financial situation did not improve; its August 1899 issue was its last.

Throughout the run of the *American Jewess*, Sonneschein advocated for the expansion of women's roles in the synagogue and the Jewish community. It was in this regard that she believed the NCJW could contribute. Rather than focus its main efforts on philanthropy, which, she argued, many other Jewish organizations pursued successfully, Sonneschein asserted that it should concentrate on promoting greater religious unity and observance (particularly Sabbath observance) in the American Jewish community, a task for which she believed Jewish women especially well suited.

Taking a stance that set her apart from the majority of her middle-class Jewish peers, Sonneschein also advocated for Zionism in the *American Jewess*'s pages. She viewed Zionism as a potential source of relief for oppressed Jews in Eastern Europe and a source of pride and a countermeasure to assimilation for Jews in America and Western Europe. Sonneschein attended and reported on both the First and Second Zionist Congresses in 1897 and 1898. At the former, she was one of only four American participants and twenty-one women attendees (out of approximately 250).

Rosa Sonneschein linked her advocacy of Zionism with her vision for the NCJW, arguing that by adopting Zionism as its credo, the organization could better reach out to immigrant Jewish women and thus become a truly representative, national organization. That the NCJW neither readily adopted her passion for Zionism nor pursued religious goals as its main focus disturbed Sonneschein. In her magazine's last years, she became increasingly dissatisfied with and critical of the organization, though it is unclear whether she ever completely severed ties with it.

After the demise of the *American Jewess* in 1899, Sonneschein virtually disappeared from public life. She continued to write and travel, but never again was as publicly involved in the activities of Jewish women's organizations or of the Zionist movement. After living

intermittently with her daughter Fanny, Sonneschein returned to St. Louis, where she died on March 5, 1932. Although divorced for over thirty years, she was still memorialized in her obituary as Solomon Sonneschein's widow.

By founding and editing the *American Jewess*, Rosa Sonneschein not only provided support and space for the emerging national network of Jewish clubwomen and created a forum in which to publicize her then unconventional views on Zionism, but also pioneered a professional role in journalism for American Jewish women.

SELECTED WORKS BY ROSA SONNESCHEIN

"The American Jewess." *American Jewess* 6 (February 1898): 205–208; "The National Council of Jewish Women and Our Dream of Nationality." *American Jewess* 4 (October 1896): 28–32; *The Pioneers: An Historical Essay. Read Before the Society of Pioneers, May 18, 1880* (1880); "Plucked from the Grave." *Jewish Messenger* (New York), March 6, March 13, and March 20, 1885; "Something About the Women's Congress in Brussels." *American Jewess* 6 (October 1897): 11–12; "Three Kisses." Translated from German by Mrs. Julius Wise. *American Jews' Annual* 5645 (1884–1885): 76–82; "The Zionist Congress." *American Jewess* 6 (October 1897): 13–20.

BIBLIOGRAPHY

AJYB 6 (1904–1905): 191; *AJH* 68:57–63; Binswanger, Augustus. Diaries 1870–1871. Augustus Binswanger Papers, AJA, Cincinnati, Ohio; *EJ* (1973–1982); Jacobson, Laura D. "The Pioneers." *American Jewess* 1 (August 1895): 241–242; Kraut, Benny. "A Unitarian Rabbi? The Case of Solomon H. Sonneschein." In *Jewish Apostasy in the Modern World*, edited by Todd M. Endelman (1987); Loth, David. "The American Jewess." *Midstream* 31 (1985): 43–46, and "Notes on the Marital Discord of Solomon and Rosa Sonneschein," and "Supplementary Memoir of the Sonnescheins." Small Collections. AJA; Loth, Fanny Sonneschein. "Autobiographical Questionnaire." Small Collections. AJA; Orlan, Haiyim. "The Participants of the First Zionist Congress." In *Herzl Year Book*, vol. 6, *Essays in Zionist History and Thought*, edited by Raphael Patai (1964–1965); Porter, Jack Nusan. "Rosa Sonnenschein [sic] and *The American Jewess*: The First Independent English Language Jewish Women's Journal in the United States." *AJH* 67 (September 1978): 57–63, and "Rosa Sonneschein and *The American Jewess* Revisited: New Historical Information on an Early American Zionist and Jewish Feminist." *AJA* 32 (1980): 125–131; Sonneschein, Solomon H. Letterbooks, 1882–1893. Solomon H. Sonneschein Papers, AJA; "Widow of Rabbi Sonneschein Dies." *St. Louis Globe-Democrat*, April 6, 1932; "A Woman's Cultural Club." *Missouri Historical Society Bulletin* 6 (1949–1950): 109.

JANE H. ROTHSTEIN

In her essays, or "case-studies," examining art and the "modern sensibility," Susan Sontag has covered topics from photography to illness to fascism. One of the most widely read cultural critics of her generation, she has been a lightning rod for both praise and vilification. [Library of Congress]

SONTAG, SUSAN (b. 1933)

When her essays first began appearing on the American critical scene in the early 1960s, Susan Sontag was heralded by many as the voice—and the face—of the Zeitgeist. Advocating a "new sensibility" that was "defiantly pluralistic," as she announced in her groundbreaking collection of essays *Against Interpretation*, Sontag became simultaneously an intellectual of consequence and a popular icon, publishing everywhere from *Partisan Review* to *Playboy*, and appearing on the covers of *Vanity Fair* and the *New York Times Magazine*. She rejected the traditional proj-

ect of art interpretation as reactionary and stifling, and called instead for a new, more sensual experience of the aesthetic world: "an act of comprehension accompanied by voluptuousness." Challenging what she saw as "established distinctions within the world of culture itself—that between form and content, the frivolous and the serious, and . . . 'high' and 'low' culture," Sontag stood as a champion of the avant-garde. Contemporary literature, she proclaimed, was too burdened by the weight of edification. Rather, the visual arts were "the model arts of our time."

As the only woman among the 1960s world of New York Jewish intellectuals, Sontag was both venerated and villainized, depicted as either a countercultural hero or a posturing pop celebrity. In a 1968 essay in *Commentary*, Irving Howe saw her as the "publicist" for a young generation of critics that was making its presence felt "like a spreading blot of anti-intellectualism." Focusing on the woman rather than the work, other critics dubbed her "Miss Camp" and "The Dark Lady of American Letters." Indeed, in his book *Making It*, Norman Podhoretz snidely attributed her popularity to her gender and to the fact that she was "clever, learned, good-looking, capable of writing family-type criticism as well as fiction with a strong taste of naughtiness." While Sontag's public image has shifted from that of sixties radical to nineties neoconservative, neither representation accounts for either the complexity of her views or the significance of her contribution to contemporary cultural debates.

Sontag has been the subject of intense media scrutiny throughout her career, despite her own consistent rejection of the biographical as a means of understanding a work. "I don't want to return to my origins," she has told Jonathan Cott in an interview. "I think of myself as self-created—that's my working illusion." Her distrust of the potentially reductive nature of personal criticism is magnified by her insistence that she herself does not "have anything to go back to."

Susan Sontag was born on January 16, 1933, in New York City, the older of Jack and Mildred (Jacobson) Rosenblatt's two daughters. Her early years were spent with her grandparents in New York while her parents ran a fur export business in China. When she was five, her father died of tuberculosis and her mother returned from China. A year later, mother and daughters moved to Tucson, Arizona, in an effort to relieve Susan's developing asthma. In 1945, Mildred Rosenblatt married Army Air Corps captain Nathan Sontag, the daughters assumed their stepfather's last name, and the family left Arizona for a suburb of Los Angeles. Although her parents were Jewish, Sontag did not have a religious upbringing, and she claims not to have entered a synagogue until her mid-twenties.

Sontag's one autobiographical essay, "Pilgrimage," depicts her long-standing sense of rootlessness and fragmentation as "the resident alien" in a "facsimile of family life." It also expresses her feeling of intellectual isolation and her fear of "drowning in drivel" in suburban America. "Literature-intoxicated" from a very young age, she read the European modernists to escape "that long prison sentence, my childhood" and to achieve "the triumphs of being not myself." Many of these issues—the fierce individualism of the intellect, the pleasure and nourishment to be derived from knowledge, and the question of what it means to be modern—have become central themes in Sontag's fiction and essays.

At age fifteen, Sontag discovered literary magazines at a nearby newsstand, and she describes her excitement in an interview with Roger Copeland by explaining that "from then on my dream was to grow up, move to New York, and write for *Partisan Review*." She achieved this dream in 1961, after twelve years in the academic world. Having graduated from high school at age fifteen, Sontag spent one semester at the University of California at Berkeley before transferring to the University of Chicago for the remainder of her college study. There she met Philip Rieff, a sociology lecturer, while auditing a graduate class on Freud. They married ten days later, when Sontag was seventeen and Rieff twenty-eight. Their only son, David, was born in 1952, the year Sontag entered Harvard as a graduate student in philosophy and English. After receiving master's degrees in both fields, Sontag spent two years studying at Oxford and the Sorbonne, although she did not complete a dissertation. Shortly after her return to the United States in 1959, she divorced Rieff and moved to New York City with her son. She also explains in an interview with Jonathan Cott: "I did have the idea that I'd like to have several lives, and it's very hard to have several lives and then have a husband. . . . [S]omewhere along the line, one has to choose between the Life and the Project."

In New York, Sontag began establishing herself as an independent writer while teaching philosophy in temporary positions at Sarah Lawrence, City College, and Columbia University, and working briefly as an editor at *Commentary*. She published twenty-six essays between 1962 and 1965, as well as an experimental novel, *The Benefactor*, in 1963. Although best known for her nonfiction, Sontag has worked in many creative genres. The 1960s and 1970s saw the production of a second novel, *Death Kit* (1967), a collection of short stories, *I, Etcetera* (1978), and the script and

direction of three experimental films: *Duet for Cannibals* (1969), *Brother Carl* (1971), and *Promised Lands* (1974). *Promised Lands*, a documentary on the Yom Kippur War, is Sontag's only work that deals explicitly with Jewish issues.

Sontag's career-long series of essays—or "case studies," as she calls them in *Against Interpretation*—reveals an expansive and democratic definition of art, encompassing such diverse subjects as photography, illness, fascist aesthetics, pornography, and Vietnam. A self-described intellectual generalist, Sontag explains in an interview with Roger Copeland that her overarching project is to "delineate the modern sensibility from as many angles as possible." Her essays range freely from high modernism to mass culture, from European to American artistic figures, from the aesthetics of silence to the contemporary media proliferation of images and noise. Her career as a writer is characterized by the tension between such oppositions: "Everything I've written—and done," she explains, "has had to be wrested from the sense of complexity. *This*, yes. But also *that*. It's not really disagreement, it's more like turning a prism—to see something from another point of view."

In both her fiction and her critical essays, Sontag has told Copeland, she uses such disjunctive forms of writing as "collage, assemblage, and inventory" to demonstrate her thesis that "form is a kind of content and content an aspect of form." Insisting that interpretation is "the revenge of the intellect against the world," *Against Interpretation* (1966), her first collection of essays, seeks to subvert both the style and the subject matter of traditional critical inquiry. The function of criticism should be to help us *experience* art more fully, she explains, "to show *how it is what it is, even that it is what it is*, rather than to show *what it means*." *Against Interpretation* introduced an American audience to lesser-known European figures such as Georg Lukács, Simone Weil, and Claude Lévi-Strauss. It also explored the irreverent playfulness and self-conscious artificiality of an underground camp aesthetic.

Styles of Radical Will (1969) advances Sontag's aesthetic argument by looking closely at pornography, theater, and film, and by examining the impact of self-consciousness on the modern art and philosophy of E.M. Cioran, Ingmar Bergman, and Jean-Luc Godard. But the collection suggests a political as well as an aesthetic mode of transforming consciousness. The essay "Trip to Hanoi," originally published in 1968 as a separate book, is Sontag's candid response to her trip to North Vietnam as she grapples with the limits of her own culturally formed perceptions. *Under the Sign of*

Saturn (1980), which collects seven essays of the 1970s, combines personal reflections on Paul Goodman and Roland Barthes with sustained analyses of Walter Benjamin, Antonin Artaud, and Elias Canetti. It also contains the well-known piece "Fascinating Fascism," in which Sontag uses Leni Riefenstahl's Nazi propaganda films to discuss the ways in which history becomes theater.

Sontag's award-winning volume *On Photography* (1977) analyzes how photographic images have changed our ways of looking at the world. Resistant to the acquisitive nature of photography and its consequent leveling of meaning, Sontag here displays a growing suspicion of the "sublime neutrality" of art that she had so heralded in *Against Interpretation*. Although hopeful about the value of photography when it awakens the conscience of the audience, she is also concerned about its potentially predatory nature, explaining that "[t]o photograph people is to violate them." Like *On Photography*, *Illness as Metaphor* (1978) broke new critical ground by examining the significance of a common cultural phenomenon: in this case, the discursive representation of disease. Growing out of Sontag's own diagnosis of breast cancer in 1975, the book sought to expose the fantasies and fears that are masked by the vocabulary of illness. In 1989, she elaborated on this theme in *AIDS and Its Metaphors*, which was received with some controversy. Many in the gay community criticized her efforts to disentangle the cultural metaphors of AIDS from its politics.

Most recently, Sontag has focused her efforts on fiction and theater. *Unguided Tour*, the film version of an earlier short story, appeared in 1983, and in 1985, she directed the premier production of Milan Kundera's play *Jacques and His Master*. Her own play, *Alice in Bed*, premiered in Bonn, Germany, in 1991 and was published in 1993, the same year that she directed Samuel Beckett's *Waiting for Godot* in war-besieged Sarajevo. *The Volcano Lover* (1992), her most critically acclaimed novel, brings together concerns that have long animated her writing: the relationship between style and form, the moral pleasure—and service—of art, and the psychology of collecting. A historical novel with a self-consciously modern narrator, *The Volcano Lover* is a revisionary retelling of the eighteenth-century love affair between Lady Emma Hamilton and Lord Horatio Nelson that moves away from the abstraction of Sontag's earlier fiction while still remaining a novel of ideas.

Over the course of her career, Sontag has remained committed to the idea of cultural criticism, explaining that it is "what being an intellectual—as opposed to being a writer—is." Her contributions have been recognized through numerous awards and grants, which include two Rockefeller Foundation Grants (1964, 1974), two Guggenheim Foundation Fellowships (1966, 1975), the Arts and Letters Award of the American Academy and Institute of Arts and Letters (1976), and the MacArthur Foundation Fellowship (1990). She has served as a member of the selection jury for the Venice Film Festival and the New York Film Festival, and was a founding member of the New York Institute for the Humanities. Sontag also served as president of the PEN American Center from 1987 to 1989.

Despite the fact that she is perhaps one of the most widely read intellectuals of her generation, Sontag has been largely ignored by academics, feminists, and Jews. Her cultural criticism has taken many forms. In the 1960s, it aligned her with the avant-garde; today, she is frequently criticized for aesthetic and political conservatism. While her consistent advocacy of critical autonomy does not mark a turn to the political right, her insistence that she is a universalist, and her refusal to be identified by gender, religion, or sexual orientation, do leave her outside of crucial debates that are fueling current critical discourse. "I don't like party lines," she explains in an interview published in *Salmagundi*. "They make for intellectual monotony and bad prose." This suspicion of particularist affiliations places Sontag at some distance from contemporary art and culture; however, it also stands as an unresolved tension within her own work. For example, although she does not write explicitly about Jewish issues, Jews are frequently the point of reference from which she draws analogies to other groups. Moreover, despite her disavowal of feminism as "an empty word," *The Vocano Lover* ends with the admission of a female character that "all women, including the author of this book . . . lie to [themselves] about how complicated it is to be a woman." Thus, while the "particular" is clearly a matter of concern, Sontag refuses to limit herself to any single critical perspective. What she writes of Roland Barthes applies well to her own project: "The point is not to teach us something in particular. The point is to make us bold, agile, subtle, intelligent, detached. And to give pleasure."

SELECTED WORKS BY SUSAN SONTAG

ESSAYS

Against Interpretation and Other Essays (1966); *AIDS and Its Metaphors* (1989); *Illness as Metaphor* (1978); *On Photography* (1977); "Pilgrimage." *New Yorker* (December 21, 1978): 38–54; *Styles of Radical Will* (1969); *A Susan Sontag Reader* (1982); *Trip to Hanoi* (1968); *Under the Sign of Saturn* (1980).

NOVELS AND SHORT STORY COLLECTIONS
The Benefactor (1963); *Death Kit* (1967); *I, Etcetera* (1978); *The Volcano Lover* (1992); *The Way We Were* (1991).

PLAYS
Alice in Bed: A Play in Eight Scenes (1993).

FILMS AND FILMSCRIPTS
Brother Carl (1971); *Brother Carl: A Filmscript* (1974); *Duet for Cannibals* (1969); *Duet for Cannibals: A Screenplay* (1970); *Promised Lands* (1974); *Unguided Tour* (1983).

BIBLIOGRAPHY
Aronowitz, Stanley. "Sontag versus Barthes for Barthes' Sake." *Village Voice Literary Supplement* (November 1982): 1+; Brooke-Rose, Christine. "Eximplosions." *Genre* 14:1 (Spring 1981): 9–21; Brooks, Cleanth. "The Primacy of the Reader." *Mississippi Review* 6, No. 2 (1983): 289–301; *Contemporary Authors*. Vol. 25 (1989); *EJ*; Hentoff, Nat. "Celebrity Censorship." *Inquiry* 5, No. 10 (June 1982): 8; Holdsworth, Elizabeth McCaffrey. "Susan Sontag: Writer-Filmmaker." *Dissertation Abstracts International* 42 (April 1982), Ohio State University, 1991; Hollander, Paul. *Political Pilgrims: Travels of Western Intellectuals to the Soviet Union, China, and Cuba 1928–1978* (1981); Howe, Irving. "The New York Intellectuals." *Commentary* 46 (October 1968). Reprinted in *Selected Writings 1950–1990*, by Irving Howe (1990): 267–268; Kalaidjian, Walter B. "Susan Sontag." In *The Johns Hopkins Guide to Literary Theory and Criticism*, edited by Michael Groden and Martin Kreiswirth (1994); Kendrick, Walter. "In a Gulf of Her Own." *The Nation* (October 23, 1982): 404; Kennedy, Liam. *Susan Sontag: Mind as Passion* (1995); Kramer, Hilton. "Anti-Communism and the Sontag Circle." *New Criterion* 5, No. 1 (September 1986): 1–7, and "The Pasionaria of Style." *The Atlantic* 50, No. 3 (September 1982): 88–93; Light, Steve. "The Noise of Decomposition: Response to Susan Sontag." *Sub-stance* 26 (1980): 85–94; Linkon, Sherry Lee. "Susan Sontag." *Jewish American Women Writers: A Bio-Bibliographical and Critical Sourcebook*, edited by Ann R. Shapiro et al. (1994); Nelson, Cary. "Soliciting Self-Knowledge: The Rhetoric of Susan Sontag." *Critical Inquiry* (Summer 1980): 707–729; Podhoretz, Norman. *Making It* (1967). Cited in *Susan Sontag: Mind as Passion*, by Liam Kennedy (1995): 133; Poogue, Leland, ed. *Conversations with Susan Sontag* (1995); Rich, Frank. "Stage: Milan Kundera's 'Jacques and His Master.'" *NYTimes*, January 24, 1985, C19; Sayres, Sohnya. *Susan Sontag: The Elegaic Modernist* (1990).

TRESA GRAUER

SOTHERAN, ALICE HYNEMAN (1840–1919)

Alice Hyneman Sotheran, author, lecturer, and reviewer for a variety of magazines in the late nineteenth and early twentieth centuries, wrote about women's work and women's issues. She was born in Philadelphia on January 31, 1840, the daughter of Leon and Sarah (Gumpert) Hyneman. She was the wife of Henry Rhine of Clarksville, Texas. After Rhine's death, she married Charles Sotheran in 1893, and the couple remained together until his death on June 27, 1902.

Sotheran lived in Ridgefield, New Jersey, and centered her writing efforts on magazines published mainly in New York City, where she was a member of the Society of American Authors. Sotheran profiled Gail Hamilton, "Neither Genius nor Martyr," for the *North American Review*. She also wrote extensively on women's work and contributed journalistic pieces to *Arena, Forum*, and *Popular Science Monthly*. In addition to her articles of contemporary interest, Sotheran published travel pieces such as *Niagara Park Illustrated—Descriptions, Poems, and Adventures* (1885) and other works of poetry.

Sotheran died in New York at age eighty-eight on December 16, 1919.

BIBLIOGRAPHY
AJYB 22:168; *NYTimes*, December 17, 1919, 17:2; *Who's Who in America* (1906–1907): 1672.

BARBARA L. TISCHLER

SPECTOR, BERTHA KAPLAN (1896–1938)

Bertha Kaplan Spector was a bacteriologist whose authoritative research helped to control an epidemic of amebic dysentery during the Chicago Century of Progress World's Fair. Her work contributed to a better understanding of the disease, as well as to new standards of hygiene.

Born on October 9, 1896, in Kobrin, Russia, Bertha Kaplan Spector was one of eight children of Samuel and Rose (Hausman) Kaplan. In 1905, her family moved to Chicago, where her high school education almost ended for lack of money until a family friend found her a job. She received three degrees from the University of Chicago: a B.S. (1916), an M.S. (1921), and a Ph.D. (1931) in hygiene and bacteriology.

Bertha was a research assistant with the Bussey Institute at Harvard University from 1916 to 1918. During World War I, she worked as a bacteriologist at the U.S. Base Hospital at Fort Riley, Kansas, from 1918 to 1919. After the war, she went to work in Chicago as a bacteriologist in the U.S. Veterans Hospital from 1921 to 1923 and Cook County Hospital from 1923 to 1926, contributing to several medical journal articles on streptococcal hemolytic toxins.

"Boil the water!" was the order given by scientific researcher Bertha Spector during the only known large-scale epidemic of amebic dysentery, which occurred around Chicago's "Century of Progress" in 1933. Her practical suggestion, which was unheard of at the time, not only saved lives but also led to more stringent sanitation standards. [Photo courtesy of Charlene Kanter Sales]

She concentrated her research on the study of amebic dysentery as an instructor in bacteriology and parasitology at the University of Illinois College of Medicine from 1926 to 1929. She spent 1928 at the Institut für Schiff und Tropen Krankheiten in Hamburg, Germany. In 1929, the University of Illinois awarded her the Beaumont Prize for her research on the gastrointestinal tract. Over the next decade, she published extensively on amebic dysentery.

She and Morris Spector, a patent attorney, were married on March 8, 1929. They had two children: Rosa Leah (b. 1930), and Avron Newton (b. 1933).

Soon after she married, Spector joined the research staff of the University of Chicago Department of Medicine, Douglas Smith Foundation. She also became a member of HADASSAH.

In 1933, the Century of Progress World's Fair came to Chicago, along with over eight million people. It brought with it the only known large-scale epidemic of amebic dysentery in a civilian population until that time. Poor sanitation conditions were noted as a cause of the outbreak, which involved over fourteen hundred cases and resulted in as many as ninety-eight deaths. Physicians, who were unfamiliar with the unusual presentation of the disease, did not properly diagnose or treat it, contributing to the high fatality rate. During the outbreak, the results of years of research by Spector and her colleagues moved from the pages of medical journals to a central position in saving lives, instructing physicians, and leading to more stringent sanitation standards.

Spector's precautions against water contamination are part of family lore. During her investigative work on the epidemic, she lunched on hard-boiled eggs and boiled water, and did not contract amebic dysentery, as did many coworkers. Whenever utility pipe repairs were made on the street near her home, Spector would admonish her family to "boil the water!"

Following the epidemic, Spector continued her research with the University of Chicago. In 1934, she also joined the U.S. Public Health Service as a protozoologist in charge of research work on amoebas. Her work for the government took her family to Albuquerque, New Mexico, in the summers of 1936 and 1937, where she studied dysentery in children on Indian reservations. During the summer of 1937, Spector became disabled from Hodgkin's disease, which she diagnosed herself in 1935. She succumbed to the disease and died on March 26, 1938, at age forty-one.

Spector's short life was a remarkable journey from a shtetl in Russia to the laboratories of the University of Chicago, where she made important contributions to the study of amebic dysentery and became a highly regarded diagnostician. She was a devoted mother who left a legacy of caring to her children and to future generations. Bertha Kaplan Spector was buried near her mother, along with members of K'helas Jacob Anshe Drohitzin, a congregation of immigrants from near her place of birth in Russia.

BIBLIOGRAPHY

AJYB 40 (1938–1939): 392; *BEOAJ*; Cutler, Irving. *The Jews of Chicago from Shtetl to Suburb* (1996); Geiger, J.C.,

C.S. Williamson, and B. Kaplan. "The Advance against Amebic Dysentery." In *Chemistry in Medicine: A Cooperative Treatise Intended to Give Examples of Progress Made in Medicine with the Aid of Chemistry*, edited by Julius Stieglitz (1928); Kirsner, Joseph B., M.D., Ph.D., Louis Block Distinguished Service Professor of Medicine, University of Chicago Medical Center. Interview by author, November 1996; Marcus, Jacob Rader. *The American Jewish Woman, 1654–1980* (1981); Minsk, Rosalie [daughter]. Interview by author, January 1997; Obituaries. *Chicago Tribune*, March 27, 1938, and *NYTimes*, March 27, 1938, II 6:6; Spector, Avron Newton. Interview by author, December 1996; Spector, B. K. "Amebiasis in Chicago, December 1933 to June 1936." *American Journal of Public Health* 27 (July 1937): 694–700; U.S. Treasury Department, Public Health Service. "Epidemic Amebic Dysentery: The Chicago Outbreak of 1933." *National Institute of Health Bulletin* 166 (1936); Weinstein, Chapels. Piser Weinstein Menorah Archive, Chicago; *WWIAJ* (1938).

CHARLENE KANTER SALES

SPECTOR, JOHANNA (b. 1915)

The only one of her immediate family to survive the Nazi holocaust, Johanna Spector decided in the aftermath of World War II to devote herself to the study of Jewish music. Since then, her ethnomusicological studies have documented the culture of some of the most exotic of Jewish communities.

Johanna Spector was born on March 23, 1915, to timber merchant Jacob Chayim and his wife Anna (Meyer) Lichtenberg. Johanna and her older brother, Naum, enjoyed an upper-class childhood in Libau, Latvia. She was educated at home by private tutors, who included Hebrew in her studies. She married Robert Spector in 1939; he was killed by the Nazis in December 1941. Her brother and parents were also killed. After surviving the war years in a series of concentration camps, Spector immigrated to the United States in 1947 and earned her doctorate from Hebrew Union College in 1950. She later earned a master's degree at Columbia University in 1960. Spector served as a faculty member of the Rubin Academy of Music and as a research fellow at Hebrew University in Jerusalem from 1951 to 1953, but returned to the United States and became a naturalized citizen in 1954. In that same year, she became a member of the faculty of the Jewish Theological Seminary of America, and she served as founder and director of the ethnomusicology department of the Seminary College of Jewish Music from 1962 through 1985. Spector was promoted to associate professor of musicology in 1966 and to professor in 1970. She was named professor emeritus in 1985.

Spector is a highly regarded ethnomusicologist who holds memberships in a wide variety of professional associations: the American Anthropological Association; the American Musicological Society; the International Folk Music Council; the African Musican Society; the Society for Ethnomusicology, in which she served as New York City chapter secretary-treasurer from 1960 to 1964; and the Asian Music Society, in which she served as president from 1974 to 1978 and vice president since 1964. She founded the Society for the Preservation of Samaritan Culture in 1971.

Spector is the author of several books as well as a vast number of contributions to encyclopedias and professional journals, but her most recent professional activity has been as producer of documentary films. Her earliest film *The Samaritans* (1971) was followed by *Middle Eastern Music* (1973), *About the Jews of India: Cochin* (1976), *The Shanwar Telis or Bene Israel of India* (1978), *About the Jews of Yemen, A Vanishing Culture* (1986), and *Two Thousand Years of Freedom and Honor: The Cochin Jews of India* (1992). Spector has also gathered a collection of over ten thousand recordings of religious and folk music from the various communities she has studied.

Johanna Spector has helped hundreds of students to understand the ancient cultures of non-Western Jewish communities. Her writings, recordings and film projects have documented the music of those now-shrinking communities for posterity. While interest in and performance of the music of Western communities has predominated throughout the twentieth century, Johanna Spector's pioneering studies of Eastern Jewish musical traditions have shed light on a long-neglected but fascinating segment of the Jewish world.

FILMOGRAPHY

About the Jews of India: Cochin (1976); *About the Jews of Yemen: A Vanishing Culture* (1986); *Middle Eastern Music* (1973); *The Samaritans: The People of the Sacred Mountain*. Motion picture directed by Dan Wolman. (1971); *The Shanwar Telis or Bene Israel of India* (1979); *Two Thousand Years of Freedom and Honor: The Cochin Jews of India* (1992).

BIBLIOGRAPHY

EJ; Nulman, Macy. *Concise Encyclopedia of Jewish Music* (1975); Rosenblatt, Judith Turk, ed. *Who's Who in World Jewry: A Biographical Dictionary of Outstanding Jews* (1987); *Who's Who in America* (1994).

MARSHA BRYAN EDELMAN

SPELLMAN, GLADYS NOON (1918–1988)

Gladys Noon Spellman, whose participation in American politics culminated in her service as a Democratic congresswoman for over seven years, was born Gladys Blossom Noon to Henry and Bessie G. Noon on March 1, 1918, in New York City. After attending public schools in New York and Washington, D.C., she studied at George Washington University and then at the graduate school of the United States Department of Agriculture.

Settling in Maryland, Spellman taught in Prince Georges County schools. From 1962 to 1970, she was a member of Prince Georges County board of commissioners, serving as its chair beginning in 1966. Also in the same period, she headed the board of trustees of Prince Georges General Hospital. In 1967, President Lyndon B. Johnson appointed her to the Advisory Commission on Intergovernmental Relations. She served as the county's councilwoman at large from 1971 to 1974 and was president of the national Association of Counties by 1972.

Having aligned herself with the Democratic Party (as most American Jews of the time did), Spellman was elected to the Ninety-Fourth Congress of the United States from the Fifth Maryland District and began her service on January 3, 1975. She was re-elected to the next three congresses. On October 31, 1980, Spellman was stricken with a heart attack while campaigning for a fourth term. She overwhelmed Republican Kevin R. Igoe at the polls four days later, but she remained semiconscious. On February 24, 1981, her seat was declared vacant by the House since she was unable to discharge the duties of her office.

Although she reached the pinnacle of her political career as a congresswoman, Spellman was also active in state politics. Among the numerous positions she held with the Maryland state government were chair of the Maryland State Comprehensive Health Planning Advisory Council, vice chair of the governor's Commission to Determine the State's Role in Financing Public Education, vice president of the Metropolitan Washington Council Government, and member of the governor's Commission on Law Enforcement and Administration.

Spellman lived in Laurel, Maryland, until her death at age seventy on June 19, 1988. She was married to Reuben Spellman, with whom she had three children: Stephen, Richard, and Dana Spellman O'Neill. She was buried in Arlington National Cemetery.

By the time she left Congress in 1981, Spellman was one of twenty-seven Jews in the House of Representatives—an increase of five over the previous election. Her service in the U.S. Government coincided with a period of American politics in which Jews were becoming increasingly visible, both as voters and as elected officials. As a minority figure wielding power on the political scene, Gladys Noon Spellman was a model for both Jews and women in America.

BIBLIOGRAPHY

Biographical Directory of the United States Congress 1774–1989 (1989); Temkin, Sefton P. "Spellman, Gladys Noon." EJ Decennial Book (1973–1982); Who's Who in American Politics (1981); WWIAJ (1980).

TAMAR KAPLAN

SPEWACK, BELLA (1899–1990)

"Just about the ages of 10 and 12, and even much more before then, there burns brightly in every ghetto child's brain the desire to see what lies without the ghetto's walls," playwright Bella Spewack wrote in her diary in 1922. When she made this observation, Spewack was in Berlin, Germany, with her husband, Sam Spewack, who was working there as a reporter for the New York World. She was only twenty-three years old, but already on the way to a successful career in writing and show business. These early experiences are chronicled in Streets: A Memoir of the Lower East Side.

After reading her diary, it is clear that most of Bella's childhood and youth was a struggle to leave the Lower East Side for a better life uptown. A better life did not mean simply material things, but also, perhaps even more importantly, a proper education and a career.

Bella (Cohen) Spewack was born on March 25, 1899, in Transylvania, at the time a province of the vast Austro-Hungarian Empire, now part of Romania. Jews from that region, especially those from urban areas, were generally better educated and more cultured than their brethren from the hinterlands of Poland and Russia. Unlike the shtetl Jews of Galicia and the Ukraine, the more urbanized Austro-Hungarian Jews possessed some of the sensibility of Central Europeans: They were cosmopolitan with an eye for elegance and aesthetics.

These qualities were clearly evident in Bella and in her mother, Fanny Cohen. In fact, Bella owed a great deal to her mother. Her parents were already divorced in 1902, when Bella and her mother arrived in New York. Fanny Cohen remarried in 1911. Bella's stepfather was Noosn Lang, a boarder in their apartment on Lewis Street, who was a pants presser in the garment district. A year later, her half-brother Hershey was born, but he died of an incurable disease at age five. Daniel, a second half-brother, was born in 1913. Like Bella, he too grew up fatherless because Lang, a mean, abusive husband, abandoned his family soon after Hershey's death, while Fanny was pregnant with Daniel. It would be an understatement to say that 1912 and 1913 were tumultuous years for Bella: She experienced a death, a birth, parental separation, graduation from Washington Irving High School, and the start of her career as a reporter for the *Yorkville Home News*. (Her struggle to become a writer is reminiscent of another famous immigrant author, ANZIA YEZIERSKA, who wrote of her aspirations in the autobiographical novel *Bread Givers*.) It is not surprising that Bella chose this profession—her memoir of her early teens clearly reveals a keen eye for human behavior, wit, and good writing skills. This position soon led to jobs as publicity agent and reporter for a string of newspapers, including *The Call*.

In 1922, she married Sam Spewack, a foreign correspondent for the *New York World*. After a four-year stint in Europe, the two began writing some of the most memorable lyrics in musical theater history. Two librettos, *Leave It to Me* (1938) and *Kiss Me Kate* (1948), were Cole Porter collaborations, the first play an adaptation of a 1932 Spewack drama, *Clear All Wires*, and the second, a modern version of *The Taming of the Shrew*. In addition, the Spewacks wrote screenplays for several Hollywood hits of the 1940s: *My Favorite Wife* (1940), with Cary Grant, and *Weekend at the Waldorf* (1945), with Ginger Rogers and Lana Turner. In 1948, *Kiss Me Kate*, the movie, had its premiere in New York. Their first play, *The Solitaire Man* (1927), was seen only in Boston, but *Boy Meets Girl* (1936) ran for 669 performances in New York.

Since they worked as a team, it is, of course, impossible to evaluate one without the other. However, it is widely accepted that Sam created the plot and action, while Bella wrote most of the dialogue. George Abbott, the legendary Broadway director, said that the Spewacks "know how to write lines which are not only funny to read but which crackle when spoken in the theatre." True, some of their serious drama received mixed reviews, but the negative response was mostly to the plot, not the dialogue. Anyone familiar with the Spewack comedies is struck by the liveliness of the text, the witty remarks, the biting irony, and the fast tempo.

The Spewacks' early plays—*Poppa*, *Spring Song*, and *War Song*—deal with a variety of social issues, among them problems facing new immigrants, some of whom are Jewish. They focus on the clash of cultures, the effect of Americanization on traditional ways, and disenchantment with the elusive American dream. These themes are usually built around some family crisis—failed marriages, mixed marriages, duty to parents. Who better than Bella Spewack, who has "seen it all," to write about such things? These concerns bring to mind many of the Jewish plays written in the 1920s and 1930s by such established dramatists as Clifford Odets, Elmer Rice, and Aaron Hoffman. Most of these plays failed at the box office. In times of economic hardship, people seem to prefer comedies over serious drama. The Spewacks recognized that need and devoted themselves to lighter matters, generally based on the formula: "Boy meets girl, boy loses girl, boy gets girl"—hence, *Boy Meets Girl* and *Kiss Me Kate*, their biggest hits on Broadway and in Hollywood.

Though in later works the Spewacks distanced themselves from their Jewish roots, the couple contributed time and money to a variety of Jewish causes, mostly involving children. In 1946, as representative for the United Nations, Bella Spewack covered the distribution of food in ravaged Eastern Europe, where so many Jewish communities lay in ruins. In 1960, Bella and Sam founded the Spewack Sports Club for the Handicapped in Ramat Gan, Israel.

Except for a few minor pieces, the Spewacks' creative career ceased in the mid-1950s. Occasionally, they would appear in public with a Broadway director or famous musician, but after Sam's death in 1971, Bella's activities were confined to traveling to see productions of *Kiss Me Kate* and walking the fashionable midtown neighborhoods near Carnegie Hall—not bad for a poor Hungarian girl from the crowded tenements of the Lower East Side.

Bella Spewack died on April 29, 1990.

SELECTED WORKS BY BELLA SPEWACK

Boy Meets Girl (1936); *Clear All Wires* (1932); *Kiss Me Kate*, with Cole Porter (1948); *Leave It to Me*, with Cole Porter (1938); *My Favorite Wife* [screenplay] (1940); *Poppa* (1929); *The Solitaire Man* (1927); *Spring Song* (1936); *Streets: A Memoir of the Lower East Side* (1995); *War Song* (n.d.); *Weekend at the Waldorf* [screenplay] (1945).

BIBLIOGRAPHY

Drorbaugh, Elisabeth. "Bella Spewack." In *Jewish American Women Writers*, edited by Ann Shapiro (1994); *EJ*; *UJE*, s.v. "Spewack, Samuel"; *WWIAJ* (1938). For a complete bibliography, see Drorbaugh's essay, which includes citations of media reviews, movie and television scripts, and librettos of musicals.

MICHAEL TAUB

SPIEGEL, DORA (1879–1948)

Dora Spiegel served as president of the National Women's League of the Conservative Movement for sixteen years, from 1928 to 1944, guiding it through the difficulties of the Depression and the war years.

The daughter of Rabbi Daniel Rosenberg, Dora (Rosenberg) Spiegel was born on November 27, 1879, in Hungary. The family immigrated to America when she was a young girl. In 1900, she married Samuel Spiegel, a New York physician. Spiegel's activities turned to avenues where she could serve Jewish children and their mothers. To prepare herself for meaningful service, she returned to study, earning a B.S. at Teachers College of Columbia University in 1916 and, in 1920, an M.A. with a special diploma as Advisor to Women.

Spiegel's interests and her dedication are reflected in the achievements of her lifetime. She taught the Bible to blind children, English to immigrant mothers, psychology to nurses, and literature to classes at the Educational Alliance, New York's training school for the Americanization of the teeming thousands pouring into the Golden Land. She was a teacher in the newly organized Sunday schools designed to provide at least a taste of Jewish education to the children of those who had shed their old traditions as they left their old world. She was a leader in the Zionist movement at a time when many Jews were comfortable and content with their lives and saw no need to involve themselves in the establishment of a Jewish homeland.

In the National Women's League and its program, she found a synthesis of all her goals. Service to the league and its growing membership of affiliated sisterhoods became her real life's work. She became the league's second national secretary and, at the same time, headed the New York Metropolitan branch.

By 1933, already deeply aware of and concerned with the "grievous conditions in Germany," the National Women's League asked constituent sisterhoods "to make personal sacrifices in order to be able to forward monies to the Joint Distribution Committee for Germany." Through the war years, Dora Spiegel's "President's Chats," published in *Outlook*, the league's magazine, encouraged affiliated sisterhoods to pledge themselves to participate in relief efforts. At the 1941 national convention in Detroit, Eleanor Roosevelt addressed the delegates on "Women in Defense," and within one month, league members across the country began working for a nation at war. In March 1943, Dora Spiegel reported, "Over 100,000 of our membership are working in every single branch of the war effort, giving of their blood, selling bonds, turning assembly halls into emergency hospitals,

As president of the National Women's League of the Conservative Movement (now the WOMEN'S LEAGUE FOR CONSERVATIVE JUDAISM*) during the Depression and World War II, Dora Spiegel inspired Jewish women to make sacrifices for the good of their sisters in America and abroad. [Women's League for Conservative Judaism]*

enlisting in motor corps, serving in canteens, taking first aid courses, and teaching first aid."

It was under Spiegel's direction that the National Women's League began its Torah Fund Campaign, establishing the Seminary Dormitory and Scholarship Fund that enabled rabbinical students to devote their full time to study. She encouraged the league to help create the MATHILDE SCHECHTER Scholarship Fund and the Cyrus Adler Scholarship Fund, and the idea of building a dormitory for women students began to grow during her term of office.

Dora Spiegel rendered distinguished service in many fields: in the organization of league sisterhoods, in education, and in publications that stimulated women's loyalty to the synagogue and the Jewish home. She helped found the Women's Institute of Jewish Studies at the Jewish Theological Seminary of America and influenced the lives of countless Jewish women and children.

Failing health forced Dora Spiegel to step aside before the conclusion of her last term of office. She died on February 15, 1948.

BIBLIOGRAPHY

AJYB 50:523; National Women's League of the United Synagogues of America. *Seventy-five Years of Vision and Voluntarism* (1992); Obituary. *NYTimes*, February 16, 1948, 21:4; *UJE*; Women's League for Conservative Judaism. *They Dared to Dream* (1968); *WWIAJ* (1928, 1938).

SELMA WEINTRAUB

SPIEGELBERG, FLORA LANGERMAN (1857–1943)

Flora Langerman Spiegelberg's life did not fall neatly into typical historical categories. Born on September 10, 1857, her eighty-seven years spanned nearly half of two centuries. A native of America, yet educated in Europe, Spiegelberg was a nineteenth-century settler of New Mexico and a twentieth-century progressive reformer in New York City. However, Spiegelberg did not feel that her work as a pacifist, a writer, and a founder of both nonsectarian public schools and Jewish women's organizations crossed gender boundaries. In reference to her intensive efforts to improve New York City sanitation, she remarked, "It is a womanly hobby. Unusual, if you like, but quite in the province of a woman."

Flora Langerman Spiegelberg was the daughter of Jewish New York City residents William Langerman of Bavaria and American-born Rosalia Lichtenheim. Her maternal grandfather had come from Hamburg to New York in 1820 and married a Christian descendant of a Hessian officer who had fought with the colonists in the Revolutionary War. Two months after Flora's birth, the family moved from New York City to San Francisco, spurred by her father's interest in the California gold rush. The Langermans returned to New York in 1866, a twenty-one-day journey via the Panama Canal. When William Langerman died three years later, Flora's mother took her to Nuremberg, Germany, to complete her education.

Thirty-year-old Willi Spiegelberg, one of the prosperous merchant and banking Spiegelberg brothers of Santa Fe, traveled to his German homeland in 1874. He knew of the Langermans through distant family connections. Flora succinctly related the outcome of his visit: "I was young and he was handsome and in a very short time I became Mrs. Willi Spiegelberg." Their wedding was the first in Nuremberg's

new Reform temple. In 1875, after an extensive European honeymoon, the couple arrived in New York and headed for New Mexico. The journey culminated in the arduous Santa Fe Trail. Spiegelberg later recalled her shocked reaction to one night's accommodations where she slept among numerous cowboys, separated from them by only a muslin curtain.

Once settled in Santa Fe, Spiegelberg assumed a leading social position among the area's prominent families. She frequently entertained visiting dignitaries such as Generals Grant and Sherman, President Hayes, and local officials such as the governor and archbishop. Her appreciation for diverse cultures coexisted with her strong Jewish identity. Few in number, Jewish New Mexicans had strong social and commercial ties to both Catholic and Indian communities. These relationships led to Willi Spiegelberg's election as mayor in 1880 and probate judge in 1884.

In 1889, the Spiegelbergs and their two daughters (Betty and Rose) left Santa Fe for New York, the last members of the Spiegelberg family to relocate. They were concerned about their children's education and marriage possibilities within the faith. In New York, Spiegelberg soon became a founding member of the Committee for Jewish Women, the Temple Emanu-El Sisterhood, and the Friendly Club (the first Jewish working girls club). Around 1910, she began a decades-long campaign to improve New York City garbage collection and disposal. Lectures included *A Menace to Public Health*, a film Thomas Edison made for her in 1914. Nicknamed "Garbage Can Flora," she won the praise of sanitation workers by supporting their demands for better wages and working conditions, and received successive appointments to the New York City Health Commission, the Street Cleaning Department, the Bill Board and Daylight Saving Commissions, and the Public Market Commission. Spiegelberg also promoted and gave vocational instruction, advocated her "Ten Commandments for World Peace" (1919), which called for a constitutional amendment to ensure that war could be declared only by popular vote, and published numerous children's stories.

Flora Langerman Spiegelberg died on December 8, 1943, in New York, having made substantial innovative contributions to civic welfare and Jewish life.

**SELECTED WORKS BY
FLORA LANGERMAN SPIEGELBERG**

Princess Goldenhair and the Wonderful Flower (1917, 1932, 1939); "Reminiscences of a Jewish Bride of the Santa Fe Trail." Part 1. *New York Jewish Spectator* (August 1937): 21, Part 2. *New York Jewish Spectator* (September 1937): 44; "Reminiscences of Governor Lew Wallace." *Oklahoma City*

Jewish Chronicle (February 1934): 6; "Tribute to Archbishop Lamy." *Oklahoma City Jewish Chronicle* (December 1933): 3.

BIBLIOGRAPHY

AJHQ 55 (1965):98–106, 56 (1968):371–451; *BEOAJ*; Lawson, Michael L. "Flora Langerman Spiegelberg: Grand Lady of Santa Fe." *Western State Jewish Historical Quarterly* 8 (July 1976): 291–308; Obituary. *NYTimes*, December 9, 1943, 27:1; Spiegelberg, Flora Langerman. Manuscript catalog and papers. AJA, Cincinnati, Ohio, and Microfilm No. 511. Hebrew Union College Library, Los Angeles Calif., and Papers. University of New Mexico Library, Albuquerque, N. Mex.; Tobias, Henry J. *A History of the Jews in New Mexico* (1990); *UJE*; *WWIAJ* (1938).

JILL FIELDS

SPIRITUALITY

Spirituality can be defined as life lived in the presence of God. It embraces not only traditional and formal modes of religious expression, but also more informal individual and communal efforts to remain mindful of the sacred in all aspects of experience.

Jewish women's spirituality developed historically within the confines of a patriarchal tradition. The sages understood woman's nature as more private than man's—"the entire glory of the king's daughter lies on the inside" (Ps. 45:14)—and thus the proper focus of her spiritual life was considered the home. Within this sphere, women elaborated their own customs and conventions that were passed on from mother to daughter. But even if these were distinct from or in tension with the larger male tradition, they remained constrained by its boundaries. Feminist spirituality, as it has developed since the late 1960s, represents a new phenomenon. It constitutes a *self-conscious, critical* attempt to transform Jewish tradition, for the sake of justice for women and in the name of perspectives and values said to be represented by women. It involves women *claiming* the *power* to participate fully in and actively shape Jewish religious life.

The first feminist efforts at creating a self-conscious women's spirituality revolved around claiming equal access to the (formerly male) public Jewish spaces of the synagogue and the house of study. Arguing that women should not be barred from those forms of prayer and learning that have formed the heart and soul of traditional Judaism, women in non-Orthodox denominations fought—successfully—for the rights to lead services, read from the Torah, be counted in a minyan [quorum of ten (men) necessary for a full service], and enjoy admission to the rabbinate and cantorate. Orthodox women formed women's *tefillah* [prayer] groups, in which, in the absence of men, they could lead services, read from the Torah and haftarah [additional reading for the Sabbath], and recite all prayers not requiring a minyan. Despite opposition from some segments of the Orthodox world, these groups have proliferated and flourished.

Feminists have not confined themselves, however, to laying claim to forms of spiritual expression formerly reserved for men. They have also raised questions about the existence and content of a specifically female spirituality. Should it be the goal of feminism simply to adopt traditionally male forms of study and worship? Are there uniquely female spiritual experiences and perspectives? Do women have anything distinctive to contribute to Jewish spirituality—not because they are more interior or more innately pious than men (as the tradition has sometimes claimed), but because of their long history of separation, subordination, and marginalization? What would it mean for women to begin self-consciously to explore their spiritual lives *as women*?

These questions represent a strand of feminist exploration that sometimes informs the struggle for equal access, but is also distinct from it. Such questions have most often been addressed in women-only contexts in which participants have considerable freedom to play with the boundaries of tradition. Since 1976, when Arlene Agus first wrote about rosh hodesh [the new moon] as a woman's holiday, for example, women's rosh hodesh groups have sprung up all over the country. Serving as important vehicles of feminist organizing, rosh hodesh groups have used the association of women with the moon in midrash and folk tradition as a foundation for wide-ranging spiritual exploration and liturgical inventiveness. The brief rosh hodesh liturgy has provided feminists with a jumping-off point for developing new rituals and stories that attempt to link generations of Jewish women. Rosh hodesh ceremonies appear in a number of collections, including Penina Adelman's *Miriam's Well* (1986), which draws on twenty years of feminist rosh hodesh organizing, and the newsletter *Rosh Hodesh Exchange*. Orthodox women's prayer groups, which sometimes are organized around rosh hodesh, also have begun creating and circulating new liturgy that reflects women's life experiences.

Feminist seders [Passover liturgical meals] have provided another important context for developing women's spirituality. Many college campuses and women's groups around the country have established a tradition of a third seder that uses the structures and themes of the Haggadah [Passover liturgy] to reflect

Feminist seders have provided an important context for developing Jewish women's spirituality.
Perhaps the first and certainly the most famous feminist seder began in 1976 in New York City
and is described in ESTHER M. BRONER's The Telling: The Story of a Group of Jewish Women Who
Journey to Spirituality Through Community and Ceremony. *She is shown here at the seventeenth seder*
of the group in 1991 with another of the original "seder sisters," LETTY COTTIN POGREBIN. *[Joan Roth]*

on the situation of women within Judaism. Moving from the freedom of the Jewish people to the hoped-for liberation of women, feminist seders provide opportunities for both celebrating women's history and reflecting critically on the erasures of women's experience from the Haggadah and other mainstream texts that make a third seder necessary. Such seders fall anywhere along a continuum, from those that remain fairly close to the traditional liturgy, integrating women's history and experience into the established narrative of the liberation from Egypt, to those that shift the focus of the Haggadah from the liberation of the Israelites to the liberation of women.

Another kind of separate space is provided by Jewish feminist retreats, conferences, and spirituality collectives that seek to provide special and concentrated time for exploring issues of women's spirituality. In 1981, a group of Jewish feminists founded *B'not Esh* [daughters of fire], a collective that began with the goal of reconfiguring Judaism from a feminist perspective. Meeting annually for four days over Memorial Day weekend, *B'not Esh* has generated a number of spin-offs, including *Achiyot Or* [sisters of light] and *Bat Kol* [daughter of the voice/the divine voice]. While these groups differ in tone and emphasis, they all provide opportunities for study, extensive ritual/liturgical experimentation, and exploration of the relationship among feminism, spirituality, and issues of everyday life. Taking up topics from sexuality, to politics, to cost sharing, to the meaning of women's Torah, they all attempt to imagine and create a Judaism that thoroughly integrates women's experiences. Such groups—and other conferences and retreats—are necessarily limited in the number of participants who can be directly involved, but they have generated ideas and resources that have spilled over into a larger Jewish feminist community.

While most Jewish feminist spiritual experimentation has been communal in nature, a fair amount of the ritual generated by feminist groups has revolved around the individual life cycle. The absence of a traditional ceremony for celebrating the birth of a daughter, the absence of blessings for the central moments in women's biological lives, the desire to find Jewish ways to affirm the female body and to value relationships between women have all served as important stimuli to feminist ritual inventiveness.

Birth ceremonies for girls were the earliest feminist ritual innovation, and the one most widely accepted and adopted. In the early 1970s, many couples created rituals around the births of their daughters. Daniel and Myra Leifer, for example, wrote ceremonies for the moment of birth, naming, and

pidyon habat [redemption of the firstborn daughter], while Sharon and Michael Strassfeld immersed their daugher in the *mikvah* [ritual bath] to welcome her into the covenant. Since then, others have searched hard for a symbolic act or series of acts that could match the power and significance of Brith Milah [the covenant of circumcision]. Feminists have tried or suggested a variety of rituals, from washing a girl's feet as a sign of welcome, to breaking her hymen, to offering her a ritual object (for example, a prayer shawl or Kiddush cup) that expresses her parents' hopes for her future participation in the Jewish community.

Once feminists discovered that it was possible to create effective new ceremonies, new rituals multiplied, each seeking to create some Jewish marker for a central event or crisis in women's lives. Jewish feminists have developed rituals for, among other things, menarche, childbirth, weaning, miscarriage, rape, and hysterectomy. A number of women have held "croning" ceremonies in which, on reaching sixty, they celebrate wisdom and the entry into a new phase of life. Other rituals have sought to sanctify significant non-biological turning points, such as rabbinic ordination, moving across country, becoming a vegetarian, or coming out as a lesbian. For a long time, such new rituals circulated only privately, so that women looking for new ceremonies were generally forced to invent them from scratch. Collections by Elizabeth Resnick Levine, Ellen Umansky and Dianne Ashton, and Debra Orenstein now gather at least some of these resources together, making them available to a wide audience.

The creation of new life cycle rituals poses special challenges to Jewish lesbians, who are doubly excluded from the Jewish ceremonial cycle. According to Rebecca Alpert, who has been a leader in this area, lesbians must both reconstruct those rituals they hold in common with all other Jews and create new rituals that speak to their difference. While commitment ceremonies have been the most visible area of lesbian ritual creativity, lesbians must also transform mourning rituals that do not recognize a lesbian partner as a mourner, find ways to celebrate the birth or adoption of a child in the context of a lesbian relationship, and make connections between the cycle of the year and lesbian experience of liberation. The fact that some feminist seders, for example, incorporate references to Jewish lesbians or highlight the lesbian experiences indicates that Jewish lesbians have been active and involved in leadership roles in all areas of feminist spiritual experimentation, even as they have had to remain alert to the heterosexual bias present in some feminist ceremonies.

Apart from the absence of Jewish markers for significant events in women's lives, discomfort with traditional male God-language was the most important early catalyst for the creation of feminist liturgy. Convinced that the traditional prayer book is idolatrous because it identifies the image of God with maleness, feminists tried to reimagine the sacred by speaking of God as female. The fullest early experiment with new language was Maggie Wenig and Naomi Janowitz's *Siddur Nashim* (1976), a Sabbath prayer book in English that referred to God throughout using female pronouns and imagery.

Since the 1970s, feminist experiments with imagery have broadened and deepened. Changes in the gender of God have evolved into more fundamental changes in conceptions of God, and changes in English translations of prayers have begun to be combined with changes in the original Hebrew. Feminists have focused on the *immanence* of God within the world and within women; they have called on God using a myriad of metaphors and have imagined her as moving and changing. Liturgists such as Lynn Gottlieb and Penina Adelman have drawn on female imagery from many traditions; used traditional Hebrew images for the divine, like *Shekhinah*, the feminine aspect of God in Jewish mysticism; and also created new names, like *harahamaima*, compassionate giver of life. Feminist concerns have influenced a number of community and denominational prayerbooks: the Sudbury siddur *V'taher Libenu*, which alternates male and female God-language in its English translations; P'nai Or's *Or Chadash*, which provides all Hebrew blessings in the masculine and feminine; and the Reconstructionist siddur *Kol Haneshamah*, which offers many images for God and includes numerous feminist offerings among its readings. These two lines of experimentation—with new images and new Hebrew—come together most fully in the work of Marcia Falk, whose *The Book of Blessings* (1996) entirely reworks the daily, Sabbath, and rosh hodesh liturgies from a feminist perspective.

While new forms of ritual, prayer, and God-language in many ways form the heart of feminist spiritual exploration, feminist spirituality has by no means been confined to these media. Midrash, for example, has been another important mode of feminist expression. Drawing on traditional techniques for explicating and expanding biblical texts and for resolving contradictions and filling in silences, feminists have created a host of new midrashim, focusing largely, but not entirely, on the female figures in the Bible. Where was Sarah when Abraham took the child born of her old age to offer him as a sacrifice on top of Mount Moriah? Why did Lot's wife look back as the family fled Sodom? How did Miriam feel when she was punished with leprosy for challenging Moses's authority? In classes, workshops, and women's groups, feminists have been asking new questions of traditional texts and expanding on biblical narratives in ways that connect with their own experiences. Much of the midrash written in response to new questions remains in drawers or circulates privately, but the San Diego Woman's Institute for Continuing Jewish Education has brought at least some of it together in its anthology *Taking the Fruit*.

Jewish feminist theology is a more theoretical form of spiritual expression that grows out of and attempts to reflect on the changes taking place in all these areas. What views of self, God, and world underlie feminist experiments with midrash or liturgy, and how might feminist worldviews express themselves in transformed liturgy and ritual? Where do feminist understandings of key Jewish categories converge with or diverge from traditional rabbinic conceptions? How do the new texts women are creating shape or transform the meaning of Torah? Is a feminist halakah [Jewish law] possible, and what would it be like? What makes Jewish feminist ritual/God-language/midrash *Jewish*? Feminists such as Judith Plaskow, Rachel Adler, Ellen Umansky, Drorah Setel, and Laura Levitt have produced a range of theoretical work that tries to reconceptualize central aspects of Jewish life and thought from differing feminist perspectives. Plaskow has written the only book-length systematic feminist Jewish theology, *Standing Again at Sinai*.

Other avenues of feminist creativity have been as rich and varied as the talents of feminists themselves. ALICIA OSTRIKER and E.M. BRONER have developed powerful midrash and ritual through poetry and fiction. Fanchon Shur has used dance to try to convey the spiritual power of women. Ruth Wiesberg and others have celebrated women's spiritual lives through painting and other visual arts. Many Jewish feminists see feminist activism itself as a significant mode of spiritual expression. Efforts to create a Judaism that fully incorporates the diversity of women's experiences contribute to *tikkun olam*, the healing or repair of the world.

What other shapes feminist spirituality will take and which of its innovations will become part of the mainstream, are difficult to predict. As women take on new roles, as they engage with, challenge, and transform tradition, they create a new Jewish reality that itself becomes the foundation for further evolution.

BIBLIOGRAPHY

Adelman, Penina V. *Miriam's Well: Rituals for Jewish Women Around the Year* (1986); Agus, Arlene. "This Month Is for You: Observing Rosh Hodesh as a Woman's Holiday." In Koltan, *The Jewish Woman*; Falk, Marcia. *The Book of Blessings* (1996); Haut, Rivka. "Women's Prayer Groups and the Orthodox Synagogue." In *Daughters of the King: Women and the Synagogue*, edited by Susan Grossman and Rivka Haut (1992); Koltun, Elizabeth, ed. *The Jewish Woman: New Perspectives* (1976); Levine, Elizabeth Resnick, ed. *A Ceremonies Sampler: New Rites, Celebrations, and Observances of Jewish Women* (1991); Orenstein, Debra, ed. *Lifecycles: Jewish Women on Life Passages and Personal Milestones* (1994); Plaskow, Judith. *Standing Again at Sinai*; Umansky, Ellen M., and Dianne Ashton, eds. *Four Centuries of Jewish Women's Spirituality: A Sourcebook* (1992); Wenig, Maggie, and Naomi Janowitz. *Siddur Nashim* (1976); Zones, Jane Sprague, ed. *Taking the Fruit: Modern Women's Tales of the Bible* (1981).

JUDITH PLASKOW

From her work with the NATIONAL COUNCIL OF JEWISH WOMEN *to the United Nations, Constance Sporborg devoted her energies to bettering the lives of women throughout the world.* [American Jewish Archives]

SPORBORG, CONSTANCE AMBERG (1879–1961)

Constance Amberg Sporborg was a career clubwoman who dedicated her life to the advancement of women's rights, immigrant settlement, international organizations, and world peace. As an example of her extensive involvement in local and world affairs, she once, in the mid-1940s, simultaneously held fifteen different leadership posts in local, national, and international organizations.

Born on July 11, 1879, to Louis and Rose (Winkler) Amberg of Cincinnati, Ohio, she began her long career of community service at age fifteen by volunteering at a local settlement house. She went on to attend the University of Cincinnati, and, in 1901, earned a bachelor of science degree in languages. After completing her degree she moved with her family to New York where she continued her work with settlement houses, volunteering at both the Christy House and the Henry Street Settlement. In 1902, she married William Dick Sporborg, a lawyer. They had two children, Elizabeth and William Dick, Jr.

By 1916, Constance Sporborg was already contributing much of her time to civic organizations. She served as president of the New York section of the NATIONAL COUNCIL OF JEWISH WOMEN (NCJW) from 1916 to 1921, and in 1926, she served as its national president. The NCJW dedicated much of its activities to the development of settlement houses and assistance for immigrant women. They stationed a permanent representative on Ellis Island to interview every Jewish woman who passed through in an effort to help

her assimilate more quickly to American culture and avoid prostitution. During Sporborg's years of leadership, the NCJW was expanding its efforts to reach Jews who had settled in more rural areas as well.

Sporborg was also concerned with international issues and establishing lasting world peace. Her international interests included involvement in pan-American relations, women's issues, and extensive service for and with the United Nations. In 1937, she took part in a seminar group studying conditions in Europe firsthand. In the 1940s, Sporborg began her commitment to the UN and its organizations. She served as a member of the U.S. National Committee for UNESCO from 1946 to 1949, was involved with the UNRRA, and was an accredited observer representing women's groups from 1946. In addition, Sporborg headed the women's delegation to the Pan-American Conference in Lima, Peru, in 1938.

All of this, however, was only part of her lifelong career as a social activist. In addition to her work with the NCJW, she served as president of the New York City and State Federations of Women's Clubs. She wrote articles and handbooks for women about congressional procedures, legislation, and voting. In 1933, she chaired the women's exhibit at the Chicago World's Fair.

In 1939, she was recognized for her years of outstanding community and international service, and in particular for her efforts on behalf of women, when Russell Sage College awarded her an honorary doctorate.

Constance Amberg Sporborg dedicated much of her life to bettering the lives of women and working toward a more peaceful world. While she was always active in the Jewish community, her efforts aided both Jews and gentiles at home and abroad. She died on January 2, 1961, in New York City at age eighty-one, survived by her two children and four grandchildren.

BIBLIOGRAPHY

AJYB 63:562; Obituary. *NYTimes*, January 3, 1961, 29:2; Rogrow, Faith. *Gone to Another Meeting: The National Council of Jewish Women, 1893–1993* (1993); Russell Sage College. Archives. Troy, N.Y.; *UJE*; *WWIAJ* (1938); *WWWIA* 6.

SUSAN FOX

SPORTS

A 1922 publication of the YOUNG WOMEN'S HEBREW ASSOCIATION (YWHA) of New York, "How We Serve the Community," included the theme of physical education, along with dormitory, religious work, and education in the commercial school, trade, and domestic arts. In the physical education category the YWHA emphasized "Swimming-Tournaments and Contests, Gymnastics, Athletics" at their facility at 31 West 110th Street, New York. Organizers of the YWHA and other Jewish institutions integrated

The ideology of sport and physical culture for female immigrants took on gender and class dimensions in the Progressive Era. Reformers believed that women needed physical health to fulfill domestic roles and offset the negative influence of unsanitary urban conditions. Physical exercise was the answer, as demonstrated by this evening calisthenics class. The photograph is from 1914.
[92nd Street YM-YWHA Archives]

The YOUNG WOMEN'S HEBREW ASSOCIATION *of New York's swimming pool opened in 1916 and represented a major part of promoting sport and physical culture for working girls and women. This class was photographed in 1923. [A. Tennyson Beals. 92nd Street YM-YWHA Archives]*

physical activities and sports into programs designed to enhance the experiences of women and girls. However, historians of American sport, and of American Jewish history, generally have neglected the study of sports by and for Jewish American women.

The ways females participated in the sporting life within the immigrant and larger culture reveals how women's sports activities at times promoted assimilation yet also generated discord within the generational, gender, class, and ethnic context of their lives in the United States.

For immigrant women, exposure to American life and sport and physical exercise often occurred at settlement houses and immigrant aid associations in the latter decades of the nineteenth century. In fact, as Eastern European immigrants came to America and populated urban areas like New York and Philadelphia, the earlier immigrants, usually German Jews, who by the 1880s had become wealthier and more prominent in American institutions, sought to assist the newest Jewish immigrants by promoting assimilation into American culture rather than nurturing the ethnic identities and religiosity. During the period of widespread Jewish immigration to the United States, 1880 to 1920, philanthropists organized the Young Men's Hebrew Association (YMHA), Young Women's Hebrew Associations (1902), and the Educational Alliance in New York City to provide for the educational, social, and physical welfare of Jews.

Some women participated in sports at Jewish settlement houses. At the Young Women's Union in Philadelphia, founded in 1885, Fannie Binswanger and other young women who sought to promote social services for Russian Jewish immigrants introduced recreation and sports to give children a chance to escape the congested city. Women and girls participated in calisthenics and gymnastics, and, when a new building opened in 1900, girls were instructed in gymnasium class by Caroline Massman and Sadie Kohn. Reorganized as the larger Neighborhood Centre in 1918, the director stated that the new schedule at the settlement revealed added activities in dramatics, cooking, and athletics.

Seeking to promote spiritual and bodily wellbeing for working-class females, philanthropists who founded the Irene Kaufmann Settlement House in Pittsburgh in 1895 incorporated health and recreational activities in their programs. Known as the IKS, the settlement promoted wholesome physical exercise and athletics in the girls clubs. In *I.K.S. Neighbors*, the house journal, an article revealed that, "Many of our girls have asked for use of the gymnasium and their requests have been granted." Classes were held for girls of various ages in gymnasium, swimming, basketball, and aesthetic dancing. Sporting opportunities for girls and young women at settlements, YMHAs, and YWHAs served as forerunners of organized athletic events of the Jewish community centers most popular in the second half of the twentieth century.

The ideology of sport and physical culture for female immigrants took on gender and class dimensions in the Progressive Era (1900–1920). Social reformers, alarmed at the vice and danger they affiliated with the city life of lower-class immigrants, wanted to offer an alternative and to inculcate youth into American middle-class, white cultural values. Reformers who believed that women needed physical health to fulfill domestic roles and to offset the negative influence of unsanitary urban conditions endorsed physical exercise for women. At Chicago's Jewish Training School, founded in 1888, immigrant Hilda Satt Polacheck remembered that as a young girl, "Gymnastics were taught in a real gymnasium." With calisthenics and basketball games going on at Hull House, Polacheck said that "the gymnasium was like an oasis in a desert on Halsted Street."

The Educational Alliance in New York considered physical training and sports for immigrants to be a significant component of the institutional mission. In 1895, the Educational Alliance offered in its "Physical Work" program "male and female classes, and now both young men and young women and children received the benefits of well-regulated physical exercise." The alliance's physical culture department conducted "free developing exercises, marching, fancy steps and work with bells, wands, clubs, balls, hoops, horse rings, rope and jumping" for females. The assumption of female gender-appropriate physical exercise meant the emphasis was on forms of health-building sports rather than competition. The goal of such sporting exercises in the settlement house movement centered on "the cultivation of a good carriage" and "the reproducing of better health."

Women social workers and physical culture trainers fostered the use of the gymnasium for girls for fitness and Americanization purposes. In 1911, JULIA RICHMAN suggested to the Committee on Education of the Educational Alliance that the gymnasium be opened on certain afternoons for "girls between the ages of eleven and fifteen, who are wandering aimlessly about the streets and who might be attracted to amusement halls and other places of doubtful influence." As a counterpoint to the dance halls, saloons, and street life for youth, Educational Alliance physical culture proponents seemed pleased with the Walking Club that sought to "arous[e] girls' interest in city history and at the same time stimulat[e] in them a desire for healthful outdoor exercise." Physical educational advocates, like the director of the Chicago Jewish Peoples' Institute, recognized the appeal of sports for youth, asserting, "There is, however, a possibility of injecting a Jewish influence even in the Gymnasium."

Jewish organizations convey a rich history of promoting women's basketball in intramural and team competition. But the women's basketball game differed from the men's version to accommodate concerns of basketball being too physically rough on woman's constitution. Revised rules avoided physical contact and ensured a team-oriented philosophy with more players on each team. Jewish American immigrant SENDA BERENSON, known as the "Mother of Women's Basketball," became a leading physical educator at Smith College in the 1890s and an avid supporter of women's sport. She wrote women's basketball rule books to promote physical vigor and womanly athletic skill. Women's basketball gained popularity not only in collegiate institutions but also spread to other schools, YWCAs, and YWHAs.

Basketball games took place at the Young Women's Hebrew Association of New York, in programs linking Jewishness with spiritual and physical well-being. Women were required to undergo medical examinations before participating in basketball and other sports so as to avoid potential health risks. The YWHA Physical Training classes for girls included gymnasium exercises and basketball, and when the YWHA moved to its new larger building in 1914, athletic facilities for basketball played an important role. The YWHA touted basketball as "the greatest of all indoor games." At Chicago's Jewish Peoples' Institute, girls played basketball enthusiastically and with excellent ability. They won three girls' basketball championships in the early 1920s.

Women also excelled in basketball at non-Jewish institutions. For example, Rebecca Kronman, who attended the Business High School in Washington, D.C., played on several 1920s championship basketball teams; as Betty K. Shapiro, she served as president of B'NAI B'RITH WOMEN International in the late 1960s. More recently, outstanding basketball player Nancy Lieberman dominated the women's college game during her years as an All-American at Old Dominion University in Virginia in the 1970s. Lieberman, a basketball superstar, made the 1980 Olympic squad and played in the women's professional basketball league in the early 1980s. A few Jewish players competed in the highly competitive National Collegiate Athletic Association women's basketball tournament in 1995.

Additional sports opportunities existed for some women and girls at Jewish institutions. The YWHA's new swimming pool opened in 1916 and represented a major part of promoting sport and physical culture for working girls and women. This excellent pool hosted not only recreational classes but also national competitive swimming championships featuring prominent national and Olympic champions such as Aileen Riggin and Gertrude Ederle in the 1920s. Aileen Riggin, 1920 Olympic gold medal diving champion and 1924 diving and swimming champion, recalled how as a member of the Women's Swimming Association of New York, founded by CHARLOTTE EPSTEIN, the association's manager, and also the 1920 and 1924 Olympic women's swimming team manager, she swam at the YWHA pool for a national championship. An outstanding pool regularly used for both health and competitive purposes, one commentator identified it as a key part of the New York 110th Street YWHA, which "has the most comprehensive program of physical education in the country for Jewish women and girls." Swimming meets focused on maintaining femininity and fitness while competing in athletics in the context of gender expectations. Therefore, a newspaper article described a swim meet as: "A Harlem Mermaid Scores in A Metropolitan Swimming Meet," featuring Eugenia Autonof who won the 100-yard freestyle at the YWHA Aquatic Carnival. *I.K.S. Neighbors* reported that girls ought to tell their own mothers that, "This keeps them in good form and—here's a secret—thin also." Whether or not mothers and daughters alike heeded this advice, the Irene Kaufmann Settlement organized girls' swimming teams for competition.

Jewish Ys encouraged women and girls to swim to acquire a feminine body while experiencing the excitement of competition. Women achieved victory in competitive swimming: Marilyn Ramenofsky, who broke the world record in 1964 in the 400-meter freestyle, won a silver medal in this event in the 1964 Olympics. Hillary Bergman and Wendy Weinberg of the United States each won medals in swimming events in the 1977 Maccabiah Games.

Furthermore, outdoor sports offered health dividends for working girls generally confined indoors. So around 1920 the YWHA even emphasized baseball, usually a male sport, at the Y's country house in White Plains, the forerunner to the YWHA's Ray Hill Camp in Mt. Kisco, New York. Other outdoor sports

Around 1920, the YOUNG WOMEN'S HEBREW ASSOCIATION *of New York emphasized baseball, usually a male sport, at the Y's country house in White Plains, New York. [A. Tennyson Beals. 92nd Street YM-YWHA Archives]*

Ray Hill Camp in Mt. Kisco, New York, provided outdoor exercise for the women who were a part of New York City's YWHA program. This photograph was taken in 1922. [A. Tennyson Beals. 92nd Street YM-YWHA Archives]

endorsed by the YWHA and available at various summer camps for young women were tennis, track and field, archery, croquet, and outdoor swimming. A wide range of sports for women and girls from bowling to volleyball, together with Jewish activities, provided health and enjoyment.

Some women distinguished themselves in public sporting competitions in the early decades of the twentieth century. Track and field star LILLIAN COPELAND earned Olympic medals in the 1928 and 1932 Olympic Games. Copeland was a superb athlete at the University of Southern California, playing several sports. She excelled in track and field and won

numerous national titles in the discus throw and shot put in the 1920s and early 1930s, winning the gold medal for the discus throw at the 1932 Olympic Games. Accomplished track athlete Edith Chaiken of Northwestern University won the national championship in the 440-yard dash for girls in 1914.

Tennis was early considered a suitable feminine sport. In August 1928, an article in the *American Hebrew* featured Clara Greenspan, the captain-coach-manager of the HUNTER COLLEGE tennis team and winner of the Women's New York State Doubles Championship, Eastern Clay Court Championship, and other tournaments. The article hailed Greenspan

Track and field star LILLIAN COPELAND *earned medals in the 1928 and 1932 Olympic Games. A superb athlete at the University of Southern California, she excelled in both the discus throw and the shot put.* [Library of Congress]

as fitting the feminine form and described her "fine complexion that comes with a healthy outdoor life," concluding that she "makes a picture equally attractive on the court or in a ballroom." To foster tennis participation and female fitness, in the 1920s the NATIONAL COUNCIL OF JEWISH WOMEN, Junior Auxiliary, sponsored tennis tournaments for girls in New York. In the 1940s, Helene Irene Bernhard earned the number-four ranking in United States singles, one of the highest rankings achieved by an American Jewish women. Outstanding champions also include Julie Heldman, a national junior champion and winner of the 1969 singles, doubles, and mixed doubles in the 1969 Maccabiah Games. In the late 1960s and early 1970s, Heldman achieved a number-five world ranking. The success of women in tennis championships has continued with Andrea Leand, a top junior player and winner of the tennis competition in the Maccabiah Games in 1981, who turned professional in the 1980s.

Although some Jewish female athletes gained experience in sport through collegiate and Jewish Y programs, women and girls of the middle and upper ranks participated in more elite sports like tennis and golf at Jewish country clubs. By the 1920s, several Jewish clubs had been founded by wealthy German Jews when anti-Semitism prohibited Jews from joining Anglo-Saxon, Protestant, elite country clubs. The locales became places for social, recreational, and competitive sports. The *American Hebrew* printed articles on sports at country clubs and cited the accomplishments of female golf stars, although their gender roles as wife, mother, or daughter shaped the descriptions of athletic prowess.

For example, Elaine Rosenthal Reinhart exhibited talent on the golf links, winning the Women's Western Golf Championship for the third time in 1923. As the best Jewish female golfer in the United States, however, observers in the American Jewish press tended to comment on her husband's good golf as well, emphasizing Reinhart's marriage. "How often Mr. Reinhart was a golf widower is not in the records, but that Mrs. Reinhart lost neither heart nor cunning in the games was again proved" when she was again Western Women's Golf Association champion in 1918. Other golf champions included Mrs. Louis Lengfeld, winner of the Northern California crown in 1927 and member and golf captain of San Francisco's exclusive Beresford Country Club. Mrs. Harry Grossman earned the 1929 Women's Golf Championship of Los Angeles and belonged to well-known elite Jewish Hillcrest Country Club. Today, AMY ALCOTT has earned victories and prize money on the Ladies Professional Golf Association tour.

The emergence of Jewish resorts by the sea or in the mountains provided another locale for experiencing a sports culture. Resorts and hotels in a rural atmosphere flourished in the Catskill Mountains. For working- and middle-class Jewish urbanites in Chicago and Detroit, summer vacation spots like South Haven, Michigan, provided sports and recreation.

Through the auspices of several Jewish institutions, women and girls participated in sport and physical education for enhancing health, for taking part in Americanization programs, or for engaging in physical recreation deemed appropriate for females. As sport increasingly played a significant role in American society in the twentieth century, sport also became part of Jewish women's experiences in American life. Through the years, women and girls participated in swimming, basketball, gymnastics, tennis, track, or golf in their physical pursuits in American culture.

BIBLIOGRAPHY

Addams, Jane. *Spirit of Youth and the City Streets* (1923), and *Twenty Years at Hull-House* (1910, 1960); Bellow, Adam. *The Educational Alliance: A Centennial Celebration* (1990); Blitzer, Grace Rosenberg. "Junior Jottings—and Golf and Tennis." *The American Hebrew* 115 (November 7, 1924): 853; Educational Alliance Records. YIVO Institute for Jewish Research, YIVO Archives, NYC; Eisen, George. "Sport, Recreation and Gender: Jewish Immigrant Women in Turn-of-the-Century America (1880–1920)." *Journal of Sport History* 18 (Spring 1991): 103–120; Ewen, Elizabeth. *Immigrant Women in the Land of Dollars, Life and Culture on the Lower East Side, 1890–1925* (1985); Gems, Gerald R. "Sport and the Forging of a Jewish-American Culture: The Chicago Hebrew Institute." *AJH* 83 (March 1995): 15–26; Goodman, Cary. *Choosing Sides: Playground and Street Life on the Lower East Side* (1979); Gumpert, Bertram Jay. "A Rising Tennis Star." *The American Hebrew* 123 (August 3, 1928): 389; "Highlights on Links and Polo Fields." *The American Hebrew* 123 (June 1, 1928): 94+; "Hows and Whys of Big Burg's Y's. 110th Street Y.W.H.A. Has Most Comprehensive Physical Education System of Type in Entire Country." *New York Post*, January 17, 1936; Irene Kaufmann Settlement House, Pittsburgh, Pa. *I.K.S. Neighbors*. Vols. 1–5 (1923–1927); Jewish Training School of Chicago. *Second Annual Report of the Executive Board* (1890–1891). Chicago Jewish Archives/Spertus Institute, Chicago, Ill.; Kraus, Bea. "South Haven's Jewish Resort Era: Its Pioneers, Builders & Vacationers." *Michigan Jewish History* 35 (Winter 1994): 20–25; Levine, Peter. "The American Hebrew Looks at 'Our Crowd': The Jewish Country Club in the 1920s." *AJH* 83 (March 1995): 27–49, and *Ellis Island to Ebbets Field: Sport and the American Jewish Experience* (1992); "Lillian Copeland, 59, Dies; Won Olympic Medal in 1932." *NYTimes*, July 8, 1964, 35:1; Meites, Hyman L. ed. *History of the Jews of Chicago* (1927); "Miss Epstein Dead; Olympics Official." *NYTimes*, August 27, 1938, 13:4; "New Home for Girls' Club." *NYTimes*, April 26, 1914; Peiss, Kathy. *Cheap Amusements: Working Women and Leisure in Turn-of-the-Century New York* (1986); Polacheck, Hilda Satt. *I Came A Stranger: The Story of a Hull-House Girl*. Edited by Dena J. Polacheck Epstein (1989); Postal, Bernard, Jesse Silver, and Roy Silver. *Encyclopedia of Jews in Sports* (1965); Rabinowitz, Benjamin. *The Young Men's Hebrew Association (1854–1913)* (1948); Riess, Steven A. *City Games: The Evolution of American Urban Society and the Rise of Sports* (1989), and "Sport and the American Jew: A Second Look." *AJH* 83 (March 1995): 1–14; Rosenberger, Ruth. "Personalities in the World of Golf and Tennis." *The American Hebrew* 124 (May 3, 1929): 966+; Seman, Philip L. "The Problem of the Leisure Hour, A Challenge: One Way of Meeting It." Jewish Peoples' Institute Annual Report, Chicago (1927); Slater, Robert. *Great Jews in Sports* (1983. Rev. ed. 1992); Soule, Aileen Riggin. Interview with author, June 16, 1996. Department of History, Western Michigan University, Kalamazoo, Mich; Spears, Betty. "Senda Berenson Abbott: New Woman, New Sport." In *A Century of Women's Basketball: From Frailty to Final Four*, edited by Joan S. Hult and Marianna Trekel (1991); "Thrice Western Women's Golf Champion." *The American Hebrew* 117 (November 6, 1925): 828); Wald, Lillian D. *The House on Henry Street* (1915, 1971); Young Women's Hebrew Association. Records. 92nd Street Young Men's-Young Women's Hebrew Association Archives, New York; Young Women's Union of Philadelphia. Neighborhood Centre Records. Philadelphia Jewish Archives Center, Balch Institute, Philadelphia, Pa.

LINDA J. BORISH

STEIMER, MOLLIE (1897–1980)

Mollie Steimer, a leading anarchist and advocate for the rights of political prisoners, was a codefendant in one of the most publicized antiradical trials in American history.

Born on November 21, 1897, in Dunaevtsy, Russia, Steimer arrived in New York City at age fifteen, along with her father, her mother Fannie Steimer, and five brothers and sisters. To help support her family, she worked in a garment factory, where she was first exposed to radicalism. In 1917, she became an anarchist and joined a group of Jewish radicals calling itself *Frayheyt* [Liberty]. The group supported the Russian Revolution and, in addition to publishing a Yiddish journal, secretly distributed leaflets and other propaganda materials that were banned by wartime legislation. Among these materials were two brochures—one in English and one in Yiddish—opposing American intervention in the Russian Revolution and strongly criticizing the U.S. Government.

The two brochures soon got *Frayheyt* in trouble with government authorities. One of the group's members was arrested for distributing the leaflets. After he agreed to cooperate with military intelligence, six other members, including Steimer, were arrested and charged with conspiring to violate the Sedition Act.

The subsequent trial became a *cause célèbre*, notable as the first major prosecution under the Sedition Act and for the blatant infringement of the defendants' rights. Steimer and her codefendants were represented by Harry Weinberger, a well-known advocate for conscientious objectors, pacifists, and radicals. The two-week trial began on October 10, 1918. Weinberger argued that, since the actions of the defendants did not directly interfere with the war effort, they were not punishable under the provisions of the Sedition Act. Despite his defense, all but one of the defendants were found guilty, and four were given major sentences. Jacob Abrams, Hyman Lachowsky, and Samuel Lipman were each sentenced to twenty years in prison and fined $1,000, while Steimer received fifteen years and a fine of $5,000. All four appealed their case to the Supreme Court.

Released on bail, Steimer continued her radical activities. She was befriended by anarchist EMMA GOLDMAN, who had just been released from prison herself. Goldman admired Steimer's uncompromising attitude toward anarchist ideals and called her "a sort of Alexander Berkman in skirts." Steimer's continued radical activities resulted in at least eight arrests while her case was on appeal, and finally led to her imprisonment on Blackwell's Island in the East River toward the end of 1919. While she was there, the Supreme Court upheld her conviction and those of her colleagues. Steimer was transferred to a prison in Jefferson City, Missouri, where she was put to work sewing garments.

Meanwhile, Harry Weinberger continued his efforts to free the four anarchists, this time hoping to obtain a pardon, a decree of amnesty, or deportation to Russia. He was able to elicit a groundswell of support for the group, not only among Jewish radicals but also among a number of leading lawyers and intellectuals who were convinced that they had not received a fair trial. Despite such support, Steimer refused to sign a petition for amnesty or to request deportation to Russia. "I do not want any pardon," she wrote to Weinberger. "The word 'pardon' drills my ears and affects my sense of right, which is bad already." She objected to deportation on the basis of her belief that "each person shall live where he or she chooses," and that "No individual has the right to send me out of this, or of any country!" Despite these objections, Weinberger secured the group's release. In 1921, the four anarchists were permitted to be deported to Soviet Russia at their own expense, and received a full pardon on the condition that they never return to the United States.

After arriving in Russia, Steimer was disappointed to find that anarchists were little more welcome than in the United States. Goldman and Berkman, who had been deported a few months before her, had already left the country in disillusionment. The new communist regime tolerated no opposition to state policy and viewed the anarchists as a threat to its authority. Promising to "advocate my ideal, anarchist communism, in whatever country I shall be," Steimer started spreading propaganda for anarchist causes and on behalf of Soviet political prisoners.

Not long after her arrival in Russia, Steimer met and fell in love with fellow anarchist Senya Fleshin, a Russian-born Jew who had immigrated to the United States and returned after the Revolution. Although the two never married, they became devoted companions. Like Steimer, Fleshin was disillusioned with the Soviet regime, and the two joined forces in their work to help political prisoners. In 1922, Steimer and Fleshin were arrested by the Soviet secret police, accused of having anarchist connections in Europe and the United States. They were sentenced to two years' exile in Siberia, but were released when they staged a hunger strike. After being arrested a second time and staging another hunger strike, the two were expelled from the Soviet Union, leaving for Germany in 1923.

During the next fifteen years, Steimer and Fleshin moved between Berlin and Paris, aiding political prisoners and anarchist exiles. They maintained contacts with countless prisoners—to whom they sent care packages—and with radicals in several countries, many of whom they received as guests. The couple also took part in the major debates of the day concerning radical politics, including the controversy surrounding Peter Arshinov's *Organizational Platform*. Arshinov proposed the creation of a central executive committee to guide the anarchist movement, a move that Steimer and Fleshin felt would lead to authoritarianism and a subversion of anarchist principles.

At the beginning of World War II, Steimer and Fleshin were living in Paris. With the invasion of France by the Nazis they faced danger both as radicals and Jews. In 1940, Steimer was arrested and taken to an internment camp, while Fleshin fled to the unoccupied sector. Able to negotiate her release, Steimer was reunited with Fleshin in Marseilles, and the two fled to Mexico City, where they opened a photographic studio and became part of a growing group of political exiles. In 1963, they retired to the town of Cuernavaca. Steimer spent her final years corresponding with fellow radicals and receiving many visitors who admired her as a veteran of the international anarchist movement. She died on July 23, 1980, at age eighty-two.

BIBLIOGRAPHY

Avrich, Paul. *Anarchist Portraits* (1988); Szajkowski, Zosa. "Double Jeopardy—The Abrams Case of 1919." *American Jewish Archives* 23 (April 1971): 8–32.

ERIC L. GOLDSTEIN

STEIN, GERTRUDE (1874–1946)

Gertrude Stein, the American modernist writer, was an international celebrity, an artistic iconoclast, and a self-proclaimed genius. Her experiments in poetry and prose still puzzle structuralist, deconstructionist, and feminist critics. Her contribution to American literature, however, is not in doubt: Scholars consider Stein an important innovator whose attention to language and questioning of narrative conventions influenced such writers as Ernest Hemingway and Sherwood Anderson. But even those who never read Stein's works are familiar with Stein as a legendary personality. From the early 1900s, when she first arrived in Paris, until her death in 1946, she reigned at the center of a flourishing Parisian salon whose guests included Pablo Picasso and Henri Matisse, Edith Sitwell and Harold Acton, F. Scott Fitzgerald and Thornton Wilder, and scores of other writers, artists, and musicians.

Gertrude Stein was born on February 3, 1874, in Allegheny, Pennsylvania, the youngest of five children—three boys and two girls—of Daniel, a businessman, and Amelia (Keyser) Stein. Both parents were of German Jewish descent. Her father had been born in Bavaria and immigrated to the United States in 1841. The Steins recognized their cultural roots in Judaism, but although Daniel and Amelia Stein were members of a synagogue throughout Gertrude's childhood, the Stein children were not raised to be practicing Jews. Nevertheless, Stein grew up believing strongly that Jews shared certain personal traits, such as superior intelligence, financial acumen, and loyalty to one another.

When Gertrude was an infant, the Stein family left Pennsylvania and traveled back to Europe. Stein spent her early years in Austria and later in France. In 1879, the Steins returned to America, settling first in Baltimore, where Amelia Stein had relatives, and then, in 1880, moving to Oakland, California, where Stein spent the rest of her youth. Of Oakland she was later to utter the famous remark, "There is no there there." Claiming that the community provided little cultural stimulation, she countered the lack by reading voraciously. Shakespeare, Scott, Richardson, Fielding, and Wordsworth were among her favorite authors.

After both parents died—her mother in 1888 and her father in 1891—Stein's eldest brother, Michael, moved his four siblings to San Francisco, where he directed a street railway company. In 1892, with her brother Leo and sister Bertha, Stein moved to Baltimore to live with an aunt. Throughout Stein's youth, Leo was her closest companion and confidante. When he decided to leave Baltimore to enroll at Harvard, Stein followed without hesitation.

Because Harvard was closed to women, in the fall of 1893 Stein enrolled at the Harvard Annex, the precursor to Radcliffe College, where she studied for four years, graduating in 1897. She studied with William

James, George Santayana, Josiah Royce, and Hugo Munsterberg, among others, and later cited James as the most significant influence of her college years. Stein worked in James's psychology laboratory, carrying out experiments in automatic writing that became the basis of her first publication, "Normal Motor

A startling innovator in style, in both prose and poetry, Gertrude Stein left a lasting mark on American literature. Her life in Paris with lover ALICE B. TOKLAS, *surrounded by the great artists and writers of the time, inspired the same sort of bafflement and admiration as her work. [Library of Congress]*

Automatism" (coauthored with a classmate, Leon Solomons), which was published in the *Psychological Review* in 1896.

Although some critics later connected Stein's experimental writings to these laboratory experiments, it is more likely that the experiments inspired Stein's interest in subconscious layers of personality. In early notebooks and various literary portraits, one can see Stein attempting to discover the "bottom nature," as she put it, of her friends, acquaintances, and her own personality. Because Stein expressed an interest in studying psychology, James suggested that she continue her education at the Johns Hopkins Medical School. Following his advice, she began to study at Johns Hopkins in the fall of 1897. But her enthusiasm for scientific coursework soon waned, and her grades plummeted.

Besides disappointment in her studies, Stein, not for the first time, suffered in her personal life. Her occasional writings during her undergraduate years at Radcliffe reveal a troubled and depressed young woman, unable to envision herself fitting into such prescribed roles as wife and mother. Her "red deeps," as she termed her tumultuous feelings, became exacerbated at Johns Hopkins, where her love for another woman was not reciprocated. This emotional crisis made its way into her first extended piece of fiction, *Things As They Are* (1903), which was published posthumously.

Lonely and despondent, Stein decided to leave Johns Hopkins and follow her brother Leo to Europe, where he had recently settled. The two lived first in London in 1902 and then in Paris in 1903, where Stein joined him in his flat at 27 rue de Fleurus, in the Montparnasse district of the city. Soon their brother Michael, his wife, Sarah, and their son, Allan, took up residence nearby.

Although the Steins' expatriation was not unusual at a time when many artists, writers, and intellectuals found a more hospitable environment in Europe than in the United States, Stein sought in Paris a liberation from the strictures of American society that made her feel like an outcast. In a community of artists and writers who were trying to invent a new language in painting, poetry, and prose, Stein was able to create her own identity as a literary pioneer. In a community that accepted and even affirmed a wide range of sexual identities, Stein did not need to fear censure.

Stein began writing earnestly in Europe. Her two early works, *Three Lives*, a collection of stories loosely modeled on Flaubert's *Trois Contes*, and *The Making of Americans*, a novel, are based largely on her own life, concerns, and struggles. The protagonist of each story in *Three Lives* is a woman who does not conform to mainstream society because of ethnic or racial difference. The setting of Baltimore serves to represent America at large. Of the three stories, "Melanctha" has received most attention, partly because it is the longest story, and partly because Melanctha, the central character, and her lover, a physician, are African American. In depicting their troubled love affair, Stein pits the sexually impulsive Melanctha against the more cerebral Jeff Campbell to portray the pain and frustration both feel as they try, but fail, to understand each other. Alienated from white society because of their color, they cannot find a sense of community with each other. Written with the pain of her own thwarted affair still afflicting her, Stein was concerned less with exploring racial issues than with reconsidering her own feelings of loneliness.

The Making of Americans, written from 1906 to 1911, was not published in its entirety until 1966. More than *Three Lives*, this book is stylistically unconventional, reflecting Stein's interest in creating a sense of "continuous present" that represents our experience of time. Even an abridged version that appeared in 1934 seemed to most readers bloated and inaccessible because of its long, rambling, repetitious sentences and paragraphs. In her effort to explore the shaping of American identity, she used herself and her family as representative Americans. The main characters, the Herslands, are barely fictionalized versions of the Steins, with Gertrude Stein appearing as the depressed and unhappy Martha. Much of the book describes and reiterates autobiographical episodes. While it has served some of Stein's biographers as a source for documenting her life, it has not won Stein many admirers.

Nevertheless, writing these two works persuaded Stein that she had found her vocation. Her growing confidence, however, was not evident to visitors at the rue de Fleurus. Friends who remember Stein in the first years after her arrival in Paris describe a quiet, reticent woman who sat in the shadows of her loquacious brother. Leo, eagerly engaged in art collecting and formulating his own aesthetic theories, claimed the role of family intellectual. Unfortunately, he had no admiration for his sister's writing.

But Stein soon found ample encouragement from her new friend ALICE B. TOKLAS, who arrived in Paris in 1907 and soon replaced Leo in Stein's affections and in her life. When Leo moved out of the rue de Fleurus apartment, Toklas moved in, becoming Stein's lifelong companion. They continued to make their home in Paris and later spent part of the year at Bilignin in the south of France, where they rented a house.

With Toklas as appreciative reader, Stein felt free to experiment more boldly than she had before. In *Tender Buttons* (1912), she created verbal collages that have been compared, in effect, to the cubist paintings of her friends Picasso, Georges Braque, and Juan Gris. Stein aimed in these pieces, and also in many later works, to revitalize language by stripping words of their historical and cultural connotations. Sometimes she believed that merely by repeating a word, she could divest it of its contextual barnacles. The most familiar line that demonstrates this technique comes from the poem "Sacred Emily": "Rose is a rose is a rose is a rose." In her attempt to achieve an accurate representation of her own experienced reality, she juxtaposed words and phrases in an order that defied conventional logic and readers' expectations. Most of Stein's experimental works were published in small literary magazines or by vanity presses. Toklas often took upon herself the task of arranging for the publication of Stein's works.

During World War I, Stein and Toklas left Paris for Mallorca. During this period of isolation, Stein wrote short pieces in which she developed further the technique she had used in *Tender Buttons*, juxtaposing mundane descriptions (of weather conditions and food, for example), bits of conversation, and random reflections. Yet these works reflect Stein's interest not only with artistic experimentation, but with exploring her feelings about Alice Toklas, their relationship, and their future together. The Mallorcan pieces include many exclamations of exuberant love, sometimes expressed in private code, as well as feelings of jealousy and insecurity. Although some biographers portray the Mallorcan period as an idyllic honeymoon, a careful reading of Stein's works suggests that the atmosphere often was tense and even volatile.

When Stein and Toklas returned to France in 1916, the two women volunteered their services for the American Fund for French Wounded. Stein learned to drive, and she and Toklas delivered hospital supplies throughout the south of France. The sight of the two atop their Ford truck has been recalled vividly in the memoirs of many of their contemporaries.

In the 1920s, Stein's lively literary and artistic salon attracted a growing population of young American expatriates whom Stein called the Lost Generation—lost, she said, because they had been too young to fight in World War I and therefore had found no political or social cause to inspire them. Among these lost young men, the most notable was Ernest Hemingway, whose attentions to Stein inspired Toklas's jealousy. Toklas eventually succeeded in banning Hemingway from the rue de Fleurus, but not before

Hemingway took Stein's words for the epigraph of his first novel, *The Sun Also Rises*.

In 1926, when Stein was invited to lecture at Oxford and Cambridge, she offered her first sustained discussion of the theoretical basis for her experimental prose. In "Composition As Explanation," she argues that cultural and artistic contexts affect the way a literary work is both written and read. But writer and reader sometimes do not share the same context at the same time. When writers bring to their works new patterns of thinking and perceiving, readers may deem their creations avant-garde and, sometimes, impenetrable. Stein cited her own invention of the "continuous present" as a technique that was "natural" to her, but difficult for some of her readers. "Composition As Explanation" was followed by such pieces as "Sentences and Paragraphs" (1930) and *What Are Masterpieces and Why Are There So Few of Them* (1935), both of which served as guides for understanding modernist literary experiments. These cogent, thoughtful works testify to the deep and complex intellectual basis of Stein's literary productions.

By the 1930s, Stein had gained a reputation as a literary innovator, but her works were read only by a small audience: the writers who frequented her salon, the readers of the "little magazines" in which she was published, and her circle of Parisian friends. She longed for wider recognition, however, and decided to take the advice of some American friends—the music critic Carl Van Vechten and the publisher Bennett Cerf, among them—and write her memoirs. When *The Autobiography of Alice B. Toklas* was published in 1933, Gertrude Stein at last found the fame that she had sought for so long. This witty, gossipy, and irreverent memoir created the public legend of Gertrude Stein.

Suddenly, Stein became a sought-after personality on both sides of the Atlantic. The literary lion who landed in New York in October 1934 for a much-publicized lecture tour bore no resemblance to the vulnerable young woman who had left three decades before. Reporters thronged the ship, interviewers and photographers followed her everywhere, and her fans packed auditoriums to hear her talk.

Yet as delighted as she was with recognition and accolades, privately Stein wondered if her identity as a writer had been compromised. In experimental pieces written in the 1930s, she questioned the effect of publicity and readers' expectations on her ability to be true to her own aims as a writer. Although she continued to produce popular books, including *Everybody's Autobiography* (1937) (a sequel to *The Autobiography of Alice B. Toklas*); *Paris, France* (1940), an homage to her adopted city; and *Brewsie and Willie* (1945), an affectionate tribute to the American soldiers who fought in World War II, she never stopped writing experimental prose.

Because Stein never confined herself to any genre, some readers may know her through her plays, which sometimes find their way into the repertory of experimental or college theatre groups. Although many of her plays were not written to be staged, two were set to music by Stein's close friend Virgil Thomson: *Four Saints in Three Acts*, an opera featuring Saint Theresa of Avila, and *The Mother of Them All*, which celebrates the life and work of Susan B. Anthony. Their repetitious lyrics, lack of character development or plot, and unremarkable score have not earned them wide acclaim.

Stein's reputation as an avant-garde writer is based largely on her experimental, hermetic works: pieces that have been collected in eight volumes published by Yale University Press and in several other collections. In evaluating criticism of these works, it is important to remember that Stein often wrote hermetic pieces in order to veil her lesbian relationship with Toklas and to explore personal issues that she did not want outsiders to understand. Although Stein defended her work by asserting that she wanted to challenge her readers' preconceptions about language and narrative, she also used her writing to dissect and probe her own "bottom nature." While it is tempting to explain Stein's experimental writing as her rebellion against a literary patriarchy, or her creation of a literary cubism, no single explanation is viable for all of her works.

Stein and Toklas remained in France during World War II. Their American friends feared for the safety of the two Jewish women and encouraged them to flee. But they fled only as far south as Bilignin, where they waited out the war and scrounged for food and necessities. It is likely that they were protected by a few French friends with ties to the Vichy government. Stein herself never spoke out on behalf of the persecuted Jews.

After the war, Stein, who had suffered from stomach problems throughout her life, was diagnosed with stomach cancer. She died on July 27, 1946, at the American Hospital at Neuilly-sur-Seine. Gertrude Stein is buried at the Père-Lachaise Cemetery in Paris.

SELECTED WORKS BY GERTRUDE STEIN

The Autobiography of Alice B. Toklas (1933); *Everybody's Autobiography* (1937); *The Making of Americans* (1966); *Paris, France* (1940); *Three Lives* (1909); *Wars I Have Seen* (1945); *The Writings of Gertrude Stein*, Yale edition. 8 vols. (1951–1958).

BIBLIOGRAPHY

AJYB 49:618; *BEOAJ*; Bridgman, Richard. *Gertrude Stein in Pieces* (1970); Brinnin, John Malcolm. *The Third Rose: Gertrude Stein and Her World* (1959), and *Selected Operas and Plays*, editor; DeKoven, Marianne. *A Different Language: Gertrude Stein's Experimental Writing* (1983); *DAB* 4; *EJ*; Haas, Robert Bartlett, ed. *How Writing is Written* (1974), and *A Primer for the Gradual Understanding of Gertrude Stein* (1971), and *Reflections on the Atom Bomb* (1973); Mellow, James. *Charmed Circle: Gertrude Stein and Company* (1974); Meyerowitz, Patricia, ed. *Gertrude Stein: Writings and Lectures 1911–1945* (1967); *NAW*; Obituary. *NYTimes*, July 28, 1946, 40:6; Simon, Linda. *The Biography of Alice B. Toklas* (1977, reprint 1991); Simon, Linda, ed. *Gertrude Stein Remembered* (1994); Stein, Gertrude. Papers. American Literature Collection. Beinecke Library, Yale University, New Haven, Conn.; *UJE*; Vechten, Carl Van, ed. *Selected Writings of Gertrude Stein* (1962); Walker, Jayne. "Gertrude Stein." In *American Women Writers* (1983), and *The Making of a Modernist: Gertrude Stein from* Three Lives *to* Tender Buttons (1984); White, Ray Lewis. *Gertrude Stein and Alice B. Toklas: A Reference Guide* (1984); *WWIAJ* (1938); *WWWIA* 2.

LINDA SIMON

STEIN, HANNAH (1920–1973)

Hannah Stein wrote "The ultimate need is the need for a meaning of existence. We can only be understood, and thus respected by others, if we are clear as to the purpose of our own existence," quoted in *Six Citizens in Search of a Cause* by John R. Coleman (1974). She found her own purpose, and renown, as an advocate for the economically disadvantaged in the United States and Israel. During her fourteen-year tenure as the executive director of the NATIONAL COUNCIL OF JEWISH WOMEN (NCJW), Stein worked to establish job-training programs for poor women as well as day care for their children.

Born in Berlin, Germany, on May 30, 1920, Stein was nearing adolescence when Hitler began his rise to power. Her father, an attorney, had both the means and the foresight to send her to London to study in 1933. She stayed there until the end of World War II, earning a degree in journalism at St. Andrews College. During this time, she aligned herself with the Zionist movement and was elected president of the Zionist Youth of Great Britain in 1943. Immediately after the war, she worked as a journalist, reporting on war refugees in western Europe and Palestine. Soon after the war, her parents separated. Her father sought refuge in Palestine, while Stein accompanied her mother to the United States. There, she worked as a fund-raiser for the Zionist Organization of America from 1946 to 1958. She then began her professional association with the NCJW.

Working in cooperation with other advocacy organizations, including the National Council of Negro Women and the United Church Women, Stein helped to establish the Women in Community Service (WICS) coalition, mobilizing volunteer-service programs in aid of disadvantaged women. In her role as executive director, she instituted the NCJW's first public fund-raising campaign, soliciting donations for both the WICS and an NCJW educational research center in Jerusalem. She was also involved in NCJW investigations of American day-care and juvenile-justice facilities.

Hannah Stein died of cancer on September 11, 1973, in New York City. The impact of her life's work survives her. Friends and comrades remember her as a "creative, dynamic, women's libber." As a self-proclaimed feminist and a Jewish professional who looked beyond her own people, Stein's infuence was felt by Jewish and non-Jewish individuals in needy communities throughout the western world.

BIBLIOGRAPHY

AJYB 75:657; Coleman, John R. *Six Citizens in Search of a Cause: Hannah Stein Memorial Lecture* (1974); Groiziani, Bernice. *Where There's A Woman: Seventy-Five Years of History as Lived by the National Council of Jewish Women* (1967); Obituary. *NYTimes*, September 13, 1973, 52:3; Powers, Helen. Interview by author, 1995; *WWWIA* 6.

JESSICA BERGER

STEINEM, GLORIA (b. 1934)

She was born to a rebellious Scotch Presbyterian mother, raised in Theosophy, and baptized in a Congregational church at the age of ten because her mother thought she should be old enough to remember it. She lost what little interest she had in religion when she became a feminist and started "wondering why God always looks like the ruling class," but she still loves the pagan parts of Christmas—the tree, presents, and midnight Mass. With all this, what is Gloria Steinem doing in a Jewish women's encyclopedia?

She is included here because her father was a Jew, because she considers herself an outsider and sees Jews as the quintessential out-group, and because she feels drawn to the spirituality and social justice agenda of Jewish feminism. She is here because, as she puts it, "Never in my life have I identified myself as a Christian, but wherever there is anti-Semitism, I identify as a Jew." Finally, she is here because in the eyes of the

world she is Jewish, and thus whatever she does is associated with Jews and Judaism, for good or for ill.

When historians distill the essence of the women's movement known as the Second Wave (as opposed to the suffrage campaign, the First Wave), they often embody it in two names—Betty Friedan and Gloria Steinem—both ground-breaking pioneers, both identified as Jews. By the same token, when extremists of the ultra-right excoriate feminism, they name Steinem (along with Friedan and former Congresswoman Bella Abzug) as a leader of the "Jewish conspiracy" to destroy the Christian family. They claim that the struggle for abortion rights is a Jewish plot to kill Christian babies, or that empowering children, women, and minorities is a threat to the God-given hegemony of white Christian men. If Steinem is their Jew, she is ours.

Although she is recognized around the world as a writer, speaker, political activist, and feminist visionary, the facts about Gloria Steinem's Jewish origins, tenuous and meager though they may be, are virtually unknown. To recognize those connections here is not to exaggerate their significance but merely to acknowledge the unacknowledged and to suggest that even without full-fledged Jewish identity—one forged by affiliation or halakic legitimacy (religious law)—this is a woman who acts Jewishly in the world.

Gloria Steinem was born on March 25, 1934, in Toledo, Ohio, to Ruth and Leo Steinem. Her father, an itinerant antique dealer, spent winters selling his wares from a house trailer, usually with his family in tow; as a result, Gloria did not spend a full year in school until she was twelve years old. In the summers, Leo owned and operated a beach resort at Clark Lake, Michigan, where little Gloria apprenticed herself to the nightclub entertainers and learned to tap-dance.

Steinem's appreciation of Judaism, such as it was, came at the hands of her non-Jewish mother. A former journalist, Ruth Steinem took some pains to make sure both Gloria and her older sister, Susanne, understood the evils of anti-Semitism and knew about the horrific crimes of the Holocaust. Steinem remembers that when she was eight or so, her mother encouraged her to listen to a radio dramatization of Jewish torment under the Nazis and the story of a mother who could not get enough food for her little girl. "This is going on in the world," Ruth Steinem said, "and we must know about it." She also taught her daughters that being Jewish was a proud heritage.

PAULINE PERLMUTTER STEINEM, Gloria's paternal grandmother, was born in Germany after her family's escape from Russia and grew up in Munich, the daughter of a cantor. She achieved the equivalent of a college education in order to become a teacher, then married Joseph Steinem and immigrated to America. Pauline Steinem died when Gloria was five, but she left her granddaughter with vivid "sense memories" of an intelligent, calm, well-organized woman who remains a strong role model. A well-known women's rights activist, chair of the educational committee of the National Woman Suffrage Association, a delegate to the 1908 International Council of Women, and the first woman to be elected to the Toledo Board of Education, Pauline Steinem was also a leader in the movement for vocational education. She was deeply distressed by the gathering stormclouds in Germany. In the mid-1930s, during the early years of the Nazi terror, when it cost five hundred dollars to get a Jew out of Germany and into Palestine, Pauline Steinem managed to rescue many members of her family.

Despite having the benefits of a hard-won education at the University of Toledo and a career as a journalist at a time when she first had to write under a man's name, Ruth Steinem's spirit was broken by the conflict between work and family that caused her to give up the career she loved. In response to this and other strains, she suffered incapacitating depressions and hallucinations. She and Leo divorced in 1945, and eleven-year-old Gloria became housekeeper, cook, and caregiver to her mother during a period that, at best, can be called cheerless and at worst, spiritually and financially impoverished. In her early teens, Gloria performed at local clubs for ten dollars a night, hoping to tap-dance her way out of Toledo. When she was sixteen, she worked as a salesgirl after school and on Saturdays. The following year, she was rescued by Susanne, who persuaded their father, despite the divorce, to take over Ruth's care for one year so that Gloria could get away and live with her sister in Washington, D.C.

In 1952, after graduating from Washington's Western High School, Steinem entered Smith College, where she danced in college productions and majored in government. She spent her junior year in Geneva and a summer in Oxford, earned a Phi Beta Kappa key, and graduated magna cum laude. A Chester Bowles Fellowship sent her to India, where for nearly two years she immersed herself in the culture of a people she grew to love and would often write about, first in a government guidebook, *The 1000 Indias*, and later in essays on the relevance of Gandhian principles to grassroots organizing, especially for the women's movement.

Back in the United States in 1958, she moved to Cambridge, Massachusetts, and worked for Independent Research Service, a group that tried to persuade American students to attend communist youth festivals then being held in Europe. Hoping for a career as a writer, she moved to New York City in 1960, a time when women were expected to be Gal Fridays and gossip columnists, not serious journalists. She managed to cobble a modest living from odd scraps of assignments—working with Harvey Kurtzman, creator of *Mad* magazine, on his new project, *Help!*, a journal of political satire, and contributing short articles to *Glamour*, *Ladies' Home Journal*, and other women's magazines. She also did unsigned pieces for *Esquire*, which eventually published her first bylined piece, a story about the then-new contraceptive pill. A year later, in 1963, Steinem herself made headlines when she got an assignment from *Show* magazine for which she took a job as a Bunny at the Playboy Club and wrote an exposé of the unglamorous working conditions of the club's glorified waitresses—sex objects in rabbit ears and cotton tails.

Regardless of her new celebrity and proven investigative skills, Steinem could not persuade editors to let her cover the political subjects that interested her. Still, rather than be relegated to the girl ghettos of food and fashion, she got as far as writing profiles of people such as Truman Capote and James Baldwin. Simultaneously, she volunteered with Cesar Chavez's United Farm Workers and Robert F. Kennedy's presidential campaign, experiences that amounted to a hands-on political education.

In 1968, she became a founding editor of *New York* magazine, where she was finally able to graft her writing to her political interests in a column that established her as a voice for the voiceless and a force for change. Suddenly the magazine gave her other assignments—political profiles, coverage of the 1968 presidential campaign, the New York City mayoral race, the civil rights, antiwar, and migrant workers' movements, the first moon landing—and with them came the long-awaited satisfaction of being taken seriously. But it was a public hearing on abortion, then illegal in the United States, that radicalized Steinem's perception of what makes an issue "serious." Covering this event made her question why women's lives are rarely considered important enough for media attention and public discourse. It also led her to research the fledgling feminist movement and discover that feminism made sense of her own life.

In 1969, she began what would become a second career as a spokesperson for the women's movement. Often pairing herself with one of her African-American friends—usually Dorothy Pitman Hughes, Flo Kennedy, or Margaret Sloan—Steinem talked on campuses, in community centers, union halls, and

An icon of the women's movement, Gloria Steinem helped to redefine the American woman through her magazine, Ms., her activism in the women's movement, and her personal style. She is a source of fascination for those who apparently cannot reconcile her feminist beliefs with her style and appearance. She is shown here at a women's rights march in New York City in August of 1977. [Bettye Lane]

corporate boardrooms, at sit-ins and street rallies. She talked about the shared origins of race and gender caste systems, how the cultural equation of masculinity with dominance feeds the roots of violence, how sex rules stunt the development of children and suffocate the aspirations of both women and men. She touched women's hearts, blew their minds, and mobilized them to start consciousness-raising groups, lawsuits, legislative strategies, and social change organizations to advance the cause of women's liberation. Generally speaking in those years, her analysis of shared oppression did not extend to the experience of the Jewish people, nor did she then, as she would later, make the analytical connection among sexism, racism, and anti-Semitism.

In 1971, she cofounded *Ms.*—the magazine that roared—the first feminist periodical with a national readership and the first mass-market women's magazine with a revolutionary agenda. In the decades since, her writing has appeared in innumerable magazines, newspapers, anthologies, television commentaries, political campaigns, and film documentaries in

America and internationally. She has been the subject of many media profiles and has appeared on the cover of *Newsweek, McCalls, People, New Woman, Ms.,* and *Parade.*

Never again a pen for hire, she has become a brilliant advocacy journalist whose definition of objectivity includes the overt promotion of justice and whose pursuit of truth is aided, not compromised, by her empathy for the oppressed. What she writes about is what she believes in—women's empowerment and feminist solidarity, racial and economic equality, reproductive freedom, nonsexist child rearing, multicultural education, stopping violence, especially the sexual abuse of women and children, and more recently, preserving the cultures of indigenous peoples and disseminating their lessons of gender balance and balance of nature.

The titles of her books suggest both the evolution of her ideology and her state of mind at the time each was written. *Outrageous Acts and Everyday Rebellions* (1983) is a collection of twenty years of her most enduring, powerfully argued essays, from the Playboy Bunny story to her satirical classic, "If Men Could Menstruate"; from her probing interviews of Patricia Nixon and Jacqueline Kennedy Onassis to the searingly confessional "Ruth's Song," a tribute to her mother. *Marilyn: Norma Jean* (1986) is a warm, sympathetic rendering of the life of Marilyn Monroe, revisited from the perspective of feminist analysis. *Revolution From Within: A Book of Self-Esteem* (1992) describes Steinem's efforts to link internal and external change into a full circle of revolution, partly through a reconsideration of her childhood and the inner life that she had repressed in her lifelong effort to be "useful to people in the outside world"—first her mother, then all of womankind and every other marginalized group. *Moving Beyond Words* (1994), an idiosyncratic compendium of original and previously published works, ranges from a scathing send-up of Freud to a paean to women muscle builders; from an exposé of the censoring power of advertisers to her epiphanies at turning age sixty.

Not content to limit herself to words when action is called for, Steinem has been an indefatigable fundraiser for women's causes and the cofounder of several still-thriving organizations: the Women's Action Alliance (1971), the first national clearinghouse for information and technical assistance on women's issues and projects; the National Women's Political Caucus (1971), a bipartisan organization devoted to getting pro-equity women into elected and appointed office; the Ms. Foundation for Women (1972), which was originally founded to channel the (nonexistent) profits

of *Ms.* magazine into women's activities, and which now raises and distributes funds for grassroots projects that empower women and girls; the Coalition of Labor Union Women (1974), a national group devoted to equalizing women's position in the labor movement; and Voters for Choice (1979), a bipartisan political action committee that supports candidates pledged to protect reproductive freedom.

She has played a major role—as speaker, delegate, organizer, commissioner, journalist, or scribe—at many important public events, among them every Democratic convention since 1968, a conference of journalists at the united Nations Women's Conference in 1975 in Mexico City, and the 1977 National Women's Conference convened by Congresswoman BELLA ABZUG and others as a kind of Constitutional Convention for Women. She has also been involved in innumerable electoral campaigns, most notably the presidential bids of Robert F. Kennedy, George McGovern, Shirley Chisholm, and Walter Mondale and his running mate Geraldine Ferraro, as well as the congressional campaigns of Colorado representative Patricia Schroeder, Maryland senator Barbara Mikulski, Texas governor Ann Richards, and Illinois senator Carol Moseley-Braun.

Steinem does have at least one meaningful current Jewish connection. Every Passover for nearly twenty years, she has joined a small group of "seder sisters"—E.M. BRONER, PHYLLIS CHESLER, Lilly Rivlin, Michelle Landsberg, Bea Kreloff, Edith Isaac-Rose, and LETTY COTTIN POGREBIN—Jewish women in New York City who plan and perform a women's seder, usually on the third night of Passover. The founding premise of this seder is that women matter, that women must be acknowledged for their roles in the Exodus story and their current struggle for equality in Jewish life. Using traditional ritual objects and a nontraditionalist Haggadah written by Broner and Naomi Nimrod, the group, led first by Chesler and then by Broner, also draws upon poetry, song, prayer, and personal testimony to honor Jewish women and make room for female expressions of spirituality that have been ignored or eclipsed by traditional manmade, male-led ceremonies. Over the years, Steinem has sung "Dayenu" and "Miriam Ha'Neviah" [Miriam the Prophet], shared in discussions of "The Ten Plagues of Women" and "The Four Questions of Women," and helped to make modern midrash about our Jewish foremothers.

Of her participation in this unique revisionist tradition, Steinem says: "The women's seder introduced me to ritual. It was the first spiritually-centered occasion in my feminist life. Other feminist gatherings had a consciousness-raising component but it was more about the politics of the here and now; it didn't admit of the past or one's spiritual needs. When I feel most drawn to Judaism it's not the law part that attracts me, it's the mystical part, the Kabbalah, the Shechinah [female aspect of God]. I do feel socially drawn to Jewish warmth, sensuality, expressiveness."

Not long ago, Steinem's sister, Susanne, a gemologist, came across a catalog listing items of jewelry that belonged to victims of the Nazis, items that were auctioned to aid Jewish survivors when no one could locate the original owners or their heirs. Today, that catalog rests in the library of the Holocaust Memorial Museum in Washington, D.C. Its bookplate reads: "Donated in honor of Pauline Perlmutter Steinem by Susanne Steinem Patch and Gloria Steinem."

LETTY COTTIN POGREBIN

STEINEM, PAULINE PERLMUTTER (1866–1940)

Pauline Perlmutter Steinem was born on August 4, 1866, to Bertha (Slisower), a homemaker, and Hayman Perlmutter, a cantor, just after the couple left Russia to live in Germany. According to family lore that was passed down to me as her granddaughter, they left as part of the Reform wave of Judaism, and also because Hayman Perlmutter wanted to write operas, a secular interest the Orthodoxy had opposed.

Thinking about this grandmother who died when I was five years old, I imagine that the liberal spirit of Reform Judaism helped her achieve a higher education than was usual for a Jewish female. At a time when young women were told that intellectual activity was a danger to their reproductive systems, my grandmother graduated from the teachers' seminary at Memmington, Bavaria, with a teacher's diploma. Perhaps this spirit also opened the way to her later work as a suffragist—after all, the Reform Movement had broken the prohibition against women and men worshiping together—and to her discovery of Theosophy, a movement that gave an Eastern spiritual base to Reform Judaism's belief in social justice and the moral life. Together with her dedication to her family and the Jewish community, these remained Steinem's lifetime interests: education, universal adult suffrage, and Theosophy.

From samplers of fine embroidery that were passed down to me, however, I also know she learned the traditional arts. At age seventeen or eighteen she was a new graduate, when Joseph Steinem returned to his native Germany to find a suitable wife. While

A suffragist who encouraged newly enfranchised women to go to the polls together to avoid harassment, Pauline Perlmutter Steinem was the first woman elected to the Toledo Board of Education. Her legacy of social activism can be seen in her granddaughter, GLORIA STEINEM. *[American Jewish Archives]*

waiting in the family parlor to meet her older sister, this man in his early thirties, a hardworking immigrant in Toledo, Ohio, saw and fell in love with Pauline Perlmutter. In order to secure her hand, he made two promises: first, that he would send her home every few years to visit her family, and second, that he would sell the small brewery that, together with a few rental properties, was the source of his livelihood. Though her family made the first request, my grandmother herself insisted on the second. She was so opposed to alcohol that only paste vanilla went into her cooking. As a strict vegetarian, she kept both customs, even though she cooked meat for her sons and tolerated wine for others.

They married in 1884. After their first son, Edgar, was born in Germany, they returned to Ohio when Steinem was age nineteen. Three more sons were born in Toledo: Jesse, Clarence, and Leo, who was the youngest and my father.

By all historical evidence, Steinem was a remarkable activist. Over the years, she served as president of the Toledo section of the NATIONAL COUNCIL OF JEWISH WOMEN, national chair of the Sabbath School Committee, president of the Hebrew Associated Charities and Loan Association, president of the Federation of Women's Societies, and on the Ohio Board of Charities.

Given her abiding interest in education, she also helped to develop the Ohio Juvenile Court, was the first woman elected to the Toledo Board of Education, and founded Macomber Vocational High School, the first public school for vocational education. (According to some, the choice between naming the school after her or after Macomber, its financial benefactor, was made by the flip of a coin, but according to others, by anti-Semitism.) She was also an active suffragist, and in the early years of the twentieth century, she became one of the few women listed in *Who's Who in America.*

In the years after my grandmother's death at age seventy-three in January of 1940, I always understood that the woman I had known as "Mama Einie" was admirable. My mother's stories praised her community leadership, her perfect housekeeping, her unaccented English and excellent writing style (which she learned within a few years of arriving in America), and, most of all, her deep love of Theosophy—an interest my mother shared. Though marriage between my middle-class Jewish father and working-class Protestant mother had been opposed by both families, my mother and my mother-in-law gradually grew to love each other. I knew that the Bible passage, "Whither thou goest, I will go . . . thy people shall be my people," had been said by one woman to another, because my mother said it to her mother-in-law, just as the biblical Ruth had said it to Naomi.

Active statewide in the Ohio Woman Suffrage Association, Steinem also headed the educational committee of the National Woman Suffrage Association, traveled abroad in 1908 as one of two U.S. delegates to the International Council of Women, and marched and testified in Washington, D.C. (She wrote a letter of complaint to her senator about the absence of police protection for marchers in 1913.) My family had not concealed these events, but they saw the ways my grandmother served her family and community as more praiseworthy than the ways she tried to transform them. For instance, I knew she had been elected to the school board, but not that she was the first woman elected to any public office in Toledo—perhaps the first in Ohio—or that she was elected on a coalition ticket with the socialists and the anarchists.

There are many stories I cherish. Here are two I've learned only in recent years.

After my grandfather died—either from pneumonia or despair at losing most of his money in the crash of 1929—my grandmother's income was about $500 a month. Before World War II, when ransoming Jews from Nazi Germany was still possible, the price of sending one person to Israel was also $500. Despite opposition from some of her family at spending her money this way—and despite her position as a universalist, not a Zionist—she sent as many relatives as she could.

Women did not yet have the vote nationally when my grandmother ran for the board of education, and many resented the newly won right in Ohio. To frighten women out of the "unnatural" act of voting, gangs of men and boys surrounded the polls, and indulged in what we would now call sexual harassment. My grandmother won by organizing women to go to the polls—together.

It was this sense of unity—with other people and with all living things—that I find inspiring in Pauline Perlmutter Steinem.

BIBLIOGRAPHY

AJYB 7 (1905–1906):105; *NYTimes,* January 7, 1940, 49:3; *WWWIA* 4.

GLORIA STEINEM

STEREOTYPES

Jews, like all minorities, serve the dominant cultures in which they live as a nearly empty canvas on which others imagine their own fears, longings, power, and anxieties. The process of projecting ideas and fantasies is called stereotyping. Scholars have repeatedly demonstrated that stereotypes, in fact, have more to teach about the "stereotyper" than the "stereotyped." In relations between minorities and majorities, particularly when a dominant group suppresses and limits another, those stereotypes play a crucial role in rationalizing the rights of the powerful over the powerless and in justifying why a group is despised.

As complex as the psychological and power dimensions of stereotypes are, they are further complicated by the fact that stereotypes often shape the reality of their objects as well. Stereotypes circulated widely enough and repeated frequently enough become confused with accurate information for both their objects and perpetrators.

In the nineteenth and twentieth centuries, when Americans and their nation were undergoing dramatic transformations—a massive influx of immigrants, industrialization and the rise of corporations, the integration of women, ethnics, and minorities in the workforce, and urbanization—American culture became obsessed with crude and often cruel racial and ethnic stereotypes in literature, popular arts, and the press. Racism and anti-Semitism were powerful forces in American culture, affecting all parts of the political spectrum. European Jews who immigrated by the millions from the mid-nineteenth century to the mid-1920s, along with many other racial and ethnic minorities, were prominent objects of these stereotypes. Freed from the terrors of pogroms and the inability to make a living, Jews in America were nevertheless greeted by a steady stream of anti-Semitism, as evident in entertainment as it was in politics. These stereotypes made them believe that their safety was always tenuous and that their rights in America had to be vigilantly guarded. Jewish immigrants bore the task of becoming American Jews in a nation that was undeniably hostile to them, even as it offered them (limited) economic opportunity. The process of becoming American Jews required them and their children to alter their most basic assumptions about their lives and to join a radically different culture.

From the perspective of the dominant culture, there was little acknowledgment of the many differences among Jews. The "Jew" of anti-Semitic stereotypes—avaricious, unrefined, and menacing—described those who lived in America's urban tenements as well as those whose elegant homes graced the boulevards of large cities.

In truth, the Jews who lived in the United States, primarily in urban centers, were separated from one another by a wide gulf of class, political, cultural, and religious distinctions. In an American society that was exceptionally hostile to racial and ethnic differences in general, and to Jews in particular, Jewish newcomers reflected on their differences from one another in terms of their own Americanization. American Jews, then, were objects of anti-Semitic stereotypes at the same time that they generated stereotypes of one another. What united these two processes was Americanization itself. The ideal of a pure and unified American people created the vicious stereotypes of "outsiders" who many perceived as "invading" the nation. Similarly, the privileged position of even slight acculturation became a powerful tool with which Jewish Americans might chisel fine distinctions about who among them was an American and who was not.

For example, young Jews understood themselves to be American in contrast to their parents who were mired in the Old World. German Jews believed that their "refinement" and wealth made them "really" Americans, unlike the "coarser" Jews of the working class from Eastern Europe who didn't belong. Radical Jews, working men and women from Eastern Europe's Pale of Settlement, claimed to embody more fully the ideals of American life than upper-class German Jews, who lacked the democratic spirit.

These divisions, along with many others, were in part expressed through Jews' recourse to highly developed stereotypes that they themselves elaborated. Most of these stereotypes traveled with them from Europe, and others blossomed in the soil of American Jewish life. All of them drew on some of the anti-Semitic caricatures that literally threatened European Jews' lives and well-being. The ineffective immigrant father, the vulgar and noisy Eastern European Jewish woman, and the smothering but loving Jewish mother—all, in large measure, stereotypes created by Jews of different generations and genders—are popular examples.

These stereotypes served American Jews as a language, albeit a distorting one, to communicate about their future, their past, and their place in the nation. Young Jews' anxieties about how to become Americans were quickly summarized, for example, in their attempt to distance themselves from one of the most popular stereotypes of the time—the failed patriarch, a pious Jewish man who did not embrace the values of capitalism. Masculinity, Americanization, aspirations for mobility, extended family obligations, and Jewishness were each understood in relation to this diminished patriarchal image. Many of these stereotypes, such as the patriarch, faded quickly from collective memory, no longer serving the needs of acculturated Jews. Others have proved remarkably persistent, even when their specific content underwent change. Long-lived stereotypes, such as the Jewish American Princess and the Nice Jewish Girl, reflect Jews' continuing underlying anxieties about American Jewish life.

These stereotypes are frequently linked to gender, and women are far more likely to fill the canvas of others' imaginations than are men. The prominence of gender and family stereotypes (in contrast with some of the classic anti-Semitic stereotypes that focus on economic relations) suggests that American Jews most intimately experienced Jewishness in the private domain of family, love, and marriage. That intimacy, however, became a focus for Jews' self-rejection when those relationships became vehicles for stereotypes of undesirable Jewish behavior.

Throughout the century, these stereotypes have continued to provide each generation of American Jews with highly condensed images of their place in American society as members of families, as participants in the economy, and as sexual and emotional persons. American Jews have left behind the generations of those who had to adjust to an alien physical and cultural terrain, but they continue to negotiate a society that remains uncomfortable for those who stand apart from the majority.

These stereotypes circulate among Jews and are drawn from and appear in jokes and comedy, film, literature, the Jewish press, and daily life. They have no specific origin, belonging instead to a mass culture shared by Jews with the larger society. They do not persist because they embody even a "grain" of truth. To the contrary: The "truth" of these canvases is their ability to reveal that Jews experience their world from the point of view of a majority culture and their place within it.

Stereotypes do not present an agreed-upon reality. Instead, they often express contradictions, such as the belief that a Jewish American Princess is a woman who is both sexually withholding and insatiable. Stereotypes are contradictory because they condense a large number of traits in the person of a single figure, and as expressions of prejudice they draw on irrational processes. They sometimes allow their purveyors to emphasize different features. The same figure, the Jewish Mother or Ghetto Girl, for example, meant different things to different groups of Jews. German and Eastern European Jews, women and men, Jewish professionals and immigrants, literally saw different things as they characterized Jewish experience in terms of their own Americanization.

IMMIGRANT STEREOTYPES— THE GHETTO GIRL

During the early decades of the twentieth century, American Jewish stereotypes drew most consistently upon the differences between the foreign and native born, class distinctions, and women and men. In this period, when millions of Jews lived close to one another in a small number of neighborhoods and cities, their intensely intertwined cultures also drew upon differences of birthplace and religious practice. However, by sheer frequency, gender, class, and generation served as the most consistent sources for common stereotypes.

Many of the stereotypes are unfamiliar to Jews today. With upward mobility, new stereotypes rapidly replaced the old. However, from the 1900s to the 1920s, images of the Ghetto Girl appeared in letters, advice columns, and articles in both the Yiddish- and English-language press of American Jews, in novels, and in the descriptions of more acculturated, as well as professional, Jews, who were social workers, probation officers, and experts on immigrant life.

The stereotype of the young, unmarried Jewish immigrant woman as the Ghetto Girl was an image that had a variety of meanings to the many communities of American Jews. At first, it referred to the significant number of young Jewish working women who lived and worked in the ghetto of New York's Lower East Side. By the 1920s, they may have moved out of the ghetto and worked as clerical workers, retail salespeople, or, for the most ambitious and fortunate, teachers.

The stereotype took on a different meaning for those who wrote about the Ghetto Girl, scolding her and expressing through her their worries about the Americanization of Jews. The Ghetto Girl was consistently associated with desires judged inappropriately excessive. Her clothing was criticized as cheap and exaggerated. Jewish social reformers and commentators described, among her failures, a fondness for bright colors, large paste jewels, and outlandish hairstyles. At the same time, others writing for the mainstream press, not always Jewish, ridiculed these women for wearing the latest fashions that they copied from the garments they sewed for the rich. One New York journalist wrote in 1900 for the *New York Tribune*, "Does Broadway [upper New York] wear a feather? Grand Street [the Lower East Side] dons two, without loss of time. If my lady wears a velvet gown, put together in an East Side sweat shop, may not the girl whose tired fingers fashion it rejoice her soul by wearing a copy of it on the next Sunday?" (Jacob R. Marcus, "Even Solomon in All His Glory Was Not Arrayed Like One of These," *The American Jewish Woman: A Documentary History*, 1981, p. 497).

Some journalists and professionals used the Ghetto Girl's stylishness to prove that immigrant social welfare needs were exaggerated. At the same time, others explained the dangerous sacrifices young women made in order to own fashionable clothing, even "starving" themselves to save for a garment (Interested Reader letter to "Just Between Ourselves Girls," *Jewish Daily News*, vol. 19, January 17, 1904: English page), leading others to worry that working women would abandon their financial responsibility to their families in the process ("Just Between Ourselves Girls," *Jewish Daily News*, vol. 18, December 22, 1903: English page). This fear was not born out. Women provided essential economic support for their households.

The Ghetto Girl's appearance on the canvas of Jewish anxiety elaborated her role as a woman who transgressed boundaries. The stereotype cast these young Jewish women as working consumers who aspired to own and wear things that imitated the rich. Ghetto girls' consumption challenged the hierarchy of American life that placed immigrants close to the bottom. Americanization, to immigrants and the native-born, was visible in what a woman owned and wore. The stereotype suggests that working Jewish women crossed and blurred the boundaries between refined and vulgar American womanhood. By labeling someone a Ghetto Girl, those acculturated Jews outside of the ghetto could proclaim that American society was right to keep rigid boundaries between the foreign- and the native-born, and between those who had good taste and those who lacked it.

At the same time, women whom some called Ghetto Girls were also accused of excessive consumption by the Jewish men they would most likely want to marry. The Yiddish press, particularly its English language pages directed at young Americanizing Jews, focused on the young Jewish woman as an excessive consumer. Headlines about young Jewish women in the *Jewish Daily Forward* screamed, "What's the Matter with the Modern Girl?" (Nathaniel Zalowitz, vol. 26, May 27, 1923: 3), "Trolly Car Girls with Rolls Royce Tastes? (Leo Robbins, vol. 26, May 13, 1923: 3), and "Is the Modern Girl a Mercenary?" (Thelma Kaplan, vol. 9, July 17, 1927: E4). These articles asserted that women's economic dependence on men, and their desire to join the middle-class with its expanded opportunities for consumption, created difficult burdens for Jewish men. Women's desires had to be contained.

Although the stereotypes about young Jewish women were more varied and developed, young Jewish men were subject to stereotyping by other Jews as well. If excessive consumption was the irreducible core of Jewish women's caricature, then failing to be productive, a key quality of the successful American man, powered the image of young Jewish men. The Jewish press often referred to them as "Swells," "Hot Sports," and "Stiffs." Like the Ghetto Girls, these men were consistently criticized for wearing clothing that was too colorful and extreme and were condemned for their extravagance.

Stereotypes that Jews themselves created about young Jewish women and men centered on the relationship between those who made money and those who spent it. These issues appeared to be virtually inseparable from Americanization itself and drew upon the oldest anti-Semitic themes. As Jews aspired to become Americans and enter the middle class, they often foundered on insufficient economic means. Women needed to marry in order to join the middle class. Until well into the 1930s, married women did not work for reasons other than virtual destitution. Immigrant men and their sons who joined the middle class were expected to be the family's sole breadwinners. These men and women then shared the same goals, but their means put them in conflict and generated stereotypes of dangerous consumption and inadequate productivity.

These twin stereotypes were by no means the only ones of their era elaborated by Jews. Jewish male and female anarchists, with specific styles of clothing, hair, personality, and politics, found their way into the drama, literature, and the press of their day. Their radicalism, sometimes admired but most often feared, created for Jews further barriers to membership in the American nation.

At the other end of the political spectrum was the Alrightnik, the vulgar Jew whose economic success gave him undeserved power and standing in the United States. His wife was often the paradigm of conspicuous consumption. These figures too readily absorbed Americanization, abandoning all values of the Old World. Anarchist and Alrightnik were bookends of immigrant experience, extreme comments on Americanization.

The Vulgar Jewish Woman, the other most common stereotype of the period, bore an uncanny resemblance to the Ghetto Girl despite her apparent difference by such measures as class and age. This stereotype was shared by the sexist and anti-Semitic dominant culture, as well as by many Jewish men of different classes. The dominant press portrayed the Vulgar Jewish Woman as greedy, miserly, and lacking taste. Jewish male writers of fiction and journalism caricatured her by her excess of jewelry, her fatness, the brightness of her clothing, and her insatiable desire to own as much as possible. For example, in his novel *Jews Without Money* (1930), the socialist writer Mike Gold described the Vulgar Jewish Woman as betraying her own humble working-class roots through her repulsive consumption. The Anglo-Jewish press also attacked her excess in order to express the fear of how Jews would be seen by America's "better classes." Jewish women of the same class and acculturation constantly warned other women of their "natural" inclination for such distasteful behavior, for loud and nasal voices, and for an absence of good manners. Rather than condemning the image, women's page writers exhorted their readers to monitor these behaviors, which endangered their families' social standing.

JEWISH MOTHERS AND FATHERS: THE CHANGING STEREOTYPES

Even more significant than the stereotypes of young Jewish men and women was the stereotype of the Jewish Mother, which served as the most powerful vehicle for expressing Jews' relationship to American life. Jewish Fathers served as an important immigrant stereotype only to disappear by mid-century.

These stereotypes were no less complex than those of young American Jews. The specific features of the contradictory meanings attributed to the Jewish Mother stereotype may best be understood by examining those who created them. The children who wrote memoirs, songs, films, and novels usually portrayed the Jewish Mother as emotive and caring. Professionals and philanthropists far more often portrayed her as the root of her children's problems.

"Mother" for American Jews, as in most immigrant traditions, was the figure who evoked home. The earliest name for the Jewish Mother stereotype was the *yidishe mame* in Yiddish, the language of home. This Jewish Mother was characterized by devotion, hard work, selflessness, and concern for her family. Her cooking, both because of her skill at making special dishes from "home" and because poverty demanded ingenuity, was definitive. She was also portrayed as pious. The immigrant mother lighting ritual candles was a popular image in American Jewish life through the 1920s.

Paradoxically, many images of the *yidishe mame* from film, memoirs, and the press portrayed her not only as the anchor to the old world but the bridge to the new one. Elizabeth Stern's memoir *My Mother and I* (1917) recounts her mother's willingness to allow her to go to college and begin a life totally alien to their shared world, to which she will never return. Hollywood's Jewish Mothers encouraged their sons in their pursuit of Americanization. *His People*, produced in 1925, and the 1927 *Jazz Singer* featured mothers who encouraged their sons to pursue boxing and jazz singing, each a symbol of a new American leisure culture that broke with the Old World. Similarly, Sara Smolinksy, ANZIA YEZIERSKA's alter ego in her novel *The Breadgivers: The Struggle Between an Old World Father and His New World Daughter* (1975), had a loving, if passive, mother who never forbade Sara to pursue her desire to live on her own as a writer.

These Jewish Mothers are the work of 1920s Americanized Jews. They are variations on the "classic" *yidishe mame* of the Old World. The immense popularity of these films and fictions suggests that they spoke to Jews, in addition to many other groups of acculturating Americans. The Jewish Mother stereotype revealed that the Old World persisted and was even accessible through New World nostalgia. Contained in her home, and even in her kitchen, the Old World, in the persona of the Jewish Mother, had not disappeared but remained to nurture the next generation. She was not of the New World, but in it. The stereotype could be reassuring only if it promised a different future for her children.

The Jewish Mother often served as a contrast to the Jewish Father, a term that never took on comparable cultural significance. Portrayed as a stern patriarch, a man unable to adapt, a dreamer, or some combination, the father was virtually never portrayed as a bridge to the New World, and was most often frozen in time. That inability to move forward was sometimes shown with dignity, but more often as weakness. This stereotype had a short life. Once the dominant image of the Jewish Father was placed in the world of work, something that often eluded the patriarch, he was shorn of the patriarchal features associated with Judaism. Work Americanized Jewish fathers and men.

Another stereotype of the Jewish Mother that reigned in this period was the cultural opposite, the Acculturated Mother. When the *American Hebrew*, a popular English-language paper, asked in 1916, "Who is to blame if there is nothing Jewish about a Jewish home?" the answer was "Find the woman" (Anonymous, November 24, 1916: 84). The husbands of these women were so thoroughly associated with the world of work and profit that, in keeping with the sentiments of the day, they were lost as a source of religion and morality. Addie Richman Altman's 1917 novel *The Harmons: A Story of Jewish Home Life* was a morality tale of failed Jewish motherhood. The Harmon family sang hymns around their piano on Sabbath evening. The Solomons, however, lacked such a pious home and charitable mother. Their son Richard, who slipped into a life of crime and women, explained to Mr. Harmon:

> I don't want to blame my mother, but I cannot help thinking some of my hatred of the Jew is due to her indifference to her religion and her satisfaction in hearing she does not look like a Jewess. . . . Can't you understand I never had a faith to which I could cling? (pp. 67–68).

The successfully Americanized mother stereotype posed as sure a threat to her children as did the nonliterate immigrant. Often associated with card playing and a love of leisure that took her out of the kitchen and away from her family, she failed to provide "Jewishness" for her family.

Neither the good nor the bad Jewish Mothers offered more than the width of a balance beam to negotiate Americanization. Attachment to the Old World threatened to block access to Americanization, and a wide embrace of the new nation threatened to create a vulgar and un-American Jew. The Jewish Mother stereotype constantly cautioned Jews that their access to America was under scrutiny and they were found wanting.

The greater complexity of the stereotyped mother is explained, at least in part, by America's obsession with mothers during this time. Jews' anxieties, like those of the nation, evoked a reassertion of the importance of the domestic hearth for assuring stability. The more avidly mothers were made to be the answer to social and economic change, the more they could be blamed for those victimized by the new urban life—the poor, out-of-wedlock mothers, and youth, for example. Immigrant mothers throughout the nation were associated with nostalgia for the Old World and castigated when they sought to Americanize themselves.

ACCULTURATED POSTWAR JEWS— THE JEWISH MOTHER IS REBORN

Through the dark years of World War II and the incremental steps toward the middle class, American Jews drew upon the stereotypes of the century's first decades. The *yidishe mame* persisted, with more poignancy, to express the mounting awareness of the loss of the Old World. Fathers continued to appear as unable to enter the American economy or to join in effectively. The economic anxieties of the Depression and the disruptions of the war years certainly limited much of the expressions of consumerism and other themes of the more optimistic 1920s.

The major shift in stereotypic images of Jews began in the 1950s and flowered fully in the subsequent decades, taking one direction in the 1960s, and then veering quite differently in the 1970s and 1980s. Jewish women so dominated the easel of American Jewish anxiety that, until the last decade, they virtually eclipsed men for certain periods. The birth of television and the expansion of the film industry intensified the circulation of publicly identified Jewish characters who embodied these stereotypes. Even as anti-Semitism decreased in the United States, ethnic stereotyping persisted. Particularly in the media, the presence of Jewish stereotypes is entirely the work of Jews in the industry.

The years following World War II were the culmination of Jews' efforts to join the middle class. Their strategies for mobility, in combination with America's support for its white population through financing suburban development and home ownership, allowed Jews access to a new form of life. Disproportionate to their numbers, Jews lived in new suburban areas outside of the nation's major urban centers. Their life in the middle class allowed Jewish women to remain at home during their child-rearing years in greater numbers than white women of comparable ages. Jews were participating in higher education in unprecedented numbers, and young Jewish men began to pursue different occupations than in previous generations. They were increasingly bound for professions, whereas their fathers had been self-employed or managers.

Not surprisingly, this rapidly changing world created new images for negotiating American life for the children and grandchildren of immigrants. The Jewish Mother (no longer the *yidishe mame*) became the central image of that era, characterized by nurturance gone awry. She continued to share the *yidishe mame*'s key features, but they were understood in dramatically different terms. The Jewish Mother fed her children to excess, forcing on them food they did not want in quantities that were out of proportion. Her nurturance was suffocating, keeping her sons from developing into "normal" American males. Rather than offered out of concern and responsibility, her caretaking served her own needs. She induced guilt. She gave in order to obligate. She loved because she wanted. She suffered in order to be compensated. Rather than sustaining, she destroyed. Jokes as mild as, "How many Jewish mothers does it take to change a light bulb? None, I'll sit in the dark," captured this meaning. At the same time, the novelty humor books, greeting cards, stand-up nightclub routines, comics, and stationery that appeared over a two-decade period offered portraits that were less than mild. Television programs as diverse as *Saturday Night Live*, *The Mary Tyler Moore Show*, its spinoff *Rhoda*, and *The Nanny* introduced the character to mass audiences. Molly Goldberg, the lovable and wise, but ethnically denuded, Jewish Mother of early television and radio was replaced by meddlesome and oppressive mothers who set about ruining the lives of their children.

Several Jewish male novelists were particularly set on introducing the stereotype in their 1960s fiction. Sophie Portnoy, Philip Roth's nightmare Jewish Mother, left all competitors in the dust in his 1969 best-seller *Portnoy's Complaint*. Alexander, the novel's protagonist, was made into a morally corrupt, emotionally damaged, but successful lawyer by his Jewish mother. The novel was so popular that, for decades,

Jewish women, rabbis, and professionals debated its veracity and defended Jews against its "accusations."

The Jewish Mother was a relational image. She played against a weakened and incompetent Jewish Father. He provided little more than a background to the foregrounded consuming Mother. The suffocating Mother was also linked negatively to her children, who were acculturated and straining to get away from her to a life of adventure and risk.

Sociologists claim the 1950s and 1960s was a period when anti-Semitism was at an all-time low, particularly in contrast with the 1930s and 1940s. Yet studies demonstrate that in the suburbs non-Jewish parents did experience concern for the influence of Jewish children on their own. Jewish children were accused of having excessive freedom, resources, attitudes, and values found repugnant by non-Jewish neighbors. They were "lacking in refinement, materialistic, hedonistic, and aggressive" (Benjamin Ringer, *The Edge of Friendliness: A Study of Jewish Gentile Relationships*, 1967, pp. 71–73; Albert Gordon, *Jews in Suburbia*, 1959). The concerns that non-Jews had about their relatively new proximity to Jews was translated by Jews into anxiety over what was holding them back from further acceptance in the United States. The Jewish Mother was neither anchor nor bridge. As the Jewish Mother dominated the canvas of American life, her image clarified the anxieties created by the dominant culture's ambivalence about incorporating Jewish Americans.

As mother and wife, the Jewish Mother literally embodied the continuity of the Jewish people and the inaccessibility of the dominant culture. It was left to Roth's Alexander Portnoy to make the connection clear. He extolled the *shvitz* [the sweat bath] as the ideal world of Jewish masculinity, "a place without goyim and women" (Philip Roth, *Portnoy's Complaint*, 1969, p. 40).

CONSUMPTION AND PRODUCTIVITY— YOUNG JEWS' STEREOTYPES RE-EMERGE

The Jewish American Princess may well be the first stereotype to compete with the Jewish Mother in postwar American Jewish life. She shares a strong family resemblance to the Jewish Mother by inversion and to the Ghetto Girl by extension.

The Jewish American Princess (JAP), sometimes married and sometimes unmarried, is always portrayed as childless, underscoring her unduly demanding nature. She does not nurture or take domestic responsibility. The JAP is obsessed with her physical attractiveness, but is most often portrayed as unwilling to give sexual pleasure. Instead, her purpose for living is to consume and to adorn her otherwise passive body. She is inseparable from the consumer culture of late twentieth-century United States. The JAP is found in the company of two different generations—her father and her husband/boyfriend. They are portrayed as indulging and enabling her behavior and whims. Their devotion to her needs is essential for her to obtain what she wants. She never produces for herself.

The earliest contemporary Jewish American Princesses appeared in the fictional works *Marjorie Morningstar* by Herman Wouk (1955) and *Goodbye Columbus* by Philip Roth (1959); the former was one of the best-selling books when it was published. Unlike contemporary JAPs, each of these women was beautiful, sexually active, and desirable. Each was also indulged by parents whose social-class mobility was rapid (in Marjorie's case, reversed) and recent. These daughters, more than any other feature of family life, symbolized success. If their daughters married well and entered suburban Jewish life, their parents' work was complete. Each novel's plot turned on the conflict of a Jewish man who, by resisting the demands of American Jewish respectability, lost the Princess and was liberated.

By the early 1980s, the JAP stereotype was widespread throughout the United States. Without hesitation, any group of Jews, particularly young ones, and any group of Americans who lived in areas with a high population of Jews, could reel off her defining characteristics. This well-mapped identity became the butt of hundreds of jokes. *The Official J.A.P. Handbook* by Anna Sequoia (1982), based on *The Preppy Handbook*, designed to identify classically WASP qualities, intensified the "accuracy" of this stereotype. JAP items proliferated—necklaces, bracelets, dolls, and greeting cards—and reinforced the image of the young Jewish woman as a symbiotic consumer, dependent on Jewish men who received nothing from her in return—not love, sex, nurturance, or approval.

Well after *Marjorie Morningstar* and *Goodbye Columbus* were made into popular films, the American film industry presented a trickle of films about Jewish women. *The Heartbreak Kid* (1972), ELAINE MAY's adaptation of Bruce Jay Friedman's story of a vacuous Jewish man who left his repulsive Jewish wife to pursue the embodiment of a gentile goddess in Minnesota, provided a low point in the representations of Jewish women. The years that followed slowly introduced the JAP to viewers. *Private Benjamin* (1980) glorified the ability of a young woman to transcend her

Princess role. *Dirty Dancing* (1987) and *Baby It's You* (1983) depicted relationships between Jewish women and working-class non-Jewish men that liberated them from the middle-class world of Jewish "royalty." *White Palace* (1989) transformed this strategy by allowing a wealthy young Jewish man to escape the grasp of his Jewish world through his love affair with a considerably older working-class waitress. Hollywood has had few enough Jewish women's roles, and while they do not all portray Princesses, none allowed a mutual and loving relationship with a Jewish man.

The images of young Jewish womanhood embodied by the JAP suggest a new relationship between Jews and American culture. Because women are the target of JAP stereotypes, these stereotypes must be understood from the point of view of young men. Mothers are no longer their entrappers; now their future wives are. The JAP's body—her sexuality, adornment, and passivity—serves as a map of American Jewish experience. Placed on the canvas of American Jewish anxiety it demonstrates that Jews are inseparable from their location in the middle class. If the middle class is characterized as a consuming class, then Jews personify consumption.

The 1980s was a period of increased acculturation for Jews. Intermarriage, which began in the 1960s, grew dramatically. Many college quotas limiting Jewish enrollments had been dropped in the 1970s, leading to increased admission of Jews to elite institutions. Jews were entering into professions and work settings once thought unattainable. This openness, rather than reassuring Jews, seemed to intensify the anger and frustrations embodied in the JAP stereotype. The JAP was portrayed as holding the harness that would enslave Jewish men to work, produce, and succeed more—in short, to join the middle-class in the 1980s.

The Jewish men of the baby boom generation, no longer tethered to the more ethnically homogenous world of their youth, now expressed anxiety about being middle class, the quintessentially Jewish identifier, by projecting those desires onto Jewish women. Not unlike the Ghetto Girl, the JAP was portrayed as excessive in wants and desires. But, unlike the working Ghetto Girl, the JAP not only wanted, she withheld and denied, rendering her Jewish partner a slave. The culture's attack on Jewish masculinity, the generalized middle-class anxiety about the accessibility of their class to their children, and a consumer culture that narrowed its definitions of attractiveness and desirability conspired to create the JAP. She was so hateful that separating from her—even destroying her—

promised liberation by self-erasure. To reject the JAP freed Jews from family and class, the most important foundations of postwar American Jewish life.

A Jewish American Prince did appear on the scene, though the stereotype was never elaborated in mass culture to the extent of the JAP. On the other hand, the Prince's characteristics are amazingly consistent with slurs directed at him in the Jewish press as early as the 1920s. He is arrogant, unaware of the needs of others, and unkind to Jewish women. In the persistent, classical anti-Semitic stereotypes of Jewish men, Princes are feminized, incompetent, dishonest, and neurotic—in all cases incomplete men. JAP humor, so apparently antifemale, is all the more complex because the teller of the joke is also its victim. The Prince and Princess remain, nevertheless, hopelessly entwined in representing Jewishness as unacceptable to one another.

For more than a century, American Jews have negotiated the various stages of acculturation through gendered images that define links to and barriers between themselves and the dominant culture. Nothing, in the end, explains these complex cultural images as fully as a nation fundamentally hostile to cultural heterogeneity. American Jews' enormous adaptability to that culture determined that their vulnerability as outsiders would be symbolized by intra-Jewish stereotypes that expressed their fears that Jewishness itself was a barrier to the nation.

BIBLIOGRAPHY

The works on American Jewish women that provide historical and sociological grounding for this discussion of stereotypes are:

Baum, Charlotte, Paula Hyman, and Sonya Michel. *The Jewish Woman in America* (1974); Fishman, Sylvia Barack. *A Breath of Life: Feminism in the American Jewish Community* (1993); Glenn, Susan. *Daughters of the Shtetel: Life and Labor in the Immigrant Generation* (1990); Heinze, Andrew. *Adapting to Abundance: Jewish Immigrants, Mass Consumption, and the Search for American Identity* (1990); Hyman, Paula E. *Gender and Assimilation in Modern Jewish History: The Roles and Representations of Women* (1995); Prell, Riv-Ellen. *Fighting to Become Americans: Jewish Women and Men in Conflict in the Twentieth Century* (forthcoming).

Works on anti-Semitism, Jewish stereotypes, and the overlap of race and gender stereotypes are:

Dinnerstein, Leonard. *Anti-Semitism in America* (1994); Gilman, Sander. *The Jew's Body* (1991); hooks, bell. *Black Looks: Race and Representation* (1992); Roediger, David. *The Wages of Whiteness: Race and the Making of the American Working Class* (1991); Wallace, Michele. *Black Macho and the Myth of the Superwoman* (1978; reprint 1990).

The most significant discussions of Jewish Mothers and Fathers are:

Bellman, Samuel I. "The Jewish Mother's Syndrome." *Congress Bi-Weekly* (December 22, 1965), 3–5; Bienstock, Beverly Gray. "The Changing Image of the American Jewish Mother." In *Changing Images of the Family*, edited by Virginia Tufte and Barbara Myerhoff (1979); Blau, Zena Smith. "In Defense of the Jewish Mother." *Midstream* 13 (1967): 42–49; Eren, Patricia. *The Jew in American Cinema* (1984); Hertzberg Arthur. *The Jews in America: Four Centuries of an Uneasy Encounter* (1989); Howe, Irving. *The World of Our Fathers: The Journey of the East European Jews to America and the Life They Found and Made* (1976); Rothbell, Gladys. "The Jewish Mother: Social Construction of a Popular Image." In *The Jewish Family: Images and Reality*, edited by Steven Cohen and Paula Hyman (1986); Slobin, Mark. *Tenement Songs: The Popular Music of the Jewish Immigrants* (1982).

The most significant works on stereotypes of Jewish women and men, as well as issues of Jewish masculinity, and Jewish relationships are:

Beck, Evelyn Torton. "From 'Kike' to 'JAP': How Misogyny, Anti-Semitism and Racism Construct the "Jewish American Princess." In *Race, Class, and Gender: An Anthology*, edited by Margaret L. Anderson and Patricia Hill Collins (1992); Berger, Maurice. "The Mouse That Never Roars: Jewish Masculinity on American Television." In *Too Jewish? Challenging Traditional Identities*, edited by Norman L. Kleeblatt (1996); Breines, Paul. *Tough Jews: Political Fantasies and the Moral Dilemma of American Jewry* (1990); Chyat, Sherry. "JAP-Baiting on the College Scene." *Lilith: The Jewish Women's Magazine* 17 (1987): 42–49; Dundes, Alan. "The J.A.P. and the J.A.M. in American Jokelore." *Journal of American Folklore* 98 (1985): 456–475; Gilman, Sander L. *Jewish Self Hatred: Anti-Semitism and the Hidden Language of the Jews* (1986); Kennedy, Mopsie Strange. "The Jewish American Prince." *Moment* (May/June 1976): 12; McClain, Ellen Jaffe. *Embracing the Stranger: Intermarriage and the Future of the American Jewish Community* (1995); New, Elisa. "Killing the Princess: The Offense of a Bad Defense." *Tikkun* 2 (1989): 17–18; Pogrebin, Letty Cottin. *Deborah, Golda, and Me* (1989); Prell, Riv-Ellen. "Rage and Representation: Jewish Gender Stereotypes in American Culture." In *Uncertain Terms: Negotiating Gender in American Culture*, edited by Faye Ginsburg and Anna Lowenhaupt Tsing, and "Why Jewish American Princesses Don't Sweat: Desire and Consumption in Postwar American Jewish Culture." In *The People of the Body: Jews and Judaism From An Embodied Perspective*, edited by Howard Eilberg-Schwartz (1992); Schneider, Susan. "In a Coma! I Thought She Was Jewish: Some Truths and Some Speculations about Jewish Women and Sex." *Lilith: The Jewish Women's Magazine* (1979): 5–8; Schnur, Susan. "When a J.A.P. Is Not a Yuppie? Blazes of Truth." *Lilith: The Jewish Women's Magazine* 17 (1987): 10–11; Weinstein, Judith Klein. *Jewish Identity and Self-Esteem: Healing Wounds through Ethnotherapy* (1989).

RIV-ELLEN PRELL

STERN, BESSIE CLEVELAND (1888–1979)

Bessie Cleveland Stern is most recognized for her work as statistician for the Maryland Board of Education. She collected and interpreted data about the Maryland school system from 1921 through 1948, and school officials turned to her for information to support appropriations measures and proposed changes in state laws relating to the schools. Miss Bessie, as she was known, was also active in civic and musical affairs. She led the business and professional unit of the Baltimore League of Women Voters from 1949 to 1964.

Bessie Cleveland Stern was born in Hornell, New York, on February 14, 1888. Her parents, Leopold and Julia (Mehlinger) Stern were Jewish. They moved their family to Buffalo, New York, when Bessie was twelve years old. She began studying piano at age six, studied at the Peabody Conservatory, and continued to give recitals after she was eighty years old. Bessie attended high school in Buffalo, then won a scholarship to Cornell University, where she received her B.A. in 1909 and was elected to Phi Beta Kappa. She taught German and French from 1909 to 1910 at the Silver Creek (New York) High School before beginning her long career as a statistician, using her talents for educational reform and improvement. From 1911 to 1918, she was examiner and statistician for the New York City Board of Estimates and Apportionment and the Committee on Education. Near the end of World War I, she moved to Washington, D.C., as statistician for the U.S. Shipping Board (1918–1919). She was office manager at a silk mill, Arthur & Walter Price, in Paterson, New Jersey, from 1919 to 1920 before returning to school, receiving a master's in education from Harvard University in 1921. Other education included Goucher College, Columbia University, and the University of Chicago. She taught statistics and educational administration at Johns Hopkins University.

In 1921, Stern began her tenure with the recently created Bureau of Measurements of the Maryland State Board of Education. She was director of finance, statistics, and educational measurements at the Maryland State Department of Education until her retirement in 1948. She instituted an annual statewide reporting system for attendance, age level, and study progress to assess the twenty-three-county public school system.

In addition to the League of Women Voters, Stern's civic activities included serving as treasurer for the National Association for the Study of Platoon Schools (1928–1931), member of the Maryland Conference on

Social Work, and secretary of the State Directors of Educational Research (1932–1934). She was also active in the United Nations Association, the city and state libraries, the Central Scholarship Bureau, and the Public Administration Society.

Stern belonged to many other civic organizations. Professional memberships included the American Association of School Administrators, the Department of Superintendence of National Education Association, Maryland State Teachers Association, American Education Research Association, and the American Statistical Association. Hood College awarded her a citation in 1951.

After a long illness, Bessie Cleveland Stern died on March 29, 1979, at a nursing home in Towson, Maryland.

BIBLIOGRAPHY
Maryland Department, Enoch Pratt Free Library, Baltimore; *Who's Who in World Jewry* (1972; *WWIAJ* (1938).

AUDREY J. LYKE

STERN, EDITH MENDEL (1901–1975)

A prolific writer as well as an activist in the mental health field, Edith Stern authored four novels and many guides for laypeople on the subjects of mental illness, aging, and handicapped children. She also wrote numerous articles for popular magazines, including *Collier's*, *Reader's Digest*, the *Saturday Evening Post*, *Literary Digest*, and *Redbook*.

Born Edith Mendel in New York on June 24, 1901, she received a B.A. from Barnard in 1922. She joined the staff of the Alfred A. Knopf publishing house, then, after a few years with the editorial departments of other houses, published the first of a series of novels, *Purse Strings* (1927). This was followed by *Scarlet Heels* (1928), *Men Are Clumsy Lovers* (1934), and *Escape from Youth* (1935).

Edith Mendel married William A. Stern II, who was a lawyer with the Justice Department. Her interest in later life turned to technical books on the subject of mental health, the best known being *Mental Illness: A Guide for the Family*, which was published in 1942. Immensely popular, the book was revised five times before her death. Her other how-to books include *The Attendant's Guide* (1943); *The Housemother's Guide* and *The Mental Hospital: A Guide for the Citizen* (1947); *The Handicapped Child: A Guide for Parents* (1950); *You and Your Aging Parents* with Mabel Ross (1952, revised in 1965); *Notes for After 50* (1955); and *A Full Life After 65* (1963).

Edith Stern was a member of the Maryland Board of Mental Hygiene and a consultant to the National Institute of Mental Health, as well as a director of the Epilepsy League. After her husband's death, she remained in the Washington area, where she died on February 8, 1975, at age seventy-four.

BIBLIOGRAPHY
Obituary. *NYTimes*, February 14, 1975, 35:3; *UJE*; *WWIAJ* (1938); *WWWIA* 6.

MARION SHULEVITZ

STERN, EDITH ROSENWALD (1895–1980)

Edith Rosenwald Stern, philanthropist, community leader, and civil rights activist, was born in Chicago, but resided in New Orleans after marrying business and community leader Edgar Stern. It was in New Orleans and beyond that she left her legacy of commitment to social justice.

Born into the Rosenwald family on May 21, 1895, she inherited more than financial resources from her father, Julius Rosenwald, builder of the Sears, Roebuck retail empire, and her mother, Augusta Nusbaum Rosenwald, matriarch of formidable clan. With her personal involvement, resources, and energy, Edith Rosenwald Stern perpetuated her father's deep interest in social justice, particularly the support of educational institutions serving African Americans. Julius Rosenwald believed in using his wealth and personal influence to address societal inequities and to empower those most distressed by the structural inadequacies of American society. Although there have been much greater American fortunes, the personal commitment of the Rosenwald-Stern family increased the value of their philanthropy exponentially.

When Edith Stern identified a need, she created a solution and engaged others in her cause. The Newcomb School was started when she sought a nurturing but stimulating preschool environment for her own children and their peers. Later, with similar dedication, she gathered other parents to establish The Country Day School.

As a Jew, she had empathy for other persecuted peoples, at the same time encouraging responsibility and empowerment with her philanthropy. Both she and Edgar Stern, in partnership with the African-American community, helped build Dillard University in New Orleans into a premier educational institution, extending the opportunity for high-quality education to four generations of black leaders. By leveraging their contributions with challenge grants, they engaged African-American churches and major American foundations. That technique, at once giving and challenging others to contribute, helped build many institutions in New Orleans and beyond.

Voter education and registration provided another means for Stern to contribute to social justice and equality. Intolerant of the abuses in voting rights in New Orleans, she spearheaded the cleanup of the voting lists, actively organized voter registration, and brought voting machines into the public high schools so that the next generation of voters would be familiar with voting procedures.

Her involvement in civil rights could also be personal. Learning that there was an extraordinary singer in the choir at her cook's church, she went to hear for herself. Determined to advance the young woman's career, she invited the elite of New Orleans to a society dinner party in her home with singer Marian Anderson as guest of honor. No one declined her invitation.

With the same passion and strategy, she led the Jewish community in its philanthropy, encouraged her grandchildren to pursue their own charitable interests, and strongly supported Israel. In a 1973 interview for a video documentary, she attributed her attitude toward giving to her Jewish heritage, saying that "one is permitted to glean one's field only once. Thereafter, others can partake.... One has to tithe." She died in New Orleans on September 11, 1980.

BIBLIOGRAPHY

AJYB 82:373; Hess, Anne [granddaughter]. Interview by author; Hess, Bill [grandson]. Interview by author; Klein, Gerda Weissmann. *A Passion for Sharing* (1984); Obituary. *NYTimes*, September 12, 1980, 3:2; Sosland, Jeffrey. "A School in Every County." In *A Partnership of Jewish Philanthropist Julius Rosenwald and American Black Communities* (n.d.).

SHARON BURDE

STERN, ELIZABETH (1889–1954)

"If I am truly part of America it was my mother, she who does not understand America, who made me so." This description of a young woman's identity formation, offered in the final chapter of Elizabeth Stern's autobiographical *My Mother and I* (1917), observes a poignant irony. Stern's work is notable for its focus on ironies and ambiguities in the lives of young and middle aged American women as they make transitions from one set of generational and cultural expectations to another. Evident in the quoted

passage and in the title of her second autobiographical novel *I Am a Woman—and a Jew* (1926) is a concern with the struggle common to second-generation Jewish immigrant women in the early twentieth century—defining an identity within seemingly mutually exclusive familial, cultural, religious, and national boundaries. In her own life, Elizabeth Stern achieved success within a number of realms and balanced a number of competing roles: fiction writer, journalist, social worker, wife, mother, and an American woman leading a secular life who examined the importance of cultural heritage. She worked for a variety of social service organizations.

Elizabeth Gertrude Levin was born on February 14, 1889, in Skedel, Poland, to Sarah Leah (Rubenstein) and Aaron Levin. Her family immigrated in 1892 to Pittsburgh, where her father was a rabbi. She earned her B.A. from the University of Pittsburgh, then moved to New York and attended the New York School of Social Work, where she met Leon Thomas Stern, who was to become a well-known penologist. They married in 1911 and had two sons, Thomas, in 1913, and Richard, in 1921. They lived in New York City, Galveston, and Philadelphia. She and her husband collaborated in research together on several occasions.

Stern was a writer for the *Philadelphia Sunday Record*, the *New York Times*, the *New York Evening World*, and the *Philadelphia Public Leader*. Written under the pen name "Leah Morton," *I Am a Woman—and a Jew* is the work that focuses most directly on themes of Jewish life in the United States. Telling the story of Leah's early adulthood and middle age, the novel addresses questions of assimilation and position within "the melting pot." Leah must confront a number of culturally inscribed perspectives: her husband's ambivalence about his wife's career, her parents' disapproval of her secular values, a one-time boss's anti-Semitism, and the opinion of some Jewish friends that her marriage to a gentile is "criminal." The meaning of her cultural identity becomes increasingly important to Leah, and the book concludes with this statement: "I belong to my own people. My life is only a tiny atom of their long history." Stern's own sense of identification with Judaism was less definitive than Leah's. She was affiliated first with the Philadelphia Ethical Society and later became active in Quakerism.

In addition to her two autobiographical full-length narratives, Stern published five novels. These books address social relationships and the family dynamic. Several focus on women's roles and a mother's influence on her daughter. Beginning in 1943, Stern turned to biographies and wrote three:

one of business woman Margaret McAvoy Scott, another of inventor Josiah White, and finally *The Women Behind Gandhi*. Only *My Mother and I* and *I Am a Woman—and a Jew* have been reprinted, and Stern has received significantly less recent critical attention than two contemporaries with whom she is sometimes grouped, MARY ANTIN and ANZIA YEZIERSKA. Elizabeth Stern died in Philadelphia in January 1954, at age sixty-four.

SELECTED WORKS BY ELIZABETH STERN

A Friend at Court, with L.T. Stern (1923); *Gambler's Wife* (1931); *I Am a Woman—and a Jew* (1926; reprint 1969, 1986); *Josiah White: Prince of Pioneers* (1947); *A Marriage Was Made* (1928); *Memories: The Life of Margaret McAvoy Scott* (1943); *My Mother and I* (1917); *Not All Laughter: A Mirror to Our Times* (1937); *This Ecstasy* (1927); *When Love Comes to Woman* (1929); *The Women Behind Gandhi* (1953).

BIBLIOGRAPHY

Bannan, Helen M. "Elizabeth Gertrude Levin Stern." *American Women Writers: A Critical Guide From Colonial Times to the Present*, edited by Lina Mainero. Vol. 4 (1980): 272–274; Baum, Charlotte, Paula Hyman, and Sonya Michel. *The Jewish Woman in America* (1976); *BEDAJ*; Kamel, Rose Yalow. *Aggravating the Conscience: Jewish-American Literary Mothers in the Promised Land* (1988); Obituary. *NYTimes*, January 10, 1954, 86:14; Uffen, Ellen Serlen. *Strands of the Cable: The Place of the Past in Jewish American Women's Writing* (1992); *UJE*; Umansky, Ellen M. "Introduction." *I Am a Woman—and a Jew* (1986); *WWIAJ*, 1928, 1938.

KIRSTEN WASSON

STERN, FRANCES (1873–1947)

Frances Stern's experience as a second-generation American Jew dedicated to social reform, interested in education, and having the good fortune to come into contact with several prominent women engaged in various aspects of social work led her to a career in scientific nutrition, applied dietetics, and home economics.

Frances Stern was the fourth daughter and the last of seven children born to Louis and Caroline (Oppenheimer) Stern, who had immigrated to the United States from Rheinfels, German. Frances Stern was born in Boston on July 3, 1873. Upon completion of a grammar school education, Stern volunteered to teach in the Sunday school for girls founded by LINA FRANK HECHT that attempted to bridge the divide between older Jewish immigrants from Central Europe and new arrivals from Eastern Europe. In 1890, as an expansion of the work of the Sunday school, Hecht encouraged and financed the establishment of the

Hebrew Industrial School for Girls. Stern quickly became involved in the new enterpise, and, in 1895, with her friend Isabel Hyams, opened the Louisa May Alcott Club in Boston's South End to teach homemaking to the poor young women of the neighborhood. In 1895, as a result of her emerging career as a social worker, Stern enrolled in graduate courses in kindergarten training, which ignited her interest in teaching nutrition to children. From her experience teaching nutrition grew the belief that, "if children were properly trained in home-making, they could help to lead the world to the 'art of right living.'"

As a teacher of dietetics, Stern encountered the scientific analyses of several foods carried out at Pratt Institute under the direction of Ellen H. Richards, a pioneer in the chemical analysis of food, an advocate of the social benefits of applied science, and a graduate of MIT. Due to their shared interests, Stern went to work in Richards's lab, became her assistant, and accompanied her to the home economics conferences held in Lake Placid, New York. The conferences eventually led to the establishment of the American Home Economics Association in 1908, and Richards became its first president.

While associated with Richards, Stern became a special student at MIT, enrolling in courses on the chemistry and sanitation of foods to meet her interests in nutrition. Her training and commitments led her to develop visiting housekeeping programs for the Boston Association for the Relief and Control of Tuberculosis and the Boston Provident Association. This work placed Stern in contact with underfed patients on low incomes, which motivated her to investigate the diet of the factory worker. Her research culminated in her book *Food for the Worker*, published in 1917, and led to her appointment as Industrial Health Inspector for the Massachusetts Board of Labor and Industries. During World War I, Stern served with the Food Conservation Division of the United States Food Administration as an investigator of food adequacy for industrial workers for the Department of Agriculture, and with the American Red Cross in France. In 1918, in association with Dr. Michael Davis, Director of the Boston Dispensary, who shared her belief that diet and adequate nutrition were essential elements of social welfare, Frances Stern founded the Food Clinic as an component of the Dispensary.

The Food Clinic, as one manifestation of the emerging home economics movement, served not only as a center for dispensing practical advice on food and meal preparation for outpatients and their families, but also as a center for research on the relationships among health, nutrition, class, and ethnicity. Typical of many enterprises associated with the reforms of the Progressive Era (1900–1920), the Food Clinic effectively combined scientific methods with a moral commitment to social betterment. The emphasis on food and nutrition as essential elements of health provided women opportunities to participate in the progressive movement, which combined their traditional tasks as homemakers with new public roles as scientific experts.

Significantly, under Stern's direction, the Food Clinic operated with a broad understanding of the environmental influences that determined patterns of food consumption, including mental and emotional factors, income, religion, and ethnicity. The fruits of Stern's teaching, research, and practical experience were brought together in her last publication, *Applied Dietetics*, first published in 1936, with a second edition in 1943. The preface to the second edition, in which she reflected on the impact the new knowledge of vitamins had on the understanding of the chemical value of foods, illustrated Stern's commitment to remain at the forefront of her field.

The Food Clinic was quickly recognized for its contributions to patient care and earned an international reputation. The Rockefeller Foundation selected the Food Clinic as a training center for the hospital dieticians it brought over from Europe and Asia. Stern was rewarded with an honorary degree from Tufts Medical School and appointed a special instructor in dietetics and social work at Simmons College in Boston.

While establishing a career that would bring her worldwide fame as a nutritionist, Frances Stern was also active in the Boston Jewish community as a social worker and role model for a younger generation of Jewish activists. In 1914, she was appointed to the Welfare Committee of the Boston Federated Jewish Charities, charged with studying the agency's needs and making suggestions for reform. The committee's report recommended that the Boston Federated adopt the concepts of scientific philanthropy, the professionalization of charity, and organizational bureaucracy—all important components of Stern's career as a social worker. These suggestions were adopted and catapulted the Boston Federated into the forefront of Jewish communal service.

Frances Stern died in Boston on December 23, 1947, at age seventy-four.

SELECTED WORKS BY FRANCES STERN

Applied Dietetics (1936. 2d ed. 1943); "Dietetics and the Food Clinic Development." In *The American Jewish Woman: A Documentary History*, edited by Jacob Rader Marcus (1981): 721–727; *Food for the Worker* (1917).

BIBLIOGRAPHY

AJYB 50:523–524; Ebert, Susan. "Community and Philanthropy." In *The Jews of Boston*, edited by Jonathan D. Sarna and Ellen Smith (1995): 211–237; Obituary. *NYTimes*, December 25, 1947, 21:6; *NAW*; Solomon, Barbara Miller. *Pioneers in Service: A History of the Associated Jewish Philanthropies of Boston* (1956); Weigley, Emma Seifrit. "It Might Have Been Euthenics: The Lake Placid Conferences and the Home Economic Movement." *American Quarterly* 26 (1974): 79–96.

JOHN LIVINGSTON

STERN, JEAN GORDON *see* GORDON, JEAN

STERNBERGER, ESTELLE (1886–1971)

Estelle Sternberger fought for social justice as an activist, a writer, and a radio commentator. Her interpretation of the moral and ethical code of Judaism informed her vision of a world where the masses would hold power and women would work outside of the home. Despite her own bourgeois background, she added her own powerful voice to the early twentieth-century clamors for reform.

Born in 1886 in Cincinnati to Hannah (Greeble) and Abraham Miller, Estelle was educated at the University of Cincinnati and the School of Jewish Philanthropy in Cincinnati. Upon completion of her studies, she joined a number of civic movements and began to lecture and write on left-wing concerns.

In 1923, while executive secretary of the NATIONAL COUNCIL OF JEWISH WOMEN, she compiled information about the careers of contemporary Jewish American women. She was very active in the Jewish community and held key posts in a number of Jewish women's organizations.

In the 1930s, Sternberger became the executive director of World Peaceways. Her book *The Supreme Cause: A Practical Book About Peace* (1936) is an impressive analysis of military and economic issues that have an impact on peace.

In time, Sternberger turned from activism to commentary. She was an outspoken personality on radio, discussing noteworthy political and cultural events. She retired from this second career in 1965.

Estelle Sternberger and her husband, Harry Sternberger, raised a daughter, Minnette, while working and

Estelle Sternberger emerged from bourgeois beginnings to become a powerful voice for left-wing social causes, first as a writer and later as a successful radio commentator. [American Jewish Archives]

living in New York City. A second marriage to Rabbi J. Max Weiss ended when he died in 1968.

Estelle Sternberger died on December 23, 1971.

BIBLIOGRAPHY

BEOAJ; "Estelle Sternberger dies at 85: Radio Commentator on Politics." *NYTimes*, December 24, 1971, 28:5; Marcus, Jacob Rader. *The American Jewish Woman: A Documentary History* (1981); Rogow, Faith. *Gone to Another Meeting: The National Council of Jewish Women, 1893–1993* (1993); Sternberger, Estelle. *A Practical Book About Peace* (1936); *UJE*; *WWWIA* 5; *WWIAJ* (1928, 1938).

JESSICA BERGER

STERN COLLEGE FOR WOMEN

In September 1954, an inaugural class of thirty-two students enrolled at Stern College for Women, as Yeshiva University opened the first liberal arts college in America for women under Jewish auspices. The school was named in honor of the parents of Max Stern, one of the university's major benefactors. Situated in the Murray Hill section of Manhattan, Stern College offered baccalaureate programs in the arts and sciences and religious education with a heavy emphasis on Judaic studies. Its dual curriculum of Jewish and general disciplines was modeled after Yeshiva College, the university's men's undergraduate school that had been established fifteen years earlier. The creation of Stern was an outgrowth of Yeshiva University's postwar endeavor to both meet the changing needs of its Orthodox constituents and to expand Orthodoxy's impact upon American Jewry and the larger national scene. During this same era (c. 1945 to 1955), Yeshiva established a medical school, graduate schools of Jewish social work, education, and psychology, a community service department, and an undergraduate program for men with limited backgrounds in Judaica from both Orthodox and non-Orthodox homes.

Stern was designed to attract the increasing number of young Jewish women from both Orthodox and non-Orthodox Jewish homes who were then beginning to desire college training. In the previous generation, since few Orthodox families had contemplated sending their daughters to universities, Yeshiva had felt no pressure or obligation to provide women with a comfortable higher education environment where they could study secular and religious studies together and where no one would attempt to undermine their religious commitments.

In the mid-1950s, Yeshiva saw Stern's particular niche as its offer to its students of preparation for careers, graduate study, and "management of a Jewish home and family." Implicit too in that message was the understanding that this women's college, placed within the world's largest Jewish community, would provide its students, particularly those from smaller Jewish communities, with abundant opportunities for social engagements with potential marriage mates. From its inception, Stern College enrolled women from within and without the metropolitan area in almost equal numbers, a trend that continues to this day.

During its first score of years, Stern enrollment rose to five hundred students as the school attracted not only graduates from its own Manhattan and Brooklyn Central girls' high schools (established in 1948) and from other New York day schools, but those youngsters from "out of town" who had only Talmud Torah or Sunday school religious training. Under the leadership of Deans Dan Vogel, Norman E. Frimer, and David Mirsky, Stern College accommodated the diversified educational needs of a religiously heterogeneous student body that hailed from

*In September 1954, an inaugural class of thirty-two students enrolled at Stern College for Women,
as Yeshiva University opened the first Jewish liberal arts college for women in America.
This early photograph of students includes manual typewriters. [Yeshiva University]*

Conservative as well as from Orthodox Jewish homes through a multitiered Jewish studies program. Meeting the general educational needs of this first generation of students was a less challenging task because so many of the students wanted to be schoolteachers, either in the public or Jewish school system. This was a career that melded well with the students' equally heartfelt desire to be wives and mothers.

In September 1977, Karen Bacon was appointed dean of Stern College, The first woman to occupy that post, this 1964 alumna of Stern had earned a Ph.D. in microbiology from UCLA and had served as an assistant professor of biology at the university before assuming the deanship. During her tenure (she is still in office), the size of the student body grew to 764 in 1996, the educational and religious profile of those who enroll has changed, and their range of Judaic studies and professional interests has diversified

further, even as Stern College graduates still attempt to harmonize careers with family lives.

Increasingly, the women drawn to Stern are graduates of Orthodox day schools. Those from nonmetropolitan areas who choose Stern have significantly better Jewish educations than their sisters of a generation ago since they have been the beneficiaries of the proliferation of secondary Jewish schools in every area of the United States. Most students at Stern College spend a year of study in a women's yeshivah in Israel, which has only intensified their ardor for intensive Judaic learning and strengthened their commitment to Orthodoxy. Conversely, in 1996, less than 15 percent of Stern freshmen had only gone to Hebrew school or Sunday school, some of which were affiliated with the Conservative Movement.

Responding to a more learned student body's desire for the most advanced training in Judaica, in

1980 Stern College reorganized its multitiered Jewish studies department to provide its students with greater facility in analyzing classical Jewish texts. The study of Talmud and allied rabbinic literature, the bedrock of learning in the traditional yeshivah and a discipline that some Orthodox Jews withhold from their women, was intensified and has since been pursued by some of the best students at Stern. This high-level program has begun to produce woman scholars who serve as intellectual resources for the Orthodox community in schools and women's yeshivahs in both the United States and Israel. These women's elevated Jewish expertise has not, however, led most students to advocate for a greater participatory role for themselves in Orthodox ritual life. Though Stern professors Rabbis Saul Berman and Avraham Weiss have been outspoken supporters of women's *tefilla* [prayer] groups, their enthusiasm for this innovation in the Orthodox synagogue has not engendered widespread interest within the school's student body.

Finally, Stern College students of this most recent generation are training for a variety of careers since teaching school, primarily in Orthodox day schools, has become but one of several professional pursuits attractive to Orthodox young women who seek still to combine professions with traditional Jewish family lives. In 1996, psychology was the most popular major at Stern College; biological sciences was second, with education and Jewish studies—the two fields that often attract teachers in training—running third and fourth respectively. In 1996, 122 of the students enrolled at Stern College majored in business and accounting at the university's Sy Syms School of Business, an undergraduate school that since 1987 has offered a business alternative to Stern College's own liberal arts and sciences curriculum.

BIBLIOGRAPHY

Commentator and *Observer*, Yeshiva University undergraduate student newspapers (1955–1995). File in Public Relations Office, Yeshiva University; Gurock, Jeffrey S. *The Men and Women of Yeshiva: Higher Education, Orthodoxy and American Judaism* (1988); Papers. Registrar's Office, Yeshiva University.

JEFFREY S. GUROCK

STERN-TAEUBLER, SELMA (1890–1981)

A sage once said: "What one can understand, one can endure." This adage became the watchword of Selma Stern-Taeubler over the course of her lengthy and productive career as historian and archivist. In the preface to her book *The Court Jew* (1950), Stern-Taeubler charged her fellow Jews in the aftermath of World War II to use the "tragedy and inexorableness of our present experience . . . to view our past more objectively than before . . . [because] understand[ing] our road through the centuries can make our destiny easier to bear." She herself had been a refugee who escaped Berlin, on the last ship headed to America in 1941.

Selma Stern-Taeubler was born on July 24, 1890, in Kippenheim (Baden), Germany, to Dr. Julius and Emilie (Durlacher) Stern. In 1901, the bourgeois family moved to Baden-Baden, where her father developed a medical practice with a swelling international clientele. The middle of three daughters, Selma used the pages of her teenage diary both to ponder weighty philosophical issues such as the existence of God and to try her hand at poetry on themes as wide-ranging as young love and premature death. Her precociousness led her, in 1904, to become the first girl to be accepted to the Baden-Baden humanities gymnasium, from which she graduated in 1908 with honors.

That same year, despite her father's untimely death, Selma's mother provided for her daughter to continue her studies in history at the University of Heidelberg. Shortly before the outbreak of World War I, she graduated summa cum laude and moved to Frankfurt-am-Main to live with her mother and younger sister. Her reactions to World War I are captured in her diary. While retaining her admiration for German culture, history, and literature, she also expressed her growing alienation from German politics. Jews like herself, she claimed, were strangers in Germany as well as being estranged from Jewish culture and religion. And, in fact, she ultimately would shift the focus of her studies from German history to German-Jewish history.

To this end, she accepted an invitation to become a research fellow at the newly founded Akademie für die Wissenschaft des Judentums in Berlin. She became intrigued with its director, Eugen Taeubler, and his novel historical approach that sought to understand the particularities of the Jewish experience by examining the political and cultural context out of which it emerged. Eventually the two were married in 1927. A series of diary entries from 1944 reveals, however, that as the years passed, Stern-Taeubler felt "psychologically separated" from her husband. Devoted years of service to him had been met with a "lack of love and fits of anger." As she put it: "What I had initially perceived [in him] to be self-confidence was really selfishness; what I had initially perceived to be the shy disguise of insecurity and apprehension was really arrogance."

Stern-Taeubler began to compose the first two volumes of her magnum opus *Der preussische Staat und die Juden* [The Prussian state and the Jews], a study of Jewry in eighteenth-century Prussia, in the late 1920s—a period when the liberalism she described in her book still persisted in Germany. By the time she began work on the third volume, though, her world had changed radically and her belief in tolerance and emancipation could no longer withstand contemporary historical reality. In 1938, when the Nazis forbade Stern-Taeubler to study in the library and archives in Berlin, Leo Baeck and other friends assisted her in copying documents that had become inaccessible to her, as well as helping to salvage her manuscripts from destruction. She immigrated to the United States in 1941 with her husband.

The two became part of the academic community at Hebrew Union College in Cincinnati, he as a professor of history, she as the founding director of the American Jewish Archives of the college. Seeking perhaps to comprehend the tragic events occurring in Europe, Stern-Taeubler turned temporarily to belles lettres, producing a novel set in the period of the Black Death (1348–1349), entitled *The Spirit Returneth* (1946). (The original German title is better translated as "You Are My Witnesses.") She dedicated the book to the "martyrs of my people" and explained elsewhere that "it [was] possible to draw a parallel between the host desecration and ritual murder accusations . . . and the horrors of the gas chambers and concentration camps" (preface to *Josel of Rosheim*, 1965).

In 1956, Eugen Taeubler died, and Stern-Taeubler received an honorary degree from Hebrew Union College. Four years later, upon retiring from the American Jewish Archives, Stern-Taeubler moved to Basel, Switzerland, where she continued to write until her death on August 17, 1981.

American-Jewish academe has largely undervalued Stern-Taeubler's contribution to Jewish history. It would seem that Eugen Taeubler's highly regarded scholarship unfairly overshadowed Selma Stern-Taeubler's scholarly achievements.

**SELECTED WORKS BY
SELMA STERN-TAEUBLER**

The Court Jew: A Contribution to the History of the Period of Absolutism in Central Europe (in German). Translated by Ralph Weiman (1950); *Josel of Rosheim: Commander of Jewry in the Holy Roman Empire of the German Nation* (in German). Translated by Gertrude Hirschler (1965); *Jud Suess: Ein Beitrag zur deutschen und zur jüdischen Geschichte* (1929); *Der preussische Staat und die Juden* (1962–1975); *The Spirit Returneth* (in German). Translated by Ludwig Lewisohn (1946).

BIBLIOGRAPHY

EJ; Rickertsen, Ulf. "Selma Stern." In *Die Beucherkommentare* (1980); Stern-Taeubler, Selma. Archives. Leo Baeck Institute, NYC.

CAROLE B. BALIN

STETTHEIMER, FLORINE (1871–1944)

The career of Florine Stettheimer, painter, poet, and designer, disproves the myth of the artist as a lonely and misunderstood genius, struggling to produce works that transcend his (and less frequently, her) own historical time and place. Stettheimer's paintings are lively, diarylike accounts of her life, but also acute examinations of upper-class ways in New York between the wars. Her decorative, figurative style, often characterized as feminine, offers an alternative to prevailing modes of contemporary modernist painting.

Born on August 29, 1871, in Rochester, New York, to Rosetta (Walter) and Joseph Stettheimer, Florine Stettheimer was the second youngest of five children. The members of her extended family were wealthy and influential assimilated Jews who were comfortable moving between Europe and America. By 1883, the Stettheimers were living in Germany, where Florine received her elementary schooling. It was during this time that their father abandoned the family for reasons that are unclear. Rosetta Stettheimer never remarried, and the three youngest daughters, Carrie, Florine, and Ettie, remained single and lived with their mother until her death in 1935, forming a distinctly matriarchal household. Florine began her formal art training in 1892 at New York's Art Students League, where she studied with the idealist Kenyon Cox and the realist Robert Henri. Her early work reflects academic training tempered by a bright palette and pronounced brushstroke that attest to her exposure to postimpressionism during her family's extensive travels in Europe. But shortly after World War I forced the Stettheimers' return to New York in 1914, Florine began to paint in a stylized and richly colored manner that owed as much to popular illustration as it did to fine art.

Stettheimer's paintings from 1917 on form an unprecedented pictorial category that is part portraiture, part history painting, and part genre painting. Many works, such as *La Fête à Duchamp* (1917) and *Asbury Park South* (1920), commemorate outings and parties organized by her family, and can be read as biographical. But these real events and their protagonists are described in a style so fantastic in its miniaturization and decorative excess that they take on a theatrical aspect that betrays the critical distance of their author. For, in spite of the lively art salon cultivated by the three sisters, Florine Stettheimer maintained the stance of the detached observer, recording events for the private pleasure of friends and family. Except for an early solo exhibition at the Knoedler Gallery, she seldom showed her work, and never sold it. And although she painted many portraits, whimsical works that describe their subjects less by resemblance than by attributes, they were always of friends: artists and writers such as Marcel Duchamp, Alfred Stieglitz, and Carl Van Vechten.

Stettheimer was a member of the American Society of Painters, Sculptors, and Engravers, and entered work annually in the exhibitions of the Society of Independent Artists. In 1934, she made her most public appearance when she designed the sets and costumes for the premiere production of *Four Saints in Three Acts*, the avant-garde opera by Gertrude Stein and Virgil Thomson. Her best-known works, however, are four paintings celebrating modern life in New York: *Cathedrals of Broadway* (1929), *Cathedrals of Fifth Avenue* (1931), *Cathedrals of Wall Street* (1939), and *Cathedrals of Art* (1942), all now housed in New York's Metropolitan Museum of Art. These paintings are historical documents at once public and private, and are presented with wit and irony in a style whose ornamental superfluity celebrates the popular culture of her own time.

Florine Stettheimer died in New York on May 11, 1944, while still at work on the last of the *Cathedrals* paintings. She was seventy-three years old. Following her death, her sister Ettie published a volume of Florine's poetry, entitled *Crystal Flowers* (1949). Her reputation, though eclipsed by the rise of abstract expressionism in the 1950s, has continued to grow, particularly since her paintings share in many concerns that occupy postmodernist art. In her poems and in her paintings, Stettheimer described a world in which people define themselves by the things that surround them, rather than by their internal values or beliefs. Through the form and content of her work, she criticized the high-mindedness of modern art and the course of modern life.

BIBLIOGRAPHY

Bloemink, Barbara. *The Life and Art of Florine Stettheimer* (1995); Nochlin, Linda. "Florine Stettheimer: Rococo Subversive." *Art in America* 68 (September 1980): 64–83; Stettheimer, Florine. *Crystal Flowers* (1949), and Exhibition File. Museum of Modern Art Archives, NYC, and Papers. Columbia University, Rare Book and Manuscript Library, NYC; Stettheimer, Florine, and Ettie Stettheimer. Papers. Collection of American Literature, Beinecke Rare Book and Manuscript Library, Yale University, New Haven, Conn.; Sussman, Elisabeth, and Barbara J. Bloemink. *Florine Stettheimer: Manhattan Fantastica*. Exhibition catalog (1995); Tyler, Parker. *Florine Stettheimer: A Life in Art* (1963).

SUSAN LAXTON

STOKES, ROSE PASTOR
(1879–1933)

Most accounts of Rose Pastor Stokes begin with the events leading to her controversial and sensational marriage to the millionaire James Graham Phelps Stokes. In her autobiography, however, she locates herself in the context of work, opening her story with the humble statement, "I slipped into the world while my mother was on her knees, scrubbing the floor." This juxtaposition reveals the contradictions of identity that Rose Pastor Stokes negotiated throughout her life.

Born Rose Harriet Wieslander in Augustova, Poland, on July 18, 1879, she was the first child of a loveless marriage. At age three, she moved to England with her mother, leaving her father (whom she knew only as "Jacob the Learned Bootmaker") and the pogrom-threatened shtetl behind. Living with relatives in the squalid slums of London's East End, Rose was compelled by necessity to leave school at age eight and join the workforce. In England Rose's mother, Hindl, married Israel Pastor, who soon decided to resettle the family in America. In 1890, Hindl, Rose, and the new baby Maurice joined Pastor in Cleveland, where Rose found work in a "buck-eye," the cigar-sweatshop in which many Jews labored. She worked as an unskilled "stogey-roller" for twelve years. After Israel Pastor abandoned the family, she became the sole supporter of six. For those who later popularized her character in the media, this period of her life often faded to an idealized working-class experience, but for Rose herself, it stood out as formative for her identity.

Her love of reading impelled her to respond to a call for letters in the *Yidishes Tageblat* [Jewish daily news]. In 1901, her first letter was published on the *Tageblat's* English page, and she soon became a regular contributor. Her column gained such popularity that the editor offered her a full-time position as a resident columnist in New York City for the enticing salary of $15 per week. She settled in the Lower East Side in January 1903, within a few months joined by her mother and some of her siblings.

Her work at the *Tageblat* provided her with a forum to explore political themes and brought her into contact with ghetto intelligentsia. It was also through the *Tageblat* that she met her future husband. As part of a series on settlement workers, Rose interviewed James Graham Phelps Stokes, a reform-minded millionaire from a prominent family. After the publication of this interview, Pastor and Stokes became fast friends. Their relationship took a more intimate turn at the end of the summer of 1904, and they began to discuss marriage.

The news of this unlikely engagement broke on the front page of the *New York Times* on April 6, 1905, with a headline reading "J.G. Phelps Stokes to Wed Young Jewess—Engagement of Member of Old New York Family Announced—Both Worked on East Side." The article sensationalized the romantic story and the sharp contrasts in background between the two, calling her the "Cinderella of the sweatshops."

Although the great disparity in class background between Pastor and Stokes was to become the central—and divisive—issue in the course of their marriage as well as in historical hindsight, the issue of religion provoked the most concern at the time of their engagement. The class distinction between them, however, constituted material for romantic fantasy. A love that overcame social barriers appealed to the public as a living fairy tale, as well as an example of the classic American success story.

From the first time that Stokes and Pastor discussed marriage, they determined to remain in the world of the Lower East Side, yet she joined his world of philanthropic reformism. Both quickly became disillusioned with settlement work, however, and in 1906, they joined the Socialist Party of America. She became one of the most prominent speakers on the Intercollegiate Socialist Society tour.

Stokes defined her new role as the voice of the worker, with the responsibility to use her newfound influence to help the working class. Although she stated, "I believe . . . that the Jewish people, because of the ancient and historic struggle for social and economic justice, should be fitted to recognize a special mission in the cause of the modern Socialist movement," she resisted ethnic specificity and association with Jewish organizations, defining allegiance only along class lines.

After devoting herself to the lecture circuit for ten years, Stokes applied her political energy to labor activism and to organizations outside the formal structure of the Socialist Party. She led the movement in support of Patrick Quinlan, a strike leader of the radical Industrial Workers of the World. In New York in 1912, she spearheaded a campaign to organize chambermaids into a branch of the International Hotel Workers' Union and to encourage them to strike. Stokes also garnered a great deal of attention for her birth control activism, serving as a leader of the groups that agitated in support of Margaret Sanger during the time of her arrest and trial, and writing two pro–birth control plays, *The Woman Who Wouldn't* and *Shall the Parents Decide* (cowritten with Alice Blache). Stokes became involved in the cause of birth control because it provided a means of doing direct, concrete work for the benefit of the working class. Her distinctive position made her particularly successful in this cause, for her working-class background gave her argument a personal legitimacy, while her upper-class position protected her from arrest.

Public attention to Stokes reached its peak over her antiwar activism, culminating in her arrest on March 22, 1918, for an antiwar speech in Kansas City, Missouri, and a letter to the local paper in which she declared, "No government which is for the profiteers can also be for the people, and I am for the people, while the government is for the profiteers." Stokes's conviction was appealed twice before the decision was reversed in March 1920, on the grounds that the charge to the jury was prejudicial against the defendant.

The arrest and trial of Stokes attracted a great deal of notoriety and only exacerbated the tension within her marriage, which ended in divorce in 1926. Stokes had moved toward a radicalism increasingly incompatible with her husband's position as a millionaire socialist. She was present at the 1919 socialist convention in Chicago, at which the Communist Party of America was founded, and she held a position on the CP Central Executive Committee. As an American delegate to the Comintern's Fourth World Congress in Moscow in 1922, Stokes submitted a minority report on the "Negro question." Although she had been wary of separate organizations for women during her involvement in the Socialist Party, she began to advocate a special organization for women in the Communist Party and took on the job of managing the Women's Work Department of the Central Executive Committee.

While she remained devoted to radical activism, the last ten years of Stokes's life were filled with emotional and financial strain. Making no financial demands on her ex-husband except for a monthly stipend for her mother, Stokes depended on her writing as her primary source of income. She remarried in 1927, to Jerome Isaac Romain (who later changed his name to Victor J. Jerome), a Russian-Polish Jew active in the Communist Party. Due to their financial needs, Romain lived and worked in New York, while Stokes remained at her house in Westport, Connecticut, taking care of Romain's young son and continuing her political activism.

In 1930, Stokes was diagnosed with a malignant breast tumor, which she attributed to having received a blow on the breast from a policeman's club during a demonstration—claiming martyrdom for the proletarian cause. Her health rapidly declined; even so, she maintained her radical, fighting spirit. Although her illness prevented her from remaining active in the Communist Party during the last years of her life, she continued to assert her allegiance to it. On June 20, 1933, she died in Germany, where she had sought medical care at an experimental clinic.

She was called the "Cinderella of the sweatshops" when, as a young reporter, Rose Pastor Stokes met and married millionaire James Graham Phelps Stokes. The fairy tale romance, however, did not last. Stokes became increasingly radical, adopting antiwar and pro-abortion stands and joining the Communist Party. This photograph was taken in December of 1913. [Library of Congress]

Stokes's complicated identity continued to confound historians, writers, and thinkers after her death. Some have located her importance in her sensational marriage, emphasizing her connection to the Phelps-Stokes family over and above her political significance and activism. In contrast, the Communist Party, as the custodian of her memory after her death, sought to construct from her character and experiences a model for the party that fit neatly—more neatly than Stokes did herself during her lifetime—into party ideology.

Stokes used her autobiography, which she began in 1924, as a forum to negotiate these tensions in her identity, rewriting her own background and balancing the visions that others had of her life and mission. When she became too ill to continue writing, she entrusted the project of its completion to Samuel Ornitz, a communist writer, friend, and later member of the blacklisted Hollywood Ten, who finally abandoned it in 1937. In her autobiography as in her life, Stokes fused American values of self-improvement with immigrant and socialist ideals of community.

**SELECTED WORKS BY
ROSE PASTOR STOKES**

"I Belong to the Working Class": The Unfinished Autobiography of Rose Pastor Stokes. Edited by Herbert Shapiro and David L. Sterling (1992); *Shall the Parents Decide*, with Alice Blache; *The Woman Who Wouldn't* (1916).

BIBLIOGRAPHY

AJYB 24:207, 35:129; *DAB*; *EJ*; *NAW*; Obituary. *NYTimes*, June 21, 1933, 17:1; Stokes, Rose Pastor. Papers. Manuscripts and Archives, Sterling Memorial Library, Yale University, New Haven, Conn., and Tamiment Institute Library, New York University, NYC; *UJE*; *WWIAJ* (1928); *WWWIA* 1; Zisper, Arthur, and Pearl Zisper. *Fire and Grace: The Life of Rose Pastor Stokes* (1989).

JUDITH A.H. ROSENBAUM

STONE, HANNAH MAYER (1893–1941)

A pioneering physician and advocate of birth control, Hannah Stone defied both New York City police and the federal government in her efforts to make contraception legal and available to American women. Her attempts to circulate birth control information landed her in a New York City police paddy wagon after a raid on the clinic where she was director.

Born in New York City in 1893 to Jewish parents, Max and Golda Rinaldo Mayer, Hannah (Mayer) Stone earned a pharmacy degree from the Brooklyn College of Pharmacy in 1912, after which she attended Columbia University. New York Medical College together with Flower Hospital granted her a medical degree in 1920. She married another doctor, Abraham Stone, an associate of the New York Department of Health. They had one child, Gloria.

Stone was an early associate of Margaret Sanger, the founder of the movement to legalize birth control. She became medical director of Sanger's Birth Control Clinical Research Bureau of New York in 1923. Six years later, she was arrested along with her medical staff in a police raid on the clinic, for disseminating contraceptive information in violation of the law. After hearing the charges, the presiding magistrate dismissed them. In addition, the police were criticized for taking the staff to the police station in a patrol wagon.

The following year, in another attempt to halt her activities, the U.S. Government sued Stone for importing contraceptive devices from Japan, which it alleged was in violation of the Tariff Act of 1930. The Circuit Court of Appeals dismissed the suit, holding that the law was not designed to prevent the importation, sale, or use of devices that conscientious and competent physicians might employ for the purpose of saving life or promoting the well-being of patients.

In addition to her work at the clinic, Stone and her husband opened the first Marriage Consultation Center in New York in 1931, followed by a second one somewhat later. She also was the coauthor of two books, one with her husband and the other with Margaret Sanger.

Hannah Stone did not live to see the fruits of her labors. She died on July 10, 1941, at age forty-eight.

The courage and daring that Hannah Stone displayed throughout her life—from her resoluteness in graduating from medical school in an era when few women could succeed in becoming physicians, to her struggle for the emancipation of women—make her a true heroine and role model.

BIBLIOGRAPHY

AJYB 44:344; Obituary. *NYTimes*, July 11, 1941, 15:4.

MARION SHULEVITZ

STRAKOSCH, CELIA (1879–1961)

Before her death at age eighty-three, Celia Strakosch could look back on a lifetime of social work, which led her from an affluent California town to the older (and poorer) traditionally Jewish neighborhoods in the Bronx and the Lower East Side of New York City. Her career after her marriage centered around a number of social organizations, some of which she founded and others to which she lent her considerable organizational skill.

She was born on November 14, 1879, in Truckee, California, to Jacob and Mary Lewison. She graduated from the Normal School in San Francisco, where she taught from 1900 to 1906. As was the case with most middle-class women of her generation, her marriage signaled the end of her employment. On June 3, 1906, she married Edgar H. Sigismund Strakosch, with whom she had one daughter, Frances S. Alexander.

The couple moved to New York in 1913, where Strakosch quickly became involved in volunteer social work. From 1914 to the beginning of the active United States involvement in World War I, Strakosch was the director of the Emanu-El Employment Bureau for Jewish Girls. During the war, she served as the assistant director of the Mayor's Committee on Unemployment. At the war's end, she returned to Jewish social work, joining the Emanu-El Sisterhood Settlement House in Brooklyn in 1920. Although she remained on the Settlement House's staff until the beginning of the Great Depression, she also became the director of the Reconstruction Unit of the NATIONAL COUNCIL OF JEWISH WOMEN, in order to help the Jewish communities in Europe devastated by the general destruction and pogroms of World War I.

During the 1930s, Strakosch joined the legions of social workers—mostly female—hoping to mitigate the effects of extreme poverty. In 1930, she rejoined the Emanu-El Employment Bureau (renamed the Federation Employment Bureau for Jewish Girls) as assistant director. However, most social workers, no doubt including Strakosch, realized the futility of large-scale social work during the Depression. Increasingly, she turned her attention to the plight of Jewish children. From 1923 to 1944, she was the owner and director of Camp Awanee for Girls, a low-cost camp providing outdoor experiences for poor Jewish girls.

Following World War II, Strakosch continued her work in children's social service. Between 1946 and 1948, she was the executive director of the Brightside Day Nursery. In the 1950s, she served on the board of the Bronx House Emanu-El Camps.

By the time Strakosch died on May 9, 1961, her career in social work had spanned five decades. Her particular focus on Jewish issues and organization was typical of Jewish American women from affluent backgrounds. Social work represented not only a benevolent dedication—untainted by direct political involvement—to the larger Jewish community but also an empowering position beyond the potentially restrictive limits of middle-class domestic existence.

BIBLIOGRAPHY

AJYB 63 (1962): 562; Obituary. *NYTimes*, May 10, 1961, 45:3; *WWIAJ* (1938).

DANIEL BENDER

STRAUS, DOROTHY (1888–1960)

Over the course of her life, Dorothy Straus was active as a lawyer, college lecturer, Democrat, member of the League of Women Voters, and member of several municipal and state government committees. In her writings, public statements, and activities, she demonstrated a commitment to efficient, socially active government policies, especially regarding the protection and advancement of women.

The daughter of Philip and Sarah (Strauss) Straus, Dorothy was born on April 12, 1888, in New York City, where she lived for most of her life. She began her education at Normal College (later known as HUNTER COLLEGE), which she attended from 1897 to 1901. From 1901 to 1904, she was enrolled at Dr. Julius Sachs' School for Girls, and subsequently obtained an A.B. from Bryn Mawr College in 1908 and an LL.B. from New York University Law School in 1911. She practiced law with Hays, Kaufman, and Lindheim (1911–1917); with Coleman, Stern, and Ellenwood (1917–1923); in private practice (1923–1930); and, finally, as a partner in the firm of Straus and (Dorothy) Kenyon.

In addition to her legal work, Dorothy Straus served as an organizer and, from 1914 to 1917, as treasurer of the League for Business Opportunities for Women. She was chair of the New York League of Women Voters' municipal affairs committee from 1922 to 1926 and, in 1928, became the sole woman appointee to the subcommittee on budget, finance, and revenues of Mayor James J. Walker's Committee on Plan and Survey. Straus's involvement with the League of Women Voters led to her being chosen to represent the United States on the Committee on Nationality of Married Women of the International Alliance of Women for Suffrage and Equal Citizenship. As a delegate at the alliance's 1929 summer congress in Berlin, Straus endorsed the principle of gender equality in laws regarding nationality rights and the retention of citizenship. At that time, many nations, including the United States, revoked a woman's citizenship if she married a foreign national and resided in her spouse's country for a specified period of time. Such restrictions did not apply to married men. Straus believed that a woman's nationality should not be subject to change on the basis of marital status and that citizenship laws should apply to men and women equally.

On a local level, Straus was appointed by Mayor Fiorello LaGuardia to the mayor's committee investigating unemployment relief for the years 1934 and 1935. She was appointed to the New York State Planning Council in 1935 and reappointed in 1936, was named a special lecturer of law at Bryn Mawr's Graduate Department of Social Economy and Social Research in 1936, and was one of the first twelve women to be admitted in 1937 to the Bar Association of New York City. As the only female member of the newly created State Planning Council, Straus viewed her position as an opportunity to improve the efficiency of both government building projects and the use of natural resources. In addition, she hoped to educate women's organizations about the work of the council, and of government in general, in order to increase their participation in civic and political activities.

While Straus advocated an expanded public role for women, she opposed the Equal Rights Amendment, which would have placed men and women legally on an equal footing. Her writings and congressional testimony of the late 1930s and early 1940s indicate that she feared, as did labor unions and the League of Women Voters, that minimum wage and maximum hour protections for working women would be repealed by the passage of the ERA. More specifically, she criticized the lack of a clear definition of "equal," believing that the legal system would become chaotic as numerous of laws were reexamined and modified without clear constitutional or legislative guidelines.

Straus was part of the first generation of urban professional women in America. She helped break down gender barriers in professional organizations and government and, despite her opposition to the ERA, advocated the improvement of women's status. As an assistant secretary for the 1938 New York State Democratic convention, she was guided by her party affiliation and a progressive belief that government should actively protect the disadvantaged. One of her last public acts was her resignation in 1944 from the state's Committee on Discrimination, citing delays in the passage of key legislation and the group's lack of power. Dorothy Straus died on July 22, 1960, in Bar Harbor, Maine.

SELECTED WORKS BY DOROTHY STRAUS

"I Swear Allegiance to . . ." *The Woman's Journal* 15, no. 1 (January 1930): 28–29; "Independent Nationality Through National Laws." *The Congressional Digest* 9, no. 11 (November 1930): 281–282; "Librarians Underpaid." Letter. *NYTimes*, August 28, 1925, 12; "The President's Work." Letter. *NYTimes*, November 6, 1916, 10.

BIBLIOGRAPHY

AJYB 63 (1962): 562; "Bar Group Turns to Noted Women." *NYTimes*, October 24, 1937, sec. 6, p. 7; "'Equal Rights' Held a Peril to Women." *NYTimes*, August 8, 1937, 1–2; Eustis, Grace Hendrick. "Meeting for Discussion and Explanation of Revised City Document Will Be Held Tomorrow—Many Groups Aid." *NYTimes*, October 18, 1936, sec. 6, p. 7; "Foe Tells Views On Women's Pact." *NYTimes*, December 21, 1933, 18; "The Legislative Journey of the Equal-Rights Amendment 1923–1943." *The Congressional Digest* 22, no. 4 (April 1943): 105–128; McLaughlin, Kathleen. "New Opportunity for Women Seen." *NYTimes*, December 15, 1935, sec. 2, p. 6, and "Quiet Mrs. Lehman Avoids Spotlight." *NYTimes*, September 30, 1938, 17, and "Roosevelt 'Purge' Upheld by Hopkins." *NYTimes*, August 31, 1938: 6, and "Women Argue 'Equal Rights.'" *NYTimes*, February 13, 1938, sec. 4, p. 7, and "Women Condemn Equal Rights Plan." *NYTimes*, February 8, 1938, 7, and "Women Democrats Praise Court Bill." *NYTimes*, June 15, 1937, 15, and "New Body Takes Up Fight on Bond Issue." *NYTimes*, October 22, 1925, 5; Petersen, Anne. "Campaign is Begun by 10 Women Here." *NYTimes*, February 27, 1938, sec. 6, p. 5, and "Converts Sought by the Opposition." *NYTimes*, March 27, 1938, sec. 6, p. 5, and "Delay in Naming Frieda Miller Stirs Protests." April 2, 1939, sec. 2, p. 5; "Quitting Bias Unit, 8 Criticize Dewey." *NYTimes*, March 27, 1944, 19; "Renamed to State Boards." *NYTimes*, February 10, 1937, 10; "Topics of the Times: Bar is Lifted." *NYTimes*, October 22, 1937, 22; "Woman Legislator Spurns Smartness." *NYTimes*, May 21, 1942, 22; "Woman Wins Suit for Commission." *NYTimes*, March 11, 1925, 4; *WWIAJ* (1938).

JOE KOMLJENOVICH

STRAUS, SARAH LAVANBURG (1861–1945)

Warm friendship, a brilliant mind, breadth of interests, remarkable energy, and a sense of humor even in the heart of Africa: this is how one close friend described Sarah Lavanburg Straus.

Sarah Straus was born in 1861 in New York City to Hannah (Seller) Lavanburg and Louis Lavanburg, an investment banker. She had one brother, Frederick, a merchant and philanthropist interested in housing issues. She was educated in private schools and married Oscar Solomon Straus on April 19, 1882, in New York City. Oscar Straus, born in Otterburg, Bavaria, was a jurist, diplomat, cabinet member, philanthropist, and member of the merchandising family that operated R.H. Macy & Company. They had three children: Mildred (b. 1883), Aline (b. 1889), and Roger Williams (b. 1891), who became an industrialist, communal leader, and philanthropist.

Oscar Straus was involved in his family's business when the couple married. In 1887, he was appointed United States ambassador to Turkey, and Sarah Straus accompanied him on this overseas assignment, which lasted until 1889. Upon their return, they built a home in Manhattan, in which each of the major rooms was furnished in the style of a different Near Eastern country.

With the help of philanthropist Baroness Clara de Hirsch, Sarah Straus helped to establish two homes for immigrant girls in New York City early in the twentieth century. [Library of Congress]

During the sojourn in Turkey, the Strauses met Baron Maurice de Hirsch, a German industrialist and philanthropist. Oscar Straus was instrumental in persuading the baron to establish the Baron de Hirsch Fund (1891), which aided Jewish immigrants relocating from Russia. Baroness Clara de Hirsch continued to support the fund after her husband's death in 1896.

Early that year, when the baroness decided to establish a home for immigrant girls in the United States, she sought the advice of the Strauses. The baroness and the Strauses corresponded and spoke in Paris about the home. Sarah Straus investigated the existing institutions for women in New York, Boston, and Philadelphia. With this report and previous correspondence in mind, in 1897 the baroness established the CLARA DE HIRSCH HOME FOR WORKING GIRLS. Sarah Straus was the first president, and, with the exception of the years from 1898 to 1900, when she again accompanied her husband to Turkey, she served as president until she died.

Sarah Straus took an active interest in all aspects of the home, located at 225 East 63rd Street. By 1906, the home also had a downtown facility, the Clara de Hirsch Home for Immigrant Girls. In 1915, the Immigrant Home's operation was taken over by Sarah Straus and her brother, and incorporated as the Hannah Lavanburg Home in honor of their deceased mother.

After her husband's death on May 3, 1926, in New York City, Sarah Straus continued a busy life of philanthropy, recreation, and travel. In 1929, she financed and accompanied a four-month expedition to central Africa for the American Museum of Natural History to obtain birds in Uganda, Kenya, and Nyasaland, from which region the museum previously had no collections. In 1934, she financed and participated in an eight-month expedition to West Africa for the Field Museum of Chicago to collect bird specimens in Senegal, French Sudan, and the Niger territory. With her musical background, she was enthusiastic about recording tribal music on these expeditions.

She served on the board of the Fred L. Lavanburg Foundation and was a member of Temple Emanu-El. Sarah Lavanburg Straus died on November 9, 1945, at her home in New York City.

BIBLIOGRAPHY

AJYB 48: 500; *American Hebrew* (June 7, 1929): 106; *American Jewess* (June 1895): 148; "Mrs. Oscar Straus African Expedition." (1929) Photograph Collection, American Museum of Natural History; Obituary. *NYTimes*, November 10, 1945, 15:3; Straus, Oscar S. Papers. Library of Congress; *UJE*.

STEVEN SIEGEL

STRAUSS, ANNETTE GREENFIELD (b. 1924)

Annette Greenfield Strauss made history in the spring of 1987 when she was elected as the first female and first Jewish mayor of Dallas. By then, she had already served on the city council since 1983 and as mayor pro tem since 1984.

A tireless worker for civic and religious causes, Annette Louise Greenfield Strauss was born in Houston, Texas, on January 26, 1924. Her parents were Edith and J.B. Greenfield, the son of a rabbi. After graduating from Houston public schools, Annette attended Rice University in her hometown for one year before transferring to the University of Texas at Austin. While at college, she was named Outstanding Woman Speaker in the Southwest. She graduated, Phi Beta Kappa, with a bachelor's degree in sociology in 1944. The following year, she earned a master's degree in sociology and psychology at Columbia University, while working as a fashion model for the John Robert Powers agency. In 1946, she married Theodore H. Strauss. Three months later, the newlyweds moved to Dallas.

Unable to get a paying job, Strauss began to volunteer for the United Jewish Appeal Drive. This first effort led to her remarkable career as Dallas's most effective fund-raiser. To date, she has raised over $20 million as the leader of many citywide campaigns and projects. At the University of Texas Health Science Center, she established a chair in geriatrics. She has also raised funds for the women's division of the United Jewish Appeal, the Dallas Symphony Orchestra, the women's division of the United Way, and the Dallas County Heart Fund Campaign.

Her honors include an honorary doctorate of humane letters from Southern Methodist University, an honorary doctorate of public service from the University of North Texas, the NATIONAL COUNCIL OF JEWISH WOMEN's Hannah Solomon Award for Outstanding Volunteer Service, the National Mother's Day Committee "Mother of the Year" Award, the Dallas Council of World Affairs Neil Mallon Award for Distinguished Civic Service, the Jewish National Fund's "Person of Valor" Award, and *Town and Country* magazine's Honor Role of Volunteer Women in the United States, and the John F. Kennedy Commitment to Excellence Award. In addition, an annual humanitarian award is named in her honor.

Strauss is currently an ambassador at large for the city of Dallas. She is chair of the board of the John G. Tower Center for Political Studies at South-

Starting as a volunteer fund-raiser for the United Jewish Appeal, Annette Greenfield Strauss has raised more than twenty million dollars for various institutions in a career that has included her election as the first female and the first Jewish mayor of Dallas.

ern Methodist University and of the Dallas Council of World Affairs. She also serves on the development boards of the University of Texas and the Dallas Institute of Humanities and Culture. She is a director or trustee for numerous other organizations.

Her Judaism has been the springboard to her career. While she began as a volunteer for Jewish causes, she has since then reached out to help all people.

BIBLIOGRAPHY

Biography Index. Vol. 12 (1984), and Vol. 15 (1988); Castleberry, Vivian Anderson. *Daughters of Dallas: A History of Greater Dallas Through the Voices and Deeds of Its Women* (1994); *Who's Who in American Politics* (1993); *Who's Who of Women in World Politics* (1991); *Who's Who in Advertising* (1990); *Who's Who of American Women* (1993); *Who's Who in the South and Southwest* (1988); Winegarten, Ruthe, and Cathy Schecter. *Deep in the Heart: The Lives and Legends of Texas Jews* (1990).

JANE BOCK GUZMAN

STRAUSS, LILLIAN LASER
(1889–1946)

Lillian Laser Strauss performed pioneering work in public health and child welfare in Pennsylvania, became a lawyer at age fifty, and, in the midst of active legal advocacy for public health, died suddenly of a heart attack at age fifty-six.

She was born on February 22, 1889, in Little Rock, Arkansas, and graduated from Bryn Mawr College in 1909. She was in charge of publicity at the Bureau of Municipal Research in New York City and was editor of their *Field Reports* from 1911 to 1913. In 1914, she married Berthold Strauss, a textile manufacturer in Philadelphia, with whom she had two children: Bella (b. 1918), and Richard (b. 1919).

Strauss pioneered preventive health care in Pennsylvania and was the first president of the Community Health Center, which became a constituent of the Federation of Jewish Charities. In 1930, she became secretary of the committee on health centers for President Herbert Hoover's Child Welfare Conference. She coauthored a study on child health centers emerging from that conference, which was published in 1932.

In 1937, at age forty-seven, Strauss entered the University of Pennsylvania Law School, and she received her law degree three years later. Filling out a Bryn Mawr alumna form in 1940, she answered yes to the question, "Do you administer the household?" and no to the question, "Is it your chief occupation?"

In 1943, Strauss coauthored with Edwin P. Rome, a prominent Philadelphia attorney, *The Child and the Law in Pennsylvania*, a survey of all laws regarding children and child welfare at that time. She became a lecturer in medical jurisprudence at the Women's Medical College in Philadelphia (now called the Medical College of Pennsylvania). During World War II, she handled the legal cases of servicemen through the Legal Aid Society in Philadelphia.

Strauss served on the board of the Public Charities Association of Pennsylvania. As a member of the board of directors of the Bryn Mawr College Summer School, she helped to establish several county nutrition clinics with Dr. Samuel Hamilton. She was also the director of the Bryn Mawr Summer School for Workers in Industry.

Lillian Laser Strauss died in her home in Elkins Park, a suburb of Philadelphia, on October 6, 1946, one week after suffering a heart attack. She had just finished writing a book dealing with medical legislation in Pennsylvania.

SELECTED WORKS BY LILLIAN LASER STRAUSS

The Child and the Law in Philadelphia, with Edwin P. Rome (1943); *Child Health Centers: A Survey*, with James Hall Mason Knox and Philip Van Ingen (1932); *A Survey of Opportunities for Vocational Education in Pennsylvania*, compiled with Meribah Delaplaine and Rosa Stein De Young (1929).

BIBLIOGRAPHY

AJYB 48:501; Bryn Mawr College. Register of Alumnae and Former Students; *Evening Bulletin*, October 8, 1946; *Philadelphia Inquirer*, October 8, 1946; *Philadelphia Record*, October 8, 1946.

LINDA HERSKOWITZ

STREISAND, BARBRA (b. 1942)

From the moment she burst on the Hollywood scene in *Funny Girl*, winking as she uttered the immortal "Hello, gorgeous" to her mirror image, until the release of her 1996 film, *The Mirror Has Two Faces*, there was and has been no one quite like Barbra Streisand.

She was born off-off-off Broadway, in Brooklyn, the second child of Emmanuel and Diana (Rosen) Streisand, on April 24, 1942. Fifteen months later, Emmanuel Streisand died of a cerebral hemorrhage and the family immediately plunged to an economic level just above poverty. Diana Streisand took a job as a bookkeeper to support her daughter Barbara Joan and son Sheldon, leaving her little time for her children. The situation was only exacerbated when, in 1949, she married Louis Kind, who was, according to Streisand, "allergic to kids." The couple had one child together, Rosalind (later changed to Roslyn). They then separated, reconciled, and finally divorced.

Streisand graduated from Erasmus High School in 1959 with a love of the theater and an impressive A average. Her formal education may have ended in Brooklyn, but her academic rewards are ongoing. In May 1995, she received an honorary doctorate from Brandeis, and earlier that year she had delivered a lecture at the John F. Kennedy School of Government at Harvard.

As soon as she graduated from high school, despite her mother's protests, she left home to pursue her chosen career in Manhattan. Streisand worked odd jobs while preparing for stardom. She tried to enter the famous Actors Studio, but failed, so she took acting lessons from a friend, Alan Miller, instead, working hard at perfecting her craft. She then moved in with another actor friend, Barry Dennen, who steered her toward singing, helping her shape a song into a theatrical event. Streisand's first venue for this combined approach was the weekly talent show at the Lion Club, one of the premier gay clubs in New York.

The underground bar scene fostered a sense of self and a sense of humor that readily warmed to Streisand: The kooky outsider finally found a place where her persona was appreciated and applauded. Journalist Shaun Considine recalls, "with the release of the final note from the song she was treated to her first ovation; and to her first victory." Hired for a one-week engagement, Streisand stayed at the Lion Club for three, building an idiosyncratic songbook and perfecting a wacky delivery style of impromptu one-liners. By word of mouth alone, the Lion Club was mobbed every evening to hear Streisand. She had become a gay icon overnight, and has remained so ever since.

Following her success at the gay cabaret, Streisand was offered a job by the nearby Bon Soir club, at double her weekly salary. Once again, her engagement was quickly extended, from three weeks to thirteen. She was working hard on her act, and the audience responded appreciatively wherever she was booked: New York, Detroit, Cleveland, and St. Louis. In 1961, she made her television debut on *The Jack Paar Show*, but it was her role of Miss Marmelstein in Broadway's *I Can Get It for You Wholesale* at age nineteen that put Streisand on the fast track to superstardom.

The part of Miss Marmelstein was enlarged for her, and new songs were added. The show ran for nine months, garnering much praise. Streisand won more than rave reviews for *Wholesale*—she also won the heart of the male lead, Elliott Gould. The two married in 1963. In 1966, they had a son, Jason Emmanuel. In 1969, they separated, and in 1971 they divorced, although they later hosted Jason's bar mitzvah celebration together.

Although Streisand's show-stopping turn as Miss Marmelstein gave her national media exposure, it took months for Columbia Records to sign her to a contract. She was, it seems, too much of everything for their taste: too Brooklyn, too Broadway, too Jewish, too special, too eccentric, too unattractive. Her songs were too old and too obscure, and her style was too homosexual. Finally, in the spring of 1964, *The Barbra Streisand Album* was released and made history: it remained on the charts for nearly eighteen months, establishing Streisand as one of the most popular American singers of all time.

The path from Barbara to Barbra, Manhattan to Malibu, has been neither linear, nor always successful. Following her astounding movie breakthrough in

Funny Girl in 1968, Streisand snatched *Hello, Dolly!* from Carol Channing, who had made Dolly Levy a household name. Playing a middle-aged matchmaker was not a wise career move, however, and the film flopped. Its album peaked at number forty-nine on the chart, a dismal placing for a star. Having won an Oscar for *Funny Girl*, Streisand was not even nominated for *Hello, Dolly!* Her next film, *On a Clear Day You Can See Forever*, was nearly not released, and the soundtrack sold poorly—until the release of *The Owl and the Pussycat* in 1970 made it almost look passable.

On opening night of the musical Funny Girl, *twenty-one-year-old Barbra Streisand received twenty-three curtain calls. Through a career that has encompassed tremendous successes in singing, acting, directing, and producing, the enthusiasm of the public has not diminished, despite the covert discrimination that often comes to aggressive and successful women. She is shown here in a scene from the movie.*

Then came *What's Up, Doc?* with Ryan O'Neal (they would team up again in *The Main Event*—and jump-start the fitness craze). She was back in orbit. In 1973, *The Way We Were* would bring her not only more money, fame, and fans, but also her first number-one hit song. By then, she had also participated in her first political fund-raiser, for George McGovern (an act that would place her on Richard Nixon's enemies list). By the end of the 1970s, Streisand had starred in a rock remake of *A Star Is Born* with Kris Kristofferson and collaborated with singer-songwriter Barry Gibb on her best-selling album *Guilty*. She was on her way to superstardom.

In September 1981, idolized and iconized, Streisand recorded "Memory" from the Andrew Lloyd Webber hit show *Cats*. According to Considine, then at Columbia Records, she declined to record "Don't Cry for Me Argentina" from *Evita* because Eva Perón "was a fascist." The album *Memories* went platinum even though it featured only two new songs.

But her next project took a lot of chutzpah, and won for her both accolades and condemnation. Streisand both directed and starred in the film version of Isaac Bashevis Singer's story *Yentl*. Even though the movie made money, garnered good reviews, and inspired women's groups, she did not receive an Academy Award nomination (the film did win an Oscar for its music). Nor did Singer find the film treatment faithful to his original text.

Briefly crushed, Streisand was soon back in the limelight again, in her own way, on her own terms, with *The Broadway Album*. The first cut on the recording is Streisand speaking with two advisers, who tell her the record won't sell—yet it peaked at number one on the charts and won two Grammys. In 1991, she tried her hand again at directing and starring (as well as producing) a film, Pat Conroy's *The Prince of Tides*. And again, despite the movie's good reviews and box office success, Streisand was snubbed by the Academy of Motion Picture Arts and Sciences. She turned her energies to helping elect Bill Clinton. In November 1996, she released another film in which she starred as well as directed and produced, *The Mirror Has Two Faces*. The movie was a hit with the fans, but the reviews were generally unfavorable.

To date, then, Streisand has appeared in sixteen movies, mastering each genre—comedy, drama, musical—in turn. Whatever the plot, however, Streisand is decidedly, defiantly, Jewish. She portrays many undeniably Jewish characters: FANNY BRICE in *Funny Girl* and *Funny Lady*; Dolly Levy in *Hello, Dolly!*; the teenaged yeshivah boy who is really a girl in *Yentl*; and a Jewish psychiatrist in *The Prince of Tides*. In fact,

Barbra Streisand is more than another consumer-culture icon. She is a diva. A superstar. A sensation. Since the 1960s, she has won more varied awards (Emmy, Grammy, Oscar, special Tony) than anyone else in show business and has sold more records than any singers except the Beatles. [New York Public Library]

even when she plays a non-Jew, she is Jewish nonetheless, acting the part with courage and conviction. She even made the lead role in the classic *A Star Is Born* Jewish, and insisted on playing a Jewish Rose in *The Mirror Has Two Faces*, formerly a French farce.

Before Streisand, conventional wisdom stated that looking Jewish, for an actress, meant being relegated to supporting roles. Now, thirty years after Streisand, looking Jewish, ethnic, or in any way different has become chic. Streisand's Jewishness is not a role, but a life-style. She has been generous to Jewish causes and philanthropies in the United States and in Israel, honoring the memory of her late father, an educator.

When asked why she performs, Streisand has indicated that it is not for the money. "I have enough money, thank God, and the only reason I want it is to give it away. There's nothing more I need," she told the *New York Times* in 1983.

She champions environmental projects and is a dedicated Democratic fund-raiser; she raised so much money for Bill Clinton's 1992 election campaign that she was invited to his inauguration. She later spearheaded a boycott of Colorado ski resorts when that state passed Proposition 2 to deny gay men and lesbians any legal recourse against even the most blatant homophobia: "We must now say clearly that the moral climate in Colorado is no longer acceptable, and if we're asked to, we must refuse to play where they discriminate."

Streisand's often courageous stands earn her the unswerving respect and loyalty of fans all over the world. At Harvard, she explained her philosophy:

> I know that I can speak more eloquently through my work than through any speech I might give. So, as an artist, I've chosen to make films about subjects and social issues I care about, whether it's dealing with the inequality of women in *Yentl*, or producing a film about Colonel Grethe Cammermeyer, who was discharged from the army for telling the truth about her sexuality.

Yet in public performances and on the screen as the singer and actress, Streisand has a carefully constructed persona. She is touted as a natural talent, but she has taken many acting lessons. She sings to standing-room-only crowds, but she rarely performs in public because of her stage fright. She has a reputation with Hollywood insiders for arrogance, but is deeply insecure. Streisand is a perfectionist, pouring all her time and energy into her film projects, but Hollywood loves to snub her.

Streisand, unapologetic about her insistence on total control over her movies and albums, believes the criticism is indicative of sexism. "Of course I want utter and complete control over every product I do. You know, the audience buys my work because I control it, because I am a perfectionist, because I care deeply."

Streisand's fans think they know better; they love her. In her long career, Streisand has spawned a legion of fans, including singer Tony Bennett, whose 1995 album *Here's to the Ladies* begins with a tribute to Streisand and her signature song, "People": "From her humble beginnings to her triumph in the theater, no one has been more successful than Barbra. She is at the pinnacle of her art." Her films, albums, and rare public performances continue to break records. Fans are united in their love of the multitalented star and their hatred of what they perceive to be sensation-seeking critics. There are Streisand fan clubs, Streisand fanzines, Streisand cyber-fansites, Streisand collectors, Streisand groupies, and just plain Streisand aficionados. The most notable of these just opened a Streisand boutique in California called, appropriately, Hello Gorgeous. To her fans, Streisand is a trailblazer who has developed her own unique sense of style and beauty. Her lifework, as expressed in her music and movies, as well as in her political activism, is a defiant reexamination and redefinition of these terms—beauty, style, woman, activist—on her own terms.

Fans and critics alike agree that Streisand is extraordinarily gifted as a performer. Marvin Hamlisch, who in 1962 was Streisand's rehearsal pianist and in 1973 wrote the music for her hit movie *The Way We Were*, recalled his awe and surprise at her acumen for musical phrasing: "There was nothing she couldn't do with that voice, and she had an instinctual music taste that brought genius to everything she sang." She is equally at home singing ballads and rock, playing a harlot and a Hasid, directing a movie or producing one, creating her image or decorating a house.

Designer Isaac Mizrahi, in the March 1997 issue of *Out* magazine, recalls that in his youth, Streisand was "one of my icons. She was kind of a misfit, and yet she convinced everyone she was beautiful, including me. She *is* beautiful, but she's not the prototypical ideal of female beauty."

She has recorded fifty albums—thirty went gold and twenty went platinum, making her one of the most popular singers of all time. Moreover, many of her albums have produced hit singles. She has starred in sixteen major movies, three of which she directed. She consistently draws sell-out crowds to her live performances. Her television specials brought her to living rooms from Burbank to the Bronx. In addition, her innumerable philanthropic contributions to a wide variety of worthy causes are a testament to the fact that Streisand is much more than just an exceptionally talented and accomplished entertainer.

Barbra Streisand is more than another consumer-culture icon. She is a diva. A superstar. A sensation. Since the 1960s, she has won more varied awards (Emmy, Grammy, Oscar, special Tony) than anyone else in show business, and has sold more records than any singers but the Beatles. She is timeless, enduring, phenomenal. She has triumphed as herself in a town that thrives on make-believe, and she has done it all without mirrors.

FILMOGRAPHY

All Night Long (1981); *For Pete's Sake* (1974); *Funny Girl* (1968); *Funny Lady* (1975); *Hello, Dolly!* (1969); *The Main Event* (1979); *The Mirror Has Two Faces* (1996); *Nuts* (1987); *On a Clear Day You Can See Forever* (1970); *The Owl and the Pussycat* (1970); *Prince of Tides* (1991); *A Star Is Born* (1976); *Up the Sandbox* (1982); *The Way We Were* (1973); *What's Up, Doc?* (1972); *Yentl* (1983).

BIBLIOGRAPHY

Considine, Shaun. *Barbra Streisand: The Woman, The Myth, The Music* (1985); *EJ*; Hamlisch, Marvin, with Gerald Gardner. *The Way I Was* (1992); Mr. Showbiz. http://www.mrshowbiz.com; Pimentel, David. Barbra Streisand Web site on the Internet: http://acs2.bu.edu:8001/~pimentel/bjsweb.html; Riese, Randall. *Her Name Is Barbra: An Intimate Portrait of the Real Barbra Streisand* (1993); Robertson, Pam. "A Star is Born Again: Imitation and Difference in Streisand's Image." Paper presented at the Film and Performance Conference, University of New South Wales, Australia, September 1996; Spada, James. *Streisand: Her Life* (1995); *Time.* CD-ROM (1994); Zec, Donald, and Anthony Fowles. *Barbra: A Biography of Barbra Streisand* (1981).

LIORA MORIEL

STROOCK, HILDA WEIL
(1876–1945)

Hilda Weil Stroock was a sponsor of the first Women's Conference on Jewish Affairs held in 1938 at the Jewish Theological Seminary of America. This pioneering event reflected her lifelong interest in the welfare of women and children and the condition of the Jewish community.

Hilda Stroock, a daughter of Max and Gertrude Williamson Weil of New York, was born in 1876. She graduated from HUNTER COLLEGE, an institution in which she continued to take an active interest throughout her life. She married Solomon Marcuse Stroock, a well-known corporation lawyer who was a member of a distinguished family of lawyers and businessmen known for their philanthropic contributions to the general and Jewish communities. They had two children, a daughter Minette and a son Allan.

In the tradition of her husband's family, Hilda Stroock became a leader in organizational and philanthropic activities. When her family lived in Ossining, New York, she was vice president of the Westchester County Children's Association. Her special concern for children led her to sponsor a cardiac clinic for youngsters at the Montefiore Hospital, of which she later became a trustee. Prior to that, she was head of the Women's Auxiliary, a position more typical of women's volunteer work of the time.

Hilda Stroock was a trailblazer for women volunteers in community service. She served as vice-chair of the New York City Work and Relief Administration, created by Mayor John P. O'Brien in 1933 to administer all relief work in New York City. At its first meeting, the committee drew up a plan to transfer needy persons from home relief to work relief projects. She also served on the board of directors of the State Conference of Social Work, and, in 1931, as chair of the Women's Division in the emergency appeal of the Federation for the Support of Jewish Philanthropic Societies.

Hilda Stroock died in July 1945, having served as a leader in philanthropic and welfare programs directed to the needs of children in the general and Jewish communities.

BIBLIOGRAPHY

AJYB 48:501; *EJ* 15 (1972): 442, s.v. "Stroock"; *NYTimes*, July 30, 1945, 19: 4.

GLADYS ROSEN

STROOCK, REGINA D.
(1875–1948)

Born in New York City, in 1875, to a life of privilege, Regina Stroock parlayed her talents and wealth into a career of philanthropy and civic leadership. The daughter of jeweler Jacob Dreicer, Stroock graduated from Barnard College. She married Maurice C. Sternbach, son of the founder of Herrman and Sternbach, a dry-goods concern, who died in 1923. In 1927, she married her second husband Joseph Stroock, president and chief executive officer of S. Stroock and Company, a successful woolen mills and goods enterprise.

Active in Jewish and in New York City philanthropy, Stroock was a member and one-time chair of the Women's Division of the Joint Distribution Committee and National Refugee Service. She was also the honorary chair of the Women's Divisions of both the New York and the Brooklyn Federations of Jewish Charities. For many years, she devoted herself to helping young people, as a member of the board of the Hebrew Orphan Asylum and its successor, the Jewish Child Care Association of New York City. Mayor Fiorello LaGuardia appointed her to the board of the Children's Center of New York. In 1933, Stroock founded the Girls Home Club, a residence for working girls. She also began a boys' home, which did not succeed. A tireless worker, Stroock was involved in many fund-raising campaigns for the American Red Cross.

The mother of Maurice C. Dreicer and step-mother of Stephen J. Stroock, Regina Stroock died on August 15, 1948, in Scarsdale, New York.

BIBLIOGRAPHY

EJ, s.v. "Stroock"; *NYTimes*, August 15, 1948, 60:2.

JUDITH FRIEDMAN ROSEN

STRUNSKY, MANYA GORDON
(c. 1882–1945)

Manya Strunsky, better known under her maiden name of Manya Gordon, was a social activist and a respected writer on political and social issues.

Born in Kiev around 1882, she and her family immigrated to New York City in 1896. In her early years, she was educated at home; she later attended history and drama classes at Columbia University.

As a young woman, she was active in the American branch of the Russian Socialist Revolutionary Party, advocating the overthrow of the czar. More important, she became involved in the effort to bring Jews from czarist Russia to the United States during the peak years of Eastern European Jewish immigration. Once the immigrants were on American soil, Strunsky helped them to become settled and find employment.

After the Bolshevik Revolution in 1917, she wrote a number of articles about the new communist nation for such prestigious journals as *Harper's*, the *North American Review*, and the *Forum*. In later years, she was a literary critic for the *Saturday Review of Literature*.

She married journalist Simeon Strunsky, a member of the editorial board of the *New York Times*. The couple had two children, Robert and Frances.

Strunsky's scholarly reputation (or, more accurately, notoriety) largely rested on two major works that she published toward the end of her life. *Workers Before and After Lenin* (1941) is a highly readable account of the economic conditions prior to and following the Russian Revolution. Strunsky's sympathies for the aims of the communists are obvious; however, the book is empirical and objective, and she spares no harsh criticism of Lenin and Stalin's repressive tactics. Her second book, *How to Tell Progress from Reaction*, was published in 1944.

She died in New Canaan, Connecticut, on December 28, 1945.

SELECTED WORKS BY
MANYA GORDON STRUNSKY

How to Tell Progress from Reaction (1944); *Workers Before and After Lenin* (1941).

BIBLIOGRAPHY

AJYB, 48:501; Obituary. *NYTimes*, December 29, 1945.

JEROME S. LEGGE, JR.

SUBURBANIZATION

Few Jews participated in the first wave of suburbanization during the final decades of the nineteenth century, when streetcar suburbs were built around such cities as Boston, Philadelphia, and Chicago. In their early years, Brookline in Massachusetts, the Main Line in Pennsylvania, and the North Shore in Illinois did not offer new homes to Jews. In contrast to the close proximity of the rich, middle class, and poor in large cities, class stratification characterizes suburban districts. Moving to a newly created suburban utopia allowed people to be selective in their neighbors. Many suburbanites expressly kept Jews from living in their neighborhoods through individual residential covenants or through corporate regulations of planned communities.

Nonetheless, the children and grandchildren of Jewish immigrants embraced the American dream of home ownership and suburban living. Like other Americans, Jews wanted the cleanliness, quiet, and security that comes from living in a relatively homogeneous, middle-class community. Thus, Jewish suburbs were built, often by Jewish developers, during the second wave of suburbanization prior to World War II. Most American cities with large Jewish populations had at least one such suburban district, usually within the city's boundaries. This area was considered Jewish because of the presence of Jews (often as much as 30 percent of the district's population) and Jewish institutions, including large, modern synagogues.

Most Jews, however, did not opt for suburban living until the mass-produced suburbs of the 1950s and 1960s brought home ownership within the reach of millions of middle-class Americans. In 1948, the Supreme Court had declared restrictive residential covenants to be illegal, invigorating the efforts of such organizations as the AMERICAN JEWISH CONGRESS to eliminate anti-Semitic discrimination in housing. Gradually, many suburbs were opened to Jews, allowing them to benefit from generous provisions in the GI bill as well as federal mortgage, tax, and highway policies encouraging suburbanization. Unlike their predecessors, the new suburbs were designed for automobiles and were built beyond a city's boundaries. Like their predecessors, they were residential enclaves, stratified by class and race, where women and children spent their days while men worked in the nearby cities.

Jewish women responded in diverse ways to suburban living. When the occasional well-to-do immigrant families first moved to Jewish suburbs, the women were initially disoriented by the isolation of the individual homes and the lack of public culture, so different from the bustling conditions of the city. By contrast, most native-born Jewish women appreciated the freedom from paid employment and the opportunity to devote themselves to child rearing and housekeeping. Many extended their understanding of family responsibilities to include a larger, Jewish public sphere. Jewish women's organizations, from the NATIONAL COUNCIL OF JEWISH WOMEN to HADASSAH to the synagogue sisterhoods, successfully recruited suburbanites. Jewish women also participated in non-Jewish civic and cultural organizations. However, they rarely socialized with their gentile neighbors, despite socioeconomic similarities between the two groups. The Jewish suburb, sometimes called a "gilded ghetto"—a term evoking the wealthy yet exclusively Jewish character of these enclaves—supported many Jewish social and leisure-time organizations, including country clubs. Jews pursued suburban leisure and recreation activities almost exclusively with other Jews, behavior that came to be seen as typically Jewish. Ethnic sociability was replacing religious or political affiliation.

Jewish girls growing up in the suburbs sometimes found them stifling. Despite the good secular education they received in public schools, they faced a narrow choice of gender roles. Most were expected to marry and raise children without even a short interlude of paid employment. Few acquired more than a minimal Sunday school Jewish education, although their parents often provided them with many material comforts. In the postwar period, stereotypes and popular culture often ridiculed pampered suburban Jewish daughters like the fictitious Brenda Patimkin in Philip Roth's novel, *Goodbye Columbus*. Despite her Radcliffe education, Brenda is shallow and immature, more concerned with getting her nose fixed to conform to gentile standards of beauty than with any aspects of intellectual or political life. As a minority growing up in a world shaped by middle-class, American values, suburban Jewish daughters often struggled to attain a sense of Jewish self-esteem in the face of widespread negative attitudes toward Jews. A few rebelled by pursuing political activism to achieve social justice or by adopting a bohemian life-style that rejected the conformity and materialistic values of suburbia.

After World War II, the Jewish middle class moved to the suburbs en masse. As a result, different types of Jewish suburbs developed. For example, in the 1970s and 1980s, Syrian Jews and Iranian Jews each had their own suburban areas. Jews also began settling in integrated suburbs, where they remained a small minority—under 10 percent of the population. Around New York City, which was home to roughly 40 percent of the American Jewish population prior to World War II, Jews settled in suburbs in Westchester county and northern New Jersey, and especially on Long Island.

Suburbanization and postwar affluence stimulated an extensive period of synagogue building. Conservative Judaism, especially, benefited from this growth in congregations. Jewish girls, in turn, benefited from the expanded educational opportunities provided by Conservatism, including the adoption of the Bat Mitzvah, marking a Jewish girl's coming-of-age. Nevertheless, materialism and concern for gentile standards of beauty characteristic of prewar suburbanization persisted even as the social barriers between Jews and gentiles diminished. Rebellious Jewish daughters coming of age in the 1960s often identified these characteristics of suburban life not as typically American middle class, but as essentially Jewish.

Postwar middle-class Jewish women raising their families in the suburbs adopted similar strategies to their predecessors before the war. They turned to a wide range of volunteer activities to take them out of their secluded homes and enhance their lives. These activities included political action, usually on a local scale. Jewish women brought liberalism to the suburbs, supporting taxation to build strong public schools, the antinuclear peace movement, and laws guaranteeing civil rights for minorities. They also advocated specifically Jewish concerns, especially championing the new State of Israel and efforts to free Soviet Jewry. Many suburban Jewish women supported the feminist movement's political agenda, including equal rights for women and legalization of abortion, and encouraged their daughters' fight for equality in public schools. After their children left home, some Jewish mothers decided to look for jobs or go to college or professional school.

Today, suburbs are the popular residential choice of most Americans. No longer exclusively residential, suburbs house industry and technology as well as businesses. Despite their increasing diversity, they still lack the population density, poverty, and public culture of urban centers. Suburbs have offered Jewish women mixed blessings. On the positive side are material comforts, good schools, and a safe environment in which to raise a family. On the negative side are standards of femininity and beauty that weaken

Jewish self-esteem, narrow gender roles, materialistic values, and reduced access to Jewish, intellectual, and cultural pursuits.

BIBLIOGRAPHY

Baldassare, Mark. *Trouble in Paradise: The Suburban Transformation of America* (1986); Baum, Charlotte, Paula Hyman, and Sonya Michel. *Jewish Women in America* (1976); Binzen, Peter. "A Place to Live." In *Philadelphia Jewish Life 1940–1985*, edited by Murray Friedman (1986); Ebner, Michael. *Creating Chicago's North Shore* (1988); Fishman, Robert. *Bourgeois Utopias: The Rise and Fall of Suburbia* (1987); Gans, Herbert. "Park Forest: Birth of a Jewish Community." *Commentary* 11 (April 1951): 330–339, and "Progress of a Suburban Jewish Community." *Commentary* 23 (February 1957): 113–122; Gordon, Albert. *Jews in Suburbia* (1959); Jackson, Kenneth. *Crabgrass Frontier: The Suburbanization of the United States* (1985); Kramer, Judith, and Seymour Leventman. *Children of the Gilded Ghetto* (1961); Rosenthal, Erich. "This Was North Lawndale: The Transplantation of a Jewish Community." *Jewish Social Studies* 23, no. 2 (April 1960): 67–82; Sklare, Marshall, and Joseph Greenblum. *Jewish Identity on the Suburban Frontier: A Study of Group Survival in the Open Society* (1979); Warner, Sam Bass, Jr. *Streetcar Suburbs: The Process of Growth in Boston 1870–1900* (1969).

DEBORAH DASH MOORE

SULZBERGER, ELSIE K. (1884–1977)

Elsie K. (Elsepet Kohet) Sulzberger had an important public career through her leadership in the NATIONAL COUNCIL OF JEWISH WOMEN (NCJW) and in the early twentieth-century birth control movement.

She was born in Hungary, on September 5, 1884, to Rabbi Alexander and Elsepet (Elizabeth) Kohet and was educated at HUNTER COLLEGE and Barnard College, receiving her B.A. in 1906. She married Mayer B. Sulzberger in 1910, and they had one daughter, Evalyn.

Sulzberger lived the majority of her adult life in Detroit, Michigan, maintaining an active and diverse volunteer career in both Jewish and secular organizations. Her Jewish organizational leadership was primarily on the local level as the vice president of the Detroit section of NCJW and the Detroit League of Jewish Women. However, she achieved national recognition at the 1923 meeting of the NATIONAL FEDERATION OF TEMPLE SISTERHOODS concerning "The Jewish Problem in the Larger World." In a speech, she protested the modern Jewish attitude of condescension based on the ancientness of Judaism, adding that "the glories of which we boast become mere crutches to a limping self-esteem." Sulzberger then urged modern Jews to seek their own laurels and "not snatch them from the heads of our progenitors." Specifically, she called for increased volunteer activity on the part of American Jewish women, emphasizing that a "good name in man or woman ... comes with doing public chores," adding that "as the Jewish woman is seen attending energetically to the world's work, the prejudice that is a suspicion of her aloofness will disappear."

Outside the Jewish organizations, Sulzberger unquestionably practiced the volunteerism she preached. Her chosen secular cause was the early birth control movement as a member of the Michigan Birth Control League and as vice president of the Detroit Maternal Health Section. Her most important contribution, however, was the establishment of birth control clinics in the Detroit area, beginning with the Mother's Health Clinic in 1927. The Mother's Health Clinic, of which Sulzberger was both the founder and first president, was reputed to be the only birth control clinic between New York and Chicago in the late 1920s. In 1933, she established two more local birth control clinics, one within the North End Clinic and the other at the Dunbar Hospital, the latter then a segregated, all-black hospital. She also had an active literary career as the editor of the *Detroit Club Woman Magazine* from 1921 through 1931 and as the author of many poems, essays, and short stories.

Elsie K. Sulzberger died on November 17, 1977.

BIBLIOGRAPHY

BEOAJ; "Reform Judaism Program Discussed." *NYTimes*, January 26, 1923, 11; Rogow, Faith. *Gone to Another Meeting: The National Council of Jewish Women, 1893–1993* (1993).

SUSAN ROTH

SULZBERGER, IPHIGENE OCHS (1892–1990)

Iphigene Ochs Sulzberger was the daughter, wife, mother, and grandmother of four publishers of the *New York Times*.

Born on September 19, 1892, to second-generation German Jewish immigrants in Chattanooga, Tennessee, she was the granddaughter of the renowned Reform rabbi Isaac Mayer Wise. She moved to New York City when her father, Adolph Ochs, purchased the *New York Times* in 1896. Her childhood in New York was spent in the company of New York power brokers and cultural leaders. Sundays were often spent visiting the Carnegies or the Schiffs, or walking with her father in Central Park. She writes in her memoirs that "The city's cultural institutions were my

Her position as part of the New York Times *publishing dynasty allowed Iphigene Ochs Sulzberger to move comfortably among the luminaries of the twentieth century and to become an important contributor to numerous social and educational causes. She is shown here at the American Jewish Archives. From left to right: Dr. Abraham Peck, now director of the archives; Susan Dryfoos; Sulzberger; and the dean of American Jewish historians, Jacob Rader Marcus. [American Jewish Archives]*

classroom." After being educated at private schools, including the exclusive Bejamin-Dean School, she entered Barnard College in 1910. She performed well in college and graduated in 1914 with majors in economics and history. She attributed her commitment to social causes in part to her Barnard education, and volunteered weekly at the famous Henry Street Settlement throughout college.

She married Arthur Sulzberger, a cotton merchant, in 1917. She had met Sulzberger briefly while he attended Columbia University, but their relationship blossomed while he was in the armed forces. After they married, Iphigene Sulzberger focused on building a family. Her four children were all born between 1918 and 1926. The youngest, Arthur, would eventually succeed his father as editor of the *New York Times*. As her family grew, she shifted her focus from the home to civic and philanthropic causes. She became president of the Parks Association in 1934,

and served until 1950, when she began serving as chairman, in which capacity she remained until 1957.

She became a trustee of the *Times* upon her father's death in 1935. At this time, her husband became publisher of the newspaper. She avoided using her personal influence to affect editorial positions within the paper, although she claimed in her memoirs to have suggested and encouraged many stories with social justice and community service themes. Her civic activities revolved around educational institutions. She served on the board of Barnard College from 1937 to 1968, and raised funds for the construction of a library. She also served as a trustee of the Hebrew Union College–Jewish Institute of Religion, which awarded her an honorary doctorate of humane letters in 1973. She served as a trustee for the University of Chattanooga as well. Not limiting herself to universities, she sat on the board of the CEDAR KNOLLS SCHOOL FOR GIRLS, where she had once worked.

Sulzberger won numerous awards for her public service, and received several honorary degrees. In 1951, Columbia University granted her a doctor of laws degree. In 1978, she received an honorary doctorate of humanities from Bishop College in Dallas, which noted that she had been the largest single contributor to the United Negro College Fund over the previous decade. The Jewish Theological Seminary awarded her an honorary doctorate of letters in 1968.

Her family continued to shape the *Times* for the rest of the century. Her son-in-law, Orvil Dryfoos, became editor upon her husband's retirement in 1961. After Dryfoos died in 1963, Arthur Ochs Sulzberger succeeded him as publisher. His son, Arthur Ochs Sulzberger, Jr., became publisher in 1992. Iphigene Sulzberger's memoirs, *Iphigene*, were published in 1981. They provide an amusing and insightful look at the *Times*'s history, and many of the famous figures of the twentieth century.

Iphigene Sulzberger died in her sleep at age ninety-seven on February 26, 1990.

BIBLIOGRAPHY

Obituary. *NYTimes*, February 27, 1990. Sulzberger, Iphigene Ochs. *Iphigene: The Memoirs of Iphigene Ochs Sulzberger*, as told to Susan W. Dryfoos (1981, 1987); *WWIAJ* (1938).

DAVID KAHAN

SULZBERGER, RACHEL HAYS (1861–1938)

Rachel Hays Sulzberger maintained an active volunteer career in public service, in both Jewish and secular organizations. She is best remembered, however, as the second president of the New York section of the NATIONAL COUNCIL OF JEWISH WOMEN (NCJW), from 1894 to 1900. As section president, Sulzberger was a strong proponent of the NCJW as a moral and spiritual force in America's big cities.

Rachel Hays Sulzberger was born in 1861 in New York City, the daughter of David Hays and Judith Piexotto Hays. Her father was a descendant of Jacob Hays, one of the founders of Shearith Israel, the first organized Jewish congregation in America. Her mother was descended from the Piexottos, one of the oldest American Sephardi Jewish families. Rachel Hays was educated in New York City and graduated from the Normal College Training School (now Hunter College). Prior to her marriage, she taught for four years, both at the Normal College and in the public schools. In 1884, Rachel Hays married Cyrus L. Sulzberger. Their children included Arthur Hays Sulzberger, who became the publisher of *The New York Times*.

In a speech at the national convention in 1896, she proclaimed that the NCJW's greatest success was not its vast charitable works, but that the organization had "quickened the religious feeling of the community" through the influence of the religiously inspired women of the NCJW within their homes. She also justified the leisure-time activity of the Bible circles as a means of spiritual elevation for the Jewish woman. Despite this emphasis on a woman's home-bound moral influence, Sulzberger also exhorted the NCJW members to take up outside volunteer work and even recommended that every member who was not already thus engaged and "whose home duties permit" be required to do volunteer work for a few hours a month.

Both within and beyond the National Council of Jewish Women, Sulzberger herself invested her time as well as her money in volunteer activities. As NCJW president, she founded the Recreation Rooms and Settlement, popularly known as "The House on Christie Street," and served as its president for 25 years following its independence from NCJW. She remained on the board until she died.

Beyond the NCJW, Rachel Hays Sulzberger was the vice president of the United Neighborhood Houses, an association of settlement houses, and chaired its Parks Anti-Litter Committee, formed at her suggestion. As committee chair, she worked in cooperation with the mayor for the installation of trash receptacles in New York City's public parks. She was also the first woman trustee of the Aguilar Library Association, which was later part of the New York Public Library System, as well as a member of the New York Urban League and founder and honorary director of the Jewish Working Girls Vacation Society. She was a member of the Daughters of the American Revolution as well.

Rachel Hays Sulzberger died on February 10, 1938.

BIBLIOGRAPHY

AJYB 7 (1905–1906): 107, 40:392; Birmingham, Stephen. *The Grandees: America's Sephardic Elite* (1971); Dryfoos, Susan W. *Iphigene: Memoirs of Iphigene Ochs Sulzberger of The New York Times Family, as Told to Her Granddaughter, Susan W. Dryfoos* (1991); "Mrs. Sulzberger Dies at Her Home." *NYTimes*, February 11, 1938, 23:3; National Council of Jewish Women. *Proceedings of the National Council of Jewish Women, 1896* (1896); Rogow, Faith. *Gone to Another Meeting: The National Council of Jewish Women, 1893–1993* (1993).

SUSAN ROTH

SUMMER CAMPING

In the winter of 1945, Elsie Reich and her husband Harry bought seven acres of land in Salisbury, Connecticut. She had "pawned her diamond ring" and convinced him to borrow money against his business to finance this purchase. The deed of sale lists Harry Reich as the owner of the grounds. But Elsie Reich managed the property. She employed homeless people recommended to her by a New York City clergyman. Their names were Joe, Turk, the Swede, and Dutch.

In the spring of 1946, Reich drove "her men" up from the Bowery to Connecticut. They constructed cabins and carved out a waterfront in exchange for room and board. Berkshire Hills Camp opened that summer. It provided Jewish children with "amusement, recreation, entertainment and instruction," and Elsie Reich with the prospect of financial independence.

Neither the camp nor Reich's activities were unique. Berkshire Hills was one of thousands of summer camps established in the American Northeast (a directory published in 1949 listed 1,783 camps for New York, Connecticut, Massachusetts, and Maine alone). Its campers were among the millions of Jewish children who attended summer camp. And Elsie Reich was one of the many Jewish women who became involved with summer camping in the first half of the twentieth century.

Summer camp became an American institution in the aftermath of World War I. It evolved within a society that was concerned with children and believed in reform. In the early 1920s, social commentators and ordinary people were convinced that "crass materialism" and "cheap amusements" were turning American youth into juvenile delinquents. These beliefs echoed throughout the decade and were augmented with a fear of "idle hands" and "latchkey children" during the Great Depression and World War II. The radio series "Are These Our Children?" articulated these anxieties. This weekly show reenacted the stories of "real life young criminals" and located their vice in overindulgent mothers, unchaperoned leisure, jazz, and cigarettes.

Summer camps were frequently run by women. This photo of a scene from Berkshire Hills Camp in the 1940s includes the "camp mother" (left, ladling milk) and the camp codirector. [Photograph courtesy of Nancy Mykoff]

This scene from an unidentified camp depicts campers (several in bathing suits) lighting candles in the dining hall. The "Camp for Living Judaism" sign on the back wall refers to "300 years of American Jewish Life." [American Jewish Archives]

Summer camp was presented as a cure for these social dilemmas. Camp brochures and news releases pledged to prevent delinquency and vowed to transform "physically and spiritually illiterate" boys and girls into "able bodied" and "morally upright" American citizens. The plan for accomplishing this feat centered on removing children from their urban environments and placing them in the "great school out-of-doors."

The federal government, along with private individuals and institutions, adopted this approach. During the New Deal Era, it established camps for transient workers, union members, and unemployed boys and girls. These camps were informed by the communal and patriotic ideals expressed by Jewish camping women and articulated in summer camp promotional literature.

The summer camp was a site of Americanization. Separate and isolated from the larger society, it provided the opportunity to transmit specific values and ideologies to children. The activities and programs that structured daily life were central to this citizen-making process.

Jewish institutions of a variety of ideological stripes perceived the summer camp as a means of mediating between ethnic and American identities. The desire to rear moral American citizens while instilling specific ideas about Jewish culture fueled their camping activities. Jewish Federations of Philanthropy were among the many organizations that established culturally defined summer camps. They were driven by the need to counteract the "missionary efforts" of non-Jewish camping organizations and by the belief that poor urban children would benefit from a vacation in the country.

Other Jewish organizations also became involved with summer camping. The Central Jewish Institute of New York City, for instance, established camp Cejwin shortly after World War I. BERTHA SCHOOL-MAN was an instrumental figure in its operation. The camp was conceived as an "educational enterprise, not just a fresh-air place for poor children." The 1,300 children who attended Camp Cejwin in the summer of 1961 were divided into gender and age groups. This division fostered a sense of independence in Cejwin's male and female campers.

Zionists, Hebraists, Yiddishists, Socialists, and Communists all viewed the "total environment" of the summer camp as an unparalleled venue for the transmission of values. Dr. Samson Benderly, head of the New York City Bureau of Jewish Education, established the first Hebrew-speaking camp in America in 1927. It was followed by Camp Massad in 1941, Camp Yavneh in 1944, and Camp Ramah in 1947.

Camp Ramah was established in Wisconsin by the Jewish Theological Seminary (JTS). This camp, an expression of Conservative Judaism, became a movement in itself. A prominent JTS educator, SYLVIA ETTENBERG, was an active promoter of the six Ramah camps which would dot the American landscape. These camps attempted to bridge the gap between "what the school was teaching and what the Jewish child was experiencing in the home, by providing a new milieu which could act as a surrogate home."

The Reform Movement also instituted a network of summer camps that defined and conveyed Jewish culture. Unlike their Conservative counterparts, however, these camps were not Hebrew speaking. Orthodox Judaism also entered into the summer camp fray. HADASSAH, for instance, sponsored the Young Judaea Zionist summer camps. Like the Conservative and Reform camps, the more Orthodox camps provided opportunities for girls to study

Jewish texts and culture alongside boys, thereby redefining the gendered construction of Jewish education. These definitions influenced the campers' young and adult lives. Mrs. Barbara Levine, for example, framed the picture of her bat mitzvah at summer camp. The fifty-five-year-old image hangs among pictures that chart the turning points in her family history.

Within the Conservative Movement, the Ramah camps introduced the notion of egalitarianism in religious ritual. In 1972, the camp directors issued a report endorsing *aliyot* for women and their chanting of the Torah and prophetic portions. This report also suggested that camp directors be granted the right to hold ancillary services where post–bat mitzvah girls could have *aliyot* and function as *shelihot zibbur* [leaders of the service].

Not all explicitly Jewish summer camps were religious or Zionist in their orientation. Yiddish cultural organizations such as the Workmen's Circle and the Sholem Aleichem Institute also became involved with summer camping. Yiddishists established the nonpolitical Boiberik and the Socialist Kinder Ring camps. Yiddish culture was also mobilized to teach Communist ideology. According to Irving Howe, the children at Camp Kinderland were "dutifully herded into thirty-six little Soviet Republics."

Sports were an essential part of summer camping. This archery class is at Camp Watitoh in Becket, Massachusetts. The photograph was taken in 1950. [American Jewish Historical Society]

Jewish women promoted and participated in a variety of Jewish camps, ranging from the secular to the political. Ethnic issues informed their deep involvement with these diverse forms of summer camping. Anti-Semitism, for example, raged throughout the interwar period. It fueled nativist policies that denied Jewish-Americans access to educational institutions and social clubs. It was also expressed in immigration legislation that effectively barred Jews from entering the country.

Summer camp provided a means of coping with this racism. Anti-Semites claimed that Jewish people were physically unfit to be (or become) American citizens. Camps undermined this accusation with rigorous exercise and nutritious foods. They designed competitive sports and "milk squads," for example, for both male and female campers. This focus on the physical developed a "muscular Judaism." It also fostered ethnic pride.

Although Jewish camps varied in terms of their religious and political orientations, all of them catered to Jewish children. Staff members crafted and conveyed "Jewish" traditions that shaped the experiences of childhood. They conducted flag-raising ceremonies that began with the Pledge of Allegiance and ended with the singing of Hebrew songs. They also led religious ceremonies in the woods. In the summer of 1934, "Miss Sunny conducted services" while "Miss Jean kindled the Sabbath candles" at Camp Council. And like "Aunt Mickey" at Camp Woodmere, they told "moral" tales after conducting the Sabbath prayers. Campers' letters and memories reveal that these new rituals "instilled a proud Jewish identity which lasted beyond the closing of camp itself."

Camp owners and organizers rallied support for their business ventures by presenting summer camp as a "public family" of motherly and fatherly directors and staff. This familial (and therefore familiar) presentation was embodied in the "camp mother." Like Mrs. Ruth Steinbach Steppacher, known to Woodmere campers as "Aunt Dolly," the camp mother prefaced her name with "Aunt" and treated the campers as if they were her own children. These women "dried tears, sewed buttons," and were the object of the campers' love and affection.

Female counselors were encouraged to relate to "their" campers in a "motherly way." Letters written to their own mothers show that they took this directive to heart. Marie Rothschild was a counselor at Camp Tripp Lake. In the summer of 1921, she and two other counselors took a group of campers on a canoe trip. Although they suffered from an "unmerciful sun, hunger, dirt and fatigue," these dedicated young women "wouldn't say die." They tended to and inspired their campers, and returned to camp "dead tired but thrilled at the trip" and "singing hymns of Joy."

Camping women assumed the role of "female fathers" as well as nurturing mothers. Sometimes, the two roles converged. Miss Carrie Kuhn and Miss Estelle Goldsmith, two Sunday school teachers, directed life at Camp Woodmere throughout the early twentieth century. They signaled the beginning of the day by "ringing the old school bell." And with "proper shoes and pursed lips," they oversaw the daily activities. "Aunt" Shulamit was the head counselor at Berkshire Hills Camp in the 1940s. Like the "directresses" of Camp Woodmere, she inspired deference and sometimes fear. "Aunt Minna," on the other hand, embodied both "masculine" and "feminine" characteristics. This camp dietitian is remembered as imposing yet nurturing. She was "gutsy enough to buy from the meat man, yet loving enough to comfort any home-sick camper."

Although many Jewish women were employed as directors or dieticians, some shaped summer camp from afar. Social reformers and educators, including JENNIE FRANKLIN PURVIN, presented lectures and wrote articles that encouraged parents to send their children "off to camp." Purvin also worked as the "camp adviser" of Mandel Brothers Department store. Her skill at recommending appropriate summer camps for individual children earned her the gratitude of satisfied parents and the praise of the department store from the 1930s to the mid-1950s. The president of Mandel Brothers described Jennie Purvin's work as a "great contribution" to the store's "prestige and reputation," as well as to its camp and sporting goods sales.

Purvin made financial contributions to individual camps as well to the department store. The few dollars she donated to Camp Council in 1924 were eclipsed by the "main building, large dining porch and store room" bestowed by a female philanthropist a few years later. Nevertheless, her donation testifies to the myriad ways reformers and philanthropists embraced and developed summer camping throughout the decades.

When Elsie Reich opened Berkshire Hills Camp in 1946, she was perpetuating a female tradition that had existed for thirty years. In 1916, Miss Kuhn and Miss Goldsmith founded Camp Woodmere. The "fundamentals of good citizenship" structured life at this summer camp. Democracy and patriotism were conveyed on the fields, within the cabins, and around the campfires that were central to the camping experience. Elsie

What would summer camp be without swimming?
This "girls' swim" was photographed at Surprise Lake Camp
in Cold Spring, New York, in the early 1950s.
[Ike Vern. 92nd Street YM-YWHA Archives]

Reich carried these ideals and customs into the second half of the twentieth century.

Throughout the century, Jewish women justified their camping activities in terms of extending their child-rearing duties to a more public sphere. This enabled them to journey to summer camp without crossing traditional gender boundaries. Many women were compelled to camping by financial need. Others, however, did not receive wages. They worked at camp so that their children could enjoy a vacation in the country.

But women's less traditional camping activities suggest that they challenged, as well as confirmed, contemporary ideas about male and female behavior. Camp's very location in "the wilderness" illustrates this point. The wilderness has featured in historical narratives as a male territory. Be it virginal or savage, it is often described as an object that is either conquered or tamed by men. Camping women ventured into the woods. Neither conquering nor taming it, they transformed pieces of the "great out doors" into prototypes of the American home.

BIBLIOGRAPHY

Borish, Linda. "Jewish American Women, Jewish Organizations and Sports, 1880–1920." In *Sports and the American Jew* (1997); Eisen, George. "Sport, Recreation and Gender: Jewish Immigrant Women in Turn-of-the-Century America (1880–1920)." *Journal of Sport History* (1991): 103–121; Erenberg, Lewis A., and Susan E. Hirsch. *The War in American Culture: Society and Consciousness During World War II* (1996); Glenn, Susan A. *Daughters of the Shtetl: Life and Labor in the Immigrant Generation* (1990); Hyman, Paula E. *Gender and Assimilation in Modern Jewish History: The Roles and Representation of Women* (1995), and "The Unfinished Symphony: The Gerson Cohen Years." In *Tradition Renewed: A History of the Jewish Theological Seminary*, edited by Jack Wertheimer (1997); Joselit, Jenna Weissman, and Karen S. Mittleman, eds. *A Worthy Use of Summer: Jewish Summer Camping in America* (1993); Norwood, Vera. *Made from This Earth: American Women and Nature* (1993); Peiss, Kathy. *Cheap Amusements: Working Women and Leisure in Turn of the Century New York* (1986); Riess, Steven A. "Sport and the American Jew: A Second Look." *American Jewish History* (1995): 1–15; Sorin, Gerald. *Tradition Transformed: The Jewish Experience in America* (1997); Wenger, Beth S. *New York Jews and the Great Depression: Uncertain Promise* (1996).

NANCY MYKOFF

SWERDLOW, AMY (b. 1923)

An active participant for Women Strike for Peace (WSP) since its inception, Amy G. Swerdlow—teacher, scholar, writer, and social activist—has written the following about this organization:

> By stressing the global issues and international cooperation rather than private family issues, WSP challenged the key element of the feminine mystique: the domestication and privatization of the middle class white woman. By making recognized contributions to the achievements of an atmospheric test ban, WSP also raised women's sense of political efficacy and self-esteem.

Amy Miriam Galstuck Swerdlow was born on January 20, 1923, in New York City, the daughter of Joseph J. and Esther (Rodner) Galstuck. In 1949, she married Stanley H. Swerdlow and the couple had four children: Joan, Ezra, Lisa, and Thomas. Swerdlow holds a B.A. from New York University (1962), an M.A. from Sarah Lawrence College (1973), and a Ph.D. from Rutgers University (1984).

Before marriage, Swerdlow worked briefly in publishing, and has been a member of the board of directors of the Feminist Press since 1973. A delegate to the National Women's Conference in 1977, she has

focused on women's history. From 1976 to 1979, she was director of the American Historical Association's Institute for Women's History in Secondary Schools. In 1981, she was appointed professor of women's and American history at Sarah Lawrence College. Swerdlow is director emerita of the Women's Studies Program at Sarah Lawrence, a post she "inherited" from GERDA LERNER, who introduced her to United States women's history and encouraged her to dig into the field. She has edited feminist publications and contributed articles and essays to journals and books. She is the author of *Women Strike for Peace: Traditional Motherhood and Radical Politics in the 1960's*.

SELECTED WORKS BY AMY SWERDLOW

"Abolition's Conservative Sisters: The Ladies' New York City Anti-Slavery Societies, 1834–1840." In *The Abolitionist Sisterhood*, edited by Jean Fagan Yellin and John C. Van Horne (1994); "'Clean Bombs' and Clean Language." In *Women, Militarism, and War: Essays in History, Politics, and Social Theory* (1990); "The Congress of American Women: Left-Feminist Peace Politics in the Cold War." In *U.S. History as Women's History: New Feminist Essays*, edited by Linda K. Kerber, Alice Kessler-Harris, and Kathryn Kish Sklar (1995); *Women Strike for Peace: Traditional Motherhood and Radical Politics in the 1960's* (1993).

BIBLIOGRAPHY

Contemporary Authors 105 (1982); *Who's Who in America*. 49th ed. (1995).

MOIRA REYNOLDS

SYLVIN, FRANCIS *see* SEAMAN, SYLVIA BERNSTEIN

SYMS, SYLVIA BLAGMAN (1917–1992)

"When you perform, it's a one-to-one love affair with the people out there. That's how it has to be," stated Sylvia Syms before her death in 1992. Syms's dynamic saloon performances were characterized by an intimate storytelling style and a grainy contralto voice combined with honesty, a "been-there" aura, and a genuine love of the connection with her audience. She was touted as one of the best contributors to her genre by such noteworthy peers as Cy Coleman, Billie Holiday, Frank Sinatra, and Duke Ellington.

The eldest of three children, Syms was born on December 2, 1917, in New York City to a poor Russian immigrant father, Abraham Solomon Blagman, and a New York–born, devoutly Jewish mother, Pauline

A nightclub and Broadway singer whose schooling was listening to jazz greats on 52nd Street, Sylvia Blagman Syms was discovered by Mae West and died during a standing ovation she was receiving at the Algonquin Hotel. [New York Public Library]

(Weiss) Blagman. Both parents had minimal formal education, and Syms's own was limited.

Syms nursed her growing musical passion by sneaking out to stand in saloon coatrooms when she was underage to listen to jazz greats such as Mildred Bailey, Billie Holiday, Art Tatum, and Lester Young. Fifty-second ("Swing") Street became Syms's musical "classroom." By the mid-1940s, she was appearing regularly in several clubs and had recorded her first single, "I'm in the Mood for Love." Syms married Bret Morrison in 1946 and divorced in 1953 due to differences in life-styles and goals.

In 1949, she was discovered by Mae West, who became a significant teacher and influence on Syms's performing style. Syms participated in musical theater throughout much of her career, appearing in *Diamond Liz*, *South Pacific*, *Camino Real* (her favorite role), and *Hello, Dolly!*

In 1956, she recorded her major hit, a double-tempo version of "I Could Have Danced All Night," which sold more than one million copies. Also, in the mid-1950s, she married dancer Ed Begley, whom she also later divorced. She had no children. Although her health began to fail from emphysema and lung cancer in the 1960s, she continued to perform both in clubs and musical theater.

In the 1980s, Syms taught master classes on musical theater singing at Northwood Institute in Dallas, Texas. Considering herself a historian, she enjoyed passing on her musical knowledge, especially that of 52nd Street. She was indeed a living monument to an era of New York music; her nightclub career spanned fifty-one years.

Syms recorded fifteen albums. Successful songs included "In Times Like These," "Dancing Chandelier," and "It's Good to be Alive." She toured the United States and eventually performed throughout the world.

Syms was a dynamic personality with a sharp, analytical eye. She was barely five feet tall and was perennially plump, giving her a distinctive, round face that prompted loving nicknames such as "Buddha" (Sinatra) and "Moonbeam Moscowitz" (Tatum). Her presence was said to be immediately commanding and a joy to behold.

Judaism was not an active part of Syms's life; as she said in 1974, "her religion [was] people." Singing became a "total cleansing" for Syms, which helped her feel young and full of life. She did show respect for her mother's Jewish faith, however, by giving generously to her mother's synagogue.

Syms died of a heart attack on May 10, 1992, while receiving a standing ovation after a performance at the Algonquin Hotel in New York City.

SELECTED DISCOGRAPHY

After Dark, Version VLP 1D3 (1954); *The Fabulous Sylvia Syms*, 20th Century-Fox TFS 4123 (1964); *A Jazz Portrait of Johnny Mercer*, DRG Records, AHB-3281 (live 1984, 1995); *Lovingly*, Atlantic SD 18177 (1976); *Sings*, Atlantic 1243 and Decca DL 8188 (1956); *Songs of Love*, Decca DL 8639 (1958); *Sylvia Is . . .*, Prestige 7439 (1966); *Then Along Came Bill*, DRG Records, ocm23234338 (1990); *Torch Songs*, Columbia CS 8243 (1961); *You Must Believe in Spring*, ELBA 5004.

BIBLIOGRAPHY

Bailey, Muriel (née Blagman). Telephone conversation with author, May 5, 1996; Balliet, Whitney. *American Singers* (1988); *Biography Index*. Vols. 10–12; Blagman, Burton. Telephone conversation with author, May 6, 1996; "Died, Sylvia Syms." *Time* (May 25, 1992): 23; Gavin,

James. *Intimate Nights: The Golden Age of New York Cabaret* (1991), and "Sylvia Syms, One of Pop's Greatest Storytellers." *NYTimes*, May 17, 1992, 29; Holden, Stephen. "Our Perennial Songbirds." *NYTimes Magazine*, November 15, 1987, 47–48, and "Sylvia Syms, Singer, Dead at 74; Cabaret Artist with Saloon Style." *NYTimes*, May 11, 1992, D10; Koenig, Rhoda. "Nightlife: Fall Preview." *New York* (September 18, 1978): 56–57; Palmer, Robert. "The Women of Jazz: Where They Are Singing." *NYTimes*, November 5, 1982, 12; Wilson, John S. "Sylvia Syms, Singer from Swing Street." *NYTimes*, August 10, 1979, 21.

INGERLENE VOOSEN

SYRKIN, MARIE (1899–1989)

Marie Syrkin is best known as a polemicist for the State of Israel, whose keen arguments appeared in a wide range of publications for a period of almost seventy years. It is not a very well-known fact, however, that she recorded both the public and private aspects of her life and career in poetry written over the course of her lifetime. In her eightieth year, she published a volume of poetry called *Gleanings: A Diary in Verse* (1979), which brings together the public aspects of her career—her commitment to Israel, her social commentary, and her devotion to literature—with profoundly moving expressions of intimate emotions, private struggles, and personal sorrows. For Marie Syrkin, the personal and the Jewish people were ineluctably intertwined. The close of her most intensely personal poem, "Memorial For A Child," an excruciating reflection upon the death of her son in his second year, brings together personal life and experience through the people:

I have never gone back to Ithaca,
Afraid of the small headstone, the weed-choked
   plot.
Now there is a plaque with your name
In a kindergarten in Jerusalem.
In Jerusalem
In a house for children
With eyes dark as yours,
Prattling in Hebrew
And laughing,
I took heart to face your name:
Benyah.

Marie Syrkin was born in Switzerland on March 23, 1899. She was the only daughter of Nachman Syrkin, the theoretician of Socialist-Zionism, and Bassya Osnos Syrkin, a feminist revolutionary activist. By the time Syrkin was ten she had lived in five coun-

tries, finally moving to the United States in 1908 because, as she herself quipped, "Papa was always getting exiled—so we travelled a lot." The Syrkins treated their unusually beautiful and exceptionally intelligent child, who at age ten was fluent in five languages—Russian, French, German, Yiddish, and English—as a prodigy. Hebrew, however, was not among the languages she learned, and, blaming it on her father's inept and sporadic pedagogic attempts, she later claimed this lack as a major reason for her failure to immigrate to Israel.

Educated in the American public school system, Marie Syrkin showed sensitivity to the nuances of language in poetry that she began to write at a very early age. When she was fifteen, her mother, who suffered from chronic tuberculosis, died at age thirty-six. When Marie was eighteen she eloped with the writer and future Zionist activist Maurice Samuel, who, then twenty-two, had enlisted in the army and was about to leave for France. Nachman Syrkin, however, to his daughter's everlasting resentment, had the marriage annulled, claiming that his daughter was underage.

In 1918, Marie Syrkin went off to Cornell University to pursue her literary studies. There, in 1919, she met and married Aaron Bodansky, a biochemist. They had two sons, the older of whom tragically died in 1924, only two months before the death of Nachman Syrkin and three months before the birth of their second son, David, who was to become a physicist. By this time, Marie Syrkin's insistence upon pursuing her own career led to a divorce from Aaron Bodansky. She left Cornell with an M.A. degree and returned to New York City with her infant son. In order to support herself and her child, she took a position as an English teacher at Textile High School in Manhattan, a job she disliked intensely but held for over twenty years. During these years, she also earned extra money by translating Yiddish poetry into English. She was among the first to do so.

The mid-1920s marked the low point of her life, both personally and professionally. But in 1927, she met the objectivist poet Charles Reznikoff, whom she married in 1930, and she lived with him on and off until his death in 1976.

Meanwhile, she began to become increasingly involved in Zionist activities. Just after her first trip to Palestine, in 1934, she joined the staff of the *Jewish Frontier*, the new English-language Labor-Zionist publication. This was the beginning of a sustained and remarkable career: a lifelong contribution to Zionism, American and Jewish cultural life, as a responsible journalist who would be published in a wide range of publications from the *New York Times* to the *Jerusalem Post*.

Among the first to understand and write about the true extent of Hitler's Final Solution, Marie Syrkin's polemical works in defense of Israel made her a giant of her time. She was also a poet and journalist and, as English professor at Brandeis University, she established the first course in the literature of the Holocaust. [YIVO Institute]

In the pages of the *Jewish Frontier*, she exposed the truth about the Moscow Trials of 1937, the first exposé to appear in English. From 1937 through 1942, Syrkin reported on critical events regarding the Nazi persecutions in Europe, although she later admitted that at this point she and her colleagues did not yet understand their full implications. In August of 1942, however, Marie Syrkin learned of a cable that had been sent from the Geneva representative of the World Jewish Congress to be forwarded to Rabbi Stephen Wise, president of the American Jewish Congress. The message contained information about the ongoing Nazi murder of European Jewry. In the first editorial in the American press to report that the systematic extermination of the Jews was already in progress, Syrkin wrote in the *Jewish Frontier*: "It is a policy of systematic murder of innocent civilians which in its ferocity, its dimensions and its organization is unique in the history of mankind . . ." (November 1942).

During these disastrous war years, Syrkin continued her multifaceted activities on behalf of the Jewish community in a flow of editorials, articles, and poems pressing for the opening of the immigration gates of Palestine, demanding liberalization of immigration quotas in America and elsewhere, trying to find havens for refugees, and writing speeches for such famous figures as Chaim Weizmann and GOLDA MEIR. During this time, she also found time to write a widely acclaimed book on the American public school system, *Your School, Your Children* (1944). Based upon Syrkin's experience in the system, the book was to play a substantial role in the coming focus on American educational reform.

When the war was over, Marie Syrkin went once more to Palestine to collect material for her book on Jewish resistance—the first of its kind—*Blessed Is the Match* (1947). In 1947, she was sent to the displaced persons camps in the American Zone of Germany to help find suitable candidates for Hillel Scholarships to American universities. She returned to the new State of Israel in July 1948, just after the siege of Jerusalem. Her task was to draw up an official report on the continuing Arab exodus and on the accusation that the new government of Israel had destroyed mosques and other holy places. Her study was the basis for the official Israeli government report to the United Nations. The trip also resulted in several closely argued essays on the subject of Arab refugees and the nature of Arab-Palestinian nationalsim.

In 1950, at age fifty-one, Marie Syrkin began a new career. She became the first female professor of an academic subject at the newly established Brandeis University, where she was appointed to the English faculty. Here, she developed the first university course in the literature of the Holocaust and in American Jewish fiction. During her sixteen years at Brandeis, Syrkin wrote a memoir of her father and a biography of her close friend Golda Meir, edited an anthology of the writings of Hayim Greenberg, edited the *Jewish Frontier*, served on the editorial board of *Midstream*, and was editor of the Herzl Press. She continued to write polemical pieces on political and cultural issues in the pages of many publications. Perhaps one of her most controversial public appearances was her bitter attack on HANNAH ARENDT's book *Eichmann in Jerusalem*. This occurred at a debate on the book sponsored by *Dissent*. In this period she also served as an elected member of the World Zionist Executive.

Marie Syrkin retired as professor emerita from Brandeis University in 1966. She then returned to New York, where she held a position at the Jewish Agency. After the death of Charles Reznikoff in 1976, she moved to Santa Monica, California, to be near her sister, the daughter of Nachman Syrkin and his second wife, and closer to her son and his family. There she continued to write, lecture, comment publicly on the current scene, be an active member of the board of *Midstream*, and confound her critics on the Left by signing the first Peace Now statement, but resigning for ideological reasons from the board of *Tikkun* magazine after the first issue.

The recipient of numerous awards and prizes, including Israel's prestigious Bublick Prize and of honorary degrees from both American and Israeli institutions, Marie Syrkin died on February 2, 1989, one month short of ninety years. Her life touched almost every significant aspect of Jewish life in America and Europe in the twentieth century with the exception of the religious. She is among the most important American Jewish women of the twentieth century, a peer of Golda Meir and HENRIETTA SZOLD.

SELECTED WORKS BY MARIE SYRKIN

Blessed Is the Match: The Story of Jewish Resistance (1947); *Gleanings: A Diary in Verse* (1979); *Golda Meir: Israel's Leader* (1970); *Golda Meir Speaks Out: The Speeches of Golda Meir*, editor (1973); *Hayim Greenberg Anthology* (1968); *Nachman Syrkin: Socialist Zionist* (1960); *The State of the Jews* (1980); *Your School, Your Children* (1944).

BIBLIOGRAPHY

EJ; Kessner, Carole S. "In Memoriam: Marie Syrkin, An Exemplary Life." *Midstream* (May 1989):3–10, and "Marie Syrkin: An Exemplary Life." In *The "Other" New York Jewish Intellectuals* (1994), and "On Behalf of the Jewish People; Marie Syrkin at Ninety." *Jewish Book Annual, 1988–89* 42 (1988): 206–220, and "The Poems of Marie Syrkin." *Reconstructionist* 45 (July 1979): 25–27; "Marie Syrkin; A Tribute by her Friends, Colleagues, and Students." *Jewish Frontier*, special issue (January/February 1983); "Marie Syrkin and Trude Weiss-Rosmarin: A *Moment* Interview," *Moment* 8, no. 8 (September 1983): 37–44; Syrkin, Marie. Papers. AJA, Cincinnati, Ohio.

CAROLE KESSNER

SZOLD, HENRIETTA (1860–1945)

Henrietta Szold was a woman of many contradictions. She was a family person who lived largely in the public arena. Possessed of only a high school diploma, she edited and published some of the monuments of modern Jewish scholarship and later helped to shape the educational system in Palestine. American to the core, she devoted herself to Zionism and lived the last quarter century of her life in Palestine. Her work

in rescuing children from the Holocaust and rehabilitating them earned her the sobriquet "mother of the *yishuv*" [the Jewish community in Palestine before 1948].

Educator, essayist, editor, social and communal worker, Zionist organizer, and politician, first in the United States and then in Palestine, Szold was born in Baltimore, Maryland, in 1860 at the outbreak of the American Civil War and died in Jerusalem during the closing months of World War II. Her life was touched

Henrietta Szold's first trip to Palestine was in 1909, when she was forty-nine years old. She had found her life's vocation—the re-creation of the Jewish homeland. She is shown here in 1921, clearly dressed for the job. [Hadassah Archives]

by some of the most momentous events of modern American, Jewish, and world history. Her prodigious capacity for work and unwavering sense of duty, her powerful intellect and ability to meet new challenges, the breadth of her activities, and her singular contributions to American Jewish culture, to Zionism, and to the *yishuv* mark her as an extraordinary human being.

Szold was the oldest child of liberal-minded Rabbi Benjamin Szold and his wife Sophie (Schaar), who had come to the United States from Central Europe a year before Henrietta's birth. Although a Lincoln supporter in a city with southern sympathies, Benjamin Szold was a traditionalist in Jewish matters and a scholar well versed in both sacred and secular studies. His firstborn was her father's spiritual and intellectual heir. Her record at Western Female High School was never equaled, but it was at home that she learned German and Hebrew, as well as Jewish sacred texts. In her teens, she served her father as amanuensis, translator, and editor.

A born teacher, Szold was hired straight out of high school to teach French, German, and algebra at the Misses Adams's English and French School for Girls and Judaism at the school of her father's congregation, Oheb Shalom. When, in the 1880s, waves of Jewish immigration from Eastern Europe brought to Baltimore a large number of Russian and Polish Jews, she assisted the immigrants in establishing a night school in which to learn English and civics. To her, Americanization was not "the opposite . . . to Jewish living and thinking" but rather the process of empowering the disfranchised. By 1894, over nine hundred immigrants, both Jews and gentiles, were registered in her night school. Some years later while a student at the Jewish Theological Seminary in New York—upon enrolling, she was required to sign an undertaking that she did not aspire to the rabbinate, which was then a male preserve—Szold assumed a more unusual pedagogical assignment: teaching English to her instructors, most of whom were recent immigrants from Europe. From 1918 to 1920, she played a national role in education, heading the Education Department of the Zionist Organization of America.

About the same time she began to teach, Szold embarked upon a career as an essayist and editor. As "Shulamith" and under her own name she wrote in an increasingly fluid style for the New York *Jewish Messenger* and other journals on a variety of issues of concern to the American Jewish community. In 1888, she was invited to be one of nine members—and the only female—of the publications committee of the new Jewish Publication Society (JPS), which would rapidly establish itself as one of the premier cultural institutions of American Jewry. Two years later, she collaborated with the young Cyrus Adler, a Semitics scholar who was to become head of the Jewish Theological Seminary, the American Jewish Committee, and Dropsie College, in writing a section on the United States for JPS's first publication, Lady Katie Magnus's *Outlines of Jewish History*. It was "the first ever textbook summary of its kind covering American Jewish history," and it set out clearly the young authors' sunny view of their native country. "No spot in the land can be connected with bitter or painful reminiscences," they wrote, "a proud boast, which America alone . . . may utter." Szold also assisted JPS in the editing of the classic *History of the Jews* by Heinrich Graetz, the German Jewish historian.

In 1893, she became the first full-time (executive) secretary of the publications committee, serving until 1916. Her pioneering, hardworking, and meticulous stewardship inaugurated a new era in the history of JPS. Szold, however, received less than her share of recognition, partly because of her diffidence and politeness, but perhaps, too, because of her gender. Among the works she translated were Simon Dubnow's *Jewish History: An Essay in the Philosophy of History* (1903) and Nahum Slouschz's *The Renascence of Hebrew Literature* (1905). From 1898 to 1909, she was instrumental in producing the *American Jewish Year Book*, which quickly became the indispensable record of American Jewish organizations and affairs. She translated, edited, and indexed much of the monumental *Legends of the Jews* compiled by Jewish Theological Seminary scholar Louis Ginzberg, as well as his other works. At her urging, the publications committee began seriously to consider Yiddish literature. During her tenure, the Schiff Library of Jewish Classics was launched, and the JPS Bible translation project, which resulted in the publication of the Jewish *Revised Standard Version*, was begun and completed.

Szold was drawn to Jewish nationalism in its earliest days, becoming a charter member of the Baltimore Hevras Zion in 1893 together with her friend Dr. Harry Friedenwald, an early president of the Federation of American Zionists (FAZ). In fact, Zionism became her third American "career." In a speech delivered a month before the publication of Theodor Herzl's *Der Judenstaat* in 1896, Szold outlined her philosophy of Zionism, which included not only the ingathering of the exiled Jews in their ancient land but also the revival of Jewish culture. Two years later, she became a member of the FAZ executive committee, the only woman in the group; later she agreed to serve as secretary—a post often reserved for women in male-dominated organizations—and set about trying to bring order to the chaotic affairs of the federation. During World War I, she served as secretary of the Provisional Executive Committee for General Zionist Affairs headed by Louis D. Brandeis, which assumed the leadership of the world movement rent asunder by the war. There, too, she was the only woman in the group.

In 1909, in the company of her mother, she traveled to Palestine for the first time and visited the Zionist agricultural settlements as well as the holy sites. During that trip, when she was already forty-nine years old, Szold found her life's vocation: the health, education, and welfare of the *yishuv*. The next year, she became secretary of the board of the new Agricultural Experiment Station established in Palestine by Aaron Aaronsohn. It was her first official connection with the reconstruction work in the Jewish homeland.

Of her American activities, that which had the greatest and most lasting influence was the creation of HADASSAH, the women's Zionist organization. In 1896,

Szold had argued that "sexless [gender-free] work is the great desideratum." Later, however, she eagerly accepted certain tasks as especially appropriate for women and all-women's groups as appropriate settings for the accomplishment of those tasks.

In 1907, at the invitation of Rabbi Judah Magnes, who was to become a close friend and coworker, Szold joined a small women's gathering called the Hadassah Study Circle, one of several such groups in New York where she was then living. In 1912, she and some friends formed the Daughters of Zion-Hadassah Chapter, which had enlisted 122 members by the fall of that year. Some of the FAZ members expected the new society to serve as a ladies' auxiliary of their own group. Szold envisioned an independent social service organization modeled along the lines of the women's agencies, which had recently proliferated in the United States. She sought to bring into being a group guided by the principles of American progressivism: project orientation; "trained and willing forces; [and a] . . . tested organization." It was to be altogether different

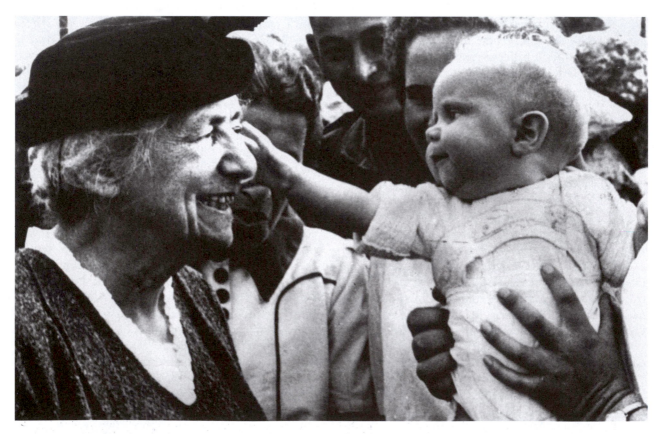

What was perhaps most astonishing about Henrietta Szold was the breadth of her activities. Teacher, translator, essayist, editor, organizer, politician, administrator, and humanist, she will always be remembered for founding HADASSAH, the American Women's Zionist Organization. She is shown here with a young admirer. [Hadassah Archives]

from the predominantly male Zionist societies, such as the FAZ. They were infused with the very different spirit of Eastern Europe; they were romantic and amateurish, not scientific and businesslike. Under her direction, Hadassah became the largest and most powerful Zionist group in the United States. And, despite its founder's avowedly nonpartisan Zionism, the organization became a major political force in the American and world movements.

The first major project undertaken by Hadassah was the establishment of an American-style visiting nurse system in Jerusalem in 1913. Its success earned Szold the praise of Jane Addams, the pioneer American social worker. Five years later, Hadassah organized and helped to fund the American Zionist Medical Unit, which brought American medical personnel and a field hospital to Palestine. The unit began the reformation of medical care in the Holy Land with the establishment of a nursing school, dental, medical, and X-ray clinics, hospitals, a hygiene department, infant welfare stations, and the medical sanitary expedition. From the 1920s, Hadassah supported medical services and education in the *yishuv*. Its medical institutions exemplified American efficiency and showcased American technology, bringing to Palestine, and then Israel, a standard of medicine equal to that of the wealthy Western nations. In the 1930s, at Szold's behest, Hadassah assumed the support of Youth Aliyah programs for refugee and problem children in Palestine.

In 1920, Szold herself arrived in Palestine to take charge of the Medical Unit, soon to be renamed the Hadassah Medical Organization (HMO). As a woman and an American, she was doubly an outsider in the *yishuv*, which was dominated by Eastern Europeans. She remained for three stormy but productive and innovative years, although her insistence on American standards and work habits was stoutly resisted, and labor circles resented what they perceived to be medical imperialism. Gradually, however, coworkers and the public were won over. After a lengthy home leave, Szold returned to Palestine in 1925 as resident mentor to the new HMO director, and in subsequent years played a supporting, but still significant, role in the affairs of the organization.

In 1927, Szold was appointed by the World Zionist Congress to its three-member Palestine executive, with responsibility for the health and education portfolios. The executive was charged with bringing the budget of the *yishuv* into balance, a thankless task that created constant friction with the indigenous *yishuv* leadership. Szold became a special target of attack because it was felt that her American friends were failing to meet their financial commitments to Zionism.

This 1934 photograph shows a characteristically dynamic Szold speaking to Youth Aliyah children. [Hadassah Archives]

She agreed but believed that the existence of the *yishuv* would be endangered if its financial affairs were not put in order. The schools, which had no money for supplies or teachers' salaries, she saw as a case in point.

To survey the educational system, Szold brought to Palestine Isaac B. Berkson, an American Jewish educator who was a disciple of W.H. Kilpatrick and John Dewey. Berkson remained on as director of the executive's Department of Education, first working with Szold to balance the education budget and to ensure that teachers would be paid on time, then embarking on bringing a measure of American educational reform to *yishuv* schools. By the time Szold was removed from the executive when it was reorganized in 1930, she had succeeded, Berkson remarked, in setting the schools "on the way to orderly and effective administration and financing." The educational publisher and Tel Aviv municipal counsellor Shoshana Persitz claimed that Szold had singlehandedly succeeded in gaining legitimacy for education in a community that then viewed manual labor as the only noble occupation. In fewer than three years she had made a major impact on the *yishuv* educational system and, despite the economic restraints she helped to impose and the earlier disapproval with which she and the HMO were regarded, had gained the respect of a wide public. The laborites came to appreciate her progressive American sympathy for the underdog, endorsement of the trade union ideal, and suspicion of wealth as the marks of an ally.

Social work was the third area of *yishuv* life to which Szold made a significant and lasting contribution. While still in America, she had perceived the need to improve the lot of Palestine's women. She proposed that American "settlement workers" teach the women pioneers "modern housework and other domestic industries," and at the same time "rouse a noble discontent among them" to spark demands for "better sanitation and better living conditions." Once on the scene, she realized that the men of the *yishuv* also lived a harsh life, and she began to investigate ways to ease the burdens of all.

During her first year in the country, she helped to organize the Federation of Hebrew Women to engage in social work activities. While sitting on the Zionist executive, she tried to bring to the *yishuv* the American concepts of scientific social work and casework through her involvement with local charitable agencies such as the Nathan Straus Soup Kitchen. Her most important contributions in this area, however, were made between 1931 and 1939 when she held the social welfare portfolio of the *Knesset Yisrael*, the semi-autonomous legislative body of the *yishuv*, which had called her back to Palestine from America in 1931.

Already in 1930, she had produced the report "The Future of Women's Work for Palestine," which outlined a plan for systematizing social work throughout the *yishuv*. She sought to replace, as she put it, "the old Lady Bountiful system, based on hysteria and not on justice to the unfortunate." With aid from wealthy American friends, she succeeded by 1934 in establishing modern social service agencies in Jerusalem, Tel Aviv, Haifa, and Petah Tikva, as well as the Social Service Department of the *Knesset Yisrael*. The next year she opened the country's first school of social work, which later became the School of Social Work of the Hebrew University.

Captured waiting to begin a radio broadcast, this elegant photograph of Szold shows her with a beautiful, uncharacteristically pensive, expression. [Hadassah Archives]

Her perceptiveness regarding Hitler's threat—she traveled to Nazi Germany for Youth Aliyah and met with Jews and gentiles including dissidents such as the artist Käthe Kollwitz—led her to believe that the *yishuv* would face an unprecedented wave of immigration in the 1930s. Remembering her experiences with the Eastern Europeans in Baltimore, Szold endeavored to convince the *yishuv* leadership that immigrants required special "emotional and intellectual support." Although she encountered opposition to immigrant-aid work in general, there was more receptivity to the notion of assisting children.

It was not she who first conceived of Youth Aliyah as a means of rescuing young people from Nazi Europe. But she was the person who understood the administrative complications and how to cut through them, and the social and emotional problems the children would have and how to solve them. Because of her "cabinet" position in the *yishuv* administration, she was able to ensure that the children would be properly looked after, and she had the connections with Hadassah, which provided most of the funds. Moreover, Szold genuinely cared for children. Her work with Youth Aliyah made hers a household name in her native country. Public recognition came in the form of regular birthday tributes from the famous and from ordinary people, especially children (she painstakingly answered every letter), and in the award of an honorary degree by Boston University in 1944, her only university degree.

When warclouds gathered in 1939, many of the Americans in Palestine returned home. Szold might well have followed. She was very attached to her sisters Rachel Jastrow, Adele Seltzer, and BERTHA LEVIN and to their families. (Rachel had died in 1926, and Sadie, to whom she was not close, had died earlier.) A life member of the International Longfellow Society from 1916, she remained American in her sensibilities and culture to a considerable extent. (At her last Passover seder in 1944, she sang African-American spirituals.) She had come to Palestine at the age of sixty, after all! Moreover, she was a pacifist and troubled by the increasing militancy of the *yishuv* in its dealings with Britain and the Arabs. She participated in both the *Brith Shalom* and the *Ihud*, associations of intellectuals mostly of American, British, or Central European background such as Rabbi Magnes and Martin Buber, which promoted the notion of Palestine as a binational, Arab-Jewish state. But Szold did not return to the United States. She thought "it right and proper" to "stay with the community" where she had lived for two decades.

Her early objective for the *yishuv* had been to reform it along the lines of the Progressives' vision for America. As time went on, however, she moved away from her former associates and friends in America, although not from her family. Her values became less American. She never rejected her homeland and always thought of it in positive, although not uncritical, terms. From an apostle of Americanism in Palestine, she developed into an interpreter of the *yishuv* to America. She strongly believed that one day "Palestine, resplendent intellectually," would repay "to the Diaspora its whole investment . . . in terms of spiritual succor, stimulation and strength." In 1936, she told her former colleagues in the Zionist Organization of America that, "philosophically considered, there is nothing but Zionism . . . to save us." She died in Jerusalem, at the modern medical center that Hadassah had erected, on February 13, 1945.

BIBLIOGRAPHY

Brown, Michael. *The Israeli-American Connection: Its Roots in the Yishuv, 1914–1945* (1996); *Current Biography* (1940): 785–786; Dash, Joan. *Summoned to Jerusalem: The Life of Henrietta Szold* (1979); *DAB* 3 (1973): 756–758; *Dictionary of Jewish Biography* (1991): 512–514; *EJ*; Kutscher, Carol Bosworth. "The Early Years of Hadassah." Ph.D. diss., Brandeis University, 1976, and "From Merger to Autonomy: Hadassah and the ZOA, 1918–1921." *Herzl Yearbook* 8 (1978): 61–78; Lowenthal, Marvin. *Henrietta Szold, Life and Letters* (1942); *NAW*; *New Encyclopedia of Israel and Zionism* (1994); Sarna, Jonathan D. *JPS: The Americanization of Jewish Culture, 1888–1988* (1989); Szold, Henrietta. Papers. Central Zionist Archives, Jerusalem.

MICHAEL BROWN

T

TAMIRIS, HELEN (1902–1966)

Helen Tamiris was a pioneer of American modern dance. She brought a social consciousness to the concert hall and went on to become the director of the Dance Project for the Works Progress Administration (WPA) and later an acclaimed Broadway choreographer. Her works were uniquely American, dramatically depicting important social issues of the time such as racism, poverty, and war. In 1928, she wrote the following manifesto in her concert program: "Art is international but the artist is a product of a nationality. . . . There are no general rules. Each original work of art creates its own code."

She was born Helen Becker on April 23, 1902, into a poor but cultured Orthodox family on New York City's Lower East Side. Her parents, tailor Isor and Rose (Simonov) Becker, had come with their son Maurice to New York in 1892 from Nizhni Novgorod, Russia, where they had fled from pogroms and czarist military oppression. Maurice Becker became a cartoonist and painter. Two other brothers were born in New York: sculptor Samuel Becker and art collector Peter Becker.

She attended New York public schools and later studied economics and labor statistics at the Rand School (1918–1920). At age eight, she began to study Isadora Duncan–style dance at the Henry Street Settlement, and at age fifteen her professional dance career began when she auditioned for the Metropolitan Opera Company Ballet. She danced for three seasons at the Met, toured with the Bracale Opera Company as a ballerina, and performed in the Music Box Review in 1924. Early in her career she took the name of Tamiris, a ruthless amazonian queen of Persia who overcame all obstacles.

In 1927, she presented her first solos in a concert called *Dance Moods* at the Little Theater in New York. The following year, a new concert at the same theater attracted excellent notices, and she was described as being in the forefront of the younger dancers of the "new dance." This concert included *Prize Fight Studies* and the seminal and dramatic *Negro Spirituals*. Later in 1928, Tamiris became the first American dancer since Isadora Duncan to tour Europe, where the critics hailed her as the outstanding interpreter of American life. In 1929, she founded the School of American Dance and her company, Tamiris and Her Group, which she directed until 1945. From 1930 to 1932, Tamiris banded together with Martha Graham, Doris Humphrey, and Charles Weidman to found and direct the Dance Repertory Theater, a cooperative in which the four companies shared productions and expenses.

During the WPA, Tamiris became a spokesperson for American modern dance. In 1935, she went to Washington, D.C., as the head of the American Dance Association to lobby for the inclusion of a separate Dance Project in the organization of the Federal Theater Project under the WPA. The Federal Theater

Project operated from 1935 to 1939, and Tamiris became the director and main choreographer of its Dance Project. She also acted as the organization's representative in Washington. Her major productions during this period were *Salut au Monde* (1936), *How Long Brethren?* (1937), *Trojan Incident* (1938), and *Adelante* (1939). She continued to perform *Negro Spirituals*, which contained strong elements of protest against prejudice, violence, and human suffering, and could be considered a metaphor for Jewish oppression. From 1935 to 1945, Tamiris created many modern dance works.

As she began to perform less, Tamiris moved into musical theater. She had taught movement for actors and directors and was skilled at moving large groups effectively in her own dance works. She began to create and perform musical theater material with her partner Daniel Nagrin, whom she married on September 3, 1946. She went on to choreograph over eighteen Broadway musicals with Nagrin as her assistant. These included *Up in Central Park* (1945), *Annie Get Your Gun* (1946), *Touch and Go* (1950), *Plain and Fancy* (1955), and *Fanny* (1955). Outstanding dancers who performed for Tamiris in these shows were Daniel Nagrin, Talley Beatty, Valerie Bettis, Dorothy Bird, PEARL LANG, and Pearl Primus.

Tamiris and Nagrin continued their partnership by forming the Tamiris-Nagrin Dance Company

Helen Tamiris was one of the pioneers of American modern dance. As a choreographer, she explored her Jewish roots in her 1959 work Memoir *and women's roles in society and the dehumanizing devastation of the Holocaust in* Women's Song *(1960).*

(1957–1964), with Nagrin as codirector. Tamiris was also active as a teacher at various colleges. Notable works from this final period in Tamiris's life were *Memoir* (1959), which explored her Jewish roots, and *Women's Song* (1960), about women's roles in society and the dehumanizing devastation of the Holocaust. She received many awards for her work.

Helen Tamiris died of cancer in New York on August 4, 1966. From her cultured Jewish upbringing, Tamiris developed an active social consciousness. Highly aware of political and religious persecution through her heritage, Tamiris brought her activism to bear on all spheres of her life. From her first works protesting racism and oppression, through the WPA years when she fought to bring dance that spoke directly about social issues to a broad public, Tamiris was in the forefront of modern dance. She worked to create jobs for dancers during the Depression and made dances calling for international cooperation and peace as World War II approached. While few of her works were explicitly Jewish in theme, her Jewishness and strength as a woman echo throughout all her works.

SELECTED WORKS BY HELEN TAMIRIS

Adelante (1939); *Dance Moods* (1957); *How Long Brethren?* (1937); *Memoir* (1959); *Negro Spirituals* (1928); *Prize Fight Studies* (1928); *Salut au Monde* [Salute to the world] (1936); *Trojan Incident* (1938); *Women's Song* (1960).

BIBLIOGRAPHY

Arbeit, Ida. Telephone interviews with author; Becker, Bruce. Telephone interview with author; Becker, Paul. Telephone interview with author; *DAB* 8; *EJ*; Nagrin, Daniel. Telephone interview with author; Obituary. *NYTimes*, August 5, 1966, 31:1; *NAW* modern; Schlundt, Christena L. *Tamiris, A Chronicle of Her Dance Career, 1927–1955* (1972); Tamiris, Helen. Scrapbooks (1944–1967). Dance Collection, New York Library for the Performing Arts, NYC; Tish, Pauline. "Remembering Tamiris." *Dance Chronicle* 17, no. 3 (1994); Zurier, Rebecca. *Art for the Masses* (1985).

PAULINE TISH

TANZER, HELEN (1876–1961)

"This book / to my students / yesterday today tomorrow." Translated from the Latin, Helen Tanzer's dedication of *The Letters of Pliny the Younger* sums up her principal contribution, namely, her legacy as an educator in classical studies.

Helen Henrietta Tanzer was born in New York City in February 1876 to German-speaking Jewish parents Arnold and Ida Tanzer. She had a brother, Lawrence (b. 1874), and a sister, Edith (b. 1877). She graduated from Barnard College in 1903, with a senior thesis titled "English Usage, as shown by the Recent revision of the Bible." She taught Greek and Latin at HUNTER COLLEGE, New York, and received her doctorate from Johns Hopkins in 1929. In that same year, she began teaching classics and archaeology at Brooklyn College, where she remained until her retirement. She spent much time abroad, studying at the American School of Classical Studies in Rome and working for the Belgian Information Service (1918–1919) and as editor of the *Belgian Bulletin*. Named to the Chevalier Order of Leopold II by Belgium, she also held the post of honorary attaché to the Belgian embassy in Washington.

As an author, her first known published work is "Juvenal on Education," in *Essays in Honor of M.B. Wilson* (1922). In 1948, Tanzer received the Medal of Merit at the bicentennial celebration of the excavation of Pompeii. Her book *The Common People of Pompeii: A Study of the Graffiti* (1939) examines that city in the context of everyday life, thus foreshadowing the interest of students at the end of the twentieth century.

Tanzer's most important role, however, may have been as a propagator of classical and archaeological texts through her work as a translator. Her introduction to and translation of *The Villas of Pliny the Younger* (1924) familiarized generations of students with these villa/garden complexes. Because Pliny's letters describing in detail his Laurentine and Tuscan villas are the only contemporary comprehensive documents of this ancient Roman type of habitation—a prototype for Renaissance country houses—Tanzer's modest book became an important source. Enhanced by descriptions of earlier classical references for this building type, it contains fifty-six plates showing the varied reconstructions of Pliny's summer and winter villas. Included are the well-known plans of Scamozzi (from 1615), Félibien, Castell, Schinkel, and Bouchet. Also featured is the author's own reconstruction with a clay model built by her students in 1912: Tanzer notes "with unbecoming lack of modesty [that it is] in every respect much better than that made by any other student of Pliny ... [drawn] from the text alone." Refreshing too is Tanzer's critique of Schinkel's 1841 perspective for introducing "gratuitously, features which were not mentioned in Pliny." Almost as useful to the student is Tanzer's edition of *The Letters of Pliny the Younger* (1936), which was designed to serve as a companion guide to the author's epistles.

Tanzer's literary skills were not limited to classical languages, as is evident in her translation from the German of Erasmus's *In Praise of Folly* (1931) and her introduction to the facsimile edition of the work, with Holbein's marginal drawings. She also translated Christian Hüelsen's first edition of *The Forum and the Palatine* (1928). Despite the plethora of documentation on the latter subject in the decades since, this small volume with its sixty-five plates and folding plan still serves as a valuable compendium of the complicated history and topography of these sites.

Contributing to the dissemination of classical and archaeological works, Tanzer well fulfilled the rigorous requirements of scholar and teacher. Her pioneer endeavors may be exemplified in her role as creator and editor of *Latin Visualized*, a series of films with manuals. Tanzer was a fellow of the American Geographical Society, the American Philological Association, the History of Science Society, and AAAS, and a member of the New York Classics Club and the Archaeological Institute of America.

Helen Tanzer died on December 23, 1961.

SELECTED WORKS BY HELEN TANZER

The Common People of Pompeii: A Study of the Graffiti (1939); Erasmus. *In Praise of Folly* (1931), and Hüelsen, Christian. *The Forum and the Palatine* (1928), translated by Helen Tanzer; *The Letters of Pliny the Younger* (1936), selected and edited by Helen Tanzer; *The Villas of Pliny the Younger* (1924).

BIBLIOGRAPHY

American Women: The Standard Biographical Dictionary of Notable Women 3 (1939): 892; Obituary. *NYTimes*, December 24, 1961, 36: 6; *UJE*.

NAOMI MILLER

TAUSSIG, HELEN BROOKE
(1898–1986)

Helen Brooke Taussig was one of the most celebrated physicians of the twentieth century. Starting in the 1920s, her early work focused on the clinical and anatomic manifestations of rheumatic fever. Later, in the mid-1940s, her ideas about the treatment of so-called blue babies led to the development of one of the first surgical procedures for treating infants with congenital cardiac defects. Through her research and teaching she was a leader in the development of the medical specialty of pediatric cardiology. In the 1960s, she was responsible for investigating the epidemic of serious congenital limb malformations in European children. She documented that the malformations were caused by the use of thalidomide by their mothers when pregnant. She continued to publish articles in the medical literature long after her 1963 retirement

and, at the time of her death at age eighty-seven, was actively engaged in research on the avian heart.

Helen Brooke Taussig was born in Cambridge, Massachusetts, on May 24, 1898. On her father's side she came from a distinguished St. Louis, Missouri, family. Taussig's father, Frank William Taussig, held the Henry Lee chair in economics at Harvard University. Her mother, Edith Thomas Guild of Boston, had been a student at Radcliffe College and maintained an interest in zoology and other natural sciences. They had four children: William Guild, Mary Guild, Catherine Crombie, and Helen Brooke. Taussig's mother died of tuberculosis when Taussig was eleven.

Suffering from lifelong dyslexia, Taussig was sometimes regarded by teachers as being retarded. Her father helped her learn to read, write, spell, and do numbers. Reading was never easy for Taussig, complicating any lengthy reviews of the literature for scientific articles. Taussig attended Radcliffe for two years before transferring to the University of California at Berkeley, where she graduated in 1921, Phi Beta Kappa. School policy prevented her from entering the then all-male Harvard Medical School. She was, however, allowed to study histology on a noncredit basis at Harvard, sitting in a remote corner of the hall during lectures and viewing slides in a separate room. It was at Boston University that Taussig became interested in the heart, having been encouraged to study the muscle bundles of the ox heart. In 1923, she matriculated at Johns Hopkins University School of Medicine, graduating in 1927 and maintaining her association with Hopkins for sixty years.

Following her graduation from medical school, she was appointed a fellow at the Heart Station at Hopkins and went on to develop the pediatric cardiology clinic there. At age thirty-one, she started to go deaf and by age thirty-five was using a hearing aid and an amplified stethoscope. She was able to compensate for the loss of her hearing through the use of her hands for palpation of patients' chests. Otologic surgery in the 1960s substantially improved Taussig's hearing.

One of Taussig's greatest contributions to medical science lay in the development, with surgeon Alfred Blalock, of the Blalock-Taussig procedure, a surgical technique that corrects cyanosis in certain types of congenital cardiac abnormalities. This operation launched the modern era of pediatric cardiac surgery. In her 1947 textbook *Congenital Malformations of the Heart*, Taussig made clear the results of her extensive anatomical and clinical work and provided a classic text for the developing fields of pediatric cardiology and pediatric cardiac surgery. She was one of

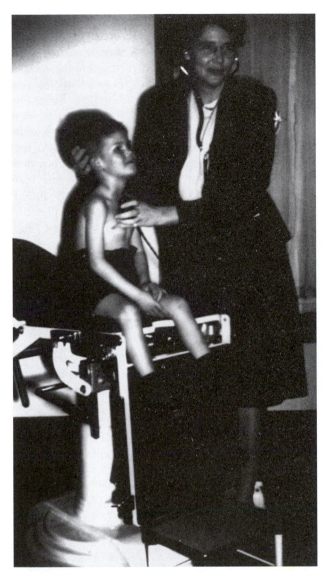

One of the most celebrated physicians of the twentieth century, Helen Brooke Taussig did groundbreaking work in the treatment of rheumatic fever and infants with congenital cardiac defects. [Alan Mason. Chesney Medical Archives, Johns Hopkins University]

only six physicians chosen by the American Board of Pediatrics to head the Sub-Board of Pediatric Cardiology, the official certifying body for the new subspecialty.

In 1962, following reports of an outbreak of serious congenital deformities in Europe, Taussig traveled throughout West Germany to investigate the situation. Concluding, as had German physicians, that the sedative thalidomide was responsible, Taussig authored an article in the *Journal of the American Medical Associ-*

ation describing her findings. Her testimony before Congress and her scientific articles persuaded the Food and Drug Administration to disallow the sale of thalidomide in the United States.

Numerous honors came her way. Like her father before her, she was honored as a chevalier in the French Legion of Honor (1947). President Lyndon B. Johnson awarded her the Presidential Medal of Freedom (1964). Johns Hopkins, however, was not so generous. For the first sixteen years at Hopkins, she was an instructor; for the next thirteen, an associate professor. She held the rank of professor only for the four years preceding her 1963 retirement. She was, however, the first woman to hold a full professorship at the medical school.

Taussig never really retired. Of the more than one hundred scholarly articles she authored, she wrote approximately forty after retirement. At age sixty-seven, she became the first woman president of the American Heart Association. She remained active in her research until her death.

Taussig was not religious, although she described herself as Unitarian, as her mother had. She did not consider herself to be Jewish, although she told friends on occasion that she was of Jewish extraction on her father's side.

Despite the many honors she received, her accomplishments as a physician and the respect she was accorded by her students and patients, Taussig's life was complicated by serious adversity: her father's mental illness during her childhood, her mother's death, sex discrimination as she tried to educate herself, envy she experienced at her fame in the man's world of medicine, insecurity about her Hopkins appointment, deafness, and dyslexia. She was a Democrat, pro-choice regarding abortion, and was a proponent of national health insurance.

Helen Brooke Taussig was killed in an automobile accident on May 21, 1986, three days shy of her eighty-eighth birthday.

SELECTED WORKS BY HELEN BROOKE TAUSSIG

Congenital Malformations of the Heart (1947. Revised 1960); "Difficulties, Disappointments, and Delights in Medicine." *Pharos of Alpha Omega Alpha Honor Medical Society* 42 (1979): 6–8; "Little Choice and a Stimulating Environment." *Journal of the American Medical Women's Association* 36 (1981): 43–44; "A Study of the German Outbreak of Phocomelia." *Journal of the American Medical Association* 180 (1962): 1106–1114; "The Surgical Treatment of Malformations of the Heart in Which There Is Pulmonary Stenosis or Pulmonary Atresia," with Alfred Blalock. *Journal of the American Medical Association* 128 (1945): 189–202.

BIBLIOGRAPHY

"At 67, Another First." *NYTimes*, October 20, 1965, 31; Burgess, Patricia, ed. "Helen Brooke Taussig." In *The Annual Obituary 1986* (1989); *Concise Dictionary of American Biography* (1977), s.v. "Frank William Taussig" and "William Taussig"; *Current Biography Yearbook 1946*, s.v. "Helen Brooke Taussig"; *Current Biography Yearbook 1966* (1966, 1967), s.v. "Helen Brooke Taussig"; *DAB* (1935, 1936), s.v. "William Taussig"; *DAB* (1958), s.v. "Frank William Taussig"; Dietrich, Herbert J. "Helen Brooke Taussig, 1898–1986." *Transactions and Studies of the College of Physicians of Philadelphia* 8, 4 (1986): 265–271; "Dr. Taussig at 66; As Busy as Ever." *NYTimes*, December 20, 1964, 72; Engle, Mary Allen. "Dr. Helen Brooke Taussig, Living Legend in Cardiology." *Clinical Cardiology* 8, 6 (1985): 372–374; "Helen Brooke Taussig, 87, Pioneer in the Field of Pediatric Cardiology." *Philadelphia Enquirer*, May 22, 1986; Henderson, Mary Taussig. "Mrs. Frank Taussig." *Radcliffe Memorial Biographies*, vol. 4 (unpublished); Hyde, William, and Howard L. Conard, eds. "Ethical Society of St. Louis." In *Encyclopedia of the History of St. Louis* (1899); McNamara, Dan G. "Helen Brooke Taussig: 1898–1986." *Pediatric Cardiology* 7 (1986): 1–2; McNamara, Dan G., et al. "Helen Brooke Taussig: 1898–1986." *Journal of the American College of Cardiology* 10, 3 (1987): 662–671; Neill, Catherine A. "Dr. Helen Brooke Taussig, May 24, 1898–May 21, 1986, International Cardiologist." *International Journal of Cardiology* 14 (1987): 255–261; "Noted Heart Doctor Killed in Crash." *Philadelphia Enquirer*, May 21, 1986; Ross, Richard S. "Presentation of the George M. Kober Medal (Posthumously) to Helen B. Taussig." *Transactions of the Association of American Physicians* 100 (1987): cxii–cxxv; Self-Culture Hall Association. *22d Annual Report* (1910).

RICHARD JAMES FORDE

TAUSSKY-TODD, OLGA (1906–1995)

Olga Taussky-Todd called herself a "torchbearer for matrix theory." Her subject originated in the mid-nineteenth century, remaining a province of mathematicians until physicists reinvented it in the 1920s to interpret quantum mechanics. Her work and passion helped shape matrix theory and draw other talented mathematicians to its development. A century after its inception, matrix theory joined calculus as an essential component of a scientist's education.

She was born on August 30, 1906, in Olümz, Austro-Hungary (later Olomouc, Czechoslovakia). She came from a well-to-do, cultivated Jewish family, the second of three daughters of Julius David and Ida (Pollach) Taussky. The family settled in Linz in 1909, where her father worked as an industrial chemist and journalist. All three sisters pursued scientific careers. Olga entered the University of Vienna in 1925 to study mathematics and chemistry, but after a year left chemistry to study the philosophy of mathematics. It was the time of Moritz Schlick's famous Vienna Circle, which attracted philosophers and scientists from around the world. Kurt Gödel, whose work at age twenty-five shook the foundations of mathematics, became her mentor and friend.

When Olga finished her dissertation on algebraic number theory in 1930 with Philip Fürtwangler, Richard Courant brought her to the world renowned Göttingen Mathematics Institute for a one-year appointment to edit Hilbert's manuscript on number theory. There she met EMMY NOETHER, the preeminent woman mathematician of the century, and Princeton geometer Oswald Veblen. Courant, who in 1932 cautioned Olga about the volatile political situation in Germany, left Göttingen two years later for New York University, where he was to found a major mathematics institute. When Noether found refuge at Bryn Mawr, she and Veblen arranged a fellowship for Olga during 1934 and 1935.

Two lonely but productive years in Vienna followed, where she supported herself by tutoring and an assistant's stipend from Hans Hahn and Karl Menger. She spent the next two years at Girton College, Cambridge, England, and then, with mathematician G.H. Hardy's help, she found a junior post at a women's college in London University. In 1938, she married the Irish mathematician John Todd.

During World War II, Taussky-Todd worked on aircraft design at the National Physical Laboratory near London. This work turned her away from her first love, number theory, to her second, matrix theory.

In 1947, her husband received a year's appointment at the National Bureau of Standards in Washington. The matrix theorists assembled there and stirrings of the embryonic computer revolution made the offer appealing. Both were hired, traveling to America on a liberty ship with a hundred war brides. They remained until 1957, when they were lured to the California Institute of Technology, Todd to be a professor of mathematics, and Taussky-Todd to be a research associate. She received tenure in 1963, but had to wait until 1971 for a professorial appointment, well after she had become internationally known. She published two hundred papers in her lifetime, most during her fertile thirty-eight years at Cal Tech, where she guided fourteen doctoral students.

Among her many honors and awards were the *Los Angeles Times* Woman of the Year (1963) and the Mathematical Association of America's Ford Prize (1970). She served on the councils of both the London and the American Mathematical Societies, and was vice president of the latter in 1986–1987. Both the journals *Linear Algebra and Its Applications* and *Linear and Multilinear Algebra* published issues dedicated to her.

Taussky-Todd was visiting professor at the University of Vienna in 1965, accepted the Austrian government's Cross of Honor in Science and Art in 1980, and later became a corresponding member of the Austrian and the Bavarian Academy of Sciences. Historians and others puzzle over the warm feelings some Austrian Jews, Taussky-Todd among them, retained for their country of origin in the face of Austria's long tradition of virulent anti-Semitism. Her writings ascribe her career difficulties to academe's prejudice against women, not to anti-Semitism. Though of Jewish birth, she identified herself with an international intellectual community, not a specifically Jewish one.

Olga Taussky-Todd died on October 7, 1995, in Pasadena, California, survived by her husband of fifty-seven years.

SELECTED WORKS BY OLGA TAUSSKY-TODD

"An Autobiographical Essay." In *Mathematical People: Profiles and Interviews*, edited by Donald J. Albers and G.L. Alexanderson (1985); "How I Became a Torchbearer for Matrix Theory." *American Mathematics Monthly* 95 (1988): 801–812.

BIBLIOGRAPHY

Berkley, George. *Vienna and Its Jews* (1988); Brewer, James W., and Martha K. Smith. *Emmy Noether* (1981); Davis, Chandler. "Remembering Olgo Taussky-Todd." *The Mathematical Intelligencer* 19, no. 1 (1997): 15–21; Grinstein, Louise S., and Paul J. Campbell. *Women of Mathematics* (1987); Luchins, Edith H., and Mary Ann McLoughlin. "In Memorium: Olga Taussky-Todd." *Notices of the American Mathematical Society* 43, no. 8 (1996); Reid, Constance. *Courant in Gottingen and New York* (1976); Schneider, Hans. "On Olga Taussky-Todd's Influence on Matrix Theory and Matrix Theorists." *Linear and Multilinear Algebra* 5 (1977/8): 197–224.

SEYMOUR KASS

TAYLOR, SYDNEY (1904–1978)

Like three of her predecessors—Louisa May Alcott, Margaret Sidney, and Laura Ingalls Wilder—Sydney Taylor created a fictional family of such endearing character and loving spirit that her young readers clamored for more titles. In all, five books about the *All-of-a-Kind Family* were written between 1951 and 1978. The values of family love, charity, wisdom, compassion, and social justice that define Taylor's *All-of-a-Kind Family* owe their particular flavor to Jewish culture.

After graduating in drama from New York University, she became first an actress with the Lenox Hill Players in New York City from 1925 to 1929, and then a professional dancer with the Martha Graham Dance Company from 1930 to 1935. Despite her successful career, she became a full-time wife and mother ten years after her marriage to businessman Robert Taylor in 1925 and the birth of their only child, Joanne (Jo), in 1935. When Jo was seven, Taylor resumed her interest in the arts, serving as a dance and dramatics counselor at the nonprofit Cejwin Camps.

Although she was to write several other children's stories as well as plays (which she also directed and choreographed), nothing equaled the invention stimulated by her recollection of her own childhood as the middle child in a household rich in love, learning, and tradition. Eager to comfort Jo, who felt lonely at nighttime in bed, Taylor told her daughter stories about her own growing up in a family where loneliness was unheard of, since five sisters shared the same bedroom. Perhaps it is no irony that Taylor's daughter was given the same nickname as the beloved heroine Jo March in *Little Women*, another American classic about sisters in a warm, loving family.

As Taylor related her stories to Jo, she was flooded with nostalgia for her childhood, growing up on New York's Lower East Side, where she was born in 1904. She found herself wanting to record her early history as the child of immigrant parents struggling to make a life for themselves among the many eager, hopeful newcomers to America in the early 1900s. The documentation was entirely personal; as she stated, "Satisfied, I promptly put the manuscript away and the years rolled over it." Forgotten, too, was her childhood response to the inevitable question, "What do you want to be when you grow up?" She had then answered, "A writer."

It remained for Taylor's husband, Robert, president of Caswell-Massey Company, a firm of chemists and perfumers, to unearth the manuscript when he heard about the Charles W. Follett Award for writing. Unknown to his wife, he submitted *All-of-a-Kind Family*, which was published in 1951, received the award, and launched Sydney Taylor's career as writer of children's fiction. The book also won the 1952 Jewish Book Council Award.

In *All-of-a-Kind Family*, Mama and Papa love their girls dearly and teach them to be good to one another, to their parents, to their neighbors and friends, and to their faith. Taylor gently integrates the rich traditions and heritage of Judaism into this family's life: The reader learns about the celebration of Purim, Passover, Sukkoth, and Hanukkah not as an aside but as a central part of religious Jewish life. Such activities as attending shul, making a sukkah, and celebrating the weekly Sabbath are interspersed with all of the kitchen activities typical of an Orthodox Jewish household—rolling dough for *teyglekh*, making gefilte fish, baking challah. When the family moves uptown to the Bronx into a predominantly gentile community, Papa and Mama remind their daughters that America promises an opportunity to advance as well as the freedom to retain one's Jewish roots. If this attention to heritage and learning sounds plodding, Taylor enlivens it always with generosity of spirit and humor. Mama reassures the family by telling them, "You don't have to worry. . . . We'll still be able to buy *bagel* and *lox* for Sunday morning breakfast."

A contemporary reader may approach these books about this kind and gentle family with skepticism. The characters act with predictable innocence and goodness, there is little character development, and stereotypical family roles predominate. World events, including World War I, intrude only slightly into this sunny home. Mama's place is still in the kitchen, while Papa goes out to work. The birth of a long-awaited son somewhat eclipses the importance of the family's five energetic, engaging daughters. Even modern trends, such as the entry of women into the work force, cannot change the importance of family. The eldest sister, Ella, who is the focus of the final book in the series, ultimately chooses family over a career, believing that "there's a kind of contentment in such homely tasks [as washing dishes]." What stands the test of time is Taylor's magical evocation of a past age when spirituality was a central part of life. We may even grieve that this era is no more.

Sydney Taylor died of cancer on February 12, 1978. The final *All-of-a-Kind Family* book was published posthumously later that year. It received the first annual Sydney Taylor Body-of-Work Award, established by the Association of Jewish Libraries in 1979.

**SELECTED WORKS
BY SYDNEY TAYLOR**

All-of-a-Kind Family Downtown. Illustrated by Beth and Joe Krush (1972); *All-of-a-Kind Family Uptown.* Illustrated by Mary Stevens (1958); *All-of-a-Kind Family.* Illustrated by Helen John (1951); *Danny Loves a Holiday.* Illustrated by Gail Owens (1980); *The Dog Who Came to Dinner.* Illustrated by John E. Johnson (1966); *Ella of All-of-a-Kind Family.* Illustrated by Gail Owens (1978); *More All-of-a-Kind Family.* Illustrated by Mary Stevens (1954); *Mr. Barney's Beard.* Illustrated by Charles Geer (1961); *Now That You Are Eight.* Illustrated by Ingrid Fetz (1963); *A Papa Like Everyone Else.* Illustrated by George Porter (1966).

BIBLIOGRAPHY
A Book of Children's Literature. 3d ed. Edited by Lillian Hollowell (1966); *Contemporary Authors.* Vols. 77–80. Edited by Frances Carol Locher (1979); Himmel, Maryclare O'Donnell. *Children's Books and Their Creators.* Edited by Anita Silvey (1995); Hopkins, Lee Bennett. *More Books by More People* (1974); Hoyle, Karen Nelson. *Twentieth Century Children's Writers.* 4th ed. Edited by Laura Stanley Berger (1995); *More Junior Authors.* Edited by Muriel Fuller (1963); *Something about the Author.* Vols. 26, 28. Edited by Anne Commire (1982); Ward, Martha E., et al. *Authors of Books for Young People.* 3d ed. (1990).

SUSAN P. BLOOM

TEACHING PROFESSION

Jewish women in America became professional teachers to an extent unprecedented in Jewish history. Throughout the nineteenth and twentieth centuries, female Jewish teachers flocked into both public and Jewish education, causing the teaching profession to emerge as a primary occupational niche for Jewish women in America. This emergence is remarkable considering that, in the premigration world of most Jewish immigrants, women were virtually excluded from teaching in any official capacity. The notion of a female teacher charged with the task of educating both boys and girls was inconceivable for most Central and Eastern European Jews. The very act of learning had been traditionally reserved for men, and teaching, an occupation saturated with religious overtones, remained indisputably a male domain. Although in Eastern Europe Jewish women often taught young girls rudimentary skills such as reading and writing Yiddish, the official teachers of the Jewish community were always male. Only in the last quarter of the nineteenth century did Jewish women in Eastern Europe manage to establish and teach in their own private schools.

The official exclusion of women from the teaching profession began to change dramatically at the beginning of the twentieth century. European Jews began to reconfigure traditional female Jewish education in an attempt to combat the erosion of traditional values and observance. New Jewish schools for girls were opened in such places as Vilna, Warsaw, Istanbul, and Rhodes, and each school demanded an increased number of Jewish female teachers. While the number of Jewish female teachers increased throughout the world in the early twentieth century, their rise was most spectacular in America, where they predominated in both secular and Jewish schools. In the New York City school system—the largest public school system in the world—Jewish women comprised 56 percent of the new teaching staff in 1940 and were the majority of the public school teaching staff until 1960. By 1982, female teachers in Jewish schools comprised approximately 80 percent of the teaching staff. The increased involvement of Jewish women in the teaching profession had a formative impact on both public and Jewish education in America.

JEWISH WOMEN AND THE PUBLIC SCHOOL SYSTEM

Jewish female teachers have played an active and important role in the New York City public school system for the last 150 years. Starting in the nineteenth century, teaching in the system became feminized through the efforts of a group of young middle-class women. The life of JULIA RICHMAN, a member of this vanguard group of teachers, exemplifies the critical role played by Jewish women in the feminization of the New York City school system. Like other female educators of her generation, Richman worked for over a decade as an elementary school teacher before she became the superintendent for the Lower East Side school district. The child of middle-class immigrants from Bavaria, Richman remained single throughout her career, like many of her contemporary female educators. Her experiences suggest that the lives of Jewish female teachers in the late nineteenth century were strikingly similar to their Christian sisters. A teaching career was the only appropriate profession for a single middle-class woman.

Many nineteenth-century women, like Julia Richman, were drawn to teaching for its respectability, prestige, and perhaps as an appropriate substitute for marriage, but these factors appear to have been of less significance for Jewish women in the next century. By the twentieth century, few Jewish female teachers remained single. The majority combined marriage and child rearing with their teaching careers. This new type of teacher became the norm as a result of several court decisions that forced the public school system to abolish its "marriage bar," which tacitly prohibited women's employment after marriage. Moreover, these legal decisions mandated that the New York City public school system allow female teachers to return to work even after childbirth.

In addition to this new legislation, most twentieth-century Jewish teachers were Eastern European immigrants whose financial needs required a combination of work and marriage. Entering the United States with little money, Eastern European Jewish women wanted to find a respectable profession, but were focused primarily on earning a living. They sought an occupation, like teaching, that was socially acceptable and provided a stable income. Although teacher training required considerable financial and time commitments, the eventual stability of a teaching career appears to have outweighed all the sacrifices in the minds of many young Jewish women. As one teacher claimed in Ruth Markowitz's study of female Jewish teachers in New York City public schools, Jewish immigrant mothers in the early twentieth century often advised their sons to marry teachers, since they could then rely on their wives to bring home a steady, significant income. The importance of a stable income was even more critical for many Jewish women who entered the teaching profession during the Depression era when securing ongoing employment was a primary concern.

Family social aspirations combined with these practical economic needs to further encourage Jewish women to pursue teaching careers. Many Jewish immigrant parents hoped that their children would be able to move up the economic and social ladders. In the eyes of most immigrant parents, white-collar work provided the most desirable way to achieve such mobility. However, Jewish women who tried to pursue careers in white-collar work were met by overt discrimination, particularly evident during the Depression era when companies regularly advertised clerical positions for non-Jews only. Since most avenues of white-collar work were closed to Jewish women in this era, public education emerged as the ethnic niche for second-generation Jewish women who desired social mobility.

Economic factors and the social aspirations of Jewish families played an important role in drawing Jewish women to teaching, but many were also drawn to this profession as a result of their own personal experiences, goals, and dreams. The favorable experiences of young Jewish immigrant girls in the New York City public school system appear to have played a crucial role in their future career paths. Sydney Stahl Weinberg notes that Jewish girls sought free secular education in the United States, because they rarely had such opportunities in Eastern Europe. Consequently, young Jewish women were more enthusiastic about education, and later about teaching, than young women from any other ethnic group. From their entrance into school, Jewish girls held their teachers in particularly high esteem, for teachers helped them transform from immigrants into Americans. This esteem and enthusiasm for school encouraged many Jewish women to continue their education, and often attracted them to a professional career in teaching.

Whether a Jewish woman was drawn to teaching in search of prestige, personal fulfillment, or economic stability varied according to each individual. What is quite clear, however, is that Jewish women flooded this occupation at an extraordinary rate. The preponderance of Jewish women in the system had a formative impact on the organization of the New York City school system. Ruth Markowitz suggests that the activities of Jewish women helped bring about the unionization of public school teachers in New York City. Female Jewish teachers flocked to join the Teachers Union—Local 5 of the American Federation of Teachers—and provided it with much-needed membership and support. Jewish women also provided these unions with innovative leadership. As early as 1925, half of the Teachers Union executive board were Jewish women. Rebecca Coolman Simonson is just one example of a Jewish woman who played an important leadership role in the New York City teachers' unions. Joining the Teachers Union soon after she began teaching in 1921, Simonson would later join the Teachers Guild, a teachers' union founded in 1935. Simonson not only served as president of the Teachers Guild from 1941 to 1953, but she was also a vice president of the American Federation of Teachers and a member of the board of examiners.

Aside from facilitating the unionization of the New York City school system, female Jewish teachers and their experiences illustrate one of the ways in which second-generation Eastern European Jews became entrenched in the middle class. Their experiences demonstrate how women, rather than men, were often the first members of Jewish immigrant families to enter the professional class. Traditionally, scholars have utilized male earnings to chart and assess Jewish immigrant mobility. However, the experiences of Jewish women in the field of public education clearly illustrate the critical role played by women in this process. Jewish women entered the professional field of teaching almost a generation earlier than their male coreligionists entered other professional fields such as law or medicine. Thus, female Jewish teachers were the harbingers of Jewish class mobility, and their experiences suggest that gendered notions of mobility have obscured remarkable trends in the first-generation of immigrants.

JEWISH FEMALE TEACHERS AND JEWISH EDUCATION

When Jewish Eastern European immigrant women became teachers in the New York City public school system in the early twentieth century, they brought about radical changes in the ethnic composition of the teaching staff. They did not, however,

introduce any alterations to the gender composition of the teaching staff, for they had entered a profession that had already undergone the process of feminization. In sharp contrast, American Jewish women who entered the Jewish teaching profession were pioneers who helped transform this field. While they comprised a majority of teachers in Jewish educational institutions by the end of the twentieth century, their dominance in this field did not seem likely at the beginning of the century, and their rise did not occur in a gradual or consistent manner.

It is difficult to assess the gender composition of Jewish teachers before the early twentieth century, for no surveys exist concerning the status of the Jewish teaching profession. Surveys from the first several decades of the twentieth century reveal the increase of female teachers in Jewish schools between 1916 and 1930. Women comprised between one-fifth and one-fourth of the teaching staff in Jewish educational institutions in 1916. By 1930, female teachers constituted one-third of this profession. The most significant increase of Jewish female teachers occurred in once-a-week supplementary schools. In 1916, women constituted one-half of the teaching staff, and by 1930, they comprised over two-thirds.

A revolutionary change in attitude complemented the increased participation of female teachers in Jewish schools. An article written by Mordecai Kaplan in 1932 demonstrates this change: The Jewish woman was not only considered an acceptable teacher for American Jewish children, but now emerged as the ideal Jewish educator. Kaplan argued that Jewish women's "lack of tradition" made them better able to reevaluate their Jewish heritage. Thus, Kaplan asserted, only Jewish women had the innate skills to help the Jews of America become an important factor in "the spiritual destiny of world Jewry." As suggested by Kaplan's article, leaders of the American Jewish community developed a radically new conception of the female Jewish teacher that elevated female teachers in America above their European forebears or even contemporary counterparts. Furthermore, Kaplan's conception of the centrality of Jewish women to Jewish education suggests an ideological transformation that occurred in America concerning the relationship between gender and Jewish education.

Between the 1930s and 1960s, no significant shifts occurred in the gender composition of the Jewish teaching profession, possibly as a result of the influx of European refugee rabbis who arrived after World War II and who devoted themselves to Jewish education. A 1953 survey confirms that the gender composition of the Jewish teaching profession had barely

*Jewish women in America became professional teachers to an unprecedented extent.
In terms of percentages, most of them taught in New York City, but they were spread out
through the country, as well. This 1909 photograph shows Belle Zimmerman with her
grade school class in a small Wisconsin town. [Jewish Historical Society of the Upper Midwest]*

changed since 1930. In twenty-seven communities throughout the United States, 62 percent of the teachers in Jewish educational institutions were male, while only 38 percent were female. While throughout the 1940s and 1950s the feminization of the Jewish teaching profession slowed significantly, by the 1960s and 1970s this process of feminization surged forward once again. The extent of this surge is evidenced by the fact that one 1967 study found that the typical Jewish school teacher was a young, single Jewish woman. By the 1980s, women constituted the vast majority of teachers in Jewish schools, as confirmed by a 1982 statistical study where women comprised 98 percent of the teaching staff in Jewish elementary schools, 75 percent of the teaching staff in supplementary schools, and 70 percent of the staff in day schools.

Throughout the twentieth century, the feminization of Jewish education was most directly influenced by religious denomination. As early as 1930, studies demonstrated that the gender composition of the teaching staff was directly correlated with the denominational affiliation of the school. For example, in once-a-week Jewish schools belonging to the Reform Movement, two-thirds of the teaching staff was female in 1930, while in communal and congregational Talmud Torahs, male teachers still predominated. By 1944, the typical Reform religious school teacher was a twenty-one-year-old female. While communal and Orthodox schools were still dominated by male teachers in the 1950s, the Reform school teaching profession had already been completely feminized.

In addition to religious denomination, the feminization of the teaching staff in Jewish schools was also facilitated by the new place of Jewish education within the lives of American Jews. As supplementary education grew to be the primary medium through which Jewish education was conveyed to Jewish children, men—for whom part-time work was not acceptable—were forced to pursue more lucrative "full-time" work. As a 1964 study claimed, each year 75 percent of young Jewish men left the Jewish teaching profession for other professions. They saw Jewish education only as "a temporary economic springboard." For Jewish women, on the other hand, part-time work was extremely attractive, for it allowed them to combine work with family responsibilities. Furthermore, as Jewish men moved up the economic ladder throughout the 1950s and 1960s, it became unnecessary—and in some cases, even socially inappropriate—for Jewish women, as middle-class wives, to work full-time. Thus, the "part-timeness" of Jewish education, which became particularly prevalent during the 1960s, caused the Jewish teaching profession to emerge as an extremely appropriate occupation for women and an almost implausible one for men.

In the second half of the twentieth century, with the rise of supplementary schools, Jewish education more often focused exclusively on younger children—another factor that encouraged the feminization of Jewish education. In the Old Country, it was acceptable for men to educate young Jewish boys. In America, however, secular cultural trends reserved elementary education for women. Consequently, female Jewish teachers predominated in this field from the early 1930s and continued to dominate throughout the century. As Jewish elementary school programs grew throughout the course of the late twentieth century, female teachers began to comprise a larger percentage of the Jewish teaching profession.

With the exception of ultra-Orthodox yeshivahs and some Orthodox day schools, most teachers today involved in Jewish education are female. The feminization of the Jewish teaching profession would not have been possible if not for the part-time nature of this profession and the commensurately low salaries paid to its teachers. The feminization of the Jewish teaching profession has recently become a topic of scholarly inquiry, as Jewish educators have turned their attention to the correlation between this occurrence and the general devaluation of Jewish education in the latter half of the twentieth century.

Concern over this devaluation has spurred the development of several innovative educational organizations over the last several decades, and Jewish women have played a major role in shaping these agencies. Of these organizations, the Conference on Alternatives in Jewish Education (CAJE), renamed the Coalition for the Advancement of Jewish Education in 1987, provides one of the best examples of the creative and critical contributions that female Jewish teachers continue to make to the field of Jewish education. Founded in 1977 as a result of the tireless efforts of Cherie Koller-Fox and Jerry Benjamin, this grass-roots organization of Jewish teachers has been enriched greatly through the leadership of many accomplished female Jewish educators, most notably Betsy Dolgin Katz, Carol Starin, and Sylvia Abrams. Awarded numerous prizes for its programming, curriculum banks, and conferences, CAJE continues to bring together both lay and professional Jewish educators from across the ideological spectrum for their annual conferences; it has become the main support agency for Jewish teachers throughout North America.

Through Jewish educational organizations, Jewish schools, and public schools, female Jewish teachers have played an important role in shaping the North American teaching profession. Over the last 150 years, American Jewish women have been drawn to teaching in both public and Jewish schools by a multitude of factors. The massive influx of Jewish women into teaching was clearly informed by the larger global feminization of the teaching profession. Throughout this period, however, numerous social, cultural, and economic factors distinctly shaped the experiences of Jewish female teachers in America. These unique circumstances allowed Jewish female teachers to play a formative role in shaping both public and Jewish education in America.

BIBLIOGRAPHY

Brooks, T. *Towards Dignity: A Brief History of the UFT* (1967); Chipkin, Israel. "The Jewish Teacher in New York City and the Remuneration for His Services." *Jewish Education* 2, no. 3 (Fall 1930): 165–175; Cohen, J. *Jews, Jobs and Discrimination: A Report on Jewish Non-Employment* (1937): 13–18; Dellapergola, S., and A. Dubb, A. *First Census of Jewish Schools in the Diaspora, 1981/2–1982/3* (1986); Dushkin, Alexander. "Supply and Training of Teachers for Jewish Schools in the Diaspora." *Jewish Education* 35, no. 1 (Fall 1964): 22–37; Ingall, Carol. "The Feminization of Jewish Education." *The Melton Journal* (Fall 1987): 11; Jaffe, Philip. "Study of Two Hundred and Forty Teachers in the Reform Religious Schools of New York." *The Jewish Teacher* 12, no.

2 (January 1944): 23–35; Janowsky, Oscar, ed. *The Education of American Jewish Teachers* (1967); Kaplan, Mordecai. "What the American Jewish Woman Can Do for Jewish Education." *Jewish Education* 4, no. 3 (Fall 1932): 139–147; Markowitz, Ruth. *My Daughter, the Teacher: Jewish Teachers in the New York City Schools* (1993); Monson, Rela Geffen. "What We Know About Women and Jewish Education." In *What We Know About Jewish Education: A Handbook of Today's Research for Tomorrow's Jewish Education*, edited by S. Kelman (1992); Weinberg, Sydney Stahl. "Longing to Learn: The Education of Jewish Immigrant Women in New York City, 1900–1934." *Journal of American Ethnic History* 8 (Spring 1989): 108–126.

REBECCA KOBRIN

TEC, NECHAMA (b. 1931)

"My research about the Nazi annihilation of European Jews alerted me to a serious omission and an equally serious distortion," begins Nechama Tec in the preface to her sixth book, *Defiance: The Bielski Partisans* (1993). Tec's determination to address the silences and inaccuracies surrounding the Holocaust and to reveal the untold stories of righteousness and rescue epitomize her work as an American Jewish scholar. Tec brings to Holocaust studies the training of a sociologist and the insight of a survivor. Her in-depth studies of Jewish and Christian rescuers during World War II have added a new dimension to the understanding of heroism and the Holocaust.

Nechama Tec's interest in rescue and resistance is rooted in her own experiences as a hidden child in Nazi-occupied Europe. Born in Lublin, Poland, in 1931 to Roman Bawnik, a businessman, and Esther (Hachamoff) Bawnik, Nechama lived for three years during World War II under an assumed Christian identity. With the aid of Catholic Poles, her sister and parents also survived the war by hiding in homes and evading Nazi detection.

Immediately following the war, Nechama was determined to put her Holocaust experiences behind her. She married Leon Tec, a child psychiatrist, in 1950 and immigrated with her husband to the United States in 1952, where they had two children, Leora and Roland. Tec embarked on a career in academia, earning her bachelor's (1954), master's (1955), and doctoral (1963) degrees in sociology from Columbia University.

In 1975, Tec's memories of the war reemerged, and she began to write her Holocaust memoir. The result was *Dry Tears: The Story of a Lost Childhood* (1982), a vivid account of Tec's life in Poland from 1939 to 1945. *Dry Tears* represents a turning point in Tec's career. By recalling her own story of Christian protection, Tec raised questions about rescue and sur-

vival, namely, why did certain Christian Poles help save Jews and what were the experiences of other Jews who, through passing and hiding, survived? Tec's subsequent book, *When Light Pierced the Darkness: Christian Rescue of Jews in Nazi-Occupied Poland* (1986), is a systematic exploration of these issues.

Based on archival material and in-depth personal interviews with rescuers and survivors, *When Light Pierced the Darkness* examines Jews under Christian protection and the background and motives of righteous gentiles. Tec challenges previous theories that characterize rescue behavior as either inexplicable or rooted in class, friendship patterns, or political or religious affiliation. Instead, she explains altruistic rescue by the presence of several characteristics: individuality that approximates marginality, independence to act according to one's beliefs despite external pressures, long-standing commitment to aiding the helpless,

Nechama Tec's sociological work, informed by her experience as a Holocaust survivor, addresses the silences and inaccuracies surrounding the Holocaust and reveals untold stories of righteousness and rescue. [Shlomo Arad. Courtesy of Oxford University Press]

perception of rescue as a necessary response to circumstances and not an act of heroism, unplanned initiation of rescue, and universalistic view of Jews as needy human beings reliant on others' aid.

Focusing on relatively unknown but extraordinary cases, Tec's subsequent books continue to explore passing and rescue. *In the Lion's Den: The Life of Oswald Rufeisen* (1990) recounts the experiences of a young Jew who survived the Holocaust by passing as half German and half Polish. Rufeisen's story is particularly remarkable because of his role as a rescuer of hundreds of Jews and Christians. *Defiance: The Bielski Partisans* makes an important contribution by showing that many other Jews could be both rescuers and survivors. *Defiance* presents the story of Tuvia Bielski, a Belorussian Jew who organized a band of partisans that helped save over twelve hundred lives. In recounting the Bielski fighters' heroic actions, Tec corrects the distorted view that Jews were passive victims of Nazi persecution and demonstrates that Jewish altruism, courage, and resistance helped save Jewish lives.

Tec has been a professor of sociology at the University of Connecticut at Stamford since 1974. She is a member of the advisory board of the Braun Center for Holocaust Studies of the Anti-Defamation League of B'nai B'rith and its International Advisory Board of Directors of the Foundation to Sustain Righteous Christians. She is the author of over thirty articles in such journals as *Adolescence*, *Contemporary Sociology*, *Journal of Marriage and Family*, *Journal of Social Problems*, *Journal of Social Science and Medicine*, *Social Forces*, *Eastern European Quarterly*, and *Polin*. Tec is also the recipient of numerous awards, including a Pulitzer Prize nomination, a First Prize for Holocaust Literature by the World Federation of Fighters, Partisans and Concentration Camp Survivors in Israel, a Christopher Award, and an International Anne Frank Special Recognition Prize.

SELECTED WORKS BY NECHAMA TEC

Defiance: The Bielski Partisans (1993); *Dry Tears: The Story of a Lost Childhood* (1982. Reprint, with new epilogue, 1986); *Gambling in Sweden* (1964); *Grass Is Green in Suburbia: A Sociological Study of Adolescent Usage of Illicit Drugs* (1974); *In the Lion's Den: The Life of Oswald Rufeisen* (1990); *When Light Pierced the Darkness: Christian Rescue of Jews in Nazi-Occupied Poland* (1986).

BIBLIOGRAPHY

Ash, Timothy Garton. Review of *When Light Pierced the Darkness: Christian Rescue of Jews in Nazi-Occupied Poland*, by Nechama Tec. *The New York Review of Books* 32 (December 19, 1985): 26–28+; Baumgarten, Murray. "Nechama Tec's *Dry Tears* and the Sociological Imagination." In *Expectations and Endings: Observations on Holocaust Literature. Working Papers in Holocaust Studies* 3 (September 1989): 1–78; Bronner, Ethan. Review of *Defiance: The Bielski Partisans*, by Nechama Tec. *Boston Globe*, August 22, 1993, B16; *Contemporary Authors*; Gross, Jan Tomasz. Review of *When Light Pierced the Darkness: Christian Rescue of Jews in Nazi-Occupied Poland*, by Nechama Tec. *NYTimes Book Review* 91 (January 12, 1986): 37; Kirsch, Jonathan. Review of *Defiance: The Bielski Partisans*, by Nechama Tec. *Los Angeles Times*, September 22, 1993, E6; Lyons, Gene. Review of *When Light Pierced the Darkness: Christian Rescue of Jews in Nazi-Occupied Poland*, by Nechama Tec. *Newsweek* 107 (January 27, 1986): 62; *NYTimes*, February 6, 1994, C1; Pease, Neal. Review of *In the Lion's Den: The Life of Oswald Rufeisen*, by Nechama Tec. *The Catholic Historical Review* 77 (April 1991): 323; Tec, Nechama. Interview by author. Tape recording. Westport, Conn., June 8, 1995; *Who's Who of American Women*. 9th ed.

RONA SHERAMY

TEITELBAUM, FAIGE (b. 1913)

Faige Teitelbaum is the widow of the late Satmarar rebbe, Rabbi Joel Teitelbaum (died 1979). She is a leader of the Satmarar Hasidic community and often performs the role of a Hasidic rebbe. In this powerful role, she is undoubtedly the best-known woman in the Hasidic world.

Faige (Shapiro) Teitelbaum was born in 1913, in Czenstichov, Poland, the daughter of a well-known Polish Hasidic leader, Rabbi Avigdor Shapiro, a scion of the Kosnitz Hasidic dynasty. In 1936, she married Rabbi Joel Teitelbaum, thereby becoming the Satmarar *rebbetzin* [traditional title given to the wife of an orthodox rabbi]. Rabbi Teitelbaum's first wife, with whom he had three daughters, had died several years earlier. The Teitelbaums were rescued from the Nazi regime of Hungary in 1944 and relocated to the Williamsburg section of Brooklyn, New York, in 1947.

While the outside world best knows the Satmarar Hasidim for their rigid opposition to Israel and political Zionism, the Satmar community has developed a vast institutional structure, composed of religious, educational, and social welfare institutions. While the chief centers of Satmar are in Monroe, New York, and Williamsburg, other Satmar communities are found in Borough Park, Brooklyn; Monsey, New York; Lakewood, New Jersey; Montreal; London; Buenos Aires; Melbourne; Vienna; Antwerp; and a number of cities in Israel.

Teitelbaum was particularly active in various charitable activities in the Satmar community. She collected and distributed enormous amounts of money to Jewish people in need around the globe. Because of her particular interest in assisting brides and young mothers, she was instrumental in establishing several rest homes for women with young children. These hostels were located in the metropolitan New York area and were open to all Orthodox mothers at little or no cost. Because of Teitelbaum's charitable work, many followers of the Satmarar rebbe regarded her as a saintly woman in her own right.

As her husband aged and his health deteriorated, Teitelbaum came to be regarded by her husband's followers as a conduit to their rebbe. With a small group of loyal assistants, she controlled access to her ill husband and often had a strong say in major decisions regarding the Satmar community.

Following Joel Teitelbaum's death in 1979, many Satmarar Hasidim regarded Teitelbaum as a spiritual leader and as a symbol to preserve the memory of their beloved rebbe. Hasidim refused to accept the authority of the new Satmarar rebbe, Rabbi Moses Teitelbaum, a nephew of the late rabbi. They firmly believed that no new rebbe was necessary at this point and were supported in their belief by Joel Teitelbaum's chief administrative aide, Rabbi Joseph Ashkenasi. Rather, Faige Teitelbaum, with a group of loyal male aides, would speak for the dead rebbe and control access to his grave site in Kiryas Joel [Joel's village], the autonomous Satmar village in Monroe, New York.

Since 1979, the leadership struggle in the community has continued. While Rabbi Moses Teitelbaum has retained control of the majority of the Satmarar people, a small group called B'nai Joel [children of Joel] has remained loyal to Teitelbaum's memory of her late husband. These groups have clashed, often violently, chiefly in Kiryas Joel. At the same time, Teitelbaum has continued her charitable activities, distributing large amounts of money in the United States and Israel. Supporters and admirers regard Teitelbaum as a Hasidic leader and a sort of rebbe in her right. Many Satmarar Hasidim regularly petition her for blessings and advice. Teitelbaum is thus unique in the post–World War II period, as the only woman in the Hasidic world who functions de facto as a Hasidic rebbe and leader.

While modern society might regard Teitelbaum's powerful position as a throwback to leadership roles played by women in the nineteenth and early twentieth centuries, she is clearly a major influence in her own society. In the Hasidic community in general and the Satmarar community in particular, Feige Teitelbaum is revered.

BIBLIOGRAPHY

Alpert, Zalman. "Satmar Rebbe: Joel Teitelbaum." In *Jewish-American History and Culture: An Encyclopedia* (1992): 562–563; Kranzler, George. *Hasidic Williamsburg: A Contemporary American Hasidic Community* (1995); Mintz, Jerome. *Hasidic People: A Place in the New World* (1992); Rubin, Israel. *Satmar: An Island in the City* (1972).

ZALMAN ALPERT

TELEVISION

American Jewish women have a complex history of association with the medium of television. Since emerging as a mass medium in the early post–World War II years, television has figured prominently in the careers of a number of American Jewish women working both before and behind the camera. Moreover, television has provided a distinctive venue for contemporary American Jewish portraiture, in which women play a strategic role.

PERSONAS AND PERSONALITIES

Jewish women have appeared on American television over the past half-century in diverse capacities—from children's puppeteer SHARI LEWIS (*The Shari Lewis Show*, 1961–1963) to daytime talk-show host

Jewish women have appeared on American television over the past half-century in widely diverse capacities and sometimes unusual roles. Puppeteer SHARI LEWIS *[The Shari Lewis Show, 1961–1963] often had to play second fiddle to Lamb Chop. [New York Public Library]*

Two other puppeteers stayed completely behind the cameras. Bil and CORA BAIRD *produced
biweekly fifteen-minute programs in the 1950s entitled* Life with Snarky Parky
and The Bil Baird Show. *Their creations also appeared regularly on*
The Morning Show *and* The Ed Sullivan Show.

Sally Jessy Raphael (*Sally Jessy Raphael*, 1985–), from an interview with Nobel Prize–winning scientist ROS-ALYN YALOW (on *Jewish Voices and Visions*, 1985) to a documentary on the life of real estate magnate Leona Helmsley (on *A&E: Biography*, 1995). Regular appearances on television have helped a number of American Jewish women become national celebrities. Among the first is GERTRUDE BERG, who, as the writer, producer, and star of one of the medium's earliest comedy series, *The Goldbergs* (1949 to 1955), figures as the doyenne of Jewish women on American television. The series' portrait of a lower-middle-class family living in a Bronx apartment house became an archetype of New York Jewry for the first American television watchers.

Berg's pioneering career in broadcasting has perhaps only recently been matched among American Jewish women by former stand-up comic ROSEANNE, producer and star of the eponymous situation comedy since 1988. Berg's ingenuous, amiable public persona, fused with the character of Molly, contrasts strongly with the provocative, often caustic Roseanne (who in the series plays Roseanne Conner, a nominally half-Jewish wife and mother in a small-town, midwestern, working-class family). Nonetheless, the two women—as well as their respective careers and personas—make for an interesting measure both of the dynamics of women as powerful figures in the largely male broadcasting industry and of Jewish women's presentation of self in American popular culture.

As iconic as Berg's portrait of Molly, the Goldberg family matriarch, was in early postwar American television, it was only one image of Jewish womanhood offered by the medium at this time. However, during a period when most American Jews stressed the Americanness that they shared with fellow citizens over their distinction as Jews, these other Jewish women (along with their male counterparts) generally appeared unmarked as Jews before the television camera. MARY LIVINGSTONE performed with husband Jack Benny in a semiautobiographical situation comedy (*The Jack Benny Program*, 1950–1965), in which the

Most Jewish women on television generally appeared unmarked as Jews. Mary Livingstone performed with her husband, Jack Benny, in a semiautobiographical situation comedy (The Jack Benny Program, *1950–1965), in which their Jewishness was never mentioned.*

Rhoda from 1974 to 1978, superseded Molly as American television's longest-running fictional portrait of an American Jewish woman. Rhoda, who grew up in the Bronx before moving to Minneapolis, where *The Mary Tyler Moore Show* was set, figured as the earthy, comically displaced foil to WASP protagonist Mary Richards (played by Moore). When Rhoda was transformed into the title character of the eponymous spin-off series, a comic foil—Rhoda's younger sister, Brenda (played by Julie Kavner)—was introduced. Brenda took up what had been Rhoda's comic trope of self-deprecation, centered on her physical appearance and lack of romance.

Most American Jewish female performers who have become prominent on television have done so in comedy, whether appearing in continuing roles on situation comedies—BEA ARTHUR (*Maude*, 1972–1978; *The Golden Girls*, 1985–1992), Sandra Bernhardt (*Roseanne*), Mayim Bialik (*Blossom*, 1991–) Fran Drescher (*The Nanny*, 1993–), Barbara Feldon (*Get Smart*, 1965–1970), Carol Kane (*Taxi*, 1978–1983), Julie Kavner (*Rhoda*; *The Tracy Ullman Show*, 1987–1990; *The Simpsons*, 1990–), LINDA LAVIN (*Alice*, 1976–1985), Rhea Perlman (*Taxi*, 1978–1983; *Cheers*, 1982–1993; *Pearl*, 1996–)—or making regular appearances as sketch or stand-up comics on variety, quiz, and talk shows—Totie Fields, GOLDIE HAWN (a regular cast member of

Jewishness of the protagonists was never mentioned. The same was true of DINAH SHORE, who demonstrated both her talent as a popular singer and aplomb as a television host on variety shows *The Dinah Shore Show* (1951–1957) and *The Dinah Shore Chevy Show* (1956–1963). (In the latter program's theme song, she exhorted the nation to "see the U.S.A. in your Chevrolet.") But for the viewer who knew that these and other women were Jews, their on-screen attributes could be understood as emblematic of American Jewish womanhood. The celebrity quiz shows *I've Got a Secret* (1952–1967) and *To Tell the Truth* (1956–1967), for example, featured among their panelists former Miss America BESS MYERSON, opera singer Kitty Carlisle, and actress Phyllis Newman, who offered an image of American Jewish women as witty and cosmopolitan.

Recent decades have seen more Jewish women as characters and as public figures on television, although few have matched the iconic stature of Molly Goldberg. The character of Rhoda Morgenstern (portrayed by Valerie Harper), who appeared on *The Mary Tyler Moore Show* from 1970 to 1974 and on

The character of Rhoda Morgenstern (portrayed by Valerie Harper), who appeared on The Mary Tyler Moore Show *from 1970 to 1974 and on* Rhoda *from 1974 to 1978, superseded Molly Goldberg (*GERTRUDE BERG*) as American television's longest-running fictional portrait of an American Jewish woman.*

Laugh-In, 1968–1970), Marilyn Michaels, GILDA RADNER (a regular cast member of *Saturday Night Live*, 1975–1980), JOAN RIVERS, Rita Rudner. The comic performances created by American Jewish women project a wide spectrum of images of womanhood—ranging from the slinky, adventurous Agent 99 portrayed by Feldon on the parody espionage series or Lavin's Alice Hyatt, a savvy, working-class, single parent, to the self-effacing stand-up humor of the corpulent Fields or the reedy Rivers.

For many American Jewish women performers, television has played an occasional, variable role in their careers. Veteran Yiddish actress MOLLY PICON, for example, briefly hosted her own variety show on ABC in 1949. In the 1960s, she made guest appearances as a Jewish matron on situation comedies such as *Gomer Pyle* and *Car 54, Where Are You?* and appeared in the 1970s as a recurring character, Sarah Briskin, on the soap opera *Somerset*. In other instances, the medium has provided Jewish female performers with a distinctive venue for self-portraiture. SELMA DIAMOND began her career in television in the 1950s as one of the few women writers for the medium, working on *The Milton Berle Show*. A writer for Jack Paar when he hosted *The Tonight Show* in the late 1950s and early 1960s, she made occasional guest appearances on the talk show. Besides serving as the model for comedy writer Sally Rogers—a character on *The Dick van Dyke Show* (1960–1966) created by Carl Reiner, a fellow veteran of Sid Caesar's comedy-variety series of the 1950s—Diamond appeared on panel shows and acted in situation comedies (including *Night Court*) in the 1970s and 1980s. Joan Rivers has not only brought her self-reflexive humor to television audiences as a guest on variety, quiz, and talk shows, but has hosted her own talk shows (including Fox's *The Late Show*, 1986–1988) and has produced and played herself (as did her daughter, Melissa Rosenberg) in *Tears and Laughter* (1994), a television drama about the aftermath of her husband's suicide. Although BARBRA STREISAND's appearances on the medium have been infrequent, her occasional television specials and televised concerts (1965, 1966, 1967, 1995) offer an evolving self-portrait as performer and as public figure.

While many American Jewish women have worked behind the scenes in news, cultural and public affairs broadcasting, relatively few of them gained a national on-camera presence on these programs. Most prominent among them is BARBARA WALTERS, whose

Two of the most popular and influential women on American television today are not fictional characters but themselves. They are such a part of America culture that they are identified by their first names: BARBARA [WALTERS] *and Oprah Winfrey.*

career spans several decades as a correspondent, news anchor, and host of a news magazine series (*20/20*, 1984–) and of celebrity interview specials. A highlight of Walters's career as a television journalist came in 1977, when she interviewed Israeli prime minister Menachem Begin and Egyptian president Anwar Sadat on the occasion of Sadat's first visit to Israel. In recent years, American Jewish women who have reported regularly on network newscasts include Andrea Mitchell, Jessica Savitch, Lynn Sherr, and Nina Totenberg. Among the more prominent Jewish women involved in American cultural programming are BEVERLY SILLS, who has hosted numerous public television broadcasts of operas and concerts, following her career as an opera singer, and Judy Kinberg, a producer of arts programming for public television since the 1970s.

ABSENT AND CRYPTO-JEWISH WOMEN

The complexities of identifying a person or a character as a Jew in the modern world have further complicated the range of portraits of Jewish women on American television. Given that the signs of Jewishness in American culture are anything but simple or consistent, and that there is no consensus as to what these markers are, an examination of the presence of Jewish women on American television must also consider figures who are oblique, cryptic, even absent. This is particularly important, given that the majority of American television's portraits of Jewish women are the work of male writers, directors, and producers.

Indeed, even as American Jewish women come to play a larger role in shaping their self-portraiture on television as performers, writers, and producers, much of the medium's representation of Jewish women ought to be read as the visions of men (who are often Jewish). For example, one of the most memorable discussions of Jewish women aired on television—a 1970 installment of *The David Susskind Show* devoted to the topic of Jewish mothers—featured the observations of comedians Mel Brooks, Dan Greenburg, and David Steinberg, along with other men, but no women. One of the most popular portraits of a Jewish woman on American television in the mid-1990s is the character of Linda Richman (who has made the Yiddish term *farklemt* something of an American household word), created and performed by comedian Mike Myers on *Saturday Night Live*.

Another complicating factor in the dramatic portraiture of Jewish women on American television is the frequent disparity between the Jewish identity of characters and of the women who perform them.

Among the Jewish characters in continuing series played by non-Jewish performers are Rosalie Goldberg (*The Goldbergs*), played by Arlene McQuade; Rhoda Morgenstern and her mother, Ida (*The Mary Tyler Moore Show*, *Rhoda*), played by Valerie Harper and Nancy Walker; and Phyllis Silver (the mother on *Brooklyn Bridge*, 1991–1993), played by Amy Aquino. This common phenomenon suggests that Jewishness is not regarded as an innate identity, but a performative one that can be realized (through accent, gesture, etc.) by non-Jews as easily as by Jews.

Conversely, Jewish actresses frequently portray characters identified as non-Jews. In some instances— Elaine Bennett (*Seinfeld*, 1990–), portrayed by Julia Louis-Dreyfus; Dorothy Zbornak and Sophia Petrillo (*The Golden Girls*), played by Bea Arthur and Estelle Getty; Simka Gravas (*Taxi*), played by Carol Kane— these characters are often understood by some viewers as "crypto-Jews"—that is, characters who, while nominally identified as having some other ethnicity or religion, are nonetheless regarded as Jews in disguise. They are regarded as such not only by virtue of the performer's identity, but also because of character attributes (such as being aggressive, neurotic, clever, or talkative) understood as signs of female Jewish behavior. This phenomenon suggests a larger sense of ethnic relativism distinctive to American culture.

Of special interest along the spectrum of Jewish women on American television is their strategic *absence* as characters. A salient example is American television's frequent presentations of Jewish/non-Jewish intermarriages in more recent years, beginning with the short-lived and controversial *Bridget Loves Bernie* (1972–1973) followed by a spate of examples since the mid-1980s: *thirtysomething*, *Northern Exposure*, *Chicken Soup*, *Anything but Love*, *Mad About You*, *A Year in the Life*, *Murphy Brown*, among others. Following a convention established earlier in Broadway plays (notably *Abie's Irish Rose*, 1924) and Hollywood films (for example, *His People*, 1925), these all entail relationships between a Jewish man and a non-Jewish woman. Only occasionally is the reverse situation presented—for example, Rhoda's marriage to Joe Gerard on *Rhoda*; Frasier Crane's wife Lilith Stern (played by Bebe Neuwirth) on *Cheers*; the romance between Melissa Steadman (played by Melanie Mayron) and Gary Shepherd on *thirtysomething*. (Significantly, all of these relationships end in separation or divorce during the course of their series.) The comic and dramatic possibilities of interfaith families has also been explored in the situation comedy *All in the Family* (1971–1983), when archetypal working-class WASPs Archie and Edith Bunker become guardians of a half-Jewish niece, Stephanie Mills (played by Danielle Brisebois). The dramatic series *Sisters* (1991–1996) included the character of Frankie Reed Margolis (played by Julianne Phillips), a non-Jew married to a Jew, who converts to Judaism.

Television's frequent presentation of Jews in intermarriages may reflect a concern by producers that an entirely Jewish family would be of limited interest to an American mass audience. Since *The Goldbergs*, the only all-Jewish family identified as such at the center of a prime-time series has been the Silvers of *Brooklyn Bridge*. Aside from providing a ready subject for domestic conflict, television intermarriages sometimes constitute an autobiographical exercise. This was the case for *thirtysomething* producers Ed Zwick and Marshall Herskovitz, both of whom are Jews with non-Jewish wives. Moreover, dramas of marriage between a Jew and a non-Jew also become emblematic of intermarriage (religious, ethnic, class, regional, etc.) in general. Indeed, by using the family unit as a symbolic setting in which to investigate Jewish integration into American culture, these dramas of intermarriage can serve as case studies of the challenge of cultural integration in general.

PERFORMING JEWISH WOMANHOOD

While the most common appearances of Jewish women on American television figure in comic performances or in dramas about contemporary family life, the medium has also offered a wider range of portraits of Jewish womanhood in other programming genres. Of particular interest are episodes of ecumenical series from the late 1940s to the early 1980s, produced in conjunction with the Jewish Theological Seminary (*Frontiers of Faith*, *Lamp unto My Feet*, *The Eternal Light*, *Directions*) or other mainstream Jewish religious institutions. These public service series have occasionally presented dramas based on the lives of women such as HENRIETTA SZOLD, EMMA LAZARUS, and Jessy Judah, one of the first Jewish settlers of the New World; performances by the likes of choreographer PEARL LANG and folksinger MARTHA SCHLAMME; and interviews with American Jewish women ranging from opera singer ROBERTA PETERS to SALLY PRIESAND, the first woman ordained by the Reform rabbinate.

Occasional prime-time dramatic specials have dealt with the lives of Jewish women, both historical (*A Woman Called Golda*, a 1985 miniseries starring Ingrid Bergman as Israeli prime minister GOLDA MEIR) and fictitious (*Evergreen*, a 1985 miniseries based on a popular novel by Belva Plain, which follows Anna, played by Leslie Ann Warren, a Polish Jewish immigrant to the United States, from the 1900s to the

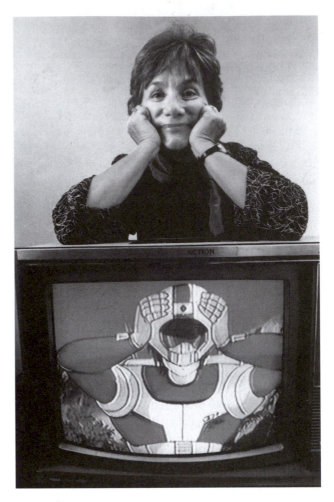

One highly influential Jewish woman in the television industry was never in front of a camera or listed in the credits for a show. Peggy Charren founded Action for Children's Television and forced the government to link television licensing to children's educational programming. [Photograph courtesy of Peggy Charren]

1960s). As is true of American television's presentations of Jews in general, the medium has devoted more broadcasts to the experiences of Jewish women during the Holocaust than in any other historical period. Among the earliest of these was the appearance of Hannah Block Kohner, a survivor of four Nazi concentration camps, on a 1953 episode of *This Is Your Life*. More recently, women Holocaust survivors have been the subject of documentaries—such as *Kitty: Return to Auschwitz* (1981), in which Kitty Felix Hart revisits the camp in a film originally made by Yorkshire Television in 1979; *One Survivor Remembers*, a portrait of GERDA WEISSMANN KLEIN, made by Home Box Office in conjunction with the U.S. Holocaust Memorial Museum in 1995—and dramatic specials—

such as *Playing for Time* (1980), which created considerable controversy when Vanessa Redgrave, an actress known for her anti-Zionist activism, was cast as Auschwitz survivor Fania Fénelon; *Miss Rose White*, 1992, based on Barbara Lebow's play *A Shayna Maidel*. Gina Sloan, an Italian Jewish survivor of the Holocaust and widow of an American GI, appeared as a regular character on the dramatic series *Homefront* (1991–1993), set in a midwestern small town in the late 1940s.

Anne Frank, the young author of a diary kept while in hiding in Nazi-occupied Amsterdam, has been the subject of numerous documentaries and dramas on American television—more than any other Jewish woman. The earliest of these was a half-hour play by Morton Wishengrad presented in 1952 on *Frontiers of Faith*, followed by made-for-television versions of Frances Goodrich and Albert Hackett's authorized stage version of *The Diary of Anne Frank* in 1967 (starring Diane Davila as Anne) and 1980 (with Melissa Gilbert in the title role), and *The Attic*, a 1988 television movie based on the memoirs of Miep Gies, the Dutch woman who hid the Frank family. The diarist even survives the war in Philip Roth's novella *The Ghost Writer*, adapted for television by *American Playhouse* in 1984, which explores her iconic stature in American Jewish culture.

Since the mid-1970s, a growing number of Jewish women have become documentary filmmakers, many of them presenting their work on public television, which has become the main venue for this genre in America. These women have made documentaries dealing with a wide array of subjects, including those of special interest to Jews and women (for example, Gina Blumenfeld's *In Dark Places: Remembering the Holocaust*, 1978; Lynn Littman's *In Her Own Time*, a portrait of anthropologist BARBARA MYERHOFF, 1985). A number of Jewish women video artists (including Eleanor Antin, Beryl Korot, Ilene Segalove) have used American television images as a point of departure in their work. The Jewish Museum in New York has been an important venue for their exhibition, and the museum's National Jewish Archive of Broadcasting houses many examples of American Jewish women on television.

While the broadcasting industry has provided fewer professional opportunities for women, both Jewish and non-Jewish, than it has for men, increasing numbers of American Jewish women work in television, whether behind the scenes as producers, directors, writers, and technicians, or in front of the camera. Television has also presented some of the most widely familiar images of contemporary American Jewish women, yet it remains to be seen how this continually expanding and diversifying medium might serve them as a community.

BIBLIOGRAPHY

Berlin, Charles, comp. *Guide to Judaica Videotapes in the Harvard College Library* (1989); Brooks, Tim, and Earle Marsh. *The Complete Directory to Prime Time Network TV Shows, 1946–Present* (1988); Brown, Les. *Les Brown's Encyclopedia of Television*. 3d ed. (1992); Fox, Stuart, comp. *Jewish Films in the United States: A Comprehensive Survey and Descriptive Filmography* (1976); Jewish Museum of New York. *National Jewish Archive of Broadcasting: Catalog of Holdings*. 2d ed. (1995); MacNeil, Alex. *Total Television* (1991).

JEFFREY SHANDLER

THEATER

For over a hundred years, Jewish women have been making their lives in the American theater as writers, actors, directors, designers, and producers. The vitality of the Yiddish theater, the splendor of Broadway, the rich tapestry of the regional theater—and everything in between—all owe a debt to the Jewish women who have given of their talents, their energy, their drive, and their dreams. From the classical performances of ROSE EYTINGE in the 1860s to the radical experiments of JUDITH MALINA in the 1960s, Jewish women have found in the American theater opportunities to express themselves, to challenge audiences, and to take the art of theater to new heights.

THE RICH LEGACY
OF THE YIDDISH THEATER

With the great wave of Jewish immigration in the late nineteenth century, the Yiddish theater in America was thriving. In a broad range of styles, from lively musical revues to intellectual avant-garde performances, the Yiddish theater was a center of community life for many Jewish immigrants. It was entertaining *and* educational. It was a way to feel a sense of belonging in a strange place, to understand life in a new world, and to preserve the culture of the homeland. It was a first step on the bridge between being foreign and being American. With a rich and vast legacy to the English-language theater, it also served as a conduit for new European plays, cultivated a community of passionate theatergoers, and produced an array of fine actors whose influence is still felt today.

SARA ADLER was genuine Yiddish theater royalty. First married to actor Moishe Heine-Haimovitch, later to flamboyant Yiddish theater impresario Jacob P. Adler, she was known for her dark beauty and the depth of her emotional power. The great Yiddish playwright Jacob Gordin wrote several plays especially for her, including *Without a Home*, in which she played an immigrant woman who suffers and finally goes mad because her husband and son can succeed in adjusting to American life, while she fails. Sara Adler's achievements—along with those of Yiddish actors such as BERTHA KALICH, Ester Kaminska, and Keni Liptzin—contributed to the recognition of women as serious actors. Her daughter STELLA ADLER built on her mother's accomplishments and went on to change the face of acting in America.

CELIA ADLER, daughter of Jacob Adler and his second wife Dina Shtettin Feinman, appeared in the Yiddish theater from childhood. As Nahma Sandrow describes it, "Throughout her career she specialized in playing romping, innocent young hoydens and, enormous eyes brimming with tears, sensitive girls and wildly weeping mothers." Celia Adler was a founding member of the Jewish Art Theater, dedicated to the new trend toward realism in drama, a literary repertoire, serious rehearsals, and professional directors and designers. In contract negotiations, she turned the spotlight on the difficulty faced by a woman alone in a business dominated by and designed for men. And while her long, rich career was built almost exclusively in the Yiddish theater, she was among the first of the serious actors to appear in an English-language production on Broadway.

Actors such as BERTA GERSTEN and Bertha Kalich dedicated themselves primarily to the Yiddish theater but found success on the English-language stage as well. So did the charming MOLLY PICON, whose first major role in the English-language theater was in the Broadway production of *Morningstar* by Sylvia Regan and who found that, from then on, all doors were open to her.

These actors did more than merely open doors for themselves, however. They popularized the image of the Jewish woman on stage and paved the way for others to follow in their footsteps. They bestowed upon a nation the rich gifts of their talents. And they nurtured Jewish culture, maintaining a centuries-old theatrical tradition while creating a rich legacy for new generations.

THE COMMERCIAL THEATER

Actors

In the nineteenth century, two major stars of the American stage were Jewish women. The great French actress Sarah Bernhardt made her American debut in 1880 as the tragic title character in *Adrienne Lecouvreur.* In her nine tours of America, she swept audiences away with her tragic grandeur and majestic passion. This was a time when audiences came to the theater not to see the play but to see the star, and ROSE EYTINGE was a notable attraction. She performed with such luminaries as Edwin Booth, touring major cities, performing for President Lincoln, even visiting the White House. Of her performance in *Rose Michel* (1875), one critic said that she "attained to the exalted pitch of perfect truth, in delineation of horror and agony, and it swept to this apex with the spontaneity of perfect ease." Her fierce, dark passion thrilled audiences, many of whom never knew that she was Jewish. Eytinge concealed her ethnicity, allowing herself to appear exotic while not admitting to being Jewish. Others who blazed the trail into the commercial theater took a variety of different approaches.

ADAH ISAACS MENKEN, for example, made her name in American theater history by donning a flesh-toned body stocking and strapping herself to a horse in the melodrama *Mazeppa* (1861). She "is the sensation of the New York stage," gushed one reviewer. "Her rare beauty and the tantalizing audacity of her performance defy description. She must be seen to be believed; anyone who misses her at the Broadway Theater will be denying himself the rarest of exhilarating treats." The truth of her background is obscure—Menken told so many conflicting stories that it is impossible to know what is fact and what is fiction—but this woman made certain that she was noticed and remembered.

In burlesque and vaudeville, some Jewish women adopted the conventions of the already-accepted outsiders in America—blacks—in order to gain a foothold in show business. SOPHIE TUCKER began her career wearing blackface and singing songs in black dialect—she was billed as "the red-hot mamma." LOUISE DRESSER employed a chorus of African-American children in her act. And BELLE BAKER found her early vaudeville success by playing the sexy, sensual image that white audiences associated with black women.

There was fame, if not fortune, for those lucky enough to be chosen for the Ziegfeld Follies, and that included Sophie Tucker, Belle Baker, NORA BAYES, and the incomparable FANNY BRICE. Born Fania Borach in New York's Lower East Side, Brice was a natural mimic with a sharp sense of humor and an excellent singing voice. Although early in her career she tried to appear less "ethnic" by changing her name to Brice (after all, she didn't even speak Yiddish), she found early on that it was her comic specialty numbers—

such as Irving Berlin's "Sadie Salome, Go Home" sung with a Yiddish accent—that won her audiences. A certain kind of ethnic humor, based largely on stereotypes, was popular early in the twentieth century, and Brice was able to catch the wave and ride it all the way to eventual stardom.

For many years on Broadway, the success of Jewish actresses seemed to depend on the degree to which they could downplay their Jewishness. Trained for a career in opera, VIVIENNE SEGAL made her early career playing the ingenue in musicals such as *Oh, Lady! Lady!* (1918) and *The Desert Song* (1926), later returning to Broadway in the roles of sultry older women in shows such as *Pal Joey* (1952) and *A Connecticut Yankee* (1943, 1952). LIBBY HOLMAN was an alluring torch singer who appeared on Broadway in *Garrick Gaieties* (1925). The superb comedienne JUDY HOLLIDAY made her New York debut in *Kiss Them for Me* (1945), became a star with her portrayal of mob moll Billie Dawn in *Born Yesterday* (1946), and earned a Tony award for her turn as the meddling telephone operator in *Bells Are Ringing* (1956).

Broadway was also the biggest, brightest showcase for a woman who has come to be considered one of America's biggest, brightest stars: BARBRA STREISAND. As the klutzy Miss Marmelstein in *I Can Get It for You Wholesale* (1962), she introduced her own brand of energy, brass, and humor to the Broadway stage. But it was Streisand's portrayal of Fanny Brice in *Funny Girl* that made her a star. Perhaps what's most significant about Streisand's success is that she did it by being herself. She did not change her last name or her nose. Her upbringing was Jewish—she neither flaunted nor hid it. She simply lived it.

Writers

American Jewish playwrights, composers, and lyricists have contributed their talents to the Broadway stage in abundance. William Goldman's claim that "without Jews, there simply would have been no musical comedy to speak of in America" is not far off. Irving Berlin, George and Ira Gershwin, Richard Rodgers, Lorenz Hart, Yip Harburg, and Stephen Sondheim are but a few of those whose talents essentially *made* the American musical theater. And Jewish women are right up there with Jewish men.

DOROTHY FIELDS was a lyricist and librettist whose work is best known for fresh turns of phrase and zesty humor. She wrote the lyrics to such popular songs as "I Can't Give You Anything But Love" and "On the Sunny Side of the Street," and she wrote librettos for popular shows such as *Annie Get Your Gun* (1946) and *Sweet Charity* (1966). Even after her death, her lyrics

were featured on Broadway in productions of *Ain't Misbehavin'* (1978) and *Sugar Babies* (1979).

BELLA SPEWACK and her husband Sam were one of Broadway's best-known husband-and-wife writing teams. Together they wrote twelve plays—mostly madcap comedies and social satires—including *Boy Meets Girl* (1935) and the book for Cole Porter's Tony Award–winning musical *Kiss Me Kate* (1948).

The team of BETTY COMDEN and Adolph Green won fame on Broadway for fast-paced, wisecracking lyrics and librettos. They wrote *On the Town* (1944) with Leonard Bernstein and Jerome Robbins, *Wonderful Town* (1953) with Leonard Bernstein, and *Bells Are Ringing* (1956) with Jule Styne. Their partnership was one of the longest and most successful in Broadway history, continuing through *Applause* (1970) and *Singin' in the Rain* (1985).

Among the significant American Jewish writers of the nonmusical Broadway theater—Elmer Rice, Clifford Odets, Paddy Chayevsky, and Arthur Miller—are a host of great women, including EDNA FERBER, ROSE FRANKEN, Sylvia Regan, and LILLIAN HELLMAN.

Edna Ferber was a celebrated novelist as well as an acclaimed playwright, known for her keen ear for dialogue and her sharp wit. She created her great Broadway successes in collaboration with George S. Kaufman: *Minick* (1924), *The Royal Family* (1927), *Dinner at Eight* (1932), and *Stage Door* (1936). Two of her novels were made into popular Broadway musicals: *Showboat* (1927) and *Saratoga* (1959).

Novelist and short story writer Rose Franken crossed over into the theater with the surprise hit of her play *Another Language* in 1932. Her sharp-eyed observations about the American family gave tang to her domestic dramas *Claudia* (1941) and *The Hallams* (1947). Social concerns such as anti-Semitism, homophobia, sexism, and war fueled her other plays such as *Outrageous Fortune* (1943), *Doctors Disagree* (1943), and *Soldier's Wife* (1944).

Sylvia Regan was a press agent for Orson Welles's Mercury Theatre before she made her mark as a Broadway playwright with the 1940 production of her Jewish family drama *Morningstar*, featuring Molly Picon and Sidney Lumet. In 1953, she topped her earlier success with the production of her comedy about the garment industry, *The Fifth Season*.

But no discussion of American playwrights—male or female, Jewish or gentile—would be complete without Lillian Hellman. Like her male counterparts Clifford Odets and Arthur Miller, Hellman expressed through her plays a strong belief in ethics, morality, truth, and responsibility. *The Children's Hour* (1934)— Hellman's drama about the destructive power of a lie—won her the accolades of critics, who called her a "second Ibsen" and "the American Strindberg." In tightly constructed, powerful dramas such as *The Little Foxes* (1939), *Another Part of the Forest* (1947), *The Autumn Garden* (1951), and *Toys in the Attic* (1960), Hellman took audiences on rigorous emotional journeys and left them drained, horrified, uplifted, angry, sorrowful . . . but never bored.

Designers

As a young woman, ALINE BERNSTEIN planned to put her artistic abilities to use as a portrait painter, but the lure of the theater turned her into a costume and scenic designer. At the Neighborhood Playhouse, she designed *The Little Clay Cart* and *The Grand Street Follies* (1924). On Broadway—in addition to her work on *Grand Hotel* (1930)—she is remembered for her designs for Lillian Hellman's powerful dramas *The Children's Hour* and *The Little Foxes*.

When JEAN ROSENTHAL went to work for the Federal Theater Project in 1935, there was no such thing as a lighting designer. Lighting was handled by an electrician, whose goal was simply to make sure that the audience could see the stage. But it all changed with Rosenthal, who saw the power of light to evoke mood, draw focus, and express ideas. Her lighting design for Orson Welles's production of *Julius Caesar* (1937) brought her to prominence, and she went on to design extensively for modern dance pioneer Martha Graham. Rosenthal designed such well-known Broadway productions as *West Side Story* (1957), *Hello, Dolly!* (1964), and *Fiddler on the Roof* (1964).

Producers

The ultimate power in the American commercial theater is held by producers. It is a profession that demands, as Cheryl Crawford once said and Helen Krich Chinoy quotes, "a ton of nerves" and "the philosophy of a gambler." It is a field largely dominated by men, but that hasn't stopped Jewish women from taking on the challenge. With savvy, drive, a passion for quality, and a knack for leadership, a number of Jewish women have beaten the odds in this demanding profession.

HELEN MENKEN turned her substantial energy to producing after a successful career as an actress. She is best known as producer of the *Stage Door Canteen*, Broadway's contribution to the war effort from 1942 to 1946, and was president for many years of the American Theater Wing, the organization responsible for Broadway's top honor: the Antoinette Perry Award (the Tony).

One of the most important American theater producers of the 1920s, 1930s, and 1940s was THERESA HELBURN, president of the Theatre Guild. She spearheaded Guild efforts to raise the artistic level of Broadway production, to present challenging plays in the commercial theater, to build audience support, and to nurture the work of talented theater artists. The Guild's achievements over time include legendary productions of plays by Elmer Rice, John Howard Lawson, Robert Sherwood, Maxwell Anderson, and Eugene O'Neill. Helburn was responsible for uniting Alfred Lunt and Lynn Fontanne (1924), for bringing *Oklahoma!* to the stage (1943), and for producing *Othello* with Paul Robeson (1943).

IRENE MAYER SELZNICK—daughter of MGM founder Louis B. Mayer and the wife of producer David O. Selznick—learned about producing from some of the best in the business and went on to produce *A Streetcar Named Desire* (1947), *Bell, Book and Candle* (1950), and *The Chalk Garden* (1955). Wrote *New York Times* drama critic Mel Gussow, "When she produced *Streetcar* and other plays, she worked hand in glove with the playwright in insuring that the work was seen absolutely to its best advantage."

NEW PASSION, NEW APPROACHES

Jewish women have often been the trailblazers in American theater, seeing the problems with modern ways of working and envisioning new methods, challenging their creative collaborators, and pushing the bounds of the theatrical art. Stella Adler—daughter of Yiddish theater legends Jacob and Sara Adler—was such a trailblazer.

She was one of a group of young theater artists in the 1930s who found Broadway's endeavors sorely lacking. Productions at the time could be haphazard affairs, with little effort to achieve a unified style of design and performance and no sense of having grown out of a common need of the artists to express an idea or feeling. "This produced positive results when the elements thrown together were based on the rather primitive appetites of a large number of people," wrote Harold Clurman. "Action melodrama, a leg show, a conventional musical, or a knockabout farce was generally more satisfactory from the standpoint of completeness or unity of style than were the more ambitious efforts of the highbrow theater."

So a group of committed young theater artists— Stella Adler among them—chose to forge their own path. Theirs would be a theater that valued content *and* form, where artists were continually nurtured in the development of their technique, and where technique was used to express a shared response to the world around them. The approach was group oriented, so they named themselves the Group Theatre.

Founded in 1931 by Harold Clurman, Cheryl Crawford, and Lee Strasberg, the Group Theatre dedicated itself to training and nurturing actors and to building a sense of ensemble performance in which everyone contributed equally to the success of a production. In addition to Stella Adler, the company included talented young actors such as Sanford Meisner, Morris Carnovsky, Franchot Tone, and Phoebe Brand. Together, they explored the methods of Russian acting teacher and director Konstantin Stanislavsky, developing an approach to acting that emphasized spontaneity and emotional authenticity. Claimed one reviewer enthusiastically in response to the Group's first production, "They are not only earnest and skillful, but inspired. . . . Their group performance is too beautifully imagined and modulated to concentrate on personal achievements. There is not a gaudy, brittle or facile stroke in their acting." Noted another, "Jaded Broadway seems finally to have found the young blood and new ideas for which many of us have been praying."

But despite the success, Stella Adler was dissatisfied with the company's acting methods. She wanted techniques that were more reliable, more tangible, and less personally intrusive, so she took up the matter with the great Stanislavsky himself when she met him in Paris in 1934. Intrigued by Adler's boldness, the master invited her to study with him and to learn more about how his ideas about acting had changed over time. "He understood," said Adler later, "that asking the actor to recall his personal life could produce hysteria, so he had abandoned that. He believed now that the actor must rely on his imagination." Adler recorded the sessions in her diary over the six-week period that she and Stanislavsky worked together, and shared her findings with the members of the Group Theatre upon her return to America.

The results of Adler's work with Stanislavsky significantly altered the Group's approach to acting. Although these ideas were never fully embraced by Lee Strasberg, the dynamic tension between Adler's understanding of Stanislavsky and that of Strasberg resulted in some of the finest ensemble performances ever recorded in the American theater. In Clifford Odets's *Awake and Sing* and *Waiting for Lefty*, the ideals of the Group Theatre were magnificently realized.

In 1949, Adler carried her work forward by founding the Stella Adler Conservatory of Acting where, until her death in 1992, she trained a generation of up-and-coming actors: Marlon Brando, Robert De Niro, Ellen Burstyn, Elaine Stritch, and many others.

Stella Adler's high standards, her passion for excellence, her willingness to challenge the status quo, and her love of theater itself inspired and influenced a vast array of actors, directors, and acting teachers. This indomitable Jewish American woman, daughter of Yiddish theater royalty, changed American acting fundamentally and forever.

VISIONARIES, ICONOCLASTS, AND RULE BREAKERS

During the turbulent 1960s, virtually every aspect of American society was called into question, and that included the American theater. As Ellen Schiff says, it was a time of experimentation, and Jewish women were among those with "plenty to say, bursting with a passion for performance and new ideas for using the stage, heady with the opportunity to pursue artistic, rather than monetary or even critical, success."

Among the most influential of the experimental groups was the Living Theatre, a collective founded by Jewish American actor/director JUDITH MALINA and her husband Julian Beck. Originally devoted to producing the poetic works of writers such as Federico Garcia Lorca and GERTRUDE STEIN, the company's aesthetic began to evolve with its hyperrealistic productions about drug addiction (*The Connection*) and the rituals of life in a military prison (*The Brig*). However, it was in 1963—when the company went into exile in Europe to avoid taxes—that the Living Theatre truly found its style. According to Renfreu Neff, "Its primary impetus was a need for a common language in which to communicate with its audiences as it traveled from country to country across the Continent. A non-verbal dramatic idiom had to be found that would go beyond words and reach the public on a level that transcended the need for language." Intrigued by the radical acting theories of Antonin Artaud, Malina and Beck developed a unique performance style that sought to shatter the restraints of realism, break down the boundaries between audience and performer, blur the distinction between art and real life, and create a communal ritual experience of the moment. Wrote critic Robert Brustein, "By stirring up a kind of theatrical anarchism wilder than anything that has been seen here or abroad, the Living Theatre has literally given life to theater." They returned to the United States in 1968 and, at Brustein's invitation, presented four spectacular performances at Yale University—*Mysteries and Smaller Pieces*, *Antigone*, *Frankenstein*, and *Paradise Now*—that bedazzled, enraged, and inspired audiences. Especially provocative was *Paradise Now*, Brustein recalled, at the end of which "everyone was exhorted to leave the theater and convert the police to anarchism, to storm the jails and free the prisoners, to stop the war and ban the bomb, and to take over the New Haven streets in the name of the People."

Meanwhile, other Jewish American women were rocking the foundations of the theater establishment as well. Playwright Susan Yankowitz scripted the Open Theater's landmark 1969 production of *Terminal* and lent her bold imagery and avant-garde sensibility to works such as *The Ha-Ha Play, Slaughterhouse Play*, and *Boxes*. ROSALYN DREXLER skewered sex and violence in satires such as *Home Movies* and *The Line of Least Existence*. And Karen Malpede wrote *Lament for Three Women, The End of War*, and *Making Peace* even as she cofounded the New Cycle Theater in Brooklyn.

In the revolutionary spirit of the 1960s and 1970s, theater companies began to emerge with the mission to support artists of specific ethnic and cultural backgrounds, to explore ethnic and cultural identity, and to create theater based on that exploration. New theaters devoted to the American Jewish experience sprang up in this creative climate, including American Jewish Theater and Jewish Repertory Theater in New York, and A Traveling Jewish Theater in San Francisco.

Actor/director Naomi Newman, together with Corey Fischer and Albert Greenberg, founded A Traveling Jewish Theater "out of a desire to create a contemporary theater that would give form to streams of visionary experience that run through Jewish history, culture, and imagination." In brilliantly evocative productions, using masks, puppets, music, movement, sound, and silence, A Traveling Jewish Theater has explored a range of concerns, including isolation, exile, and assimilation. And when Naomi Newman takes the stage in her play *Snake Talk: Urgent Messages from the Mother*, she speaks to the very heart with passion and eloquence.

DREAMING OF A REGIONAL THEATER— AND MAKING IT HAPPEN

As early as the 1920s, Jewish women recognized that there was an American theater beyond New York. Outside professional structures, in community and regional drama groups, in art theaters and little theaters all over the country, theater was being created purely for the love of the art. Often this work celebrated community, bringing people together in the collective experience of producing a play and providing opportunities for the community itself to share in the event. Jewish American critic EDITH ISAACS, the influential editor of *Theatre Arts* magazine, referred to this kind of theater as "the tributary theater," feeding the mainstream with a wealth of talent, energy, and

ideas. She rejected the commercialism of the New York theater and called on Americans to go to "the four corners of the country and begin again, training playwrights to create in their own idiom, in their own theaters." All over the country, people responded to Isaacs's call, dedicating themselves to developing and nurturing a nationwide, grassroots theater movement.

One of those who took up the call was Zelda Fichandler. Like Isaacs before her, Fichandler rejected the commercialism of the New York theater. She saw the joblessness of American theater artists as a tragic waste of talent and the centralization of American theater in New York as a denial of the vast cultural potential of a diverse nation. "Some of us looked about and saw that something was amiss," says Fichandler. "What was essentially a collective and cumulative art form was represented in the United States by the hit-or-miss, make-a-pudding, smash-a-pudding system of Broadway production. What required by its nature continuity and groupness, not to mention a certain quietude of spirit and fifth freedom, the freedom to fail, was taking place in an atmosphere of hysteria, crisis, fragmentation, one-shotness, and mammon-mindedness." So Fichandler and two other pioneering women decided to do something about it. In 1947, Margo Jones founded Theater 47 in Houston and Nina Vance founded the Alley Theater in Houston, and in 1950, Zelda Fichandler founded the Arena Stage in Washington, D.C.

The common goal of these theaters was to put art before money. Jones, Vance, and Fichandler envisioned theaters that would nurture professional artists, provide opportunities for artistic risk-taking, set high professional standards for the production of new plays as well as classics, and embrace the idea that long-term success may mean short-term failure. Wrote Henry Hewes in the *Saturday Review*, "The great bright hope of the [regional theater] movement is that these organizations will be able to tackle large, serious works that would be financially prohibitive in the current Broadway economy."

And that's just what happened at the Arena Stage under Zelda Fichandler's deft direction. She surrounded herself with consummate professionals, including a skillful administrative and production staff and a dynamic company of actors, designers, and directors. She devoted her considerable drive, artistic vision, and business acumen to the success of the Arena Stage, giving classics by Oscar Wilde and Oliver Goldsmith a place alongside modern plays by Arthur Miller and Tennessee Williams.

In 1967, when Fichandler produced Howard Sackler's sprawling new play *The Great White Hope—*

guiding the development of the play from its unwieldy original form into a finely honed and powerful epic, and giving it a first-class production starring James Earl Jones—she made the entire theater profession stand up and take notice. Suddenly, people began to realize the potential power of the regional theater. This was a place where plays could be carefully nurtured over time, given the care and support they needed, and allowed to develop, before being subjected to the fierce scrutiny of the commercial theatrical marketplace. "It all happened because of the whimsical and radical genius of Zelda Fichandler," said director Edwin Sherin. "Zelda has the vision of a seer."

Fichandler's success inspired others. Soon, her Arena Stage was just one of a vast network of regional theaters all across the United States, including the Guthrie Theater in Minneapolis, the Mark Taper Forum in Los Angeles, the American Conservatory Theater in San Francisco, the Long Wharf in New Haven, Connecticut, the Seattle Repertory Theater, and many others. In 1965, Ella Malin noted that regional theaters illustrate "the slow but growing acceptance of theater as a permanent cultural institution worthy of community support in much the same way as museums, libraries, and symphony orchestras." Today, there are over three hundred nonprofit professional theater companies in the United States, consistently offering a broad range of high-quality productions and providing artistic homes to countless professional actors, directors, designers, technicians, and administrators. Thanks are largely due to Zelda Fichandler: a woman with a dream—and the chutzpah—to make it come true.

Among those who have followed in Fichandler's footsteps are Emily Mann, artistic director of the McCarter Theater Center in Princeton, New Jersey; Libby Appel, artistic director of the Oregon Shakespeare Festival in Ashland, Oregon; and Susan Medak, managing director of Berkeley Repertory Theater in Berkeley, California. Outspoken, ambitious, and idealistic all, these Jewish women are keeping alive the dream of an American regional theater and preparing the path for the next generation of leaders.

Over the past thirty years, the American regional theater has been fertile ground for the production of new plays by Jewish women, offering a supportive environment where plays can grow and change for artistic, rather than business, reasons. Emily Mann's *Annulla, An Autobiography* premiered at the Guthrie Theater in Minneapolis; Barbara Damashek's *Quilters* (cowritten by Molly Newman) was first presented by the Denver Center for the Performing Arts; Barbara Lebow's *A Shayna Maidel* was developed at the Academy Theater in Atlanta and received its first professional production at Hartford Stage Company; and WENDY WASSERSTEIN's Pulitzer Prize–winning play *The Heidi Chronicles* was workshopped at Seattle Repertory Theater and later presented at Playwrights Horizons in New York.

Wendy Wasserstein's success is indicative of the progress made by Jewish American women playwrights in recent years. Wasserstein doesn't hide her Jewish identity behind bland de-ethnicized character names and vague attempts to make characters' family backgrounds seem generically American, as her forebear Lillian Hellman did. The Jewish characters are unabashedly, quirkily, wonderfully Jewish. And Wasserstein's wit and her off-kilter insight on the experiences of contemporary American women make her plays appealing to audiences of all backgrounds. In plays such as *Uncommon Women and Others, Isn't It Romantic?, The Heidi Chronicles*, and *The Sisters Rosensweig*, Wendy Wasserstein's identity simply proclaims itself: as woman, as Jew, as American. And theater is richer as a result.

CONCLUSION

Throughout the history of the American theater, Jewish women have contributed their many talents, pushing the art of the theater to greater heights and giving strength and depth to its intellectual and creative foundations. They have written great plays. They have performed onstage with skill, strength, and sensitivity. They have been innovators in lighting, costume, and scenic design. They have directed productions. They have challenged and inspired with their critical writing. They have founded and run their own theater companies. And they have nurtured talent as teachers. Jewish women have been there from the beginning, and they have performed with distinction. They continue to do so today.

BIBLIOGRAPHY

Adler, Stella. *The Technique of Acting* (1990); Bigsby, C.W.E. *A Critical Introduction to Twentieth Century Drama* (1985); Bordman, Gerald, ed. *Oxford Companion to American Theatre* (1992); Brock, Pope. "Stella Adler: The Fiery First Lady of American Acting." *People Weekly* 32, no. 3 (July 17, 1989): 66; Brustein, Robert. *Making Scenes: A Personal History of the Turbulent Years at Yale, 1966–1979* (1984), and *The Third Theatre* (1970); Chinoy, Helen Krich, and Linda Walsh Jenkins, eds. *Women in American Theatre* (1987); Clurman, Harold. *The Fervent Years: The Story of the Group Theatre and the Thirties* (1957); Cohen, Sarah Blacher, ed. *From Hester Street to Hollywood: The Jewish-American Stage and Screen* (1986); Croyden, Margaret. *Lunatics, Lovers and*

Poets: The Contemporary Experimental Theatre (1974); Goldman, William. *The Season* (1970); Guernsey, Otis L. *Curtain Times: The New York Theatre, 1965–1987* (1987); Hewes, Henry. *Saturday Review* (December 30, 1967): 18; Lifson, David S. *The Yiddish Theatre in America* (1965); Lynes, Russell. *The Lively Audience: A Social History of the Visual and Performing Arts in America, 1890–1950* (1985); Malin, Ella A. "The Season around the United States with a Directory of Professional Regional Theatres." *The Best Plays of 1965–1966* (1966): 42; Malina, Judith. *The Diaries of Judith Malina, 1947–1957* (1984); Neff, Renfreu. *The Living Theatre: USA* (1970); Picon, Molly, and Jean Bergantini Grillo. *Molly!* (1980); Sandrow, Nahma. *Vagabond Stars: A World History of Yiddish Theater* (1977); Schiff, Ellen. *Awake and Singing: Seven Classic Plays from the American Jewish Repertoire* (1995), and *Fruitful and Multiplying: Nine Contemporary Plays from the American Jewish Repertoire* (1996); Sherin, Edwin. "In the Words of Edwin Sherin." *Cue* (May 24, 1969): 15; *Theatre Profiles 9* (1990); Wilmeth, Don B., and Tice L. Miller. *Cambridge Guide to American Theatre* (1996); Zeigler, Joseph Wesley. *Regional Theatre: The Revolutionary Stage* (1973).

CHRISTINE SUMPTION
JUDITH NIHEI

THEATER, YIDDISH *see* YIDDISH MUSICAL THEATER; YIDDISH THEATER

THOMASHEFSKY, BESSIE (1873–1962)

Bessie Thomashefsky, Yiddish actor and comedian, delighted audiences for over thirty years with leading roles in New York, and later on tour throughout the United States, in London, and in Toronto.

Born Brukhe Baumfeld-Kaufman in Kiev, Ukraine, Bessie Thomashefsky and her family arrived in America and settled near Baltimore in 1883. She attended school for two years until she was twelve, and then went to work in a stocking factory and a sweatshop. At fourteen, she saw a Yiddish play that starred the young Boris Thomashefsky, who was then performing the women's roles in the company. A few years later, she joined the Thomashefsky Players and married Boris in 1891. Although she was overcome with fright the first time she appeared onstage, she soon became the star of the company, playing the parts she had first seen her husband perform.

Her husband opened the People's Theater in New York City, intending to bring Chekhov and Shakespeare to Yiddish-speaking audiences. Bessie Thoma-shefsky starred in melodramas such as *The Kreutzer Sonata* and *The Broken Fiddle*, and created the character of Beynishl in *The Yeshiva Boy* by Zolatarevsky.

As immigrants demanded more and more to see American plays, in 1901 the People's Theater staged a Yiddish version of *Uncle Tom's Cabin*. Along with Irving Berlin, Boris Thomashefsky wrote songs such as "Der Yidisher Baseball Game" and "Der Yidisher Yankee Doodle," many of which Bessie Thomashefsky made famous. In 1911, she starred in *Das Meydl fun West*, a Yiddish version of David Belasco's *Girl of the Golden West*. In 1915, her husband wrote *Di Sheyne Amerikaner* [The beautiful American] for Thomashefsky, who shocked and delighted audiences by playing an emancipated woman in a riding costume.

Three of her most famous roles were in plays with strong suffragist and women's rights themes: *Minke, the Housemaid*, a Yiddish *Pygmalion* in which the maid-transformed-into-lady rejects Henry Higgins; *Chantzie in America*, a musical about an immigrant girl who assumes a male identity in order to be allowed to drive a car; and *Jennie Runs for Mayor*, a play about the first woman candidate for mayor.

In an extraordinary move, Thomashefsky took over the management of the People's Theater in 1915, and the following season the theater was renamed Bessie Thomashefsky's People's Theater. She starred in the Yiddish version of *Hamlet*, joining Sarah Bernhardt, who startled audiences when she first appeared in that role. She was also an accomplished comedian, taking roles formerly performed by the comic genius Mogulesko. These included the hugely popular *Green Boy* and *Green Girl* plays. Bessie Thomashefsky starred in so many of these Green roles that she was, for a time, called the "Salad Queen of Second Avenue."

One of her most popular roles was as "Suzi Bren" in Zolatarevsky's play of the same name, a part that may have reflected SOPHIE TUCKER's fame as the "Red Hot Mama." There can be little doubt that Thomashefsky served as a model for FANNY BRICE and MOLLY PICON.

In 1919, her name was removed from the People's Theater, and she separated from Boris Thomashefsky in 1922. She continued to appear in both Yiddish- and English-language plays and in vaudeville, touring the United States, and performing in London and Toronto. She retired in 1930. She had two sons, Harry and Teddy, and was the grandmother of Michael Tilson Thomas. Bessie Thomashefsky lived in California until her death on July 6, 1962. Her memoir, *Mayn Lebens Geshikht*e [My life's history: The joys and tribulations of a Yiddish star actress], as told to A. Tennenholz, was published in 1915.

THE EMINENT JEWISH ARTIST
BESSIE
THOMASHEFSKY

The hugely popular actor Bessie Thomashefsky played a wide variety of roles. She was in so many of the Green Girl *and* Green Boy *plays ("green" referring to newly arrived immigrants) that she was called the "Salad Queen of Second Avenue."*

Few if any accounts of Bessie Thomashefsky's professional career exist in English, where she is described only as "wife of" and "mother of." The history of her career in the *Lexicon of the Yiddish Theatre* is probably the only account of her stage career in print today.

BIBLIOGRAPHY
AJYB 65:438; *EJ*, s.v. "Thomashefsky, Boris"; *Lexicon of the Yiddish Theatre*. Edited by Zalman Zylbercwajg. Vol. 2 (1934): 840–845; Obituary. *NYTimes*, July 8, 1962, 65:2; *UJB*, s.v. "Thomashefsky, Boris."

LILLIAN SCHLISSEL

THOMSON, JUDITH JARVIS
(b. 1929)

In her thirty-five-year career as a philosopher, Judith Jarvis Thomson has published important papers in ethics, metaphysics, and the philosophy of law, including the widely anthologized essays "A Defense of Abortion" (1971) and "The Trolley Problem" (1985), both of which apply the techniques of analytic philosophy to questions of morality.

Born in New York City, on October 4, 1929, Judith (Jarvis) Thomson was the second child of Theodore Jarvis (Javitz), an accountant, and Helen (Vostrey) Jarvis, an English teacher. Her mother was of Catholic Czech extraction, and her father was descended from a line of Eastern European rabbis, including Rabbi Hayyim Eliezer Wachs of Kalish and Rabbi Jacob Emden. Raised in an observant family on the Lower East Side, Theodore Javitz changed his name to Jarvis in 1918. His relationship with his wife, which began at socialist summer camp, was a source of tension for both their families.

Helen Jarvis died when Judith was six, and Theodore Jarvis remarried two years later. His second wife was Jewish and had two children. She was a successful interior designer and an arts and antique dealer and importer.

Judith's parents placed no religious pressure on her, but she officially converted to Judaism at age fourteen, when she was confirmed at Temple Israel in Manhattan. Though her adult involvement with organized religion has been minimal, she feels concern for Israel and for the future of the Jewish people.

She attended elementary school in New York City and in Yonkers, graduating from Hunter High School in January 1946. She went on to receive a B.A. from Barnard College in 1950, a second B.A. from Cambridge University in 1952, an M.A. from Cambridge

in 1956, and a Ph.D. from Columbia in 1959, all in philosophy.

In 1962, she began teaching at Barnard College, and in 1962 she met and married the British philosopher James Thomson, who was a visiting professor at Columbia University. After spending 1962–1963 at Oxford, the couple moved to Boston, where James Thomson was appointed professor of philosophy at MIT. Judith Thomson taught for a year at Boston University and, in 1964, was appointed to the faculty at MIT, where she is currently Laurence S. Rockefeller Professor of Philosophy. The Thomsons were separated in 1976 and divorced in 1980; they remained colleagues until James Thomson's death in 1984.

Judith Thomson has been visiting professor at the University of Pittsburgh (1976), the University of California at Berkeley Law School (1983), and Yale Law School (1982, 1984, 1985), and has held fellowships from the Fulbright Foundation (1950–1951), the American Association of University Women (1962–1963), the National Endowment for the Humanities (1978–1979, 1986–1987), the Guggenheim Foundation (1986–1987), and the Center for Advanced Study in Oslo, Norway (1996). In 1989, she was elected to the American Academy of Arts and Sciences, and in 1992–1993 she served as president of the American Philosophical Association, Eastern Division.

Judith Jarvis Thomson has published countless philosophical articles, a number of which were collected into her well-respected anthology *Rights, Restitution, and Risk*. In addition, Thomson is the author of *Acts and Other Events*, *The Realm of Rights*, and *Moral Relativism and Moral Objectivity*, (with Gilbert Harman).

BIBLIOGRAPHY
Philosophy and Phenomenological Research 53, no. 1 (March 1993): 159–194. Symposium on *The Realm of Rights*; Thomson, Judith Jarvis. *Acts and Other Events* (1977), and *The Realm of Rights* (1990), and *Rights, Restitution, and Risk* (1986); Thomson, Judith Jarvis, and Gilbert Harman. *Moral Relativism and Moral Objectivity* (1996).

TAMAR SZABÓ GENDLER

TOBACH, ETHEL (b. 1921)

Despite the enormous number and range of her contributions to psychology, Ethel Tobach appears to have slipped through the net even of those historians of psychology who are interested in reaffirming women's contributions to the field. One possible reason for this neglect is that many of Tobach's scientific contributions have been in comparative and physiological psychology—areas that are not well understood by many psychologists and that attract few women.

Ethel Tobach was born in Miaskovka, a small village in the Ukraine, On November 7, 1921. Her mother came from a Jewish family that owned the village's mill and general store. Her father was an orphan who made his living tutoring students in villages without proper schools. As Labor Zionists, they planned to stay in her village after the Russian Revolution and cultivate the land that the Red Army had offered them. Shortly afterward, however, the village was captured by the White Army, which was carrying out pogroms against the Jews. Ethel was born during this period, and her parents escaped to Palestine when she was two weeks old.

Her father died in Palestine when Ethel was nine months old, and her mother immigrated with her to Philadelphia, where she became an activist in the garment workers' union. She attributes her radical politics to her mother's socialism.

She also worked at blue-collar occupations while studying at HUNTER COLLEGE, from which she graduated Phi Beta Kappa in 1949. Shortly after World War II she met and married Charles Tobach, a radical man who belonged to the same union as she did. He encouraged her to go on for a Ph.D. in psychology at New York University. At this time, NYU was not very enthusiastic about enrolling married women because they did not "stay in the field," but "in her innocence," Tobach succeeded in convincing her interviewer that her husband "was very supportive." She obtained her Ph.D. in comparative psychology in 1957, working under the supervision of a leader in the field, T.C. Schneirla.

Tobach began her professional career at the American Museum of Natural History, where she remains. From 1957 to 1961, she was a research fellow in its department of animal behavior. She became associate curator of that department in 1964 and curator from 1969 to 1981. Tobach has had a few full-time appointments at various universities in the New York City area and continues to teach graduate courses at the City College of the City University of New York. However, most of her career has been spent as a full-time researcher.

It is impossible to describe adequately Tobach's research, which has been both voluminous and broad in scope. She has written or edited 117 professional articles, book chapters, and books. She regards her major contributions to comparative psychology as showing links between stress and disease in rats and demonstrating that newborn rats are olfactorily sensitive (can smell) at birth. She has also contributed extensively to the study of emotionality in rats and mice, the biopsychology of development, and the evolution of social behavior.

Tobach has been a consistent critic of genetic determinism as it is expressed in psychological theory in general, in comparative psychology, and in societal racism and sexism. In 1978, she and Betty Rosoff initiated a book series, Genes and Gender, the first such series of its kind. These books are an important contribution to a field that is relatively unsophisticated about the interactions between biological and social processes.

Tobach's leadership activities within psychology illustrate her commitment to both science and social activism. She was vice president of the New York Academy of Sciences in 1972, president of the Division of Comparative and Physiological Psychology of the American Psychological Association in 1984–1985, and president of the Eastern Psychological Association in 1987–1988. She has also been actively involved in the American Psychological Association's Society for the Psychological Study of Social Issues and received that organization's Kurt Lewin Award in 1993.

SELECTED WORKS BY ETHEL TOBACH

Behavioral Evolution and Integrative Levels, edited with G. Greenberg (1984); *The Biopsychology of Development*, edited with Lester R. Aronson and E. Shaw (1971); "The Biopsychology of Social Behavior in Animals," with T. Schneirla. In *The Biologic Basis of Pediatric Practice*, edited by R.E. Cooke (1968): 68–82; *Challenging Racism and Sexism: Alternatives to Genetic Explanations*, edited with Betty Rosoff (1994); "Development of Olfactory Function in the Rat Pup," with Y. Rouger and T. Schneirla. *American Zoologist* 4 (1967): 792–793; "Effects of Stress by Crowding Prior to and Following Tuberculosis Infection," with H. Bloch. *American Journal of Physiology* 187 (1956): 399–402; "Eliminative Responses in Mice and Rats and the Problem of 'Emotionality,'" with T. Schneirla. In *Roots of Behavior*, edited by E.L. Bliss (1962): 211–231; "Evolution of Behavior and the Comparative Method." *International Journal of Psychology* 11 (1976): 185–201; "Evolutionary Aspects of the Activity of the Organism and Its Development." In *Individuals as Producers of Their Development: A Lifespan Perspective*, edited by Richard M. Lerner and N.A. Busch-Rossnagle (1981); *The Four Horsemen: Racism, Sexism, Militarism, and Social Darwinism*, editor (1973); *Genes and Gender I: On Hereditarianism and Women*, edited with Betty Rosoff (1978); *Genes and Gender III: Genetic Determinism and the Child*, edited with Betty Rosoff (1980); *Genetic Destiny, Scientific Controversy, and Social Conflict*, edited with Harold M. Proshansky (1976); *Historical Perspectives and the International*

Status of Comparative Psychology, editor (1987); "If It Was Easy, It Would Have Been Done: Genetic Processes Are a Hard Row to Hoe." *European Bulletin of Cognitive Psychology* 10 (1990): 681–685; "The Methodology of Sociobiology from the Viewpoint of a Comparative Psychologist." In *The Sociobiology Debate*, edited by Arthur Caplan (1978): 423–441; *On Peace, War and Gender: A Challenge to Genetic Explanations*, edited with Betty Rosoff (1991); "Personal Is Political." *Journal of Social Issues* 50 (1994): 221–244; "Some Evolutionary Aspects of Human Gender." *Journal of Orthopsychiatry* 41 (1971): 710–715; "Some Guidelines to the Study of the Evolution and Development of Emotion." In *Development and Evolution of Behavior: Essays in Memory of T.C. Schneirla*, edited by Lester R. Aronson, Ethel Tobach, Daniel S. Lehrman, and J.S. Rosenblatt (1970): 238–253; "A Study of the Relationship Between Behavior and Susceptibility to Tuberculosis in Rats and Mice," with H. Bloch. *Advances in Tuberculosis Research* 6 (1955): 62–89; *Violence Against Women*, edited with Susan Sunday (1985).

BIBLIOGRAPHY

Tobach, Ethel. Communication with author, March 12, 1997; *Who's Who of American Women* (1997–1998).

RHODA K. UNGER

TOKLAS, ALICE BABETTE
(1877–1967)

Alice Babette Toklas, cookbook author and memoirist, is an indelible figure in modern cultural history. With GERTRUDE STEIN, she served as host to one of the liveliest literary and artistic salons in Paris, from 1907 until Stein's death in 1946. In the last decades of her life, she was sought after for her many stories about her famous friends and acquaintances—and enemies—including F. Scott Fitzgerald, Ernest Hemingway, Pablo Picasso, Henri Matisse, Thornton Wilder, and scores of other writers, artists, and musicians.

The trajectory of Toklas's life could not have been predicted from her early years. She was born in San Francisco on April 30, 1877, the first child and only daughter of Ferdinand and Emma (Levinsky) Toklas, and she grew up in San Francisco and Seattle, where her father was a merchant. On both sides of the family, Toklas was descended from Polish immigrants. Her father came to America in 1865. Her maternal grandfather, Louis Levinsky, and his brothers joined the waves of forty-niners who came to California in search of gold. Instead of finding gold, however, the Levinskys discovered that they could prosper as merchants, and their dry-goods store in Jackson, California, soon yielded enough capital to finance a more substantial store in San Francisco.

The Levinskys were observant Jews. In Jackson, John Levinsky, one of Louis's brothers, became president of the first synagogue established in the town. Louis and two other brothers served on the board of trustees. There is no evidence, however, that Toklas was taught the tenets of Judaism, nor did she practice the religion later in her life. In fact, after Stein's death, Toklas converted to Catholicism in the hopes, she explained, of meeting Stein in heaven.

Toklas was educated in private schools and attended the University of Seattle. She studied piano and apparently showed sufficient talent to consider becoming a concert pianist. Although she never pursued music, she was attracted to the arts and had friends in the San Francisco arts community. Her favorite author was Henry James, whose fictional worlds she longed to experience for herself by traveling to Europe.

Her chance came when, after the devastating San Francisco earthquake of 1906, Michael and Sarah Stein, the brother and sister-in-law of Gertrude, returned to the city from Paris to assess damage done to their property. Toklas listened eagerly as the Steins described their life abroad, convincing her to journey to France. She had little to keep her in California: Her mother had died on March 10, 1897, just weeks before Toklas's twentieth birthday, and since then she had been serving as housekeeper to her father, younger brother, and assorted male relatives. Moreover, realizing that she felt sexually attracted to several women friends, she was convinced that she would not marry and fulfill the roles of wife and mother that her family expected of her. She longed for escape.

Toklas arrived in Paris in September 1907 and immediately met Gertrude Stein. At the time, Stein, thirty-three, was not the literary lion she would become but rather a lonely woman unsure of her talents as a writer, troubled by her sexuality, living in the shadow of her loquacious and domineering brother Leo. Stein found a sympathetic spirit in Alice Toklas, and the two women quickly became friends and then lovers. Toklas, for her part, claimed that a bell rang for her each time she encountered a genius, and she heard distinct chiming when she met Gertrude Stein. Stein, who had been residing unhappily with Leo, suggested that sharing her life with Toklas would be more satisfactory. She proved to be right.

Toklas has been described as Stein's housekeeper, cook, typist, secretary, and friend. She was all of these. She kept the household running smoothly, typed all of Stein's writings, helped to publicize and publish her works, and served as gatekeeper to weed out friend from foe. Sometimes her assessments did not coincide

Known primarily as the lifetime companion of writer GERTRUDE STEIN, *Alice B. Toklas is an intriguing figure to anyone with an interest in the artistic life of Paris in the first half of the twentieth century. The salon she hosted with Stein drew the greatest artists, writers, and musicians of the time. This remarkable photograph shows her (left) and Janet Flanner* (The New Yorker's *Paris writer under the name Genêt) admiring Picasso's painting of Stein.*
[Library of Congress]

with Stein's—but Toklas prevailed. She doted upon F. Scott Fitzgerald, who was welcome at the salon. She feared that Hemingway was trying to seduce Stein, and he was barred. Many who visited the salon remember Stein talking with the more famous male artists and writers, while Toklas took on the task of talking with their wives.

Although she dominated their personal relationship, Toklas was reticent about competing with Stein as a writer. Stein, after all, was the acknowledged genius. But Toklas gained considerable notoriety in 1934, when Stein published *The Autobiography of Alice B. Toklas.* Despite its title, the book centers around Stein: her adventures, opinions, and view of life. Friends of the couple, however, testify that in the dry humor and droll anecdotes we can hear Toklas's voice.

After the book was published in America, Toklas's name became a household word.

Stein wrote about Toklas in her more hermetic works as well. Many poems, prose pieces, and plays offer glimpses of the couple's daily life together. Some of Stein's works read as love letters to Toklas; some reflect Stein's unhappiness and discomfort caused by her concern about Toklas's possible disloyalty or even infidelity. Although these works have been mined for biographical references by some scholars, the task has by no means been completed.

Toklas wrote her own works only after Stein's death. *The Alice B. Toklas Cookbook* (1954) contained recipes from many of the couple's famous friends; artist Brion Gysin contributed the famous recipe for hashish fudge. Although Toklas claimed that she never tested the recipes and was not aware of the surprising ingredient. Critics pounced on the opportunity to explain some of Stein's strange writing. The cookbook offers many anecdotes centering around Stein's culinary likes and dislikes, her eccentricities, and her adventures. Similarly, Toklas's memoir *What Is Remembered* largely perpetuates Stein's public image. A second cookbook, *Aromas and Flavors of Past and Present*, although it bears Toklas's name as author, was largely the work of the book's editor, Poppy Cannon.

Toklas suffered from arthritis and cataracts during the last years of her life. Buoyed only by her memories, she hardly could see the paintings that she and Stein had collected, and the landlord of the Paris apartment in which she lived alone would not allow her to drive a nail into the wall to hang them.

Alice Babette Toklas died on March 7, 1967, and is buried beside Stein in the Père-Lachaise cemetery in Paris.

**SELECTED WORKS BY
ALICE BABETTE TOKLAS**

The Alice B. Toklas Cookbook (1954); *Aromas and Flavors of Past and Present* (1958); *What Is Remembered* (1963).

BIBLIOGRAPHY

Burns, Edward, ed. *Staying On Alone: Letters of Alice B. Toklas* (1973); *DAB* 8: 655; Obituary. *NYTimes*, March 8, 1967, 45:1; *NAW* modern; Simon, Linda. "Alice B. Toklas," *Dictionary of Literary Biography* (1980): 391–394, and *The Biography of Alice B. Toklas* (1977. Reprint 1991), and *Gertrude Stein Remembered* (1994); Stein, Gertrude. *The Autobiography of Alice B. Toklas* (1933), and *Everybody's Autobiography* (1937); Toklas, Alice B. Papers. Bancroft Library, University of California at Berkeley, and Beinecke Library, Yale University, New Haven, Conn.

LINDA SIMON

TOUREL, JENNIE (1900–1973)

Jennie Tourel is universally regarded as one of the most distinguished vocalists of her time.

She was born in Russia in the early years of the twentieth century. Her birth year is generally given as 1900. Her father was a merchant who, during the Russian Revolution, took his family first to Berlin, then to Paris. From this period dates her remarkable command of French and German, which stood her in good stead later in her career.

In Paris, Tourel came under the influence of Emil Cooper, who later became a well-known conductor at New York's Metropolitan Opera House. He coached her in her earliest roles. When he thought she was ready, he brought her to the Opéra Comique. She was engaged to sing Carmen, a role in which she had spectacular success. For the next ten years, she was star of the Opéra Comique, where she also sang the role of Charlotte in Massenet's *Werther* and the title role in Thomas's opera *Mignon*.

This chapter in Tourel's life was brought to an abrupt end by the Nazi invasion. With her longtime companion, the gifted painter Yakob Michaelson, she escaped just a week before the Germans entered Paris. Along with other desperate refugees, they set out on a hair-raising journey, part of it by foot, that brought them to Portugal. An epidemic of typhoid was raging in Lisbon, and Tourel became very ill. She had the good fortune to be admitted to a nunnery, where she was taken care of until she recovered. After many difficulties, Tourel and Michaelson obtained the necessary visas for Havana, from which they made their way to Canada and finally reached New York.

Tourel's American career did not get under way at once. She was unknown in the United States, she did not have a manager, and she had barely recovered from the trauma of her abrupt departure from Europe. She tried to make her way into the musical world of New York, at first with no success. Then she made the acquaintance of Friede Rothe, a musical agent who was deeply impressed by the beauty of her voice and became her personal representative. Rothe persuaded Toscanini to give Tourel an audition. The great conductor engaged her to sing with the New York Philharmonic. Soon she also appeared with Koussevitzky and the Boston Symphony and with Stokowski and the Philadelphia Orchestra. In these performances, she was revealed as a star of the first magnitude.

Tourel made her debut at the Metropolitan Opera House singing Adelgisa to Zinka Milanov's Norma. She also sang Mignon at the old Met. In fact, her voice was not ideally suited to the huge space of the Met. Her subtle art was at its best in the concert hall. As she approached fifty, Tourel became active as a song recitalist. Her recitals became unique events eagerly awaited by an ever larger circle of fans. Her voice, a coloratura mezzo-soprano, was brilliant and agile in the upper register, deeply expressive in the middle range, and with a darkly somber sheen in the lower. She had superb vocal technique and sense of style. Each song she sang became a miniature tone drama that she shaped as closely as possible to the composer's intention. Her repertory spanned the French, German, and Russian literature. Her extraordinary recordings of Mussorgsky's *Songs and Dances of Death*, Debussy's settings of Verlaine's poems, Ravel's

Just a week before the Germans entered Paris, Jennie Tourel fled to escape persecution. In America, she continued her career as a concert singer, becoming a valued performer for Arturo Toscanini and, later, Leonard Bernstein, who wrote his Jeremiah Symphony *with her voice in mind.*
[New York Public Library]

Shéhérazade, and the masterpieces of Schubert and Schumann have become collectors' items.

Tourel, having left Europe as a Jew fleeing from Hitler, remained intensely interested in Jewish affairs. In her later years, she became increasingly involved in the musical life of Israel, and alternated her teaching at the Juilliard School in New York with an annual master class at the Samuel Rubin Academy of Music in Jerusalem. With her first visit in 1949, she was one of the earliest artists of international stature to go to Israel. Her teaching introduced new standards of artistic performance and musicianship to her Israeli students.

Tourel was extremely close to Leonard Bernstein, who wrote his *Jeremiah Symphony* with her voice in mind. She performed the work with him all over the world. Together they flew to Israel for a historic performance on Mt. Scopus to celebrate the triumphal end of the Six-Day War. Because she had been careful never to force her voice beyond its natural capacity, it retained its sheen when she was past seventy. Indeed, she gave some of her most memorable concerts at an age when many other singers have long since retired.

Tourel was an intense woman of vivid personality and powerful temperament. Up to her last years she maintained the highest standards, judged people accordingly, and from herself she expected nothing less than perfection.

Jennie Tourel died on November 23, 1973, at the Lenox Hill Hospital in New York City, of lung cancer aggravated by emphysema. Joseph Machlis established a scholarship in her name at the Samuel Rubin Academy, where she had taught so brilliantly. Leonard Bernstein delivered the eulogy at her funeral. No one who treasures the memory of Tourel, her total artistry, and the enormous impact she had on the art of singing, will ever forget the final words of his tribute: "When Jennie opened her mouth, God spoke."

BIBLIOGRAPHY

NAW modern; Obituary. *NYTimes*, November 28, 1973, 84:5; *WWWIA* 6.

JOSEPH MACHLIS

TRIANGLE SHIRTWAIST FIRE

One of the worst industrial disasters in the history of New York City, causing 146 deaths and an unknown number of injuries, took place on March 25, 1911, at the Triangle Shirtwaist Company. The workplace occupied the eighth, ninth, and tenth floors of the Asch Building located on the corner of Greene Street and Washington Place, off Washington Square. Isaac Harris and Max Blank, the Jewish owners of the factory, employed almost a thousand workers in busy seasons. On the day of the fire approximately five hundred workers were present. Victims of the fire were mostly recent immigrant Jewish women aged sixteen to twenty-three. The Triangle Shirtwaist Company was an anti-union shop and the site of the famous 1909 UPRISING OF THE 20,000 for union recognition organized by the International Ladies Garment Workers Union (ILGWU) that swept the

*In less than twenty minutes, 146 workers at the Triangle Shirtwaist Company lost their lives
in one of the worst industrial disasters in the history of New York City. Most of those who
died were young Jewish women who were recent immigrants. Many leapt to their death
from the ninth floor rather than face the unbearable flames. This newspaper photo
was captioned "bodies on sidewalk." [Brown Brothers]*

industry. Though some firms settled with the workers, the Triangle Shirtwaist Company refused to grant their demands, and most union members were discharged.

The fire probably started as a result of a lighted match dropped accidentally into a bin full of fabric scraps. It spread rapidly throughout the densely packed area of the shop. While many of the workers on the eighth floor escaped through the staircase, and those on the tenth floor escaped onto the roof, workers on the ninth floor were trapped by the fire. The employers had kept the escape exits locked to prevent theft and "stealing time," and to keep out union organizers and prevent spontaneous walkouts. The sole existing fire escape bent in the heat and under the weight of those fleeing the fire, while the firefighters who arrived on the scene were not equipped with ladders of sufficient height. The desperate workers tried to escape by jumping onto nets, trampolines, and blankets extended below, which collapsed under the weight of many women jumping at once. Others leaped from windows, their clothes ablaze, and were killed on impact, while the rest were burned to death.

The trial of the proprietors resulted in acquittal. The owners, who collected their insurance and soon reopened their shop at a new address, offered to pay one week's wages to the families of the victims.

To the Jewish community, the unprecedented scope of the tragedy and its horrors were evocative of the pogroms that were the greatest disaster to befall Jewry in modern times. A special relief fund distributed money, collected within the Jewish community and by outside organizations, to dependents living in New York, Russia, Austria, and even Palestine. The outrage and the grief galvanized the Jewish community and the progressive public into action. The first protest meeting, organized by the Women's Trade Union League (WTUL)—a traditionally important ally of ILGWU since the days of the 1909 strike—was attended by leaders of civic and labor organizations who demanded that a committee be appointed to study the tragedy and draft proposals for health and safety legislation. At a meeting of the Local 25, ILGWU, with a number of survivors in attendance, there were calls for drastic measures against those guilty of imposing intolerable work conditions. The largest meeting, organized by Anne Morgan of the WTUL, took place at the Metropolitan Opera House on April 2, 1911, and was attended by civic leaders, representatives from an array of institutions and progressive organizations, and union representatives. The meeting called for public pressure for legislation to ensure safety in the workplace. In her impassioned speech, however, ROSE SCHNEIDERMAN, the leader of the strike in the Triangle factory, railed against the civic leadership and their neglect, and called on all working people to organize and take action. The culminating event took place on April 5, the day designated for the funeral of seven unidentified victims. A huge march sponsored by Local 25, ILGWU, was a silent but powerful demonstration that drew a crowd of 500,000 mourners.

In the wake of public protest and the wave of sympathy for working women, the New York State Committee on Safety was established. Among its participants were forerunners of the New Deal, including Frances Perkins, Henry L. Stimson, and Henry Morgenthau, Sr. Following the committee's recommendations, the New York State Legislature set up a Factory Investigating Commission chaired by Robert F. Wagner, Sr., and Alfred E. Smith. In its four-year

This march mourning the victims of the Triangle Shirtwaist fire and protesting working conditions drew more than 500,000 people. This photograph was published in the International Socialist Review *under the heading "The Murder of the Shirt Waist Makers." [Tamiment Library]*

term, the commission investigated work conditions in shops, factories, and tenement houses, and was instrumental in drafting new factory legislation. These measures limited the number of occupants on each factory floor relative to the dimensions of staircases, prescribed automatic sprinkler systems, and drafted employment laws to protect women and children at work.

Ever since then, the site of the fire has become the focus for labor activity. The tragedy is still being commemorated by annual demonstrations, by gatherings of women workers, and by union events, emphasizing the importance of the Occupational Safety and Health Act.

BIBLIOGRAPHY

Stein, Leon. *The Triangle Fire* (1962); Triangle Fire file. Wagner Labor Archives, Tamiment Institute Library, New York University, NYC.

HADASSA KOSAK

TRILLING, DIANA (1905–1996)

The life of Diana Trilling encompassed the rise and fall of the Jewish intellectual community centered in New York, and the literary and political journals that arose there after the Depression. Although often identified as the wife of Lionel Trilling, soul of the Columbia University English department from 1929 until his death in 1975, Diana Trilling was an intellectual voice in her own right, writing literary criticism and autobiography into her nineties. Trilling's formidable reviews and commentary, as well as her position among the liberal anticommunist critics of the *Partisan Review*, the *Nation*, and the *New Republic*, reflect an influential period of American social critique.

Diana Rubin Trilling was born on July 21, 1905, the youngest of three children, to Joseph and Sadie (Forbert) Rubin. Although her parents were both Polish Jews, their exposure to Judaism was different. Joseph Rubin was raised in the Warsaw ghetto, while Sadie Forbert grew up fifty miles from Warsaw in the Polish countryside, knowing little of Yiddish or of Jewish culture. Like her mother, Diana did not have a typical Jewish childhood. Until 1914, when the Rubin family moved to Brooklyn, Diana and her siblings, Cecilia and Samuel, lived in Westchester, far from the hub of Eastern European Jewish culture. Joseph Rubin owned a factory that produced silk braid for hats, and then manufactured silk stockings when styles changed. In a generation of intellectuals whose devo-

tion to learning began in deeply religious homes, Diana was an exception. Of the relationship between religion and American society, she wrote, "Increasingly, one's religious choice has become the equivalent of a political statement. On the left, to advertise oneself as a Jew is to claim honorific status as a member of a minority; minorities are presumed to be genetically virtuous. On the right, it implies that one's religious commitment falls into line with other well-tested moral and social attitudes." Trilling likened her upbringing to her husband's: "the childhood of an American who happened to be a Jew, not that of a Jew who happened to be an American."

She graduated from Radcliffe in 1924. She considered her undergraduate experience inferior to her husband's Columbia education because of the differing assumptions underlying men's and women's collegiate preparation. Even though Radcliffe women were not expected to be merely decorative, she asserted, "our college educations would not only help us be more efficient housekeepers but also provide us with something to occupy our minds as we went about our domestic chores . . . drying our dishes, we could recite to ourselves our favorite poems of Shelley or Keats. . . . Success as women was still measured by our success as wives." The limitations of this gender gap would remain part of her life. She gained entry to the circle of New York critics as the wife of Lionel Trilling, whom she married on June 12, 1929.

Trilling's first professional ambition, to become a vocalist, was thwarted by a nervous condition she attributes to her childhood. Her career as a writer did not begin until 1941, when Margaret Marshall of the *Nation* asked Lionel Trilling to recommend someone to write unsigned reviews of recent fiction for the magazine. Diana Trilling suggested herself for the position, although she admits she was unqualified and, until that moment, had never considered becoming a critic. Her *Nation* reviews, later collected under the title *Reviewing the Forties*, gave her a chance to examine the most important authors of the day, including Sartre, Bellow, Welty, Marquand, Lewis, Capote, Rand, Priestley, Warren, Hersey, Maugham, Wouk, Waugh, McCullers, and Orwell. Although she was still invited to *Partisan Review* parties as a wife, her prominence as a *Nation* critic gave her a visibility denied to other women in the Trillings' progressive intellectual circle.

The Trillings were often criticized for deracination and for the betrayal of the Left that marked their staunch anti-Communist position of the 1940s. In largely Jewish circles of fellow travelers, these two

The life of Diana Trilling encompassed the rise and fall of the Jewish intellectual community centered in New York and the literary and political journals that arose there after the Depression. [UPI/CORBIS-BETTMANN]

traditions were often related. Yet Trilling made herself a political book critic; as she asserted in her autobiography, "my anti-Communism was seldom far from the surface of my reviews." Although her husband was the first Jewish tenured professor of English at Columbia, critics often accused him (unjustly) of inventing his mellifluous name to distance himself from the Eastern European culture of communists and fellow travelers.

As she approached her forty-second birthday, she decided that she and her husband had been squander-

ing their lives. "We were afraid to be full grown up and to be in command of ourselves and others." And so she became pregnant. Their only child, James, was born shortly thereafter, in 1947.

In 1948, Diana Trilling left the *Nation* to become an independent critic. The topics that occupied her in later years were not bound by any formal discipline. Her subjects—the Oppenheimer, Profumo, and Hiss cases, Edith Wharton, Beat Generation authors, and Timothy Leary, among many others—can be called, in her words, "adversaries to our society." *Mrs. Harris*, a full-length book on the murderer of Herman Tarnower of Scarsdale Diet fame, written in 1981, gave Trilling an opportunity to contemplate a middle-class woman on trial for murder after the first wave of 1970s feminism. Trilling's work always granted her the "life of significant contention" for which she hoped to be remembered. In her writing, she examined those who elected or were relegated to social expatriation during the many moments of the twentieth century when social upheaval interrogated the status quo.

Trilling's last book was *The Beginning of the Journey* in 1993, a chronicle of her marriage. Although it follows their lives as Depression era children through the fall of 1930s radicalism and the campus unrest of the 1960s, between the lines lies a lingering sadness at the critical voices no longer heard. Trilling's age was one of criticism, and she was connected to its most influential voices for decades when intellectual work was not limited to the university. Indicting current academics for their preference of expertise over significant contention, Diana Trilling placed herself at the final boundary of a generation of intellectuals who commanded social criticism for much of the twentieth century. She died on October 23, 1996.

SELECTED WORKS
BY DIANA TRILLING

The Beginning of the Journey: The Marriage of Diana and Lionel Trilling (1993); *Claremont Essays* (1964); *Mrs. Harris: The Death of the Scarsdale Diet Doctor* (1981); *The Portable D.H. Lawrence*, editor (1947); *Reviewing the Forties* (1978); *Selected Letters of D.H. Lawrence*, editor (1958); *We Must March, My Darlings* (1977).

BIBLIOGRAPHY

Bosworth, Patricia. "Diana Trilling: An Interview." *Paris Review 35* (Winter 1993): 234–270; *EJ*, s.v. "Trilling, Lionel"; Weissman, Judith. "A Straight Back and an Arrogant Head." *Georgia Review 48* (Spring 1994): 181–187.

PETER TABACK

TROMMER, MARIE (1895–1971)

Marie Trommer was an early twentieth-century writer, poet, artist, art critic, and contributor to American Jewish newspapers.

She was born in Kremenchoug, Ukraine, on September 29, 1895 (although at least one reference suggests her year of birth to be 1901), and came to the United States in 1905. She was the daughter of Bernard and Betha (Yedlin) Trembitsky. A graduate of Women's Art School and Cooper Union Art School in 1914, Trommer became known as an artist and art critic in New York, specifically as a staff member of the *Jewish Tribune*. Her many articles on art and Jewish artists for the English-Jewish press can be found in the archives of the *Jewish Tribune*, *The Jewish Daily News*, and the *Boston Jewish Advocate*.

Her own work as an artist was first exhibited at the Society of Independent Artists in 1924. Subsequent exhibitions took place in New York City for the next thirty years, at such diverse locations as the American Museum of Natural History, the Grant Galleries, and even at a hobby show at the Lemberg Home for the Aged (1957–1958), where she worked as an occupational therapist. Trommer specialized in landscapes and figures, working in oils and watercolors.

As a writer she is most remembered for her translations of Russian nature poems into English and her translations of American and British poetry into Russian. She was also the editor and publisher of the *American Russian Review*, a photo-litho bimonthly publication. Two of her own published works include "Sketches from My Childhood" and a poem in *Avalon Anthology*. Trommer received prizes for her writing, two in 1947 for an essay titled *World in Books*, and one in 1960 from the Avalon organization.

Marie Trommer was a member of the Creative Writers Group, Society of Independent Artists, Salons of America, and Art Alliance of America. She died in New York City on February 6, 1971.

BIBLIOGRAPHY

Cooper Union Alumni Association. Records (1971); *WWIAJ* (1926, 1928, 1938); *Who's Who of American Women* (1964, 1958, 1972).

ANNETTE MUFFS BOTNICK

TUCHMAN, BARBARA W. (1912–1989)

Barbara W. Tuchman was one of America's foremost popular historians and winner of two Pulitzer Prizes for *The Guns of August* and *Stilwell and the American Experience in China*.

She was born into a prominent New York family on January 30, 1912. Her father, Maurice Wertheim, was a international banker, president of the American Jewish Congress, honorary trustee of the Federation of Jewish Philanthropies and fund-raising chairman in 1947, trustee of Mount Sinai Hospital in New York, owner of *The Nation*, art collector, sportsman, and a founder of the Theatre Guild. Her mother, Alma, was the granddaughter of diplomat Henry Morgenthau, Sr., who served as ambassador to Turkey and Mexico under President Woodrow Wilson. She was the second-born of three daughters; her sisters were Josephine (Pomerance), who became active in the peace movement and died in 1980, and Anne W. Werner, who died in 1996.

Growing up she was influenced by the Twin Series of children's books by Lucy Fitch Perkins; George A. Henty, who wrote swashbuckling imperial adventures; Sir Arthur Conan Doyle, author of the Sherlock Holmes mysteries; Jane Porter; and the historical novels of Alexandre Dumas. She spent childhood summers in Europe with her parents. She attended Walden School before entering Radcliffe College. Her studies there concentrated on history and literature, and she received her bachelor's degree in 1933. She studied under Irving Babbitt and C.H. McIlwain, writing an honors thesis entitled "The Moral Justification for the British Empire."

Tuchman lived a very privileged life. Upon graduation, she accompanied her grandfather to the World Economic Conference in London. She volunteered as a researcher and editorial assistant at the American Council of the Institute of Pacific Relations from 1933 to 1935. At age twenty-four, she contributed to the prestigious journal *Foreign Affairs*. In 1934, she went to Tokyo for a year. She spent a month in Peking and returned to America in late 1935 via the Trans-Siberian Railway, Moscow, and Paris.

Tuchman became staff writer and foreign correspondent for *The Nation* from 1933 to 1937, a journal owned by her father until 1937. As a correspondent for *The Nation*, she went to Valencia and Madrid, reporting on the Spanish Civil War. This led, in 1938, to her first book, *The Lost British Policy: Britain and Spain since 1700*, about British policy toward Spain and the western Mediterranean. During World War II, she worked at the Office of War Information. Traveling in Asia and Spain during major military conflicts prefigured Tuchman's interest in the history of the world of war.

Though she wrote about historical events, Tuchman's relations with professional academic historians were uneasy. According to her, her lack of academic

Translated into thirteen languages, the eminently readable, meticulously researched histories by Barbara Tuchman won two Pulitzer Prizes and a loyal audience that made them best-sellers. [American Jewish Historical Society]

title and graduate degree was a benefit: "It's what saved me. If I had taken a doctoral degree, it would have stifled any writing capacity." She accused historians of producing overdetailed studies that were unreadable.

Instead, she preferred the literary approach. She was regarded by some as more of a summarist than an explorer of fresh sources, ideas, and methods. She was not a historian's historian; she was a layperson's historian who made the past interesting to millions of readers. Her prescription for writing was "the writer's object is—or should be—to hold the reader's atten-

tion." She visited the battlesites involved in her histories to increase realistic detail. But she chided, "historians who stuff in every item of research they have found, every shoelace and telephone call of a biographical subject, are not doing the hard work of selecting and shaping a readable story."

However, she was given some professional recognition. The authoritative *Guide to Historical Literature* says that *The Guns of August* (1962) is the "classic account of July and August 1914, military men, and diplomats, as Europe slid into World War I." *The Proud Tower: A Portrait of the World before the War, 1890–1914* (1966), a "vivid portrait of explosive tension in society and politics at close of long nineteenth century" includes a chapter on the Dreyfus Affair, a significant episode of late nineteenth-century anti-Semitism. A world history textbook described *A Distant Mirror* (1978) as "a riveting account, with a focus on the life of a French knight."

She married Dr. Lester Reginald Tuchman, a New York internist in 1940. He later became emeritus professor of clinical medicine at Mount Sinai School of Medicine. The Tuchmans had three daughters: Lucy Tuchman Eisenberg, Jessica Tuchman, and Alma Tuchman.

From 1945 to 1956, she raised her daughters and did the research for *Bible and Sword: England and Palestine from the Bronze Age to Balfour* (1956) in which she "expressed strong sympathy for the Zionist cause and an appreciation of Palestine's role in world history." A member of the elite, she could not have written while raising her daughters "if I hadn't been able to afford domestic help." From 1956 onward she produced a new book about every four years.

Tuchman's books have been translated into thirteen languages. A reviewer of *The Zimmermann Telegram* captured the essence of Tuchman's historical method: She made "brilliant use of well known materials." But most of all, she told a good story. *The Guns of August*, awarded the Pulitzer Prize (general nonfiction), provided the basis for the movie of the same name released in 1964. In 1972, she received her second Pulitzer Prize for *Stilwell and the American Experience in China, 1911–1945*. She also wrote *Notes from China* (1972). Her 1981 publication *Practicing History: Selected Essays* was a retrospective of her essays that she identified as weathering the tests of time. It is also useful for her comments on the reasons that some of her essays were consciously excluded. *The March of Folly: From Troy to Vietnam* (1984) indicates realism or disillusionment with politics and politicians as they made self-destructive choices despite a knowledge of superior options. In an interview in 1962, she said,

"Anyone who wants to talk of the stupidity of 1914 has only to remember the Bay of Pigs in 1961."

Tuchman was a member of the Society of American Historians (president, 1970–1973), Authors Guild (treasurer), Authors League of America (member of council), American Academy of Arts and Letters (president, 1979), and American Academy of Arts and Sciences. She served as a trustee of her alma mater, Radcliffe College. In 1979, she was the first woman selected as the Jefferson Lecturer for the National Endowment for the Humanities.

Although she never earned a doctorate, she received honorary degrees from Yale University, Columbia University, New York University, Williams College, University of Massachusetts, Smith College, Hamilton College, Mount Hollyhock College, Boston University, and Harvard University. Despite the honor, she did not like making commencement addresses. She had a firm rule against commencement speeches, because "I have no idea what to tell the young people and no desire merely to fill a required occasion with generalities." She did lecture at Harvard University, the University of California, and the U.S. Naval War College as well as contributing articles to numerous serious and popular publications.

Barbara W. Tuchman died at age seventy-seven, on February 6, 1989, in Greenwich, Connecticut, from complications of a stroke. Her last book, *The First Salute* (1988), setting the American Revolution in international perspective, had been on the *New York Times* best-seller list for seventeen weeks and was number nine in the week preceding her death. According to Max Lerner, Tuchman's idea of heaven was the National Archives and the manuscript division of the Library of Congress.

**SELECTED WORKS BY
BARBARA W. TUCHMAN**

Bible and Sword: England and Palestine from the Bronze Age to Balfour (1956); A Distant Mirror: The Calamitous Fourteenth Century (1978); The First Salute (1988); The Guns of August (1962); The Lost British Policy: Britain and Spain since 1700 (1938); The March of Folly: From Troy to Vietnam (1984); Notes from China (1972); Practicing History: Selected Essays (1981); The Proud Tower: A Portrait of the World before the War, 1890–1914 (1966); Stilwell and the American Experience in China, 1911–1945 (1971); The Zimmermann Telegram (1958).

BIBLIOGRAPHY

Contemporary Authors. New Revision Series 24: 444–445; EJ: 1973–1982; Guide to Historical Literature. 3rd ed. (1995).

OLIVER B. POLLAK

TUCKER, SOPHIE (1884–1966)

Sophie Tucker was an international star of vaudeville, music halls, and later film, performing in both Yiddish and English in a career that spanned over fifty years. She was born Sophie Kalish in Russia as her parents were preparing to immigrate to the United States. While immigrating, her father, who feared repercussions for having deserted the Russian military, adopted the name "Abuza" for the family. When she was three months old, the family settled in Hartford, Connecticut, where they ran a successful kosher diner and roominghouse that catered to many show business professionals. Tucker recalled waiting on Yiddish theater greats such as Jacob Adler, Boris and BESSIE THOMASHEFSKY, and Madame Lipsky, exclaiming, "the thrill I got when I took an order from BERTHA KALICH!"

Theater people intrigued her, but her parents, wary of the vaudeville *paskudnyacks* [scoundrels] who traveled through their town, encouraged her to marry and settle in Hartford. In her autobiography *Some of These Days*, Tucker wrote that her mother believed "that marriage, having babies, and helping her husband get ahead were career enough for any woman. I couldn't make her understand that it wasn't a career that I was after. It was just that I wanted a life that didn't mean spending most of it at the cookstove and the kitchen sink."

By way of compromise, she began singing for the customers she waited on. She recalled, "I would stand up in the narrow space by the door and sing with all the drama I could put into it. At the end of the last chorus, between me and the onions there wasn't a dry eye in the place."

She eloped to Holyoke in 1903 with local beer cart driver Louis Tuck. Upon her return, her parents arranged a proper Orthodox wedding for the couple. They had a son, Burt (b. 1906), shortly before she asked her husband, who she asserted wasn't working hard enough, for a separation. Soon afterward, Willie Howard of the Howard Brothers, who had admired her singing, gave her a letter of introduction to well-known composer Harold Von Tilzer. She left Hartford for New York City and changed her name to Tucker.

While Von Tilzer was not immediately impressed with her talents, Tucker soon gained employment in New York's cafés and beer gardens such as the German Village, singing for meals, weekly pay, and "throw money" from customers. Tucker sent much of the money she earned home to her family.

In 1907, Tucker got her first break in vaudeville, singing at Chris Brown's amateur night. After her initial

The last of the Red Hot Mamas, Sophie Tucker was funny, risqué, and full of life, but she could also evoke tears with "My Yiddishe Mama." Recordings of that song, which had the power to evoke a reverence for Jewish culture, were ordered smashed in Germany after Hitler gained power. [American Jewish Archives]

audition, she overheard Brown muttering to a colleague, "this one's so big and ugly, the crowd out front will razz her. Better get some cork and black her up." Despite her protestations, producers insisted that she could be successful only in blackface. Quickly booked into Joe Woods's New England circuit, she became known as a "world renowned coon singer," a role that she couldn't bear to let her family know she had taken. A stroke of luck befell her when her costume trunks were lost while touring; she debuted onstage in Boston without blackface, declaring to the shocked audience: "You-all can see I'm a white girl. Well, I'll tell you something more: I'm not Southern. I'm a Jewish girl and I just learned this Southern accent doing a blackface act for two years. And now, Mr. Leader, please play my song."

It wasn't long before Tucker was performing out of blackface to increasingly adulating audiences. Songs like "A Good Man Is Hard to Find," "I'm Living Alone and I Like It," "I Ain't Takin' Orders from No One," and "No Man is Ever Gonna Worry Me" were hits with female and male audiences alike, at venues such as Tony Pastor's Palace, Reisenweber's supper club, vaudeville houses throughout the United States, and music halls throughout Europe. In 1910, African-American composer Shelton Brooks wrote her immensely popular signature song "Some of These Days." This, like many other songs, Tucker purchased exclusive rights to sing.

In 1925, Jack Yellen penned perhaps her most famous song, sung in Yiddish and English, titled "My Yiddishe Momme." The song was mostly played in large American cities where there were sizable Jewish audiences. Tucker explained, "Even though I loved the song and it was a sensational hit every time I sang it, I was always careful to use it only when I knew the majority of the house would understand Yiddish. However, you didn't have to be a Jew to be moved by 'My Yiddishe Momme.' 'Mother' in any language means the same thing."

Tucker never forgot her Jewishness, even as she performed for broader, gentile audiences. On her 1922 tour of England, Tucker was welcomed by a London audience with a sign reading "WELCOME SOPHIE TUCKER, America's Foremost Jewish Actress." Tucker noted, "I was prouder of that than of anything." During the tour, Tucker got to know many Jewish actors in London, and took pleasure, at a Palladium benefit for the Lying-in Hospital, in singing "Bluebird, Where Are You," in her words, "as a hazan would." Tucker was immensely popular in England, amusing eager crowds with songs like "When They Start to Ration My Passion, It's Gonna Be Tough on Me" and "I'm The Last of the Red-Hot Mamas." Hanan Swaffer of London's *Daily Express* described her as "a big fat blond genius, with a dynamic personality and amazing vitality." Tucker's reminiscences of several tours provide unique insights into pre- and postwar European culture.

Tucker described the terrible tension of playing for a 1932 French audience that included many Jews. Throughout her performance, they sent notes and called out requests for her to sing "My Yiddishe Momme." Tucker was wary but finally decided to sing the song, feeling that its emotion would touch everyone. Tucker then began the song in English to a fairly receptive house. However, when she reached verse two, which is in Yiddish, anti-Semites began to boo and other audience members responded with shouts, begging for quiet. Tucker remembered, "The noise was so great I couldn't hear my own voice, nor could I hear Teddy at the piano. I thought: in a minute there'll be a riot. Quick as a flash I turned to Teddy and said 'Switch!' Before the audience knew what the hell was happening I was singing 'Happy Days Are Here Again.' My God, I only hoped they were!"

By contrast, the song was generally well received in Vienna. Tucker was recognized at a record store and asked to sing "My Yiddishe Momme" to an audience that seemed hungry for the images the song evokes. She reflected, "It is a commentary on Berlin in 1931 that . . . it was 'My Yiddishe Momme' that the Berlin Broadcasting Company asked for. That for the Paris mob!"

Several years after Hitler came into power, Tucker's recordings of "My Yiddishe Momme" were ordered smashed and the sale of them banned by the Reich. The song had the power to evoke a reverence for Jewish culture and a cultural memory of more peaceful times and was thus threatening to Hitler's regime. Shortly after the war broke out, Tucker talked with actress Elizabeth Bergner, a German in London exile, who informed Tucker, "There isn't one of us in Germany who hasn't this record of yours."

Tucker was known for her reverence of the Hebrew principle of *tzedaka*, charity and acts of good will toward others. In 1945, she established the Sophie Tucker Foundation, donating time, energy, and resources to an ecumenical assortment of causes. Tucker contributed to the Jewish Theatrical Guild, of which she was a life member, the Negro Actors Guild, and the Catholic Actors Guild, as well as the Will Rogers Memorial Hospital, the Motion Picture Relief Fund, synagogues, and hospitals. She supported Israel Bonds, and her foundation endowed a Sophie Tucker chair at Brandeis University in 1955. In 1959, on the first of several trips to Israel, Tucker dedicated the Sophie Tucker Youth Center at Beit Shemesh in the Judean Hills. Two years later, she sponsored another youth center at Kibbutz Be'eri in the northern Negev near Gaza. In 1962, she sponsored the Sophie Tucker Forest near the Beit Shemesh amphitheater and raised money for another forest. She also donated time and money to numerous hospitals and homes for the aged.

Tucker used her economic independence to empower herself and others, which created tensions in her personal life. Early in her career, Tucker had helped many of the prostitutes who lived in the same rooming houses as she, stashing money from their pimps, noting that, "Every one of them supported a family back home, or a child somewhere." While on tour, she brought her band to play in houses of prostitution for women who'd taken the night off in her honor. Tucker felt that it was her economic independence that doomed her marriages to Tuck, accompanist Frank Westphal, and manager Al Lackey, all of which ended in divorce. As she explained it: "Once you start carrying your own suitcase, paying your own bills, running your own show, you've done something to yourself that makes you one of those women men like to call 'a pal' and 'a good sport,' the kind of woman they tell their troubles to. But you've cut yourself off from the orchids and the diamond bracelets, except those you buy yourself."

In her humorous raciness, Sophie Tucker could be viewed as a precursor of today's strong female singers. Indeed, Tucker is directly evoked by BETTE MIDLER in a portion of her performances under the persona "Soph." Throughout her life, however, she insisted, "I've never sung a single song in my whole life on purpose to shock anyone. My 'hot numbers' are all, if you will notice, written about something that is real in the lives of millions of people."

Despite this fact, or perhaps because of it, the self-described "King-sized Lollabrigida" was removed from the stage in 1910 for singing "The Angle-Worm Wiggle." The judge, however, threw out the case, and the theater held her over two weeks to sold-out houses with lines around the block.

Tucker's performance was a complex critique of ethnic, gender, and class codes of morality. Songs like "I'm the 3-D Mama with the Big Wide Screen" and "I May Be Getting Older Every Day (But Younger Every Night)" were challenges to age, size, and gender stereotypes of women's sexuality couched in the humor that provided an antidote to puritanism.

As vaudeville gave way to cinema, Tucker had parts in several films, including *Honky Tonk* (1929), *Broadway Melody of 1938* (1937), *Thoroughbreds Don't Cry* (1937), and *Follow the Boys* (1944). She was, however, critical of the movie industry, asserting that film had usurped the power of performance from performers themselves. Without a live audience, the director was "the only critic to be pleased."

Tucker preferred performing in Broadway hits such as Cole Porter's *Leave It to Me* (1938) and *High Kickers* (1941), which toured in London in 1948. But live theater work was harder to find in an era of sparkling celluloid faces, much to the chagrin of Tucker and others. In 1953, *Sophie*, a Broadway musical based on Tucker's life, ran for only eight performances.

Tucker performed at the last show at Tony Pastor's Palace in New York City, which marked the end of an era: "Everyone knew the theater was to be closed down, and a landmark in show business would be gone. That feeling got into the acts. The whole place, even the performers, stank of decay. I seemed to smell it. It challenged me. I was determined to give the audience the idea: why brood over yesterday? We have tomorrow. As I sang I could feel the atmosphere change. The gloom began to lift, the spirit which formerly filled the Palace and which made it famous among vaudeville houses the world over came back. That's what an entertainer can do."

Sophie Tucker always used her power as an entertainer both to lift spirits and provoke thought in her audiences. Describing a command performance before King George V and Queen Mary at the London Palladium in 1926, a critic wrote, "In her bespangled gown, a hairdo in layers, and wearing a long string of orchids, she made a dazzling and towering theatrical figure whose love for the audience was returned to her in waves."

Tucker never retired, working until weeks before her death on February 9, 1966, in New York City, from a lung ailment and kidney failure at age eighty-two. Three thousand mourners attended her funeral at Emanuel Synagogue Cemetery in Weathersfield, Connecticut; striking teamsters' union hearse drivers temporarily called off their picket in her honor. Tucker's legacy exists in her generous contributions to charity, her influence on images of Jewish culture and women's sexuality, and her role as an entertainer who thoughtfully interpreted the chaotic and beautiful world around her.

BIBLIOGRAPHY

Allen, Robert C. *Horrible Prettiness: Burlesque and American Culture* (1991); *AJYB* 68:534; Brown, Janet. "The 'Coon-Singer' and 'Coon-Song': A Case Study of the Performer-Character Relationship." *Journal of American Culture* 7, 1–2 (Spring/Summer 1984): 1–8; Cohen, Sarah Blacher, ed.

From Hester Street to Hollywood: The Jewish-American Stage and Screen (1983), and *Jewish Wry: Essays on Jewish Humor* (1987); *DAB* 8; *EJ*; "500 at Funeral of Sophie Tucker." *NYTimes*, February 14, 1966; Fricker, Karen. "Experience the Divine Bette Midler. *New York Financial Times*, October 4, 1993; Gilbert, Douglas. *American Vaudeville: Its Life and Times* (1963); Green, Abel. "Two in One Week: Sophie Tucker Dies at 82, Billy Rose Succumbs at 66." *Variety* (February 16, 1966); Kaplan, Mike, ed. *Variety Who's Who in Show Business* (1985); Lifson, David S. *The Yiddish Theater in America* (1985); Loy, Pamela, and Janet Brown. "Red Hot Mamas, Sex Kittens and Sweet Young Things." *International Journal of Women's Studies* 5, no. 4 (September–October 1982): 338–47; Nachman, Gerald. "'Hudl Mitn Shtrudl' and Other Stage Delicacies." *San Francisco Chronicle*, December 2, 1990, 17; *NAW* modern; "A Nip of Tucker." *San Francisco Chronicle*, January 12, 1997; Rogin, Michael. "Making America Home: Racial Masquerade and Ethnic Assimilation in the Transition to Talking Pictures." *Journal of American History* (December 1992); Rosenberg, Joel. "Jewish Experience on Film." *AJYB* (1996); Sandrow, Nahma. *Vagabond Stars: A World History of Yiddish Theater* (1977); "The Singing Yiddishe Momma." *Israel Post*, February 11, 1966, 5A; Slide, Anthony. *The Encyclopedia of Vaudeville* (1994); Sochen, June. "Fanny Brice and Sophie Tucker: Blending the Particular with the Universal." In *From Hester Street to Hollywood: The Jewish-American Stage and Screen*, edited by Sarah Blacher Cohen (1983); "Sophie Tucker Dies Here at 79 [sic]." *NYTimes*, February 10, 1966, 1:8; Tucker, Sophie. *Some of These Days* (1945); Unterbrink, Mary. *Funny Women: American Comediennes 1860–1985* (1987); Vicinius, Martha. "Happy Times … If You Can Stand It: Women Entertainers During the Interwar Years in England." *Theater Journal* 31 (1979): 358; *WWIAJ* (1926, 1928, 1938); *WWWIA* 4; Yellen, Jack. "My Yiddishe Momme." *The Lawrence Wright Song and Dance Album* (1925).

ANNE S. BORDEN

TURECK, ROSALYN (b. 1914)

When she was a child, Rosalyn Tureck's father would tell her about her grandfather, a famous cantor in Russia. Each year, before the High Holidays, a coach with eight white horses came to the door to take him on tour. Pianist Rosalyn Tureck has toured the world as a consummate interpreter of the keyboard music of Johann Sebastian Bach, drawn by the white horses of lifelong commitment.

Tureck was born in Chicago on December 14, 1914, the third of three daughters of Russian immigrants Samuel and Monya (Lipson) Tureck (née Turk—Rosalyn's father was of Turkish descent). Of modest means, her family observed the Sabbath and major Jewish holidays in a warm atmosphere. Surrounded by music from infancy, she blossomed under fine piano teachers Sophia Brilliant-Liven and Jan Chiapusso, winning a full scholarship to the Juilliard School of Music at sixteen. At her audition, she amazed the distinguished piano faculty by presenting a list of prepared works that included sixteen of Bach's Preludes and Fugues.

At Juilliard, she studied with Olga Samaroff, graduating with distinction in 1935. She made her Carnegie Hall debut on October 18, 1935. At age twenty-two, in 1937, she gave an extraordinary series of six weekly all-Bach Town Hall recitals, earning the Town Hall Young Artist Award. For the next fifteen years, Tureck was based in New York, performing, teaching, and touring. Her first European tour was in 1947, and her London debut in 1953. Subsequently, she divided her time between living in England and in the United States.

Besides her frequent performances in Europe and the United States, Tureck has toured in South America, Israel, Turkey, South Africa, Australia, and the Far East. Undaunted by age, she appears radiant in a video of a 1992 concert in Buenos Aires, played to superlative reviews in Florence and Munich in 1993, and made a particularly poignant debut in an all-Bach program in St. Petersburg in 1995. In the program notes, she described her childhood in a circle of emigré Russians and the deep debt she felt to the rigorous and passionate training that characterized the Russian school of music.

Although her special relationship with the music of Bach developed early, she did not at first limit herself to the all-Bach programs for which she is particularly known. Her early repertoire included numerous Romantic works, including concertos. She also actively supported and performed contemporary music, premiering such works as William Walton's Piano Sonata and the William Schuman Piano Concerto. After four decades of performing almost exclusively Bach, Tureck once again began presenting a broader repertoire in the 1990s, while still maintaining her Bach focus.

Rosalyn Tureck performs mainly on the piano, yet she also excels on the harpsichord, clavichord, and organ, and sometimes performs on more than one instrument in a recital, relishing the differences in sonority and in technical requirements. Her most striking accomplishment of this kind is her performance of the Bach Goldberg Variations on the harpsichord, then on the piano. Tureck's interpretation of Bach is based on meticulous scholarship, going back to all extant versions of the text and to works on performance practice, particularly on ornamentation, together with a finger technique she has evolved. The

A magnificent interpreter of the works of Bach, Rosalyn Tureck performs on the piano, the harpsichord, the clavichord, and the organ. In 1994, she founded the Oxford-based Tureck Bach Research Institute, which in 1995 offered its first symposium on structure in science and music. [New York Public Library]

goal is that all ten fingers articulate separately and are equally well developed, a triumph over the anatomy of the hand. While occasional critics have found her approach lacking in spontaneity, the great majority have acclaimed her accomplishments.

Tureck has received numerous awards and five honorary doctorates, including one from Oxford University in 1977. She has taught at the Mannes School of Music (1940–1944), Juilliard (1943–1955), the University of California at San Diego (1966–1972), and Yale (1991–1993). She has lectured at a range of institutions, including the Smithsonian, the Hebrew University, and the Royal Institution of Great Britain. In 1994, she founded the Oxford-based Tureck Bach Research Institute, which in 1995 offered its first symposium; the topic was structure in science and music.

Her publications include a three-volume *Introduction to the Performance of Bach* (1960) and many articles on performing and teaching. She has edited a number of Bach's works, including his Italian Concerto. Her playing has been captured on LPs, cassettes, television, video, film, and CDs. Many performances have been issued in retrospective collections such as *Rosalyn Tureck: The Young Firebrand*.

Tureck married twice; her first marriage, to Kenneth Klein, ended in divorce in 1945. The couple had no children, but Tureck played a satisfying maternal role for Klein's two children by a previous marriage. Her second marriage was to scientist George Wallingford Downs; he died in 1965.

Rosalyn Tureck credits the Jewish values of her upbringing for her lifelong focus on inner spiritual and intellectual life, her deep regard for scholarship, and her lack of concern with external rewards.

SELECTED WORKS BY ROSALYN TURECK

An Introduction to the Performance of Bach. 3 vols (1960); *Rosalyn Tureck Live at St. Petersburg,* VAIA 1131. Compact disc; *Rosalyn Tureck Live at Teatro Colon,* VAI 69081. Video; *Rosalyn Tureck: The Young Firebrand,* VAI 1058. Compact disc.

BIBLIOGRAPHY

Dubal, David. "Rosalyn Tureck." In *Reflections from the Keyboard* (1984); Gillespie, John, and Anna Gillespie. "Rosalyn Tureck." In *Notable Twentieth-Century Pianists: A Bio-Critical Sourcebook.* Vol. 2 (1995); Lepage, Jane Warner. "Rosalyn Tureck." In *Women Composers, Conductors, and Musicians of the Twentieth Century: Selected Biographies* (1980); Mach, Elyse. "Rosalyn Tureck." In *Great Pianists Speak for Themselves* (1980); Tureck, Rosalyn. Letter to author, and Rosalyn Tureck Collection. Special Collections, Mugar Memorial Library, Boston University, Boston, Mass., and Tureck Bach Research Institute, Oxford University, and Rosalyn Tureck Collection. New York Public Library for the Performing Arts, Lincoln Center, NYC.

HARRIET FEINBERG

TUSSMAN, MALKA HEIFETZ (1893–1987)

Although she declared the natural rhythms of speech and breath as her poetic credo, at the peak of her powers the Yiddish poet Malka Heifetz Tussman introduced into Yiddish one of the most rigid verse forms, the triolet, and mastered another, the sonnet corona. A teacher of Yiddish language and literature in the Midwest and the West, Tussman was awarded the Itsik Manger Prize for Yiddish poetry in Tel Aviv in 1981.

Born around the holiday of Shavuot, Tussman herself disputed the exact year, stating it variously as 1893, 1895, or 1896. She considered May 15 her American birthday. Her father was the third generation of the Hasidic Heifetz family to manage an estate in the village of her birth, Khaytshe or Bolshaya-Chaitcha, in the Ukrainian province of Volhynia.

The second of eight children, Malka, like her siblings, was educated in Hebrew, Yiddish, Russian, and English, initially by private tutors and later in the Russian schools in the nearby towns of Norinsk and Korostyen. As a young child, she began to write poems in Russian about the poverty of the neighboring peasants.

She came to America in 1912 and joined family members in Chicago. "Under terrible conditions she pursued her learning," as Tussman once wrote about herself. Her first Yiddish short story appeared in 1918, and her first poem was published in 1919. She also wrote in English for the Chicago anarchist publication *Alarm* in 1914.

After her marriage to the cantor Shloyme Tussman, when she was eighteen years old, and the birth of her two sons (in 1914 and 1918), the family lived in Milwaukee, Wisconsin. In 1924, Tussman began to teach in a Yiddish secular school; at the same time, she studied at the University of Wisconsin. She also studied briefly at the University of California at Berkeley. In 1941 or 1942, the family moved to Los Angeles, where Tussman taught Yiddish elementary and high school students at the Workmen's Circle School in Boyle Heights. In 1949, she became an instructor of Yiddish language and literature at the University of Judaism. After her husband's death in 1971, she lived for a year in Israel. Upon her return, she moved to Berkeley, where she resided until her death.

Although she lived far from the centers of Yiddish letters, Tussman's poems, short stories, and essays appeared in the leading Yiddish newspapers and journals from 1918 onward. These publications included the New York papers *Fraye Arbeter Shtime* and *Der Vokh,* as well as the journals *Oyfkum, Inzikh, Yidisher Kemfer, Svive, Kinder Zhurnal,* and *Di Tsukunft,* the Warsaw weekly *Literarishe Bleter,* the Toronto literary magazine *Tint un Feder,* and the Tel Aviv quarterly *Di Goldene Keyt.* Her poems were represented in collections of Yiddish poetry, such as *Antologye—Mitvest-Mayrev* [From Midwest to North Pacific] (1933) and *Amerike in Yidishn Vort* [America in Yiddish literature] (1955). She published six volumes of poetry between 1949 and 1977. Until her death, Tussman continued to work on a seventh, *Un Ikh Shmeykhl* [And I smile], which is unpublished.

Throughout her career as a poet, Tussman sustained literary friendships and extensive correspondences with Yiddish writers in the United States, Canada, Poland, France, and Israel, including the poets Kalman Marmor, Yankev Glatshteyn, H. Leyvik, Rokhl Korn, KADYA MOLODOWSKY, Melekh Ravitsh, and Avraham Sutzkever. She read poetry of many languages, modern and ancient, and exercised her poetic voice by translating poems by writers as various as Yeats, Rossetti, Auden, and Tagore into Yiddish. By maintaining a ferocious poetic independence from any school or movement, Tussman achieved a compressed lyrical style noted by the critic M. Littvin for

Originally from the Ukraine, Yiddish poet Malka Heifetz Tussman lived most of her life in Milwaukee and Los Angeles, sustaining friendships with Yiddish writers all over the United States and in Canada, Poland, France, and Israel. Her work was marked by a compressed, lyrical style and an explicitly female sensuality. [YIVO Institute]

its elliptical syntax and free verse rhythms that render the strophe inconspicuous but dense. Avraham Sutzkever praised her poetry for asserting an ever more flexible, youthful voice, the older the poet herself grew.

Tussman has significance as a woman poet in Yiddish. Although she did not believe that poetry should be read or written in terms of gender, her poems are fueled by an explicitly female sensuality. Denying any feminist orientation, she nonetheless acknowledged how difficult it was for women writing poetry in Yiddish, even in the heyday of Yiddish poetry in America, to publish their poems in periodicals or to find sponsors for the publication of their books. In an interview

she expressed her sense that women who excelled in writing poems for children, such as Kadya Molodowsky, were often categorized by the Yiddish literary establishment as "merely children's poets," so that their other work remained unacknowledged. In her later years, she taught informally and befriended a number of younger poets, many American-born and writing in English, who helped disseminate her poetry through their translations, including Eli Katz, Marcia Falk, Kathryn Hellerstein, and Daniel Marlin. She also served as a mentor for some younger Yiddish poets, of whom an Israeli recipient of the Manger Prize, Rokhl Fishman, was the best known. Malka Heifetz Tussman thus served as a bridge between the generations of Yiddish poets who emigrated from Eastern Europe and of those American-born Jewish poets who have taken up the task of making Yiddish poetry known to a readership that knows little Yiddish.

SELECTED WORKS BY
MALKA HEIFETZ TUSSMAN

Am I Also You? Translated by Marcia Falk (1977); *Bleter Faln Not* [Leaves do not fall] (1972); *Haynt Iz eybik: Lider* [Now is ever: Poems] (1977); *Lider* [Poems] (1949); *Mild Mayn Vild: Lider* [Mild my wild: Poems] (1958); *Shotns fun Gedenkn* [Shadows of remembering] (1965); *Unter Dayn Tseykhn: Lider* [Under your sign: Poems] (1974); *With Teeth in the Earth: Selected Poems.* Translated, edited, and introduced by Marcia Falk (1992).

BIBLIOGRAPHY

Bankier, Joanna, Carol Cosman, Doris Earnshaw, et al., eds. *The Other Voice: Twentieth-Century Women's Poetry in Translation* (1976); Diamant, Zeynvl. "Kheyfets-Tuzman, Malke." In *Leksikon fun der Nayer Yidisher Literatur*. Vol. 3 (1960): 744–745; Harshav, Benjamin, and Barbara Harshav, eds. *American Yiddish Poetry: A Bilingual Anthology* (1986); Hellerstein, Kathryn. "From Ikh to Zikh: A Journey from 'I' to 'Self' in Yiddish Poems by Women." In *Gender and Text in Modern Hebrew and Yiddish Literature*, edited by Naomi B. Sokoloff, Anne Lapidus Lerner, and Anita Norich (1992): 113–143; Howe, Irving, Ruth R. Wisse, and Khone Shmeruk, eds. *The Penguin Book of Modern Yiddish Verse* (1987); Littvin, M. "Dos Poetishe Verk fun Malke Kheyfets-Tuzman." *Di Goldene Keyt* 89 (1976): 80–88; Sutzkever, Avraham. "Haynt Iz Eybik (Tsum Toyt fun Malke Kheyfets Tuzman)." *Di Goldene Keyt* 122 (1987): 52.

KATHRYN HELLERSTEIN

TUVIM, JUDY *see* HOLLIDAY, JUDY

U

UDIN, SOPHIE A. (1896–1960)

An intelligent, determined, career woman, Sophie A. Udin was a feminist leader and activist who sought equality between the sexes, including equal pay for equal work and equal representation for women. Channeling her campaign for autoemancipation for all women and support of working women in Palestine through PIONEER WOMEN, she used her organizational, public relations, speaking, writing, and librarian skills to build the organization and the Zionist movement in America and to aid Israel.

Born on August 31, 1896, in Zhinkov, Ukraine, Udin emigrated as a young girl with her socialist parents to Pittsburgh, Pennsylvania. At the early age of fourteen, she became active in the American branch of the Poale Zion movement, which combined socialism, Zionism, and the struggle against assimilation. Upon graduation from Pittsburgh Central High School in 1913, she moved to New York, enrolling in the Library School of the New York Public Library. She received her certification in 1914, a B.S. in education at Columbia University's Teachers College in 1928, and an M.L.S. from Columbia University School of Library Science in 1929.

Udin chose library science because it was one of the few vocational professions open to women. She served on the staff of the New York Public Library system from 1914 to 1929, specializing in foreign collections. Meanwhile, on March 13, 1918, she helped organize the American Mogen David Adom and served as its first national secretary from 1918 to 1919.

Taking a leave from the New York Public Library in 1921 and 1925 to 1927, she went to Palestine where she joined the fledgling Jewish National and University Library. At the library, she convinced the director, Dr. Hugo Bergmann, to keep the library open for longer reading hours, replace the German cataloging system with the Dewey decimal system and Anglo-American cataloging, and adopt American-style library education for the staff. While living in Jerusalem, she became involved in clandestine work for the Haganah.

Udin married Pinhas Ginguld, a Poale Zion officer and head of the network of secular Yiddish Folk Schools and Teacher's Seminary, in New York in 1922. They had two children, a son, Yehuda, and a daughter, Marcia. In 1924, she raised funds from America to produce the first Kiryat Sefer, the bibliography of Jewish and Hebrew publications of the National Library in Jerusalem.

Responding to a letter from her friend Rahel Yanait Ben-Zvi, who asked her to help raise money for a well to water trees at a tree nursery near Jerusalem, she founded, with the assistance of six wives of Poale Zion members, the Women's Organization for the Pioneer Women of Palestine (also known as Pioneer Women, subsequently Na'amat U.S.A.), incorporating it in December 1925.

An intelligent, determined career woman, Sophie Udin was a feminist leader and activist who sought equality between the sexes, including equal pay for equal work and equal representation for women. This photograph was taken in 1940.
[Na'amat Woman]

Udin established and directed the Zionist Archives and Library in New York, where she collected documentation of the Zionist movement and edited important reference materials such as the four-volume *The Palestine Year Book* annual (1945–1949) and the three-volume *Palestine and Zionism* (1947–1948). In 1948, she published the important bibliographical listing "A List of References Leading to the Establishment of the Jewish State of Israel" in *The Journal of Educational Sociology*.

Udin made aliyah in 1949 when she was appointed by David Ben-Gurion to set up and direct the Israel State Archives, now the National Archives. She directed the classification and listing of archival material that had already been collected. In an effort to ease the absorption of American immigrants to Israel, she helped establish the Association of Americans and Canadians in Israel in 1951.

Sophie A. Udin died in Jerusalem on April 24, 1960.

SELECTED WORKS BY SOPHIE A. UDIN

"A List of References Leading to the Establishment of the State of Israel." *Journal of Educational Sociology* 22 (November 1948): 239–247; *Palestine and Zionism*, editor (1947–1948); *The Palestine Year Book*, editor (1945–1949).

BIBLIOGRAPHY

AJYB 62:453; Keren, Thea. *Sophie Udin: Portrait of a Pioneer* (1984); Levitats, Tamar Schultz. "In Memoriam: Sophie Udin." *Pioneer Women* (May–June 1960): 12–13; Obituary. *NYTimes*, April 28, 1960, 35:4; Sokoloff, Judith. "Na'amat U.S.A. Through the Decades." *Na'amat Woman* (September–October 1995): 17–21; *WWIAJ* (1938).

JUDITH FRIEDMAN ROSEN

ULMANN, DORIS MAY (1882–1934)

One of America's most accomplished but enigmatic pictorialists, Doris Ulmann is often mistakenly hailed as a pioneering documentary photographer. Ulmann's interest in folk archetypes, her tableaux portraiture of impoverished rural Americans, and her life-long affiliations with Progressive Era institutions suggest that she never transcended her Victorian class biases. As a critic once described Ulmann's significance for the *New York Times:* "It is the tension between her romantic vision and these little unintended bits of the present that give her photographs their haunting power."

Born May 29, 1882, on New York City's Upper East Side, Doris May Ulmann was the second daughter of Reform Jewish parents, Gertrude (Maas) and Bernhard Ulmann, a German immigrant who amassed a fortune in America as a woolen manufacturer. As members of the Ethical Culture Society of New York, the Ulmann family embraced a nonsectarian faith in secular humanism, a sensibility reflected in Doris Ulmann's later choice of destitute black southerners and Appalachian mountaineers as portrait studies.

In 1903, Ulmann received a teaching degree from the Ethical Culture School, but went on to take courses in law and psychology at Columbia University. At Teachers College, she pursued her childhood interest in photography with Clarence White, a cofounder in 1902 with Alfred Stieglitz of the Photo-Secession, a select group of pictorialists committed to

From 1925 to 1932, photographer Doris Ulmann searched America for vanishing cultures, recording Mennonites, Shakers, and Kentucky mountaineers as well as rural African Americans. [University of Oregon Library]

establishing photography as a fine art form. Inspired by the Impressionist painters, pictorialist photographers used large-format view cameras and soft-focus lenses to lend a painterly, dreamy quality to their idyllic landscapes and portraits. So dedicated was Ulmann to Clarence White and the pictorialist genre that she and her surgeon husband, Charles H. Jaeger, joined him as as cofounders of the Pictorial Photographers of America shortly after the end of World War I.

From 1920 to 1925, Ulmann augmented her Victorian oeuvre with three published volumes of photos of prominent physicians and magazine editors, but her divorce from Jaeger seems to have marked a turning point in her career. Ulmann's first photographs of rural Mennonites, Shakers, and mountaineers appeared in *The Mentor* in 1927 and *Scribner's* in 1928, while her portraits of such modernist giants as Ansel Adams, Albert Einstein, Martha Graham, Edna St. Vincent Millay, José Orozco, and Thornton Wilder were carried by *Bookman*, *Vanity Fair*, and the gravure sections of Sunday newspapers.

During the late 1920s, Ulmann befriended the Pulitzer Prize–winning writer Julia Peterkin, who invited her to photograph a large community of African-American laborers living at Lang Syne, Peterkin's South Carolina plantation. From 1929 to 1932, Ulmann photographed black southerners there and in coastal Alabama and Louisiana, producing what may be the most extensive documentation of the southern plantation. When asked in 1931 by Allen H. Eaton of the Russell Sage Foundation to photograph native craft production in Appalachia, Ulmann hired Kentucky balladeer John Jacob Niles to assist with the transport of her cumbersome equipment and heavy glass plates.

She fell ill while working in the North Carolina mountains during the summer of 1934 and died shortly after her return to New York City on August 28. Doris Ulmann endowed the John C. Campbell Folk School in Brasstown, North Carolina, and established the Doris Ulmann Foundation at Berea College, Kentucky.

BIBLIOGRAPHY

AJYB 37:262; *The Appalachian Photographs of Doris Ulmann* (1977); Banes, Ruth A. "Doris Ulmann and Her Mountain Folk." *Journal of American Culture* 8 (1985): 29–42; Coles, Robert. *The Darkness and the Light: Photographs by Doris Ulmann* (1974); *Contemporary Photographers* (1982); Davis, Keith F. *An American Century of Photography* (1995); *Doris Ulmann: Photographs from the J. Paul Getty Museum* (1996); Eaton, Allen H. *Handicrafts of the Southern Highlands* (1937); Featherstone, David. *Doris Ulmann, American Portraits* (1985); Hagen, Charles. "Rural Social

From 1929 to 1932, Ulmann photographed black southerners at Lang Syne, Julia Peterkin's South Carolina plantation, and in coastal Alabama and Louisiana, producing what may be the most extensive documentation we have of the southern plantation. The above is one of the photographs from this series. [University of Oregon Library]

Commentary with a Difference." *NYTimes*, November 4, 1994; Lamuniere, Michelle C. "*Roll Jordan Roll*: The Gullah Portraits of Doris Ulmann." Master's thesis, University of Oregon, 1994; Lovejoy, Barbara. "The Oil Pigment Photos of Doris Ulmann." Master's thesis, University of Kentucky, 1993; Obituary. *NYTimes*, August 29, 1934; Ulmann, Doris. Collection of African-American studies and artist portraits. New-York Historical Society, NYC; Photographs. Berea College, Berea, Kentucky; Proof prints. University of Oregon, Eugene; Warren, Dale. "Doris Ulmann, Photographer-in-Waiting." *Bookman* 72 (October 1930): 129–144.

ELIZABETH ROBESON

One of the leading Jewish philanthropists of the second half of the twentieth century, Joy Ungerleider-Mayerson left an indelible mark on a broad array of Jewish cultural, scholarly, and religious endeavors and institutions. [The Jewish Museum, New York]

UNGERLEIDER-MAYERSON, JOY (1920–1994)

One of the leading Jewish philanthropists of the second half of the twentieth century, Joy Ungerleider-Mayerson left an indelible mark on a broad array of Jewish cultural, scholarly, and religious endeavors and institutions. She accomplished much of this work as president the Dorot Foundation, which she established in 1972.

Born Joy Gottesman in 1920, she was educated at New York University, where she received a B.A. in 1942 and an M.A. in Hebrew studies in 1971. She was married to Samuel Ungerleider, Jr., from 1945 until his death in 1972. In 1976, she married Philip Mayerson.

Ungerleider-Mayerson focused on projects and institutions dealing with Jewish education, Jewish museums, biblical archaeology, and Jewish pluralism. She was a curator of the Jewish Museum from 1967 to 1969. During that period she was responsible for bringing to the museum the Masada exhibition, which documented the excavations at that site. In 1972, she was appointed director of the museum and served in that position until 1980. At the time of her appointment, the museum was the subject of severe criticism for neglecting its Judaica collection and concentrating on contemporary and avant-garde art. It also faced serious financial difficulties, and many people felt its future was in doubt. Before Ungerleider-Mayerson's appointment as director, in fact, the museum had been closed for a year. Ungerleider-Mayerson is widely credited with saving the museum from both its financial and curatorial problems. She convinced a series of prominent philanthropists to support and become involved in the museum's activities and eventually recruited some of these people to serve as chairs of the museum's board of directors.

Of equal, if not greater, significance was her role in reorienting the museum's agenda by giving renewed attention to its Jewish mandate. Under her tutelage, the Jewish Museum began to mount exhibitions with specific Jewish content, both secular and religious. The art critic Arthur C. Danto noted in a Jewish Museum exhibition catalog that the museum's decision at the time of Ungerleider-Mayerson's ascendancy to the directorship to "retreat from the frontier of avant-garde culture was perceived by many . . . as the willed destruction of a vital institution." In retrospect, however, Danto observed, it should be considered as "precocious in terms of the cultural particularism that was destined to overtake American and world culture in the post modern era." Under Ungerleider-Mayerson's direction, the museum mounted a number of exceptionally important shows, chief among them *Danzig: Treasures of a Destroyed Community*. The Danzig materials and artifacts had been shipped to the museum in 1939 when the Danzig community was disbanded in the face of Nazi persecution. They had sat in the museum storehouse until, under Ungerleider-Mayerson's direction, they were cataloged and the show mounted. The exhibit attracted massive crowds both in New York and in the other cities it visited.

Ungerleider-Mayerson wrote two books, *Jewish Folk Art from the Biblical Period to Modern Times* and, with Nitza Rosovsky, *Museums of Israel*. In addition to her impact on the world of Jewish museums, Ungerleider-Mayerson, working through the Dorot Foundation, left her mark on the field of Jewish studies in both the United States and Israel. In 1994, a Dorot professorship of modern Jewish and Holocaust studies was established at Emory University in Atlanta. In addition, the foundation set up a Dorot teaching professorship and fellowship program at New York University and a Dorot chief librarian and bibliographer of the Jewish Division at the New York Public Library. There is also an Ungerleider chair of Judaic studies and two professorships in related disciplines at Brown University.

Ungerleider-Mayerson expressed her love of Israel and its history through the Dorot Foundation's active support of a series of archaeological projects both in Israel and abroad. The organization established a Dorot professor in residence at the Albright Institute for Archaeological Research in Jerusalem and a professorship in the archaeology of the land of Israel at Harvard University. But Ungerleider-Mayerson not only endowed projects in biblical archaeology, she took a personal interest in the field. At the time of her death, she was the chair of the Albright Institute and had personally participated in a number of archaeological digs in Israel. In addition, the Dorot Foundation has long supported the excavations at Tel Migne-Ekron and the American School of Oriental Research.

Because of Ungerleider-Mayerson's interest in folklore, the Dorot Foundation established the Museum of Bedouin Culture at Kibbutz Lahav. Among the foundation's most innovative projects is its fellows program, established in 1990, which selects college graduates to spend a year in Israel, where they study Hebrew and attend seminars on a wide range of topics relating to Israeli culture, politics, and society. In addition, each fellow designs a part-time program of Jewish studies and a part-time internship in his or her own field of professional interest. For over a decade, the Dorot Foundation has also provided approximately ten American universities with travel grants, used to help between 180 and 230 students travel and study in Israel every year. As well, the foundation supports a series of Israel-based institutions that cater primarily to American students interested in studying Judaica in an Israeli setting. Among those institutions are Pardes, an institute for advanced textual study for men and women in Jerusalem; Livnot U'Lehibanot, a program for young men and women with limited backgrounds in Judaica; and Elul, an organization that engages in scholarly projects designed to enhance pluralism within the Jewish community. Beit Shmuel, named after Samuel Ungerleider, Jr., and built with funds provided by Ungerleider-Mayerson and other foundations attached to Hebrew Union College, is attached to the Jerusalem campus of the college. It is designed both to strengthen Reform Judaism in Israel and to expose and link secular Israelis to aspects of Jewish tradition. During the last years of her life, Ungerleider-Mayerson, who spent part of each year living in Israel, became a strong backer and active member of Kol HaNeshamah, an innovative, liberal congregation in Jerusalem. She was particularly gratified that the synagogue attracted a broad array of congregants, including both those with an intensive Jewish background and those with none.

She also contributed to a range of American-based Jewish institutions, among them the Conference on Learning and Leadership (CLAL). She was the primary supporter of CLAL's program for enhancing Jewish pluralism and dialogue among various religious sectors of the Jewish community.

As the representative of the Gottesman family, Ungerleider-Mayerson played a critical role in the design and construction of the Shrine of the Book, the home of the Dead Sea Scrolls at the Israel Museum in Jerusalem. In so doing, she was continuing a role begun by her father, D.S. Gottesman, who provided the Israeli government with the funds to purchase the scrolls.

Ungerleider-Mayerson was a vice-chair of the Institute for Social and Economic Policy in the Middle East at Harvard University. She was also an active benefactor of a program that enabled Arabs and Israelis to study together at the university.

Joy Ungerleider-Mayerson died in 1994. One of the foremost Jewish philanthropists of the second half of the twentieth century, she was a model of the involved and active donor. In her work, she changed the face of Jewish learning, culture, and scholarship in both the United States and in Israel.

SELECTED WORKS BY
JOY UNGERLEIDER-MAYERSON

Jewish Folk Art from the Biblical Period to Modern Times (1986); *Museums of Israel*, with Nitza Rosovsky (1989).

DEBORAH LIPSTADT

UNTERMEYER, JEAN STARR
(1886–1970)

Jean Starr Untermeyer's memoir, *Private Collection* (1965), recalls a childhood blighted by "fear of the loss of love." The fear and the loss—and the love—shadowed her life, but they illuminated her art.

The eldest of three children, born May 13, 1886, in Zanesville, Ohio, to Abram and Johanna (Schonfeld) Starr, she delighted in music, books, and the German spoken by her hardy immigrant grandparents. After their storm-delayed passage had depleted the family's kosher provisions, one pious grandmother had sewn a shroud and prepared to starve rather than eat *traif*. When land was finally sighted, the weakened but indomitable woman was carried onto American soil. For Jean, Germany was the enchanted land "Mamma came from." However, advancing mental illness rendered her mother increasingly erratic and remote. Solace lay in her father, her piano, and (despite occasional anti-Semitic taunts in the schoolyard) her studies. She was sent to New York, where she attended Kohut College Preparatory School and took courses at Columbia University. In New York, on January 23, 1907, she married aspiring writer Louis Untermeyer; eleven months later, she bore a son, Richard.

Jean Untermeyer envisioned a career as lieder singer, but intimacy with writers—Sara Teasdale, Amy Lowell, Carl Sandburg, Robert Frost—led her to absorb poetry (as she put it) "by osmosis." Hearing Edna St. Vincent Millay recite a new piece inspired her to begin writing poems. Her husband discovered them, submitted them to periodicals, and pressed for the publication of her first two volumes of poetry, *Growing Pains* (1918) and *Dreams out of Darkness* (1921).

Though music remained Untermeyer's passion, her 1924 debuts in Vienna and London were discouraging, and more profound personal disappointments loomed. The Untermeyers returned to the United States at the end of 1924, enrolled their son at Yale, and spent the summer of 1925 at the MacDowell Colony. Also at MacDowell was a young woman Louis would marry the next year after obtaining a Mexican divorce. In January 1927, Louis and Jean's son, Richard, hanged himself in his room at Yale.

Death is immutable; divorce is not. Indeed, Mexican divorces had only questionable validity in American courts and could be successfully contested by a nonconsenting partner. Jean, however, had not contested either the divorce or Louis's marriage. When that second marriage ended, the Untermeyers reunited, adopted two boys, and moved to the Adirondacks. Unfortunately, the reconciliation failed and, because Jean was overwhelmed by the prospect of trying to raise two children by herself, Louis reluctantly accepted custody of the boys. He then obtained another Mexican divorce to marry a third wife, then yet another Mexican divorce to marry a fourth. When his third wife challenged in court the validity of the Mexican divorce that presumably dissolved her marriage (challenging, by implication, the validity of Louis's latest marriage), Jean, hoping for yet another reconciliation, testified in favor of Louis: She asserted that she, the first wife, had not consented to any Mexican divorce—and her testimony allowed the court to rule the first marriage still in effect and all subsequent marriages invalid. In 1951, having abandoned all hope of reconciliation, Jean agreed to a Nevada divorce: Her marriage was finally over.

Nevertheless, her work continued. She had published a third volume of poems, *Steep Ascent* (1927), translated Oscar Bie's *Schubert, the Man* (1928), and published a fourth volume of poems, *The Wingèd Child* (1936). She returned to the MacDowell Colony in 1938, in 1940 (when she published a fifth book of poems, *Love and Need*), and in 1941. At Yaddo in 1939, she met Hermann Broch; later she translated for publication his novel *The Death of Virgil* (1946). She published essays and book reviews, taught at Olivet College (1936–1937) and the New School for Social Research (1948–1951), and joined W.H. Auden, Archibald MacLeish, and others on the board of the Poetry Guild. She published her memoirs; a sixth volume of poems, *Job's Daughter* (1967); and a volume of poems translated from French, German, and Hebrew, *Re-Creations* (1970).

Though she experimented, her strongest poems are traditional in form; their subtle but complex harmonies—that inner movement of poetry she called "the fuel that feeds my fire"—reflect her passion for music. Her June 1923 *Bookmark* essay defended a woman's right to use personal experience in her art, yet her poems are never confessional. Laced with motifs of betrayal and abandonment, they trace the struggle to renounce desire, transcend resentment, transmute suffering into insight. Her early work draws from nature, war, and closely observed domestic experience. Her later poems explore love, death, and loss, seeking regeneration through reflection and self-discipline, revealing, as Amy Lowell asserted, "the heart of a woman, naked and serious, beautiful and unashamed."

Jean Starr Untermeyer died on July 27, 1970, in New York.

SELECTED WORKS BY JEAN STARR UNTERMEYER

A Bunch of Sweet Peas: Including Poetry, Prizes, Politics, Principles, Patriarchs, Puns, Personal Preferences, and A Few Cues [1949?]; *Dreams out of Darkness* (1921); *The Flowering of Lane Field* (1933); *Growing Pains* (1918); *Jean Starr Untermeyer Reading Her Poems at the City College of New York, March 28, 1941*. Sound recording (1941. Copied 1953 for Archives of Recorded Poetry and Literature, Library of Congress); *Jean Starr Untermeyer Reading Her Poems, with Comment, at the Pathé Sound Studios, New York, N.Y.: January 5, 1961*. Two sound cassettes (1961); *Job's Daughter* (1967); *Later Poems* (1958); *Love and Need: Collected Poems, 1918–1940* (1940); *Poetry in a Prosaic World*. Presented at Boston Jewish Book Week, Boston Public Library, December 22, 1940. Microform (1940); *Private Collection* (1965); *Re-Creations* (1970); *Steep Ascent* (1927); *The Wingèd Child* (1936).

Jean Starr Untermeyer wrote lyrics to the following music: Adler, Samuel. *The Passionate Sword: A Prayer for Baritone Solo, Flute, Clarinet, Violin, Cello, and Percussion* (1979); Bie, Oskar. *Schubert, the Man*. Translated by Jean Starr Untermeyer (1928); Broch, Hermann. *The Death of Virgil*. Translated by Jean Starr Untermeyer (1995); Hyson, Winifred. *Song's* [sic] *of Job's Daughter: For Soprano with Piano Accompaniment* (1983); Leonhard, Rudolf. *Christmas Song*. Translated by Jean Starr Untermeyer (1939); Read, Gardner. *Lullaby for a Man-child: Medium Voice Op. 76, No. 1*. Words by Jean Starr Untermeyer (1957).

BIBLIOGRAPHY

BEOAJ; Broch, Hermann. Papers and book collection. Hermann Broch Archive. Bienecke Rare Book Collection, Yale University Library, New Haven, Conn.; Dobbs, Jannine. "Jean Starr Untermeyer." In *American Women Writers: A Critical Reference Guide from Colonial Times to the Present in Four Volumes*, edited by Lina Mainiero. Vol. 4 (1982); *EJ*, s.v. "Untermeyer, Louis"; Farano, Michel. Papers. University of Delaware Library, Newark; Obituary. *NYTimes*, July 29, 1970, 39:2; *UJE*; Untermeyer, Jean Starr. Papers. Yale University Library, New Haven, and State University of New York Library at Buffalo; Untermeyer, Louis. *Bygones: The Recollections of Louis Untermeyer* (1965), and *From Another World: The Autobiography of Louis Untermeyer* (1939), and *These Times* (1917); Untermeyer, Richard Starr. *By Richard Starr Untermeyer* (1927); *WWIAJ* (1926, 1928, 1938); *WWWIA* 5, 7.

FRANCESCA TILLONA

UPRISING OF THE 20,000 (1909)

On November 23, 1909, more than twenty thousand Yiddish-speaking immigrants, mostly young women in their teens and early twenties, launched an eleven-week general strike in New York's shirtwaist industry. Dubbed the Uprising of the 20,000, it was the largest strike by women to date in American history. The young strikers' courage, tenacity, and solidarity forced the predominantly male leadership in the "needle trades" and the American Federation of Labor to revise their entrenched prejudices against organizing women. The strikers won only a portion of their demands, but the uprising sparked five years of revolt that transformed the garment industry into one of the best-organized trades in the United States.

Designed in the early 1890s, the shirtwaist (or blouse) arrived at a time when production of women's clothing moved from the household to the factory. By 1909, six hundred shops operated in New York City (the center of garment manufacturing in the United States), employing thirty thousand workers and producing fifty million dollars in merchandise annually. The relatively newer shirtwaist factories—generally of medium to large size, employing roughly fifty to three hundred people during the busy seasons—provided slightly better working conditions and wages than the older suit and cloak shops, which employed mostly Jewish men.

In the shops, the internal subcontracting system trapped about a quarter of the women in unskilled, poorly paid jobs. These "learners," so-called even after they mastered their tasks, earned three to four dollars per week (during the busy seasons) while semiskilled "operators," about 50 to 60 percent of the workforce, earned seven to twelve dollars per week. At the top of the hierarchy stood highly skilled sample makers, cutters, and pattern makers who earned fifteen to twenty-three dollars per week and subcontracted work to "learners." They were almost exclusively male and the most likely segment of the workforce to be unionized before the uprising. The division of labor along skill and gender lines reinforced biases among conservative trade unionists against organizing women and unskilled laborers. Although the INTERNATIONAL LADIES GARMENT WORKERS UNION did not officially discriminate against women, its conservative leadership (replaced by socialists in 1914) dismissed women as an ephemeral part of the workforce, interested primarily in marriage and motherhood—an opinion shared by Samuel Gompers and many of the AFL's craft unions. Jewish women did quit working after marriage in significantly higher numbers than their Italian coworkers, but this did not prevent militancy in the workplace or in the community. (Conversely, Italian woman proved difficult to organize.) In fact, an emergent tradition of activism among women (punctuated by the 1902 kosher meat boycott, the 1907 rent strike, and sporadic labor struggles) played a key role in sustaining the 1909 uprising.

The movement that culminated in the uprising of the 20,000 began with spontaneous strikes against the Leiserson Company, the Rosen Brothers, and the Triangle Shirtwaist Company (New York's largest manufacturer of shirtwaists) during the summer/fall busy season of 1909. Although prompted by different incidents, workers shared a common set of underlying grievances about wages, hours, workplace safety, and workplace indignities suffered specifically by women (such as unwanted sexual advances, threats, and invasions of privacy). The Rosen Brothers settled with their employees after five weeks, but Leiserson and Triangle remained intransigent.

From the outset, the young strikers faced three-way opposition from the manufacturers, the police, and the courts. Triangle and Leiserson hired thugs and prostitutes to abuse strikers, often with aid from policemen who then arrested strikers on trumped-up charges of assault. In court, strikers faced hostile magistrates who upbraided the young women ("You are striking against God and nature," scolded one enraged judge), fined them, and, in some cases, sentenced them to the workhouse. In an attempt to curb abuses, the fledgling Local 25 of the ILGWU, which represented shirtwaist makers, asked the Women's Trade Union League (WTUL) (established by upper-class suffragists in 1904 to promote the welfare of working women) to monitor the picket lines. After police arrested Mary Dreier, head of the WTUL, for allegedly harassing a scab, strikers won the sympathy of a previously indifferent public. The WTUL proved a valuable ally; its members walked the picket lines, raised funds, and pleaded the strikers' case to the general public. The *Forverts*, the United Hebrew Trades, the *Arbeter-ring* (Workmen's Circle), and the Socialist Party and its weekly *The Call* also provided important logistical and financial support.

Nonetheless, by early November, Local 25 had almost depleted its strike fund, and many strikers chose to return to work rather than suffer arrest, harassment, and personal injury. Furthermore, Triangle and Leiserson partially circumvented the strike by subcontracting work to smaller shops (though, on at least one occasion, subcontracted workers went on a sympathy strike). Instead of conceding defeat, Local 25's fifteen-member executive committee (six of whom were women and all socialists) called for a general strike to shut down production entirely in the shirtwaist industry. On November 22, thousands of young women packed into Cooper Union to discuss Local 25's recommendations. Samuel Gompers and Mary Dreier spoke, along with a number of luminaries of the Jewish labor movement, including Meyer London, labor lawyer and future Socialist Party congressman; Benjamin Feigenbaum, the meeting's chairman and popular *Forverts* writer; and Bernard Weinstein, head of the United Hebrew Trades. In speech after speech, speakers offered support, but urged caution. Frustrated after two hours, CLARA LEMLICH [SHAVELSON]—a leader of the Leiserson strike and a member of Local 25's executive committee—demanded the floor and delivered what the press termed a "Yiddish philippic." In words now legendary, the impassioned twenty-three-year-old declared, "I am a working girl, one of those who are on strike against intolerable conditions. I am tired of listening to speakers who talk in general terms. What we are here to decide is whether we shall or shall not strike. I offer a resolution that a general strike be declared—now." Lemlich ignited the audience. In unison, the crowd pledged support for the general strike by reciting a secularly adapted Hebrew oath chanted by Feigenbaum.

The following morning, approximately fifteen thousand shirtwaist workers took to the streets. By evening, the number swelled to more than twenty thousand. According to some estimates, almost thirty thousand workers participated in the strike during its eleven-week duration, 90 percent of whom were Jewish and 70 percent women. "Learners" and "operators" made up the bulk of the strikers, but male craftsmen (who themselves employed "learners" and occupied a critical position in the production process) also marched on the picket line, thereby guaranteeing a complete work stoppage. Pandemonium reigned during the uprising's initial days as thousands of workers rushed to meetings, swarmed union locals, and milled the streets. In the confusion, some workers returned to their jobs, demoralized. At the same time, a number of small shops quickly negotiated with the union to gain an edge on their larger competitors. Thus, hundreds of workers returned to their shops, even as hundreds of others joined the picket lines.

Throughout the uprising, arrests and harassment continued unabated. In one month, 723 people were arrested and 19 sentenced to the workhouse. Bail averaged $2,500 per day, and court fines totaled $5,000. Overall, the strike cost $100,000. Clara Lemlich suffered six broken ribs and was arrested a total of seventeen times. In one egregious miscarriage of justice, a ten-year-old girl was tried without testimony and sentenced to five days in the workhouse for allegedly assaulting a scab. In response to such outrages, the WTUL organized mass rallies at the Hippodrome, Carnegie Hall, and City Hall in which the strikers' plight was connected to the suffragist cause. Although a degree of mutual suspicion existed behind the scenes, this alliance produced a new perspective that merged class consciousness with feminism (later named "industrial feminism").

"Learners" and "operators" conducted much of the uprising's daily legwork. These bold young women—malnourished and poorly clad in the bitter winter cold—handed out leaflets, raised funds, distributed strike benefits, scheduled meetings, and maintained the crowd's morale. Some of the outstanding organizers, such as Clara Lemlich, PAULINE NEWMAN, and ROSE SCHNEIDERMAN, had been active in radical politics even before their emigration from Russia. Hundreds of other women assumed leadership roles spontaneously, only to disappear after the strike.

For much of the eleven-week strike, workers and manufacturers were locked in a stalemate. The Associated Waist and Dress Manufacturers, representing the large employers, rejected the closed union shop. Exhausted, but determined, workers refused to budge on this point, fearing that an open shop would leave the union powerless to enforce agreements. However, the strikers (represented at the negotiating table by Socialist Party leader Morris Hillquit and John Mitchell of the United Mine Workers) could not hold out. The general strike was called off unceremoniously on February 15, 1910, with about a thousand workers still on the picket line.

Though not a complete victory, the uprising achieved significant, concrete gains. Out of the Associated Waist and Dress Manufacturers' 353 firms, 339 signed contracts granting most demands: a fifty-two-hour week, at least four holidays with pay per year, no discrimination against union loyalists, provision of tools and materials without fee, equal division of work during slack seasons, and negotiation of wages with employees. By the end of the strike, 85 percent of all shirtwaist makers in New York had joined the ILGWU. Local 25, which began the strike with a hundred members, now counted ten thousand. Furthermore, the uprising laid the groundwork for industrial unionism in the garment industry. Inspired by the shirtwaist makers, sixty thousand cloak makers—men, this time—launched the Great Revolt in the summer of 1910, and other garment strikes ensued across the country. After five years of unrest, the "needle trades" emerged as one of the best organized in the United States.

Less tangible, but equally important, the general strike convinced conservative veterans to accept women as capable union activists. The young women themselves discovered their own self-worth through the ideological ferment and economic struggles of 1909–1910. Many of them remembered the Uprising of the 20,000 as the formative event of their adult lives.

BIBLIOGRAPHY

Baum, Charlotte, Paula Hyman, and Sonya Michel, eds. *The Jewish Woman in America* (1976); Epstein, Melech. *Jewish Labor in USA: An Industrial, Political and Cultural History of the Jewish Labor Movement* (1969); Glenn, Susan A. *Daughters of the Shtetl: Life and Labor in the Immigrant Generation* (1990); Hyman, Paula. "Immigrant Women and Consumer Protest: The New York City Kosher Meat Boycott of 1902." *AJH* 70, no. 1 (September 1980): 68–90; Kessler-Harris, Alice. "Organizing the Unorganizable: Three Jewish Women and their Unions." *Labor History* 17, no. 1 (Winter 1976): 5–23; Levine, Louis. *The Women Garment Workers: A History of the International Ladies' Garment Workers' Union* (1924); McCreesh, Carolyn Daniel. *Women in the Campaign to Organize Garment Workers 1880–1917* (1985); Orleck, Annelise. *Common Sense and a Little Fire: Women and Working Class Politics in the United States, 1900–1965* (1995); Seller, Maxine Schwartz. "The Uprising of the Twenty Thousand: Sex, Class and Ethnicity in the Shirtwaist Makers' Strike of 1909." In *'Struggle a Hard Battle': Essays on Working-Class Immigrants*, edited by Dirk Hoerder (1986); Tax, Meredith. *The Rising of Women: Feminist Solidarity and Class Conflict, 1880–1917* (1980); Tyler, Gus. *Look for the Union Label: A History of the International Ladies' Garment Workers' Union* (1995); Waldinger, Robert. "Another Look at the International Ladies' Garment Workers' Union: Women, Industry Structure and Collective Action." In *Women, Work and Protest: A Century of U.S. Women's Labor History*, edited by Ruth Milkman (1985).

TONY MICHELS

V

VAN BUREN, ABIGAIL (DEAR ABBY) (b. 1918)

In 1990 alone, advice columnist "Dear Abby" and her staff received over fifty-five thousand letters from men and women of all ages, classes, nationalities, sexual orientations, and religions. With a clear, witty, and informative writing style and a readership of 150 to 200 million, Pauline Esther Friedman Phillips, known professionally as Abigail Van Buren or Dear Abby, has influenced American life and culture since the inception of her column in the mid-1950s. Openly revealing her opinions concerning anti-Semitism, sexism, and racism while responding to her readers' diverse queries, Dear Abby has actively championed Jewish and non-Jewish women's rights both in the United States and internationally.

Pauline's parents, Abraham and Rebecca Friedman, were Russian Jewish immigrants who arrived in United States in 1908. They moved to Sioux City, Iowa, in 1910, giving birth to Helen and then Dorothy soon after. Like many Russian Jewish immigrants of that time, the family slowly earned enough money to leave the poorer sections of the city, first by peddling chickens from a pushcart and then, by 1911, by amassing enough earnings to buy into a grocery store. When Pauline was born, her parents owned a small house. Her father became part owner of a movie and vaudeville theater when she was in her early teens. Active in the Jewish community of Sioux City, Abraham Friedman's civic stature grew as he acquired other theaters and diversified his business interests.

Nicknamed "Popo," Pauline was born on July 4, 1918, only seventeen minutes apart from her twin, Esther Pauline (later known as columnist ANN LANDERS). The two girls shared similar interests, dressed in like styles, attended the same high school (Central High School, from which they graduated in 1936), and matriculated at the same small college nearby. Pauline met her future husband, Mort Phillips, at a University of Minnesota dance. Mort Phillips's father, like the girls' father, was a Russian Jewish immigrant, born in Minsk. Just as the twins had experienced other important events simultaneously, soon after Pauline became engaged, Esther met her future husband, Jules Lederer. The sisters had a double wedding on July 2, 1938, at their synagogue in Sioux City. The Phillipses had two children, Jeannie and Eddie.

When the Phillipses moved to Hillsborough, California, from Eau Claire, Wisconsin, in 1955, Pauline contacted an editor with the *San Francisco Chronicle* to express her displeasure with their newly established Molly Mayfield lovelorn column. She offered the *Chronicle* a radical departure from the paper's previous features. Her column was to be humorous, helpful, and filled with one-liners. The paper hired her and she rapidly became a success, adopting the name Abigail Van Buren. Pauline contracted for the rights to

Pictured above are two of the most influential women in America, and they just happen to be twins—Abigail Van Buren (Dear Abby) on the right and Ann Landers on the left. For forty years, "Dear Abby" has championed the rights of women, Jews, African Americans, and other "minorities" in her column. She is active in both national and local Jewish organizations. [UPI/CORBIS-BETTMANN]

the names Abigail Van Buren and Dear Abby, a move that gave her great control over her column and a large share of its profits.

In the past forty years, Abigail Van Buren has counseled her readership, as well as shared with them her political, moral, and social views. Championing the rights of women, Jews, African-Americans, and others, she has published advice columns that newspapers have threatened not to print. On July 29, 1991, for example, she reissued a letter in favor of women's rights to control their bodies, even though a number of papers threatened not to run it.

Because she became Dear Abby three months after her twin assumed the Ann Landers column, the sisters attempted to curb any acrimony between them by agreeing not to vie for the same city's newspaper. However, their competition intensified after Ann Landers signed a one-year contract with the *Sun Times* and appeared on *What's My Line?* In 1956, Abigail Van Buren allegedly offered "Dear Abby" at a reduced rate to the twins' hometown paper, *Sioux City*

Journal, as long as it promised not to run "Ann Landers." *Life* magazine informed the public of their acrimony in April 1958. Although the sisters publicly reconciled in 1964 for their twenty-fifth wedding anniversaries, their competition continued.

Abigail Van Buren has lived in Sioux City, Eau Claire, Los Angeles, and St. Paul. In all these locations, she has continually remained active in citywide and national Jewish and non-Jewish organizations. Volunteering with synagogues, old age homes, and the Jewish National Fund, her largest contribution lies in her ability to make public issues of concern to Jewish and non-Jewish women.

BIBLIOGRAPHY

Pottker, Jan. *Dear Ann, Dear Abby: The Unauthorized Biography of Ann Landers and Abigail Van Buren* (1987); "Queen of Hearts." *Psychology Today* 26 (May/June 1993): 56–60+; Rottenberg, Dan. "Ann and Abby's Lessons for Journalists." *The Quill* 72 (January 1984): 20–24.

ROBIN JUDD

VAN VORT, ROSA ZIMMERN (1876–1944)

A member of Virginia's first generation of trained nurses, Rosa Zimmern Van Vort devoted her career to the training and education of nurses.

The daughter of Isaac and Hettie (Zimmern) Van Vort, Rosa Zimmern Van Vort was born in Richmond, Virginia, on August 6, 1876. Her family belonged to Temple Beth Ahabah, Richmond's second-oldest congregation. She attended public schools, graduated from Richmond High School, and at age twenty-one, entered the Old Dominion Hospital Training School for Nurses at the Medical College of Virginia in Richmond. This training school, organized by Sadie Health Cabaniss in 1895, was modeled on the Nightingale plan. Van Vort herself said that she was a "student of Florence Nightingale four times removed."

Her two-year course of study consisted of eight-hour shifts in the hospital and special-duty service during weekends, with little time for formal instruction. This experience made a lasting impression on Van Vort and she sought to improve the quality of training and reduce work hours for student nurses throughout her career. Following her graduation from the hospital training school in 1899, Van Vort attended courses at the Philadelphia Orthopedic Hospital and Teachers College, Columbia University, where she came into contact with M. Adelaide Nutting, a prominent leader in nursing education.

Van Vort returned to Old Dominion Hospital and served as acting superintendent in the final months of its operation. In 1903, she moved with the training school to the Medical College of Virginia's new teaching facility, the Memorial Hospital. She subsequently became superintendent of nurses and principal of the training school in 1904, serving until 1913. Following her experience at Memorial Hospital, Van Vort organized a training school at the newly established Stuart Circle Hospital in Richmond. She served as superintendent and principal of the training school from 1913 until 1924. After a brief stint as superintendent at St. Elizabeth Hospital in Richmond, Van Vort moved to Knoxville, Tennessee, where she reorganized the nursing school at the city's General Hospital. She returned to Virginia a year later and appears to have retired.

During World War I, Van Vort served on the state and city councils of defense, where she was responsible for recruiting nurses. The national Red Cross selected her and two other Richmond women to enroll nurses in Red Cross service. For these efforts, she received a special award in 1922.

Her most significant contribution to professional nursing and nursing education was her leadership in the organization of the Virginia State League of Nursing. The league was organized in January of 1918, and the members elected Van Vort as the first president. She served for four terms, stepping down following the 1922 annual meeting. During her tenure as president, the league successfully fought legislation requiring a compulsory eight-hour day for student nurses. Van Vort was also a charter member of the Virginia State Association of Nurses.

Plagued by ill health for the last decade of her life, Van Vort was forced to limit her professional activities, but she maintained her interest in the profession and periodically attended meetings.

Rosa Zimmern Van Vort died at her home on February 13, 1944.

BIBLIOGRAPHY

McLeod, Josephine S. "Nurse Practice in Action In Virginia," *Bits of News* 5 (July 1936): 18–29; Obituaries. *Bits of News* 12 (April 1944): 14–15, and *Richmond Times-Dispatch*, February 14, 1944; School of Nursing, Medical College of Virginia, Virginia League for Nursing, and Virginia Nurses' Association. Records. Special Collections and Archives, Tompkins-McCaw Library, Virginia Commonwealth University, Richmond; *WWIAJ* (1928, 1938).

JODI KOSTE

VAUDEVILLE

When hearing or reading the phrase "Jewish women in vaudeville," one is likely to think first of the headliners SOPHIE TUCKER and BELLE BAKER, chief among those who placed their ethnicity at the center of their acts. (FANNY BRICE might be added, although her early career focused more on the Ziegfeld Follies than on the vaudeville circuit per se.) One might also remember those headliners who were Jewish but kept their Jewish identity offstage, such as NAN HALPERIN and NORA BAYES. Still to be added would be the visitors from other venues, such as MOLLY PICON, star of Yiddish theater, and Sarah Bernhardt, star of the stage. But as rich as this list would be, it would introduce us only to the canonical history, the biographies of the familiar, established stars. It would only begin to tell the larger story of how and why Jewish women and vaudeville came to intersect as they did in the early decades of the twentieth century.

That story, first of all, included a much larger and more diverse company of participants. Generally left out of vaudeville histories have been the performers in Yiddish vaudeville, a circuit distinct from both the American vaudeville houses and Second Avenue's Yiddish theater. In beer halls and saloons across New

York City, such Jewish women as Nellie Casman, MIRIAM KRESSYN, and Vera Rosanko performed sketches and skits mainly in Yiddish, identifying themselves more directly with *yiddishkeit* than did the performers of mainstream vaudeville. Equally unheralded have been the lesser-known performers on all the circuits—the second-billers, chorus girls, and female members of teams. One finds them mentioned in contemporary daily papers such as the *New York Dramatic Mirror*—performers such as Sadie Fields, Belle Gold, Annie Goldie, Leah Russell, Lillian Shaw, and Fannie Woods (Grossman 31). One finds recordings by singers such as Rhoda Bernard ("Yiddishe Matinee Girl" and "Rosie Rosenblatt"). For the most part, however, even their names have been lost, and their contributions elided from the histories.

This expanded list does not stop here, for participation in the business was not limited to performers. Behind the curtain were the Jewish mothers who supported both daughters and sons in the business, such as Sarah Glantz, Milton Berle's mother and manager. And in front of the curtain were the Jewish women in the audience, constituting perhaps a third of the house in Jewish neighborhoods and areas such as Brooklyn.

What brought all of these performers and participants together is also a largely untold story—the story of a struggle over representation. Enacted on the vaudeville stage was the emergence of the American Jew. The Jews who played the central role in this process were the immigrants who had arrived from Eastern Europe between 1880 and 1910 and settled in the urban Northeast. During this period and in this area, an unprecedented intermingling of men and women from different races, ethnicities, and classes forged not only many of the expressive conventions of vaudeville, but also the foundations for representing ethnic American identity. The criteria for ethnic representation, particularly the representation of Jews, did not arise without debate. Many points of view entered the process, registering the attitudes of Jews of different generations and places of origin, of non-Jews, of men and women, of people from different social classes. Despite these differences, however, the debate was often pursued through a common frame of reference: the representation of the Jewish woman. Jewish women were drawn to the center of this debate on a number of levels: as participants in assimilation, as vehicles for the expression of attitudes about assimilation, and as speakers in their own right.

The figures of the *yidishe mame* and the ethnic vamp, the "dumb Dora" and the nagging wife, served to express the anxieties and ambivalences attending assimilation in all its aspects, from the preservation of the community to the allocations of authority over issues of gender. The same process was at work in the celebration and vilification of the female Jewish vaudevillians themselves. That the battleground for these mixed feelings would be women's bodies, specifically the construction and spectacular display of those bodies on stage, is not surprising: Women's bodies are often the site where cultural disputes are enacted. In this case, the focus on Jewish women's bodies in particular is also not surprising. During this period, Jewish women did, of course, play a significant role in the process of assimilation, through their entry into the workplace (a workplace that included the vaudeville stage as well as the sweatshops), their exposure to new notions of sexual desire and autonomy, and the reconfigurations of filial and personal responsibilities that accompanied these changes. But the actions and attitudes of the Jewish immigrant women themselves were rarely the focus of these debates. On the vaudeville stage, these women became representations of the enticements, dangers, and emancipatory promises of assimilation. One finds figures of Jewish women representing divided attachments to both the Old World (the *yidishe mame* invoked almost nightly in Sophie Tucker's stage act) and the New (the ethnic vamp cajoled in Irving Berlin's 1909 "Sadie Salome").

Yet Jewish women did not allow themselves to be only the objects of this debate. They also entered the discussion as subjects in their own right. Female vaudeville performers in particular, mainly recent immigrants and children of immigrants, found the vaudeville stage to be one of the few places where they could act out their concerns and dramatize their often divided feelings about both assimilation and their assigned roles as women. Through, and often against, the conventions of vaudeville, they fought to represent themselves, offering their own commentaries on the positioning of the Jewish woman in America. On a typical night on the stage, for instance, Sophie Tucker would follow a highly sentimentalized performance of "My Yiddishe Momme" with a highly sexualized performance of the ribald song "You've Got to See Mama Ev'ry Night." She then complicated the picture further by drawing both personae together to create the fantastic figure of the Jewish "red hot mama."

Such performances constituted not an abandonment of Jewish identity but rather an attempt to create something new: an American Jewish identity specifically available to women. The drive toward this identity is evident even in the performers' names—or, rather, the name changes through which these women marked their transformation into performers. Sophie Tucker began her life as Sophie Abuza, adopted the name Tuck after her husband's name, and then finally changed it to Tucker. Belle Baker began as Bella Becker, and Fanny Brice as Fanny Borach. While these changes to, or abandonments of, given names indicated the control that the women exerted over their professional lives in America, the new names hardly demonstrated the women's desire to erase or hide their Jewish identity.

The beginnings of this struggle over representation can be traced back to the 1882 introduction of the first female "Hebrew" figure on the American stage. The routine was titled "Our Pawnshop," and it was performed by the male-female team of William Hines and Earle Remington. One might expect to find that the participation of Jewish women vaudevillians dated back to this early period. Yet many years passed before Jewish women began to appear onstage, and at least twenty years before a few of them began to acquire the status of headliners. Remington, for instance, although the writer of the team, was not Jewish.

This lag was partly the result of repressive attitudes toward women, and Jewish women in particular, that were as common onstage as off. Most of the early onstage "Hebrew" figures were male. In virtually all of the early routines about Jews, female characters were either absent altogether, as in such classic monologues as "Cohen at the Telephone" and "Levinsky at the Wedding," or constructed only as offstage foils, as in the very first "Hebrew" routine, an 1878 number by the team of Burt and Leon entitled "The Widow Rosenbaum," a parody of a popular Irish song. But if Jewish women themselves were largely excluded from the stage as performers or subjects in their own right, the "Jewish woman" was not so difficult to find: nagging but voiceless, feared but powerless.

This anxiety about women, and the containment of women, was evident in all levels of early performance conventions. It was present in the content of the routines, the extent and nature of the roles allotted to women performers, the positioning of the women on stage (alone and in relation to men), the wardrobe, the display of types of language and language proficiency, and the concrete dimensions of the voice itself. In addition, men were generally the ultimate curators and controllers of these conventions: the owners, managers, and booking agents, the fathers and husbands at home, and the men in the audience. Even the very appearance of women on stage was at first considered scandalous, a sign of a public exposure that, in the case of the Jewish woman, amounted to nothing less than the woman casting aside her fidelity to her "people," her "place." Indeed, Jewish women were not encouraged to sing even offstage, and so had few models to draw upon as performers. In European Jewish society at the time, singers, both religious and secular, were invariably men, and America offered few models of its own (the remarkable burlesque performer ADAH ISAACS MENKEN was one of the few exceptions).

Sexism was not the only obstacle to the opening of the stage to Jewish women. Whether male or female, Jews in general faced conflicting and constraining stereotypes of themselves as Jews, figures muffled in dialect and confounded by greed or incompetence, icons of ridicule and nostalgia. Jewish women during this early period were thus subject to a double negation, as women and as Jews.

Such denigration and displacement did not end with the new century. But it would be wrong to argue that these stage representations succeeded in wholly repressing Jewish women. Certainly they did not keep Jewish women off the stage after the turn of the century, nor did they prevent these women from critiquing the representations themselves. One of the remarkable features of the Jewish female vaudevillians was their ability to claim cultural authority in such an inhospitable environment.

What made their entry onto the stage possible? A number of factors could be cited. Toward the end of the century, the vaudeville stage began to become "respectable," largely through the efforts of performer and stage entrepreneur Tony Pastor. Pastor wanted to "clean up" vaudeville, to make it an arena of acceptable entertainment for women and families as well as men. Larger theaters were built to supplement the beer halls and cabarets, and certain risqué and male-directed conventions of the stage that had been common for fifty years began to change. Women performers were no longer represented in advertisements or on the stage itself merely as sources of illicit pleasure. At the same time, a female performer could respectably perform her own sexual desirability. By the second decade of the twentieth century, the effects of these changes could partly be measured by the makeup of the audience, which had been transformed from mostly men to roughly two-thirds men and one-third women and children.

Jewish women performers were now better able to enter the battleground of representation on their own terms. They could use their stage personae to explore their roles as women and particularly as Jewish women. Through the alterations of old routines and inventions of new ones, and through displays of visual and verbal dexterity, they articulated the intersections of Jewish and female identity, most notably with regard to their own previously suppressed sexual desires. Thus Sophie Tucker could become all things to all men—kept woman, nice Jewish girl, flippant flapper, beckoning Jewish mother—yet still manage to claim self-possession. ("I ain't takin' orders from no one," she sang in a 1927 song.) While such flirtation with transgressive desire was occasionally criticized as "vulgar," it was just as often celebrated as a sign of exuberant self-confidence. Indeed, in the theater columns of local newspapers, Tucker and others were granted a kind of "high society" status, their flamboyant show of sexuality and wealth reconfigured as a demonstration of refinement. Their every public gesture was loftily reported, from their appearances at public events to their displays of the latest fashions and their contributions to charities. Tucker was especially shrewd in coordinating the media's presentation of her as the royalty of a now noble profession.

Not all female vaudevillians were as straightforward as Tucker in their use of their sexuality or as devoted to claiming class status as a sign of respectability. Performers such as Molly Picon and Fanny Brice explored more indirect avenues of self-expression and thus offered somewhat different commentaries on the positioning of Jewish women. Picon often played a young girl in man's clothing, a performance recorded in the 1937 Yiddish film *Yiddle with His Fiddle*, and Fanny Brice began developing her Baby Snooks character, a mischievous child undermining all sorts of authority, including her own. Nor were spectacle and indirection the only performative modes pursued by women in vaudeville; their acts also included material that directly addressed the kinds of experiences Jewish women encountered in America. In "The Song of the Sewing Machine," for instance, Fanny Brice sang about her mother's work in the garment district.

As is evident from these examples, the performance of gender and sexuality was only one sphere in which Jewish women explored their identity. In keeping with vaudeville conventions of the time, Jewish identity was also articulated through racial and ethnic impersonation. Such impersonations were wide-ranging in their choice of objects. Sophie Tucker began her career as a "coon shouter," while Molly Picon first auditioned for vaudeville by impersonating a Hawaiian maiden, complete with short skirt and ukulele. Belle Baker was exemplary in this area. She might begin her act in the character of Sadie Cohen, an aging Jewish woman begging her boyfriend to marry her. Then she would sing another plea to a lover, only this time in minstrel-Italian dialect ("Come Back Antonio"). Then would come her version of "My Mother's Rosary," followed, perhaps, by a song with black minstrel overtones, such as "How I Wish I Could Sleep 'Til My Daddy Comes Home." Finally, she would begin the song for which she became famous, "Eili, Eili," sung entirely in Yiddish (Snyder 112).

While ethnic impersonation was not itself unusual on the early vaudeville stage, female performers were rarely involved. Aside from a few exceptional women such as Sophie Tucker, the blackface performers were men, in part because blackface operated as a mode of licensed transgression, a license deemed too dangerous to grant to women. But the female vaudevillians found ways around this prohibition. As in Belle Baker's act, they performed through the personae of many ethnicities, even though ultimately anchoring their stage presence in their Jewishness. The meanings of such routines as enactments of Americanization were characteristically varied. The acts were sometimes a means of forging a hybrid American identity, born of the urban experience of the Northeast. They were also a means of displacing anxieties about the changing nature of Jewishness itself. In this latter case, one might argue that, by the second decade of the twentieth century, Jewish vaudevillians had begun to perform their own ethnicity on stage. Fanny Brice, for instance, did not know Yiddish when she began her career, but chose to learn it as a way of defining her stage persona. Finally, these routines were a way for Jewish women in particular to engage in the transgressions that such hybridity seemed to require. Baker's modulating impersonations of a sexy Italian woman, a minstrel "coon," a devout Catholic girl, and a Yiddish lover were a means of defining herself as an American Jewish woman, as was Fanny Brice's self-naming "confession" in her hilarious "I'm an Indian."

This struggle over the representation of the Jewish women did not end with the closing of the vaudeville houses in the 1930s. While the actual reign of the Jewish female vaudevillians ended about this time, many of the headliner performers continued to raise these issues in their acts in other venues. They also left a rich and varied legacy, as can be seen in the works of entertainers from Ethel Merman, who began her career at the end of the vaudeville era, to such contemporary figures as BETTE MIDLER. Through them the voices of the Jewish vaudevillians continue to be heard, making their artful claims upon a still heatedly debated identity: the American Jewish woman.

BIBLIOGRAPHY

Allen, Robert C. *Horrible Prettiness: Burlesque and American Culture* (1991); Antelyes, Peter. "Red Hot Mamas: Bessie Smith, Sophie Tucker, and the Ethnic Maternal Voice in American Popular Song." In *Embodied Voices: Representing Female Vocality in Western Culture*, edited by Leslie C. Dunn and Nancy A. Jones (1994); Cohen, Sara Blacher, ed. *From Hester Street to Hollywood: The Jewish-American Stage and Screen* (1986); DiMeglio, Joe. *Vaudeville, U.S.A.* (1973); Erenberg, Lewis. *Stepping Out: New York Nightlife and the Transformation of American Culture, 1890–1930* (1981); Gilbert, Douglas. *American Vaudeville: Its Life and Times* (1940); Grossman, Barbara W. *Funny Woman: The Life and Times of Fanny Brice* (1991); Isman, Felix. *Weber and Fields* (1924); Laurie, Joe, Jr. *Vaudeville: From the Honky-Tonks to the Palace* (1953); Matlaw, Myron, ed. *American Popular Entertainment* (1979); Picon, Molly, with Jean Bergantini Grillo. *Molly!: An Autobiography* (1980); Slide, Anthony. *The Encyclopedia of Vaudeville* (1994); Slide, Anthony, ed. *Selected Vaudeville Criticism* (1988), and *The Vaudevillians: A Dictionary of Vaudeville Performers* (1981); Smith, Bill. *The Vaudevillians* (1976); Snyder, Robert W. *The Voice of the City: Vaudeville and Popular Culture in New York* (1989); Staples, Shirley. *Male-Female Comedy Teams in American Vaudeville, 1865–1932. Theater and Dramatic Studies* 16 (1984); Stein, Charles, ed. *American Vaudeville as Seen by Its Contemporaries* (1984); Tucker, Sophie, with Dorothy Giles. *Some of These Days: The Autobiography of Sophie Tucker* (1945); Wilmeth, Don B. *Variety Entertainment and Outdoor Amusements: A Reference Guide* (1982).

PETER ANTELYES

VOCATIONAL TRAINING SCHOOLS

In the years prior to World War I, few institutions enchanted the members of American Jewry's philanthropic community as much as that "aladdin's lamp" of upward mobility, the vocational training school. Combining education with charity and moral uplift with sociology, the vocational school (also known as the technical, manual, or industrial training school) spread from coast to coast. Beginning in the 1880s and continuing well into the 1930s, exemplars of "beautiful, clean, happy little technical school homes" took root everywhere, from Portland's Industrial Sewing School and Cleveland's Kitchen Garden School to New York's Hebrew Technical School for Girls. "All the tendencies of the age are towards vocational school," exclaimed the *American Hebrew* in 1915, noting how the possibility of making "happy and honored artists and artisans" out of what might otherwise have become "drudges and drones," or worse still prostitutes and misfits, fired the collective imagination of the civic-minded.

For nearly fifty years, these institutions enabled immigrant women and their single daughters to aspire to, and in many instances actually attain, a higher standard of living. Ranging in scale from after-school programs and evening classes to a rigorous, uninterrupted eighteen-month course of study, "trade train-

For nearly fifty years, vocational training schools enabled immigrant women and their single daughters to aspire to, and in many instances actually attain, a higher standard of living. Pictured above is a sewing class in 1892 at the Jewish Manual Training School in Chicago.
[American Jewish Historical Society]

HEBREW TECHNICAL SCHOOL FOR GIRLS

Annual Benefit
New York Theatre
Thursday, December 28, 1911
at 2.15 P. M.

Thanks are given to M. J. Roth, Esq.,
who has printed this Programme
without charge to the School.

The Hebrew Technical School for Girls in New York was a major educational institution, as the size of their building indicates. [Peter Schweitzer]

ing" sought to outfit those women poised to enter the workforce with a set of marketable skills. All too many working girls, observed their great advocate Rose Sommerfeld, director of New York's CLARA DE HIRSCH HOME FOR WORKING GIRLS, are "entirely unfitted to enter the great field of labor." Inexperienced and unskilled, they "drift from one branch of industry to another, incapable of doing anything well." By providing women with a trade, be it dressmaking, millinery, or stenography, Jewish vocational schools sought to prevent "drift" while at the same time raising wages and generating self-reliance and independence. "Our aim," explained the president of New York's Hebrew Technical School for Girls, "is not merely to enable our girls . . . to become self-supporting, but we are constantly trying . . . to dignify them, to refine them, to ennoble them."

At first, institutions like the Hebrew Technical School for Girls concentrated their efforts on encouraging Jewish immigrant women to take up the broom and the dust rag. With cooks, laundresses, and housekeepers in short supply, a career in domestic service,

explained educator JULIA RICHMAN, one of its most ardent champions, was of inestimable utility. It not only provided a secure job but also enabled young immigrant women to acquire "habits of greater refinement and culture. Table manners and personal habits will improve and with their improvement a long stride will have been taken away from the old landmarks of ignorance and vulgarity." More to the point, perhaps, the emphasis placed on domestic service reflected the belief that housekeeping had as much to do with moral order as with physical disorder. "Home is the foundation of society," declared a leading social worker. "We will have better homes when every woman is trained to be a thoroughly competent cook, dressmaker, designer, milliner or whatever it may be, because through this training habits of industry will be developed which will make a finer type of character."

Despite such lofty rhetoric, record numbers of Jewish students turned a deaf ear to claims that domestic service was truly a noble profession. Housework, they insisted, was a "wretched occupation," too low-paying, too onerous and a brake on their independence.

"Did I come to America to make from myself a cook?" a character in ANZIA YEZIERSKA's acclaimed short story "How I Found America—Part Two" exclaims, giving voice to the immigrant Jewish woman's objections to working as a servant, objections widely noted both within and without the philanthropic world. "Almost without exception, [they] prefer the hard work combined with the freedom of the factory, to the easy toil of domestic service, which deprives them of liberty," editorialized the *American Hebrew*, its sympathies more with the servantless mistress than with the working girl.

Like the newspaper, the philanthropic community appeared vexed, even irritated, by the lack of enthusiasm displayed by working girls for domestic service, which they interpreted as a show of arrogance and (unseemly) ambition. In time, however, its members conceded that their attempts to promote domestic service had completely failed. Many went a step farther, agreeing with SADIE AMERICAN who, in 1911, wrote: "We can no more in these days undertake to make girls into servants because they are poor than we can undertake to make girls into beauties if the Lord has not built them that way. We have got to wake up to this."

Eventually, social workers and educators did just that, abandoning their commitment to domestic service. What they did not abandon, however, was their fidelity to gendered notions of work or, as MINNIE

LOUIS, the founder of the Hebrew Technical School for Girls, would have it, the "effeminate employments." Hailing the needle as "woman's industrial sceptre," Louis and her colleagues enthusiastically promoted sewing, dressmaking, and millinery as appropriate forms of female employment. As office work became increasingly respectable, even glamorous, instruction in stenography, bookkeeping, and the newfangled skill of typewriting was added to the curriculum.

In later years, beauty culture, yet another example of "effeminate employment," was enthusiastically promoted as well. A growth industry in America of the 1920s, beauty culture, explained Samuel Turchin in his textbook *Barbering and Beauty Culture*, "is an occupation in which a trained person dresses the hair, manicures the fingernails, pedicures the toenails, and beautifies the face by mean of cosmetics. . . . A person in this occupation," he went on to explain, "is often termed a hairdresser, dermatician or cosmetologist. However, the term most acceptable . . . is a beautician." By whatever name, beauty culture took hold in the classroom. Drafting tables made way for emery boards as students were now encouraged to meet the "growing demands of beautification" by studying its secrets.

For all their concern with the workplace, Jewish vocational schools firmly believed that working women ought not to be "mere adjuncts of machinery" but ladies who worked or, as the president of one such school put it, "wage-earners with an appetite—indeed a hunger—for intellectual advancement." To whet that appetite and, in the process, to "implant in the character all the elements that go to make up the perfect woman," students were taught penmanship and "personality," music, geography, hygiene, and "house-wifely wisdom." They were also actively encouraged to get out from behind the workbench and the desk to experience the finer things in life: Trips or self-styled "pilgrimages" to museums and concerts, day-long outings to the country, and opportunities to "meet and mingle with those more favored" filled the days of the female Jewish vocational student.

An estimable success, the Jewish vocational training movement quickly took hold. "What a boon!" exclaimed one observer as early as 1907, noting its contribution to America's urban economy. Hundreds of girls "annually to enter [the] labyrinths of labor bringing the standard of ability, purity and aspiring womanhood." Louis couldn't agree more. "Already is the change fast coming," she related. "Dainty, alert, intelligent, earnest Jewesses sit at the bookkeeper's desk and at the typewriter's machine." Well trained

We don't know what the students in this class at one of Chicago's Jewish training schools studied, but they clearly enjoyed themselves when it came time for the class photograph to be taken. [Chicago Historical Society]

and well mannered, her students and those of sister institutions had little trouble securing positions and were often sought by manufacturers. "When I finished my education," recalled one alumna of the Hebrew Technical School for Girls, "I got a job. Very easily, because people used to call up Hebrew Tech to ask for their girls, because they knew how bright we were."

Still, the enterprise was not without its critics. Some, like HENRIETTA SZOLD, writing in 1903, wondered why practical skills were taught at the expense of Jewish cultural literacy. The "salvation of Jewish girls as Jewesses and, for the present at least, as fine specimens of womanhood, depends upon a proper alignment of their Jewish education with their secular education," she counseled, but to little avail. A generation later, officials of New York's Federation of Jewish Philanthropies, investigating conditions at the Hebrew Technical School for Girls, put forth much the same claim. "It seems strange," they declared, "that a school that recruits its student body exclusively from Jewish homes should do absolutely nothing to acquaint these girls with the basic tenets of Jewish faith and with the most dramatic incidents and characters of the Old Testament and of Jewish history." Still other critics, like the redoubtable Sadie American, questioned both the meaning and the efficacy of thinking about work in rigidly gendered terms. "But all girls no more like to sew and are no more fitted to sew than boys like to be sailors. It is a curious thing," she added, "that the world has classified all women together, not realizing that they [are] made differently just as men are."

Ahead of her time, Sadie American would ultimately be proved right. By the 1940s, increasing numbers of American Jewish women, many the daughters of vocational school alumnae, set their sights on higher education. Enrolling in college rather than a technical school, a new generation of Jewish women began to expand its horizons. Concomitantly, the world of the Jewish technical school began to contract. Meanwhile, increased competition from the public sector, which, by the 1920s, had actively committed itself to building a network of vocational high schools, exacerbated matters, forcing many private Jewish facilities to acknowledge that they had "outlived their usefulness."

In the end, the Jewish vocational movement was a victim of its own success. Enabling thousands of "aspiring" women to make good, it placed within reach the promise of America.

BIBLIOGRAPHY

Annual Report, Hebrew Technical School for Girls, 1900–1919; Joselit, Jenna Weissman. *Aspiring Women: A History of the Jewish Foundation for Education of Women* (1996); Richman, Julia. "Women Wage Earners." *Papers of the Jewish Women's Congress* (1894); Szold, Henrietta. "The Education of the Jewish Girl." *The Maccabaean* 5, no 1 (July 1903): 8–10.

JENNA WEISSMAN JOSELIT

VON MISES, HILDA GEIRINGER
see GEIRINGER, HILDA

W

WAELSCH, SALOME GLUECKSOHN (b. 1907)

How does the fertilized egg generate the entire mammalian body with its hundreds of cell types arranged in an orderly fashion? Until the 1930s, there were two distinct disciplines studying this question. Genetics focused on the inherited genes whose mutations caused variations in adults. Embryology stressed the changing populations of cells that interacted with each other to form the mammalian body. Salome Gluecksohn Waelsch combined these two sciences to form a new discipline, developmental genetics, a science that investigates the genetic mechanisms of development. For over sixty years, Waelsch has made fundamental discoveries in mammalian development and cancer research. In 1993, she received the National Medal of Science from President Bill Clinton.

Salome Gluecksohn Waelsch overcame numerous obstacles in becoming a scientist. Born in Danzig Germany, on October 6, 1907, to Ilyia and Nadia Gluecksohn, she lost her father during the influenza epidemic of 1918. The family's wealth disappeared in the inflation following World War I, and as a young girl she had to endure anti-Semitic taunts from her schoolmates.

Salome had originally intended to pursue the classics, but as a socialist Zionist she switched to biology, a discipline she thought would be more practical in Palestine. She received her Ph.D. in 1932 from the laboratory of Hans Spemann, the embryologist who would receive the Nobel Prize three years later. Despite being so well trained, there was no place in German (or any other) biology for a person of her gender and religion. "You—a woman and a Jew—forget it," said one potential employer. She was able to obtain employment as a research assistant at the University of Berlin, and there she met an eminent young biochemist, Rudolf Schoenheimer, whom she married that year.

In 1933, the couple fled Hitler's Germany to come to Columbia University, where Rudolf Schoenheimer had found a position. Because Columbia University's policies would not allow Salome a faculty position, she worked first as an unpaid laboratory assistant to Samuel R. Detwiler, a developmental neurobiologist, and then with Leslie C. Dunn on a project that would combine her new knowledge of genetics with her training in embryology. In 1938, she published her first paper on the genes involved in forming the mouse embryo.

Waelsch still could not get a faculty appointment at Columbia University. In 1955, however, Ernst and Berta Scharrer were recruiting for the newly formed Albert Einstein College of Medicine, and Waelsch found a place where competent Jewish women were welcome. By 1958, she had become a full professor, and in 1963 she became chair of the genetics department. Although retiring officially in 1978, she continues working in her laboratory. Above her desk are photographs of Albert Einstein and LILLIAN HELLMAN. In 1979, Waelsch was elected to the National Academy of Science, and in 1982 she was awarded a gold diploma from her alma mater, the University of Freiburg in Germany. Memories of the Holocaust caused her to decline this latter award.

Rudolf Schoenheimer died in 1941, a suicide. Waelsch married Heinrich Waelsch, a biochemist, in 1943. They had two children, Naomi and Peter. Heinrich Waelsch died in 1966. Salome Gluecksohn Waelsch remains a vital force in developmental biology and serves as a model for Jews and non-Jews, men and women, who wish to combine excellent science with freedom of the spirit, humor, and family.

SELECTED WORKS BY SALOME GLUECKSOHN WAELSCH

"The Causal Analysis of Development in the Past Half Century: A Personal History." *Gastrulation*, edited by Claudio Stern and Phil Ingham (1992); "The Development of Two Tailless Mutants in the House Mouse." *Genetics 23* (1938): 573–584.

BIBLIOGRAPHY

Deichmann, Ute. "Gluecksohn-Waelsch, Salome." In *Jüdische Frauen im 19. und 20. Jahrhundert: Lexikon zu Leben und Werk*, edited by Jutta Dick and Marina Sassenberg (1993); Gilbert, Scott F. "Induction and the Origins of Developmental Genetics." In *A Conceptual History of Modern Embryology*, edited by Scott F. Gilbert (1991); Newton, David E. "Salome Waelsch." In *Notable-Twentieth Century Scientists*, edited by Emily J. McMurray (1995); Talan, Jamie. "The Mouse Lady: 60 Years of Genes." *Newsday*, September 30, 1993; Voss, Julianne. "Salome Glueckson Waelsch." Available from http://web.mit.edu.afs.athena.mit.edu/org/w/womens-studies/www/dev-bio/waelsch3.html; Zuckerman, Harriet, Jonathan Cole, and John T. Bruer, eds. "Interview with Salome Waelsch." *The Outer Circle: Women in the Scientific Community* (1991).

SCOTT F. GILBERT

WALD, LILLIAN D. (1867–1940)

In 1934, one year after she retired from her position as headworker of Henry Street Settlement House on New York's Lower East Side, Lillian D. Wald recalled the lesson of her years there. "We have found," she wrote, "that the things which make men alike are finer and stronger than the things which make them different, and that the vision which long since proclaimed the interdependence and the kinship of mankind was farsighted and is true."

Wald began her voyage toward this vision in 1893, when she discovered the need for health care among New York's largely Jewish immigrant population. Her solution to this problem, in the form of public health nursing, served only as the foundation of her life's work, which spanned local, national, and international efforts to bring health care and, on a broader scale, social justice to people throughout her ever-expanding "neighborhood." Wald's dedication to the causes of nursing, unionism, tenement reform, woman suffrage, child welfare, and antimilitarism demonstrated her strong progressive faith in the ability of democratic institutions to realize the vision of a unified humanity.

Lillian D. Wald was born on March 10, 1867, in Cincinnati, Ohio, the second daughter and third of four children of Max D. Wald and Minnie Schwarz Wald. The Walds and Schwarzes descended from rabbis and merchants in Germany and Poland, both families having left Europe after the Revolutions of 1848 to seek economic opportunity. Max Wald prospered as a successful optical goods dealer, first in Cincinnati, then in Dayton, and finally in 1878, settling in Rochester, New York, which Lillian Wald considered her hometown. Wald recalled her mother, who married at sixteen, as friendly, warm, and kind; Max Wald was distant, practical, and quiet. The family home overflowed with books and music, and Wald recalled fondly the indulgence of her Grandfather Schwarz, himself a successful merchant, who told her stories and often brought the children presents. Though the Walds were members of Rochester's Reform Temple Berith Kodesh, Lillian Wald received no Jewish education and was raised in a liberal Jewish atmosphere.

Wald received her education at Miss Cruttenden's English-French Boarding and Day School in Rochester. Demonstrating great skills in languages, the arts, math, and science, she applied to Vassar College at age sixteen but was refused because of her age. Wald continued in her studies and led an active social life until she felt the need for more serious work. In 1889, she enrolled in the nursing program of the New York Hospital training school. Upon her graduation two years later, she worked for a year as a nurse at the New York Juvenile Asylum but eventually left institutional nursing to become a doctor. Shortly after she began taking courses at the Women's Medical College in New York, she accepted an invitation to organize classes in home nursing for immigrant families on the Lower East Side.

Wald experienced a "baptism of fire" into reform work during one of her classes, when a child led her to a sick woman in a dilapidated tenement. She saw "all the maladjustments of our social and economic relations epitomized in this brief journey," and she became intent on her own "responsibility" to bring affordable health care to those on the Lower East Side. She left medical school and, with her friend and colleague Mary Brewster, moved to the College Settlement House on Rivington Street and then to a tenement house on Jefferson Street. In 1895, Wald took up residence at 265 Henry Street where she founded the Nurses' Settlement.

Making health care her first priority, Wald pioneered public health nursing—and coined the name of the profession—with the idea that the nurse's "organic relationship with the neighborhood should constitute the starting point for a universal service to the region." The nurses operated on a sliding fee scale, so that all city residents might have access to medical attention. Nurses responded to calls from physicians, charitable agencies, and individuals in need. They kept daily records and offered educational classes. In 1905 alone, Henry Street nurses had eighteen district centers and cared for forty-five hundred patients. Wald also worked to extend the services of public health nurses. In 1902, she initiated the first American public school nursing program in New York City. In response to her idea, in 1909, Metropolitan Life Insurance Company began a nursing service for its industrial policyholders; other insurance companies soon followed that example. In 1910, as a result of a series of nursing lectures she organized, Teachers College of Columbia University established a department of nursing and health. The National Organization for Public Health Nursing, an association for a profession she herself had founded, chose Wald as its first president in 1912.

Though she was not familiar with the work of Jane Addams when she moved to the Lower East Side, Wald led the Nurses' Settlement in the direction of a full-fledged settlement house—eventually changing the name to Henry Street Settlement—as she saw the social causes of poverty in the neighborhood. She supplemented the nursing service with programs for neighborhood improvement. Working with members of the neighborhood, the house residents organized girls' and boys' clubs as well as classes in arts and crafts, English, homemaking, and drama; they held social events; and rented out the newly built Clinton Hall for union meetings. The house provided vocational guidance and training, and Wald established a scholarship to allow talented boys and girls to remain in school until age sixteen. She spearheaded campaigns for playgrounds and parks, better housing, and to eliminate tuberculosis, called the "tailors' disease" for its preponderance among Jewish immigrants, many of whom were garment workers.

Lillian Wald's life's work encompassed local, national, and international efforts to bring health care and social justice to the people of her ever-expanding "neighborhood." She virtually created the profession of public health nurse, founded the Henry Street Settlement, cofounded the National Child Labor Committee, and campaigned fiercely for both peace and woman suffrage. [Library of Congress]

Wald's work with Eastern European Jewish immigrants appealed to the benevolence of New York's German Jewish elite. Betty Loeb, who had funded the East Side nursing classes, and her son-in-law Jacob Henry Schiff, banker and philanthropist, provided Wald with the funds to move into 265 Henry Street. Many of New York's prominent German Jewish families were benefactors of Henry Street, which relied on voluntary contributions for support.

While Henry Street was strictly nonsectarian, Wald saw her settlement work as suffused with spirituality, a "new impulse to an old gospel." As a member of Felix Adler's Ethical Culture Society, she subscribed to the idea of an evolution of organized religion to a code of ethical precepts. She saw her work as part of this gradual evolution in its strivings toward good will and humanitarianism. She expressed no particular religious connection between herself and the Jewish immigrants with whom she worked, but she embraced the contributions all immigrants made to society. Wald spoke out against Americanization programs that demanded the shedding of native cultures. She considered the newcomers' traditions, art, and ideas "new life and new blood for America." Wald came to see her primary task as that of an interpreter: In the movement toward "the fundamental oneness of humanity," the settlement bridged boundaries of ethnicity, race, class, and immigrant generations.

Wald served as an advocate for her neighbors, speaking with the authority of one with "long and intimate acquaintance" with immigrants. In public and private correspondence, she upheld the immigrants' rights to free speech and spoke of immigrant radicalism as another instance of their "passion for progress and justice." Wald defended the character of the new immigrants and asked the mainly German Jewish upper-class audience to consider their own responsibility toward the swelling urban populations at the first convention of the NATIONAL COUNCIL OF JEWISH WOMEN in 1896. "If there is a strike," she urged, "try to discover both sides of the question . . . not rejoicing in the workingman's failure without understanding what was behind the discontent."

Wald dedicated much of her time and energy to serving her neighbors' interests through public institutions. With the approval of New York's peddlers, who considered her their representative, she served on the Mayor's Pushcart Commission in 1906. In 1908, she worked on the New York Commission on Immigration, which Governor Charles Evans Hughes formed upon her recommendation to investigate the living and working conditions of New York's immigrants. The commission's report led to the creation of the State Bureau of Industries and Immigration. The next year, Wald worked with Mary Ovington, Florence Kelley, Henry Moskowitz, and others to found the National Association for the Advancement of Colored People, offering up Henry Street for the organizing conference. During the garment strikes of 1910 to 1912, she worked alongside Schiff, Adler, Moskowitz, Louis Brandeis, and Morris Hillquit in arbitration efforts. In 1912, she served as one of three "representatives of the public" on the Joint Board of Sanitary Control of the Cloak, Suit, and Skirt Industry. The board's report called for fire safety and sanitation measures, as well as protective legislation for pregnant workers.

Wald often focused her political energies on the interests of children and working women. In 1903,

she supported organizing the National Women's Trade Union League. A lifelong member of the New York Child Labor Committee, Wald, together with Adler, Kelley, and others, founded the National Child Labor Committee in 1904 to fight against child labor. Wald originated the idea for a national Children's Bureau within the Department of Labor and worked unceasingly for its creation from 1906 until 1912. She turned down President Taft's offer to be bureau chief in 1912, believing herself more useful at Henry Street. Though not a militant suffragist, Wald believed women had a "special contribution to make" to government as coordinators of "that portion of the political life that is related to human happiness"—the home and family. As honorary vice-chair of the New York State Woman Suffrage Party, she campaigned for the woman suffrage referendum in 1915, citing in editorials the overwhelming support among her working-class immigrant neighbors for the right to vote.

Wald feared the increasing nationalism and anti-foreigner sentiment that accompanied the campaign for American entry into World War I. She viewed war as opposed to her vision of a unified humanity. As president of the American Union Against Militarism, she, along with Kelley, Addams, Amos Pinchot, Max Eastman, and others, lobbied the Wilson administration toward mediation and away from active involvement. She held fast to her pacifism even when some contributors to Henry Street protested her platform and withdrew support. After the United States entered the war, she fought against abridgments of civil liberties, especially those of immigrants during wartime. She served as chair of the committee on home nursing of the Council of National Defense and headed the Red Cross Nurses Emergency Council, formed in response to the 1918 influenza epidemic. Under her direction, Henry Street cleared all cases of influenza and mobilized the efforts of thousands of volunteers.

Wald's political activities continued after the war. Her work with the American Union Against Militarism led her to contribute to the founding of the League of Free Nations Association, a forerunner of the Foreign Policy Association. She remained loyal to the Democratic Party's progressive vision, though in 1912 Wilson's refusal to support woman suffrage, and Wald's belief that Progressive Party membership exacted "too great a price," led her to reject both platforms. Wald supported Alfred E. Smith throughout his career—despite his opposition to Prohibition—as someone whose stand on social issues approached her own. She was friends with Eleanor Roosevelt and was enthusiastic about Franklin Roosevelt's policies and his administrative appointments of many former

Henry Street residents, including Adolph A. Berle, Jr., Frances Perkins, Henry W. Morgenthau, Jr., and Sidney Hillman. She believed that the ideas formulated experientially at Henry Street were being put to use in government. In 1936, in her final major involvement in an election, Wald cochaired the Good Neighbor League, which attracted independents to the Democratic ticket.

By 1936, periodic heart trouble and chronic anemia began to take their toll on Wald's health. Her travels, which had included a world tour in 1910, a trip to discuss public health measures in Russia in 1924, and a vacation with Jane Addams in 1925, grew less frequent. In 1933, she resigned as headworker of Henry Street Settlement and retired to her house-on-the-pond in Westport, Connecticut. There, in 1934, she wrote the second of her two books—the first was an anecdotal autobiography, *The House on Henry Street* (1915)—a collection of her thoughts on her life experiences titled *Windows on Henry Street.* In 1936, she voiced her opinions on the growing anti-Semitism in Europe, stating that "wrong inflicted upon any one is a wrong done to all," and reasserting her optimism that "common interests" would triumph over ignorance and hatred.

Wald's work has been memorialized throughout the twentieth century. She was chosen as honorary chair or adviser to nearly thirty state and national public health and social welfare organizations and won the gold medal of the National Institute of Social Sciences in 1912. To honor her role in founding the public health nursing profession, both Mount Holyoke College and Smith College granted her honorary doctorates in law. On her seventieth birthday, in 1937, a public gathering was held in her honor: Laudatory words from President Roosevelt and Governor Lehman were read, and Mayor LaGuardia granted her the city's distinguished service certificate.

Lillian Wald died in Westport on September 1, 1940, at age seventy-three, after a long illness brought on by a cerebral hemorrhage. She was buried in Rochester, New York.

Wald's compassion and good humor drew admirers and supporters from individuals in the many circles in which she traveled. Her confidence, administrative talent, and understanding of the social causes of poverty, together with her membership in the neighborhood she had chosen to join, inspired her to link efforts with her network of women and work toward a vision of a unified humanity. Public figures continue to memorialize Wald and her work. In late 1940, hundreds of her friends gathered in Carnegie Hall to honor her memory. In 1965, she was elected to the Hall of Fame of Great Americans at New York University. In 1993, she was inducted into the National Women's Hall of Fame in Seneca Falls, New York. Wald's vision of a universal "brotherhood of man"—applicable to all peoples, of all backgrounds—allowed her to assume greatness among a generation of Progressive Era figures in the fields of public health nursing, settlement work, and social reform.

Her greatest living memorial—Henry Street Settlement—still stands on New York's Lower East Side in its three original buildings. Now serving the neighborhood's largely Asian, African-American, and Latino population, the settlement continues Wald's pathbreaking work with Jewish immigrants in the 1890s, working toward the realization of her vision of social justice and a unified humanity.

SELECTED WORKS BY LILLIAN D. WALD

House on Henry Street (1915); Windows on Henry Street (1934).

BIBLIOGRAPHY

AJYB 7 (1905–1906): 111, 24:211, 43:365; *BEOAJ*; Cook, Blanche Wiesen. "Female Support Networks and Political Activism: Lillian Wald, Crystal Eastman, Emma Goldman." *Chrysalis* 3 (Autumn 1977); Coss, Clare, ed. *Lillian D. Wald: Progressive Activist* (1989); *DAB* 2; Daniels, Doris Groshen. *Always a Sister: The Feminism of Lillian D. Wald* (1989); Davis, Allen F. *Spearheads for Reform: The Social Settlements and the Progressive Movement, 1890–1914* (1967); Duffus, R.L. *Lillian Wald: Neighbor and Crusader* (1938); *EJ*; Langemann, Ellen Condliffe. A *Generation of Women: Education in the Lives of Progressive Reformers* (1979); *NAW*; Obituary. *NYTimes*, September 2, 1940, 15:1; Resnick, Allan Edward. "Lillian Wald: The Years at Henry Street." Ph.D. diss., University of Wisconsin at Madison (1973); Siegel, Beatrice. *Lillian Wald of Henry Street* (1983); *UJE*; Wald, Lillian. Papers. Butler University Library, Indianapolis, Ind., and Rare Books and Manuscripts Division, Columbia University Library, NYC; *WWWIA* 1; *WWIAJ* (1926, 1928, 1938).

MARJORIE N. FELD

WALDBAUM, JULIA (1897–1996)

Julia Waldbaum was a philanthropist and businesswoman. In every context, whether personal, professional, or philanthropic, she had a gift for making each individual with whom she came in contact feel special.

She was born in Manhattan on July 4, 1897, to Harry and Anna Leffel. She was the second of three daughters and the third of six children. She grew up in the Bedford-Stuyvesant section of Brooklyn.

At twenty-one, she married Israel (Izzy) Waldbaum, an Austrian immigrant seven years her senior who owned the local butter and egg store. The marriage, which produced three children—Shirley, Phyllis, and Ira—lasted until Israel's death at age fifty-five in 1947.

By that time, the family had a chain of seven stores, and the "personal touch," which Julia Waldbaum brought to every aspect of life, including the marketing of groceries, was evident. The expanding chain of stores had over four hundred products bearing its private label by the 1960s, and Waldbaum's picture—with recipes she tested at home—appeared on virtually all those labels except, as she once joked to a reporter, "the dog food and the bathroom tissue."

In 1986, gross revenues of $1.37 billion a year from 140 stores in New York, Connecticut, and Massachusetts made the chain an attractive acquisition for the Great Atlantic and Pacific Tea Company, which purchased most of the family stock. Even after transferring control, however, Waldbaum still made some thirty surprise visits to Waldbaum's stores every month. She was concerned with quality, cleanliness, and service, and her pet peeves included bruised fruit and dusty shelves. Checkout clerks who could not be bothered to thank patrons for their business particularly drew her ire.

That attention to detail led Waldbaum to insist upon keeping her home telephone number in the directory for years after her family wanted her to get an unlisted number. She explained that customers should be able to reach her so that they would not think that "Mrs. Waldbaum [was] an imaginary person like Betty Crocker."

Although raised in an Orthodox household, Waldbaum became a Reform Jew in later life. Her profound commitment to the Jewish principle of *tzedaka* [righteous works] was expressed both through personal and monetary participation in a vast and ecumenical array of philanthropies as diverse as foster homes and opera companies. She was also the honoree at numerous fund-raising dinners given by charities ranging from the Anti-Defamation League to Brooklyn's Catholic Charities. On those occasions, Waldbaum greeted every subscriber personally and attendance often broke records.

Despite a calendar crowded with work and philanthropic obligations, Julia Waldbaum always made time for her family. She shared with a son-in-law the upbringing of three of her grandchildren after the untimely death of her daughter Phyllis left them motherless. Frequent Friday dinners at Waldbaum's home were a time for all the extended family to gather and recount the events of the week.

In her ninety-ninth year, Julia Waldbaum died in her sleep on September 30, 1996, at her home in Queens, New York City. She was survived by two siblings, two children, ten grandchildren and twenty-four great-grandchildren.

BIBLIOGRAPHY
Malinsky, Randie [granddaughter]. Telephone interview by author, 1996; Obituary. *NYTimes*, October 3, 1996; Waldbaum, Nancy [granddaughter]. Telephone interview by author, 1996.

NAOMI GESCHWIND

WALLING, ANNA STRUNSKY (1879–1964)

Anna Strunsky Walling, author, lecturer, and socialist activist, was born in Russia on March 21, 1879. The family fled Europe in 1893, so that Anna's three older brothers would not be forced into Russian military service. Impoverished, Anna's father Elias and mother Anna (Horowitz) Strunsky, daughter of Rabbi Lasser Horowitz, first settled for a few years in New York. They relocated to San Francisco when Anna was fourteen years old. Elias supported the family with his liquor business and placed a heavy emphasis on his children's education.

During her last year in high school, fifteen-year-old Anna joined the American branch of the Socialist Labor Party (SLP). Reminiscing in a 1960 taped interview, she recalled the older members of the SLP thinking she was a bit young to become a socialist. She told them: "You are born a socialist. You are born with music, or poetry or painting or science. You can't really become a socialist unless you're born that way." But she also attributed her early socialist ideas to the personal suffering her family had endured in Europe.

In December 1899, at an SLP celebration of the Paris Commune, Anna, then attending Stanford University, met the young writer Jack London. They spent a great deal of time together discussing social and political issues, and they were part of a wider group of San Francisco intellectuals known as "The Crowd." Although at times it appeared Anna and Jack's friendship might blossom into marriage, London surprised Anna by marrying Bess Maddern.

Anna graduated from Stanford in 1900. Three years later, she and London published a collaborative project anonymously—a novel in the form of letters, *The Kempton-Wace Letters* (1903). The book is devoted to a debate on the nature of love in which the woman correspondent, Dane Kempton, defines the ideals of love as romantic, while the man, Herbert Wace, contends love is essentially biological.

Between 1900 and 1905, she traveled to New York and England, attempted to write another novel, *Windlestraws*, and gave public lectures on Russian subjects. In 1905, she helped establish the group Friends of Russian Freedom in San Francisco. Just before the outbreak of the 1905 Russian Revolution, she traveled by herself to Vilna, Minsk, and Hommel. After visiting Hommel, she published an article of an interview she had held with General Orlov, who had recently perpetrated a pogrom against Jews in that city.

During this stay in Russia, she became engaged to William English Walling, an American socialist and labor leader. Walling's maternal grandfather, William Hayden English, had been the Democratic vice presidential candidate in 1880 and an uncle served in Congress. His father, Willoughby Walling, a physician, had amassed a fortune in real estate, and his mother, Rosalind English Walling, was a member of the Daughters of the American Revolution. Although neither the Strunsky nor the Walling family was happy about the match because of religious and social differences, they were married in Paris in 1906, with Anna's sister Rose and Jean Lonquet, Karl Marx's grandson, as witnesses to a civil ceremony. Anna's first child, born in 1908, died when only five days old. The following year she had a miscarriage. Between 1910 and 1918, Anna Walling gave birth to four children, Rosamond, Anna, Georgia, and William Hayden English.

In 1915, her novel *Violette of Père Lachaise*, which she had started ten years earlier, was published. It is the story of a young flower seller who becomes an actress involved in social revolution.

Walling's political involvement in the socialist movement, her career in journalism, and her creative writing were curtailed by her household duties and the raising of her children. Meanwhile, her marriage began to falter. With the advent of World War I, Anna and William Walling developed seemingly irreconcilable political differences. While she concurred with the American Socialist Party's view of the war, he broke with the party. While she was enthusiastic about the Russian revolution, he was highly critical of the Bolsheviks. By the 1920s, the couple were also having serious financial problems. In 1932, William filed for a Mexican divorce, but Anna refused to recognize the end of the marriage. William Walling died in Amsterdam in 1936.

During the last thirty years of her life, Anna Walling helped edit a memorial volume on her husband; she wrote memoirs about the Jack London years; she participated in Quaker social actions and followed the activities of the War Resisters League, the League for Mutual Aid, the American League to Abolish Capital Punishment, the League for Industrial Democracy, and the National Association for the Advancement of Colored People, which she and her husband had helped found. Her sense of respect for the socialist movement and its significance motivated her to preserve her own and her husband's extensive correspondences with family, with friends, and with the wide array of important political and cultural people who had enriched their lives.

Anna Strunsky Walling died in February 1964.

BIBLIOGRAPHY

AJYB 6 (1905–1905): 199, 24: 211; Kaplan, Diane, John Espy, and Jon Waldner. "Finding Aid" to the Anna Strunsky Walling Papers. Manuscripts and Archives, Yale University Library, New Haven, Conn.; Obituary. *NYTimes*, February 26, 1964, 35:4; Walling, Anna Strunsky. Interview, June 6, 1960. Oral History of the Left, Tamiment Library, New York University, and Papers. Bancroft Library, University of California, Berkeley, and Huntington Library, Pasadena, Calif; *WWIAJ* (1928, 1938); *WWWIA* 4.

NORMA FAIN PRATT

WALTERS, BARBARA (b. 1931)

"She is like the autumn cherry tree," said *Time* magazine in 1995, "in full flower." When a hard-edged news magazine waxes this lyrical about a woman, one would expect her to be a movie star. In this case, the object of the admiration is a journalist with a reputation for integrity, professionalism, and, at times, unscrupulous competitiveness. But then, Barbara Walters has always elicited extreme responses.

Barbara Walters was born on September 25, 1931, in Boston and grew up in Boston, Miami, and New York City. Her father, Lew Walters, was a well-known nightclub owner whose life was filled with celebrities, excitement, and financial success. Barbara attended both public and private schools before attending Sarah Lawrence College, from which she graduated in 1953. "Until I was about 23 or 24," she told interviewer Tabitha Soren in 1996, "we were very rich. I can go around New York and show you all the penthouses we lived in. And then in my later 20s it was all gone." From that point on, Walters focused on supporting herself and helping to take care of her family.

Walters worked briefly for a New York advertising agency before taking her first position in television. She began not as a broadcaster but as assistant to the publicity director for the NBC-affiliated television

In 1976, Barbara Walters became the first woman to cohost a network news show—the ABC Evening News. *Her million-dollar-a-year salary and five-year contract made her the highest-paid journalist, male or female, in history. She is shown here speaking at the "Women of the Year" award ceremony at Lincoln Center, New York City, on April 8, 1976.* [Bettye Lane]

station in New York City. She was soon the youngest person ever to become a producer at the station. After going from there to another local station, she joined the CBS network staff as a news and public affairs producer and as a writer.

Walters took a break from television to work for a theatrical public relations firm, but she was back in broadcasting by 1961. Working as a writer for NBC's successful morning show *Today*, she began for the first time to make occasional appearances on the air. These feature-story appearances led to an opportunity to try out as the "Today Girl." Walters took the role of the pretty, smiling small-talker and turned it into an essential part of the program. Before long she was reading news and acting as a commentator. She also worked in the field, going in 1972 to China as part of the NBC News team covering President Richard Nixon's historic visit.

It was at *Today* that Walters began doing interviews, an area of broadcasting that would become her specialty. Her interviews with such eminent figures as GOLDA MEIR, Robert Kennedy, and Coretta Scott King led to a reputation as a serious interviewer of serious people.

Walters's professionalism—along with her remarkable intelligence and presence—elicited a powerful response from audiences. In 1974, she became the show's cohost, working beside veteran Hugh Downs. In 1975, she won an Emmy for her work on the show. She also acquired her own syndicated talk show, *Not for Women Only*. This spectacular rise peaked in 1976 when she became the first woman to cohost a new network show—the *ABC Evening News*. So convinced were they that Walters was the woman for the job, the network offered her a record-breaking million-dollar annual salary and a five-year contract. It made her the highest-paid journalist, male or female, up to that time. That fact was trumpeted in the press, and Walters was suddenly a bigger celebrity than many of the people she interviewed.

This particular triumph, however, did not last. Her cohost, Harry Reasoner, did not cooperate. "Harry did not want a partner," Walters says. "It was very painful. Definitely the worst year of my life." Only a year and a half after she took the job, she was out of the anchor desk—but not off the air. The highest-paid journalist in history fulfilled her contract with ABC by producing her own television specials.

Under attack in the press as a five-million-dollar bomb, Walters suffered considerable anguish, but the disaster led to even greater success. Her interviewing skills made *The Barbara Walters Specials* legendary. According to broadcaster Mike Wallace, a friend and rival, "She's the best damn interviewer in the business. It's taken all this time to perfect her craft, and she never stopped working at it. Everything she has invested—the phone calls, the contacts, the letters, the knowledge—has paid off. For a long time, people didn't understand what a good journalist she is."

Walters herself had doubts after the conflict with Reasoner, and her work in the 1970s reflected it. "There was a long time when I was working my way back from the tough times in the '70s and I felt I had to prove myself journalistically." During that time Walters developed a reputation for stealing interviews and fawning over celebrities. Certainly she has been intensely competitive. Once, Diane Sawyer was set to interview Katharine Hepburn when Walters reportedly called to say, "Strike the lights, turn off the cameras. I'll be right there to do it myself." It is impossible to say, however, how much of the resentment was due to Walters's personality or to her success.

In any case, Walters earned the respect of those celebrities and political figures everyone in journalism wanted to interview. She was able to obtain one exclusive interview after another. Princess Grace of Monaco agreed to talk to Walters, as did Henry Kissinger. She conversed on the air with Prince Philip, Fred Astaire, and Mamie Eisenhower. She has interviewed every president since Richard Nixon and every first lady since Lady Bird Johnson. In 1977, she arranged the first joint interviews with President Anwar Sadat of Egypt and Prime Minister Menachem Begin of Israel. She also interviewed President Fidel Castro of Cuba.

In 1982 and 1983, Walters won Emmy awards for her interviewing. In 1984, she was back on a regularly scheduled show. With old friend and cohost Hugh Downs, she helped to develop one of the first, and still one of the best, investigative news shows, *20/20*.

Personally, Walters has sometimes suffered for her success. After two divorces and an annulment, she is now happily unmarried. Her relationship with daughter, Jacqueline Guber, has survived many difficult and painful times. She reminded *USA Weekend* interviewer Tabitha Soren that the world was very different when her daughter was growing up. "There were women leaving their husbands and children because they had to fulfill themselves. It's no longer like that. Joan Lunden or Katie Couric can bring her kids to work. [If I'd brought my baby] into the studios, people would have looked at me like I was bringing in a puppy that wasn't housebroken."

Walters has collected virtually all of the broadcasting industry's highest awards. In 1988, she was honored with the President's Award by the Overseas Press Club and was given a retrospective at the Museum of Broadcasting. In 1990, she was inducted into the Television Arts and Sciences Hall of Fame and received the Lowell Thomas Award for journalistic excellence. In 1991, the International Women's Media Foundation granted her their lifetime achievement award.

In 1994, Walters made the news when another ABC broadcaster, Diane Sawyer, was offered a contract worth an extraordinary $7 million a year. As always, Walters was the standard against which any woman journalist was measured. The press immediately reported that Walters made $10 million, but that the production costs of her specials cut into that figure. Her agent was soon renegotiating her contract.

In recent years, Walters has helped to keep *20/20* at the top of the newsmagazine shows, in spite of the proliferation of rivals. She has won acclaim for her interviews of General Colin Powell and actor/director Christopher Reeve. Hugh Downs explains her success this way: "Barbara has operated on the premise that her first allegiance is to the person tuning in. She represents the viewer and does it without hostility." From someone who has himself mastered the art of nonconfrontational interviewing, that is praise indeed. And according to *Time*, Walters often elicits praise from the specialists. "Walters is a terrific editor, say her editors. She is a great writer, say her writers. She is her own best booker, say her producers. She is her own best publicist, say her publicists. She works us hard, but she works harder than we do, they say."

BIBLIOGRAPHY

"Barbara Walters." *Her Heritage: A Biographical Encyclopedia of Famous American Women* (1995); "Barbara Walters Talks Back." *USA Weekend;* "The Big Time! 8 Who Got Where Only Men Got Before." *Cosmopolitan;* "Singing Walters' Praises." *USA Today.*

KATHLEEN THOMPSON

WARBURG, FRIEDA SCHIFF (1876–1958)

An astute, generous, and well-read woman, Frieda Schiff Warburg's life was an example both of the opportunities made possible by great wealth and the educational and vocational limitations imposed on women of her time. Her pattern of giving was more a reflection of her desire to carry on her family's philanthropic tradition—particularly her father's—than an expression of interests she developed on her own. It also served as a kind of substitute for the religious

The opportunities made possible by great wealth and the limitations imposed on women of her time were both reflected in the life of Frieda Schiff Warburg. Denied both education and career, she carried on her family's philanthropic tradition with grace and generosity. She is shown here with her five children: Left to right, Carola (and her dog, Yenny), Paul, Frederick, Gerald, and Edward. [The Jewish Museum, New York]

observance that had been important to her father, but that she did not feel moved to carry on in her own life.

Frieda Schiff Warburg was born on February 3, 1876, into the privileged world of New York City's German Jewish elite. She was the daughter of Jacob Schiff, head of the Kuhn, Loeb banking firm and one of the preeminent Jewish communal leaders of his day. Her mother was THERESE LOEB SCHIFF, daughter of the firm's founder.

While the principal focus of Frieda's life was on her home and family, in her public life she followed the model established by her father. Her grandmother, Betty Loeb, who, along with Jacob Schiff, was the original backer of LILLIAN WALD's Henry Street Settlement and Visiting Nurse Service, also served as a model for her charitable giving.

Frieda Warburg contributed sizable sums and held largely honorary positions in many, mostly Jewish, organizations in which her family had already set the pattern of involvement. During the last two

decades of her life, when her children were occupied with their own lives, and her father, husband, and brother, Mortimer Schiff, had all died, nearly the full weight of the family's philanthropic and communal responsibilities fell on her shoulders.

Frieda Schiff was poorly prepared for any kind of public career. While both her brother and husband became partners in Kuhn, Loeb, the firm cofounded by her grandfather Solomon Loeb and headed by Jacob Schiff, no such career could be contemplated for a woman of Frieda's time and social milieu. Her upbringing was opulent—including private lessons in piano, French, Bible, horseback riding, dancing, and fencing—but her formal education ended with her graduation from the exclusive all-girl Brearley School.

In 1895, Frieda Schiff married Felix Warburg, the Hamburg-born son of the M.M. Warburg and Company banking family. They had five children, Carola (b. 1896), Frederick (b. 1897), Gerald (b. 1901), Paul (b. 1904), and Edward (b. 1908).

Warburg began her philanthropic work after her marriage as a director of the Brightside Day Nursery. In 1911, she became a director of the YOUNG WOMEN'S HEBREW ASSOCIATION (YWHA) and later its president (1929–1942).

In 1938, following a tradition established by her father, husband, and brother, Frieda Warburg became a member of the board of directors of the Jewish Theological Seminary of America, and served until her death. As the first and, during most of her tenure, only woman on the seminary's board, she was consulted about the seminary's programs for women.

In 1944, she contributed her Fifth Avenue mansion to the seminary. In 1947, it opened in the former Warburg house as the Jewish Museum.

Other organizations she supported include the Henry Street Settlement and Visiting Nurse Service, the American Jewish Joint Distribution Committee, the Women's Division of the Federation of Jewish Philanthropies of New York, HADASSAH, and the Jewish Welfare Board. Between 1943 and 1945, she served as honorary vice president of the New York City Welfare Council.

Although both Frieda and Felix Warburg maintained their position as non-Zionists, their first trip to Palestine in the early 1920s, made with the encouragement of Chaim Weizmann, turned them into enthusiastic supporters of development there. In 1936, Frieda Warburg was honorary chair of the building fund campaign for the Hadassah Hospital in Jerusalem. In 1949, she established a $100,000 fund for medical scholarships at the hospital, and in 1951, she contributed $650,000 to the United Jewish Appeal to house and educate new immigrants to Israel. She also supported the Hebrew University, as had her husband, and she served as the honorary vice president of the International Youth Aliyah Committee.

In 1935 the Warburgs founded the Felix M. and Frieda Schiff Warburg Foundation. With Frieda Warburg as president and her five children as members, the foundation chiefly supported Jewish causes but, reflecting the interests of the Warburg children, also funded health, education, civic, art, music, and African-American organizations.

During the Nazi era, Frieda Warburg responded by helping rescue friends and family members caught in Germany, housing many of these refugees at her homes in Manhattan and White Plains, New York.

She received honors during her later years, among them honorary degrees from the Jewish Theological Seminary and Hebrew Union College, both in 1945.

Frieda Schiff Warburg died at her home in White Plains on September 14, 1958. In her estate of more than $9 million, she left bequests to her family and to the many organizations she had supported during her lifetime.

BIBLIOGRAPHY

Adler, Cyrus. *Felix M. Warburg: A Biographical Sketch* (1938), and *Jacob Schiff. His Life and Letters* (1928); *AJYB* 61 (1960): 419; Chernow, Ron. *The Warburgs: The Twentieth-Century Odyssey of a Remarkable Jewish Family* (1993); *EJ*; JTS Records, R.G.1 and R.G.11. JTS; Miller, Julie. "Planning the Jewish Museum, 1944–1947." *Conservative Judaism* 47 (Fall 1994): 60–73; Obituary. *NYTimes*, September 15, 1958, 21:3; *UJE*; Warburg, Frieda Schiff. *Reminiscences of a Long Life* (1956); "Warburg Estate Put at Nine Million," *NYTimes*, September 23, 1958; Weber, Nicholas Fox. *Patron Saints: Five Rebels Who Opened America to a New Art, 1928–1943* (1992); *WWIAJ* (1938); Young Women's Hebrew Association. Records, R.G.5. YM-YWHA Archives, 92nd Street YM-YWHA, NYC.

JULIE MILLER

WARNER, MARIE PICHEL LEVINSON (1895–1979)

"Contraception is a health problem of importance to the patient and to the physician and involves the welfare of not only the individual but also of society," concluded Marie Pichel Warner in a 1940 article in the *Journal of the American Medical Association*. Warner pursued that health problem, as well as infertility, in research and in practice, as assistant medical director at Margaret Sanger's Clinical Research Bureau from 1927 to 1936, and medical director of the Family Planning Clinic in Harlem (beginning in 1933), run in conjunction with the New York Urban League.

Marie Pichel Levinson Warner was born on June 30, 1895, in Cincinnati, Ohio, one of five children of Isaac and Lily (Loeb) Pichel. She earned a B.S. from the University of Cincinnati (1919), working as a social investigator at Cincinnati General Hospital (1916–1917) and as a case worker for the American Red Cross (1917–1918). She married Louis J. Levinson in 1922 in Cincinnati, and earned an M.D. from the College of Medicine of the University of Cincinnati the next year. She interned at Deaconess Hospital (1923–1924). After her husband's untimely death, she moved to the East Coast. In 1933, she married Dr. Benjamin W. Warner. The couple lived in New York City and Scarsdale, New York.

Reflecting the limited employment opportunities for women physicians of the era, she held various positions in education and social service in addition to running a private practice. She served as assistant medical examiner for the University of Cincinnati's Department of Hygiene (1923–1924); physician for the public schools in New Britain, Connecticut (1924–1926), and in New York City (beginning in 1928); and director and camp physician at Camp Eagle Point and Camp Stimson in Rumney, New Hampshire (1924 to 1932).

The bulk of Warner's professional commitments focused on the birth control movement. Historian Carole McCann maintains that Sanger chose Warner as medical director of the Harlem clinic because of Warner's good rapport with its African-American clients. Warner claimed to have founded the birth control clinic at the Recreation Rooms Settlement House in Manhattan in the 1930s; in 1940, she became medical director there. She also served as medical director of contraceptive clinics at New York City's Jewish Memorial Hospital and as a member of the committee on the prevention of venereal disease of the Bronx Tuberculosis and Health Association, and lectured on the topic at New York University (1934–1936). Recognizing the value of the nonprint media, Warner gave talks about birth control over radio station WEVD, under the auspices of the New York City Young Men's Christian Association (1933–1936), and produced a film on the subject in the 1930s. She took the cause to the road and traveled throughout the United States, lecturing and visiting other clinics. In 1934, as an American delegate, Warner spoke at the meeting of the International Medical Women's Association in Stockholm, Sweden.

In addition to these activities, she ran a private practice and published articles and books on contraception and infertility. She also held various assistant or adjunct hospital appointments, at New York City's Mount Sinai and Jewish Memorial hospitals, for example. Beginning in the early 1950s, Warner was visiting obstetrician at the New York Infirmary of Beth Israel Medical Center. Her professional memberships included the American Medical Association, the New York State Medical Society, and the American Social Hygiene Association. She also belonged to the Alpha Epsilon Iota, Order of the Eastern Star.

Warner maintained a full-time medical practice on Fifth Avenue through the 1960s and 1970s. Ill health finally forced her to retire at age eighty-four, only a few months before she died on November 3, 1979.

SELECTED WORKS BY MARIE PICHEL LEVINSON WARNER

Artificial Insemination in Cases of Incurable Sterility (1948); "Contraception: A Study of Five Hundred Cases from Private Practice." *JAMA* 115 (July 27, 1940): 279–285; *The Couple Who Wanted a Baby* (1961; Revised edition, 1968, as *Modern Fertility Guide*); *A Doctor Discusses Breast Feeding*, with Miriam Gilbert (1981); *Social Hygiene Problems of Childhood and Family Concerns.* (1934).

BIBLIOGRAPHY

American Medical Directory (1925–1969); Cincinnati Medical Heritage Center. University of Cincinnati, Cincinnati, Ohio; Kopp, Marie E. *Birth Control in Practice* (1933); McCann, Carole R. *Birth Control Politics in the United States, 1916–1945* (1994); Obituary. *NYTimes*, November 5, 1979, D7; Sanger, Margaret. Collection. Library of Congress, Washington, D.C., and Sophia Smith Archives, Smith College, Northampton, Mass.; *WWIAJ* (1938): 1104.

JIMMY E. WILKINSON MEYER

WASSERSTEIN, WENDY (b. 1950)

In the 1960s, at the Calhoun School on the Upper West Side of Manhattan, Wendy Wasserstein discovered that she could get out of gym class if she wrote skits about the mother-daughter fashion show. In 1989, with *The Heidi Chronicles*, she would win a Pulitzer Prize and become the first woman to receive the Tony Award for Best Play.

Wasserstein was born in Brooklyn on October 18, 1950, to Morris and Lola (Schleifer) Wasserstein. Her wealthy and sophisticated grandparents on her mother's side came from a Polish resort town. Suspected of being a spy, her grandfather Simon Schleifer left Poland for America, where he became a high school principal in Paterson, New Jersey, and wrote Yiddish plays. Her father owned a textile factory with his brother, where he patented velveteen. Her mother, a housewife with a passionate interest in dance and theater, took Wendy to weekly lessons at the prestigious June Taylor School of Dance. She has two sisters and a brother. The family lived in Brooklyn until Wendy was twelve, when they moved to the Upper East Side of Manhattan.

Wasserstein was a history major at Mount Holyoke College in South Hadley, Massachusetts, but when she found herself falling asleep over *The Congressional Digest* as she was preparing to become a summer intern for Congress, she seized a friend's suggestion that they take a course in playwriting at Smith instead. After graduating from Mount Holyoke, she studied creative writing with Joseph Heller and Israel Horowitz at City University of New York, where she wrote her first play, *Any Woman Can't*, as her master's thesis in 1973, about a girl who gives up on a dancing career and gets married after blowing an audition for tap-dancing class.

Still uncertain about her direction in life, Wasserstein almost went to law school, business school, and medical school before deciding to try something she really enjoyed and entering the playwriting program at the Yale School of Drama. There, she studied no plays by women, nor did she meet one woman director. In fact, at the first reading of *Uncommon Women* at Yale, a male student remarked that he did not know if he could "get into" her play because it was about women. Wasserstein thought, "Well, I had 'gotten into' *Hamlet* and *Lawrence of Arabia*, so why don't you try this on for size?" Equally disturbed by Hollywood's negative and stereotypical representation of women, Wasserstein was determined to prove that a woman need not be insane, desperate, or crazy in order to be stageworthy. Consequently, she has devoted her entire playwriting career to exploring the lives of intelligent, talented women.

The production of her first play happened as serendipitously as her first playwriting course. When her mother's friend asked how Wendy was doing, her mother started hyperventilating and exclaimed desperately, "She's not a lawyer. She's not married to a lawyer. And now she's writing plays." The friend asked for one of Wendy's plays in order to show it to director Robert Moss at Playwrights Horizons, an Off-Broadway theater. Ever since, Playwrights Horizons has been her artistic home, and she now serves on its artistic board.

PLAYS

Uncommon Women and Others, first produced in 1975 as her thesis at Yale, then presented at the Phoenix Theater in New York City in 1977, and later televised for public television's *Great Performances* series in 1978 and revived in the fall of 1994 at the Lucille Lortel Theatre in New York with an updated ending, introduces five women as they meet at a New York restaurant, then travels back six years to their senior year at Mount Holyoke, where they discuss their future careers, men, sex, marriage, and the fact that society is patriarchal. *Uncommon Woman* was a landmark, the first play that treated contemporary women's issues with seriousness. The *New York Times* critic John O'Connor complimented the play's "insights into the challenges and crises confronting modern women." Critics also praised her ear for dialogue and her wicked sense of humor.

In a slightly different key, her 1983 one-act play *Tender Offer*, produced at the Ensemble Theater, explores poignantly the relationship between a girl and her father.

"When your name is Wendy Wasserstein and you're from New York, you are the walking embodiment of 'too Jewish'," says the Pulitzer Prize and Tony Award winning playwright in response to one type of criticism of her plays. Yet she doesn't shy away from that theme, declaring that *The Sisters Rosensweig is, among other things, "about being Jewish."* [New York Public Library]

Like *Uncommon Women and Others, Isn't It Romantic*, presented by Playwrights Horizons in New York in 1983, explores upper-middle class, expensively educated, single women, but Janie and Harriet are six years older than their counterparts in *Uncommon Women*, and they are out in the world, searching for love and professional fulfillment in Manhattan in the face of changing values. While Janie is the daughter of overprotective Jewish parents who desperately want her to get married, Harriet is the daughter of a WASP professional woman who encourages her to pursue her career.

Isn't It Romantic received mixed reviews from New York critics. Some had trouble with the play's episodic structure, and Douglas Watt found its conclusion, with Janie's "dance of joy," to be "hollow and unconvincing." Others argued that the characters were underdeveloped. In some quarters, the play was criticized as "too Jewish"—but then, as Wasserstein wryly notes, "when your name is Wendy Wasserstein and you're from New York, you are the walking embodiment of 'too Jewish.'" Among the favorable reviews was *Variety's*, which acknowledged Wasserstein as "a hawk-eyed observer of urban professional foibles [who] knows how to construct jokes."

Wasserstein's Pulitzer Prize–winning play, *The Heidi Chronicles*, was workshopped at the Seattle Repertory Theater, then presented by Playwrights Horizons, before moving to Broadway's Plymouth Theater, where it also won the New York Drama Critics Circle Award, the Drama Desk Award, and the Susan Blackburn Prize, in addition to the Tony. In 1995 it appeared on TNT television. The play explores the wistful character of Heidi Holland, a witty, unmarried art history professor at Columbia University approaching middle age and becoming disillusioned with the collapse of the idealism that shaped the 1960s. Spanning twenty-three years, the play begins with Heidi's slide lecture in which she affirms the neglect of women artists, and then it skates back to a 1965 Chicago high school dance and on to college, where Heidi and her friends become ardent feminists and radicals. We see them at a 1968 Eugene McCarthy rally in New Hampshire, a 1970 Ann Arbor consciousness-raising session when Heidi is a Yale graduate student, and a 1974 protest for women artists at the Art Institute of Chicago.

Heidi's friends become swept by the materialism and narcissism of the Reagan eighties. Heidi, however, remains adamantly committed to the ideals of feminism and feels stranded. At her high school alumni luncheon, the climax of the play, she delivers a long, impromptu confession concerning her feelings of abandonment and her disappointment with her peers. "I thought the point was we were all in this together," she exclaims. By the end of the play in 1988, Heidi adopts a daughter as a single parent, hoping that the daughter will feel the confidence and dignity that were the aims of the women's movement.

Many feminist critics assaulted the play, insisting that Heidi "sells out" in the end by adopting a baby and that the true cause of her depression was her not having a man. While it is clear that the play is not radically feminist, it is a mistake to read the ending so literally. Wasserstein, who resists being labeled a "feminist" playwright, arguing that men are not subject to such labels, says that Heidi adopts a baby because that choice is consistent with her character.

Heidi and her daughter become icons for future generations of women who will have a stronger sense of self in a more equal society.

Wasserstein affirms that her 1992 Broadway comedy hit, *The Sisters Rosensweig*, set in London at the moment of the 1989 Soviet coup, is "about being Jewish." It dramatizes the disparate lives of three sisters, Sara, Pfeni, and Gorgeous, as they congregate to celebrate Sara's fifty-fourth birthday. Wasserstein wanted to write a play that celebrated the possibilities of a middle-aged woman who, unlike her other protagonists, does not end up alone. In addition, each sister comes to terms with her Jewish heritage differently. Indeed, Wasserstein says that her notion of theater derives from her Jewish identity: "I think in many ways my idea of show business comes from temple, not that I really practice, but that sense of community, melancholy, and spirituality is there." Furthermore, *The Sisters Rosensweig* also reflects the profound impact of Chekhov on her imagination, specifically *The Three Sisters*. Chekhov's ability to capture the quotidian aspect of life as he balances humor and sorrow particularly appeals to Wasserstein. *Sisters* moved from the Greenwich Theatre in London to the Old Vic in the fall of 1994.

Her 1997 play, *An American Daughter*, appearing at Lincoln Center, takes place in Washington and was inspired by what Wasserstein calls "the blatant unfairness" of what happened to Zoe Baird, Lani Guinier, and Kimba Wood in the wake of being nominated for government office. Once the media exposes the fact that Dr. Lyssa Dent Hughes, the great-granddaughter of Ulysses S. Grant and the daughter of a conservative Republican senator, neglected to do jury duty, she is forced to resign as nominee for surgeon general. Not only does the play expose the sexism to which women are subjected in the public arena, but it is also Wasserstein's first play to take a hard look at the problems of liberalism. The most overtly political play of her career, *An American Daughter* was also her first play to move directly from the Seattle Repertory Theater to Broadway. While some critics felt the play lacked direction, others thought it cleverly combined the features of a social problem play, a comedy of manners, and a political satire.

ADAPTATIONS

Wasserstein has also adapted the works of other writers, including Chekhov's short story "The Man in a Case," which examines the relationship between a stuffy classics professor and his vivacious fiancée (1985). With Christopher Durang, a friend and collaborator from the Yale days, she adapted Charles

McGrath's short story "Husbands" for the screen as *The House of Husbands* (1981), which comically explores gender conflict in divorced couples but ultimately celebrates the possibilities of marriage. Hollywood is currently negotiating a production of Wasserstein's 1990 adaptation of the British comedy *Antonia and Jane*. The film explores Wasserstein's canonical concerns of friendship and rivalry between single women with identity crises, who are frustrated in their romantic and professional lives. In 1994, with choreographer Kevin McKenzie, she adapted *The Nutcracker Suite* for the New York City Ballet, focusing on Clara's coming of age. Their ballet reached New York during the company's 1994 May season at the Metropolitan Opera House.

MUSICALS

She has also written three musicals. The first was a parody about the Miss America pageant, *When Dinah Shore Ruled the Earth*, cowritten with Durang while they were at Yale (1975). *Happy Birthday, Montpelier Pa-zazz*, containing the seeds of Wasserstein's concern about frustrated relationships between men and women, opened at Playwrights Horizon in 1976. Playwrights Horizons also presented her 1985 musical, *Miami*, about a brother and sister coming of age as America grows out of the Red Scare of the Eisenhower fifties into the promise of liberalism in the sixties.

TELEVISION

In 1984, Wasserstein began writing comedy skits for the television series *Comedy Zone*. For KCET-TV in Los Angeles, she wrote *"Drive," She Said*, a comedy about a woman learning to drive late in life as she struggles with her identity. *Kiss, Kiss Dahlings*, a 1992 teleplay for public television, humorously depicts three generations of actresses, two of whom sell out to popular culture. *Uncommon Women and Others* and *The Heidi Chronicles* have also been adapted for television.

ESSAYS

Wasserstein's essays have appeared in the *New Yorker, Esquire, New York Woman, and Harper's Bazaar, among others. A collection, Bachelor Girls*, was published in 1991; its subjects are as diverse as the three influences that shaped her imagination in her youth—Richard Halliburton's *Complete Book of Marvels*, the HELENA RUBINSTEIN Charm School, and Broadway musicals—but the unifying subject is young, unmarried women, who support themselves and often live alone. She currently has a column called "The Wendy Chronicles" in *Harper's Bazaar* and began as a columnist for *New Woman* magazine in 1994.

Wasserstein has made a special place for herself in the American theater by being one of the first women to stage women's issues with the astute and comic eye of a social critic. As her characters, accomplished women who are trying to find fulfillment in their personal and professional lives, discover that it is impossible to "have it all," they gain a better understanding of who they are. Although she resists being labeled a "feminist" playwright, arguing that men are not subject to such labels, she is seriously troubled by the unjust inequities based on gender she sees in American society. Therefore, her plays continue to focus on women struggling to define themselves in a "postfeminist" America that still suffers from the backlash of sexism, homophobia, and traditional values but also from the problem of liberal entitlement. Her writing not only reflects her passionate interest in women but also reveals the fact that she is Jewish and a New Yorker.

Her most recent work, however, depicts men more generously than her earlier did. Indeed, Wasserstein is quick to point out that she owes a great deal to two men who have been instrumental in her career: the artistic director of Lincoln Center, Andre Bishop, the former artistic director of Playwrights Horizons, who produced her early plays; and director Dan Sullivan. While her plays continue to expose the brutal reality of sexism, they always maintain a comic, wistful, Chekhovian tone, and at the same time have an unmistakable Jewish urban quality.

BIBLIOGRAPHY

For a complete bibliography of works by and about Wendy Wasserstein, see Jan Balakian, *The Dramatic World of Wendy Wasserstein* (1998). Wasserstein's manuscripts are collected at the Mount Holyoke Archives, South Hadley, Mass.

JAN BALAKIAN

WEIL, GERTRUDE (1879–1971)

Gertrude Weil's career provides a rare example of southern Jewish social activism during the first half of the twentieth century. She was the first Jewish woman to lead a statewide secular women's movement in North Carolina. Beginning with the controversial campaign for woman suffrage in 1915, Weil lobbied for numerous social causes such as protective labor legislation for women and children, voter education, and election reform. Gertrude Weil believed that women could be more influential social reformers

Gertrude Weil's life is a rare example of southern Jewish social activism during the first half of the twentieth century. She was the first Jewish woman to lead a statewide secular women's movement in North Carolina. She began her activist career in 1915 fighting for woman suffrage and carried through to the civil rights movement of the 1960s. [Courtesy of the North Carolina Division of Archives and History]

through the direct means of politics rather than indirect influence. Her decision to associate herself with a relatively radical social and political agenda was unusual for a southern woman and even more uncommon for a southern Jew. Historically, southern Jews had stayed away from political or social causes that challenged southern norms for fear of anti-Semitic backlash. Weil, however, strayed from this norm,

because she believed that women had a responsibility to participate in the political process.

Born in Goldsboro, North Carolina, on December 11, 1879, she was the oldest daughter of immigrant Henry Weil and first-generation American Mina (Rosenthal) Weil. The Weils had three other children, Leslie, Herman, and Janet. Of German Jewish descent, the Weils were prominent business and civic leaders in Goldsboro.

Gertrude Weil received a progressive formal education, which was unusual for a southern woman of her time. In 1894, at age fifteen, she was sent to New York City to attend the Horace Mann High School at Teachers College. After high school, she attended Smith College. In 1901, Gertrude Weil became the first North Carolinian to graduate from Smith.

Although she wished to pursue a teaching career in New York City, family pressure persuaded her to return home to Goldsboro, where Weil first became involved in the women's club movement. Continuing a family tradition, she was an active leader in her local sisterhood at Temple Oheb Shalom. In 1906, Weil joined the North Carolina Federation of Women's Clubs, a nondenominational umbrella organization for the state's clubwomen.

Over the next ten years, Weil became increasingly visible in the women's club movement. In 1915, she was simultaneously offered executive positions in the North Carolina Federation of Women's Clubs and the North Carolina Equal Suffrage League. Weil decided to devote her time and energy to the more controversial latter organization.

In the southern states, the argument for women's direct participation in politics struck at the heart of southern, white cultural assumptions about womanhood and white supremacy. Antisuffragists argued that only "militant" women who wished to destroy American family life could support woman suffrage. They also exploited white southerners' fears of enfranchising African Americans. And they appealed to the legislators on the basis of the states' rights tradition. In response to these arguments, Gertrude Weil shrewdly based her pro-suffrage arguments on appeals to women's responsibility as moral guardians of the home. Weil maintained that the mothers of America had a responsibility to participate in government for the sake of their children. The suffragists were ultimately unsuccessful. North Carolina was not among the four southern states that ratified the Nineteenth Amendment.

Weil's role in the suffrage campaign set her apart from the majority of her fellow clubwomen. However, her leadership in this movement and those that she subsequently joined distinguished her from other southern Jews to an even greater degree. Although Jews in the South had always maintained a low political profile, this attitude was especially pervasive after the 1913 trial and lynching of Leo Frank, a Jew from Atlanta. Thus, it is surprising to find that only two years after Frank's sensational murder, a Jewish woman from North Carolina directed a bitterly contested and high-profile suffrage campaign. Weil's dedication to social reform, however, was a unique product of her education, her family position, and the strength of her personal conviction. These factors enabled and inspired Gertrude Weil to stand beside her beliefs despite adverse public reaction.

Throughout the next five decades of her life, Weil led organizations as varied as the North Carolina chapter for the League of Women Voters, the Goldsboro Community Chest (a Depression Era relief agency), the North Carolina Association of Jewish Women, and the North Carolina Interracial Committee. In 1964, Smith College recognized Weil's "lifetime of service to the cultural, charitable, religious and political welfare" of North Carolina.

Gertrude Weil continued to be involved in North Carolina affairs until May 3, 1971, when she died, at age ninety-two, in the same Goldsboro home in which she had been born.

BIBLIOGRAPHY

Geisberg, Heather. "Universal Sisterhood and Gertrude Weil: The Secular and Religious Organizational Activities of a Southern and Jewish Social Activist." Honors thesis, Dartmouth College (1995); Hyman, Bob. Obituary. *Goldsboro (North Carolina) News-Argus,* May 31, 1971; Rountree, Moses. *Strangers in the Land: The Story of Jacob Weil's Tribe* (1969); Weil, Gertrude. Papers. College Archives, Smith College, Northampton, Mass., and State Department of Archives and History, Raleigh, N.C.

HEATHER GEISBERG

WEIL, HELEN (1902–1992)

"Who can explain the searching smile that flies across your wrinkled face upon my gentle touch? . . . No worded answer tells me, but I can feel the hidden presence of an eternal spark." These words, written by Helen Weil, illuminate her sensitivity and commitment to older people that she developed during a long and active career in gerontology and social services.

Born near the French border in Breisach, Germany, on January 3, 1902, Helen (Kahn) Weil was the middle child of Nathan Kahn, a leather salesman, and Bertha (Levi). Siblings included an older brother Joseph and a younger sister Margaret (Gretel) and four half sisters and a half brother from her father's first marriage. She received her early education from Ursuline nuns who respected and nurtured her Jewish heritage. She studied social work and teaching at St. Ursula's in Breime, Germany, before marrying Julius Weil, a clinical psychologist, in 1924. In a pattern of mutual professional collaboration that persisted throughout their sixty-four-year marriage, Helen Weil became the social worker at a Munich institution for delinquent boys that her husband directed for nine years. Active in the Blue and White, a Zionist Youth Organization, Weil served as president of the Women's International Zionist Organization (WIZO). She left Nazi Germany in 1937 with her daughters, Naomi (Feil) and Gabriele (Hays).

Weil worked at the New York Refugee Relief Center before settling in Cleveland, Ohio, in 1940, when her husband became the director of a Jewish home for the aged. She continued her education at John Carroll University, University Heights, Ohio, where she majored in sociology and philosophy, wrote her thesis on German refugees, and received a Ph.B. in 1943. She graduated with a master's degree in social work from the School of Applied Social Sciences at Western Reserve University in 1945.

Julius Weil, as executive director from 1941 to 1968, and Helen Weil, as head of social services from 1945 to 1968, transformed Cleveland's Montefiore Home from a traditional shelter for elderly Jewish residents to a model facility with an array of medical, therapeutic, psychological, rehabilitative, and social services. During a transitional period in gerontological history, the Weils initiated staff social workers, a day care service (1944), a sheltered workshop (1944), a special department for senile residents (1945), a psychiatric unit (1947), and an out-resident program based on the concept of foster care (1943). In 1947, Montefiore became a training site for graduate students interested in caring for the aged, one of the earliest geriatric facilities to offer such placement.

Weil's extensive publications on aging and institutional care include articles in the *Jewish Social Services Quarterly* and the *American Journal of Orthopsychiatry.* In the 1960s, she was an adjunct professor at Western Reserve University and taught aging and family life, a course that introduced gerontology into the general studies program. She spoke at local and regional workshops, seminars, and national conferences on topics such as the changing nature of the Jewish family, parental/child relationships, and institutional and social services for the aged. Her volunteer activities included work with the Cleveland Council on Mental Health, the Cleveland Welfare Federation, and the Institute on Care of the Aged and Chronically Ill in Philanthropic, Private and County Homes.

In 1968, the Weils left Montefiore Home to form and direct the Cornelia Schnurmann Foundation and develop Schnurmann House, a residential compound for senior citizens in Mayfield Heights, Ohio. Weil remained active in the administration until her death on August 20, 1992.

Helen and Julius Weil were honored by the local chapter of the National Conference of Christians and Jews (1955), named Senior Citizens of the Year by the Cuyahoga Senior Citizens Council (1972), and inducted as charter members in the Ohio Senior Citizens Hall of Fame (1978). In recognition of her service to the university, the community, and her family, John Carroll University awarded Helen Weil the Alumni Medal in 1990. She belonged to Shaarah Tikvah, "Gates of Hope," and Temple Beth El in Shaker Heights, Ohio.

BIBLIOGRAPHY

Dictionary of Cleveland Biography. Edited by David D. Van Tassel and John J. Grabowski (1996): 474; Ettore, John, "'I'm Still Not in a Laughing Mood,' Helen Weil. A Pioneer in Social Services Carries Holocaust Pain." *Carroll Alumni Journal*, John Carroll University (May 1990): 3; Montefiore Home Records, MSS 3835. Western Reserve Historical Society, Cleveland, Ohio; Weil, Julius and Helen. Papers, MSS 4499. Western Reserve Historical Society, Cleveland.

BETH DiNATALE JOHNSON

WEINBERG, GLADYS DAVIDSON (b. 1909)

Gladys Davidson Weinberg's pioneering archaeological work on ancient and medieval glass and its manufacture in the Mediterranean world sheds light on the trade and technology of preindustrial societies.

Born in New York City on December 27, 1909, the first of two daughters of Hebrew literary scholar Israel Davidson and CARRIE (DREYFUSS) DAVIDSON, Gladys Davidson Weinberg's archaeological interest was spurred by her study of Greek in high school. She received her bachelor's degree from New York University in 1930 and her Ph.D. five years later from Johns Hopkins University for her dissertation on the excavations at Corinth. In 1931, she began her archaeological career with the Johns Hopkins University expedition to Olynthus. From 1932 to 1938, she stud-

ied at the American School of Classical Studies at Athens, after which she became assistant curator of ancient art at the Princeton Art Museum, a post she held for four years. During her tenure there, in 1942, she married fellow archaeologist Saul Weinberg, who later became cofounder and chairman of the department of art history and archaeology at the University of Missouri–Columbia. They had one daughter, Susanna Miriam.

From 1943 to 1945, Weinberg served as a translator and librarian in the Foreign Service Auxiliary of the U.S. Department of State in Istanbul and Athens. She then worked as assistant librarian from 1946 to 1947 and acting librarian from 1947 to 1948 at the American School of Classical Studies in Athens.

As editor of *Archaeology* magazine from 1952 to 1967, Weinberg conducted several excavations in search of ancient glass factories in the Mediterranean. In 1959, she directed an excavation in Crete sponsored by the Corning Museum of Glass. Several years later, the Corning Museum joined with the University of Missouri–Columbia to focus on the early centuries when glass vessels first became household products in the eastern Mediterranean. With Weinberg as field director, the team at Jalame, Israel (near Haifa), studied glassmaking technology, examining the types of tools, fuels, and furnaces used, and the form of the raw materials needed for glassmaking.

As curator of ancient art (1962–1973), assistant director (1973–1977), research fellow (1977–), and cofounder of the Museum of Art and Archaeology at the University of Missouri, Weinberg promoted the study and appreciation of ancient objects. While at the museum, she also founded and became editor of *Muse, Annual of the Museum of Art and Archaeology* (1966–1977).

Gladys Davidson Weinberg is an honorary life member of the American Association of University Women and of the Archaeological Institute of America. In 1985, she and her husband received the Gold Medal for Distinguished Archaeological Achievement from the Archaeological Institute of America. A year later, she received the Percia Schimmel Award for Archaeological Exploration in Biblical Lands from the Israel Museum.

SELECTED WORKS BY GLADYS DAVIDSON WEINBERG

The Antikyhera Wreck Reconsidered (1965); *Corinth: The Minor Objects* (1952); *Excavations at Jalame* (1988); *Glass Vessels in Ancient Greece* (1992); *Small Finds from the Pnyx: I,* with Dorothy Thompson and Lucy Talcott (1943–1956).

BIBLIOGRAPHY

"Ancient City Found on Coast of Crete by U.S. Explorers." *NYTimes*, December 20, 1959, 4:8; "Archaeological Institute of America Award for Distinguished Archaeological Achievement." *American Journal of Archaeology 90* (April 1986): 173; *Biography Index*; "Coins of 350 B.C. Found in Sicily." *NYTimes*, December 29, 1966, 28:4; De Bat, Donald. "Columbia Archaeologists Discover Glass Slab on Israeli Expedition." *Columbia Missourian*, May 15, 1966: 9; *Directory of American Scholars*; "Dr. Weinberg Awarded Research Fellowship." *Columbia Missourian*, May 14, 1963; *EJ*, s.v. "Weinberg, Saul S."; LaHue, Jill. "Broken Glass Helps Reconstruct Past." *Columbia Missourian*, April 27, 1974; Ricchiardi, Sherry. "M.U. to Display Old Roman Glass." *Columbia Missourian*, November 12, 1965; *Who's Who in World Jewry*; *Who's Who of American Women*.

ALEISA FISHMAN

WEISS-ROSMARIN, TRUDE (1908–1989)

Trude Weiss-Rosmarin was one of the foremost Jewish intellectuals of the twentieth century. She was the editor of the *Jewish Spectator*, author of many books, and a woman of intense passions and commitment to Jewish life, with very strong and often provocative opinions. A dynamic speaker backed by broad-ranging Jewish scholarship and a prodigious memory, she was a popular lecturer at synagogues and Jewish centers across the United States and a foremost critic of American Jewish life and institutions.

She was born in Frankfurt-am-Main on June 17, 1908, daughter of Jacob and Celestine (Mullings) Weiss. Her father was a successful wine merchant. As a young girl, Trude joined the Blau-Weiss, the German Zionist youth movement, and studied at the Hebraische Sprachschule, the Zionist Hebrew school, under Yosef Yoel Rivlin. For a brief time, she ran away from home to a *hakhshara* training farm near Berlin that prepared young people for agricultural life in Palestine, but a bout of pneumonia forced her to give up those plans. When only seventeen, she established and ran a Hebrew-language school in Duisburg. She continued her studies of Jewish texts, both by herself and at the Frei Judische Lehrhaus established by Franz Rozenzweig, while preparing herself for her final school examinations and university entrance. In later years, she noted that the Blau-Weiss, the Hebraische Sprachschule, and the Frei Judische Lehrhaus were the three focal points of her Jewishness.

Trude studied first at the University of Berlin (1927–1928) and then at Leipzig (1929). In 1931, at age twenty-two, she completed her doctorate in Semitics,

For more than fifty years, Trude Weiss-Rosmarin edited the Jewish Spectator, *where her controversial opinions regarding subjects such as feminism and Palestinian nationalism made the magazine influential beyond its circulation. Her passion, however, was Jewish culture, and she used her editorials, articles, and lectures to encourage Jewish education. [American Jewish Archives]*

archaeology and philosophy at the University of Würzburg. Her thesis, a collection of Babylonian-Assyrian references to Arabia and the Arabs, was later published as *The Mention of the Arabs in Assyrian-Babylonian Texts*.

She married Aaron Rosmarin, a Russian Jewish scholar who was an American citizen, and they came to New York in 1931. They had one son, Moshe. She and Aaron Rosmarin were divorced in 1951. She later married Nissim Sevan.

When Weiss-Rosmarin was unsuccessful in finding a teaching position in Assyriology, she and her husband established the School of the Jewish Woman on the Upper West Side of Manhattan in October 1933. In the beginning, the school was under the auspices of HADASSAH. Weiss-Rosmarin modeled the school on the Frankfurt Lehrhaus. She believed that Jewish women were being shortchanged by not getting an adequate Jewish education and she wanted to remedy this with adult education. Weiss-Rosmarin was the director and taught two classes every day; her husband was the registrar, and Albert Einstein was the honorary chairman. Classes were taught in Hebrew, Bible, Jewish history, and Yiddish. The school continued until 1939.

At the end of 1935, Weiss-Rosmarin introduced a newsletter, *News from the School of the Jewish Woman*, and in February 1936, the newsletter became the *Jewish Spectator:* "a typical family magazine, with a special appeal to the woman." She became sole editor in 1943. It was through the *Jewish Spectator*, as well as through her extensive and popular lecture tours, that Weiss-Rosmarin had her extraordinary impact on the thinking of rabbis and Jewish professionals for over five decades. The paper appeared monthly until 1974, and then became a quarterly. In 1978, Weiss-Rosmarin moved to Santa Monica, California, and continued publishing the *Spectator* there. Shortly before her death in 1989, she passed the editorship over to Robert Bleiweiss. While the *Spectator* never had a mass circulation, it was always very influential. During the more than fifty years that Weiss-Rosmarin was editor, it remained independent and unsubsidized. The magazine covered a wide range of Jewish topics and included both original fiction and poetry, but the most important part for readers was "The Editor's Quarter," which included Weiss-Rosmarin's editorials.

Writing in 1988, Weiss-Rosmarin considered that "what gives publishers/editors of controversial and struggling little magazines the will and strength to continue, is that some of their far out opinions of yesteryear have become the 'in' opinions of today."

A strong Zionist from her youth, Weiss-Rosmarin made Israel a major focus of her concerns. She came to believe that the Palestinians had a legitimate case and believed in the reality of Palestinian nationalism (although she said that, emotionally, she would want Israel to extend from the Euphrates to the Nile). In the midst of the general euphoria following the Six-Day War in 1967, she had already written an article titled "Toward Jewish-Muslim Dialogue." She felt that Zionist organizations had become obsolete after the establishment of the state and considered the Jewish Agency, in particular, rife with bureaucratic waste.

In other columns, she attacked the lack of accountability in the fund-raising drives of Jewish organizations and condemned the misuse and abuse of communal funds. At a time when federations were considered the primary Jewish organizations in the United States, she emphasized the primacy of the synagogue.

Weiss-Rosmarin repeatedly stressed the need for Jewish education at all levels. She was a strong advocate of Jewish day schools when other Jews considered them un-American. Recognizing the inadequacy of supplementary Jewish education in America, she advised delaying bar and bat mitzvah ceremonies in Reform and Conservative congregations until the age of fifteen or sixteen, so that youngsters would have more years of Jewish education.

For Weiss-Rosmarin, the key to Jewish survival was Jewish education, and she promoted it in every way. In 1940, she launched a series of inexpensive Jewish books called *The Jewish People's Library*, issued by the Jewish Book Club. Some of her own books, dealing with topics as diverse as Jewish women through the ages and Jewish expressions on Jesus, were included in this series.

Besides teaching for periods at New York University and the Reconstructionist Rabbinical College in Philadelphia, Weiss-Rosmarin was one of the most popular lecturers on a vast range of Jewish topics in the United States. She was passionate about Jewish culture and Jewish life and was immensely learned in Jewish sources. Her editorials, articles, and lectures were full of biblical and Talmudic quotations. At the same time, she had a mind free of conventional views and was prepared to follow the logic of an argument wherever it led. She never pandered to audiences or feared being controversial.

Weiss-Rosmarin held very strong but carefully nuanced views on the role of women in Jewish life. She was prepared to say that while Judaism denied women many legal rights, it offered them a uniformly high, even privileged, social position. In many ways, she believed, Judaism honored women and assigned them great importance. She considered that the position and status of Jewish women had to be looked at in the context of each historical period. For example, she considered that the social and legal status of Jewish women in biblical times "was incomparably higher and in every respect, more favorable" than that of other women.

Weiss-Rosmarin strongly advocated changes in Jewish family law, railing against inequities in marriage and divorce, particularly in the treatment of the *agunah*. She called for transferring authority in matters of divorce from the husband to the *Bet Din*, many years before the Conservative Movement called for this change.

Yet she was prepared to disagree with Jewish feminists on many issues. She was opposed to women's prayer groups and women's minyans, because she considered them a revival of the "woman's synagogue"—the "*weibershe shul*"—of the Middle Ages. Instead, she advocated egalitarian minyans of women and men. Her belief that the future of Jewish women lay in integration, not segregation or separation, led her to dismiss Jewish women's studies. For her, what was important was equal access for Jewish women both in the marketplace and in places of worship. Self-segregation, she warned, was as misguided and wrong as segregation by others.

Her sensitivity to linguistic sexism distinguished between what she considered genuinely offensive and what she felt women often objected to out of ignorance. That the prayer book referred to God in male terms did not bother her especially, because the Torah, Shekhinah, and Shabbat were all seen in feminine terms. While believing that the liturgy should address God as God of the foremothers as well as God of the forefathers, she considered that many progressive contemporary writers committed the same offense in their book titles by referring to "fathers and sons." She attributed the greater prevalence of linguistic sexism in English and other Germanic languages to the lack of the feminine form for nouns.

Weiss-Rosmarin was one of the first to raise the issue of discrimination against women in Jewish public life. In an August 1936 editorial, she wrote that "In every institution whether it is a synagogue, a Hebrew school, a hospital—we find the identical situation. The women members are allotted no say and almost no representation at all when it comes to basic decisions affecting the policy of the institution." Through the decades, she continued to speak and write against the underrepresentation of women.

While she was determined that her role in bringing up her son would not interrupt her professional life, Weiss-Rosmarin felt that Jewish women should be free to be homemakers and be respected for their choice. She wrote, "The real challenge of women's liberation is not taking women out of the home but emancipating the homemaker as homemaker by placing dignity on her work, instead of derogating it. . . . [Women] must be liberated in their selfhood as women and in fulfillment of their femininity—not by assimilation and imitation of men."

While editing the *Spectator*, Weiss-Rosmarin sent articles to other Jewish newspapers and periodicals worldwide, including a regular column, "Letters from New York," in the London *Jewish Chronicle* from 1963 to 1966. She served as vice president of the National Association of Biblical Instructors. From 1947 to 1951, she was national cochair of education for the

Zionist Organization of America. She sat on the advisory board of the National Jewish Curriculum Institute and the Jewish Book Council, and was a member of the American Academy of Religion and the Society for the Scientific Study of Religion.

Trude Weiss-Rosmarin died of cancer on June 26, 1989, at age eighty-one. Her combination of scholarship, iconoclasm, and absolute commitment to Judaism and its future had made her a unique figure in American Jewry.

SELECTED WORKS BY TRUDE WEISS-ROSMARIN

The Hebrew Moses: An Answer to Sigmund Freud (1939); *Highlights of Jewish History* (1941); *Jerusalem* (1950); *Jewish Expressions on Jesus: An Anthology* (1977); *Jewish Survival* (1949); *Jewish Women Through the Ages* (1940); *Judaism and Christianity: The Differences* (1943); *New Light on the Bible* (1941); *The Oneg Shabbath Book* (1940); *Religion of Reason: The Philosophy of Hermann Cohen* (1936); *Saadia* (1959); *What Every Jewish Woman Should Know* (1940).

BIBLIOGRAPHY

Dellenbach, Carolyn. "An Inventory to the Trude Weiss-Rosmarin Papers (1908–1989)." AJA, Cincinnati, Ohio; *EJ* 14 (1965); Gertel, Elliot B. "My Friend, Trude Weiss-Rosmarin." *Jewish Spectator* (Fall 1989): 11–17; Gilson, Estelle. "Trude's a Holy Terror: Scholar, Critic, Rebel, Gadfly." *Present Tense* (Winter 1978): 33–36. Reprinted in *Jewish Spectator* 54 (Fall 1989): 6–10; Moore, Deborah Dash. "Trude Weiss-Rosmarin and the *Jewish Spectator*." In "*The Other New York Jewish Intellectuals*," edited by Carole S. Kessner (1994); Reed, Barbara Strauss. "Trude Weiss-Rosmarin: Rebel with a Cause." *New Jersey Journal of Communication* 3 (1995): 58–76; *UJE* 10:494; Weiss-Rosmarin, Trude, and Marie Syrkin. Interview. *Moment* 8 (September 1983): 37–44; *WWIAJ* (1938).

JENNIFER BREGER

WEITZENKORN, IRMA *see* MAY, IRMA

WELTMAN, ESTHER ZISKIND (1901–1994)

Trustee and philanthropist Esther Ziskind Weltman was instrumental in giving shape and focus to Jewish philanthropy in the United States in the post–World War II years. As a trustee of the Jacob Ziskind Trust, she oversaw the contribution of buildings and funds to major Jewish institutions both in the United States and Israel.

Born in Lowell, Massachusetts, on June 21, 1901, she was one of six children of Rose (Elkin) and David Ziskind, Lithuanian Jews who had immigrated to the United States in 1898. She graduated from Smith College in 1922 and the Harvard Graduate School of Education in 1924. After her marriage to Sol Weltman, she lived in Springfield, Massachusetts, where she was a founder of the NATIONAL COUNCIL OF JEWISH WOMEN's Springfield Scholarship Clearing House. She was also a charter trustee of the Massachusetts Board of Higher Education and served at one time or another on the boards of twelve colleges in Massachusetts. She had a daughter, Elienne (Squire), and a son, David.

In 1951, she became a trustee of the Jacob Ziskind Trust for Charitable Purposes, created by her brother at his death. Under her leadership, the trust established buildings at the Weizmann Institute and the Technion in Israel, and buildings named after her brother at Smith College and the New England Medical Center. The trust also endowed programs at Brandeis University, Brown University, Colby College, the Jewish Theological Seminary, Dartmouth College, Harvard University, and Yale University. In 1976, Weltman was awarded the Smith College Medal for her leadership in supporting higher education. She received a degree of honorary doctor of laws from Colby College.

Esther Ziskind Weltman died on April 30, 1994.

BIBLIOGRAPHY

Weltman, David L. Letter to author, 1996.

NANETTE STAHL

WERTHEIMER, BARBARA MAYER (1932–1983)

Barbara Mayer Wertheimer's guiding passion in life was to empower workers, especially union women. She recognized the barriers that union women face from management and from male-dominated union structures. As a result, she built a remarkable environment of support, encouragement, learning, and skill training at Cornell University's New York State School of Industrial-Labor Relations by establishing the Institute for Women and Work and trade union women's studies programs. She always believed that it was women who "will be the ones to organize other women, . . . to transmit enthusiasm and confidence in trade unionism."

The trade union women's program, initiated under her leadership in 1972, gave many New York women unionists their first opportunity to meet, network, and explore issues of leadership within their respective unions. Wertheimer inspired the New York Trade Union Women's Conference in January 1974, which built a strong foundation for a new organization, the Coalition of Labor Union Women (CLUW). At CLUW's founding convention, Wertheimer expressed faith in the organization's educational potential to "provide a training ground for women." She said that it made her "blood boil to see what women have to put up with and how long they have had to wait for justice."

Wertheimer revived working women's summer schools, modeled after earlier summer schools for working girls at Bryn Mawr College. These schools, which now operate under the auspices of the University and College Education Association, bring hundreds of union women together from across the United States for a one-week intensive study session of trade union leadership. The summer schools also help to renew union women's extraordinary spirit of sisterhood and solidarity.

At the Institute for Women and Work, Wertheimer developed academic programming, such as the career women's studies program, and undertook research on nineteenth-century women organizers, including Lavinia Waight of the New York Tailoresses Union, Kate Mullaney of the Troy, New York, Collar and Laundry Union, Augusta Lewis of the Typographical Union, and countless others who worked as union activists. The research turned into a book, *We Were There*, which documents the history of working women in America, their roles in the American workplace, and their efforts to unionize.

Barbara Mayer Wertheimer died on September 20, 1983, at age fifty-one, survived by her two children. Her husband, Val Wertheimer, a vice president with the Amalgamated Clothing and Textile Workers union, had died in 1978. Lane Kirkland, the former head of the AFL-CIO, said that Wertheimer's death was "a loss for all of organized labor" and noted that "generations of working women will continue to benefit from her work." Her rich legacy of activism, female empowerment, and education lives on at Cornell's Institute for Women and Work and the summer schools she founded for union women.

BIBLIOGRAPHY

NYTimes, September 22, 1983; Wertheimer, Barbara Mayer. *We Were There* (1977).

FRANCINE MOCCIO

WERTHEIMER, MILDRED
(1896–1937)

A brilliant scholar of international relations and member of the research staff of the Foreign Policy Institute, Mildred Wertheimer made significant contributions to political science at a pivotal time in world history.

Born in San Diego, California, to Monroe and Annette Wertheimer, Mildred, one of two children, went east for her education. A 1917 graduate of Vassar College, Wertheimer pursued several more degrees. She was a member of the International Law Division of the Colonel House Commission of Inquiry until 1919, and in 1921 continued her studies at the University of Berlin. In 1924, she received her doctorate from Columbia University. In the *Foreign Policy Bulletin* of 1937, her colleagues described her published thesis *The Pan-German League* as "a distinct contribution to diplomatic history."

That year she joined the research department at the Foreign Policy Association (FPA) as an expert on Germany and Central Europe. She traveled often to Geneva, closely following the League of Nations' operations. In 1929, she was the FPA's representative at the First Hague Reparation Conference. In 1933, she helped organize the High Commission for German Refugees.

Wertheimer authored over forty articles and two books, *New Governments in Europe* (1934) and *Germany Under Hitler* (1935) for the FPA. Her expert knowledge of foreign languages and political systems combined with her "sound judgment, keen sense for news, and warm interest in people" ensured close contacts and friendships with statesmen, journalists, and diplomats in London, Paris, Geneva, Berlin, and Washington, D.C. Her study of Germany under the Third Reich consisted of perceptive observations and analysis of how suppressive Nazi control increased relative to the country's economic difficulties. In *Germany Under Hitler*, she cautiously reminded her readers that "the ultimate aims of Nazi foreign policy as expounded in *Mein Kampf* have never been retracted."

Mildred Wertheimer did not live to see how eerily accurate was her sense of foreboding. She died on May 6, 1937, in San Diego, after a long illness. In the 1920s, few women worked in the field of foreign policy, and even fewer achieved her level of scholarship and reknown. Lauded for her intelligence and sensitivity, her obituary in the *Foreign Policy Bulletin* described her as someone who "was dominated by a desire to assist in the making of a better world."

BIBLIOGRAPHY

AJYB, 39:599; *Foreign Policy Bulletin* 16, no. 29 (May 14, 1937); *NYTimes*, May 7, 1937, 30:3.

MICHELE SIEGEL

WESSEL, BESSIE BLOOM
(1889–1969)

Bessie Bloom Wessel was unique in her contributions to life in New England, both as an active citizen and as a scholar. A charter member of Temple Beth-el of New London, Connecticut, Wessel served on many important committees and published numerous studies of ethnic issues in the region.

She was born on April 22, 1889, in Ukraine to Max and Celia (Sergei) Bloom. The Bloom family came to the United States in 1891. Bessie Wessel earned a B.A. from Brown University in 1911, and an M.A. (1924) and a Ph.D. (1935) from Columbia University. From 1911 to 1915, she served as director of the Immigrant Educational Bureau of Providence, Rhode Island. In 1918, she began as an instructor in economics and sociology at Connecticut College in New London; twenty years later, she became a professor and the chair of the department of social science. While on a leave of absence from Connecticut College between 1925 and 1928, she lectured and directed a study of ethnic issues in community life at Brown University's graduate school, and continued that study until 1930. In 1945, she became a professor in and chair of the department of social anthropology, a position she held until her retirement in 1953. Wessel also taught classes for immigrants at the Doyle Avenue School.

She served on many committees, including the Committee of Public Welfare (an advisory committee to the city manager of New London) from 1932 to 1935; on the New London Community Forum, as a member of the Conference on Jewish Relations and on the National Conference of Christians and Jews; and the American Association of Social Workers (sitting on the National Housing Committee from 1934 to 1936). Wessel was a member of the American Sociological Society and a member of the executive committee of the Eastern Sociological Society, and served a term as president of the Connecticut State Conference of Social Work in 1934. In 1938, she was a member of the advisory committee of the Red Cross Disaster Program.

Bessie Bloom Wessel was married to Morris J. Wessel, and had one child, a son, David Edward, who was born in 1915. Wessel died on April 11, 1969. Among her many ethnic studies, the best known is *An Ethnic Survey of Woonsocket, R.I.*, published in 1931 by the University of Chicago Press.

BIBLIOGRAPHY

BEOAJ; *Rhode Island Herald*, April 25, 1969; Rhode Island Jewish Historical Association, Providence, R.I.; *UJE*; *WWIAJ* (1938).

MARLA BRETTSCHNEIDER

WESTHEIMER, RUTH (b. 1928)

In the last two decades of the twentieth century, there were many reasons not to celebrate sex. The fear of AIDS brought to the surface the connection between passion and death that has always been a dark strain in the human mind. A fundamentalist Christian reaction against the sexual revolution threatened to re-enthrone Puritan values. On the other side of the coin, millions of children were bearing children, many of them damaged by drug and alcohol abuse. Against this desolate background, a cheerful Jewish grandmother who called herself Dr. Ruth marched forward and said, with undeniable sincerity and forthright common sense, that sex was good, indeed "heavenly." To the astonishment of many Americans, who tend to associate religion with sexual repression, Ruth Westheimer declared that her message of liberation had its origin in Orthodox Judaism.

Karola Ruth Siegel was born in Germany on June 4, 1928, the daughter of Irma Hanauer, a housekeeper, and Julius Siegel, a notions wholesaler and son of the family in which Irma worked. Julius Siegel gave his daughter an early grounding in Judaism, taking her regularly to the synagogue in Frankfurt, where they lived. When Karola was ten years old, shortly after the infamous *Kristallnacht*, her father was taken to a detention camp. Her mother and grandmother then sent the little girl to Switzerland, where she lived in an orphanage for six years.

After the war, unable to find any other members of her family, sixteen-year-old Karola went to Palestine. There, she lived on a number of kibbutzes and joined the Haganah, the underground army. Later, she taught kindergarten, before going with her first husband to Paris, where she studied at the Institute of Psychology at the Sorbonne. After a divorce, she came to the United States.

In New York, she entered the New School for Social Research, on a scholarship for victims of the Holocaust. While studying, she married her second husband and gave birth to her first child, Miriam. After a second divorce, she met Manfred Westheimer. They were married in December of 1961, and their son Joel was born in 1964. The next year, Ruth Westheimer became an American citizen and, in 1970, received her Ed.D. from Columbia University.

After working in a number of positions involving sex education, family planning, and sex therapy, Westheimer found her niche when she did a guest appearance on a local radio show. The audience response was so positive that she was soon hosting her own show, *Sexually Speaking*. Beginning in 1980 as a fifteen-minute embellishment to the station's schedule, it quickly expanded to an hour and finally to two hours.

Westheimer proved to have a real genius for communicating joy in human sexuality while at the same time informing her audiences about responsibility, sexually transmitted diseases, and safe sex. The diminutive woman with her appealing accent was equally successful on television. She hosted her own program—variously called *Good Sex! with Dr. Ruth Westheimer*, *The Dr. Ruth Show*, and *Ask Dr. Ruth*—but her national reputation came from appeareances on such network programs as *Nightline*, *CBS Evening News*, the *Tonight Show*, and *Late Night with David Letterman*.

In 1983, Westheimer published her first book, *Dr. Ruth's Guide to Good Sex*. Since then, she has written more than a dozen others, including her autobiography, *All in a Lifetime* (1987).

In 1995, Westheimer coauthored *Heavenly Sex: Sexuality in the Jewish Tradition*, with Jonathan Mark. Drawing on traditional Judaic sources, it grounds the famous sex therapist's philosophy in Orthodox Jewish teaching. While some have suggested that the authors ignored the darker side of the classical Jewish dialectic on the subject, it is difficult to ignore the cultural significance of both the book and Dr. Ruth.

As David Biale asked, "What does it mean for America's best-known sex therapist to make Judaism the basis of a contemporary sex ethic? If Freud had claimed to have created the science of sexuality by destroying the 'illusion' of religion, Dr. Ruth reverses the course: It is precisely on the basis of religion—Judaism—that a truly healthy contemporary science of sexuality might be constructed."

In 1994, Westheimer entered cyberspace with *Dr. Ruth's Encyclopedia of Sex* on CD-ROM. Two hundred and fifty entries deal straightforwardly with all areas of sex and sexuality. Westheimer followed it up with *Sex for Dummies*, in the famous series of how-to manuals. She told *USA Today* that her first reaction to the idea of the book was negative. "When they approached me, I said, 'Absolutely no, I do not talk to dummies.

To the astonishment of many Americans, who tend to associate religion with sexual repression,
sex therapist Dr. Ruth Westheimer has declared that her message of liberation had its
origin in Orthodox Judaism. This photograph was taken at the 1996 national convention
of the NATIONAL COUNCIL OF JEWISH WOMEN, *where she was a featured speaker.*
[National Council of Jewish Women]

I talk to intelligent people.'" She changed her mind, however, when she recognized the irony of the titles and their disarming appeal to a wide segment of the population. "And then I said, hold it, if I can prevent one unintended pregnancy, one person from getting AIDS, one person from getting a sexually transmitted disease, it will be worth it."

This determinedly optimistic, affirmative, and wholesome approach leaves Westheimer open to criticism and satire. It is a testament to the endurance of the human spirit that someone who was exposed to the horrors of humanity and experienced great sorrow at an early age is able to look away from the darkness and toward the light. As she told a Reuters interviewer at the 1995 Frankfurt Book Fair, "I was kicked out in 1939 by being placed on a train right here in Frankfurt.... I never saw my parents again. Every time I am sad I just have to think about my five-year-old grandson. Hitler didn't want me to have that grandson. I put the picture of my grandson in my mind and

say—You see, we did triumph. So I do therapy on myself."

In 1997 she coauthored a book expressly for grandchildren, *Dr. Ruth Talks About Grandparents: Advice for Kids on Making the Most of a Special Relationship.* And more books are on the way. Her *Pregnancy Guide for Couples: Romance, Sex, and Medical Facts* (with Dr. Amos Grunebaum) will be published by Routledge, Inc., as will a book on grandparenting *for* grandparents.

SELECTED WORKS BY RUTH WESTHEIMER

All in a Lifetime, with Ben Yagoda (1987); *Dr. Ruth's Encyclopedia of Sex* (1994); *Dr. Ruth's Guide to Good Sex* (1983); *Heavenly Sex: Sexuality in the Jewish Tradition*, with Jonathan Mark (1995); *Sex for Dummies* (1995).

BIBLIOGRAPHY

Biale, David. "Dr. Ruth's 'Heavenly Sex': Are Jews 'A Sexual Light Unto the Nations'?" *Forward*, October 6, 1995, and "Review of *Heavenly Sex*," *Ethnic Newswatch*,

October 1995; Haas, Nancy C. "Everything You Ever Wanted to Know About Sex . . . And a Few Things You Didn't Are Spelled Out in Westheimer's Latest Tome." *Forward*, July 29, 1994; Majendie, Paul. "For Sex Therapist Dr. Ruth, Homecoming Is Agony." Reuters, October 12, 1995; Painter, Kim. "How Dr. Ruth Was Seduced into Writing 'Sex For Dummies.'" *USA Today*, September 10, 1995; Schwartz, Bruce. "Dr. Ruth Brings Therapy to Cyberspace." *USA Today*, November 11, 1994.

KATHLEEN THOMPSON

WETSTEIN, MARTHA A. (b. 1880–?)

Contributions to society are sometimes made by women who then disappear from recorded history because they change their name at marriage, change their occupation, or simply never reply to requests for information. Martha A. Wetstein is one of those women. Born in Philadelphia on May 10, 1880, daughter of Herman and Anne (Witkoff) Wetstein, she was educated in the local public schools and the Free Hebrew Academy. Quickly and briefly, she became a bright star in prison reform.

At twenty-two, Wetstein was a delegate to the National Prison Congress of 1902. By the time she was twenty-five, she is said to have been the second Jewish probation officer in the United States and the first to supervise all the Jewish cases in Philadelphia. Here the trail ends, but the Jewish men and women Martha A. Wetstein supervised benefited from her ability to speak their language and assist them in reestablishing themselves in society.

BIBLIOGRAPHY
AJYB 7 (1905–1906): 115.

DOROTHY THOMAS

WHITMAN, RUTH (b. 1922)

"I keep my clocks a little fast / so time won't take me by surprise," wrote Ruth Whitman in "Round," one of her early poems collected in *Laughing Gas* (1991). That collection of poems, chosen from thirty years of lyrical writing, records a life lived as a race against the clock. Whitman wrote her first poem when she was age nine and sold her first poem when she was age eleven. At age seventy, in *Hatshepsut, Speak to Me*, her eighth volume of poetry, she wrote, "I'm racing to leave behind / a few words arranged in a pattern / that will touch the living."

Her autobiographical poems are about her journey through life, inspired by her experiences as a daughter, granddaughter, wife, and mother of two daughters and a son. Ruth (Bashein) Whitman, oldest daughter of Meyer David and Martha H. (Sherman) Bashein, was born on May 28, 1922, in New York City. Her brother, Harry Bashein, was born in 1927, and her sister, Nancy Baker Coe, in 1929. She has memories of her Russian-born grandfather singing Yiddish and Russian lullabies to her. As an adolescent, she read poetry avidly and was encouraged by her teachers in high school and college to write. She graduated from Radcliffe College magna cum laude in 1944 with a degree in Greek and English and received her M.A. in classics from Harvard University in 1947.

In 1941, she eloped with Cedric Whitman, a brilliant young classicist poet at Harvard University, and the couple had two daughters, Rachel and Lida. The marriage ended in divorce in 1958. A shorter marriage to Firman Houghton, during which her son David was born, ended in divorce in 1964. In 1966, she married Morton Sachs, the painter. She wrote of that marriage as her "homecoming."

Late in life, Whitman learned Yiddish, and a year as writer-in-residence at the Hebrew University (1984–1985) added yet another dimension to her Jewish life. There are Jewish poems in all her collections, but she has received special acclaim for her translations of the work of Yiddish poets Jacob Glatshteyn and Abraham Sutzkever. Her excellent *Anthology of Modern Yiddish Poetry*, first published in 1966, was reissued with additional poems in 1995.

In the 1970s, Whitman began her series of narrative poems written in the voices of women from the past. Lizzie Borden, the repressed nineteenth-century rebel; Tamsen Donner, who lost her life during an ill-fated trek west in 1864; Hanna Senesh, who was executed by firing squad after trying to rescue Hungarian Jews, including her mother, in 1943; and Hatshepsut, the only woman pharaoh in ancient Egypt. Whitman's *Hatshepsut, Speak to Me*, a dialogue across twenty-five centuries, describes the problems with sexual identity, love, work, and motherhood that she and Hatshepsut share. She speaks to Hatshepsut as if she were her contemporary and tries to learn how to use her strength without fear.

Whitman's subjects stem from her obsession with survival—her questions about how she would behave under life-threatening stress, whether she would be a victim or a survivor. She has earned her living as a teacher and reader of poetry, and has received many awards, grants, and fellowships. Her teaching career began at the Cambridge Center for Adult Education in 1964. Since 1969, she has lectured on poetry at the Radcliffe Seminars and has been a poet-in-residence on many campuses.

*Noted poet Ruth Whitman's series of narrative poems are written in the voices of women from the past,
including accused murderer Lizzie Borden; Tamsen Donner, a member of the ill-fated Donner party;
and Hatshepsut, the only woman pharaoh in ancient Egypt. Whitman has also been acclaimed
for her translations of Yiddish poets. [Martha Stewart]*

Ruth Whitman lives in Newport, Rhode Island, where the view of the Atlantic from her window provides peace and inspiration, and in Brookline, Massachusetts, accessible to students from the Radcliffe Seminars and M.I.T., where she is a visiting professor of poetry.

SELECTED WORKS BY RUTH WHITMAN

Anthology of Modern Yiddish Poetry, 3d ed. (1995); *The Fiddle Rose: Poems by Abraham Sutzkever* (1990); *Hatshepsut, Speak to Me* (1992); *Laughing Gas* (1991); *The Marriage Wig and Other Poems* (1968); *The Passion of Lizzie Borden* (1973); *The Selected Poems of Jacob Glatstein* (1973); *Tamsen Donner: A Woman's Journey* (1977); *The Testing of Hanna Senesh* (1986).

BIBLIOGRAPHY

Contemporary Poets; Rothchild, Sylvia. "Interview with Poet Ruth Whitman." *The Jewish Advocate*, January 24, 1992; *Who's Who in America.*

SYLVIA ROTHCHILD

WHITNEY, ROSALIE LOEW (1873–1939)

In 1901, Rosalie (Rose) Loew became acting attorney in chief of the New York Legal Aid Society. She was the first woman to hold that post. Born May 4, 1873, she was the second daughter and third child of Hungarian-born attorney William Loew and milliner Lottie (Wechsler) Loew's three daughters and three sons. Her paternal grandfather was Reform rabbi Leopold Loew, influential in the emancipation of Magyar Jews in 1867.

Rosalie, who often helped in her mother's store, was educated in the public schools and earned a B.A. from HUNTER COLLEGE (1892) and an LL.B from New York University (1895). After she was admitted to practice, her father made her his law partner in Loew and Loew.

In 1897, she moved to the Legal Aid Society. Most of the cases were wage claims. Fluent in German,

Yiddish, and Hungarian, she also understood other languages, and judges allowed her to act as interpreter as well as counsel. She was enthusiastic, energetic, and tireless; her arguments were made in a "low, clear voice" with "wit and sense."

Travis Harvard Whitney, an Indiana-born (June 22, 1875) Methodist who graduated from Harvard Law School in 1903, was assistant secretary of the young New York City Citizens Union. He went to Legal Aid as one of Rosalie's volunteer assistants. They were married in 1903. It is known that she converted to Protestantism, although records of the details are not available. The Whitneys may not have been wholly estranged from her family: Travis gave a speech in synagogue, and in the 1930s, Rosalie helped her parents' relatives resettle in the United States.

The couple practiced law as Loew & Whitney from 1903 until 1907. In 1903, while president of a local women lawyer's association, she applied for admission to the Association of the Bar of the City of New York, trying to break the barrier for women, but withdrew her application in 1904. However, she was in the first group of women admitted to membership in 1937. During the three-year period when her sons were born she practiced part time. The sons were Travis Jr. (b. 1904), John L. (b. 1905), and William T. (b. 1907).

Travis and Rosalie Whitney's professional lives were marked by appointment to state and local public office. Travis, a transportation specialist, practiced privately between positions. In 1933 Mayor Fiorello La Guardia appointed him civil works administrator. Intense and dedicated, Travis labored until he collapsed and, on January 8, 1934, died at fifty-nine after complications from emergency surgery for a bleeding ulcer.

Rosalie Whitney joined the Brooklyn Woman Suffrage Party in 1917 and was the New York congressional chair in the Woman's Federal Equality Association and a speaker for the National American Woman Suffrage Association at the House of Representatives suffrage amendment hearing in 1918. She was a Republican Party statewide campaigner in 1920 and developed Republican women's organizations. A founder of the New York Women's National Republican Club, she was an officer and its attorney.

Republican governor Nathan Miller appointed her commissioner of the State Department of Labor in 1921; she served more than a year. In May 1930, as volunteer director of the Neighborhood Laundry Association in Brooklyn, Whitney was described as the "first woman dictator of an American industry." She quickly cleaned out the racketeers.

Following Travis Whitney's death in 1934, Mayor LaGuardia appointed Rosalie Whitney first deputy license commissioner of New York City and, in 1935, a justice of the Domestic Relations Court. Rosalie Loew Whitney sat until her death at sixty-six on September 3, 1939, from leukemia. After a large funeral in Holy Trinity Protestant Episcopal Church, she was buried in Greenwood Cemetery, Brooklyn, New York.

BIBLIOGRAPHY

AJYB 6 (1904–1905): 206; Anthony, Susan B., Elizabeth Cady Stanton, et al., eds. *History of Woman Suffrage* Vol. 5 (1922): 578, 580; Harkness, LeRoy T. "Memorial of Travis Harvard Whitney." *Association of the Bar of the City of New York Yearbook, 1934; NYTimes*, January 9, 1934; Obituary. *NYTimes*, September 4, 1939, 19:3; Sicher, Dudley F. "Memorial of Rosalie Loew Whitney." *Association of the Bar of the City of New York Yearbook, 1940.*

DOROTHY THOMAS

WIERNIK, BERTHA (1884–c. 1951)

Writer and translator Bertha Wiernik, the younger sister of American journalist and essayist Peter Wiernik by nineteen years, was born to Hirsch Wolf and Sarah Rachel (Milchiger) Wiernik in Vilna, Lithuania, on March 21, 1884. Her father was a *magid* [itinerant preacher], and her mother was a merchant. Wiernik arrived in the United States in 1887, two years after her brother. She grew up in Chicago, where she attended public school and studied Hebrew and the Bible privately with a rabbi. She obtained a job setting type for the Chicago Hebrew weekly *Ha-Tehiyah*. In 1903, she moved to New York City, where she worked for various relief organizations and businesses.

She began writing in 1899 under the pseudonym "Shulamit." Her poems were published in *Der Kol* and the *Jewish Courier*. She also translated Yiddish literary classics for the *Jewish Herald, Tageblat*, and other English-language Jewish periodicals. Among her translations was Isaac Meir Dick's 1868 Yiddish book *Slavery or Serfdom*, a Jewish version of Harriet Beecher Stowe's *Uncle Tom's Cabin*. Wiernik was also a contributor and translator for the *English-Yiddish Encyclopedic Dictionary*, edited by Paul Abelson (1915).

She wrote and produced several dramatic works, which were staged under the auspices of various New York charitable societies. Her dramas include *Lomir Makhn a Pshoreh* [Let us compromise], *Di Teyveh* [The ark], *Mrs. Peddler, Nokh Nisht* [Not yet], and *Gaystige Atomen* [Spiritual atoms].

After her brother's death in 1936, Wiernek withdrew from the public scene and became religious. Her last written work, *Gaystige Atomen*, was a religious drama that was published in New York in 1946.

The date and place of Bertha Wiernik's death are uncertain. The *Leksikon fun der Nayer Yidisher Literatur* states that "in 1946, she moved to California where, according to reports, she died lonely and forgotten." According to her nephew Harris Wiernik she died in Brooklyn in 1951.

BIBLIOGRAPHY

Niger, Shmuel, ed. *Leksikon fun der Nayer Yidisher Literatur* (1956–1981). Vol. 3, s.v. "Viernik, Basiah (Berte)"; Reisen, Zalman. *Leksikon fun der Yidisher Literatur, Prese, un Filologye* (1927–1929). Vol. 1, s.v. "Viernik, Basiah (Berthe)"; Wiernik, Harris. Letter to Roger S. Kohn, March 28, 1988. Yeshiva University Archives, NYC; Yeshiva University Archives. *An Inventory to the Peter Wiernik and Bertha Wiernik Collection, 1886–1950* (1990); Zylbercwaig, Zalman. *Leksikon fun Yidishn Teater* (1931–1969). Vol. 1, s.v. "Viernik, Basiah."

ROGER KOHN

WILKE, HANNAH (1940–1993)

The body is omnipresent in the work of Hannah Wilke. Her typically nude body and its self-representation became the vehicle by which Wilke exposed personal, political, and linguistic themes. Like the work of her feminist peers of the 1970s, Wilke's art has often been oversimplified by critics, yet it continues to influence the complex art of postmodern artists today.

Wilke was born in New York City on March 7, 1940, as Arlene Hannah Butter to Selma and Emanuel, a lawyer. Wilke's maternal grandparents, the Fabians, emigrated to the United States from Hungary and her paternal grandparents from Poland. She earned two degrees from Temple University in Philadelphia: a bachelor of fine arts from Tyler School of Art in 1960 and a B.S. degree in 1961. After her marriage to designer Barry Wilke ended, she returned to New York City in 1965. Here Wilke would be represented by Ronald Feldman Fine Arts and later teach at the School of Visual Arts for nearly two decades.

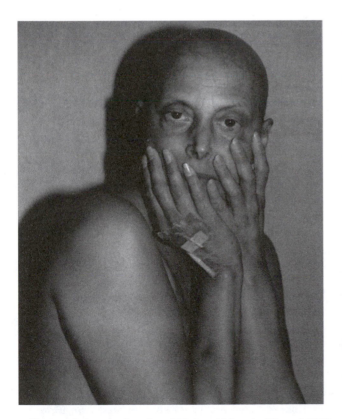
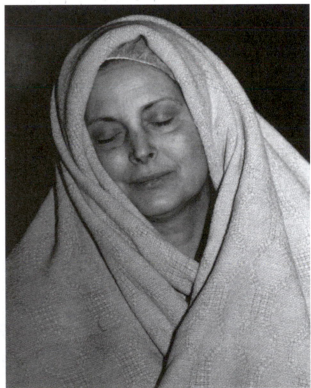

Her own body was often the vehicle by which artist Hannah Wilke explored the personal and the political, parodying and dismantling stereotypical representations of "femininity." Her last series, Intra-Venus, *is a painfully profound series using photographs and mixed media to reveal the gradual deterioration of her once-familiar body caused by lymphoma. The two panels from the series reproduced above are entitled* July 26, 1992/February 19, 1992. #4. *[Dennis Cowley. Photograph courtesy Ronald Feldman Fine Arts, Inc.]*

Wilke's elder sister, feminist therapist Marsie Scharlatt, observes that one of her sister's first artistic joys was the folding of triangular pastries with their mother (*Intra-Venus*, 18). This process is echoed in Wilke's signature fortune cookie-like works, such as *Teasle Cushion* (1967), which combines the artist's interest in human gesture and sexuality with word-play. These folded forms are ever-present in Wilke's oeuvre—made of terra cotta, latex, lint, chewing gum, etc.—and are consistently vaginal in shape. "My concern," asserted Wilke, "is with the word translated into form, with creating a positive image to wipe out the prejudices, aggression, and fear associated with the negative connotations of pussy, cunt, box" (Frueh, 139). Similarly, Wilke reclaimed disposable materials, such as lint, thereby transforming the "negative" into "art."

Although Wilke continued to produce both sculpture and drawings, by the early 1970s she had begun to focus on photography, video, and performance art. In *S.O.S.—Starification Object Series* (1974–75), Wilke presents a collection of "performalist self-portraits," in which she both parodies and dismantles stereotypical representations of "femininity." She disrupts the pleasure of the gaze by covering her semi-nude body with vaginal-shaped chewing gum, which appears as scars on her flesh. For Wilke, this "scarification" links beauty with vulnerability and death, via such references as numbered tattoos on Holocaust victims and African cicatrization.

Nudity assumes a different role in Wilke's *Venus Pareve* (1982–1984), a group of small self-portrait figures that were originally cast in chocolate. As she related the consumption of food with that of women, Wilke explored ideas concerning beauty and Jewish identity. The Hebrew dietary term *pareve* [neither meat nor dairy] is used to convey the concept of the universal. Thus, Wilke offered her classically nude body as a "universal" Jewish goddess of love, while examining myths of the ideal woman.

In 1987, Wilke was diagnosed with lymphoma. She had been painting abstract watercolors of her face that were later exhibited as *B.C.* meaning *Before Consciousness* (of her cancer). In 1991, Wilke began to document the effects of her illness/treatment. With the help of her husband, writer and editor Donald Goddard, she produced *Intra-Venus*, a painfully profound series using photographs and mixed-media to reveal the gradual deterioration of her once-familiar body. Goddard explains that the works were originally to be part of her *Cured* show, but that title could not be used (*Intra-Venus*, 16).

Hannah Wilke died on January 28, 1993.

BIBLIOGRAPHY

"Artist Hannah Wilke Talks with Ernst." *Oasis d'Neon* 1, nos. 1 and 3 (1979): 1–5; Broude, Norma, and Mary D. Garrard, eds. *Power of Feminist Art* (1994); Frueh, Joanna. *Hannah Wilke: A Retrospective*. Edited by Thomas H. Kochheiser (1989); Huestis, Chris, and Marvin Jones. "Hannah Wilke's Art, Politics, Religion and Feminism." *New Common Good* (May 1985): 1+; Jones, Amelia, Donald Goddard, Marsie Scharlett, et al. *Intra-Venus* (1995); Margolin, Ruth. "An Interview with Hannah Wilke." *Forum* (November/December 1989): 9–11; Robins, Corinne. "Why We Need 'Bad Girls,' Rather than 'Good' Ones!" *M/E/A/N/I/N/G* 8 (November 1990): 43–48; Ronald Feldman Fine Arts, Inc. Archives. NYC; Rose, Barbara. "Vaginal Iconology." *New York* (May 20, 1974): 59; Siegel, Judy. "Between the Censor and the Muse? Hannah Wilke: Censoring the Muse?" *Woman Artists News* (Winter 1986): 4+; Smith, Roberta. "Hannah Wilke, 52, Artist, Dies: Used Female Body as Her Subject." *NYTimes*, January 29, 1993, A18; *Too Jewish? Challenging Traditional Identities*. Edited by Norman L. Kleeblatt (1996); Wacks, Debra. "Feminism/ Humanism in Hannah Wilke's *S.O.S.—Starification Object Series*." Master's thesis, Institute of Fine Arts, New York University, 1992.

DEBRA WACKS

WILLEN, PEARL (1904–1968)

Pearl Willen was a social and human welfare activist and communal leader with a love for the Jewish heritage. She had a lifelong record of service for such causes as civil rights, women's rights, and the rights of workers.

Born in Chicago, Illinois, on January 2, 1904, Pearl (Larner) Willen was the daughter of Sarah and Mayer Larner, the oldest of four brothers and one sister. She graduated from Washington University and came to New York on a fellowship at the Graduate School of Jewish Social Work. It was there, in 1925, that she met and married Joseph Willen. Her husband, who died in 1985, was the executive vice president of the Federation of Jewish Philanthropies, and they had two children, Paul Willen, an architect, and Deborah Meier, an educator. Willen received an M.A. degree from Columbia University in 1935. She began her career as a case worker in child care at the Foster Home Bureau in New York in 1927 and was a field organizer and group leader for the Parent Education Council in Westchester, New York. Involved in many social programs, she helped organize the Southern School for workers (a resident workers' school), which emphasized the principles of unionism. Here she taught and encouraged workers to read and write.

A dynamic and dedicated leader in political as well as communal settings, Pearl Willen was chair of the

A dynamic and dedicated leader in political as well as communal settings, Pearl Willen was chair of the Women's Division of the American Labor Party, which backed the trade unions and introduced liberal idealism in New York politics. From 1963 to 1967, she served as president of the NATIONAL COUNCIL OF JEWISH WOMEN.

Women's Division of the American Liberal Party, which backed the trade unions and introduced liberal idealism in New York politics. She was involved in many organizations including the Southern Camp of Pioneer Youth, an organization supporting two camps for children of trade unionists, where she served as chair. She served as secretary to the Labor Education Service, a national organization in the field of workers' education, as a member of the Executive Board Union for Democratic Action, as a member of the Board of Editors of the Jewish Welfare Board Women's Division Journal, and as vice chair of the State Administrative Committee of the Liberal Party. She ran for the City Council of New York in 1943, stating that "democracy means wide participation by all people, especially in New York, where we have to break down its bigness into units that reach everybody."

Willen was appointed in 1951 by the State Department to participate in a panel of American women to visit and study organizational life in West Germany. She was on the board of governors for the Hebrew University in Jerusalem and on the board of directors of the American Friends of the Hebrew University, as well as on the board of governors for the American Red Cross. She led the International Council of Jewish women for three years and traveled throughout Europe, Asia, and South America to help Jewish women develop their leadership skills. She led many programs dealing with human rights and social welfare in the NATIONAL COUNCIL OF JEWISH WOMEN, and, because of her outstanding service, was chosen as its president from 1963 to 1967.

Her children remember her as an articulate and dedicated leader who fought for the underdog, as well as a humorous and warm mother and grandmother. She lived life to its fullest and was not only a leader in liberal social causes but also an inspirational speaker, a talented pianist, gardener, and athlete.

Pearl Willen met an untimely death at age sixty-four in March 1968, while on an African safari when the vehicle she was in overturned. Willen had a life-long record of service and worked to advance human welfare and democracy. A great humanitarian, she actively worked for freedom from oppression and poverty for all people.

BIBLIOGRAPHY

AJYB, 70:526; *American Examiner* (July 7, 1966): 10; *EJ* s.v. "Willen, Joseph"; Levine, Sue. Interviews with Paul Willen [son] and Deborah Willen Meier [daughter]; Obituary. *NYTimes*, March 18, 1968, 45:1; Willen, Pearl. Biographical sketch; *WWWIA*, 5.

SUE LEVINE

WIMPFHEIMER, HENRIETTA SCHEUER (1836–1939)

An extraordinarily active woman who lived to be 103, Henrietta Scheuer Wimpfheimer's life was representative of many nineteenth-century urban Jewish women.

Henrietta Scheuer Wimpfheimer, born on June 21, 1836, to Bernhardt Baruch and Rosa Scheuer in Mainz, Germany, married Max Wimpfheimer when she was eighteen. In 1854, Henrietta Scheuer Wimpfheimer and her husband joined the wave of German Jews who left their homeland for religous freedom and economic opportunity in the United States. Unlike most Jewish immigrants, the Wimpfheimers settled in rural Somersworth, New Hampshire. There they raised a family of five daughters and four sons. Twelve years later, the Wimpfheimers moved to New York City, where Max opened a velvet business with his brother Abraham.

Max Wimpfheimer died at age forty-seven, leaving Henrietta Wimpfheimer with over half her life remaining to be lived. She filled the next fifty years participating in local Jewish community groups. She was a member of Temple Beth-El and Central synagogues, and an active member in a number of Jewish women's benevolent associations. Wimpfheimer joined Unabhaengiger Treue Schwestern [United Order of True Sisters]—a female equivalent of B'nai B'rith—as a charter member. This New York–founded organization with lodges in nearby cities merged benevolence with social functions. Following the lead of Protestant secret societies such as the Masons, the United Order of True Sisters included rituals in their meetings and special codes for their members, while they assisted Jews in need.

Wimpfheimer was a member of many other New York benevolent societies including the New York Guild for the Blind, the Amelia Relief Society, the Montefiore Home, and the Godmothers' League.

Besides her benevolence work, Wimpfheimer led an active social life. Her obituary in September 1939 in *The New York Times* characterized her as a strong-willed and well-loved woman. She was known to drink champagne with dinner and to smoke a cigarette on occasion. A practical and resourceful woman, she managed her own finances after her husband's death. Shortly before she died, a reporter asked Wimpfheimer her secret for a long and productive life. Her answer, printed in her obituary, was, "I didn't do anything extra. I had my three meals a day—I had fresh air and I worked."

BIBLIOGRAPHY

Diner, Hasia R. *A Time for Gathering: The Second Migration, 1820–1880* (1992); Obituary. *NYTimes*, September 17, 1939, 49:1; *WWIAJ* (1938): 1141–1142.

AMY DeROGATIS

WINESTINE, BELLE (1891–1985)

Belle Winestine is best remembered as Jeannette Rankin's legislative assistant, though she served in this capacity for only one year (1916–1917). Nonetheless, her work with Rankin served as an important apprenticeship that created a lasting friendship, profoundly influenced her understanding of the legislative process, and solidified what became her lifelong commitment to reform. For over seventy years, she devoted time, money, and energy to support and enforce legislation pertaining to women's rights and children's issues.

Initially, her reform interests directly challenged the gendered conventions that governed her family's life. Her parents, Herman and Minnie Fligelman, were Jewish immigrants who moved to Helena, Montana, from Romania in 1889. Minnie died two weeks after giving birth to Belle. Herman became a successful businessman and married Getty Vogelman in 1895. Together, they raised Belle and her older sister, Frieda, in the Jewish faith and planned for them to attend finishing school, marry, and have children.

Belle Winestine's aspirations were not limited to religious or domestic proscriptions for women. She studied journalism at the University of Wisconsin, Madison, a center of new ideas about government legislation and labor reform. She used her journalistic talents as the editor of the women's page of the student newspaper to express her interests in labor laws, health insurance, the exploitation of workers in industry, and women's rights. Her peers recognized her outspoken, energetic, and affable personality by electing her president of the Women's Student Government Association, voting her the most prominent coed in the university, and selecting her as the first woman commencement speaker. Her popularity extended beyond campus life. Members of the State Headquarters for Woman Suffrage in Wisconsin selected her as the student representative to address a joint session of the state legislature, thus marking her entrance into the suffrage movement.

In 1914, one year after graduating with a bachelor's degree in philosophy, she helped to launch the woman suffrage movement in Montana. To capture the public's attention, the suffragists drove up and down Main Street waving banners and handing out literature. These demonstrations culminated in street speeches that electrified the community and put women's political demands at the forefront of public debate. While making significant contributions to the suffrage movement, Winestine also worked as the first woman reporter for the *Helena Independent*. That summer, the paper's editor assigned her to report on Jeannette Rankin's speech at a meeting of the local Federation of Women's Clubs in Lewistown, Montana. Winestine immediately became Rankin's most devoted follower, traveling with her and other suffragists throughout the state. Rankin's leadership and Winestine's capable assistance enabled Montana suffragists to achieve their quest—woman suffrage.

Winestine also played a key role when Rankin ran for Congress in 1916, writing publicity pieces for newspapers, lobbying potential supporters, and helping to organize her campaign strategies. She moved to Washington, D.C., after Rankin won the election to work as her legislative secretary and ghostwriter. As Rankin's most active staff member, Winestine supported legislation that included civil service reform, pay equity, and infancy and maternity laws.

Though Belle Winestine eagerly pursued professional aspirations, she also enjoyed a sixty-seven-year marriage to Norman Winestine. They raised three children, Mina (b. 1918), Judy (b. 1919), and Henry (1924–1989). She served as the state president of the League of Women Voters in the 1920s, leading the campaign that gave women the right to serve on juries. She also lobbied for the Child Labor Amendment and the Equal Rights Amendment and for the creation of a state Children's Bureau. In 1932, she unsuccessfully ran for the Montana Senate under the slogan "Smaller and Better Senators."

As a member of the women's movement, Belle Winestine believed that she contributed to the historical process that encouraged women to seek public employment and to pursue professional lives. She identified herself as a professional journalist and writer of short stories, plays, and children's books. She did not see herself as a politician but rather as an individual with the responsibility to help ameliorate the problems of her community. As a politically active woman, she advocated legislation that regulated working conditions in industry, ensured pay equity between men and women, and challenged discriminatory attitudes that strictly relegated women to the domestic sphere. Winestine successfully balanced the responsibilities of family life with the rigors of her reform activism and journalism career. Her family and friends remember her for her generosity, tenacity, sense of humor, and ability to live life to its fullest extent.

Belle Winestine died in a nursing home in Helena, Montana, on April 21, 1985, following complications from a stroke in 1984.

BIBLIOGRAPHY

Berson, Robin Kadison. *Marching to a Different Drummer: Unrecognized Heroes of American History* (1985); Hewes, Minna. Interview with author, 1996; Rochlin, Fred, and Harriet Rochlin. *Pioneer Jews: A New Life in the Far West* (1984); Schaffer, Ronald. "The Montana Woman Suffrage Campaign, 1911–1914." *Pacific Northwest Quarterly* 55 (January 1964): 9–15; Winestine, Belle. Belle (Fligelman) and Norman Winestine Collection, 1882–1985. Manuscript Collection, Montana Historical Society Archives, and Interviews with George Cole (1976) and Bill Lang (November 2, 1979). Montana Historical Society, Special Collections, and "Mother Was Shocked." *Montana: The Magazine of Western History* (Summer 1974): 70–79, and Papers. M-136, Reel B 38, AW767. Schlesinger Library, Radcliffe College, and "A Time for Women," April 5, 1973, Montana Historical Society Archives, Special Collections; Winestine, Zachary. Interview with author, 1996; Wolf, Judy. Interview with author, 1996; *WWIAJ* (1938).

AMY BUTLER

WINETZKAJA, MARIA (c. 1888–1956)

Maria Winetzkaja was a renowned opera singer, whose international career spanned twenty years, and a rebellious, independent woman. She was born to Woolf and Naomi (Nemeroff) Kleiner in Kishinev, Bessarabia (now Moldova), probably around 1888 or 1889; the exact date is unknown. She was the seventh of ten children, and the fifth of six girls. Her father was a cantor in a synagogue in Kishinev. Her love for his voice may have influenced her choice of a career, but she wanted nothing to do with Judaism, calling it ridiculous and foolish. She was particularly angered by what she perceived to be Judaism's attitude toward women: "Women are nothing." She informed her family early on that she would have no part of it.

When Maria was ten years old, she won a piano scholarship to the Russian Imperial Conservatory of Music. Around 1904, following progroms in Kishinev, her family came to the United States. She received an artist's degree in 1913 from the Institute of Musical Art in New York, and made her professional singing debut in 1917 with the Boston Opera Company. She eventually spoke eight languages through the study of opera.

Winetzkaja was a leading mezzo soprano with the Boston National Grand Opera Company in 1917 and 1918, and toured Central and South America with the Bracale Opera Company from 1919 to 1921. She performed in many cities in the United States throughout her career, as a member of several opera companies, including the Puccini Opera Company of Philadelphia and the New York Grand Opera and Cosmopolitan Opera companies in New York. Winetzkaja also gave recitals at Town Hall, Aeolian Hall, and Carnegie Hall in New York, as well as in other major American cities. She never sang at the Metropolitan Opera, the pinnacle of success for American singers: the reason, she said, was that she refused to sleep with one of the Met's directors.

Winetzkaja had a very rich, beautiful mezzo-soprano voice, and was an excellent musician. A spontaneous singer, she rarely marked her scores. During

At an early age, Maria Winetzkaja rejected her family's Judaism for what she regarded as a lack of respect for women. It was that strength of character that allowed her to become an international opera star renowned for her rich, mezzo-soprano voice.
[Photograph courtesy of Steven Winnett]

the 1920s, a reviewer wrote that her voice, "which ranges from big chest tones almost masculine in timbre to quite high tones, which have a clear silvery ring, is much like her person. It shows the same richness and powerful magnetism" (Dorothy J. Teall, *Musical America*). *The Musical Leader* reported, "Mme. Winetzkaja's dramatic quality served her as well in recital as it did in the impersonation of a role. She showed extraordinary musicianship and versatility in English, French, Italian and Russian songs."

She was also an excellent dramatic actress, and the roles she sang encompass some of the most dramatic in the mezzo repertoire. Her favorite roles were Carmen *(Carmen)* and Delilah *(Samson and Delilah)*, and she routinely sang the Witch/Mother in *Hansel and Gretel*, Amneris in *Aïda*, Azucena in *Il Trovatore*, and Suzuki in *Madama Butterfly*.

Winetzkaja lived as a modern woman in an age that did not encourage such behavior. She was a common-law wife to her husband, Schai Winett, although they claimed a wedding date for appearances. She also took the feminine version of his Ukrainian name, Winetsky, which he had anglicized when he arrived in the United States. Winett was a civil engineer and architect for the city of New York, and also managed much of his wife's career. He had immigrated to the United States in 1903, from Ukraine.

Winetzkaja had her children late in her life, given the times: Ralph and George were born in 1915 and 1923, respectively. The demands of her career meant that she was often distracted or simply not at home. Although it sometimes seemed she lacked the mothering instinct, she loved her family fiercely. For instance, she rejected the wisdom of doctors who suggested she allow George to die when, as a newborn, he threw up all food fed to him. She dragged the infant from doctor to doctor until she found one who correctly diagnosed and treated him for pyloric stenosis, a closure of one of the main gastrointestinal valves. George grew up to be a chemist; Ralph, a writer.

After retiring from the stage, Winetzkaja taught, both privately and on the Juilliard faculty, and traveled extensively. She was very active in her students' lives, and several of them lived with her at various times. Her husband died in 1941, when she was in her early fifties.

Winetzkaja died in 1956 of the cancer she had had for several years. Despite her illness, she was energetic in her final years, traveling around Alaska a year before her death. She also remained feisty. When her first grandchild was born in 1954, her parents had to cope with the difference between the norms of cleanliness in the old and new worlds. Concerned for their newborn's health, the parents would drape a towel over my grandmother's shoulder and chest to "prevent the baby from drooling on her clothes." Winetzkaja was not fooled. On one memorable visit, she stalked wordlessly into the apartment carrying a large bag and disappeared into the bathroom. She emerged dressed in a spotlessly clean nurse's uniform. "*Now* can I hold your baby?" she asked.

Winetzkaja's desire for an equal footing for women may have been unusual for her time, but she influenced her descendants. In terms of women's roles, the daughter of her son Ralph currently practices medicine. Her son George married a professional musician and orchestra conductor; their daughter is a professor of feminist and comparative literature. The music lives on, too. Steven Winnett is not only a professional forester but also a singer and bassoonist.

BIBLIOGRAPHY

Obituary. *NYTimes*, May 23, 1956, 31:4; Recital programs of Maria Winetzkaja, 1918–1929, in author's possession; Winnett, A. George, and Elaine S. Winnett. Interview with author, February 1996; *WWIAJ* (1928, 1938).

STEVEN WINNETT

WINSLOW, THYRA SAMTER
(1893–1961)

Author Thyra Samter Winslow's sketches of women's lives reflect her combined feelings of fondness for and restless impatience with small-town life, and later her attraction to the big city.

Born to Louis and Sara (Harris) Samter on March 15, 1893, she began writing as a child, and like many of her young female characters, yearned for life beyond her hometown of Fort Smith, Arkansas. She eventually left to attend the University of Missouri School of Journalism and later moved to Chicago where she worked as a chorus girl, actress, and dancer—experiences she depicts in her novel *Show Business* (1926). Finally Samter secured a position as a feature writer with the *Chicago Tribune* from 1915 to 1916, and during this time began publishing stories and articles for newspapers and magazines such as *The Smart Set* and *American Mercury*. She briefly attended Columbia University and the Cincinnati Art Academy.

In the early 1920s, she married John Seymour Winslow. They were divorced in 1927, and she married Nelson Waldorf Hyde the same year. Her career as a fiction writer blossomed in the 1930s when she began to publish stories in *The New Yorker*, and gained the attention of critics such as Carl Van Doren. In 1937, Winslow and Hyde divorced, and she began working as a screenwriter with Columbia, RKO, and later with Warner Brothers and NBC. She lived the rest of her life in Hollywood and New York City.

When considered together, Winslow's fictional works comprise a loose and fragmented scrapbook of women's struggles and choices. While she glamorizes marriage as a means to happiness, she often parts the curtains of social convention, revealing troubled inner lives. Beneath their decorum and "soft blond exteriors," many of her characters—both country and city women—harbor feelings of anger, boredom, and oppression, and even thoughts of suicide. The "happy endings" of several stories (poor country girl marries rich city man) are nevertheless tinged with a hollow, ambiguous quality. Many of Winslow's female characters long for success and adventure, but remain locked into the routine of marriage and family, helplessly wait for "something to happen." While Winslow clearly established a place for herself in cosmopolitan society, in her fiction she often looked back on provincial life with nostalgia. Her collection of sketches (*Picture Frames*, later released as *Window Panes*) affectionately depicts local idiosyncrasies, and dignifies the closeness of small-town life.

That few of her stories are directly about Jewish characters is a choice which in itself indicates Winslow's desire to assimilate into American "high society." In "A Cycle of Manhattan," she traces the progression of a family of Lithuanian Jewish immigrants from poverty to economic security in America. Following in the pattern of Winslow's other "rags to riches" stories, this tale of bittersweet success hints at the losses and costs of assimilation into mainstream urban life. Like her "country girls" who endeavor to transform themselves culturally, her Jewish characters pressure one another to discard their *sheytl* [traditional Jewish women's head coverings or wigs], to shave their beards, to soften their manners, and to change their names. As the family relinquishes traditions and ceases to speak Yiddish, it loses its closeness. Talk of old times and memories is forbidden. The grandmother becomes alienated, silent and isolated, while the children grow increasingly self-centered and insensitive.

Winslow portrays the urge to assimilate and achieve social and economic success in modern American urban life. At the same time, she offers a window into the emotional dilemmas accompanying this quest for cosmopolitan sophistication and prosperity.

Thyra Samter Winslow died in New York on December 2, 1961, a year after suffering a paralyzing fall.

SELECTED WORKS BY THYRA SAMTER WINSLOW

Blueberry Pie and Other Stories (1932); *Chorus Girl* (1945); *Four Daughters* (1938). Dialogue and motion picture; *My Own, My Native Land* (1935); *People Round the Corner* (1927); *Picture Frames* (1923. Reprinted as *Window Panes*, 1945); *The Sex Without Sentiment* (1954); *She Married Her Boss* (1935). *Show Business* (1926); *Think Yourself Thin: The New Mental Outlook to Help You Lose Weight* (1951).

BIBLIOGRAPHY

BEOAJ; Blanck, Jacob Nathaniel. *Bibliography of American Literature*. Vol. 9 (1955–1991); *EJ* 15 (1971): 1584;

Maugham, William Somerset, ed. *Tellers of Tales* (1939); Obituary." *NYTimes*, December 3, 1961, 88:4; Van Doren, Carl. *Modern American Prose* (1934); *WWWIA* 4; *Who's Who in America* 30: 1958–1959 (1938): 3024; *WWIAJ* (1928, 1938): 1144.

JOAN MOELIS

WINTERS, SHELLEY (b. 1924)

Shelley Winters's acting career has ranged from a fairy in a local pageant at age four to the eccentric Grandma Harris on television's *Roseanne*. She has performed in over 100 movies, 50 stage plays, and countless television programs, and has won two Academy Awards and an Emmy.

Shelley Winters was born Shirley Schrift on August 18, 1924, in St. Louis, Missouri. She was the second of two children, born five years after her sister Blanche. Her mother, Rose Winter, was also born in St. Louis after her parents emigrated from Grymalow, Austria. Winters's father, Jonas Schrift, also emigrated from Grymalow, marrying his third cousin Rose in America. When Shirley needed a stage name, she took her mother's maiden name. Later, Universal Studios added the *s* at the end, resulting in Winters.

The Schrifts moved to New York in the late 1920s, as Jonas Schrift attempted to work his way up into the middle class. But when Shelley was nine, her father was jailed for arson, a conviction for which he was exonerated after spending a year in prison. In New York, Shelley's Jewish education consisted of attending the Jamaica Jewish Center, as well as learning pioneer Hebrew songs at her Brooklyn public school. She dropped out of high school to earn money and to act.

When Winters first went to Hollywood in the early 1940s, she was made into a blonde bombshell, although she resisted the nose job they suggested. With age and experience, she has made the transition to character actor. She personally considers her best role in any medium to have been Charlotte in the film *Lolita*.

Winters has written a play, *One Night Stands of a Noisy Passenger*, which was produced in 1971. She has also published two volumes of her autobiography and is at work on the third. She has practiced the Stanislavsky Method of acting for most of her acting life and still teaches the method at the Actors Studio in New York.

It was Winters's *zeideh* [grandfather] who taught her the lesson of the talmudic Rabbi Hillel when she was only three: "If I'm not for myself, then who am I for? But if I am only for myself, what am I?" Sparked by her grandfather's teaching, fourteen-year-old Shel-

The enormously talented Shelley Winters has appeared in more than one hundred movies, fifty theatrical performances, and countless television programs. She has won two Academy Awards and an Emmy and written two volumes of an autobiography that reveals her to be a woman of great compassion, wit, and insight. [New York Public Library]

ley organized a strike at the local Woolworth's at which she was working. She later participated in civil rights movement activities and campaigned for presidential candidates Adlai Stevenson and John F. Kennedy. Soon after World War II, she engaged in a three-month tour for the United Jewish Appeal.

Winters has been married three times. Her first marriage was to a man she always refers to by a pseudonym. Because he is not a public figure, she prefers to safeguard his privacy. Her second husband was the

Italian actor Vittorio Gassman. They were married in 1952 but divorced in 1954 because neither of them was willing to move to the other's country. They had a daughter, Vittoria. Her third husband, Tony Franciosa, was also an actor. They were married in 1957 and divorced in 1960.

While the majority of her roles have had no Jewish connection, Winters has played a few Jewish roles, such as the hysterical Jewish mother in *Next Stop Greenwich Village*. In 1950, while on a publicity tour, she visited the two-year-old State of Israel. In the early 1950s, she refused to travel to Germany to film the exterior scenes of the movie *I Am a Camera* because she couldn't reconcile the thought of doing so with the image of her Holocaust-survivor uncle Yaekel, who spent the rest of his life searching for his wife and family, even though the Jewish Agency reported that they had starved to death in a boxcar left on a siding. Instead, a double was used for her in the footage in Germany.

In 1959, Winters won an Oscar for her role as Mrs. Van Daan in the film version of *The Diary of Anne Frank*. As preparation, she and the rest of the cast watched films of the concentration camps taken by American soldiers who liberated the camps. Since then, she has been unable to read or watch anything Holocaust-related. During the filming, she met Anne's father, Otto Frank, and promised him that if she won an Oscar for that role, she would donate it to the Anne Frank Museum in Amsterdam. She did win, and her Oscar is mounted on the wall of the museum.

SELECTED WORKS BY SHELLEY WINTERS
Shelley: Also Known as Shirley (1980); *Shelley II: The Middle of My Century* (1989).

BIBLIOGRAPHY
Ragan, David. *Who's Who in Hollywood 1900–1976* (1977).

SONIA ZYLBERBERG

WISCHNITZER, RACHEL
(1885–1989)

Rachel Wischnitzer was a pioneer in the fields of Jewish art history and synagogue architecture. Her wide-ranging scholarship included books, articles, book reviews, and exhibition catalogs on ancient, medieval, and modern Jewish art.

Rachel Bernstein Wischnitzer was born in Minsk, Russia, on April 14, 1885, to Vladimir and Sophie (Halpern) Bernstein. Her family, while acculturated, celebrated Jewish holidays. They lived in comfortable circumstances. She had one younger brother. Her father was an insurance agent and supported her while she pursued her studies. She graduated from high school in Warsaw in 1902, and studied art at the University of Heidelberg in 1902–1903, and the University of Munich in 1910–1911. She spent 1903 to 1905 at the School of Architecture at the Brussels Royal Academy, then transferred to the École Spéciale d'Architecture in Paris and received an architect's diploma in 1907, one of the first three women in Europe to attain that degree.

She married Mark Wischnitzer, a historian, in St. Petersburg in 1912. They had one child, Leonard, born in 1924. In 1920, the couple moved to London, where she was one of the first scholars to work on illuminated Hebrew manuscripts at the British Museum, London, and at the Bodleian Library, Oxford. This work led to later publications in the field.

The Wischnitzers moved to Berlin in 1921. Friends helped them found *Rimon* [Hebrew] and *Milgroim* [Yiddish], companion journals that each included a literary and art section. Rachel Wischnitzer was art editor of the short-lived (1922–1924) but beautiful periodicals. While in Berlin, she was also the art and architecture editor of the *Encyclopedia Judaica* (Berlin) from 1928 to 1934 and served the Jewish Museum in various capacities, including a curatorial one, from 1928 to 1938. A major achievement during this period was the publication of her first book, *Symbole und Gestalten der Jüdischen Kunst* [Symbols and forms of Jewish art] (1935).

The Wischnitzer family left Nazi Germany in the spring of 1938 and resided in Paris temporarily, where Rachel Wischnitzer took a course with Comte Robert du Mesnil du Buisson, excavator of the Dura-Europos synagogue (built A.D. 244–245) in Syria, an educational experience that significantly influenced the rest of her career.

Upon moving to New York in 1940, she resumed her formal studies at New York University's Institute of Fine Arts and completed her M.A. in 1944. At the same time, she was a research fellow at the American Academy for Jewish Research. Her master's thesis was published in 1948 as *The Messianic Theme in the Paintings of the Dura Synagogue*.

Her study of the synagogue continued with her book *Synagogue Architecture in the United States*, published in 1955, the year her husband died. The following year, at age seventy-one, she established the fine arts department at the STERN COLLEGE FOR WOMEN in New York, and taught there until her retirement in 1968. *The Architecture of the European Synagogue*, her final book-length work, was published in 1964.

Yeshiva University awarded her an honorary doctorate of humane letters at its commencement in 1968, and the *Journal of Jewish Art* dedicated an issue to her in 1979. This special issue included an autobiography and a bibliography of Wischnitzer's writings on both Jewish and general art, with a total of 344 entries. A later publication was an article on Picasso's *Guernica* that appeared in 1985, the centenary of her birth. She died four years later, at age 104. Her son, Leonard James Winchester, an engineer, survived her.

Rachel Bernstein Wischnitzer was a seminal figure in the development of a new scholarly discipline. The breadth of her contributions to the history of Jewish art and architecture is exemplified in her lifelong dedication to her work as editor, author, educator, lecturer, curator, and scholar.

SELECTED WORKS BY RACHEL WISCHNITZER

The Architecture of the European Synagogue (1964); *From Dura to Rembrandt* (1990); *The Messianic Theme in the Paintings of the Dura Synagogue* (1948); *Symbole und Gestalten der Jüdischen Kunst* [Symbols and forms of Jewish art] (1935); *Synagogue Architecture in the United States* (1955).

BIBLIOGRAPHY

AJYB 91 (1991): 568–569; *Artibus et Historiae* 9, no. 17 (1988). Special issue in honor of Rachel Wischnitzer; Elliott, Roberta. "Centenarian Thrives on Her Synagogue Architecture Work." *Jewish Week* (May 24, 1985): 22; *EJ*, s.v. "Wischnitzer, Mark"; Feil, Katharina. "A Scholar's Life: Rachel Wischnitzer and the Development of Jewish Art Scholarship in the Twentieth Century." D.H.L. thesis, Jewish Theological Seminary, 1994; *Journal of Jewish Art* 6 (1979); *Leksikon fun der Nayer Yidisher Literatur* [Biographical Dictionary of Modern Yiddish Literature] (1956–1981), s.v. "Vishnitser-Bernshteyn, Rahel"; Mayer, L.A. *Bibliography of Jewish Art* (1967); *NYTimes*, November 22, 1989, D18; *UJE*, s.v. "Wischnitzer-Bernstein, Rachel"; *Who's Who in World Jewry* (1973), s.v. "Wischnitzer, Rachel"; Winchester, Leonard James. Telephone interviews with author, May 29 and June 2, 1997; Wischnitzer, Rachel. File. Public Relations Department, Yeshiva University Archives, NYC.

SHULAMITH Z. BERGER

WISE, LOUISE WATERMAN
(1874–1947)

Philanthropist and charity worker Louise Waterman Wise was likely the first American Jewish woman to be awarded the Order of the British Empire, the equivalent of a knighthood. She was, without doubt, the first to decline the honor. How an ardent Zionist and outspoken critic of Britain's "ruthless conduct" with respect to Jewish settlement in Palestine could, nevertheless, perform such outstanding service to the British people as to merit official praise, is just one aspect of the "legend of Louise."

Were it not for the fact that she was married to America's most renowned rabbinic leader, Wise would be remembered today as one of the most prominent women in the history of Jewish America. For although most historians view her as simply the wife of Stephen S. Wise, her influence as a tireless advocate for the care and protection of children, the development of communal health care, refugee resettlement, and the establishment of the State of Israel was unparalleled. The introduction to the classic biographical collection *Notable American Women* clearly states that women (except for the wives of American presidents) were not included merely on the basis of their husbands' credentials. Significantly, the entry on Wise appears prominently in the pages of that book. And though the writer called her a "Jewish Eleanor Roosevelt," unintentionally diminishing her accomplishments, it was a comparison that Wise herself would have appreciated, since she considered her position as the wife of Stephen S. Wise to be her most valued role in life.

Born on July 17, 1874, in New York City, Louise Waterman was the daughter of Julius and Justine (Meyer) Waterman, wealthy aristocrats of German Jewish origin. Her mother was a woman of considerable education and refinement. Her father, a respected and successful businessman, valued education and the arts, though he himself was largely self-taught.

Louise was the youngest of three children, and her high spirits and boundless enthusiasm soon earned her the family nickname "Quicksilver." She was educated at the exclusive Comstock Finishing School and attended an Episcopalian Sunday school for a time, despite her parents' nominal membership at New York's Temple Emanu-El. In the 1890s, she met Felix Adler, founder of the Ethical Culture Society, and through him began her charitable work, teaching art at settlement houses in New York's slums.

Her parents did not approve of her charitable work, fearing her association with undesirable people. Their fears were confirmed when, in 1899, she met and fell in love with a young rabbi named Stephen Samuel Wise. To say that her parents disapproved of her wish to marry him would be an understatement of gigantic proportions. Stephen Wise's Hungarian heritage was considered a "serious impediment," his relative lack of wealth made him unsuitable, his choice of profession was a "major catastrophe," and his radical politics were scandalous. Finally, his Zionism was literally more than the Watermans could bear. Since

Louise Waterman Wise was probably the first American Jewish woman to be awarded the Order of the British Empire. She was certainly the first to decline the honor. Her reason— she was an outspoken critic of Britain's "ruthless conduct" with respect to Jewish settlement in Palestine. She is shown here with her daughter, JUSTINE WISE POLIER. *[American Jewish Historical Society]*

their family's reputation was at stake, they sent Louise on an extended vacation in Europe, in the hope that she would meet a more appropriate mate. But the young couple's struggle and separation only served to cement their relationship. Despite all objections, they were married the following year.

They spent the next six years in Portland, Oregon, where Stephen Wise had accepted a position as the rabbi of Temple Beth Israel. In Portland, Louise Wise established the Free Nurses' Association and bore two children. James (b. 1901) became a writer and his mother's principal biographer; JUSTINE WISE POLIER (b. 1903) became a lawyer and, later, a judge of a domestic relations court. In 1907, the family

returned to New York, where Stephen Wise established his Free Synagogue and rose to national prominence as an outstanding rabbi and political leader in American Jewish life.

Louise Wise continued her charitable work, taking on in 1916 the ambitious project of helping Jewish orphans. She learned that Jewish children left to the care of the state were routinely placed in asylums, since no agency existed to care for them. She therefore established the Child Adoption Agency of the Free Synagogue. The agency was a massive undertaking, which involved searching for literally thousands of Jewish orphans, gaining custody of them, and then placing them in Jewish homes all across the country.

During the 1920s, Wise studied painting and translated several French works on religion and Zionism into English. Her paintings show considerable talent, even though she never had enough time to truly develop her craft. Her eloquent translation of Edmond Fleg's "Why I am a Jew" is now a fixture of the Haggadah and the prayer books of Reform Judaism.

In 1931, she began working on behalf of Jewish refugees fleeing Europe, through the women's division of the AMERICAN JEWISH CONGRESS. The women's division provided information, refugee housing, and, later, hostels for Allied soldiers during World War II. Congress House was the first home welcoming untold thousands of refugees escaping Nazi persecution. Wise and her committed corps of volunteers greeted these immigrants as honored guests and long-lost kin, personally caring for their needs until appropriate housing and support could be found for them.

When the United States entered the war and the flood of Nazi refugees was cut off, Congress House became Defense House, a hostel accommodating more than a quarter of a million servicemen from nearly every nation of the Allied armies. Soldiers and sailors of all faiths were lovingly cared for by Wise's volunteers, drawing the praise and support of many, including Eleanor Roosevelt. The first lady was astonished by the thousands of women who attended the women's division annual luncheon at which she had been invited to speak.

Wise was an ardent Zionist for all of her adult life. She traveled many times to what was then British Mandate Palestine. She worked closely with HENRIETTA SZOLD in founding HADASSAH, the women's Zionist organization. With Hadassah, Wise worked to provide health care and support for the many immigrants to Palestine. She accompanied her husband to Palestine, lending her own strong voice to the negotiations that would result in both the Balfour Declaration after World War I and the United Nations call for the establishment of an independent Jewish state after World War II. Though she did not live to see that dream fulfilled, she did witness its birthing pains.

Louise Waterman Wise died on December 10, 1947, of pneumonia at her home in New York City.

BIBLIOGRAPHY

AJYB 24:215, 50:525; *BEOAJ*; *EJ*, s.v. "Wise, Stephen S."; *NAW*; Obituary. *NYTimes*, December 11, 1947, 33:1; Rapport, Joe Rooks. "Notable American Jewish Women: A Computer Aided Study in Collective Biography." Rabbinic thesis, Hebrew Union College (1984); *UJE*; Wise, James Waterman. *Legend of Louise* (1949); Wise, Stephen S. *Challenging Years: The Autobiography of Stephen Wise* (1949), and *Servant of the People* (1969); *WWIAJ* (1926, 1928, 1938); *WWWIA* 2.

JOE ROOKS-RAPPORT

WISSE, RUTH R. (b. 1936)

As a scholar and a literary and social critic, Ruth R. Wisse is a unique figure in American Jewish letters. She bridges the worlds of Yiddish and American culture, of literature and politics, and of Israel and the diaspora.

Born in Czernowitz, Romania, on May 13, 1936, Ruth, her older brother, and her parents Masha and Leo Roskies were admitted into Canada in 1940. The Roskieses' home in Montreal was a salon for Yiddish writers, actors, and artists. All four children (two were born in the New World) received a rigorous Hebrew and Yiddish education. Her brother David G. Roskies is a professor of Jewish literature at the Jewish Theological Seminary, and her sister Eva Raby is a professional storyteller and Jewish children's librarian in Montreal.

At McGill University, where she received a B.A. in 1957, Ruth studied with poet Louis Dudek, who was also a mentor to Leonard Cohen. But it was the Yiddish poet Abraham Sutzkever who played a pivotal role in her career by suggesting that she pursue a graduate degree in Yiddish studies at Columbia University. Upon her marriage to Leonard Wisse, she did just that, studying with both Max Weinreich and his son Uriel Weinreich, and received her M.A. at Columbia with an award-winning thesis on Sutzkever's prose poem *Green Aquarium*. After returning to Montreal, Wisse began raising a family while she completed her Ph.D. under Dudek's supervision. Published as *The Schlemiel as Modern Hero* (1971), this study traces the evolution of the schlemiel from Yiddish to American Jewish fiction.

Academically, Wisse was a pioneer. In 1968, she began teaching Yiddish literature and helped found the program, later the Department of Jewish Studies, at McGill University. In 1993, she became a professor of Yiddish at Harvard University. Intellectually, however, Wisse found her home in the political culture of the 1970s magazine *Commentary*. Here she measured the actual accomplishments of American Jewish fiction against its promise; introduced giants of twentieth-century Yiddish culture such as Moyshe-Leyb Halpern, Chaim Grade, I.B. Singer, and Abraham Sutzkever; and, like her close friend LUCY S. DAWIDOWICZ, refused to allow the destruction of Eastern European Jewish culture to cloud her historical judgment. Out of her engagement with Yiddish culture grew an interest in modern Jewish politics and its difficulty adjusting to the reality of Jewish statehood.

Wisse is best known in literary circles for her collaborative anthologies with Irving Howe: *The Best of Sholom Aleichem* (1979) and, together with Khone Shmeruk, *The Penguin Book of Modern Yiddish Verse* (1987). Her most sustained works of literary history are *A Little Love in Big Manhattan: Two Yiddish Poets* (1988) and her monographic study *I.L. Peretz and the Making of Modern Jewish Culture* (1991). She was also the first editor-in-chief of the Library of Yiddish Classics. In addition to her political essays, which appear regularly in *Commentary*, *The New Republic*, and *The Jerusalem Report*, Wisse has published a Zionist critique of the American Jewish political climate, *If I Am Not for Myself . . . : The Liberal Betrayal of the Jews* (1992).

SELECTED WORKS BY RUTH R. WISSE

The Best of Sholom Aleichem, edited with Irving Howe (1979); "A Golus Education." *Moment* (January 1977): 26+; "Hura! Hura!" *Moment* (December 1975): 21–23; *I.L. Peretz and the Making of Modern Jewish Culture* (1991); *I.L. Peretz Reader* (1990); *A Little Love in Big Manhattan: Two Yiddish Poets* (1988); "The Most Beautiful Woman in Vilna." *Commentary* (June 1981); "My Life Without Leonard Cohen." *Commentary* (October 1995): 27–33; *The Penguin Book of Modern Yiddish Verse*, edited with Irving Howe and Khone Shmeruk (1987); "What My Father Knew." *Commentary* (April 1995): 44–49.

DAVID G. ROSKIES

WOLF, FRANCES (1873–1957)

Of the approximately eighty women who were instrumental in opening up the legal profession for women in the United States, Frances Wolf was the first Jewish woman in that very select group.

She was born in Memphis, Tennessee, on June 18, 1873, the oldest of Tobias and Kate (Klein) Wolf's eight children. Only Wolf, two sisters, and three brothers survived to maturity. Frances was a second mother to her siblings, breadwinner and caregiver all her life, most importantly after her father's death in 1906.

Wolf's mother, Kate Klein, who was born in Baltimore, the daughter of a storekeeper, came to Memphis with her parents and met Tobias Wolf, an office worker. The Wolfs were a typical southern Jewish family: Reform in religion and southern in culture, keeping only the High Holy Days and cooking southern-style food.

After graduating from Memphis High School and a business school, Wolf was employed as a clerk. Sent by her employer to work in a booth at the World's Columbian Exposition in Chicago, she became interested in women's rights and the law when she visited the Woman's Pavilion. On her return, she began to read law and went to work for the law firm of John P. Houston. In 1903–1904, she attended the University of Tennessee law department, but not as a degree candidate. As the state of Tennessee would not admit her to practice law, she went to St. Louis and was admitted to the Missouri bar in 1904, returning to Houston's office to work as a law clerk. Meantime, Marion Griffin, who worked in Judge T.M. Scruggs's office in Memphis, left to study law at the University of Michigan. She graduated in 1906 and was admitted to the Michigan bar.

Wolf and Griffin knew each other through their association with Judge Scruggs's office. Griffin had been lobbying for a woman's bar admission statute since 1900. When she came back to Memphis in 1906, Wolf joined her, and together they promoted the passage of the bar admission bill. Its enactment in 1907 was the result of their joint effort. The story is told that the two women planned to be admitted at the same time, but Griffin's friends prevailed upon her to move immediately for admission without telling Frances Wolf. Griffin was admitted in February 1907, and Wolf, after struggling to get over her disappointment, was admitted on July 11, 1907. It was not the first time that two women working together to secure enabling legislation were caught up in a battle for the honor of being the first. The local bar association, however, always recognized both women as pioneers.

Wolf worked as a title lawyer and trial lawyer with John Houston and John Johnson, practicing in all the state's courts. She was the first woman lawyer to argue before the Court of Civil Appeals. Houston named her executor of his will, and when he died in the late 1920s, Wolf successfully administered his estate with its large real estate holdings. After her mother died in 1934, Wolf retired to take care of an invalid sister.

A woman with a keen sense of humor, she loved music, nature, children, and her ever-growing collection of books, many on Napoleon. Her devotion to her family was exemplary.

Frances Wolf died at age eighty-three of arteriosclerosis and pulmonary edema on January 28, 1957. She is buried in Temple Israel Cemetery in Memphis.

BIBLIOGRAPHY
Bench and Bar of Memphis Memorial Record. Memphis, Tenn. (n.d.); *Memphis Commercial Appeal*, July 12, 1907, and Obituary. January 29, 1957; Watkins, Emma. Interview, July 1961.

DOROTHY THOMAS

WOLF, SALLY RIVOLI (b. 1899)

During World War I, Sally Rivoli Wolf joined the United States Navy as a Yeoman F, first class, and served from 1918 to 1919, as one of 2,324 women from the state of New York. This year of wartime service to her country and the camaraderie and patriotism it engendered determined the interests and activities to which she devoted the next twenty years of her life. As a professional journalist, she used her writing skill to record the history of the veterans' organizations she helped establish, and served as editor and associate editor for their publications. She was an organizer and active participant in the Women War Veterans Association, the American Legion, the Jewish War Veterans of the United States, and the National Yeoman F, an association of the women who had served in the U.S. Navy organized to preserve the historical significance of their service. She worked actively with both the Jewish War Veterans of the United States and the American Legion in positions promoting good will among Americans of all faiths and developing patriotic programs to perpetuate American ideals.

Sally Rivoli Wolf was born in New York City on November 6, 1899, the daughter of Charles and Anna Wolf. She studied journalism at New York University and appears to have spent her entire career in the New York City area. Between 1920 and 1936, she worked as the New York correspondent for several newspapers, and on the staff or as a special news writer for other newspapers. These included *Motion Picture News* (Oregon), the *New York Globe*, *Augusta Chronicle* (Georgia), *Pleasantville Journal* (New York), and *Bronx Home News*. As part of her volunteer work for veterans' organizations, she wrote *History of Bronx*

County American Legion, 1919–27 (1927) and "Women War Veterans" in *The Jewish Veteran* (1935). She was editor of the *Department Bulletin* for Jewish War Veterans of the United States in 1932 and, in 1933, associate editor of *The Jewish Veteran*, their monthly magazine.

She was a charter member of American Legion Post 43 and was adjutant from 1924 to 1927 and from 1930 to 1936. She was also chair of the Americanism Committee. In 1935, as a member of the American Legion, Hunts Point Post 58, she received a medal for a decade of service. She was a charter member of the Jewish War Veterans of the United States, where she served as a member of the national Americanism Committee, as adjutant in 1922 and from 1930 to 1932, New York State adjutant from 1931 to 1933, assistant national adjutant from 1931 to 1933, and judge advocate in 1936. She was awarded a Silver Cup for service in 1923 by the Colonel Harry Cutler Post 3. She served as chair of the Bronx-Westchester district from 1934 to 1937.

Sally Rivoli Wolf was a woman who took positive steps to advance her interests and talents. She joined the U.S. Navy during the World War I as soon as women were admitted, worked on newspapers when few women did, and spent many years as an active member and officer of three largely male veterans' advocacy groups. She worked to promote veterans' concerns, Jewish and American ideals, and women veterans' place in history.

SELECTED WORKS BY SALLY RIVOLI WOLF

History of Bronx County American Legion, 1919–27 (1927); "Women War Veterans." *The Jewish Veteran* (February 1935).

BIBLIOGRAPHY

Ebbert, Jean, and Mary-Beth Hall. *Crossed Currents: Navy Women from W.W. I to Tailhook* (1993); *UJE* 6:147, s.v. "Jewish War Veterans of the United States"; *WWIAJ* (1938).

HELENE L. TUCHMAN

WOLFENSTEIN, MARTHA (1869–1906)

Heralded as a great literary discovery—compared in her day to Grace Aguilar and EMMA LAZARUS, hailed by Israel Zangwill and a host of other critics, and described near the end of her life as "the best Jewish sketch writer in America"—Martha Wolfenstein is today a forgotten figure in American Jewish literature.

Martha Wolfenstein

Martha Wolfenstein is today a forgotten figure in American Jewish literature, but critics of the late nineteenth century believed the young writer had great promise. Before her death at age thirty-six, she wrote with charm, learning, and a distinctive woman's perspective. [American Jewish Archives]

She was born in Insterburg, Eastern Prussia, Germany, on August 5, 1869, the second child and eldest daughter of Bertha (Brieger) and Rabbi Samuel Wolfenstein. In 1870, her father immigrated to America to assume the pulpit of Congregation B'nai El in St. Louis, Missouri, and a year later the family followed. Martha attended the public schools, first in St. Louis and later in Cleveland, Ohio, where the family moved in 1878 following Rabbi Wolfenstein's appointment as superintendent of the Cleveland Jewish Orphan Asylum. From age nine until her death, she resided at the orphanage. On her mother's death, in 1885, she became her father's housekeeper and confidante; she idolized him.

Wolfenstein studied with her learned father and imbibed his stories of village life in Moravia, where he was raised. Young "Shimmele," the "wonder-child" in her novel *Idyls of the Gass* (1901), was modeled upon these stories. Her dedication—"to the original Shimmele, the precious source of all I have accomplished or may accomplish in this life"—is telling.

Wolfenstein's talent as a writer emerged early, but her first published works consisted of translations from German. She was especially influenced by Leopold Kompert's stories of Jewish life in the *Judengasse*, the "Jewish Street." In the 1890s, she published her own stories of Jewish life in "the Gass" both in Jewish newspapers and in general periodicals like *Lippincott's Monthly Magazine*. These led to her moving novel *Idyls of the Gass*, which, like much of her writing, featured a strong and appealing female hero. Maryam, Shimmele's grandmother, was not only a "smart woman" who could "*pasken* [answer ritual questions] as well as any rabbi," she was also modern enough to read "German books with not a word of *Yiddishkeit* [Judaism] in them." The novel, as a whole, was unusually sympathetic to ghetto Jews and their highly ethical way of life, even as it was conscious of impending change. It garnered positive reviews, but never achieved the commercial and critical success of Israel Zangwill's ghetto tales.

Bereft of literary acquaintances, Wolfenstein lacked self-confidence: "I have never yet finished a bit of writing that I was not wholly depressed with," she admitted in a 1901 letter to HENRIETTA SZOLD. Her writing displayed charm, learning, and a distinctive woman's perspective, but was sentimental and often shallow. Still, contemporaries considered her full of promise, and she achieved more recognition than most American Jewish women writers of her day.

Tragedy struck in 1902 when she was felled by tuberculosis, the disease that had earlier killed her mother and two brothers. She lingered for four years, during which time the Jewish Publication Society published a collection of her short stories, *A Renegade and Other Tales* (1905). She also wrote a play that remains unpublished. Martha Wolfenstein died, at age thirty-six, on March 17, 1906. Martha House, a home for wayward girls in Cleveland, was named in her memory.

SELECTED WORKS BY
MARTHA WOLFENSTEIN

Idyls of the Gass (1901); *A Renegade and Other Tales* (1905).

BIBLIOGRAPHY

AJYB 4 (1902–1903): 208, 218, 226, 310–311; 6 (1904–1905): 208–209; 8 (1906–1907): 225; Gartner, Lloyd P. *History of the Jews of Cleveland* (1978); *JE*; "Martha Wolfenstein, Sketch Writer." *Maccabean* 10 (1906): 16; Polster, Gary Edward. *Inside Looking Out: The Cleveland Jewish Orphan Asylum, 1868–1924* (1990); Sarna, Jonathan D. *JPS: The Americanization of Jewish Culture, 1888–1988* (1989); *UJE*; Wolfenstein, Martha. Letters and papers. AJA, Cincinnati, Ohio, and Jewish Publication Society, Philadelphia Jewish Archives Center.

JONATHAN D. SARNA

WOLFSON, THERESA (1897–1972)

Theresa Wolfson, economist and educator, taught at Brooklyn College from 1929 until her retirement in 1967. A prolific writer, she published in the fields of labor economics and industrial relations. As early as 1916, Wolfson studied barriers to the advancement of women in the workplace and the unequal treatment of women within trade unions. Because she cared about the education of workers as well as of college students, she taught adult students for the educational department of the INTERNATIONAL LADIES GARMENT WORKERS UNION (ILGWU) and Headgear Workers Union (1921–1927); and at the Summer School for Office Workers (held 1925–1936, 1949 at Bryn Mawr, Oberlin, Northwestern, and in Columbus, Ohio); and, after retiring from Brooklyn College, at the continuing education program at Sarah Lawrence College.

Born in Brooklyn, New York, on July 19, 1897, Theresa Wolfson was the eldest child and only daughter of Adolph and Rebecca (Hochstein) Wolfson. Her brother Martin became an actor; her brother Victor became a playwright and novelist. Victor Wolfson's *My Prince! My King!* (1962) is a fictionalized account of the family.

Wolfson attended Eastern District High School in Brooklyn, and then earned her B.A. from Adelphi College (1917). While at Adelphi, she helped organize a chapter of the Intercollegiate Socialist Society (later the League for Industrial Democracy). During the summer of her junior year, she began her long career in labor relations by investigating wage standards in New York City's garment industry. She was a health worker in New York City from 1917 to 1918. From 1918 to 1920, as a field agent for the National Child Labor Committee, she investigated child labor in North Carolina, Arkansas, Michigan, Louisiana, and Oklahoma. From 1920 to 1922, as executive secretary of the New York State Consumers League, Wolfson lobbied for minimum wage and eight-hour-day legislation.

Wolfson's 1922 to 1924 studies of posture, lighting, and fatigue in the garment factories of New York City led to her M.A. from Columbia University in

1923. From 1925 to 1927, she directed education at the Union Health Center of the ILGWU. *The Woman Worker and the Trade Unions*, her Ph.D. dissertation (Brookings Institution, 1926), examined barriers to organizing women workers. It was published in 1926.

Wolfson's first marriage, to Iago Galdston on July 19, 1920, ended in divorce in 1935. Galdston was beginning a career in public health when he and Wolfson met. Later, he worked in psychiatry at the Union Health Center of the ILGWU. Galdston and Wolfson had two children: Richard (b. 1926) and Margaret Beatrice (b. 1930), who stayed with Wolfson after the divorce. In 1938, Wolfson married Austin Bigelow Wood, professor of psychology at Brooklyn College, and they were separated only by her death in 1972.

Wolfson's Jewish background helps explain the importance she always placed on education and training. In her Ph.D. dissertation, when discussing cultural influences on the psychology of women workers in the United States, she writes: "The patriarchal Jew would have his daughters helpmates to their mothers in the home. Education and training are given the sons, discipline and housework, the daughters. In Russia, however, Jewish families were compelled to change their ideas about women's work. The revolutionary movements of that country fed upon the idealism and enthusiastic activity of these same Jewish daughters who became self-supporting and economically independent." As Wolfson's parents had immigrated to the United States from Russia in 1894, her observations may stem in part from her own experiences. Wolfson also published the article "Jews in Labor and Industry" in 1928. Aside from these references to her background, Judaism does not seem to have played a dominant role in her life. Although her spiritual strength is mentioned repeatedly in tributes and eulogies Judaism is mentioned only in terms of her parents' immigrant status.

In 1928, Wolfson joined the faculty of the Brooklyn branch of HUNTER COLLEGE, which later became Brooklyn College. As a pioneer member of the Brooklyn College faculty, she helped with curriculum design and departmental organization. She taught graduate and undergraduate courses in labor economics, served on numerous committees over the years, and chaired committees on student activities (1939–1941), student aid (1943–1944), Honors Day (1944–1946), and tenure. While Wolfson was still alive, her students established a collection of books on labor-management relations at Brooklyn College Library in her honor. After her death, an annual scholarship was established for a student to pursue graduate study in labor economics.

Wolfson was a member of the public panel of the War Labor Board from 1942 to 1945, of the national panel of arbitrators of the American Arbitration Association, of the New York State Board of Mediation (1946–1953), of the Kings County Council Against Discrimination (1949–1953), and of the executive board (president, New York chapter) of the Industrial Relations Research Association. In 1957, Wolfson was corecipient of the John Dewey Award of the League for Industrial Democracy in recognition of her mediation of industrial disputes.

Theresa Wolfson died on May 14, 1972.

SELECTED WORKS
BY THERESA WOLFSON

"Aprons and Overalls in War." *Annals of the American Academy of Political and Social Science* (September 1943): 46–55; *Frances Wright, Free Enquirer: The Study of a Temperament*, with A.J.C. Perkins (1939); "Industrial Unions in the American Labor Movement," with Abraham Weiss. *New Frontiers* (February 1937): 3–52; "Jews in Labor and Industry." *Immigrant* 7, nos. 8–9 (May-June 1928): 16–18; "Labor's Role in Post War Reconstruction." *Free World* (February 1943): 142–159; "People Who Go to Beets." Pamphlet (1920), also in *Am. Child* (November 1919): 217–239; "Posture and Fatigue." *Survey* (April 8, 1922): 52–53; "The Recent Social Climate." In *Workers' Education in the United States*, the Fifth Yearbook of the John Dewey Society, ed. Theodore Brameld (1941); "The Right to Fair Pay." *Frontiers of Democracy* (Summer 1942): 232–233; "Role of the ILGWU in Stabilizing the Women's Garment Industry." *Industrial and Labor Relations Review* (October 1950); "Should White Collar Workers Organize?" *Independent Woman* (November 1936); "Trade Union Activities of Women." *Annals of the American Academy of Political and Social Science* (May 1929); "The Trade Union and Economic Control." *Planned Society: Yesterday, Today, Tomorrow*, edited by Findlay MacKenzie (1937); "Union Finances and Elections." *Annals* of the American Academy of Political and Social Science (November 1946): 31–37; "Where Are the Organized Women Workers?" *American Federationist* (June 1925): 455–457; *The Woman Worker and the Trade Unions* (1926).

BIBLIOGRAPHY

Brooklyn College Special Collections; Library of Congress Hebraic studies database; Obituary. *NYTimes* (May 15, 1972), 38:5; *NAW* modern; *UJE*; *WWIAJ* (1938); *Who's Who of American Women (and Women of Canada)*, 5th ed. (1968–1969); Wolfson, Theresa. Papers. Labor-Management Document Center, Catherwood Library, Cornell University, Ithaca, N.Y.; Wolfson, Victor. Papers. Twentieth-Century Archives, Boston University; *Women, Work & Protest*, ed. Ruth Milkman (1985).

AUDREY J. LYKE

WOLLSTEIN, MARTHA (1868–1939)

In 1908, Martha Wollstein declared before the Women's Medical Society of the State of New York that the current generation of women physicians had "entered societies and laboratories for the benefit of all." Indeed, responding to the public health crisis of the early twentieth century, she herself had just begun an exemplary career path in pathology and the experimental study of childhood diseases.

Martha Wollstein was born to Louis and Minna (Cohn) Wollstein in New York City on November 21, 1868. Information about her family background is scarce. Her parents, both Jewish, had been born in Germany. She had one brother named Isaac.

From 1886 to 1889, Wollstein attended the Women's Medical College of the New York Infirmary. The college and its hospital offered women students education and training dedicated to the highest standards of professional excellence. It became part of Cornell University Medical School in 1909. The influence of this educational experience is clearly apparent in Wollstein's publication of one of the earlier narratives written by American women physicians about their historical role in medical education and practice. She extolled the specific achievements of "medical women" in the past and cataloged women's struggles to enter medical school, to find teaching, hospital, or laboratory positions, and to gain admittance to medical societies.

Following graduation, Wollstein completed a two-year internship at the Babies Hospital in New York City and was immediately awarded an appointment there as a pathologist. Her career with this institution would span forty-three years. She began her laboratory science career at a time when the medical community was beginning to believe in the possibility that diseases could be explained logically by discovering specific microorganisms. Wollstein conducted research on infant diarrhea, malaria, tuberculosis, and typhoid fever. Her work on infant diarrhea was recognized by the distinguished pathologist Simon Flexner, and the results of her research were published through the Rockefeller Institute for Medical Research. In 1906, she received an appointment as an assistant at the Rockefeller Institute, and in 1907, she began experimental studies in Flexner's laboratory on the transmission of polio. Her efforts to find "evidence of a micro-parasitic origin of the disease" in research with infants and children were unsuccessful, but they contributed to future polio research on humans and monkeys.

Between 1910 and 1920, Wollstein studied a variety of infectious diseases at the Rockefeller Institute. She looked at possible causal relationships between different bacteria and differing types of pneumonia with the physiologist Samuel Meltzer. With Harold Amoss, she contributed to developments in serum treatment for meningitis. In an independent experimental study of mumps, Wollstein used saliva filtrate from sick children and from soldiers in Army camp hospitals near New York City. She was able to inject the disease from these groups of patients into cats and then from cat to cat, suggesting, but not proving, the viral nature of mumps. She was the first researcher at the Rockefeller Institute to publish a scientific study that described the significance of the bacteriophage discovered by Felix D'Herelle.

From 1921 until her retirement in 1935, Wollstein pursued research on children's diseases, including tuberculosis and leukemia, at the Babies Hospital. Over several generations, her pathological studies supported the work of clinical physicians and public health workers in their common struggle to ascertain the ways bacteria were transmitted, diagnose patient illness, and mount effective campaigns to eliminate infectious disease.

In 1928, Wollstein was appointed head of the pediatric section of the New York Academy of Medicine. In 1930, she became the first woman awarded membership in the American Pediatric Society. While Wollstein worked with and for male Jewish colleagues who were among the early members of the Rockefeller Institute, she was not given this privilege. Indeed, only one woman received this acknowledgment in the institute's first fifty years.

By the time Martha Wollstein retired to Grand Rapids, Michigan, in 1935, she had authored eighty scientific papers. However, professional acclamation did not follow her death on September 30, 1939, at Mount Sinai Hospital in New York City. Her *New York Times* obituary stated merely that she "was also known as a pathologist . . . " Yet Wollstein's achievements clearly merit recognition beyond the "also known" distinction. Her prominence among the first group of American women physicians to conduct original research in pathology at distinguished American hospitals and research institutes is undeniable.

SELECTED WORKS
BY MARTHA WOLLSTEIN

"A Biological Study of the Cerebro-Spinal Fluid in Anterior Poliomyletis." *Journal of Experimental Medicine* 10 (July 1908): 476–483; "An Experimental Study of Parotitis." *Journal of the American Medical Association* 71 (1918): 639–644; "The History of Women in Medicine." *The Woman's Medical Journal* 18 (1908): 65–69; "Studies on the Phenomenon of D'Herelle with Bacillus Dysenteria."

Journal of Experimental Medicine 34 (November 1921): 467–476; "A Study of Tuberculosis in Infants and Young Children." *American Journal of Diseases of Children* 21 (January 1921): 48–56.

BIBLIOGRAPHY

BEOAJ; Hurd-Mead, Kate Campbell. *Medical Women of America* (1933); Kagan, Solomon R. *Jewish Contributions to Medicine in America* (1939); Kaufman, Martin, et al., eds. *Dictionary of American Medical Biography* (1984); Marcus, Jacob R. *The American Jewish Woman, 1654–1980* (1981); Morantz-Sanchez, Regina. *Sympathy and Science: Women Physicians in American Medicine* (1985); *NAW*; Obituary. *NYTimes*, October 1, 1939, 53:2; "Reports to the Board of Scientific Directors." Rockefeller Institute for Medical Research (1907–1920); *WWIAJ* (1938).

JENNIFER TEBBE

WOMEN OF REFORM JUDAISM— THE FEDERATION OF TEMPLE SISTERHOODS *see* NATIONAL FEDERATION OF TEMPLE SISTERHOODS

WOMEN'S AMERICAN ORT

THE FOUNDING OF ORT

ORT (initials of Russian Obshchestvo Rasprostraneniya Truda Sredi Yevreyev), the Organization for Rehabilitation through Training, was founded in Russia in 1880 to promote vocational training of trades and agriculture among impoverished Jews. Craftsmen received aid to move from the Pale of Settlement to the Russian interior and to establish small trades workshops, trade schools, and vocational courses. ORT gradually expanded to create Jewish agricultural colonies, model farms, and agricultural schools. During World War I, ORT helped Jewish refugees resettle and find employment. After the 1917 Revolution, ORT helped Jewish farmers and craftsmen in Russia, the Ukraine, Belorussia, Bessarabia, and elsewhere in the Soviet Union.

In 1921, ORT was established in Berlin as an international organization, the World ORT Union, which quickly became active throughout Poland, Lithuania, Latvia, Bessarabia, Germany, France, Bulgaria, Hungary, and Romania. ORT spread the idea of manual work among Jews and stressed the need for a change in the economic structure of Jewish life. ORT organizations were established in the United States, South Africa, Canada, South America, and elsewhere.

American ORT was founded as a males-only organization in 1922, when a program of activities and financing was agreed upon with the Joint Distribution Committee. The new organization was supported by the Workmen's Circle, followed by large sections of the Jewish labor movement. This initial response proved critical to the development of ORT and Women's American ORT as broad-based community organizations.

WOMEN'S AMERICAN ORT

Women's American ORT (WAO) was founded October 12, 1927, to assist ORT in providing financial support to the ORT program serving Eastern European Jews. Most of the founders were wives of ORT leaders: FLORENCE DOLOWITZ was the wife of the treasurer of American ORT; ANNA BOUDIN was the wife of lawyer Louis Boudin, who was also vice president of American ORT. Their marital connections were critical factors in creating an auxiliary organization to assist their husbands' work.

The women's early support for ORT was limited to bazaars and concerts spearheaded by the wives of ORT leaders and their friends, led by Fannie Shluger and Mrs. Jacob Panken. A glamorous recital by Efram Zimbalist at Carnegie Hall in 1928 to help the Jews in Eastern Europe launched their activities as a women's auxiliary. The concert program listed as patrons some of the leading American Jewish women of German origin. Supporters also included Eastern European Jewish wives and leaders of the INTERNATIONAL LADIES GARMENT WORKERS UNION, reflecting the close support between the labor movement and ORT that would continue throughout its history.

In its first years, the women helped raise funds for the ORT Reconstruction Committee, designed to help Eastern Europe's Jews recover from World War I. Only one woman sat on the ORT National Committee at that time: Louise C. Taussie.

Women's support of ORT reflected Jewish women's emergence into public life by creating their own organizations to meet community needs. After World War I, some women were becoming increasingly independent due to their service in the war and activism in such causes as obtaining votes for women. Many middle-class women, however, remained cautious about public activism and preferred to put their energies into more traditional social service. Although a few Jewish women's organizations, such as the NATIONAL COUNCIL OF JEWISH WOMEN, were independent of men in the 1930s, many remained as auxiliaries. WAO, still a brand-new organization of women finding its way, fit that pattern of social service in connection to larger, male-run groups.

By 1933, the women's auxiliary was large enough to put on a pageant, *Activities of ORT*, at the 44th Street Theater in New York City, demonstrating the various skills taught by ORT in different countries. A year later, the women raised money to rescue six hundred workshops in Poland that trained five thousand workers. Women's ORT soon branched out beyond Manhattan to Long Island, and then to other cities, from San Antonio to Chicago.

The pioneers were not content to limit their organizing efforts to the United States. A Women's ORT was organized in Poland in 1935, launched by Anna and Louis Boudin, leaders of women's and men's American ORT. WAO increased its assistance to Jews in Poland as their intense poverty worsened in the years before the Nazi invasion.

By 1937, as war became imminent, WAO raised funds for the relief of German refugees and intensified its efforts for Polish Jewish workers. WAO created study groups to educate women on the situation in Eastern Europe. WAO strongly supported ORT's work in Germany and Eastern Europe, as it precariously maintained training schools after the Nazi anschluss and invasion of Poland in 1938. During this period in Germany, for example, ORT opened a vocational high school in Berlin that survived until 1943.

At this critical juncture, WAO's prestigious honorary chairman, Mrs. Albert Einstein, died. Her loss made it harder to fulfill WAO's 1938 pledge to raise fifty thousand dollars, but they met their goal. In doing so, WAO established itself as a vital element in the survival of the World ORT Union at an especially perilous time in its history. Einstein's place remained vacant until 1950, when the Baroness Pierre de Gunzbourg became WAO's honorary national president, remaining in that post until her death in 1969.

WORLD WAR II

As war neared in 1940, Women's American ORT was created as an independent organization at ORT's first annual convention in thirteen years, with the theme "A Trade Is a Refugee's Passport." WAO was no longer content to remain a women's auxiliary to men. Their fund-raising prowess and critical influence in ORT affairs had apparently convinced the women that they had the skills and experience to act independently. The urgent need to raise money for imperiled European Jews who were now less able to raise funds themselves appears to have compounded their belief that they needed to act quickly. This demanded independence from men's American ORT, caught up in the multitude of contrasting demands from their members, clients, and supporters. Above all, they were guided by the example of other Jewish women's organizations, such as the National Council of Jewish Women, which were tackling refugee problems with vigor and distinction.

As the Nazis conquered Europe, WAO funded ORT accommodations for refugees in various ORT installations in France, vocational courses in Swiss camps and internment homes, and maintenance of ORT workshops in Polish ghettos that managed to be kept alive until the ghettos were destroyed.

By the end of the war, ORT had transformed itself into an emergency organization primarily serving adult displaced persons (DPs) about to migrate or in transit. WAO was a vital element in funding ORT's postwar vocational training in the DP camps, as well as the rehabilitation of DPs in the United States, Israel, Holland, Belgium, Greece, and elsewhere in free Europe. In Israel, WAO was particularly instrumental in establishing vocational and agricultural schools for refugees. In the process, WAO leaders became skilled in fund-raising for postwar needs.

A NEW ERA

By 1950, Women's American ORT's membership had climbed to more than twelve thousand, and the organization had become a financial mainstay of the World ORT Union. Among all World ORT Union members, "By far the most spectacular expansion was registered by Women's American ORT," notes Jack Rader in ORT's official history.

Women of the 1950s who had worked or run wartime volunteer efforts returned to the home as men returned from the war. Still, these women had acquired skills during wartime that they did not wish to abandon in peacetime. Volunteerism filled that gap, as it had for women after World War I.

By the mid-1950s, WAO was helping to fund ORT's growing network of vocational and technical high schools in Western Europe and North Africa, Iran, India, and Israel. Technical schools and schools for special needs were established across the developing countries as well.

WAO boasted of a "distinctive and unique role" in world Jewish life by 1958. It funded scholarships for teacher training, social assistance to needy students, preventive medical care, maintenance of vocational training schools, and support of Tel Aviv's Aaron Syngalowski Center. It also helped fund the establishment of a network of large ORT apprentice training centers throughout Israel.

The need to educate American Jewish communities so they could raise money for refugees propelled WAO into a new position in American life. WAO immersed itself in American Jewish life, spreading the ORT message in several ways. Viewing the education of American communities about ORT as part of its mission, it produced public programs and study groups. WAO reinforced its image and influence by supporting the major Jewish fund-raising campaigns: United Jewish Appeal, local welfare funds, and Israel Bonds. Its Americanization of ORT became a critical factor in WAO's membership growth and its growing power within the World ORT Union.

WAO also generously contributed to the Joint Distribution Committee's budget, increasing the effect of its financial support to the overseas operations of the World ORT Union.

WAO took care to infuse new meaning to the personal lives of WAO members. Understanding that its growth as a membership organization depended on its appeal to women, WAO provided programs that linked education and social activity. Combining informal meetings, classes, and casual and glamorous social functions made the organization more attractive and fulfilling to women living in the suburbs of the 1950s who wanted to make congenial friendships as well as to fund a social cause.

ADAPTING FOR THE FUTURE

The tactics succeeded. By 1970, Women's American ORT boasted nearly ninety thousand members organized into seven hundred chapters across the United States. Educating communities about ORT's purpose, WAO brought ORT into every substantial community across the United States, rooting ORT into American Jewish communal life as never before.

WAO was now the World ORT Union's central financial backbone, contributing almost $2 million annually. From the postwar years to 1970, it provided over $15 million to the parent organization, an astonishing sum raised through membership activities alone. Today, WAO remains the World ORT Union's largest affiliate organization, with a WAO representative serving on the union's executive committee.

Continuing to fund ORT's basic projects, WAO expanded its aid into programs of accelerated adult training; scholarships for teacher training; medical and health services to students; apprenticeship; social assistance to help provide meals, clothing, cultural and recreational facilities; and school construction and equipment.

But the women's movement has changed the way American women approach volunteerism. As more and more women moved out of the home and into careers, WAO found it necessary to change its membership tactics as well. The results influence the organization's methods and approach. Like other women's groups, WAO now must appeal to growing numbers of young career women, either single women or young mothers juggling jobs and child care. Programs include fewer luncheons and more evening meetings, and fund-raising causes focus not only on vocational needs abroad but also on issues at home in America: public education, literacy, combating anti-Semitism, and support for women's rights.

Facing the threat of declining membership that affects all volunteer women's organizations, WAO is attempting to adapt to the needs and constraints of working women by developing special chapters that appeal to single women and young mothers. WAO also focuses on issues of concern to women, such as a conference on the genetics of breast cancer. It participates in the campaign to stop domestic abuse by the Conference of National Jewish Women's Organizations. WAO takes positions supporting women's equality, as well as freedom from harassment and physical and mental abuse.

Attempting the difficult task of engaging busy young women, WAO is devoting more staff on working with this group of women. Programs are being designed to enrich their personal lives. At the same time, WAO is cultivating young leadership, involving them intellectually, socially, and financially in the organization's goals. The effort is meeting with some success. The president's Young Leadership Council involves a core of young women who are making a significant impact and revitalizing Women's American ORT to meet the needs of today's women.

Even the approach to technical education has expanded to reflect younger members' interests. The Bramson ORT Technical Institute in Queens, New York, opened in the 1970s, not only provides vocational education but also hosts broader educational projects, such as a conference for educators from Jewish educational institutions. WAO has also opened schools in Los Angeles, New York, and Chicago, where it has a two-year program for adults that teaches English as a second language, computers, and robotics to refugees and American citizens. These schools operate independently, supported by WAO and its member-volunteers. WAO also operates programs in Jewish day schools in Atlanta and Miami.

BIBLIOGRAPHY

Abramson, Rosina K. "The Millennium Is Only Three Years Away" (unpublished speech); *EJ* 12: 1482–1486; *Focus:*

The Women's American ORT Leadership Newsletter; Kaufman, Mrs. Ferdinand. *History of Women's American ORT: From Auxiliary to Movement*; *ORT Reporter*; Rader, Jack. *By the Skill of Their Hands: The Story of ORT*; Women's American ORT. *QuORTerly Briefing: Issues and Trends.*

LINDA GORDON KUZMACK

WOMEN'S LEAGUE FOR CONSERVATIVE JUDAISM

Women's League for Conservative Judaism is the national organization of Conservative sisterhoods established by MATHILDE SCHECHTER in 1918 as the National Women's League of the United Synagogue. Schechter continued the work begun by her husband, Solomon Schechter, who had called for women to assume a role in the newly established United Synagogue of America. As founding president (1918–1919), she envisioned an organization that would be the coordinating body of Conservative synagogue sisterhoods and inspired Women's League to promote an agenda whose mission was the perpetuation of traditional Judaism in America through the home, synagogue, and community. The early leaders disseminated their message through the publication of educational materials in English, which helped young women through the process of acculturation and Americanization. One of Schechter's first projects adopted by Women's League was the opening of a students' house offering a homelike atmosphere with room and kosher board to Jewish students in New York. After succeeding in New York, the project was expanded to other cities, including Philadelphia, Boston, Denver, and Detroit.

By 1925, Women's League had grown from the founding hundred women in twenty-six sisterhoods to a membership of 230 sisterhoods in six branches in the United States and Canada with twenty thousand members. In 1939, six additional branches were added, contributing to a total of over 100,000 members. By 1968, the Women's League reached a peak of 200,000 members affiliated with eight hundred sisterhoods represented in twenty-eight branches. After a consolidation resulting from changing demographics, Women's League in 1997 has 150,000 members affiliated with seven hundred sisterhoods in twenty-five branches.

EDUCATION

The Education Department of Women's League has operated on the premise that "Education is the lifeline of sisterhood" and includes people who work in the areas of adult education, books, libraries, creative handicrafts, Jewish family living, Judaica shops, music, and programming. The goal of all these efforts is to make members more knowledgeable and better equipped to educate others. Early publications provided guidance and instruction for Sabbath and holidays, with *The Three Pillars: Thought, Worship and Practice* (1927) by DEBORAH MELAMED serving as the cornerstone of educational programs. Women's League also published the popular *Jewish Home Beautiful* (1941) by Betty D. Greenberg and Althea O. Silverman. This book, based on a popular pageant of the same name, included descriptions, traditional recipes,

MATHILDE SCHECHTER *saw the need for an organization that would coordinate all the sisterhoods of the Conservative synagogues. The agenda of the national organization would be the perpetuation of traditional Judaism in America through the home, synagogue, and community. True to the activist tradition begun by Schechter, the league has been involved in all the critical issues of twentieth-century American Jewish life. Particularly, it has played a leadership role in promoting and protecting the rights of women, from aliyah to abortion. [Women's League for Conservative Judaism]*

illustrations of table settings, and music, all of which illustrated the potential for creating a Jewish home filled with beauty and spirituality.

The league's continuing concern with enhancement of Jewish ritual and observances is perhaps best symbolized by the magnificent sukkah at the Jewish Theological Seminary. After Schechter's death, ADELE GINZBERG, founder and active member, took charge of this project for decades, decorating the sukkah with fresh fruits, vegetables, and greenery. In the 1970s, the National Women's League dedicated a Sukkah Endowment Fund in the name of "Mama G" to underwrite the increasing costs associated with it. Women's League together with the seminary continues to be responsible for the decoration of the sukkah, which is named in Ginzberg's memory.

After World War II, Women's League's educational activities expanded tremendously in response to the increased pace of growth of the Conservative Movement. Adele Ginzberg initiated a Girl Scout project in 1946 that led to the establishment of the Menorah Award for Jewish Girl Scouts in order to stress the importance of Jewish education and encourage Jewish scouts to participate in synagogue activities (and to parallel the Ner Tamid Award for Jewish Boy Scouts). The Judaism-in-the-Home project introduced in the 1950s, and chaired by ROSE GOLDSTEIN and Anna Bear Brevis, produced instructional materials to teach sisterhood women the meaning of Jewish holidays and rituals in order to promote family observance. A series of Oneg Sabbath programs based on the weekly Torah portions were published under the leadership of Education Department chairs EVELYN GARFIEL, Rose Goldstein, and Adina Katzoff. In 1952, the newly created Ceremonial Objects and Gift Shop Department made Jewish ritual objects and other ceremonial items, including New Years cards, accessible to all members. In 1959, Hadassah Nadich initiated the first calendar diary. Issued annually until 1986, these calendar guides promoted Jewish activities in the home, synagogue, and community. They were distributed to all sisterhoods so that local leaders could incorporate educational elements into their projects.

Intensive Jewish study for its own sake has also long been a priority. In 1931, the Women's Institute of Jewish Studies of the Jewish Theological Seminary of America was initiated through the league's Metropolitan Branch in cooperation with other leading Jewish women's organizations, including HADASSAH, the NATIONAL COUNCIL OF JEWISH WOMEN, Ivriah, the Federation of Jewish Women's Organizations, and Women's League for Palestine. The purpose of the

In the 1950s, the league introduced the Judaism-in-the-Home Project, which produced instructional materials to teach sisterhood women the meaning of Jewish holidays and rituals in order to promote family observance. The program was chaired by ROSE GOLDSTEIN and Anna Bear Brevis. Goldstein is shown here at the 1966 Jubilee Convention, leading morning services. [Women's League for Conservative Judaism]

institute was "to offer women attending its classes an opportunity to equip themselves for making a constructive approach to the problems of contemporary Jewish life, and a broad perspective of modern Jewish problems." Since 1977, Women's League has organized its own annual institute consisting of two semesters of classes taught by seminary faculty members. In recent years, similar programs have been developed in Philadelphia, Washington, D.C., and east and west coast Florida. In 1993, Women's League, under the chair of Lynne Heller, sponsored its first Elderhostel program at the University of Florida in Gainesville, and this has since become a regular part of its educational offerings.

Women's League members have long sought out additional opportunities to advance their knowledge and observance of Jewish ritual. Inspired by the burgeoning Jewish feminist movement, many women chose to undertake the necessary studies to become bat mitzvah as adults. *Kolot Bik'dushah* was formed in 1993 and consists of over 250 women nationwide who have the ability to lead a religious service and/or read from the Torah.

Women's League's magazine *Outlook* has been published since 1930. Its initial mission was to keep sisterhood members in touch with each other and with the other organizations with which the league was affiliated. It was also meant to be a means for members to voice their opinions. CARRIE DAVIDSON served as editor from 1930 to 1942 and then again from 1945 to 1953 and, together with Hanna Marx, SARAH KUSSY, and Fanny Minkin, she shaped its initial tone. Davidson was especially interested in helping women learn how to influence the preservation of traditional Judaism. Articles focused on Jewish cultural subjects and contemporary issues as well as on the achievements of the seminary and United Synagogue. Each issue carried a president's message and messages from National Activity chairpeople and branch presidents. One of the most popular features was the Children's Corner, which introduced thousands of readers to Sadie Rose Weilerstein's fictional character K'tonton beginning in 1935. Leading spokespersons for the Conservative Movement are frequent contributors to the magazine, which has a current readership of 150,000.

FUND-RAISING

Women's League has been closely linked not only to the Conservative Movement but especially to the Jewish Theological Seminary of America. It has always been particularly concerned with the welfare of its students. Beginning in 1934, this interest was formalized through the establishment of an educational fund to which members would contribute an annual amount to assist the seminary in its work; it was renamed Torah Fund after 1942. Initially it was suggested that each member contribute a minimum of $6.11 (the Hebrew numerical equivalent of the word "Torah"). Building on the success of this campaign, in 1945, the Chai Club was formed to encourage women to increase their annual contributions to eighteen dollars. Since 1957, thousands of contributors in a special gifts category have proudly worn Torah Fund pins, which are designed annually to enable Women's League members to symbolize their dedication to the seminary. Monies were raised to support the seminary with scholarships and, after 1958, for a dormitory for women students through the Mathilde Schechter Residence Hall campaign. The annual goal was raised to $100,000, and different giving categories were established both to encourage grass-roots giving and to recognize large donors. In 1963, the Torah Fund campaign was expanded to support all of the seminary's schools and well as other seminary facilities and programs.

The Mathilde Schechter Residence Hall opened as a dormitory for seminary undergraduates in 1976. In response to changing needs, it has always been a coeducational residence hall. After this goal was reached, the fund was used to provide support for all seminary residence halls (including those at the University of Judaism), bookshelves and study carrels in the new seminary library, the beautification of the quadrangle of the seminary building, and increased financial aid for promising students. The most recent fund-raising project was the refurbishing of the seminary synagogue, which was named the Women's League Seminary Synagogue at its dedication in October 1995. The league is currently raising funds to refurbish the Residence Hall. As of 1997, the annual fund-raising goal was $2.6 million; it is noteworthy that league campaigns have always reached or surpassed their goals.

SOCIAL ACTION

As part of its commitment to further traditional Judaism, Women's League has long been involved with social action on issues of social justice, human rights, and care for the poor, hungry, and homeless. The league has also been especially active in helping the Jewish blind through the Jewish Braille Institute. League women served as transcribers of Braille for the Jewish blind, and the first Hebrew-English prayer book in Braille was underwritten by the league in 1954.

During World War II, the league was active in the Supplies for Overseas Survivors Drive and in collecting food and clothing for the Joint Distribution Committee. Members were also trained to assume needed tasks in many different areas, including serving as Red Cross instructors and air raid wardens. Sisterhoods in areas of war industry turned their social rooms into emergency hospitals, and some organized kosher kitchen units for civilian populations in the event of a catastrophe. Concerned about the deteriorating condition for Jews in Nazi Germany and its occupied territories, beginning in 1933, Women's League called for personal sacrifice on the part of its members to aid the war efforts.

After the war, Women's League continued its involvement with issues of public concern. The first resolution adopted in 1950 advocated the elimination of discrimination in public places. Over the decades, Women's League has supported a liberal political and social agenda, zealously guarding civil liberties in the McCarthy era, advocating the separation of church and state, and calling for government funding to

This photograph from the 1992 Biennial Convention of the league includes, from left to right:
Debra Togut, cantorial student; Dr. Ismar Schorsch, chancellor of the Jewish Theological Seminary,
receiving an aliyah; Hadassah Blocker, reading the Torah; Lynne Heller; and, Paula Victor, cantorial student.
[Women's League for Conservative Judaism]

ameliorate deteriorating social conditions of the poor and the aged. Especially concerned with women's issues, the league passed resolutions urging the adoption of the Equal Rights Amendment as well as laws to protect battered women and abortion rights. This commitment also affected Women's League's policies toward Jewish religious life. Women's League was an early and vocal advocate for egalitarianism in Conservative Jewish religious life. At its national convention in 1972, women were called to the Torah for an aliyah; they also voted to remove their husbands' names from the official roster. An opinion poll taken at that time revealed that an overwhelming majority of members believed that women should be elected to congrega-tional boards, be permitted to read from the Torah, and be able to initiate divorce proceedings. Over 60 percent also called for women to be counted in the minyan [quorum of ten] and called to the Torah for an aliyah. In subsequent years, delegates voted three-to-one for the ordination of women by the Jewish Theological Seminary (1980) and the acceptance of women as cantors (1990). Resolutions throughout the period forcefully called for equality in Jewish life.

Israel has always been a high priority for the orga-nization. In 1923, National Convention delegates voted unanimously "for unqualified support of all agencies engaged in the upbuilding of Palestine." By 1926, the league had embarked on a project to raise funds for the construction of the Yeshurun Synagogue in Jerusalem. Since the creation of the State of Israel, Women's League has continued its unwavering support, passing resolutions supporting the need for foreign aid and security and criticizing the Arab boycott and propaganda and United Nations discriminatory policies.

In recent years, attention has shifted to religious issues with Women's League asserting the need for religious pluralism and for the recognition of the Masorti (Israeli Conservative) movement. It has fought vigorously against calls to amend the Law of Return and has supported Masorti congregations as well as the Conservative Kibbutz Hanaton and Conservative Moshav Shorashim. Overseas groups of women in Masorti congregations were formed in 1972, and since 1979, individual sisterhoods in each of the league's branches have offered financial support to these groups. This project serves to link Women's League members with Israel in a more direct manner. Concern for world Jewry resulted in resolutions of advocacy on behalf of the Jews of Ethiopia, the Soviet Union, and Syria. On the broader international scene, Women's League has opposed apartheid, the communist takeover in Hungary in 1956, and international terrorism. It has called for nuclear arms control and support for emerging democracies in Eastern Europe.

Beginning with an invitation to the White House Mid-Century Conference on Youth in 1950, Women's League has been included in all such major assemblies of the nation's leading organizations. Its presidents have been invited to conferences on civil rights, children and youth education, and racial equality. Since 1952, Women's League has also been an accredited nongovernmental observer at the United Nations. Within the Jewish world, Women's League has been a member of the Conference of Presidents of Major American Jewish Organizations since the 1960s, and its president and executive director serve as representatives to the group. The 1965 Women's League Convention was the first international conclave of synagogue women to be held in the State of Israel. During the 1970s, the presence of Women's League expanded to the international scene as it became an active member in its own right of the World Council of Synagogues. In 1980, it gained autonomous affiliation with the National Jewish Community Relations Advisory Council. Women's League has also had an increasingly independent voice as one of the constituent arms of the Conservative Movement. Convening a joint leadership conference for Women's League, the United Synagogue, and the Federation of Men's Clubs in 1986, the league paved the way for the establishment of the Leadership Council of the Conservative Movement.

By the mid-1970s, Women's League had come of age, an attitude symbolized by two important events. First, in 1969, it moved out of the seminary, where it had been housed since its inception, to new offices on Seventy-fourth Street in New York City. Three years later, the organization changed its name to Women's League for Conservative Judaism, signifying what had been increasingly the case, that it was not a subsidiary of United Synagogue but rather an independent arm of the Conservative Movement.

Women's League in the 1990s continues to be involved in all of the critical issues of twentieth-century American Jewish life, both Jewish and secular. It remains firmly committed to the enhancement of Jewish educational programs on all levels while also continuing to promote a broad spectrum of interests. For the past ten years, Women's League has sponsored a biennial Capital Conference in Washington, D.C., that promotes public policy debates with the nation's leaders on issues such as women's health, foreign policy, and immigration. Its most recent project is its involvement in President Clinton's "Read*Write*Now," a national literacy program, with league volunteers across the country tutoring children individually. Women' League remains a vital force in accenting the pivotal role played by women in the preservation and promotion of Judaism and broader Jewish interests in America, and it has been a critical factor in contributing to that goal.

PRESIDENTS OF WOMEN'S LEAGUE FOR CONSERVATIVE JUDAISM

Mathilde Schechter 1918–1919; Fanny Hoffman 1919–1928; Dora Spiegel 1928–1946; Sarah Kopelman 1946–1950; Marion Siner 1950–1954; Helen Sussman 1954–1958; Syd Rossman 1958–1962; Helen Fried 1962–1966; Evelyn Henkind 1966–1970; Selma Rapoport 1970–1974; Ruth Perry 1974–1978; Goldie Kweller 1978–1982; Selma Weintraub 1982–1986; Evelyn Auerbach 1986–1990; Audrey Citak 1990–1994; Evelyn Seelig 1994–.

BIBLIOGRAPHY

Nadell, Pamela S. *Conservative Judaism in America: A Biographical Dictionary and Sourcebook* (1988); *Seventy-Five Years of Vision and Voluntarism* (1992); *The Sixth Decade: 1968–78* (1978); United Synagogue of America. National Women's League. *They Dared to Dream: A History of National Women's League, 1918–68* (1967); *Women's League Outlook* (1930–).

SHULY RUBIN SCHWARTZ

WOMEN'S STUDIES

What we have at present is a man-centered university, a breeding ground not of humanism, but of masculine privilege.

ADRIENNE RICH
On Lies, Secrets, and Silences

Women's studies has variously been called "a process, a field of inquiry, a critical perspective, a center for social action, and/or the academic arm of the Women's Movement." As an academic discipline, women's studies examines and produces scholarship simultaneously in several fields. Early formulations that women's studies was by, for, and about women have changed as varieties of feminism, the substantive basis for women's studies scholarship, and "new" scholarship influence the debates considered central to feminist thinking.

The National Women's Studies Association notes that as an academic field of inquiry, women's studies grew out of the women's movement. Both faculty and students saw that "women's social and political inequality was reflected in and partly produced by the invisibility of women's experience in the curricula, research priorities, and methodologies in higher education." The late 1960s are often called the second wave of the women's movement to distinguish it from the first wave, which began with the Women's Rights Conference in 1848 at Seneca Falls and ended with the passage of women's right to vote in 1920. A survey by the American Council on Education reveals that 68 percent of all universities, 49 percent of all four-year colleges, and 27 percent of two-year colleges offer women's studies courses. The number of institutions offering graduate work in women's studies rose from 55 in 1988 to 102 in 1990.

Jewish women have played an impressive part in creating women's studies as an academic discipline. Generally, because they operate on restrictive budgets, women's studies programs are often considered marginal to mainstream liberal studies. This view, from the boundaries of conventional academic disciplines, provides women's studies with the theoretical perspective of the "other." The academic tension generated by its interdisciplinary perch and marginal placement creates the very conditions of women's studies' intellectual strength. Jewish women may be visible within the field of women's studies because they have experienced the world from the margins, as women and as women within the Jewish tradition.

Jewish women have been critical not only as political activists and administrators, as editors and contributing editors of the key women's studies journals, but also as prominent thinkers in the intellectual debates within the field of women's studies. As heads of women's studies programs, they help shape the angle of vision for scholarship, maintain the programs' credibility on campuses through curricula and research development in the field, and support and recruit other scholars. Their efforts represent an immeasurable and often undervalued task on many campuses.

SCHOLARSHIP

In her intellectual history of feminist thought, Hester Eisenstein outlines the chief argument of the first phase of women's studies scholarship: The socially constructed differences in power and opportunity between the sexes were judged to be the chief source of female oppression. In this phase, discussions emphasized the distinctions between sex and gender (biology and the social construction of sex) and how to minimize differences between men and women. Eisenstein views the work in this early period as pointing, explicitly or implicitly, to the replacement of gender polarization with some form of androgyny. CAROLYN HEILBRUN's *Toward a Recognition of Androgyny* (1973), underscored this premise. As activist, educator, scholar, and publisher (the editor of Feminist Press), FLORENCE HOWE played a critical part in legitimating women's studies scholarship by establishing a place for the publication of women's studies monographs. Similarly, in 1981, Barbara Haber brought together the scholarly work of the first phase of second-wave feminism by editing *The Woman's Annual: 1980 Year in Review* and *Women in America: A Guide to Books, 1963–1975, with an Appendix on Books Published 1976–1979.*

Pioneer work by psychologists such as Roz Barnett, Grace Baruch, Sandra Bem, Nancy Datan, Lois Hoffman, Alexandria Kaplan, Jean Lipman-Blumen, MARTHA MEDNICK, Sandra Tangri, and Rhoda Unger rooted women's difference from men in the social psychological attributes and attitudes found in the cultural construction of femininity.

Whether a class, a caste, or a minority (Helen Mayer Hacker, in 1951, was among the first to discuss women as a minority group), women generally were described as a generic grouping despite differences in class, race, ethnicity, and/or nationality. Florence Howe saw this generic grouping as the groundwork for the field of women's studies, since once defined as a group, women could then become an analytic category of study. The other premise of this first phase of women's studies was that women's experiences were different from those of men because of different educational and institutional opportunities, socialization processes, and the social constructions of "femininity" and "masculinity." Janet Saltzman Chafetz was among the first to analyze, in 1974, the gender effects of early gender-role socialization. Differences focused on in this first phase were sociohistoric and/or social psychological in origin, not biological.

Liberal feminism of this period, first voiced and best expressed in BETTY FRIEDAN's landmark *The Feminine Mystique* (1963), stressed the similarity between the sexes and the lack of equal opportunity to explain women's poorer achievements in the public spheres of education and the labor market. Some of the major contributions to "liberal feminist" thinking in this initial stage of the second wave came from the social sciences, especially sociology and psychology. Although less interdisciplinary in their focus than their counterparts representing women's studies journals, the editors, contributing editors, and consultants of such journals as *Journal of Sex Roles*, *Psychology of Women Quarterly*, and, later, *Gender & Society* have made important contributions to women's studies scholarship by providing a critique of their respective disciplines through a gender analysis.

The pioneering work of several sociologists early in this first phase of women's studies scholarship raised issues about the invisibility of women in research, scholarship, and the creation of theory and methodology. Scholars recognized that traditional definitions of knowledge were derived from, and set by, the experiences of men and a masculinist tradition of inquiry. Women's studies as a discipline needed to focus on female experience, not only to expand knowledge but also to understand better how social life and behavior actually worked.

Pauline Bart recast research on menopause (and thereby on life cycle studies for both men and women) by focusing on role loss as more important than biological changes in explaining depression among midlife women. Preceding the "fear of success" research by more than a decade, as early as 1946 Mirra Komarovsky wrote of cultural contradictions and women's roles, suggesting that women often had to "play dumb" to attract males. Cynthia Fuchs Epstein legitimated and made the study of gender pivotal in the sociology of the professions with her formative book, *Woman's Place* (1970). This book gave new meaning and focus to the sociological adage that how people behave, feel, and what they "know" is affected by their particular location in the social structure. Epstein's research focused on the social structure of the professions. Her network analysis of the "old boy"

system launched scores of doctoral dissertations. Debra Renee Kaufman, coauthor of *Achievement and Women*, (1982), offered a critique of the sociological and psychological research on achievement by looking at the masculinist assumptions and techniques that legitimate the limited scope and findings about women and achievement in both disciplines. This book not only provided a critique of the disciplinary assumptions and methods that underestimated and undervalued women's achievements but also anticipated the next phase of women's studies scholarship, which criticized the American culture of competitive success. Shulamit Reinharz broke new ground with *On Becoming a Social Scientist* (1983), which laid the groundwork for her later work, *Feminist Methods in Social Research* (1992).

In *Another Voice: Feminist Perspectives on Social Life and Social Sciences* (1975), Marcia Millman and Rosabeth Moss Kanter brought together work that posed some of the critical questions for sociology from a feminist perspective. By attending primarily to the formal, official action and actors in the social organization of social life, the editors argued that sociologists have ignored large chunks of social life. Contributors to this trailblazing anthology suggest that knowledge of the social world and social behavior could be expanded if we included the realities and interests of women in our social science theories, paradigms, substantive concerns, and methodologies. Summarizing her work on organizational theory and behavior, Kanter argues that sociologists had overlooked important support structures that house large cadres of women (secretaries, clerks, wives) in their analyses of organizational behavior. In addition, she noted that the male managerial model works against the upward mobility of female employees.

With the provocative title "She Did it All for Love: A Feminist View of the Sociology of Deviance" (1975), Marcia Millman demonstrates how the focus on dramatic events and incidents that occur in official locations have prevented sociologists from understanding the effects of deviance on victims, family members, and other individuals closely involved but having no place in formal procedures. Summarizing the work of Arlene Kaplan Daniels, the editors note how Daniels keeps her feminist politics and academic scholarship together by demanding that feminists not only do research on the conditions of women's lives and the causes and consequences of their oppression but also identify how to improve the quality of their lives. Daniels and Rachel Kahn-Hut, her sometime coauthor, not only were vocal about the development of gender studies in the field of sociology but also focused on the relationship between the women's movement and women's studies scholarship.

For feminist political science scholars Berenice Carroll, Ethel Klein, and Virginia Sapiro, like the sociologists, the points of origin for differences between men and women were firmly located in the organization and institutionalized patterns of social life in both public and private spheres and/or in the assumptions inherent in the theories and methods used to measure those differences. Anthropologist Michelle Zimbalist Rosaldo anchors differences between the sexes in the sexual division of labor that associated women with "nature" and assigned them to the lesser-valued private sphere of life. In a critical anthology, *Toward an Anthropology of Women* (1975), Rayna Reiter Rapp marks the importance of the political uses of academic research, reiterating the need for new studies that will focus on women because of the biases that have traditionally trivialized and misinterpreted female roles. Her goal is to "redefine the important questions, reexamine all previous theories, and be critical in . . . [the] acceptance of what constitutes factual material." The contributors to this volume, many of them Jewish women anthropologists, such as Lila Leibowitz and Ida Susser, address her cautions. For instance, Leibowitz examines the popular belief that the physical differences between the sexes are directly responsible for social-role differentiation, concluding that "biology is not social destiny, even for monkeys and apes." Susser, in one of the first major urban ethnographies, offers an analysis of women's grassroots organization on a neighborhood level. All the contributors offer a critical reanalysis of cultural and biological evolution, data on the productive roles of women, and the complexities of male supremacy.

This first phase of feminist thinking within the field of women's studies was profoundly affected by women who had their political roots in the women's movement and whose works set the stage for some of the key debates in the field and for feminist theory. SHULAMITH FIRESTONE's *The Dialectic of Sex: The Case for Feminist Revolution* (1971), Susan Brownmiller's *Against Our Will: Men, Women and Rape* (1975), and Andrea Dworkin's *Our Blood: Prophecies and Discourses on Sexual Politics* (1976) were central to the first phase of women's studies scholarship and feminist theory in that they addressed the relationship among women's reproductive roles, sexual violence, and the physical and psychological oppression of women. Dworkin stressed that sexual violence enables men to control women. All put forward a radical, historical critique of reproduction and sexual violence that highlights the extent to which reproduction and sexual violence are a result of masculine social power, not female biology.

JOURNALS

Similarly, many of the women responsible for editing the first feminist academic journals and airing some of the major debates were not only tied closely to the feminist movement and the New Left publishing model but also were central in defining the discipline and the content of women's studies within the university. In 1981, Annette Kolodny won the Modern Language Association's Florence Howe Award for her article with the political point that academic journals must stay responsible to the community of feminists outside the academy as well as within. The *National Women's Studies Association Journal*, founded in 1988, best expresses the ambivalence, exemplified in the voice of Robin Leidner, about the conflicts between feminist activism and feminist scholarship within women's studies.

Frontiers, Feminist Studies, and *SIGNS* were among the three earliest academic journals that covered, through an interdisciplinary perspective, feminist scholarship and research throughout the field of women's studies. Perhaps because it initially drew on women from a consciousness-raising group organized around Columbia University's women's liberation group, a women's studies lecture series at Sarah Lawrence College, and community activists in New York City, *Feminist Studies* has since its inception had a clear presence of Jewish editors, contributing editors, and consultants. Its association with the prestigious Berkshire Conferences makes it the leading publication of social history and materialist feminist analysis. Therefore, it is not surprising that its editorial staff was primarily staffed by historians or historical sociologists who had their roots in the New Left.

The politically informed scholarship of Marxist-oriented social historians in the pages of *Feminist Studies* was best formulated by such scholars as Nancy Cott, Linda Gordon, Robin Miller Jacoby, Alice Kessler-Harris, GERDA LERNER, Sherry Ortner, Rosalind Petchesky, Elaine Showalter, Kathryn Kish Sklar, and Judith Stacey. All later published their work with mainstream scholarly presses and became leading women's studies scholars in their respective fields. They focused on such issues as the division of labor into public and private spheres, the family as a unit of production, housework and mothering as unpaid labor, and society's control of female sexuality and reproduction. Even those who were not historians emphasized how women's experiences and oppression were shaped by their relations to historically specific contexts.

Frontiers, founded in 1975, had as its mission to heal the breach between feminists in the university and in the community. Renee Horowitz was on the founding editorial collective. Initially, *Frontiers* was characterized as regional (the West); however, its focus on community and regional interests led to two very important special issues on women's oral history. In 1977, the first volume was published under special guest editor, Sherna Gluck. Its success prompted "Women's Oral History Two" in 1983, with a contribution by Sydney Stahl Weinberg about the world of Jewish immigrant women. *Frontiers* consistently underscored the diversity of female experience, especially from the lesbian perspective, and in 1979, guest editor Judith Schwarz did a special issue on lesbian history.

In 1973, the University of Chicago Press published a special issue of the *American Journal of Sociology* entitled "Changing Women in a Changing Society." Impressed with the number of copies sold, the press agreed to publish *SIGNS: Journal of Women in Culture and Society*. From its inception, the editors wanted academic recognition and legitimation for feminist scholarship. The first editor of *SIGNS* used the Barnard, Columbia, Sarah Lawrence, Rutgers, and New York City network of feminist scholars. The editorial staff reflects the clear presence of Jewish women: Sandra L. Bem, JESSIE BERNARD, Barbara R. Bergmann, Francine Blau, Joan Burstyn, Nancy Chodorow, NATALIE ZEMON DAVIS, Cynthia Fuchs Epstein, Estelle B. Freedman, RUTH BADER GINSBURG, Linda Gordon, Carolyn Heilbrun, Lois Wladis Hoffman, Florence Howe, Mirra Komarovsky, Gerda Lerner, Ruth B. Mandel, RUTH BARCAN MARCUS, Elaine Marks, Ellen Messer-Davidow, Hanna Papanek, Harriet Presser, Estelle R. Ramey, Rayna Rapp, Michelle Zimbalist Rosaldo, Margaret K. Roseheim, Neena B. Schwartz, Elaine Showalter, Myra Strober, Sheila Tobias, Gaye Tuchman (guest associate), Naomi Weisstein, and Froma Zeitlin.

SECOND PHASE

By the mid-1970s, the debates considered central to feminist thinking shifted. Feminist thinking adopted a woman-centered focus that located specific virtues in the historical and psychological experiences of women. Describing this as the beginning of the second phase of the second wave, Hester Eisenstein notes that instead of seeking to minimize the polarization between masculine and feminine, current scholarship sought to isolate and to define those aspects of female experience that were potential sources of strength and power for women. In contrast to the first phase, where differences between the sexes were seen as an obstacle to achievement and as a means of keeping women in their devalued and domestic place, this second phase viewed female differences as positive.

Two books helped to usher in this woman-centered focus: PHYLLIS CHESLER's *Women and Madness* (1972) and Gerda Lerner's *The Majority Finds Its Past* (1979). In addition, Adrienne Rich, a lesbian feminist poet and philosopher, transformed feminist thinking with her writings on sexuality and mothering. In *Of Woman Born* (1976), she directs our attention to the difference between institutionalized motherhood and mothering. Unlike some feminists, she saw a woman's capacity to bear children as a strength rather than an incapacity. In her work on sexuality she builds on Simone de Beauvoir's premise that women are originally homosexual, then argues that women's experience, history, culture, and values are distinct from the dominant patriarchal and heterosexual culture.

With the publication of *Reproduction of Mothering* (1978), Nancy Chodorow became one of the most influential feminist psychoanalytic theorists of sexual difference. Chodorow argues that the mother is the central element in identity formation. Given female parenting, girls develop relational capacities by internalizing the role of caring and by identifying with their mothers. Boys, on the other hand, learn to reject the female aspects of themselves such as nurturing and empathy in order to adopt a masculine gender identity. Adult women are able to empathize with other people's needs and feelings, whereas men develop a defensive desire for autonomy based on the abstract model of the absent father. Chodorow revises Freudian theory by focusing on mother relations, not the Oedipus complex, to explain gender differences.

CAROL GILLIGAN's *In a Different Voice* (1982) explores moral development theory from a woman-centered perspective and introduces new thinking about the place of care within a moral developmental framework focusing solely on abstract concepts of justice. Her work brings into focus the methodological biases and the conceptual weaknesses of moral developmental theories based on traditional male interests and formulations.

In the introduction to *The Future of Difference*, Hester Eisenstein notes that this woman-centered perspective raises questions about "maleness" and "femaleness." Citing the work of DOROTHY DINNERSTEIN, Eisenstein asks if "masculinity" is an "outmoded, or even a dangerous construct." Eisenstein argues that the move toward a woman-centered perspective had a liberating effect on many women's studies scholars, encouraging them "to contemplate the varieties of female experience."

A spate of books in this period addressed varieties of women's experiences, including religious differences. Older works were recovered for use in women's studies courses. *The Jewish Woman in America* (1976) by Charlotte Baum, Paula Hyman, and Sonya Michel and, later, the readings from *On Being a Jewish Feminist* (1983) edited by Susannah Heschel were incorporated into women's studies curricula and syllabi. *Womanspirit Rising* (1979), an important feminist reader in religion, with contributions from Aviva Cantor, Naomi Goldenberg, Rita Gross, Naomi Janowitz, Judith Plaskow, and Maggie Wenig, as well as Carol Ochs's *Women and Spirituality* (1983) became widely used in introductory women's studies courses.

In the spring of 1980, *Feminist Studies* published a scholarly debate entitled "Politics and Culture in Women's History" that was important to the second phase of women's studies scholarship. While addressing the nineteenth-century "female homosocial world," it raised the controversial question about the origins of feminism and whether it could develop outside of a female world. This symposium marked the beginning of a host of debates about "women's culture" in academic journals. Some feared that the affirmation of gender differences and the celebration of traditionally feminine qualities, particularly those associated with mothering, might obscure the power differences between the sexes and the fight against male domination.

The shift from the first to the second phase of contemporary feminist thought is highlighted further in the sexuality debates of the 1980s. A major conference at Barnard College in 1982, "The Scholar and the Feminist IX: Toward a Politics of Sexuality," clarified some of the key splits among feminists on the issue of sexuality. The event featured forty participants who represented a wide variety of analytic perspectives, including the two polarized critiques that had evolved from the radical insights of sexual politics in the 1960s. One analyzed how patriarchy shapes female sexuality, extending this analysis of male dominance to include rape, degrading images of women in advertising, the myth of the vaginal orgasm, and pornography. The second explored female sexuality when free of patriarchal distortion and looked to alternative expressions of female sexuality and erotica.

THE THIRD PHASE

The debates in the late 1980s anticipate the third phase of women's studies scholarship in which several interrelated issues become paramount: woman as a universal category, multiculturalism, and how to link feminism to other existing or emerging sociopolitical approaches and poststructuralist criticism. Similarities between feminist and poststructuralist analysis came in the recognition of the links between the public and private realms of experience, of the existence and authority of patriarchy, and of women's voice in the construction of the cultural categories of female and male. However, poststructuralism questions the category of woman as a unit of analysis, thereby undercutting the field of women's studies. In the important anthology *Feminism/Postmodernism* (1990), theorists critical in formulating the points of tension and accord between postmodernism and feminism frame the debates. Feminists prominent in the fields of philosophy, literary theory, Romance languages, and history, such as Annette Kolodny and Susan Mosher Stuard, are among spokespersons for the arguments in this third phase of the second wave of feminist scholarship. Wini Breines brings together many of these approaches in her book, *Young, White and Miserable: Women in the 1950s* (1992).

New journals, such as *differences: A Journal of Feminist Cultural Studies* and *Genders*, address the need to incorporate analyses from poststructuralism, cultural studies, and critical studies into feminist analysis. For *differences* editor Naomi Schor, the title connotes not so much "pluralism" as "multiple subjectivities." The use of difference as a form of cultural criticism rather than the focus on woman or gender as the unit of analysis characterizes this turn in the third phase of feminist scholarship. *Genders* focuses on constructions of gender within the arts and humanities as its principal concern. Each journal reconfigures the category of woman. Joan Wallach Scott, another *differences* editor, theorizes that gender signifies relationships of power. Literary theorist Rita Felski observes that "feminism as a critique of values is also engaged in a more general and public process of revising and refuting male-defined cultural and discursive frameworks." Moving away from a thematized focus on women to gender opens the field of women's studies to investigations of male subjectivities and the construction of male-defined culture. The debates raise the provocative question of whether women's subjective position will remain the privileged focus for women's studies analysis.

The meaning and the use of the term *feminist* and the question of what comprises feminist scholarship provide the basis of an ongoing discussion about the range of theories and methods that belong to women's studies. Jewish women have contributed significantly to this unrestricted field of study, which is continuously making and remaking itself.

BIBLIOGRAPHY

Bart, Pauline. "Middle Aged Women and Depression." In *Women in Sexist Society*, edited by V. Gornik and B. Moran (1971); Baum, Charlotte, Paula Hyman, and Sonya Michel. *The Jewish Woman in America* (1976); Bernard, Jesse. "My Four Revolutions: An Autobiographical History of the ASA." *American Journal of Sociology* (1973): 791–804; Breines, Wini. *Young, White and Miserable: Women in the 1950s* (1992); Broverman, I., et al. "Sex Role Stereotypes: A Current Appraisal." *Journal of Social Issues* (1972): 59–78; Brownmiller, Susan. *Against Our Will: Men, Women and Rape* (1975); Chafetz, Janet Saltzman. *Masculine/Feminine or Human?* (1974); Chesler, Phyllis. *Women and Madness* (1972); Chodorow, Nancy. *Reproduction of Mothering* (1978); Christ, Carol, and Judith Plaskow. *Womanspirit Rising* (1979); Davidman, Lynn. *Tradition in a Rootless World: Women Turn to Orthodox Judaism* (1991); Dinnerstein, Dorothy. *The Mermaid and the Minotaur* (1976); Dworkin, Andrea. *Our Blood: Prophecies and Discourses on Sexual Politics* (1976); Eisenstein, Hester. *Contemporary Feminist Thought* (1983); Eisenstein, Hester, and Alice Jardine, eds. *The Future of Difference* (1980); Epstein, Cynthia Fuchs. *Woman's Place* (1970); Felski, Rita. *Beyond Feminist Aesthetics: Feminist Literature and Social Change* (1989); Firestone, Shulamith. *The Dialectic of Sex: The Case for Feminist Revolution* (1971); Friedan, Betty. *The Feminine Mystique* (1963); Gilligan, Carol. *In a Different Voice* (1982); Ginsburg, Faye. *Contested Lives* (1990); Haber, Barbara. *The Woman's Annual: 1980 Year in Review* (1981), and *Women in America: A Guide to Books, 1963–1975, with an Appendix on Books Published 1976–1979* (1981); Hacker, Helen Mayer. "Women as a Minority Group." *Social Forces* (1951): 60–69; Heilbrun, Carolyn. *Toward a Recognition of Androgyny* (1973); Heschel, S. *On Being a Jewish Feminist* (1983); Kanter, Rosabeth Moss, and Marcia Millman, eds. *In Another Voice* (1975); Kaufman, Debra Renee. *Rachel's Daughters* (1991); Kaufman, Debra Renee, and Barbara Richardson. *Achievement and Women* (1982); Keller, Evelyn Fox. "Gender and Science." *Psychoanalysis and Contemporary Thought* 1 (1978): 409–433; Klatch, Rebecca. *Women of the New Right* (1988); Koedt, Anne. "The Myth of the Vaginal Orgasm." In *Radical Feminism*, edited by A. Koedt, E. Levine, and A. Rapone (1973); Kolodny, Annette. "Dancing Between Left and Right: Feminism and the Academic Minefield in the 1980s." *Feminist Studies* 14 (1988): 455–461; Komarovsky, Mirra. "Cultural Contradictions and Sex Roles." *American Journal of Sociology* 52 (1946): 184–189; Lerner, Gerda. *The Majority Finds Its Past: Placing Women in History* (1979); McDermott, Patrice. *Politics and Scholarship* (1994); National Women's Studies Association. *Liberal Learning and the Women's Studies Major* (1991); *NWSA Directory of Women's Studies Programs, Women's Centers and Women's Research Centers: a Publication of the National Women's Studies Association* (1990); Ochs, Carol. *Women and Spirituality* (1983); Rapp, Rayna Reiter, ed. *Toward an Anthropology of Women* (1975); Reinharz, Shulamit. *Feminist Methods in Social Research* (1992), and *On Becoming a Social Scientist* (1983); Rich, Adrienne. *Of Woman Born* (1976), and *On Lies, Secrets and Silences: Selected Prose 1966–1978* (1995); Rosaldo, Michele, and Louise Lamphere, eds. *Women, Culture and Society* (1974); Ruth, Sheila. *Issues in Feminism* (1985); Stacey, Judith. *Brave New Families* (1993); Stuard, Susan Mosher. "The Annales School and Feminist History: Opening Dialogue with the American Stepchild." *SIGNS* 7 (1981): 137–148; Unger, Rhoda. *Woman: Dependent or Independent Variable?* (1975).

DEBRA KAUFMAN

WOMEN'S *TEFILLA* MOVEMENT

HISTORY

Orthodox women's *tefilla* [prayer] groups consist of women who want to stay within the halakic parameters of the Orthodox community and who meet regularly to conduct prayer services for women only.

The first women's *tefilla* group began in the late 1960s on the holiday of Simhat Torah at Lincoln Square Synagogue in Manhattan. Simhat Torah had proved to be a particularly frustrating experience for Orthodox women as all of its customs and celebrations are tied to the synagogue and formal prayer. Perhaps even more critical was the fact that celebration focused on carrying, dancing, and rejoicing with the Torah scrolls, a practice from which women were excluded. With the support of Rabbi Shlomo Riskin of the Lincoln Square Synagogue, the women were given the Torah scrolls for the celebration and permitted to convene a separate Torah reading. Subsequently, it was seen as a major step forward when women in other Orthodox synagogues were also granted the privilege of holding the Torah and taking it to the women's section. Many groups progressed to conducting full-fledged Simhat Torah services for women only—services in which women read the Torah portion aloud and gave aliyahs to every woman present.

By the late 1970s, a number of groups began to meet monthly. Some of these prayer services were tied to *rosh hodesh* [the beginning of the month] and the new moon cycle and met on weekdays, while others met once a month on Shabbat. In 1978 and 1979, *tefilla* groups were formed in Baltimore, Maryland; in St. Paul, Minnesota; and in Riverdale and Washington Heights, New York. In the early 1980s, the first women's *tefilla* group in Canada was founded, shortly followed by the Flatbush group in Brooklyn, New York.

During this period, most women's *tefilla* groups met in private homes, as Orthodox synagogues were

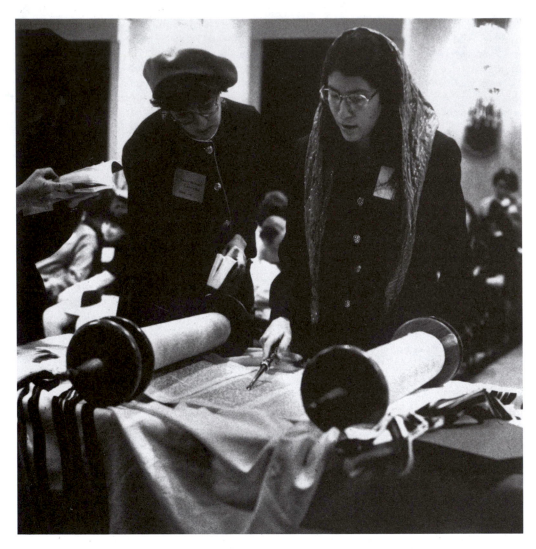

Orthodox women's tefilla *groups consist of women who want to stay within the halakic parameters
of the Orthodox community and who meet regularly to conduct prayer services for women only.
The above photograph was taken at a 1997 conference in New York City on Feminism and
Orthodoxy, the first of its kind. [Joan Roth]*

not prepared to sanction the practice. Two notable exceptions were the Riverdale group, which was invited by Rabbi Avi Weiss to meet in the Hebrew Institute of Riverdale, a major Orthodox synagogue and an East Side group which met in Kehillat Jeshorun under the guidance of Rabbi Haskel Lookstein. Mainstream modern Orthodox rabbis and community leaders rejected women's *tefilla* groups for reasons that ranged from the halakic to the sociological. This issue came to a head in 1985 with publication of the "teshuva: responsa" by five highly regarded Yeshiva University rabbis. The position paper viewed the movement as stemming from, and copying, the feminist movement in America with no serious spiritual or religious basis. It prohibited all organized women's prayer groups in any form.

The reaction to this public statement was dramatic. Although some rabbis used the statement to justify their prohibition of these prayer groups, a number of well-respected Orthodox rabbinic leaders viewed the document as totally subjective and without serious halakic basis. This spurred them to take more public roles and action in support of the growing movement. Subsequently, a book was published by Rabbi Weiss entitled *Women and Prayer*, which analyzed and supported women's *tefilla* from a halakic perspective. Also as a response, the Women's Tefilla Network was born. The network serves as a support and resource center for new and existing groups, publishes regular newsletters, counsels groups, and provides groups with written and taped prayer guides.

By the late 1980s, women's *tefilla* groups proliferated throughout New York and spread to isolated venues throughout North America. It is difficult to ascertain the exact number of groups. Since the climate was so hostile, many existed "underground." By 1988, it was estimated that there were twenty groups, and in January of 1997 there were over forty identifiable groups in the United States, Canada, Israel, England, and Australia. These represented nearly four thousand women.

STRUCTURE

Women's prayer groups meet monthly to pray, read Torah, and study together. Most groups meet on Shabbat mornings, while others meet on Shabbat afternoons or *rosh hodesh* weekdays. Generally, full Torah and haftarah portions are read. The women conduct a full service based on guidelines set by their local rabbis. For the most part, women's *tefilla* groups do not function as a *minyan*. This means that they omit specific prayers for which a *minyan* is required. Thus the status of these groups remains different from that of their male counterparts.

Women's *tefilla* groups have become a new arena for women's life cycle events within the Orthodox community. Celebrations include *simhat bat* ceremonies celebrating the birth of a baby girl, bat mitzvah ceremonies, and *ufrufs* [calling to the Torah] for women about to be married. Among the unique practices that have resulted from these groups is the inclusion of a prayer for *agunot*, women denied religious divorce.

The *tefilla* groups are attended by women of every age and religious background. Young mothers with babies, older women, preadolescents, teenagers, and college students all participate. This forum allows each of them unique entry into the world of prayer. For some women it affords the opportunity to learn and practice new synagogue skills; for some it provides an opportunity to serve as role models for their children; for some it is a doorway back to the Orthodox community; for some it is a natural extension of leadership that they experience in other areas of their lives.

As feminism continues to influence American Orthodoxy, women's *tefilla* groups will remain a viable alternative for Orthodox women who desire a fuller worship experience without leaving Orthodoxy.

RONNIE BECHER
BAT SHEVA MARCUS

WOMEN'S ZIONIST ORGANIZATION OF AMERICA *see* HADASSAH

WOODWARD, HELEN ROSEN (1882–1950)

Helen Rosen Woodward is best known for her contribution to the world of advertising and is generally believed to be the first female account executive in the United States. Born in New York City to Polish and German immigrants Louis and Frederika (Sachs) Rosen, she attended the Girls' Latin School in Boston and in 1913 married William E. Woodward, a non-Jewish writer and historian. She was largely self-taught, read voraciously, was excited by new ideas, and was imbued with a bristling patriotism.

Woodward recounts the challenges she faced as a young working woman in a variety of businesses in her forthright autobiography *Through Many Windows*. Her keen observations about office life in the early part of the century make fascinating reading. She explains that "girls in offices" in this period were nearly all opposed to suffrage "except for an occasional Jewish girl." Gradually, women began to change as their self-respect and self-reliance grew.

In 1907, Woodward began her long career in advertising and her long association with women's magazines, including *Pictorial Review*, *Woman's Day*, and *McCall's*. She later wrote a lively social history titled *The Lady Persuaders* about how women's magazines transformed women's place in American society.

After she met her husband, Woodward realized that she had two ambitions: "To write novels and do something for the good of mankind." She proceeded to join the Women's Trade Union League and became active in encouraging the formation of labor unions among female workers. In her later years, Woodward reflected on her experience as a Jewish woman in business and dismissed the notion that her Jewishness had anything to do with how she was treated. "I have certain talents they want and they like me as a person," she explained. Indeed, her Jewishness figures little in her autobiography. She writes that she never went to any religious service and that the exclusively Jewish social life of her brother and sister held no interest for her whatsoever.

Woodward left advertising after twenty years, because she wanted to travel with her husband and write. During this time, she wrote books both alone and in collaboration with other authors, including a two-part memoir with a Russian ex-soldier about his experiences in the Bolshevik Revolution. She was a passionate woman and a prolific author who was committed to social justice and delighted by life's possibilities.

Helen Rosen Woodward died in New York City in 1950.

SELECTED WORKS BY
HELEN ROSEN WOODWARD

The Lady Persuaders (1960); *Lances Down*, with Richard Boleslavski (1932); *Through Many Windows* (1926); *Way of the Lancer*, with Richard Boleslavski (1932).

BIBLIOGRAPHY

Applegate, Ed, ed. *Ad Men and Women: A Biographical Dictionary of Advertising* (1994); Burke, W.J., and Will Howe. *American Authors and Books, 1640 to the Present Day.* 3rd ed. (1972); *Contemporary Authors: A Bio-Bibliographical Guide to Current Writers in Fiction, General Non-Fiction, Poetry, Journalism, Drama, Motion Pictures, Television and Other Fields* (1969); *UJE; WWIAJ* (1938); *WWWIA 7.*

SUSAN MARTHA KAHN

WORKING WOMEN'S EDUCATION

In the early twentieth century, young Jewish Eastern European immigrant women needed to work but wanted to learn as well. Expected to work until they married, Jewish daughters wanted an education to advance themselves economically and to take advantage of opportunities denied them in the Old Country. Jewish women formed a high proportion of students in evening schools, settlement houses, and vocational training courses that taught them to be more proficient workers, to speak better English, and to be more American. Jewish working women also served as the leaders and members of the largest attempt to educate women as workers, the workers' education movement. Begun by the predominantly Jewish INTERNATIONAL LADIES GARMENT WORKERS UNION (ILGWU) in the 1910s and continued by other union leaders and reformers, workers' education programs taught workers to develop a sense of class consciousness and a desire to promote social justice. Organizers designed these programs specifically for the needs of women workers but always allied with the labor movement over feminism when forced to choose. This article discusses the many types of education Jewish working women received, focusing on the 1910s through the 1930s, the height of the workers' education movement in the United States.

Mostly single Jewish women sought education. Married women, with dual responsibility for the household and family income, tended not to take advantage of educational opportunities. Once a Jewish woman married, she generally stopped working outside the home. As in Eastern Europe, married women contributed to the family income by taking in boarders, helping in their husbands' businesses, or sewing and finishing garments in the home.

While Jewish families expected married women to stay at home, they expected their single daughters to work to supplement family income, to keep brothers in school, and to bring over relatives from the Old Country. Although they worked in a variety of trades, most Jewish women spent some part of their young adult life working with a needle and thread. In 1900, 53.6 percent of all employed Jewish women in New York City worked in the garment industry.

Conditions in both garment sweatshops and factories were bad. In sweatshops, the contractor, usually a slightly more established immigrant, obtained precut, unsewn garments from the manufacturer. The contractor either supervised basting, pressing, finishing, zipper installing, buttonhole making, and pocket making himself, or gave some of the work to a subcontractor, who then gave that work to people to finish at home. This system encouraged exploitation. Workers labored in crowded sweatshops for long hours. Contractors had small profit margins and so paid their sweatshop workers low wages. In addition, the system created a vicious cycle: Immigrants became contractors whenever possible; they competed with former employers by offering lower bids and speedier deliveries; and they exploited the latest group of newcomers.

Factories, or "inside shops," were not much better than sweatshops. Frequent speedups; dangerous work; fees for needles, irons, lockers, chairs, and electric power to run machines; and fines for damaging garments, breaking needles, and arriving late all made for miserable work conditions.

Even though young Jewish immigrant women in the early twentieth century worked in demanding jobs, they reserved time and energy for education. Why? What did they expect in terms of education? Women who immigrated as teenagers knew how to read and write because Jewish culture considered such skills acceptable for girls. In the United States, these young women grabbed opportunities for education newly available to them in such a way that they could continue to work. Unlike in the Old Country, education in America was compulsory and free. Even poor girls could attend high school. However, economic

In 1921, the INTERNATIONAL LADIES GARMENT WORKERS UNION *(under the direction of* FANNIA COHN)
established Brookwood College, the first coeducational labor college in the United States, in Katonah, New York.
The classes were structured to help students understand societal problems, with the understanding that they would
go back to their shops to "spread the word" to their coworkers. This photograph is from the 1935 commencement.
Fannia Cohn is in the front row, fifth from the right. [Kheel Center, Cornell University]

realities dictated that many immigrant girls left school for full-time jobs as young as nine or ten. In 1914, the New York State Factory Investigating Commission reported that 75 percent of women working in factories had left school before completing the eighth grade.

For most girls, learning job skills was the first priority. Many had to attend evening school because they worked during the day. The New York City Board of Education, the Industrial School for Girls, and the Educational Alliance offered vocational courses in dressmaking, sewing, and hat trimming, among other subjects. Jewish girls already proficient in English sometimes took typing or bookkeeping courses to obtain coveted office positions. In addition to vocational training, settlement houses such as the Educational Alliance offered classes in English and Yiddish on history, literature, religion, music, art, hygiene, "virtue," and American nationalism. By 1898, New York City's Board of Education ran sixty-one elementary schools and four high schools in the evening. By 1906, Jews constituted the majority of students enrolled in elementary, high school, and Americanization classes in New York City, and the Board of Education sponsored lectures in Yiddish. Forty percent of the Jewish students were female. However, earning a high school degree at night was very difficult for working women, who lacked the time and energy for the advanced classes, which met for five three-hour sessions weekly. Despite registering in large numbers, Jewish girls attended high school classes only sporadically. Still, the high proportion of Jewish women in the evening school system shows their avid desire for learning and economic advancement.

While public schools and settlement houses offered vocational training and academic courses, workers' education programs also attempted to teach women workers about social activism. In the 1910s and 1920s, the workers' education movement tried simultaneously to convince workers of the need to build a new and better social order and to moderate their more radical impulses by instructing workers on the principles of trade union participation and leadership. Many of the middle-class intellectuals, radicals, and reformers who started the movement and many of the workers who benefited from it were Jewish women.

The workers' education movement began in 1915, when Juliet Stuart Poyntz, a middle-class, non-Jewish, college-educated midwesterner, established the first unity house in the Catskills to serve as a vacation house for members of the ILGWU Local 25. Poyntz went on to organize unity centers at local public schools, where workers could attend union meetings and take courses in English and physical education. Inspired by these activities, the ILGWU created a national education department in 1916.

Before Poyntz resigned in 1918, she directed the ILGWU's education department. The ILGWU opened more unity houses and unity centers and established the Workers' University at Washington Irving High School in New York City. At this university, workers took classes in American history and government, labor problems, economics, literature, and psychology; these classes continued well into the 1970s.

The education department was to act as both a radical and a moderating influence on its workers. It aimed to "enlighten our members upon all matters concerning labor, and make of them a well-disciplined and reliable body of men and women, who cannot be misled and incited by anybody who desires to do so." The ILGWU wanted to teach the responsibilities and duties of unionism and express its deep commitment to social unionism, a philosophy that connected the growth of a union to the building of a new social order in which workers' economic, social, and spiritual needs would be fulfilled. According to social unionism, workers needed higher wages and shorter hours, but they also needed education, health care, housing, and recreation. This philosophy had practical benefits: If a union met its members' needs, then members would feel more loyalty to the union.

The most urgent of the immigrant workers' needs was for education. FANNIA COHN, a Russian Jewish immigrant who replaced Poyntz, believed that age, lack of formal schooling, or class should not deprive workers of a liberal education. At the Workers' University, workers studied art, literature, philosophy, or history on the weekends from the same professors who lectured to the upper classes at Columbia University during the week. The ILGWU's education department arranged for New York City public school teachers to teach reading, writing, and arithmetic to workers at night and on the weekends.

Cohn, who had worked in a garment factory despite her middle-class background, argued that workers' education would make for a stronger union. While "individual education" inculcated students with individualistic values and "Knowledge for Knowledge's sake," workers' education, Cohn explained, inspired workers to serve the labor movement. The ILGWU's curriculum, while including a wide variety of course offerings, reflected Cohn's goals. For example, in the early 1920s, the Workers' University offered more classes in trade union history, political science, and economics than in music, literature, art, and remedial subjects. The ILGWU workers' education program was to enable immigrant workers to restructure American society through a greater awareness of society's problems and possible solutions.

In addition to teaching their worker-pupils how to remake the social order, Cohn and Poyntz recognized that women workers wanted a place to have fun. To the many women who had thought of trade unions as a group of middle-aged men smoking, drinking, and arguing, the unity center offered an alternative—a comfortable place for women. At a unity center, women workers could take courses, attend shop meetings, or enjoy a cup of coffee with friends. Thus, workers' education programs provided women not only with an education in economic justice but also a sense of community.

After World War I, the lofty goal of the ILGWU to create a new social order through education seemed within reach. The Russian Revolution, revolts in Germany and Eastern Europe, the rise of the British Labour Party, and the wave of strikes across the United States in 1919 all gave hope to and helped nourish the workers' education movement. Beginning in 1921, several colleges opened summer schools for women workers. The ILGWU's education department and its Jewish members played an important role in the development of all of these institutions.

Like the ILGWU's education department, the summer schools wanted workers to learn the principles of trade unionism. Unlike the ILGWU, they also aimed to teach women workers to be union leaders by removing them from their jobs for a period of weeks or even months to receive intensive education in trade union history, politics, and economics. Several hundred women workers gave up pay and risked losing their jobs to attend these summer schools, located on college campuses or in quiet country homes. These schools had a precursor: the Women's Trade Union League's Training School for Women Organizers. Although it lasted only from 1914 to 1926 and educated a small number of students, this Chicago-based school succeeded in its goal of training young women for leadership positions in the union movement through several months of academic work and then several of fieldwork. Fannia Cohn was a member of the school's first class.

The Women's Trade Union League sponsored the first summer school at Bryn Mawr College in 1921. Each summer until 1938, at least sixty staunch union women spent about seven weeks at the Bryn Mawr Summer School for Women Workers. A preponderance of students were Russian Jewish immigrants. One notable Jewish graduate of the school was ROSE PESOTTA, who became a leading trade unionist in the 1930s and 1940s and the only woman vice president of the ILGWU's executive board. The school encouraged participation and discussion and expected the students to take knowledge of critical thinking back to their fellow workers and lead working women to change their lives.

Other residential summer schools followed. The Barnard College Summer School, the Summer School for Workers of the University of Wisconsin, and the Southern Summer School all began in the mid-1920s. These schools formed a coordinating body for workers' education programs for women, the Affiliated Schools for Women Workers, in 1928. Students generally appreciated the summer schools. They enjoyed uninterrupted freedom to learn and, as alumnae, stated that the understanding stimulated at the schools led them to various types of labor and union activities. Former students developed workers' education programs in their local areas and promoted better working conditions for women by speaking out on issues such as labor standards, unemployment insurance, and labor legislation. Alumnae expressed a few complaints: Several were disappointed about the lack of courses in socialist theory, and others noted the ironic difference between the tranquil campus and their daily working lives.

In 1921, the ILGWU and Cohn established Brookwood College, the first coeducational labor college in the United States, in Katonah, New York. As with other workers' education programs, Brookwood classes, especially in the social sciences, helped students to understand societal problems and encouraged them to go back to the shops to disseminate their new knowledge. Also in 1921, Cohn helped found the Workers' Education Bureau to coordinate workers' education programs and activities and develop a philosophy of workers' education.

Most women who led the workers' education programs, such as Fannia Cohn, rejected the label of feminist. They argued that they were not trying primarily to improve the status of women but instead to reform working conditions within industrial society. Yet, they worked specifically to improve women's lives and felt that a better society would not allow women to be victims of long hours, low wages, and poor working conditions. Like the prominent women of the New Deal, the women leaders of the workers' education movement were social feminists who believed that women had a special role to play in creating a more just society, rather than feminists who believed in equal rights for women.

In many ways, workers' education was an enormous success. Shaped in large part by Jewish women, the movement prepared a generation of women trained in the principles of trade unionism. Many of these women moved into union leadership and demanded improvements in working conditions. When, in the late 1930s, the Congress of Industrial Organizations made efforts to organize women, it found ready support from women schooled in workers' education.

However, by the mid-1920s, the ILGWU's education department began to decline. Automation, seasonal unemployment, and stagnant wages and benefits hurt the ILGWU. Employers waged campaigns against the unions, and within unions communists and socialists competed bitterly for control. Finally, young workers became increasingly concerned with acquiring the contraptions of consumer culture rather than with saving society through workers' education. The ILGWU and its education department revived during the New Deal but in a different form. The ILGWU's new workers' education, known by the 1930s as "labor education," dismissed the special concern for women workers developed and nurtured by Fannia Cohn and Juliet Poyntz and instead focused only on creating good union members. The 1930s education department no longer paid attention to workers' economic, social, and spiritual needs. It taught workers to serve the union, not to remake the social order. In addition to transforming the education department, the changing political tides of the 1930s forced the closing of two other major enterprises in workers' education, Brookwood Labor College and the Bryn Mawr Summer School.

At the beginning of the twentieth century, young Jewish working women flocked to evening school, vocational training courses, and settlement house programs, hoping to learn more than had been permitted to them in Eastern Europe. Immigrant daughters also led the way in a unique experiment in education, the workers' education movement. This movement drew

Jewish working women as leaders and participants because of its commitment to learning, social justice, and social feminism. Angered by their working conditions, young Jewish women sought education, which they believed would help them to improve their own lives and to remake the world.

BIBLIOGRAPHY

Altenbaugh, Richard J. *Education for Struggle: The American Labor Colleges of the 1920s and 1930s* (1990); Baum, Charlotte, Paula Hyman, and Sonya Michel. *The Jewish Woman in America* (1976); Brumberg, Stephan F. *Going to America, Going to School: The Jewish Immigrant Public School Encounter in Turn-of-the-Century New York City* (1986); Bryn Mawr School for Women Workers. Papers. Institute of Management and Labor Relations, Rutgers University, New Brunswick, N.J.; Cohn, Fannia. Collection. New York Public Library, NYC; Feingold, Henry L. *A Time for Searching: Entering the Mainstream, 1920–1945* (1992); Glenn, Susan A. *Daughters of the Shtetl: Life and Labor in the Immigrant Generation* (1990); Hill, Helen D. *The Effect of the Bryn Mawr Summer School as Measured in the Activities of Its Students* (1929); Kessler-Harris, Alice. "Organizing the Unorganizable: Three Jewish Women and Their Union." *Labor History* 17, no. 1 (Winter 1976): 5–23, and *Out to Work: A History of Wage-Earning Women in the United States* (1982); Smith, Hilda W. Collection. Schlesinger Library, Radcliffe College, Cambridge, Mass.; Sorin, Gerald. *A Time for Building: The Third Migration, 1880–1920* (1992); Starr, Mark and Helen. Collection. Archives of Labor and Urban Affairs, Brookwood Labor College, Wayne State University, Detroit, Mich.; Tamiment Library. New York University, NYC; Weinberg, Sydney Stahl. *The World of Our Mothers: The Lives of Jewish Immigrant Women* (1988); *The Women of Summer*. Film. (1975); Wong, Susan Stone. "From Soul to Strawberries: The International Ladies' Garment Workers' Union and Workers' Education, 1914–1950." In *Sisterhood and Solidarity: Workers' Education for Women, 1914–1984*, edited by Joyce L. Kornbluh and Mary Frederickson (1984).

LAURA E. ETTINGER

WORTIS, ROSE (1895–1958)

Rose Wortis was an Eastern European immigrant needleworker who devoted her life to working-class organizing and the Left.

The fourth of six daughters of Samuel Shadduck and Chia Wortis, she was born in August 1895 in the village of Krasilov in the Ukraine, then the Pale of Settlement. She came to Brooklyn, New York, in 1908, living in a household with her mother's relatives, working in a blouse factory, and attending school at night, including evening high school from 1911 to 1915. Wortis worked as an operator in the needle trades at least until 1925, and like many other immigrant Jewish women needleworkers, she joined Local 25 of the INTERNATIONAL LADIES GARMENT WORKERS UNION (ILGWU), where she later served as an elected official of the complaints department. In 1925, she began to work as an organizer for the ILGWU.

In the 1910s, Wortis, like many other Jewish men and women in her Williamsburg, Brooklyn, neighborhood, was active in the Socialist Party until it fragmented due to political differences regarding the implications of the Bolshevik Revolution and the role of foreign-language federations. At that point (1919), Wortis became a charter member of the Communist Party of the United States of America. From 1915 to 1925, Wortis struggled to create a leftist presence within the ILGWU, attempting to return union leadership to the shop floor (with more guidance from communist activists), and to mobilize against the ILGWU's attempts to expel leftist militants from union locals.

When leftist activists convened the Trade Union Unity League in 1929 to promote the organization of industrywide unions, Wortis was elected secretary. She also served as secretary in the leftist Needle Trades Workers Industrial Union during the years in which this organization competed with the ILGWU. In 1934, Wortis ran for New York State Controller on the Communist Party ticket. Other communists active in the labor movement and in the needle trades remembered her in the 1930s as "always foremost on the picket lines . . . always coming up with constructive advice, how to work in strikes, how to organize." Wortis became well known as a public speaker and as a writer in Yiddish and English, especially on labor issues. Her articles appeared in the Communist Party's daily paper, the *Daily Worker*, the party's theoretical journal, *The Communist*, and in the Yiddish communist daily newspaper, *Oifrayheyt*.

In an entry in *Who's Who in American Jewry* (probably based on a questionnaire she filled out), Wortis suggested how she wanted to present herself to the Jewish community in 1938. She identified herself foremost as a labor organizer, supported by her membership in the Dressmakers Executive Board and on the strike committee of the ILGWU. She positioned herself on the left of the labor movement by noting her activities in the leftist Trade Union Educational League and its affiliated Needle Trades Workers Industrial Union. Making use of the Communist Party's new public openness after 1935 as part of its participation in New Deal and labor coalitions, she noted her own party leadership as secretary of the labor department for the New York District Communist Party. Her listing of her membership in the International Workers Order (IWO), a fraternal association with leftist ties, was probably an indication of her activity in the Jewish People's Fraternal Order, the IWO's huge Jewish section.

In the 1940s, Wortis was probably active in the Communist Party's attempt to encourage left-wing and antiracist union activity, although after 1947, the emergence of red-baiting made it harder to work publicly as a communist. In the 1950s, communist activists like Wortis had to spend most of their time defending themselves and their organizations from anticommunist legal and political attack. By the early 1950s, Wortis was increasingly disabled by rheumatoid arthritis, and after several years "on a bed of anguish," she died in New York in 1958.

BIBLIOGRAPHY

"Communists Pick Ticket," *NYTimes*, August 25, 1934, 2; Dixler, Elsa. "The Woman Question: Women and the American Communist Party, 1929–1941." Ph.D. diss., Yale University, 1974; *Encyclopedia of the American Left*. Edited by Mari Jo Buhle, Paul Buhle, and Dan Georgakas (1990), s.v. "Communist Party," and "International Ladies Garment Workers Union," and "International Workers Order," and "Rose Wortis (1886–1958)," and "Trade Union Unity League"; Foner, Philip. *Women and the American Labor Movement: From the First Trade Unions to the Present* (1979); Hardy, Jack. *The Clothing Workers: A Study of Conditions and Struggles in the Needle Trades* (1935); Isserman, Maurice. *Which Side Were You On? The American Communist Party During the Second World War* (1982); Keeran, Roger. "National Groups and the Popular Front: The Case of the International Workers Order." *Journal of American Ethnic History* 14 (1995); Klehr, Harvey. *The Heyday of American Communism: The Depression Decade* (1984); North, Joseph. "Memories of Rose Wortis Bloom Among Her Friends." *Daily World*, March 10, 1972; Ottanelli, Fraser M. *The Communist Party of the United States: From the Depression to WWII* (1991); "Rose Wortis: In Memoriam. *Jewish Currents* 13 (February 1959): 28; *WWIAJ* (1938).

JUDITH SMITH

WUNDERLICH, FRIEDA (1884–1965)

Frieda Wunderlich, a prominent economist and politician in Germany, became the only woman faculty member of the New School for Social Research in New York when it was established in 1933 as a haven for academic refugees from Nazism. She achieved international recognition for her research and publications on labor and social policy, including women's work.

Born into a middle-class Jewish family in Berlin in 1884, she was the older of two sisters. Her father, David Wunderlich, owned a wholesale textile business. After completing a girls' high school in 1901, Frieda worked in her father's firm for several years. In 1910, she passed her matriculation examination and began studying economics at the University of Berlin and then in Freiburg. In 1919, she received her doctorate in political science summa cum laude from the University of Freiburg with a dissertation on Taylorism.

During World War I, Frieda Wunderlich interrupted her studies to head a division of the National Women's Service dealing with public and private welfare work. Thereafter, she worked for the Brandenburg War Department for Labor and Welfare as a specialist in industrial protection of women and employment counselling and then for the Central Board for Foreign Relief, responsible for the distribution of food and textiles from abroad. She later served as judge in the German Supreme Court for Social Insurance. From 1923 to 1933, she edited the political journal *Soziale Praxis* and published numerous books and articles on social policy and economic theory. She lectured at a variety of educational institutions, including the Women's School for Social Welfare and the Graduate School for Civil Administrators, and in 1930 became a professor at the Vocational Pedagogical Institute in Berlin.

Elected on the German Democratic Party ticket, she served as a member of the Berlin City Council for eight years and in the Prussian Diet from 1930 to 1932. She was also involved in the Commission for Women's Work of the International Labor Office. In 1933, having been dismissed from her academic position as both a Jew and a woman, Wunderlich decided to go into exile, resigning from the City Council upon her departure.

Wunderlich was extremely fortunate to receive a job offer from the New School for Social Research, which she accepted with a heavy heart; she was the only woman among the foreign scholars hired. In 1939, she was elected dean of the graduate faculty of political and social science and served as professor of economics, labor, and sociology until her retirement in 1954. She was highly regarded as an effective and warmhearted teacher, as well as a gifted researcher. While in the United States, she continued to publish widely on labor and social policy in Germany and Britain. In 1954, the University of Cologne awarded her an honorary doctorate in political science in recognition of her distinguished contribution to the social sciences.

In her later years, Frieda Wunderlich lived with her younger sister, Dr. Eva Wunderlich, who was a professor of German at Upsala College in New Jersey. She died in their home in East Orange in December 1965, at age eighty-one. The New School established the Frieda Wunderlich Prize for outstanding foreign graduate students in her memory.

SELECTED WORKS BY FRIEDA WUNDERLICH

British Labor and the War (1941); *Farm Labor in Germany, 1810–1945* (1961); *German Labor Courts* (1946); *Labor under German Democracy: Arbitration 1918–1933* (1940).

BIBLIOGRAPHY

Backhaus-Lautenschläger, Christine. *Und standen ihre Frau: Das Schicksal deutschsprachiger Emigrantinnen in den USA nach 1933* (1991); *International Biographical Dictionary of Central European Emigres.* Vol. 1 (1980): 837; Kaznelson, Siegmund, ed. *Juden im Deutschen Kulturbereich* (1959); Krohn, Claus-Dieter. *Intellectuals in Exile: Refugee Scholars and the New School for Social Research* (1992); Lowenthal, Ernst G. *Juden in Preussen: Biographisches Verzeichnis* (1981); *NYTimes*, September 2, 1933, 13, and Obituary. December 31, 1965, 21; Preller, Ludwig. "In Memoriam Frieda Wunderlich." *Sozialer Fortschritt*, 15, no. 2 (1966): 45–46; Wunderlich, Frieda. Frieda Wunderlich Collection, AR-C1288-3230, Leo Baeck Institute, NYC.

HARRIET PASS FREIDENREICH

WYLER, MARJORIE (b. 1915)

Marjorie Wyler is a pioneer in the presentation of Judaism to the American public. Her involvement in religious broadcasting, coupled with decades of public relations work, has made her an advocate for the ethics of social justice inherent to Judaism.

Marjorie Goldwasser Wyler was born on September 23, 1915, in New York City, the eldest child of Israel and Edith (Goldstein) Goldwasser. Her parents were Americans of German Jewish descent. She had a brother, Edwin, and a sister, Joan. The Goldwassers were upper middle class. Israel Goldwasser held a Ph.D. in education and served as a public school superintendent before becoming the first executive director of the Jewish Federation in 1915. Edith Goldwasser was a teacher who was active in child welfare issues. The Goldwasser home was secular, and Marjorie received no Jewish education as a child.

She attended the Horace Mann School. She went on to Bryn Mawr, where she earned both her B.A. and M.A. in philosophy. It was at the Quaker-run college that she first began to explore her faith. With Jews as a tiny minority of the student body, she was forced to confront her identity. She took general courses in religion and supplemented them with independent reading. She returned to New York, where she did graduate coursework in philosophy and psychology at the University in Exile at the New School.

In 1938 she married Wilfred Wyler, an accountant. The couple has two daughters: RUTH MESSINGER, now the Manhattan borough president, and Barbara Gold, a pediatrician. Wyler became more observant in her own home and began keeping Shabbat. The family also affiliated itself with the Conservative movement, a connection it has maintained for over fifty years.

Also in 1938, Wyler began her professional relationship with the movement when she accepted her first position at the Jewish Theological Seminary of America. For $1,300 a year, Wyler was the second employee in what would become the Department of Public Information. While researching and writing public relations materials, Wyler received additional exposure to Judaica.

In October 1944, *Eternal Light Radio* debuted under the eye of Milton Krenz, whom Wyler assisted. This weekly radio program revolutionized the use of mass media for Jewish education. As Wyler explains it, its double goal was to show that "Judaism was the best-kept secret going and to explain [it] in a non-evangelical, non-emotional way." *Eternal Light* expanded to television in 1948. Programming varied from dramatic shows about great Jews in history to episodes about the holidays.

Over the ensuing decades, Wyler was involved with all aspects of *Eternal Light*, eventually serving as its executive producer. Using new technology to transmit traditional Jewish values worked wonders. For thousands of people, *Eternal Light* was their only connection to their heritage. The television series continued, although in a reduced annual format, until 1993.

Wyler's work at JTSA encompassed all public presentation, ranging from speechwriting to fostering friendly relations with the press. In every task, she functioned as an astute and articulate liaison between the Jewish and secular worlds. Since leaving the seminary in 1993, Wyler has remained active in the religious and communications fields. She serves as a consultant for religious television programming. She is also involved with many organizations, including the UJA-Federation and the Mayor's Commission on Foster Care. Wyler lives in Manhattan and continues to view Judaism as a source of ethical inspiration. As she puts it, "We become more secure of our place in the scheme of things as we mend the world."

BIBLIOGRAPHY

Department of Radio and Television, Jewish Theological Seminary of America, NYC; Wyler, Marjorie. Interview with author, December 6, 1995.

EDNA FRIEDBERG

WYMAN, ROSALIND WIENER (b. 1930)

Rosalind Wiener Wyman was, in her words, "born a Democrat." She was the youngest person ever elected to the Los Angeles City Council and one of the youngest elected officials of a major United States city.

She was born on October 4, 1930, in Los Angeles, the second child and only daughter of Oscar and Sarah (Selten) Wiener. Her mother, a significant role model, studied pharmacy at night during the Depression so she could share professional duties in the family drugstore with her pharmacist husband. Sarah and Oscar were avid New Deal Democrats, introducing their daughter to political life at an early age.

Rosalind Wiener Wyman graduated from Los Angeles High School in 1948 and the University of Southern California in 1952, with a B.S. in public administration. She became politically active in college, leading to the council nomination the year of her graduation. She was the first woman council member in thirty-seven years and the first Jew in fifty-three years.

In 1954, she married attorney Eugene Wyman, a graduate of Northwestern University and Harvard Law School and fellow Democratic activist. Their children are Betty Lynn (b. 1958), Robert Alan (b. 1960), and Brad Hibbs (b. 1963).

While on the city council, Rosalind Wyman was the first female acting mayor, and she played a pivotal role in bringing the Dodgers baseball team from Brooklyn to Los Angeles in 1957. Controversies over the arrangements contributed to Wyman's defeat for a fourth term in 1965, as did the opposition of conservative Democratic mayor Sam Yorty.

After leaving office, Wyman continued her involvement in political and public affairs. She responded to her husband's unexpected death in January 1973 by redoubling her political work. During the 1974 congressional campaigns, she became the first woman to head a major party's fund-raising efforts. Popular with rank-and-file Democrats, she was chair and chief executive officer of the 1984 Democratic National Convention in San Francisco, the first woman to fill this position for a major party. She has been a convention delegate every presidential year (except one) since 1952. Always interested in increasing political opportunities for women, Wyman cochaired the senatorial campaigns of DIANNE FEINSTEIN.

Wyman's national appointments include the UNESCO Commission and the National Endowment for the Arts. She was employed as a movie industry executive and consultant to Los Angeles mayor Tom Bradley. She has been a board member of many arts, social services, educational, and health organizations, and has received numerous awards.

Rosalind Wiener Wyman is a strong, even controversial, personality. Naming her Woman of the Year for 1958, the *Los Angeles Times* called her "not a namby-pamby, self-sacrificing, 'unselfish' woman—[but] a woman who believes people should have what they enjoy." In addition to pioneering female activism in traditional party politics, she helped open the southern California political establishment to people, many Jewish, from the entertainment industry.

Wyman has received many Jewish community awards, chaired fund-raising events, and served on the board of American Friends of the Hebrew University. In harmony with her political commitments, Wyman's deepest Jewish involvements have concerned intergroup relations. Vice-chair of the Community Relations Committee of the Los Angeles Jewish Community Council, Wyman has advocated Jewish community engagement with the widest range of civic affairs.

BIBLIOGRAPHY

Berges, Marshall. "Home Q & A: Rosalind Wyman." *Los Angeles Times*, December 10, 1978, sec. 2C, p. 74+; Chall, Malca. "'It's a Girl': Three Terms of the Los Angeles City Council, 1953–1965, Three Decades in the Democratic Party, 1948–1978." Oral history. Transcript, Regional Oral History Office, Bancroft Library, University of California, Berkeley; "A 'Born Democrat' Plans the Party." *NYTimes*, July 16, 1984 (reprinted in *NYTimes Biographical Service*, 1984 ed., 1043–1044); Hicks, Cordell. "Woman of the Year: Rosalind Wyman, a Civic Force at 28." *LATimes*, January 18, 1959, sec. 4, p. 1; Lewine, Frances. "Democrats Count on Rosalind." *LATimes*, April 20, 1973, sec. 4, p. 13; Moore, Deborah Dash. *To the Golden Cities* (1994); Vils, Ursula. "Convention Chair Another in Life of Firsts." *LATimes*, July 7, 1983, sec. 5, p. 1+; *Who's Who in American Politics*, 13th ed. (1991); *Who's Who of American Women*. 12th ed. (1981).

AMY HILL SHEVITZ

WYNER, GUSSIE EDELMAN
(1870–1949)

Gussie Edelman Wyner was an early leader of the Boston Jewish community and a national leader of HADASSAH who is credited with creating the idea of life memberships in women's organizations and with establishing the first chapter of Junior Hadassah.

Gussie Wyner was one of six children born in Minsk to Rabbi Abraham and Esther Edelman. The Edelman family immigrated to New York in the 1880s, where the young Gussie managed a home-based garment manufacturing business. In 1890, she married George Wyner, a merchant who had migrated from Vilna to South Africa, whom Gussie had met when he was visiting relatives in the United States. She agreed to emigrate to Malmsbury, South Africa, on the condition that, if she did not like it there after ten years, they would return permanently to the United States. After a stop in London, the Wyners returned to Boston in 1899, one year before the required ten years agreed to.

Gussie and George Wyner had five children: Frances, Isidore A. ("I.A."), Rudolph, Edward, and Maurice. While raising her five children and managing an extensive household, Gussie Wyner became one of the pioneers in women's leadership and made significant contributions to the women's Zionist movement and Boston Jewish communal life.

Wyner's devotion to Zionism grew out of the Edelman family's attachment to Palestine as a religious homeland. In the later years of their lives, both Gussie Wyner's grandfather and father had moved to Palestine to study and, eventually, to die. In the 1920s, Wyner traveled to Palestine several times, once in the company of HENRIETTA SZOLD, the founder of Hadassah, for the joint purpose of assessing the medical needs of in the land and of visiting her father. He died in 1927, and Gussie Wyner arranged his burial on the Mount of Olives, where her grandfather was also interred.

In the main, however, Wyner's Zionism was lived out in America. She was an early officer of the Boston chapter of Hadassah. On her initiative, the Boston chapter established what is believed to be the first Junior Hadassah chapter, and her daughter-in-law Sara Goldberg Wyner served as its first president. The success of the Boston Junior Hadassah chapter inspired the creation of other chapters around the United States.

Gussie Wyner took an active role in raising funds for the first Hadassah Hospital in Jerusalem and was especially proud of her work in supporting the treat-

Gussie Wyner was an early leader of HADASSAH, *and she created the idea of life memberships in women's organizations. She is shown here in a photograph taken in July of 1931, turning the first shovel of dirt for a new maintenance building and power plant at Beth Israel Hospital, Boston. The building was paid for by the proceeds of the Life Membership Fund of the Beth Israel Women's Auxiliary, which she founded. [American Jewish Historical Society]*

ment of eye disease in the Jewish and Arab children of Palestine. A memorial resolution adopted by the Boston chapter of Hadassah on the occasion of Wyner's death said:

> A full decade before National Hadassah had even planned the magnificent Rothschild Hadassah University Hospital on Mt. Scopus, Mrs. Wyner organized fund-raising functions . . . for a research hospital in Palestine. When Palestine asked Hadassah to build a teaching-clinical university hospital, the Boston Chapter was the first to respond with fifty thousand dollars because Mrs. Wyner, the builder, had been assembling the bricks.

Wyner left her most indelible mark as an officer of the Women's Auxiliary of Boston's Beth Israel Hospital. As treasurer of the Women's Auxiliary in 1927, she proposed the creation of the new concept, the Life Membership Fund, as a way to raise needed capital gifts and endowment funds for the hospital. She insisted that the proceeds of the Life Membership Fund be used for "tangible improvements" to the hospital's facilities, such as a new maternity ward, a surgical research lab, housing for hospital interns, an electric generator, and a children's pavilion. Wyner held the post of treasurer of the auxiliary until her death in 1949. She also served on Beth Israel's Board of Trustees. Her devotion to Beth Israel was continued through the service of her son Rudolph as president and her grandson Justin on the Board of Trustees.

The Life Membership Fund concept proved to be an attractive means for soliciting funds to meet long-term goals, and under Wyner's direction as treasurer it was subsequently adopted by the Boston chapter of Hadassah, which called it Perpetual Membership, followed by many Jewish and non-Jewish charitable organizations around the United States.

Gussie Wyner's funeral was attended by prominent communal, organizational, civic, and state officials, including Massachusetts governor Paul Dever, who honored her efforts to improve the social welfare of Boston. She was eulogized by Rabbi Irving Mandel as having "made philanthropy and community endeavor her spiritual vocation," as well as for being the "architect and engineer, strategist and tactician" of the Jewish organizations to which she had devoted her adult years. TAMAR DE SOLA POOL wrote of Gussie Wyner: "Often when I sat beside her at conventions, Hadassah meetings and in her home, I would say to myself, 'It is this which has assured the survival of the Jewish people, this innate knowledge of what it means to be a Jew, and this unswerving determination to live a Jewish life on the highest plane of our heritage.'"

BIBLIOGRAPHY

Fifty Years of Jewish Philanthropy in Greater Boston, 1895–1945: 50th Anniversary Yearbook of the Combined Jewish Appeal (1945); Solomon, Barbara Miller. *Pioneers in Service: The History of the Associated Jewish Philanthropies of Boston* (1956).

HOLLY SNYDER

Y

YAKUBOVITCH, RUZHA *see* SHOSHANA, ROSE

YALOW, ROSALYN (b. 1921)

A Jewish woman whose father-in-law is a rabbi, who keeps a kosher home, who invites her lab assistants to Passover seders, and worries about them catching colds is not the typical image of a Nobel Prize winner. But it is the image of Rosalyn Yalow, the first woman born and educated in the United States to win a Nobel Prize in a scientific field.

Rosalyn (Sussman) Yalow was born July 19, 1921, in the South Bronx, a working-class area of New York City. Her father, Simon Sussman, owned his own small business selling cardboard and packing twine. Her mother was Clara (Zipper) Sussman. Both parents were immigrants from Eastern Europe and urged Rosalyn and her brother Alexander to get the education that had been denied to them. Yalow gives credit to her father for having instilled in her the idea that girls could do anything that boys could do.

An honor student at school, Rosalyn excelled in math and chemistry, and her teachers encouraged her. She graduated from Walton Girls High School at age fifteen and went directly to HUNTER COLLEGE, a free city university for women. As a freshman, she listed her major as chemistry, but when she took her first course in physics, professors recognized her potential as a physicist and guided her into that discipline.

In the 1940s, the standard assumption was that Rosalyn Sussman would be a career woman rather than a housewife. In those years, there was little possibility of combining the two. Rosalyn, however, had her own ideas. Even before her high school graduation, she had decided on both marriage and a career and never doubted her ability to achieve those two goals.

She graduated from Hunter College Phi Beta Kappa, magna cum laude, with a B.A. in chemistry and physics, in 1941. She was the perfect candidate for a graduate fellowship, but she was turned down by one university after another. Only one admissions office was honest enough to admit the real reason: As a Jew and a woman, they believed that she would never get a job in the field.

She was well prepared for these setbacks. In college, she had been warned to take typing and steno courses so she could support herself as a secretary while going to school. It was simply an alternative way to work toward a doctorate. The Sussmans did not have the money required for their daughter's graduate tuition without some kind of financial aid. If she worked at a university, she would be permitted to take courses without charge. Rosalyn accepted a secretarial job at Columbia University and prepared to take night classes.

At the end of the summer, just before she was scheduled to begin working, she received an offer from the University of Illinois at Urbana. No clear explanation was given for this late acceptance, but it was assumed that places in the graduate program in physics were vacant as a result of the draft for World War II. Even more crucial, Rosalyn Sussman was offered a teaching assistantship and would be able to support herself while studying.

At Urbana, twenty-year-old Rosalyn was the only woman among four hundred faculty and teaching assistants and one of only three Jews. One of the other Jews was Aaron Yalow. Aaron was from upstate New York and was the son of an Orthodox rabbi. He had entered the program at the same time as Rosalyn. The two struck up a friendship that developed into a romance. On June 6, 1943, they were married.

The Yalows received their doctorates in physics together in 1945. They returned to the Bronx and both found employment at the Federal Telecommunications Laboratory. After the laboratory closed, Aaron took a position as a researcher in medical physics at Montefiore Hospital and Rosalyn returned to Hunter College where she taught physics. Although she also wanted a research position, such jobs were not routinely offered to women.

It was through her husband's encouragement and help that she made contact with Bernard Roswit of the Bronx Veterans Administration Hospital. In 1947, the Veterans Administration hospitals had launched a research program to explore the use of radioactive substances for the diagnosis and treatment of disease. One of the hospitals chosen for this nuclear medicine project was the Bronx VA Hospital. Roswit was impressed with Rosalyn Yalow's ability and determination and offered her laboratory space and a small salary as a consultant in nuclear physics. She held that position, together with her faculty position at Hunter, for three years. In 1950, she was appointed physicist and assistant chief of the hospital's radioisotope service and left her teaching post for full-time research.

Yalow experimented with the safe use of radioisotopes in humans. Radioisotopes were considered an inexpensive substitute for radium and were being used to treat cancer. Yalow wanted to find other uses for them as well, but she needed more medical expertise than a physicist ordinarily had. She began a search for a research partner who had medical experience and found Solomon Berson, a young doctor at the VA hospital. The two began a close and successful partnership that lasted for twenty-two years. People who knew how they worked reported that they sometimes

Rosalyn Yalow had two strikes against her in her effort to become a physicist: She was a Jew and a woman. She persevered and not only earned a career in science and many awards—including a Nobel Prize—but also changed the medical world with the introduction of radioimmunoassay (RIA). [American Jewish Archives]

finished each other's sentences; they even joked about believing in telepathy.

Yalow and Berson started by measuring radioactive iodine in the diagnosis and treatment of thyroid disease. They went on from there to the measurement of blood volume and then to measure insulin and other hormones and proteins in adult diabetics. These initial experiments led to the discovery of radioimmunoassay (RIA), an ingenious application of nuclear physics in clinical medicine. RIA makes it possible to use radioactive tracers to measure pharmacological or biological substances with radioisotopes. The system can be used on humans, animals, or plants and is sensitive enough to measure any trace material, even in the most minute amounts. Using this technique, endless varieties of hormones, viruses, and chemicals could be measured.

During those early years of research, Rosalyn and Aaron Yalow had their first child, a son, Benjamin, born in 1952. The young mother was back in her laboratory a week later, together with her baby. She continued her lab work while she nursed the baby, managing it all on very little sleep. When she gave birth to her daughter, Elanna, in 1954, she followed the same procedure. She was conscious of the responsibilities of motherhood and tried hard not to neglect her children. While they were in school, she came home every day to give them lunch and maintained a kosher home in deference to her husband's wishes. She was home in time to prepare dinner every evening, sometimes returning to her laboratory afterward, working long into the night. In an interview with the *New York Post* many years later she said, "It's true that women are different from men. If you want to be a good wife, you have to work a little harder." She routinely maintained a work schedule of sixty to eighty hours per week.

After nine years of careful research, Yalow and Berson publicly presented their discovery. It was first used in 1959, but it took several more years before the scientific community realized its ramifications. Ultimately, RIA created "an explosion of knowledge" in every aspect of medicine and was used in thousands of laboratories in the United States and abroad.

Yalow's work was recognized throughout the medical field, and she was inundated with prizes, appointments, and honorary degrees. In the mid-1950s, she was already serving as a consultant at Lenox Hill Hospital. In 1961, she was given the American Diabetes Association's Eli Lilly Award; in 1968 she was named acting chief of the radioisotope service at the Bronx VA Hospital and was also a research professor in the department of medicine at Mount Sinai School of Medicine, a position that she held until 1974. She was a member of the President's Study Group on Careers for Women in 1966–1967. In 1969, she was appointed chief of the RIA reference laboratory. In 1970, she became chief of the nuclear medicine service and, in 1972, was named senior medical investigator of the Veterans Administration. Unfortunately, Yalow's partnership with Berson ended before the two researchers could enjoy the ultimate success for their discovery of RIA. Solomon Berson died of a heart attack in 1972.

After Berson's death, Yalow continued alone, publishing sixty papers on RIA in an attempt to publicize the discovery and its uses. In 1973, she assumed the directorship of the newly established Solomon A. Berson Research Laboratory and earned several more medical awards, including a Commemorative Medallion in 1972, the A. Cressy Morrison Award in Natural Science, the VA Exceptional Service Award, and the Scientific Achievement Award of the American Medical Association, all in 1975.

The most prestigious of her awards was the Albert Lasker Prize for Basic Medical Research, which she won in 1976 at age fifty-five. She was the first woman to receive this prize. It was followed in 1977 by the Nobel Prize, the crowning achievement of her career. She was only the second American woman to receive the Nobel Prize in the fields of physiology or medicine. (The first was Gerty T. Cori in 1947, who shared it with her husband.)

At the Nobel Prize presentation ceremonies in Oslo, Norway, Rosalyn Yalow commented on her achievements as a woman:

We still live in a world in which a significant fraction of people, including women, believe that a woman belongs and wants to belong exclusively in the home; that a woman should not aspire to achieve more than her male counterparts and particularly not more than her husband.

Discussing equality of opportunity, she explained:

We cannot expect in the immediate future that all women who will seek it will achieve [it]. But if women are to start moving toward that goal, we must believe in ourselves or no one else will believe in us; we must match our aspirations with the competence, courage and determination to succeed, and we must feel a personal responsibility to ease the path for those who come after us. The world cannot afford the loss of the talents of half its people if we are to solve the many problems that beset us.

Returning to her laboratory at the VA Hospital after she was awarded the prize, she was deluged with calls from well-wishers, friends, and reporters. In an interview for *People* magazine she was asked what she planned to do with the $74,500 that was her half of the prize money. (The other half went to two male scientists who had done research on the hypothalmic area of the brain.) She replied that she had simply put it in the bank. "I can't think of anything I want," she said. "I wasn't handed college or graduate school or anything else on a silver platter. I had to work very hard, but I did it because I wanted to. That's the real key to happiness." (Some colleagues felt that Yalow should have shared the prize money with the family of Solomon Berson, and they see this as a major moral lapse.)

After the excitement and publicity of the Nobel Prize, the tireless Yalow continued to work in her modest laboratory in the Bronx and remained in her home in nearby Riverdale, New York. She collected a growing number of honorary degrees, including those from Yeshiva University and Hunter College, her alma mater. In 1978, the Rosalyn S. Yalow Research Development Award was established. For the second time, she was given the VA Exceptional Service Award, then the Torch of Learning award by the American Friends of the Hebrew University. She even found time to host a five-part dramatic series for Public Broadcasting on the life of Marie Curie, one of Yalow's own early role models. Through it all, she refused to allow fame to change her life-style.

Yalow continued writing papers (a total of over five hundred as of 1996) and doing research. In 1988, she was awarded the National Medal of Science. In 1992, at age seventy-one, she became senior medical investigator emerita at the VA Hospital and claimed to be still cooking dinners nightly for her husband, a physics professor at Cooper Union College in New York City. Her grown children are both successful professionals in their own right. Benjamin is a computer systems analyst, and Elanna has a Ph.D. in psychology from Stanford University.

Rosalyn Yalow is proud of her accomplishments and never regretted not patenting RIA. Had she done so, she would be a rich woman. However, she still feels uncomfortable having "more money than I can spend usefully." As she told a *New York Post* reporter, "I have my marriage, two wonderful children. I have a laboratory that is an absolute joy. I have energy. I have health. As long as there is anything to be done, I am never tired."

BIBLIOGRAPHY

American Jewish Biographies (1982); *Current Biography* (1978); Dash, Joan. *The Triumph of Discovery: Women Scientists Who Won the Nobel Prize* (1991); *EJ* (1973–1982); Taitz, Emily, and Sondra Henry. *Remarkable Jewish Women: Rebels, Rabbis and Other Women in History from Biblical Times to the Present* (1996); *Who's Who* (1996).

EMILY TAITZ

YEZIERSKA, ANZIA (c. 1885–1970)

"My one story is hunger." So declared the protagonist of Anzia Yezierska's novel *Children of Loneliness* (1923). Having immigrated with her family from Eastern Europe, Yezierska chronicled the hunger of her generation of newly arrived Jewish Americans around the turn of the century. Her novels, short stories, and autobiographical writing vividly depict both the literal hunger of poverty and the metaphoric hunger for security, education, companionship, home, and meaning—in short, for the American dream.

Born in the Russian-Polish village Plinsk, near Warsaw, between 1880 and 1885, the youngest of nine children, Yezierska arrived in the United States with her family in the early 1890s. The year of her birth is uncertain not only because Yezierska did not recollect the exact date but also, according to her daughter, because she perpetually reinvented her history in interviews, frequently claiming to be younger to compensate for her relatively late start as a writer. Her oldest brother Meyer preceded the family by several years. Immigration officers americanized his name into Max Mayer, replacing his last name with a version of his first. When Anzia landed in United States at Castle Garden, the entire family was given the surname Mayer, and Anzia was renamed Harriet, later shortened to Hattie. She reclaimed the name Anzia Yezierska when she was about twenty-eight. The family settled into a cramped tenement apartment in the Lower East Side of Manhattan.

Her father, Baruch (Bernard), a talmudic scholar, engaged in full-time study of sacred books and was not gainfully employed. Her mother, Pearl, worked at menial jobs to support the family. Pressured to help support her struggling family in a cultural climate that did not legitimate the educational aspirations of girls, Yezierska attended elementary school for two years before working at a succession of domestic and factory jobs. Four of her brothers studied pharmacy, another became a high school math teacher, another an army colonel. Young Anzia clashed frequently with her father, whose poverty, religious observance, and Eastern European ways she saw as barriers to full entry into American life. Eventually, she left her parents' apartment and moved into the CLARA DE HIRSCH HOME FOR WORKING GIRLS. She pursued her ambition for education with a single-minded determination. According to her daughter, Yezierska promised patrons to become a domestic science teacher to help better her people, inventing a high school education for her application to Columbia University. Continuing to support herself by menial work, Yezierska attended Columbia University's Teachers College on scholarship from

1901 to 1905. She then taught elementary school from 1908 to 1913, with a brief leave of absence to attend the American Academy of Dramatic Arts. In 1913, she began to write fiction.

In 1910, Yezierska married Jacob Gordon, a lawyer, but applied for an annulment the following day. She explained that while she valued his friendship, she was unprepared for the physical aspect of marriage. The following year, she married Arnold Levitas, a teacher and textbook writer, in a religious but not a civil ceremony. Their daughter, Louise Levitas (Henriksen), was born in 1912. In 1916, Yezierska moved to San Francisco with Louise and worked as social worker, the last of several flights from her marital home. Because Yezierska could not support herself and her daughter, Louise was sent to live with Levitas in New York when she was five. The couple divorced in 1916. Yezierska's relationship with her daughter remained close but troubled. Years later, Louise Levitas described Yezierska as a vibrant, daring, and courageous person, but one whose extreme mood swings and egoism affected all her personal interactions.

Yezierska's fiction focuses on Jewish immigrant life at the turn of the century, and she sees herself as giving voice to her people. Her work features female protagonists and explores the transition from "greenhorn" to American; the struggle against patriarchy, poverty, and restrictive Jewish practice; the striving for acceptance, independence, and prosperity in the New World; and the cultural and personal gain and loss inherent to assimilation. Yezierska pays particular attention to the hardships of poverty for women saddled with child care and crowded conditions, and utterly financially dependent on husbands. In contrast to the ineffectual or exploitative Jewish immigrant man, her fiction frequently features a liaison with a sophisticated WASP or assimilated Jewish man who functions as the protagonist's mentor. While Yezierska rejected her father's Orthodox way of life and opinions, she absorbed and loved the cadences of the Bible, was interest in God and the spirit, and replaced Judaism with faith in the intellect. Her first publication, "Free Vacation House" (1915), exposes the humiliation inflicted on poor women by well-intentioned charitable organizations. Based on her sister Helena's experience, the story's free country house for poor mothers and their children is so rule-bound that the guests, who are forbidden to sit on the comfortable chairs in front of the house or on the porch, experience it as a prison. Social workers repeatedly ask them intimate questions in public. "The Fat of the Land" was published in Edward J. O'Brien's *Best Short Stories of 1919*, which was dedicated to Yezierska. The story depicts the loneliness and anomie of an elderly immigrant Jewish woman whose successful, Americanized children support her in luxury but are ashamed of her Old World ways. Housed in an affluent neighborhood, the woman yearns for the intimacy and cultural vibrancy of the tenement world.

In 1917, Yezierska met John Dewey, who was to be the great romance of her life despite the difference in their ages—he was fifty-eight, she was in her midthirties. Yezierska audited his seminar in social and political thought at Columbia University. Dewey was attracted by Yezierska's outspokenness, emotionality, and passion, she by his erudition and intellect. Dewey wrote several poems about Yezierska (in 1917–1918), while he served in her writing as the prototype of the Anglo-Saxon gentile mentor/lover. Yezierska treated the relationship fictionally in *All I Could Never Be* (1932). According to her daughter, Yezierska used his poems and phrases from his letters uncredited in her writing. Their relationship was fictionalized in Norma Rosen's *John and Anzia: An American Romance* (1989). The breaking point in their relationship came when he made a sexual overture to her.

Yezierska was catapulted briefly to fame and fortune when *Hungry Hearts* (1920) caught the attention of Samuel Goldwyn, who based a 1922 silent movie on it. In 1925, Sidney Alcott directed a silent film based on Yezierska's *Salome of the Tenements*. Although Goldwyn brought Yezierska to Hollywood as a screenwriter, she found her writing blocked amid wealth and removed from the culture she knew. Refusing a $100,000 contract, she returned to economic struggle in New York. In the early 1930s, she worked for the WPA Writer's Project, cataloging trees in Central Park. Beginning in the 1950s, she wrote book reviews for the *New York Times*, primarily on Jewish or women's themes whose import she universalized. Her autobiography *Red Ribbon on a White Horse* is considered both vibrant writing and factually unreliable. During the 1950s and 1960s, she wrote of the plight of Puerto Rican immigrants in New York, and, during the last decade of her life, she explored the theme of aging—the diminution of one's faculties, the lack of dignity and respect, the loss of independence. Yezierska's last published story, "Take up Your Bed and Walk" puts forth the perspective of an elderly Jewish woman.

Critical assessment of Yezierska's work has fluctuated since her earliest publications. Initially lauded as an authentic voice of the tenements—Cinderella of the sweatshops—by the 1940s, Yezierska had fallen into obscurity. Seen by the American mainstream as "too Jewish," within the Jewish community her writing was offensive to both immigrant and Americanized Jews who felt mocked and exposed. Because of the growing interest in both ethnic and women's writing, the 1980s saw a resurgence of appreciation for her writing. *Breadgivers* was reissued in 1975, followed by editions of many of her other works. Most contemporary critics approach her work sociologically rather than aesthetically, drawn by her compelling depictions of cultural and geographic displacement, the American dream and the harsh reality of immigrant life, and the struggle to acculturate.

In the main, she has been seen as aesthetically inferior to other writers of the Jewish immigrant and assimilation experience. Many critics praise the raw power of her writing but see in it no real artistry. They cite the proliferation of stock characters—the overworked mother, the ineffectual father, the intellectual gentile or assimilated male savior, the cold WASP, the rootless Americanized Jew, the condescending social worker, the passionate and intelligent young Jewish immigrant woman. Often, readers read the work as veiled autobiography, taking the voice of her protagonists as her own.

But there has been a renewed appreciation for her oeuvre as a crafted literary work. In a biography of Yezierska, her daughter discusses her mother's imaginative inventiveness and also contrasts the stylized "Yinglish" dialect of the fiction with her mother's more proper, standardized English. Some contemporary readers note Yezierska's artful use of metaphor, her ability to present multiple points of view, and the broad humor of her exaggerated types.

Anzia Yezierska died of a stroke on November 21, 1970, in Ontario, California.

SELECTED WORKS BY ANZIA YEZIERSKA

All I Could Never Be (1932); *Arrogant Beggar* (1927); *Breadgivers: A Struggle between a Father of the Old World and a Daughter of the New* (1925. Reprinted 1975 and 1984); *Children of Loneliness* (1923); *How I Found America: Collected Stories of Anzia Yezerskia* (1991); *Hungry Hearts* (1920); *Hungry Hearts and Other Stories* (1985); *The Open Cage: An Anzia Yezierska Collection* (1979); *Red Ribbon on a White Horse* (1950. Reprint, 1981); *Salome of the Tenements* (1992).

BIBLIOGRAPHY

AJYB 24:217; *BEOAJ*; *EJ*; Gornick, Vivian. Introduction to *How I Found America: Collected Stories of Anzia Yezierska*, by Anzia Yezierska (1991); Henriksen, Louise Levitas. Afterword to *The Open Cage: An Anzia Yezierska Collection*, by Anzia Yezierska (1979), and Introduction to *Red Ribbon on a White Horse*, by Anzia Yezierska (1981); Henriksen, Louise Levitas, with Jo Ann Boydson. *Anzia Yezierska: A Writer's Life* (1988); Levin, Tobe. "Anzia Yezierska." *Jewish American Women Writers: A Bio-Bibliographical and Critical Sourcebook*, edited by Ann Shapiro et al. (1994); *NAW* modern; Obituary. *NYTimes*, November 23, 1970, 40:2; Rosen, Norma. *John and Anzia: An American Romance* (1989); Schoen, Carol. *Anzia Yezierska* (1982); Stinson, Peggy. "Anzia Yezierska." *American Women Writers* 4 (1982): 480–482; *UJE*; *WWIAJ* (1926, 1928, 1938); *WWWIA* 7.

SARA R. HOROWITZ

YGLESIAS, HELEN (b. 1915)

Twice married, once divorced, mother of three and a grandmother, very much the wife of my husband, a distinguished writer, whose person entirely filled the landscape of my emotions, I, born poor and without an easy entrance into the world where I coveted a place, I had crawled somehow, into a little corner.

In *Starting: Early, Anew, Over and Late* (1978), Helen Yglesias recollects her own life and presents the lives of others in terms of renewal. In the process, she describes those circumstances that lead to self-definition. Yglesias discovered that her own nature was buried, and that only a transformation of her life would allow her to become a novelist. Similarly, a process of self-recognition leads her protagonists, all of them women, to accept responsibility for their lives and values.

While currently residing in Maine, Yglesias is very much a daughter of New York. She was born in New York on March 29, 1915, the youngest of seven children. Her parents, Solomon and Kate (Goldstein) Bassine, had left Russia and Russia-Poland respectively, spent several years in England, and came to America. Solomon Bassine, a grocer in America, was not a success and the Bassine children were numerous: in birth order, Harry, Minnie, Cecile, Charles, Louis, Rose, and Helen. In "A Way In and a Way Out," Yglesias remembers her parents and siblings living in a cold-water, four-room tenement in Brooklyn. At the age of sixteen, she graduated from James Monroe High School in the Bronx and thought that writing a novel would help lift her parents out of poverty. However, one of her brothers humiliated her efforts and she destroyed her manuscript. When she was seventeen, this same brother, who later became a prominent businessman and philanthropist, paid her way for a trip to Europe and Palestine. An avid reader, she was soon introduced to the works of D.H. Lawrence, William Faulkner, GERTRUDE STEIN, and Marcel Proust. Working in nondescript jobs, she also began to read Henry James while at the New York Public Library. Yglesias became a member of the Young Communist League in 1936. (She left the Communist Party in 1952.) In 1937, she married Bernard Cole. The couple had two children, Tamar and Lewis. In the 1940s, she reviewed books and for a short time helped edit the cultural section of *The Daily Worker.* She also became a member of the Newspaper Guild. In 1950, she and Cole divorced, and that year she married José Yglesias. They had one child, Rafael. They divorced in 1992.

In 1965, Helen Yglesias joined the staff of *The Nation* and shortly thereafter became its literary editor. At age fifty-four, she left her job to dedicate herself to becoming a writer. *How She Died,* her first novel, was published in 1972. This book was followed by *Family Feeling* (1976), *Starting: Early, Anew, Over, and Late* (1978), *Sweetsir* (1981), *The Saviors* (1987), and *Isabel Bishop* (1989).

Except for in *Sweetsir,* her protagonists come from the variable Jewish life of New York. Yglesias binds their private lives to their public environment, for these women are assimilated but concerned with utilizing the morals of the Jewish past and its prophetic ethic—a concern for justice and dignity. Moreover, her main characters concern themselves with the civic education of those around them—family members as well as a larger public. They gain their autonomy as they reassess the mores and politics that prevent them from understanding and acting upon their environment. Yglesias's realism makes a distinctive contribution to American Jewish writing.

SELECTED WORKS BY HELEN YGLESIAS

Family Feeling (1976); *How She Died* (1972); "Invoking America: A Gitche Gumee Memoir." *NYTimes Book Review,* July 5, 1987, 1: 22; *Isabel Bishop* (1989); *The Saviors* (1987); *Starting: Early, Anew, Over, and Late* (1978); *Sweetsir* (1981); "A Way In and a Way Out." *New York Times Book Review,* June 14, 1981: 3: 24–25.

BIBLIOGRAPHY

Avery, Evelyn. "Oh My 'Mishpocha'! Some Jewish Women Writers From Antin to Kaplan View the Family." *Studies in American Jewish Literature* 5 (1986): 44–53; Brown, Rosellen. "Breaking the Circle of Destructive Love." *NYTimes Book Review,* April 5, 1981, 3: 28–29; Bunge, Nancy. "Helen Yglesias." *Finding the Words: Conversations with Writers Who Teach* (1985); Chevigny, Bell Gale. Review of *Family Feeling. New Republic* 174 (May 8, 1976): 27–29; Fried, Lewis. "Helen Yglesias." *Jewish American Women Writers: A Bio-Bibliographical and Critical Sourcebook,* edited by Ann Shapiro et al. (1994); Haynes, Muriel. Review of *How She Died. Saturday Review* 55 (March 18, 1972): 74–75; Kapelovitz, Abbey Poze. "Mother Images in American-Jewish Fiction." Ph. D. diss., University of Denver, 1985; Ryan, Bryan. "Yglesias, Helen." *Contemporary Authors,* edited by Linda Metzger, New Revision Series, vol. 15 (1985): 471–474.

LEWIS FRIED

YIDDISH FILM

During the early half the twentieth century, feature films in the Yiddish language were produced in and around New York City. A direct offshoot of the Yiddish theater, these films, as well as those produced in Poland, Russia, and Austria, ranged from farce and musical comedy to melodrama and tragedy. The films presented an unusual body of ethnic images and were produced, financed, and directed by a handful of male entrepreneurs hoping to capitalize on the burgeoning film industry. During the "Golden Age" of Yiddish film, 1936 to 1939, more than two dozen films opened in New York City to encouraging box-office income, only to be curtailed abruptly by the onset of World War II. The films capture the language and life-style, as well as the values, dreams, and myths of the world of Yiddish culture and immortalize some of the greats of the Yiddish theater.

The films follow by several decades the height of the thriving Yiddish theater that played such a significant role in the life and culture of the immigrant communities. The earliest films produced after World War I and in the 1920s have not survived, and written reports are notoriously inaccurate, so it is difficult to secure any definitive information. The first surviving film, *East and West* (1923) was actually filmed in Vienna; it starred MOLLY PICON and was produced by an American filmmaker, Sidney Goldin, together with Picon and her husband, Jacob Kalich. The film is a hilarious depiction of a young American secularized Jewish woman in conflict with the traditions of her European Jewish family she is visiting. The film provides a marvelous vehicle for the impish comedian to cross-dress, satirize parochial religious practices, and strut her way into a new medium. Picon later recreated similar characterizations of the independent, feisty, secular young Jewish woman in *Yiddle with His Fiddle* (1936) and *Mamele* (1938).

The most prevalent image of Jewish women to be presented in American Yiddish films is that of the immigrant woman struggling to overcome the adversities of the difficult immigrant experience: Judith Abarbanel in *Uncle Moses,* Lucy Levin in *His Wife's Lover,* JENNIE GOLDSTEIN in *Two Sisters,* Yetta Zwerling in *Motl the Operator,* and CELIA ADLER in *Where Is My Child?* All these roles attracted large audiences and were immensely popular, especially among immigrants in the large metropolitan areas.

Only a few women were involved in the behind-the-scenes creation of films. Sheyne Rokhi Simkoff wrote *His Wife's Lover* (based on Molnar's *The Guardsman*, a 1931 Academy Award–winning feature film with Lunt and Fontanne). This first Yiddish talkie opened September 25, 1931, at the Clinton Theatre on the Lower Fast Side to favorable reviews in the Yiddish and English press. Shirley Castle Alexander (Ulmer) wrote the screenplay for *American Schadchen*, as well as assisted her husband, Edgar G. Ulmer, with his four Yiddish film productions. Judith Berg was the choreographer and featured performer in the dance of death sequence for *The Dybbuk*, and Molly Picon and Jacob Kalich were co-producers of Picon's 1923 film shot in Vienna, *Mizrakh un Mayrev* (East and West)

Women were the stars of many of the Yiddish features: BERTA GERSTEN as *Mirele Efros;* Celia Adler, doyenne of the Yiddish stage, as the bereaved mother in *Where Is My Child?* (1937); Miriam Riselle as the rebellious daughter Khava in *Tevye* (1939); Lili Liliana as the beautiful, ethereal Leah in *The Dybbuk;* Jennie Goldstein as the long-suffering, sacrificing sister in *Two Sisters;* Helen Beverly in *Green Fields* and *The Light Ahead;* Judith Abarbanel in *Uncle Moses* and *Americaner Schadchen;* and Florence Weiss in *The Singing Blacksmith.* Yetta Zwerling, a marvelous comedian from the vaudeville stage, starred in eight Yiddish features. One genuine Hollywood star, Lila Lee, who starred with Rudolph Valentino in *Blood and Sand* (1922), returned to the East in 1926 to make *Broken Hearts* with Maurice Schwartz. Otherwise, female roles were drawn from the cadre of talent available in the Yiddish theater in the New York area.

A few of the stars tried to cross over to the American film scene in Hollywood, but other than Molly Picon (*Come Blow Your Horn*, 1963, and *Fiddler on the Roof*, 1971), most of the women featured in Yiddish films remain relatively unknown beyond the world of Yiddish theater. A few exceptions are Reizl Bozyk, who played the grandmother in *Crossing Delancey*,

In Jacob Kalich's film Ost und West *(1923), Molly Picon is an American girl who, when not disguised as a Hasidic boy, mistakenly marries a Talmudist, played by Kalich, eventually happily secularized. Viewing a restored version with Yiddish dubbing and sound effects added, a critic opined that "it breathes Jewish character, but does not satisfy . . . thank God . . . high literary expectations." [American Jewish Historical Society]*

CELIA ADLER *appeared in two films:* Abe's Imported Wife *and the 1937 production (from which the above still is taken)* Vu Iz Mayn Kind? *[Where is my child?]. As might be surmised from this image, it was described as "a reprise of the melodramatic tearjerkers of her earlier years."* [National Center for Jewish Film]

Helen Beverly, who performed on stage and screen (*The Master Race* and *The Robe*); Berta Gersten, who appeared in *The Benny Goodman Story* (1956) and *A Majority of One* (1959); and Dina Halpern, who performed on stage frequently in the Chicago area.

SELECTED YIDDISH ACTRESSES AND FILMS
Prepared by Miriam Saul Krant

Abarbanel, Judith
Uncle Moses, 1932; The Cantor's Son, 1937; Americaner Schadchen, 1940.

Adler, Celia
Where Is My Child?, 1937.

Appel, Anna
Broken Hearts, 1926; The Eternal Prayer, 1929; The Holy Oath, 1937; Green Fields, 1937; The Singing Blacksmith, 1938.

Beverly, Helen
The Cantor's Son, 1937; Green Fields, 1937; The Light Ahead, 1939; Overture to Glory, 1940.

Drute, Dina
Green Fields, 1937.

Gersten, Berta
Mirele Efros, 1939; God, Man, and Devil, 1949.

Goldstein, Jennie
Two Sisters, 1938.

Halpern, Dina
The Dybbuk, 1937; The Vow, 1938.

Kressyn, Miriam
Sailor's Sweetheart, 1930; Purimshpiler, 1937.

Liliana, Lili
The Dybbuk, 1937; Kol Nidre, 1939; Mazel Tov Yidden, 1941.

Picon, Molly
Das Judenmadel [The Jewish Girl], 1921; East and West, 1923; Yiddle with His Fiddle, 1936; Mamele, 1938.

Riselle, Miriam
Tevye, 1939; The Singing Blacksmith, 1938.

Weintraub, Rebecca
Tevye, 1939.

Weiss, Florence
   The Cantor's Son, 1937; *The Singing Blacksmith*, 1938;
   Overture to Glory, 1940.
Zwerling, Yetta
   I Want to Be a Mother, 1937; *I Want to Be a Boarder*,
   1937; *Living Orphan*, 1939; *Kol Nidre*, 1939; *The Great
   Advisor*, 1940; *Motl the Operator*, 1940; *Jewish Melody*,
   1940; *Her Second Mother*, 1941; *Mazel Tov Yidden*, 1941.

BIBLIOGRAPHY

Hoberman, J. *Bridge of Light: Yiddish Film Between Two Worlds* (1995); National Center for Jewish Film. Films, videotapes and files. Brandeis University, Waltham, Mass.

SHARON PUCKER RIVO

YIDDISH LITERATURE

"Ikh bin geven a mol a yingling" [I was once a lad] begins a Yiddish poem of the same name. Transgression—the sense of identity as permeable and unfixed—is announced in this line written by ANNA MARGOLIN, one of the few American women noted for writing in Yiddish. *Yingling* is not a word in Yiddish. It is a combination of *yingl* [boy] and *yung* [young], with an opaque suffix more familiar in English than Yiddish. In a language whose nouns are gendered, *yingl* may be either masculine or neuter (just as *meydl*—girl—is feminine or neuter), signaling at the outset of this poem the problem of claiming any stable rules or essential characteristics governing gender. However, the poem is not only linguistically transgressive. It invokes sexual transgressions as well, suggesting both homosexual and incestuous love and confusing the reader who sees the poet's feminine name next to the word *yingl*. This poem, now known primarily in English translation (where *yingling* may be translated as youth, lad, boy, youngling), begins as though it were looking back, perhaps nostalgically, to the speaker's youth. This youth could never have been experienced by the poet. Defying space, time, and sexuality, the speaker lays claim to several shifting identities in this twelve-line poem: male, Greek, Roman, Christian, at once a student of Socrates and a libertine. But never a woman or a Jew.

Recent considerations of Yiddish women's texts privilege Margolin's iconoclastic voice, seeing in it the tone and role women have assumed in the Yiddish literary tradition. Margolin is an ideal representative of such a voice: the peripatetic divorcee who left her infant son in the custody of his father, took lovers and eventually married the poet Reuben Iceland, wrote under a pseudonym (her real name was Rosa Lebensboim), was known as an intellectual aggressive woman, and in later years, was a recluse reported to be too

huge and too despondent (she suffered from obesity and severe depression) to emerge from her apartment.

It is an exaggeration to claim transgression as the identifying characteristic of Yiddish literature by women, but it is an understandable exaggeration that seeks to redress the equally exaggerated, conventional claims that women have been the conservative force in Yiddish life and letters, the mothers holding home and tradition intact even when they have worked outside the home or have been involved in radical politics. Like other Jewish women in America, Yiddish writers have often been understood in terms of these mythic representations. They have been regarded as women who have had to overcome various hardships (poverty, child-rearing responsibilities, immigration) that impeded their writing, or as lonely women unable to find fulfillment in love or family. They had neither a room of their own nor even a corner of the kitchen table on which to write.

Writers of a broad range of texts—passionate and erotic lyrical verse, social realist fiction, affecting descriptions of immigrant life, nostalgic paeans to their Eastern European homes, dirges to those murdered in the Holocaust—these women are more accurately understood as modernists and traditionalists, romantics and realists, prose writers and poets. They represent, in short, no single school or line of development but rather the range of women's voices contained in Yiddish literature.

The history of women writing Yiddish in the United States has yet to be written. It could be organized chronologically, thematically, or generically. A more controversial and more provocative approach would consider the status of Yiddish in Jewish cultural life and the extent to which Yiddish, the *mame-loshn* [mother tongue], has been feminized and domesticated. Scholars have launched this work, and it is now possible to list perhaps a hundred women who published prose and poetry in the United States in the last hundred years. Still, the prominent story is one of absence and the lack of basic biographical or bibliographical information about writers—even of the very names of women whose works are yet to be uncovered in the pages of scores of unindexed journals and newspapers, or who never found their way into print at all. Some of this is particular to the situation of women in Yiddish letters, but much of it is a reflection of the state of Yiddish literature in America more generally.

The women who immigrated to the United States before 1924 (when changes in immigration laws made it harder to enter this country)—including such major writers as CELIA DROPKIN, MIRIAM KARPILOVE, MALKA LEE, Anna Margolin, Anna Rapaport, YENTE

SERDATSKY, FRADEL SHTOK, MALKA HEIFETZ TUSSMAN, Rashelle Veprinski, Hinde Zaretsky—never conceived of themselves as a literary group. Whether they wrote deliberately political socialist texts or lyrical poetry, they were equally cut off from one another and from the centers of Yiddish publication. Most immigrant women were educated in Eastern Europe, receiving for the most part a better secular education but a less complete religious education than their brothers. Many became radicals and also began writing in Eastern Europe. If they are known today, it is largely through the efforts of English translators of the last decade.

An outgrowth of the *haskalah* [Jewish Enlightenment], modern secular Yiddish literature began in the mid-nineteenth century, spreading to all the corners of the world to which Eastern European Jews immigrated in the next hundred years. Among its early practitioners there are no familiar names of women, although women had certainly written Yiddish texts—primarily *tkhines* [petitionary prayers in prose and verse]—since the medieval period. Yiddish literary production in the United States is commonly understood to follow a generational pattern, beginning with the socially conscious poetry and prose of the "proletarian" or "sweatshop" writers of the 1880s–1900s. These primarily socialist writers were followed, in quick succession, by the rhymed and metered verses of *Di yunge* [The youth] who, in 1907, announced an "art for art's sake" credo that elevated mood and tone over social relevance. In 1919, the Inzikhistn [Introspectivists] declared that free verse and social realities must be combined, that the poet's craft required that he [sic] look into the self [*in zikh*] and thus present a truer image of the psyche and the world. The 1930s were marked by an expansion of socialist and communist journalism and the literature such politics inspired. With the Holocaust, the Hitler-Stalin Pact, and the destruction of Eastern European Jewish life came a literature primarily of consolation and mourning. More recent interest in Yiddish has resulted in the emergence of a small number of new writers, including women, born primarily in the United States or Western Europe.

There are several problems with this chronological paradigm, not least of them the observation that literary epochs in Yiddish last about a decade, often overlap with one another, never correspond to the literary career of any writer, and rarely refer to more than a handful of writers at any period. Moreover, female writers seldom make their way into this schematic account except as the wives or sisters of male writers. Indeed, demanding that women be included in such accounts is highly problematic since any sense of what constitutes the Yiddish literary canon is contested. European and, especially, American feminist literary criticism of the 1970s and beyond insisted on the place of women within established canons, which, supple as the definitions of such canons might be, traditionally overlooked women. Such an enterprise has been attempted in Yiddish as well, but with less success since it has entered a field whose boundaries have not been as well-defined, that is reaching closure, is unlikely to acquire significant new writers for much longer, and is increasingly known only in translation.

Critics have frequently noted that the greatest experiments and accomplishments in Yiddish literature in America took place in poetry rather than prose. Unlike their European and American contemporaries, women writing Yiddish have certainly been more prominent as poets. The reasons for this are social and generic, relying on the status of each genre in Jewish life as well as on the social conditions in which women found themselves. Poetry, some might argue, can sometimes be written despite hectic schedules that include the responsibilities of earning a livelihood and raising a family; the expansive form of the novel requires time and publishing resources rarely available to women. It is, however, difficult to imagine any poet making such an argument. A related explanation is that, despite their crucial economic roles, Jewish women did not have the kind of grounding in an expansive and cohesive social world that storytelling demands. Religious life may have played a less central role in modern America than in nineteenth-century Eastern Europe, but neither as Jews nor as Americans were women and men similarly rooted. The status conferred by economic success in America, like the earlier status conferred by religious learning, one's place in the synagogue, or ritual life among Jews, has always figured in masculine terms. The cultural effect of exclusion from these areas needs to be considered in any analysis of women's literary production in Yiddish. So, too, must the Jewish storytelling tradition, associated as it is with religious learning, haggadah, and midrash. Men, in other words, could associate storytelling with tradition; they could tell their stories in the prayer house, between prayers, even as prayers. Women, for the most part, could not, and the different valence of their stories—told primarily in the kitchen, the parlor, or on the front stoop—no doubt affects the way they might have regarded stories and poems.

Whatever the genre, the status of Yiddish as a literary medium also influenced women's creative endeavors and the possibilities for publication. In its ongoing struggle for respectability, *mame-loshn* has had to distinguish itself from the feminized and the matrilineal. This is, of course, not to say that Yiddish was ever a "woman's language," but rather that it was seen in the context of both Hebrew with its patrilinear religious authority and also as an indigenous national language that carried secular authority. Yiddish was increasingly figured as the language of home in the modern, post-*haskalah* period and especially in America. "To be a Jew in the home and a human being in the street," as the *haskalah* enjoined, meant confining the distinctive customs, appearance, and language of the Jew to the home, while appearing and sounding like everyone else in public. Once Yiddish is identified with the maternal, the familiar, nurturing home, it also becomes, like that home, the place from which one sets forth into the mature world. Even when it was still the language of the Jewish masses, its use was often taken as a sign of their ignorance. Religous texts (the most famous example is the early-seventeenth-century *Tsene Urena*) in Yiddish carried subtitles explaining that they were designed for women or ignorant men; Enlightenment writers turned to Yiddish because too few could read their Hebrew texts; in America, Yiddish could be seen as a necessary tool en route to English and acculturation (as suggested by Abraham Cahan and the most important Yiddish daily, the *Forverts*). Sh. Niger published an often-cited essay in 1913 ("*Di Yidishe Literatur un di Lezerin*" [Yiddish literature and the female reader]) in which he asserted the significant role of women in Yiddish letters as readers and writers, contrasting it with the role Hebrew assumed for male readers. It was difficult to disassociate Yiddish letters from these disparaging feminized images. Men writing in Yiddish might claim some distance from them, as Sholem Aleichem did when he established a patrilineal Yiddish literary genealogy that began with Mendele Moykher Sforim, whom he called *der zeyde* [grandfather]. Women could, it seems, primarily serve as a reminder of the limitations associated with Yiddish.

In light of these concerns, the sheer numbers of female authors and their texts should perhaps surprise us more than the dearth of information about them. Interest in women and Yiddish literature, while limited in scope, can be traced from the early decades of this century. In 1917, M. Bassin's *500 Yor Yidishe Poezye* [500 years of Yiddish poetry] anthologized ninety-five modern poets, the majority of them Americans. His volume included only eight women. In 1928, Ezra Korman's *Yidishe Dikhterins* [Yiddish women poets] included the work of seventy poets. This was less than a quarter of the number included in Reyzen's definitive *Leksikon fun der Yidisher Literatur*

(1928), but Korman's book was noteworthy both because it was published in the United States and, primarily, because it focused exclusively on women's poetry. It also entered into a series of debates about women in Yiddish that were sometimes witty, sometimes vituperative. Several of the exchanges that represent this debate took place in the pages of the Warsaw journal *Literarishe Bleter*. In 1927, Melekh Ravitsh published an article whose critical stance can be discerned in its title: "*Meydlekh, Froyen, Vayber— Yidishe Dikhterins*" [Girls, women, wives—Yiddish poetesses]. Ravitsh sexualized the discussions about women, referring to chastity, seduction, flirtation, fecundity. He was taken to task by two young women, both of whom were Yiddish teachers and were to become among the most noteworthy of the modernist poets in America: KADYA MOLODOWSKY and MALKA HEIFETZ TUSSMAN. The combined presence of Ravitch, the most itinerant of Yiddish writers, Molodowsky, still living in Warsaw, and Tussman, writing from her home in Milwaukee, attests to the international character of Yiddish literature at this time. Writers in America cannot be neatly separated from their peers in Europe since the lines of communication, publication, and debate remain open in both directions with writers on both continents reading and writing in the same journals.

These debates about the role of women in Yiddish are perhaps best epitomized in two essays, one written in 1915 by the renowned (male) poet A. Glants, the other written twenty years later by Kadya Molodowsky, the equally renowned (female) poet. Glants, lamenting the absence of a female presence in Yiddish literature, called for a new era. He claimed that Yiddish literature would stagnate if only men's voices were heard in it. Based partly on essentialist notions of masculinity and femininity—the latter, predictably, seen as more intuitive and emotive—Glants insisted that the inclusion of women was necessary if Yiddish was to live up to its full cultural potential. When Kadya Molodowsky turned to the question of women poets, she echoed parts of her earlier argument with Ravitsh and wrote a sarcastic dismissal of the very concept of "women poetesses." Molodowsky, who had arrived in the United States in 1935, was an acclaimed teacher and writer (of poetry, prose, drama, children's stories). She was to go on to serve as the editor of *Svive* (1943–1944, 1960–1974), an important literary-cultural journal. No female cultural figure could boast of such a position, although some had written regular columns in other journals. In 1936, responding to a number of articles and cultural events honoring women writers, she dismissed such events as condescending, another way of marginalizing the work of poets and women. The very concept of the "female poetess" showed a kind of intellectual laziness on the part of critics, an inability to grapple with the real differences among writers, a way of essentializing women's voices and relegating them to the status of "*tsarte, oftmol ekzotishe blumen in literarishn gortn*" [dainty, often exotic flowers in the literary garden]. Without referring to her own poetry, but reflecting its themes and tones, Molodowsky dismissed the notion that women were more sensitive than men or more likely to write love poetry. Such beliefs recalled the function of the women's gallery in synagogues through which women might peer at the public roles men assumed but from which their voices were never to emerge. For all their differences, Glants and Molodowsky were arguing for the same thing: an honorable position for women in the Yiddish literary canon. Their entreaties and warnings seem to have gone unheeded. Increasingly frightening events in Europe—events culminating in the Stalinist purges and the Holocaust—overshadowed questions about the role of women or of Yiddish.

It would take decades before critics returned to these questions. In 1966, Shmuel Rozhansky published *Di Froy in der Yidisher Poezye* [The woman in Yiddish poetry] as volume 29 of his *Musterverk fun der Yidisher Literatur*, a monumental project of canon formation intended to run to 100 volumes containing representative works of Yiddish literature. Previous volumes had focused on individual authors or a group of two or three, but this one included 136 poets of whom about one-third were women. In 1973, Ber Grin published a series of articles presenting short biographical and bibliographical information about women poets in various countries. Hearkening back to Korman's title (which was his own as well) and the significance of that volume, Grin went on to list the names of twenty-four women who constituted a new generation of American Yiddish women writers. He referred to *yidishe dikhterins* with none of the irony or self-consciousness that Molodowsky's 1936 essay or the earlier essays by her and Tussman might have encouraged. Grin divided his entries by country, including the biographies of twenty-seven women under the heading "American Yiddish poetesses."

More recently, however, the story of women in Yiddish literature, like that of Yiddish literature in general, must be understood primarily as one of translation and analytical essays. Still, as Irena Klepfisz has observed, few women appear in English anthologies: 1 out of 14 writers in Betsky's *Onions, Cucumbers and Plums* (1958); 12 out of 141 in Leftwich's *The Golden Peacock* (1961); 3 out of 57 in Dawidowicz's *The Golden Tradition* (1967); 1 out of 82 in Leftwich's *Great Yiddish Writers of the Twentieth Century* (1969); 6 out of 58 in Howe and Greenberg's *A Treasury of Yiddish Poetry* (1969); 1 out of 7 in Harshav's *American Yiddish Poetry* (1986); 5 out of 39 in Howe, Wisse, and Shmeruk's *The Penguin Book of Modern Yiddish Verse* (1987). Women fare better in volumes devoted entirely to them. This takes into account neither the increasingly frequent appearance of Yiddish translations in journals nor the work of major Canadian writers such as Rokhl Korn or Chava Rosenfarb.

The significance of the poetry and prose produced by women in Yiddish cannot be understood in terms of these counting exercises, revealing though they may be. Such assessments will emerge only from the ongoing work of translation, criticism, bibliography and, above all, reading.

BIBLIOGRAPHY

Glants, A. "Kultur un di Froy" [Culture and women]. *Di Fraye Arbeter Shtime* (October 30, 1915): 4–5; Grin, Ber. "Yidishe Dikhterins" [Yiddish poetesses]. *Yidishe Kultur* (December 1973, January 1974, March 1974, April–May 1974); Hellerstein, Kathryn. "Canon and Gender: Women Poets in Two Modern Yiddish Anthologies." *Shofar* 9, no. 4 (Summer 1994): 9–23, and "In Exile in the Mother Tongue: Yiddish and the Woman Poet." In *Borders, Boundaries, and Frames*, edited by Mae G. Henderson (1995), and "A Question of Tradition: Women Poets in Yiddish." In *Handbook of American-Jewish Literature*, edited by Lewis Fried (1988); Klepfisz, Irena. "Queens of Contradiction: A Feminist Introduction to Yiddish Women Writers." *Found Treasures: Stories by Yiddish Women Writers*, edited by Frieda Forman, Ethel Raicus, Sarah Silberstein Swartz, and Margie Wolfe (1994): 21–62; Korman, Ezra. *Yidishe Dikhterins* (1928); Molodowsky, Kadya. "Meydlekh, Froyen, Vayber, un . . . Nevue" [Girls, women, wives, and prophecy]. *Literarishe Bleter* (June 3, 1927), and "A Por Verter vegn Froyen Dikhterins" [A few words about women poets]. *Signal* 6 (June 1936): 23; Niger, Sh. "Di Yidishe Literatur un di Lezerin" [Yiddish literature and the female reader]. *Der Pinkes* (1913); Norich, Anita. "Jewish Literatures and Feminist Criticism: An Introduction to Gender and Text." *Gender and Text in Modern Hebrew and Yiddish Literature*, edited by Naomi Sokoloff, Anne Lapidus Lerner, and Anita Norich (1992); Pratt, Norma Fain. "Culture and Radical Politics: Yiddish Women Writers, 1890–1940." *American Jewish History* 70 (September 1980): 68-91; Ravitsh, Melekh. "Meydlekh, Froyen, Vayber—Yidishe Dikhterins" [Girls, women, wives—Yiddish poetesses]. *Literarishe Bleter* (May 27, 1927); Rozhansky, Shmuel, ed. *Di Froy in der Yidisher Poezye* [The woman in Yiddish poetry] (1966); Tussman, Malka Heifetz. "An Entfer Melekh Ravitshn af 'Meydlekh, Froyen, Vayber—Yidishe Dikhterins'" [A response to Melekh Ravitsh]. [unpublished?].

ANITA NORICH

YIDDISH MUSICAL THEATER

From 1876 to the early 1880s, a newly hatched phenomenon of Yiddish theater, "operettas," could be found in Jewish communities in Russia, Romania, Austria, and Poland. Abraham Goldfaden, father of Yiddish theater, had devised operettas for his troupes of singer-players and instrumentalists. This new genre of theater gradually featured women rather than young boys in female roles and soon included special set pieces for female performers. By the 1880s, operettas and their artists began to immigrate to America, where both male and female entertainers rapidly adopted the qualities and societal patterns of their American counterparts. Male artists became matinee idols, while female artists became role models who reflected the diversity of women's lives and conditions in America.

Jewish women on stage in America took on a variety of musical roles and performed all kinds of songs, including religious hymns and liturgical chants. Sophie Karp (formerly Sara Siegel Goldstein), who had been discovered and trained for the stage by Goldfaden, became a popular soubrette in Yiddish revues and shows at the Bowery theaters on the Lower East Side of New York City. In 1896, she introduced a Yiddish ballad written especially for her by a musician named Peretz Sandler. That song, "Eili, Eili," was a dramatic arietta that became an immediate favorite and soon became a featured solo of many other female performers of the day, even those in general entertainment. Operatic sopranos SOPHIE BRASLAU and Rosa Raissa sang it at the old Metropolitan Opera House and in concert halls. BELLE BAKER featured it in her touring vaudeville presentations, and her photograph adorns several published editions of the song. When Yossele Rosenblatt made it part of his repertoire, "Eili, Eili," originally a Yiddish stage tune of female singers, evolved into a Jewish hymn considered in the domain of male singers.

One of the singers of "Eili, Eili" was BERTHA KALICH, a famous dramatic actor whose performances were acclaimed by English as well as Yiddish critics. She started her career on Bowery stages and then moved to Second Avenue theaters and Broadway, playing Yiddish versions of heroines in plays by Tolstoy, Dostoyevsky, Schiller, Ibsen, and Shakespeare. All of Kalich's roles involved music—so important to Jewish productions. Goldfaden had shaped that format, set that distinctive artistic pattern. Songs were the dominating element in drama as well as comedy, and everyone on the Jewish stage had to sing.

The earliest female singer-actor, for whom Goldfaden himself wrote many operettas featuring heroic women, was Regina Prager. In the course of her long career, she introduced heroines such as Shulamith, the gallant girl of the Second Temple era, and Dinah, the warrior consort of hero Simeon Bar Kokhba. Over the years, Prager went from lovely soubrette and romantic lady to a formidable matron with the leading role in Boris Thomashefsky's musical *Di Khazinte* [The lady cantor]. Her photographs adorned the covers of an entire series of special solo song selections. Indeed, it became customary for female performers to be featured on theater posters and commercial sheet music, usually in costumes and scenes from a particular show.

By 1910, resourceful Yiddish theatrical entrepreneurs were presenting their own versions of "uptown" American musicals. BESSIE KAUFMAN THOMASHEFSKY starred as the "Jewish American Beauty" in her husband Boris Thomashefsky's production of *The Yiddish Yankee Doodle*. For advertisements and covers on sheet music from that show, Bessie is clad in a riding costume that makes her resemble BARBRA STREISAND! Indeed, in those early years Bessie Thomashefsky favored pants and other "advanced" fashion ideas. After her marriage dissolved, she moved on to have a busy theatrical life—directing, producing, and acting in her own shows.

While Jacob P. Adler was the abiding theatrical star of his day, the Adler women constituted an array of exceptional talents. His daughter CELIA (Cili Feinman) ADLER enjoyed a long and varied stage career, as did the widely acclaimed performer and teacher STELLA ADLER, daughter of Jacob Adler's third wife, SARA HEINE ADLER, who also appeared in dramatic roles well past her eightieth birthday.

In its heyday, the Yiddish stage mirrored life, depicting many issues and problems that directly affected the audiences. Family matters had particular importance in that era of immigrant accommodation and acculturation to American life. The nobility of motherhood was celebrated in legions of stories and songs. How could it be possible, all balladeers sang, that one mother could take care of ten children and yet ten children would not take care of one mother? An amazing range of women's woes were highlighted, discussed, and often resolved across the footlights, presenting reality to an extent not paralleled in the general theatrical world of those years. Some theatricals were comic, as in songs and stories about suffragettes and women's rights issues, where the idea of women as doctors or politicians, even rabbis or cantors, was mocked. Other theatricals, however, were serious expositions, for example, those on behalf of movements for women's labor regulations that followed upon the TRIANGLE SHIRTWAIST FIRE in 1911 where 146 people lost their lives and numerous others were maimed.

JENNIE GOLDSTEIN was a particular favorite of the Yiddish stage, as she portrayed in her dramatic performances a great range of lonely women struggling to survive despite great adversity. Goldstein's stage song was always a version of: "The sun shines but never for me." She began her career portraying a vulnerable immigrant waif, then a wronged maiden who had to give away her baby, a girl with a "stained past," and an exhausted working girl pleading "take me away from the sewing machine." Over the years, she played the victim of a bad husband, or a deserted wife with sickly children who became an unappreciated self-sacrificing middle-aged mother, and finally in old age, abandoned and penniless. Her photographs in those roles appeared on numerous sheet music covers and souvenir programs, and she filled crowded theaters with teary women and sympathetic men.

Two highly popular comic-soubrettes who enjoyed long and illustrious careers were Nellie Casman and MOLLY PICON. Casman, who had a particular type of humorous style, somewhat naughty yet wise, wrote much of her own theatrical material, including songs. One of her tunes, "Yosel, Yosel" [Joseph, Joseph], and its English version "Joseph Make Your Mind Up" continues to be sung by non-Jewish as well as Jewish performers worldwide. In late 1939, Casman concluded a successful year-long European tour, fleeing by train from Berlin after a performance in that city. It was an experience she would vividly recall to the end of her life. Picon was likely the most beloved performer on both the Yiddish and the general stage. She exploited the idea of a girl-boy *Yankele* [Little Jackie] persona and played a variety of such roles in productions throughout the world. Her delightful characterizations were shaped by a petite physical appearance and warm personal charm. The songs she presented on stage and in recordings were written by three leading composers of Yiddish music theater: Joseph Rumshinsky, Sholom Secunda, and Abraham Ellstein. She made two Yiddish movies, filmed in Poland in 1937 and 1938. Almost to the end of her life, she appeared on stage, in films, and on television, ever a gifted and versatile star.

Although their performances were often associated in style, genre, and content with the Yiddish theatricals, neither FANNY BRICE nor SOPHIE TUCKER appeared formally on the Yiddish stage. There were some women, such as Rhea Silberta, who composed songs for the Yiddish musicals, generally for their own performances. One leading female composer was Mana-Zucca (Augusta Zuckerman), who also had a long career in the general music field. Among her selections of specific Judaic content were "Rakhem" [Mercy] and "Sholem Aleichem" [Greetings/Peace to you], the published editions of which were dedicated to soprano Rosa Raissa.

By the second half of the twentieth century, the distinctive qualities of Yiddish theater had mainstreamed into American life. While the artists and their artistry found new audiences in radio, movies, and television, the special qualities of Yiddish theater abided and were even strengthened in the much broader venues of entertainment and cultural expression. Nevertheless, a number of highly talented performers and creative figures stayed within the ranks of Yiddish-focused arts. Many were women, acting and singing, composing and writing, directing and producing.

The older style of Yiddish theatricals and popular songs remains a special legacy from an era rich in innovative ideas and notable personalities. Women from that heyday all did yeoman service and helped bring other women into the forefront of Jewish artistic self-expression.

BIBLIOGRAPHY

Green, Stanley. *Encyclopaedia of the Musical Theatre* (1976); Heskes, Irene. *The Music of Abraham Goldfaden: Father of the Yiddish Theater* (1990), and *Passport to Jewish Music: Its History, Traditions, and Culture* (1994), and *Yiddish American Popular Songs, 1895 to 1950* (1992); Landis, Joseph C., ed. *Memoirs of the Yiddish Stage* (1984); Lifson, David S., trans. and ed. *Epic and Folk Plays of the Yiddish Theatre* (1975); Sanders, Ronald. *The Downtown Jews: Portraits of an Immigrant Generation* (1969); Sandrow, Nahma. *Vagabond Stars: A World History of Yiddish Theater* (1977); Rosenfeld, Lulla Adler. *Bright Star of Exile: Jacob Adler and the Yiddish Theatre* (1977. Rev. ed., *The Yiddish Theatre and Jacob P. Adler*, 1988); Slobin, Mark. *Tenement Songs: The Popular Music of the Jewish Immigrants* (1982).

IRENE HESKES

YIDDISH THEATER

During the Middle Ages and for most of the centuries since then, Ashkenazim—the Yiddish-speaking Jews of central and Eastern Europe—produced virtually no theater at all. Since ancient times, rabbinic Jewish tradition had disapproved of theater, for men and women alike. Moreover, it was specifically considered immodest for women to perform for men. Men were prohibited from hearing women's voices singing, and women were prohibited from dressing as men. Finally, unlike other Western cultures, in many of whose theaters men played women's roles up into early modern times, Jewish men were permitted to dress as women only as part of the topsy-turvy merrymaking of the Purim holiday. For that reason, it was only during

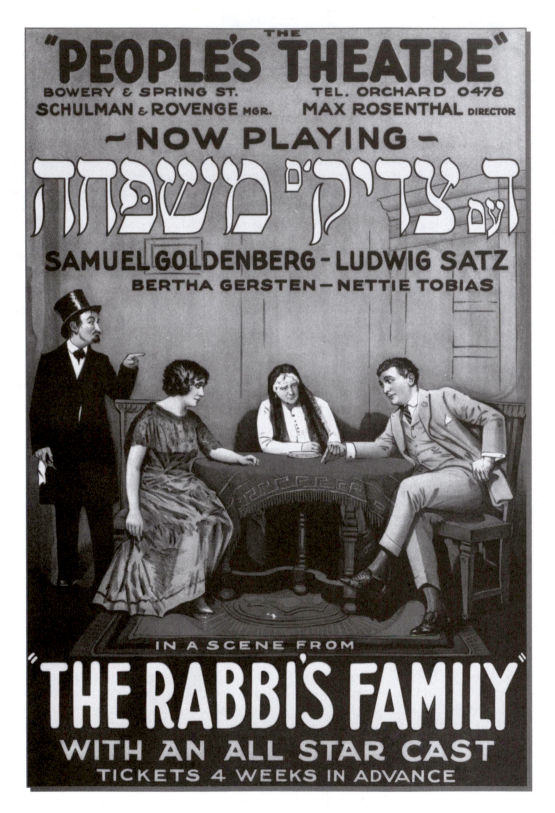

*The American capital of Yiddish theater was New York City, where at times as many
as fourteen theaters were filled simultaneously, not counting vaudeville and cabaret.
This production at the People's Theatre advertised "Tickets 4 Weeks in Advance."
[John D. Woolf. Photograph courtesy of the American Jewish Historical Society]*

Purim, in early spring, that lively amateur entertainments were produced, and even then women participated only as spectators. Professional Yiddish theater did not exist until 1876. Until then there were only groups of wandering acrobats, among whom, however, two women's names are recorded: Ruza and Feygele.

During the late-nineteenth-century *haskole* [Enlightenment], period, when Eastern European Ashkenazi culture was becoming more modern and cosmopolitan, some Yiddish plays were written to be read at home as sophisticated literary entertainment. The first recorded actual performance of one of these plays was organized in 1862 by Madame Slonimsky, wife of the new headmaster of the Zhitomer Academy for boys in Zhitomer, Poland. Her husband's students played all the roles. The play was *Serkele*, by Shlomo Etenger. The title role, a strong-willed female character, was played by a boy named Avrom [Abraham] Goldfadn, who grew up to establish the first professional Yiddish troupe.

Goldfadn's troupe, formed in Jassy, Romania, in 1876, was one manifestation of a general loosening of governmental restrictions on Jewish culture from the outside, as well as a loosening of traditional rabbinic restrictions from inside. The first company consisted of Goldfadn plus one actor. He soon hired a second actor, Sakher Goldstein, to play women's roles as well as men's. Goldfadn's wife, Paulina, served the enterprise as the translator of French and German popular plays into Yiddish.

Probably the first woman to perform on the Yiddish stage was Sara Segal, a sixteen-year-old seamstress with dark eyes and a sweet soprano voice. However, her mother refused permission until Goldstein, being the only unmarried company member, married her and took her along on their wandering life. She changed her name to the European-sounding Sophie, becoming Sophie Goldstein. Later, in New York, she married another actor, making her name Sophie Goldstein-Karp, or Sophia Karp. Karp was the first woman whose profession was Yiddish theater, and she was typical of the many hundreds who followed. She was an actress, known for glamour and charm. She occasionally participated in a venture as producer or even director as well as star. (Karp is said to have died of a theatrical dispute. In an effort to prove her claim on a certain theater, she refused to leave the building, even sleeping on the unheated stage, until she caught pneumonia and died.) But this was minor, and in fact women in Yiddish theater were primarily performers.

The Golubok company was the first to arrive in the United States, in 1882, at the start of the great wave of Jewish immigration. Their prima donna was a Madame Sara Krantsfeld. Sophie Karp and many other actresses and actors came shortly afterward. For a decade and more, most American Yiddish actresses were immigrants, as were their audiences, but Yiddish theater was so new that many who were born in Europe made their debuts in the new land. Others started careers in the Old Country and then immigrated; by 1900, talent scouts were aggressively importing actresses whose reputations had arrived at Ellis Island along with other news from home.

Most of the qualities associated with Yiddish actresses were already clear in the 1880s. Theatergoers favored fiery temperament and emotionalism in drama, and "quicksilver" energy in comedy, for actresses and actors alike. As the theater acquired serious playwrights and discriminating audiences, truthfulness and sensitivity became highly valued. Types, in the styles of the period, included queenly lovers, strong heroines, glamorous villainesses, saucy soubrettes, and devoted mammas. And since music was interpolated in most shows, even including serious straight dramas, a good singing voice was also important.

From the beginning, many actresses married men in the theater community, and their names were and have remained linked in pairs with their husbands'. Eventually there came to be many actors' daughters as well. Often families played in the same company. Companies generally formed for a season, or for a tour, and touring companies moved not only around the United States but also back and forth to Eastern Europe and Russia. It was also not unusual to visit Western Europe, South America, or South Africa. On tour many actresses took along their children, who soon learned to perform. The American capital of Yiddish theater was New York City, where at times as many as fourteen theaters were filled simultaneously, not counting vaudeville and cabaret. But there were also professional theaters in other cities around the country, such as Philadelphia, Detroit, and Providence.

Because the Yiddish public was passionate about theater, they generally were aware of actresses' private lives, including romances, which were matters of comment in theater columns and critiques in the press. Although respectable families were not pleased if their daughters went on the stage, actresses committed to intellectual or political ideals were highly respected by the intelligentsia, and for the community at large the presence of actresses lent dash and style to café life. Actresses, like other performers, customarily contracted for one night a season to be played for their own benefit. In this practice, not unique to Yiddish theater, the performer picked and cast the play. On these benefit nights, the house might be filled with an actress's enthusiastic fans, and the box office take came to a significant yearly bonus. She might also receive gifts in addition to money profits.

In this early period began the long career of Bina Abramovich, who fifty years later was still known affectionately as the "mother" of Yiddish theater, both because she had always been there and because the roles she was associated with were folksy Old Country mammas. Pretty, lively Dina Shtettin played with her husband Jacob Adler in London en route to America, and finished her career here married to Seymour Feinman, after which she became known as Dina Feinman. Regina Prager was known for her operatic singing and dignified carriage.

BESSIE THOMASHEFSKY met her husband, Boris, when she was a girl in Baltimore and he came there to start a Yiddish theater. Through her long, successful career, she played many roles, both comic and deeply dramatic, light and intense. She even played mischievous little boys. Her many enthusiastic fans extolled her acting as "natural," a term of particularly high praise.

Starting in 1890, some actresses were known not only for their work in popular theater but also in association with the playwright Jacob Gordin, whose literary repertory dominated the more intellectually ambitious Yiddish theater between roughly 1890 and 1905. Among Gordin's political causes was women's rights, and among his dramatic talents was writing juicy roles, often with certain stars in mind. Gordin was the first, though certainly not the last, professional Yiddish dramatist to create thoughtful and intelligent female characters. Keni Liptzin, BERTHA KALICH, and SARA ADLER remained permanently associated with Gordin roles.

Keni or Kenia Liptzin ran away from home to join one of Goldfadn's earliest troupes and played in many companies in Eastern Europe and London before she settled in New York and encountered Gordin. Tiny and elegant, she was known for her uncompromising high standards for Yiddish literary repertoire. She was able to play only those plays she respected because she was married to a successful publisher, making her perhaps the only Yiddish theater producer ever who could be financially independent of whether or not her vehicles sold tickets. The role she was best known for was Gordin's *Mirele Efros; or, The Jewish Queen Lear*. This tells the story of a woman who loses everything to a scheming daughter-in-law and to her own pride. When the Polish Yiddish star Ester Rokhl Kaminska toured in New York in that same role, the Yiddish press called it a duel of rival champions.

Bertha Kalich began as a chorus lovely in Lemberg, Poland, and though she also played on the non-Yiddish Polish stage, talent scouts soon brought her to America. She was known for her grace and femininity. Gordin is supposed to have written his popular play of thwarted love, *The Kreutzer Sonata*, because once, as he sat in her dressing room, she flirted with him, brushing her long dark hair and coaxing, "Write a play for my hair." She subsequently played the role in English translation on Broadway. She also created the female lead in his *Sappho*, a photographer who dares to bear a child out of wedlock because the father turns out to be unworthy, and in *God, Man, and Devil*, an unhappy wife. She played for many years in Yiddish and English even after she became totally blind.

For Sara Adler, Gordin wrote *Without a Home*. Adler, who began her career as Sara Heine-Haimovitch, rose to fame while married to Jacob Adler. Her fiery temperament delighted her many fans, onstage and off, and she remained a star—possibly the most successful of her generation—for many years. Her daughters Frances, Julia, and STELLA ADLER all became actresses; Stella soon transferred to the English-language stage, where she was an influential performer and teacher.

Yiddish theater participated in the art theater movement in the United States, as well as in Western Europe and Russia. In 1917, New York acquired the Yiddish Art Theater, organized by Maurice Schwartz, and the following year the Jewish Art Theater organized by Jacob Ben-Ami. There were others in the New York area and elsewhere. Several actresses were associated with this movement, which emphasized text, direction, and ensemble work as opposed to the star system. CELIA ADLER, raised in traditional Yiddish theater and known for her delicacy and vulnerability, was an enthusiastic reformer, later recalling the period as a "golden era." So was the glamorous BERTA GERSTEN.

The popular theater in the first half of the twentieth century had many skilled and energetic female performers in a variety of styles. The following are some of the best known. Nellie Casman sang and recorded songs, some of which (like "Yosel, Yosel") she wrote herself. JENNIE GOLDSTEIN starred in tearjerkers and later turned to comedies. Henrietta Jacobson and Yetta Zwerling were popular comediennes. Anna Appel and Malvina Lobel were known in dramas. Vera Rosanka billed herself as the Jewish Gypsy. Clara Young was a frilly coquette. MOLLY PICON, whose mother sewed costumes backstage, began in English-language vaudeville. Her husband, Jacob Kalich, groomed her for stardom—even tutoring her in Yiddish—and helped make her the darling of Yiddish musical theater, cabaret, and films. She was especially popular in gamin roles, even boy roles such as Yankl, the mischievous yeshivah student. Picon ended her career back on the English-language stage, playing in American musical comedies.

By mid-century, new names drew audiences to the theaters. Mina Bern played *kleynkunst*, charming musical revues that included art songs and scenes of literary value, with her husband, Ben Bonus. Clever Reizl Bozyk, who was actually born onstage on her mother's benefit night, performed with her husband, Max, and alone, and in old age was highly praised for her role in the Hollywood film *Crossing Delancey* written by Susan Sandler. Dina Halpern acted and also gave solo literary performances known as "word concerts." Betty and Jacob Jacobs were a perennial song-and-dance duo. MIRIAM KRESSYN played Yiddish dramas and musicals and in films. Shifra Lerer, trained in Argentinean theater, acted with her husband, Ben Zion Vitler, and appeared in Yiddish films. Lillian Lux, with her husband, Pesach Burstein, and son, Mike Burstyn, had her biggest international success in *The Megile of Itsik Manger.*

A number of these actresses also appeared in one or more of the Yiddish films made in the United States, though film acting was generally less respected than stage productions. Some are better remembered for their film work than from stage appearances: Helen Beverly, Judith Abarbanel, Gertrude Bullman, Lucy Gehrman, Lila Lee, Lucy Levine, Miriam Riselle, Mae Simon, and Florence Weiss. Yiddish radio programs were widespread and popular; Esther Field was a prominent personality. With her husband, Seymour Rexsite, Miriam Kressyn presented a long-running series of radio shows evoking the history of the Yiddish theater.

There was another venue for Yiddish performance: the resorts of the Catskills. The most famous was Grossinger's, run by the hotel keeper JENNIE GROSSINGER. Here Yiddish performers did their routines in a mixture of Yiddish and English for increasingly assimilated audiences. There were also opportunities to perform at summer camps like Nit Gedayget.

By the 1970s and 1980s there were a number of new women on the professional Yiddish stage in America. Ida Kaminska, the intelligent and dignified daughter of Ester Rokhl Kaminska, spent some years heading her own company here between the time she left Poland and settled permanently in Israel. Just as she played with her famous mother, so too her daughter Ruth Kaminska in turn played with her.

Mary Soreanu, born in Romania and based in Israel, spent a number of seasons in New York starring in light musical vehicles designed to show off her strong voice, easy good humor, and good looks. Rita Karen Karpinovitch, trained in the Moscow Art Theater, gave "word concerts." Vivacious American-born Eleanor Reissa understudied Soreanu early in her career but went on to star in Yiddish, English, and bilingual shows, and to choreograph them as well. Besides her stage appearances here, dark-voiced Raquel Yossiffon has taught university courses about Yiddish theater in Israel. Other young performers of the 1980s and 1990s included Joanne Borts, Adrienne Cooper, Shira Flam, Rosalie Gerut, Ibi Kaufman, and Suzanne Toren.

Amateur theater groups have always been active in Yiddish cultural communities, encouraging new dramatists and providing social cohesiveness. Many were associated with political or social positions, and many provided a congenial venue for artistically ambitious Yiddish dramas. Chayele Ash and Dina Halpern were professional actresses who organized and sustained such groups. But there were many unknown heroines who gave enormous time and energy to organize and sustain these theaters. At the moment, the major established Yiddish theater company in the United States is the Folksbiene, in New York City. The oldest continuously performing Yiddish theater company in the world, the Folksbiene was amateur through most of its years, though now it employs professional artists as well, and its most active member is the popular veteran Zypora Spaisman.

Women in professional Yiddish theater have been almost exclusively performers. In the early period, when male stars often headed their own companies, it was rare for women to do so. Keni Liptzin was a major exception, but she was subsidized by her husband; Bessie Thomashefsky, Sara Adler, and Jennie Goldstein were also intermittently company heads, as was Ida Kaminska. Playwrights and songwriters created vehicles for the well-known female performers, but although Molly Picon wrote songs, women rarely wrote their own material; there were no professional women writers or directors. Rose Pivar worked in the Hebrew Actors Union administrative office, and other women were active in the Hebrew Actors Guild. More recently, Renee Solomon served as musical director and piano accompanist for many productions, and Ruth Vool handled theater business as well as performing. Bessie White translated several volumes of Yiddish short plays. Celia Adler and Bessie Thomashefsky wrote their memoirs.

There are women connected with professional Yiddish theater in creative capacities other than performing. Miriam Hoffman has created several plays. The best known are *Songs of Paradise*, with cowriter Rena Berkowicz Borow and composer Rosalie Gerut, and *A Rendezvous with God*, about the poet Itsik Manger.

Hoffman is the executive director of the Joseph Papp Jewish Theater and teaches Yiddish language at Columbia University. Miriam Kressyn adapted a number of classics for contemporary productions and wrote lyrics for them. Bryna Wasserman Turetsky adapted *Mirele Efros* for productions at the Folksbiene and the Saidye Bronfman Centre in Montreal. Rina Elisha and Bryna Wasserman Turetsky directed Folksbiene productions. Eleanor Reissa won a Tony for choreographing the bilingual *Those Were the Days*. JOAN MICKLIN SILVER produced the Hollywood feature films *Crossing Delancey* and *Hester Street*; the latter, based on the Yiddish story *Yekl*, incorporated a great deal of Yiddish dialogue. Tova Ronni, of the Folksbiene's board, organized the installation of devices for simultaneous translation—an innovation that has helped the Folksbiene continue to draw audiences. The United States has also seen numerous tours by the Yiddish Theatre of the Saidye Bronfman Centre of Montreal, founded and directed by Dora Wasserman, who when she suffered a stroke was succeeded by her daughter Bryna Turetsky.

Women have also been active historians of the Yiddish theater. Diane Cypkin, besides performing in Yiddish theater, was curator of the Yiddish theater collection of the Museum of the City of New York. Sharon Pucker Rivo is executive director of the National Center for Jewish Film, which has rescued, preserved, and made available to viewers more Yiddish films than any other institution. Faina Burko has written a major study of the Moscow Yiddish Art Theater, and Edna Nahshon has chronicled the left-wing avant-garde theater ARTEF. Nahma Sandrow translates Yiddish plays, and created several original shows out of Yiddish theater material. Lulla Rosenfeld wrote a biography of her grandfather, Jacob Adler. EVELYN TORTON BECK wrote about the influence of Yiddish theater on Franz Kafka's work. The scholar RUTH WISSE taught a course in Yiddish theater at Harvard University.

Women have always been important as Yiddish theater audiences. In the early sweatshop days, working girls spent hard-earned pennies for tickets. Girls went to the theater in friendly groups or on dates. It was the custom for fraternal organizations to buy out a performance and sell tickets to raise money, and women often went to such performances in order to meet people from back home in the Old Country. Mothers could bring along their children, with picnic lunches to keep them fed during long matinees. Dramas of life in America provided them with ways to learn about the new country and try out, vicariously, new ways to cope. Translations of world classics or of Broadway hits were glimpses of the outside world. Escapist operettas and comedies offered relief from the hardships of immigration and poverty. And women's tastes influenced the theater world. Actors whom women found handsome played leading roles; there are many tales of women swooning in the aisles and running after Adler or Thomashefsky. Actresses whom women admired, whose styles they copied, became stars and remained stars long past their youth. Now, as Yiddish theater is attenuated, the loyalties and memories of women are important for its survival.

BIBLIOGRAPHY

For a detailed overview of Yiddish theater see *Vagabond Stars: A World History of Yiddish Theater*, by Nahma Sandrow (1977). The volume includes an extensive bibliography of sources in both Yiddish and English.

NAHMA SANDROW

YOUNG WOMEN'S HEBREW ASSOCIATION

Judging by the name alone, it might seem that the Young Women's Hebrew Association (YWHA) was the women's version of the Young Men's Hebrew Association (YMHA) and nothing more. But just as the YMHA was no mere knockoff of its Christian namesake, so too was the idea of the YWHA both a borrowing and an innovation. As a communal agency run entirely by and for women, the YWHA provided an important political arena for Jewish women in the early part of the twentieth century. As a pioneering Jewish institution combining social and religious services, the YWHA became one of the principal sources of the Jewish community center movement.

The Young Men's Christian Association (YMCA), certainly a key inspiration for the YMHA movement, was introduced to America in 1851. Four years later, a women's analogue—the YWCA—was instituted as well. Spreading rapidly across the country, the YM-YWCA movement provided young men and women with an ecumenical social center. Yet it also came to function as a young people's church and virtually became a Protestant denomination of its own. YMHAs, on the other hand, were first established during the 1850s on the model of Jewish young men's literary associations and benevolent societies. The first major YMHA institution was founded in New York City in 1874. It too eschewed religious services and emphasized the cultural uplift of young men, that is, the YMHA grew out of educational precedents in its own community and was furthermore distinct from the YMCA in its secular orientation. Rather than resting on a religious basis, the YMHA movement sprang

The YWHA was dedicated to the uplift—both social and spiritual—of young Jews. To quote Bella Unterberg, the best way to reach young people was, ". . . by placing before them opportunities of pleasant and refined social pleasures to attract them gradually to better, nobler and more spiritual ideals." The above scene of the "reading hour" at the Y's summer camp at the Warburg estate in White Plains, New York, could hardly be more "pleasant and refined." The photograph was taken in 1920.
[A. Tennyson Beals. 92nd Street YM-YWHA Archives]

from ethnic and cultural motives and was integral to the late nineteenth-century revival of Jewish life.

Following the onset of mass immigration in the 1880s, the YMHA came to be employed as an agency of Americanization. Hence in 1883, the New York YMHA established a branch downtown in the immigrant district of the Lower East Side, said to be "the first Jewish neighborhood center in America for immigrant groups." Six years later, the downtown YMHA joined with two other educational agencies to form the Hebrew Institute. Soon renamed the Educational Alliance, it became the premier Jewish settlement of the Lower East Side and the flagship institution of a nationwide movement. The YMHA thus played a significant role in the emerging settlement movement, an institutional trend largely led and staffed by women. Thus the first Young Women's Hebrew Association was founded in New York City in 1888 for the purpose of immigrant education. Under the presidency of public school educator JULIA RICHMAN, this early YWHA—the first time the name appeared—remained for only a few years and was never more than auxiliary to the YMHA.

The immediate precursor of the YWHA movement, therefore, was the participation of women in the life of the YMHA. Early on, women were admitted to some YMHA activities on a limited basis, such as the "musical and dramatic corps which included young ladies" at the YMHA in Lafayette, Inidana, in 1868 and the class in elocution and English literature of the Philadelphia YMHA, which permitted women to join in 1876. Whereas the New York YMHA voted against the admittance of women in 1874, other YMHAs proved more liberal. The YMHAs of Chicago and Philadelphia voted to admit women as full members in 1877 and 1880 respectively, and in 1878, a YMHA in Wisconsin changed its name to Madison Hebrew Association in order to include women. Following the 1888 establishment of the YWHA auxiliary in New York, similar women's auxiliaries were organized in cities around the country, including Louisville, Kentucky; Denver, Colorado; New Orleans, Louisiana; Columbus, Ohio; Birmingham, Alabama; and Washington, D.C. Women's participation in YMHA activities soon expanded, as when the Louisville YMHA instituted gymnasium classes for women in 1891.

A truly independent women's association did not appear until after the turn of the century, when a new YWHA was established in New York City in early 1902. Its principal founder and guiding spirit was Bella Unterberg (née Epstein), the wife of shirt manufacturer and Jewish philanthropist Israel Unterberg. Born in 1868 to a Russian Jewish immigrant family (her father had arrived in the United States in 1855 and fought in the Civil War), Unterberg received both a New York City public school education and a sound Jewish upbringing. As a young woman in her twenties, she was profoundly affected by the efflorescence of Jewish women's social activism during the 1890s. Supporting and supported by the parallel efforts of her husband, Unterberg became a communal leader in her own right, directing campaigns for the Ladies' Fuel and Aid Society and the Women's Committee of the Council for National Defense. But it was the YWHA that became her foremost concern and "favorite child." She became so closely identified with the YWHA, in fact, that her biographer could quite rightly state: "The story of the YWHA is from the beginning the story of Mrs. Unterberg, its record Mrs. Unterberg's record, its triumphs and achievements, her triumphs and achievements."

The institution had its beginnings in a meeting called by Unterberg on February 6, 1902, and held in her home at 143 West 77th Street. The eighteen women present elected Unterberg as president, Mrs. Henry Pereira Mendes as vice president, and Mrs. Simon Liebovitz as treasurer. Mendes was the wife of the hazan of the Spanish and Portuguese synagogue, Shearith Israel, and in addition to the vice presidency was elected "religious guide" of the organization. Regarding its mission, Unterberg recommended "that the Society establish an institution akin in character to the YMHA but combining therewith features of a religious and spiritualizing tendencies." The minutes conclude: "After considerable discussion on the question of the Society's name, it was agreed that it be called and known as the Young Women's Hebrew Association."

So the new institution would be modeled after the YMHA as a community center dedicated to the uplift—both social and spiritual—of young Jews. In Unterberg's view, the best way to reach young people was "by thoroughly fraternizing and associating with them and by placing before them opportunities of pleasant and refined social pleasures to attract them gradually to better, nobler and more spiritual ideals." By the beginning of 1903, the YWHA had rented a building at 1584 Lexington Avenue and soon established itself as a vital community center in the burgeoning Jewish neighborhood of Harlem. From the start, its primary aim was to provide social recreational activities for Jewish working girls. As such, it was an immediate success, recording a total attendance of over twenty-one thousand in its first year alone. Unterberg soon recognized the need for larger quarters and in 1906 rededicated an expanded and renovated facility. The building could now house eighteen female residents and would henceforth become a boarding home as well as a community center. At the dedication, Unterberg asked those assembled: "Can you imagine doing a greater good than supplying hundreds of hard working girls with a chance of bettering their condition and of helping them, in many cases, from a condition of want and necessity to a place in the world where they can become independent and self-supporting?" Under her beneficent direction, the new YWHA was a kind of social settlement house for young working Jewish women.

The essential factor setting the new YWHA apart from the YMHA was its pronounced Jewishness. While the YMHA movement had given some attention to the observance of Jewish religion and the preservation of Jewish identity, its guiding ethos was not Judaism but Americanism. Following the turn of the century, many Jewish women rebelled against this emphasis and made their version of the settlement house a positive force for Jewish life. This was part of a general backlash against the assimilationist tendency of the first quarter century of mass immigration, but it was also part of a women's movement for the "Judaization" of American Jewry. In her address at the dedication ceremony of the YWHA building in February 1903, REBEKAH KOHUT "laid stress upon the necessity of having religion as the foundation stone of the new organization, and paid a tribute to the religious work now being done by the YMHA." A 1912 newspaper article quoted Sophia Berger, superintendent of the YWHA: "Back of all that we do, is the thought of preserving the essential Jewishness of our people. As Jews we want to save our Judaism. As Jews we bring these girls in here that they may find shelter and help and find, too, the God of their fathers." And at the dedication exercises of the new YWHA building in 1914, Augusta Wolf, representing the younger members of the organization, urged that "the new home be made distinctly a center for the propagation of Jewish ideals, Jewish traditions, Jewish culture and Jewish religion." The special care of the association, she declared, was "to make Jewish girls grow up into Jewish women."

All agreed that the keynote of the YWHA was Judaism, and thus the YWHA included a synagogue on its premises from early in its history. The YWHA synagogue functioned as an independent congregation catering to the surrounding community, not as a women's congregation as such. To suit the constituents of that highly Americanized immigrant neighborhood, it offered a modernized Orthodox service—the traditional liturgy but with an English sermon, mixed seating, and choral music—a new religious mix that soon would be called Conservative Judaism. Apparently, such innovation could be accepted more readily in a women's institution. In the new building of 1914, the auditorium doubled as the synagogue, and services were conducted every Friday night, Saturday morning, and on Jewish holidays. The other major Jewish aspect of the YWHA was its curriculum consisting of classes in Hebrew, Bible study, and Jewish history. This was coordinated with an experimental Hebrew school for girls conducted at the YWHA by the Bureau of Jewish Education (of the New York City Kehilla).

Of course, the YWHA offered far more than religious services and Hebrew classes. In 1917, a few years after the completion of its new eight-story facility on 110th Street overlooking Central Park, the New York YWHA was described as "the only large institution of its kind in America." The description of the modern social center continued: "Besides being a most comfortable home for one hundred and seventy girls, the building is also a true center for the communal interests of the neighborhood; it houses a Commercial School, a Hebrew School, Trade Classes in Dressmaking, Millinery, Domestic Science, classes in Hebrew, Bible Study, Jewish History, Art, English to Foreigners, Advanced English, French, Spanish, and Nursing. There is a completely equipped modern gymnasium and swimming pool." Serving both its residential population and the larger community, the YWHA became a full-service Jewish center. Housing both a synagogue and a swimming pool, the YWHA was nothing less than a "shul with a pool"—an early exemplar of the synagogue center movement (Mordecai Kaplan's Jewish Center did not appear until three years later).

Additional amenities included "musical salons" held on Sunday evenings and weekly dances for young women and men on the outdoor roof garden, which proved to be especially popular. The roof was also used during the summer for day care programs for "anemic and cardiac children, and the children of poor families."

YWHA centers existed all around the country. This 1915 photograph was taken in San Francisco.
[Western Jewish History Center]

The YWHA also sponsored summer camping, including hiking, canoeing, and all manner of sporting activities. Back in the city, athletics was fostered in classes in swimming, tennis, fencing, and so on. Dance was especially popular, being offered in several varieties. An employment bureau was provided for young women in need of jobs, and during World War I, the YWHA cooperated extensively with numerous war relief efforts. Finally, the earlier emphasis on immigrant adjustment was retained but from a more sympathetic point of view: "An important work to which a great deal of attention has been paid is the formation of Americanization Classes for Aliens, to help lessen the tragedy in the social evolution of the immigrants."

Following the success of the New York YWHA, new YWHAs were soon established around the city: the West Side YWHA in 1914, the YWHA of Brooklyn in 1916, and the YWHA of Brownsville in 1917. Around the country, the women's auxiliaries of the earlier period began to be replaced by independent YWHAs. The spread of the movement was so rapid that regional federations of YWHAs began to appear. The first was the Associated YWHAs of New England, organized in 1913. The Metropolitan League of YWHAs of New York City and the New Jersey Federation of YWHAs soon followed. Partly as the result of the acceleration of the YWHA activity, the YM-YWHA movements were organized on a national basis when the Council of Young Men's Hebrew and Kindred Associations (CYMHKA) was established in 1913. The development came at the expense of YWHA independence, however, as YWHAs began to merge with their male counterparts.

In 1919, the CYMHKA listed 294 constituent organizations, of which some 127 were YWHAs—the majority being in New York, New Jersey, Pennsylvania, and Massachusetts. As above, most of these existed alongside YMHAs. Out of a total 127 YWHAs, 46 shared the same address with YMHAs, 19 were ladies' auxiliaries to YMHAs, and 8 were listed as part of a combined YM-YWHA. On the other hand, 23 YWHAs enjoyed their own separate facilities and 15 were independent institutions without a neighboring YMHA (though some were affiliated with the local Jewish settlement). Cities thus monopolized by a YWHA included Los Angeles, California; Atlanta, Georgia; Lewiston, Maine; Baltimore, Maryland; Fitchburg, Massachusetts; Cincinnati, Ohio; Johnstown, Pennsylvania; and Galveston, Texas.

The turning point was the 1921 absorption of CYMHKA by the Jewish Welfare Board (JWB), which took as its mission the formation of all-inclusive Jewish community centers. Independent agencies such as the YWHA were thereafter encouraged to merge with similar institutions. With the prompting of the JWB staff, no fewer than fifty-three YWHAs merged with their brother associations to form combined YM-YWHAs during the years 1921 to 1923, a pattern that continued in the years to come. The original independent YWHA of New York City resisted the trend until 1942, when its building on 110th Street was leased to the United States Army as a barracks and its activities were moved to the YMHA building at Ninety-second Street and Lexington Avenue. Three years later, the two groups merged by reincorporating the YMHA as the Young Men's and Young Women's Hebrew Association. The former YWHA was reincorporated as the Jewish Association of Neighborhood Centers, a local version of the JWB.

The New York YWHA had existed as an independent institution for over forty years and during that time it gave rise to a national movement. Unterberg founded the movement in 1902 and served conspicuously as the lone woman on the CYMHKA and on the board of the JWB. She remained the president of the YWHA until 1929, when she was succeeded by vice president FRIEDA SCHIFF WARBURG (daughter of Jacob Schiff, the main benefactor of the YWHA, and wife of Felix Warburg, the president of the YMHA, among their many other philanthropic activities). Under the leadership of these two remarkable women, the independent YWHA gave thousands of young Jewish women a home of their own in the big city, creating a women's sanctuary in a male world—no small achievement. Resting on the foundations of the YM-YWCA, the YMHA, the settlement house, and other philanthropic agencies, the YWHA was innovative in its own right. Its integrated program of religious, education, and social services became a principal model for the synagogues and Jewish centers of today. The Young Women's Hebrew Association was, it might be claimed, the original Jewish community center.

BIBLIOGRAPHY

Goldwasser, I.E. "The Work of Young Men's Hebrew and Kindred Associations in New York City." *Jewish Communal Register* (1917); *Israel and Bella Unterberg—A Personal and Communal Record* (1932); Kaufman, David. "The YMHA as a Jewish Center." In " 'Shul with a Pool': The Synagogue Center in American Jewish Life, 1875–1925." Ph.D. diss., Brandeis University, 1994; Ninety-Second Street Y. Archives. Record group 5, Young Women's Hebrew Association, NYC; Rabinowitz, Benjamin. "The Young Men's Hebrew Associations," *PAJHS* 37 (1947).

DAVID KAUFMAN

Z

ZEISLER, FANNIE BLOOMFIELD (1863–1927)

"She plays like a man" was a near-refrain in critiques of Fannie Bloomfield Zeisler, a brilliant pianist who emerged in the young, male-dominated American concert world of the 1880s. With magnetic energy and articulate technique, Zeisler broke out of the "lady pianist" molds to become a virtuoso revered for her musical intellect, expressivity, bravura, and scintillating touch in a wide range of concert repertoire. Her popularity peaked in the late 1890s, following highly acclaimed European tours, and continued into the first two decades of the twentieth century. Through much of her life the pianist juggled fifty-engagement seasons with teaching (at Chicago's Bush Temple of Music and in a private studio) and family duties; in her fifties, her career began to subside, affected by deaths in her family and health setbacks.

Fannie Bloomfield Zeisler was born on July 16, 1863, in Bielitz, Austrian Silesia, the youngest of three children of Bertha (Jaeger) and Salomon Blumenfeld. Her brothers were Sigmund and Moritz, later known as Maurice Bloomfield, a renowned Sanskrit scholar. In 1867, the four-year-old Fannie moved with her family from war-depressed Austria to Appleton, Wisconsin, where her father entered into a store partnership, then to Milwaukee, and, in 1870, to Chicago. In the family's Chicago home, first located near the Blumenfelds' dry-goods store in the city's Jewish neighborhood, Fannie absorbed German Jewish values and traditions from her kosher-keeping grandmother Jaeger, her father, a Talmudic scholar, and her mother, an avid reader of German literature.

An intelligent and serious child, Fannie excelled in public school and early music study. She graduated with honors from Chicago's Dearborn School for Girls, where she stood out as the only Jewish girl of her class. At seven, after being taught piano informally by her brother Moritz, she began three years of formal study with the theorist Bernhard Ziehn before working with the charismatic teacher Carl Wolfsohn. Following a debut at age eleven at a concert of Wolfsohn's Beethoven Society on February 25, 1875, and reappearances with the organization, she auditioned for the touring Russian virtuoso Annette Essipoff in 1877 and, at her urging, set off for Vienna the following year to study with Theodor Leschetizky, accompanied by her mother and grandmother, and partially subsidized by local banker Henry Greenebaum. After one year at the Vienna Conservatory, Fannie began a rigorous course of study, lasting from 1879 to 1883, with Leschetizky. She became one of a luminous roster of pianists who would emerge from his studio.

Shortly after "graduation" performances in Vienna, Fannie returned to America and secured Henry Wolfsohn, brother of her early Chicago teacher, as her manager. Her American debut as a professional, on January 11, 1884, with Chicago's Beethoven Society,

Fannie Bloomfield Zeisler broke out of the "lady pianist" mold to become renowned for her musical intellect, expressiveness, and bravura. Performing for the great conductors and with such concert artists as Pablo Casals, Mischa Elman, and Fritz Kreisler, she expanded the standard repertoire to include the compositions of her contemporaries, including Amy Cheney Beach, Cécile Chaminade, and Edward MacDowell. [New York Public Library]

was in essence a return engagement; her New York debut came on January 31, 1885, with a performance of Anton Rubinstein's Concerto in D Minor conducted by Frank Van der Stücken. During the 1884–1885 season, she also appeared in a series of concerts with the Boston Symphony Orchestra under Wilhelm Gericke and the New York Symphony under Walter Damrosch.

On October 18, 1885, she married her second cousin Sigmund Zeisler. Sigmund Zeisler had met the pianist during her early Vienna years and, after completing a J.D. at the University of Vienna, followed her to Chicago. He then earned an LL.B. at Northwestern University before acting as defense cocounsel in the explosive trial of the Haymarket Riot "anarchists." The couple had their first child, Leonard, in 1886, followed by sons Paul, born in 1897, and

Ernest, born in 1899. The Zeislers maintained a German American home in which High German was spoken. Although they were nonpracticing Jews, both belonged to Jewish clubs, associated with prominent Jewish leaders and artists, and supported Reform Judaism.

Despite her husband's wishes that she settle down to a domestic life, Zeisler returned to Vienna by fall 1888 for a five-month "refresher course" with Leschetizky. Her determination to excel paid off within the next decade, when she solidified artistic relationships with the orchestras of New York, Boston, Chicago, and Pittsburgh, performed at the Columbian Exposition of 1893, toured Europe, and appeared in numerous recitals throughout the United States, including an 1896 West Coast tour that featured seven different programs in eighteen days.

Although "nervous prostrations" had cut short her first European tour of 1893–1894, her triumphs during this and the following season in Europe marked a career turning point. By 1896, American writers were dubbing her "America's greatest virtuoso" and, at times, the "Sarah Bernhardt of the piano." Zeisler performed in England in 1898 and returned to the Continent in 1902 and 1912.

By the end of her career, Zeisler had appeared with major American and European orchestras under the prominent conductors Camille Chevillard, Walter Damrosch, Victor Herbert, Artur Nikisch, Anton Seidl, Leopold Stokowski, Richard Strauss, and Theodore Thomas. She had given regular solo recitals in major American concert halls, including annual appearances at Carnegie Hall, and had shared the stage with prominent concert artists. In addition to the then-standard concert repertoire, some of which she recorded for the Welte-Mignon and Ampico recording pianos, she promoted works of contemporary American and European composers. Two imposing programs put the final touches on an eminent career. In February 1920, in a single evening at Chicago's Orchestra Hall, she overwhelmed her audience with three concertos (Mozart's C Minor, Chopin's F Minor, and Tchaikovsky's B-flat Minor). She did a repeat performance at Carnegie Hall. On February 25, 1925, she celebrated the fiftieth anniversary of her early debut with performances of the Schumann A Minor and Chopin F Minor concertos with the Chicago Orchestra.

As performer and teacher, Zeisler was a central transmitter of Leschetizky's high standards of pianism and artistry (preceding the Leschetizky-trained Paderewski on the American scene) and a widely publicized role model for two generations of young American musicians, many of them female. Her successes, built on her Viennese training, were buttressed by an uncannily strong will and by ideals of hard work and achievement instilled by her family.

Fannie Bloomfield Zeisler died of a heart attack on August 20, 1927, at age sixty-four. She was eulogized as a "truly great and noble woman" whose vigorous, intense life was filled with "idealism, indomitable courage, remitless industry, [and] absolute sincerity."

SELECTED WORKS BY FANNIE BLOOMFIELD ZEISLER

"Appearing in Public." In *Great Pianists on Piano Playing*, edited by James Francis Cooke (1913); "Public to Blame for Blind Worship of European Fetish." *Musical America* (October 1914); "Woman in Music." *American Art Journal* 58 (1891): 1–3.

BIBLIOGRAPHY

Allais, Paul, Ella Snell Gara, Nellie Killiam, Rose H. Mergentheim, and Ernest Moeller. *Fannie Bloomfield Zeisler Appreciation* (1927); Ammer, Christine. *Unsung: A History of Women in American Music* (1980); Cohn, Harriet. "The Life and Career of Fannie Bloomfield Zeisler." Research paper, University of Cincinnati (1960); Cole, Rossetter. "Fannie Bloomfield Zeisler." *Studies in Musical Education, History and Aesthetics: Music Teachers' National Association Proceedings* 12 (1927): 26–38; *DAB*; Ehrlich, A. *Celebrated Pianists of the Past and Present* (1894); Fay, Amy. "Fannie Bloomfi[e]ld-Zeisler," *Music* 9 (1895): 224–225; Ffrench, Florence, comp. *Music and Musicians in Chicago* (1899); Gerig, Reginald R. *Famous Pianists and Their Techniques* (1974); Hallman, Diana R. "Bloomfield Zeisler: American Virtuoso of the Gilded Age" (in progress), and "The Pianist Fannie Bloomfield Zeisler in American Music and Society." Master's thesis, University of Maryland (1983); Lahee, Henry C. *Famous Pianists of Today and Yesterday* (1901); Mathews, William S.B. "A Great Pianist at Home." *Music* 9 (1895): 1–10; *New Grove Dictionary of Music and Musicians* (1980), *NAW*; Saville, Richard. "Madame Bloomfield-Zeisler." *Musician* 9 (January 1904): 5; Schonberg, Harold C. *The Great Pianists* (1963); Tracey, James M. "Some of the World's Greatest Women Pianists." *The Etude* 25 (December 1907): 773; *UJE*, s.v. "Fanny Bloomfield-Zeisler"; *Who's Who in America* (1899 and subsequent editions); Zeisler, Sigmund. "Fannie Bloomfield Zeisler." Biographical draft. AJA, Cincinnati, Ohio.

DIANA HALLMAN

ZIEGLER, DOROTHY MIRIAM (1922–1972)

Dorothy Miriam Ziegler's lifelong musical career began with violin lessons at age two. Actually, she had played the triangle in her father's municipal band even earlier. "I can't remember any time when I wasn't playing something," she said in a 1967 *Miami Herald* interview. During her distinguished career, she made her mark as an orchestral trombonist, pianist, opera coach, and conductor.

She was born in Muscatine, Iowa, on July 20, 1922, the first child of Elmer Ziegler and Wilma Busch, who were both of German descent. Her father was a musician, bandmaster, and music store owner. Her mother taught music and played piano, clarinet, and oboe. Her younger brother, Frederic, played the tuba and drums while serving in the United States Navy.

Her parents taught her to play many instruments, but as a teenager Ziegler excelled at trombone and piano, winning honors at state and national music conventions. After graduating from Muscatine High

School in 1939, she attended the Eastman School of Music in Rochester, New York, where in 1943 she earned a bachelor of music degree with distinction, with a double major in trombone and piano.

Her performances on trombone in the All-America Youth Orchestra under Leopold Stokowski during 1940 and the Tanglewood Music Center Orchestra under Serge Koussevitzky from 1941 to 1942 paved the way to her first professional job as trombonist with the National Symphony Orchestra, in Washington, D.C., for the 1943–1944 season.

In 1944, she won the principal trombone position with the St. Louis Symphony. At the same time, she continued to study with pianist Earl Wild, and in 1946 she received a master of music degree as a piano major from the University of Southern California. In 1947, she earned a performance certificate from the American Conservatory, France, where she studied with Robert and Gaby Casadesus.

A turning point in Ziegler's career came in 1947, when she was hired as the St. Louis Grand Opera Guild's accompanist. Thereafter, her most significant work was as a vocal coach and conductor, primarily of opera. In 1955, she became the guild's conductor and artistic director, a post she held until 1964. She also directed the Washington University Opera Theater from 1951 to 1958 and the Kirkwood, Illinois, Symphony Orchestra from 1963 to 1965. Her innovative "music minus one" recording, *Your Rehearsal Accompanist* (1962), was widely used by instrumental and vocal soloists.

In 1957, she attended the Juilliard Institute for Opera Conductors, and in 1961 she won an American Symphony Orchestra League Award to study with conductor Max Rudolph.

During her twenty years with the St. Louis Symphony, Ziegler taught at the St. Louis Institute of Music, Washington University, and the University of Southern Illinois, but in 1964 she left St. Louis to teach at Indiana University, where she directed the Indiana University Opera Theater. During the 1965–1966 season, she was the vocal coach for the Metropolitan Opera National Company. At various times, she coached such opera stars as Grace Bumbry, Robert Rounseville, and Eugene Holmes.

In 1966, she accepted a teaching position at the University of Miami, Florida, primarily to direct the University of Miami Opera Theater from 1966 to 1971. While in Florida, she played trombone in the University of Miami faculty brass quintet, the Fort Lauderdale Symphony, the Miami Opera Guild, and the Miami Beach Symphony, and often served as accompanist for the Israeli soprano Shoshana Shoshan.

In 1970, Ziegler went to Moscow to accompany three opera singers in the Tchaikovsky International Competition. She was a member of Sigma Alpha Iota music fraternity, the National Society of Arts and Letters, the National Association of Teachers of Singing, the American Symphony Orchestra League, and the American Federation of Musicians.

Ziegler's most significant achievements were in areas in which women are rarely seen: as orchestral trombonist and opera conductor. Overcoming such gender stereotypes took prodigious talent and tireless dedication to music. Dorothy Miriam Ziegler died of cancer on March 1, 1972, in South Miami, Florida at age forty-nine.

BIBLIOGRAPHY

Madison Capital Times, October 7, 1967; Obituary. *Miami Herald*, March 2, 1972; Reno, Doris. *Miami Herald*, November 12, 1967; Weatherly, Robert. Telephone interview with author, 1996; Weldon, Constance. Telephone interview with author, 1996; Ziegler, Dorothy. *Your Rehearsal Accompanist*. (1962), and Ziegler file. School of Music Archives, University of Miami; Ziegler, Frederick [brother of Dorothy Ziegler]. Letter to author, April 13, 1996.

SUSAN FLEET

ZIONISM

The modern movement of Zionism began in the nineteenth century and had as its goal the return of the Jewish people to the Land of Israel. Scholars have often noted that the cultural and political contexts of the United States shaped and informed the particular directions and boundaries of the American branch of the movement. American Zionism, unlike its European counterpart, tended to shun political activity, for the conditions that propelled political Zionism elsewhere—Jewish homelessness and persecution—did not apply to American Jews themselves. American Zionists never subscribed to the European Zionist emphasis upon *shelilat ha-golah* [the negation of the diaspora]. Instead, American Zionism consistently portrayed the movement as faithful to democratic and social ideals and argued that the highest ideal of Zionism—social justice for the persecuted remnants of the Jewish people in Europe and elsewhere—was identical with the ethos that animated the American nation.

The American setting caused most early American Zionists to regard education and philanthropy and not immigration to *Eretz Yisrael* or Jewish statehood as the decisive Zionist acts, and through the influence of men such as Solomon Schechter and Mordecai Kaplan many also came to regard Zionism as a crucial bulwark against American Jewish assimilation.

In these accounts of the American Zionist narrative, sufficient attention has seldom been paid to the distinctive roles occupied by women. However, novel ways for understanding and defining the nature of the American movement emerge through the adoption of a more inclusionary approach that focuses upon the historical experiences of women as well as one that employs the category of gender—the socially and culturally constructed aspects of the divisions of the sexes—as a decisive variable in the historical analysis of American Zionism. For even as American Zionist women shared a common Jewish heritage with their fathers, husbands, brothers, and sons, they also constructed an approach to American Zionism that reflected their own unique position in American and Jewish society. A complex interplay of gender, social class, and religio-ethnic culture shaped the ways in which women helped to direct the course of Zionism in America, and a proper history must take all these factors into account in presenting developments and trends that marked the movement.

While scholars have frequently labeled mid-nineteenth-century European men such as Moses Hess and Rabbi Zvi Hirsch Kalischer as *m'vasrei tziyon* [forerunners of Zionism], the American Jewish poet and writer EMMA LAZARUS surely merits this appellation as well. Stirred to Jewish consciousness by the Russian pogroms of the early 1880s and the subsequent plight of Eastern European Jewry, the aristocratic Lazarus, whose familial roots in America extended back to the 1700s, called for the rebirth of the Jewish nation on its ancestral soil in both poetry and prose. In her 1882–1883 prose work "An Epistle to the Hebrews," published in the *American Hebrew*, Lazarus promoted a proto-Zionist vision that predated and paralleled the Zionist position adavanced a decade later in the writings of Theodor Herzl. Lazarus wrote, "What we need to-day . . . is the building up of our national, physical force. . . . For nearly nineteen hundred years we have been living on an idea. . . . Our body has become starved and emaciated beyond recognition. . . . Let our first care to-day be the re-establishment of our physical strength, the reconstruction of our national organism, so that in the future, where the respect due to us cannot be won by entreaty, it may be commanded, and where it cannot be commanded, it may be enforced."

ROSA SONNESCHEIN, publisher and editor of the *AMERICAN JEWESS* between 1895 and 1899, echoed many of the Zionist themes that Lazarus had articulated and became one of the earliest supporters of Herzl on American soil. In the April 1897 issue of her journal, Sonnenschein wrote an article entitled "What Jew Has Not Dreamed of Seeing Israel Restored as a Nation—Of a New, Free, Great, and Glorious Judah?" Later that year, she was invited by Herzl to attend the First Zionist Congress in Basel as the representative of the *American Jewess*.

As Zionism began to attract a growing number of American adherents, the bulk of American Jewish women Zionists expressed their support of the nascent Zionist movement through organizations that were by and large—though not exclusively—segregated by gender. Shortly after the 1913 establishment of the American branch of the Orthodox Zionist organization Mizrachi, Orthodox Zionist women formed the Mizrachi Women's Organization of America and sought to rebuild the Jewish homeland on the basis of traditional Orthodoxy by serving "the physical, social, educational, and spiritual needs of refugee and native youth." In 1926, American women committed to the cause and principles of Labor Zionism established PIONEER WOMEN and attempted to "arouse public opinion on behalf of the rescue of our people" by advancing a humanitarian and "progressive social vision." By engaging in these activities, the women in these organizations championed causes that were consonant with the image the larger society held of women as nurturers.

Foremost among all these groups was HADASSAH. The goals and objectives of Hadassah were akin to those that animated the other groups, and an analysis of the methods and style that Hadassah women employed to achieve their organizational aims reveals the distinctive role that women's organizations came to play in the unfolding and development of American Zionism. Hadassah had its origins in study circles organized by EMMA LEON GOTTHEIL, the wife of Richard Gottheil, an ardent Zionist and Columbia University professor of Semitics. Gottheil accompanied her husband to the Second Zionist Congress in 1898 and was charged by Herzl himself to organize American Jewish women on behalf of the Zionist cause. She responded by establishing chapters of the Daughters of Zion as an affiliate of the Federation of American Zionists. These study groups soon dotted the New York area and attracted to their ranks outstanding young women such as JESSIE ETHEL SAMPTER and LOTTA LEVENSOHN, who were destined in later decades to become prominent American Zionist figures. The women who participated in these study circles saw their devotion to Palestine and Zionism as a means of redress for the problems of social inequality that dominated the Progressive agenda and spirit of the time.

In 1907, the well-known and highly regarded HENRIETTA SZOLD became an active member of the

Harlem study group known as Hadassah Circle. Szold traveled to Palestine in 1909. There she obtained a firsthand understanding of conditions in *Eretz Yisrael*. Appalled by the lack of medical and sanitary facilities in the nascent and growing *yishuv* [Jewish settlement], Szold resolved upon her return to the United States to alleviate the effects of disease, starvation, and homelessness that existed there by establishing health programs and facilities for Jews and Arabs alike. Though Szold served in 1910 as honorary secretary to the male-dominated American Federation of Zionists, that group's financial chaos caused her to ignore it and to turn instead to women Zionists in Daughters of Zion and Hadassah study circles for support. A constitution for the Hadassah organization was drawn up in 1912. While formally affiliated with the Federation of American Zionists, Hadassah insisted upon maintaining control of its own affairs—much to the consternation of several male critics who found it inappropriate that women express their independence in this way.

Hadassah ignored these critics and built its programs and activities on a heritage of Jewish philanthropy as well as upon the charitable and organizational model provided by the U.S. women's club movement of the Progressive Era. Chapters were soon formed throughout the United States, and memoirs authored by women throughout the country during these years testify to the universal success and status Hadassah enjoyed throughout the American Jewish community. Membership in Hadassah and participation in its projects and activities became a fixed part of the civic duties in which thousands of American Jewish women engaged.

With the financial support of Nathan and Lina Straus, Hadassah sought to offer preventive health care to Jewish settlers and natives alike by sending two nurses—ROSE KAPLAN and RACHEL [RAE D.] LANDY—to Palestine in 1912. Bertha Landsmen, a public health nurse trained in New York, followed in the footsteps of Kaplan and Landy; she sought to reduce the soaring infant mortality rates that then obtained in Palestine by offering free layettes and pasteurized milk to parents who gave birth in Rothschild Hospital as well as by improving sanitary conditions at childbirth by educating midwives.

The success of these early endeavors caused the Federation of American Zionists to charge Hadassah in 1916 with responsibility for raising the then seemingly insurmountable sum of twenty-five thousand dollars for the creation of an American Zionist Medical Unit (AZMU) in Palestine. Undaunted by the challenge, Szold called on each Hadassah woman throughout the country to save on carfares and contribute fifteen cents in support of the project. Her fund-raising technique mobilized thousands of women on behalf of the Zionist enterprise, and Hadassah soon exceeded its goal by contributing thirty thousand dollars for the AZMU.

The participatory and grass-roots model of philanthropy established by this activity served as a model for the fund-raising projects of other organizations as well as for Hadassah itself. For example, Mizrachi Women held frequent luncheons where individuals offered small donations for the support of religious institutions and orphanages as well as children's homes and religious kibbutzim in Palestine. The Women's League for Palestine, established in the early 1920s by Emma Gottheil, also utilized comparable fund-raising techniques for the creation of vocational schools and residences for young Jewish refugee women when they arrived in Palestine.

However, Hadassah retained its position as the preeminent organization of Zionist women in America throughout this entire period. In 1921–1922, Hadassah made an appeal to religious school pupils in the United States to "give a penny so a child in Jerusalem can eat." By 1923, schools in Jerusalem were able to provide hot lunches for all their students. In the 1930s, Hadassah likewise garnered financial support for the Youth Aliyah project designed to bring Jewish refugee children to Palestine by gathering its membership together in hundreds of weekly or monthly chapter tea or parlor meetings throughout the United States. At these meetings, each woman was asked to donate a few dollars until the chapter goal of $360 was achieved. In this way, Hadassah quickly reached its national goal of sixty thousand dollars. All of this reflects the central role women now occupied in American Zionism, and Hadassah became arguably the most powerful Zionist organization in the world by the 1930s.

The humanitarian and social concerns these organizations addressed were viewed as logical public extensions of traditional female domestic responsibilities, and through Hadassah and other groups women were allowed to take their skills and talents out of the home in a socially approved manner. Participants in these organizations eroded the boundaries between public and private domains by transforming issues originally of private concern into matters of societal import, in a particularly Jewish and political arena.

To be sure, such expansion did not receive universal approbation. From the outset, Hadassah had more

The story of how American women participated in and shaped Zionism in America has yet to be fully told. What is clear, however, is that they were active and vocal participants from the earliest years of the movement. The Women's Organization for the Pioneer Women of Palestine was officially founded in 1925. (It changed its name to PIONEER WOMEN *in 1939 and is today called Na'amat.) This early photograph of its leaders includes: left to right, standing—Leah Brown, Goldie Meyerson (*GOLDA MEIR*), Miriam Meltzer, and Nina Zuckerman; seated—Leah Biskin, Rahel Siegel, Fiegel Berkinblitt. Insert, Chaya Ehrenreich.*

than its share of male critics who were outraged by the independence it displayed. This attitude reached its zenith in 1926–1928, when Louis Lipsky, president of the Zionist Organization of America (ZOA), was enraged by the refusal of Hadassah and its president, IRMA LEVY LINDHEIM, to cosign a bank loan for the United Palestine Appeal of the ZOA. Lindheim publicly criticized the ZOA for what she regarded as its poor organization and fiscal irresponsibility, and she demanded increased Hadassah representation to the Congress of the ZOA. In response, Lipsky called for the National Board of the ZOA to rebuke Lindheim. The board rejected his request and even went so far as to express a vote of public confidence in Lindheim. Lipsky then turned to the pages of the Zionist journal *New Palestine* to attack Hadassah; he accused Lindheim of abandoning the principles of Henrietta Szold,

"who recognized the proper role of women within the ranks of the ZOA." Such gender-based critique caused Szold herself to respond, and she asserted that she saw nothing "unwomanly" in the positions Lindheim championed. Szold maintained that Hadassah had every right to play an independent role in Zionist affairs. In affirming their right to speak out autonomously on public issues, Lindheim and Szold expanded the range of appropriate public behavior for females. The entire affair testifies to the strength and power of Hadassah as well as the public role of authority conferred upon women in the American movement.

So empowered, other women claimed positions of public responsibility and leadership within American Zionist circles. Minette Baum, trained at Jane Addams's Hull House, served as president of the Fort Wayne

Zionist District from 1919 to 1935, one of the first women in America to occupy such a position in a male-dominated Zionist organization. Others such as Lotta Levensohn and Jesse Sampter did not hesitate to defend publicly the institution of the kibbutz from the critiques of more conservative American men in the 1920s and 1930s who attacked it as a source of socialism and immorality. Indeed, Sampter, in the pages of *New Palestine*, boldly called for groups of American *halutzim* [pioneers] to make aliyah and join the pioneers already there in the formation of a new society based on equality, justice, and cooperation.

These women were animated by a dual Jewish-American heritage that was often informed and shaped by a specific feminine sensibility. Lindheim herself, the daughter of an affluent German-American Jewish anti-Zionist family, described the moment of her conversion to the Zionist cause in 1923 in the following way: "I am an American. . . . I am a Jew. . . . Instead of an enigma to myself, am I therefore not doubly blessed, doubly responsible? What better fulfillment than to take my place with those who have suffered for centuries for their beliefs? To share in rebuilding a national life in the land where our forefathers held that very concept of freedom, equality, brotherhood on which the greatness of America—my America?—is built? . . . In that moment, . . . Zionism reached out to me and took my hand." Sampter expressed similar sentiments in her poetry, and other American Jewish women—both foreign- and native-born—shared their vision. Eastern European native GOLDA MEIR, informed by the tenets and visions of Labor Zionism, left America to join Kibbutz Merhavyah in 1921. Twenty-five-year-old American-born Hannah Hoffman, the daughter of a New Jersey Conservative rabbi and a graduate of Smith College, traveled to Palestine in 1925 over the objections of her family and became a pioneer at Tel Joseph; when asked to explain what motivated her decision to become perhaps the first native American *halutzah* [female pioneer] in Palestine, she stated, "It was a question of youth, an American tradition, 100 percent pure American tradition. I felt that I was a Pioneer. The early settlers went West to build up the country—I would go to Palestine. I see many things similar in the thoughts and traditions of America and Israel. Pioneerism and interest in the Bible influenced me to come to Palestine."

By the 1930s, the integral role that women had come to occupy in American Zionism was assured. The impact Zionism had upon the lives of these women, young and old alike catapulted such women as SHOSHANA CARDIN into positions of prominence in American Jewish life. The role these women had come to play in the life of the American movement is captured in the memoirs of former New York congresswoman BELLA ABZUG, who recalled that in 1932, "when I was 12, I joined Hashomer Hatzair [the Young Guard], a Zionist Youth Organization. From then on, I was an enthusiastic Zionist who dreamed of working in a kibbutz, helping to build a Jewish national home in what was then called Palestine. Dressed in brown uniforms and ties, my friends and I rode the subways and stood in the cold on street corners, collecting pennies for our cause. It was my first venture into political campaigning, and also my first experience as a leader."

Jewish women were active participants in American Zionism from the earliest years of the movement on these shores. From the time of Emma Lazarus, women expressed the greatest yearnings of the movement, and others such as Hannah Hoffman and Jesse Sampter participated in and described the pioneering dimensions of the Zionist cause. These women moved fluidly between private and public life, and they placed areas of great concern to their own lives as American Jewish women onto the Zionist public and political agenda. Informed by Jewish and American values, and conscious of their place as women in society, they often made their greatest contributions to the Zionist cause through gender-specific Zionist organizations, and the political success they enjoyed through these organizations frequently allowed them to bend the public course of American Zionism to their wills and voices. At the same time, figures ranging from Henrietta Szold and Minette Baum through Mary Ann Stein, president of the New Israel Fund in the 1990s, occupied leadership positions in general Zionist organizatons as well. The full story of how American women participated in and shaped the American contours of Zionism has yet to be fully told.

BIBLIOGRAPHY

Fineman, Irving. *Woman of Valor: The Life of Henrietta Szold, 1860–1915* (1961); Geller, L.D. *The Alice L. Selisberg and Rose G. Jacobs Papers in the Hadassah Archives, 1918–1957* (1984), and *The Henrietta Szold Papers in the Hadassah Archives, 1875–1965* (1982); Hoffman, Leon F. *Ideals and Illusions: The Story of an Ivy League Woman in 1920s Israel* (1992); Levin, Marlin. *Balm in Gilead: The Story of Hadassah* (1973); Marcus, Jacob R. *The American Jewish Woman: A Documentary History* (1981); Miller, Harriet. *The Biography of Minette Baum* (1975); Udin, Sophie A., ed. *The Palestine Year Book*. Vol. 1 (1944–1945); Umansky, Ellen M., and Diane Ashton, eds. *Four Centuries of Jewish Women's Spirituality* (1992); Urofsky, Melvin. *American Zionism from Herzl to the Holocaust* (1975).

DAVID ELLENSON

ZOLOTOW, CHARLOTTE (b. 1917)

Charlotte Zolotow's over seventy books for children have established her as an influential twentieth-century author. Her best-known story is *William's Doll*, which was produced as a short film and as a song for the popular children's album *Free to Be . . . You and Me*.

Zolotow makes an effort to see, hear, and think as a child, an empathetic skill she calls "a common respect for the child." Though some of Zolotow's books do approach difficult topics such as gender roles, death, single parents, and conflict, her literary prowess is most apparent in her ability to capture a sensory or emotional experience and translate it into a dynamic, poetic story.

As an editor, Zolotow works with books for all ages of children, but she prefers to write picture books. She is excited by the additional dimension of storytelling that an illustrator can add, and she has an editorial talent for matching illustrators and authors. Her own books have been illustrated by accomplished artists including Garth Williams, Maurice Sendak, and H.A. Rey.

Judaism does not play an obvious role in Zolotow's writing. She does, however, feel that the warm extended families who populate her books are echoes of the Orthodox Jewish culture of her own family.

Charlotte (Shapiro) Zolotow, born to Louis J. and Ella (Bernstein) Shapiro on June 26, 1915, in Norfolk, Virginia, grew up in New York City. She studied literature at the University of Wisconsin from 1933 to 1936, worked briefly at a collector's bookshop, then joined Harper & Row, where she was Children's Division senior editor from 1938 to 1944 and from 1962 to 1976. In 1938, she married writer Maurice Zolotow (whom she divorced in 1969). The couple had two children, Stephen and Ellen (children's author Crescent Dragonwagon). Harper published her first book, *The Park Book*, in 1944. Zolotow was Junior Books Division vice president and associate publisher from 1976 to 1981 and became Charlotte Zolotow Books Division consultant and editorial director in 1981. She has lectured at writers' conferences at the University of Colorado and Indiana University, and is a member of the PEN Authors League.

Zolotow's awards include *The New York Herald Tribune* Spring Festival Honor for *Indian, Indian* (1952); Caldecott honors for *The Storm Book* and *Mr. Rabbit and the Lovely Present* (1953 and 1963, respectively); American Library Association notable citations for *Mr. Rabbit and the Lovely Present, William's Doll, My Grandson Lew,* and *Do You Know What I'll Do?; New York Times* outstanding book of the year and *School Library Journal* best book of the year awards for *William's Doll* (1972); *Redbook* awards for *William's Doll* and *I Know A Lady* (1984 and 1985 respectively); the Christopher Award for *My Grandson Lew* (1984). Zolotow also received the LMP Award, R.R. Bowker (1990); and the American Library Association tribute (1991). Her newest title is *Who Is Ben?*

SELECTED WORKS BY CHARLOTTE ZOLOTOW

For an extensive bibliography of writings by Charlotte Zolotow, see *Something about the Author,* volume 78.

BIBLIOGRAPHY

American Women Writers: A Critical Reference Guide from Colonial Times to the Present. Edited by Lynne Langdon Faust (1983); Arbuthnot, May Hill, and Zena Sutherland. *Children and Books.* 4th ed. (1972); Bader, Barbara. *American Picturebooks from Noah's Ark to the Beast Within* (1976); Carpenter, Humphrey, and Mari Prichard. *Oxford Companion to Children's Literature* (1984); *Children's Literature Review.* Vol. 2 (1976); *Contemporary Authors, New Revision Series.* Vol. 38 (1993); *Dictionary of Literary Biography.* Vol. 52, *American Writers for Children since 1960: Fiction* (1986); Hopkins, Lee Bennett. *Books Are by People* (1969); Huck, Charlotte. *Children's Literature.* 3d ed. (1978), and *Children's Literature in the Elementary School* (1976); Rudman, Masha K. *Children's Literature.* 2d ed. (1976); *Something about the Author: Facts and Pictures about Authors and Illustrators of Books for Young People.* Vol. 78. Edited by Kevin S. Hile (1994); *Twentieth-Century Children's Writers.* 4th ed. Edited by Laura Standley Berger (1995); Wintle, Justin, and Emma Fisher. *The Pied Pipers: Interviews with the Influential Creators of Children's Literature* (1974).

LEAH OPPENHEIM

ZUNSER, MIRIAM SHOMER (1882–1951)

Miriam Shomer Zunser, journalist, playwright, and artist, was an important promoter of Jewish culture in America during the period before World War II. Born Manya Shaikevitsch in Odessa on November 25, 1882, she was the daughter of the well-known novelist and playwright Nokhem Mayer Shaikevitsch (Shomer) and Dinneh Bercinsky. The family immigrated to New York in 1889, where Miriam attended public school. After graduation, she worked as a librarian while studying drawing and art at the Jewish Educational Alliance under Henry McBride. In Europe, and later in America, she was surrounded by the leading lights of the Yiddish literary world. She became a contributor to publications such as the

Yidishes Tageblat [Jewish daily news] and *American Weekly Jewish News*, where she wrote for the women's pages, often on feminist themes and in support of suffrage. In 1905, she married Charles Zunser, the son of the folk bard Eliakum Zunser. The couple had three children.

Later in life, Zunser began a career as a Yiddish playwright, usually in collaboration with her sister Rose Shomer Bachelis. In 1921, they authored *Ayne fun Folk*, billed in English as *One of the Many*, which was among the first Yiddish plays written by women. Starring BERTHA KALICH, it was received with critical acclaim. They followed with two more Yiddish plays, *Sirkus Meydl* [Circus girl, 1928], which starred MOLLY PICON, and *In di Hent fun Gezets* [In the hands of the law] as well as an operetta, *Der Zingendiker Ganef* [The singing thief], starring Ludwig Satz. Zunser also wrote several plays in English, including *Goldenlocks and the Bears*, which appeared on Broadway.

Active in Zionist affairs, Zunser founded a Brooklyn chapter of HADASSAH. She was also a delegate to the first AMERICAN JEWISH CONGRESS, convened by her brother Abraham Shomer. In 1932, she founded MAILAMM, an organization designed to promote Jewish music in Palestine and the United States, which became the Jewish Music Forum in 1942. Her memoir *Yesterday* appeared in 1939. She died in October 1951.

SELECTED WORKS BY
MIRIAM SHOMER ZUNSER

Yesterday: A Memoir of a Russian Jewish Family (1939. 2d ed. edited by Emily Wortis Leider, 1978); *Unzer Foter Shomer*, with Rose Shomer Bachelis (1950).

BIBLIOGRAPHY

WWIAJ (1938); Zunser, Miriam Shomer. Papers. New York Public Library.

ERIC L. GOLDSTEIN

Appendices

Annotated Bibliography and Guide to Archival Resources on the History of Jewish Women in America

Phyllis Holman Weisbard

This bibliography concentrates on books, chapters in anthologies, and periodical articles on the collective history of American Jewish women as well as archival resources on individuals and women's organizations. While much relevant information can be found in publications from collateral branches of American history that focus on women, Jews, labor, immigrants, radicals, ethnicity, organizations, the early twentieth century working class and the mid-century middle class, as well as from the fields of women's studies and American literature, these can only be hinted at below. For citations to material in American history periodicals, see *America: History and Life* (Santa Barbara, CA: ABC-CLIO Press and computer file). For coverage of Jewish communal studies and other relevant research in American Jewish history, consult *Judaica Americana: An Annotated Bibliography of Publications From 1960–1990*, by Nathan M. Kaganoff (Brooklyn, NY: Carlson, 1995), compiled from columns by Kaganoff that appeared in *American Jewish History*; the "Judaica Americana" column since 1994, compiled by Jonathan D. Sarna; and *Judaica Americana: A Bibliography of Publications to 1900*, by Robert Singerman (New York: Greenwood, 1990); as well as *Index to Jewish Periodicals* (Cleveland: 1963–, print and online publication). Similarly, the recent outpouring on contemporary Jewish women's lives, writings, and role in American Judaism is beyond the scope of this bibliography. Developments in this area are best followed by reading *Lilith: The Independent Jewish Magazine, Bridges: A Journal for Jewish Feminists and Our Friends, Hadassah Magazine*, and denominational periodicals aimed at women. The view from women's studies can be traced by using *Women Studies Abstracts* (New York: Rush Publishing Company, 1972–present in print and online for citations since 1984 in *Women's Resources International* [Baltimore, NISC], *Feminist Periodicals: A Current Listing of Contents* (Madison: University of Wisconsin System Women's Studies Librarian, 1980–present), and other indexes to the field in print and online. For material on individual women, see the bibliographic suggestions at the end of their entries.

The bibliography begins with annotated entries for books, followed by a section of articles published in periodicals and anthologies. In general, articles that were subsequently incorporated into books described in the first section are not listed. A third section covers collective works that sample the autobiographical and creative writings and record the oral histories of Jewish women since their arrival in America. Major archival resources are described in the last section.

BOOKS

Antler, Joyce. *The Journey Home: Jewish Women and the American Century*. New York: Free Press, 1997. 410 p.

Recounts the lives of more than fifty high achievers involved in major public issues of the twentieth century:

immigration, social reform, political radicalism, Zionism, emergence of popular culture, professionalism, internationalism, Cold War culture and politics, feminism, and post-feminism. Antler weaves a social history from the fabric of women's lives, from iconoclastic *American Jewess* editor Rosa Sonneschein to Ruth Bader Ginsburg, who accepted nomination to the United States Supreme Court by saying that she hoped to be all her mother would have been had she been born in an age when women could aspire and daughters were cherished as much as sons. Each of these accomplished writers, activists, and entertainers had to confront the Jewish, American, and female aspects of her identity, and they arrived at different resolutions. Antler asserts that Jewish feminism has made it possible for many Jewish women to be both assertively Jewish and imbued with a feminist consciousness. This is a lively cross-over book that can be read and enjoyed both by scholars and general readers.

Balka, Christie, and Andy Rose, eds. *Twice Blessed: On Being Lesbian, Gay, and Jewish.* Boston: Beacon Press, 1989. 305 p.

Part Two, "Reclaiming Our History," includes an oral history by Jeffrey Shandler of Gerry Faier, a great-grandmother who was involved with the gay liberation movement of the 1970s and at the time of the interview was active with SAGE (Senior Action in a Gay Environment). The interview reveals her personal devotion to her Jewish cultural heritage. Other essays cover new ways to approach traditional Jewish texts and the absence of lesbian and gay experience from recorded Jewish history.

Baskin, Judith R., ed. *Women of the Word: Jewish Women and Jewish Writing.* Detroit: Wayne State University Press, 1994. 382 p.

A companion to *Jewish Women in Historical Perspective* (1991), also edited by Baskin, this volume explores the lives of women in different times and places through literature. Many deal with American Jewish writers. Norma Fain Pratt provides an abridged and somewhat altered version of her article originally published in *American Jewish History* and reprinted in *Decades of Discontent* recovering the names and work of more than fifty Yiddish women writers. The meager number of poets and poems by women in the canonical anthology *Finf Hundert Yor Yidishe Poezye* [Five hundred years of Yiddish poetry], by M. Bassin (1917) are compared by Kathryn Hellerstein to the seventy poets and range of poetry found in *Yidishe Dikhterins: Antologye* [Yiddish women poets: An anthology], by Ezra Korman (1928). Janet Burstein examines three women's writings from the 1920s (Rebekah Kohut's autobiography *My Portion* [1925], Elizabeth G. Stern's fictive memoir *I Am a Woman—and a Jew* [1926], and Emanie Sach's novel *Red Damask* [1927]) that bring the experience of the mother to center stage, and Laura Wexler demonstrates why Anzia Yezierska deserves to be better known. Sarah Blacher Cohen calls Cynthia Ozick a "prophet of parochialism," while Carole S. Kessner probes

the zealous identification with the Jewish people exhibited by Emma Lazarus and her spiritual daughter, Marie Syrkin, with reference to Ozick as well. Sara Horowitz respectfully considers the meaning of memory and testimony in the memoirs and oral histories of women Holocaust survivors, many of whom settled in America. These essays, while fully grounded in feminist theory, literary criticism, and Jewish sensibilities, are written to be read by anyone interested in understanding the writers and writing of *Women of the Word*.

Baum, Charlotte, Paula Hyman, and Sonya Michel. *The Jewish Woman in America.* New York: Dial Press, 1976. 290 p.

Groundbreaking study that made many American Jewish women aware of their rich history but received little attention from the academic Jewish studies community ostensibly because it was aimed at a popular audience and lacked footnotes. It does makes use of memoirs, contemporary newspapers and reports, archival material, interviews, and especially literary sources, all of which are listed in an extensive bibliography. Chapters examine the traditional Jewish attitude toward women, assimilationist German Jewish immigrants, robust working women of the Eastern European migration and the life they made in America, union activism, the complex and ambiguous relationship between "Uptown" German Jewish women and the "Downtown" Eastern Europeans, and the evolving image of Jewish women in literature, including the shift from veneration of the *Yiddishe mame* to vituperation for the overbearing Jewish mother and her materialistic Jewish American Princess daughter. Concludes that no single set of characteristics does justice to American Jewish women, who should draw upon the strength of the heritage of Jewish womanhood to fight stereotypes and face modern challenges.

Burstein, Janet Handler. *Writing Mothers, Writing Daughters: Tracing the Maternal in Stories by American Jewish Women.* Urbana: University of Illinois Press, 1996. 205 p.

Analyzes successive generations of twentieth-century authors writing in English on the mother-daughter theme. In her first four chapters, Burstein focuses on psychological dimensions; in the fifth and final chapter, her emphasis shifts to the influence of the history of Jewish women's political activism on the daughters. Chapters one and two are daughter-centered. The first describes literature by daughters of immigrants (by Mary Antin, Anzia Yezierska, Emma Goldman, and Kate Simon) in which the protagonists confront the effects of the gender imbalance within their immigrant families. The daughters desperately want to be subjects of their own lives rather than the subordinate objects their mothers are, yet they remain connected to the mothers and translate the mothers' stories into English. Chapter two concentrates on writers of the 1920s and 1930s, principally Tess Slesinger, Edna Ferber, and Fannie Hurst, who detach from home in order to differentiate themselves from their mothers and for whom the American part of their identity is critical. Mothers recover their own voices in the writing by Rebekah Kohut, Leah Morton, Tillie Olsen, and others discussed in the next chapter. Daughter-writers of the 1960s and 1970s (Cynthia Ozick, Anne Roiphe, Erica Jong, etc.), though influenced by the feminist movement, see their stories as mirroring their mothers. They do not like what they see and try to break away through sexual encounters and romantic love, which fail them. The last chapter reveals an integration of American/Jewish/woman aspects of identity in the writing of contemporary writers who look to the activist history of Jewish women as a source of inspiration and mothering.

Braunstein, Susan L., and Jenna Weissman Joselit, eds. *Getting Comfortable in New York: The American Jewish Home, 1980–1950*. New York: Jewish Museum, 1990. 110 p.

Catalog from 1990 exhibition at the Jewish Museum includes a personal reminiscence by Irving Howe and articles by Barbara Kirshenblatt-Gimblett and Joselit. Kirshenblatt-Gimblett's "Kitchen Judaism" is a careful reading of Yiddish and English cookbooks that demonstrates how food shapes social life and cultural values. She discusses books with non-kosher recipes, especially *Aunt Babette's Cookbook*, first published in 1889, kosher cookbooks, food columns in the Jewish newspapers and their subsequent compilation into books, and charity cookbooks, such as *The Settlement Cook Book*, revised and reprinted numerous times since its original appearance in 1901. Joselit focuses on the social implications of a communal reliance on domestic rituals as a vehicle for acculturation in "'A Set Table': Jewish Domestic Culture in the New World, 1880–1950." In her view (developed further in her *Wonders of America*), attention centered first on the physical aspects of domesticity (table settings, cleanliness of homes, etc.), then shifted to the promotion of home-based rituals to strengthen the family and appeal to children. Her evidence includes manuals on home observance directed at middle-class Jewish housewives, such as *The Jewish Woman and Her Home*, by Hyman Goldin (New York: Montauk Bookbinding, 1941), and *The Jewish Home Beautiful*, published that same year by the National Women's League of the United Synagogue of America. Copious photographs of material in the exhibition throughout.

Ewen, Elizabeth. *Immigrant Women in the Land of Dollars: Life and Culture on the Lower East Side, 1890–1925*. New York: Monthly Review Press, 1985. 303 p.

Examines the lives of two generations of working-class Jewish and Italian "unwitting pioneers" who were confronted with a rapidly expanding mass-production economy and consumer culture in America, conditions that devalued family and group bonds important in the Old Country, particularly to women. Daily life became a "theater of cultural conflict" for them, with criticism from social workers and Americanized children alike. Ewen is interested in the interplay of class with the status of belonging to an immigrant ethnic group, less in distinctions between the Jewish and Italian communities.

Feingold, Henry L., gen. ed. *The Jewish People in America*. 5 v. Baltimore: Johns Hopkins University Press, 1992.

This series of five separately authored books covering successive historical periods synthesizes much of the research on American Jewish women and incorporates it into a general history of Jews in America. The two volumes dealing with German and Eastern European immigration, which have received the most attention from historians of women's history, do an especially good job of integrating the research. These are *A Time for Gathering: The Second Migration, 1820–1880*, by Hasia R. Diner, and *A Time For Building: The Third Migration, 1880–1920*, by Gerald Sorin.

Fink, Greta. *Great Jewish Women: Profiles of Courageous Women From the Maccabean Period to the Present*. New York: Menorah, 1978. 197 p.

An example of efforts in the 1970s to restore women to history through discovering the lives of exceptional women. Women included (who lived some or all of their lives in America) are an eclectic bunch—from founders of Jewish women's organizations (Hannah G. Solomon and Henrietta Szold) and anarchist Emma Goldman to artist Louise Nevelson and cosmetic mogul Helena Rubinstein.

Fishman, Sylvia Barack. *A Breath of Life: Feminism in the American Jewish Community*. New York: Free Press, 1993. 308 p.

Based on analysis of the 1990 National Jewish Population Survey, interviews, and keen observations, Fishman argues that since the 1960s feminism has invigorated the American Jewish community. She covers the impact of the growing number of women rabbis and cantors in non-Orthodox branches of Judaism, new liturgy and life cycle rituals created by women, and options available to contemporary Jewish women. Also useful are the extensive appendices of statistical data from the survey, broken down by gender. Her earlier essay, "The Impact of Feminism on American Jewish Life," in the *American Jewish Year Book* 89 (1989): 3–62, was one of few in *Year Book* history to assess the role of Jewish women in American Jewish society, with Rebekah Kohut's "Jewish Women's Organizations in the United States," in the 1931/1932 *Year Book* (vol. 33, pp. 165–201) being another.

Foner, Philip S. *Women and the American Labor Movement: From Colonial Times to the Eve of World War I*. New York: Free Press, 1979. 621 p.

Eminent labor historian Foner traces the history of working women from colonial times to World War I. The contributions of Jewish women such as Clara Lemlich, Pauline Newman, Rose Schneiderman, Rebecca Saul, and Dora Landburg are critical to the development of the movement.

Excellent, detailed coverage of the succession of strikes that brought the women to the fore.

Friedman-Kasaba, Kathie. *Memories of Migration: Gender, Ethnicity, and Work in the Lives of Jewish and Italian Women in New York, 1870–1924.* Albany: State University of New York Press, 1996. 242 p.

Newest of several works (see Krause, Ewen, and Smith) on immigrant Jewish and Italian women. Sociologist Friedman-Kasaba draws from many disciplines—migration studies, feminist scholarship on gender, and ethnicity/race concerns—to demonstrate the complexity of what immigration meant for these women. The main question she poses is, "Was the experience empowering or disempowering?" She found there was no single unifying "immigrant experience." For married women and/or women with children in both groups, immigration disempowered most, while single women took more control over their own lives. Russian Jewish women had the advantage over the Italian women of assistance with vocational and Americanization training provided by German Jewish "co-ethnics," dubious though this help may have been at times. Whatever their background, Friedman-Kasaba regards immigrant women as active participants in migration and acculturation, engaged subjects rather than reactive objects of these processes. The academic prose and theoretical concerns make this a more difficult work to read than the earlier assessments.

Gay, Ruth. *Unfinished People: Eastern European Jews Encounter America.* New York: Norton, 1996. 310 p.

A mixture of personal remininiscences and material from published accounts, the chapter "Girls" vividly captures the persistence of negative attitudes toward girl children and women among the immigrant Jewish community.

Glantz, Rudolf. *The Jewish Woman in America: Two Female Immigrant Generations, 1820–1929.* Vol. 1, The Eastern European Jewish Women. Vol. 2, The German Jewish Woman. New York: Ktav for the National Council of Jewish Women, 1976–1977.

Published at the same time as the Baum-Hyman-Michel book by the same name, Glantz's two volumes are the inferior work, hampered by disconnected chapters, little attention to chronology, and inconsistent style. Yet his descriptions of nineteenth-century Jewish social life are instructive, and his use of contemporary periodicals, letters, and material from Jewish organizations, cited in extensive notes and bibliographies, provides historians with a glimpse into the primary sources available for the study of Jewish women in America.

Glenn, Susan A. *Daughters of the Shtetl: Life and Labor in the Immigrant Generation.* Ithaca, NY: Cornell University Press, 1990. 312 p.

Glenn's thesis is that Jewish women garment workers developed their own version of "new womanhood" activism based on cooperation and partnership with men, unlike middle-class Progressive "new women" who operated separately. She finds the roots of the Jewish brand of new womanhood in the conflicting shtetl legacy of the woman who could be breadwinner but not a leader in the shtetl power structure, because such roles were exclusively reserved for men; the socialist Bund, which tended toward gender equality; and the influence of the American notion of domesticity. This backdrop helps her explain convincingly why young Jewish women workers could be strike leaders one day, then nonworking wives and mothers the next, yet champions of full education and work roles for their daughters. Her argument is complex, knitting the strands of gender, ethnicity, labor, and the immigrant experience. Generous use of quotations from memoirs and oral histories personalizes the social history.

Goldman, Anne E. *Take My Word: Autobiographical Innovations of Ethnic American Working Women.* Berkeley: University of California Press, 1996. 237 p.

Goldman is interested in women's writing that falls outside the traditional boundaries of the literary canon or even literature as commonly understood. About a third of this study focuses on autobiographical writing of working-class Jewish women, in particular assessing how the women balance their need to present themselves as individuals yet represent Jewish culture. In contrast to the assimilationist narratives of Mary Antin, Elizabeth Stern, and others, Goldman finds that Jewish labor activists took a different approach. In effect, they substituted the language of class consciousness for ethnic affiliation. Her principal examples are Rose Pesotta's *Bread Upon the Waters* and Rose Schneiderman's *All for One*, with their intertwining histories of labor and self. Couched in the discourse of cultural studies, this is a difficult but rewarding read.

Gurock, Jeffrey S. and Marc Lee Raphael, eds. *An Inventory of Promises: Essays on American Jewish History in Honor of Moses Rischin.* Brooklyn: Carlson, 1995. 436 p.

This anthology is an excellent illustration of a sensitivity to women's history in recent scholarship. Unlike collections from earlier eras that ignored women's experiences and contributions to American Jewish life, or those more recent ones that sport a token women-focused essay, this one explicitly includes several. Jenna Weissman Joselit describes the vocational training of American Jewish women before the Depression, while Allon Gal tackles the political characteristics of Hadassah, the Women's Zionist Organization of America. Pamela S. Nadell discusses how rabbinic ordination for women was achieved, distinguishing between the "top-down" direction in which it came about in the Reform Movement from the "bottom-up" path taken among Conservatives. Norma Fain Pratt rediscovers "lost" first-generation immigrant Yiddish women writers who published poems and prose in the Yiddish press on themes ranging from sweatshop work to yearnings for full lives. William Toll looks at settlement work in western cities in the United States conducted by Jewish women trained in social work.

Heinze, Andrew. *Adapting to Abundance: Jewish Immigrants, Mass Consumption and the Search for American Identity.* New York: New York University Press, 1990. 276 p.

Particularly in Chapter Six, "Jewish Women and the Making of an American Home," Heinze demonstrates the critical role of women as "rulers of domestic consumption" in the successful adjustment of Jews to America. Makes virtues of the *balebosteh's* keen observation of American social standards for home decor, festive meals, and use of modern appliances, along with her sharp eye for bargains.

Henry, Sondra, and Emily Taitz. *Written Out of History: Our Jewish Foremothers.* New York: Biblio Press, 1990. 303 p.

First published by Bloch in 1978 under the title *Written Out of History: A Hidden Legacy of Jewish Women Revealed Through Their Writings and Letters*, this collection introduces general readers (including those fortunate to receive a copy as a bat mitzvah present) to the life stories of illustrious Jewish women throughout history. The biographies of only four Americans are among them, however: Rebecca Gratz, Penina Moïse, Emma Lazarus, and Rebekah Kohut. A new concluding chapter touches on events and new research on women's lives published since 1978.

Hyman, Paula. *Gender and Assimilation in Modern Jewish History: Roles and Representations of Women.* Seattle: University of Washington Press, 1995. 197 p.

General purpose of this book is to reclaim the experiences of Jewish women as they accommodated to modernity in Europe and the United States and to explore the role of ideas about gender in the construction of Jewish identity. Chapter 3, "America, Freedom, and Assimilation," analyzes how the patterns of assimilation of women and men immigrants differed in significant ways. Women were specific targets for socialization in respectability, whether taught in institutions like the Educational Alliance or instructed in manners and fashion by advice manuals. Their newfound work outside the home introduced single women to union issues and socialist ideas, yet they were also expected to find their principal fulfillment as married homemakers, as they had in Europe.

Jensen, Joan M., and Sue Davidson, eds. *A Needle, A Bobbin, A Strike: Women Needleworkers in America.* Philadelphia: Temple University Press, 1984. 304 p.

Jensen's introduction to the middle section of the book, "The Great Uprisings 1900–1920," is a clearly written schematic overview of the unions involved in the garment workers' strikes in Rochester, Chicago, Cleveland, and New York. Jewish women strikers are described in essays on each strike. They include Rochester strikers Ida Brayman (who was shot to death during the strike), Libbie Alpern, and Fannie Gor-

don; Hannah Shapiro and Bessie Abramowitz in Chicago; national union organizer Pauline Newman in the Cleveland strike; and numerous women in New York. Ann Schofield's essay "The Uprising of the 20,000: The Making of a Labor Legend" is a good review of the varying interpretations of the events by feminist and other historians.

Joselit, Jenna Weissman. *The Wonders of America: Reinventing Jewish Culture 1880–1950.* New York: Hill and Wang, 1994. 349 p.

Examines the fashioning of American Jewish culture through three generations of American Jews: immigrants, first generation, and the Jews of the suburbs. What they created was a "domesticated Jewishness" centered around the home and family—its objects, meals, and observances—with women at its core. This entertaining, richly illustrated text constructs a culture from the likes of the Maxwell House Haggadah, a mah-jongg tile menorah, ritual guidebooks for the Jewish home, and Yiddish press food columns. While the role of Jewish women is implicit on every page, the discussion of immigrant Jewish motherhood in Chapter Two ("Yidishe Nachas") is particularly noteworthy. Here Joselit discerns the origins of the Jewish mother stereotype in the works of health professionals ("The Jewish mother betray[s] an unusual amount of concern about the problem of feeding her children," states Ethel Maslansky in a 1941 article in *Medical Woman's Journal*) and anthropologists. Joselit's enthusiasm for the wonders of "domesticated Jewishness" is infectious. Even those who equate "culture" with fine arts and highly intellectual pursuits will be engaged by the telling.

Kamel, Rose Yalow. *Aggravating the Conscience: Jewish-American Literary Mothers in the Promised Land.* New York: P. Lang, 1988. 194 p.

A study of the narrator-persona created by five Jewish American women writers (Maimie Pinzer, Anzia Yezierska, Tillie Olsen, Grace Paley, and E.M. Broner). The women writers developed autobiographical personae who share six common characteristics: All are first-generation immigrant daughters, working-class, secular and self-educated; they live in cramped city surroundings; their relationships with men range from uneasy to antagonistic; mother-daughter relationships are tense, leading them to find literary foremothers for themselves; they identify with all victims of social injustice; and their texts are replete with Yiddishisms. The antihero pariah created by American Jewish male writers was quite different.

Kessner, Carole S., ed. *The "Other" New York Jewish Intellectuals.* New York: New York University Press, 1994. 382 p.

Considers the lives and contributions of intellectuals who were highly involved in Jewish concerns as compared to the better-known but disaffected Jewish literati of the 1930s and 1940s. Only two of the fifteen essays are on women, because it was rare for Jewish women to devote themselves to lives of writing and lecturing on Jewish topics in that era. But both the chapters on Labor Zionist poet and *Jewish Frontiers* editor Marie Syrkin (by Carole S. Kessner) and German-born Trude Weiss-Rosmarin, who founded and spent half a century editing *The Jewish Spectator* (by Deborah Dash Moore), tantalize readers with glimpses into the lives of exceptional women worthy of book-length biographies.

Koltun, Elizabeth, ed. *The Jewish Woman: New Perspectives.* New York: Schocken, 1976. 294 p.

Expanded version of the 1973 anthology, adding other role models from Jewish women's past and sections on women in Jewish literature and the status of Jewish women in modern society. Stephen M. Cohen, Susan Dessel, and Michael Pelavin advocate a stronger role for women in Jewish communal organizations in their "The Changing (?) Role of Women in Jewish Communal Affairs: A Look Into the UJA." In "Mothers and Daughters in American Jewish Literature: The Rotted Cord," Sonya Michel discusses the conflict between immigrant mothers and American-born daughters in autobiographies and novels, as well as the less frequently found theme of reconciliation. She speculates that the second generation kept some of their mothers' traits that were reviled by the culture to which they aspired, leading to the negative stereotype perpetrated by *their* sons and (to a lesser extent) daughters. Says that the rotted (umbilical) cord may yet fall away if the condemned values come to be respected.

Koltun, Elizabeth, et al., eds. "The Jewish Woman: An Anthology." *Response* no. 18 (Summer 1973), 192 p.

Influential first collection of writing from Jewish feminists committed to achieving equality for women *within* Judaism. Essays cover women's spirituality, Jewish law and texts, life cycle events, Israel, the Jewish community, and Jewish history. Charlotte Baum's contribution, "What Makes Yetta Work? The Economic Role of Eastern European Jewish Women in the Family," examines figures on female labor force participation from the 1900 and 1910 United States censuses. She provides reasons why female labor in general and Jewish women's work in particular were underrepresented.

Krause, Corinne Azen. *Grandmothers, Mothers, and Daughters: An Oral History Study of Ethnicity, Mental Health, and Continuity of Three Generations of Jewish, Italian, and Slavic-American Women.* New York: Institute for Pluralism and Group Identity of the American Jewish Committee, 1978. 176 p.

The author found a continued importance of ethnicity as expressed in food, holidays, and family closeness in all three groups. Observed that Jewish grandmothers valued their independence, and Jewish mothers were deeply empathetic with their children. The third generation of Jewish women studied wanted both families and careers, and their self-esteem was influenced by their level of educational attainment.

Kuzmack, Linda Gordon. *Woman's Cause: The Jewish Woman's Movement in England and the United States, 1881–1933.* Columbus: Ohio State University Press, 1990. 280 p.

Traces the role of Jewish women in the secular women's movement on both sides of the Atlantic while creating a "feminist movement that was distinctively Jewish" as well. The latter led to the founding of the National Council of Jewish Women and efforts to enhance the position of women in the synagogue. Kuzmack's research is based on newspaper accounts, diaries, and other archival material.

Lebeson, Anita Libman. *Recall to Life: The Jewish Woman in America.* South Brunswick, NJ: Yoseloff, 1970. 351 p.

The first history of Jewish women in America, Lebeson's work is based on various secondary sources on American Jews, published memoirs, the author's prior publications (*Pilgrim People: Jewish Pioneers in America*), and her personal experiences in the National Council of Jewish Women. There was then virtually no critical historical research on Jewish women on which Lebeson could rely. She is bent throughout on giving untempered praise both to the anonymous Jewish woman, who kept the faith and worked tirelessly on behalf of worthy causes, and to Rebecca Gratz, Emma Lazarus, Rosa Sonneschein, Henrietta Szold, and a few other named women, better known because they left a written record.

Lichtenstein, Diane. *Writing Their Nations: The Tradition of Nineteenth-Century American Jewish Women Writers.* Bloomington: Indiana University Press, 1992. 176 p.

First book-length critical treatment of the subject. Lichtenstein's thesis is that nineteenth-century Jewish women writers shared a tradition combining two ideals: the pious, domestic, Christian "Cult of True Womanhood" and the protective, assertive "Mother in Israel." According to Lichtenstein, these Sephardic and German Jewish women used their writing to achieve respectability and to integrate their Americanism and Jewishness. The twenty-five writers surveyed range from Rachel Mordecai Lazarus, who started writing early in the century, to twentieth-century writer Edna Ferber.

Marcus, Jacob R. *The American Jewish Woman, 1654–1980.* New York: Ktav, 1981. 231 p.

One of two companion volumes written by the eminent historian of American Jews and founder of the American Jewish Archives. This narrative history of American "Jewesses" begins in seventeenth-century New Amsterdam with the contributions women made to the first synagogue in the colony and ends more than three centuries later when Jewish women were at the forefront of the women's movement. Marcus highlights the lives of individuals rather than the social forces at work in the Americanization process. His excellent bibliographic essay at the end of the book, pointing to many avenues for further research, is an important bequest he bestowed on his successors.

Marcus, Jacob R. *The American Jewish Woman: A Documentary History*. New York: Ktav; Cincinnati: American Jewish Archives, 1981. 1047 p.

Marcus was the first to bring together an array of primary source material for the study of American Jewish women. He provides introductions to 177 selections or groups of selections, which are arranged chronologically. They include such items as eighteenth-century letters by Abigail Franks and Rachel Gratz; epitaphs; an ethical will from Deborah Moses (1837); poems by Rebekah Hyneman and Emma Lazarus; documents from Hebrew ladies benevolent societies; Civil War remembrances of Clara L. Moses (Old Natchez); recollections of life with her husband Wyatt by Josephine Sara Marcus Earp; excerpts from speeches at the Jewish Women's Congress (1893); statements of purpose from labor leaders, suffragists, and Zionists; and selections from scores of additional memoirs, autobiographies, and essays.

Markowitz, Ruth Jacknow. *My Daughter, the Teacher: Jewish Teachers in the New York City School*. New Brunswick, NJ: Rutgers University Press, 1993. 224 p.

Using interviews with sixty-one retired teachers as well as Board of Education records and union archives, Markowitz recounts how and why Jewish women in New York flocked to teaching in the 1920s and 1930s. Encouraged by their immigrant mothers, the women obtained college educations, typically at Hunter College, and positions teaching in New York City. They married, had children, and continued their teaching careers, because the New York City board did not force married women to quit and because they found satisfaction in their profession. Markowitz is especially interested in the extensive involvement of these women in unionization. She does not deal with their lives as Jews except insofar as they were subjected to anti-Semitism.

McCreesh, Carolyn Daniel. *Women in the Campaign to Organize Garment Workers, 1880–1917*. New York: Garland, 1985. 298 p.

Reviews and analyzes the role of women workers and members of the Women's Trade Union League in unionizing activities, tactics, goals, and gains. Believes that Eastern European immigrant Jewish women were able to withstand the rigors of picket lines and rise to Union leadership due to their idealism and heritage of fighting oppression. Furthermore, unlike native-born American women, they remained outside the constraints of "domesticity," the view that women's sphere should be confined to the home, and were therefore less reluctant to take on public roles. Describes the parts played by Rose Schneiderman, Fannie Zinsher, Bessie Abramowitz, and other Jewish women.

Metzker, Isaac, ed. *Bintel Brief: 1: Sixty Years of Letters from the Lower East Side to the "Jewish Daily Forward"; 2: Letters to the Jewish Daily Forward 1950–80*. New York: Doubleday, 1971–1981; repr. New York: Behrman House, 1982.

The best-known primary source for gaining an appreciation of the problems encountered by immigrants is this translated collection from the advice column in the *Forward*. Many of the letters came from women struggling in poverty with added burdens such as husbands who deserted them or employers who harassed them.

Moore, Deborah Dash. *To the Golden Cities: Pursuing the American Jewish Dream in Miami and L.A.* New York: Free Press, 1994. 358 p.

In the course of discussing spiritual life in Los Angeles in the post–World War II era, Moore takes note of the high proportion of adult women students in the University of Judaism and Brandeis Camp Institute programs. They were welcomed by Jewish educators who recognized that educated mothers held the key to the future of Judaism in America. Favoring experiential learning over traditional study, these women also influenced the curricula.

Myerhoff, Barbara. *Number Our Days*. New York: Dutton, 1978. 306 p.

Influential ethnographic study of some three hundred aged Jews (mostly women) living in Venice, California, who are members of the Aliyah Senior Citizens' Center. Myerhoff looks for clues to successful aging, which she finds in their collective sense of being one people and their individual sense of themselves. The women are the backbone of the center, although the men hold the ceremonial positions. The women continue performing "woman's work," which maintains a sense of worth that the men seem to have lost with retirement. Filled with anecdotes from the personal histories of the informants.

Orleck, Annelise. *Common Sense and a Little Fire: Women and Working-Class Politics in the United States, 1900–1965*. Chapel Hill: University of North Carolina Press, 1995. 384 p.

Collective biography of four labor leaders: Fannia Cohn, Clara Lemlich Shavelson, Pauline Newman, and Rose Schneiderman, whom Orleck calls "industrial feminists." Each confronted sexism in the factory and the union, elitism from their middle- and upper-class allies, and anti-Semitism from all sides, yet all persevered to achieve great victories for labor and women. Deals with their personal as well as work lives.

Pinzer, Maimie. *The Maimie Papers*, ed. Ruth Rosen and Sue Davidson. Old Westbury, NY: Feminist Press, 1977. 439 p.

The unusual twelve-year correspondence (from 1910–1922) between a Jewish former prostitute and a Boston society woman is a rich source of information on poor immigrant women who chose prostitution over menial labor or marriage. By the time of the letters, Maimie had been "saved" by a social worker, and during their exchange she founded a home for wayward girls. The introduction by Ruth Rosen does not dwell on Maimie's Jewishness.

Rogow, Faith. *Gone to Another Meeting: The National Council of Jewish Women, 1893–1993.* Tuscaloosa: University of Alabama Press, 1993. 300 p.

This history of the first national organization of Jewish women emphasizes how the notion of separate spheres for men and women, shared by American "true womanhood" and traditional Jewish societal values, influenced the rhetoric and activities of the council. Maternalism allowed the women to move beyond the home into the public sphere to shelter and instruct immigrant daughters, offer classes on parenting, and promote protective legislation for women and children. Initially the organization provided Jewish education for its members as well as a vehicle for social and philanthropic work, but the religious divisions within the Jewish community and the great success of the council's social service program led to its increasing secularization. The book is especially strong on the founding and early years of the council but summarizes the period from the 1920s to the present in one final chapter.

Schloff, Linda Mack. *'And Prairie Dogs Weren't Kosher': Jewish Women in the Upper MidWest Since 1855.* St. Paul: Minnesota Historical Society Press, 1996. 256 p.

Companion to an exhibition at the Minnesota Historical Society and written by the curator, who hopes to dispel the notion that all Jews settled on the East Coast and worked in the garment industry. This richly illustrated book describes Jewish women homesteaders in Minnesota and the Dakotas who worked alongside their husbands whether on the farm or in their dry goods "Jew stores," took in boarders, started organizations, and interacted with their neighbors at all levels. Schloff also analyzes Minneapolis/St. Paul data in the 1910 manuscript census to contrast the occupational pattern of Jewish women residents with other European immigrants in the area and to Jewish women elsewhere. Bibliography lists relevant manuscripts held in the Minnesota Historical Society, the Jewish Historical Society of the Upper Midwest, other repositories in the region, and the American Jewish Archives.

Schreier, Barbara A. *Becoming American Women: Clothing and the Jewish Immigrant Experience, 1880–1920.* Chicago: Chicago Historical Society, 1994. 154 p.

Accompanying an exhibition organized by the Chicago Historical Society, this lavishly illustrated text documents the primacy of clothing in the acculturation process. Young Jewish women, especially those in the needle trades, were sensitive to fabrics and fashion and quickly adopted American styles. Their mothers were not so quick to abandon their *sheytl* [wig], the most tangible sign of Old World customs and the underlying religious values it symbolized.

Seltzer, Robert M., and Norman J. Cohen, eds. *The Americanization of the Jews.* New York: New York University Press, 1995. 468 p.

Includes a section on the impact of the women's movement on American Judaism, with essays by Ellen M. Umansky on Reform Judaism, Paula E. Hyman on the Ezrat Nashim feminist organization, and Judith Hauptman on Conservative Judaism. All three chart major advances made by women since the early 1970s but also mention areas resistant to change, including liturgical language, adding women's voices to the midrash [interpretation] of Jewish texts, and acceptance of egalitarianism as a warranted halakic [legal] development.

Shapiro, Ann, Sara Horowitz, Ellen Schiff, and Miriyam Glazer. *Jewish American Women Writers: A Bio-Bibliographical and Critical Sourcebook.* Greenwood Press, 1994. 557 p.

The only reference work to date that combines biographical information, critical analysis, and bibliographic citations about historical and contemporary Jewish American women writers. Mary Antin and Anzia Yezierska typify those who wrote of the generational conflicts among the immigrant generations, while Ilona Karmel, Irena Klepfisz, and Lore Segal are three who write as survivors of the Holocaust. The fifty-seven writers studied include women estranged from Judaism early in their lives who subsequently returned to their Jewish roots for inspiration. A separate chapter by Barbara Shollar discusses the disproportionate number of autobiographies by Jewish women in what is a major genre of women's writing in America. Shollar describes some of the two hundred such twentieth-century writings in which ethnicity and gender are important themes.

Shepherd, Naomi. *A Price Below Rubies: Jewish Women as Rebels and Radicals.* Cambridge, MA: Harvard University Press, 1993. 336 p.

While mainly on European women, Shepherd's chapter "I Need a Violent Strike" focuses on Rose Pesotta and other Jewish immigrant unionists.

Smith, Judith E. *Family Connections: A History of Italian and Jewish Immigrant Lives in Providence, Rhode Island, 1900–1940.* Albany: State University of New York Press, 1985. 228 p.

Discusses the work, kinship, and communal patterns established in Providence by immigrant Jews and Italians. Although the majority of both Jewish and Italian women did not then work outside the home, some took in boarders or were shopkeepers. Smith attributes divergence between the two ethnic groups to the skills brought with them from Europe rather than to cultural differences.

Sochen, June. *Consecrate Every Day: The Public Lives of Jewish American Women, 1880–1980.* Albany: State University of New York Press, 1981. 167 p.

Sochen's thesis is that Jewish American women have been prominent in three areas—unionism, volunteerism, and literature—precisely because of the "ambivalent richness of their dual background," which gave them fresh perspective, an "agonizing need to redefine themselves," and "an impetus to move outside predictable forms." Besides detailed treatment of union leaders, radical activists, mainstays of organizations, and writers, Sochen includes some fascinating variations on the theme of successful mergers of Jewish and American identities, from Yiddish actresses to rabbis. Given the brevity of the volume, its contribution is also to reveal the fertile, untilled ground remaining for further analytic ploughing. The book's title comes from Hannah Greenbaum Solomon, founder of the National Council of Jewish Women and a Reform Jew, in answer to a challenge to her leadership from traditional women because she did not consecrate the Sabbath in an Orthodox manner.

Sorin, Gerald. *The Prophetic Minority: American Jewish Immigrant Radicals, 1880–1920.* Bloomington: Indiana University Press, 1985. 211 p.

Seeks to explain the connection between radicalism and being Jewish by exploring the lives of 170 Jewish immigrants active in socialist unions or politics. Sorin's view of the prominence of women in this history is evident from page one, where Pearl Halpern is the first activist to be mentioned by name. Women are featured throughout the book, and a separate chapter examines their special situation as female radicals. Sorin discusses discrimination they encountered as women within the unions, sexual harassment of women in the shops, and complicated relationships with feminist organizations. He also offers interesting information on the ways women radicals differed from other immigrant Jewish women. They often had received more education in Europe, were more apt to continue their education at night schools in America, and almost half had already been in socialist groups before emigrating. Women radicals were also more likely to have had parents with relatively egalitarian marriages. Unlike most Jewish women who stopped working at marriage, these women either continued working after marriage or never married.

Tax, Meredith. *The Rising of the Women: Feminist Solidarity and Class Conflict, 1880–1917.* New York: Monthly Review, 1980. 332 p.

The chapter "The Uprising of the Thirty Thousand" in this study of socialist feminists pays particular attention to the role of Clara Lemlich in the shirtwaist makers' strike of 1909–1910 and to the temporary unity of socialists, feminists, and trade unionists.

Tenenbaum, Shelly. *A Credit to Their Community: Jewish Loan Societies in the United States, 1880–1945.* Detroit: Wayne State University Press, 1993. 204 p.

Especially in the section "Women as Leaders" but interspersed throughout, Tenenbaum provides data and analysis of the operations of Jewish women's free loan societies in numerous places in America. In her view, women formed their own organizations not because they wanted to give loans exclusively to women but rather because they wanted control of disbursements, since they were rarely granted leadership positions in the general (male-led) Jewish loan societies and credit cooperatives. One notable exception discussed is Pauline Perlmutter Steinem, president of the Jewish Free Loan Association of Toledo, and grandmother of second wave feminist leader Gloria Steinem. Also covers the reasons women applied for loans, which included paying for rent, household expenses, medical bills, and education for themselves and their children. By contrast, most loans to men were for business ventures.

Toll, William. *Women, Men and Ethnicity: Essays on the Structure and Thought of American Jewry.* Lanham, MD: University Press of America, 1991. 240 p.

Pulls together a series of studies on women and the formation of Jewish communities in the South and West. Reassessing their role, Toll finds the informal social network created by women to be the very essence of defining a *community;* indeed, until women form an organization in a locale, it can be called only a *settlement.* The organizations were established to meet traditional religious needs, later serving as proving grounds for civic activism and professional training. Makes novel use of census tract information as well as organizational reports and minutes and oral histories.

Uffen, Ellen Serlen. *Strands of the Cable: The Place of the Past in Jewish American Women's Writing.* New York: P. Lang, 1992. 193 p.

A chronological presentation of selected Jewish women writers beginning with the immigrant generation (Antin, Stern, and Yezierska), followed by Tess Slesinger and Beatrice Bisno in the 1930s, Jo Sinclair as representative of 1940s and 1950s, Zelda Popkin and Marge Piercy who started writing in the 1960s, and Cynthia Ozick for her work beginning in the 1970s. A concluding chapter covers contemporary writers. All are concerned with Jewish identity and the double-edged sword that is assimilation. Their characters turn to the past for understanding of their place in the present. Unlike male writers and their characters who seek to shed Jewish identity, women writers search for new ways to be Jewish in the New World.

Wagenknecht, Edward. *Daughters of the Covenant: Portraits of Six Jewish Women.* Amherst: University of Massachusetts Press, 1983. 192 p.

Biographies of Americans Emma Goldman, Rebecca Gratz, Emma Lazarus, Henrietta Szold, and Lillian D. Wald and British writer Amy Levy that focus on their personal qualities, relationships to Judaism, and public accomplishments.

Weatherford, Doris. *Foreign and Female: Immigrant Women in America, 1840–1930.* New York: Schocken, 1986. 288 p.

Although no separate chapter is devoted to Jewish women immigrants, this text draws on many diaries, letters, and memoirs of Jewish women. It is a good introduction to the common problems encountered by immigrant women of all backgrounds but is less helpful on considering the influence of ethnicity on the solutions adopted.

Weinberg, Sydney Stahl. *The World of Our Mothers: The Lives of Jewish Immigrant Women.* Chapel Hill: University of North Carolina Press, 1988. 325 p.

Offers a redress to Irving Howe's *World of Our Fathers* (1976) in which "immigrant Jews" means *males* and the treatment of women is generally patronizing. This work concentrates on the day-to-day lives of Jewish women who immigrated to New York before 1925. Based on interviews with forty-six such women and augmented by reference to other memoirs, oral interviews, and secondary sources, Stahl builds a collective, chronological history out of the personal stories. Reverence for education and the burden of breadwinner role foisted on oldest daughters are two themes that emerge. While not as sweeping as the Howe book, it demonstrates how the values carried from Europe interacted with conditions in America for women.

Wenger, Beth. *New York Jews and the Great Depression: Uncertain Promise.* New Haven: Yale University Press, 1996. 369 p.

Includes documentation of the financial contribution Jewish women made through earnings and careful management of the family budget during a difficult era.

Zaborowska, Magdalena. *How We Found America: Reading Gender Through Eastern European Immigrant Narratives.* Chapel Hill: University of North Carolina Press, 1995. 359 p.

Compares the experiences of Jewish immigrants (Mary Antin, Elizabeth Stern, Anzia Yezierska, and Eva Hoffman) to one another and to non-Jewish immigrant writers (Maria Kuncewicz, Vladimir Nabokov, and herself). Explores the conflicts in gender expectations in the Old World and New and the complex identities of transplanted writers.

ARTICLES

Abrams, Jeanne. "Unsere Leit ('Our People'): Anna Hillkowitz and the Development of the East European Jewish Woman Professional in America." *American Jewish Archives* 37 (November 1985): 275–278.

Puts Hillkowitz's career forward as typical of the volunteer turned paid professional communal worker. Hillkowitz served the Denver Jewish Consumptive Relief Society in the early 1900s. Her activities are well documented through two hundred letters preserved in the Archives of the JCRS.

Albert, Marta. "Not Quite 'A Quiet Revolution': Jewish Women Reformers in Buffalo, New York, 1980–1914." *Shofar* 9, no. 4 (Summer 1991): 62–77.

Takes issue with William Toll (below) that Jewish women's social welfare work in the late nineteenth century was a gradual expansion of women's sphere. In Buffalo, Albert found a more assertive challenge to notions of women's proper sphere among women who fought for recognition in their community and synagogues.

Antler, Joyce. "Between Culture and Politics: the Emma Lazarus Federation of Jewish Women's Clubs and the Promulgation of Women's History, 1944–1989." In *U.S. History as Women's History*, ed. Linda K. Kerber, Alice Kessler-Harris, and Kathryn K. Sklar, 267–295. Chapel Hill, University of North Carolina Press, 1995.

Founded in the 1940s by Clara Lemlich Shavelson (who had rallied the shirtwaist workers to strike in 1909) and other radical activists like her, the Emma Lazarus Federation fought anti-Semitism and racial injustice; promoted women's rights, the State of Israel, world peace, and consumer issues; and supported the remembrance of secular progressive Jewish women's history. Antler argues that, like their namesake, the Emmas successfully integrated the female, radical, and Jewish aspects of their identities. Fills a gap in understanding what radical Jewish women did *after* the worker battles of the first part of the century.

Antler, Joyce. "A Bond of Sisterhood: Ethel Rosenberg, Molly Goldberg, and Radical Jewish Women of the 1950s." In *Secret Agents: The Rosenberg Case, McCarthyism, and Fifties America*, ed. Marjorie Garber and Rebecca L. Walkowitz, 197–214. New York: Routledge, 1995.

Contrasts the media representation of Gertrude Berg's character Molly Goldberg, the public persona of Ethel Rosenberg, and their actual selves. Molly Goldberg was much-beloved and the epitome of a good Jewish mother. She stayed home, worried about her family and neighbors, leant a sympathetic ear, and was a fixer-upper par excellence. What the public perceived of Ethel Rosenberg was a cold, controlling woman who could abandon her children with ease. In reality, Gertrude Berg was a superb professional, who created her character, wrote the scripts, and directed and produced her show; and Ethel Rosenberg was intensely concerned about her parenting and her sons. Antler also discusses the defense of Rosenberg mounted by the leftist Emma Lazarus Federation of Jewish women, who were convinced of her innocence—or at least considered her fate to be marked by political persecution tinged with anti-Semitic overtones.

Ashton, Dianne. "Souls Have No Sex: Philadelphia Jewish Women and the American Challenge." In *When Philadelphia Was the Capital of Jewish America*, ed. Murray Friedman, 34–57. Cranbury, NJ: Associated University Presses, 1993.

Demonstrates how several nineteenth-century Jewish women who remained unmarried (including Rebecca Gratz, Emily and Ellen Phillips and others) engaged in significant benevolent activity while maintaining firm commitments to Judaism and defending it against evangelists.

Avery, Evelyn. "Oh My Mishpocha! Some Jewish Women Writers From Antin to Kaplan View the Family." In *Studies in American Jewish Literature 5: The Varieties of Jewish Experience*, ed. Daniel Walden, 44–53. Albany: State University of New York Press, 1986.

Finds similarities between two immigrant works (Mary Antin's *The Promised Land* and Anzia Yezierska's *The Bread Givers*) and contemporary family sagas (Helen Yglesias's *Family Feeling* and Joanna Kaplan's *O My America!*). Both the earlier and later works are rooted in the Yiddish past and explore the effects of assimilation on Jewish families, and all pay tribute to the Jewish mother as the mainstay of the family and repository of tradition. Critical of the vacuous, materialistic second and third generations, the contemporary novels are much more negative about the bargain struck by the immigrants in giving up traditional values in the interest of becoming fully Americanized.

Bergland, Betty. "Ideology, Ethnicity, and the Gendered Subject: Reading Immigrant Women's Autobiographies." In *Seeking Common Ground: Multi-disciplinary Studies of Immigrant Women in the United States*, ed. Donna Gabaccia, 101–121. Westport, CT: Praeger, 1992.

Uses the concept of chronotope (time/space) to compare and contrast the positioning of the subjects/authors of three Jewish women's autobiographies. Mary Antin is the most Americanized of the three, yet she never has to deal with the problems of an adult woman since her autobiography ends in adolescence. Hilda Satt Polacheck, Hull House resident, identifies with the traditional Jewish role of wife and mother but remains critical of American values. The third, Emma Goldman, challenges prevailing American and Jewish ideologies alike, moving to a place (the public arena) unoccupied by many adult Jewish women of the time.

Berrol, Selma. "Class or Ethnicity: The Americanized German Jewish Woman and Her Middle Class Sisters in 1895." *Jewish Social Studies* 47, no. 1 (Winter 1985): 21–35.

Compares Rosa Sonneschein's *The American Jewess* to magazines aimed at the average middle-class American woman of the time.

Bienstock, Beverly Gray. "The Changing Image of the American Jewish Mother." In *Changing Images of the Family*, ed. Virginia Tufte and Barbara Myerhoff, 173–191. New Haven: Yale University Press, 1979.

Interested in why the image of the solid immigrant Jewish mother of early twentieth-century novels by men degenerates into a "maternal vampire" by the 1960s. Attributing the shift to adaptation to America, Bienstock says that mothers came to epitomize the bourgeois materialism that 1930s writers revolted against. By the postwar era, writers treated the Jewish mother with condescension, parodied her, or blamed her for the sexual maladjustment and other inadequacies of her sons. Aside from the heroic mother in Anzia Yezierska's *The Bread Givers* (1925), Bienstock takes no notice of the portrayal of mothers in Jewish women's writings.

Blicksilver, Edith. "The Bintl Briv Woman Writer: Torn Between European Traditions and the American Life Style." *Studies in American Jewish Literature* 3, no. 2 (Winter 1977–78): 36–49.

Discusses the types of problems women wrote about to the *Forward* editor between 1906 and 1911, especially dealing with family matters. Cautions that the *bintl* letters have limitations as a research source because they were written by unhappy women, who may not be representative of all immigrant Jewish women at the time. Furthermore, only some of the thousands of letters sent to the newspaper were actually published, and many were heavily edited. Praises editor Abraham Cahan for his thoughtful responses.

Bodek, Evelyn. "'Making Do': Jewish Women and Philanthropy." In *Jewish Life in Philadelphia, 1830–1940*, ed. Murray Friedman, 143–162. Philadelphia: Institute for the Study of Human Issues, 1983.

Describes the leadership role played by a handful of German Jewish women in founding and maintaining charitable institutions. They were especially attuned to the needs of poor women. The philanthropic women became highly adept at the political process and administration of organizations yet were passed over for communal leadership when the Philadelphia Jewish community created a federation of the various charities in 1901.

Braude, Ann. "The Jewish Woman's Encounter With American Culture." In *Women and Religion in America*. Vol 1, *The Nineteenth Century*, ed. Rosemary Radford Ruether and Rosemary Skinner Keller, 150–192 (essay and documents). San Francisco: Harper, 1981.

Discusses how the Enlightenment prepared German Jewish immigrants for the individualistic, voluntary model of religious life in America, where Reform Judaism opened most doors to women (except ordination) but denigrated the commandments that had been specifically designated for women to perform. Covers the 1893 Congress of Jewish Women at the World Parliament of Religions.

Braude, Ann. "Jewish Women." In *In Our Own Voices: Four Centuries of American Women's Religious Writing*, ed. Rosemary Skinner Keller and Rosemary Radford Ruether, 109–152 (essay and documents). New York: Harper, 1995.

Provides an overview of the status and practices of women in traditional Judaism and summarizes the changes wrought by feminists who challenged exclusions. Regards the formation of Orthodox women's prayer groups as more "radical" in its context than the achievement of equality in non-Orthodox branches of Judaism. Also mentions the attraction for some formerly secular women of the strictly prescribed Orthodox way of life. Useful to readers unfamiliar with Jewish tradition.

Braude, Ann. "Jewish Women in the Twentieth Century: Building a Life in America." In *Women and Religion in America*. Vol. 3, *1900–1968*, eds. Rosemary Skinner Keller and Rosemary Radford Ruether, 131–174 (essay and documents). San Francisco: Harper, 1986.

Overview of religious conflicts for Jewish women seeking to move beyond the sphere of home and family.

Brav, Stanley R. "The Jewish Woman, 1861–1865." *American Jewish Archives* 17, no. 1 (April 1965): 34–75.

Draws on memoirs collected by Jacob R. Marcus in *Memoirs of American Jews 1775–1865* (Philadelphia: Jewish Publication Society, 1955–1956), newspaper accounts, letters, and other material to demonstrate the acculturation of Jewish women in America at the time of the Civil War. Discusses their education, household duties, social life, employment, and support for the war effort in both the North and South.

Brodsky, Naomi. "The First 100 Years of the National Council of Jewish Women." *Rhode Island Jewish Historical Notes* 11, no. 3 (1993): 359–369.

A decade-by-decade review of the accomplishments of the Providence, Rhode Island, section of the Council.

Chevat, Edith. "In For the Long Haul: Edith Chevat in Conversation With Annette & Friends." *Bridges* 6, no. 1 (Summer 1996): 7–30.

Chevat converses with three Jewish women activists then in their eighties: literary critic and American Labor Party officer Annette Rubinstein, civil rights and anti–Vietnam War activist Beatrice (Bd) Magdoff, and social worker Sherry (Elizabeth) Most, who was also active in the anti–Vietnam War movement. They discuss their involvements, careers, and what being Jewish means to them.

Clar, Reva. "Women in the Weekly *Gleaner*, Part I." *Western States Jewish History* 17, no. 4 (July 1985): 333–346; Part II: *WSJH* 18, no. 1 (October 1985): 44–57.

Rabbi Julius Eckman, editor of the San Franciso Jewish newspaper founded in 1857, was sympathetic toward women. In the *Gleaner*, he offered advice to women and covered their involvement in the community.

Cohn, Josephine. "Communal Life of San Francisco: Jewish Women in 1908." *Western States Jewish History* 20, no. 1 (October 1987): 15–36.

Reprint of 1908 article by a school principal and Hebrew teacher that provides details on Jewish women's organizations shortly after the San Francisco earthquake.

Drucker, Sally Ann. "'It Doesn't Say So in Mother's Prayerbook': Autobiographies in English by Immigrant Jewish Women." *American Jewish History* 79 (Autumn 1989): 55–71. Somewhat different version published as "Wandering Between Worlds: Autobiographies in English by Immigrant Jewish Women." In *Women in History, Literature and the Arts: A Festschrift for Hildegard Schnuttgen*, ed. Lorrayne Y. Baird-Lange and Thoman A. Copeland, 275–294. Youngstown, OH: Youngstown State University, 1989.

Identifies nineteen autobiographies by fifteen women authors who achieved prominence later in life. Most chose to dwell on their early years in Europe and America in their autobiographies rather than their subsequent public roles. Discusses the importance of the genre and treats in more detail the autobiographies of four fiction writers: Mary Antin, Rose Cohen, Elizabeth Stern, and Anzia Yezierska.

Eisen, George. "Sport, Recreation and Gender: Jewish Immigrant Women in Turn-of-the-Century America (1880–1920)." *Journal of Sport History* 18, no. 1 (Spring 1991): 103–120.

Discusses the increase in consciousness of sports and recreation due to the efforts of settlement houses, self-help organizations for the working girl, and the realization among the women that such activities could provide an avenue for self-expression and a break from traditional role expectations.

Frank, Dana. "Housewives, Socialists, and the Politics of Food: The 1917 New York Cost-Of-Living Protests." *Feminist Studies* 11, no. 2 (Summer 1985): 255–285.

Spontaneous demonstrations and boycotts characterized the reaction of Jewish housewives to rising prices for staples. In contrast, male socialists directed their energies at advocating for higher wages.

Fridkis, Ari Lloyd. "Desertion in the American Jewish Immigrant Family: The Work of the National Desertion Bureau in Cooperation with the Industrial Removal Office." *American Jewish History* 71 (December 1981): 285–99.

Similar to Friedman's article (below), with greater emphasis on the relationship between the National Desertion Bureau and the Industrial Removal Office. Reports that the Bureau handled more than twelve thousand cases of desertion from its founding in 1902 through 1922. Disagrees with Irving Howe who, in *World of Our Fathers*, viewed desertion as a less significant problem than conflict between generations. In Fridkis's eyes, such desertions must have wreaked havoc in families, not just marriages. Most common reasons given for desertion according to a 1912 report: insufficient dowry, another woman, and "bad habits."

Friedman, Reena Sigman. "The Jewish Feminist Movement." In *Jewish American Voluntary Organizations*, ed. Michael N. Dobkowski, 575–601. Westport, CT: Greenwood, 1986.

Chronicles Jewish feminist events from the late 1960s through the mid-1980s, including the creation of Ezrat Nashim in 1971. This group began by studying traditional Jewish sources in order to evaluate the position of women in Judaism and moved to activism in 1972 when it submitted a position paper calling for change to a convention of Conservative rabbis. Ezrat Nashim also organized the first national Jewish women's conference in 1973, with subsequent conferences in 1974 and 1975. Discusses the formation of the Jewish Feminist Organization, which grew out of second conference, the founding of *Lilith Magazine* (1976), and successful openings in religious roles.

Friedman, Reena Sigma. "'Send Me My Husband Who Is in New York City': Husband Desertion in the American Jewish Immigrant Community, 1900–1926." *Jewish Social Studies* 44, no. 1 (Winter 1982): 1–18.

Similar in scope to Fridkis's article (above), this study uses archival material from the National Desertion Bureau, established by the National Council of Jewish Charities, to chart the extent and impact of desertion. More details than in Fridkis on the causes and impact of desertion. Cites studies that found marital infidelity to be the principal cause, followed by economic hardship, cheerless existences, poor health, and incompatibility. The total economic dependence of wives made many unwilling to testify against their husbands when they were apprehended. Some even turned to prostitution. Concludes that desertion was probably underreported and that a fuller picture would emerge with an analysis of female-headed households in the Jewish population, combined with figures from orphanages and other sources of data.

Generations (Jewish Historical Society of Maryland) 5, no. 1 (June/July 1984).

Includes "The Origins of Jewish Women's Social Service Work in Baltimore," by Cynthia H. Requardt, and several articles on individual Jewish women in Maryland.

Goldman, Karla. "The Ambivalence of Reform Judaism: Kaufmann Kohler and the Ideal Jewish Woman." *American Jewish History* 79, no. 4 (Summer 1990): 477–99.

Reform rabbinical leader Kohler saw women as embodying an idealized Jewish past when Judaism was centered in homes imbued with Jewish values and customs. Even though Kohler championed equality for women in the synagogue, Goldman makes a convincing case that he still wanted them to maintain the Jewish home of yore and did not see the contradiction.

Goldman, Karla. "Not Simple Arithmetic." *Shofar* 14, no. 1 (Fall 1995): 101–105. Somewhat modified version published as "When the Women Came to Shul." In *Judaism Since Gender*, ed. Miriam Peskowitz and Laura Levitt, 57–61. New York: Routledge, 1997.

Discusses the salience of gender to the molding of American Judaism as seen through changes in architectural features of synagogue design as well as other accommodations to the dominant presence of women at Sabbath services. Fully articulated in Goldman's dissertation, "Beyond the Gallery: The Place of Women in the Development of American Judaism" (Harvard University, 1993).

Golomb, Deborah Grand. "The 1893 Congress of Jewish Women: Evolution or Revolution in American Jewish Women's History?" *American Jewish History* 70 (September 1980): 52–67.

Although revolutionary in form, as the first such national gathering of Jewish women, the congress is to Golomb more evolutionary in substance. The women involved were not associated with the women's rights movement, and the antecedents for the National Council of Jewish Women, which grew out of the congress, were women's clubs, not suffrage organizations. Nevertheless, Golomb concludes that the congress was a pivotal event, providing a model for a national organization that went on to expand the sphere of women's endeavors.

Harris, Joanna Gewertz. "From Tenement to Theater: Jewish Women As Dance Pioneers: Helen Becker (Tamiris), Anna Sokolow, Sophie Maslow." *Judaism* 45 (Summer 1996): 259–276.

Enlightening look at three children of Eastern European Jewish immigrants who became modern dance innovators. Each took part in the Neighborhood Playhouse of the Henry Street Settlement (New York) and drew inspiration for her choreography from her Jewish heritage in different ways. Tamiris advocated racially mixed companies and was dedicated to encompassing multicultural elements. Sokolow created dances around social concerns, and Maslow used Sholem Aleichem stories as a motif along with other folk elements.

Hauptman, Judith. "The Ethical Challenge of Feminist Change." In *The Americanization of the Jews*, ed. Robert M. Seltzer and Norman J. Cohen, 296–308. New York: New York University Press, 1995.

Attributes the rapid acceptance of Jewish feminism to the liberalism of the American Jewish community, the openness of American society to new ideas, the coming of age of the Jewish community, and its pluralistic denominational structure. Hauptman focuses primarily on developments in the Conservative Movement. The way was eased by the fact that decades earlier the Conservative Movement had made a number of radical changes in ritual, such as removing the *mehitzah* [separation] and allowing men and women to sit together in the synagogue. The movement's Committee on Jewish Law and Standards readily voted to sanction local rabbis who permitted women in their congregations to be counted in the minyan [prayer quorum] to lead prayers and to function as witnesses. Rabbinic ordination was a thornier matter, but it too eventually succumbed, and women candidates for the rabbinate were admitted to the Movement's seminary beginning in 1983. Hauptman ends by calling for a recognition that halakah [Jewish law] can and does evolve in light of new ethical understandings. Egalitarianism is such a principle and therefore should be regarded as a halakically sanctioned development.

Hellerstein, Kathryn. "A Question of Tradition: Women Poets in Yiddish." In *Handbook of American-Jewish Literature: An Analytic Guide to Topics, Themes, and Sources*, ed. Louis Fried, 195–237. New York: Greenwood, 1988.

Reviews the literary history of Yiddish poetry and its anthologizing, with a detailed examination of Ezra Korman's 1928 *Yidishe Dikhterins Antologye* [Yiddish women writers anthology], which included poetry going back to the sixteenth century written in *Yidish-Taytsh* [old Yiddish] but emphasized twentieth-century immigrant women's work. While their poems reflect the same modernist shift from political and collective themes to more personal statements found in poetry by men, the women's writings show their special stance as women Jews writing in Yiddish. According to Hellerstein, evaluation and reevaluation of the women poets is just beginning.

Herscher, Uri D., guest ed. "The East European Immigrant Jew in America (1881–1981)." *American Jewish Archives* 33, no. 1 (April 1981).

Entire issue devoted to memoirs of the immigrant experience, including Ida R. Feeley on growing up on the East Side of New York; remarks by Lillian Wald to an 1896 convention of the National Council of Jewish Women concerning crowded districts; and the experiences of being raised in Arkansas, by Jeannette W. Bernstein, and in North Dakota, by Bessie Schwartz.

"History Is the Record of Human Beings: A Documentary." *American Jewish Archives* 31, no. 1 (April 1979).

Entire issue devoted to memoirs expressing the many different life experiences of American Jews. Includes Margaret Sanger on the misery she saw in the tenements, an autobiographical sketch of Nobel Prize winner Rosalyn Yalow, a nineteenth-century mother (Rebecca Cohen) coping with the loss of her infant, a 1931 report on a tragic voyage by Lena Pearlstein Berkman, and thoughts concerning "The Jewish Woman, The Jewish Home, and the Ideal Achieved," by Jennie R. Gerstley of Chicago (1931).

Horvitz, Eleanor F. "The Years of the Jewish Woman." *Rhode Island Jewish Historical Notes* 7, no. 1 (1975): 152–170.

Discusses the benevolent organizations established by Jewish women in Rhode Island from the 1870s onward.

Horvitz, Eleanor F. "The Jewish Woman Liberated: A History of the Ladies Hebrew Free Loan Association." *Rhode Island Jewish Historical Notes* 7, no. 4 (1975): 501–512.

Focuses on an organization founded in 1931 that existed until 1965, which provided free loans to Jewish women.

Hyman, Paula. "Culture and Gender: Women in the Immigrant Jewish Community." In *The Legacy of Jewish Migration: 1881 and Its Impact*, ed. David Berger, 157–168. New York, Columbia University Press, 1983.

Focuses on the intersection of gender, class, and Jewishness in standards for social and political behavior, extent and nature of employment, and formation of informal support networks of immigrant women. Identifies areas in need of further research.

Hyman, Paula. "Ezrat Nashim and the Emergence of New Jewish Feminism." In *The Americanization of the Jews*, ed. Robert M. Seltzer and Norman J. Cohen, 284–295. New York: New York University Press, 1995.

As a participant-observer of American Jewish feminism, Hyman reflects on the reasons why early goals enunciated by religiously committed Jewish feminists in Ezrat Nashim were so readily accepted and why later, more profound calls have met with less success. Besides the general receptivity of the Jewish community to claims based on equality and steps such as mixed seating in synagogues that had prepared the way, equal education for boys and girls created a cadre of educated Jewish women who cogently argued the case for equality. The Ezrat Nashim members were products of the best Jewish education offered by the Conservative Movement. Firmly rooted in Judaism, they functioned from within the community. Similarly, educated

Orthodox feminists could often find local rabbis supportive of women's prayer groups. Reform Judaism, having no halakic [Jewish law] constraints, had decided to admit women to rabbinical study before the Jewish feminist movement had crystalized. But liturgical changes and the incorporation of women's experiences into ritual and midrash have been harder to achieve. Feminists themselves are divided in the need for such changes, and many Jews remain emotionally attached or fear changes in the nature of Judaism. Hyman urges feminists to challenge those who regard feminism itself as a threat to Jewish survival.

Hyman, Paula. "Feminist Studies and Modern Jewish History." *Feminist Perspectives on Jewish Studies*, ed. Lynn Davidman and Shelly Tenenbaum, 120–139. New Haven: Yale University Press, 1994.

Reviews the beginning steps in Jewish historiography toward recognition of gender as an analytic tool. From subsuming women under the universal (male) experience or ignoring their womanly activities entirely, historians influenced by twenty years of feminist historical scholarship started to add prominent women and the treatment of women to their work. More recently, historians have begun to use concepts of gender analysis to reexamine Jewish history as a whole. The supposed split between public and private spheres is challenged by women's involvement in social welfare and philanthropy, which grew out of familial and group relationships. The notion that assimilation in America was a rapid, sharp break with the past does not hold up when women's roles as consumers and domestic managers are examined. Hyman raises several areas for further research, among them the implications of transferring principal responsibility for Jewish cultural transmission to mothers, the meaning of community for women, and the impact of female entrance into the rabbinate. Closes with a challenge to her fellow historians to enrich the understanding of Jewish history with attention to gender.

Hyman, Paula. "Gender and the Immigrant Jewish Experience in the United States." *Jewish Women in Historical Perspective*, ed. Judith R. Baskin, 222–242. Detroit: Wayne State University Press, 1991.

Uses gender as an analytical category with which to rethink the conventional views of historians about the acculturation of American Jews. Jewish women experienced America differently from Jewish men and from other women. Many came alone as single women, distinguishing their trajectory from that of other ethnicities where husbands and single men invariably emigrated first. Their work options were restricted to jobs considered suitable for women, but they embraced unionism and the fight for suffrage as opportunities to exercise their independence. Unlike other immigrant women, married Jewish women generally stopped working outside the home. Although their economic situation was dependent on their husbands, when their income was comfortable, the women turned their attention to social and communal philanthropies.

Hyman, Paula. "Immigrant Women and Consumer Protest: The New York City Kosher Meat Boycott of 1902." *American Jewish History* 70 (September 1980): 91–105. Reprinted in *The American Jewish Experience: A Reader*, ed. Jonathan D. Sarna, 135–146. New York: Holmes & Meier, 1986.

Shows how the Jewish, female, and Americanized aspects of the immigrant identities coalesced into collective action against the price of kosher meat. While short-lived, the effectiveness of collective action by women was not lost on their sisters, daughters, or unions. Hyman considers the protest a prelude to the garment workers' strikes a decade later.

Hyman, Paula. "The Introduction of the Bat Mitzvah in Conservative Judaism in Postwar America." *YIVO Annual* 19 (1990): 133–146.

Anshe Emet Congregation in Chicago made the bat mitzvah a regular occurrence in the 1940s and held a service in 1952 conducted by women, at which women were called to the Torah for all the *aliyot*. The Brooklyn Jewish Center had its first bat mitzvah in 1955 with the impetus coming from the Education Committee of the Hebrew School desirous of keeping girls in the School.

Joselit, Jenna Weissman. "Saving Souls: The Vocational Training of American Jewish Women 1880–1930." In *An Inventory of Promises: Essays on American Jewish History in Honor of Moses Rischin*, ed. Jeffrey S. Gurock and Marc Lee Raphael, 151–169. Brooklyn: Carlson, 1995.

On the mission and operations of the Louis Downtown Sabbath School, later called the Hebrew Technical School for Girls, established in 1880 by Minnie Louis and other "Uptown" Jewish women who wished to Americanize the "Downtown" masses. The school added industrial education five years later, with a curriculum that included cutting and fitting of dresses, sewing, millinery, bookkeeping, "typewriting," business penmanship, and housework. The girls themselves rejected outright domestic service as a career and preferred commercial to manual training, but their ultimate goal was marriage. Neither the school nor the students moved beyond a gendered view of options.

Joselit, Jenna Weissman. "The Special Sphere of the Middle Class American Jewish Woman: The Synagogue Sisterhood, 1890–1940." In *The American Synagogue: A Sanctuary Transformed*, ed. Jack Wertheimer, 206–230. New York: Cambridge University Press, 1987.

Studies the common pattern of sisterhood activities and attitudes in three New York synagogues of different denominations and concludes that they in no way challenged the assumption that women's sphere was the home. Sisterhoods during the era examined were religious housekeepers of the synagogues, with responsibilities extending from decorating a sukkah in an aesthetically pleasing manner to providing food at youth events. In Joselit's view, the sisterhoods were only negligible forces for change.

Karsh, Audrey R. "Mothers and Daughters of Old San Diego." *Western States Jewish History* 19, no. 3 (April 1987): 264–270.

Principally about Hannah Solomons Jacobs, the first Jewish woman to settle in San Diego (1851), her daughters, and Hannah Mannasse and her daugher Celita.

Kessler-Harris, Alice. "Organizing the Unorganizable: Three Jewish Women and Their Union." *Labor History* 17, no. 1 (Winter 1976): 5–23. Reprinted in *Class, Sex and the Woman Worker*, ed. Milton Cantor and Bruce Laurie, 144–165. Westport, CT: Greenwood, 1977.

The three indefatigable organizers of the International Ladies Garment Workers Union studied are Pauline Newman, Fannia Cohn, and Rose Pesotta. Each saw her options as either career with the union or marriage and children, and each chose the union. Kessler-Harris credits the high value American Jewish culture placed on self-sufficiency with influencing their decisions.

Kirshenblatt-Gimblett, Barbara. "The Kosher Gourmet in the Nineteenth-Century Kitchen: Three Jewish Cookbooks in Historical Perspective." *Journal of Gastronomy* 2, no. 4 (Winter 1986–87): 51–89.

Puts cookbooks forward as a source full of information on social, religious, and domestic life, particularly of women. Discusses *Jewish Cookery*, by Esther Levy, the first Jewish cookbook in the United States (Philadelphia, 1871).

Klingenstein, Susanne. "'But My Daughters Can Read the Torah': Careers of Jewish Women in Literary Academe." *American Jewish History* 83 (June 1995): 247–86.

Describes the professional paths of five Jewish female professors of literature: Susan Gubar, Carolyn Heilbrun, Marjorie Garber, Carole Kessner, and Barbara Herrnstein Smith. None received a Jewish education as a child comparable to that of boys of their generation, yet both gender and Jewishness affect their lives and careers. A groundbreaking study of Jewish women in a profession.

Korelitz, Seth. "A Magnificent Piece of Work: The Americanization Work of the National Council of Jewish Women." *American Jewish History* 83 (June 1995): 177–203.

Argues that the NCJW differed from other Americanizing organizations in its support for the expansion of women's role into the public sphere.

Kramer, William M., and Norton B. Stern. "A Woman Who Pioneered Modern Fundraising in the West." *Western States Jewish History* 19, no. 4 (July 87): 335–45.

On Anna Myers, wife of the founding rabbi of the oldest Conservative synagogue in Los Angeles.

Krause, Corinne Azen. "Urbanization Without Breakdown: Italian, Jewish, and Slavic Immigrant Women in Pittsburgh, 1900–1945." *Journal of Urban History* 4, no. 3 (May 1978): 291–306. Excerpted in *Immigrant Women*, ed. Maxine Schwartz Seller, 62–67. 2d ed. Albany: State University of New York Press, 1994.

Based on interviews with forty-five women who on the whole succeeded in adjusting to America, helped by family, neighbors, churches and synagogues, and ethnic communities.

Lamoree, Karen M. "Why Not a Jewish Girl? The Jewish Experience at Pembroke College in Brown University." *Rhode Island Jewish Historical Notes* 10, no. 2 (1988): 122–140.

Discusses admissions policy and campus life of Jewish students admitted during the period 1897–1949.

Lederhendler, Eli. "Guides for the Perplexed: Sex, Manners, and Mores for the Yiddish Reader in America." *Modern Judaism* 11, no. 3 (October 1991): 321–341.

Examines the advice manuals and journals written in or translated into Yiddish that sought to Americanize immigrant Jews through instructing them in manners, hygiene, fashion, parenting, sexuality, and birth control. Since most of these topics fall within the traditional sphere relegated to women, the literature was often addressed to them specifically.

Lerner, Anne Lapidus. "'Who Has Not Made Me a Man': The Movement for Equal Rights for Women in American Jewry." *American Jewish Year Book* 77 (1977): 3–38.

Discusses the effect feminism has had on Orthodox, Conservative, and Reform Judaism in America.

Lerner, Elinor. "American Feminism and the Jewish Question, 1890–1940." In *Anti-Semitism in American History*, ed. David Gerber, 305–328. Urbana: University of Illinois Press, 1986.

Indicts American feminism for "non-recognition of Jewish existence." The movement took no stand in the 1930s on mounting persecution of Jews in Europe, and Jewish support for feminism was rendered invisible.

Lerner, Elinor. "Jewish Involvement in the New York City Woman Suffrage Movement." *American Jewish History* 70, no. 4 (June 1981): 442–461. Reprinted in *Women and the Structure of Society: Selected Research From the Fifth Berkshire Conference on the History of Women*, ed. Barbara J. Harris and JoAnn K. McNamara, 191–205. Durham, NC: Duke University Press, 1984.

Demonstrates that Jewish women regarded woman suffrage as a civil rights issue completely in accord with American notions of equality. Discusses the roles played in the movement by Ernestine Rose, Maud Nathan, and Rose

Schneiderman and the legions of immigrant Jewish women in the victorious quest for voting rights.

Litt, Jacquelyn. "Mothering, Medicalization, and Jewish Identity, 1928–1940." *Gender & Society* 10, no. 2 (April 1996): 185–198.

Uses narratives of twenty Jewish women who gave birth to their first child between 1928 and 1940 to examine the relationship between mothers and medical discourse. The women were eager to adopt medicalized mothering practices as a sign of their advancement from immigrant culture into the American middle class.

Monson, Rela Geffen. "The Impact of the Jewish Women's Movement on the American Synagogue: 1972–1985." In *Daughters of the King: Women and the Synagogue, a Survey of History, Halakhah, and Contemporary Realities,* ed. Susan Grossman and Rivka Haut, 227–236. Philadelphia: Jewish Publication Society, 1992.

Credits the feminist movement and gains made by educated, professional Jewish women in the outside world with awakening their desire for change within Judaism. Sparked by the actions of Ezrat Nashim, a Jewish women's study group turned activist, in the early 1970s religiously committed Jewish women focused their energies on obtaining equality within the synagogue, the locus of Jewish life. Life cycle rituals were affected next, including in the Orthodox community, which introduced the *simchas bat* [naming ceremony for a baby girl] and extended the concept of bat mitzvah to mark the coming of age for Orthodox girls. Orthodox women's prayer groups formed as well. The impact on the Conservative Movement has been considerable, from ordaining women rabbis since 1985 to ceding to women many leadership positions within congregations. Developing gender-neutral liturgical language became an interest of Jewish women in the Reform Movement. Essay is followed by personal vignettes from women across the religious spectrum with varying views of the changes wrought.

Moore, Deborah Dash. "Studying the Public and Private Selves of American Jewish Women." *Lilith* 10 (Winter 1983): 28–30.

Summarizes the state of historiography of Jewish women's history as of that date.

Nadell, Pamela S., guest ed. *American Jewish History* 83, no. 2 (June 1995).

Thematic issue on American Jewish women's history, with articles by Dianne Ashton on nineteenth-century Philadelphia community leader Mary M. Cohen; Seth Korelitz on the National Council of Jewish Women; Norma Baumel Joseph on Rabbi Moshe Feinstein's view of Jewish education for women; Shuly Rubin Schwartz on the rebbetzin in twentieth-century America; Susanne Klingenstein on careers of Jewish women in literary academe; and reviews of two books on Jewish women. In the introduction, Nadell

reviews the course of incorporation of women and gender into Jewish historiography.

Nadell, Pamela S. "A Land of Opportunities: Jewish Women Encounter America." In *What is American About American Jewish History,* ed. Marc Lee Raphael, 73–90. Williamsburg, VA: Department of Religion, College of William and Mary, 1993.

Nadell extends to women's experiences a three-factor paradigm (freedom-frontier-immigration) used by Abraham J. Karp to explain what in the American national character most influenced the American Jewish community. For women, freedom of religion led to the establishment of synagogues and associated organizations where women were allowed increasing roles, particularly in Reform congregations. Frontier communities educated girls and boys together, and a dearth of traditional leaders opened up opportunities for women that included acting as rabbis in some instances. The immigration of Eastern European Jews created Conservative institutions that permitted women to become leaders more slowly than did the Reform movement yet also gradually allowed women such roles.

Nadell, Pamela S. "Rereading Charles S. Leibman: Questions From the Perspective of Women's History." *American Jewish History* 80, no. 4 (Summer 1991): 502–516.

Gracious comments on sociologist Liebman's body of work give way to chiding for his failure to include women in his studies. Provides examples where Liebman generalized about American Jewish life from exclusively male samples and calls gender an essential category of history. In a rejoinder ("A Perspective On My Studies of American Jews," pp. 517–534), Liebman retorts that he does not think his results would have been any different had he surveyed women, and that gender, like class and ethnicity, is not salient in every place and at all times.

Nadell, Pamela S. " 'Top Down' or 'Bottom Up' " Two Movements for Women's Rabbinic Ordination." In *An Inventory of Promises: Essays on American Jewish History in Honor of Moses Rischin,* ed. Jeffrey Gurock and Marc Lee Raphael, 197–208. Brooklyn: Carlson, 1995.

Contrasts the "top-down" direction in which rabbinical ordination of women became sanctioned in the Reform Movement with the "bottom-up" pathway taken by the Conservative Movement.

Nadell, Pamela S. "The Women Who Would Be Rabbis." In *Gender and Judaism: The Transformation of Tradition,* ed. T.M. Rudavsky, 123–134. New York: New York University Press, 1995.

Situates the movement for women's rabbinic ordination within the historiography of women in the professions and focuses on the handful of women who enrolled in rabbinical school courses, raising the issue of ordination in concrete terms. The story of Irma Levy Lindheim, a well-to-do New

York matron and mother of five who became an ardent Zionist and full-time student in the Jewish Institute of Religion in the 1920s, is a particularly compelling one. Although she did not complete her studies, she went on to become the second president of Hadassah, which she wrote made her feel more truly ordained than if she had been confirmed as a rabbi. Laura Geller's essay in this anthology is a useful companion piece because it examines the nature of women's rabbinical leadership in the 1990s, after hundreds of women have been ordained.

Nadell, Pamela S., and Rita J. Simon. "Ladies of the Sisterhood: Women in the American Reform Synagogue, 1900–1930." In *Active Voices: Women in Jewish Culture*, ed. Maurie Sacks, 63–75. Urbana: University of Illinois Press, 1995.

The founding of the first Reform sisterhood in 1905 by Carrie Simon, wife of the rabbi of Washington Hebrew Congregation, was influenced by a history of general benevolence performed by Hebrew ladies aid societies, the growth of synagogues as central institutions of American Jewish life, and parallel women's organizations in churches. Once established, individual sisterhoods and their umbrella organization, the National Federation of Temple Sisterhoods, moved beyond supporting activities to involvement in shaping the customs and role for women in Reform Judaism. Differs with Joselit, who views sisterhoods as negligible factors of change.

Neu, Irene D. "The Jewish Businesswoman in America." *American Jewish Historical Quarterly* 66, no. 1 (1976): 137–154.

Describes several Sephardic women merchants and shopkeepers in the eighteenth century, when it was not unusual for women to engage in business, particularly if they were unmarried or widowed. This is followed by discussion of fewer acceptable options for nineteenth- and early twentieth-century German and Eastern European immigrant married women, who could join their husbands in shopkeeping and small manufacturing ventures but rarely set out on their own. Single women might work as domestics or in factories, but they did not pursue business ventures. Neu recounts stories of some Eastern European women who showed marked entrepreneurial ability and were more enterprising than their husbands within familial businesses. After the immigrant generation, few Jewish women were engaged in business, expending their energies instead on volunteer work.

Pratt, Norma Fain. "Culture and Radical Politics: Yiddish Women Writers, 1890–1940." *American Jewish History* 70, no. 1 (1980): 68–90. Reprinted in *Decades of Discontent: The Women's Movement, 1920–1940*, ed. Lois Scharf and Joan M. Jensen, 131–152, Westport, CT: Greenwood, 1983, and in *Women of the Word: Jewish Women and Jewish Writing*, ed. Judith R. Baskin, 111–135. Detroit: Wayne State University Press, 1994.

Deals with the lives and works of some fifty writers virtually ignored by historians until Pratt rediscovered them. They shared a proletarian Eastern European Jewish background and poorly educated parents (with many of the mothers being close to illiterate). They too received little advanced formal education yet became journalists, poets, and fiction writers in their own language in America. Their writing appeared in radical, secular Yiddish newspapers and literary journals and spoke of female, Jewish, and working-class concerns and adjustments to life in America. Pratt discusses the experiences that brought many of the women to writing, and the lives of several of the writers, including Hinde Zaretsky, Esther Luria, Anna Rappaport, Fradel Stock, Yente Serdatzky, Celia Dropkin, Anna Margolin, Rachel Holtman, and Kadya Molodowsky. An appendix lists the poets, with their birth and immigration dates.

Pratt, Norma Fain. "Immigrant Jewish Women in Los Angeles: Occupation, Family and Culture." In *Studies in American Jewish Experience*, ed. Jacob R. Marcus and Abraham J. Peck, 78–89. Cincinnati: American Jewish Archives, 1981.

Takes issue with Irving Howe's view in *World of Our Fathers* that Eastern European Jewish women lost their importance in the family economy and had only marriage, motherhood, and "ladylike passivity" as roles. Pratt found a more complex situation when she examined their experiences in Los Angeles between 1900 and 1940. Like men, women were expected to work and to move from working to middle class through education for middle-class occupations, which for women meant clerical work.

Pratt, Norma Fain. "Transitions in Judaism: The Jewish American Woman Through the 1930s." *American Quarterly* 30, no. 5 (Winter 1978): 681–702. Reprinted in *Women in American Religion*, ed. Janet Wilson James, 207–228. Philadelphia: University of Pennsylvania Press, 1980.

Explains the Orthodox, Conservative, and Reform movements in American Judaism as background to discussion of changes in the type and degree of participation by women in the 1920s. In Reform and Conservative branches, only actual religious services stayed in the realm of the sacred, while Jewish education, philanthropy, social services, and culture moved outside the orbit of Talmudic/rabbinic regulation. These areas, therefore, became open to women, who availed themselves of the opportunities for involvement. Also discusses *Der Yidisher Froyen Zhurnal* [The Jewish ladies journal], 1922–1923, memoirs, poetry, and other writings by women, their organizations, and the education of girls.

Pratt, Norma Fain. "Women Moving Forward: Dreamers, Builders, Leaders: A History of Jewish Women in Southern California." *Legacy* [Southern California Jewish Historical Society] 1, no. 3 (Spring 1989), entire issue (61 p.).

Captures some significant names, events, and experiences of Jewish women settlers in Southern California from the mid-nineteenth century to the present. Like immigrants elsewhere, Jewish women in California attended schools, worked at least until marriage, and were active in Jewish women's organizations. Hollywood, however, is another story. Anzia Yezierska became an instant celebrity—the "Immigrant Cinderella"—when she was brought out to turn *Hungry Hearts* into a movie (she quickly fled), and silent screen star Carmel Myers refused advice to change her name to something not so recognizably Jewish.

Pratt, Norma Fain. "A Working Girl With a Mind of Her Own." In *An Inventory of Promises: Essays on American Jewish History in Honor of Moses Rischin*, ed. Jeffrey S. Gurock and Marc Lee Raphael, 209–222. Brooklyn, NY: Carlson, 1995.

Rediscovers lost first-generation immigrant Yiddish women writers including "sweatshop poets" Berta Nagle and Dora Mogilanski, whose themes were similar to their male working-class counterparts, and others whose writing centered on the yearnings of the working girl. Publishing in Yiddish newspapers in the first decade of the twentieth century were poet Anna Ziv, novelist Toybe Segal, and short story writers Yente Serdatsky, Miriam Karpilove, and Rokl Lurie. These writers touched on important life issues—work, sex, family, education, and justice—as seen from the eye of the working woman and may have contributed to the collective action aimed at bettering working conditions spearheaded by Jewish women not long thereafter.

Quint, Ellen Deutsch. "Women in Leadership Roles in Federations: An Historic Review." *Journal of Jewish Communal Service* 72, no. 1/2 (Fall/Winter 1995/1996): 96–101.

Reviews the progress in involvement of lay and professional women leaders in federations since the early 1970s when the issue was first put on national and local federation agendas. Surveys in 1972 of volunteer decision makers and in 1975 of professional positions found women severely limited in their participation rate. Subsequent surveys noted improvements, due to active steps taken by the federations to make their boards and upper-echelon staff positions more inclusive, yet a 1993 survey still found few women at the very top of federations in large cities. Quint calls for continued efforts to attract women philanthropists, volunteers, and professional leaders.

Rochlin, Harriet. "Riding High: Annie Oakley's Jewish Contemporaries: Was the West Liberating for Jewish Women?" *Lilith* 14 (Fall 1985/Winter 1986): 14–16.

Equivocating on a firm answer to her question, Rochlin offers examples of successful Jewish women pioneers of the West, then asks a series of quantitative, comparative, and Jewish questions awaiting further research.

Rogow, Faith. "Why Is This Decade Different From All Other Decades? A Look at the Rise of Jewish Lesbian Feminism." *Bridges* 1, no. 1 (Spring 1990): 67–79.

Explores the hints of Jewish lesbian history present in the lives of early twentieth-century social reformers and labor organizers and the fiction of Jo Sinclair. Traces developments in the 1970s including the founding of gay synagogues, networks of Jewish lesbian consciousness-raising groups, and the rise of a distinctive literature. Finds increased acceptance of gays and lesbians in congregations and rabbinical training in the 1980s but also considerable remaining homophobia, ignorance, and ignoring of lesbians by the organized American Jewish community. Criticizes Jewish feminist historical scholarship that ignores lesbians.

Sanua, Marianne. "From the Pages of 'The Victory Bulletin': The Syrian Jews of Brooklyn During World War II." *YIVO Annual* 19 (1990): 283–330.

The Victory Bulletin was a monthly published during the war by a group of young Syrian Jewish women. Besides keeping Syrian American Jewish soldiers apprised of what was going on in the community, it also advocated changes in women's roles.

Schwartz, Shuly Rubin. "'We Married What We Wanted To Be': The Rebbetzin in Twentieth-Century America." *American Jewish History* 83 (June 1995): 223–246.

Using published sources from the Conservative Movement in particular, Schwartz elevates the position of *rebbetzin* [rabbi's wife] to one of religious and communal leadership in the days before women could become rabbis.

Seller, Maxine S. "Defining Socialist Womanhood: The Women's Page of the *Jewish Daily Forward* in 1919." *American Jewish History* 76, no. 4 (June 1987): 416–438.

Analyzes the advice given women by socialist newspaper columnists, who favored involvement in unionism, woman suffrage, and the feminist movement yet required them to be true to traditional roles of Jewish women in home and family.

Seller, Maxine S. "Putting Women Into American Jewish History." *Frontiers* 5, no. 1 (Spring 1980): 59–62; and variant published as "Reclaiming Jewish Herstory" in *Lilith* 7 (1980): 23–24.

Written version of presentation made at the 1979 National Women's Studies Association. Describes issues of content, format, conceptualization, materials, and student reaction addressed by her effort to add women to a survey course on "The American Jewish Experience."

Seller, Maxine S. "World of Our Mothers: The Women's Page of the *Jewish Daily Forward*." *The Journal of Ethnic Studies* 16, no. 2 (Summer 1988): 95–118.

Demonstrates that the *Forward's* women's page emphasized politics and public affairs, as did the rest of the newspaper, along with Americanization.

Seller, Maxine Schwartz. "The Uprising of the Twenty Thousand: Sex, Class, and Ethnicity in the Shirtwaist Makers Strike of 1909." In *Struggle a Hard Battle: Essays on Working Class Immigrants*, ed. Dirk Hoerder, 254–279. DeKalb, IL: Northern Illinois University Press, 1986.

After summarizing the working conditions that led to the strike, Sellers discusses how the coincidence of class and ethnicity within the Yiddish-speaking community created the climate in which Jewish women had no conflict becoming union activists. One of the long-term impacts of the strike was that several Jewish women who came to leadership stayed active thereafter in unions, woman suffrage campaign, and other political work.

Sinkoff, Nancy B. "Educating for 'Proper' Jewish Womanhood: A Case Study in Domesticity and Vocational Training, 1897–1926." *American Jewish History* 77, no. 4 (June 1988): 572–599.

German Jewish women associated with the Clara de Hirsch Home for Working Girls in New York City helped train young Eastern European immigrant women for work and domestic life in America. Their attitude was compassionate but patronizing.

Sochen, June. "Happy Endings, Individualism, and Feminism in American Jewish Life." *American Jewish History* 81 (Spring/Summer 1994): 340–345.

Included in a thematic issue of *American Jewish History* devoted to the American dimension of American Jewish history, Sochen speculates on the influence on Judaism of the American regard for individual autonomy and attention to gender. Jewish feminists in her view provide a model of successful integration of Jewish commitment to social justice and American respect for individual rights.

Sochen, June. "Some Observations on the Role of the American Jewish Women as Communal Volunteers." *American Jewish History* 70, no. 1 (1980): 22–34.

Stresses that insufficient attention has been paid by either the Jewish community or historians to the importance of women volunteers, in particular the "professional board ladies," who are professional in all senses of the word except remuneration.

Sochen, June, guest ed. *American Jewish History* 70, no. 1 (1980).

Thematic issue on American Jewish women's history, including articles by Deborah Grand Golomb on the 1893 Congress of Jewish Women; the New York City Kosher Meat Boycott of 1902, by Paula Hyman; volunteer activists, by June Sochen; Julia Richman's work, by Selma Berrol; Yiddish women writers, by Norma Fain Pratt; images of Jewish women in modern American drama, by Ellen Schiff; and Henry Hurwitz's mother remembered.

Stern, Norton B. "The Charitable Jewish Ladies of San Bernadino and Their Woman of Valor, Henrietta Ancker." *Western States Jewish Historical Quarterly* 13, no. 4 (July 1981): 369–376.

Discusses the Henrietta Hebrew Benevolent Society, founded in 1880, and its original guiding light and namesake, Henrietta Ancker. Says that this is the only instance of a Jewish charitable group in the West being named for a person.

Stern, Norton B. "The Jewish Community of a Nevada Mining Town." *Western States Jewish Historical Quarterly* 15, no. 1 (1982): 48–78.

Includes discussion of six Jewish women entrepreneurs who owned grocery stores, a millinery shop, a restaurant, and a boardinghouse in Eureka, Nevada, in 1878.

Tenenbaum, Shelly. "The Ways We Were: Buying Chickens, Paying Bills: Jewish Women's Loan Societies." *Lilith* 16, no. 3 (Summer 1991): 32+.

Highlights information about Jewish women borrowers and lenders that is analyzed thoroughly in her *A Credit to Their Community: Jewish Loan Societies in the United States, 1880–1945* (Detroit: Wayne State University Press, 1993).

Toll, William. "The Domestic Basis of Community: Trinidad Colorado's Jewish Women, 1889–1910." *Rocky Mountain Jewish Historical Notes* 8, no. 4/9, no. 1 (Summer/Fall 1987). Reprinted in *Women, Men and Ethnicity: Essays on the Structure and Thought of American Jewry*, by William Toll, 59–70. Lanham, MD: University Press of America, 1991.

After the founding of the Hebrew Ladies Aid Society in 1899, Trinidad's women gradually became the organizing force for the Jewish community, raising funds for needy members and others and sponsoring social events.

Toll, William. "The Female Life Cycle and the Measure of Jewish Social Change: Portland, Oregon, 1880–1930." *American Jewish History* 72, no. 3 (1983): 309–332.

Applies sociological methods to Jewish history. Examines changes in indicators from the life cycle of women, including age at marriage, differential age between wife and husband, number of children, and work history to understand how the Jewish community develops over time. While differences exist between women of German or Eastern European origin, American-born daughters of both groups shared a marked decline in family size and increase in work participation.

Toll, William. "A Quiet Revolution: Jewish Women's Clubs and the Widening Female Sphere, 1870–1920." *American Jewish Archives* 41, no. 1 (Spring/Summer 1989): 7–26.

How middle-class American Jewish women regarded themselves and their sense of purpose underwent a major shift during this time period. At first Jewish women, like their Protestant counterparts, did "instinctive nurturing"—informal, sisterly work on behalf of needy Jews, as part of their religious obligation. When specialized institutions took over these general benevolent functions, this role faded. By the 1890s they were attempting to better the lives of the less-fortunate Jews and non-Jews by applying principles from the new field of social science. They formed settlement houses and educated themselves to become politically astute, informed advocates for improvements in public health and a variety of social issues.

Umansky, Ellen. "Feminism and American Reform Judaism." In *The Americanization of the Jews*, ed. Robert M. Seltzer and Norman J. Cohen, 267–283. New York: New York University Press, 1995.

Discusses why it took Reform Judaism until the late 1960s to decide to ordain women rabbis even though the movement from its mid-nineteenth-century inception espoused an egalitarian philosophy. According to Umansky, the stance was more theoretical than practical. It required impetus from social changes in the 1960s to create a climate of receptivity. Those changes included more Protestant denominations ordaining women, actual qualified women who were considering the rabbinate, a shortage of rabbis in the movement, and some indication that congregations would be willing to accept women rabbis. While the decision to admit women to rabbinical study was made before the modern women's movement had gotten off the ground, it subsequently influenced developments in all aspects of Reform Judaism. The nature of the rabbinate and cantorate began to change in response to feminist notions of balance, intimacy, and empowerment. Lay leadership, religious education, liturgy, receptivity to women's midrashim [textual interpretations], acceptance of patrilineal descent, and endorsement of ordination for gay and lesbian Jews are all attributable in whole or in part to feminism.

Umansky, Ellen M. "Spiritual Expressions: Jewish Women's Religious Lives in the Twentieth-Century United States." In *Jewish Women in Historical Perspective*, ed. Judith R. Baskin, 265–288. Detroit: Wayne State University Press, 1992.

Examines the nature of Jewish women's religious lives beyond the study of religious texts and participation in communal worship, which constitute the traditional definition of Judaism. Umansky finds philanthropic and educational endeavors by Jewish women to be steeped in religious values and spiritual meaning. Likewise, literary writers like Elizabeth Stern and Anzia Yezierska evidenced struggles with religious identity, and Josephine Lazarus wrote an explicitly

theological tract, *Spirit of Judaism* (1896). In the 1920s, Martha Neumark sought ordination from the Reform movement, arguing that women were in fact better suited for a Reform rabbinate than men, since most of the people attending services were women who could better identify spiritually with a woman rabbi. In the last twenty years, women rabbis have added a personal approach to sermons, and many Jewish feminists have created new rituals. These themes are further explored and documented in her *Four Centuries of Jewish Women's Spirituality* (with Diane Ashton; Boston: Beacon Press, 1992).

Walden, Daniel, ed. *Studies in American Jewish Literature*, no. 3. Albany: State University of New York Press, 1983.

Entire issue devoted to Jewish women writers and the portrayal of women in American Jewish literature, with contributions by June Sochen ("Identities Within Identity: Thoughts on Jewish American Women Writers"); Norma Fain Pratt ("Anna Margolin's *Lider*: A Study in Women's History, Autobiography, and Poetry"); articles by Susan Kress, Rose Kamel, Ellen Golub, and Susan Hersh Sachs on Anzia Yezierska; considerations of Grace Paley (by Dena Mandel) and Cynthia Ozick (by Deborah Heiligman Weiner); and the image of women in the writings of twentieth-century male Jewish authors.

Watkins, Susan Cotts, and Angela D. Danzi. "Women's Gossip and Social Change: Childbirth and Fertility Control Among Italian and Jewish Women in the United States, 1920–1940." *Gender & Society* 9, no. 4 (August 1995): 469–490.

Through interviews with elderly Jewish and Italian women in New York and Philadelphia, Watkins and Danzi find differences in their acceptance of birth control and of hospitals as desired places for births. The authors attribute the variation to differences between Jewish and Italian social networks. Jewish women had a larger and more varied circle with whom to exchange ideas, and the greater number of Jewish medical professionals in their personal networks also influenced their ability to accept new practices. An interesting contribution to the study of ethnic differences in the acceptance of new health care practices that listens carefully to what the women were saying.

"We Honor Our Founding Mothers," *Na'amat Woman* 5, no. 4 (September/October 1990): 4–10+ and 5, no. 5 (November/December 1990): 16–20.

In celebration of the sixty-five birthday of Na'amat USA (formerly Pioneer Women), several members offer reminiscences of their mothers who worked tirelessly for the organization. "Pioneer Women/Na'amat USA was her life," say Edith Gates, daughter of Rose Brooker, but it could have been said about all the women mentioned. They lived in New York, Milwaukee, Sioux City, Iowa, and many other places but shared a common vision of bettering the lives of women and children in Israel and the United States.

Wenger, Beth S. "Jewish Women and Voluntarism: Beyond the Myth of Enablers." *American Jewish History* 79, no. 1 (Autumn 1989): 16–36.

Attributes the persistence of the view of women as only facilitators whose actions empowered others, even after they had become activists in their own right, to the fact that thinking of women as "enablers" meant there was no need to redefine gender roles.

Wenger, Beth S. "Jewish Women of the Club: The Changing Public Role of Atlanta's Jewish Women (1870–1930)." *American Jewish History* 76, no 3 (March 1987): 311–333.

Argues that clubs moved Jewish women out of the home and into public life in Jewish institutions and the general community of Atlanta earlier than this happened in northern communities.

Zandy, Janet. "Our True Legacy: Radical Jewish Women in America." *Lilith* 14, no. 1 (Winter 1989): 8–13.

Recalls the strikers, union leaders, and women's rights activists who can serve as models of "applied spirituality and courageous disobedience."

COLLECTIONS OF MEMOIRS, ORAL HISTORIES, AND CREATIVE WRITINGS

For full editions of published memoirs by individuals, see their entries in the *Encyclopedia*. Numerous other unpublished memoirs by women are found in archives throughout North America.

Antler, Joyce, ed. *America and I: Short Stories by American Jewish Women Writers*. Boston: Beacon Press, 1990. 355 p.

Arranged historically, this anthology takes readers on a tour through Jewish women's experience in America as registered by the creative imagination of twenty-three gifted authors, from Mary Antin and Edna Ferber writing in the second decade of this century through Cynthia Ozick, Grace Paley, and others in the 1980s. Antler's introductory essay reviews the recurrent Jewish themes in the writing (assimilation versus tradition, loss of identity, unfamiliar cultures, quest for moral meaning in Judaism, antisemitism, marginality, generational conflict, social commitments, and the importance of writing) and provides a historical/biographical context for the selections.

Blicksilver, Edith, ed. *The Ethnic American Woman: Problems, Protests, Lifestyle*. Rev. ed. Dubuque, IA: Kendall/Hunt, 1989, 471 p.

Jewish women's voices chime in throughout this anthology, with selections ranging from union leader Rose Schneiderman on her childhood to Judith Plaskow's 1973 address on Jewish feminism at a National Jewish Women's Conference.

Fishman, Sylvia Barack, ed. *Follow My Footprints: Changing Images of Women in American Jewish Fiction*. Hanover, NH: University Press of New England for Brandeis University, 1992. 506 p.

Anthology of short stories and excerpts from novels that trace the development of the self-sacrificing mother in nineteenth-century Yiddish literature (from I.L. Peretz, Sholem Aleichem, and others) into the domineering, overprotective mother and her materialistic princess daughter in twentieth-century American works most associated with Philip Roth. Adds section by contemporary women writers (from Tillie Olsen, Grace Paley, Cynthia Ozick, and more) who write of the struggles of women protagonists balancing American and Jewish values. Fishman opens with an essay on the historical position of women in Jewish life and provides brief introductions to each selection.

Frommer, Myrna Katz, and Harvey Frommer. *Growing Up Jewish in America: An Oral History*. New York, Harcourt, 1995. 264 p.

Almost half the voices of teachers, writers, librarians, administrators, businesspeople, Jewish communal workers, and other twentieth-century Jews in this entertaining collective memoir are women's.

Kaye/Kantrowitz, Melanie, and Irena Klepfisz, eds. *The Tribe of Dina: A Jewish Women's Anthology*. Boston: Beacon Press, 1989. 360 p.

Diverse collection of poems, stories, interviews, and essays by Jewish women past and present from the United States, Europe, and Israel. Irena Klepfisz's essay on secular Jewish identity ("Yidishkayt in America"), Melanie Kaye/Kantrowitz's "To Be a Radical Jew in Late Twentieth Century," and Bernice Mennis's "Jewish and Working Class" are moving statements of their Jewish connections. Other contents of historical interest include a story and poem by immigrant Yiddish writer Fradel Shtok, translated by Klepfisz, an interview with long-term political activist Lil Moed, and Sarah Schulman's "When We Were Very Young: A Walking Tour Through Radical Jewish Women's History on the Lower East Side, 1879–1919." An earlier version of *The Tribe of Dina* appeared as issue 29/30 of *Sinister Wisdom* in 1986.

Kramer, Sydelle, and Jenny Masur, eds. *Jewish Grandmothers*. Boston: Beacon Press, 1976. 174 p.

Gripping oral histories of ten elderly women in Chicago, whose collective lives stand for the experiences of thousands of "ordinary" Jewish immigrants. What emerges from the narratives are portraits of risk takers, rebels against traditional attitudes, and women fiercely committed to education.

Krause, Corinne Azen. *Grandmothers, Mothers and Daughters: Oral Histories of Three Generations of Ethnic American Women*. Boston: Twayne, 1991. 231 p.

Based on oral histories conducted for the study "Women, Ethnicity, and Mental Health," sponsored by the American Jewish Committee in the 1970s, this is a highly accessible book for the general reader. In assessing the interviews with successive generations in the same families, Krause found that what each grandmother thought and said affected how her daughter and granddaughter lived their lives. Jewish grandmothers in the study often had worked in factories before marriage and in husband-wife businesses afterward, yet they did not consider their role in the businesses as "work." Instead, they "helped out," but their real focus was on their children. The daughter generation was better educated but also centered on raising families and on the accomplishments of their children. The granddaughters had still more education than their mothers and, influenced by feminism, careers that they valued. Includes edited narratives of three generations of two Jewish families, with similar chapters for Slavic and Italian women. Krause reinterviewed the women still alive in 1989 and added updated information. The Jewish women's family lines are Sylvia Sacks Glosser–Naomi Cohen–Cathy Droz and Eva Rubenstein Dizenfeld–Belle Stock–Ruth Zober.

Marks, Marlene Adler, ed. *Nice Jewish Girls: Growing Up in America*. New York: Plume, 1996. 292 p.

Collection of more than forty coming-of-age stories by established writers such as Vivian Gornick, Erica Jong, and Grace Paley, and newer writers Carolyn White, Karen Golden, and others. Engagement with Judaism and Jewishness characterizes the stories as a whole. Sections of the book focus successively on events in early childhood, memories of Jewish rituals, adolescent experiences, and encounters with the non-Jewish world.

Matza, Diane, ed. *Sephardic-American Voices: Two Hundred Years of a Literary Legacy*. Hanover, NH: University Press of New England for Brandeis University Press, 1997. 363 p.

Recovers the words of a minority-within-a-minority, whose works are at the margins of both mainstream and Jewish American writings. According to Matza, Sephardic literature is marked by its cosmopolitanism, the confidence of its women writers, and the examination of patriarchal culture by both men and women. Fourteen of the thirty writers included are women. Descendants of colonial Sephardim, Penina Moïse, Emma Lazarus, and Annie Nathan Meyer represent "insiders" who feel quite at home in America,

while Gloria De Vidas Kirchheimer, Rosaly DeMaios Roffman, Emma Adatto Schlesinger, Rae Dalven, and Ruth Behar are twentieth-century writers who display attachments to the world left behind. The only anthology of its kind, this collection is an eye-opener to the unrecognized contribution of Sephardic women and men to American Jewish literature.

Mazow, Julie Wolf, ed. *The Woman Who Lost Her Names: Selected Writings of American Jewish Women*. San Francisco: Harper, 1980. 222 p.

Selections were chosen in which the writers reveal positive views of themselves as women and as Jews (unlike the image of Jewish women found in literature by Jewish men), replete with examples of the importance to them of tradition and family. Most are contemporary writers, but Anzia Yezierska, and Emma Goldman are included as well.

Moskowitz, Faye, ed. *Her Face in the Mirror: Jewish Women on Mothers and Daughters*. Boston: Beacon Press, 1994. 314 p.

Stories, poems, essays, and novel excerpts written since 1945 on facets of the complex relationship between Jewish mothers and daughters. The mother-daughter theme captures the differences between two postwar generations (more limited lives for the mothers; more dangers for the daughters) of American Jewish women. Many of the writers are assimilated Jews who write as outsiders to Jewish life. A few are returning from nonobservant backgrounds to tradition. Good mix of all types of women, working class to wealthy, heterosexual and lesbian.

Niederman, Sharon, ed. *Shaking Eve's Tree: Short Stories of Jewish Women*. Philadelphia: Jewish Publication Society, 1990. 279 p.

This is the first short story collection of works consciously both Jewish and feminist. The stories explore what it means to be a Jewish female and probe the depths of Jewish identity in America today. Like *Her Face in the Mirror* (above) mother-daughter relationships are also an important theme in this anthology by contemporary American Jewish women writers.

Rubin, Steven J. *Writing Our Lives: Autobiographies of American Jews, 1890–1990*. Philadelphia: Jewish Publication Society, 1991. 347 p.

Combines in one volume characteristic excerpts from twenty-six autobiographies, including eleven by women. The book is divided into three historical periods, with the earliest featuring writers born around the turn of the century. The immigrant writers Mary Antin, Rebekah Kohut, and Golda Meir sought ways to define themselves within a new culture; their stories become the collective experience of the Jewish people. Edna Ferber is the only American-born writer included from that period. Her experience differs from the others because she deals with small-town Jewish life in the Midwest. The second section includes selections from the children of immigrants, now more assimilated into American culture but aware of the losses of tradition. Feminists Kate Simon and Faye Moskowitz and historian of the Holocaust Lucy Dawidowicz are the women contributors from this period. The three females in the last section have had very different lives. Vivian Gornick's emphasis on understanding the bond between her immigrant mother and herself epitomizes the experience of a generation of contemporary Jewish women. Holocaust survivor Isabella Leitner's *Saving the Fragments: From Auschwitz to New York* (1985) is representative of many survivor autobiographies that deal with unspeakable memories of concentration camps as well as adjusting to life afterward. Eva Hoffman was born in Poland at the close of the war and came to Canada as a thirteen-year-old. She, too, must adjust to a new life, but her focus is on the relationship between identity and lost language. These excerpts are well chosen from published autobiographies; eloquent unpublished accounts preserved in archives await a similar treatment.

Rubin-Dorsky, Jeffrey, and Shelley Fisher Fishkin, eds. *People of the Book: Thirty Scholars Reflect on Their Jewish Identity*. Madison: University of Wisconsin Press, 1996. 507 p.

Richly textured autobiographical accounts by contemporary academics reflecting on their connections to Jewishness, in particular inquiring of themselves how their scholarship is influenced by being Jewish. Sixteen of the thirty are women. These feminist literary critics, anthropologists, and others have achieved the pinnacle of secular intellectual success, beyond the dreams of their mothers, immigrant grandmothers, and earlier forebears. Each must confront the meaning of gender as well as ethnicity in her search for identity.

Seller, Marine Schwartz, ed. *Immigrant Women*. 2d ed. Albany: State University of New York Press, 1994. 378 p.

Jewish women's writing featured includes that of Golda Meir, Emma Goldman, and Anzia Yezierska, as well as excerpts from scholarly writing on Jewish women: "Urbanization Without Breakdown," on adaptations to America by Italian, Slavic, and Jewish women, by Corinne Azen Krause; and "Strategies for Growing Old: Basha is a Survivor," from *Number Our Days*, by Barbara Myerhoff (New York: Dutton, 1978). The first edition of *Immigrant Women* contains additional essays from Jewish women, including statements by Ernestine Rose and Rose Schneiderman, and excerpts from *The Jewish Woman in America*, by Charlotte Baum, Paula Hyman, and Sonya Michel (New York: Dial, 1976).

Umansky, Ellen M., and Dianne Ashton, eds. *Four Centuries of Jewish Women's Spirituality: A Sourcebook*. Boston: Beacon Press, 1992. 350 p.

Since Umansky and Ashton have an expansive definition of spirituality, encompassing thoughts and deeds of social reformers, literary authors, and Jewish communal leaders imbued with spiritual feelings, this anthology has numerous selections of relevance to all aspects of Jewish women's history. Although the book begins in the sixteenth century, most of the voices heard are nineteenth- and twentieth-century Americans. Umansky's essay, "Piety, Persuasion, and Friendship: A History of Jewish Women's Spirituality," characterizes women's spirituality historically as private, spontaneous, and emotional, and it introduces the forms of spiritual expression: diaries, memoirs, letters, speeches, sermons, creative writing, and, in late twentieth century, new rituals marking events in women's lives.

ARCHIVAL RESOURCES

By their very nature, archival resources are unique, and finding them presents unique problems. The principal tool for locating cataloged archival collections in the United States is the *National Union Catalog of Manuscript Collections (NUCMC)*, published in print by the Library of Congress through 1993, and available on-line through the Research Libraries Information Network (RLIN)'s Archival Catalog, which is also accessible through the NUCMC Internet site (http://lcweb.loc.gov/coll/nucmc/nucmc.html). Some research libraries also have *The National Inventory of Documentary Sources in the United States (NIDS US)*, a compilation of thousands of finding aids from hundreds of repositories (microfiche set published by Chadwyck-Healey), and *ArchivesUSA*, a database from Chadwyck-Healey that combines *NUCMC*, the *NIDS US* Index, and other material. Unfortunately, many collections languish uncataloged and unreported to *NUCMC*. Compounding the problem, material relevant to Jewish women, and women in general, has long been obscured within the very repositories themselves, subsumed within family collections, those named for male relatives, and institutional or communal records combining various committees and organizations. The Social Welfare History Archives at the University of Minnesota spearheaded a project from 1975 to 1979 that surveyed repositories in the United States for sources on women. This effort resulted in *Women's History Sources: A Guide to Archives and Manuscript Collections in the United States*, edited by Andrea Hinding (2 vols., New York: Bowker, 1979), which described more than 18,000 collections in 1,586 repositories. Several collections of Jewish women's organizations are included, and the index term "Jews" as well as the names of various Jewish organizations point to the papers of individual women with Jewish activities. However, since there was no systematic attempt to index as Jewish all Jewish women in the *Guide*, there are actually more collections of Jewish women's papers present than appear at first glance.

Since 1979, the interest in recovering the role of women in the Jewish community has intensified, leading to the acquisition and description of much relevant print material within archives under Jewish auspices and elsewhere. In addition, many women whose accomplishments might have been lost to history because they kept no written records have been interviewed by oral history projects, and the tapes and transcripts from the projects are available in archives. Besides those listed below, there are numerous ongoing projects taping the testimony of women and men who survived the Holocaust and settled in America. For a description of the Holocaust projects, including a breakdown by gender, see *A Catalogue of Audio and Video Collections of Holocaust Testimony*, by Joan Ringelheim, 2d ed., Westport, CT: Greenwood Press, 1992. The US Holocaust Memorial Museum Archives is a source for written testimonies by women, described on the museum's Internet site (http://www.ushmm.org).

Thus, it is apparent that information about archival resources on Jewish women remains scattered and incomplete. The Jewish Women's Archive is a recently established organization whose plans include a much-needed project of identifying material on Jewish women in archives across the country and creating a database that will unify access to the information. Until that project is completed, the best current sources of information are published guides to repositories, available in many research libraries, and unpublished finding aids for individual collections, available through *NIDS US* or at the repositories. At present, many archival institutions are moving rapidly to establish presences on the Internet, and some have begun mounting their finding aids and, occasionally, actual documents from their collections. This development can raise awareness of the priceless holdings throughout America documenting the contributions of Jewish women to all endeavors.

What follows is a preliminary list of significant repositories for researching Jewish women's history, with information on published guides, the location of records of national offices of Jewish women's organizations, and selected examples of collections of personal papers and oral histories. The absence of an institution from the list should not be taken to mean there are no relevant holdings in that repository. Preserved records of local affiliates of Jewish women's organizations as well as papers of individual women

active in their communities are apt to be in state or local historical societies, synagogues, or nearby Jewish historical museums and archives where they exist. University archives are a potential resource for finding papers and oral histories of Jewish women associated with universities.

Note: All dates pertain to the span of coverage within collections rather than birth and death dates for individuals, unless otherwise specified.

American Jewish Archives
Hebrew Union College
3101 Clifton Avenue
Cincinnati, OH 45220

Guide:

Clasper, James W., and M. Carolyn Dellenbach. *Guide to Holdings of the American Jewish Archives*. Cincinnati: American Jewish Archives, 1979.

Catalog:

Manuscript Catalog 1991 (51 fiche)

Organizations:

Association for the Relief of Jewish Widows and Orphans, 1854–1938

B'nai B'rith Women national records, 1947–1985

Emma Lazarus Federation of Jewish Women's Clubs

National Federation of Temple Sisterhoods, District Nine, Ohio Valley Federation, 1913–1978 (later called Women of Reform Judaism)

Major holdings of records for congregations, sisterhoods, and local women's benevolent societies ("Hebrew Ladies Aid Society of . . .")

Personal Papers (a sampling demonstrating the range of material from women in hundreds of collections):

Amy Blank, letters, autobiography, and poems, 1922–1967

Fannie Bloomfield-Zeisler, 1882–1925; concert pianist

Alice B. Citron, 1933–1979; educator, civil rights worker

Lillian Adlow Friedberg, 1913–1970; executive director Jewish Community Relations Council of Pittsburgh

Sophie G. Friedman, 1897–1953; lawyer in Memphis, TN

Jennie R. Gerstley, 1859–1934; founder Chicago Woman's Aid; notes by Sarah Nunes Falter on Gerstley's trip across the Atlantic in the 1850s

Rose Bogen Gold, 1905–1941; nurse, autobiography

Anna M. Kross, 1910–1974; judge

Tehilla Lichtenstein, 1929–1970; sermons, correspondence, etc., from leader of the Jewish Science Movement

Adah Isaacs Menken, 1832–1860; poet, actress

Annie Nathan Meyer, 1858–1950; founder, Barnard College, social activist, anti-suffragist, active in home economics movement

Martha Neumark Montor; rabbinical school applicant in 1920s (correspondence file)

Jennie Franklin Purvin, 1868–1958; executive of Mandel Brothers Department Store, Chicago

Rena M. Rohrheimer, 1935–1950; efforts to get Jews out of Nazi-occupied Europe; travels

Marjorie Rukeyser, 1965–1967; president, National Federation of Temple Sisterhoods

Clara Lemlich Shavelson; labor activist

Hannah Greenebaum Solomon; founder, National Council of Jewish Women (biographies file)

Frances Stern, 1921–1967; nutritionist

Sophie Tucker, 1911–1966; actress

Ida Uchill, 1913–1950; from Denver, CO

Weiss-Rosmarin, Trude, 1962–1975; scholar, editor *The Jewish Spectator*

Miscellaneous:

Women authors of histories of local communities

American Jewish Committee. Oral History Library
Jewish Division
New York Public Library
Fifth Avenue and 42 Street
New York, NY 10018

Guide:

American Jewish Committee. Oral History Library. *Catalogue of Memoirs* v. 1–3. New York: The Committee, 1978–1993.

Oral Histories:

American Jewish Women of Achievement series, 1970s–
Ongoing collection of interviews with women from all walks of life who discuss their backgrounds, careers, voluntary activities, and families. Included among the scores of women interviewed are Bella Abzug, politician; Celia Adler, Yiddish actress; Georgette Bennett, banker, criminologist, journalist; Rachel B. Cowan, rabbi, foundation director; Midge Decter, author; Ariel Durant, author; Estelle S. Frankfurter, labor relations specialist; Ellen Futter, college president, lawyer; Hortense W. Gabel, judge; Helen Galland, retailer; Manya Gersen, dentist; Temima Gezari, artist, teacher; Elinor Guggenheimer, civic planner and leader; Charlotte Jacobson, community leader; Melanie Kahane, interior and industrial designer; Grace LeBoy Kahn, composer; Lillian Vernon Katz, entrepreneur; Bel Kaufman, teacher, author; Sylvia Fine Kaye, producer; Madeleine Kunin, Vermont governor; Esther R. Landa, civic leader; Edith Davis Lyons, Planned Parenthood leader; Vivian Mann, art historian, Judaica curator; Ellen Stettner Math, cantor; Herta Mayer, Jewish communal worker; Harriet F. Pilpel, attorney; Belva Plain, author; Letty Cottin Pogrebin, author; Justine Wise Polier, judge; Shirley Polykoff, advertising executive; Anna Maximilian Potok, furrier; Bernice Resnick Sandler, researcher, editor, women's advocate; Claudia Weill, filmmaker; Rosalyn S. Yalow, medical physicist, Nobel Prize winner; and many more.

Women of Achievement, Atlanta (Tapes are also in the Jewish Heritage Center of Atlanta)
Interviews with more than fifty women.

Women of Achievement, Cleveland (Tapes are also in the Western Reserve Historical Society)
Nineteen interviews.

Other oral history series by the committee also include women.

American Jewish Historical Society
2 Thornton Road
Waltham, MA 02154

Organizations:

American Jewish Congress, Women's Division

Columbia Religious and Industrial School for Jewish Girls, 1905–1944; records of New York school founded in 1888

Federation of Jewish Women's Organizations (NY), 1912–1982 (formerly Federation of Sisterhoods)

Jewish Reconstructionist Foundation, Women's Organization

National Conference on Soviet Jewry, Women's Plea, 1971–1978

Union of Orthodox Jewish Congregations of America, Women's Branch, 1923–1968

Personal Papers:

Sadie American, social worker

Lucy Dawidowicz, historian

Cecilia Razovsky Davidson, 1922–1968; social worker, National Refugee Service leader

Bilhah Abigail Levy Franks, 1733–1748; colonial correspondent

Rebecca Gratz, 1794–1869; Philadelphia educator

Emma Lazarus, 1869–1887; poet, essayist

Ray Frank Litman, 1871–1957; lecturer, journalist, first "girl rabbi"

Mordecai Family, 1771–1907; includes correspondence of several women members of the family

Molly Picon, 1876–1967; actress

Grace Seixas Nathan, 1805–1830; poet, author

Emily Solis-Cohen, 1923–1936; author, educator, active in the National Jewish Welfare Board

Leona G. and David A. Bloom
Southwest Jewish Archives
1052 N. Highland Avenue
Tucson, AZ 85721

Doll Collection:

Ten Jewish women pioneers; background descriptions found in *Some Amazing Arizonan Jewish Women of the Past*, available on the Internet (http://dizzy.library.arizona.edu/images/swja/dolls.html).

Internet Exhibit:

http://dizzy.library.arizona.edu/images/swja/swja.list
(Internet site contains photographs, memoirs, and other documents from additional southwestern Jewish women, indexed by individual or family name.)

Boston University.
Mugar Memorial Library Special Collections
Boston, MA 02215

Personal Papers:

Margaret Gene Arnstein, 1929–1972; professor and dean of public health nursing

Bella Fromm (Steuerman), 1917–1971; journalist, social columnist

Helen Deutsch, 1890s–1960s; theatrical press agent, film writer

Emma Goldman, 1907–1939; anarchist, writer

Joanne Goldenberg Greenberg, 1950s–; writer

Maxine Kumin, 1940s; poet

Libby Holman, 1860s–1970; singer, actress

Lenore Guinzburg Marshall, 1935–1971; poet, novelist

Sylvia Rothchild (Sylvia Rossman), 1945–; author

Ruth Seid (Jo Sinclair), 1922–1960s; writer

Irene Mayer Selznick, 1910–; theatrical producer

Theresa Wolfson, 1953–1970; economist

Anzia Yezierska, 1922–1970; writer

Canadian Jewish Congress. National Archives
1590 Docteur Penfield
Montreal, Quebec H3G 1C5
Canada

Organizations:

National Council of Jewish Women of Canada, 1916–1975

Central Zionist Archives
Jerusalem, Israel

Organizations:

Hadassah

Personal Papers:

Rose G. Jacobs, 1910–1960; Hadassah leader

Jessie Sampter; writer, Zionist

Alice Seligsman, 1917–1942; Hadassah leader

Henrietta Szold; Hadassah founder, writer, editor

Chicago Historical Society
North Avenue and Clark Street
Chicago, IL 60614

Organizations:

National Council of Jewish Women Chicago Section, 1898–1968 (includes material on founder Hannah Greenebaum Solomon)

Personal Papers:

Julia and Alice Gerstenberg; social leaders

Lillian Herstein, 1920–1958; teacher, union leader

Chicago Jewish Archives
Spertus College
618 S. Michigan Avenue
Chicago, IL 60605

Organizations:

Jewish Federation of Metropolitan Chicago, Women's Division, 1933–1964

Personal Papers:

Spiegel Family, 1945–1956 (includes Lizzie Barbe, first president of the Jewish Manual Training School of Chicago)

Columbia University.
Oral History Collection
Box 20 Butler Library
New York, NY 10027

Oral Histories:

Theresa Goell, 1965; archaeologist

Dorothy Gordon, radio pioneer

Pauline Newman, 1965; labor activist

Sheba Skirball, 1976; librarian

Columbia University.
Rare Book and Manuscript Library
Butler Library
New York, NY 10027

Personal Papers:

Bella Savitsky Abzug, 1970–1976; congresswoman

Rose Franken, 1925–1966; novelist, playwright

Emma Lazarus, 1868–1887, correspondence; poet, essayist

Bella (and Sam) Spewack, 1920–1980; writer

Cornell University.
Catherwood Industrial
and Labor Relations Library.
Labor Management Document Center
229 Ives Hall
Ithaca, NY 14853

Organizations:

National Consumers League, 1911–1947, includes material from Josephine Goldmark

Teachers Union of the City of New York, 1916–1964, includes material about Jewish women active in the union and defendants in cases

Personal Papers:

Theresa Wolfson, 1919–1970; labor arbitrator

Cornell University Library. Department of Manuscripts and University Archives
Ithaca, NY 14853

Personal Papers:

Stonehill/Schwartzkopf Family, 1904–1909, includes Elsie B. Schwartzkopf, teacher; Theresa Stonehill, memoir, 1904

Ellis Island Immigration Museum
Statue of Liberty National Monument
Liberty Island
New York, NY 10004

Oral Histories:

Ellis Island Oral History Project
Many Jewish women immigrants are among the interviewees.

Hadassah Women's Zionist Organization of America. Archives
50 West 58 Street
New York, NY 10019

Guide:

Geller, L.D. *The Henrietta Szold Papers in the Hadassah Archives, 1875–1965.* N.P.: Hadassah: 1982.

Organizations:

Numerous series of records for Hadassah and its divisions, 1912–

Personal Papers:

Denise Tourover Ezekiel, 1935–1981; attorney, national Hadassah Board member

Rose G. Jacobs, 1910–1940; Hadassah president

Henrietta Szold, 1875–1982; Zionist leader, editor, translator, founder of Hadassah

Historical Society of Pennsylvania
1300 Locust Street
Philadelphia, PA 19107

Guide:

Ashton, Dianne. *The Philadelphia Group and Philadelphia Jewish History: A Guide to Archival and Bibliographic Collections.* Philadelphia: Center for American Jewish History, Temple University, 1993 (covers archives in Philadelphia and elsewhere).

Personal Papers:

Mary Fels, 1907–1952; writer, community leader

Gratz Family, 1825–1891; includes material from Louisa, Caroline, and Elizabeth Gratz

Historical Society of Western Pennsylvania
4338 Bigelow Blvd.
Pittsburgh, PA 15213

Oral Histories:

Tapes and transcripts from the "Women, Ethnicity, and Mental Health" study conducted by Corinne Azen Krause sponsored by the American Jewish Committee, 1975. Includes seventy-five interviews with three generations of women in Jewish families in Pittsburgh area.

Jewish Community Library
6505 Wilshire Blvd.
Los Angeles, CA 90048

Organizations:

Various community records, including the Jewish Mothers Alliance

Oral Histories:

Jewish Oral History interviews include five women descendants of prominent Jewish families in the area.

Leo Baeck Institute
129 East 73 Street
New York, NY 10021

Personal Papers (the institute focuses on German Jewry but contains collections from German Jews who immigrated to the United States):

Hannah Arendt, 1958–1965; philosopher, political scientist

Alice Salomon, 1746–1761; social worker

Selma Stern (Taubler); German Jewish historian

Lesbian Herstory Archives
P.O. Box 1258
New York, NY 10116

Guide:

"Special Collections," *Lesbian Herstory Archives News* 6 (July 1980): 3–4, and "Recent Acquisitions" in subsequent issues. The archives holds memoirs, interviews, musical recordings, unpublished manuscripts, and photographs of Jewish lesbians.

Personal Papers:

Liza Cowan, 1970–1989; broadcaster, publisher, founder of White Mare Archives

Deborah Edel, 1971–; child psychologist, cofounder of Lesbian Herstory Archives

Maxine Feldman, 1970–1989; composer, singer, music producer

Joan Nestle, 1968–; writer, teacher, cofounder of Lesbian Herstory Archives

Adrienne Rich, 1950–1978; writer

Sarah Schulman, 1980–; writer, cofounder of Lesbian Avengers

Sonny Wainwright, 1972–1985; writer, breast cancer activist, cofounder of Feminist Writers Guild

Maxine Wolfe, 1974–; teacher, activist, cofounder of Lesbian Avengers

Library of Congress. Manuscripts Division
Washington, DC 20540

Guide:

Kohn, Gary. *The Jewish Experience: A Guide to Manuscript Sources in the Library of Congress.* Cincinnati: American Jewish Archives, 1986.

Organizations:

National Council of Jewish Women, national office, 1929–1981

Personal Papers:

Hannah Arendt, 1898–1976; philosopher, political scientist

Berta Bornstein, n.d.; psychoanalyst

Jo Davidson, n.d.; sculptor

Lillian Evarts, 1933–1956; poet

Anna Freud, 1954–1969; psychoanalyst

Pauline Goldmark, 1865–1941; social worker

Rebecca Gratz, n.d.; educator

Rose Pastor Stokes, 1913–1915; unionist

Minnesota Historical Society
Archives and Manuscripts
345 Kellogg Blvd.
St. Paul, MN 55102

Organizations:

National Council of Jewish Women, Minneapolis Section, 1917–1970

Personal Papers:

Fanny Fligelman Brin, 1896–1958; civic leader, pacifist

National Archives of Canada
395 Wellington
Ottawa, Ontario K1A 0N3
Canada

Guide:

Tapper, Lawrence. *Archival Sources for the Study of Canadian Jewry*, 2d ed. Ottawa: The Archives, 1987.

Organizations:

Hadassah-WIZO Organization of Canada, 1912–1975

Personal Papers:

Nina Fried Cohen, 1925–1981; Jewish community leader

Sharon Drache, 1978–1983; journalist

Sarah Fischer, 1874–1975; opera singer

Phyllis Gotlieb, 1949–1974; poet

Sarah Gotlieb, 1932–1983; Jewish community leader

Suzann Cohen Hutner, 1921–1981; copublisher of *Canadian Jewish Review*

Ethel Ostry, 1945–1947; welfare officer with UN relief organization

National Center for Jewish Film
Lown Building
Brandeis University
Waltham, MA 02254-9110

Holds numerous films in English and Yiddish portraying Jewish women.

National Jewish Archive of Broadcasting
Jewish Museum
1109 Fifth Avenue
New York, NY 10128

Guide:

Subject Guide to the Collection of the Jewish Museum's National Jewish Archive of Broadcasting. New York: Jewish Museum, 1988.

Audio- and videotapes of programs with Jewish themes and characters, including Jewish women.

New York.
92nd Street YM-YWHA
1395 Lexington Avenue
New York, NY 10128

Organizations:

Clara de Hirsch Home for Working Girls, founded 1897

New York.
Federation of Jewish Philanthropies
130 East 59 Street
New York, NY 10022

Guide:

Oral History Collection of the Federation of Jewish Philanthropies of New York. New York: the Federation, 1985.

Oral Histories:

Many women are among the civic leaders and social service executives active in the New York Federation interviewed in the 1980s, including Helen L. Buttenwieser, Elinor Guggenheimer, Lucy G. Moses, Dorothy F. Rodgers, and several others.

New York Public Library.
Lincoln Center Performing Arts
Research Center
40 Lincoln Center Plaza
New York, NY 10023

Personal Papers:

Helen Tamaris, 1939–1966; dancer, choreographer

New York Public Library.
Manuscripts and Archives
Fifth Avenue and 42 Street
New York, NY 10018

Personal Papers:

Fannia Mary Cohn, 1919–1962; union official, educator

Babette Deutsch, 1923–1941; poet, critic, author

Emma Goldman, 1906–1940; anarchist, editor

Bel Kaufman, n.d.; author, teacher

Rose Pesotta, 1922–1965; unionist, official of the International Ladies Garment Workers Union

Lillian D. Wald, 1918–1940; Henry Street Settlement House founder

New York University. Tamiment Library
New York, NY 10012

Guide:

Guide to the Manuscript Collection of the Tamiment Library, compiled by the staff of the Tamiment Collection, Dorothy Swanson, Librarian. New York: Garland, 1977.

Personal Papers:

Emma Goldman, 1924–1940; anarchist, editor, activist

Rose Schneiderman, 1904–1975; president National Women's Trade Union League

Rose Pastor Stokes, 1905–1933; socialist and communist activist, writer

Oral Histories:

Immigrant Labor History Project

Oral History of the American Left Collection
Both of these collections include interviews with Jewish women.

Oregon Jewish Oral History and Archive Project
Mittleman Jewish Community Center
6651 S. Portland
Portland, OR 97219

Oral Histories:

Interviews documenting the history of Jews in Oregon. About half the seventy interviews were with women.

Philadelphia Jewish Archives Center
Balch Institute
18 South Seventh Street
Philadelphia, PA 19106

Guides:

Nauen, Lindsay B. *A Guide to the Philadelphia Jewish Archives Center*. Philadelphia: the Center, 1977.

Ashton, Dianne. *The Philadelphia Group and Philadelphia Jewish History: A Guide to Archival and Bibliographic Collections*. Philadelphia: Center for American Jewish History, Temple University, 1993 (covers archives in Philadelphia and elsewhere).

Organizations:

Association for Jewish Children and its predecessors, including the Jewish Foster Home and Orphan Asylum, founded by Rebecca Gratz

Hebrew Sunday School Society, 1838–1976; founded by Rebecca Gratz with an all-female board of directors

Na'amat USA [formerly Pioneer Women], Philadelphia Council, 1949–1990

Women's League for Conservative Judaism, Philadelphia, 1964–1978

Personal Papers:

Rita Gerstley, 1950–1969, civic activist

Arline Lotman, 1971–1974; *Jewish Exponent* columnist

Sybil Richman Margolis, 1922–1957; active in the American Jewish Congress, Philadelphia

Sarah Newhoff, 1915–1958; philanthropist

Lena Schleindlinger, 1937; customhouse broker

Anne Smilowitz, 1926–1946; secretary

Research Foundation for Jewish Immigration
570 7th Avenue, 11th floor
New York, NY 10018

Guide:

Lessing, Joan C. *Jewish Immigrants of the Nazi Period in the U.S.A.* vol. 3/1, *Guide to the Oral History Collection of the Research Foundation for Jewish Immigration*. New York: K.G. Saur, 1981.

Oral Histories:

Oral History Collection

Women interviewed in the 1970s included social workers, entrepreneurs, housewives, physicians, journalists, artists, librarians, political leaders, and others.

Arthur and Elizabeth Schlesinger Library on the History of Women in America
Radcliffe College
Harvard University
Cambridge, MA 02138

Catalog:

The Manuscript Inventories and the Catalogs of Manuscripts, Books and Periodicals, 2d rev. ed. Boston: G.K. Hall, 1984; also available as *Women in the U.S.: Collections of the Schlesinger Library, Radcliffe College* (CD-ROM). Palo Alto: Dialog, 1994.

Personal Papers:

Jennie Loitman Barron, 1911–1969; judge

Judy Chicago, 1970–1996; artist

Ethel Cohen, 1918–1977; medical social worker

Helene Deutsch, 1900–1984; psychoanalyst

Betty Friedan, 1952–1993; author, feminist leader

Theresa Goell, 1920–1985; archaeologist

Bertha Sanford Gruenberg, 1898–1985; lecturer, journalist, director of camp using John Dewey's progressive principles

Elinor Coleman Guggenheimer, 1959–1980; day care and planning advocate

Frances Fineman Gunther, 1915–1963; journalist

Gerda Lerner, 1955–1981; historian, author

Maud Nathan, 1890–1938; social reformer, Consumers' League leader

Pauline Newman; labor movement activist

Justine Wise Polier, 1892–1990; lawyer, judge, juvenile justice advocate, daughter of Rabbi Stephen and Louise Waterman Wise

Rebecca Hourwich Reyher, n.d. (lived 1897–1987); writer, lecturer, suffragist

Adrienne Rich, 1933–1984; poet, teacher

Beatrice Sadowsky, 1928–1984; transportation executive

Barbara Seaman, 1920–1983; women's health activist

Barbara Miller Solomon, 1936–1988; historian, university dean

Smith College. Sophia Smith Collection
Northampton, MA 01063

Guide:

Murdock, Mary-Elizabeth. *Catalog of the Sophia Smith Collections, Women's History Archive*, 2d ed. Northampton, MA: Smith College, 1976.

Catalog:

Catalogs of the Sophia Smith Collection. Women's History Archive. 7 v. Boston: G.K. Hall, 1975.

Personal Papers:

Anna Moskowitz Kross, n.d.; New York City commissioner of corrections

Florence Rena Sabin, 1871–1953; physician, medical researcher

Geraldine Stern, n.d.; artist, author

Stanford University Libraries. Department of Special Collections
Stanford, CA 94305

Personal Papers:

Tillie Olsen, 1930–1990, writer

State Historical Society of Wisconsin
816 State Street
Madison, WI 53706

Guides:

Guide to the Wisconsin Jewish Archives at the State Historical Society of Wisconsin, 2d ed. Madison: the Society, 1992.

Leuchter, Sara, with the assistance of Jean Loeb Lettofsky. *Guide to Wisconsin Survivors of the Holocaust: A Documentation Project of the Wisconsin Jewish Archives.* Madison: SHSW, 1983.

Personal Papers:

Lizzie Black Kander, 1875–1960; author, *Settlement Cook Book* (housed in the Area Research Center, Milwaukee)

Myrtle Baer, 1854–1963; social worker and editorial staff member of the *Settlement Cook Book* (housed in the Area Research Center, Milwaukee)

Edna Ferber, 1910–1977; author

Myra Hess, 1950–1969; concert pianist

Elizabeth Brandeis Raushenbush (and Paul A.), 1918–1980; economist

Adele Szold, 1895–1996; letters by University of Wisconsin freshman to her sister Henrietta; other letters

Oral Histories:

Documenting the Midwestern Origins of the Twentieth Century Women's Movement Project, 1987–1992, includes Gene Boyer, businesswoman.

Wisconsin Jewish Oral History Interview Project, 1954–1974, includes fourteen women from around the state.

Evelyn Torton Beck, professor, 1975 interview

Syracuse University Library. Manuscripts Collection
Syracuse, NY 13244

Personal Papers:

Gertrude Berg, 1930–1962; radio and television actress

Jan Gelb (and Boris Margo), 1915–70; artist

Tulane University. Howard-Tilton Memorial Library Special Collections Division. Manuscripts Department
New Orleans, LA 70118

Guide:

Collections related to Southern Jewish history are described on the Internet (http://www.tulane.edu/~lmiller/JewishStudiesIntro.html), and based on work by Andrew Simons, 1995.

Personal Papers:

Doris Laurie Chesky, 1950–1975; music teacher

Mathilde Dreyfous, 1952–1971, civil rights activist

Ida Weiss Friend, 1837–1963; social and civic activist (finding aid on the Internet site)

Amelia Greenwald, 1908–1966; nurse

Miriam Levy, 1920s–1950s; artist, jeweler

Clara Lowenburg Moses, 1870s–1920s; Natchez, MS memoir

Oral Histories:

Lucy Ater, 1974; caterer

Renee Samuel Bear, 1974; nurse

University of California, Berkeley. Bancroft Library Manuscripts Division
Berkeley, CA 94720

Personal Papers:

Ellise Stern Haas (includes letters from Alice B. Toklas)

Clara Garfinkle Shirpser, 1948–1973; Democratic National Committeewoman, California

Oral Histories:

California Jewish Community
Project conducted by the Regional Oral History Office, Bancroft Library, University of California, Berkeley, from 1968 to the 1980s and underwritten by the Western Jewish History Center; interviewed several women civic leaders from around the state.

Los Angeles City Council member and Democratic Party activist Rosalind Weiner Wyman is one of the women interviewed for the *Women in Politics Oral History Project*. Other oral histories in the division feature Jewish women who were early residents of California with a range of interests, from a 1985 interview with poet and teacher Flora Jacobi Arnstein to suffragist and National Woman's Party activist Rebecca Hourwich Rayher (in the *Suffragists Oral History Project* Collection, 1977).

University of California, Berkeley.
Emma Goldman Papers Project
2372 Ellsworth Street
Berkeley, CA 94720

Project has collected tens of thousands of documents by and about anarchist, birth control advocate, lecturer, editor Goldman from libraries and other sources around the world. Much of this is published in the Project's *Emma Goldman Papers: A Microfilm Edition* (Chadwyck-Healey, 1991). Exhibits from the project can be viewed on the Internet (http://sunsite.berkeley.edu/Goldman/).

University of Illinois at Chicago Library
801 South Morgan Street
P.O. Box 8198
Chicago, IL 60608

Personal Papers:

Helen Aaron, 1942–1972; Chicago civic leader

Rose Greenbaum Hass Alschuler, 1916–1973; philanthropist, nursery school expert

Esther Loeb Cohen, 1896–1965; social worker

Hilda Satt Polacheck, 1910–1958; resident of Hull House neighborhood, writer

Esther Saperstein, 1949–1975; Chicago alderperson

University of Michigan—
Wayne State University.
Institute of Labor and Industrial Relations.
Programs on Women and Work
Victor Vaughan Building
1111 East Catherine Street
Ann Arbor, MI 48109

Oral Histories:

The Twentieth Century Trade Union Woman: Vehicle for Social Change Oral History Project, 1970–79, includes interviews with Mollie Levitas, Pauline Newman, and other Jewish labor leaders.

University of North Carolina.
Wilson Library.
Manuscripts Department.
Southern Historical Collection
Chapel Hill, NC 27514

Inventories:

Many collection descriptions are mounted on the Internet (http://www.unc.edu/lib/mssinv/).

Personal Papers:

Rachel Lyons Heustis, 1859–1965; resident of South Carolina, correspondence with authors and soldiers

Miriam Gratz Moses, 1824–1864; letters from her aunt Rebecca Gratz and others

Mordecai Family, 1783–1947; correspondence of female seminary director Jacob Mordecai with family members

Phillips-Myers Collection includes material from Confederate Eugenia Levy Phillips and her daughter Caroline Phillips Myers

University of Pennsylvania.
Center for Judaic Studies
420 Walnut Street
Philadelphia, PA 19106

Guide:

Ashton, Dianne. *The Philadelphia Group and Philadelphia Jewish History: A Guide to Archival and Bibliographic Collections.* Philadelphia: Center for American Jewish History, Temple University, 1993 (covers archives in Philadelphia and elsewhere).

Personal Papers:

Mary M. Cohen (and Charles J.), 1846–1920; journalist, poet, civic leader

Emily Solis-Cohen (Solis-Cohen Family Papers), 1857–1948; writer and activist (Additional papers held privately, at Wolf, Block, Shorr and Solis-Cohen law firm, Philadelphia.)

University of Pittsburgh Libraries.
Archives of Industrial Society
Pittsburgh, PA 15260

Organizations:

Records of Pittsburgh chapters of Hadassah (1917–1968) and the National Council of Jewish Women (1893–1967), and for the Pittsburgh Conference of Jewish Women's Organizations (1923–1963)

University of Texas.
Harry Ransom Humanities
Research Center
P.O. Drawer 7219
Austin, TX 78713

Personal Papers:

Lillian Hellman, 1931–1970; playwright

Fannie Hurst, 1927–1960; novelist

University of Washington Libraries.
Archives and Manuscripts Division
Seattle, WA 98195

Personal Papers:

Jeanette Schreiber, 1956–1980; active in Jewish women's organizations in Seattle

Bella Kracower Secord, 1898–1925; pharmacist

Oral Histories:

Jewish Archives Project, 1849–1975
Includes some records of Jewish women's organizations in Washington State and many interviews with women covering the first half of the twentieth century. Several were members of Seattle's Sephardic community.

Western Jewish History Center
Judah L. Magnes Museum
2911 Russell Street
Berkeley, CA 94710

Guide:

Rafael, Ruth Kelson. *Western Jewish History Center Guide to Archival and Oral History Collections.* Berkeley: WJHC, Judah L. Magnes Memorial Museum, 1987.

Organizations:

California Alliance of Jewish Women (college students), 1922–1958

Emanu-El Sisterhood for Personal Service (San Francisco organization that sponsored a residence home for young Jewish working women for over forty years), 1894–1969

Records of various congregational sisterhoods and local chapters of national women's organizations

Personal Papers:

Flora Jacobi Arnstein, 1884–1974; poet, author, teacher

Selma Ruth Miguel Cohn, 1881–1971; soprano, concert vocalist

Jennie Harris, 1902–1972; businessperson, songwriter

Lila B. Hassid, 1959–1971; translator of Yiddish works, Jewish folklore radio program host, Jewish community center director

Florence Prag Kahn (and Julius Kahn), 1852–1948; teacher, congresswoman

Estelle Goodman Levy, 1850–1973; active in organizations in the Southwest

Miriam Fligelman Levy, 1943–; human rights and peace activist, youth advocate

Hattie Mooser and Minnie Mooser, 1877–1967; hostesses for gatherings of people in the arts, proprietors of San Francisco's first supper club

Fanny Jaffe Sharlip, 1880–1960s; factory worker, shopkeeper

Rosalie Meyer Stern, 1842–1977; San Francisco civic and social leader

Oral Histories:

Jewish Lives in Perspective
Interviews by Vista College, University of California, Berkeley, students, sponsored by WJHC. Women interviewed include a welder, bus driver, language teacher, weaver, and pharmacist.

Northern California Jews From Harbin, Manchuria
Includes two women.

San Francisco Jews of Eastern European Origin, 1880–1940.
Project conducted 1976–1978, sponsored by the WJHC and the American Jewish Congress, San Francisco; included ten women.

Miscellaneous additional oral histories with Bay Area women leaders

Western Reserve Historical Society
10825 East Blvd.
Cleveland, OH 44106

Guide:

Pike, Kermit J. *A Guide to Jewish History Sources in the History Library of the Western Reserve Historical Society.* Cleveland: the Society, 1983.

Organizations:

Cleveland chapters of Hadassah, National Council of Jewish Women, and Women's American ORT

Personal Papers:

Mary B. Grossman, 1921–1966; lawyer

Jeanette Sheifer, 1921–1979; nursery school administrator

Selma H. Weiss, 1926–1946; social worker

Yale University.
Beinecke Rare Book and Manuscript Library
New Haven, CT 06511

Personal Papers:

Gertrude Stein and Alice B. Toklas, 1901–1987; authors

YIVO Institute for Jewish Research
555 West 57 Street, 11th floor
New York, NY 10019

Organizations:

National Desertion Board (dealt with thousands of cases of desertion by immigrant Jewish husbands)

Pioneer Women [later Na'amat] national records, 1913–1952; Zionist organization

United Hebrew Immigrant Aid Society, 1907–1950 records preserve HIAS's efforts on behalf of immigrant women (and men)

YIVO holds the records for numerous individual landsmanshaftn [organizations of immigrants from a particular area], which often include women's divisions. For example, the American Federation for Polish Jews [federation of landsmanshaftn] records include the Women's Division, Ezra, founded in 1931.

Personal Papers:

Diana Blumenfeld (and Jonas Turkow), c. 1930–1961; Yiddish actors

Ida Hoffman, c. 1900–1966; nurse, social worker

Sarah Liebert, 1920–1955; president, Sholem Aleichem Women's Organization

Lilian Lux (and Paul Burstein), 1930–1979; Yiddish comedians and actors

Rina Opper (pen name of Rayne Opoczyski), 1921–1969; Yiddish writer

Anna Shomer Rothenberg, 1916–1951; singer and community activist

Rose Schwartz,1900–1974; officer of the women's division of the a landsmanshaftn federation

Dora Weissman (and Anshel Shor) papers, 1906–1966; Yiddish actors, owned talent agency

Oral Histories:

Amerikaner-Yiddishe Geshichte Bel Pe Collection
Includes labor leader Pauline Newman (1965) and several more women.

Oral History transcripts of interviews conducted 1974–1975 for the book *Jewish Grandmothers* by Sydelle Kramer and Jenny Masur

Notes on Editors and Contributors

THE EDITORS

Paula E. Hyman is the Lucy Moses Professor of Modern Jewish History at Yale University. Born in Boston in 1946, she is the oldest of three daughters of Sydney and Ida (Tatelman) Hyman, both American-born children of Eastern European immigrants. She was given a Jewish education at a five-day-a-week Hebrew school and then at Boston's Hebrew Teachers College. After graduating from Radcliffe College with a B.A. in 1968, she earneded a Ph.D. from Columbia University in 1975. While a graduate student, she joined the New York Havurah, a Jewish fellowship that combined religious observance, study, and social action. She has been a feminist activist within the Jewish community for more than twenty-five years. Hyman married Stanley Rosenbaum, a physician, in 1969; their two daughters, Judith and Adina, were born in 1973 and 1976. After several years of teaching at Columbia, in 1981 Hyman joined the faculty of the Jewish Theological Seminary of America. There she also served as dean of the Seminary College of Jewish Studies, the first female dean in the seminary's history. In 1986 she moved to Yale, where she chairs the Program in Judaic Studies. Hyman's publications have focused on the social history of French Jewry and on Jewish women's history. Her books include the coauthored *The Jewish Woman in America*, *From Dreyfus to Vichy: The Remaking of French Jewry, 1909–1939*, *The Emancipation of the Jews of Alsace: Acculturation and Tradition in the Nineteenth Century*, and *Gender and Assimilation: The Roles and Representation of Women*.

Deborah Dash Moore is a fourth-generation American who has devoted most of her academic career to interpreting the history of American Jews. She was born in New York City in 1946, the first child of Irene Golden and Martin Dash. They raised her and her sister, Deena, in the Reconstructionist Movement. After receiving her B.A. from Brandeis University, she married MacDonald Moore in 1967. She combined graduate studies at Columbia University, where she received her Ph.D. in 1975, with motherhood. Her two sons, Mordecai and Mikhail, were born in 1971 and 1974. In 1976, Moore joined the Religion Department of Vassar College, becoming a full professor in 1988. From 1992 to 1995, she served as director of the American Culture Program. Her first book, *At Home in America: Second Generation New York Jews*, examined New York Jews in the years between the world wars; her most recent book, *To the Golden Cities: Pursuing the American Jewish Dream in Miami and L.A.*, followed New Yorkers in their postwar migrations. She is currently researching American Jewish GIs in World War II.

EDITORIAL ADVISORY BOARD

Joyce Antler is the Samuel Lane Professor of American Jewish History and Culture at Brandeis University, where she chairs the American Studies Department. Her works in women's history include *The Journey Home: Jewish Women and the American Century* and, as editor, *America and I: Short Stories by American-Jewish Women Writers* and *Talking Back: Images of Jewish Women in American Popular Culture*.

Dore Ashton is an art historian and cultural critic who has written twenty-five books on the visual and performing arts and has curated a number of exhibitions. She is professor of art history at the Cooper Union in New York City.

Adrienne Fried Block, a musicologist, specializes in the music of American women. Her *Women in American Music: A Bibliography of Music and Literature* remains a standard reference work in its field, and she is author of *Amy Beach, Passionate Victorian: The American Composer and Her Music*.

Ze'eva Cohen was born in Tel Aviv, Israel, and studied at New York's Juilliard School, subsequently performing with the Anna Sokolow Dance Company for several years. Cohen was a founding member of the Dance Theater Workshop, where she worked as a choreographer and dancer until 1971, when she initiated her pioneering solo dance repertory program that toured throughout the United States, Canada, Europe, and Israel. In 1983, she founded Ze'eva Cohen and Dancers, and in recent years she has choreographed works for the Boston Ballet, the Munich Tanz project, Batsheva Dance Company of Israel, and Alvin Ailey Repertory Ensemble. Currently, Cohen is setting two of her works on Inbal Dance at the Theater of Israel, while continuing her performances. She is professor of dance at Princeton University, where she founded the Dance Program and is its coordinator.

Hasia R. Diner is the Paul S. and Sylvia Steinberg Professor of American Jewish History at New York University. Her books include *In the Almost Promised Land: American Jews and Blacks, 1915–1935*, *Erin's Daughters in America: Irish Immigrant Women in the Nineteenth Century*, and *A Time for Gathering: The Second Migration, 1820–1880*.

Patricia Erens is professor of film studies in the department of comparative literature at the University of Hong Kong. Her publications include *The Jew in American Cinema*. She is also the editor of *Sexual Stratagems: The World of Women in Film* and *Issues in Feminist Film Criticism*.

Sylvia Barack Fishman is assistant professor in the Near Eastern and Judaic Studies Department at Brandeis University, specializing in contemporary Jewish life and the sociology of American Jews. She also serves as associate director of the International Research Institute on Jewish Women at Brandeis. She is the author of *Follow My Footprints: Changing Images of Women in American Jewish Fiction*, *A Breath of Life: Feminism in the American Jewish Community*, and *American Jewish Lifestyles in Cultural Context*. Fishman received her Ph.D. in English literature from Washington University in 1980 and the Samuel Belkin Distinguished Professional Achievement Award from Yeshiva University, her undergraduate alma mater, in 1991.

Jenna Weissman Joselit, who received her B.A. from Barnard College and her Ph.D. from Columbia University, is a historian who lectures and writes on American Jewish culture and history. Her many publications include *Our Gang: Jewish Crime and the New York Jewish Community, 1900–1940* and *The Wonders of America: Reinventing Jewish Culture, 1880–1950*, which won the National Jewish Book Award in History in 1995. She has received grants and fellowships from the University of Pennsylvania's Center for Judaic Studies and Princeton University's Center for the Study of American Religion. Joselit has also curated or contributed to more than twenty exhibitions throughout the United States and Israel, such as *Getting Comfortable in New York: The American Jewish Home, 1880–1950*, *A Worthy Use of Summer: Jewish Summer Camping in America*, and *The Glitter and the Gold: Fashioning America's Jewelry*. She is currently at work on a social history of clothing in nineteenth- and twentieth-century America.

Alice Kessler-Harris is professor of history and former director of women's studies at Rutgers University, where she received her M.A. and Ph.D. Among her numerous publica-

tions are *Out to Work: a History of Wage-Earning Women in the United States*; *A Woman's Wage: Historical Meanings and Social Consequences*; and *U.S. History as Women's History: New Feminist History*, edited with Linda Kerber and Kathryn Kish Sklar. A graduate of Goucher College (A.B.), Kessler-Harris has won a number of fellowships, awards, and honorary degrees. Her current work examines the gendered construction of social policy and culture.

Anne Lapidus Lerner is vice chancellor at the Jewish Theological Seminary, the first woman to hold that post and the highest-ranking woman at the institution. She teaches in the Department of Jewish Literature and serves as program adviser of the newly created M.A. Program in Jewish Women's Studies. Previously, she served as dean of the seminary's List College for seven years. Lerner's scholarly interests include the study of modern Jewish literature, particularly poetry. She is author of "Who Has Not Made Me a Man: The Movement for Equal Rights for Women in American Judaism" and *Passing the Love of Women: A Study of Gide's 'Saul' and Its Biblical Roots*. She is one of the editors of *Gender and Text: Feminist Approaches to Modern Hebrew and Yiddish Literature*. Lerner holds a Ph.D. in comparative literature from Harvard University and master's and bachelor's degrees from both Harvard University and Hebrew College.

Deborah Lipstadt is Dorot Professor of Modern Jewish and Holocaust Studies at Emory University, where she directs the Graduate Program in Jewish Studies. Her latest book, *Denying the Holocaust: The Growing Assault on Truth and Memory*, won the Jewish Honor Book award in 1994. She was a consultant to the United States Holocaust Memorial Museum and participated in designing the section of the museum dedicated to the American response to the Holocaust. In June 1994, she was appointed by President Clinton to the United States Holocaust Memorial Council, where she serves as a member of the council's Executive Committee and chairs the museum's Education Committee. Lipstadt is currently writing a book based on the Holocaust in the postwar American political, religious, and social imagination, and is the author of *Beyond Belief: The American Press and the Coming of the Holocaust*.

Pamela S. Nadell is associate professor of history and director of the Jewish Studies Program at American University and cochair of the women's caucus of the Association for Jewish Studies. She holds a Ph.D. from Ohio State University. In addition to articles on Jewish immigration and American Jewish women, she is the author of *Conservative Judaism in America: A Biographical Dictionary and Sourcebook* and is working on a book on the history of women's rabbinic ordination.

Anita Norich is a scholar of Yiddish literature who has taught American Jewish and Yiddish literature and literature of the Holocaust at the University of Michigan since 1983. Born in 1952 in a displaced persons camp near Munich, Germany, she immigrated to the United States in 1957 with her parents and brother. She attended New York City public schools and graduated from Barnard College in 1973. She earned her Ph.D. in Victorian literature from Columbia University in 1979 and studied Yiddish literature at the YIVO Institute for Jewish Research in New York and the Hebrew University in Jerusalem. Norich has published numerous articles exploring contemporary Jewish and Yiddish culture and is the author of *The Homeless Imagination in the Fiction of Israel Joshua Singer* and coeditor of *Gender and Text in Modern Hebrew and Yiddish Literature*.

Norma Fain Pratt has written extensively on American Jewish political history, immigration, and women's history, focusing especially on the late nineteenth and early twentieth centuries. Her works include *Morris Hillquit: A Political Biography of an American Jewish Socialist, Women Moving Forward: Dreamers, Builders, Leaders,* and "Culture and Radical Politics: Yiddish Women Writers, 1880–1940." Pratt has also published fiction and translations.

Elisabeth Israels Perry holds a Ph.D. from the University of California at Los Angeles. Among her recent books are *Belle Moskowitz: Feminine Politics and the Exercise of Power in the Age of Alfred E. Smith, The Challenge of Feminist Biography: Writing the Lives of Modern American Women,* and *American Women in Political Parties, 1880–1960*. She has also published articles on Eleanor Roosevelt's early career, American Girl Scouting, and the political choices of women in postsuffrage New York.

Riv-Ellen Prell is associate professor of American studies at the University of Minnesota, where she is also associated with women's studies and Jewish studies. She received her Ph.D. in anthropology from the University of Chicago. She is the author of *Prayer and Community: The Havurah in American Judaism* and coeditor with the Personal Narratives Group of *Interpreting Women's Lives*. She has published articles about ritual, gender relations, and the development of twentieth-century American Jewish life and culture.

Sheila M. Rothman is a senior research scholar at the College of Physicians & Surgeons of Columbia University. She is the author of *Woman's Proper Place: A History of Changing Ideals and Practices 1870 to the Present* and *Living in the Shadow of Death: Tuberculosis and the Social Experience of Illness in American History*. Her current research focuses on the ethical implications of the genome project. She also directs the program in human rights and medicine, which trains medical students about the social and medical needs of vulnerable populations and provides opportunities for them to care for new immigrants to New York City and refugees and displaced persons overseas.

Nahma Sandrow is a professor at Bronx Community College, City University of New York. She has written prize-winning musicals based on Yiddish theater material, including *Kuni-Leml* and *Vagabond Stars*. Sandrow is the author of *Vagabond Stars: A World History of Yiddish Theater* and *Surrealism: Theater, Arts, Ideas*. She also reviews Yiddish theater and translates plays.

Shelly Tenenbaum is associate professor of sociology and adjunct associate professor of Jewish Studies at Clark University. She is currently a visiting scholar in the Department of Sociology at the University of California at Berkeley. A graduate of Antioch College (B.A.) and Brandeis University (M.A., Ph.D.), Tenenbaum specializes in American Jewish studies, race and ethnicity, and Jewish women's history. Her publications include *A Credit to Their Community: Jewish Loan Societies in the United States, 1880–1945* and *Feminist Perspectives on Jewish Studies*, edited with Lynn Davidman. Tenenbaum has won a number of fellowships and awards and has

been an editorial board member of the *Journal of Race, Sex, and Class*.

Ellen M. Umansky is the Carl and Dorothy Bennett Professor of Judaic Studies at Fairfield University. Umansky received her B.A. in philosophy from Wellesley College, her M.A. in religion from Yale University, and her Ph.D. from Columbia University. Among her publications are *Four Centuries of Jewish Women's Spirituality: A Sourcebook* (coeditor) and *Lily Montagu and the Advancement of Liberal Judaism: From Vision to Vocation*, as well as numerous articles on women and Judaism and on modern Jewish history and thought. Umansky is a contributing editor of *Sh'ma: A Journal of Jewish Responsibility*, a member of the advisory board of the *Reconstructionist*, and a member of the editorial board of the *Journal of Feminist Studies in Religion*.

CONTRIBUTORS

Pnina Abir-Am is the author of more than thirty publications in the history of molecular biology and related fields, including *From Collective Memory to History in Molecular Biology: Commemorating the Secret of Life in the United States, United Kingdom, and France*. She is the coeditor of *Creative Couples in the Sciences* and *Uneasy Careers and Intimate Lives: Women in Science, 1789–1979*, for which she received an award from the History of Science Society for outstanding research. She has taught at Johns Hopkins University, the Hebrew University of Jerusalem, and the University of Ottawa, where she currently holds the joint chair (with Carelton University) in women's studies. In August 1997, she became a National Science Foundation visiting professor in history of science and women's studies at the University of California at Berkeley.

Naomi Abrahami is a writer, performer, and choreographer. She received her B.A. in art history from Brown University and her M.A. in dance from the University of California at Los Angeles. Her articles on dance, art, and music have appeared in *Dance Magazine, Jewish Week, Hadassah Magazine,* and *Jewish Journal*.

Jeanne Abrams is director of the Rocky Mountain Jewish Historical Society and Beck Archives of Rocky Mountain Jewish History at the Center for Judaic Studies at the University of Denver. Among her publications are *Historic Jewish Denver, Colorado Jewish History: A Guide for Teachers,* and *Blazing the Tuberculosis Trail in Colorado*, as well as articles on Colorado Jewish history. Abrams received her Ph.D. in American history from the University of Colorado. She is currently working on a manuscript titled "Children Without Homes: The Plight of Orphans in Denver, 1880–1930."

Ruth Abusch-Magder is working on a Ph.D. in modern Jewish history at Yale University. She has a B.A. from Barnard College and is coauthor of *The Jewish Women's Awareness Guide*. She writes and speaks about cookbooks.

Martha Ackelsberg, a graduate of Radcliffe College (B.A.) and Princeton University (M.A., Ph.D.), is professor of government at Smith College. With research interests that include feminism, anarchism, and Jewish ethics, Ackelsberg has published numerous articles as well as *Free Women of*

Spain: Anarchism and the Struggle for the Emancipation of Women and *Women, Welfare, and Higher Education: Toward Comprehensive Policies*, edited with Randall Bartlett and Robert Buchele. She has won a Bunting Institute fellowship from Radcliffe.

Alan Ackerman is completing his doctorate in English at Harvard University. His dissertation explores the relationships between theater and other forms of literature in nineteenth-century America.

Eliyana R. Adler is a doctoral student in Jewish history at Brandeis University. She holds a B.A. in history and Jewish studies from Oberlin College and a joint master's degree in women's studies and Judaic studies from Brandeis University.

Joseph S. Alper is professor of chemistry and director of the Center for Genetics and Public Policy at the University of Massachusetts at Boston. He received his B.A. from Harvard and his Ph.D. from Yale. Alpert has published articles on theoretical chemistry as well as on the ethical, political, legal, and social implications of human genetics research and technology.

Sara Alpern received her Ph.D. from the University of Maryland. She is associate professor of history at Texas A&M University, where she teaches the history of American women. Alpern is the author of *Freda Kirchwey: A Woman of the Nation* and is a contributor to and coeditor of *The Challenge of Feminist Biography: Writing the Lives of Modern American Women*. She has written on the effects of woman suffrage and the history of eating disorders among women, and she is at work on a manuscript on the history of women in business.

Rebecca T. Alpert is codirector of the women's studies program and assistant professor of women's studies at Temple University. She is the rabbi and the former dean of students at the Reconstructionist Rabbinical College. Alpert has taught and published extensively in the areas of women in religion, medical ethics, contemporary Judaism, and gay and lesbian studies. She is the coauthor of *Teaching Medical Ethics to Theological Students* and *Exploring Judaism: A Reconstructionist Approach* and is now completing *The Outsider Within: Jewish Lesbians and the Jewish Community*.

Zalman Alpert is reference librarian at the Mendel Gottesman Library of Yeshiva University.

Julie Altman is a Ph.D. candidate in history and education at Columbia University. Her dissertation is "Expert Women, Expert Wives: the Association of Collegiate Alumnae and American Higher Education, 1883–1918."

Donald Altschiller is the history bibliographer at Mugar Memorial Library at Boston University. He has edited several books and was a contributor to *The Jewish Almanac*. In addition to writing articles for Jewish periodicals, he reviews books for library journals.

Ziva Amishai-Maisels holds the Alice and Edward G. Winant Chair for Art History and is head of the Robert and Clarice Smith Center for Art History at the Hebrew University of Jerusalem, where she received her Ph.D. She has written extensively on modern art, concentrating on modern Jewish art and on Gaugin. One of her recent publications is *Depiction and Interpretation: The Influence of the Holocaust on the Visual Arts*.

Gannit Ankori is a lecturer in art history at the Hebrew University of Jerusalem. She specializes in modern art, aesthetics, and feminist art theory and has published on modern Jewish and Israeli art, on contemporary Palestinian art, and on Frida Kahlo.

Peter Antelyes is an associate professor at Vassar College, where he teaches in the English Department and the American Culture Program. Author of *Tales of Adventurous Enterprise: Washington Irving and the Poetics of Western Expansion* and essays on ethnic literatures and cultures, he is currently at work on a study of multiracial literatures in the United States.

Joyce Antler is on the Editorial Advisory Board of the *Encyclopedia*. See the beginning of this list for a biographical note.

Cindy Aron is associate professor of history at the University of Virginia. She is author of *Ladies and Gentlemen of the Civil Service: Middle-Class Workers in Victorian America* and is currently writing a history of vacations in the United States, 1820–1940.

Isa Aron is professor of Jewish education at the Rhea Hirsch School of Education, Hebrew Union College, Los Angeles.

Elliot Ashkenazi received his B.A. in history from the University of Pennsylvania, his J.D. from Harvard University Law School, and his Ph.D. in history from George Washington University. He has taught history at American, George Mason, and George Washington universities and was an associate editor of *Documentary History of the Supreme Court, 1789–1800*. Ashkenazi is the author of *The Civil War Diary of Clara Solomon, Growing Up in New Orleans, 1861–1862* and *The Business of Jews in Louisiana, 1840–1875*.

Dianne Ashton is associate professor of philosophy and religion at Rowan College of New Jersey. She received her Ph.D. in religion from Temple University, and her book *Unsubdued Spirits: Rebecca Gratz and Women's Judaism in America* grew out of her dissertation on Gratz. Ashton is also the author of *Jewish Presence in Pennsylvania* and editor, with Ellen M. Umansky, of *Four Centuries of Jewish Women's Spirituality: A Sourcebook*.

Hillary Mac Austin was for many years director of the Chicago Actors Ensemble and is now a writer. She was a major contributor to *Encyclopedia of Black Women*, as well as assistant to the editor in chief. Most recently, she assisted Darlene Clark Hine and Kathleen Thompson on *A Shining Thread of Hope*. She is currently working on a history of women in American entertainment.

Maria T. Baader is a Ph.D. candidate in Jewish history at Columbia University, working on issues of gender in the process of the emergence of modern Judaism and of Jewish cultural and social embourgeoisement in Germany between 1800 and 1870.

Peter B. Baird is director of the Baird Marionettes and a partner in the Children's Video Theatre. He is the son of Cora and Bil Baird.

Paula Eisenstein Baker, Houston cellist and musicologist, is an authority on the early twentieth-century Society for Jewish Folk Music in St. Petersburg, Russia. She has published one article on composer and society member Leo Zeitlin in *Strings* magazine and has two more forthcoming in *YIVO*

Annual and the *International Journal of Musicology*. Baker has spoken and performed works by the members of the society for audiences throughout the United States.

Zachary M. Baker is head librarian at the YIVO Institute for Jewish Research. He is a regular contributor to *Avotaynu, The Jewish Book Annual*, and *Judaica Librarianship*. Baker also coedited, with Bella Hass Weinberg, the five-volume *Yiddish Catalog and Authority File of the YIVO Library*.

Jan Balakian received her Ph.D. from Cornell University. She is assistant professor of English at Kean College of New Jersey. She has published articles and interviews about Arthur Miller and Tennessee Williams and a book on Wendy Wasserstein's work.

Carole B. Balin is a doctoral candidate in the History Department of Columbia University and a Mellon Fellow in the humanities. Her field of concentration is modern Eastern European Jewish history. Balin is currently writing a dissertation on Jewish women writers in late Imperial Russia, 1850–1917. She was ordained a rabbi at Hebrew Union College–Jewish Institute of Religion in New York, where she is an instructor of history.

Robert Bannister is Scheuer Professor of History at Swarthmore College. His publications include *Darwinism: Science and Myth, Sociology and Scientism: The American Search for Objectivity 1880–1940*, and *Jessie Bernard: The Making of a Feminist*.

Pamela Barmash is a rabbi at Temple Shaare Tefilah in Norwood, Massachusetts, and a Ph.D. candidate at Harvard University. She received her bachelor's degree from Yale University and her master's degree from the Jewish Theological Seminary, where she also was ordained as a rabbi.

John Baron is professor of musicology at Newcomb College of Tulane University, where he holds the Schawe professorship and is chair of the department. He is one of the founders of the Jewish Studies Program at Tulane, in which he regularly teaches courses on Jewish music. Baron has written on chamber music, baroque music, the music of New Orleans, and Jewish music and is the editor of a biography of Amy Beach. He is currently preparing a history of Jewish music.

Lois Baer Barr is professor of Spanish at Lake Forest College. Educated at Georgetown University's Institute of Languages and Linguistics (B.S.), Middlebury College (M.A.), and the University of Kentucky (Ph.D.), Barr formerly taught Spanish language and literature at Northwestern University. She is the author of *Isaac Unbound: Patriarchal Traditions in the Latin American Jewish Novel* and numerous articles on Latin American Jewish authors.

Betty Barrer is a free-lance writer and editor. She specializes in writing articles on technical subjects for lay audiences and nonprofit groups, such as the *Bulletin* of Temple Israel in Boston. A graduate of Kirkland (now Hamilton) College, Barrer was a managing editor of the journal *Law, Medicine & Health Care* for many years.

Nancy L. Barth is a library cataloger at the law firm Graham and James in Los Angeles. A graduate of the University of California at Los Angeles (B.A.) and the University of

Chicago (M.L.S.), she researched and helped to write *The Jews of Los Angeles, 1849–1945: An Annotated Bibliography* for the Magnes Memorial Museum in Berkeley, California. In addition to having worked as a librarian at a number of law firms, Barth has directed a one-person library specializing in transportation safety.

Judith R. Baskin is chair of the Department of Judaic Studies at the State University of New York at Albany. She received her Ph.D. in medieval studies from Yale University in 1976. She is the author of *Pharaoh's Counsellors: Job, Jethro and Balaam in Rabbinic and Patristic Tradition*, which compares Jewish and Christian views of gentiles in late antiquity, and the editor of *Jewish Women in Historical Perspective*. She is also the editor, with Shelly Tenenbaum, of *Gender and Jewish Studies: A Curriculum Guide* and is the author of articles on aspects of Jewish culture in late antiquity and the Middle Ages.

Ronnie Becher is educational director of the Gananu Early Learning Center in Manhattan. Chair of the Women's Tefillah of Riverdale, she also serves as executive vice president of the Hebrew Institute of Riverdale. She is a former Wexner Heritage Fellow.

Karen Bekker studied Judaic studies and art at Oberlin College and at Ben-Gurion University. She has been actively involved in Jewish community organizations and in the feminist movement for several years. Her writing includes several articles in *Lilith*.

Roselyn Bell is publications coordinator for the Coalition for the Advancement of Jewish Education (CAJE). She edited *Hadassah Magazine* for ten years, working as senior editor for five years. Bell also edited and wrote a number of chapters in *The Hadassah Magazine Jewish Parenting Book*. She received her B.A. from Pomona College, her M.A. in comparative literature from the University of California at Berkeley, and her M.S. in Jewish education from Yeshiva University. She founded and is now the managing editor of CAJE's *Jewish Education News*.

Carl Belz is the Henry and Lois Foster Director of the Rose Art Museum at Brandeis University. He has organized many exhibitions of the work of living artists, among them Helen Frankenthaler, Frank Stella, Katherine Porter, and Joan Snyder.

Tobin Belzer is a Ph.D. candidate in sociology at Brandeis University. She received her M.A. in women's studies from Brandeis and her B.A. in business and social issues from the University of Judaism in Los Angeles. Belzer founded the Brandeis University Graduate Student Women's Studies Association, and she has given a number of conference papers on women, gender, and feminism.

Daniel Bender is a Ph.D. candidate in American labor history at New York University. A graduate of Yale University (B.A.), Bender has received the Andrew Mellon fellowship in humanistic studies and the Henry Mitchell MacCracken fellowship at NYU.

Aviva Ben-Ur is a Ph.D. candidate in Brandeis University's Near Eastern and Judaic Studies Department. She specializes in Ladino and Sephardic studies and is completing her dissertation on the New York immigrant experience of early twentieth-century Ladino-speaking Jews. In 1990, she was awarded a Fulbright fellowship to study Ladino at the Hebrew University of Jerusalem and in the same year was named a Mellon fellow for graduate studies in the humanities.

Jessica Berger received her B.A. in psychology from Vassar College. She has worked as an executive assistant to Bella Abzug at the Women's Environment and Development Organization and as Israel Programs Registrar at Young Judaea/Hadassah in New York City.

Shulamith Z. Berger is archivist at Yeshiva University. She has an M.S. from the School of Library Service at Columbia University and an M.A. in modern Jewish history from the Bernard Revel Graduate School of Yeshiva University. Among her articles are "Tehines: Women and Prayer" and "Madison Avenue Comes to East Broadway: Advertising and the Jewish Immigrant Meet." She has lectured on these topics for Jewish groups in New York.

Gershon Berkson is professor of psychology at the University of Illinois at Chicago.

Miriam H. Berlin is a specialist in Russian history who has taught at Wellesley College and Harvard University. Berlin is a graduate of Smith College (B.A.) and Harvard (M.A., Ph.D.). She has published articles in *American Scholar* and *Yale Review*.

Reena Bernards is director of the Center for Organizational Development. She is a consultant and trainer in conflict resolution, leadership development, and multicultural awareness. Her clients include the League of Women Voters, the Ms. Foundation for Women, and the National Wildlife Federation. Bernards is the founder of the Dialogue Project Between American Jewish and Palestinian Women. She has trained leaders in dialogue in North America, the Middle East, and Eastern Europe. She holds a master's degree in public administration from the John F. Kennedy School of Government at Harvard University and a bachelor of arts degree from Brandeis University.

Anne Bernays, Doris Fleischman Bernays's daughter, is the author of eight novels, among them the award-winning *Growing Up Rich* and *Professor Romeo*. With Pamela Painter, she is the coauthor of *What If?*, a book of writing exercises for fiction writers. Bernays also coauthored *The Language of Names*, with her husband, Justin Kaplan. Bernays has taught fiction since 1975 at a number of schools, including the University of Massachusetts and Boston College. In addition, for three years, Bernays occupied with Kaplan the Jenks Chair in Contemporary Letters at the College of the Holy Cross.

Selma Berrol taught at Baruch College for twenty-seven years, serving many years as chair of the department and assistant dean of liberal arts, before becoming professor emerita in 1995. A graduate of Hunter College (B.A.), Columbia University (M.A.), and the City University of New York (Ph.D.), Berrol is the author of *Immigrants at School: New York, 1898–1914, East Side/East End: Eastern European Jews in London and New York,* and *Growing Up American: Immigrant Children in the United States.*

Janet Beyer has contributed entries to *American Women Writers* and *Notable American Women.* She is a columnist for the *Concord Journal* in Concord, Massachusetts, as well as a free-lance writer and editor. She has lived in Concord for thirty years and is active in town and state politics.

Adele Sarah Bildersee is a school media specialist for the Great Neck public schools, in Great Neck, New York, and an adjunct professor at the Palmer School of Library and Information Science of Long Island University. She has a B.A. in history and an M.S. in library science from Queens College and has published a book of library skills for elementary school students.

Dorothy Bilik teaches comparative literature, Yiddish language and literature, and Holocaust literature at the University of Maryland. Her publications include *Immigrant Survivors: Post-Holocaust Consciousness in Recent Jewish-American Fiction* and entries on Yiddish language and literature in the *World Book Encyclopedia.* She has contributed to *Studies in Philology* and *Comparative Literature Studies,* among other journals.

Ruth Ann Binder is coordinator of the Jewish Women's Resource Center and the Pregnancy Loss Support Program, both projects of the National Council of Jewish Women, New York section. Binder received her B.A. in anthropology and women's studies from the University of California at San Diego and has taught outdoor education to children in Montana and New Hampshire. She is pursuing graduate work on the effects of gender on culture.

Emily Bingham is a Ph.D. candidate in American history at the University of North Carolina. Her dissertation, "When We Were Children: Gender, Identity, and Faith in a Nineteenth Century American Family," focuses on the three generations of a Southern Jewish family. With Thomas Underwood, Bingham coedited *The Social Writings of the Southern Agrarians.* A graduate of Harvard University (B.A.), she is associate editor of the *Southern Historian.*

Adrienne Fried Block is on the Editorial Advisory Board of the *Encyclopedia.* See the beginning of this list for a biographical note.

Susan P. Bloom teaches graduate courses in children's literature and also administers the nation's only graduate program in children's literature. She has coauthored, with Cathryn M. Mercier, *Presenting Zibby Oneal* and *Presenting Avi.* A guest contributor to the *Horn Book* magazine, Bloom writes articles and reviews for a variety of books and journals. She served as chair of the 1992 *Boston Globe–Horn Book* Award Committee and was a member of the 1997 Newbery Award Committee.

Laurie Blunsom is a Ph.D. candidate in musicology at Brandeis University. She studied piano performance and musicology at Nebraska Wesleyan University (B.M.) and the New England Conservatory of Music (M.M.), as well as Brandeis (B.A.). Her dissertation is "Gender, Genre, and Professionalism: Five Boston Women Composers and Their Songs, 1870–1925."

Lesley Bogad is a doctoral student in the Cultural Foundations of Education Program at Syracuse University. Her research focuses on the intersection of gender, education, and popular culture. She also teaches Hebrew school and advises a youth program at a synagogue in Syracuse.

Judith Bolton-Fasman is books editor for the *Baltimore Jewish Times*. Her work has appeared in the *Washington Post*, the *Christian Science Monitor*, the *Jerusalem Report*, and the *Forward*.

Marlene Booth is an award-winning filmmaker who has worked in film since 1975, both as an independent filmmaker for her own company, Raphael Films, and for public television station WGBH-TV in Boston. A graduate of Beloit College (B.A.) and Yale University (M.F.A.), Booth has produced and directed several major documentary films, including *When I Was 14: A Survivor Remembers*, *The Double Burden: Three Generations of Working Mothers*, and *The Forward: From Immigrants to Americans*. Currently she is producing *Yidl in the Middle*, a documentary film about growing up Jewish in Iowa.

Anne S. Borden holds an M.A. in American studies from the State University of New York at Buffalo and a B.A. in Afro-American studies from the University of Wisconsin. She has published poetry as well as the article, "Heroic 'Hussies' and 'Brilliant Queers': Genderracial Resistance in the Works of Langston Hughes." Borden is the coeditor of the Women in Dialogue Page of *The Black World Today*. At SUNY-Buffalo, she coedits the *Graduate Quill* and is vice president of the *Buffalo Americanist Digest*.

Linda J. Borish is associate professor of history at Western Michigan University. Borish received her Ph.D. in American studies from the University of Maryland. Her work focuses on nineteenth-century American history, women's history, and the history of sport, and she has published articles in journals such as the *Journal of American Culture*, *Agricultural History*, and *The International Journal of the History of Sport*. Borish is currently completing a book titled *"The Lass of the Farm": Perceptions and Reform of Women's Well-Being in Rural New England, 1820–1870*.

Sandra K. Bornstein is pursuing a master of arts degree in Jewish studies at the Spertus Institute in Chicago. Her area of concentration is Jewish women in America, with a focus on Chicago Jewish women. She contributed an article on Lizzy Spiegel Barbe to the *Historical Encyclopedia of Chicago Women*.

Annette Muffs Botnick received her B.A. from Columbia University and has earned advanced degrees from the Jewish Theological Seminary, Adelphi University, and Rosary College. She is a reference librarian at the library of the Jewish Theological Seminary and is preparing two bibliographies for publication.

Jennifer Breger holds a B.A. and an M.A. from Oxford University and an M.A. from the Hebrew University. She has published articles on Jewish women's liturgy and literature, Jewish women's printing, and the history of Hebrew printing in *Antiquarian Bookman*, the *Jewish Book Annual*, *Judaism*, and other publications. She has been cultural correspondent of the Swiss magazine *Shalom* since 1988. She has curated and written catalogs for several museum exhibits on Holy Land maps. Breger also conceived and cocurated an exhibit on Switzerland and the Jews for the B'nai B'rith Museum in Washington and wrote essays for the accompanying catalog on Hebrew printing in Switzerland and on Zionist history.

Barbara Brenzel is professor of education at Wellesley College. She is the author of *Daughters of the State: A Social Portrait of the First Reform School for Girls in North America, 1856–1905* and is writing a book on destitute children and the institutions that cared for them in the late nineteenth and twentieth centuries.

Marla Brettschneider is professor of political philosophy with a joint appointment in political science and women's studies at the University of New Hampshire. Her books include *Cornerstones of Peace: Jewish Identity Politics and Democratic Theory*, *The Narrow Bridge: Jewish Views on Multiculturalism*, and *Race, Gender, and Class: American Jewish Perspectives*.

Nancy Brody is a psychologist in private practice in Scottsdale, Arizona, where she provides psychotherapy for adults and children and does psychodiagnostic and psychoeducational testing. She also writes a monthly column on psychological and parenting issues for the *Jewish News of Greater Phoenix*. Brody is the former clinical director of Jewish Family and Children's Service in Scottsdale, and she has worked in Phoenix schools as a licensed school psychologist. Brody earned her Ph.D. in psychology at Loyola University of Chicago, did master's work in counseling at Northeastern Illinois University, and received her undergraduate degree in French from the University of Illinois.

Constance W. Brown, who holds a master's degree in social work, is a psychotherapist in private practice in New York City. She is on the faculty of the Harlem Family Institute in New York.

Michael Brown teaches humanities and Hebrew and directs the Center for Jewish Studies at York University in Toronto. He holds degrees from Harvard University, Columbia University, the Jewish Theological Seminary of America, and the State University of New York at Buffalo. Brown is the author of *Jew or Juif? Jews, French Canadians and Anglo-Canadians, 1759–1914* and *The Israeli-American Connection: Its Roots in the Yishuv, 1914–1945*.

Stephan F. Brumberg is professor of education and head of the Program in Education Administration at Brooklyn College. He has written articles on immigrants in American schools and is the author of *Going to America, Going to School: The Jewish Immigrant Public School Encounter in Turn-of-the-Century New York City*.

Elly Bulkin is coauthor, with Minnie Bruce Pratt and Barbara Smith, of *Yours in Struggle: Three Feminist Perspectives on Anti-Semitism and Racism*. She edited *Lesbian Fiction: An Anthology* and coedited, with Joan Larkin, *Amazon Poetry* and *Lesbian Poetry: An Anthology*. She was a founding editor of *Conditions: A Magazine of Writing by Women with an Emphasis on Writing by Lesbians* and of *Bridges: A Journal for Jewish Feminists and Our Friends*.

Sharon Burde is executive director of the American Friends of Neve Shalom/Wahat al-Salam [Oasis of peace]. She is a mediator who has been influenced by the confluence of American democratic values and Jewish commitment to social justice.

Patricia M. Burnham, lecturer in American studies and art history at the University of Texas, received her doctorate in art history from Boston University in 1984. She writes and lectures widely on American art, particularly nineteenth-century American history painting. She first met Theresa Bernstein in 1988.

Alice M. Burstein is a niece of Judith Pinta Mandelbaum, a daughter of her sister Miriam Pinta Burstein. She grew up in a Young Israel community and graduated from Central Yeshiva (Yeshiva University) High School for Girls. Burstein is a market research analyst for Pfizer and is on the Executive Committee of the Pharmaceutical Business Intelligence Group. She is a life member of Amit.

Janet Burstein is professor of English at Drew University in New Jersey. She has published articles on Victorian literature in *Victorian Studies* and *Nineteenth-Century Fiction* and on American Jewish literature in *American Literature* and *Studies in American Jewish Literature*. Her latest book is *Writing Mothers, Writing Daughters: Tracing the Maternal in Stories by American Jewish Women*.

Barbara Burstin is an instructor at both the University of Pittsburgh and Carnegie-Mellon University, where she teaches courses on the Holocaust in American Jewish history. She has published articles on the Holocaust, as well as a book, *After the Holocaust: The Migration of Polish Jews and Christians to Pittsburgh*. Through the Pittsburgh Holocaust Center, Burstin has taught courses for local high school teachers on the Holocaust. Currently she is writing the history of the Jewish community of Pittsburgh.

Joan N. Burstyn is professor of cultural foundations of education and of History at Syracuse University. Formerly dean of the School of Education at Syracuse, she has also served as president of the History of Education Society and of the American Educational Studies Association and on the Board of Directors of the Syracuse Jewish Federation. Her most recent publications are *Educating Tomorrow's Valuable Citizen* (editor) and *Past and Promise: Lives of New Jersey Women* (editor in chief).

Jan Butin studied history of science at the University of Kansas, where she is now employed by the division of continuing education. In 1980–1981, she received a Fulbright for research at the Naples Zoological Station archives. Her work on Ida Hyde is part of a larger project on the Naples Table Association for Promoting Scientific Research by Women, 1897–1932, which Hyde founded.

Amy Butler is a Ph.D. candidate in United States history at the State University of New York at Binghamton. Butler's research interests include legal and women's history, and she has taught these subjects as an adjunct professor in the history department at SUNY-Binghamton. A graduate of the University of California at Los Angeles (B.A.), Butler contributed an entry on Alice Paul to *Significant Contemporary Feminists: A Biocritical Sourcebook*.

Deidre Butler is a doctoral student in religion at Concordia University in Montreal. She is working in the areas of modern Jewish philosophy, feminist ethics, and women and religion. Her interest in Holocaust studies focuses on women and the Holocaust and philosophical responses to the Holocaust. She is the editor of the *Journal of Religion and Culture* and is currently coediting a book of Canadian scholarship in the area of women and Judaism with Norma Baumel Joseph.

Suzanne Campbell received her B.A. and M.A. in history from Angelo State University. She is a member of the board of directors of the Texas Jewish Historical Society and has written numerous articles on Jewish history in West Texas. Campbell is currently library assistant for the West Texas Collection, the historical and archival collection at Angelo State University.

Greg Caplan is a Ph.D. candidate in German history at Georgetown University. He received his M.A. in European studies from Georgetown and his B.A. in political science from the University of Georgia. Caplan's research interests center around modern German Jewish history.

Steven Carr is an assistant professor at Indiana University–Purdue University, Fort Wayne. He teaches film and television studies in the Department of Communication. His work has appeared in *Cinema Journal* and the anthology *Shared Differences: Multicultural Media and Practical Pedagogy*. He is writing a book on the allegation of Jewish control over Hollywood.

Susan Chambré is professor of sociology at Baruch College, City University of New York. Her publications focus on the link between adolescent pregnancy and welfare dependency, the cultural and social determinants of volunteering, and the role of nonprofit organizations in the formation and implementation of social policy.

Judith Chasin is a clinical audiologist in private practice in Brookline, Massachusetts. She received her M.A. in audiology from Western Reserve University and her B.A. in speech therapy from the University of Michigan.

Noah Chasin is a Ph.D. candidate in architectural history at the Graduate Center of the City University of New York.

Ellen Chesler, a fellow of the Twentieth Century Fund in New York, is the author of the award-winning *Woman of Valor: Margaret Sanger and the Birth Control Movement in America*. A graduate of Vassar College (B.A.) and Columbia University (M.A., Ph.D.), Chesler has taught history and women's studies at Barnard College and Hunter College and has served as campaign manager and chief of staff for former New York City Council president Carole Bellamy. Chesler is currently writing a biography of Betty Friedan.

Susan Chevlowe is assistant curator of fine arts at the Jewish Museum in New York. She was coeditor, with Norman L. Kleeblatt, of *Painting a Place in America: Jewish Artists in New York, 1900–1945* and is the curator of the museum's 1998 centenary exhibition of the art of Ben Shahn. She received an M.Phil. degree from the Graduate Center of the City University of New York, where she is also a Ph.D. candidate in art history.

Robin Clark is an art historian specializing in American and European art of the 1960s and 1970s. She has worked as a research assistant at the J. Paul Getty Museum in Malibu, the Phillips Collection in Washington, D.C., and the Museum of Contemporary Art in Los Angeles. Clark is collections curatorial assistant at the Solomon R. Guggenheim Museum in New York and a student in the art history Ph.D. program at the Graduate Center of the City University.

Erin Elizabeth Clune received her B.A. from Stanford University and her M.A. from New York University, where she is a Ph.D. candidate in twentieth-century American history.

Sara Coen received her B.A. from the University of Pennsylvania and is working toward a master's degree in teaching high school English at the Harvard University Graduate School of Education. She has taught Jewish and United States history at the Solomon Schechter Day School in Newton, Massachusetts.

Debra Nussbaum Cohen is a staff writer at the Jewish Telegraphic Agency, a wire service for Jewish newspapers worldwide. She writes about religious issues and interreligious affairs, intergroup relations, and issues related to Jewish continuity and identity. Cohen has won four awards from the American Jewish Press Association for her coverage of issues related to Jewish identity and religion. She was awarded a grant from the Lilly Endowment to write about how women have changed the nature of the ministry and the rabbinate.

Ilene Cohen has been a children's librarian, a branch manager, and an audiovisual librarian with the Santa Monica Public Library since 1970. She received her B.A. in English from California State University at Northridge in 1968 and her M.L.S. from the University of Southern California in 1970. She has served on the Board of Trustees at Leo Baeck Temple in Los Angeles.

Lynn Cohen is a musician, social worker, and writer who lives in New Hampshire. She has degrees from the New England Conservatory and Simmons School of Social Work and is currently working on a master of fine arts in creative writing at Emerson College.

Selma Jeanne Cohen received her A.B. and Ph.D. in English literature at the University of Chicago and received her dance training with the choreographer and teacher Eugene Loring. Cohen is the founding editor of the quarterly *Dance Perspectives*, and her publications include the *International Encyclopedia of Dance*, *The Modern Dance: Seven Statements of Belief*, and *And Next Week: Swan Lake*. She has taught dance at the University of California, Riverside, the University of Chicago, and Sarah Lawrence College.

Seth Aloe Cohen practices gastroenterology in New York City and is a sixth-generation Jewish American.

Tamara Cohen is the program director of Ma'yan: The Jewish Women's Project of the JCC on the Upper West Side of Manhattan. She graduated from Barnard College in 1993 with a B.A. in women's studies and English and is a writer, educator, and activist on Jewish feminism and Jewish lesbian and gay issues.

Alyson Cole is a Ph.D. candidate in political science at the University of California at Berkeley, where she received her master's degree. She received her bachelor's degree from Smith College. Cole's areas of specialization include political theory and public law and jurisprudence. Her dissertation is "The Victim in American Political Discourse."

Irma Commanday attended New College, Columbia University. She was administrative director at Indian Hill, a summer workshop in the arts in Stockbridge, Massachusetts, from 1952 to 1976. Marjorie Guthrie taught dance at Indian Hill for six summers; in 1978, Commanday joined Guthrie as her associate at the Committee to Combat Huntington's Disease and as coordinator of the Woody Guthrie Archive. With her husband, Mordecai Bauman, Irma Commanday produced *The Stations of Bach*, a television biography of Johann Sebastian Bach, for PBS.

Cynthia Connolly is a Ph.D. candidate in nursing history at the University of Pennsylvania as well as a clinical instructor at the Johns Hopkins University School of Nursing. She has worked as a pediatric nurse for sixteen years.

Thomas F. Connolly teaches in the English Department of Suffolk University. He is the North American review editor for *Theatre Research International* and an advisory editor of *The Eugene O'Neill Review*. He is currently a Fulbright Scholar in the Czech Republic.

Blanche Wiesen Cook is distinguished professor of history and women's studies at the John Jay College and the Graduate Center of the City University of New York. She was chosen as Scholar of the Year in 1996 by the New York State Council on the Humanities. Her biography *Eleanor Roosevelt: Volume One* received the 1992 Biography Prize from the *Los Angeles Times* as well as the Lambda Literary Award. Among her other books is *The Declassified Eisenhower*. She has served as vice president for research of the American Historical Association and as vice president and chair of the Fund for Open Information and Accountability and was cofounder and cochair of the Freedom of Information and Access Committee of the Organization of American Historians. She produces and hosts her own program for Radio Pacifica, *Women and the World in the 1990's*. She is working on Volume Two of *Eleanor Roosevelt*.

Ruth Schwartz Cowan studied biology at Barnard College and history at the University of California at Berkeley, and she received her Ph.D. in the history of science from Johns Hopkins University. She is a professor in the History Department of the State University of New York at Stony Brook, where she has also served as the director of women's studies. Cowan's publications include *More Work for Mother: The Ironies of Household Technology from the Open Hearth to the Microwave; Our Parents' Lives: Everyday Life and Jewish Assimilation*, with Neil M. Cowan; and *A Social History of American Technology*. Cowan's current projects are a history of American women engineers and a history of prenatal diagnosis.

Jenifer Craig is associate professor and chair of the Department of Dance at the University of Oregon. Craig earned her Ph.D. from the University of Southern California, where she also taught in the Dance Department. She is director of Daugherty Dance Theatre and has been associated with the Bella Lewitzky Dance Foundation of Los Angeles since 1976. Craig is a member of the board of directors of the Society of Dance History Scholars and serves on the editorial board of the Congress on Research in Dance.

Kate Culkin is an archival assistant and master's student in American history at New York University. A graduate of Middlebury College (B.A.), she writes a regular column for the journal *Verbivore* and has published an article in *Ladies Start Your Engines*. Culkin has also worked as a project archivist at the Brooklyn Museum.

Catherine Daligga, a doctoral candidate in the Program in American Culture at the University of Michigan, plans to write her dissertation on American and French autobiographical narratives about World War II written between 1960 and 1980.

Enid Dame is a writer and poet who teaches at Rutgers University and the New Jersey Institute of Technology. Her latest book of poems is *Anything You Don't See.* She is the coeditor of an anthology of Jewish women's writings about Lilith, Adam's transgressive first wife.

Marilynn Danitz, founder and artistic director of High Frequency Wavelengths, Inc., a dance/theater/video/art company, has toured her works throughout the United States and abroad. Collaborating with other artists, such as poet Allen Ginsberg, Danitz has choreographed ballets for international competition, and she has taught at ballet companies throughout the world. She is currently working on a video documentary, *Hadassah, Kissed by the Gods.*

Irene G. Dash received her Ph.D. from Columbia University and now teaches at Hunter College. She is the author of *Wooing, Wedding, and Power: Women in Shakespeare's Plays* and *Women's Worlds in Shakespeare's Plays.* Her articles in literary journals such as *Shakespeare Studies* and *Modern Language Studies* bring together the fields of literary scholarship, theater history, and feminist criticism. Dash has been awarded fellowships by the National Endowment for the Humanities and the Folger Shakespeare Library.

Michael Dashkin is a free-lance writer and photographer in New York City. He has published on art and photography and was the curator of an exhibition on computers and art that was exhibited in New York and Boston. He received a B.A. from the University of California at Berkeley, an M.F.A. from New York University, and is completing an M.S. in library and information studies at Queens College, with an emphasis on image information systems.

Joseph W. Dauben is professor of history and the history of science at Herbert H. Lehman College of the City University of New York. He is a fellow of the New York Academy of Sciences and a *membre effectif* of the International Academy of History of Science. He has been editor of *Historia Mathematica,* an international journal for the history of mathematics, and chairman of the International Commission on the History of Mathematics. He is the author of *Georg Cantor, His Mathematics and Philosophy of the Infinite* and *Abraham Robinson: The Creation of Nonstandard Analysis, a Personal and Mathematical Odyssey.* A graduate of Claremont McKenna College (A.B.) and Harvard University (A.M., Ph.D.), Dauben won a Guggenheim Fellowship and was named Outstanding Teacher of the Year at Lehman College.

Lynn Davidman received her Ph.D. from Brandeis University. She is an associate professor of Judaic studies and Sociology at Brown University. Davidman won a National Book Award for *Tradition in a Rootless World.* She has published two other books, *Feminist Perspectives on Jewish Studies,* coedited with Shelly Tenenbaum, and *Feminist Methods in Social Research,* cowritten with Shulamit Reinharz. Davidman is on the advisory committee of the Center for the Study of American Religion at Princeton University. She is currently working on *Motherless Daughters and Sons* and is coediting the book series *Explorations in Religion.*

Amy DeRogatis is a graduate student in the Department of Religious Studies at the University of North Carolina.

Leila Diamond is professor emeritus of the Wistar Institute of Anatomy and Biology in Philadelphia. Diamond received her B.A. in medical microbiology from the University of Wisconsin and her Ph.D. in biology from Cornell University Medical College, Sloan-Kettering Division. She has served on the advisory committee for the National Institutes of Health and has been a member of the editorial board of *Journal of the National Cancer Institute.*

Thea Diamond is a Ph.D. candidate in English at the University of Pennsylvania, and she is also director of education of the Annenberg Center. Diamond received her B.A. in English from Yale University and her M.A. in English and creative writing from the University of Pennsylvania.

Hasia Diner is on the Editorial Advisory Board of the *Encyclopedia.* See the beginning of this list for a biographical note.

Miriam Dinerman received her Ph.D. and M.S.W. from Columbia University and has taught social welfare, social work policy, and history at Rutgers University since 1968. She has published numerous articles in the areas of public policy regarding women, social work education, and the history of social work. With Ludwig Geismar, she is coauthor of *A Quarter-Century of Social Work Education* and is currently researching the life and career of Sophonisba Breckinridge.

Joan Ditzion is a founder of the Boston Women's Health Book Collective and coauthor of all editions of *(The New) Our Bodies Ourselves* and *Ourselves and Our Children* and a contributor to *The New Ourselves Growing Older.* She is a clinical geriatric social worker and serves as an adjunct faculty member at Lesley College.

Judith E. Doneson received her B.S. in film from Boston University and her M.A. and Ph.D. in contemporary Jewish history from the Hebrew University of Jerusalem. She has taught at Tel Aviv University, worked on a filmed course for the Institute of Contemporary Jewry at the Hebrew University, and lectured at the Yad Vashem seminar. Doneson was a fellow at the Center for Jewish Studies at the University of Pennsylvania and is currently a visiting professor of history at Washington University. Doneson is the author of *The Holocaust in American Film.*

George Dorris is associate professor of English at York College, City University of New York, and a coeditor of *Dance Chronicle.* He is an editor of *International Encyclopedia of Dance* and contributes regularly to *Ballet Review, Dance Now,* and *Dancing Times.*

Thomas Dublin is professor of history at the State University of New York at Binghamton. Among his publications are the award-winning *Women at Work, Transforming Women's Work: New England Lives in the Industrial Revolution,* and *Immigrant Voices: New Lives in America, 1773–1986.* Dublin received his B.A. in chemistry from Harvard College and his Ph.D. in American history from Columbia University. Among his current projects is research on gender and deindustrialization in the anthracite region of Pennsylvania.

Marsha Bryan Edelman is associate professor of music and dean for academic affairs at Gratz College. Educated at Columbia University (B.A., M.Ed., Ed.D.) and the Jewish Theological Seminary of America (B.H.L., B.S.M., M.S.M.), Edelman is a lecturer and writer on topics relating to the nature and history of Jewish music. She is also a singer and conductor of Jewish choral music and has served the Zamir Choral Foundation in various musical and managerial capacities.

J. Michele Edwards, professor of music at Macalester College, specializes in twentieth-century women musicians and composers. She has contributed numerous articles to textbooks such as *Women and Music: A History*, edited by Karin Pendle, and to reference books such as the *International Dictionary of Black Composers*, edited by Samuel A. Floyd, Jr. In addition to being a musicologist, Edwards is conductor for the hundred-voice Macalester Festival Chorale and Harmonia Mundi, a professional woodwind and keyboard ensemble.

Jay M. Eidelman, a native of Montreal, is assistant professor of religious studies at Hobart and William Smith Colleges. He holds a Ph.D. in religious studies from Yale University. His dissertation, "'In the Wilds of America': The Early Republican Origins of American Judaism, 1790–1830," was completed in 1997.

Tanya Elder is a librarian, archivist, storyteller, and actor. She received her B.F.A. in theater from the Tisch School of the Arts at New York University and her M.I.S. in library science from Wayne State University. Currently, Elder is an M.A. student in history and archival management at NYU. She has worked as a librarian at the Free Library of Philadelphia and the Queens Borough Public Library and has also performed several one-woman shows in New York City. Elder has published an essay about being a new children's librarian in *In Our Own Voices: The Changing Faces of Librarianship.*

Meira Eliash-Chain holds a B.A. in the history of theater from Hebrew University in Jerusalem, and an M.A. in theater arts from Tel Aviv University. She also studied at the City University in London. Eliash-Chain has served as an art administrator in Israel and the United States. Currently she is executive director for the internationally recognized dance company Jennifer Muller/THE WORKS. She has published poetry in Israeli periodicals and has also written for cultural publications in England and Israel.

Judith Laikin Elkin is founding president of the Latin American Jewish Studies Association and a research associate of the Frankel Center for Judaic Studies at the University of Michigan. A graduate of the University of Michigan (B.A., Ph.D.), Columbia University (M.A.), and the London School of Economics (Ph.D.), Elkin was also educated at the Detroit Public Schools and Farband Folk Schule and Mittelshule, and she attended performances at Littman's People's Theatre with her family's houseguest, Jacob Ben Ami.

David Ellenson is the I.H. and Anna Grancell Professor of Religious Thought at Hebrew Union College–Jewish Institute of Religion, Los Angeles, and an adjunct faculty member at the Center for Jewish Studies at the University of California at Los Angeles. He has written extensively on diverse topics in modern Jewish history, ethics, and thought.

Ruth Andrew Ellenson was born in Jerusalem, raised in California, and is currently a graduate student at Columbia University in New York City.

Shulamith Reich Elster is executive director of Hillel of Greater Washington. She was an associate professor of Jewish education at Baltimore Hebrew University, chief education officer for Initiatives in Jewish Education, and served as headmaster of the Charles E. Smith Jewish Day School from 1982 until 1991.

Sue Levi Elwell is a founding staff member of Ma'yan: The Jewish Women's Project of the JCC on the Upper West Side of Manhattan. She serves as assistant director of the Pennsylvania Region of the Union of American Hebrew Congregations. She is the compiler of *The Jewish Women's Studies Guide*, coauthor of *Jewish Women: A Mini-course for Jewish Schools*, and coeditor of *The Jewish Calendar 5746*. She has edited acclaimed feminist haggadot, including *The Journey Continues: The Ma'yan Haggadah* and *And We Were All There: A Feminist Passover Haggadah.*

Judith E. Endelman is director of the Historical Resources business unit at the Henry Ford Museum and Greenfield Village in Dearborn, Michigan. Endelman has written *The Jewish Community of Indianapolis, 1849 to the Present; Religion in Indiana: A Guide to Historical Resources*, coedited with L.C. Rudolph; and *Americans on Vacation*, coauthored with Donna R. Braden.

Lisa Epstein received her Ph.D. in Jewish studies from Yale University and is a research fellow at the YIVO Institute for Jewish Research. She formerly taught modern Jewish history at Vassar College. Epstein is currently working on issues of health care, medical politics, and Judaism.

Marc Michael Epstein is coordinator of Jewish Studies at Vassar College. He writes on various topics in the relationship between the history of Jewish art and cultural production and Jewish mentalités. His most recent book is *Dreams of Subversion in Medieval Jewish Art and Literature.*

Shifra Epstein is an assistant professor at Emory University. Her areas of research and publication are Jewish folklore and ethnology. She is the author of a book on the Daniel-Shpil and has produced two documentary films.

Patricia Erens is on the Editorial Advisory Board of the *Encyclopedia*. See the beginning of this list for a biographical note.

Sylvia C. Ettenberg is dean of educational development and lecturer in Jewish education at the Jewish Theological Seminary of America. In her former position as associate dean of the seminary's undergraduate school, Ettenberg was the first woman in the seminary's academic administration. A graduate of the Teachers Institute of the seminary, Ettenberg cofounded the seminary's Ramah camps.

Laura E. Ettinger received her B.A. from Vassar College and is a doctoral candidate at the University of Rochester. Specializing in women's history and the history of medicine, Ettinger is completing a dissertation titled "The Birth of a New Professional: The Nurse-Midwife in the United States, 1925–1955."

Anne S. Evans is an independent clinical social worker in private practice in Boston. She is a graduate of Syracuse University (A.B.) and the Simmons College School of Social Work (M.S.W.). Evans coedited *Drugs and Social Therapies in Chronic Schizophrenia* and is the author of articles about volunteer case aides and chronic schizophrenia. She is currently working on a biography of Maida Herman Solomon.

Eli N. Evans is president of the Charles H. Revson Foundation in New York City. He graduated from the University of North Carolina (B.A.) and Yale Law School (J.D.) and served as a speechwriter on the White House staff of President Lyndon B. Johnson. A native of Durham, North Carolina, Evans is the author of *The Provincials: A Personal History of Jews in the South, Judah P. Benjamin: The Jewish Confederate*, and *The Lonely Days Were Sundays: Reflections of a Jewish Southerner*. He is the son of Sara N. Evans.

Eli Faber is professor of history at John Jay College in New York. He received his Ph.D. in American history from Columbia University and is the author of *A Time for Planting: The First Migration, 1654–1820* as well as a history of Jews and slavery.

Candace Falk is editor and director of the Emma Goldman Papers. She is author of *Love, Anarchy, and Emma Goldman*.

Esther Farber is a free-lance writer and public relations specialist. She previously worked in marketing and communications for New York UJA-Federation and for CLAL, the National Jewish Center for Learning and Leadership. She received a master's degree in public communications from Fordham University.

Harriet Feinberg worked as project associate for *Jewish Women in America*. She taught English and codirected the student-teaching program in secondary-school English at the University of Massachusetts at Boston. Feinberg edited *Memories*, the autobiography of the Dutch physician, feminist, and pacifist Aletta Jacobs, and coedited *Poemmaking: Poets in Classrooms*, with Ruth Whitman. She also has a longstanding involvement with Middle East peace activities, including a women's dialogue group and the "Playing for Peace" project of the Apple Hill Center for Chamber Music.

Marjorie N. Feld is a Ph.D. candidate in the history of American civilization at Brandeis University. She is currently a research associate for an exhibit on American Jewish women at the American Jewish Historical Society. Her research interests center around Jewish women's work with immigrants in the early twentieth century.

Michael Feldberg is executive director of the American Jewish Historical Society. He received his Ph.D. in history from the University of Rochester and is the author, coauthor, or editor of five books in history and in criminal justice.

Lori A. Ferguson received a B.A. in political science from Indiana University and an M.A. in history from Pennsylvania State University. She is currently a Ph.D. student in the social policy history program at Case Western University. Her research interests are in the areas of rural history and the Midwest, particularly in the twentieth century.

Kirsten Fermaglich is a Ph.D. candidate in American history at New York University. A graduate of Columbia University (A.B.) and Washington University (M.A.), she is writing her dissertation on memories of Nazi Germany in American political culture.

Jill Fields received her B.A. in history and women's studies from the University of California at Santa Cruz and her Ph.D. in history from the University of Southern California. Specializing in women's history, social history, and feminist theory, Fields wrote her dissertation on "The Production of Glamour: A Social History of Intimate Apparel, 1909–1952."

Arthur Fine is the John Evans Professor of Philosophy at Northwestern University, past president of the Philosophy of Science Association, and president-elect of the Central Division of the American Philosophical Association. His works include *The Shaky Game: Einstein, Realism and the Quantum Theory*.

Lori Finkelstein is a Ph.D. candidate in United States history at New York University, where she also earned her M.A. A graduate of McGill University (B.A.), Finkelstein is writing her dissertation on Revolutionary War widows between 1790 and 1840. Her interests include public history, women's history, and the history of aging.

Carol Fippin is president of an architectural firm in Cambridge, Massachusetts. She holds degrees from Boston University and the Harvard Graduate School of Design. Her professional work over the past twenty-two years has involved the design of public and private projects throughout the United States and Canada.

Jerilyn Fisher is assistant professor of English and coordinator of writing and literature at Hostos Community College, City University of New York. She is coeditor of *Analyzing the Different Voice: Feminist Psychological Theory and Literary Works*. Her current areas of research include fairy tales and cooperative learning in the writing and literature classrooms.

Tessa Fisher, a native of South Africa, graduated from the University of Cape Town with a B.A. in English and political science. After immigrating to the United States, she worked as a copywriter and associate creative director at international advertising agencies.

Aleisa Fishman is assistant director of academic publications at the United States Holocaust Memorial Museum, where she helps to edit the *Journal of Holocaust and Genocide Studies*. Fishman received her bachelor's degree from Duke University and her master's degree in American history from American University. She is in the Ph.D. program at American University.

Sylvia Barack Fishman is on the Editorial Advisory Board of the *Encyclopedia*. See the beginning of this list for a biographical note.

Susan Fleet is a trumpeter and a professor at Berklee College of Music in Boston. She formerly taught at Brown University and Wheaton College. Her CD *Baroque Treasures for Trumpet and Organ* was released in 1993. Fleet has written entries on Oscar Levant, Thomas Schippers, and E. Power Biggs for the *Dictionary of American Biography*.

Susan Fleming is a senior lecturer at Lesley College, where she teaches children's literature. She earned her Ed.M. at

Harvard Graduate School of Education and her Ph.D. at Lesley College. A former primary grade teacher and editor of teaching manuals, Fleming is also the author of numerous professional articles and three novels for young readers. Her research interests include gender differences in children's writing and the lives of nineteenth-century women educators.

Richard James Forde is staff psychiatrist at the Naval Medical Center in San Diego, California. He is active in the medical student teaching program at the University of California at San Diego School of Medicine.

Frieda Forman established and heads the Women's Educational Resources Centre at the Ontario Institute for Studies in Education at the University of Toronto. Her publications include *Taking Our Time: Feminist Perspectives on Temporality; Feminism and Education: A Canadian Perspective*, edited with Mary O'Brien; and *Found Treasures: Stories by Yiddish Women Writers*, coedited with Ethel Raicus, Sarah Silberstein Swartz, and Margie Wolfe. Forman attended Hebrew Teachers College in Boston and Yiddish programs at Oxford Summer Institute and the Hebrew University in Jerusalem.

R. Lori Forman is director of Jewish resources for the United Jewish Appeal-Federation of New York. She has worked extensively in Jewish education, with both adults and children, and in the area of interreligious affairs. She was ordained in 1988 by the Jewish Theological Seminary of America.

Susan Fox works in cultural programming and teaching in New York City. She holds an M.A. in English from George Mason University and has published poetry and fiction.

Glenda Frank received her B.A. and M.A. in American literature and her Ph.D. in American drama from the City University of New York. She teaches at the Fashion Institute of Technology, the State University of New York, and City College. A former drama critic for two New York weeklies, Frank has published scholarly articles and reviews in *Theatre Journal* and *Shakespeare Bulletin*. Currently revising her dissertation on Eugene O'Neill, Frank recently received a grant from the National Endowment for the Humanities to study the stage images of American Jews.

Ellen Frankel is editor in chief of the Jewish Publication Society. Frankel is the author of *The Five Books of Miriam: A Woman's Commentary on the Torah; The Encyclopedia of Jewish Symbols*, with Betsy Teutsch; and *The Classic Tales: 4000 Years of Jewish Lore*. A professional Jewish storyteller, she has also written two young adult books, *Choosing to Be Chosen* and *Tell It Like It Is*, with Sarah Levine. Frankel received her B.A. from the University of Michigan and her Ph.D. in comparative literature from Princeton University.

Oz Frankel is a Ph.D. candidate in history at the University of California at Berkeley. Frankel received both his master's and bachelor's degrees from the Hebrew University in Jerusalem. He has won a number of fellowships for his research on social investigations in the United States and Britain. Frankel has also been a journalist for *The Jerusalem Post* and Galey-Zahal, an Israeli radio station.

Gwen Nefsky Frankfeldt is a painter and graphic designer in Cambridge, Massachusetts. She is senior book designer at Harvard University Press and exhibits her paintings in the Boston area. She has won awards for book design from the New England Book Show and the Association of American University Presses. Frankfeldt holds a B.A. in history, literature, and philosophy from Swarthmore College and an M.A. in modern European intellectual history from the University of Chicago.

Karen S. Franklin is director of The Judaica Museum of the Hebrew Home for the Aged at Riverdale and director of the Family Research Program at the Leo Baeck Institute. Mrs. Franklin is a past chair of the Council of American Jewish Museums and vice president of the International Association of Jewish Genealogy Societies.

Janet Freedman is dean of library services and professor of education at the University of Massachusetts at Dartmouth. Her research and teaching interests include women's studies and feminist theory, as well as library management and educational administration. She has won grants and awards from the American Library Association and the National Endowment for the Humanities. Freedman is the coauthor of *Information Searching: A Handbook for Designing and Creating Instructional Programs*, with Harold Bantly.

Harriet Pass Freidenreich is professor of history at Temple University. She has a Ph.D. in Eastern European and Jewish history from Columbia University and teaches European and Jewish women's history. She is the author of *The Jews of Yugoslavia* and *Jewish Politics in Vienna, 1918–1938*. Her current research project is a collective biography of Jewish women who studied at German and Austrian universities before the Nazi era.

Lewis Fried is professor of American literature at Kent University. He was editor in chief of *The Handbook of American-Jewish Literature*.

Edna Friedberg is a Ph.D. candidate in modern Jewish studies at the Jewish Theological Seminary. She received her B.A. from the University of Illinois, Champaign-Urbana.

Natalie Friedman is a graduate student in English at New York University. She received her B.A. in English and French from Vassar College and has also studied at the Sorbonne in Paris.

Rachelle E. Friedman received her Ph.D. in American history from the University of California at Los Angeles. Her fields of research are early American history and women's history. She has worked at Harvard University as both a tutor and a manuscript arranger and is currently a high school teacher who has taught at the Winsor School and Milton Academy in Massachusetts.

Reena Sigman Friedman is a contributing editor to *Lilith* as well as an instructor in modern Jewish civilization and modern Jewish thought at the Reconstructionist Rabbinical College in Pennsylvania. She is the author of *These Are Our Children: Jewish Orphanages in the United States, 1880–1925*. She received degrees in American history from Columbia University (Ph.D., M.A., M.Phil.) and Cornell University (B.A.).

Rita Berman Frischer is a writer, reviewer, and instructor of juvenile and young adult literature, specializing in Jewish children's books. Director of library services at Sinai Temple in West Los Angeles, she has lectured at the University of

Judaism and Hebrew Union College and given workshops for the Association of Jewish Libraries and for Jewish educational boards and library organizations in the United States and abroad. She has served as a judge for numerous book awards, and her articles, reviews, and bibliographies have appeared in journals, periodicals, and books in the United States, Israel, and elsewhere.

Myrna Katz Frommer, visiting assistant professor of liberal studies at Dartmouth College, is the coauthor of the oral histories *Growing Up Jewish in America, It Happened in Brooklyn,* and *It Happened in the Catskills.* She is at work on *It Happened on Broadway.* Frommer has lectured on cultural history and Jewish life in America throughout the nation. She is also a professor of speech at the City University of New York.

Elinor Fuchs is adjunct associate professor of theater at Columbia University School of the Arts and lecturer at the Yale School of Drama. Her books include *The Death of Character: Perspectives on Theater After Modernism, Plays of the Holocaust: An International Anthology,* and the award-winning *Year One of the Empire: A Play of American Politics, War, and Protest.* Fuchs is artistic adviser to the Fund for New American Plays of the Kennedy Center and is a member of the executive committee of the Ibsen Society of America. She received her Ph.D. from the Graduate Center of the City University of New York; has won Rockefeller, Bunting, and Swedish Institute fellowships; and has taught at Harvard and Emory universities. She is the daughter of Lillian Ruth Kessler.

Jane Gabin is assistant director of undergraduate admissions and an adjunct professor of English at the University of North Carolina. She is the author of *A Living Minstrelsy: The Poetry and Music of Sidney Lanier.* She is currently pursuing an independently funded study of expatriate American women writers in Britain.

Michael Galchinsky received his Ph.D. in English from the University of California at Berkeley. He is the author of *The Origin of the Modern Jewish Woman Writer: Romance and Reform in Victorian England* and coeditor of *Jews and Multiculturalism in America.* Galchinsky teaches at Millsaps College.

Alyssa Gallin is a doctoral student in the Department of Cinema Studies at New York University. She is also the special projects editor at *Scenario: The Magazine of Screenwriting Art* and a program adviser to the Edinburgh International Film Festival.

Lloyd P. Gartner is professor emeritus of European Jewish history, Faculty of Humanities, Speigel Family Foundation, at Tel Aviv University, Israel. He is author or editor of eight books, including *The Jews in the United States.*

Rela Mintz Geffen is professor of sociology at Gratz College, where she also coordinates the program in Jewish Communal Studies. Previously, she served Gratz as dean for academic affairs. She is a fellow of the Jerusalem Center for Public Affairs and has served as vice president of the Association for Jewish Studies and as president of the Association for the Social Scientific Study of Jewry. Geffen's major research interest is the sociology of religion, which includes her book *Jewish Women on the Way Up.* Her latest study, coauthored with Egon Mayer, is *The Ripple Effect: Interfaith Couples Speak Out.* She has just been named editor of *Contemporary Jewry.*

Heather Geisberg graduated from Dartmouth College, where Gertrude Weil was the subject of her undergraduate thesis. She currently studies at the Hebrew University of Jerusalem as a Raoul Wallenberg Scholar.

Tamar Szabó Gendler holds a B.A. in mathematics and philosophy from Yale University and a Ph.D. from Harvard University. She currently teaches philosophy at Yale University. Gendler is coauthor of several publications in the area of education policy, including *High Schools with Character* and *The Teaching Internship,* as well as articles in philosophy, including "On the Possibility of Feminist Epistemology."

Jane S. Gerber is professor of Jewish history at the Graduate Center of the City University of New York, where she also directs the Institute for Sephardic Studies. She is the author of *Jewish Society in Fez,* the award-winning *The Jews of Spain,* and *Sephardic Studies in the University.* She is past president of the Association for Jewish Studies and vice president of the American Society for Sephardic Studies.

Naomi Geschwind is a monthly columnist with the Philadelphia *Jewish Exponent.* She has also written for the *Forward* and such diverse publications as *Cats* and *Videography.* Geschwind founded Hudson River Wine Tours and has written and lectured on kosher wine for the International Wine Center. She has worked for the New York University Hillel and as program director at Manhattan's Congregation Ansche Chesed. Geschwind holds an A.B. from Vassar College and an M.A. in journalism from New York University.

Celia Gilbert is a poet and printmaker in Cambridge, Massachusetts. She is the author of two books of poetry, *Bonfire* and *Queen of Darkness.* Among her honors are a Discovery Award and two prizes from the Poetry Society of America. Her monoprints are in public and private collections. Gilbert holds a B.A. from Smith College and an M.A. in creative writing from Boston University.

Scott F. Gilbert is professor of biology at Swarthmore College. He received his B.A. in biology and religion from Wesleyan University and his M.A. in the history of science and his Ph.D. in biology from Johns Hopkins University. In his postdoctoral work on developmental biology at the University of Wisconsin, Gilbert worked in the laboratory of a student of Salome Waelsch. He has published numerous works on embryology and its history, including the textbook *Developmental Biology* and *A Conceptual History of Modern Embryology.*

Anne S. Glickman is an education writer and editor in Boston. She is a graduate of Mount Holyoke College (B.A.) and Harvard University (Ed.M.).

Idana Goldberg received a B.A. in archaeology from Barnard College. She has worked at the Andrew W. Mellon Foundation in New York and is coauthor of *Crafting a Class: College Admissions and Financial Aid, 1955–1994.* Goldberg is currently a Ph.D. candidate in history at the University of Pennsylvania, concentrating on Jewish history and women's history.

Myrna Goldenberg received her B.S. in education from the City College of New York, her M.A. in English from the University of Arkansas, and her Ph.D. in the history of higher education from the University of Maryland. Goldenberg is currently a professor of English at Montgomery College, and she also serves as an adjunct faculty member at the University of Maryland, Baltimore County, and at Johns Hopkins University/School of Continuing Studies. Goldenberg has published articles on pedagogy, women in higher education and women in the Holocaust. Her dissertation focused on Annie Nathan Meyer.

Karla Goldman is assistant professor of American Jewish history at Hebrew Union College–Jewish Institute of Religion in Cincinnati. She received her Ph.D. in American history from Harvard University.

Shalom Goldman is in the Department of Near Eastern Judaic and Hellenic Languages and Literatures Department at Ohio State University.

Eric L. Goldstein holds a B.A. from Emory University and an M.A. from the University of Michigan, where he is a doctoral candidate in modern Jewish history. His publications include a book on Jewish settlement in Maryland and a study of Henrietta Szold's Zionist ideology. Goldstein's dissertation explores the ways that American understandings of race helped to shape Jewish identity in the United States between 1880 and 1945.

Marcia Tremmel Goldstein is a Ph.D. candidate at the University of Colorado. She works as an instructor at Arapahoe Community College and the Metropolitan State College of Denver, where she received her B.A. Goldstein has worked as a machine operator at the Redfield Gunsight Company and was a union steward in the United Steelworkers of America, local 5550. She has published articles on the American West, labor, and women's history in a number of Colorado historical journals and has also served as a consultant for *One Woman, One Vote*, part of the PBS series *American Experience*.

Helen Goodman is assistant professor of history at the Fashion Institute of Technology. Her research interests center on American art at the turn of the twentieth century, particularly women illustrators and photographers. Goodman has won several grants from the National Endowment for the Humanities and has contributed articles to a number of journals and reference books. She received her B.A. from the University of Michigan, her M.A. in art history from Wayne State University, and her Ph.D. in art education from New York University.

Naomi Goodman is a peace activist and historian concerned with biblical women. She is an officer of the Jewish Peace Fellowship and the Fellowship of Reconciliation. Goodman is coauthor of *The Goodbook Cook Book*, a biblical cookbook, and coeditor of *The Challenge of Shalom: The Jewish Tradition of Peace and Justice*. She is working on a book about Eve and Lilith.

Ruth R. Goodman began her dance studies at the Metropolitan Opera School of Ballet and the Ballet Russe School of Dance. She is the cofounder and director of the Israeli Dance Institute and editor of *Nirkoda* magazine. Involved with the annual Israel Folk Dance Festival since 1969, she succeeded Fred Berk as its director in 1978. Goodman is the founder and director of the Parparim Ensemble of Israeli Dance and Song and has directed a variety of dance programs on university campuses, for the New York City Department of Cultural Affairs, and for the major television networks in the New York metropolitan area.

Eric A. Gordon holds a doctorate in history from Tulane University. He is the author of *Mark the Music: The Life and Work of Marc Blitzstein*, and he collaborated with composer Earl Robinson on the autobiography *Ballad of an American*.

Julie K. Gordon is the co-rabbi at the Temple of Aaron, a Conservative synagogue in St. Paul, Minnesota, with her husband, Jonathan H. Ginsburg. She is a member of the Rabbinical Assembly and the only Conservative woman rabbi in Minnesota. Gordon is an adjunct faculty member at the College of St. Catherine, serves as the Jewish chaplain to a local hospital, and develops adult education courses for local Jewish organizations. She is on the Executive Committee of National UJA Rabbinic Cabinet and has served as the rabbi to the National UJA Women's Division March of the Living Mission to Poland and Israel.

Sherry Gorelick, associate professor of sociology and women's studies at Rutgers University, is the author of *City College and the Jewish Poor* and articles on Jewish subjects. She has lectured on Jewish feminism, the Israeli/Palestinian women's peace movement, and related topics. She was an observer at meetings of the Israeli/Palestinian women's peace movement and at the historic Women's International Conference for Israeli/Palestinian Peace at Geneva, Switzerland, in May 1991. She is completing a book on Jewish feminists and the Israeli/Palestinian conflict.

R. Pamela Jay Gottfried is director of religious life at the Solomon Schechter School of Westchester in White Plains, New York. Gottfried received her rabbinic ordination and a master's degree in Jewish education from the Jewish Theological Seminary of America. She has also served as the rabbinic intern of the Hillel Foundation of Stanford University and as assistant to the dean of List College at the Jewish Theological Seminary.

Amy Gottlieb is a fiction writer and editor who worked on the editorial staff of *Jewish Women in America* and is currently managing editor of *Conservative Judaism*. She received her B.A. in English from Clark University and her M.A. in comparative literature from the University of Chicago and has published numerous short stories and book reviews.

Jane Gottlieb is head librarian and a member of the graduate faculty at the Juilliard School. She received her B.A. in music from the State University of New York at Binghamton and her M.S.L.S. from Columbia University. Gottlieb has edited *Guide to the Juilliard School Archives* and the three-volume *The Musical Woman: An International Perspective*, and she has published articles in a number of journals, including *Notes: Quarterly Journal of the Music Library Association*.

Lois Gould is the author of eight novels, most recently *No Breaks*. A frequent contributor to the *New York Times*, she has taught at Boston University, New York University, Wesleyan University, and University College, Dublin. Her entry on her mother, Jo Copeland, is adapted from her forthcoming memoir, *Mommy Dressing*.

Wendy Graham, assistant professor at Vassar College, is writing a book on Henry James and nineteenth-century theories of creativity, sexuality, and race. Her work has appeared most recently in the journals *Genders* and *Modern Fiction Studies.*

Lauren B. Granite received her Ph.D. in sociology and the anthropology of religion from Drew University. Granite has been a visiting fellow at the University of Maryland's Meyerhoff Center for Jewish Studies and an adjunct professor at the American University and at Drew. Her dissertation was "Tradition as a Modality of Religious Change: Talmud Study in the Lives of Orthodox Jewish Women."

Tresa Grauer received her B.A., M.A., and Ph.D. from the University of Michigan. Her dissertation is "One and the Same Openness: Narrative and Tradition in Contemporary Jewish American Literature." She has won a grant from the National Endowment for the Humanities and has published an article on Jerome Badanes's work in *Studies in American Jewish Literature.*

Carol Hurd Green is associate dean of the College of Arts and Sciences at Boston College. She is coauthor of *American Women in the 1960s: Changing the Future* and coeditor of *Notable American Women: The Modern Period* and *American Women Writers,* Volume 5.

Joann Green was founder and artistic director of the Cambridge Ensemble, where she adapted and directed plays and chamber operas ranging from the *Oresteia* and *Gulliver's Travels* to writings of Peter Handke and Shakespeare. Green has served on the artistic staffs of the American Repertory Theater, the Boston Shakespeare Company, and the American National Theater at the Kennedy Center and has directed and taught at theaters and universities around the country. She has directed several plays in American Sign Language and English, one of which was a selection of the first conference on Deaf Language, History, and Culture at Gallaudet University. Green is a recipient of the Boston Critics' Circle Award for continued excellence in directing. She is the author of *The Small Theatre Handbook* and a contributor to *Working It Out.*

Cheryl Greenberg is associate professor of history at Trinity College. She has been a fellow at the W.E.B. Du Bois Institute and Charles Warren Center for Studies in American History at Harvard University. She is the author of *"Or Does It Explode?" Black Harlem in the Great Depression.*

Dan Greenberg is a critic, teacher and scholar of film. He received a B.A. in English, an M.A. in theater, and a Ph.D. in radio-television-film. He has published numerous articles and reviews, many of them while employed as a film critic for thirteen suburban Detroit newspapers. For the past thirty-two years he has taught film history, appreciation, and production at Oakland Community College in Farmington Hills, Michigan.

Joshua Greenberg received his B.A. in history from the University of California at Santa Cruz. He is currently in a graduate program at American University, where he studies American history.

Mark I. Greenberg received his Ph.D. from the University of Florida, his M.A. from the University of Western Ontario, and his B.A. from the University of Toronto. His dissertation is "Creating Ethnic Identity in Dixie: The Jews of Savannah, Georgia, 1830–1900." A former assistant editor of *Florida Historical Quarterly,* Greenberg has published articles on Southern Jewish history. He is resident historian at the Museum of the Southern Jewish Experience in Jackson, Mississippi.

Janet Wells Greene is a Ph.D. candidate in American history at New York University. She recently completed a year as a Smithsonian Fellow at the National Museum of American History in Washington, D.C., and is at work on her dissertation, "Camera Wars: Coal Miners and the Politics of Photography in the Truman Era." Greene is an archivist at the Robert F. Wagner Labor Archives at New York University. Her publications include Volume 1 of *From Forge to Fast Food: Child Labor in New York State, From Colonial Times to the Civil War.*

Charlotte Greenspan is an author and pianist in Ithaca, New York. She holds a B.A. from Queens College, an M.M. from the University of Illinois, and a Ph.D. from the University of California at Berkeley. She has taught at the University of Wisconsin and Cornell University. Her most recent publications include a cotranslation, with the author, of Laszlo Somfai's *The Keyboard Sonatas of Joseph Haydn* and "Rhapsody in Blue: A Study in Hollywood Hagiography," which will appear in *The Gershwin Style,* edited by Wayne Schneider. She is at work on a biography of Dorothy Fields.

Jill Wexler Greenstein is manager of volunteer and visitor services at the National Museum of Women in the Arts in Washington, D.C., where she lectures on women's art history to docents and members of the community. Greenstein holds a B.A. in art history from the University of California at Los Angeles and has taken classes in Judaic studies at Hebrew Union College–Jewish Institute of Religion in Los Angeles.

Catherine Gross does consulting work in fund-raising and prospect research. She received her B.A. from Barnard College, her M.A. in history and archives from New York University, and her M.L.S. from Pratt Institute.

Barbara W. Grossman is a theater historian and director. Grossman received a B.A. from Smith College, an M.F.A. from Boston University's School of Theatre Arts, and a Ph.D. from Tufts University, where she currently teaches. A Bunting Fellow at Radcliffe in 1994–1995, she was appointed by President Clinton to the National Council on the Arts, the advisory board to the National Endowment for the Arts, for a six-year term beginning in 1994. The author of *Funny Woman: The Life and Times of Fanny Brice,* her next book will focus on American actress and writer Clara Morris.

Katherina Kroo Grunfeld is an adjunct assistant professor at Hunter College, where she edits *The Echo: The Journal of the Hunter College Archives.* A graduate of New York University (B.A., M.A.) and Teachers College, Columbia University (Ed.D.), Grunfeld is also a director of English Now, a community service program designed to teach English to adult immigrants and refugees.

Jeffrey S. Gurock is the Libby M. Klaperman Professor of Jewish History at Yeshiva University. He is associate editor of *American Jewish History,* editor of the thirteen-volume series *The American Jewish Experience,* and author of *The Men and*

Women of Yeshiva: Higher Education, Orthodoxy and American Judaism.

Ruth Gursky graduated from the Benjamin N. Cardozo School of Law and received her B.A. and M.A. degrees in communications from Queens College. Gursky founded and is currently a partner in a women's law firm, Gursky and Odwak, of Brooklyn Heights, New York.

Jane Bock Guzman is a Ph.D. candidate at the University of North Texas. She is a member of the Board of Directors of both the Dallas Historical Society and the Dallas Jewish Historical Society. Guzman has published articles about Jewish and Texas history.

Beth Haber is an artist and writer whose work has been exhibited throughout the United States and Israel. She is the author of *Drawing on the Bible—Biblical Women in Art.* Haber has worked as an adjunct professor at the State University of New York at New Paltz and as a critic in residence at the Women's Studio Workshop. She has lectured, taught, and curated museum exhibits on women and art.

Malvina Halberstam is professor of law at the Benjamin N. Cardozo School of Law. She has also taught at the University of Virginia Law School and the Hebrew University in Jerusalem. A graduate of Brooklyn College (B.A.) and Columbia University (J.D., M.I.A.), Halberstam has served as an assistant district attorney in New York County and as counselor on international law in the Office of the Legal Advisor of the United States State Department. Her writings include *International Agreements on Women's Rights: An Alternative to ERA?*, coauthored with Elizabeth DeFeis, and articles on international law, human rights, terrorism, and the Arab-Israeli conflict.

Diana Hallman is a musicologist and pianist who holds a Ph.D. in music from the Graduate Center of the City University of New York, an M.M. in musicology from the University of Maryland, and a B.M. in piano performance from Wintrop College. She is assistant professor of musicology at the University of Kentucky. Hallman has written a dissertation on the French grand opera *La Juive* (1835), by Fromental Halévy and Eugène Scribe, and an M.A. thesis on the pianist Fannie Bloomfield Zeisler. She is now completing a book on the life and career of Zeisler.

Susan Halpert is reference librarian at Houghton Library, Harvard University.

Loraine Hammack is chair of the Department of English at Beachwood High School in Beachwood, Ohio.

Joanna G. Harris is a dance teacher, historian, critic, and therapist in Berkeley, California. She has taught at several California colleges and universities and now is in private practice in dance therapy and is a frequent contributor to scholarly journals. Her article "From Tenement to Theater: American Jewish Dance Pioneers" appeared in *Judaism.* She is active in San Francisco Bay area dance activities and the Jewish community.

Sandra Hartford works at the Scarborough Public Library in Scarborough, Maine. She is currently enrolled as an undergraduate history major at the University of Southern Maine. Hartford has worked as a circulation assistant at the Donald

L. Garbrecht Law Library at the University of Maine School of Law and as senior legal information specialist at Unum Life Insurance Company in Portland.

Adele Hast is co–project director and coeditor of the Historical Encyclopedia of Chicago Women, a project at the Center for Research on Women and Gender at the University of Illinois at Chicago, where she is an adjunct professor. She is also a research fellow at the Newberry Library. Hast, who received her B.A. from Brooklyn College and her M.A. and Ph.D. in history from the University of Iowa, has worked as executive editor of St. James Press and editor in chief of Marquis Who's Who, Inc. She has received research grants from the National Endowment for the Humanities and American Council of Learned Societies and is the author of *Loyalism in Revolutionary Virginia: The Norfolk Area and the Eastern Shore.*

Betty Hauck is a professional violist. She lives in southwestern New Hampshire.

Andrew R. Heinze teaches history at the University of San Francisco. He received his B.A. from Amherst College and his B.A. and Ph.D. from the University of California at Berkeley. In addition to *Adapting to Abundance: Jewish Immigrants, Mass Consumption, and the Search for American Identity*, Heinze has written articles on Jewish-American history in scholarly journals and reference books. Heinze's current works include his own reflections on American history as a Jewish historian.

Kathryn Hellerstein teaches Yiddish language and literature at the University of Pennsylvania. Educated at Wellesley and Brandeis, and with a doctorate from Stanford, Hellerstein is a poet, a translator, and a scholar of Yiddish poetry. Her books include *In New York: A Selection* and *Selected Poems of Kadya Molodowsky.* Hellerstein is a major contributor to *American Yiddish Poetry: A Bilingual Anthology.* Hellerstein's own poems and prose have appeared in periodicals such as *Bridges* and anthologies such as *Nice Jewish Girls.*

Bruce Henderson is associate professor of speech communication at Ithaca College, where he teaches performance studies. He is coauthor, with Carol Simpson Stern, of *Performance: Texts and Contexts* and is associate editor of the journal *Text and Performance Quarterly.* He has published essays on such writers as Marianne Moore, Erica Jong, Laurence Housman, and Oscar Wilde.

Mary Ellen Henry is a Ph.D. candidate in United States history at American University. She received her B.A. in English from Colby College and her M.A. in literature from the University of Hawaii. She is a writing instructor and adjunct faculty member in the Department of English at American.

Felicia Herman is a Ph.D. candidate in Near Eastern and Judaic studies at Brandeis University, where she also received her M.A. in women's studies. Herman is a research assistant at the American Jewish Historical Society, where she helped assemble a traveling exhibition on the history of Jewish women, and she has also worked as assistant to the director of the Yeshiva University Museum.

Leo Hershkowitz is professor of history at Queens College, where he is the director of the Historical Documents Collection. Hershkowitz has written books on eighteenth- and nineteenth-century New York history, including *Tweed's New*

York. Hershkowitz sits on a number of committees on archives and landmark preservation in New York, including the New York City Mayor's Committee on Archives.

Linda Herskowitz is a freelance writer. She is a former staff writer for the *Philadelphia Inquirer* and *Providence Journal* (R.I.) and received a master's in journalism from the Columbia University School of Journalism. She lives in Philadelphia with her two sons, Daniel and Ezra.

Irene Heskes is a music historian who specializes in Jewish music. She has contributed entries to *Encyclopedia Judaica*, *Musical Theater in America*, and *The Handbook of Holocaust Literature*. Among her books are *Studies in Jewish Music, Jews in Music, The Resource Book of Jewish Music, Yiddish-American Popular Songs, 1895–1950*, and *Passport to Jewish Music: Its History, Traditions, and Culture*.

Monica Hiller received her B.A. from the University of Pittsburgh and her M.A. in English from Clark University. Her academic interests include cultural narratives, literature of American immigrants, and Chinese- and Jewish-American literature. Currently, she is teaching literature, composition, and creative writing in Massachusetts. Hiller is a storyteller and collects tales from people she meets all over the world.

Rona Holub works for the Planned Parenthood Federation and is enrolled in the graduate program in women's history at Sarah Lawrence College. She is a contributing writer for *Skyjack Magazine* and a former editor and writer for the *L.E.N.D. Newsletter*. Holub has developed educational programs on the history of Brooklyn, New York, for historical organizations, including the South Street Seaport Museum. She also uses the name Raven Hall as a writer, songwriter, and performer.

Marjorie Hornbein received her B.A. and M.A. in American history from the University of Denver. She is on the Denver Planning Board, the Denver Landmark Commission, and the Colorado Commission on the Status of Women. Her articles have appeared in a number of scholarly journals.

Sara R. Horowitz is director of the Jewish Studies Program and associate professor English literature in the honors program at the University of Delaware. She is the author of *Voicing the Void: Muteness and Memory in Holocaust Fiction* and is completing a book titled "Gender, Genocide, and Jewish Memory." She has published on Holocaust literature, women survivors, Jewish American fiction, and pedagogy. Horowitz is founding coeditor of *KEREM: A Journal of Creative Explorations in Judaism*, and she coedited *Jewish American Women Writers: A Bio-Bibliographical and Critical Sourcebook* with Ann Shapiro, Ellen Schiff, and Miryam Glazer.

Marsha Hurst is associate director of research at the Children's Village in Dobbs Ferry, New York. She is also a faculty member in the health advocacy program at Sarah Lawrence College, where she teaches health care policy and the history of health care in America. A graduate of Brown University (A.B.) and Columbia University (Ph.D. in political science), Hurst received a postdoctoral fellowship from Mount Sinai Medical School in New York. She has published numerous articles in women's health, recently presenting a lecture on breast cancer at the Berkshire Conference on the History of Women.

Ann Hurwitz teaches early childhood development at Kingsborough Community College in Brooklyn, New York. She has also worked as an adjunct professor of teacher education at the Bank Street College of Education in New York and as director of the Park Avenue Synagogue Early Childhood Center. Hurwitz is the author of *One Mezuzah: A Jewish Counting Book* as well as articles and poems.

Paula E. Hyman is an editor of the *Encyclopedia*. See the beginning of this list for a biographical note.

Judith Brin Ingber is a dancer and independent scholar. She received her B.A. in dance from Sarah Lawrence College and has lectured at Princeton University and the University of Minnesota. Ingber is the author of a biography of Fred Berk titled *Victory Dances*, a monograph on Israeli folk dance in *Dance Perspectives*, and numerous articles. She was editor of a special edition of *Dance Research Journal* titled "Dancing into Marriage." Ingber is the founder, choreographer, and dancer for Voices of Sepharad.

Daniel Itzkovitz is a visiting assistant professor of English at Stonehill College and is completing his doctoral studies in the Program in Literature at Duke University. Itzkovitz is coeditor of *Queer Theory and the Jewish Question*.

Naomi Jackson teaches at Arizona State University. She received her M.A. from the University of Surrey, England, and her Ph.D. in performance studies from New York University. She has published in *Dance Research Journal, Dance Research*, and *The Dance Connection*.

Andrew Jacobs is a candidate for rabbinic ordination at the Reconstructionist Rabbinical College in Philadelphia. He received a B.A. in religion from Vassar College and an M.A. in Jewish art and material culture from the Jewish Theological Seminary in consortium with the Jewish Museum and Columbia University. Jacobs studied rabbinic literature at the University of Judaism in Los Angeles and was a member of the Tel Migne-Ekron excavation team while studying at the Hebrew University in Jerusalem.

Barbara C. Johnson, a cultural anthropologist, was coauthor with Ruby Daniel of *Ruby of Cochin: An Indian Jewish Woman Remembers*. This book grew out of Johnson's many years of research on the Cochin Jews in India and Israel, the subject of her master's thesis and dissertation. She lived for four years in south India, made numerous research trips to Israel, and served as an ethnographic consultant for the Israel Museum in Jerusalem. A graduate of Oberlin and Smith colleges and the University of Massachusetts, Johnson is assistant professor of anthropology at Ithaca College.

Beth DiNatale Johnson received her Ph.D. from Case Western University with the dissertation "Through the Rose Window: Rehabilitation and Long-Care of the Elderly at the Benjamin Rose Hospital, Cleveland, Ohio, 1953–1968." Johnson worked as a research associate at the Corinne Dolan Alzheimer Center in Ohio and has published a number of studies in the *American Journal of Alzheimer's Care and Related Disorders and Research*, as well as contributing to *Aging Policy Interest Groups*, edited by D.D. Van Tassel and J.W. Meyer.

Robert Johnston is assistant professor of history at Yale University. Johnston received his Ph.D. from Rutgers University. His dissertation was "The Radical Middle Class:

Popular Democracy and Anticapitalism in Progressive Era Portland, Oregon, 1883–1926." Johnston has contributed an article to *Suburbia Re-Examined*, edited by Barbara Kelly.

Jenna Weissman Joselit is on the Editorial Advisory Board of the *Encyclopedia*. See the beginning of this list for a biographical note.

Robin Judd is a Ph.D. candidate in history at the University of Michigan, where she received her master's degree. Judd, who received her B.A. from Wellesley, specializes in Jewish, German, and gender history. Her dissertation is "Turning German Citizens Into Jewish Outcasts: Jewish Rituals and Alleged Blood Practices, 1871–1914."

David Kahan received his B.A. in American history from the University of Pennsylvania in 1995. He taught at the Manhattan Day School for two years and is attending law school at Columbia University.

Ava F. Kahn is director of the oral history program at the Western Jewish History Center of the Judah Magnes Museum. She received her Ph.D. from the University of California at Santa Barbara, and her dissertation explored American immigrant voluntary associations in Israel. Her most recent research focuses on the Jewish community of Northern California. Kahn helped research materials for a documentary video titled "Birth of a Community: Jews and the Gold Rush" and is the author of *A Gold Rush Legacy: A Documentary History of Jewish Life in the Bay Area and the Foothills of Northern California, 1849–1880*.

Catherine Kahn is archivist of Touro Infirmary, the oldest (1852) private hospital in New Orleans. She was for many years in the manuscripts division of the Historic New Orleans Collection. She is a board member and chair of the archives committee of the Southern Jewish Historical Society and involved in the preservation of the history of the New Orleans Jewish community. Her most recent publication is *Legacy: The History of the Community Chest and the Greater New Orleans Foundation*, and she is editing a *Guide to Jewish Collections in New Orleans Repositories*. She was recently appointed to the Mayor's Holocaust Memorial Committee, charged with the selection of a site and sculpture to honor New Orleans's Holocaust survivors.

Susan Martha Kahn received her Ph.D. in social anthropology from Harvard University. She writes about reproductive technology and Jewish kinship in Israel.

Debra Newman Kamin is the principal rabbi of Am Yisrael Conservative Congregation of the North Shore in Northfield, Illinois. Kamin received her B.A. in Judaic studies from the University of Michigan and received her rabbinic ordination from the Jewish Theological Seminary of America. She has also studied at the Hebrew University in Jerusalem. Kamin has lectured throughout the Midwest and her publications include a chapter in the book *Lifecycles*, edited by Rabbi Debra Orenstein.

Jane Kamine is a painter and art educator in Cambridge, Massachusetts. She has exhibited her work throughout the country. She received her M.F.A. from the University of California at Berkeley and teaches at the Massachusetts Institute of Technology.

Elana Kanter was ordained as a rabbi by the Jewish Theological Seminary. She has served as an administrator for the Solomon Schechter Schools of Atlanta and Providence, Rhode Island. Kanter is director of the Institute for Jewish Communal Leadership in Birmingham, Alabama.

Justin Kaplan won the Pulitzer Prize and a National Book Award for *Mr. Clemens and Mark Twain*. His *Lincoln Steffens* and *Walt Whitman* also received National Book Awards. Kaplan is the editor of *Bartlett's Familiar Quotations*, 16th edition and a member of the American Academy of Arts and Letters. He was born in New York City and educated at Harvard University. The husband of Anne Bernays, he recently coauthored *The Language of Names* with her.

Marion Kaplan is professor of modern European history at Queens College and the Graduate Center of the City University of New York. Her research and teaching interests include the history of Jews in Germany and modern European women's history. She is the author of *The Jewish Feminist Movement in Germany: The Campaigns of the Juedischer Frauenbun, 1904–1938*; *When Biology Became Destiny*, coedited with Atina Grossman and Claudia Koontz; and the award-winning *The Making of the Jewish Middle Class: Women, Family, and Identity in Imperial Germany*.

Tamar Kaplan is a first-year doctoral student in Jewish history at the University of Pennsylvania.

Seymour Kass is professor of mathematics in the engineering program at the University of Massachusetts at Boston. A graduate of Brooklyn College (B.A.), Stanford University (M.S.), the University of Chicago (S.M.), and the Illinois Institute of Technology (Ph.D.), Kass has published a number of articles in mathematics journals.

Amy L. Katz is director of leadership development at the Combined Jewish Philanthropies of Greater Boston. She holds a B.A. from Stern College for Women, Yeshiva University, and an M.A. in social work from the Wurzweiler School of Social Work. She has worked as a professional in the field of Jewish communal service for twenty years.

Martha Katz-Hyman received her B.A. in American studies from Simmons College and her M.A. in museum studies from the Cooperstown Graduate Program of the State University of New York at Oneonta. She is an associate curator in the department of collections at Colonial Williamsburg in Virginia, where she works primarily with the musical instrument, kitchen equipment, and mechanical arts collection and specializes in the material culture of eighteenth-century Tidewater Virginia slaves. Katz-Hyman has also worked as assistant librarian at the American Jewish Historical Society, where she was research coordinator for the traveling exhibition, *On Common Ground: The Boston Jewish Experience, 1649–1980*.

Anne Kaufman is a mathematics and English teacher at the Sidwell Friends School and a Ph.D. candidate at the University of Maryland. Kaufman received her A.B. in women's studies from Smith College and her M.A. in English from the University of Montana. Her scholarly interests include nineteenth- and twentieth-century American women's writers, Canadian literature, American legal history, and literature of the West.

Deborah Kaufman was founder and former director of the San Francisco Jewish Film Festival, the first and largest festival of its kind in the world. She is a partner in Snitow-Kaufman Productions, producing and directing films on social and cultural issues, including the feature-length documentary *Blacks and Jews*.

Debra Kaufman is Matthews Distinguished Professor in the Department of Sociology and Anthropology at Northeastern University. She has written widely in the areas of the family, feminist methodology and theory, gender roles, and women's studies, and is the author of *Rachel's Daughters: Newly Orthodox Jewish Women*.

Jan Caryl Kaufman is director of special projects for the Rabbinical Assembly, International Association of Conservative Rabbis. Kaufman was a founder and principal of the Solomon Schechter High School at the Jewish Theological Seminary of America and has worked at a number of Jewish institutions as administrator, librarian, and rabbi. Kaufman was ordained as a rabbi at the Hebrew Union College–Jewish Institute of Religion in New York, where she also received her M.A. She received her J.D. from George Washington University.

Ellen Kellman is completing her Ph.D. in Yiddish studies at Columbia University. Her dissertation is "Popular Novels in the American Yiddish Press, 1900–1940." A graduate of Goddard College (B.A.), the University of Michigan (M.A.), and Columbia University (M.A., M.Phil.), Kellman has taught Yiddish at the University of Toronto, Columbia, YIVO Institute, and the Jewish Theological Seminary. She has also helped to curate an exhibit on Sholem Aleichem for the YIVO Institute.

Alice Kessler-Harris is on the Editorial Advisory Board of the *Encyclopedia*. See the beginning of this list for a biographical note.

Carole Kessner is professor of comparative studies in the programs of Judaic studies and women's studies at the State University of New York at Stony Brook. She received her B.A. from Brandeis University and her Ph.D. from Stony Brook. Kessner is the author of *The Other New York Intellectuals* as well as articles on a wide range of subjects, such as the poetry of John Milton, the egalitarianism of Mordecai Kaplan, and anti-Semitism in American literature. Kessner is working on a biography of Marie Syrkin.

M. Alison Kibler is assistant professor of social change and development and women's studies at the University of Wisconsin at Green Bay. She has written essays on female vaudeville performers and has received grants from the National Endowment for the Humanities and the Andrew Mellon Foundation.

Clare Kinberg was a founding editor and is currently managing editor of the biannual *Bridges: A Journal for Jewish Feminists and Our Friends*. Her essay "Challenges of Difference at Bridges" was published in *The Narrow Bridges: Jewish Views of Multiculturalism*, edited by Marla Brettschneider.

Joy A. Kingsolver is archivist at the Chicago Jewish Archives, Spertus Institute of Jewish Studies. She received an M.A. in history and an M.S. in library science from Indiana University. Her research focuses on the history of Jewish libraries. She is coauthoring a bibliography of Judaica librarianship and is researching the life of Fanny Goldstein, founder of Jewish Book Week.

Arthur Kiron is a Ph.D. candidate at Columbia University, specializing in American Jewish history. He received his A.B. in politics and women's studies from Brandeis University and his A.M. in religious studies from Stanford University, and he has also studied at the Hebrew University and the Pardes Institute for Jewish Studies in Jerusalem. Kiron has worked as manuscripts curator and assistant archivist at the Annenberg Research Institute in Philadelphia, currently the Center for Judaic Studies at the University of Pennsylvania.

Louise Klaber, founder and president of Greenwood Associates, is a consultant who works with business, educational, and public sector organizations. A graduate of Barnard College (B.A.) and Columbia University (M.A.), Klaber is an adjunct professor at the University of Hartford and has published articles on organizational development. She has worked as an internal consultant at Northeast Utilities and as an associate professor at the University of Connecticut, Institute of Public Service.

Melissa Klapper, a graduate of Goucher College (B.A.), is a graduate fellow studying American and women's history at Rutgers University. As a curatorial assistant at the Jewish Historical Society of Maryland, she helped to develop the largest exhibition ever mounted on an American Jewish woman, *Daughter of Zion: Henrietta Szold and American Jewish Womanhood*. She was also one of the contributors to the exhibit catalog. Klapper's research interests center on American Jewish women during the nineteenth and early twentieth centuries.

Kim Klausner has completed coursework for an M.A. in history at San Francisco State University. She is writing a biography of Tima Ludins Tomash. Klausner was one of the founders of *OUT/LOOK: National Lesbian and Gay Quarterly*.

Katherine Kleeman is a senior program associate at the Center for the American Woman and Politics, a unit of the Eagleton Institute of Politics at Rutgers University. She writes and edits many of the center's publications and coordinates development of many of its new projects. She has directed programs to educate young women about politics and organized many national and international conferences.

Suzanne Kling is pursuing a Ph.D. in Jewish literature at the Jewish Theological Seminary of America. She graduated with a B.A. in English from Barnard College and a B.A. in Jewish literature from List College of the Jewish Theological Seminary.

Susanne Klingenstein is assistant professor of writing and humanistic studies at the Massachusetts Institute of Technology. She is also the book review editor of *Modern Jewish Studies*. In addition to *Jews in the American Academy, 1900–1940: The Dynamics of Intellectual Assimilation*, Klingenstein has written articles on Jewish American intellectuals, Jewish women, and the Holocaust. A graduate of the University of Heidelberg (M.A., Ph.D.), Brandeis University (M.A.), and the University of Mannheim (B.A.), Klingenstein's most recent work focuses on Jewish American literary scholars from 1930 to 1990.

Ann Kneavel is a professor at Goldey Beacom College, where she teaches writing, literature, philosophy, and communications. She received her Ph.D. in modern British literature from the University of Ottawa. Her academic interests include pedagogy and the representation of psychoanalysts in Hollywood films.

Rebecca Kobrin received her B.A. from Yale University and is a Ph.D. candidate in history at the University of Pennsylvania as well as a Wexner Graduate Fellow. Her specialty is Eastern European Jewish immigration. She is a coeditor of *From Written to Printed Text: The Transmission of Jewish Tradition.*

Lisa Kogen is a doctoral candidate in Jewish history at the Jewish Theological Seminary of America.

Roger Kohn is Reinhard Family Curator of Judaica and Hebraica Collections at Stanford University Libraries, where he is also bibliographer for religious studies. Kohn has worked as an archivist at the Jewish Theological Seminary of America and as an assistant professor of history at Gratz College. He received a B.A. in history and geography and a B.A. in art history and archaeology from the Sorbonne, as well as a B.A. in modern Hebrew from the University of Sorbonne-nouvelle. He is the author of *Les Juifs de la France du nord dans la seconde moitié du XIVe siècle* as well as archival inventories, exhibit catalogs, and articles on modern and medieval Jewish history.

Joe Komljenovich is a Ph.D. candidate in United States history at New York University, where he received his M.A. and his certificate in archival management and historical editing. A graduate of Hofstra University (B.A.), Komljenovich has worked at the New York Transit Museum Archives and the New York City Municipal Archives.

Pauline Koner was a solo concert dancer for fifteen years. She pioneered in television and was a guest artist for José Limon for fifteen years. Koner has conducted workshops in Japan, India, Singapore, and Korea. She has directed her own company, received the *Dance Magazine* Award and an honorary degree from Rhode Island College, and published two books. Koner has appeared throughout the world, and her works have been performed by many companies.

Seth Korelitz is graduate student in Near Eastern and Judaic studies at Brandeis University. Korelitz received his B.A. from the Eugene Lang College of the New School for Social Research in New York City. His research interests focus on American Judaism, and his article on the National Council of Jewish Women appears in *American Jewish History.*

Hadassa Kosak is professor of history at Yeshiva University in New York. She teaches American and Jewish history.

Jodi Koste is an archivist at Tompkins-McCaw Library at Virginia Commonwealth University. Her academic interests are nursing history and Civil War medicine. She received her B.A. and M.A. in history from Old Dominion University.

Debbie Kram is director of Ma'ayan: Torah Studies Initiative for Women in Brookline, Massachusetts. A graduate of City College (B.A.) and Simmons College Graduate School of Library and Information Sciences (M.S.), Kram has also worked as a cataloger at Brandeis University and a librarian at the Massachusetts Institute of Technology. She has won several awards for Jewish communal service.

Corinne Azen Krause is a research associate in the History Department of the University of Pittsburgh. She received a B.A. from the University of Michigan, an M.A. from Carnegie-Mellon University, and a Ph.D. from the University of Pittsburgh. Krause's work focuses on Jewish communal history in Pittsburgh, particularly on Jewish women. Among her publications are *Grandmothers, Mothers, and Daughters,* an oral history study of three generations of Jewish Italian and Slavic women, and *Los Judios en México,* a Spanish translation of her dissertation on Jews in Mexico.

Linda Gordon Kuzmack is an adjunct assistant professor of history at Baltimore Hebrew University and a foundation officer at the Public Citizen Foundation in Washington, D.C. Previously, she was director of oral history for the United States Holocaust Memorial Museum. Her books include *Woman's Cause: The Jewish Woman's Movement in England and the United States, 1881–1933* and *To Save a Life: Christian Rescuers and Jewish Survivors During the Holocaust.*

Diane Lada is a graduate student at New York University, where she received her M.A. in 1997. She is a member of the Costume Society of America and was cocurator of *Nude Up,* an exhibition on fashion and the body at New York's Rosenthal Gallery. She is currently writing a series of essays about fashion theory and criticism, under the working title "In Response."

Annie LaRock is director of institutional advancement at Audrey Cohen College.

Kristine Larsen is associate professor of physics and astronomy at Central Connecticut State University. In addition to her astronomical research, Larsen has published articles in reference books and scholarly journals on women and minorities in astronomy. Larsen participates in public outreach programs designed to educate public school children and the lay public about astronomy.

Leslie Lautin received a B.A. in English literature from Washington University. She was an Eisendrath Legislative Assistant at the Religious Action Center of Reform Judaism, and then a recipient of a Dorot Fellowship to Israel, which enabled her to study at Pardes Institute of Jewish Studies and work as a community artist. Lautin is currently communications coordinator for both the Drisha Institute for Jewish Education and She'arim, a fellowship for future day school educators.

Susan Laxton is a Ph.D. candidate in art history at Columbia University, completing her dissertation on surrealism. She was cocurator of a Florine Stettheimer exhibition at Wallach Gallery at Columbia.

Paulana Layman is finishing her master's degree in Judaic studies at Concordia University in Montreal. Her specialization is Jewish women's ritual and liturgy. Her article "The Creation of Liturgy for Jewish Women" focuses on the phenomenon of the women's seder. She is also working as an interviewer for the Survivors of the Shoah Visual History Foundation.

Karen Trahan Leathem is museum historian and director of interpretive services at the Louisiana State Museum in New Orleans, where she recently curated *Jews in Louisiana before 1877*. She received a Ph.D. in American history from the University of North Carolina and is working on a book on Mardi Gras and gender in New Orleans.

Mary LeCroy is senior scientific assistant in the department of ornithology at the American Museum of Natural History. She received her B.S. in biology from Columbia University. LeCroy has published numerous papers in scholarly journals, many of them based on her extensive field studies of birds of Papua, New Guinea.

Eli Lederhendler is senior lecturer in American Jewish history at the Institute of Contemporary Jewry of the Hebrew University in Jerusalem.

Sarah Henry Lederman received her Ph.D. in history from Columbia University. She is currently writing a biography of Mary C. Richmond.

Richard B. Lee is professor and graduate coordinator in the Department of Anthropology at the University of Toronto.

Jerome S. Legge, Jr. is professor of political science at the University of Georgia, where he also teaches in the Carl Vinson Institute of Government. He received his Ph.D. in political science from Emory University in 1975. Legge specializes in comparative German politics and is interested in American and German anti-Semitism as well as Jewish immigration and Orthodox and Traditional Judaism.

Marjorie Lehman graduated from Wellesley College and received her Ph.D. in religion and Jewish studies from Columbia University. Her field of concentration is rabbinics, and she wrote her dissertation on an early sixteenth-century collection of Talmudic Aggada. She served as a senior research associate at the Melton Research Center of the Jewish Theological Seminary and is currently a professor of rabbinics at the Reconstructionist Rabbinical College.

Sondra Leiman has been a teacher of social studies at SAR Academy in Riverdale, New York, a modern Orthodox day school, for thirty years. She is the author of *America: The Jewish Experience*, a textbook for grades five to seven, and is working on *Atlas of Great Jewish Communities*, designed for students of the same age. Leiman's paper "Practical Techniques and Methods in Teaching American Jewish History" was presented at the 1995 CAJE conference.

Carolyn Gray Lemaster is a Little Rock, Arkansas, native and author of the award-winning *A Corner of the Tapestry: A History of the Jewish Experience in Arkansas, 1820s–1990s* and *The Ottenheimers of Arkansas*. Lemaster lectures on Bible and Jewish history and serves on the boards of a number of local historical institutes, including the Southern Jewish Historical Society.

Lisa Lepson is an administrator at the Hillel at the University of California at Berkeley. She is a graduate of Brown University, and her articles have appeared in *Lilith*.

Linda P. Lerman is the officer of library, bibliographic, and member services at the Research Libraries Group in Mountain View, California. Lerman has also worked as Judaica curator at Yale University Libraries, as administrative librarian at the Jewish Theological Seminary of America, and as Judaica librarian at Hebrew Union College–Jewish Institute of Religion in Cincinnati. A graduate of the Jewish Theological Seminary (B.A.) and the University of Michigan (M.B.A., M.L.S.), Lerman has written articles and prepared exhibits relating to Judaica.

Anne Lapidus Lerner is on the Editorial Advisory Board of the *Encyclopedia*. See the beginning of this list for a biographical note.

Laura J. Levine is a graduate of Harvard Law School. After clerking in the federal district, she worked as a litigation associate with a large New York law firm. She lives in New York and is involved with a variety of volunteer activities.

Sue Levine is a psychotherapist in private practice. A graduate of the University of Wisconsin (B.A.) and Rutgers University (M.S.W.), Levine is a member of the National Council of Jewish Women and Hadassah. She has been an active volunteer for Meals on Wheels, Women Helping Women, and Planned Parenthood.

Judd Kruger Levingston is principal of the Jewish Theological Seminary Prozdor. A graduate of Harvard College (A.B.), Levingston is a doctoral candidate at the Jewish Theological Seminary of America, where he received his M.A. and was ordained as a rabbi. He is a member of the editorial board of *Jewish Education News*.

Sherry Levy-Reiner is project coordinator for the Decade of the Brain in the Office of Scholarly Programs at the Library of Congress. She has a Ph.D. in English literature from the University of Cincinnati, where she taught for several years. Levy-Reiner has served as editor of publications at the Menninger Foundation, special projects editor at the University of Chicago, and director of publications and public information at the Association of American Colleges.

Rhoda Lewin earned B.A. and M.A. degrees in journalism and a Ph.D. in American studies at the University of Minnesota. After a career in publishing and public relations, she taught at the University of Wisconsin at Superior and at the University of Minnesota. Lewin is now an independent oral historian, editor, and writer. She is the author of *Witnesses to the Holocaust: An Oral History* and *Stereotype and Reality in the Jewish Immigrant Experience*. Lewin writes a monthly column for the *American Jewish World*, edits *Identity*, a literary magazine, and reviews books for several scholarly journals.

Adina Lewittes is assistant dean of the Rabbinical School of the Jewish Theological Seminary of America, where she also received her master's degree and rabbinic ordination. She graduated with a B.A. from York University in Toronto.

Amy Lezberg is associate director for the Commission on Institutions of Higher Education of the New England Association of Schools and Colleges. She has lectured and published on quality assessment and accreditation. Lezberg received her Ph.D. in English from Boston University and has worked as professor of English and associate dean for academic affairs at Massachusetts College of Pharmacy and Allied Health Sciences. She is the author of *Interpersonal Communication in the Health Professions*.

Diane Lichtenstein is associate professor and chair of the English Department at Beloit College. She received her M.A. and Ph.D. in English from the University of Pennsylvania and her A.B. in classics from Brown University. She is the author of *Writing Their Nations: The Tradition of Nineteenth-Century American Jewish Women Writers*. Her research and teaching interests include American literature, women's studies, and multiculturalism.

Andrea Beth Lieber is a Ph.D. candidate in religion at Columbia University. She is an adjunct assistant professor at Vassar College, where she received her bachelor's degree in religion. Lieber also serves as a contributor to and research consultant for the interactive CD-ROM edition of *Heritage: Civilization and the Jews* and is a member of the editorial board of *Response: A Contemporary Jewish Review*. Her special field is Judaism and Christianity of late antiquity.

Laura Lieber is in rabbinical school at Hebrew Union College–Jewish Institute of Religion in Cincinnati. She received her undergraduate degree in English from the University of Arkansas at Fayetteville.

Victor Lipari, executive director of Dance Films Association, is a writer and filmmaker. He is currently working on a video documentary, *Igor Youskevitch: Ballet Forerunner in America*. Lipari is also collaborating with the Film Society of Lincoln Center in presenting Dance Films Association's annual Dance on Camera Festival.

Robert Lipsey is a research associate and director of the New York office of the National Bureau of Economic Research and professor emeritus of economics at Queens College and the Graduate Center of the City University of New York.

Deborah Lipstadt is on the Editorial Advisory Board of the *Encyclopedia*. See the beginning of this list for a biographical note.

John Livingston is chair of the History Department at the University of Denver. He received his B.A. in history from Harvard College and his M.A. and Ph.D. in history from the University of Wisconsin. He is the author of *Clarence Darrow: Sentimental Rebel* and *Jews of the American West*, coedited with Moses Rischin, Livingston is currently editor of *Rocky Mountain Jewish Historical Notes*.

Howard Loewith was Sadie Loewith's nephew by marriage. A lifelong resident of Fairfield, Connecticut, he graduated from the University of Connecticut with a B.A. after serving in the U.S. Army of Occupation. Loewith worked as the controller of Glen Gate Corporation. He is active in Congregation Beth El in Fairfield and volunteers in the Bridgeport Public Schools.

Claudia Logan is a children's book author. Her most recent book is about an archaeological dig in Egypt. She is also a consultant in the Education Department of the Boston Museum of Fine Arts. She lives in Cambridge, Massachusetts, with her husband and son.

Joseph Lowin, executive director of the National Center for the Hebrew Language, is managing editor of the *Jewish Book Annual*. He received a Ph.D. in French literature from Yale University and has held faculty positions at Yale and Touro College. He has been education director at Hadassah and program director at the National Foundation for Jewish Culture. Lowin's publications include a book about Cynthia Ozick as well as a monthly feature in *Hadassah* magazine, "About Hebrew," which formed the basis for his book *HebrewSpeak*. A series of essays on the Midrashic Mode in Jewish narrative is his ongoing project.

Audrey J. Lyke is a researcher in environmental and natural resource economics. She received her B.A. from Williams College and her M.S. in economics and her Ph.D. in agricultural economics from the University of Wisconsin. Lezberg helped to write the Water Quality Economics handbook for the Natural Resources Conservation Service of the United States Department of Agriculture, and her dissertation was cited in the Great Lakes Water Quality Initiative. She has taught economics at Franklin and Marshall College and statistics at Goldey Beacom College.

Saunders Mac Lane was professor of mathematics at the University of Chicago for thirty-five years and Max Mason Distinguished Service Professor for almost twenty of those years. A graduate of Yale University (Ph.B.), the University of Chicago (M.A.), and Gottingen University in Germany (Ph.D.), Mac Lane has served as vice president of the National Academy of Sciences, and he has also helped to edit several scholarly journals, including the *Journal of Algebra*. His books include *Sheaves in Geometry and Logic: A First Introduction to Topos Theory*. Mac Lane was awarded the National Medal of Science in 1989.

Joseph Machlis is professor emeritus of music at Queens College. He currently teaches in the graduate division of the Juilliard School. Among his books are the *The Enjoyment of Music* and *Introduction to Contemporary Music*. Machlis has also written several novels, including *The Career of Magda V.* and *Lisa's Boy*. His English version of Francis Poulenc's opera *Dialogues of the Carmelites* was presented at the Metropolitan Opera. He was a close friend of Jennie Tourel.

Shulamit Magnus is an affiliated scholar with the Stanford University Institute for Research on Women and Gender. A graduate of Barnard College (B.A.) and Columbia University (M.A., Ph.D.), Magnus has taught at Stanford and the University of Pennsylvania and has directed the Program in Jewish Civilization at the Reconstructionist Rabbinical College. She is the author of *Jewish Emancipation in a German City: Cologne, 1798–1871*.

Sarah S. Malino is associate professor of history at Guilford College. Her research and teaching interests center around race, gender, and labor in American history. She has published several articles and is working on "A Promising Future: Women's Employment in American Department Stores, 1870–1920."

Ruth Mandel is director of the Eagleton Institute of Politics and Board of Governors Professor of Politics at Rutgers University. She writes and speaks widely on the topics of women, leadership, and politics and is the author of *In the Running: The New Woman Candidate*. Since 1991, Mandel has been a member of the United States Holocaust Memorial Council, and she was named vice-chair of the board by President Clinton in 1993.

Bat Sheva Marcus is executive director of the Union for Traditional Judaism and chair of the International Women's Tefillah Network. She served as the New York metropolitan campaign director for the UJA-Federation. Earlier she held the position of director of young leadership for the New York Federation. She holds a master's degree in social work from Columbia University and a master's degree in Jewish studies from the Jewish Theological Seminary.

Judith Margles is curator of the Oregon Museum of Science and Industry. A graduate of the University of Toronto (B.A.) and New York University (M.A.), she has served as a consultant for a number of exhibits in Oregon.

Kim Marra is associate professor of theater arts at the University of Iowa, where she teaches theater history, dramatic literature, and performance theory. She has published numerous articles on women in turn-of-the-century American theater. With Robert A. Schanke, she is coediting a three-volume series on gays, lesbians, and bisexuals in pre-Stonewall American theater history. Marra is a member of the Executive Committee of the American Society of Theatre Research, book review editor of *Theatre Survey*, and editorial consultant for *Theatre History Studies*.

Angela Wigan Marvin is a writer of fiction and nonfiction in New York who has written for *Time* magazine and the Museum of Modern Art. She is at work on a short history of New York City with Jane Mushabac.

Glenna Matthews received her Ph.D. from Stanford University. Among her major publications are *"Just a Housewife": The Rise and Fall of Domesticity in America* and *The Rise of Public Woman: Woman's Power and Woman's Place, 1630–1970*. Matthews's works in progress examine California as a region and women's labor in Silicon Valley. She has been associate professor at Oklahoma State University and a visiting associate professor at Stanford and the University of California at Berkeley and at Los Angeles.

Pamela Matz is exhibition curator at Widener Library, Harvard University. She has mounted exhibitions centering on nineteenth-century United States social history and literature. She holds a B.A. from Radcliffe College.

Naomi Burstein Max is a graphic designer and a niece of Judith Pinta Mandelbaum, daughter of her sister Miriam Pinta Burstein. She grew up in a Young Israel community and is a graduate of Central Yeshiva (Yeshiva University) High School for Girls, Bar-Ilan University in Israel, and the Cooper Union School of Art and Architecture. Max is a life member of Amit, serving on the Board of Directors and as secretary and volunteer cochair of the Communications Department.

Susan Mayer is a nursing instructor and supervisor of nurses at Jacobi Medical Center in New York City. She received her B.A. in nursing from Hunter College, her M.A. in nursing from New York University, and her Ed.D. from Teachers College, Columbia University. Mayer has published a number of articles about nursing and Jewish nursing. Her dissertation is "The Jewish Experience in Nursing in America, 1881–1955."

Louise Mayo is professor and chair of the Department of History and Political Science at the County College of Morris, where she has instituted black and women's history programs, a local history center, and an annual Holocaust memorial program. She is the author of *The Ambivalent Image: Nineteenth Century America's Perception of the Jew*.

Julia Mazow is a writer, editor, and lecturer in Houston, Texas. Her work has appeared in *Bridges*, *Lilith*, and *Midstream*. She compiled and edited *The Woman Who Lost Her Names: Selected Writings of American Jewish Women*. Mazow has taught women's literature, including a course called "From Lilith to Laura Z," inside and outside the university. In 1985, she met Laura Z. Hobson; an account of that meeting appeared in *Lilith*, where Mazow was fiction editor for more than ten years.

Mary McCune is a doctoral student at Ohio State University. She is working on her dissertation, "'Charity Work' as Nation-Building: American Jewish Women's Activism and the Crises in Europe and Palestine, 1914–1929."

Linda F. McGreavy is professor of art history and criticism at Old Dominion University and is a member of the International Association of Art Critics. She has written extensively on contemporary art and on the German artist Otto Dix.

Andra Medea was coauthor, with Kathleen Thompson, of the feminist classic *Against Rape*. She is an instructor at both Northwestern and DePaul universities. She has been an educational writer for twenty years, contributing most recently to *Encyclopedia of Black Women*, and she writes a syndicated column about conflict management. Medea is also author of *Working It Out*.

Rafael Medoff is visiting scholar in the Jewish Studies Program at Purchase College, State University of New York. He has taught Jewish history at Ohio State University, Denison University, and the Graduate School of Touro College. His essays and reviews have appeared in *American Jewish History*, *American Jewish Archives*, the *Journal of Israeli History*, *Holocaust and Genocide Studies*, and *Menorah Review*, of which he is a contributing editor.

Susan Medyn is a social worker at the Deaconess Waltham Hospital and Medical Center Early Intervention Program and a psychotherapist in private practice in Massachusetts. She received her B.S.W. and M.S.W. from the State University of New York at Albany.

Jean Ulitz Mensch, an independent historian, was born to an immigrant Jewish family. She received her Ph.D. in history from Columbia University, writing her dissertation on crime and vice in the Eastern European Jewish community in New York from 1882 to 1914. Mensch also contributed several articles to *The Encyclopedia of New York City*.

I. Scott Messinger received his B.A. from Williams College and graduated from Syracuse University Law School. He is a graduate student in American legal history at New York University. His article, "Legitimating Liberalism: The Real

Image Makers and Oliver Wendell Holmes, Jr.," appeared in the *Journal of Supreme Court History*.

Adam Meyer is assistant professor of English at Fisk University. In addition to a full-length study of Raymond Carver, he has written articles on Grace Paley, Paule Marshall, Mike Gold, and Daniel Fuchs. He is at work on an examination of Black-Jewish encounters in the fiction of contemporary African-American and Jewish American writers.

Jimmy E. Wilkinson Meyer, Ph.D., is assistant editor of the *Wooster,* the alumni magazine at the College of Wooster. She also codirects the research effort "Women and Health Care in Cleveland, 1796–1996." Coeditor of *U.S. Aging Policy Interest Groups,* Meyer served as associate editor and contributor for the *Encyclopedia of Cleveland History* and the *Dictionary of Cleveland Biography.* She was a 1995 history fellow at the American College of Obstetricians and Gynecologists history library.

Noa Meyer graduated from Vassar College in 1996, where she received her B.A. in international studies. Meyer worked on the Democratic presidential campaign and is now working in the Clinton administration.

Tony Michels is a Ph.D. candidate in Jewish history at Stanford University, writing a dissertation titled "Yiddish Culture, Socialist Politics, and the Shaping of Immigrant Jewish Identity in New York City, 1890–1917." He is managing editor of *Jewish Social Studies: History, Culture, and Society.*

Rochelle L. Millen is associate professor of religion at Wittenberg University, where she teaches Jewish studies. She holds a Ph.D. in religious studies and an M.A. in philosophy from McMaster University in Canada and has published articles on women and Jewish law, Martin Buber, and Holocaust studies. She is the editor of *New Perspectives on the Holocaust: A Guide for Teachers and Scholars.* Currently, she is editing a book on the spectrum of Jewish feminism and writing a manuscript on feminism and Judaism.

Adinah S. Miller is studying for her Ph.D. in Jewish history at Yale University, where she received her M.A. in 1996. In 1991, she earned her B.A. in history, with a concentration in feminist and gender studies, from Haverford College. She taught Jewish history and *tanakh* at the Solomon Schechter Day School of Essex and Union, New Jersey, of which she is a graduate.

Avis Dimond Miller is associate rabbi at Adas Israel Congregation in Washington, D.C., the largest and oldest Conservative congregation in the Washington metropolitan area. She graduated from the Reconstructionist Rabbinical College in 1986. Miller is the first woman in the United States to assume pulpit responsibilities in a major Conservative congregation. As chair of the Rabbinical Assembly's Committee on Outreach and Conversion, Miller was also the first and so far the only woman to be appointed to head a national committee of the RA. She serves on the Rabbinical Assembly's Executive Council.

Julie Miller is a graduate of Music and Art High School in New York City and Oberlin College and is working on a doctorate in American history at the Graduate Center of the City University of New York. She is the archivist of the Ratner

Center for the Study of Conservative Judaism at the Jewish Theological Seminary of America, and her articles have appeared in *Conservative Judaism* and *New York History.*

Naomi Miller is professor of art history at Boston University. She received a B.S. from City College, an M.A. from Columbia University, and a Ph.D. from New York University. Among her publications are *French Renaissance Fountains, Heavenly Caves,* and *Renaissance Bologna.* Miller has edited the *Journal of Society of Architectural Historians* and has won a number of fellowships, including from the Center for Advanced Study in Visual Arts.

Rose Ann Miller is working toward an M.F.A. in fiction at Warren Wilson College. She received her B.A. in English and American literature from Brown University and her M.A. in creative writing at Hollins College. Miller works at Harvard University Press and as an assistant editor at the *Journal of Neurophysiology.*

Ann Mann Millin is completing her Ph.D. at Hebrew Union College in Cincinnati. Millin's research interests center around modern Jewish history and European history; her dissertation examines Jewish social welfare work in Germany between 1933 and 1943. She is a research assistant for the Leo Baeck Institute *Gesamtgeschichte* project and teaches adult education courses in Jewish history.

Francine Moccio received her Ph.D. from the New School for Social Research in cultural anthropology and political economics. She is director of the Institute for Women and Work at Cornell University's School of Industrial-Labor Relations, a national and statewide program that provides education, training, and research to advance women's position in the workplace. She is working on a book on women's coalition building in the American union movement.

Joan Moelis received a Ph.D. in English from the University of Massachusetts at Amherst. Her dissertation, "Writing Selves: Constructing American Jewish Feminine Identity," focuses on the writings of Grace Paley, Cynthia Ozick, and E.M. Broner. Moelis is currently writing a book on African-American and American Jewish women's literary identity. She teaches at De Anza College.

Gary Mokotoff is publisher of *Avotaynu,* the magazine of Jewish genealogy; past president of the Association of Jewish Genealogical Societies; and on the board of directors of JewishGen, the principal Internet Jewish genealogical resource. Mokotoff writes and lectures on Jewish and Eastern European genealogy.

Deborah Dash Moore is an editor of the *Encyclopedia.* See the beginning of this list for a biographical note.

Mik Moore is director of the Jewish Student Press Service in New York City. He graduated with a B.A. in history from Vassar College, where he was cofounder and editor of the school's first Jewish publication, *Ra-ashan: A Journal of Jewish Culture.* He currently edits *New Voices,* the national bimonthly magazine of JSPS.

Mordecai Moore received his B.A. in politics and history from Oberlin College in 1993. He served as editor in chief of the *Hi-O-Hi* college yearbook for two years.

Ewa Morawska is a professor in the Departments of Sociology and History at the University of Pennsylvania. Her numerous publications include *Insecure Prosperity: Jews in Small-Town Industrial America, 1880–1940*; "In Defense of the Assimilation Model"; and "The Sociology and Historiography of Immigration," in *Immigration Reconsidered: History, Sociology, and Politics*, edited by Virginia Yans-McLaughlin.

Joyce Morgenroth is associate professor of dance and dance program coordinator at Cornell University. Morgenroth is the author of *Dance Improvisations*, and she has conducted improvisation workshops in the United States and abroad. She received an A.B. in theoretical mathematics from Cornell University, an M.A. in French literature from Johns Hopkins University, early dance training at the School of American Ballet, and modern dance training with Peggy Lawler, Dan Wagoner, and Viola Farber. Morgenroth has performed with Among Company in New York and in works of numerous contemporary choreographers.

Henry Morgenthau is an author and television and radio producer. Among the television series he has produced are the award-winning *South African Essay* and *Eleanor Roosevelt, Prospects of Mankind*. The son of Henry Morgenthau, Jr. and Elinor Fatman Morgenthau, he has written *Mostly Morgenthaus: A Family History*, which won a National Jewish Book Award. A graduate of Princeton University (B.A.), Morgenthau is also the author of "Dona Quixote: The Adventures of Frieda Hennock" in *Television Quarterly*.

Liora Moriel is a graduate student in comparative literature and women's studies at the University of Maryland. She received her B.A. in sociology and psychology from the Hebrew University in Jerusalem. Moriel has worked as a public relations coordinator for the Baran Group in Israel, as a reporter for Kol Israel Radio News and the *Jerusalem Post*, and as a freelance writer. She is the editor of the anthology *Laila Lohet* and the author of the play *Monologue With a Cast of Thousands*.

Bonnie J. Morris earned her Ph.D. in women's history from the State University of New York at Binghamton. As a visiting scholar at Harvard University Divinity School, Morris taught Harvard's first graduate seminar on Hasidic women. She has taught women's history and women's studies at St. Lawrence University, Northeastern University, and the University of Pittsburgh; currently, Morris teaches at George Washington University. Her essays and articles have appeared in more than thirty journals and books, including *New World Hasidim: Ethnographic Studies of Hasidic Jews in North America*.

Marian J. Morton is a professor at John Carroll University. She received her B.A. in classics from Smith College and her M.A. and Ph.D. in American studies from Case Western University. She is the author of *And Sin No More: Social Policy and Unwed Mothers in Cleveland, 1855–1990, Emma Goldman and the American Left: "Nowhere at Home,"* and *The Terrors of Ideological Politics: Liberal Historians in a Conservative Mood*.

Andrea Most is a Ph.D. candidate at Brandeis University in Jewish studies and English literature. She is the recipient of the Jacoby Fellowship at Brandeis and the Fein-Pinanski-Shain Fellowship from the CJP in Boston. She studied drama at Yale University and has worked as a film and theater producer in Boston and New York with companies such as the Wooster Group, the American Repertory Theater, and the Pepsico Summerstage festival.

Yocheved Herschlag Muffs, an educator, editor, and writer, served the Anti-Defamation League in a number of positions for more than twenty-five years. She received the Milton Senn Award for Professional Excellence in 1982. She is the author of *The Holocaust in Books and Films: A Select and Annotated Bibliography* and writes essays and book reviews.

Carla Munsat is the founder, copublisher, and editor in chief of *Art New England* magazine. A painter who specializes in organic abstraction, Munsat has also worked as an actress, an art writer, and an art educator. She did graduate work in art history and studio art at New Castle upon Tyne Polytecnic in England, as well as at the University of California at Los Angeles, where she received her B.F.A.

Priscilla Murolo teaches history at Sarah Lawrence College, where she received her B.A. A member of the editorial collective of the *Radical History Review*, Murolo has edited several issues of the journal as well as publishing a number of articles and the book *"The Common Ground of Womanhood": Class, Gender, and Working Girls Clubs, 1884–1928*. She received her Ph.D. in American studies from Yale University.

Jane Mushabac has written for National Public Radio and the *Village Voice* as well as scholarly publications. She received her B.A. from Cornell University, her M.A. from Harvard University, and her Ph.D. from the Graduate Center of the City University of New York. She currently teaches at John Jay College, CUNY. Mushabac has won numerous grants and awards for her fiction, her scholarship, and her teaching. She is writing a short history of New York City, with Angela Wigan Marvin.

Nancy Mykoff is a graduate student at New York University, where she is writing her dissertation on Jewish women and summer camps in the period 1920 to 1945.

Pamela S. Nadell is on the Editorial Advisory Board of the *Encyclopedia*. See the beginning of this list for a biographical note.

Joan Nathan is the author of a number of cookbooks, including the award-winning *Jewish Cooking in America, The Children's Jewish Holiday Kitchen, The Jewish Holiday Kitchen,* and *The Flavor of Jerusalem*. Nathan wrote for the *Washington Post* for eight years and currently contributes to publications such as the *New York Times* and *Food Arts*. She was also senior producer of an award-winning documentary, *Passover: Traditions of Freedom*, sponsored by Maryland Public Television.

Jennifer Nelson is a Ph.D. candidate in history at Rutgers University, writing a dissertation titled "From Abortion Rights to Reproductive Freedom: Second Wave Feminism and the Politics of Identity." Nelson received her B.A. in modern culture and media from Brown University.

Judith Nihei is a director, actor, and writer and has been involved with the development of Asian-American theater for twenty-five years. Nihei has written for stage and television and is on the writing staff of the children's series *The Puzzle Place*. Her short story "Koden" is featured in *American Dragons: Twenty-five Asian American Voices*, edited by Laurence

Yep. She is artistic director of the Northwest Asian American Theatre in Seattle and a faculty member of the Theater Department at Cornish College of the Arts.

Anita Norich is on the Editorial Advisory Board of the *Encyclopedia*. See the beginning of this list for a biographical note.

Jane Nusbaum is a graduate student in the Ph.D. program in history at the Graduate School and University Center of the City University of New York. She is the program coordinator of the graduate program in women's history at Sarah Lawrence College.

Mark Oehlert is a Ph.D. candidate in American history at American University. He received his B.A. from West Georgia College and his M.A.I.S. from Oregon State University.

Leah Oppenheim graduated from Smith College, where her fiction appeared in several literary magazines. She is working in the curatorial department of the Museum of Television and Radio.

Annelise Orleck is assistant professor of history at Dartmouth College. She is the author of *Common Sense and a Little Fire: Women and Working Class Politics in the United States, 1900–1965* and editor, with Alexis Jetter and Diana Taylor, of *Radical Motherhood: Activist Voices from Left to Right*. Orleck received her B.A. from Evergreen State College and her Ph.D. from New York University. She has been a consulting historian for documentary films and museum exhibitions, and she cofounded the Nelson A. Rockefeller Center Institute for Women and Social Change at Dartmouth.

Suzanne Oshinsky received her B.A. in Asian and Middle Eastern cultures, with a focus in Hebrew literature and culture, from Barnard College. She is a free-lance writer and translator who tutors students in English, writing, and math at John Jay College, CUNY. Oshinsky has also taught Hebrew in Russia and Israel.

Beth O'Sullivan studied mathematics at the Massachusetts Institute of Technology. She is a member of the Congregation Eitz Chayim in Cambridge, Massachusetts, and teaches at its Hebrew School, the Harvard Hillel Children's School.

Harriet L. Parmet is professor emerita in the Department of Modern Foreign Languages and Literature at Lehigh University, where she has taught Hebrew since 1976. She specializes in modern Israeli literature, particularly the work of women writers. Parmet coauthored a study of feminist religious reviews on reproductive technologies and an article on Haviva Reik, a heroine of the Holocaust. Cofounder of Lehigh University's Jewish Studies Program and founder of the Jewish Colloquia series, Parmet's work has appeared in journals such as *Midstream* and *Journal for Feminist Studies in Religion*.

Joanne Passet is the author of *Cultural Crusaders: Women Librarians in the American West, 1900–17*. She is currently working toward her second doctorate in history at the University of Wisconsin. Passet received her first Ph.D. from Indiana University, her M.A. in history from Bowling Green State University, and her B.A. from Bluffton College.

Peggy K. Pearlstein is the area specialist in the Hebraic Section of the Library of Congress. She has an M.S. in library science from Southern Connecticut State College, an M.A. in Jewish studies from Baltimore Hebrew University, and a Ph.D. in American studies from George Washington University. She has written for *Judaica Librarianship* and *Avotaynu, the International Review of Jewish Genealogy*.

Shulamit Peck is a clinical psychologist in Massachusetts who specializes in psychological and spiritual development. She has an M.S.W. in psychiatric social work.

Elisabeth Israels Perry is on the Editorial Advisory Board of the *Encyclopedia*. See the beginning of this list for a biographical note.

Paula F. Pfeffer is associate professor of American history at Loyola University of Chicago. She received her B.A. and M.A. from Northeastern Illinois University and her Ph.D. from Northwestern University. She is the author of *A. Philip Randolph: Pioneer of the Civil Rights Movement* as well as articles on black and women's history.

Karen Philipps is a writer and editor who also works extensively in event planning and outreach programs. Philipps is a telephone counselor at the helpline Recruiting New Teachers and a business manager for Voiceworks, a women's a cappella group that sings for community service. She received her B.A. in English from Williams College and her M.A. in English from Boston College. She is the author of a biography of Rosa Sonneschein.

Harry T. Phillips was born in Cape Town, South Africa. He received his M.B., Ch.B., D.P.H., and M.D. degrees at the University of Cape Town. In 1939, he and Eva Salber, a medical school classmate, were married. They immigrated to the United States in 1956. He has held positions at the Harvard School of Public Health, the City of Newton, Massachusetts, the Massachusetts Department of Public Health, and the University of North Carolina. He retired in 1983 as emeritus professor of public health.

Erika Piola received her B.A. in history from Haverford College and her M.A. in United States history from the University of Pennsylvania.

Judith Plaskow is professor of religious studies at Manhattan College who specializes in feminist theology. She received her B.A. from Clark University and her Ph.D. from Yale University. Among her publications are *Sex, Sin, and Grace: Women's Experience and the Theologies of Reinhold Niebuhr and Paul Tillich* and *Standing Again at Sinai: Judaism from a Feminist Perspective*. Plaskow has also coedited, with Carol P. Christ, *WomanSpirit Rising: A Feminist Reader in Religion* and *Weaving the Visions: New Patterns in Feminist Spirituality*. With Elisabeth Schussler-Fiorenza, Plaskow cofounded the *Journal of Feminist Studies in Religion* and coedited it for its first ten years.

Letty Cottin Pogrebin, a founding editor of *Ms.* magazine, is the author of eight books including *Deborah, Golda, and Me: Being Female and Jewish in America* and *Getting Over Getting Older: An Intimate Journey*.

Lee S. Polansky is a doctoral candidate in American history at Emory University. His dissertation is " 'For It Made Me a Lady': The Delinquent Girl and the Georgia Training School for Girls, 1914–1935." A graduate of the University of Pittsburgh (M.P.I.A.) and Brandeis University (B.A.), Polansky works as a researcher at the Martin Luther King, Jr. Papers Project at Emory.

Susan Kahnweiler Pollack, a political activist, serves as assistant Western director of Handgun Control, Inc., where she organizes gun control coalitions. She received a B.S. in journalism from Northwestern University and worked first as a financial writer for United Press International, then on the staff of the *Chicago Daily News.* Pollock later became a producer and writer for the public television station KPBS in San Diego, where she won two local Emmys and a number of national awards for her science-related documentaries. She is on the boards of Jewish Family Service and the Woman's Institute for Continuing Jewish Education.

Oliver B. Pollak earned his doctorate in history at the University of California at Los Angeles and his law degree from Creighton University. He has published widely in American Jewish history, on Southern Africa, Burma, legal history, and three bibliographic studies. He is cofounder of the Nebraska Jewish Historical Society and Professor of History at the University of Nebraska.

Emily Meyer Pomper received her B.A. from Bryn Mawr College, her M.A. from Columbia University, and her Ph.D. from Boston College. She has taught at the University of Chicago High School, Laney College, Merritt College, and the University of Massachusetts at Boston, where she directed the Writing Proficiency Program and was an adjunct associate professor of English. She currently teaches in the Graduate Liberal Studies Program at Wesleyan University. She is coauthor of *The Practical Tutor.*

Jack Nusan Porter is a sociologist, anthologist, and writer. His books include *Jewish Radicalism, The Sociology of American Jewry, The Jew as Outsider, Kids in Cults, Confronting History and Holocaust, Jewish Partisans,* and *The Agunah.* He is an adjunct professor of sociology and genocide studies at the University of Massachusetts at Lowell and Stonehill College.

Susan Porter is an associate professor of history at Simmons College, where she directs the graduate program in history and archives management. She is the author of *Women of the Commonwealth: Work, Family, and Social Change in Nineteenth-Century Massachusetts* and *Gendered Benevolence: Orphan Asylums in Antebellum America.* Porter is a graduate of Smith College (A.B.), the University of Massachusetts (M.A.), and Boston University (Ph.D.).

Norma Fain Pratt is on the Editorial Advisory Board of the *Encyclopedia.* See the beginning of this list for a biographical note.

Riv-Ellen Prell is on the Editorial Advisory Board of the *Encyclopedia.* See the beginning of this list for a biographical note.

Paula Rabinowitz is associate professor in the English Department at the University of Minnesota, where she is affiliated with the Center for Advanced Feminist Studies and Critical Studies in Discourse and Society. She is the author of *They Must Be Represented: The Politics of Documentary, Labor and Desire: Women's Revolutionary Fiction in Depression America,* and *Writing Red: An Anthology of American Women Writers.* A graduate of Brandeis University (B.A.) and the University

of Michigan (Ph.D.), she has been a visiting scholar in the Program in American Culture at Michigan and an Andrew Mellon fellow at Wesleyan University.

Mark A. Raider is assistant professor of modern Jewish history at the State University of New York at Albany. He received his B.A. from the University of California at Santa Cruz and his M.A. and Ph.D. from Brandeis University. He is the author of *Papers of Admiral Lewis L. Strauss: Manuscript Collection, 1908–1973* and is at work on *American Jews and the Zionist Movement.*

Ruth Raisner is a public relations and editorial consultant. Her clients include Eichler's Books, the Scleroderma Society, and the Yeshiva of Central Queens. She has worked as public relations director and director of communication and information at Amit Women, as well as the executive editor of the organization's magazine. Raisner received her B.A. from Barnard College.

Antonio Ramirez worked in the 1960s on the education staffs of the Amalgamated Clothing Workers of America and the International Ladies Garment Workers Union. He retired in 1994 after serving twenty-five years as an editor of the *New York Teacher,* the publication of the New York State United Teachers, American Federation of Teachers, AFL-CIO. He is a member of the boards of directors of the New York State Labor History Association and the Association for Union Democracy.

Harriett Ranney is music librarian at the University of Montana and a clarinetist with the Missoula Symphony Orchestra. She is a graduate of Temple University (B.Mus.Ed.), Wichita State University (M.Mus.), and Drexel University (M.L.S.). Her articles have appeared in *Clarinet.*

David Rego is an M.A. candidate in American history at Tufts University. A graduate of the University of Massachusetts, he has worked as a research assistant for a documentary on the civil rights work of Clifford and Virginia Foster Durr for the PBS series *American Experience.*

Helen Rehr received her B.A. from Hunter College and her D.S.W. from the Columbia University School of Social Work. She is professor of community medicine emerita and a consultant to the Department of Social Work Services and the Division of Social Work at the Mount Sinai School of Medicine and Medical Center. Rehr is author, coauthor, and editor of more than one hundred studies, reports, monographs, articles, chapters, and books; recently she coauthored *Social Work Issues in Health Care.* Among her awards are an honorary doctorate from Hunter College and election as fellow to the New York Academy of Medicine.

Gail Twersky Reimer is the founder and director of the Jewish Women's Archive. She is the coeditor of *Reading Ruth: Contemporary Women Reclaim a Sacred Story* and *Beginning Anew: A Women's Companion to the High Holy Days.* Reimer received her B.A. from Sarah Lawrence College and her Ph.D. in English and American literature from Rutgers University.

Shulamit Reinharz is professor of sociology and director of the women's studies program at Brandeis University, where she received her M.A. and Ph.D. Reinharz has written four books and more than sixty articles on a wide range of topics, most of which relate to women's lives. Much of her research on Jewish women concerns the life of Manya Wilbushewitz Shohat. Reinharz has served as the chair of the National Commission on American Jewish Women and is currently developing the International Research Institute on Jewish Women, which is sponsored by Hadassah and located at Brandeis.

Harriet Reisen has directed, produced, and developed new programs in various facets of media, including television, radio, print, and publicity. Her writing has spanned comedy, drama, nonfiction, documentary, magazine journalism, radio commentary, film criticism, children's books, and songs.

Susan M. Reverby is professor of women's studies at Wellesley College. She received her Ph.D. in American studies from Boston University and has taught at Wellesely since 1982. Reverby is the author of the prize-winning *Ordered to Care: The Dilemma of American Nursing* and the editor of volumes in medical, nursing, and women's history. Her current research focuses on nursing and ethics in the Tuskegee syphilis experiment.

Moira Reynolds received her B.A. from Dalhousie University and her A.M. and Ph.D. from Boston University. She has worked as a medical technologist and cancer researcher and is now a free-lance writer. Among her publications are *The Outstretched Hand: Modern Medical Discoveries, Uncle Tom's Cabin and Mid-Nineteenth Century United States: Pen and Conscience, Women Advocates of Reproductive Rights,* and *How Pasteur Changed History.*

Elana Shever Ripps is an undergraduate at Brown University, majoring in anthropology and Hispanic studies. She is an active member of the Brown-RISD Hillel, where she is chair of Kol Isha, the Jewish women's organization, and coordinator of Jewish Women's Week.

Sharon Pucker Rivo is a cofounder and executive director of the National Center for Jewish Film. She cocurated *Yiddish Film between Two Worlds,* the retrospective of Yiddish feature films that premiered at the Museum of Modern Art in New York in 1991. Rivo received the first Annual Jewish Cultural Achievement Award from the National Foundation for Jewish Culture in 1990.

Paul Roazen is professor emeritus of sociology and political science at York University in Toronto. He is a member of the Royal Society of Canada. Among his books are *Brother Animal, Freud and His Followers, Helene Deutsch,* and *How Freud Worked.*

Sandra Robbins, a graduate of the Manhattan School of Music, is a violist who has been a member of the Ysaye Quartet, the Paganini Trio, and the Bronx Arts Ensemble.

Elizabeth Robeson is a doctoral candidate in American history at Columbia University. Her article, "The Ambiguity of Julia Peterkin," appeared in *The Journal of Southern History.*

Harriet Rochlin, authority on Western Jewish history, is author of *Pioneer Jews: A New Life in the Far West.* She has also written novels on Western Jewish pioneers, including *So Far Away* and *The Reformer's Apprentice: A Novel of Old San Francisco.* She founed the Rochlin Collection of Western Jewish

History, part of the University Research Library, at the University of California at Los Angeles.

Gillian Rodger is a Ph.D. candidate in ethnomusicology at the University of Pittsburgh. She is working on her dissertation, "Male Impersonation on the American Variety and Vaudeville Stage, 1868–1930." Her M.A. thesis examined music in the Yiddish films of Joseph Green, and her doctoral work centers on musical theater forms and gender in nineteenth- and twentieth-century North America.

Faith Rogow, author of *Gone to Another Meeting: The National Council of Jewish Women, 1893–1993,* earned her Ph.D. in women's history from the State University at Binghamton. In addition to her current work as a consultant on issues related to children and television, Rogow writes on gay and lesbian history. She is also producer, composer, and performer on a cassette of original Jewish feminist music, *The Courage to Dare.*

Joe Rooks-Rapport is associate rabbi and director of religious education at The Temple in Louisville, Kentucky. He is a graduate of the Hebrew Union College (1984) and received his Ph.D. in American Jewish history from Washington University in 1988.

Dawn Robinson Rose is a visiting assistant professor at the Jewish Theological Seminary of America and director of the Center for Jewish Ethics at the Reconstructionist Rabbinical College in Philadelphia. A graduate of the University of California at Berkeley (B.A., M.A.) and the Jewish Theological Seminary (Ph.D.), Rose specializes in Jewish philosophy, mysticism, and ethics, as well as feminist and liberation theologies.

Gladys Rosen served for thirteen years as executive associate of the American Jewish History Center at the Jewish Theological Seminary of America and for twenty years as program associate of the Jewish Communal Affairs Department at the American Jewish Committee. Rosen is editor of *Jewish Life in America: Historical Perspectives* and coeditor of *The Jewish Family and Jewish Continuity.*

Judith Friedman Rosen is a research fellow at the Graduate Center of the City University of New York and an interviewer at the Survivors of the Shoah Visual History Foundation. A graduate of Stern College for Women (B.A.) and the Bernard Revel Graduate School (M.A.) at Yeshiva University, Rosen received her Ph.D. in modern Jewish history from the Skirball Institute of Hebrew and Judaic Studies. Her articles have appeared in many Jewish periodicals.

Nancy Rosen is an assistant editor at Hachette Filapacchi Magazines. A graduate of Cornell University, Rosen was previously an assistant editor at Miller Freeman PSN and did free-lance work for Rolling Stone Press.

Judith A.H. Rosenbaum graduated from Yale University with a B.A. in history. She spent the 1995–1996 academic year in Jerusalem as a Fulbright Fellow and is currently a graduate student in American civilization at Brown University. She wrote a prize-winning senior essay at Yale College on Rose Pastor Stokes.

Jennifer Rosenberg is assistant director for government relations at the UJA-Federation of New York. She holds an M.S.W. from Columbia University and an M.A. in Jewish studies from the Jewish Theological Seminary of America. Rosenberg has received the Jewish Communal Service Association Louis Kraft Award for young professional workers in Jewish communal service.

Jessica Rosenfeld is a poet and Jewish educator in Berkeley, California. She received her M.F.A. in poetry from Mills College and her B.A. in English literature from Oberlin College. She was poet-in-residence on the Arad Arts Project in Israel, and while living in Israel she was awarded the Reuben Rose Memorial award. She has also been granted awards from the American Academy of Poets and the Bay Area Poets Coalition.

Moishe Rosenfeld is the founder and president of Golden Land Connections, a national entertainment company based in New York. Among the many shows he has produced is the Itzhak Perlman concert at Lincoln Center, which was featured in the PBS documentary *In the Fiddler's House*. Rosenfeld also cocreated and produced three Yiddish-English musicals in the 1980s and has appeared in more than twenty-five plays in the Yiddish theater. For the last twenty years, he has been the writer and announcer of the daily Yiddish newscast on New York WEVD radio, the last daily Yiddish radio program in the United States. Rosenfeld attended the Jewish People's Schools, McGill University, and the New York Jewish Teachers Seminary.

Rosie Rosenzweig is a teacher, poet, and essayist whose works have appeared in a number of books and journals, including *Voices*, a psychology journal, and *Vetaher Libaynu*, the first gender-friendly prayer book in the United States. Rosenzweig is the editor and writer of the *Jewish Guide to Boston and New England*, as well as book editor of *Neshama*, Boston's Jewish women's spirituality magazine, and a columnist for *Lichnora*. She has designed and presented workshops for Hadassah and CAJE, and she founded the Jewish American Women's Poetry Festival. Rosenzweig is currently writing a book on her encounters with spiritual leaders in Southeast Asia.

David G. Roskies, professor of Jewish literature at the Jewish Theological Seminary of America, received his Ph.D. from Brandeis University. His area of specialization is Eastern European Jewry. Among his numerous publications are *Night Words: A Midrash on the Holocaust*, the award-winning *Against the Apocalypse: Responses to Catastrophe in Modern Jewish Culture*, and *A Bridge of Longing: The Lost Art of Yiddish Storytelling*. Roskies is cofounder and editor of *Prooftexts: A Journal of Jewish Literary History* and editor in chief of the Library of Yiddish Classics.

Janice Ross is a lecturer in dance history and performance art at Stanford University, where she directs the graduate program in dance education. A graduate of the University of California at Berkeley (B.A.) and Stanford University (M.A., Ph.D.), Ross is the San Francisco correspondent for *Dance Magazine* and a member of the National Endowment for the Arts Dance Panel. She has worked as the dance critic for the *Oakland Tribune* and is a past president of the Dance Critics Association.

Marion Levenson Ross earned a B.A. from the University of Michigan and an M.A. from the University of Chicago.

She is a social worker at the Jewish Family and Children's Service in Newton, Massachusetts.

Susan J. (Lief) Rotenberg is an educator who specializes in early childhood and Judaic studies. She received her M.A. in Jewish education from Baltimore Hebrew University and her B.A. in sociology and human development from the University of Maryland. Rotenberg has taught Jewish education at the preschool, elementary, secondary and adult education levels.

Susan Roth is a Ph.D. candidate in American history at the University of Iowa. She received her B.A. from Grinnell College, her M.L.S. from the University of Pittsburgh, and her M.A. from Eastern Illinois University. Her research interests include twentieth-century American cultural and social history and American Jewish history.

Sylvia Rothchild is a writer, lecturer, and adult teacher who gives seminars at Harvard University, the Massachusetts Institute of Technology, Bryn Mawr College, and other schools in the Northeast. Among her publications are *Family Stories for Every Generation;* two works of oral history, *Voices from the Holocaust* and *A Special Legacy, An Oral History of Soviet Jewish Emigres in the United States;* a novel, *Sunshine and Salt;* and a prize-winning biography of I.L. Peretz, *Keys to a Magic Door.* Rothchild's stories, reviews, and articles have appeared in *Hadassah* magazine and *Commentary.*

Jane H. Rothstein is a Ph.D. candidate in history and Hebrew and Judaic studies at New York University. She received her B.A. in politics from Brandeis University and her M.A. in history from Case Western Reserve University.

Robert A. Rothstein is professor of Slavic languages and literatures and of Judaic studies at the University of Massachusetts at Amherst. He attended the Massachusetts Institute of Technology and received his Ph.D. from Harvard University. He is the author of studies in Slavic and Yiddish linguistics, folklore, and popular culture.

Marsha L. Rozenblit is associate professor of modern Jewish history at the University of Maryland. She received her B.A. from Barnard College and her Ph.D. from Columbia University. She is the author of *The Jews of Vienna, 1867–1914: Assimilation and Identity.* Rozenblit is currently at work on a study of how the Jews of Austria-Hungary reconstructed their identities under the impact of World War I and its aftermath.

Charlene Kanter Sales received her B.A. from the University of Illinois and her J.D. from the Northwestern University School of Law. A practicing lawyer until 1986, she has since become active in community concerns, sitting on the Young Women's Board (president) and Women's Board of the Jewish United Fund of Metropolitan Chicago, the board of the Jewish Family and Community Service Agency, and Hadassah (group president). She also chairs the Sisterhood Ritual Committee at Congregation Beth Shalom in Northbrook, Illinois.

Cynthia Saltzman is a lecturer in anthropology at Rutgers University, Camden. She has been a postdoctoral fellow in Judaic studies at Yale, doing research on feminism and Judaism. She has also been a visiting assistant professor at

Barnard College and Columbia University and a visiting fellow at the Institute for Social and Policy Studies of Yale University. Saltzman received her Ph.D. in anthropology from Columbia University and is currently turning her dissertation, "Women, Unions, and Yale," into a book.

Nahma Sandrow is on the Editorial Advisory Board of the *Encyclopedia*. See the beginning of this list for a biographical note.

Susan Sapiro is an M.A. candidate in gender studies and feminist theory at the New School for Social Research. She received her B.A. from the University of Toronto and has studied at the Hebrew University of Jerusalem and the Pardes Institute of Jewish Studies in Jerusalem.

Jonathan D. Sarna is the Joseph H. and Belle R. Braun Professor of American Jewish History in the Department of Near Eastern and Judaic Studies at Brandeis University. He received his Ph.D. from Yale University. Sarna's books include *The American Jewish Experience, People Walk on Their Heads, Jacksonian Jew,* and *JPS: The Americanization of Jewish Culture, 1888–1988, A Centennial History of the Jewish Publication Society.* Sarna sits on the editorial committee of *American Jewish History,* and he edits two book series: *Brandeis Studies in American Jewish History, Culture, and Life* and the *American Jewish Civilization Series.* He is writing a new interpretive history of American Judaism.

Jeanette K. Schechter is national senior vice president of AMIT Women. She received her B.A. from Stern College for Women of Yeshiva University and her J.D. from Brooklyn Law School. She was formerly legal editor of *Trusts and Estates* magazine.

Jeanne Scheper is an independent scholar and college administrator working with young artists in Boston. She received her B.A. in liberal studies and studio art from Sarah Lawrence College and her M.A. in literature from the University of Maryland.

Lillian Schlissel is director of American studies at Brooklyn College. Her books include *Women's Diaries of the Westward Journey; Far From Home: Families of the Westward Journey,* written with Byrd Gibbens and Elizabeth Hampsten; and *Western Women, Their Land, Their Lives.* Schlissel is a member of the editorial board of *Studies in American Jewish Literature* and is working on a history of women in American vaudeville.

Linda Schloff is a Ph.D. candidate in history at the University of Minnesota and director of the Jewish Historical Society of the Upper Midwest. She was the curator of an exhibit funded by the National Endowment for the Humanities about the experiences of Jewish women in the upper midwest and is the author of a book based on the exhibit, *And Prairie Dogs Weren't Kosher: Jewish Women in the Upper Midwest Since 1855.*

Deborah Schneider holds an M.A. in modern Jewish studies from the Jewish Theological Seminary of America. She is active in the Jewish community.

Susan Weidman Schneider is a founder of *Lilith* and has been its editor in chief since the magazine's inception. She is the author of *Jewish and Female: Choices and Changes in Our*

Lives Today and *Intermarriage: The Challenge of Living with Differences Between Christians and Jews* and coauthor of *Head and Heart: A Woman's Guide to Financial Independence.*

Ruth P. Schoenberg teaches in the Department of Physical Education and Exercise Science at Brooklyn College. Her introduction to Israeli folk dance was through the American Zionist youth group Young Judaea. She is associate editor of the Israeli Dance Institute publication *Nirkoda.*

Ann Schofield is associate professor of American studies and women's studies at the University of Kansas. She is the author of *To Do and To Be: Portraits of Four Women Activists, 1893–1986.*

Debra L. Schultz, a visiting scholar at Rutgers University, is revising her dissertation, "'We Didn't Think in Those Terms Then': Narratives of Jewish Women in the Southern Civil Rights Movement, 1960–1966." Former assistant director of the National Council for Research on Women, her interests include women's activist networks; feminist oral history; intersections of gender, race, class, and ethnicity; and emerging women's movements in Eastern Europe.

Lily Schwartz is an archivist at the Philadelphia Jewish Archives Center at the Balch Institute. Schwartz received her B.A. in religion and her M.A. in liberal arts from Temple University. She gives lectures and publishes articles in Jewish newsletters on Jewish genealogy and the Jewish Archives Center.

Michael J. Schwartz is a graduate student in English at New York University. He graduated from the University of Michigan with a B.A. in English.

Shuly Rubin Schwartz is Irving Lehrman Research Assistant Professor of American Jewish History at the Jewish Theological Seminary of America, where she is dean of the undergraduate school, the Albert A. List College of Jewish Studies. Schwartz received her B.A. from Barnard College and her M.A. and Ph.D. in Jewish history from the Jewish Theological Seminary. She is the author of *The Emergence of Jewish Scholarship in America: The Publication of the Jewish Encyclopedia* and *Jewish Religion in America,* with Alan Silverstein.

Mel Scult, professor of Jewish thought at Brooklyn College, received his M.A. from Harvard University and his Ph.D. from Brandeis University. He has taught at Brandeis, Vassar College, and the New School for Social Research. Scult is the author of a biography of Mordecai Kaplan, *Judaism Faces the Twentieth Century,* and has coedited, with Emmanuel Goldsmith, *Dynamic Judaism: The Essential Writings of Mordecai Kaplan* and *The American Judaism of Mordecai Kaplan.* Scult is currently writing an essay about Solomon Schechter to be included in a multivolume history of the Jewish Theological Seminary.

Barbara Seaman, stepdaughter of Ruth Gruber and daughter-in-law of Sylvia Bernstein Seaman, holds a B.A. and an L.H.D. from Oberlin College and a Certificate in Advanced Science Writing from the Columbia University School of Journalism. She is author of *The Doctors' Case against the Pill, Free and Female,* and *Women and the Crisis in Sex Hormones.* Her most recent book is *Lovely Me: The Life of Jacqueline*

Susann. Seaman cofounded the National Women's Health Network in 1975 and has been a persistent advocate of many causes in women's health, from informed consent and patient labeling to the overthrow of female quotas in medical school admissions and the recognition of domestic violence as a major public health issue. The *New York Times* recently named her as one of twelve important leaders in the women's health movement.

Sheila Segal is the author of *Women of Valor: Stories of Great Jewish Women Who Helped Shape the Twentieth Century* and the critically acclaimed *Joshua's Dream: A Child's Journey to the Land of Israel.* Her articles and reviews have appeared in *Midstream, Hadassah,* and the *Near East Report,* of which she is a former editor. During her tenure as editor in chief of the Jewish Publication Society, she developed many books by and about Jewish women.

Micol Seigel is a graduate student in American studies at New York University, where she focuses on immigration, race, and sexuality throughout the Americas during the late nineteenth and twentieth centuries. She received her B.A. in religious studies at Yale University. Seigel currently holds a Henry Mitchell MacCracken fellowship and was awarded a fellowship for study in Argentina from the Center for Latin American and Caribbean Studies at New York University.

David Serlin is a writer, composer, and doctoral candidate in American studies at New York University, where he is completing a dissertation about experimental medical research during the 1950s. His essays have appeared in *Soul: Black Power, Politics, and Pleasure, The Encyclopedia of Homosexuality, Radical History Review,* and *Modern Language Studies,* and he is the United States editor of the Swedish arts journal *Index.*

Dennita Sewell is a collections associate at the Costume Institute at the Metropolitan Museum of Art in New York. A graduate of the Yale University School of Drama (M.F.A.), Sewell has worked as a dressmaker and costume designer and has taught graduate studies in costume history at New York University.

Jeffrey Shandler received his B.A. in literature from Swarthmore College and his Ph.D. in Yiddish Studies from Columbia University. His dissertation focused on the presentation of the Holocaust on American television. Shandler has served as the managing editor of *YIVO Annual.*

Jan Shapiro is a professional pop and jazz vocalist. She has been guest vocalist at the Boston Globe Jazz Festival, as well as a guest and performing artist on local radio shows and in advertising jingles. She has also recorded with the official jazz ensemble of the United States Air Force. Shapiro is associate professor and chair of the Voice Department at Berklee College of Music in Boston. She has presented vocal clinics throughout the country and has published articles in scholarly journals and reference books.

Linn Shapiro is a writer, editor, and historian interested in the history and culture of the North and South American Left. She is coeditor of *Red Diapers: Growing up in the American Left.*

Balia R. Shargel is a graduate of Goucher College and the Jewish Theological Seminary. She has taught at the seminary and Pace University. A social and intellectual historian, Shargel is the author of *Practical Dreamer,* a biography of Israel Friedlaender; *The Jews of Westchester, a Social History;* and a biography of Henrietta Szold.

Susanne A. Shavelson is on the faculty of the Hornstein Program in Jewish Communal Service at Brandeis University. She received her Ph.D. in American culture from the University of Michigan, where she received a Mellon Fellowship. Her dissertation was "From Amerike to America: Language and Identity in the Yiddish and English Autobiographies of Jewish Immigrant Women." Shavelson has an M.A. in American culture from the University of Michigan and a B.A. in English and American studies from Tufts University. Her areas of specialization include Jewish-American history, literature, and culture since 1881 and the experience of Jewish women in America.

Cecil G. Sheps has been a leader in the field of health administration and health services research. The Center for Health Services Research at the University of North Carolina was named in his honor. He was the husband of Mindel Cherniack Sheps.

Sam Sheps is a professor and head of the Department of Health Care and Epidemiology at University of British Columbia. He is actively involved in the field of health services research and clinical epidemiology. Sheps has served on the board of the Vancouver Peretz Institute, a Jewish organization established to foster *yiddishkeit* in Vancouver. He is the son of Mindel Cherniack Sheps.

Rona Sheramy is a Ph.D. candidate in the Department of Near Eastern and Judaic Studies and an M.A. candidate in the women's studies program at Brandeis University. Sheramy received her B.A. from the University of Michigan and is a former history teacher at the Riverdale Country School.

Amy Hill Shevitz is a Ph.D. candidate in the History Department at Oklahoma University. She received her B.A. from Smith College and an M.S. in library and information science from the Graduate School of Simmons College. Her articles have appeared in the *Reconstructionist, Western States Jewish History,* and the *Great Lakes Review.* Shevitz has worked in various library positions and in Jewish education and communal service.

Kayla Ship received her B.A. in anthropology from Dartmouth College and her master's in theological studies from Harvard University. She has taught Judaic studies and Hebrew language at Hebrew College, Prozdor division, in Brookline, Massachusetts.

Elliott Shore is head librarian at the Institute for Advanced Study at Princeton Univetsity. He received his B.A. from Temple University, his M.A. from the London School of Economics, his M.S. from Drexel University, and his Ph.D. from Bryn Mawr College. He has taught at Temple University, the New School for Social Research, Rutgers University, and Bonn University. He was a Senior Fulbright Scholar at the University of Cologne. His publications include *Talkin' Socialism: J.A. Wayland and the Role of the Press in American Radicalism* and *The German-American Radical Press: The Shaping of a Left Political Culture, 1850–1930* (coeditor).

Marion Shulevitz is a graduate of Detroit Midrasha College of Jewish Studies, Wayne State University, and the Rabbinical School of the Jewish Theological Seminary. Shulevitz has worked as a staff chaplain with the HealthCare Chaplaincy, Inc., and as Jewish chaplain for several New York hospitals. Her articles on Jewish and chaplaincy issues have appeared in *Conservative Judaism*, *Lilith*, and the *New York Times*.

Michele Siegel wrote and did research for *Jewish Women in America: An Historical Encyclopedia* through the Ford Scholars program at Vassar College. She received her B.A. in history from Vassar in 1996. She is a staff assistant in the office of the deputy chairman for grants and partnership at the National Endowment for the Arts.

Steven Siegel, library director and archivist at the 92nd Street YM-YWHA in New York City, is a graduate of Cornell University. He is a genealogist and local history researcher and has served as president of the Jewish Genealogical Society and the Archivists Round Table of Metropolitan New York. He is the compiler of *Archival Resources*, volume 1 of *Jewish Immigrants of the Nazi Period in the USA*.

Linda Simon is director of the Writing Center and a lecturer in expository writing at Harvard University. She received her Ph.D. in English and American literature from Brandeis University. Simon has written nine books, including *The Biography of Alice B. Toklas*, *Thornton Wilder: His World*, and *Gertrude Stein Remembered*. She is working on a biography of William James.

Kathryn Kish Sklar graduated from Radcliffe College in 1965 and received her Ph.D. from the University of Michigan in 1969. She has taught at the University of Michigan and the University of California at Los Angeles and is currently distinguished professor of history at the State University of New York at Binghamton. Her books focus on the history of women's particpation in social movements and public culture and include *Catharine Beecher: A Study in American Domesticity* and *Florence Kelley and the Nation's Work: The Rise of Women's Political Culture, 1830–1900*. She is coeditor of *Women and Power in American History*, *The Social Survey Movement in Historical Perspective*, and *U.S. History as Women's History: New Feminist Essays*.

Marilyn J. Sladowsky is a Ph.D. candidate at Columbia University and an adjunct lecturer in history at Hunter College, where she received her B.A. Sladowsky has been a fellow at the Center for Israel and Jewish Studies at Columbia.

Margery N. Sly is college archivist and coordinator of special collections in the Smith College Libraries. She holds a B.A. in history and German literature from Dickinson College and an M.A. in history and an M.L.S. from Case Western University. Active in archival professional organizations, she writes on a variety of archival issues.

Allen Smith is a Ph.D. candidate in American history at American University. His dissertation is "Converting America: Three Community Efforts to End the Cold War." Smith received his M.A. in American history from the University of Wisconsin and his B.A. in history from the University of the South.

Ellen Smith is curator of the American Jewish Historical Society. Her recent publications include *Portraits of a Commu-*

nity: The Image and Experience of Early American Jews and *The Jews of Boston*, coedited with Jonathan D. Sarna. Among Smith's major exhibitions are *On Common Ground: The Boston Jewish Experience, 1620–1980*, *Send Us a Lady Physician: Women Doctors in America, 1870–1920*, and *The Jews of Boston*. She is one of nine national scholar members of the Henry Luce Foundation grant project, "The Visual Culture of American Religions," and a founding advisory board member of the Center for Jewish Women's Studies at Brandeis University.

Judith Smith is associate professor and director of the graduate program in American studies at the University of Massachusetts at Boston. She received her B.A. in American history at Radcliffe College and her M.A. and Ph.D. in American civilization from Brown University. Among her publications are *Family Connections: A History of Italian and Jewish Immigrant Lives in Providence, Rhode Island, 1900–1940* and *The Evolution of American Urban Society*, with Howard Chudacoff. Smith is an editorial consultant for the journal *Feminist Studies*, and she has worked as a researcher and producer for the documentary film *Love Stories: Women, Men, and Romance*.

Kathleen Snodgrass is the author of *The Fiction of Hortense Calisher*, the first book-length study of the American fiction writer. Snodgrass's essays, reviews, and poetry translations have appeared in *Texas Studies in Literature and Language*, *The Iowa Review*, *Salmagundi*, *Trafika*, and *Artful Dodge*.

Holly Snyder is a doctoral candidate at Brandeis University in the history of American Civilization program, where she is writing a dissertation on the interrelationships between Jewish communities and urban society in British America during the colonial period. Since 1992, she has served as archivist for the American Jewish Historical Society. Snyder was previously the oral history archivist and acting director of oral history for the United States Holocaust Memorial Museum. She received her M.S.L.S. and M.A. in American history from the Catholic University of America.

June Sochen is professor of history at Northeastern Illinois University. Sochen received her B.A. from the University of Chicago and her M.A. and Ph.D. in history from Northwestern University. Specializing in American women's and American Jewish history, her books include *The New Woman: Feminism in Greenwich Village, 1910–1920*, *Consecrate Every Day: The Public Lives of Jewish American Women, 1880–1980*, and the award-winning *Cafeteria America: New Identities in Contemporary Life*. Sochen has edited a special edition of *American Jewish History* on American Jewish women.

Laurie Sokol is a graduate student in the Department of American Studies at the University of Maryland. Her research interests include contemporary Jewish women and suburban development. She is currently working on the relationship between ethnicity and identity, specifically with Jewish women in post–World War II suburbia.

Naomi Sokoloff is an associate professor at the University of Washington, where she teaches Hebrew and modern Jewish literature. She is the author of *Imagining the Child in Modern Jewish Fiction* and coeditor of *Gender and Text in Modern Hebrew and Yiddish Literature* and *Infant Tongues: The Voice of the Child in Literature*.

Gerald Sorin is chair of the History Department and director of the Jewish Studies Program at the State University of New York at New Paltz. His books include *The Prophetic Minority: American Jewish Immigrant Radicals, 1880–1920, The Nurturing Neighborhood: The Brownsville Boys Club and Jewish Community in Urban America, 1940–1990, A Time for Building: The Third Migration, 1880–1920,* and *Tradition Transformed: The Jewish Experience in America.* Sorin has also published eighty articles, essays, and reviews on aspects of ethnic identity and acculturation.

Daniel Soyer is assistant professor of history at Fordham University. A graduate of Oberlin College (A.B.) and New York University (M.A., Ph.D.), Soyer has been a curator and researcher at the Museum of Jewish Heritage, an associate archivist at the YIVO Institute for Jewish Research, and a visiting assistant professor at the University of Wisconsin. Soyer is the author of *Jewish Immigrant Associations and American Identity in New York, 1880–1939.*

David Spaner, a graduate of Simon Fraser University and Langara College in Canada, has worked as a feature writer, reporter, and editor for numerous alternative and mainstream publications. He is currently employed at the Vancouver Province newspaper and is writing a book about Canadian comedy.

Naomi Spector received her B.A. from Brandeis University and her M.A. from New York University. She has worked as manager at a number of galleries and has written extensively on the works of artists, including Eva Hesse in *Galeries Magazine.*

Michelle Spinelli is assistant to the dean of Sarah Lawrence College, where she received her M.A. in women's history and has worked as an archivist in the college library. Spinelli also works as an historical researcher and writer specializing in American women's history.

Claire Sprague received her B.A. in comparative literature, and her M.A. and Ph.D. in American literature, from the University of Wisconsin. She has taught at New York University, Brooklyn College, and the City University of New York. Sprague's publications include *Van Wyck Brooks: The Early Years, Rereading Doris Lessing: Narrative Strategies of Doubling and Repetition,* and *In Pursuit of Doris Lessing: Nine Nations Reading.*

Norma Spungen is director of the Chicago Jewish Archives, Spertus Institute of Jewish Studies. She has earned degrees in education and Jewish studies and has published articles in *Illinois Library Journal* and *Jewish Social Studies.*

Nanette Stahl is Judaica curator at the Yale University Library. She received her Ph.D. from the University of California at Berkeley in Hebrew literature and Bible. Before arriving at Yale she was head librarian at the Jewish Community Library of the Bureau of Jewish Education in San Francisco and Judaica bibliographer at the Library of the School of Law at the University of California at Berkeley, where her responsibilities included building a Jewish law collection. She is the author of *Law and Liminality in the Bible.*

Bonnie Stark is a reference librarian at the Culver City Public Library, a branch of the Los Angeles County Library. She worked previously as a special librarian in the motion picture industry, for companies such as the California Film Commission, Metro-Goldwyn-Mayer, 20th Century-Fox, and the Academy of Motion Picture Arts and Sciences. Stark is a voting member of the Academy, and she has also taught "Costuming for Hollywood" at the University of California at Los Angeles extension.

Naomi M. Steinberger is executive librarian at the library of the Jewish Theological Seminary of America. She has an M.S. in library services from Columbia University and an M.A. in musicology from Bar-Ilan University. Steinberger has written articles on library databases, particularly in the fields of music and Judaica.

Gloria Steinem has been the most prominent activist and leader in the women's movement in America for more than thirty years. She cofounded *Ms.* magazine in 1971 and has written and lectured across the United States on women's rights, feminist solidarity, social justice, and gender roles. Her most recent book is *Moving Beyond Words.*

Jennifer Stinson is working toward her Ph.D. in musicology and her M.A. in women's studies at Brandeis University. Her interests include women in music and intersections of Jewish culture and music, especially in the Yiddish theater. Her research includes work on gender roles in Molly Picon's film *Yidl mit'n Fidl* and on gender and eroticism in Italian opera.

Steven Stoll is assistant professor of history and American studies at Yale University, where he teaches environmental history and the history of the American West.

Joan Timmis Strasbaugh has written about dance for numerous publications, including *Dance Magazine,* the *Minneapolis Star Tribune,* and the *St. Paul Pioneer Press Dispatch.*

Lauren B. Strauss is a Ph.D. candidate in modern Jewish studies at the Jewish Theological Seminary, where she is focusing on American Jewish cultural history. Her dissertation explores the role of the visual arts in the immigrant Jewish community in America in the early twentieth century. Strauss holds a B.A. in politics and English literature from Brandeis University and an M.A. in international relations from Yale University. She is the author of "Staying Afloat in the Melting Pot: Constructing an American Jewish Identity in the *Menorah Journal* of the 1920s."

Christine Sumption is an instructor of theater arts at the University of Puget Sound and an administrative assistant at the Northwest Asian American Theatre. Sumption has worked as resident director of the Theatre Company Subaru in Tokyo and as a visiting associate professor of English at Toin University of Yokohama. A graduate of the University of Montana (B.F.A.) and the University of Washington (M.F.A), she has written plays, videoscripts, and articles.

Stuart Svonkin earned his Ph.D. in American history at Columbia University and is completing a J.D. at Harvard Law School. He has taught courses in American and American Jewish history at Columbia and the New School for Social Research. He is the author of *Jews Against Prejudice: American Jews and the Fight for Civil Liberties.*

Sarah Silberstein Swartz was editor in chief of *Jewish Women in America: An Historical Encyclopedia.* She is a freelance editor and writer and runs her own consulting service.

She has also worked as an editor at consulting services and publishing firms, including The Editorial Centre, Van Nostrand Reinhold, and Prentice-Hall of Canada. Swartz has written or edited *Found Treasures: Stories by Yiddish Women Writers, Lights Out for Ghosts,* and *Bar Mitzvah,* and she is editor of the quarterly journal *Communicating Together.*

Kirsten Swinth received her Ph.D. in American studies from Yale University and her B.A. from Stanford University. Her dissertation was "Painting Professionals: Women Artists and the Development of a Professional Ideal in American Art, 1870–1920." She has been a visiting assistant professor at George Washington University and an adjunct professor at the University of Maryland. Her interests include United States women's history and gender studies and the history of the American West.

Peter Taback teaches at the City College of New York. He is completing a doctoral dissertation in English on American culture after Hiroshima in fiction criticism and popular sociology at the Graduate Center of the City University.

Emily Taitz is an adjunct professor in European history and women's studies at Adelphi University's ABLE program. She received her Ph.D. in medieval Jewish history from the Jewish Theological Seminary of America. She is the author of *The Jews of Medieval France: The Community of Champagne* and, with Sondra Henry, *Remarkable Jewish Women: Rebels, Rabbis, and Other Women from Bible Times to the Present* and *Written Out of History: Our Jewish Foremothers.*

Jennifer Tammi is a Ph.D. candidate at Rutgers University. She received her B.A. in American history from Gustavus Adolphus College and her M.A. in women's history from Sarah Lawrence College. She has developed a "women's tour" for the Lower East Side Tenement Museum in New York City, and she has worked as an English instructor at the Southwest Jiaotong University in Chengdu, Sichuan, in the People's Republic of China.

Susan L. Tananbaum is assistant professor of history at Bowdoin College. She received her B.A. in Judaic studies from Trinity College and her Ph.D. in comparative European history and Near Eastern and Judaic studies from Brandeis University. Tananbaum has published and lectured on Jewish immigrant women in London.

Michael Taub teaches Israeli theater and film at Rutgers University. He is the author of *Modern Israeli Drama* and *Israeli Holocaust Drama* and coeditor of *Contemporary Jewish American Writers—A Biocritical Sourcebook.*

Jennifer Tebbe is professor of political science and American studies at the Massachusetts College of Pharmacy and Allied Health Sciences. She received her B.A. and M.A. in political science from the University of Missouri at Kansas City and her Ph.D. in American studies from Case Western Reserve University. Tebbe has written articles about women writers, health professions, and mass media, and is working on a study of the cultural history of the drugstore in American life.

Shelly Tenenbaum is on the Editorial Advisory Board of the *Encyclopedia.* See the beginning of this list for a biographical note.

Rose Anne Thom is on the faculty of Sarah Lawrence College. She also works as a critic for *Dance Magazine* and an oral historian for the New York Public Library for the Performing Arts. Thom's work has appeared in scholarly journals and reference works, such as the *International Dictionary of Ballet.* A graduate of McGill University in Canada, Thom has trained in ballet, modern dance, and choreographic studies.

Dorothy Thomas is a writer, editor, and lecturer. A graduate of Hunter College and New York University, her publications include biographies, articles on information science, and oral histories. She lectures on women and economics and women and the legal profession. Thomas is working on a history and collective biography titled *Women, the Bench and the Bar.*

Kathleen Thompson is coauthor with Andra Medea of the feminist classic *Against Rape.* With Diane Epstein, she is coauthor of *Feeding on Dreams.* Thompson was a major contributor to *Black Women in America* and was editor in chief of *Encyclopedia of Black Women.* She has worked for twenty years in education and publishing and is the author of more than one hundred books for juveniles, including *Portrait of America,* a fifty-three volume set of books that accompanied Turner Broadcasting's television series of the same name. She received Best Books for Youth award from the American Library Association in 1974 and the Gold Camera award from the United States Industrial Film Festival.

Nellie L. Thompson is a historian and senior candidate at the New York Psychoanalytic Institute, where she is also curator of the archives of the A.A. Brill Library. Thompson's research interests include the history of psychoanalysis and the role and contributions of women to the psychoanalytic movement. Thompson was guest editor for a special issue of *The Psychoanalytic Review* on early American women psychoanalysts.

Francesca Tillona is associate professor of English at the University of Massachusetts at Lowell. She received her Ph.D. from Boston University. She has taught graduate and undergraduate courses in English, American, and Continental literature in translation, as well as courses in writing fiction, professional and business writing, and editorial and publishing techniques. She is the coauthor of *Feast of Flowers,* a collection of flower recipes from the Middle Ages and the Renaissance adapted for use in the contemporary kitchen. She is working on a study of the king's two bodies—a sixteenth-century legal doctrine—and Shakespeare's development of that doctrine in his English history plays.

Barbara L. Tischler teaches history and American studies at Columbia University, where she is director of admissions and financial aid at the School of General Studies. Tischler is the author of *An American Music: The Search for an American Musical Identity* and editor of *Sights on the Sixties.* She teaches, lectures, and writes principally on culture in the contemporary United States.

Pauline Tish is professor emeritus and former chair of the Dance Department of Pratt Institute. Trained as a dancer with Martha Graham and Louis Horst, Tish performed with Helen Tamiris during the WPA Dance Project and was instrumental in the reconstruction of Tamiris's *How Long Brethren?* performed at George Mason University in 1991 and the American Dance Festival in 1993 and 1995. Tish received a B.A. from Hunter College and an M.A. in dance from New York University, where she also pursued graduate studies in anthropology.

William Toll has taught in the history departments of Oregon State University and the University of Oregon. He received his Ph.D. from the University of California at Berkeley. His publications include *The Making of an Ethnic Middle Class: Portland Jewry Over Four Generations* and *Women, Men, and Ethnicity: Essays on the Structure and Though of American Jewry.*

Brian Tress is a free-lance writer in New York City. His feature articles on Jewish issues and other subjects have appeared in several New York newspapers, as well as publishing poetry in the Jewish literary journal *Response* and essays in the travel magazine *Itinerary.* Tress is a graduate of Cornell University.

Helene L. Tuchman is librarian of the Temple Emanuel of Newton, Massachusetts, and former director of the Watertown Free Public Library. A graduate of Brooklyn College (B.A.) and the Pratt Institute (M.L.S.), Tuchman is the author of *Large Print Books of Jewish Interest.*

Miriam Tuchman is an architect at Stahl Associates Architects in Boston. Tuchman received her B.A. in urban studies and architecture at Barnard College and her M.Arch. from the Graduate School of Design at Harvard University and did course work at Hebrew University in Jerusalem. Tuchman also works as a high school teacher at Hebrew College in Brookline.

Diana B. Turk, a graduate of Hamilton College, is a doctoral candidate in American Studies at the University of Maryland. Her dissertation is "'Bound by a Mighty Vow': A Study of Sisterhood in Kappa Alpha Theta Women's Fraternity, 1870–1920."

Ellen M. Umansky is on the Editorial Advisory Board of the *Encyclopedia.* See the beginning of this list for a biographical note.

Rhoda K. Unger is professor of psychology at Montclair State University. Unger received her B.S. in psychology from Brooklyn College and her M.A. and Ph.D. in experimental psychology from Harvard University. Among her publications are *Sex Role Stereotypes Revisited: Psychological Perspectives on Women's Studies, Representations: Social Constructions of Gender,* and *In Our Own Words: Readings in Feminist Psychology,* edited with M. Crawford. Unger is a fellow of the American Psychological Association.

Bernard Unti is a Ph.D. candidate in the Department of History at American University. His interests include the history of the civil liberties movement in America and the development of concern for animals and the environment.

Jennifer Vafakos earned her B.F.A. in fashion design from the Parson's School of Design. She is an intern at the Metropolitan Costume Institute, where she monitors college classes and drafts patterns of garments in the collection.

Ingerlene Voosen has a B.A. in American cultural studies from Bates College. Interviews she conducted with female jazz vocalists are currently held in the oral history collection at the Hogan Jazz Archive at Tulane University. Voosen's academic specialties include studies of women, music, and the American South. She actively engages in field and academic research and has recently begun an affiliation with Brandeis University.

Suzanne Vromen is professor of sociology at Bard College, where she cofounded the Women's Studies Program and directed it for eight years. Her research interests include social theory and gender and collective memory, with an emphasis on commemoration, memorials, and monuments. Vromen's articles and reviews have appeared in many journals, including *YIVO Annual* and *History of European Ideas.*

Debra Wacks is a Ph.D. candidate in art history at the Graduate Center of the City University of New York. A graduate of the Institute of Fine Arts at New York University (M.A.), Wacks teaches art history at the College of Staten Island. She has published an essay on the sculptor Chryssa in *The Dictionary of Women Artists* and has given a guest lecture on Hannah Wilke at California State University at Northridge, where Wacks received her B.A.

Mel Wacks was educated as an electrical engineer at the City College of New York (B.S.E.E.) and New York University (M.S.E.E.). He later combined his interests in art and Jewish history with his hobby of numismatics to found the Jewish-American Hall of Fame at the Magnes Museum in Berkeley, California, where most of the honorees are commemorated with bas relief portraits. Wacks is the author of *The Handbook of Biblical Numismatics.*

Daniel Walden received his B.A. from the City College of New York, his M.A. from Columbia University, and his Ph.D. from New York University. Since 1966, he has taught ethnic literatures and Jewish literature at Pennsylvania State University. Among his books are *On Being Jewish* and *Twentieth-Century American Jewish Fiction Writers.* Walden has written articles on Saul Bellow, Bernard Malamud, Cynthia Ozick, and many other writers. He has edited *Studies in American Jewish Literature* since 1975 and is on the editorial boards of *The Saul Bellow Journal,* the *Bernard Malamud Newsletter,* and *MELUS.*

Karen E. Waldron is an assistant professor at the College of the Atlantic. Waldron has also taught at Boston College and Brandeis University, where she received her Ph.D. in English and American literature. Waldron has published and delivered a number of papers about black and white women writers. Her dissertation is "Coming to Consciousness, Coming to Voice: The Reinvention of Eve in American Women's Writings."

Alexandra J. Wall is a writer in New York City. She graduated with a B.A. from the University of California at Santa Cruz and with an M.A. in journalism from New York University. Wall has been published in the *New York Times, Newsday,* the *Press-Enterprise,* and many Jewish newspapers.

Joellyn Wallen is a Ph.D. candidate in American Jewish history, with a concentration in gender studies, at Brandeis University and a registration consultant at the American Jewish Historical Society. Wallen has worked as a curatorial assistant at the Hebrew Union College Skirball Museum and at the Judaica Project at the Smithsonian Institution.

Paul E. Wallner is chief of the Department of Radiation Oncology, Cooper Hospital/University Medical Center, Camden, New Jersey. He is past president of the American Cancer Society, New Jersey Division.

Susan Ware specializes in twentieth-century United States history and the history of American women. Her most recent book is *Still Missing: Amelia Earhart and the Search for Modern Feminism*. She received her Ph.D. from Harvard University, where she studied with Barbara Miller Solomon.

Lyle L. Warner has been a clinical social worker in private practice in Boston. She received her A.B. from Smith College, her M.S.W. from Washington University, and her Ph.D. from Smith College School for Social Work. She has been chair of the Friends of the Boston Psychoanalytic Society and Institute.

Nina Warnke is a lecturer in the Department of Germanic Languages at Columbia University, where she is completing her dissertation in Yiddish studies on Jewish cultural politics and the New York Yiddish theatre. Her work has appeared in *YIVO Annual* and *Theatre Journal*.

Suzanne Wasserman has a Ph.D. in American history. Her dissertation is "'The Good Old Days of Poverty': The Battle Over the Fate of New York City's Lower East Side During the Depression." Wasserman teaches at New York University in the Metropolitan Studies Program and the Museum Studies Program, where she is the internship coordinator.

Kirsten Wasson teaches American literature at Hobart and William Smith Colleges. A graduate of Wesleyan University (B.A.), State University of New York at Binghamton (M.A.), and the University of Wisconsin (Ph.D.), she is completing a book on Mary Antin, Anzia Yezierska, and Elizabeth Stern.

Steven Weiland is professor of higher education and director of the Jewish Studies Program at Michigan State University, where he teaches in the Department of English. Weiland teaches courses in adult development and aging, research methods, and the humanities. He is the author of *Intellectual Craftsmen: Ways and Works in American Scholarship, 1935–1990*.

Elliot Weinbaum graduated with a B.A. in history from Yale University. After working as a development assistant at the National Museum of American Jewish History in Philadelphia and as case manager at a social service agency working with homeless families in Trenton, Weinbaum now works as program coordinator at the Stiffel Senior Center in South Philadelphia. He spends his summers promoting cooperation between African-American and Jewish communities through his work and travels with Operation Understanding.

Sydney Stahl Weinberg is professor of history at Ramapo College of New Jersey, where she is also director of the Master of Arts in Liberal Studies Program. Weinberg received her B.A. from Barnard and her M.A. and Ph.D. in American history from Columbia University. She is the author of *The World of Our Mothers: The Lives of Jewish Immigrant Women*.

Beryl H. Weiner is the oldest member and senior partner of the law firm of Weiner, Yancey, Dempsey, and Diggs in Atlanta. He has been active in local Jewish communal activities, such as the Board of Atlanta Bureau of Jewish Education and the Jewish Educational Loan Fund. Weiner is former president of the Southern Jewish Historical Society.

Hollace Ava Weiner is a reporter for the *Fort Worth Star-Telegram*. A graduate of the University of Maryland (B.A.), Weiner is a past president of the Association for Women Journalists. She is researching a book on pioneer Texas rabbis and their wives and wrote a chapter in *The Quiet Voices: Southern Rabbis and Black Civil Rights, From the Late Nineteenth Century to the Modern Era*.

Selma Weintraub is a past national president of the Women's League for Conservative Judaism. Her articles have appeared in *Outlook Magazine*, and she has written for *The Seminary at 100*, a publication of the Jewish Theological Seminary of America.

Phyllis Holman Weisbard is women's studies librarian of the University of Wisconsin system. She graduated from the University of Wisconsin (B.S., M.A.) and Boston University (M.Ed.). Weisbard publishes *Feminist Collections: A Quarterly of Women's Studies Resources* and makes frequent presentations on electronic resources for the study of women and gender. She is the author of *Jewish Law: Bibliography of Sources and Scholarship in English*, with David Schonberg; and *The History of Women and Science, Health, and Technology: A Bibliographic Guide to the Professions and the Disciplines*, with Rima Apple.

Carol Weisbrod is Ellen Ash Peters Professor of Law at the University of Connecticut. She is author of *The Boundaries of Utopia* and coauthor of a casebook, *Family Law*. She has written law journal articles in the areas of political theory, feminist theory, church and state, and legal history.

Lee Shai Weissbach is professor of history at the University of Louisville. He received his undergraduate degree from the University of Cincinnati and his Ph.D. from Harvard University in 1975. Weissbach has worked in both French and American history, and his publications include *The Synagogues of Kentucky: Architecture and History*. His current research, supported by a National Endowment for the Humanities fellowship, concerns the history of small Jewish communities throughout the United States.

Beth Wenger teaches modern and American Jewish history at the University of Pennsylvania. She has been a visiting fellow at Princeton University's Center for the Study of American Religion. She is the author of *New York Jews and the Great Depression: Uncertain Promise*.

Sandra Wheeler has two M.A. degrees, one in medical anthropology from the University of Connecticut and one in American history from Trinity College. She is an archivist who divides her time among Hill-Stead Museum in Farmington, Connecticut, the Hartford Studies Project at Trinity, and an archival consulting practice. She is a visiting lecturer at both Trinity College and Wesleyan University. Her research interests center on the social history of Hartford from the late nineteenth to the mid-twentieth century with a special interest in the provision of services to the immigrant poor.

Stephen J. Whitfield is Max Richter Professor of American Civilization at Brandeis University, where he received his doctorate in 1972 and has taught ever since. He has also been a visiting professor at the Hebrew University of Jerusalem, the Catholic University of Louvain, and the Sorbonne. Whitfield's books include *Into the Dark: Hannah Arendt and Totalitarianism; Voices of Jacob, Hands of Esau;* and *American Space, Jewish Time.*

Ruth Whitman is the author of eight books of poetry and three translations of modern Yiddish poetry. She has received a Senior Fulbright Writer-in-Residence Award to the Hebrew University in Jerusalem, a National Endowment for the Arts Fellowship, a Radcliffe College Bunting Institute Fellowship, a Rhode Island Grant in Literature, and the Alice Fay di Castagnola Award from the Poetry Society of America. Whitman is lecturer in poetry at the Radcliffe seminars.

Estelle C. Williams is working toward a doctorate in English at the Graduate Center of the City University of New York. She teaches at Baruch College, CUNY, and at the Rosa Parks campus of the College of New Rochelle.

Steven Winnett works for the United States Environmental Protection Agency as a watershed specialist. A former senior forest policy analyst for the EPA, Winnett received his master's and doctorate degrees in forestry from Yale University School of Forestry and Environmental Studies. He has published numerous articles and government reports on forest resources.

Merla Wolk is a senior lecturer at the University of Michigan, where she teaches writing and literature. Her publications include essays on Rosellen Brown, Edith Konecky, and Henry James. Wolk is coauthor of *Arenas of the Mind: Critical Reading for Writers,* and she is at work on *Offerings: The Voices of Jewish Women Writers,* a cultural study of Jewish women writing in English around the world.

Roberta Wollons received her B.A. from the University of California at Berkeley and her Ph.D. from the University of Chicago, where she wrote her dissertation on Sidonie Gruenberg. Wollons is currently an associate professor of history at Indiana University Northwest. She has taught at Doshish University in Kyoto, where she studied American women educators in Japan. Her current research is on the spread of the kindergarten at the turn of the century, and she is the author of *Kindergarten and Culture: Twelve Studies of Nationalism.*

Susan Wyckoff is associate vice president for academic affairs at New England College. She has a Ph.D. in higher education, and her research interests include the impact of demographic shifts and economic forces on American higher education.

Alice Yelen is assistant to the director for special projects and curator of self-taught art at the New Orleans Museum of Art, where she has served as chief curator of education. Yelen curated the exhibitions and authored the related catalogs for *Passionate Visions of the American South: Self-Taught Artists from 1940 to the Present* and *Zenga: Brushstrokes of Enlightenment.* She holds a B.A. from Brandeis University and two masters degrees: one in art history from Columbia University and one in museum education from George Washington University. Yelen has been a board member of a number of museum organizations as well as of the National Foundation for Jewish Culture.

Jessica Zellner is a law student at the University of Pennsylvania. A graduate of Brown University (B.A.), Zellner founded the Committee for the Awareness and Prevention of Jewish Domestic Abuse in Providence, Rhode Island. She has worked at the Massachusetts Advocacy Center, a children's rights organization that advocates for disabled children and children who are suspended or expelled from school.

Wendy Zierler is a postdoctoral research fellow at the University of Hong Kong, where she lectures on American literature. She received her Ph.D. in comparative literature from Princeton University in 1995. Her dissertation deals with the emergence of Jewish women's writing in Israel and the United States and its relation to the immigrant experience.

Minna Pearl Ziskind is a Ph.D. candidate at the University of Pennsylvania. A graduate of Brown University (B.A., M.A.T.), she taught American history at the Charles E. Smith Jewish Day School in Rockville, Maryland.

Jane Sprague Zones, Ph.D., is a medical sociologist at the University of California at San Francisco. A long-time women's health advocate, she is former chair of the board of directors of the National Women's Health Network. She is on the steering committee of the California Women's Health Council. Author of many women's health articles, she is also editor of *The San Diego Women's Haggadah* and serves on the board of Congregation Beth Sholom in San Francisco.

Sheva Zucker holds a Ph.D. in comparative literature from the Graduate Center of the City University of New York. She teaches Yiddish and Jewish literature at Duke University and has taught at Columbia University, the University of Manitoba, and universities in Israel, Russia, and Moldova. Zucker is the author of *Yiddish: An Introduction to the Language, Literature and Culture.* Her literary research focuses on Yiddish women writers, and she has written articles on Anna Margolin, Kadya Molodowsky, and Celia Dropkin.

Sonia Zylberberg is a graduate student in the Judaic Studies Program at Concordia University in Montreal. Her master's thesis topic is woman-to-woman relationships in the Hebrew Bible. Her areas of concentrations are the Hebrew Bible, feminist Judaism, and women and religion. Zylberberg's articles have appeared in the *Journal of Religion and Culture* and *Bibliography of Women and Religion.*

Classified List of Biographical Entries

ACTIVISTS

(*see also* ANARCHISTS;
COMMUNIST AND SOCIALIST
PARTY ACTIVISTS; LABOR
ORGANIZERS/LEADERS;
ZIONISTS)

Abzug, Bella
Adler, Barbara Ochs
Adler, Helen Goldmark
Adler, Racie
Albert, Miriam
Allen, Anna Marks
American, Sadie
Arons, Jeannette
Axman, Sophie Cahn
Baerwald, Edith Jacobi
Balabanoff, Angelica
Baright, Clarice
Baruch, Dorothy
Bellanca, Dorothy Jacobs
Bernhard, Dorothy Lehman
Bernstein, Rebecca Thurman
Bettman, Meta Pollak
Borg, Madeline
Boudin, Anna Pavitt
Brandeis, Alice Goldmark
Brenner, Rose
Brin, Fanny Fligelman
Cardin, Shoshana S.
Chernin, Rose
Cohen, Nina Morais
Dalsheimer, Helen Miller
Dolowitz, Florence

Dreyfus, Sylvia Goulston
Einstein, Hannah Bachman
Engel, Katharine
Fellman, Mary Arbitman
Firestone, Shulamith
Fischel, Jane Brass
Freidan, Betty
Friend, Ida Weis
Gans, Bird Stein
Gans, Helene
Gilman, Blanche
Ginzberg, Adele
Glaser, Elizabeth
Gold, Doris Baumann
Goldman, Emma
Goldmark, Josephine Clara
Goldsmith, Edna
Gratz, Richea
Greenberg, Blu
Guggenheim, Irene Rothschild
Guggenheimer, Elinor
Guggenheimer, Ida Espen
Guthrie, Marjorie
Harris, Janet
Hartmann, Reina
Hecht, Lina Frank
Heiman, Adele Blumenthal
Herzog, Bertha Beitman
Hochfelder, Anna Weiner
Hoffman, Fanny Binswanger
Isaacs, Edith Somborn
Jacobs, Frances Wisebart
Jung, Irma Rothschild
Jungreis, Esther
Kaufman, Rhoda

Kavey, Lillian Kasindorf
Kohut, Rebekah Bettelheim
Krim, Mathilde
Kross, Anna Moscowitz
Kubie, Matilda Steinam
Lasker, Mary Woodward
Levine, Jacqueline
Levitt, Jennie Davidson
Loeb, Johanna
Loeb, Sophie Irene Simon
Loewith, Sadie
Lopez, Rebecca Touro
Lorber, Fannie Eller
Louis, Minnie Dessau
Mandl, Emma B.
May, Irma
Melton, Florence Zacks
Menken, Alice Davis
Meyer, Eugenia Goodkind
Misch, Marion Simon
Morgan, Robin
Moskowitz, Belle
Muffs, Yocheved Judith Herschlag
Nathan, Maud
Newman, Estelle
Newman, Pauline
Nirenstein, Blanche Cohen
Phillips, Rebecca Machado
Phillips, Rosalie Solomons
Pisko, Seraphine Eppstein
Pollitzer, Anita
Pomerance, Josephine Wertheim
Purvin, Jennie Franklin
Razovsky, Cecilia
Rome, Esther

Rose, Ernestine
Schechter, Mathilde
Schwartz, Felice Nierenberg
Schwimmer, Rosika
Sheftall, Frances Hart
Simon, Carrie Obendorfer
Solomon, Hannah Greenbaum
Spiegel, Dora
Spiegelberg, Flora Langerman
Sporborg, Constance Amberg
Stein, Hannah
Steinem, Gloria
Sternberger, Estelle
Strauss, Lillian Laser
Sulzberger, Elsie K.
Sulzberger, Rachel Hays
Swerdlow, Amy
Weil, Gertrude
Wetstein, Martha A.
Wyler, Marjorie

ACTRESSES

(see also COMEDIANS;
ENTERTAINERS; TELEVISION
JOURNALISTS, DIRECTORS,
PRODUCERS, AND
PERSONALITIES;
YIDDISH/VAUDEVILLE
ENTERTAINERS)

Adler, Celia
Adler, Sara
Adler, Stella
Appel, Anna
Arthur, Bea
Bacall, Lauren
Baker, Belle
Bara, Theda
Bellarina, Bella
Berg, Gertrude
Bilavsky, Glika
Blondell, Joan
Comden, Betty
Darvas, Lili
Diamond, Selma
Dolaro, Selina
Dresser, Louise
Eytinge, Rose
Gersten, Berta
Goldstein, Jennie
Gordon, Vera
Halperin, Nan
Hawn, Goldie
Held, Anna
Holliday, Judy
Kalich, Bertha
Kressyn, Miriam
Lavin, Linda
Lipman, Clara
Malina, Judith
Marinoff, Fania

May, Elaine
Menken, Adah Isaacs
Menken, Helen
Midler, Bette
Myers, Carmel
Picon, Molly
Radner, Gilda
Rainer, Luise
Rivers, Joan
Roseanne
Roth, Lillian
Segal, Vivienne
Shore, Dinah
Shoshana, Rose
Sidney, Sylvia
Streisand, Barbra
Thomashefsky, Bessie
Tucker, Sophie
Winters, Shelley

ANARCHISTS

Goldman, Emma
Pesotta, Rose
Steimer, Mollie

ARTISTS

(see GRAPHIC DESIGNERS,
PAINTERS, PHOTOGRAPHERS,
POTTER, PRINTMAKER,
SCULPTORS)

ASTRONAUT

Resnik, Judith

ATHLETES AND SPORTSWOMEN

Alcott, Amy
Berenson, Senda
Cohen, Natalie
Copeland, Lillian
Eisen, Thelma ("Tiby")
Epstein, Charlotte
Heldman, Gladys

AUTHORS

(see WRITERS)

BLUES SINGER

Holman, Libby

BUSINESSWOMEN

(see ENTREPRENEURS)

CHESS PLAYER

Karff, N. May

CHOREOGRAPHERS

Delakova, Katya
Gamson, Annabelle
Hadassah (Spira Epstein)
Lewitzky, Bella
Maslow, Sophie
Monk, Meredith
Oved, Margalit
Sokolow, Anna
Tamiris, Helen

COMEDIANS

Barth, Belle
Brice, Fanny
Goldstein, Jennie
Hawn, Goldie
Held, Anna
May, Elaine
Midler, Bette
Radner, Gilda
Rivers, Joan
Roseanne
Segal, Vivienne
Thomashefsky, Bessie

COMMUNIST AND SOCIALIST PARTY ACTIVISTS

Balabanoff, Angelica
Chernin, Rose
Malkiel, Theresa Serber
Olsen, Tillie
Rosenberg, Ethel
Shavelson, Clara Lemlich
Stokes, Rose Pastor
Strunsky, Manya Gordon
Walling, Anna Strunsky
Wortis, Rose

COMPOSERS

Bauer, Marion Eugénie
Behrend, Jeanne
Bloch, Blanche
Comden, Betty
Eisenstein, Judith Kaplan
Fields, Dorothy
Fine, Sylvia
Fuchs, Lillian
Gideon, Miriam
Jochsberger, Tziporah H.
King, Carole
Monk, Meredith
Spewack, Bella

CONCERT MUSICIANS AND SINGERS

Bauer, Marion Eugénie
Behrend, Jeanne
Bloch, Blanche
Fonaroff, Vera

Franko, Jeanne
Fuchs, Lillian
Gluck, Alma
Kisch-Arendt, Ruth
Kremer, Isa
Lhévinne, Rosina
Menuhin, Hephzibah
Raskin, Judith
Reisenberg, Nadia
Schlamme, Martha
Streisand, Barbra
Tureck, Rosalyn
Zeisler, Fannie Bloomfield
Ziegler, Dorothy Miriam

CONGRESSWOMEN

Abzug, Bella
Boxer, Barbara
Feinstein, Dianne
Fiedler, Bobbi
Harman, Jane
Holtzman, Elizabeth
Kahn, Florence Prag
Lowey, Nita M.
Spellman, Gladys Noon

DANCERS

Baird, Cora
Braun, Susan
Chochem, Corinne
Cohen, Selma Jeanne
Delakova, Katya
Gamson, Annabelle
Guthrie, Marjorie
Hadassah (Spira Epstein)
Halprin, Anna
Hayden, Melissa
Joel, Lydia
Kent, Allegra
Lang, Pearl
Lewitzky, Bella
Maslow, Sophie
Monk, Meredith
Oved, Margalit
Sokolow, Anna
Tamiris, Helen

DENTIST

Boudin, Anna Pavitt

DRAMA CRITIC

Block, Anita

EDITORS

Block, Anita
Brook, Claire
Cohen, Jessica (Jessie)
Davidson, Carrie Dreyfuss
Gay, Ruth
Joel, Lydia

Schocken, Eva
Sonneschein, Rosa

EDUCATORS

Allen, Anna Marks
Alschuler, Rose Haas
Arnstein, Margaret Gene
Bamber, Golde
Bamberger, Florence
Baruch, Dorothy Walter
Bauer, Marion Eugénie
Berkson, Libbie Suchoff
Bildersee, Adele
Brodbeck, May
Cohen, Audrey
Cohen, Helen Louise
Daum, Annette
Edelman, Lily
Elster, Shulamith Reich
Ettenberg, Sylvia
Fagin, Claire
Feingold, Jessica
Feldman, Sandra
Fine, Irene
Fizdale, Ruth E.
Furst, Norma Fields
Gamoran, Mamie
Gezari, Temima
Goldstein, Rebecca Fischel
Lazarus, Rachel Mordecai
Lee, Sara
Lieberman, Judith Berlin
Meyer, Annie Nathan
Mordecai, Rosa
Naumburg, Margaret
Peixotto, Judith
Phillips, Ellen
Prag, Mary Goldsmith
Richman, Julia
Rivkin, Nacha
Rose, Hannah Toby
Schurz, Margarethe Meyer
Scott, Miriam Finn
Solomon, Barbara Miller
Solomons, Hannah Marks
Stern, Bessie Cleveland
Wunderlich, Frieda

ENTERTAINERS

Baird, Cora
Barth, Belle
Bayes, Nora
Brice, Fanny
Dresser, Louise
Goldstein, Jennie
Gordon, Dorothy Lerner
Gorme, Eydie
Halperin, Nan
Hawn, Goldie
Holman, Libby
Joseph, Helen

Lewis, Shari
Midler, Bette
Monk, Meredith
Myers, Carmel
Roth, Lillian
Segal, Vivienne
Shore, Dinah
Streisand, Barbra
Tucker, Sophie

ENTREPRENEURS

Albert, Mildred Elizabeth Levine
Alexander, Beatrice
Arpel, Adrien
Auerbach, Beatrice Fox
Carnegie, Hattie
Gordon, Jean
Grossinger, Jennie
Halpert, Edith Gregor
Handler, Ruth Mosko
Kessler, Lillian Ruth
Lauder, Estée
LeBlang, Tillie
Leiber, Judith
Magnin, Mary Ann Cohen
Malsin, Lane Bryant
Margareten, Regina
McCluskey, Ellen Lehman
Michelson, Gertrude Geraldine
Minis, Abigail
Nassau, Lillian
Neiman, Carrie Marcus
Parnis, Mollie
Polykoff, Shirley
Rosenberg, Sophie Sonia
Rosenstein, Nettie
Rosenthal, Ida Cohen
Rubinstein, Helena
Schiff, Dorothy
Sommers, Estelle Joan
Waldbaum, Julia
Woodward, Helen Rosen

FASHION DESIGNERS

Carnegie, Hattie
Copeland, Jo
Milgrim, Sally
Parnis, Mollie
Rosenberg, Sophie Sonia
Rosenstein, Nettie

FILMMAKERS

Arnold, Eve
Brandeis, Madeline
Deren, Maya
Ephron, Nora
Hawn, Goldie
May, Elaine
Silver, Joan Micklin

FOLK MUSICIANS AND SINGERS

Elliot, "Mama" Cass
Gordon, Dorothy Lerner
Jochsberger, Tziporah H.
King, Carole
Kremer, Isa
Rubin, Ruth
Schlamme, Martha

GOVERNMENT OFFICIALS AND POLITICAL LEADERS

(*see also* POLITICIANS AND LEGISLATORS)

Bellanca, Dorothy Jacobs
Cohn, Felice
Farkas, Ruth Lewis
Flexner, Magdalen
Guggenheimer, Elinor
Henenberg, Hattie Leah
Hennock, Frieda Barkin
Kahn, Dorothy C.
Kaufman, Rhoda
Kunin, Madeleine May
Max, Pearl Bernstein
Morgenthau, Elinor
Moskowitz, Belle
Newman, Pauline
Paktor, Vera
Pomerance, Josephine Wertheim
Razovsky, Cecilia
Rosenberg, Anna Lederer
Schneiderman, Rose
Simon, Caroline Klein
Winestine, Belle

GRAPHIC DESIGNERS

Cohen, Elaine Lustig
Kruger, Barbara

INTELLECTUALS/ SCHOLARS

Adlerblum, Nima
Anshen, Ruth Nanda
Arendt, Hannah
Askowith, Dora
Bamberger, Florence
Beck, Evelyn Torton
Bernard, Jessie
Bildersee, Adele
Brodbeck, May
Bunzel, Ruth Leah
Chesler, Phyllis
Cohen, Naomi W.
Cohen, Selma Jeanne
Coser, Rose Laub
Davis, Natalie Zemon
Dean, Vera
Dinnerstein, Dorothy

Eisenstein, Judith Kaplan
Falk, Minna Regina
Farkas, Ruth Lewis
Feder-Keyfitz, Sara Rivka
Fisch, Edith
Frenkel-Brunswik, Else
Geiringer, Hilda
Gilligan, Carol
Ginsburg, Ruth Bader
Glueck, Eleanor
Goldfrank, Esther Schiff
Goldman, Hetty
Goldsmith, Luba Robin
Heilbrun, Carolyn G.
Hellman, Clarisse Doris
Himmelfarb, Gertrude
Howe, Florence
Hyde, Ida Henrietta
Jacobson, Anna
Jahoda, Marie
Karpf, Fay Berger
Landau, Sara
Landes, Ruth Schlossberg
Lerner, Gerda
Levy, Florence Nightingale
Lieber, Lillian R.
Lowenthal, Esther
Marcus, Ruth Barcan
Marmorston, Jessie
Moers, Ellen
Myerhoff, Barbara
Neugarten, Bernice L.
Noether, Emmy
Ostriker, Alicia Suskin
Peixotto, Jessica Blanche
Perlman, Helen Harris
Powdermaker, Hortense
Rand, Ayn
Rapoport, Lydia
Raushenbush, Elizabeth Brandeis
Roberts, Colette
Rosen, Gladys
Salber, Eva
Schwartz, Anna Jacobson
Shostak, Marjorie
Shuval, Judith Tannenbaum
Solomon, Barbara Miller
Sontag, Susan
Spector, Johanna
Swerdlow, Amy
Tanzer, Helen
Taussky-Todd, Olga
Tec, Nechama
Thomson, Judith Jarvis
Tobach, Ethel
Trilling, Diana
Weinberg, Gladys Davidson
Weiss-Rosmarin, Trude
Wertheimer, Mildred
Wessel, Bessie Bloom
Wisse, Ruth R.
Wolfson, Theresa

INTERIOR DESIGNERS

Lipsky, Charlotte
McCluskey, Ellen Lehman
Schaefer, Bertha

JAZZ SINGERS

Forrest, Helen
Syms, Sylvia Blagman

JOURNALISTS

Brod, Ruth Hagy
Fleischman, Doris
Frank, Lee Weiss
Frank, Ray
Gornick, Vivian
Gruber, Ruth
Jaffe, Jean
Landers, Ann
Paktor, Vera
Porter, Sylvia Field
Ross, Betty
Saarinen, Aline
Shultz, Lillie
Slott, Mollie
Stern, Elizabeth
Van Buren, Abigail
Walters, Barbara
Wolf, Sally Rivoli

JUDGES/JUSTICES

Amsterdam, Birdie
Baright, Clarice
Barron, Jennie Loitman
Brill, Jeanette Goodman
Davidson, Rita Charmatz
Ginsburg, Ruth Bader
Grossman, Mary Belle
Henenberg, Hattie Leah
Kaye, Judith S.
Kravitch, Phyllis A.
Kross, Anna Moscowitz
Polier, Justine Wise
Poritz, Deborah T.
Shapiro, Norma Levy

LABOR ORGANIZERS/ LEADERS

Balabanoff, Angelica
Bellanca, Dorothy Jacobs
Cohn, Fannia M.
Feldman, Sandra
Gans, Helene
Gay, Ruth
Goldman, Emma
Herstein, Lillian
Hillman, Bessie Abramowitz
Lang, Lucy Fox Robins
Malkiel, Theresa Serber
Newman, Pauline
Pesotta, Rose

Raushenbush, Elizabeth Brandeis
Rosenberg, Ethel
Schneiderman, Rose
Shavelson, Clara Lemlich
Wertheimer, Barbara Mayer
Wortis, Rose

LAWYERS

Abzug, Bella
Amsterdam, Birdie
Baright, Clarice
Barron, Jennie Loitman
Barsky, Evangelyn
Bullowa, Emilie M.
Buttenwieser, Helen Lehman
Cohn, Felice
Etra, Blanche Goldman
Fisch, Edith
Flexner, Magdalen
Gilbert, Susan Brandeis
Ginsburg, Ruth Bader
Grossman, Mary Belle
Harman, Jane
Hauser, Rita Eleanor
Henenberg, Hattie Leah
Hochfelder, Anna Weiner
Holtzman, Elizabeth
Holtzmann, Fanny E.
Kaplan, Aline
Kaye, Judith S.
King, Carol Weiss
Klaus, Ida
Kravitch, Phyllis A.
Kross, Anna Moscowitz
Levin-Rubin, Melba
Lewinson, Ruth
Lorber, Frieda
Lovenstein, Rebecca Pearl
Petluck, Alice A.
Pilpel, Harriet Fleischul
Polier, Justine Wise
Poritz, Deborah T.
Rock, Lillian
Shapiro, Norma Levy
Silverstein, Elizabeth Blume
Simon, Caroline Klein
Straus, Dorothy
Whitney, Rosalie Loew
Wolf, Frances

LEGISLATORS

(see POLITICIANS
AND LEGISLATORS)

LIBRARIANS, BIBLIOGRAPHERS, ARCHIVISTS

Abramowicz, Dina
Flexner, Jennie Maas
Goldstein, Fanny

Stern-Taeubler, Selma
Udin, Sophie A.

MADAM

Adler, Polly

MATHEMATICIANS

Noether, Emmy
Taussky-Todd, Olga

MUSICIANS

(see CONCERT MUSICIANS AND
SINGERS; FOLK MUSICIANS
AND SINGERS; POPULAR
MUSICIANS AND SINGERS)

NOBEL PRIZE WINNERS

Elion, Gertrude ("Trudy") Belle
Levi-Montalcini, Rita
Yalow, Rosalyn

NURSES

Arnstein, Margaret Gene
Deutsch, Naomi
Fagin, Claire
Greenwald, Amelia
Kaplan, Regina
Kaplan, Rose
Landy, Rae D.
Van Vort, Rose Zimmern

OPERA SINGERS

Abarbanell, Lina
Braslau, Sophie
Dolaro, Selina
Fabian, Mary Jacqueline
Gluck, Alma
Liebling, Estelle
Peters, Roberta
Raskin, Judith
Resnik, Regina
Sills, Beverly
Tourel, Jennie
Winetzkaja, Maria

PAINTERS

Baizerman, Eugenie
Bernstein, Theresa
Blum, Helen Abrahams
Chicago, Judy
Chochem, Corinne
Cohen, Elaine Lustig
Corcos, Lucille
Drabkin, Stella
Frank, Lee Weiss
Frankenthaler, Helen

Gezari, Temima
Gikow, Ruth
Hesse, Eva
Kohler, Rose
Krasner, Lee
Kreindler, Doris Barsky
Litzinger, Dorothea
Nevelson, Louise
Rosenthal, Doris
Stettheimer, Florine
Trommer, Marie
Wilke, Hannah

PHILANTHROPISTS

Albert, Mildred Elizabeth Levine
Alexander, Beatrice
Annenberg, Sadie Cecilia
Arpel, Adrien
Auerbach, Beatrice Fox
Blaustein, Henrietta Gittelson
Blumenthal, Florence Meyer
Cone, Etta
Freiberg, Stella Heinsheimer
Friedenwald, Jane
Fuld, Carrie Bamberger Frank
Guggenheim, Florence Shloss
Guggenheim, Peggy
Hassenfeld, Sylvia
Heller, Florence
Herrman, Esther
Ittleson, Blanche Frank
Lehman, Adele Lewisohn
Lehman, Edith Altschul
Levy, Adele Rosenwald
Lewisohn, Irene
Lewisohn, Margaret Seligman
Mastbaum, Etta Wedell
Miller, Linda Rosenberg
Naumburg, Elsie Margaret Binger
Osterman, Rosanna Dyer
Parnis, Mollie
Schiff, Therese Loeb
Schweitzer, Rebecca
Stern, Edith Rosenwald
Straus, Sarah Lavanburg
Stroock, Hilda Weil
Stroock, Regina D.
Sulzberger, Iphigene Ochs
Ungerleider-Mayerson, Joy
Warburg, Frieda Schiff
Weltman, Esther Ziskind
Wimpfheimer, Henrietta Scheuer

PHOTOGRAPHERS

Arbus, Diane
Arnold, Eve
Bing, Ilse
Jacobi, Lotte
Leibovitz, Annie
Rubin, Gail
Ulmann, Doris May

PHYSICIANS

Amir, Naomi
Baron, Sadi Muriel
Berlin, Fanny
Cohen, Elizabeth D.A.
Daily, Ray Karchmer
De Ford, Frances Allen
Finkler, Rita Sapiro
Goldsmith, Luba Robin
Kenin, Lena
Levine, Lena
Moses, Bessie Louise
Rabinoff, Sophie
Rosencrantz, Esther
Skidelsky, Rachel
Stone, Hannah Mayer
Taussig, Helen Brooke
Warner, Marie Pichel Levinson
Wollstein, Martha

PLAYWRIGHTS

Bowles, Jane
Broner, Esther M.
Caspary, Vera
Ephron, Phoebe
Franken, Rose
Helburn, Theresa
Hellman, Lillian
Jacobson, Janie
Lipman, Clara
Morton, Martha
Spewack, Bella
Wasserstein, Wendy
Zunser, Miriam Shomer

POLITICIANS AND LEGISLATORS

Abzug, Bella
Bellanca, Dorothy Jacobs
Boxer, Barbara
Feinstein, Dianne
Fiedler, Bobbi
Harman, Jane
Holtzman, Elizabeth
Kahn, Florence Prag
Kunin, Madeleine May
Lowey, Nita M.
Meir, Golda
Messinger, Ruth
Spellman, Gladys Noon
Strauss, Annette Greenfield
Wyman, Rosalind Weiner

POPULAR MUSICIANS AND SINGERS

Elliot, "Mama" Cass
Forrest, Helen
Gorme, Eydie
King, Carole
Midler, Bette
Streisand, Barbra

POTTER

Natzler, Gertrud Amon

PRINTMAKER

Grosman, Tatyana

PRIVATE DETECTIVE

Levy, Belle

PSYCHIATRISTS AND PSYCHOLOGISTS

Baron, Sadi, Muriel
Baruch, Dorothy Walter
Benedek, Therese
Bregman, Elsie Oschrin
Brothers, Joyce
Bruch, Hilde
Brunswick, Ruth Mack
Denmark, Florence Levin
Deutsch, Helene
Fraiberg, Selma
Frenkel-Brunswik, Else
Fromm-Reichmann, Frieda
Garfiel, Evelyn
Geleerd, Elisabeth Rozetta
Gilligan, Carol
Jahoda, Marie
Kenin, Lena
Levine, Lena
Mahler, Margaret
Mednick, Martha Tamara Schuch
Neugarten, Bernice L.
Sack, Sallyann Amdur
Tobach, Ethel

PUBLISHERS

Howe, Florence
Knopf, Blanche Wolf
Schiff, Dorothy
Schocken, Eva

RELIGIOUS LEADERS

Ackerman, Paula
Daum, Annette
Frank, Ray
Goldstein, Rose
Lichtenstein, Tehilla
Priesand, Sally Jane
Robbins, Betty
Teitelbaum, Faige

SCHOLARS

(see INTELLECTUALS/
SCHOLARS)

SCIENTISTS

Cohn, Mildred
Cone, Claribel

Edinger, Tilly
Elion, Gertrude ("Trudy") Belle
Finkler, Rita Sapiro
Friend, Charlotte
Hyde, Ida Henrietta
Hyman, Libbie Henrietta
Kaufman, Joyce Jacobson
Koenigsberger, Irene Caroline Diner
Krasnow, Frances
Krim, Mathilde
Levi-Montalcini, Rita
Marmorston, Jessie
Pool, Judith Graham
Resnik, Judith
Rosen, Ora Mendelsohn
Rubin, Vera Cooper
Sheps, Mindel Cherniack
Spector, Bertha Kaplan
Stern, Frances
Waelsch, Salome Gluecksohn
Wollstein, Martha
Yalow, Rosalyn

SCREENWRITERS

Caspary, Vera
Ephron, Nora
Ephron, Phoebe
Franken, Rose
Kanin, Fay
Levien, Sonya
May, Elaine
Parker, Dorothy Rothschild

SCULPTORS

Chicago, Judy
Cohen, Katherine M.
Gezari, Temima
Hesse, Eva
Kohler, Rose
Nevelson, Louise
Pollak, Virginia Morris
Wilke, Hannah

SINGERS

(see BLUES SINGER; CONCERT
MUSICIANS AND SINGERS;
ENTERTAINERS; FOLK
MUSICIANS AND SINGERS;
JAZZ SINGER; OPERA SINGERS;
POPULAR MUSICIANS
AND SINGERS; YIDDISH/
VAUDEVILLE ENTERTAINERS)

SOCIAL WORKERS

Bamber, Golde
Buttenwieser, Helen Lehman
Fizdale, Ruth E.
Fraiberg, Selma
Glueck, Eleanor

Goldmark, Pauline
Gratz, Rebecca
Greenbaum, Selina
Gruening, Rose
Hamburger, Julia Horn
Kahn, Dorothy C.
Kander, Lizzie Black
Kohn, C. Marian
Kohn, Esther Loeb
Liveright, Alice Springer Fleisher
Low, Minnie
Perlman, Helen Harris
Rapoport, Lydia
Robison, Sophia Moses
Rosensohn, Etta Lasker
Salomon, Alice
Solomon, Maida Herman
Stern, Elizabeth
Strakosch, Celia
Wald, Lillian D.
Weil, Helen
Willen, Pearl

SUPREME COURT JUSTICE

Ginsburg, Ruth Bader

TELEVISION JOURNALISTS, DIRECTORS, PRODUCERS, AND PERSONALITIES

Albert, Mildred Elizabeth Levine
Brothers, Joyce
Charren, Peggy
Fine, Sylvia
Kanin, Fay
Lewis, Shari
Myers, Carmel
Myerson, Bess
Phillips, Irna
Rivers, Joan
Shore, Dinah
Walters, Barbara
Westheimer, Ruth
Wyler, Marjorie

THEATRICAL DIRECTORS, PRODUCERS, DESIGNERS, AGENTS, AND TRAINERS

Abarbanell, Lina
Adler, Stella
Bernstein, Aline
Harris, Renee
Helburn, Theresa
Herscher, Sylvia
Menken, Helen
Nathan, Adele Gutman
Rosenthal, Jean
Schulberg, Adeline
Selznick, Irene Mayer
Shoshana, Rose
Sills, Beverly
Silver, Joan Micklin

UNITED NATIONS DELEGATE

Hauser, Rita Eleanor

WRITERS

Adler, Polly
Alschuler, Rose Haas
Antin, Mary
Arendt, Hannah
Baruch, Dorothy Walter
Berler, Beatrice
Bernays, Anne Fleischman
Blume, Judy
Bowles, Jane
Brandeis, Madeline
Brin, Ruth F.
Broner, Esther M.
Brook, Claire
Calisher, Hortense
Caspary, Vera
Chernin, Kim
Chesler, Phyllis
Cohen, Helen Louise
Cohen, Rose Gollup
Dawidowicz, Lucy S.
Decter, Midge
Deutsch, Babette
Dropkin, Celia
Dubnow-Erlich, Sophia
Durant, Ariel
Earp, Josephine Sara Marcus
Edelman, Lily
Ephron, Nora
Ferber, Edna
Firestone, Shulamith
Franken, Rose
Franks, Bilhah Abigail Levy
Franks, Rebecca
Freeman, Cynthia
Friedan, Betty
Gay, Ruth
Goldman, Emma
Gornick, Vivian
Gruber, Ruth
Gruenberg, Sidonie Matzner
Harby, Leah Cohen
Heilbrun, Carolyn G.
Hellman, Lillian
Hirschler, Gertrude
Hirsh, Marilyn
Hobson, Laura Z.
Hurst, Fannie
Hyneman, Rebekah Gumpert
Jastrow, Marie Grunfeld
Kahn, Joan
Karmel, Ilona
Karpilove, Miriam
Kaufman, Beatrice
Kaufman, Bel
Kaufman, Lyalya
Kaufman, Sue
Klagsbrun, Francine

Klein, Gerda Weissmann
Konecky, Edith
Krantz, Judith
Kumin, Maxine
Landers, Ann
Lazarus, Emma
Lazarus, Josephine
Lee, Malka
Levin, Nora
Levinger, Elma Ehrlich
Loveman, Amy
Lust, Adeline Cohnfeldt
Margolin, Anna
Marshall, Lenore Guinzburg
Merriam, Eve
Michelson, Miriam
Moers, Ellen
Moïse, Penina
Molodowsky, Kadya
Mordecai, Sarah Ann Hays
Morgan, Robin
Moss, Mary
Newman, Isidora
Olsen, Tillie
Ostriker, Alicia Suskin
Ozick, Cynthia
Paley, Grace
Parker, Dorothy Rothschild
Piercy, Marge
Pogrebin, Letty Cottin
Rand, Ayn
Reisen, Sarah
Rich, Adrienne Cecile
Riding, Laura
Roiphe, Anne
Rome, Esther
Rosen, Norma
Rubin, Ruth
Rukeyser, Muriel
Ruskay, Esther Jane
Sampter, Jessie Ethel
Schulman, Grace
Seaman, Sylvia Bernstein
Segal, Lore
Seixas Nathan, Grace
Serdatsky, Yente
Shore, Viola Brothers
Shore, Wilma
Shoshana, Rose
Shtok, Fradel
Simon, Kate
Sinclair, Jo
Slesinger, Tess
Solis-Cohen, Emily
Solis-Cohen, Judith
Sontag, Susan
Sotheran, Alice Hyneman
Stein, Gertrude
Steinem, Gloria
Steinem, Pauline Perlmutter
Stern, Edith Mendel
Stern, Elizabeth
Syrkin, Marie

Taylor, Sydney
Toklas, Alice Babette
Trilling, Diana
Trommer, Marie
Tuchman, Barbara W.
Tussman, Malka Heifetz
Untermeyer, Jean Starr
Van Buren, Abigail
Walling, Anna Strunsky
Wasserstein, Wendy
Westheimer, Ruth
Whitman, Ruth
Wiernik, Bertha
Winslow, Thyra Samter
Wolfenstein, Martha
Yezierska, Anzia
Yglesias, Helen
Zolotow, Charlotte

YIDDISH/VAUDEVILLE ENTERTAINERS

Adler, Celia
Adler, Sara
Appel, Anna
Baker, Belle
Barthe, Belle
Bayes, Nora
Brice, Fanny
Dresser, Louise
Gersten, Berta
Gordon, Vera

Halperin, Nan
Held, Anna
Picon, Molly
Thomashefsky, Bessie
Tucker, Sophie

ZIONISTS

Adlerblum, Nima
Askowith, Dora
Barron, Jennie Loitman
Bender, Rose I.
Berkson, Libbie Suchoff
Bilavsky, Glika
Brandeis, Alice Goldmark
Chesler, Phyllis
Cohen, Rosalie
Davidson, Carrie Dreyfuss
Ebin, S. Deborah
Epstein, Judith G.
Evans, Sara N.
Feder-Keyfitz, Sara Rivka
Fellman, Mary Arbitman
Fels, Mary
Freund-Rosenthal, Miriam
Friend, Ida Weis
Fromenson, Ruth Bernard
Garfiel, Evelyn
Gold, Doris Baumann
Gotsfeld, Bessie Goldstein
Gottesman, Jeane Herskovits
Gottheil, Emma Leon

Greenblatt, Aliza
Guggenheimer, Ida Espen
Halprin, Rose Luria
Herstein, Lillian
Jacobs, Rose Gell
Kaplan, Aline
Kussy, Sarah
Levensohn, Lotta
Levin, Bertha Szold
Lindheim, Irma Levy
Mandelbaum, Judith Pinta
Meir, Golda
Melamed, Deborah Marcus
Natelson, Rachel
Perlman, Florence
Phillips, Rosalie Solomons
Pool, Tamar de Sola
Prince, Jane
Resnikoff, Freda
Rosenblatt, Gertrude
Rosensohn, Etta Lasker
Sampter, Jessie Ethel
Schenk, Faye Libby
Schoolman, Bertha Singer
Seligsberg, Alice Lillie
Silverstein, Elizabeth Blume
Sonneschein, Rosa
Szold, Henrietta
Wise, Louise Waterman
Wyner, Gussie Edelman
Zunser, Miriam Shomer

Index

National Writers Union, 145
National Yeoman F, 1485
National Yiddish Book Center
  and Marjorie Guthrie, 569
  and Cynthia Ozick, 1022
  and Joan Micklin Silver, 1257
National Youth Aliyah, 354
Nation Associates, 1250
Natural Resistance and Clinical Medicine
    (Marmorston), 894
Natural Woman, A (King & Coffin), 739
NATZLER, GERTRUD AMON
  entry for, 982–983
  photograph of, 983
Natzler, Otto, 982
  photograph of, 983
NAUMBURG, ELSIE MARGARET BINGER
  entry for, 984–985
  photograph of, 984
NAUMBURG, MARGARET
  entry for, 985–986
Naumburg, Walter Wehle, 984
Naye Land, Dos, 1230
Naye Pleytim Teater, Dos, 1247
Naye Teater, 14
Naye Velt, Di (socialist weekly)
  and Celia Dropkin, 341
  and Anna Margolin, 892
  and Fradel Shtok, 1249
Nay Yidish, 892
NBC. *See* National Broadcasting Company
NCJW. *See* National Council of Jewish Women
NEA. *See* National Endowment for the Arts
Nearly Me (company), 593
Nebraska Furniture Mart (Omaha), 24
Nebraska Jewish Historical Society, 406
Nebraska Library Association, 1004
Nebraska Socialist Party, 1003
Nederlands Dance Theater, 310
Nedra (film), 893
Needle Trades Workers Industrial Union, 1510
Neff, Renfreu, 1399
Neff School of Oratory, 747
Negri, Pola, 1190
Negro Actors Guild, 1418
"Negro Jews in Harlem" (Landes), 791
Negro Spirituals (dance), 304, 1375, 1376
"Negrotarian," 664
Nehru, Jawaharlal, 584
Neighborhood Centre, 747, 1308
Neighborhood Guild, 1231
Neighborhood House (New York)
  and Carrie Bamberger Frank Fuld, 492
  and Alice Davis Menken, 912
Neighborhood Laundry Association (Brooklyn),
    1472
Neighborhood Players, 843
Neighborhood Playhouse
  and Aline Bernstein, 146, 147, 1398
  as dance venue, 307
  and Marjorie Guthrie, 568
  and Hadassah (Spira Epstein), 585
  and Pauline Koner, 303
  and Shari Lewis, 842
  and Alice Lewisohn, 302, 843, 1235
  and Irene Lewisohn, 302, 843, 1235
  and Sophie Maslow, 303, 895
  and Naima Prevots, 306
  and Jean Rosenthal, 303

  and Edith Segal, 302, 303
  and Lillian Shapero, 304
  and Anna Sokolow, 303, 1278
  and Blanche Talmud, 302
  and Helen Tamiris, 304
Neighborhood Playhouse School of the Theatre
  and Irene Lewisohn, 843, 1235
  and Jean Rosenthal, 1182
Neiman, Abraham Lincoln, 987
NEIMAN, CARRIE MARCUS
  entry for, 986–987
  photograph of, 986
Neiman Marcus (company)
  and Carrie Marcus Neiman, 986–987
  and Jo Copeland, 288
  and Estée Lauder, 800
  and Judith Leiber, 817
  and Nettie Rosenstein, 1180
Neiman Marcus family, 492
"Neither Genius nor Martyr" (Sotheran), 1295
Nelson, Esther, 306
Nelson, Pauline, 301
Nelson, Rose, 1240
Neot Kedumim, 142
Neshei Chabad Newsletter, 599
Neshei Ubnos Chabad, 599
Nessim, Maurice S., 786
Nessim, Simon S., 784
Nestle, Joan, 422
Nestor, Agnes, 625
Netherlands Dance Theater, 1279
Netherlands National Ballet, 305, 796
Netter, Esther, 950
Network, The (World Union of Jewish Students),
    199
Network Women's Conference, 296
Netzer, Sylvia, 74
NEUGARTEN, BERNICE L.
  entry for, 987–988
  and psychology, 1106
Neugass, Edwin A., 992
Neuman, Gloria, 307
Neuman, Natanya, 306
Neumark, Martha, 1117, 1137–1138
Neurological Institute of Columbia Presbyterian
    Medical Center, 47
Neuroses and Character Types (Deutsch), 331
Neuwirth, Bebe, 1393
Nevada Bar Association, 256
Nevada Federation of Business and Professional
    Women's Clubs, 257
Nevada Historical Society, 257
Nevada Native Daughters, 257
Nevada State University, 256
Neve Hadassah Youth Village (Israel), 1214
Nevelson, Charles, 989, 990
NEVELSON, LOUISE
  entry for, 988–991
  art of, 71–72
  and Colette Roberts, 1159, 1160
Nevelson-Berliawsky Gallery of 20th Century Art
    (Rockland, Me.), 991
Nevelson Brothers Shipping Company, 989
Never Cry Wolf (film), 444
Neve Shalom-Wahat Al Salaam (Dolphin &
    Dolphin), 225
New and Collected Poems (Paley), 1026
Newark Beth Israel Hospital
  and Rita Sapiro Finkler, 453

  and Carrie Bamberger Frank Fuld, 492
Newark Teachers Association, 770
Newberry Library (Chicago), 310
New Castle County Bar Association, 124
New Century Club, 124
*New Chastity and Other Arguments Against Women's
    Liberation, The* (Decter), 322
New College of California, 214
"New Colossus, The" (Lazarus), 806, 808, 1079,
    1230
Newcomb Memorial College, 242
Newcomb School, 1333
Newcomers and Colleagues (Shuval), 1251
New Cycle Theater (Brooklyn), 1400
New Dance Group
  and Fannie Aronson, 307
  and Miriam Blecher, 303
  and Nadia Chilkovsky, 303
  Ethnic Division, 585
  and Folksay, 896
  and Hadassah (Spira Epstein), 305, 585
  and Shulamite Kivel, 296
  and Marie Marchowsky, 301
  and Sophie Maslow, 303, 895, 897
  and Naima Prevots, 306
New Dance League, 302
New Dances from Israel (Freehof), 300
New Delhi Museum, 35
New Democratic Party, 1242
New Directions Books (publisher), 242, 1186
New Directions for Women, 1039
New Documents (MOMA photo exhibit), 60
New England College, 684
New England Conservatory of Music
  and Sylvia Goulston Dreyfus, 339
  and Mary Jacqueline Fabian, 389
  and Miriam Kressyn, 760
  and Ruth Laredo, 797
New England Hospital for Women and Children
    (Boston), 143, 1000
New England Medical Center, 1466
New England Poetry Club, 1069
New England Theater Conference Award, 884
New England Women's Medical Society, 143
New Faces (play), 1246
New Governments in Europe (Wertheimer), 1467
New Grove Dictionary of Music and Musicians, The,
    253
Newhall, Beaumont, 153
New Haven Hospital, 1000
New Haven Paint and Clay Club, 866
New History and the Old, The (Himmelfarb), 635,
    641
*New Illustrated Encyclopedia of Child Care and
    Guidance* (Gruenberg), 561
New International Encyclopaedia, The, 875
New Israel Fund
  and feminism, 1053
  and Letty Pogrebin, 1088
  and Mary Ann Stein, 1548
New Jersey College, 260
New Jersey Federation of YWHAs, 1540
New Jersey Law School, 1258
New Jersey Newspaper Guild, 680
New Jersey Public Health Association, 554
New Jersey State Bar Association, 1096
New Jersey State Museum Purchase Prize, 337
New Jersey Supreme Court, 1096
New Jersey Teachers Association, 770

photograph of, 582
Postcards from the Edge (novel and film), 444
Postcolonial Kinderhood (Reichek), 68
"Postemas de Mujer" (advice column), 784
Post's Literary Review, 875
Post-War World Council, 895
Potash and Perlmutter (play)
  and Louise Dresser, 338
  and Vera Gordon, 435, 540
Potato Pancakes All Around (Hirsh, illus.), 638
Potholes (musical), 566
Potter, Pauline, 208
Pound, Ezra, 1081, 1215
Poverty and Compassion (Himmelfarb), 635, 641
POWDERMAKER, HORTENSE
  entry for, 1099–1100
  as pioneer, 98
Powell, Colin, 1453
Powell, Dick, 159
Powell, Frank, 119
"Power and Horse Power" (Hurst), 663
Power, Morals, and the Founding Fathers (Koch), 641
Power of Darkness (Tolstoy), 14
Powerplay (Chicago), 219
Powers modeling agency, 1348
Poylishe Yidntum, Dos, 1247
Poyntz, Juliet
  establishes Catskills unity house, 1508
  and Fannia Cohn, 256, 1508, 1509
  and International Ladies Garment Workers
    Union, 677
PPFA. *See* Planned Parenthood Foundation of
  America
Practicing History (Tuchman), 1415
Prag, Conrad
  father of Florence Kahn, 713
  husband of Mary Goldsmith Prag, 1101
PRAG, MARY GOLDSMITH
  entry for, 1101–1102
  mother of Florence Kahn, 713
  photograph of, 1101
Prager, Regina
  and Avrom Goldfaden, 951
  in *Di Khazinte*, 202
  career in Yiddish theater, 1530, 1534
Pratt, Norma Fain, 1080
Pratt Institute (New York)
  and Clarisse Doris Hellman, 617
  and Eva Hesse, 627
  and Dorothea Litzinger, 866
  and Louise Nevelson, 989
  and Frances Stern, 1335
Prayers for the Dead (Kellerman), 428
Pre-Army Yeshivah (Israel), 49
Precious Legacy Project, 949
Prell, Riv-Ellen, 706
Premice, Josephineh, 585
Preminger, Otto, 209
Preparing for the Sabbath (Rapoport), 423
Preppy Handbook, The, 1330
Presbrey Advertising Agency, 30
Presbyterian Hospital (New York), 252
Prescott, William H., 142
Present Tense (magazine), 1162
Presidential Medal of Freedom
  Will and Ariel Durant receive, 344
  Mary Woodward Lasker receives, 798
Presidential National Medal of Science, 1188
"President's Chats" (Spiegel), 1300

President's Commission for the Study of Ethical
  Problems in Medicine and Biomedical and
  Behavioral Research, 763
President's Commission on the Status of Women,
  634
President's Committee on Mental Retardation,
  763
President's Study Group on Careers for Women
  in 1966–1967, 1519
Pressberg, Gail, 1036
Press Congress (Chicago, 1893), 40, 1290
Preussische Staat und die Juden, Der (Stern-
  Taeubler), 1340
Prevots, Naima, 306
Price, Roger, 1215
Pricket, Stacey, 896
PRIESAND, SALLY JANE
  entry for, 1102–1104
  photographs of, 1102, 1103, 1116
  leads prayer at opening of Congress, 413
  rabbinical ordination, 204, 695, 953, 1115,
    1117, 1138, 1139
  and television, 1394
Priestley, J.B., 1412
Primakoff, Henry, 257
Primakoff, Laura, 257
Primakoff, Nina, 257
Primakoff, Paul, 257
Prim-Art Series, The (Rosenthal), 1180
Primary Education, 55
Prime of Miss Jean Brodie, The (film), 444
Primitive Mysteries (dance)
  and Marjorie Guthrie, 568
  and Pearl Lang, 795
  and Sophie Maslow, 895
  and Lillian Shapero, 304
Primus, Pearl
  and Hadassah (Spira Epstein), 585
  and Helen Tamiris, 1376
PRINCE, JANE
  entry for, 1104
Prince, William, 1104
Prince Georges County (Md.) Board of
  Commissioners, 1298
Prince Georges General Hospital (Md.), 1298
Prince of the City (film), 444
Prince of Tides (film), 446, 1351
Princess Bride, The (film), 442
Princess Daisy (Krantz), 753
Princeton Art Museum, 1462
Princeton University
  admission quotas, 260
  and Hannah Arendt, 63
  and Jessie Bernard, 144
  and Ze'eva Cohen, 302
  and Natalie Zemon Davis, 316, 638
  and Helen Frankenthaler, 471
  and Ruth Kluger, 653
  and Maxine Kumin, 766
  and Ruth Barcan Marcus, 889
  and Emmy Noether, 998
  and Shirley Polykoff, 1093
  and Lore Segal, 1225
Prints with Poems (Drabkin), 337
Prison Association (New York), 12
"Prisoners, The" (Lerner), 827
Private Benjamin (film), 446, 604, 1330
Private Collection (Untermeyer), 1431
Private Matter, A (film), 1257

Private View, A (Selznick), 1228
*Private View: Inside Baryshnikov's American Ballet
  Theatre* (Arnold), 65
Prize Fight Studies (dance), 1375
Probing Our Prejudices (Powdermaker), 1100
"Problem for Purim, A" (Cohen), 1115
Professional Art Schools in the United States (Levy),
  840
Professional Children's School (New York), 496,
  1185, 1254
Professor Romeo (Bernays), 145
Programme on Medical Sociology, 1250
Progreso, El (Ladino newspaper), 783, 784, 786
"Progress and Poverty" (Lazarus), 806
Progressive Party
  and Dorothy Bellanca, 134
  and Henry Moskowitz, 944
  and Lillian D. Wald, 1448
Progressive Woman, 996
Progressive Women's Councils, 1240
Project Americana, 949
Prolegomena: Legal Fictions or Evasions of the Law
  (Askowith), 82
Prologue (dance), 897
Promenade des Anglais (Model), 1062
Promised Land, The (Antin), 55, 56, 57, 100, 101,
  350, 419
Promised Lands (film), 1293
Promise of a New Spring (Klein), 742
Propeller Club of the United States, 1025
Prophecy (Krasner), 71
Prophet (Gibran), 743
Prophetess, The (dance), 1019
Proskauer Rose Goetz and Mendelsohn (law firm),
  733
Proskurover Ladies Benevolent Society, 1051
Prospect Theater (Bronx), 536
Prosten, Ann, 778
Protest (Defiance) (dance), 1279
Protestant, Catholic, Jew (Herberg), 671
Proudhon, Pierre-Joseph, 1045
Proud Tower, The (Tuchman), 1415
Providence Association for the Blind, 931
Providence Civic and Park Association, 931
Providence District Nursing Association, 931
Providence Hospital (Washington, D.C.), 1057
Providence Plantation Club, 931
Providence Playground Committee, 931
Providence Society for Organizing Charity, 931
Provincetown Players, 920
Prozdor (high school), 385
Prudential Lines, 902
Prussian Diet, 1511
Pryor Concert Management (Council Bluffs, Ia.),
  1144
P.S. *See* Public School
Psalms (dance), 1279
Psalms, The (Raphael), 637
Psychoanalysis and the Human Situation
  (Marmorston et al.), 894
Psychoanalysis of the Neuroses (Deutsch), 330
Psychoanalysis of the Sexual Functions of Women
  (Deutsch), 329
Psychoanalytic Institute (Vienna), 194
Psychoanalytic Institute of Southwestern
  Germany, 489
Psychoanalytic Training Institute, 330
Psychological Birth of the Human Infant, The
  (Mahler), 882

SCHLAMME, MARTHA
  entry for, 1207–1209
  photograph of, 1208
  television career, 1394
Schlang, Alexander, 996
Schleifer, Simon, 1456
Schlemiel as Modern Hero, The (Wisse), 1484
Schlesinger Library on the History of Women in
    America, 968, 1282
Schlick, Moritz, 1380
Schlissel, Lillian, 1212
Schlossberg, Edwin, 555
Schmendrick (play), 1066
Schmidt, Charles P., 472
Schneemann, Carolee, 78
Schneerson, Chana, 1157
Schneerson, Chaya Moussia, 1157
Schneerson, Menachem M., 599
Schneerson, Sholom Ber, 1157
Schneider, Florence, 302
Schneider, Michael, 601
Schneider, Susan Weidman
  and *Lilith*, 695, 854, 856
  on philanthropy, 1053
  photograph of, 127
Schneider, Yael
  photograph of, 127
SCHNEIDERMAN, ROSE
  entry for, 1209–1212
  and feminism, 410, 1272
  in Hebrew Orphan Asylum, 349
  and the labor movement, 350, 772, 779, 780,
    1271, 1273
  and Pauline Newman, 993
  photograph of, 1209
  and Triangle Shirtwaist fire, 675, 1270, 1411
  and United Electrical, Radio, and Machine
    Workers, 779
  and Uprising of the 20,000, 1434
  and woman suffrage, 409
  and Women's Trade Union League, 410, 776,
    1272
Schneiderman, William, 738
Schneirla, T.C., 1405
Schnurmann House (Mayfield Heights, Ohio),
    1462
SCHOCKEN, EVA
  entry for, 1212
Schocken, Salman, 1212
Schocken, Theodore, 1212
Schocken Books, 62, 1212
Schoenfeld, Mrs. Henry
  and Lizzie Kander, 717
  The Settlement Cook Book, 717, 718
Schoenheimer, Rudolf, 1445, 1446
Schola Cantorum, 1174
"Scholar and the Feminist IX" (conference), 1502
Scholars Circle (Drisha Institute), 340
Scholarship and Guidance Association, 748
Scholarship Association for Jewish Children, 748
Schönberg, Bessie, 936
Schonthal, Ruth, 957
School and Collegiate Conference on English, 244
School Art League of New York, 840
School Children's Aid Society, 877
School for Ethical Culture. *See* Ethical Culture
    School
School for Jewish Parent Education, 46
School for the Feeble-Minded (Ga.), 731

School for the Jewish Woman. *See* School of the
    Jewish Woman
Schoolman, Albert, 141, 1213
SCHOOLMAN, BERTHA SINGER
  entry for, 1212–1214
  and Libbie Berkson, 141
  and Camp Cejwin, 1360
  photographs of, 481, 1213
School of American Ballet
  and Ruthanna Boris, 309
  and Lydia Joel, 702
  and Allegra Kent, 309, 735
  and Annabelle Lyon, 309
School of American Dance, 1375
School of Civics and Philanthropy (Chicago), 748
School of Design for Women (Philadelphia), 159
School of Jewish Philanthropy (Cincinnati), 1336
School of Jewish Studies (Pittsburgh), 608
School of Performing Arts (New York), 703
School of the Jewish Woman (Manhattan)
  dissolution of, 578
  and Trude Weiss-Rosmarin, 1463, 1464
School of Visual Arts (New York)
  and Barbara Kruger, 764
  and Bertha Wiernik, 1473
School Ties (film), 447
Schor, Naomi
  editor of *differences*, 1502
  feminist scholarship, 863
Schorr, Lev, 914
Schorr, Thelma, 1002
Schorsch, Ismar, 277
  photograph of, 1496
Schram, Peninnah, 199, 225
Schrift, Blanche, 1480
Schrift, Jonas, 1480
Schrift, Rose, 1480
Schroeder, Anne, 1232
Schroeder, Dorothy, 849
Schroeder, Patricia
  and Nita M. Lowey, 880
  and Gloria Steinem, 1322
Schubert, Franz, 740, 1409
Schubert, the Man (Bie), 1431
SCHULBERG, ADELINE
  entry for, 1214–1215
  and Ad Schulberg Agency, 440
Schulberg, B.P., 1214
Schulberg, Sondra, 448
Schulman, Arnold, 444
SCHULMAN, GRACE
  entry for, 1215
Schulman, Jerome, 1215
Schulman, Maureen
  photograph of, 582
Schulman, Naomi
  photograph of, 128
Schulman, Samuel, 623
Schultz, "Dutch," 16
Schuman, William, 1420
Schumann, Clara, 797
Schumann, Robert
  Ruth Laredo lectures on, 797
  Hephzibah Menuhin performs, 916
  Jennie Tourel performs, 1409
  Fannie Bloomfield Zeisler performs, 1543
Schurz, Carl, 1216
SCHURZ, MARGARETHE MEYER
  entry for, 1216–1217

Schuster, Joseph, 1142
Schutzman, Siegried. *See* Kyle, Steven
Schwabacher, Ethel, 71
Schwalberg, Alfred W., 960
SCHWARTZ, ANNA JACOBSON
  entry for, 1217–1219
Schwartz, Arthur, 650
Schwartz, Bertie
  and Association of Jewish Libraries, 849
  compiles *Jewish Book Annual* bibliography, 848
Schwartz, Bessie
  photograph of, 395
Schwartz, Charlotte, 1275
Schwartz, Eleanor, 982
SCHWARTZ, FELICE NIERENBERG
  entry for, 1219–1220
Schwartz, Frances, 1224
Schwartz, Hermene, 310
Schwartz, Irving, 1217
Schwartz, Irwin, 1071
Schwartz, Isaac, 1216
Schwartz, Josephine, 310
Schwartz, Lynne Sharon, 421
Schwartz, Maurice
  and Celia Adler, 13–14
  and Bella Bellarina, 136
  in *Broken Hearts*, 1524
  and Berta Gersten, 508
  and Miriam Kressyn, 761
  and Yiddish Art Theater, 13, 57, 304, 1534
Schwartz, Meyer, 1065
Schwartz, Neena B., 1501
Schwartz, Teri, 446, 604
Schwartz School of Dance, 310
Schwarz, Judith, 1501
Schweitzer, Leah, 1084
Schweitzer, Peter, 1219
SCHWEITZER, REBECCA
  entry for, 1219–1220
  photograph of, 1219
Schweitzer Memorial Hospital (Palestine), 1219
Schwerner, Michael, 226, 413
Schwerner, Rita Levant
  civil rights work, 226, 413
  photograph of, 227
SCHWIMMER, ROSIKA
  entry for, 1220–1222
  photograph of, 1221
Science, 756
"Science in the Renaissance" (Hellman), 617
Scientific Methods in Clinical Studies (Marmorston),
    894
Scorcese, Martin, 719
Scott, Joan Wallach, 638–640, 1502
Scott, Leroy, 1222
Scott, Margaret McAvoy, 1335
Scott, Marion, 302
SCOTT, MIRIAM FINN
  entry for, 1222–1223
Scott, Sir Walter, 396, 550
Scott Foresman (publisher), 125
Scottsboro Boys
  and Ida Espen Guggenheimer, 567
  and Carol Weiss King, 738
Scoundrel Time (Hellman), 619
Screen Writers Guild
  and Vera Caspary, 209
  and Tess Slesinger, 1268
Scriabin, Aleksandr, 1280

Z